Main principles

- GUI design and overall development
  - User-centered design (44)
    A design approach for building highly usable user interfaces, putting the emphasis on the user.
  - Cost-driven design (81)
    GUI design comes first, with an eye on development complexity. For example, avoid using ad-hoc components (81) in your GUI as far as possible.
  - Iterative GUI development (169)
    Iterate: GUI design and implementation, profiling, software and usability testing.
- Implementation
  - The principle of Single Functional Responsibility (227)
    Provide only one functional responsibility per class/method.
  - Object lifecycle management – a general mindset (281)
    Instantiate lazily and dispose eagerly, avoid garbage collector bottlenecks.
  - Don't go against the flow (284)
    GUI toolkits are complex beasts, so don't ignore them and implement fancy designs counter to the architecture or style of the underlying GUI toolkits and infrastructure (RCP).

Visual refactorings

Other refactorings are discussed in Chapter 5.

- Extract explicit panel (195), Extract stand-alone panel (196), and Composable units (292)
  Extract the code of an existing GUI panel into a separate implementation to enhance modularity and reusability.
- Merge panel (197)
  Merge different implementations representing the same panel into a common one.
- Add parameter to panel (197) and Remove parameter from panel (198)
  Add parameters to customize a panel and its opposite refactoring, Remove parameter from panel (198).
- Parameterize panel (199)
  Implement two slightly different panels with a unique code base.
- Replace parameter with panel (200)
  Instead of adding a parameter, separate the implementation of the two panels.
- Rename panel (201)
  Change the name of a panel.

Professional Java User Interfaces

Professional Java User Interfaces

Mauro Marinilli

John Wiley & Sons, Ltd

Copyright © 2006   John Wiley & Sons Ltd, The Atrium, Southern Gate, Chichester,
West Sussex PO19 8SQ, England

Telephone   (+44) 1243 779777

Email (for orders and customer service enquiries): cs-books@wiley.co.uk

Visit our Home Page on www.wiley.com

Other Wiley Editorial Offices

John Wiley & Sons Inc., 111 River Street, Hoboken, NJ 07030, USA

Jossey-Bass, 989 Market Street, San Francisco, CA 94103-1741, USA

Wiley-VCH Verlag GmbH, Boschstr. 12, D-69469 Weinheim, Germany

John Wiley & Sons Australia Ltd, 33 Park Road, Milton, Queensland 4064, Australia

John Wiley & Sons (Asia) Pte Ltd, 2 Clementi Loop #02-01, Jin Xing Distripark, Singapore 129809

John Wiley & Sons Canada Ltd, 22 Worcester Road, Etobicoke, Ontario, Canada M9W 1L1

Wiley also publishes its books in a variety of electronic formats. Some content that appears in print may not be
available in electronic books.

Library of Congress Cataloging-in-Publication Data

Marinilli, Mauro.
  Professional Java user interfaces / Mauro Marinilli.
      p. cm.
  Includes bibliographical references and index.
  ISBN 0-471-48696-5 (pbk. : alk. paper)
  1. Java (Computer program language) 2. User interfaces (Computer
systems) I. Title.
    QA76.73.J38M34954 2006
    005.13'3--dc22
                            2006004498

British Library Cataloguing in Publication Data

A catalogue record for this book is available from the British Library

ISBN 13: 978-0-471-48696-5

ISBN 10: 0-471-48696-5

Typeset in 10/13.5pt Palatino by Laserwords Private Limited, Chennai, India

Printed and bound in Great Britain by Bell & Bain, Glasgow

This book is printed on acid-free paper responsibly manufactured from sustainable forestry in which at least two
trees are planted for each one used for paper production.

To the person who keeps alive in his daily work
the Spirit of Wonder of the early days.

Brief Contents

Contents

Part IV User Interface Design

2 Introduction to User Interface Design   31

Part V Software Design

5 Iterative GUI Development with Java   **169**

Acknowledgements

I have been working on this book for more than five years, in one way or another. It is by no means the result of a single person (the author). A very large number of people shaped it, so many that it will be impossible to name them all.

I should first thank Sally Tickner and the management at John Wiley and Sons, for allowing me to deliver the manuscript after such a huge delay, which was mostly caused – only a partial excuse – by my never-ceasing joy of working on and taming new and complex adventures, rather than lack of interest in the subject.

It's easy to remember Steve Rickaby of WordMongers, whose expert hand made this book readable and sometimes even enjoyable. If it wasn't for his help this gigantic work would have been very different.

A special thanks too to my students, who kept the fire of honest enthusiasm and the Spirit of Wonder high, and who were extremely patient with my shameful schedule. I hope I gave them back at least a small portion of what they gave to me.

I wish also to thank the reviewers for their careful work, the many clients and colleagues for the countless lessons that I tried to put together in the book, and all the people who spent precious time out of their lives putting into written form their hard-won experience, often without any economic return.

Last but not least, my biggest thanks go to my family, my Bella, and my closest friends. Without their presence, patience, and constant support, this book wouldn't have been possible.

Introduction

This introduction is structured as follows:

The interactivity thrill talks about the magic of the first time and other things.

The organization of the book discusses the book's contents and organization.

Book readers and personas provides a more user-centered approach to the contents of the book.

The interactivity thrill

Current software technology allows developers to build graphical user interfaces (GUIs) for only the cost of the labor, and with greater simplicity than ever before. Despite that, GUIs, and Java GUIs among them, are often totally frustrating and disappointing. In the words of Alan C. Kay[1]:

> "A twentieth century problem is that technology has become too 'easy.' When it was hard to do anything, whether good or bad, enough time was taken so that the result was usually good. Now we can make things almost trivially, especially in software, but most of the designs are trivial as well. This is *inverse vandalism*: the making of things because you can. Couple this to even less sophisticated buyers and you have generated an exploitation marketplace similar to that set up for teenagers. A counter to this is to generate enormous dissatisfaction with one's designs using the entire history of human art as a standard and goal. Then the trick is to decouple the dissatisfaction from self worth – otherwise it is either too depressing or one stops too soon with trivial results."

Basically, inverse vandals don't care about their work and its impact on the lives of users and the many others affected by their work, which is a pity. Software has a sort of magic in itself, and interactive software provides a concrete, vivid example of such a magic. Whether you are a teenager playing a video game or an old guy fiddling with an early computer in your garage, there was probably a moment in your life when you were totally amazed by a piece of software – otherwise you would probably have chosen another career.

---

1.   *The Early History of Smalltalk,*
     http://gagne.homedns.org/~tgagne/contrib/EarlyHistoryST.html

Such a feeling alone, and perhaps a rather selfish and self-gratifying one, is not enough to provide reliable, professional results. There is a need to study and apply a wide array of subjects in depth, filtering user's needs through experience and the relentless application of ambitious but sensible designs and solutions, both on the GUI side and in its implementation. Despite all this hard work – or possibly because of it – the fun still remains, and I hope you can see it between the lines of this book. Finally, some words about my professional background, that could help in providing a better understanding and a more critical view of the book's contents.

My long experience is mostly on internal projects, that is, building software for customers, and also spans a few products building shrink-wrapped software. As far as Java is concerned, I started working with Java GUIs in 1998, trying to focus on client-side aspects whenever possible. I worked on a couple of large and complex GUIs, and on other projects that ranged from the weather forecasting system for the Italian air force to large multinational corporate ERPs, various Web sites, a large GUI framework for advanced enterprise clients – on various aspects still unmatched on the market – and more recently have been hopping on and off planes throughout Europe and US as a consultant while trying to find the time for a number of EU and academic research projects.

Usable GUIs and usable books

Writing a book like this is in many ways similar to GUI development[1]. The author has a target audience, at least in his mind (end users), and many little daily hindrances. He needs to work to earn his keep, trying to maintain a private life and struggle with mundane things like mastery of the English language (GUI design guidelines), the wrong dpi settings in scanned pictures (API inconsistencies), ever-newer technologies, and all the rest. Luckily he is not alone. He is the less-experienced part of a great team of professionals (the development team), good-willed reviewers (user representatives), and wonderful private-life supporters. Nevertheless, new ideas and existing content that should be better addressed seem never-ending (feature creep), and the manuscript keeps growing (deadlines shifting). The author is constrained by deadlines and wants to deliver something useful (at least within *his* definition of usefulness). There are different kinds of GUI development. There are shrink-wrapped products, where there is competition and users can easily opt for your product or a competing one, as in the case of a shareware music player, and various forms of internal projects where users have no choice but to read the

---

1. The term *development* is meant to indicate the general process of building a GUI, including GUI design and implementation.

book/use the application. A documentation manual fits the latter category[1]: unfortunately for me, this book falls into the first category.

All the above has a common denominator: the end user. The ultimate objective is to write a book that *you* would like to read, in which the message comes across as smoothly and as richly as possible and as *you* expect, saving *you* time and effort, while possibly providing *you* with a pleasant experience. This book – and the next application *you* are going to create – will be effective and useful as long as its very inception, its design and writing, focuses on end users.

The organization of the book

The book is organized in three parts. The first part introduces HCI and GUI design, starting from general concepts and concluding with recurring GUI designs. The second part, from Chapter 5 to Chapter 12, discusses general implementation advice. The third part, from Chapter 13 to Chapter 16, discusses some examples applications, from analysis and GUI design to the software architecture and the implementation – something rather rare to find in literature. Finally, two appendices provide evaluation questionnaires specifically targeted at Java GUIs.

The following gives a brief description of the book's contents.

Part	Chapter	Title	Description
	1	*Putting GUI Development into Context*	Framing GUI development in the wider context of software development, introducing a general reference functional model for GUIs, and UML diagrams.
GUI Design	2	*Introduction to User Interface Design*	A basic introduction to some key themes of HCI and user-centered, general user interface design.
	3	*Java GUI Design*	Practical GUI design for the Java platform with some practical examples, introducing the Java Look and Feel design guidelines.
	4	*Recurring User Interface Designs*	Recurring design solutions in desktop applications, with reusable code.

1. In real-world situations users have another popular choice: skip reading the manual altogether.

Part	Chapter	Title	Description
	5	*Iterative GUI Development with Java*	Building GUIs iteratively using OOP. Introducing software testing, usability testing for Java GUIs, and GUI-specific refactorings.
	6	*Iterative GUI Development with Java*	Introduction to software design strategies and OOP design patterns for GUIs.
	7	*Code Organization*	Main software architectures for GUI applications and some reusable utility classes.
	8	*Form-Based Rich Clients*	An example iterative, test-driven GUI development.
Implementation	9	*Web-Based User Interfaces*	Web GUI design basics and related Java technologies.
	10	*J2ME User Interfaces*	An introduction to J2ME GUI technologies and GUI design for wireless devices, with some example code for MIDP.
	11	*Java Tools and Technologies*	A review of the main tools and technologies available for Java application development, with particular focus on open source software.
	12	*Advanced Issues*	Some topics of interest for complex GUIs: building custom frameworks, usability applied to API design, memory management, legacy GUI code, and domain-specific languages for GUIs.

Part	Chapter	Title	Description
Examples	13	*Rich Client Platforms*	Introduction to Rich Client Platforms (RCP) and Eclipse RCP GUI design guidelines, with an example service-oriented GUI for the Eclipse RCP.
	14	*The Personal Portfolio Application*	Design and development of an example application using use cases. An alternative design using JDNC is also discussed.
	15	*An Example OO User Interface*	Using the OOUI approach to design and implement an example application, compared with the use of the Naked Objects framework.
	16	*An Example Ad-Hoc Component*	An example ad-hoc component and its comparison with the *JHotDraw* framework.
Appendixes	A	*A Questionnaire for Evaluating Java User Interfaces*	
	B	*A Questionnaire for Evaluating J2ME Applications*	

Three levels of advice

Building a usable, cost-effective, professional-quality GUI is a complex and multi-disciplinary process that involves mastery of many different skills. In this book we will cover three different perspectives: the design of the user interface, the software architecture behind it, and the tactics related to the source code, as shown in the figure below.

The three level of advice in the book

Professional GUIs are carefully designed and implemented pieces of software. For this reason special attention is given in this book to implementation details, especially at the design and architectural level – in my experience the only way to absorb reliably the sort of complexity-by-accretion that real world GUIs exhibit. Source code listings and code-level tactics are mentioned only briefly, to save space and reduce the danger of sending my copy-editor to sleep.

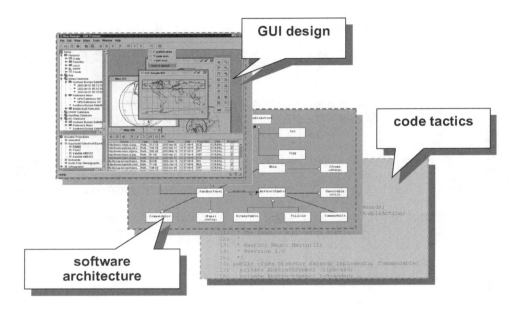

Conventions used in the book

Throughout the book notes are represented using the graphical convention below.

> This is a note.

All references are gathered in a reference section and represented following the Chicago Manual of Style, fourteenth edition, University of Chicago Press, 1993.

Source code

Source code is provided on my Web site at:

`http://www.marinilli.com/books/b1/b1.html`

or you can start from the home page at `http://www.marinilli.com` and follow the links from there. It is organized into separated bundles for each chapter, and a single file containing the code for all the chapters is also available. Sources are provided with Ant build files and with Eclipse projects.

Some of the example applications can also be launched on line using JNLP links, available at:

`http://www.marinilli.com/books/b1/b1.html`

The JNLP client will ask for authorization prior to installing the application.

Reader feedback

A book is an inherently limited means of communication, at least when compared with computer-based interactive tools. In order to balance this unfair equilibrium, a public forum will be available on my Web site for readers to give feedback, pose questions, download the source code, or start a discussion.

Book readers and personas

You might have bought this book, and I do thank you for that. Unfortunately, it is more than 707 pages long and you could not have the time or will to read it all from end to end, neither would it be a time-efficient thing to do. The objective of this section is to help you save your valuable time getting quickly to *your* point, gaining also a first glimpse of techniques for focusing the design around end users.

The book can be used in a number of ways: it is useful for experienced developers that want to explore ideas on GUI development, and can be used in courses on practical GUI design and implementation. Intermediate developers can take advantage of the many examples provided to explore sample implementations.

The book has been designed with three types of reader in mind:

i. Those that have better things to do in life than fiddling with theoretical issues, and just need to put together something that works, now.

ii. Novice readers who want to explore the complexity of professional GUI development.

iii. Those that are experienced and critical about ready-made solutions, and would like a critical and wider discussion of the major issues for GUI development in Java.

The following sections describe a set of fictitious readers, built with the persona technique[1]. If you are lucky enough to recognize yourself as one of them, or somewhere in between, their approach to the book might suit you. Alternatively, if you are one of those brave, tough, developers who think all this Lars and Melinda stuff is a bit silly, skip the following section and jump directly to the first chapter.

---

1. These user representations are called *Personae* and were introduced by A. Cooper in (Cooper 1999). They are useful for defining the user population clearly to designers, even for a book.

Lars, a Java intermediate programmer

Lars, 24, doesn't have time to waste. In his first glance at the book he sees many interesting things, but he needs to deliver a small (twenty-some screens) form-based corporate rich client application within five weeks. He needs to interface with an existing J2EE application and with a third-party Web service. After a quick look on the Web, he remains a bit confused by the many technologies and options available: he wants to look at some working code and get a clear understanding of how it works, together with some advice to help him to build a bigger picture of the best choices available, without wasting time on other fancy details.

Lars will then...

*   Take a bird's eye view of Chapter 6 and an even quicker glimpse at Chapter 7 to see about client tier architectures.
*   Perhaps take a look at Chapter 5, to see if there is some useful technique he can take advantage of in his project.
*   Read the discussion about SWT vs. Swing in Chapter 11, opting for SWT and the Eclipse RCP for his project.
*   Consequently focus his attention on Chapter 13 (RCP), and Chapter 8 (Form-based GUIs).
*   Use the quick references on the book's reverse covers as required.
*   After his project is completed, get back to the rest of the book...

Keiichi, a tech lead

Keiichi is a technical leader in a medium-sized software company in Japan who wants to explore new ideas about GUI development. He is starting a new project and has some spare time that wants to spend on refreshing his knowledge about GUI design and development. He is particularly interested in the architecture of complex desktop GUIs that provide undo/redo support, complex validation, role-based fine-grained authorization, and more.

Keiichi will then...

*   Read Chapter 1.
*   Read parts of Chapter 2 and Chapter 3 to get an idea of GUI design.
*   Browse Chapter 4 for a quick look at recurring GUI designs in desktop applications.
*   Read Chapter 5 about iterative GUI development – a subject in which he is quite interested.

- Have a look at Chapter 6 for some implementation strategies and common issues related to complex GUI development.
- Take a quick look at Chapter 7 and Chapter 8 for completing his introduction to the implementation of complex rich client GUIs with Java.
- Read Chapter 12 about advanced issues and ideas for implementing non-trivial GUIs.
- Browse the example applications in the third part of the book.
- After adding notes and bookmarks, put back the book on his shelf, promising himself to get back to it when the new project has started...

Shridhar, a professor in computer science

Shridhar is an assistant professor in a university in Kanpur, India. He is 35, married with two children. He is preparing a course on the practical development of complex GUIs. He wants to include the essentials of user interface design, advanced software design patterns, and many case studies that will form the backbone of the course. He bought the book on line to evaluate its adoption as a reference textbook for the course, integrating the parts in which he is more interested with other material. Shridhar finds some companion material for the book on line and plans to use it for his course. In particular, he is interested in using SWT for an interesting research project.

Shridhar will then...

- Organize his course content around the functional model introduced in Chapter 1.
- Plan to devote the first part of the course to GUI design issues, based on Chapters 2 and 3.
- Use Chapter 6 as the theoretical base for the second part of his course, about implementation of complex GUIs in Java.
- Use the examples in Chapters 13–16 for the case studies. He plans to extract software design patterns and architecture contents from these chapters to use in the hands-on part of his course.
- Think about creating assignments based on the ideas provided in the various chapters he has read. Because he is interested in the Eclipse RCP and SWT, he will focus on the ideas discussed in Chapter 8.

Melinda (Mellie), a manager

Mellie has a technical background and a basic overview of object-oriented technology. She wants to have an overview of current technology for GUI development with OOP, and feels that she needs to refresh her knowledge of current state-of-the-art development of client-side software. She worked in software testing back in the 1980s, and is now a senior group manager in the IT department of a medium-sized insurance company that does some in-house development. She wants to get a basic, high-level understanding of the latest trends in GUI design and development.

Mellie will then...

- Read Chapter 1 about the development context of GUI design and implementation.

- Interested by the topic of GUI design, move to study Chapter 2 for an introduction to basic user interface design.

- Read Chapter 3 for an example of an OOP GUI technology stack, showing guidelines, practical GUI design examples, and other technology-oriented topics that can also be used outside the Java world.

- Take a look at the pictures in Chapter 4, to see the most commonly-used GUI designs in real world applications, and try to match them with her daily practice of software applications (a mix of Microsoft Project, the Microsoft Office suite, and some corporate intranet applications).

- Have a look at Chapter 5 to get an idea of iterative GUI development.

- Note a few useful terms to be inserted in her next presentation, such as usability inspections, continuous profiling, and more.

- Eventually, put the book in her 'favorites' pile, hoping to have more time for it another day.

William, a first year student in a Master in CS course

William has just moved to Vancouver and is excited about starting his masters program in Computer Science and eager to become a proficient software developer. He already has some exposure to Java and the Swing toolkit, and he knows that he is going to have some courses about these topics. He wants to know more about software architectures and how complex desktop GUIs are built, possibly starting his own open source project.

William will then...

- Start reading the example applications, looking for interesting situations and trying to understand the proposed solutions.

- As he is interested in the Sandbox application discussed in Chapter 16, download and compile the source code, tweaking it to add new features.

- Jump to Chapter 6 for the theoretical background behind the implementations proposed in the example applications.
- Turn his interest to the qText application in Chapter 6, studying its simple architecture, downloading the code, and adding new commands to the editor.
- Browse the rest of the book as he needs to.

Karole, a business analyst

Karole has a degree in programming and works for a software company. While working as a full-time analyst on her current project, she discovers that she enjoys dealing with customers. She feels she would like to work more on the GUI side of software development and move into GUI design. She would like to get a wider picture of GUI development, using Java as a practical example, but also be exposed to more general concepts.

Karole will then...

- Read Chapter 1 about the development context for GUI design and implementation.
- Study Chapter 2 for an introduction to basic GUI design advice.
- Read Chapter 3 for a discussion of GUI guidelines, practical GUI design examples, and other technology-oriented topics that can also be used outside the Java world.
- Study Chapter 4, to understand the most commonly-used GUI designs and the rationale behind them.
- Perhaps read Chapters 5 and 8 to gain a better grasp of the latest iterative development techniques for client applications.
- Snoop around the rest of the book as required.

Juan, an experienced programmer

Juan is an experienced programmer in his late twenties living in Schaumburg, IL. He has just bought the book in a bookshop and is excited about it. He has some spare time, an hour or two, on a Saturday morning. He wants to browse the book for something fun, taking it easy, while sipping his favorite blend of Cappuccino in a café while waiting for his fiancé Francene, who is having her nails done. Juan is looking for cool new technologies, interesting application architectures, exciting techniques, or just a cartoon or fancy pictures before a long shopping session with Francene[1].

Juan will then...

- Browse Chapter 4 for a quick glimpse of common GUI design issues, such as choosers, area organization, and so on.
- Have a look at some of the pictures of the various look and feels in Chapter 11.
- Look at Chapter 10 for information about J2ME GUIs, and have a quick look at Chapter 9 for Web Java GUIs.
- Have a glimpse at some of the techniques discussed in Chapter 12.
- Take a look at the various pictures of the example applications in the third part of the book.
- Then, when he has more time, get back to this section to find another fictitious user who matches his needs, so that he can start seriously reading the book.

---

1. This is not a spurious use of a technical book, as it might seem at first. Establishing a positive emotional relationship with something we need in our work life is always a win-win situation. Working with something pleasant will make us feel better, being more productive, and perhaps sparing precious energy for something other than dull work.

1 Putting GUI Development into Context

This chapter provides a comprehensive introduction to the design and development of Java applications with non-trivial user interfaces. After introducing a general-purpose reference model that will guide our discussion in the remainder of the book, we introduce the organizational aspects related to UI development, discussing the role of people in the entire software lifecycle process for GUI software. We then consider the issue of early design, where we briefly introduce the delicate and often overlooked transition from analysis to UI design. A section is devoted to some interesting lifecycle models and the way they support the process of building professional user interfaces. The chapter concludes with a minimal introduction to some useful UML notation that will be used throughout the book.

The chapter is structured as follows:

1.1, Introduction briefly discusses the current state of GUI technologies and the use made of them by developers.

1.2, Focusing on users discusses user-centered design and development throughout the software lifecycle.

1.3, A functional decomposition for user interfaces introduces an abstract model for GUIs that is used throughout the book.

1.4, Tool selection: the Java singularity discusses the selection of a set of ingredient libraries technologies, many of them open source, to speed up GUI development.

1.5, Organizational aspects introduces some of the issues related to the management of the multidisciplinary teams that are common in GUI development.

1.6, Early design introduces requirements and use cases for professional GUIs.

1.7, Lifecycle models, processes and approaches briefly introduces some software lifecycle models: Rational Unified Process, Extreme Programming and other Agile approaches, the LUCID methodology, and evolutionary prototyping, focusing on GUI design and development.

1.8, UML notation introduces some UML diagrams of interest that are used throughout the book.

1.1   *Introduction*

The wealth of GUI design options provided by rich client GUI technologies is still poorly mastered by developers struggling to provide remarkable designs in a cost-effective way. This is what happens when powerful media and technologies lack widespread, deep expertise and practical support.

The same thing used to happen two thousand years ago. Pliny the Elder, an ancient Roman scholar and encyclopedist, despised his compatriots' paintings and preferred Greek classic art. His complaint was about the use of newer techniques that exploited a much wider number of colors, while Greek classic paintings used only four colors. Today we have a chance to see these much despised 'excessive' paintings, thanks to the catastrophe that buried Pompeii in 79 AD, freezing a moment of history in one of the most rich and developed areas of the age – similar to what California represents to Western civilization today – and, unfortunately, accidentally killing Pliny. Surprisingly, these miraculous survivals show a realistic and powerful use of the newer – and much harder – techniques, together with some unskillful art works.

Moving from Roman paintings to user interfaces, in the 1980s the computer industry experienced a similar mass-market technology shift in visual technologies with the introduction of powerful raster graphics with millions of colors, large dedicated memory spaces and new, ad-hoc input devices. Today, after another twenty years or more, we are in a situation no different from the Roman paintings of the 60's AD. These new technologies provided a steep increase in complexity, and developers (like the Roman painters of Pliny's age) are still struggling to tame such power for building cost-effective, usable and enjoyable GUIs.

1.2   *Focusing on users*

The most striking difference between designing and building a desktop application GUI and other software is the presence of the user. Users are those that will ultimately use the product, but in current development-centric engineering settings, they are usually completely neglected. 'Focusing on users' means focusing on human details – cognitive factors such as perception, memory, learning, problem-solving and so on – rather than implementation factors such as system and business requirements, software architecture, hardware, and so on. User-centered design is a well-established set of practices that place users at the heart of GUI design and development. This is currently the only way known to obtain software that behaves as users expect, ideally becoming transparent to them – they don't realize they are using it – and not getting in the way of getting work done. Adopting, or even merely being aware of, the user-centered approach is critical, not only in the design phase, but throughout the whole development process.

A number of practices have been established for centering the design and overall iterative development on end users:

- Understanding users, their objectives, their current working practices, and the general context in which the software will be used, all of this before starting the design of the user interface.

- As part of this, an important role is played by two deeply intertwined central issues: users and their tasks. User analysis–providing groups of users with their goals – and task analysis – breaking down tasks in smaller subtasks – are two disciplines that aim at defining these issues in useful terms.

- Involving end users or user representatives in the design from the early phases. This practice is referred to as *participatory design*.

- A useful means for understanding users is to interview and observe them while at work in their normal work environment. Techniques such as *contextual enquiries*[1] and adopting an ethnographic[2] approach to user studies are widely used in this respect.

- Usability tests help to ground an application on user's needs after various iterations of design and development.

We will see user-centered techniques applied throughout this book, but apart from these techniques, it is essential to always bear in mind that being aware of the end user – playing the role of the *advocate of the user* – is essential in producing a professional user interface, especially on fast-paced projects in which it is hard to fully apply these techniques when other, more urgent deadlines are pressing.

1.3   *A functional decomposition for user interfaces*

Graphical user interface applications are a vast class of software systems with recurring properties. In a GUI there is always a portion of the screen that is designed for interacting with users, there are various forms of reactions to user interactions, perhaps through some form of an internal representation of the business domain at hand, and so on. Decomposing these functionalities into a set of

---

1. During a contextual enquiry, several potential users of an application or a process that we want to capture in software are observed in their day-to-day work. The interviewers focus on a specific objective and adopt a partner-like approach with users, rather than being judgemental or inquisitive.
2. Ethnography is a method of studying and learning about groups of people. Typically, it involves the study of a small group of subjects in their own environment in order to develop a deep understanding of them.

layers is useful as a key to aid discussion of the various aspects of GUI development, as a reference for discussions, and as a conceptual tool to tame the complexity of GUI design and development. This is illustrated in Figure 1.1.

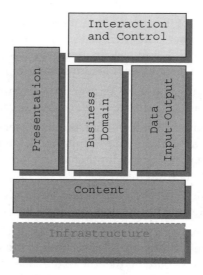

Figure 1.1   An abstract model for user interfaces

The layers in our reference model are:

- *Business Domain.* A representation of the domain of interest, separated from GUI and other non-business details.
- *Content.* The 'structure' of the GUI: widgets, windows, and navigation flow among different windows, screens, and so on.
- *Data IO.* The interface with the rest of the world other than the end user. Data formats, communication protocols and the like are represented by this layer.
- *Infrastructure.* Low-level support, runtime environment, utilities, and so on. The graphical toolkit of choice, libraries, frameworks and hardware support belong in this layer.
- *Interaction and Control.* Low-level events and control logic are gathered in this layer. Note that this layer can be thought of as the 'glue' that holds the rest of the GUI implementation together.
- *Presentation.* This layer represents graphical details that are dependent on the given presentation technology, such as pixels, colors, and fonts. This layer can be thought of as (theoretically) orthogonal to the other layers.

An example of the application of this functional model to a simple form-based GUI is shown in Figure 1.2.

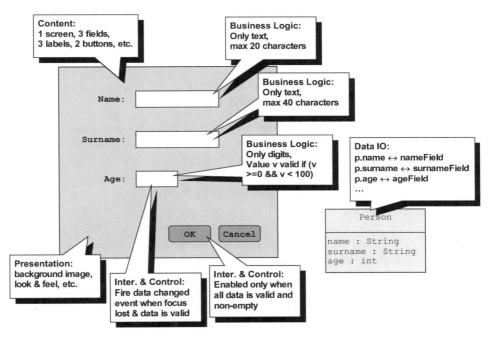

Figure 1.2   Applying the abstract model to a simple form GUI

The figure shows a very simple form-based GUI that has been decomposed using our model. Graphical aspects, no matter how implemented, belong to the presentation layer. Widgets and their layout are part of the content layer. Widget's behavior in reaction to user input – for example, the 'Age' field accepts only digits – is enforced at a low level by the interaction and control layer, but the ultimate logic lies in the business domain layer, where it is defined that an age is a numeric, integer entity with values between 0 and 100. It is the responsibility of the interaction and control layer to understand when the user has completed data input and how to handle invalid values.

This model is general – for example, it could be applied to Web GUIs, wireless device applications, touch-screen kiosks and so on – and somewhat arbitrary. It is just one of the various possible decompositions of GUI functionalities: it focuses on simplicity and practicality, and is independent of the particular implementation technology. You can use this model to represent any existing desktop application GUI, or to organize the development of new ones.

We are going to apply it to Java GUIs, which are high-level component-based user interfaces based on a strongly-typed object-oriented language and on an operating system-independent execution platform. This simple model will form the basis of our discussion about user interfaces in Java. We will analyze complex GUI implementations using this model, discussing disparate GUI technologies, and we will use it as a software architecture for one of the many examples proposed in the book.

1.4   *Tool selection: the Java singularity*

In this book we will discuss GUIs of any size and complexity, all built with Java technology. One of the most striking aspects of Java is its openness and the wide range of companies, tools, and technologies that flourish under its umbrella. This applies over a wide array of hardware, ranging from wireless devices and card readers to powerful back-end enterprise servers.

Of course, similar to Pliny's paintings, and the line of Alan Kay's 'inverse vandals' in the introduction, there are wild differences in quality. Along with open source tools with a rock-solid reputation, such as Hybernate and some good pieces of server-side facility, and in many other application domains, we have hundreds of ill-documented, partially working, hard-to-use libraries and would-be tools. Nevertheless, the whole Open Source Software (OSS) movement is a remarkable feature of Java technology, typical of the cooperative spirit that dominates this community.

A characteristic that assumes special significance for Java projects is the tool selection phase. With the sheer abundance of tools and technologies – *thousands* of OSS tools for Java development – the selection of the 'best' set of tools for a Java project can prove hard. Some choices can be changed later with acceptable cost, such as for example switching to another issue tracking system, as long as the old one provides some data export facility, but others cannot be changed without throwing away most of the work done. Choosing the right presentation technology – specifically, choosing between Swing or SWT – is a strategic choice that cannot be reversed easily. Peer opinions, Web forums and the like often provide biased opinions, or might not take your particular context and needs in account.

Commercial tools are usually better than OSS ones, but the same care in selection and evaluation should be applied. My personal experience has guided me to start with an OSS tool, and then, only if really necessary, move to a commercial one: buying a tool of which you have no previous experience can prove a costly mistake. It is wiser to start with an Open Source alternative and use it as long as possible, and this will also help to clarify your real requirements.

One thing that always strikes me when I get involved in a new project is the carelessness shown in choosing portions of the base tool set. Sentences like 'Oh, well we started off with 'X' and 'Y' together with 'Z' because they were available on the market and…' – and then usually there is a pause. Sometimes in large teams developers don't even know who started using a particular XML library or GUI testing tool, 'We just tried it, and it worked.' Then, after months of quiet work, they find themselves dealing with, perhaps, unmanageably huge XML files for acceptance tests[3].

Of running little green men and wrong choices

A little green man dashing to a door is the universal icon for emergency exits in public buildings. Similarly, alternatives and emergency plans should always be considered when choosing a project's ingredient technologies. When preparing a list of technologies for a project, let's not forget to make an alternative list with the emergency sign icon on it, because some of choices we must make are irreversible without losing much of the work already completed.

This process is like going to the forest to pick mushrooms. They are free, and they could be so tasty – but they could be poisonous. As every developer knows, tools usually work well at first, on simple tests and in recurring situations. But after some month of use, or, even worse, after more than few months, you may find that a tool can no longer support what we want to do, and you are then faced with the need to switch to another solution. Sometimes it is impossible to step back, so that there are no emergency exits for the situation. Rarely is technology the real problem, although it is always a great excuse: most of the time it is having access to the right people that will make the difference.

I have made several mistakes in tool selection. Some were inevitable at the time, others were just my fault. The most classic mistake I made was to see problems like nails to be driven in with my favorite hammers[4], the tools I was most familiar and confident with. At other times, more often than the wrong technology, the problem was a wrong adoption of a given technology.

1.5   Organizational aspects

Developing a non-trivial professional GUI is perhaps the most interdisciplinary kind of task to be found in software development. Many different roles need to interact closely: the alchemy of such interaction is so delicate that the resulting

---

3.   Chapter 11 is entirely devoted to the practice of tool selection.
4.   To paraphrase the American psychologist Abraham Maslow, *'If you only have a hammer, you tend to see every problem as a nail.'*

final outcome may be disappointingly poor, despite the dedicated people involved and the substantial resources employed.

The user interface of an application is the most visible part of a software product and the part where people external to the development team clash most. In some projects non-developers in the organization feel entitled to advise on the user interface, especially higher management. Repercussions on the UI may be not explicit or even foreseen – for example, decisions taken in database design can affect the UI, or the absence of a capable graphical artist can influence usability, thus the overall performance of users, and so also of the system, right down to the back-end servers.

People and GUIs

In this section we explore some of the issues related to the development of user interfaces and the involvement of the people who build them.

Dermaphobic and graphic hedonists

GUIs are software artifacts with a strong human component. This is apparent for end users, but it is true also for developers. In particular, there are usually two main types of developers, of which the first is the more common: the GUI-phobic developer.

There is a widespread tradition of distaste for GUI-related development. GUI toolkits are perceived as cumbersome, complex and ultimately useless – 'It's just cosmetics,' 'I've more to do than struggle with pixels.' There are a large number of implicit assumptions behind this attitude. All the 'real action' goes on the server side, and putting GUI technical skills in a resume is seen as something to avoid, like a sound engineer who has worked on lipstick design.

This implicit phobia for the 'skin' of client applications, a sort of software derma-phobia, surfaces in many ways and in various aspects of development. Sentences like 'We need to make our application totally decoupled from the GUI layer,' 'Completely hide the presentation technology,' 'I don't have the vocation for GUI stuff,' or 'Let's hand this to GUI specialists' are indicators of such ancestral fears. Of course, hiding and decoupling are good qualities for any software, and GUI toolkits tend to be complex and frustrating to master at first, but this phobic atti-tude can only harm a project. The GUI-phobic developer often puts together something that works, maybe by cutting and pasting some tutorial code found on the Web, and then rushes back to a nobler task.

Sometimes GUI specialists are just developers who find it harder than others to say 'No,' or that just don't want to be on the front line. You can hear them rationalize their phobias: 'We decoupled things so that we are GUI toolkit-independent' is the official line, but a closer inspection of the code shows that this decoupling doesn't work in practice and that is not even required at all.

The other dangerous class of developers, although much rarer, is the GUI enthusiast, such as those who can happily spend an entire working day finding the perfect gradient texture for the company's new look and feel.

Both these kinds of people tend to perceive GUI development as a developer-centric activity: the end user experience is just a by-product of a simple-to-build and possibly fun implementation.

Developers' attitude towards GUI development, and the resulting architectural choices, shape the way the final product will look. GUI-phobic developers tend to build bulky, low-bandwidth GUIs with fewer interactions, while GUI enthusiasts tend to present useless fanciness to the user while overlooking more substantial features. In both these extremes, the overall development cost is higher and the quality of the final product is compromised.

Who owns the GUI?

Apart from simple cases in which only a small number of people are involved in building simple applications, the implementation structure has social ramifications. Abstract, formal decisions about an architecture or, worse, no substantial decisions at all, affect the real nature of the implementation structure only shallowly, as mentioned in countless books[5].

If no strong force is at work in a project, developers will 'own' the development process. This can be fine for server-side applications, but needs special care for client-side applications. The most common owners of a project are its customers or other such stakeholders – although they rarely correspond to the application's final users. When a project is owned by its customers, a number of issues may arise that are specifically confined to GUI design – we detail these in Chapter 2 and 3. In these cases, though, the implementation can be designed to reflect this climate by providing effective mechanisms to absorb change at the GUI design and interaction level.

Particular care is needed in those cases in which the project will build a product or a service in a market where existing alternatives are available. Shareware software, or competing Web sites, are examples of software that is ultimately chosen by the end user, in contrast to, say, an intranet corporate portal or an ERP application, whose end users have no power of choice. In cases in which users have a low barrier to switching to a competing product or service, extra care is needed to safely ground ownership with the end users, or there is a risk of producing software that nobody

---

5.   We would just mention here two classics: (Brooks 1995) and (De Marco and Lister 1999).

will buy. This is achieved by adopting a fully-fledged user-centered design approach with extensive usability testing and feedback from users, and in which developers and the other stakeholders are constantly focused on the end user ownership.

'Ownership' dictates the overall attitude toward the implementation. If you ask a developer what a good architecture should be, they can hold forth for hours, mentioning powerful virtues like usefulness, robustness, maintainability, scalability, agility, responsiveness, extensibility, fitness to purpose, and so on. Customers, in contrast, are often dangerously vague. For a user, anything is fine 'as long as it helps with the business.'

Cost can be a major factor as well. Projects driven by cost tend to have their implementation and architecture deeply shaped by their financial climate.

An often overlooked aspect of any technical decision (languages, architectures) is the emotional connotation people attach to it. One developer may not like Swing (or SWT), while another might find it a wonderfully comfortable choice. Architectures, tools and approaches have their own advantages and drawbacks, but they are merely instruments to aid in to solving the problem at hand. It is dangerous to let our feelings drive critical choices biased by personal feelings, as choosing the wrong tool can prove disastrous in the long term.

Team composition

GUI development is a multidisciplinary activity that involves a number of diverse skills. Here are some of the roles involved in a GUI development project:

- *UI designer.* This role is responsible for driving the UI design and ensuring a UI's usability, enhanced after usability testing.

- *Analyst.* Part of the analysis phase is often performed by means of discussions about user interface prototypes.

- *Developers.* Programmers are the main resource in building a professional desktop application GUI. The wide range of scenarios and requirements make the use of GUI application frameworks and rich client platforms impractical in some situations. Developers and labor-intensive development is the only practical way to achieve professional GUI applications.

- *Application architect.* This role is perhaps the most important of all. A GUI architect must be knowledgeable about GUI design, GUI implementation technologies, programming, business and application domains, and server-side issues, as well as being capable of dealing effectively with customers and other stakeholders. Architectural decisions impact directly on the GUI. For example, the decision to adopt a Web service architecture for client–server communication dictates the kind of interaction available on the client GUI. The application architect is needed effectively to bridge the gap between customers and end users' unclear needs and the detailed information required to translate such needs into working code.

- *Usability expert.* This role oversees usability issues throughout the whole application lifecycle.

- *Graphic artist.* An artist design icons, colors and other graphics for the application. Rich client applications have a wide range of graphical possibilities, much wider than Web applications. This power can be misused, producing confusing and unusable GUIs, if not properly mastered.

- *Business domain expert.* People expert in the client's business domain should work closely with GUI developers to ensure that the GUI reflects the actual business domain terminology, skill, procedures, and so on. If a domain-driven approach has been adopted for developing a rich domain model, effort should be expended to verify with expert users that such a model doesn't remain buried behind the scenes, away from the user interface and the end users, wasting the effort required for its creation.

- *Client management.* The management of the client organization can play an important role in the development of the GUI.

- *Stakeholder.* This generic term includes any person or organization that may be affected by the success or failure of the software project. End users, developers, and managers are examples of stakeholders.

- *UI tester.* Personnel skilled in GUI testing and GUI testing tools.

Quality assurance[6] experts. The feedback from the QA team involves the user interface.

Of course, depending on the project, many of these roles might be performed by the same person or team.

The composition of the team that will design and build the GUI is also important. A multidisciplinary development team is essential to achieve a high-quality design. The contribution of people with different backgrounds and points of view is extremely important in building a professional GUI.

For example, a graphic artist is indispensable, even if only working part time as a consultant. You can see the difference a good artist can make by looking at the (very unprofessional) icons used in this book – excluding the standard ones from the graphics repositories from Sun and Eclipse.

---

6. We use the more general term 'quality assurance' without distinguishing it here from 'quality control,' although they are in fact distinct disciplines.

In very small development teams a common problem is the 'usability death spiral': if they don't try it out with external people, either other colleagues or end-users, developers get accustomed to their own design. The longer a developer – either a designer or a programmer – deals with building a GUI, the more reasonable and usable it appears to be to them!

1.6   *Early design*

Requirements are the backbone of any analysis. Requirements should be:

- *Clear* and *unambiguous*, and usually expressed in natural language.
- *Complete* – that is, covering the whole system.
- *Consistent* – they should form a consistent set of constraints for the system.
- *Testable* – for requirements than cannot be made testable, one cannot prove their fulfilment.
- *Traceable* – it's usually a good idea to establish a hierarchy among requirements, so that is possible to trace lower-level or newer system requirements to older or more general ones.

Traceability can be also done graphically. We could trace requirements or their equivalent counterpart, such as acceptance tests in XP practice, directly to screen areas in our GUI. Chapter 2 introduces a general technique, A3GUI, that can be used to tag screen areas with requirements or other useful information.

Use case diagrams and GUIs

In this book we will use UML notation extensively. This section introduces UML use cases and class diagrams, a popular analysis and documentation device. Use case diagrams are especially useful for defining functional requirements in the early stages of GUI design[7].

There are many books on UML: in particular we will refer to (Fowler 2003). Although not strictly related to user interface design, use cases are commonly used in real-world development for describing the requirements for a given application. UML use case diagrams are used as the preliminary stage to elicit the expected features of a software artifact.

---

7.   We assume that the reader is already familiar with UML notation for use cases.

Use case diagrams describe a system in terms of the functionalities provided to its users. They consist of actors and use cases. Actors are entities external to the system that interact with the use cases, such as human users, other systems, and so on. These in turn are generic functions the system provides to the rest of world.

A single function can be thought as a flow of actions. The example in Figure 1.3 shows a simple use case diagram that describes an arcade video game. We have modeled the system with one external actor only, Player, and three main use cases: join the game, play the game, and insert a high score. Possible actions could be: push the 'start' button, insert coins, push the 'fire' button, and so on.

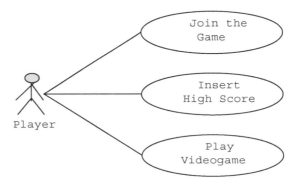

Figure 1.3   An example of use case diagram for an arcade video game

Use case diagrams are often used as inputs to the GUI design process, because they identify actors and functionalities within the system. *Scenarios* are used to represent a set of paths of possible events through single use cases. Scenarios are often described by means of natural language.

A possible scenario for the application in Figure 1.3 could the following:

- Player inserts two coins into the game console
- Player pushes the 'one player' button
- Player plays the game
- The game is over
- Player breaks the record and inserts their name into the high score list

Scenarios are also used, often in a more complex way, as a technique for identifying the typical interaction paths of a user interface. The next step could be to refine the previous scenario, including a first description of the system behavior. This is shown in Table 1.1.

Table 1.1   An example of a scenario from an arcade video game system

Player	System
The player inserts a coin into the console.	The system shows the message: 'Insert another coin and try this game.'
The player inserts one more coin into the console.	The system displays its availability to join the game by pressing the 1P button.
The player pushes the 1P button.	The player joins the video game, starting a new game.
The player plays the game.	The system engages the player in the video game.
The game is over.	The system shows the message: 'Game Over,' signaling the possibility of joining the game again by inserting more coins.
The player breaks the record and inserts their name into the high score list.	The system displays the high score list and lets the user insert their name.

Use cases can be refined into more general and more detailed ones. Use case diagrams say nothing about the implementation of the system. Use cases are not the functional modules of the system: rather, they are functionalities offered to external actors. UML does not prescribe how use cases should be represented – they can be described in any way, although usually as a list of numbered items.

Apart from narrating the user's experience of the system, use case diagrams can be helpful in understanding how use cases relate to each other, such as frequent functionalities instead of critical ones, or the possible event sequence's interactions, or as a way to expose the system analysis to customers.

For connections between use case diagrams and user interface prototyping, see for example (Elkotoubi, Khriss and Keller 1999), (Shirogane and Fukazawa 2002). Later in this chapter we will see an example of an extension to use case models to account for GUI design and usability.

1.7   *Lifecycle models, processes and approaches*

This section sets user interface development in the wider perspective of the whole software lifecycle. If we are to have usable software, it is essential to focus the whole design and development process around usability and GUI design issues.

We will introduce some different approaches to modeling the software lifecycle that take GUI design into particular consideration.

Rational Unified Process

The Rational Unified Process, or RUP, is a software engineering process made up of a number of best practices, workflows and various products (here called *artifacts*).

The key aspect of RUP lies in its iterative model for software development. RUP organizes projects in terms of disciplines and phases, each consisting of one or more iterations. There are four different phases: *inception, elaboration, construction,* and *transition*. The importance of each workflow depends on the given iteration. Using an iterative approach makes the development process more robust, with demonstrable progress and frequent executable releases.

> Don't confuse RUP with UML. UML is a modeling language for software systems, while RUP is a software engineering process that provides a controlled approach to assigning and managing tasks and responsibilities within a development organization. RUP uses UML notation extensively in its guidelines and best practices, however.

RUP supports the following best practices:

- Develop iteratively – that is, adopt an iterative lifecycle model
- Manage requirements explicitly
- Use component architectures – a wise use of OOP plays an important role
- Model visually – that is, adopt UML
- Manage change in the form of a number of best practices
- Continuously verify quality, an essential aspect for minimizing risk

RUP defines a set of roles for modeling people involved in activities. One actual person can have the responsibility for many roles. For example, a 'stakeholder' role can represent customers, end users, buyers, and so on, or anyone who represents them in the developer's organization.

A *discipline* in RUP terminology is a group of homogeneous activities that shows all the different procedures needed to produce a particular set of artifacts.

RUP considers the following disciplines:

- *Business Modeling* is a discipline that aims at comprehending the structure and the dynamics of the target organization – that is, where the system will be deployed – to understand problems and identify possible solutions within such an organization.

Business modeling aims to ensure that customers, end users, and developers have a common understanding of the target organization, produce a vision of the new target organization, and based on that vision, define the processes, roles, and responsibilities of the organization in a business use-case model and a business object model.

- *Requirements.* This discipline aims to establish and maintain an agreement with customers and other stakeholders about what the system should do, the definition of the system's boundaries, an estimate of the technical contents of iterations, and the cost and time to develop the system. Part of this discipline is to define the user interface, focusing on the needs and goals of the users. As a part of this activity stakeholders are identified, together with their requirements.

- *Analysis and Design.* The objective of this discipline is to transform the requirements into a design for the future system.

- *Implementation.* The purpose of implementation is to define the organization of the code, in terms of implementation modules, to implement classes and objects in terms of components (source files, binaries, executables, and others), to test the developed components as units, and to integrate the results produced by implementers or development teams into an executable system. Unit testing is included in implementation, while system test and integration test are part of the Test discipline.

- *Test.* This discipline oversees the proper integration of all software components. It verifies that all requirements have been correctly implemented, and tries to isolate all defects prior to software deployment.

- *Deployment.* Prior to deployment the software is tested at the development site, followed by beta-testing before it is released.

- *Environment.* This discipline focuses on the activities necessary to configure the process for a project. It describes the activities required to develop guidelines to support a project. The purpose of the environment activity is to provide the software development organization with the software development environment – both processes and tools – that will support the development team.

- *Project management.* The objective of this discipline is to provide a framework for managing software-intensive projects, providing practical guidelines for planning, staffing, executing, and monitoring projects, as well as to provide a framework for managing risk. This discipline focuses mainly on the important aspects of an iterative development process: risk management, planning an iterative project, both through the lifecycle and for a particular iteration, monitoring progress of an iterative project, metrics.

- *Configuration and change management* (CM and CRM). These disciplines involve identifying configuration items, auditing changes, restricting access to those items, and defining and managing configurations of those items. A CM system is an essential and integral part of the overall development processes. It is useful for managing multiple variants of evolving software systems, tracking which versions are used in given software builds, performing builds of individual programs or entire releases according to user-defined version specifications, and enforcing site-specific development policies.

To describe what the system will do, RUP requires that a number of documents be written: a vision document, a use-case model, a number of use cases, and eventually a supplementary specification document.

- The vision document provides a complete vision for the software system under development, and supports the contract between the customer's organization and the developer's organization. It is written from the customers' perspective, focusing on the essential features of the system and acceptable levels of quality. The vision should include a description of the features that will be included, as well as those considered but not included.

- Use cases focus on describe functional requirements. A use case describes a significant amount of functionality using narrative text. The use-case model serves as a contract between the customer, the users, and the system developers for the functionality of the system, which allows customers and users to validate that the system will become what they expected, and system developers to build what is expected.

  The use-case model consists of use cases and actors. Each use case in the model is described in detail, showing step-by-step how the system interacts with the actors, and what the system does in the use case. Use cases function as a unifying thread throughout the software lifecycle: the same use-case model is used in system analysis, design, implementation, and testing. A use case should always describe the intended functionality – what a system should do – and not *how* it will be done.

- The supplementary specifications are an important complement to the use-case model, because together they capture all software requirements, both functional and nonfunctional, that need to be described, to serve as a complete software requirements specification.

Complementing these documents, the following are also developed:

- A requirements management plan. This specifies the information and control mechanisms that will be collected and used for measuring, reporting, and controlling changes to the product requirements.

- A glossary, defining a common terminology that is used consistently across the project or organization. Note that the glossary can overlap with the Ubiquitous Language[8] document if Domain-Driven Design has been used in the project.
- Use-case storyboard and user-interface prototype, both results of user-interface modeling and prototyping, which are done in parallel with other requirements activities. These documents provide important feedback mechanisms in later iterations for discovering unknown or unclear requirements.

The RUP project structure is usually represented in two dimensions:

- The horizontal axis represents time and shows the lifecycle aspects of the process.
- The vertical axis represents the disciplines (Business Management, Requirements, Analysis & Design, Implementation, Deployment, Configuration and Change Management, Project Management, and Environment).

  This is illustrated diagrammatically in Figure 1.4. The first dimension represents the dynamic aspect of the process as it is performed. This is expressed in terms of phases, iterations (initial, elaboration, construction and transition), and milestones. The second dimension represents the static aspect of the process: how it is described in terms of process components, disciplines, activities, workflows, roles, and artifacts. The graph shows how the emphasis varies over time.

The key difference between small and larger projects is the level of formality used when producing the different artifacts: project plan, requirements, classes, and so on. Furthermore, only a limited number of artifacts can be produced by small projects.

Use cases alone do not specify user interface details. Perhaps the most common objection against RUP from GUI designers is the strong bias for requirements over design aspects.

This has been addressed in a number of ways, providing custom approaches and various extensions to the standard process. As an example of these customizations, there is an optional extension to RUP called the User Experience Model, or *UX*, for handling GUI design issues (Kruchten and Ahlqvist 2001), (Conallen 2002). Building a UX model is a non-trivial task, needed only when the GUI design needs a special focus within the whole project.

---

8.   Rather than a methodology, Domain-Driven design is an approach and a set of techniques aimed at dealing with the construction of software for complicated business domains: see (Evans 2004). 'Ubiquitous Language' is one such technique, focusing on building a language that defines the domain model and is used by all team members to connect their activities, including the construction of the software.

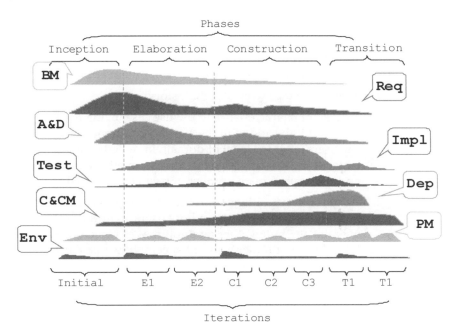

Figure 1.4   RUP Overview

User experience storyboards

The User Experience Model bridges the gap between analysis and GUI design, enriching the use case model with GUI design information. The UX model is a conceptual model that specifies visual elements (the content layer) in an abstract representation. It helps architects and GUI designers determine what will go into the UI before committing to technology details such as widget toolkits and GUI technology.

A UX model and its storyboards describe actors (user characteristics) and screens, as well as input forms, screen flows, navigation between screens, and usability requirements. The actor characteristics and usability requirements are added to the use-case descriptions. The other elements are described in UML and remain part of the UX model.

The two most important RUP disciplines relative to UX storyboards are Requirements and Analysis & Design:

- Use cases are developed in Requirements, while in Analysis & Design they are used to design the system, including the UI. RUP uses models to represent the various parts of a software system. The use-case model is the most important one to build in Requirements.

- The design models are developed in Analysis & Design. For systems with a significant amount of user interaction, the development team should also create a UX model and storyboards within that discipline. This integrates usability issues into the RUP development approach.

There are five steps to creating UX storyboards:

1. Add actor characteristics to the use case. Being non-functional, this information should be added in the special requirements section. This may include the users' average level of domain knowledge, general level of computer experience, working physical environment, frequency of use of the system, and the approximate number of users represented by an actor.

2. Add usability guidance and usability requirements to the use case. Usability guidance provides hints on how users should use the system, including average attribute values and volumes of objects, and average action use. Usability requirements might specify how fast a user must be able to do something, maximum error rates, maximum number of mouse clicks, learning times, and so on.

3. Identify UX elements. UX models use the same appearance as UML but with a different meaning: screens are rendered with UML classes, using the special stereotype «screen», navigation maps are expressed with class diagrams, screen instances with objects, and screen flow diagrams with UML sequence diagram.

4. Model the use-case flows with the UX elements.

5. Model screen navigation for the use case using UML navigation diagrams. These are essentially class diagrams with oriented links for navigation.

UX is just one possible approach to capturing GUI design and usability within the RUP.

Extreme Programming and other Agile approaches

Agile software methodologies are a radical departure from the traditional, document-heavy (usually) waterfall processes still in widespread use. These methodologies share a set of common values. They all try to find a useful compromise between informal development processes and formalized, traditional ones (Larman 2003).

Extreme Programming (Beck and Andres 2004) is perhaps the most 'extreme' of these Agile methodologies. XP is composed of the following practices:

- *Customer as a team member and on-site customer.* Development teams have one person (or a group of people) that represents the interests of the client, referred to as 'Customer.' Customer decides which features to add to the system.

- *The planning game.* Customer and developers cooperate to determine the scope of the next release. Customer defines a list of desired features for the system. Each feature is written out as a user story (see below). Developers estimate how much effort each story will take, and how much effort the team can produce in a given iteration, typically of two weeks. Customer decides which stories to implement and in what order, as well as when and how often to make available production releases of the system.

- *User stories.* These represent small features of the system that can be completed by a single developer in one iteration. Customer gives the user story a name, and broadly describes what is needed. User stories are typically written on paper cards.

- *Small releases.* Development starts with the smallest set of features that are useful. Releases are kept small by releasing early and often.

- *Simple and incremental design.* The simplest possible design that works is favored. Providing more design than is needed can be a waste of time, given that requirements can change, and is a needless cost for the project.

- *System metaphor.* Each project may have an organizing metaphor, which provides an easy to remember and guiding naming convention. This practice can be slightly confusing when adopted for GUI design: other design approaches, such as domain-driven design, suggest a focus on the core domain model to shape naming conventions and development abstractions.

- *Test-driven development (TDD).* Before writing any code, developers devise a test that defines the expected behavior of the new code, and write the test first. These are typically unit tests. Each unit test usually tests only a single class or a few classes.

- *Acceptance tests.* These are specified by Customer to test that the overall system is functioning as specified. Acceptance tests typically test the entire system, ideally automatically. When all the acceptance tests pass for a given user story, that story is considered complete.

- *Refactoring.* This is the practice of making small changes to a portion of code to improve its internal structure without changing its external behavior. This is a practice born in Smalltalk development and popularized by Martin Fowler (Fowler 1999). Refactoring fits nicely with continuous testing, because after every change, tests are run to ensure code integrity.

- *Pair programming.* All production code is written by a pair of programmers working at the same machine.

- *Collective code ownership.* No single person 'owns' a package or any portion of code. Any developer is expected to be able to work on any part of the code base at any time.

- *Continuous integration and ten-minute builds.* All changes are integrated into the code base at least daily. A build should not last more than ten minutes. A build encompasses building the whole system and running all the tests, which should be able to be run both before and after integration, and deploying the system.

- *A sustainable pace of work ('energized work').* Some XP practices advocate a forty-hour working week, to avoid the prolonged strain of work overload, usually a warning signal for a project.

- *Coding standards.* Homogeneous coding standards are applied by every member of the development team.

Official XP doctrine doesn't go into the details of user interface design, which are left to designers. A first version of the GUI design can be built up front (that is, the customer, together with developers) then used to feed the project's user stories. Alternatively, GUI design can be focused on iterations built on top of a reference framework consisting of GUI design guidelines and other constraints. Other approaches are also possible. No matter what GUI design details are chosen within the XP approach, a stable and continuous feedback loop from story creation through usability and user acceptance testing, and involving end users, is always instrumental to effective GUI design and development.

Early critics of the effectiveness of GUI designs performed with XP noted that user interface designers and usability engineers don't have a defined role within XP, and that the whole approach risks being developer-centric. However, a closer look at XP shows a number of strong points in this approach that favor sound GUI design practices. By building on the XP practices of communication, simplicity and continuous testing, usability can be achieved, not only in terms of end user acceptance and satisfaction, but also for other tenets of XP, such as implementation efficiency, developers comfort, and shared responsibility for the final product.

LUCID methodology

Classic LUCID methodology, as described for example in (Shneiderman 1998) and more recently updated, is an example of a user interface–driven approach to the whole software lifecycle, in contrast to the iterative approaches discussed previously. It is essentially a variant of the classic waterfall process, focused on usability and GUI design[9]. This is illustrated in Figure 1.5.

---

9.   See http://www.cognetics.com/lucid/

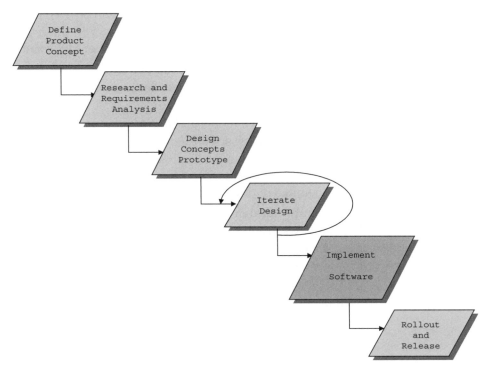

Figure 1.5   The LUCID lifecycle model

This lifecycle model can be broken down into the following elementary activities:

1. Develop the product concept:
    – Define the product concept. Begin writing down early use case diagrams.
    – Establish business objectives.
    – Set up the usability design team.
    – Identify the user population.
    – Identify technical and environmental issues.
    – Produce a staffing plan, schedule and budget.

2. Perform research and requirements analysis:
    – Partition the user population into homogeneous groups.
    – Break job activities into task units.
    – Conduct requirements analysis through construction of scenarios and participatory design.
    – Sketch the process flow for sequence of tasks.

– Identify major objects and structures that will be used in the software interface.

– Research and resolve technical issues and other constraints.

3. Design concepts and an initial prototype:
   – Create specific usability objectives based on user needs.
   – Initiate the guidelines and style guide.
   – Select a navigational model and one or more design metaphors.
   – Identify the set of key screens: log-in, major processes, and so on.
   – Develop a prototype of the key screens using a rapid prototyping tool, paper mock-ups, or other prototyping techniques.
   – Conduct initial reviews and usability tests.

4. Perform iterative design and refinement:
   – Expand key-screen prototype into a full system.
   – Conduct heuristic and expert reviews.
   – Conduct usability tests.
   – Deliver the prototype and the application specifications.

5. Implement the software:
   – Develop standard practices.
   – Manage late state change.
   – Develop on-line help, documentation and tutorials.

6. Provide rollout support:
   – Provide training and assistance.
   – Perform deployment, logging, evaluation and maintenance.

Modern software projects tend to require more flexible and rich models than this: we introduced it essentially for didactical reasons, because all main activities related to GUI development are listed in a sequentially ordered, simple arrangement.

Evolutionary Prototyping process

Many user interface design approaches use intermediate prototypes in order to produce the final GUI design more easily, reducing the risks (and costs) of the design phase[10].

The natural evolution of the prototype idea is to base the whole development around prototypes of increasing functionality. With this approach the prototype is never abandoned, but is constantly refined and expanded until it is good enough

---

10. We discuss prototyping in Chapter 3.

to be the final product. The discussion of this lifecycle approach is inspired from (McConnell 1996). The methodology is represented graphically in Figure 1.6.

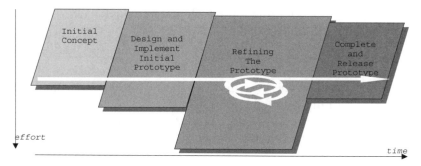

Figure 1.6   The Evolutionary Prototyping lifecycle model

This approach can be useful when requirements are changing – for example, when the customer is reluctant to commit to a defined set of requirements. It may prove useful in situations in which nobody fully understands the application domain at first, for example in advanced research projects. This model tends to produce visible progresses thanks to the steady prototype evolution.

There are however several drawbacks and potential risks when adopting this approach. First, as the application concept evolves as you develop the prototype, there are no predefined time and qualitative deadlines for ending refinement iterations. The risk is that as an important deadline approaches, the current prototype stage is declared 'good enough' to be released. Customer judgment may also not be a reliable criterion for concluding refinement iterations.

Another common risk is production of a poor-quality implementation in which code maintainability is low – if not addressed properly, continuous changes may produce code full of patches. *Feature creep* is another potential risk. When no clear and definitive requirements are set at the beginning of the development process, there is the concrete risk of adding too many new features to the prototype during its refinement.

Some guidelines help to tackle the commonest risks with this approach:

- It is essential to focus on a limited set of important aspects of the product before starting the development. These aspects will be the focus of the prototyping activity. An obvious choice is the GUI. Beginning the prototyping process with the GUI is a good way to give usability and GUI design top priority.

- The code used in evolving the prototype should be of the best possible quality, continuously refactored (Fowler et al. 2000) and enhanced, because frequent changes risk deteriorating it.

- For this reason, it is essential to avoid employing entry-level programmers when adopting this development model.

- Be sure of getting high-quality feedback from customers and end users, otherwise the prototype will prove poor and ineffective no matter what effort has been spent in refining it[11].

- Avoid evolving a throw-it-away prototype with this model. It should be clear from the initial inception of the concept whether to create a throw-it-away prototype, or to keep working on the prototype until it is refined into a final product. All members of the development team should be committed to this choice.

> Evolutionary prototyping shares many characteristics with other iterative processes, such as RUP and the family of Agile models.

1.8   UML notation

This section introduces some UML notation that will be used in the rest of the book. Readers that are knowledgeable about UML's state, interaction and class diagrams may choose to omit this section.

Class diagrams

We introduce UML class diagram notation without discussing it thoroughly: if you are not familiar with UML class diagrams, many books are available on the topic.

In this book we will use simplified class diagrams. We won't use visibility indicators ('+, #, -' symbols for showing public, protected and private fields) nor other details such as initial values.

Figure 1.7 shows a sample class diagram that illustrates the level of detail of the class diagrams used in the book.

---

11.   See the discussion on prototyping in Chapter 5.

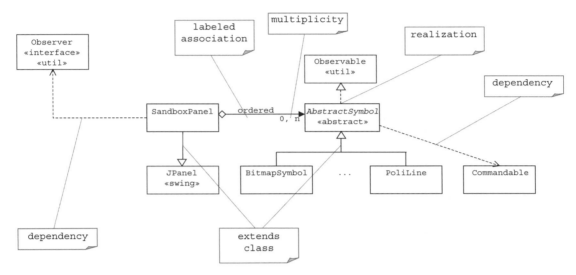

Figure 1.7   A sample class diagram

We use stereotypes – for example «swing» in the JPanel class – to represent the Java package to which the class belongs, or whether the Java type is an interface, an abstract class, or (when absent) a normal class. Figure 1.8 represents the class details we will use for documenting code.

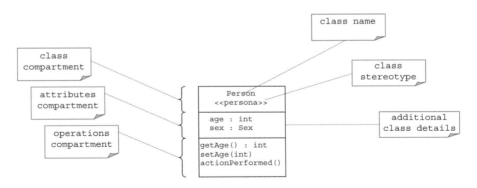

Figure 1.8   Class details

For brevity we will avoid the stereotype «abstract» for abstract classes, using only the italicized name, as in the AbstractSymbol abstract class in Figure 1.7.

We will also highlight the slight difference between realization and dependency relations:

- Realization means that a class implements behavior specified by another class. This is the common case when a class implements an interface or an abstract class.
- Dependency indicates that the implementing class *depends* on the other.

Whenever the interface Observer in Figure 1.7 changes, the SandboxPanel class may also have to change. The dependency relation is also used to express dependencies among different class packages.

Sequence diagrams

Throughout the book we will use both UML sequence and collaboration diagrams. Such diagrams, which are interchangeable, describe a behavior by means of a number of objects and the messages they exchange in a given temporal sequence.

Figure 1.9 shows an example of a sequence diagram that describes the typical behavior of a CustomListener instance that is registered for a JButton's ActionEvents.

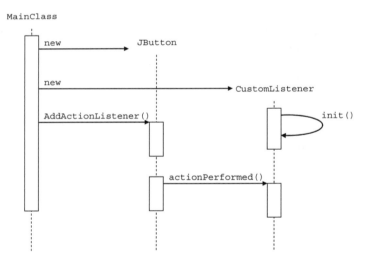

Figure 1.9   A sample sequence diagram

In the figure, an unspecified instance of the class MainClass creates a new instance of the class JButton and a new instance of the class CustomListener.

This in turn invokes the method `init()` on itself asynchronously, then invokes the method `addActionListener()` to the unspecified instance of `JButton`. After some time – not related to the previous sequence of method calls – the unspecified `JButton` instance method `init()` is invoked onto the unspecified instance of `CustomListener`.

For brevity we usually avoid indicating instance names: Figure 1.9 only specifies class names.

This section does not detail all the UML conventions used in the book for reasons of space – we have not mentioned collaboration diagrams, even though we will use them. Given the ubiquity of UML, we leave the interested reader to conssult one of the many sources available in literature or on the Web.

State diagrams

UML state diagrams are useful for describing the internal state transitions within a GUI.

Figure 1.10 shows an example of an UML state transition diagram.

As shown in the legends in the diagram, the initial state is indicated with a jagged arrow, while state transitions are indicated by arrows tagged with the event that triggers the transition from one state to the other. States are drawn as circles. Hence the state of the class described by the diagram in Figure 1.10 gets to State B after Event x happens when the class is in its initial state. Other events might change the internal state of the class, either restoring the initial state again or bringing it to a final state.

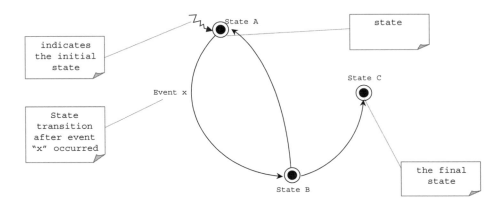

Figure 1.10   State changes within a class

1.9   Summary

This chapter has presented some introductory discussions about effective software and GUI design. In particular:

- We discussessd the important concept of focusing on end users throughout the whole development process.
- We illustrated a general decomposition of GUI implementations based on functional criteria.
- Tool selection (the topic of Chapter 11) was presented briefly.
- We briefly introduced organizational aspects related to UI development.
- We discussed lifecycle issues, showing some design methodologies focused on usability and GUI-centered development.
- We introduced UML use case diagrams as a means of documenting systems from an end user's perspective.
- We also introduced sequence and state UML diagrams.

2 Introduction to User Interface Design

The field of user interface design and human-computer interaction is complex and vast. It has many different contributors and perspectives, and still lacks a uniform descriptive language. It is fragmented into different approaches and practices, a fact that stems directly from the very nature of human-computer interaction (HCI): the presence of the human component makes it impossible to develop an exact foundational theory. HCI, its derived design guidelines and criteria are thus based mainly on empirical evidence and practical principles.

The term 'HCI' was adopted in the mid-1980s. HCI is an interdisciplinary practice that aims at improving the utility, usability, effectiveness and efficiency of interactive computer systems. SIGCHI, the special interest group in HCI, defined it as 'a discipline concerned with the design, evaluation and implementation of interactive computing systems for human use and with the study of major phenomena surrounding them[1].'

In this chapter we introduce some HCI concepts that are fundamental to the professional design of user interfaces. The chapter is structured as follows:

2.1, The human factor discusses the role of people in the design process.

2.2, Display organization introduces the esthetics of GUI design, and discusses ways in which an application can interact with its users.

2.3, Interaction styles goes into more details about human-computer interaction, and presents the five major categories of human-computer interaction.

2.4, Conceptual frameworks for UI design describes a set of coherent concepts that structure the different phases of development of UIs, and which provide a reliable and proven mindset for organizing the design, thus reducing risks and improving quality.

2.5, Assessing the quality of a GUI describes ways in which testing of user interfaces can be conducted and its results collected.

---

1. Many disciplines contribute to HCI: computer science, cognitive psychology, ergonomics, social and organizational psychology, design, engineering, anthropology, sociology, philosophy and linguistics.

For simplicity we use the term 'GUI' as a general term to refer to any graphical user interface. In this chapter we distinguish between different classes of graphical user interfaces that are gathered under the common name of GUIs when applicable.

2.1 The human factor

We begin our quick tour of HCI with end users and how they perform actions.

A model of interactive systems – seven stages and two gulfs

One of the simplest approaches to modeling interactive systems is to describe the various actions users go through when faced with the task of using an interactive system (Norman 1998). Users:

1. Form a goal
2. Form an intention
3. Specify an action
4. Execute the action
5. Perceive the system state
6. Interpret the system state
7. Evaluate the outcome

The user first forms a conceptual intention from their goal – for example, deleting an item in the application shown in Figure 2.1 – then tries to adapt this intention to the functionality provided by the user interface. From these commands, as perceived by the user, they execute the action – for example by dragging an element in the tree to delete it, as Figure 2.1 shows. The user then tries to under-stand the outcomes of the action. This is particularly important in computer systems, where the inner workings are hidden and users have to guess the internal state from few artificial hints (Norman 1998). The last three stages listed above help the user to evolve their idea of the system. The entire interaction process is performed in such cycles of action and evaluation: by interpreting the outcome of their actions, the user refines their mental model of the system.

Action and evaluation are often illustrated by means of the *gulf* metaphor, after (Hutchins et al. 1986):

- *The gulf of execution.* This phrase describes the mismatch between a user's intentions and the allowable actions: for example, a user might be used to removing items by dragging them into a wastebasket, but in some applications items may be not draggable. *Gulf of execution* describes the practical difficulty of performing tasks with a GUI.

- *The gulf of evaluation.* This phrase refers to the difference between a user's expectations and the system's representation. Referring to Figure 2.1, the user observes that even if an item can be dragged onto the wastebasket icon, the intended delete operation did not work, because the application displayed the message shown in Figure 2.2. *Gulf of evaluation* describes the difficulty users experience in evaluating the outcome of an action they perform with a GUI.

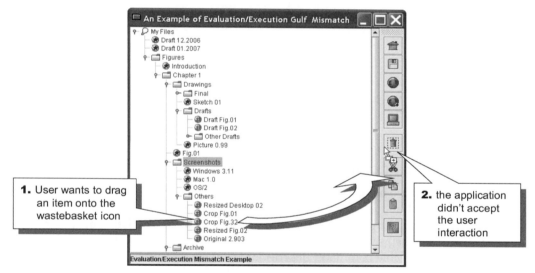

Figure 2.1   The gulf of execution: execution mismatch

The cognitive distance between two such worlds – the user's and the software's – corresponds to the potential mismatch between the way a person thinks about a task and the way it is represented in the GUI (Preece 1994). This mismatch, and the distance between the two gulfs, can be reduced by designing the user interface in a way that reduces the differences between the users' goals and the GUI's state and form.

As an aside, messages such as that shown in Figure 2.2 are rather intrusive. A better choice would be to signal the error with a less intrusive form of feedback, such as changing the mouse pointer shape or producing a beep.

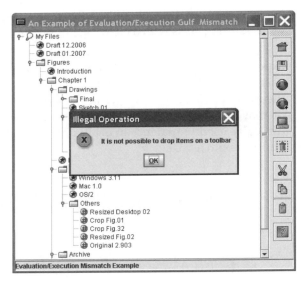

Figure 2.2   *The evaluation gulf: evaluation mismatch*

Developers are part of the design process

So far we have only described the user's perspective of the GUI. We have not yet talked about the designers and the programmers who design the application, including the user interface. Just like end users, designers and programmers also have their own vision of an application. What for the end user might be an incomprehensible command description, such as *clear action stack*, may be an 'obvious' choice for the programmer that implemented it. A graphical design inspired by some new award-winning product might represent an accolade for the designer, but a nightmare for the developer to implement and an awkward thing for an end user to work with.

Many of the problems involved in creating effective user interfaces stem from the differences between the designer's and the end user's viewpoints. Designers can sometimes become so absorbed in their work that they lose focus and overlook the importance of the user's needs.

Ideally, the designer is the mediator between users and developers. Unfortunately professional GUI designers are thin on the ground and often expensive to hire. Hence developers often fill the role of designers, especially in small and medium sized organizations. This creates a potential problem: such developers-turned-designers often adopt their habitual programmer's mental model unconsciously, producing less usable GUIs as a result. On the other hand, fortunately, the effect of good design is contagious. Design guidelines, which are often promoted by organizations that can afford a team of full-time professional designers, are slowly making their way in everyday software, not just that produced by large corporations.

The refinement of a user's model of an application is often distorted by accidental interaction, bad design or software bugs. Even developers themselves, as users of other software, sometimes struggle to understand the internal model of a buggy application. Suppose that a developer uses an application that shuts down unpredictably, corrupts data, or causes other serious trouble. They will of course try to bypass the internal states that cause such harmful behavior. To do that in the absence of implementation documentation, they must develop a mental model of the application's inner workings. Computer programs, contrary to other types of technology, are both complex and inherently abstract. A mechanic can guess from the weird noise a car makes that it probably has a problem with its suspension, but even a seasoned developer cannot determine the actual implementation behind a GUI merely by using it.

End users only have the direct experience of the GUI with which they are interacting, coupled with their previous knowledge, to work out what is going on inside an application. Humans need semantic models to enable them interact with the world sanely, and always build such models, even unconsciously. Users act like the early philosophers, trying to make sense of an incomprehensible world using only their current and past experience – it is common to hear them explaining how an application works in their own terms. As personal computers have been around for decades, many people are accustomed to concepts such as files, databases and mouse gestures[2].

In some ways this is a problem – ideally we should be able to use a complex device such as a car or a software application without having to be aware of its inner working, although a minimum coupling with the underlying technology is unavoidable. A professional GUI design should therefore start with an abstract model in the designer's head. In addition, what might seem a natural choice for the designer can later reveal awkward details that are difficult to understand and to employ by users. It is important therefore for designers to adhere to a conceptual model that is as close as possible to the prior knowledge of the intended end user population.

---

2.   The term *gesture* in HCI denotes a single basic interaction performed by the user. Usually it refers to mouse-based systems in which sequences of gestures will make the software perform certain operations. Sequences of gestures can be organized in a specific syntax, such as 'press right button-drag mouse-release right button.'

To recap, we have highlighted some important issues:

- Software is abstract. Good user interfaces are those that communicate their internal state to users effectively, encouraging the seven-stage cognitive sequence described on page 32. In computer applications, the inner workings are hidden, and human beings have to figure out the internal state from few artificial hints. Such hints should be coherent, otherwise the GUI won't be successful: it will be difficult to use, producing convoluted mental models that are hard to remember, inducing a negative response from users. Hence it is important to develop a sound conceptual model to stand behind the GUI. The basic concepts, visible items, their interaction, names and everything else should be carefully thought through at the design stage.

- People use conceptual representations of reality based on their current and past experience. Consequently, different mental models of the same application exist in the minds of its designers, its developers and its end users. It is important for designers to be aware of the different mental models involved in the development and subsequent use of a user interface as a *social artifact* – something that will be used by more than one person.

We mentioned that cognitive psychology was a contributing discipline to HCI. The next section discusses some simple cognitive models that underlie well-designed user interfaces.

Short term memory and cognitive modeling

We will now discuss some basic principles of cognitive modeling, and include some practical advice on their application to HCI design. In particular, we discuss briefly a useful – although rather crude – model of human memory, and some of its implications for interface design.

In human beings, *short-term memory* (STM) is a limited form of memory that acts as a 'buffer' for new information, used to process perceptual input. Empirical studies have shown that humans usually have an STM capacity of between five and nine items. Such items can be single objects or coherent chunks of information. The size of non-atomic pieces of information that can be stored in STM depends on the individual's familiarity with the subject, but usually the information survives no longer than 15–30 seconds.

You can try this for yourself: it is relatively easy to remember seven random colors, but it is not easy to remember seven Spanish words unless you speak Spanish – not to mention seven Urdu words. STM is very volatile. Distractions, external 'information noise' or other interrupting tasks quickly disrupt its contents.

The other type of memory is *long-term memory* (LTM), more stable and with far greater capacity, but with slower access than STM. A major problem with LTM is the difficulty of the retrieval phase. Many of us use mnemonic aids to access LTM, such as mental associations for remembering a personal code or password.

STM influences the efficiency of an HCI interaction. Interactions that can be processed using only STM are easier and faster to accomplish than those that require LTM or some external cognitive help. Complex interactions are made more difficult by the need to maintain a data context throughout the whole process, using working memory and STM.

GUIs should be designed as much as possible to let users work with STM, but this kind of memory has its own limits as well. To illustrate these ideas, here is an example of the pitfalls of placing excessive trust in STM.

An example of STM misuse

Our example GUI here is designed to allow users to reserve a train seat. It is organized as a sequence of dialog in which only partial information is shown at any one time. Such an interaction style is often referred to as a *wizard*, a term popularized by Microsoft's extensive use of it.

Our GUI has been designed only for this example, and is not intended to be an example of good user interface design – see for example our weird use of tabbed panes!

In the first dialog we are asked for the basic details for our trip, as shown in Figure 2.3.

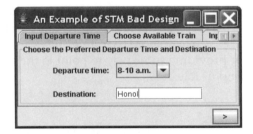

Figure 2.3   *An example of excessive STM burden: entering some data*

After some input, such as reserving a window seat, food options and so on, we are presented a reservation code, as shown in Figure 2.4. This is meant to help the user to choose between different reservations. Users can remember this sort of code for varying times.

A recap screen is then presented, and the user is asked to choose one reservation, prompting for the data of choice (as shown in Figure 2.5).

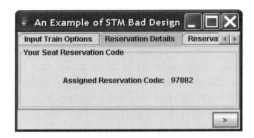

Figure 2.4   An example of excessive STM burden: memorizing the reservation code

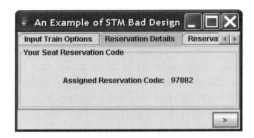

Figure 2.5   An example of excessive STM burden: retrieving data from STM

Naturally, few users can remember this information, and the wizard will probably produce the message in Figure 2.6. At this point the user's STM memory has been overloaded. Clearly, more cognitive aids, such as displaying a list of reservations made, or providing some way to point to them, would make the GUI much more robust and usable.

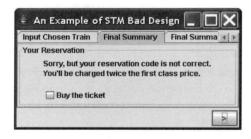

Figure 2.6   An example of excessive STM burden: negative feedback

Nobody design GUIs like this one any longer, but such design inconveniences were frequent before the widespread use of mature user interface solutions and the advent of direct manipulation techniques. In this situation the GUI shouldn't rely exclusively on the user's short term memory. But consider the case in which the client device cannot support a rich user interface, such as a mobile phone. Even in such a case, an alert message, such as 'Please print confirmation for your records…' is needed.

These problems have lead to the widely-used practice of exploiting the context for selecting and manipulating information. For example, users are now familiar with contextual menus, usually activated by right-clicking on an object, or some other platform-dependent gesture, that make all the possible commands for the selected item in the given context available. There is then no need for extra memory load on the part of the user. A designer should always try to design the user interface to make users work as much as possible with STM, as this lightens their memory load and makes the interaction speedier and less error-prone.

In contrast, something like a Unix command-line interface needs continuous access to LTM or some external cognitive aid. It is not uncommon for Unix novices users to use post-it or paper notes to remember commands and their syntax, or the sequences of commands required to carry out a certain task. With the advent of GUIs, this situation has changed. Now designers have a powerful set of tools for designing expressive, easier-to-use interfaces.

Another means of avoiding placing an excessive memory burden on users is to adopt a standard and consistent design. In this way, users can reuse the knowledge acquired from use of other parts of the GUI, or of other GUIs the adopt the same standards. Later we will show how expensive providing an arbitrary menu organization, with an incoherent command organization can be in user memory.

In conclusion, STM is a valuable aid to well-designed interfaces. STM requires concentration, so in general users should be in a proper environment for maximizing their performance. Users should feel at ease with the application, and have a predictable idea of how it works, without the fear of making catastrophic errors or of excessive time pressures. We cannot, of course, control the environment in which the application will be used, but we can consider it in our design.

UI design can be organized around basic criteria that are derived from cognitive modeling-based human psychology considerations: try to eliminate distractions, minimize user anxiety, provide feedback about task progress, and either avoid errors or handle them gracefully.

Interacting with human beings

In this section we discuss some practical issues related to interacting with users.

Response time

Even a brief introduction to cognitive modeling would be incomplete without mention of an important dimension of a user's experience when interacting with a computer system. *Response time* is a significant factor, in that slow response time is a cause of errors and user frustration. This is particularly true for Java-based applications, where performance can be a serious bottleneck[3].

Response time affects users in different ways. Their expectations and past experience play an important role in their reaction. If a user is accustomed to a task completing in a given amount of time, both excessive or too rapid a completion can confuse them. Short response times also aid more easy exploration of the GUI where such behavior is encouraged, for example by undo-able actions and low error costs.

Balancing human control and automation

It is often useful to provide automation of some features in an application, but this takes away some control from users. People become frustrated and nervous if they feel they don't have full control over the work they are doing. It is therefore important to provide the *sense* of control to end users.

In contrast, by definition a GUI should provide a high-level, easy-to-use view of an application's services and data, hiding irrelevant details from the user. A critical factor in a successful GUI design is determining the balance between automation and user control, between showing meaningful details and hiding the rest, and in doing so adaptively depending on the particular user. For example, a user may want to skip some automatic feature by taking full control of it as they become confident with the application.

It is useful to assess the levels of control that can be exerted in a GUI. This helps to make explicit in the design the layers of automation that can be provided, such as defining macros, providing wizards for most common operations, and so on. Nevertheless, a computer program is an inherently limited artifact, in that it cannot take into account all possible situations, only a restricted set of combinations thought out in advance.

Consequently, balancing human control over automation is a typical trade-off of GUI design. Providing fully-automated GUIs could be too risky, especially when the task is a critical one, such as managing a chemical plant, and there are many

---

3.   In general, interpreted bytecode and the overhead of a Java virtual machine only impacts the overall performances of Java applications to a minor degree, thanks to sophisticated technologies like 'just-in-time' compilers, garbage collectors and various other optimizations. However, GUI technologies like Swing implement low-level graphical details and infrastructure interactions as fine-grained Java objects, requiring a high number of runtime objects just to implement simple user interfaces.

independent variables that may cause unforeseen behavior. On the other hand, allowing users to have a too much control could create GUIs that are too difficult or even dangerous to use. When exposing too much detail that can be manipulated in a GUI, the risk arises that users could modify some valid data or use the interface in unanticipated ways.

To recap, in designing a correct level of automation, much depends on the user population and the nature of the application domain. For a business-oriented application, some simple rules can be applied:

- For the same application, always provide two routes through the UI: one for experienced users, with more control and less automation, and a simplified (that is, more automated) set of functions for inexperienced users.

- Provide warning messages when critical data is being manipulated directly, even by experienced users.

- Whenever possible avoid automated features and the pro-active behavior exemplified by some 'agent-like' applications ("Hi, I'm Tom, I'll check the mail for you"). This latter kind of approach hasn't proved successful and also can quite expensive to implement. Proactivity is still an untamed beast[4].

Showing the application's internal state

Users build their own system model unconsciously while interacting with the GUI. It is essential to provide the right hints and to correctly signal the system state to the user. This can be achieved using various techniques. Those most commonly used are modifying the mouse pointer or using some form of animation:

- *Changing the pointer shape*. Changes of pointer shape are widely employed for signaling an application's internal state, for example a 'busy' pointer, and currently-available operations, for example resizing a window by dragging its corner. The Java Look and Feel guidelines, which we introduce in the next chapter, prescribe the use of the 'busy' pointer for any operation that takes more than two seconds.

- *Animation*. can be used to show both the progress of an operation, often by means of a progress bar component, or generic activity, using for example an ad-hoc animation. The Java Look and Feel guidelines suggest that a progress indicator should be updated at least every 4 seconds. The example GUI in Figure 2.7 below shows a progress bar that can be set to update at various

---

4.   At a recent international conference on autonomous agents the speaker (an authority in the field, praising the many benefits of proactivity) was interrupted abruptly by his laptop crashing. It took many embarrassing minutes to recover his presentation. It turned out to be an unforeseen interaction between the screen saver (the proactive, yet unintelligent agent) and an operating system patch he had loaded the night before the presentation.

intervals in the range of 1 to 4 seconds. The task is completed in one minute. Readers are encouraged to download and try this sample GUI to directly familiarize themselves with update times.

Figure 2.7   Testing the update time for a progress indicator

One controversial notion that should be considered is the use of *modes* in an application GUI. Modes are specific states or an application that affect some of the user interface behavior. A designer or developer can think of them as contexts in which some previous user interaction changed the meaning of current actions. For example, on a cellphone the 'hang up' red button has different functionalities, depending on whether a call is in progress or not. An application can behave in a completely different way in different modes in response to the same user input. Design guidelines normally discourage the use of modal interfaces, or even ban them altogether. Modes are difficult to manage by users and easily confuse them.

It is vital to show explicitly the current mode within the GUI. This is usually done by modifying the pointer shape, for example in drawing software when a specific graphic tool is selected from the palette, or by means of toggled buttons, status bar icons or messages.

Techniques for getting the user's attention

Techniques for getting the user's attention are employed widely in user interfaces. These techniques are derived from empirical studies and can be summarized as follows:

- *Animation*. Animation is often used to express the internal state of the GUI, showing work in progress or generically signaling activity. Often this latter use is the only one suggested by official design guidelines. However, flashing items on the screen easily capture a user's attention – often too easily: this technique can be disturbing and invasive.

- *Color*. Like animation, this technique should be used carefully. As with animation, the Java Look and Feel uses few system colors. Too many colors tend to produce confusing GUIs.

- *Audio cues.* This technique, used carefully, can be very effective[5].
- *Bold fonts and other graphic adornments.* When used carefully and coherently, such graphic conventions can be effective without being disrupting. As we will see later, the Java Look and Feel design guidelines adopt some simple graphic conventions to signal importance.

Relying on professional design guidelines avoids many obvious errors. This is especially true for attention-catching devices such as flashy labels, colors and the like. All major UI design guidelines provide reliable but noninvasive mechanisms for catching user attention.

Some general principles for user interface design

Before going further it is useful to recap what we have said so far. Here we distil the previous discussions into a few high–level general principles that should always be kept in mind when designing a user interface:

- *Minimize the load on users.* Reduce the memory and cognitive load on users by providing informative feedback, memory aids and other cognitive support. Ensure that a work session can be interrupted for a few minutes without losing the work in progress, as users are only able to focus attention for a limited time.
- *Ensure overall flexibility and error recovery.* Flexibility is essential when dealing with users. Human beings make errors: providing mechanisms for reversing actions allow users to explore the GUI free from the anxiety of being trapped in an unrecoverable mistake.
- *Provide user customization.* The interface should be customizable by the user. Flexibility also includes the provision of different use mechanisms for different classes of users: novices can use wizards or other simplified means for easy interaction, while expert users can take advantage of keyboard accelerators and other shortcuts, all within the same GUI. For specific users, such as those with disabilities, such flexibility could provide the only way in which they could use the application.
- *Follow standards to preserve consistency.* Many standards and guidelines exist for interactions, abbreviations, terminology and so on, such as the Java Look and Feel Design Guidelines (Java L&F Design Guidelines 2001), (Advanced Java L&F Design Guidelines 2001). Such user interface design standards are essential for the support of consistency between applications. They ensure professional quality while reducing the design effort.

    Consistency within a single GUI is even more important than correctly adopting a set of GUI design guidelines: for example, in labeling, terminology,

---

5. Audio clues are supported in J2SE's Swing from Version 1.4.

graphical conventions, component layout and so on. In this book we will discuss many such guidelines and principles, as well as systematic approaches to software design that are oriented towards consistency.

User-centered design

Perhaps the single most cited rule in user interface guidelines is *'know thy user.'* Without a reliable model of the end-user population, a design may be too general, relying only on the designer's, possibly restricted, cognitive model of an application's use[6].

A good designer not only knows the target users, but *thinks* like them. Learning to think as a user is essential for building a high-quality GUI.

Taking the user into account in the design process leads to an approach known as *user-centered design*, in which users are central to both the early design process and to later testing and evaluation. A user-centered technique known as *participatory design* stresses the active involvement of users throughout the design process, especially in the evaluation phase.

User-centered design focuses on three concepts:

- *Users.* Usually the following general user categories apply:
  - Novice users
  - Intermediate users
  - Expert users
- Users' *tasks.* The most common categories are:
  - Frequent tasks – designers should optimize these tasks
  - Infrequent tasks – such tasks can be assigned a lower priority than frequent ones as regards design/development resources and time
  - Critical tasks – those that should be engineered most carefully in the GUI
- *Context.* In what context will users be performing their tasks?

The involvement of end users in GUI design should be carefully managed. Users are not GUI designers, and their interaction should be managed so that their role in the design process is mostly reactive, providing feedback over proposed designs rather than producing new designs from scratch. The use of a prototypes is central to early design iterations (design-evaluate-refine): such prototypes can that function both as the current GUI representation as well as its requirements documentation. Prototyping is an important activity in the design of high-quality user interfaces, and we discuss it in Chapter 5.

---

6.   The concept of 'users' should also include those whose activity is affected by the software, such as system administrators, support staff, customers, etc. We refer to these as *stakeholders*.

In the following sections we discuss the two major issues in user-centered design: users and tasks.

User analysis

User analysis is a vital part of the design process. The output of user analysis is a model of the end-user population. Such a model is usually a decomposition of the intended user population into homogeneous classes identified by some characteristic such as domain knowledge, skill level, role, system knowledge and so on. Such a model, and its underlying knowledge of the user population, is often documented by means of *user profiles*. This kind of information is always needed in any GUI design process, even at an informal level.

An example of a user profile – for a cellphone Java music player – could be the following:

- Buys a new wireless game or ring-tone at least every month.
- Buys at least one CD every two months.
- Is proficient with high-functionality cellphones.
- Is aged 16-30.
- Uses an MP3 player, possibly combined with a cellphone.
- Listens to/watches the following radio station/music shows: …

   (etc.)

As far as possible designers must study representative users directly, possibly in their workplace, to take into account their typical working environment.

Task design and analysis

The concept of *tasks* is an important one in GUI design. Tasks implicitly define users, not just the details of the actions needed to accomplish a certain result within the GUI. For example, the task of creating a sophisticated glossary in a word processor automatically underlies an expert user, while checking e-mail is a task that can be performed by any kind of user and should be thought of as characteristic of novice ones.

Tasks are used also for usability testing. To test specific parts of the GUI, designers create particular tasks the users have to accomplish in the testing environment. Task analysis studies the way in which users accomplish such tasks while using the system. This analysis produces a list of the tasks users want to achieve using the GUI, together with the information needed and the intermediate steps needed for completing them. Task analysis is be performed by interviewing users and by observing the way they complete preset tasks.

For example, suppose we are designing a music manager applet for J2ME-enabled devices, such as that shown in Figure 2.8.

Figure 2.8   A music manager applet for J2ME wireless phones

Examples of the tasks and subsequent task realizations for this kind of GUI may be:

- Convert an MP3 into a ring-tone:
  - from the main menu, select **Format Conversions**
  - in the 'Format Conversions' screen, select the input MP3 file
  - in the 'Format Conversions' screen, select the **Export** option
  - in the 'Export' screen, select the ring-tone format and rename the resulting file
- Send a piece of music to another cell phone:
  - from the main menu, select **Clipboard**
  - from the 'Clipboard' screen, select the desired file
  - from the 'Clipboard' screen, select the **Send** option
  - in the 'Send' dialog, select the **Another cell phone** option
  - in the 'Send to another cell phone' screen, select the recipient's number or type it using the numeric pad
- Configure the application preferences:
  - from the main menu, select **Preferences**

Tasks depends on the GUI – the same task performed on two different GUIs may result in completely different task realizations.

Simplified thinking aloud

This technique prescribes testing the GUI with users who are asked to express their thoughts verbally while interacting with the system. An observer can use such additional insight into user's interaction process to identify unforeseen misunderstandings in the interface design. Users are usually videotaped while interacting with a GUI, as this allows better analysis.

A simplified, more practical version of this technique involves observers who take notes while the user is interacting with the GUI. Precision and exhaustiveness are traded for economic feasibility and practicality. Even in this simplified version, this type of test can reveal extremely useful information. Testers need to be aware of the added strain on users that this type of testing usually entails, and manage it accordingly, for example by limiting the duration of individual tests to a few minutes.

Graphical user interfaces are all about the visual arrangement of information. The next section moves the focus of our discussion from the human user to the computer, discussing the visual organization of graphical user interfaces.

2.2 Display organization

The organization of the display is clearly one of the most important aspects of the design of a graphical user interface.

It can help a developer to think of display organization as a language made up of the following basic constructs, which can be combined together to produce very complex display organizations:

- *Composition*. Display organizations can be nested into others, recursively. Readers familiar with software design patterns know this mechanism as the Composite Pattern (Gamma et al. 1994).

- *Separation*. Specific portions of the display can be separated from others for semantic reasons. Static or dynamic separators, using rules or other graphic cues such as different windows, resizable areas in the same window and so on can be used. For example, a set of check boxes can be grouped and separated from other items with additional space.

- *Layout strategy*. This is the final element of our hierarchy of visually nested area organizations. We will discuss strategies for laying out the items in our GUI below.

- *Temporal sequence*. The display content depends upon external input such as user interaction or task completion. Such temporal 'screenplay' should be carefully thought through by the designer.

Layout strategies for a display area can be of two types:

- *High-density*, for conveying an high volume of information.

- Its opposite, which we call the *limited information* strategy, in which the aim is to reduce the amount of displayed data.

Such strategies are complementary and should always be used together in the design of every window or portion of it. Depending on the individual case, one or other will be dominant, but it is essential to take care with the balance of both. Interfaces that are either too cluttered, or too uncommunicative, are both hard to use. Figure 2.9 shows an example of a design in which the high density strategy is predominant. This interface has been designed mainly for expert users.

The limited information strategy is also used in the GUI in Figure 2.9 – see the use of drop-down menus, configurable areas, collapsing items and so on.

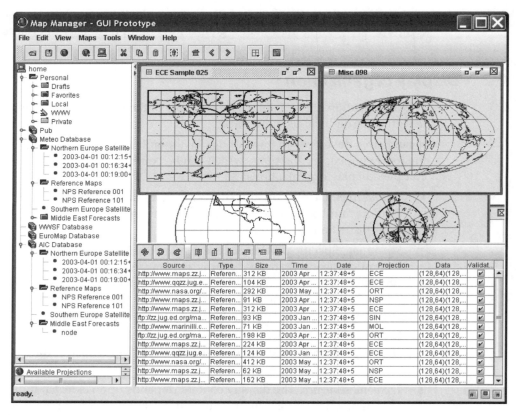

Figure 2.9   A predominantly high-density display organization

A high-density layout strategy can be usually achieved using three general mechanisms:

- *Tabular organization*. Data is organized in a list of (possibly) structured values. Typical examples are spreadsheets and database grids.

- *Hierarchical organization*. Information is structured into a tree-like hierarchy, such as in the file system's graphical representation shown on the left of Figure 2.9.

- *Graphical organization*. Data is represented graphically in the form of a chart or diagram.

A limited information layout strategy instead aims at minimizing the displayed data. There are several approaches to controlling the volume of displayed data:

- *Step-by-step interaction*. Data is serialized and shown in stages separated in time. A classic example of this approach is the wizard.

- *Details on demand*. Optional data is only shown on user request. A common example of this strategy is dialogs that have a **More details** button that enlarge the dialog to provide further information. This type of mechanism should be used with care, however, because users prefer predictable windows and may feel uncomfortable with a GUI that changes its appearance too much.

- *Minimize irrelevant information*. There are many ways to minimize data; for example by shading it. Figure 2.10 shows a contextual menu in which some commands are grayed out to signal that they are currently unavailable. We often take such features of user interfaces for granted, but think how frustrating it is for the user to select a command only to be slapped in the face with an error message because the command is currently unavailable.

Figure 2.10   Disabling unavailable information at its simplest

These general techniques can be applied to many parts of the GUI – not just to menus, but also dialogs, radio buttons and so on.

Stated in this way, however, such principles are of limited help. We will see more concrete examples of the use of these ideas in the following chapters.

Esthetic considerations

Undoubtedly, professional-designed GUIs are pleasant to look at, but wrong assumptions are often made about the meaning of the term 'pleasant.' One of the common pitfalls in GUI design is to get stuck into creating an excessively elaborate visual experience on the (wrong) assumption that more is better. GUIs should be as least astonishing as possible. A successful GUI is one that is barely noticed, that works smoothly, swiftly and predictably.

I like to call such counterproductive and 'fancy' GUIs 'Louis XIV-style user interfaces' – this is often the case with novice or amateur designers who indulge in too much baroque design. This is also a common error even for seasoned designers. In fact, given the current pace of software releases, the most obvious and visible place to add new features, and so justify the new release, is always the user interface. Hence, *feature creep* is often concentrated in the GUI[7].

> Feature creep is a well-known phenomenon, referred to as *featuritis* in the classic *The Mythical Man-Month* (Brooks 1995): 'The besetting temptation of the architect… is to overload the product with features of marginal utility, at the expense of performance and even of ease of use.'

On the other hand, esthetics *are* important. Too often developers take little interest in the visual appearance of their user interfaces, producing unusable designs as a result. Some find details of appearance such as buttons size, overall visual balance and the rest boring. Such developers are mostly implementation-driven, tending to automate the user interface as much as possible, implicitly seeing it as a dull, unnecessary activity. Unfortunately there is no substitute for human design: devices such as dialogs that automate the layout of the data they contain without semantic input can seem attractive, but produce poor user interfaces.

On the other hand, such appearance details can be hidden using wise use of object-oriented software architecture[8], in which you get all the benefits of a professional visual appearance with only a little extra work. We will show many techniques for promoting such advantages, from general approaches to practical, reusable classes.

This book promotes an *industrial* approach to user interface design, especially as regards visual appearance. Our idea of a good-looking user interface is one that adheres to official guidelines, is sober and usable as much as is economically feasible and provides extras only in a limited, 'withdrawn' fashion. This is the reason why, for example, Java libraries for advanced graphics handling, such as the 2D package, are covered only marginally. Some examples of visual details in a professional design are shown in Figure 2.11.

---

7.   You can find many examples of wrongly-designed GUIs – not only limited to the purely visual aspects – by searching the Web for 'User Interface Hall of Shame.'
8.   Alternatively, GUI layout may be done in a semi-automatic way, in which the semantic data that describes the layout of the visual components is stored externally, for example in property files or some special field derived from the class documentation or metadata.

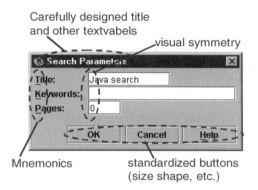

Figure 2.11   A simple dialog design

The interested reader can see (Mullet and Sano 1995) for an introduction to the art of visual design of software user interfaces, or the classic trilogy from Edward Tufte (Tufte 1990), (Tufte 1997), (Tufte 2001).

Abstract-Augmented Area for GUIs

Abstract-Augmented Area for GUIs (A3GUI or A3GUI) is a term that describes a simple approach to the definition and general management of graphical user interfaces. The key idea is to organize a GUI and all its underling dynamics conceptually – user interactions, intended behavior, design requisites, constraints, implementation and so on – by *areas*, that is, the 'real estate' of our GUIs.

A3GUI represents a GUI as a set of *augmented areas*. These areas are abstractions over the real GUI that help the design, implementation, testing or any other aspect of the GUI in which we are interested. A3GUI can be thought of as describing a general mindset that is independent of the chosen UI design approach.

By the term *real GUI*, we mean one concrete execution of our application at a given time. This will in turn depend on the surrounding context that may affect our GUI, such as the current user, the OS on which the application is running, and so on. All such context data can change the GUI's behavior and appearance for a given execution in a given situation. For example, a GUI may change depending on the given locale, or show only specific features to specific users, depending on their roles. We all deal with GUIs by managing abstractions of real executions.

Augmented areas, which for brevity we refer to merely as *areas*, are pictorial representations of specific facets of the GUI (whole windows, panels or single widgets) augmented with other information. Areas can be represented as paper sketches, in electronic form as drawings, diagrams, bundles of files, UML 2.0 diagrams and so on, or in any other convenient way. Areas can be visually nested inside other areas, can be related to other areas, and documentation attached to them, such as requirements, documents, the implementation's Java classes, and so on. The need is to provide a pictorial representation, a unique ID and an explicit or implicit set of abstractions we are representing throughout the area in the real GUI. The A3GUI concept also happens to dovetail nicely with modern OO GUI toolkits such as those used to build Java GUIs.

The type and level of abstractions really depend on our purpose. For example, Figure 2.12 shows a number of possible abstractions for a real GUI in a specific execution context.

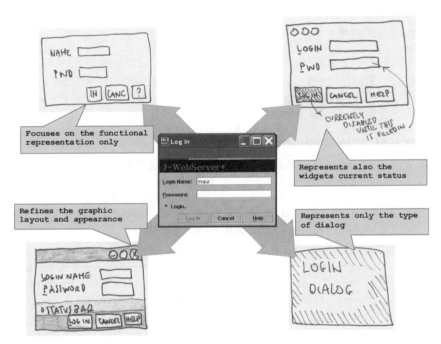

Figure 2.12   Some possible abstractions over a given GUI execution

A3GUI provides a formalized yet flexible framework for designing and managing GUIs that helps to solve the conceptual twists that we commonly face when defining GUIs at various levels of detail.

An example

Suppose we want to design a very simple GUI to display the bank accounts of specific customers. We want to provide a list of all transactions recorded for a given customer (which for simplicity are chosen outside our GUI). Only certain users may have access to transaction details: for example, if a clerk is inspecting a customer's account, we don't want to allow access to customer-sensitive data.

For simplicity we can think our GUI as having only two requirements:

- (R1) Our GUI has to show a list of all available transaction for a given customer.
- (R2) Depending on the role of the current user, only a small subset of a transaction's details can be seen.

We start by devising the following areas[9] – see Figure 2.13.

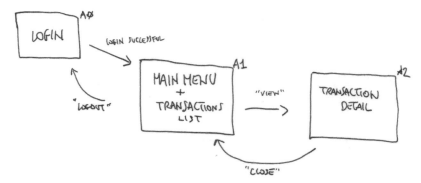

Figure 2.13   *A possible GUI representation in three areas (adopting functional abstractions)*

The following abstractions relate to each pictorial representation shown in Figure 2.13:

- A0 represents the login functionality each user has to accomplish to access the rest of the application.
- A1 represents the access to all the functionalities provided by the main menu, and also provides the list of available transactions to the user (fulfilling R2).
- A2 represents access to the transaction details, available only for the given role.

The diagram also shows some relationships between the various areas. These relationships express informally the intended navigation between the various areas. We will use the same notation to express navigational relationships between areas in the following figures also.

---

9.   In this example we use 'A' as a prefix for areas ids to specify that these areas came from analysis, and are meant to capture requisites and decompose functional behavior only.

The areas shown in Figure 2.13 were the result of a functional refinement activity – we can think these areas as roughly equivalent to the use cases for the GUI.

A further step is to refine the previous areas for the UI design, deciding whether areas will become fully-fledged windows, or parts of other areas. A possible UI design refinement step is shown in the following figure[10].

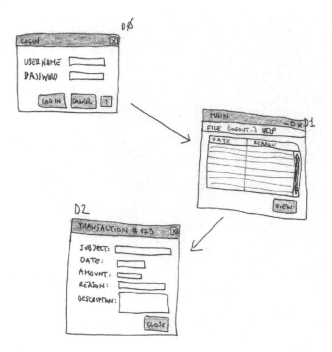

Figure 2.14   A UI design refinement step

The following abstractions related to the pictorial representation depicted in Figure 2.14:

- D0 represents the log-in dialog.

- D1 represents the main windows with the available commands and the list of all the transactions for the chosen customer. Whenever the current user (already logged in from D0) is not entitled to see transaction details, the **View** button is disabled.

- D2 represents the pop-up modal dialog that appears whenever the user has selected one transaction and presses the **View** button.

---

10. In keeping with the previous step of this example, we use 'D' to prefix areas ids, to specify that these areas arise from UI design refinements.

We have omitted some implicit relationships between the areas in Figure 2.14 and those in Figure 2.13 for simplicity. For example, D0 is the GUI design refinement of A0. These implicit relationships are useful in a number ways, as we will see in the many examples provided later in the book.

We could have provided an alternative UI design for the same area as Figure 2.13. Imagine that we provide two different windows, depending on the user's role. This design is shown in Figure 2.15, in which D0 is the same area as that shown with the same id in Figure 2.14, while the other two areas are new.

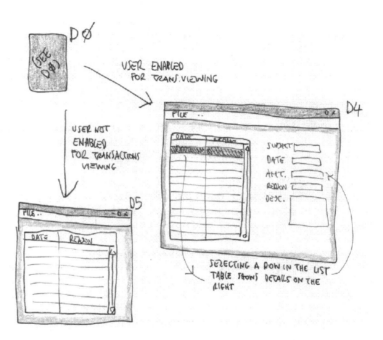

Figure 2.15   An alternative UI design

However, we decide to use the design in Figure 2.14, because it avoids having different navigation paths based on user role.

We then focus on refining area D1 in Figure 2.14 further. Now that the requirements are clearly addressed and the overall UI design is almost complete, we want to further refine the GUI for implementation reasons. This is usually performed by an experienced developer when setting out the implementation architecture for the GUI. We focus on refining area D1 into two reusable areas for technical reasons[11]. The resulting areas are shown in Figure 2.16.

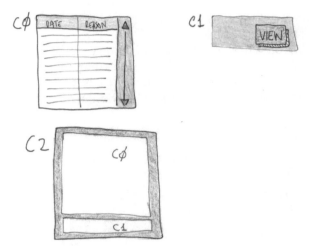

Figure 2.16   *Representing an area as composed of two other areas (adopting the visual containment abstraction)*

Note how we iteratively refined our GUI as a set of augmented areas. The areas have a number of semantic relationships between them. Figure 2.17 shows the iterative refinements we made to get to the final UI.

We have obtained the following benefits by using this conceptual approach:

*   Centralizing several notions such as functional decomposition, requisites, technical aspects and so on in one representation, organized by GUI areas at various levels of abstraction.
*   Iteratively refining our application at several levels of granularity and at several stages of the development lifecycle.
*   Clearly assigning responsibilities – for example, requirement R1 is now handled by area C1.

The A3GUI approach will be used as a common expression language throughout the book for the discussion of the various aspects of GUIs.

We go into more detail of available user interface interaction styles in the next section.

_____

11.   These areas are mapped directly to one or more Java classes to define the implementation criteria of our GUI.

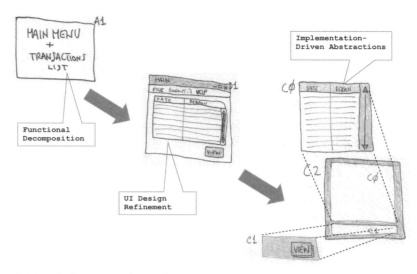

Figure 2.17   Refinement relationships among areas

2.3   Interaction styles

It is possible to identify several basic interaction styles for user interfaces (Shneiderman 1998), (Tidwell 1999).

- *Menu selection*. Here the user interacts with the system by selecting items in the UI from menu.
- *Form filling*, used for simple data input such as when inserting data in a Web form.
- *Direct manipulation*, used for example when performing operations by dragging or dropping items in a working area.
- *Language–based* interaction styles, such as interpreting users' natural language directly, or interacting by means of simple form of artificial language such as command line or scripting languages.

Such interaction styles are often combined together. Below we summarize design aspects that derive from the general principles outlined above for each style. Such styles can be thought of as abstract recurring patterns for GUIs.

Menu selection

The *menu selection* interaction style is an academic term in which a user selects items from a list of available choices. With this term we mean here a generic, abstract situation that doesn't only refer to GUIs – for example, graphical menus are only a particular case of such an interaction style – but the any type of user interface.

Menus are used for selecting items such as commands in a systematic way. The generic term 'menu' covers any selectable item, such as links in a hypertext page, commands in a drop-down menu, buttons, voice commands in voice interfaces and so on.

Figure 2.18 shows an example of a two-dimensional graphical menu implemented as a list. In the following we focus on graphical menus only, because they are the most common form of menu selection in Java user interfaces. The selection process is quick and users have a clear view of all possible choices. However, as the number of items grows, or if items lack a clear indexing organization such as a geographical or alphabetical ordering in this example, this approach reaches its limits.

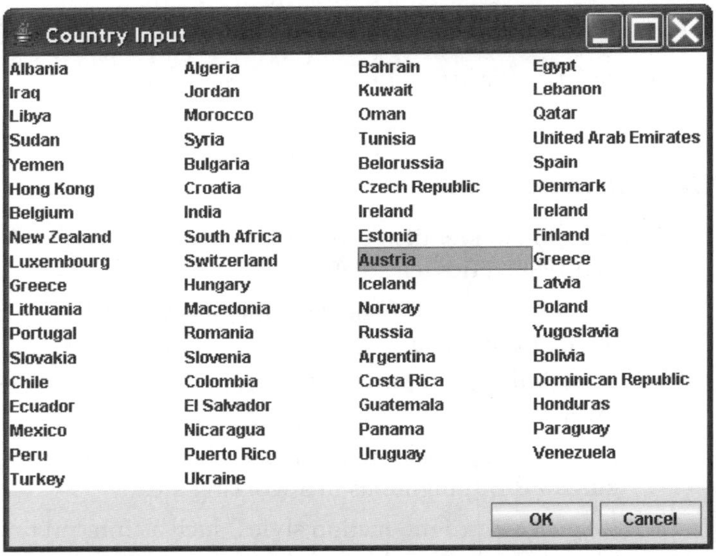

Figure 2.18   An example of a (rather unusable) two-dimensional graphical menu

Organizing menus is an important issue, especially when many items are available for selection.

The criteria mostly used are:

- *Task-related organization*. This is the single most successful strategy for organizing menu items. If items are organized at design time following some relevant semantic criteria, it greatly helps users in accessing them at runtime – as long as the semantic criteria used is clear to the end users.

- *Hierarchical grouping* in tree structures. Hierarchical menus are characterized by the number of levels (depth) and the number of items per level (breadth). Empirical studies have shown the advantage of breadth over depth in menu hierarchies. As a rule of thumb, menu hierarchies shouldn't be deeper than *three* levels. There are some practical rules for choosing the right hierarchical structure. A greater depth at the root is recommended, taking care to make sure that items are distinct and not overlapping. A broader range can be adopted on the leaves – the lowest-level items in a menu hierarchy.

- *Standardized organizations.* Adopting a standard menu organization helps users to acclimatize to new applications quickly, minimizing their required memory load when working. Later will see the Java Look and Feel guidelines prescriptions for organizing menus.

These strategies, used in combination, relieve users from the time-consuming task of finding an item in a potentially large menu space.

Figure 2.19 shows a simple **File** menu that follows the Java Look and Feel guidelines. Even in such a simple case, adhering to well-established conventions is essential. Providing non-standard, arbitrary menu structures confuses users and can wreck an application's productivity potential.

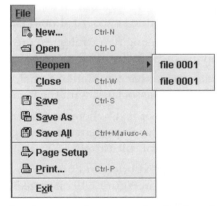

Figure 2.19   An example of commands menu using the Java Look and Feel

Form filling

Form filling is also used widely in user interface design. The general principles of a form-filling interaction style are those for general data entry (Shneiderman 1998) or (Nielsen 1993), among others. These are:

- Ensure that data-entry transactions are consistent
- Focus on minimizing end-user input actions

- Keep memory load on users as low as possible
- Ensure compatibility of data entry with data display
- Allow user flexibility and control of data entry

These criteria closely resemble the general ones discussed previously (see *Some general principles for user interface design* on page 43). There are a number of general guidelines for designing data entry forms:

- Group and sequence fields logically, for example by grouping together related items using the separation display strategy introduced on page 47.
- Supply clear instructions. Specifically, provide meaningful labels and titles for forms, and add explanatory messages for fields. This can be achieved both via contextual help and through *tooltips* – pop-up labels that appear if the mouse pointer is held over a particular item.
- Adopt consistent terminology and abbreviations. Avoid cumbersome terminology and provide names as close as possible to the business domain to which users are accustomed.
- Design the form's appearance using a visually-appealing layout – we detail one in Chapter 3 for J2SE – and by means of signaling visually which fields are mandatory and which are optional.
- Provide effective navigation focus[12]. Apart from the mouse, other navigation options such as the keyboard should be considered.
- Handle errors using two strategies: prevention, whenever possible, or displaying meaningful error messages if error states cannot be avoided.
- Provide an effective completion signal, making it clear how to complete the data entry task associated with the form.

The representation of text, wherever it appears in the GUI (buttons, menu items and so on), is another important aspect in GUI design that is not limited to form design. Some general rules apply:

- Keep labeling text brief, and preferably locate it beside the related component, as shown in Figure 2.19 on page 59.
- Use ellipses in menu items and buttons to show that another dialog will appear to accomplish the command. For commands that show a dialog as their entire result, the ellipses are redundant and should not be used. For example, an **Open** command doesn't need ellipses, because its sole purpose is to show a File Chooser dialog, while a **Print...** command does, because it

---

12. The term *focus* refers to the active area in a window or a panel where the user's next keystroke will be received. Focus represents which GUI area or widget is going to receive keystrokes.

will prompt the user with a supplementary print properties dialog, instead of directly starting printing.

To avoid visually overloading them, do not use ellipses in toolbar buttons.

- Adopt a coherent rule for titles in windows. An example of such a rule could be *object name - application name*, while titles in secondary windows could follow the format *descriptive name - application name*. This rule is adopted in several standards, including the Java Look and Feel guidelines. If you prefer to create your own rules, be sure to apply them consistently.

- All messages in English, such as command names, labels windows title, tab names and so on, should follow the *headline capitalization* rule:
  - Every word is capitalized except articles (*'the,' 'an,'* and *'a'*), coordinating conjunctions (*'but,' 'or,'* and *'and'*) and short prepositions (such as *'to,' 'in'*).
  - The first and last words in a sentence are always capitalized, no matter to what category they belong.

  These rules are not used for full sentences, where normal sentence capitalization is used instead – only the first word is capitalized. Examples of such text include alert message boxes, error or help messages, status bar messages, or general labels that indicate a status change, for example 'Download is 30% complete,' in contrast to a text label, which would follow the headline capitalization rule: 'Download Progress.'

  These rules only apply to English text. For other languages, you should refer to language-specific official guidelines, where these are available.

Creating effective forms

Creating an effective form requires some care. Figure 2.20 shows an example of a simple yet well-designed form dialog. Navigation has been enhanced and the whole interaction process smoothed with few simple details:

- Every field in the form is easily reachable using a related mnemonic – for example typing **alt+x** moves the focus to the *combo* box that indicates the gender of the person to be input. (A combo box is a GUI widget that users click to show an associated list of possible values. Some combo box options can be selected directly using the keyboard, while others allow new values to be input only through the drop-down list, thereby constraining input to the available values).

- Tab traversal – using the **tab** key to move the focus from field to field – is logical. For example, tab traversal skips the disabled **File** name field, so that if tab is pressed when the focus is on the combo box, it transfers to the **Browse...** button.

- When the dialog first appears the focus is automatically set on the **Name** field to facilitate input.

- Standard globally-applicable buttons are added at the bottom of the dialog. In this way the user knows from past experience how to dismiss the dialog.

- Effort has been spent on the visual appearance of the dialog to avoid extraneous graphics and provide a pleasant overall effect.

- Information about accessibility – providing ease of access for users with disabilities – has been added to the GUI, even if this is only partly visible. In fact, some accessibility information is stored in the GUI to allow it to be accessed by special tools such as text magnifiers or interaction facilitators. Such invisible features could be very important in some situations and should always be used.

- The field's alignment and layout of widgets provides a pleasant overall visual appearance.

Such little details greatly enhance a dialog's usability. Try it for yourself by downloading and running the relevant code.

Figure 2.20   An example of form dialog

Well-designed forms should always provide a clear completion signal. As shown in Figure 2.20, the prescribed mechanism in the Java design guidelines is to provide buttons – usually at the bottom or right-hand side of the window – with explicatory text such as **OK** and the associated behavior of closing the dialog and accepting its contents. Figure 4.15 on page 138 shows a prototype GUI that does not respect this rule, and in which the completion buttons are included within the information area, potentially confusing the user.

We will return to form design in Chapter 4.

Language-based styles

There are two other interaction styles that we will mention here for completeness, although we won't cover them extensively in this book.

- *Command language.* Using a language that must be input by users via a command line is sometimes the only solution in certain situations. For example, using a command-line user interface sometimes is the only solution in certain domains, such as a rich programming environment in which rules represented as scripts needs to be manipulated and executed. Providing a graphical UI for representing such scripts can be expensive and might ultimately result in lower usability.

- *Natural language.* Though quite complex to implement, natural language (both via text or speech recognition) can be useful in some cases.

In the next section we discuss an important interaction style for building high-quality user interfaces.

Direct manipulation

Figure 2.21 shows an example of a direct-manipulation interaction mechanism for dealing with visual objects. The items in the user interface can be dragged, edited or deleted by performing operations on them in a consistent way.

Figure 2.21   A direct manipulation interaction example

We will come across many examples of direct manipulation GUIs throughout the book. Direct manipulation is attractive from an implementation viewpoint, because it can be implemented easily using Java 2 Standard Edition (J2SE) technology, rather than another client technology such as Web pages. Direct manipulation is more difficult to implement on Java 2 Micro Edition (J2ME) devices, due to its limited pointing facilities and graphics display[13].

---

13. J2SE is the Java environment designed for desktop computers and laptops (those that provide a mouse pointer, a large graphic display, keyboard and so on), while J2ME is the Java environment for handheld and portable devices (ranging from palm top devices to wireless phones).

The appearance of the mouse cursor is often used to give some hints about the *affordances*[14] of the given items. For example, when a dragged object can be dropped onto another, the cursor appearance changes accordingly. We will see some examples of this feedback technique in the book.

2.4   *Conceptual frameworks for UI design*

In designing complex artifacts, the gap between the intended results and the chosen technology can be so wide that some conceptual structure is needed. By *conceptual framework* we mean a set of coherent concepts that structure the different phases of development – design, implementation, and so on – of UIs. Developers and designers therefore follow an abstract, principled approach to organizing the UI[15].

Conceptual frameworks provide a reliable and proven mindset for organizing the design, reducing risks and improving quality. Furthermore, by leveraging reuse, designs can be standardized and various economies derived.

Figure 2.22 shows some of the major conceptual frameworks used in today's UI design.

Various approaches to UI design are shown in the figure:

- *Entity-based.* This is a family of conceptual frameworks that structure UI development around the concept of abstract *entities*, their properties and interactions. The members of this family of conceptual frameworks vary only in the way in which the abstract concept of entity is defined. Object orientation applied to UI design is a member of this family of conceptual approaches.

- *Metaphor-based.* This approach focuses the whole design around metaphors. By leveraging those metaphors, users can use the software without having to learn the underlying system model.

---

14. The term *affordance* was introduced by Gibson and subsequently used by Donald Norman (Norman 1990) to describe the possible functions of an object. In Norman's words "a chair affords support, a pencil affords lifting, grasping, turning, poking, supporting, tapping and, of course, writing".

15. We focus this discussion on conceptual framework for UI design, and not its implementation, or other development phases. This discussion is completely separated from the actual implementation of the UI itself. Some of the approaches described here can in fact be applied to the entire software development lifecycle, not just UIs.

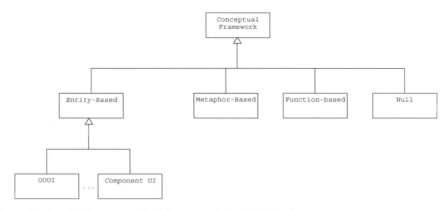

Figure 2.22   Major conceptual framework for GUI design

- *Function-based.* UIs developed using the function-based approach can be thought of as set of functions derived directly from the analysis of use cases and requirements. This UI design approach is also known as *application-oriented*. For example, we can think of a word processor as of a set of functions like 'save current document,' 'reformat selected text' and so on. The resulting UI is simply the most usable way to provide these functions given the chosen implementation technology.

- *'Null' conceptual framework.* This represents the default conceptual approach of novice designers that have never came across a sound UI design introduction.

Entity-based approaches to UI design

Entity-based approaches to UI design are characterized by the notion of the abstract concept of an entity and its relationships.

Such entities provide different views of their internal state to users, and interact with other entities within the UI environment. When designers adopt such an approach, any item in the UI is thought of as being part of an abstract entity, and users directly manipulate these entities to perform their tasks. This is usually accomplished through contextual interactions – that is, users select an entity and perform some operation on it, such as invoking a pop-up contextual menu.

A particular class of entity-based conceptual frameworks leverage object-orientation theory for defining the abstract model. We introduce this in *Object-oriented user interfaces* on page 69. Other members of this family of approaches are component-based UI design, in which the term *component* refers to a higher level of granularity than 'classic' OO objects, and various others such as the Naked Object approach to UI design – see www.nakedobjects.org.

Metaphor-based approaches to UI design

UI designs can also be shaped around the concept of metaphors. Designing a UI that resembles some real-world situation – a *metaphor* – helps users better understand the system, leveraging their knowledge of the metaphor instead of the system's actual implementation. Thus for example dragging icons could be equivalent to moving items in the physical world, and dropping an icon onto the wastebasket in the GUI is equivalent to invoking the 'delete' operation on that item. Such idioms are coherent with a desktop metaphor and do not require the user to learn implementation-dependant commands.

Historically the metaphor approach to UI design represented the first major improvement over the functional approach. Its most famous example is the desktop metaphor for operating systems originally adopted in the Xerox Star software around 1982. Metaphors can also be used at various levels in UI design even without using a fully-fledged metaphor-based conceptual framework. Examples of limited metaphors could be the wastebasket for deleting items, or using the metaphor of a restaurant menu to display the available features in a product.

> Metaphor-based approaches are different than entity-based ones in that the latter devise a generic abstract world that is applicable and repeatable in different domains. For example, one can model both a bank account and a file system directory with the same abstract concept of an 'entity.' Metaphors, in contrast, are domain-dependent, and are defined in an ad-hoc way. For example, we can model bank accounts in our UI as following a 'personal logbook' metaphor, which would not be useful for representing the file system UI.

This approach suffers from two problems:

* Good metaphors are hard to find.
* Even when a good metaphor is found, it may turn out to constrict our design.

As a trivial example of this, consider the way in which file systems are rendered in current operating system GUIs. At first it may seems that a file system is adequately modeled by means of the folder and file metaphor. However, if we had to follow the real-world metaphor of files and folders, as we know them in the physical world, we would end up of a deficient UI. First of all, real world folders cannot be nested indefinitely – this is only a mathematical abstraction that software provides us, constrained by memory resources. Second, the folder and file metaphor works fine for certain interactions such as renaming and moving, but seems a bit odd for other, such as cutting and pasting folders. It also has no parallel at all in the real-world metaphor for some operations, such as compressing the content of a folder.

Many software development approaches advocate metaphors in software design and implementation. Software documentation also benefits from the use of clear, higher-level, lifecycle-wide metaphors. Chapter 11 shows a practical example of employing an articulate metaphor in a GUI design.

Examples of metaphors used as tools can be found in different fields of computer science, such as software development (Beck and Andres 2004), with a hands-on perspective (McConnell 1993) or in the analysis process (Fowler 1997).

There are many resources available on the Web for the use of metaphors in UI design: for a critical view of such a UI design approach, see for example (Cooper 1995).

Function-based approaches to UI design

Function-based UI designs are built around the functions the system is required to perform and the interactions between them. The academic meaning of the term 'GUI' historically refers to the first generation of UIs using rich graphical technology that leveraged the underling procedural implementation approach. Menu bars, toolbars and menu items are extensively used in this approach because they help to bundle together a set of disparate *functions* the UI performs on behalf of the user. This UI design approach, as well as the 'null' approach, are the most common in current software.

'Null' approach to UI design

The so-called 'Null' approach is the approach implicitly used by developers when they do not appear using any explicit approach at all. As we said on page 35, human beings always interact with the world through semantic models, even when they are unaware of them. The Null approach, given a UI software technology, consists of putting all user requirements on the screen in one way or another, often trying to mimic other existing UIs. This is not really a bad approach in itself, but clearly lacking the backing of a sound theory, this approach has a tendency to produce confusing UI designs that do not scale well.

To better grasp the differences in the approaches described above, let's take a common example: the GUI of an OS. In order to make our point we will simplify our discussion and overlook details:

- The GUI of Windows 3.1 (Figure 2.23) can be seen an example of a functional design approach mixed with a limited use of metaphors (mainly for files and folders): the GUI was designed around a set of operations to be performed on the file system.

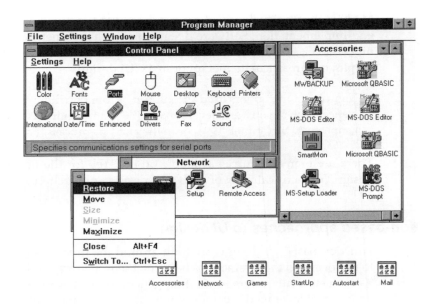

Figure 2.23   Windows 3.1

• In contrast, the original Macintosh UI (Figure 2.24) was designed following
  the desktop metaphor approach, with very few exceptions, thus providing a
  homogeneous and reliable concept model for end users.

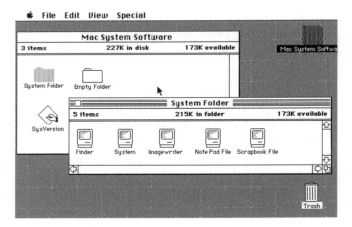

Figure 2.24   The original Apple Macintosh UI

- OS/2 (Figure 2.25) was designed completely as an entity-based GUI – every item accessible through the GUI was a conceptually well-defined entity, with its own set of available operations, properties and configuration attributes.

Despite these GUIs basically representing the same domain – the file system and basic OS functionalities – the UI design approach behind them was very different, shaping the UI in its various detail aspects.

The next section describes a particular case of entity-based approaches to UI design in detail, the Object-Oriented User Interface approach.

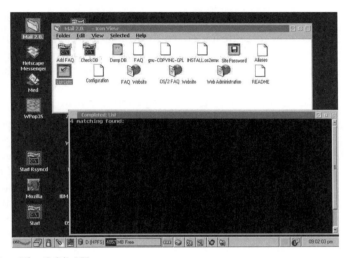

Figure 2.25   The OS/2 UI

Object-oriented user interfaces

The idea behind the Object-Oriented UI (OOUI) design approach is simple: apply OO abstract principles to UI design. An OOUI consists of a set of *abstract objects* designed following OO principles such as abstraction, implementation hiding, and so on.

> Unfortunately the term OOUI, despite widely accepted in the literature (see for example (Mandel 1997)) is rather confusing when applied in OO programming contexts such as the Java language. In fact, despite being two approaches founded on the same conceptual footing (object orientation) they are separate in practice. OOUI relates to UI design, while OOP focuses on software programming. Avoid confusing the two approaches, by ignoring for now the underlying technology on which the UI will be implemented.

OOUI focuses on defining abstract objects with which the user will interact via the user interface. Unlike the metaphor-based design approach, such 'objects' are not required to follow any metaphor from the physical world. OOUIs are a coherent collection of such objects – usually referred to as an *ecosystem* – that are available for user interaction.

The direct manipulation interaction style couples naturally with the object-oriented paradigm. Think for example of the windowing metaphor used in the Apple Macintosh, IBM OS/2, Microsoft Windows, and others, on which you can manipulate objects such as files and directories directly. A file object behaves consistently throughout many different applications, providing the same set of functionalities – move, copy, rename, and so on – like an abstract object.

Once you have designed your application GUI as a coherent object ecosystem, it is natural to interact with it by means of direct manipulation, because the UI appears as a virtual world made up of objects that can be operated on by the user. We will explore such a GUI design approach extensively, because it happens to dovetail nicely with the object-oriented nature of Java.

Java developers should be careful over some subtleties. Object-oriented programming and object-oriented user interfaces are different. One could implement an object-oriented user interface using non-OOP languages and platforms, while an OOP language like Java can be used to build any kind of user interface, command-line ones included. Furthermore, OOUI is limited to the software as it appears to the user – that is, the concepts, tasks and overall semantics exposed by the application to its users – while OOP is used to implement all of the application. A specific OOUI object, as perceived by the end-user, can be implemented with many Java classes, and, conversely (although more rarely) one Java class can implement several different OOUI objects.

Despite these differences, with thoughtful software design it is possible to bridge the two worlds systematically, providing a natural mapping between the OOUI GUI design and its underlying Java implementation.

OOUI objects are used to represent the internal state of the application and to enable user interaction. Accordingly, there is little point in providing OOUI *classes*. These are an OOP mechanism for conveniently creating objects. While interacting with an OOUI, users create new objects by manipulating existing ones.

To better grasp the OOUI concept, consider the main differences between traditional graphical user interfaces (function-based or application-oriented) and OOUIs[16]:

---

16. These differences hold also between generic entity-based UI approaches and function-based ones.

- In an OOUI users interact with objects, while in application-oriented interfaces the interaction is organized by function. In functional-based GUIs the software is rigidly organized by function. In OOUIs, in contrast, the user interacts with objects in a less structured, freer environment.

- In OOUI there are few, common objects. Combining and manipulating them produces many different results. The aspect of a coherent metaphor for object interaction is key. In traditional GUIs there are many applications, one per task, while in OOUIs the environment is common and functionalities lie within objects and their possible interactions.

- Each approach fosters different cognitive theories: traditional GUIs enforce the traditional cognitive model (a set of predefined operations that need to be learned by end users as conceived at design time by the developers), while OOUIs allow for a learning style closer to the *constructivist* cognitive approach in which users are free to interact with the system at their own pace, constructing their user experience without strongly predetermined constraints.

- Functional-based GUIs are composed of global menus. Groups of items are represented with lists. In OOUIs the objects themselves essentially convey all possible interactions.

Function-based user interfaces can be best suited for stand-alone programs, in which the user wants to accomplish one or more well-defined, circumscribed tasks. GUI designed following the OOUI approach can be useful for large applications such as operating systems, in which many functions are available and a large number of possible combinations are legal.

In this book we will combine these design approaches, with the ultimate aim of providing the most usable user interface depending on the current situation.

Object views and commands

In OOUIs, each object can be manipulated in several ways. Following Donald Norman's terminology (Norman 1990), each object has its own *affordances*. For example, some objects can be dragged, dropped onto other objects, or can provide a list of their available commands via contextual menus. Other objects cannot be dragged at all. Generally, every object provides a set of commands with which it can be manipulated. Contextual menus are the proper place to provide object command access. By convention, clicking an object on the screen with the right mouse button (or in other ways, depending on the given platform) triggers the contextual menu that contains all the valid commands for the object.

Objects can be viewed in different ways. Suppose you have a file directory. You can see it as a 2-dimensional container of icons, or as a tree in which each node can be a file or a folder. Thus the same items are viewed in different ways. You can also open a file to see its contents, providing yet another view of your file object. (Mandel 1997) mentions four basic types of object views: composed, contents, properties, and help:

- *Composed views* are views of an object obtained by combining other objects.
- *Contents views* show the contents of an object, used especially for containers objects.
- *Properties views* are used to show specific details of an object, and can also allow editing by inspecting a value and modifying it as required if this is meaningful within the application. Properties views for discrete data usually use the form-filling interaction style.
- Help views shows help data.

> We don't adopt a fully-fledged OOUI approach in this book: all the OOUI examples we provide use a simplified version of the OOUI approach. For a 'full' OOUI-driven design methodology, see for example IBM's OVID (Objects, Views, and Interaction Design).

We will see the OOUI approach implemented in Java in Chapters 14 and 15.

2.5   *Assessing the quality of a GUI*

The quality of a user interface is dependent on its *usability*. Software usability is the characteristic of a given application of being easy to use within a set of constraints such as the target user population, development budget, and so on.

Ease of use can be measured by the number of mistakes made in the use of the application by a sample user group, how quickly they can perform given tasks, users satisfaction, and how quickly the system is learned by novice users.

We won't discuss robustness and other implementation-related parameters here. An example of testing for robustness is systematically trying all combinations of buttons and other controls to see whether the GUI responds coherently, or produces unforeseen behavior.

Assessing the quality of a user interface is not a trivial task. There are many aspects to consider, and much depends upon the particular situation – the design approach followed, the end user population and other constraints. Over time several approaches have consolidated, although the fact that there are so many different criteria for GUI quality assessment underlines the complexity of such an activity.

Some of the main approaches are:

- *Expert review and survey.* Usability experts review the GUI and produce a document in which GUI weak points are identified and suggestions proposed. The review may involve a formal inspection in which the user interface is discussed with designers.

- *Usability testing*. This term encompasses all types of trial that test the GUI for usability. These involve considerations such as choosing the usability parameters to measure, the way in which such parameters will be evaluated and so on. In general usability testing is a complex discipline that need specialized personnel.

- *Acceptance testing*. Here the developer's quality assurance department define objectively measurable tests for the final GUI. A key point is the establishment of precise acceptance criteria. Acceptance tests usually cover:
  - Novice user's performance, in which the first part of the learning curve for users new to the application is measured.
  - Regular user's performance, the most commonly used acceptance tests.
  - Testing for retention, in which user expertise with the system is measured after a period of non-use of the application under test, usually of some 2–3 weeks.

- *Robustness* and other software-related tests. Usability depends on the reliability of the implementation. Buggy GUIs, no matter how well-designed, result in a poor-quality end user experience.

Other approaches to GUI assessment exist, for example Cognitive Walkthrough. The interested reader can find more details in (Nielsen 1993) or (Preece 1994).

Cognitive Walkthrough is an approach for evaluating user interfaces. A group of evaluators first determine the major tasks the system must perform. They then analyze each task, decomposing it in a sequence of steps. For each step they adopt a cognitive approach – they evaluate how difficult is for the user to identify and operate the interface element most relevant to their current subgoal, and how clearly the system provides feedback to that action. This approach is especially useful for assessing the usability of a system for users in exploratory learning mode – that is, first-time or infrequent users. Cognitive walkthrough can be performed on early prototypes as well as the final GUI.

The next section discusses a common approach to evaluate a GUI by adopting a set of rules (heuristics) that have been devised for assessing its overall quality.

Usability heuristics

When evaluating a GUI, whether in review or in usability testing, experts use this simple set of criteria in order to assess its effectiveness. The 'classic' set of such heuristics is:

- *Visibility of application status*. This involves checking whether the GUI expresses its current internal state by appropriate feedback. This is usually done by means of a status bar, mouse pointer shape, progress dialogs and so on. This criterion checks whether these means are properly used in the GUI, and whether they effective, or merely disturbing?

- *Match between application and the real world.* Terminology and the overall GUI should be as 'current' as possible. This criterion checks whether the GUI uses weird metaphors or other unnatural kinds of interaction.

- *Consistency and standards.* When checking for this evaluators should ask themselves whether the given GUI is compliant with required design guidelines, and whether any specific part of the GUI is coherent with the remainder. Evaluators look for consistency by asking themselves questions like 'Do the completion buttons always appear at the same place in a dialog?'

- *User control and freedom.* This criterion checks whether the GUI encourages exploration and error recovery. Typical hints are the effective support for undo/redo functionalities.

- *Error prevention.* This criterion checks whether the GUI is designed in such a way as to minimize user errors. A common means to achieve this is an apt use of constraints and metaphors. Another common expedient for avoiding user errors is to disable commands when they are not meaningful.

- *Helping users recognize, diagnose and recover from errors.* Not all possible errors may be prevented by clever design. This criterion checks whether the application provides helpful messages and constructive communication in the case of errors, as well as assessing the quality of error messages.

- *Recognition rather than recall.* Users need to remember specific commands or a particular interaction, and the GUI need to offer a clear visual route through all the available options. This criterion checks how effectively the users STM is exploited.

- *Flexibility and efficiency of use.* This criterion checks the extent to which it is possible to customize the GUI, and whether the GUI is suitable for expert users. It checks for the availability of accelerator keystrokes and other shortcuts that can make the GUI suitable for expert users as well as for novices.

- *Aesthetic and minimalist design.* This criterion focus on the rational and functional graphic appearance of the GUI. It checks whether the GUI is appealing visually, without being distracting or annoying.

- *Help and documentation.* This criterion checks the quality of the help system. It verifies that the supplied documentation is practical and concise, easy to search and effective in solving user needs.

Appendix A shows a simple questionnaire for evaluating Java user interfaces. This is am empirical adaptation of general questionnaires – see for example (Shneiderman 1998).

2.6   *Summary*

In this chapter we presented some introductory discussions about effective GUI design. In particular:

- We introduced some basic principles for human-computer interaction, showing how a basic understanding of human cognition can help in the design of high-quality user interfaces.

- We presented five main interaction styles. We will deal with three of these in the remainder of the book: *menu selection*, *form filling* and *direct manipulation*.

- We introduced object-oriented user interfaces (OO UIs) as a special case of direct manipulation. This approach will be adopted in some of the examples provided in the book.

In the next chapter we introduce practical GUI design for Java platforms, and introduce the Java Look and Feel guidelines.

3   Java GUI Design

In this chapter we introduce user interface design for the Java platform, focusing our attention on J2SE GUIs. The chapter is structured as follows:

3.1, Java technology for GUIs introduces the components that Java provides for building user interfaces.

3.2, Cost-driven design describes how cost constraints can be taken into account in user interface development.

3.3, Exploring the design space for a point chooser gives some examples of practical GUI design, using as an example the design of a component for selecting points on the earth surface.

3.4, Design guidelines for the Java platform introduces the idea of user interface design guidelines, specifically those for Java.

3.5, The Java look and feel design guidelines describes the Java look and feel guidelines in detail.

3.1   Java technology for GUIs

This book deals principally with graphical user interfaces composed of visual components. This kind of interface is made up of widgets and windows, following the well-established syntax of point-and-click GUIs.

Assembling the components

This section discusses the basic organization of a Java-based GUI. Java GUIs are organized in reusable units that are directly mapped onto groups of Java classes. For example, in the Swing library a visual tree component (also called an *expandable list*) is implemented as a set of more than a dozen standard classes and interfaces that can be configured or specialized as necessary. Such classes include specialized event listeners, cell renderer, and data models – see for example (Geary 1999).

In contrast, the analogous component in the SWT library is implemented using only three Java classes.

Focusing on the Swing library, even the simple dialog in Figure 3.1 below is implemented using instances of several different Java classes. Figure 3.2 shows the conceptual layering of the main user interface components that implement the dialog in Figure 3.1.

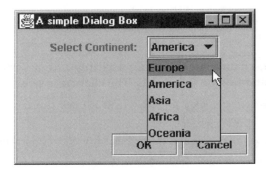

Figure 3.1   A simple dialog

The number of Java classes involved in the previous example is in fact much larger – Figure 3.2 shows only some of them. For example, the main container `JDialog` and the bottom panel use a layout manager instance that supervises to the contained widgets layout. Note that we have employed two separate panels

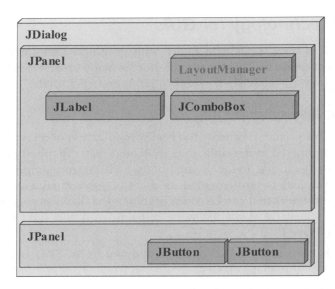

Figure 3.2   The conceptual layering behind a simple dialog using the Swing toolkit

in our design, one for the buttons at the bottom and the other one for the content area at the center. This is essentially for engineering reasons – it allows us to reuse the standard buttons panel. We discuss component reuse in *Leveraging object-oriented programming* on page 166 in Chapter 4. For a complete list of widgets available in the Swing, SWT, and AWT toolkits, refer to Chapter 11.

Three levels of component cost

In my experience I have found it helpful to distinguish between three kinds of visual component, depending on their relationship to the existing base libraries (such as Swing, AWT, or third-party ones like SWT). Categorizing GUI components in this way is useful for driving top-down development, from GUI design to software development, testing and so on:

- *Standard* components. These are standard GUI objects that are typically used with only shallow customization. These are therefore the cheapest components to use.

- *Custom* components. These are non-trivial subclasses of the standard library objects. They are also relatively inexpensive to develop, but limit designers in the degree to which they can customize existing components.

- *Ad-hoc* components. These visual components are developed to solve some special problem that cannot be solved by extending an existing component. These are of course expensive to build, as they often require additional GUI design effort, but can provide the highest quality resolution of requirements.

Figure 3.3 shows some examples of these components.

In Figure 3.3, from the left-hand side we have an example of the JTree standard component for the Swing library. Developers only need to change a few properties from the default values, and populate it with the required data. The center of the figure contains a custom JTree component, in which the same widget has been deeply customized and some of the standard classes have been extended to provide custom behavior. Finally, the right-hand side shows an example of an ad-hoc component that needed to be built from scratch because the standard library does not provide it.

This categorization is based on standard libraries such as Swing and SWT, is cost-driven and somehow arbitrary. Depending on the target Java environment, designers can rely on various GUI libraries (AWT for basic Java 1.x applets, Swing for Java 2 GUIs, and some specific toolkits for J2ME profiles).

This classification approach can be used by designers based not on standard libraries, but rather on third-party ones such as specialized set of components, or proprietary, in-house developed GUI toolkits, for example).

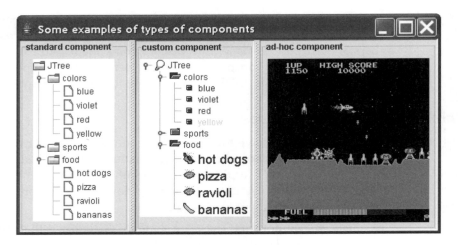

Figure 3.3   Example of the three kinds of visual component

The components in Figure 3.3 are organized by increasing development cost, from the cheapest on the left to the most expensive on the right.

This classification is however blurred, because it depends on many factors, not least the experience of the developers involved. For example, a design team that has a background in video game development may find easier to use a particular ad-hoc component than to employ a custom tree component from a complex GUI toolkit, potentially reducing development costs.

At this point some readers may wonder why, when we are discussing GUI design, we are making such an implementation-driven distinction among different visual components? The reason is because, in my opinion and experience, quality-driven industrial design cannot be separated from its implementation.

We have used three words in the latter sentence that need explanation:

* *Quality-driven* design. Quality should always drive a GUI design. Quality here means usability. For example, when it would enhance usability, a good GUI design should employ direct manipulation instead of other cheaper but more convoluted metaphors.

* *Industrial* design. As long as you are not developing your GUI for fun or for some artistic purpose, you should remain grounded in basic principles like the development cost and usefulness of the final product. No-one works in an environment of limitless resources. In real-world projects, both time and human resources are often limited, and your design cannot ignore this. The search for perfection is limited by practical industrial constraints.

- *Implementation*. Designers should always consider the final implementation, especially when developing for Java. The richness and sophistication of the platform shouldn't waylay professional designers into over-using objects and classes, degrading performance.

Generally speaking, in practice a final design is determined by the trade-offs between quality and practical constraints – this is one of the main assumptions of this book. Distinguishing visual components by their cost impacts directly on the overall GUI design, and can make the difference between an inexpensive or a costly GUI. The cost is comprised of design (plus usability testing) and the required software development, debugging and testing. A standard component is almost ready-to use: designers don't have to design its GUI from scratch or test it for usability, having only to adapt it to the current situation.

When the customization cost passes a specific threshold – for example, non-trivial subclasses need to be written – we call them *custom* components.

3.2   Cost-driven design

The term cost-driven design describes an approach to GUI design that explicitly takes into account development costs.

Ad-hoc versus custom – the difference between 'run' and 'ride'

What is the actual difference between an ad-hoc component and a customized one? When should one employ one instead of the other?

A number of parameters influence this design choice:

- *The application domain*. Sometimes the application domain dictates the kind of components used in a GUI. We will see some examples in the following sections.

- *Required GUI quality*. The quality of a GUI is a further input parameter to the design.

- *Types of users*. Depending on the user population – for example, novice users accustomed to drag-and-drop GUIs – one type of components could be preferred.

- *Practical constraints*. These include time-to-market, development costs, context-dependent constraints and so on.

In this section we discuss the difference between ad-hoc and customized components by means of practical examples.

Figure 3.4 shows the prototype GUI of a hypothetical control panel for the underground railway network in Rome, Italy.

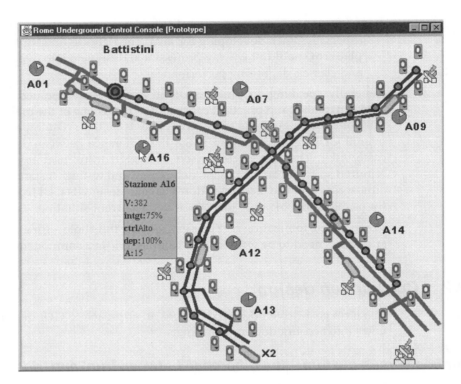

Figure 3.4   Ad-hoc prototype of the Rome underground system control console

Such a design is quite intuitive, pleasant to interact with, as it is essentially based on the direct manipulation interaction style, and relatively simple to use. Accidentally, because of its audience – it is intended for railway technicians – it is full of acronyms and technical jargon. It looks like a simple 2D-video game. Trains move on the tracks, data is queried both via tool tips for a brief summary or by double-clicking on the particular item, when a dialog pops up with the details.

This design has one major shortcoming. Such an attractive GUI is quite hard to develop. Because of the domain – complex but well-formalized – and the specialized technical audience – some of the complexity can be transferred out of the GUI to the users themselves. This can be done by a greater dependence on manuals, help support and internal training. Sadly, however, this is also often the case with badly designed GUIs.

We can imagine that such an approach might produce a much cheaper prototype like the one shown in Figure 3.5.

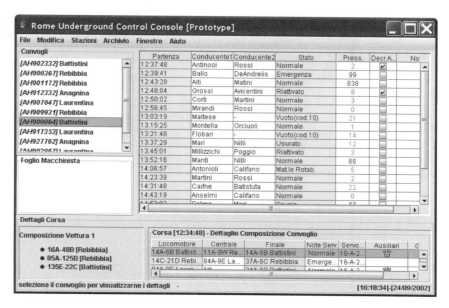

Figure 3.5   *Prototype of the Rome underground system control console using specialized components*

This second design is at first much less appealing. An additional memory burden is placed on the user, more training is needed – technicians understand technical acronyms, but would need to be specifically trained in how to use table views such as those in Figure 3.5 – and novice users can initially be lost and therefore unproductive. Even if the Rome underground system is relatively simple (consider Figure 3.4), a design such as that in Figure 3.5 gives the impression of a more complex application than does its ad-hoc counterpart: its design favors a high density layout approach over the 'lean' strategy preferred in the design shown in Figure 3.4.

When ad-hoc is the only way to go

It is not always possible to resort to a GUI composed of customized components, no matter how cleverly they are used. Consider the next two examples, illustrated in Figure 3.6 and Figure 3.7.

The first prototype is an editor for UML class diagrams. Users drop symbols on the diagram and manipulate them as needed. We will see the actual code for something similar to this in Chapter 9, but here we are interested in discussing the design issues involved in making the choice between ad-hoc versus specialized component development options.

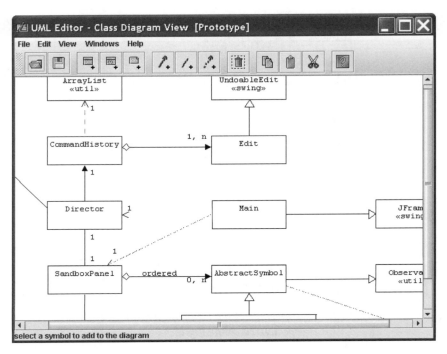

Figure 3.6   A UML class diagram editor

In this case we could imagine ways to present the same information that are simpler to develop, for example using a tree that gathers the relations of each class. Though a much poorer interaction method to the direct manipulation proposed in Figure 3.6, it is a viable and relatively usable interaction mechanism. The only problem is that one of the benefits this editor is supposed to provide lies in *the visual representation* itself. This GUI oversees the manipulation of UML class diagrams, which are themselves pictorial representations. In this case, the ad-hoc design approach, and its associated cost, is justified because it is part of the very purpose of the application. This is the case in many application domains, such as video games.

Consider another example. Even if not strictly related to graphical issues, there are domains that are intrinsically hard to manipulate via discrete widgets such as those provided by general-purpose GUI libraries. Such libraries were developed to serve well-formalized discrete domains like business management, data base manipulation and so on. The scientific domain, for example, is one such 'difficult' domain. In Figure 3.7 we show a fictitious viewer for physical data related to Oceanography. The data, rendered with an equidistant, cylindrical equatorial projection, is not a mere image, but something that can be manipulated, queried and processed (although in this prototype is a mere bitmap). There is a database behind such GUIs, but the best way to structure the interface is often radically different from those such as the underground railway network shown in Figure 3.5.

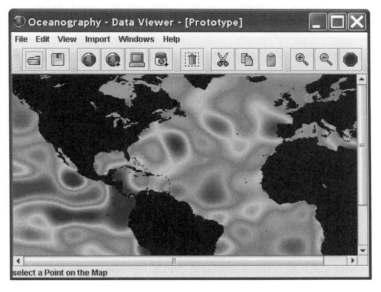

Figure 3.7   An example of a scientific data viewer and editor

Here it would be unthinkable to present the user with a set of grid views extracted from our database. It would be literally like an ocean of numbers, impossible to read, not to mention manipulate properly.

In these cases an ad-hoc development route is unavoidable. The only alternative would be to reduce the quality of the GUI by lowering interaction. In the application in Figure 3.7, for example, instead of providing complex commands to manipulate the scientific data, one can imagine an almost batch-like interaction style in which the user is prompted with a form that defines all the details of the required data manipulation, together with a **Submit** button that dismiss the dialog, launches the command and then displays an image that is the user cannot manipulate. While this interaction style might be acceptable in some cases, it can be intolerable in other contexts.

> Cost-driven design is a form of system-centered design, and as such appears to conflict with user-centered design, as described in Chapter 2. This conflict is only apparent, though. Whenever in doubt, user requirements (for usability) should prevail over system-centric considerations. If development costs are not taken into consideration, even a good GUI design can be implemented poorly, producing applications that are de-facto less usable.

3.3   *Exploring the design space for a point chooser*

In this section we examine some diverse examples of practical GUI design. We introduce practical design using the case of a simple visual component that illustrates the many possibilities the designer would consider as they relate to the chosen technology (which in the example is J2SE Swing).

Let's suppose we have to design the user interface of a component for selecting points on the earth surface, which itself forms part of a wider GUI. We will refer to this as a *Geopoint chooser*. We won't go into the details of the GUI design process here, but we will explore the design space in order to discuss few of the many design choices available, even for such a limited problem.

Of course we know that there is no absolute 'good' design. GUI design depends on many factors that include tasks[1], users, and cost. We deliberately do not commit to a fixed scenario, so that we have the freedom to discuss some more of the practical subtleties GUI designers often face in their work.

The functional requirements for our example GUI component are really simple. The related use case diagram is shown in Figure 3.8.

> Use case diagrams can also be employed for describing the details of specific parts of GUIs, such as this example. See for example the 'Complete Selection' use case above, which can be further detailed using 'Commit' or' Cancel' selection use cases independently of the given component used to implement a GUI component.

Having seen the functional requirements for our component, it's time to focus on the GUI design itself. For simplicity we focus on the selection use case only. There are established guidelines for implementing a selection completion use case, for

---

1.   By *task* we mean one of the tasks performed by the user, coinciding with the same term used during task analysis (see Chapter 2, page 45)

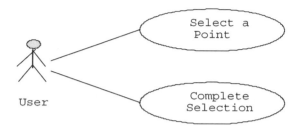

Figure 3.8   *The use case diagram for a geographic point chooser component*

example by placing **OK** and **Cancel** buttons at the bottom of a model dialog, as we will see later in this

chapter. Here we will focus on the design of the selection area only, the use of which is illustrated in the simple paper sketch[2] in Figure 3.9.

Figure 3.9   *The intended use of the Geopoint chooser*

In the following subsections we show a number of possible designs for these requirements, and introduce them in relation to their underlying implementation. Our purpose is to illustrate a number of design details that appear only in practice.

We begin with designs that are implemented by means of standard components.

_____

2.   Chapter 5 discusses paper prototypes in more detail.

Standard designs

The first and most obvious idea is to rely on existing cultural conventions, such as latitude and longitude, for selecting a point on the Earth's surface. We could adopt the form-filling interaction style, as shown in Figure 3.10. Fortunately measurements expressed in latitude and longitude are widely accepted around the world, so we don't have to worry about localization subtleties.

Figure 3.10   Using a form-filling interaction style

We can refine our simple design by leveraging the usual form-filling techniques, for example by providing a *history* facility – a drop-down window showing past input values – or by separating latitude and longitude values into degrees and minutes, as in Figure 3.11.

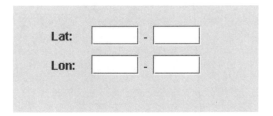

Figure 3.11   Using a form-filling interaction style – refined

Depending on whether latitude or longitude can be accessed separately in the remainder of the GUI, it could be useful to address this concept explicitly, for example by providing an icon for value. This makes sense only if such icons are used elsewhere in the GUI and with the same meaning, otherwise it is just useless visual 'noise.' Apart from additional visual clue, which might be difficult to enforce, for example in third-party components to whose GUI design we do not have access, another useful enhancement might be to use spinners for selecting input values, as shown in Figure 3.12.

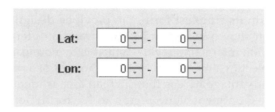

Figure 3.12   Using a form filling interaction style – even more refined

Of course we could choose to employ this sort of standard component because of the nature of our application domain, for example the required precision for latitude and longitude.

Without a proper task analysis, a design remains incomplete, because there are so many possible twists that an effective general design is often not viable.

Adopting the form-filling interaction style in our design is very cheap, as it requires only standard GUI components. It can work well if (in this case) our GUI tasks use latitude and longitude and our end-users are accustomed to such measurements. If, alternatively, we were designing a component for choosing a time zone in a non-technical GUI, or for setting locale data such as choosing a home country, clearly this design wouldn't work well.

We can use these designs to help make a point about a common situation that arises when using sophisticated GUI toolkits like Swing. Consider the following situation, which gives rise to an unexpected additional implementation cost, even for the cheap design in Figure 3.10–3.12. Suppose we are developing a GUI for a client that employs our Geopoint chooser as shown in Figure 3.10 and, somewhere else in the GUI, a date input field. Such a date input field is implemented using Swing widgets that provide extra behavior and formatting for dates. One of the features provided automatically by Swing is the ability to use arrow keys to increase days, months, and years directly in the date field (mainly through the `JFormattedTextField` class). This feature is appreciated by users, so they find it odd that the same handy mechanism is not available in our Geopoint chooser.

Thus we have an unforeseen problem of consistency with the rest of the GUI, because of the automatic facilities provided by the standard library we are using. If we decide to fill this gap, our design shifts from a standard to a custom one, as we have now to implement the behavior in our Geopoint's **Lat/Lon** text field that is available in date fields. This underlines an important point: in practice, effective GUI design is always an iterative process, no matter how simple the design may appear at first.

A geopolitical design

Even in its simplest form, the previous design is not suited to some tasks. The design shown in Figure 3.13 illustrates a different approach that uses the menu selection interaction style – which is by no means limited to commands menus – for selecting an area. This can be thought of as a point with a degree of tolerance. The advantage here is that such an area is identified by geopolitical coordinates, such as continent name, region and so forth. Depending on the user population or the nature of the task, this could be the most usable solution.

Figure 3.13   A geopolitical chooser

The design in Figure 3.13 highlights an interesting point about the low cost of building a GUI using standard components. Such cost savings relate only to the GUI's appearance, not to the remainder of the implementation. Even if we use standard components, the data needed to make this design work (countries, regions, counties, etc.) could be expensive to gather, offsetting or cancelling the cost savings.

Nevertheless, this solution is very robust: as long as the combo boxes automatically populate themselves with valid data, users cannot choose an impossible value. This is often referred to as the *power of constraints*. Well-designed GUIs should be like that – by careful design of their interaction rules, they should reduce to a minimum the possible sources of errors at the outset.

A cryptic design

An important aspect that we have not yet had the chance to discuss in detail is the importance of operational feedback. To illustrate this, we consider an absurd design choice: form filling-based selection without operational feedback.

We are usually unaware of its importance, but while we are typing into a field on a form, we actually watch what we are doing. This is a basic form of operational feedback, like seeing the mouse pointer move while we move the mouse to select a point in a GUI that employs direct manipulation. To illustrate the importance of such feedback, try out the interface in Figure 3.14, in which password fields are used for latitude and longitude input!

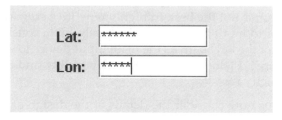

Figure 3.14   Using a cryptic form-filling interaction style

Ad-hoc designs

The simplest way to indicate a point on a map is by pointing at it with the mouse. Such as design is shown in Figure 3.15. From a technical viewpoint, this design choice needs the use of ad-hoc components, and is therefore usually more expensive to develop than those that use toolbox components.

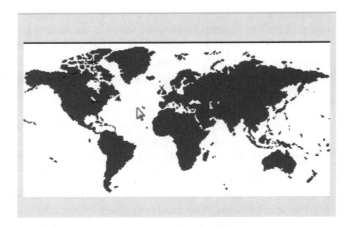

Figure 3.15   A direct manipulation Geopoint chooser

As natural and user-friendly as it may seems, there are cases in which this type of design is not the best. In highly repetitive scenarios, for example, in which users need to input many points routinely, extra consideration should be given to the use of the keyboard as the main input device to speed up selection. The design in Figure 3.15 does not provide such a facility, and this can be a serious shortcoming in such cases.

Let us now consider the details of the design of a direct manipulation Geopoint chooser.

The direct manipulation design in detail

Given the nature of the application, we assume that our users are non-occasional and skilled experts in the domain of interest.

Configuration settings such as the precision of mouse hovering and other prefer-ences are kept separate in another dialog. We won't discuss such configuration issues here.

The direct manipulation interaction employed in the design in Figure 3.15 seems a perfect choice. However, it may not be obvious to a novice user – there is nothing into the GUI that suggests the point-and-click behavior.

Instead of adding a label or a tooltip to signal the intended interaction, and so risking annoying regular users, we chose to change the cursor shape and add a label that indicates the geographical point indicates by the mouse focus, shown on the left bottom of the map, together with a label that shown any point already selected, as seen in Figure 3.16. These are all discreet hints that 'invite' the user to click on the map to see what happens. There is no need to overload the design with explicit signals – in this way both first-time and regular users are well served.

When the user selects a point, it is signaled by an 'X' on the map and represented numerically at the bottom-right of the map. On the left- hand side of the screen the point corresponding to the current mouse position is shown.

> We place the selected and the current point in the status bar, following the Java look and feel design guidelines (introduced later in this chapter), although further usability testing should be done to check that our choice is not confusing to users.

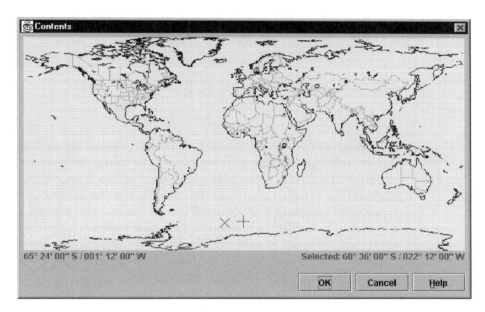

Figure 3.16   An implementation of a Geopoint chooser visual component

When the user has chosen a point on the map, they can dismiss the chooser, so committing the operation by clicking the **OK** button, or just cancel the selection operation by using the **Cancel** button.

Allowing editing of the currently selected point helps fine-tune inputs. Figure 3.17 shows a typical interaction with an enhanced version of the chooser.

This version allows users to edit latitude and longitude values directly, and so refine a chosen point more easily, to any level of precision.

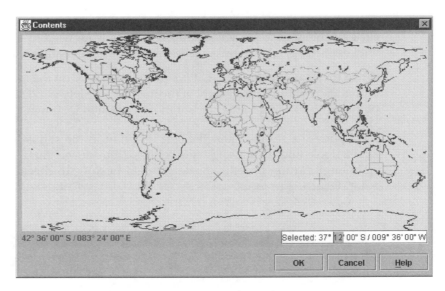

Figure 3.17   An enhanced version of the Geopoint chooser

The design in Figure 3.17 illustrates a subtlety regarding the commit behavior of the editable field for the selected point. The designers have to decide how the editing in the field is going to be committed and so change the location of the 'X' mark on the screen. One possibility is to accept the editing as soon as the user types valid numbers into the field (this is called *immediate* mode). This has the unpleasant side-effect of making the 'X' mark scatter all over the map while users are typing the digits of a coordinate. The other option is to commit the value after a special 'completion event' is performed by the user, such as pressing **Enter** or pressing a button (this is called *deferred commit* mode). A third possibility is to delay the commit for a specific time after the last user keystroke (perhaps a few seconds), giving users the time to fully input the value. This option (*delayed immediate* mode) and deferred mode are important when the commit cost could be high, for example to send data to a remote server.

Quality assurance testers love to fiddle with such subtleties. What if the chosen commit mode is delayed immediate – say after 2 seconds after last user keystroke in the field – and as soon as the user types a digit, they quickly close the dialog by pressing the **OK** button? The new value does not have time to be committed, and they developers can find themselves dealing with a new and unpleasant bug.

A further evolution of this design could involve spinners – using the `JSpinner` Swing component – instead of free text. Figure 3.18 shows such a solution.

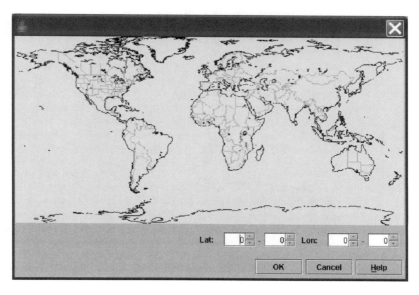

Figure 3.18   A Geopoint chooser that employs spinners

The design shown in Figure 3.18, although visually loading the chooser window a little, allows for a finer user data input. The use of spinners is also self-explanatory – users understand their actual purpose easily, so that they can use this additional control whenever a fine, but constrained, input is needed.

Figure 3.19 shows another version of our design, in which users can specify the current geographical projection adopted at the top right. Whenever the projection is changed, the underlying map and the selected point change accordingly.

Changing the map projection is an example of a configuration item that can become a part of the operational GUI, depending on the situation. If this feature is used by unskilled users, it might be distracting or even confusing. This is a common dilemma, where the user population is not easily predictable at design time[3].

---

3.   As one can imagine, designing 'catch-all' visual components isn't an easy job.

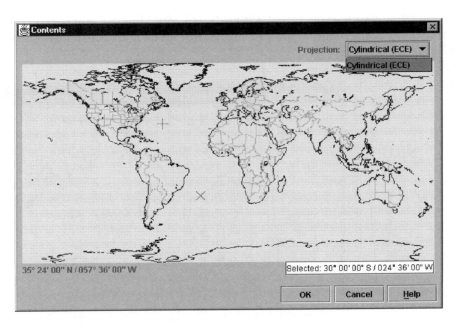

Figure 3.19   Interacting with the chooser

Finally, the class diagram related to the version shown in Figure 3.16 is shown in Figure 3.20. The implementation code for this Geopoint chooser is available on the book's Web site – see the `GeoPoint` and related classes.

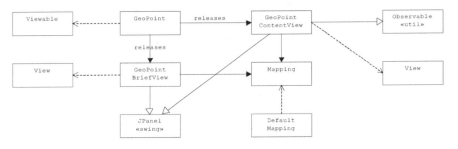

Figure 3.20   The Geopoint chooser class organization

Next we look at alternative designs that employ combinations of design approaches.

Mixed designs

As seen in the previous section, it is possible to combine direct manipulation and the use of standard components in a GUI design. These are the most expensive designs, due to the cost of building the different representations, plus the extra cost of establishing the coordination between the two. The use of such an approach should be thought through carefully, because it can actually produce more cluttered – and so less usable – designs. This is a classic phenomenon known as *feature creep*: designers feel somehow more reassured by adding extra functionalities to the GUI in a vague attempt to make it more usable.

An obvious solution for increasing the ease of use of our Geopoint chooser design is to employ two different representations of the same data simultaneously. Choosing the two representations carefully can lead to larger usable selection areas, for example one quicker to use, but less precise, together with a slower but more accurate one.

A set of different designs are possible. For example we could employ sliders for selecting the point indirectly on the map, as shown in the design in Figure 3.21.

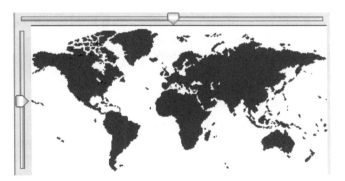

Figure 3.21   Indirect manipulation

This solution has a flaw. Depending on the projection used for the map, the sliders could indicate meaningless measurements (the geographic projection used in Figure 3.21 is only a mock-up).

One possible solution is to decouple the sliders from the visual representation of the map, as shown in Figure 3.22. This new solution has the advantage of combining the two required parameters (which may not necessarily be latitude and longitude) with the powerful visual feedback given by the chosen point indication on the map. More importantly, it does not depend on a specific map projection.

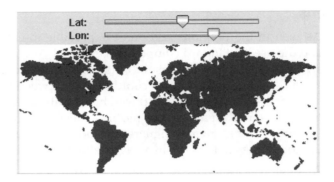

Figure 3.22   Another attempt

Like the design illustrated in Figure 3.21, this design imposes a degree of coordination between the two representation of the same data: the two sliders above being the indirect representation, and the map in the center being the direct representation of a point on the Earth's surface. When the user changes one of the sliders, the point in the map changes accordingly. This is an example of the concept of different *views* – that is, different representations – of the same data. We will see in the second part of the book how Java GUIs, by leveraging OO design pattern technology, can implement such constraints in complex applications.

Combining two designs in one

In some case is not possible to accommodate both expert and novice users with the same design without hampering one or both of the groups. In these cases one solution is to provide two slightly different versions of the same UI in combination, providing the simpler path for novice users and a more elaborate but powerful one for expert users.

Returning to our Geopoint chooser, suppose expert users want to define the information about a point on the earth surface in a more articulate way. To avoiding cluttering the UI for novice users, who are happy with point-and-click interaction, we can devise a design that conceals more complex data input in a separate area. The design in Figure 3.23 shows this solution.

We can draw a number of lessons from the design in Figure 3.23. When providing such a two-way UI differentiated by user skill, it is always a good idea to favor novices over experts, for example by starting up the GUI with the default view for novice users, or by providing simpler interactions for them. This is not always

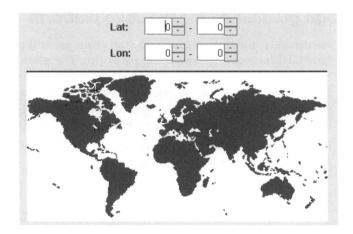

Figure 3.23   A two-way UI differentiated by user skill

possible, though. Sometime the GUI needs to be engineered for expert users over novices, for example to optimize user's interaction speed.

From a visual viewpoint, the 'expert' form-based view could be switched on and off in a number of ways, for example by means of a button, or by adding a tab pane with two tabs, one for the map and the other for the numerical representation. Two tabs would avoid confusing novice users, who can use the less precise, direct manipulation map and ignore the more elaborate form-based input area. But with two tabs, the UI loses the very useful operational feedback of seeing the point selected with spinners directly on the map.

Conclusions

Even in these simple examples we find many design choices that complicate our GUI design process. We can see how categorizing components based on their development cost can sometime be misleading, because it doesn't take account of non-GUI costs, such as data collection, such as that needed to make the design in Figure 3.13 work.

One aspect that recurs in each design we have examined is the phenomenon of *feature creep*. The more designers work on a design, the more they are tempted to add extra functionality, overloading the design beyond what is needed and potentially making it less usable.

In the next section we enter the world of user interface guidelines, introducing the official design guidelines for GUIs built with the J2SE Swing toolkit.

3.4   Design guidelines for the Java platform

Fortunately it is not necessary to start from general principles when designing a new GUI for a given computing platform[4]. The platform provides many conceptual and coding constraints that help us to build a professional GUI economically. However, many developers aren't aware of such guiding principles. This can be seen in many GUIs, in which the designer didn't understood the principles behind the visual components employed, or even misused them altogether.

Using a sophisticated and powerful GUI toolkit doesn't make one immune from gross UI design errors, as shown in Figure 3.24.

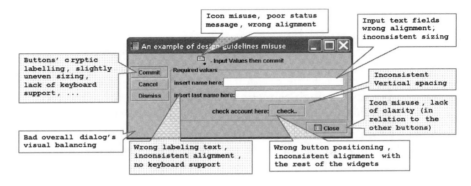

Figure 3.24   A badly-design form

What is missing from the figure is a coherent, systematic organization of the layout and intended user interaction. Such an organization is required to ensure UI consistency – users expect dialogs, panels and other GUI parts to have the same mechanisms and conventions, possibly sharing those of similar products – and ensuring the required levels of usability.

Introduction to the guidelines

Professional UI designs are the result of many contributions, ranging from the UI toolkit in use to the general UI design guidelines available for that platform, and

---

4.   Java is not only a mere development environment in the traditional sense, in that a Java runtime is also deployed with the execution code, thus providing a sort of 'Java platform' in which a minimum set of services (constantly growing with each release) are available for all Java applications. At the same time, the Java platform is not always totally independent of the underling native OS.

also comprising the general international standards and guidelines for usability, design best practices and so on. In Figure 3.25 shows some of the contributions to the final design of a simple J2ME MIDP form for a handheld device.

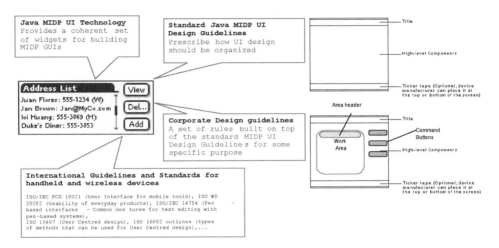

Figure 3.25   Every good design is the final result of many guidelines

Note that in general UI design guidelines are built on top of other more general ones, to provide a complex and coherent set of UI design directions – that is, guidelines that don't contradict other more general guidelines. This can be seen in Figure 3.25 above, in which the corporate UI design guidelines restrict the standard general design guidelines for MIDP GUIs. The presentation technology, including widget toolkits, is also built following standard guidelines.

Guidelines provided by the platform vendor are not exhaustive, and organizations can expand them to meet their needs, to add extra features, or to provide a 'branded' look and feel. One could provide further design guidance for a family of applications that in turn specializes corporate design guidelines. Figure 3.26 shows the general layering of user interface design constraints for any graphical interactive platform.

> The layering metaphor in Figure 3.26 is used to convey the idea of a set of *harmonized* guidelines, which, when put together, form a coherent language for building graphical user interfaces.

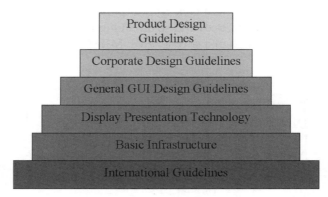

Figure 3.26   Stacking up design guidelines in general

Starting from the bottom layer:

- Basic concepts, pointing devices and the remaining items that make up the 'plumbing' of modern GUIs are based on broader and more general guidelines such as:
    - ISO 9241 (ergonomic requirements for office work with visual display terminals)
    - ISO 20282 (usability of everyday products)
    - IEC TR 61997 (guidelines for the user interfaces in multimedia equipment for general purpose use)
    - ISO/IEC 10741-1 (dialog interaction – cursor control for text editing)
    - ISO/IEC 11581 (icon symbols and functions)
    while, for J2ME other standards apply:
    - ISO/IEC 14754 (pen-based interfaces – common gestures for text editing with pen-based systems)
    - ISO/IEC 18021 (information technology – user interface for mobile tools)[5]
- Above this is the basic infrastructure for interactive GUI features provided by the platform. Such an infrastructure in modern multipurpose software environments is usually organized around the concept of component-based GUIs. These are graphical items (also called *components* or *widgets*) that can be assembled to create a large number of different GUIs. Some specialized

---

5.   There are many hardware standards too: for computer displays, keyboards, etc. For a comprehensive list of the various usability and HCI standards, see: http://www.hostserver150.com/usabilit/tools/r_international.htm.

platforms (or those with limited hardware, such as hand-held devices) may use other approaches to model the basic infrastructure of their user interface.

- The display presentation technology is built using a conceptual UI architecture and a set of basic guidelines and standards. This software allows developers to build UIs by means of specialized APIs.

- At a higher abstraction level, presentation technology alone is not enough to guarantee effective and usable UIs. A set of UI design guidelines and best practices needs to be taken into account during the UI design process. Such a set of guidelines is strictly dependent on the underling presentation technology: for example, a set of voice interfaces design guidelines is meaningless for graphical-only presentation technologies. An example of a UI design guideline for a GUI could be 'command buttons should all be the same size.' These guidelines are usually provided by the same companies that develop the related display presentation technology, or by independent standard bodies.

- Corporate design guidelines are built on top of the standard UI design guidelines by private organizations to provide a higher level of consistency for the software developed in or for the organization, and to enable other benefits such as support for a proprietary toolkit, product documentation purposes, quality assurance, UI cost estimation, and so on.

- Above corporate UI design guidelines could be further specification for single products, perhaps for providing special UI features, branding, better user targeting, and so on. Imagine for example the GUI of a software music player, as opposed to the GUI of an e-mail client built by the same company. This and the corporate level of guidelines are usually owned by organizations and not available for public use.

J2SE user interface design guidelines

The same layering of design guidelines shown in Figure 3.39 also exists for Java 2 standard edition (J2SE) too. Figure 3.27 shows how the final design of a simple J2SE Swing GUI is influenced by the different UI design guidelines layers introduced in the previous section.

The various design guidelines are compounded, enforced by the GUI technology, here Swing, to create the final result.

This layering is illustrated in Figure 3.28. The pyramid of constraints and guidelines for the design of GUIs stands on top of the same international standards mentioned above – the hierarchies in Figure 3.26 and Figure 3.28 share the same lowest level. The architects of Java adopted a common approach based on components for modeling GUIs, indicated by the *Basic Infrastructure* layer in Figure 3.26.

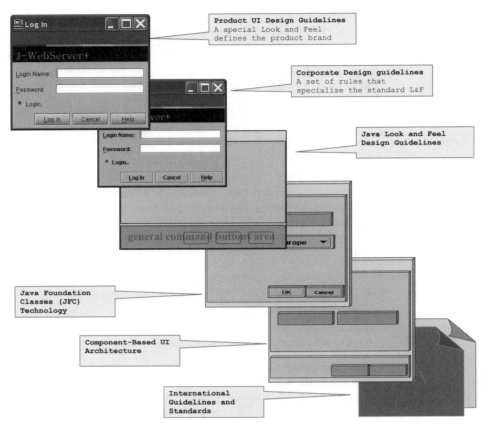

Figure 3.27   The final design of a J2SE GUI

The idea that a J2SE GUI is inherently composed of elementary, reusable components impacts both the design and implementation of GUIs. Such components can
be visual objects, such as a combo box, more abstract ones, such as a layout
manager, or non-GUI objects, such as the data model behind a list[6]. Building on
top of this conceptual model, we are offered a number of visual components that
can be combined to build GUIs.

Sun provides two, in part overlapping, toolkits created around this component
approach: Swing and AWT, plus a number of auxiliary libraries such as Java2D

---

6.   Values displayed in widgets are usually stored in runtime memory structures known as
      data models. When users modify the value in the widget through the UI the changes are
      transferred to the related data model.

and JavaHelp. These are the more popular GUI toolkits for J2SE, but there are others. At a higher level of abstraction, Sun also supplies a set of design criteria and guidelines for harmoniously composing the building blocks provided in these libraries. Finally, developers are free to add their own design constraints and guidelines by building on top of other guidelines. Figure 3.28 shows the layering of user interface design constraints for J2SE platform.

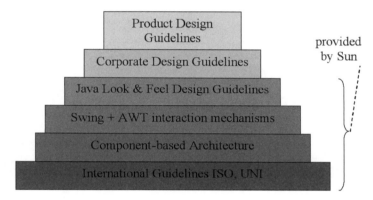

Figure 3.28   Stacking up design guidelines for J2SE

Any GUI toolkit include abstractions and mechanisms related to the use of the widgets it offers. Such interaction mechanisms may be closely linked to higher-level design guidelines. This is the case with the Java look and feel design guidelines and the underlying Swing library – in fact, the Java look and feel design guidelines have been designed specifically for the Swing toolkit. For example, the Java look and feel provides detailed guidelines for changing the visual appearance of the whole GUI at runtime, and such a feature is technically available only for Swing-based GUIs.

By taking advantage of corporate design guidelines, it is possible to create new GUI styles that highlight the product's identity, or that are specialized for some particular case. Figure 3.29 shows an example of such a custom style, built on top of the Java look and feel, used for the JetBrains IDEA[7] integrated development environment.

---

7.   IntelliJ IDEA is a trademark of IntelliJ Corp.

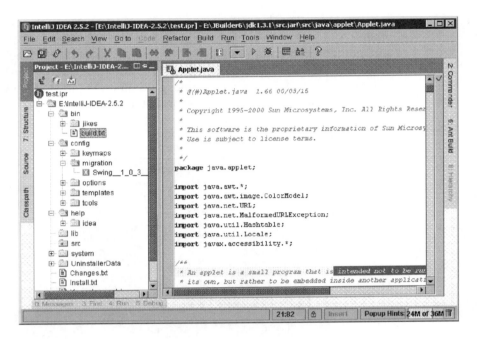

Figure 3.29   The IntelliJ IDEA GUI

As the figure shows, the designers had to solve various GUI-related problems, and resorted to adopting a specialized version of the Java look and feel style. Many of the conventions used in the standard Java look and feel were maintained, but new visual components were provided.

It is important to point out that Swing, although the most popular, is not the only toolkit available to GUI designers using Java. Developers can create their own toolkits that build on top of standard libraries, or even substitute them altogether, as IBM did for Eclipse[8]. On platforms such as Eclipse, its SWT library still offers a component-based approach to GUI building, but also provides an alternative set of widgets to developers. The design guidelines also differ from those proposed by Sun. The Eclipse design constraints are shown in Figure 3.30.

SWT design guidelines are different than Swing guidelines, as can be seen from the example GUI developed for Eclipse shown in Figure 3.31. Notice, for example, the status/message bar at the top of the dialog just below **Java Settings**. The SWT library is described in Chapter 11.

---

8.   See Chapter 11.

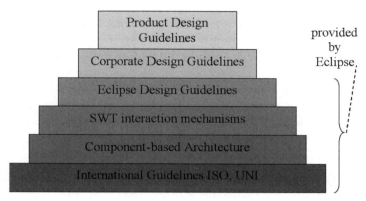

Figure 3.30   Stacking up design guidelines for the Eclipse platform

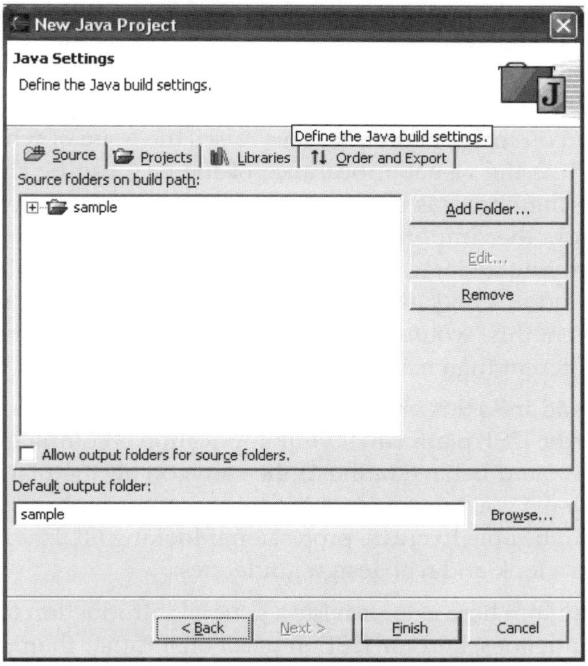

Figure 3.31   An Eclipse standard GUI

The standard Java Look And Feel design guidelines provided by Sun is not the only such set of guidelines available. The layering shown in Figure 3.26 on page 102 can be highly customized, and each guideline layer can be replaced with others. This is a powerful feature in the hands of seasoned designers, as it is expensive and time-consuming to create an original yet professional set of design guidelines. An easier and safer way is to build on top of existing guidelines. Fortunately, the Java look and feel provided by Sun is an effective set of design guidelines that fits J2SE's technical constraints and allows easily for some customization.

> In contrast to the look and feel of single components, the style (the systematic layout of widgets in windows and the set of interaction patterns recurring in the GUI) cannot be strictly enforced by a class framework no matter how clever it is devised, and it should be put into practice explicitly by designers and developers in their applications.

3.5   *The Java look and feel design guidelines*

Adhering to a particular set of design guidelines is key to the creation a professional GUI on any platform, and on Java in particular. But Java software can be run on many platforms. This raises the issue of which design guideline to adopt. While the visual appearance of the GUI can be changed easily – as long as the Swing library is used – the underlying window layouts, interaction mechanisms and other important aspects of the GUI cannot. It would be quite expensive to provide a single GUI that can look and behave like a Windows application on Windows and like an Aqua application running on an Apple Macintosh. And even this wouldn't really solve the problem, because Java applications are different than native ones, no matter how cleverly you code them.

To address this problem, Sun proposed a standard set of design guidelines specific to the J2SE platform. If your application is compliant with these guidelines, it will look and behave (almost) the same on all the platforms Java on which can run. Even if you are not planning to exploit the multi-platform capabilities of Java, you will be able to create professional-looking GUIs with little effort by adopting the Java look and feel design guidelines.

Our aim here is to provide a general introduction to the Java look and feel design guidelines, and for J2SE in particular, rather than provide a thorough exposition of topic such as how to space items in a window, how to handle raster graphics on different platforms, and so on. Readers interested in the detail can refer the official guides provided by Sun[9], *Java L&F Design Guidelines 2001*, *Advanced Java L&F Design Guidelines 2001*.

Some definitions

First, there is a small terminological twist related to two different meanings of term 'look and feel.' In Java code, 'look and feel' refers strictly to the visual appearance of GUI components, and is also known as 'Metal' in the code. In a design context, however, the same term may indicate both the visual appearance *and* a set of abstract behaviors that identify the design's style at large . We therefore use the term 'look and feel design guidelines' to describe collectively the set of abstract behaviors and design guidelines *plus* the resulting visual appearance of the GUI components.

A set of look and feel design guidelines is therefore more than a mere collection of appearances for visual components. It implies also a set of behaviors and conventions that are used throughout the applications. To take an analogy, you might build a house from bricks. and wood, but look and feel design guidelines would define the architectural style and how your constructional materials should be used to produce an effective and comfortable design. A look and feel implementation is a set of coherent components that comply with these guidelines.

The designers of the Java look and feel tried to cope with the diverse habits or users by creating a rather 'neutral' set of design guidelines that could be employed to create GUIs that could be used easily by Mac, Linux or Windows users. The Java look and feel was designed therefore as far as possible to be cross-platform. To have an idea of what such a design guideline is all about, we will examine some of its details in the following sections. As long as you employ standard or custom components in your GUI, you are not required to master all the details of the Java look and feel visual appearance, because Swing's designers have already worked them out for you. You need to be aware only of some general style guidelines – we will discuss these later in this chapter, and in the many examples in the rest of the book.

The Java 'look'

This is the most visible part of any GUI, the part that creates a user's first impressions. Three visual elements characterize the 'classic' Java look and feel:

- The *flush 3D style*. This describes the way in which component surfaces appear, making use of beveled edges. From a graphical viewpoint, component surfaces with beveled edges appear to be at the same level as the surrounding screen area.

---

9.   Available on the Web at http://www.java.sun.com/products/jlf.

- The *drag texture*. A particular graphic pattern indicates items that users can drag with the mouse.
- The *color model*. A simple set of theme colors ensures a consistent look across different platforms. The Java look and feel uses eight system colors – three primary and three secondary colors, plus two general colors for the display of text and highlights.

Figure 3.32 shows an example of an application that uses the Java look and feel, highlighting the three basic elements of the Java look and feel. To grasp the difference, Figure 3.33 shows the same application, but using the Windows look and feel.

The visual appearance of widgets is a shallow part of a GUI. Another important part of a user's experience is the way in which the GUI reacts to user manipulation – the 'feel.'

The Java 'feel'

A set of look and feel design guidelines doesn't only define the visual appearance of an application's components. An important part of the design guidelines defines the way they respond to user interaction.

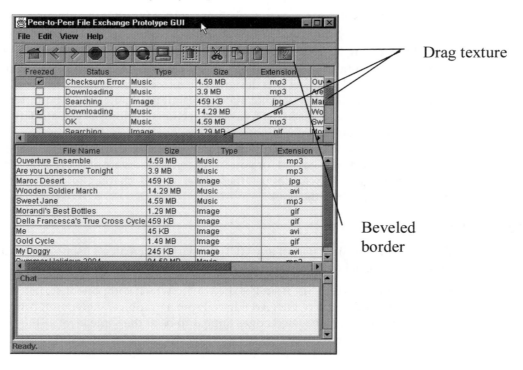

Figure 3.32   An application using the Java look and feel

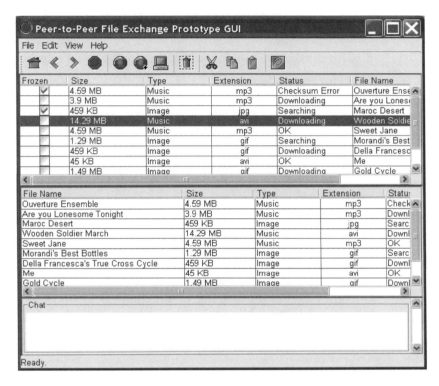

Figure 3.33   A Java Application using the Windows look and feel

Any visual component has its own interaction rules. These rules describe how components react to user manipulation. As an example, here are the rules for user selection for some of the Java widgets.

For text – multiple line or single line text-based components, such as text fields or text areas:

- A single click deselects any existing selection and sets the insertion point.

- A double click on a word deselects any existing selection and selects the word.

- A triple click on a text line deselects any existing selection and selects the whole line.

- A shift-click extends a selection by the same unit as the previous selection (single character, word, line, etc.).

- Mouse dragging deselects any existing selection and selects the currently selected range.

- Direct manipulation for cutting or copying a text selection is not provided.

While for lists and tables:

- A single click on an item deselects any existing selection and selects the object.

- A shift-click on an item extends the selection from the last selected item to the new one.

- A control-click on an item toggles its selection without affecting the previous selection.

Even from simple rules such as those above, it is clear that if you allow users to change the look and feel at runtime, you should also change the underlying behavior, terminology and standard layouts (what we called the *style*) to match the chosen look and feel. This is much trickier than simply changing the widgets' visual appearance. For this reason, if you plan to deploy your application on different target platforms, the wisest choice is to adopt the standard Java look and feel guidelines. Although technically possible, the official design guidelines strongly discourages the provision of features that allow end users to switch to a different look and feel at runtime.

Some terminology

We introduce here some terminology related to user GUI interaction that we will use throughout the book to describe the support of keyboards and other input devices.

- *Mnemonics* are look and feel and locale-dependent combinations of a letter and a modifier key such as Alt. Mnemonics are used for menu item selection and for setting the focus. They are shown by an underline under the given character. For example, the Windows or the Java look and feels allow menu items to be selected by combining the underlined letter with the Alt modifier.

  Figure 3.34 and Figure 3.37 on page 115 show examples of use of mnemonics for focus control in dialogs. Note that mnemonics are used also for command buttons.

- *Accelerators* or *keyboard shortcuts* are key combinations completely defined by the designer. For example Ctrl-x is the keyboard shortcut for activating the 'cut' command on the selected items. Figure 2.21 on page 63 shows a pop-up menu in which every command is provided with accelerators. The Java look

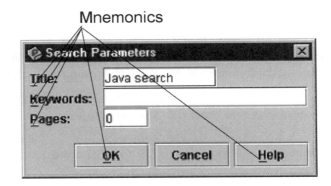

*Figure 3.34	An example of mnemonics*

and feel requires that accelerators are indicated to the right of the command label for menu items, and in the tooltip as well where relevant.

- *Focus navigation.* Using the keyboard, it is possible to switch the focus from one component to another. This provides a quick way to manipulate the GUI, and is very convenient for data entry forms.

The scope of accelerators and mnemonics is limited to the current window. When deciding which characters to use, some guidelines apply:

- Use standard accelerators whenever possible. The official guidelines[10] provide a list of the most common ones.

- If this is impossible, use the first letter, as long as it doesn't conflict with other mnemonics. In the example in Figure 3.37, 'L' is used for 'Log in.'

- If the first letter of the label is not available, resort to the next suitable consonant. For example, if 'l' is reserved, 'n' could be used. If this also fails, choose a suitable vowel. Locales with non-Latin alphabets should use the English mnemonic. (For languages other than English, internationalization guidelines are provided.)

- Finally, do not provide mnemonics or accelerators for potentially dangerous commands such as 'delete,' 'cancel,' or for the default button in a dialog, as this can be triggered merely with the Return key.

---

10. See http://www.sun.com

An example – applying the guidelines for designing dialogs

Dialogs provide a useful means delivering an application's functionalities in logical 'chunks,' which can enhance user's understanding. Dialogs also provide an indication of task completion, providing feedback to users.

We introduce some general guidelines for the design of dialogs here: in Chapter 5 we will illustrate these with coded examples.

Figure 3.35 shows a dialog designed following the Java look and feel guidelines. Some of the minor details, such as standard dimensions in pixels are also shown.

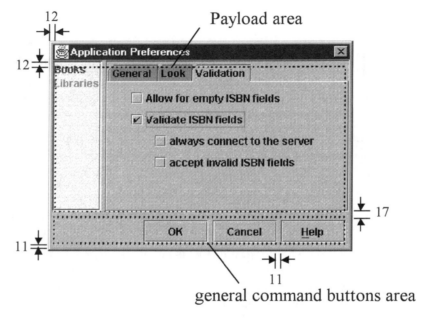

Figure 3.35   A Java look and feel guideline–compliant dialog

It is important to emphasize the prescribed structure – the *style* – for dialogs. Figure 3.36 shows the two standard arrangements for area organization within a Java look and feel compliant-dialog. Note that the second arrangement, using vertically placed buttons, is less common in practice.

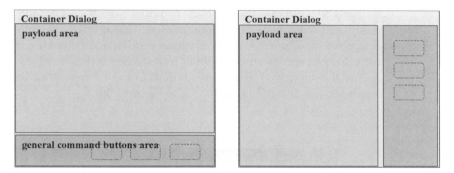

Figure 3.36   General structure for Java look and feel dialogs

Note in Figure 3.36 that buttons and other component can also be employed in the *payload* area. The general command buttons refer to the dialog as a whole, while Content-specific components will be organized within the payload area.

This simple structure guarantees a systematic and predictable layout for dialogs. Users easily discover how to dismiss a dialog or to perform the intended operation, which is always associated with the left-most button. This is illustrated in Figure 3.37, which shows an example of a log-in dialog: instead of the **OK** label, the dialog's acceptance button has a more expressive label, **Log In**.

Figure 3.37   An example of standard Java look and feel login dialog

We will see the graphic details of such a scheme when we discuss some real cases in Chapter 5.

Regrettably, not all the dialogs provided by the standard Java libraries are compliant with this simple organization. This is partly because the arrangements described in Figure 3.36 can sometimes result in inefficient use of space. Figure 3.38, for example, shows an example of a well-known JFC standard dialog that doesn't follow the suggested area organization. In the 1.4 release of J2SE, Sun's designers amended the design to that shown in Figure 3.39.

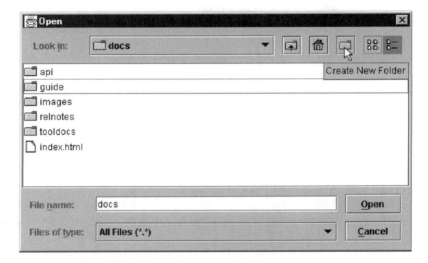

Figure 3.38   The not-so-standard file chooser of J2SE 1.3

The design in Figure 3.39 illustrates internationalization support for standard components – it shows an open file dialog for the Italian locale.

We will use a dialog classification scheme extensively in rest of this book. We group dialogs by the way they allow interaction:

- *Modal dialogs.* Users are forced to interact with the currently-open dialog. If the user wants to interact with the remainder of the application, they must first dismiss a modal dialog. Typical general commands for this kind of windows are '**OK** and **Cancel**, or some other context-dependent command such as **Log In**.

- *Modeless dialogs.* Modeless dialogs don't prevent users from interacting with other windows in the same application. Such dialogs can be used for toolbox

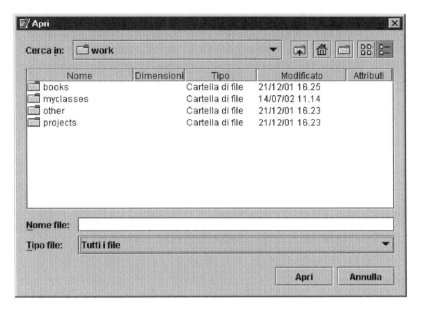

Figure 3.39   The file chooser dialog of J2SE 1.4

or other auxiliary windows that assist users with details of the operations being performed on the main window.

3.6   Summary

In this chapter we have discussed the general principles of user interface design, mentioning common aspects of user interface design, and have provided a brief introduction to the Java look and feel guidelines. We also discussed the GUI design space for a simple chooser.

Here are some of the ideas we discussed in this chapter.

- We saw that Java user interfaces for J2SE are organized into components that can be assembled to create complex user interfaces.

- We distinguished three types of visual components based on their construction complexity:

  - *Standard components* are obtained from standard library components with few adaptation to their code.

  - *Custom components* are major customizations of standard components, involving the creation of new, non-trivial specialized classes.

- — *Ad-hoc components* are components created from scratch for solving specific problems that aren't addressed by existing libraries, either those provided by Sun, or by other third-party component vendors.
- We suggested that user interface design guidelines can be visualized as a hierarchy for building a coherent framework for professional GUI design.
- We briefly introduced some of the aspects of the Java look and feel, that we will assume as the reference look and feel throughout this book.

In the next chapter we discuss some frequent GUI designs for Java GUIs.

4 Recurring User Interface Designs

This chapter illustrates some common GUI designs. We will present them in a practical way, sometimes sacrificing exactness and completeness for practical utility and intuitiveness. The idea is to make you aware of some common issues, together with their possible solutions, that have been developed and refined over recent years. Unfortunately, user interface design is a human-dependent task, and it doesn't make sense to constraint it in precise, formal rules.

Following the multidisciplinary approach of this book, we will see both GUI design and development issues together, often switching between the designer's and the implementer's viewpoints. We discuss both Sun's Java Look & Feel design guidelines, as available for Swing applications, and IBM-backed Eclipse GUI design guidelines, as available for SWT applications, although focusing more on the former: we discuss SWT extensively in Chapter 13.

This chapter is organized as follows:

4.1, GUI area organization discusses the issues related to the GUI design of screen areas in the main GUI window.

4.2, Choosers deals with a GUI design strategy that focuses on allowing users to select items and objects.

4.3, Memory components discusses the use of widgets that remember previous user choices and input, to enhance GUI usability.

4.4, Lazy initialization discusses the important approach of instantiating objects only when needed from a GUI design viewpoint.

4.5, Preference dialogs illustrates some typical GUI designs for application preferences and configuration information.

4.6, Waiting strategies introduces the most common choices for interacting with users during long-running tasks.

4.7, Flexible layout discusses the use of dynamic layout managers.

4.8, Common dialogs introduces some standard dialogs – About, Log in, and first-time dialogs, splash windows, providing reusable code.

4.9, Command components illustrates the GUI design issues related to providing toolbars, menus and buttons in GUIs.

4.10, Accessibility discusses how to provide accessibility support in Java GUIs.

4.11, Navigation and keyboard support introduces keyboard input and tab navigation to allow a GUI to be used from the keyboard.

4.12, Internationalization discusses the problems and solutions involved in internationalizing and localizing Java GUIs.

4.13, Help support describes the adoption of a help system in applications.

4.15, Leveraging object-oriented programming discusses how to employ OOP to build better Java GUIs more effectively.

4.14, Icons and images illustrates some GUI design issues related to icons and images with Java GUIs.

4.1   GUI area organization

User interfaces often need to show different information at the same time. In this case it is essential to determine a suitable organization for the screen area. Over the years several arrangements have been established for this purpose. A common layout for 'average' applications implements an area devoted to the work itself, such as the text editor pane in a RAD (rapid application development) environment, a command area, usually at the top of the frame, containing the menu bar and some toolbars, and a selection or exploration area on the left.

When there is more data to show, additional areas can be combined with these basic ones. We will see some examples of area organizations in the sections that follow.

Terminology

For container visual components, we will use the following terms in this chapter, which are taken from Swing terminology:

- A *window* is a visual container used for organizing the information that users see in an application. We will use this term to indicate both *dialogs* and *frames* (generic screens) or to indicate 'plain' windows – that is, those without the top header – used for example in splash screens.
- A *frame* is a window in which the user's main interaction takes place.
- A *dialog* is a secondary window that is dependent on a frame or on another dialog, and is used to support the main interaction that takes place in frame(s).

- Finally, a *panel* is a generic visual container that represents an area assembled with visual components. Panels can be composed within other panels or within any window.

Main frames

Essentially, except for the command area – the upper area, which gathers the menu bar and the toolbars – and a status bar on the bottom, the rest of the window is left to the designer's creativity.

A top-down design approach begins with the identification of the following standard areas in a GUI, or those of them that are required:

- *Selection area*, situated on the left of the main area. This usually contains a tree view or other selection components.

- *Work area*. the main area of the dialog, and where the user's attention is focused most of the time.

- *Secondary area*, which can be devoted to the details of the current operation, or to messages, or to some notification message not captured by the work area.

- Other areas. Depending on the GUI's complexity, additional display areas can be needed.

This type of organization has some common properties. Apart from the main area or application-specific areas, the other areas should be made visible and customizable as required by the user, and a means provided to make such settings persistent. This may be done with toggle buttons in the toolbar for the most commonly-used areas, while others may be located in a related drop-down menu. Areas other than the selection and work areas should be designed as simply as possible, in order not to distract the user's attention. For complex interactions that are not supported by the work area, a modal dialog is often the best choice.

Figure 4.1 shows a sample area organization for an application's main frame. This (fictitious) application manages a set of geographic databases containing images of the earth using different projections.

As we know from previous chapters, many design choices ultimately depend on the end user population. Their working habits, the tasks they regularly perform, and other variables all contribute to the final design. In the application above, for example, the need for comparison of different images prompts the use of a multiple document interface (MDI) display organization, implemented by using the internal frames in the main area (top right). The selection sub-area in the bottom left of Figure 4.1 has been added to accommodate the frequent task of selecting the various available projections for a given image.

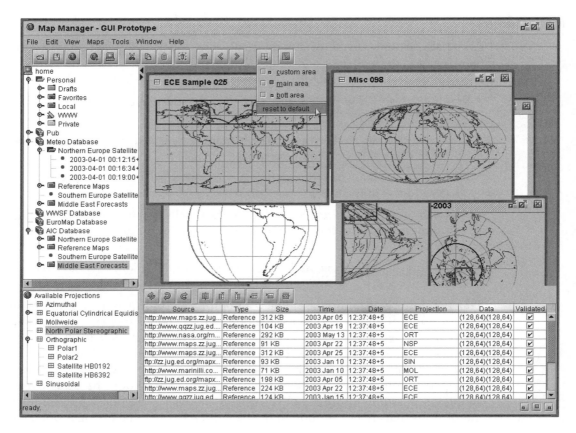

Figure 4.1   A typical main frame area organization (Compiere)

GUIs built using Eclipse can take advantage of the 'flat look' GUI library, an example of which is shown in Figure 4.2. Essentially, it exploits HTML-like widgets to save space in high-density form-based panels. It is available only within specialized panel subclasses, and it cannot be used in toolbars and other general-purpose containers.

The Eclipse 'flat look' is a valuable tool in the GUI designer's toolbox for SWT applications. As of Eclipse 3.1, though, it is still needlessly hard to use for

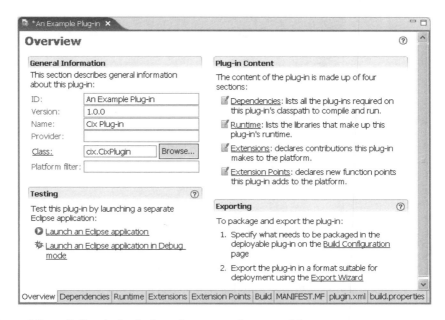

Figure 4.2   Eclipse's flat look to the rescue of crammed forms

developers. Ironically, an 'old-fashioned' desktop application GUI should take advantage of a newer and possibly more limiting technology: advanced Web forms.

Multiple document interfaces

Multiple document interfaces (MDIs) are GUIs in which several different fully-fledged internal windows are responsive to user interaction at the same time, like the application shown in Figure 4.1. MDIs can be implemented in different ways, for example as a collection of frames or non-modal dialogs in Swing.

The Swing library contains a special set of components, called *internal windows*, for providing a way to manage multiple windows that are confined inside a main window. From a usability perspective, internal frames and MDIs in general are difficult to manage for average users, and their use is usually not needed for most applications. Eclipse itself is an example of a complex GUI in which designers succeeded in minimizing the use of MDI, as shown in Figure 4.3.

Another common approach to the efficient exploitation of precious GUI real estate is to serialize it – that is, to split a long task into a sequence of simpler steps, each rendered with the same subset of the screen area. This approach has different names, but is most commonly known as a *wizard*.

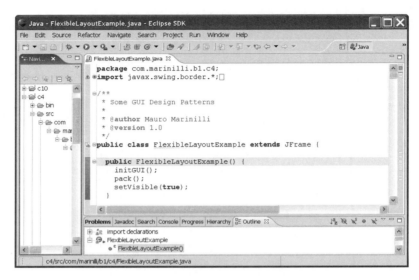

Figure 4.3   Eclipse's GUI design avoids the use of multiple document interfaces

Wizards

Wizards are a well-known and widespread way to organize GUI functionalities in order to support inexperienced users. A wizard guides the user through the features provided by the application in a simplified way, proposing only a few choices and limited information at a time. By narrowing the available choices, novice users are better guided through an interaction with the application. Historically, wizards made their debut in the mass market with Windows 95.

The (Advanced Java L&F Design Guidelines 2001) provides some useful advice on designing wizards for the Java Look and Feel, and the Eclipse guidelines also provide such advice. An example of a wizard designed to Eclipse design guidelines is shown in Figure 4.4.

The buttons at the bottom of the wizard are used for navigating through the various panels, and are disabled according to the semantic state of the current pane.

In an attempt to lower the cognitive burden needed to understand GUI interactions, all interactions should be kept localized and their context narrowed as much as possible. If user data prompts a GUI notification, this should be kept linked with the triggering cause as far as possible, so that the user will interpret it more easily. In the case of a wizard, an awkward situation arises when a data item inserted in a previous panel affects the behavior of another panel. In this case the user might not be able to notice the connection, and so fail to understand the behavior of the application.

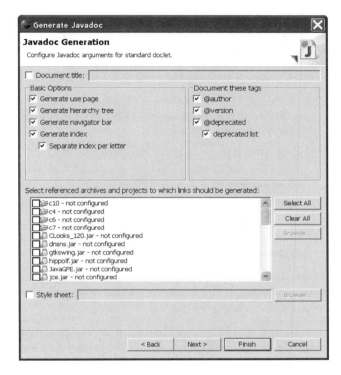

Figure 4.4   An Eclipse wizard to Eclipse design guidelines

Designing a wizard

We conclude this section by discussing some basic, general advice for designing wizard GUIs. Fortunately there is much literature and infrastructure support for building wizards in the form of high-level reusable API and classes.

Designing a usable wizard is usually not a complex task if a few simple rules are followed. Conversely, given their simplicity and the relatively cheap development cost of using a general framework to implement them, the opposite problem often the case – a proliferation of wizards in application that do not really need them. As a rule of thumb, wizards should provide an alternative interaction mechanism to an existing feature, or be employed for non-repetitive tasks for occasional users only.

Well-designed wizards clearly declare their boundaries, so that users know where the wizard begins, where it finishes, and the sequence of operations within it. The inputs and the final result should be clearly outlined, so that the user can be sure of what they are doing.

Usability studies have demonstrated some interesting aspects of this kind of user interface device. Users tend to employ a wizard only to complete a given task, and are relatively uninterested in learning new concepts in the meantime.

Wizards can be particularly useful for the following activities:

- Dividing a complex input process into many sequential steps. 'Serializing' a complex input form, such as for the creation of complex data structures, is a common case of this.

- Performing tasks that are inherently composed of a well-defined sequence of steps. By focusing on each step, correct task completion is much more likely to be achieved.

- Whenever users lack domain knowledge in some field and need to be guided through operations. Consider the integration of new hardware into an operating system, or the completion of some task involving decisions and knowledge in other fields.

Wizards for occasional, hard-to-undo operations should also provide a final recap screen where all the important data is summarized before the user leaves the wizard and completes the task.

The design ideas for organizing the application display area that we have shown in this section are rather general and can be applied to many different situations. Next we discuss another common pattern in practical GUI design – choosers.

4.2   Choosers

Principled, systematic area organization is essential in secondary windows, dialogs and choosers, as well as in any other part of the GUI. By *chooser* we mean a screen area specialized for a performing a selection task on a given item. Choosers deserve their own discussion, both because they happen to be a useful means of interaction in Java GUIs, and also because quite often their use has been misunderstood.

Figure 4.5 shows an example of a chooser with three distinct areas where the user can focus their attention:

- On the left-hand side the selection area contains a list that shows the items that can be picked.

- The right-hand side is the preview area, where the currently-selected item is shown.

- The bottom-most part of the dialog is occupied by the standard command buttons for deferred mode interaction and preview option.

Note that in choosers the main area coincides with the selection zone, because of the purpose of these components. To make the design coherent with the standard layout, the selection area is still organized on the left-hand side.

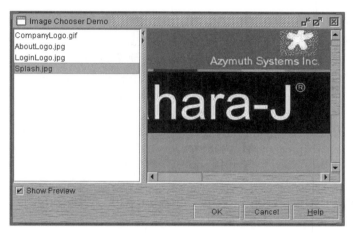

Figure 4.5   Area organization in an image chooser (Wood)

Often users need to specify one or more items while using the GUI. When this type of choice is occasional and involves a dedicated interaction because of its complexity, a chooser should be designed to accommodate it.

Choosers are often designed as pop-up dialogs that contain the information needed to specify the given item. Once the item has been chosen, the dialog is dismissed and the new value is used in the application.

Choosers are often activated by means of a button, usually a **More...** button. Such a button indicates the availability of further related data that can be showed by clicking the button. Such a behavior is signaled by the ellipsis (...) in the button's caption, together with a brief description of the planned action. For example, when selecting a file from a file chooser, instead of directly entering the file's path, a common choice for the related 'more' button label is **Browse...**

Chooser activation mechanisms

There are two main ways to show a chooser in a new window: as a pop-up window, or as a fully-fledged dialog (often a modal one).

A useful convention is to use a downward arrow to signal a pop-up chooser for buttons only, referred to as *drop-down buttons*[1]. In all other cases, a **More...** button that triggers the related chooser dialog is the most common solution.

1.   See icon images in *Graphic conventions* on page 156.

A chooser can be also contained in a lightweight pop-up such as the one used by Combo boxes, which in this respect can be seen as choosers for one text value among a list of available alternatives.

Chooser interaction styles

As we know from Chapter 3, we can have two main kinds of interaction modalities for dialogs: *immediate* and *deferred* mode.

The following two examples illustrate these two modalities and their implication for choosers: some of this discussion can be generalized for any other dialog type.

Figure 4.6 shows the standard file chooser provided by the JFC[2] in a fictitious text editor application. The file is first selected, and only when the choice is committed by hitting the **OK** button is the dialog dismissed and the new value transmitted to the underlying application. This is the deferred mode interaction style.

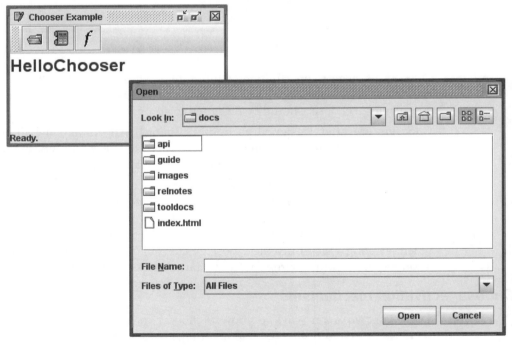

Figure 4.6   A deferred mode chooser (Smooth Metal)

---

2.   Java Foundation Classes (JFC) are the foundational libraries needed for building GUIs with Java for JSE. They comprise the AWT and Swing libraries.

Figure 4.7 shows activation of the 'choose color' button in the toolbar, causing the color chooser to appear. The difference from the previous example is two-fold: the changes made in the chooser dialog are instantly transmitted to the application, and consequently the dialog is modeless.

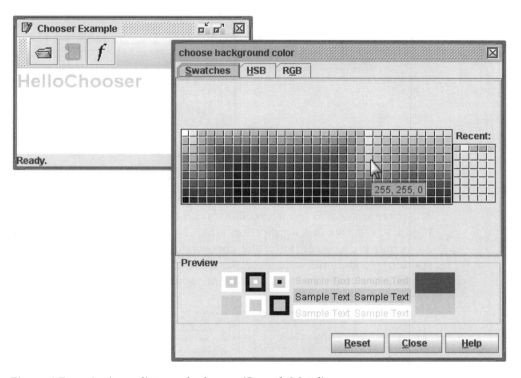

Figure 4.7   An immediate mode chooser (Smooth Metal)

There is another possible kind of interaction, which can be thought of as a combination of deferred mode – an explicit user commit action is required – and immediate mode: the window is not dismissed after user commit. In our fictitious text editor, we click the font button in the toolbar, and we are prompted with a font chooser dialog, as in Figure 4.8. Note the standard Java Look and Feel-compliant button organization.

In this example, using an immediate interaction style for the font selection could be confusing for the user and resource-consuming for the application. On the other hand, a deferred mode interaction style like the one in the file chooser is not optimal, because users prefer to see changes take place in a more interactive way. By using a multiple-use, deferred mode interaction style, we allow users to interact

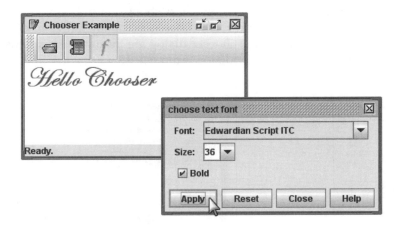

Figure 4.8   A multiple-use, deferred mode chooser (Smooth Metal)

more closely throughout the choice process at a level that is intermediate between the immediate and deferred interaction style (Figure 4.6 and Figure 4.7).

The presence of two modeless dialogs can bring some unforeseen combinations. Figure 4.9 shows our application when both modeless choosers are activated. Note that we allowed only one chooser for each kind, by disabling the corresponding command whenever the related chooser was up, although such a combination might be required in some applications.

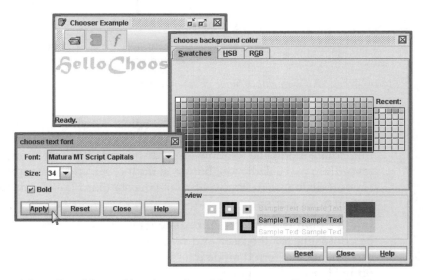

Figure 4.9   Possible combinations of modeless choosers (Smooth Metal)

Designing the interaction mode for choosers depends on several factors. The most important one is the kind of users that will be using them. Deferred mode should generally be preferred over immediate mode when the user population is made up of novices and inexperienced users. Because it provides an easier way of undoing a choice, it implies a cleaner interaction – the chooser dialog is modal, so it has to be dismissed to return to the application, hence the number of floating windows is kept under control – and keeps users more focused on the main task. Furthermore, deferred mode dialogs are more widespread in common, commercial GUIs, so users are more familiar with them. Essentially we trade usability for interaction power.

Immediate mode dialogs are used in cases in which a higher degree of interactivity is preferred and more freedom is left to the user. This happens when immediate feedback on a choice is important. Such a higher level of interactivity helps to enhance the choice process, because it allows the differences between the manipulated items to be seen immediately.

Item selection is distinct from item creation, but this is an artificial separation in practical GUIs. We discussed item selection first for clarity, but a chooser is often meant to allow users to create new items as well as selecting them from a list. In real-world choosers these two features are often blended.

Broadening the choice

From a practical viewpoint, the chooser approach is very close to the task of creating a new item. Real-world choosers frequently offer a way to create a new item as well as choosing from a list of available ones. The file chooser shown in Figure 4.10 below allows users to create a new file or folder as required.

It is always a good idea to provide an explicit way to create new items. In the case of file choosers, for example, new file creation is often obtained by entering a file name that doesn't yet exist. Unfortunately, there often is no visual hint that this is the way to do it, and users can be puzzled by this 'hidden' interaction mechanism, which often looks more like an implementation trick rather than an explicit design choice.

Other than creating new items and choosing existing ones, choosers shouldn't be overloaded with other functionalities. One of the benefits of this design solution is that it keeps the user's perception of the GUI highly structured, so that users feel comfortable and secure when interacting with it. Users *know* that they are dealing with such-and-such kind of item, and can be confused if the same chooser offers other functionalities. Real-world choosers are often polluted with management functionalities. Such features are less frequently accessed than choice-related ones, and are usually required only by experienced users.

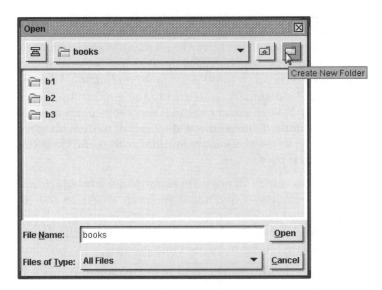

Figure 4.10   Creating new items through a chooser (Oyoaha)

More sophisticated dialogs, like management dialogs, can be built with the same design principles as choosers, but kept separate from them. In a word processor, for example, one could choose the style to be applied to a portion of text using a chooser, but the management dialog – where styles can be browsed in detail, edited, saved, imported and exported from the outside, and so on – should be kept separated from the simple chooser. A 'more' button, perhaps with a caption like **Styles...**, can be made available in the chooser if the design allows users to access the management dialog directly from the chooser.

The chooser approach can be used for selecting more than one item, as in Figure 4.11, in which users can select a list of items.

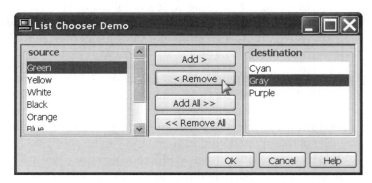

Figure 4.11   A list chooser (JGoodies Windows)

Conclusions

Choosers save GUI real estate in forms and selection screens, relegating selection to a specialized window. Choosers should be used only when the selection task is an infrequent one – in other cases, the use of a fully-fledged selection area or other more direct, faster selection mechanisms are better solutions.

Using choosers systematically in a GUI brings some benefits:

- The task of selecting an item is limited and circumscribed at a precise point, both in terms of interaction time and within the GUI.

- Completion signals indicating the end of the selection task to the user are provided automatically.

- Users understand the chooser concept, and by leveraging this repetitive interaction schema GUIs tend to be more predictable, enhancing their quality.

- Choosers are useful both for the GUI designer and for code developers.

Item creation and item selection are two conceptually separate tasks, although providing them in the same chooser is often good practice. When users are allowed to create a new item, there is usually a short-cut to such a feature within the chooser.

4.3   Memory components

Memory components are GUI components that are capable of maintaining a persistent state. This is an implementation-oriented distinction. As an example, a text field that keeps the history of previously-input strings in a drop-down can be implemented with a memory Combo box.

Memory components are usual Java visual components that can have one or more of their properties made persistent from session to session. Implementing them can be done through a specialized service provided in Service layer[3]. Designers usually need to specify only the persistent properties – in its JavaBeans meaning – of the given widgets.

There are many applications of memory components in GUI design. We will mention just a few here to better illustrate the concept.

---

3.   See Chapter 7.

Input history

Keeping track of previous user inputs is a way to record the current user's context, thereby enhancing the overall usability of the GUI. Figure 4.12 shows a simple prototype example of a text field that registers the data inserted into it persistently throughout a session, or even across sessions[4]. Searching capabilities further enhance its usability.

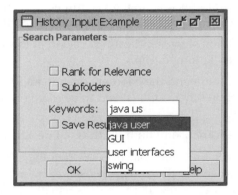

Figure 4.12   A memory combo box (JGoodies Plastic)

The field in Figure 4.12 is an example of support for user input provided automatically by the GUI. We will see in Chapter 13 that this and other stricter forms of control over user input can also be implemented for Web interfaces.

Saving user preferences

Memory components allow you to make GUI preferences persistent from session to session.

Figure 4.13 shows an example application that saves some GUI-related data persistently. The figure shows some example information that is retained for the user from session to session. Referring to the indicated areas on the figure, these are:

1. Tree structure and expanded path
2. Area separators
3. Toolbar customizations
4. Internal windows, their dimension and positions

---

4. This latter feature was implemented in the pioneering character-based GUI of Borland's TurboPascal.

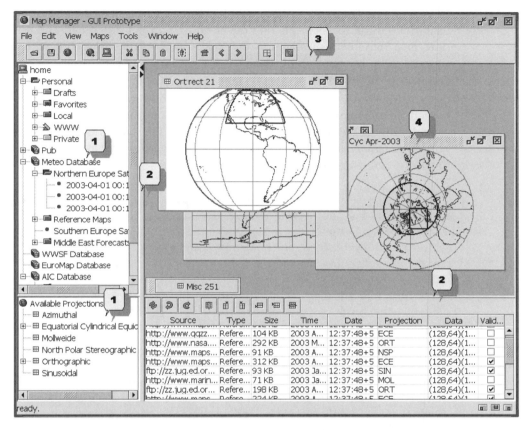

Figure 4.13   A customized application (JGoodies Plastic)

Memory components are quite important and useful in professional GUIs. They allow user customization in a way that is natural from an end user perspective, and inexpensive for developers. When the display organization becomes complex it is important to provide personalization features to allow users to customize them.

4.4   Lazy initialization

The start-up time, especially for complex GUIs, is an important aspect of GUI responsiveness and overall user experience. This is even truer for Java applications. The latest JRE technology considerably enhances start-up time, but a professional GUI can't blindly rely on the invisible hand of the Java Runtime

Environment. There are cases in which start-up time is critical to a system's usability – think for example of a never-ending applet download and initialization, or a rich client application that takes ages to fill the screen with server-sourced data. In stand-alone applications, too, snappy start-up is a feature that end users will undoubtedly appreciate.

Optimizing start-up times should be a general habit rather than a circumscribed procedure to be applied only in specific cases. It originates from implementation considerations, but involves GUI design as well. GUI designers should be aware of such considerations when designing the first window the application shows to the user.

> A note for Swing programmers. The `UIDefaults` class implements a common access point to all UI-related default values needed by Swing components. Some of these default values are rarely accessed, for example internal frame borders, so that employing a lazy instantiation mechanism make sense. Swing designers used an interface, `UIDefaults.LazyValue`, that is implemented by those classes that represent lazy values. Such an interface is composed of a single method, `createValue`, that returns an `Object` instance. The `get` method in `UIDefaults` first checks whether the type is an instance of `UIDefaults.LazyValue`. In this case the `createValue` method is invoked and the value is then returned.

Concretely, pieces of the GUI could be left hidden, and only when needed will they be instantiated on the fly[5]. Suppose we have a database management utility in which some databases are hosted on remote servers. To speed up GUI start-up, we could avoid the expensive (in time) remote connection, the application only connecting when prompted by the user.

Such an arrangement is implemented in the mock-up shown in Figure 4.14.

This prototype simulates an expensive connection time with a delay in expanding the third database node in the tree: you can try it yourself by running the prototype. To implement this mock-up we used some of the utility classes discussed in Chapter 5. What is interesting here is the addition of the connection delay simulation in the mock-up to make the prototype more realistic.

---

5. Lazy instantiation (or lazy initialization) is a strategy focused on deferring the allocation of costly resources that are not always needed until they become necessary. In this way the cost of those resources can be saved in cases where they are not required, both in terms of runtime and memory allocation.

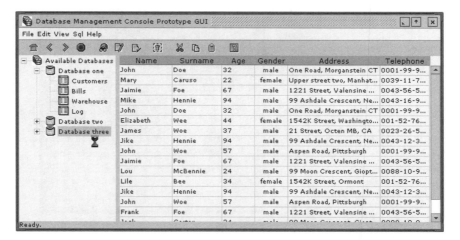

Figure 4.14   A snappy startup GUI (Hippo)

This GUI design does not need to sacrifice performance in its implementation. For example, we could keep a lightweight cache of the nodes the user expanded the last time they used the GUI. The net effect would be quick application start-up, with a delay being perceived by the end user only on node expansion. There are many possible enhancements such as this, for example keeping only few expensive nodes in memory at time, and re-adding them to the tree as needed, and so on.

4.5   Preference dialogs

User preferences are a common feature of modern GUIs. A widely-accepted practice that makes sense in terms of usability is to gather all user configuration-related commands into one configuration dialog. At design time it is important to decide what configuration information each UI object has. Usually the preference dialog is activated via a menu item and a standard button on the toolbar – see for example the Library application in Chapter 15.

Even in simple GUIs there is often a need for a preference dialog, especially when supporting a coherent means of expanding the application's features for future releases.

It is customary to organize preferences in a deferred mode dialog. To understand why, consider the application shown in Figure 4.15. This shows a fictitious GUI for a simple HTTP server. Given the simplicity of the application, operative and configuration commands are arranged together.

Figure 4.15   A confusing GUI design (Hippo)

This confuses users at first, because they can't easily understand the impact of the given commands on the application, even if they are neatly separated in different tabs. This is another case of developers dictating the GUI design. The 'catch-all' use of the tabbed pane stems directly from the implementation. Preferences should be gathered in a specialized dialog and triggered by the related option, as prescribed for example in the Java Look and Feel design guidelines.

The design choice for preference dialogs shown here of course differs from that prescribed in the official Java Look and Feel design guidelines. We discuss some of the different design choices for preference dialogs in the next section. Other visual errors demonstrated by Figure 4.15 are incorrect alignment of the check boxes and the incoherent vertical spacing between widgets.

Preference dialogs styles

Preference dialogs are an area in which designers' creativity is plentifully applied. One common design, demonstrated for example by Netscape Navigator's preference dialog, is that of using a tree to organize the selection area, like the one shown in Figure 4.18 on page 140.

In simple or medium-complexity applications particularly, using a tree results in a less usable design. It excessively burdens the user's memory (*'Where was that option?'*) and obliges users to expand the selection area to look for a specific property, when a simpler design would have been more effective. The Java Look and Feel design guidelines suggest a different design choice, one that simplifies the selection area as a non-hierarchical list. Figure 4.16 shows such a design for a fictitious Java Internet browser application.

Unfortunately, such a design doesn't scale well to complex GUIs, such as those with many options. In such cases – when the exploration area on the left doesn't

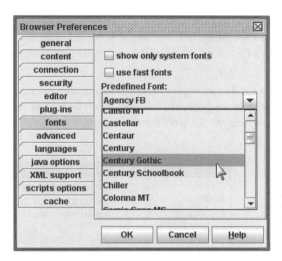

Figure 4.16   A preference dialog designed following the Java L&F guidelines (Smooth Metal)

result in sparse tree – the best solution is to organize the many options into a hierarchy. A possible solution, adopted in some of the Swing examples in this book, is shown in Figure 4.17.

The hierarchy is realized by means of a `JTabbedPane`, and the exploration area on the left-hand side, implemented with a list, points to the categories of options on the right-hand side. Icons can be used in the selection list to strengthen the mental association of label to options category, making options more recognizable for occasional users as well.

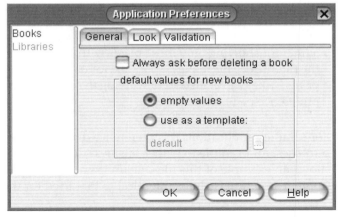

Figure 4.17   A preference dialog with a different design (Liquid)

This design isn't too dissimilar to that prescribed by the Java Look and Feel design guidelines and shown in Figure 4.16, but can accommodate more complex GUIs as well. Moreover, it forces designers to organize the options in a hierarchy at most only two levels deep.

When a GUI is complex, the previous design doesn't work well and we need to resort to a more powerful design, such as that shown in Figure 4.18, which is taken from the Eclipse 3.1 preference dialog.

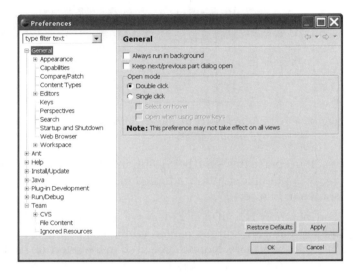

Figure 4.18   A view of the Eclipse 3.1 preference dialog

The Eclipse 3.1 preference dialog employs a search facility – the Combo box at the top of the exploration area on the left-hand side of Figure 4.18 – that acts as a filter for showing only those pages with occurrences of keywords that match the filter text. This makes it possible for users to access the required preference pages by keyword, instead of walking the exploration tree looking for the right preference page.

For complex applications this preference dialog design can be used for functional purposes, for example to gather business domain configuration data. Figure 4.19 shows an example of this idea, again from the Eclipse GUI. See how the general Content structure is almost identical to that used for the dialog in Figure 4.18.

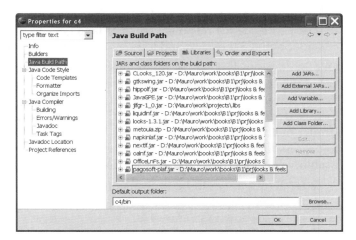

Figure 4.19   The Eclipse 3.1 project properties dialog

Despite the fact that the GUI design device is almost identical, the two previous designs are different and should be kept distinct in the GUI to avoid confusion. A useful approach is to always stick to rigorous naming conventions: 'properties' are business-domain data, with one property dialog per business domain type, such as Person, Project, and Account properties, while 'preferences' are extra functional configuration data, with one preference dialog for the whole application. Designs should also be optimized for each user type: only repetitive users should need access to preferences, while properties dialogs should be made more easily accessible and usable, for example by providing contextual menu access.

4.6   Waiting strategies

Managing user interaction while tasks are being carried out by an application is a common issue in GUI design. Responsiveness, as we saw in the first part of this book, is an important feature in modern user interfaces. Just as with people, we have the feeling that a slowly-responding person is somehow unintelligent, and, false as it may be, we call them a 'slow' person. On the other hand, gadget-laden, baroque GUIs are no more usable than sober, plainer GUIs. The Java Look and Feel favors the latter approach both as a deliberate, wise choice, and as an undeniable practical necessity.

Java desktop GUIs – mainly J2SE, but also J2EE – may suffer from responsiveness problems. Indeed, competing platforms have listed this as a major drawback of Java GUIs. However, careful design and implementation can easily produce (relatively) snappy, responsive GUIs in Java. We will see some of the little details that can enhance the responsiveness of Java GUIs in this chapter. We will again consider both GUI design and low-level implementation details.

One of these techniques is quite effective when medium–long tasks must be accomplished, and turns out to be quite common and easy to implement in practice. A common problem is to inhibit user input during computation. A solution to this when using the Swing toolkit is to use the 'glass pane' component or similar methods to divert input events from the GUI, as it is temporarily unable to process them correctly. These can be neat technical tricks, but they often lack usability considerations and a sound cost–benefit balance.

A better solution would be to focus on communicating with the user, showing them the current application state. A modal progress dialog does the trick nicely: an example is shown in Figure 4.20.

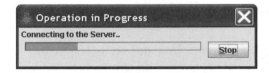

Figure 4.20   An example progress dialog (Ocean1.5)

This simple solution has a number of advantages:

i.   It shows the user what is happening.
ii.   It gives the user the option of canceling the process.
iii. As an aside, the modal progress window intercepts all the events directed to the underlying visual controls.

In practice there are many cases in which tight control over a task is not possible, for example a client–server connection to a Web service, where completion time is not known *a priori*. In this cases a simple solution is to provide an activity indicator only, using an 'indefinite progress bar,' as shown in Figure 4.21.

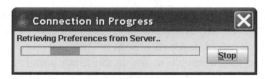

Figure 4.21   An example of a indefinite progress dialog (Ocean1.5)

Unfortunately, progress windows are not commonly seen in older Java GUIs, even in the simplistic arrangement proposed above, because of the cost of implementing them with low-level Swing components and the related threading infrastructure.

Things are simpler with SWT GUIs and the Eclipse RCP that provides a framework for supporting concurrent tasks. It is possible to choose between asynchronous (running in background) and synchronous (blocking user interaction until done) tasks, and this choice can be also offered to the end user, as shown in Figure 4.22, which is taken from Eclipse 3.1.

Figure 4.22   A progress indicator in Eclipse 3.1

Background execution basically uses the same implementation, but leaves users the ability to interact with the IDE while the task thread is running. When this is chosen, Eclipse 3.1 represent the task in the bottom right-hand side of the main frame in order to be less intrusive. Users can still interact with the task, stopping it, viewing details, and so on, by clicking on the button icon in the low-right corner, shown in Figure 4.23.

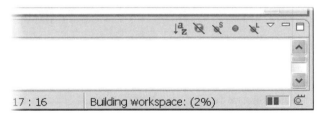

Figure 4.23   An Eclipse 3.1 progress indicator

The same indicator implemented with Flat Look is shown in Figure 4.24.

Figure 4.24   An Eclipse 3.1 Flat Look progress indicator

4.7   *Flexible layout*

Generally speaking, a well-designed window is first a usable one. Usability is frequently helped by the capability of resizing the window to enlarge it, or even to enlarge only a portion of it, according to the user's wishes.

Translating this into Java code means reconsidering our component layout philosophy. Usually designers tend to design 'static' windows, in which the widget visual organization is designed in a once-and-for-all fashion: such windows are easier and cheaper to design and build. Only for the main window or particularly critical windows is the layout is allowed to be variable, usually in the form of window resizing or using some `JSplitPane` here and there. This is easier than considering all possible user resizing needs or other related interactions, and also eases development.

Consider the fictitious GUI in Figure 4.25, which represents a hypothetical mock up for a peer-to-peer file exchange application. The first two areas list locally-available files and currently-exchanging ones. The bottom-most area represents a chat facility.

Consider the dynamic layout organization of the main frame. Allowing the window to be resizable is not a proper solution: the user might need to enlarging some of the internal lists, and this is not allowed by the design – its developers wrongly thought that a scroll pane would provide all the flexibility the user needed.

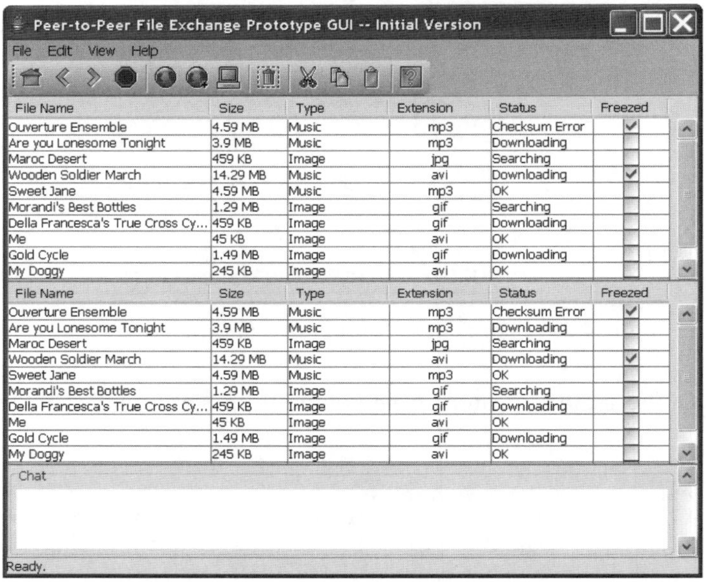

Figure 4.25   A not-so-flexible layout (Office2003)

A slightly more sophisticated design like the one in Figure 4.26 greatly enhances the usability of the application. Note that the two designs look pretty much the same from their (static) screenshots. It is in their dynamic behavior that the better quality of the second design becomes clear. Figure 4.26 shows this by using arrows.

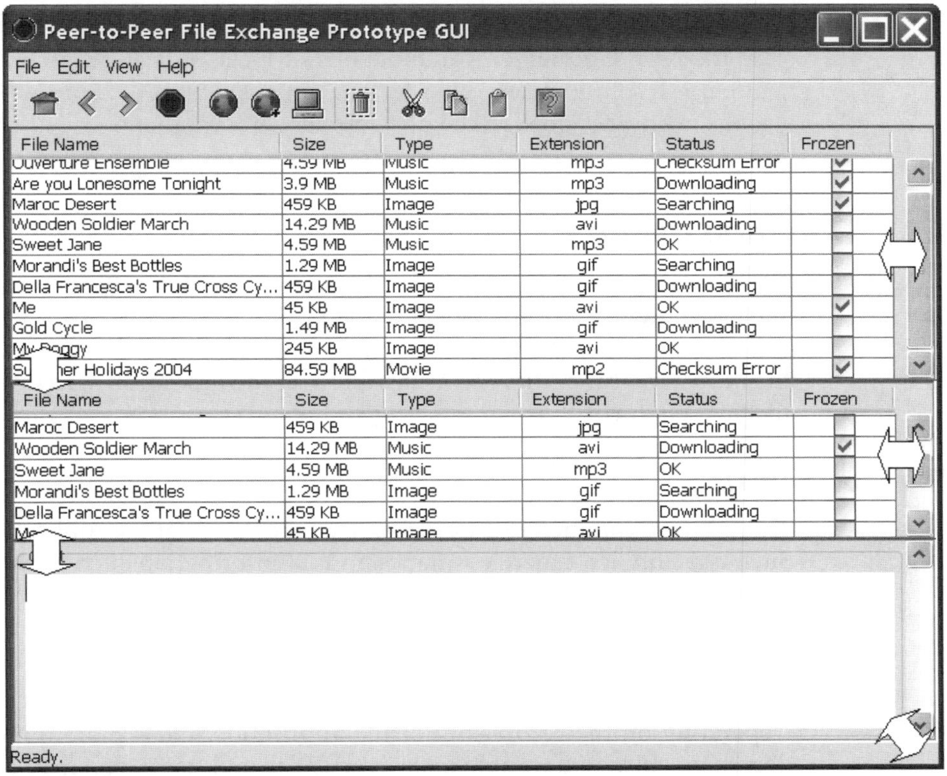

Figure 4.26   A more flexible layout (Office2003)

Any component in the window can now be enlarged as required, greatly adding to the GUI's usability. The implementation of this enhancement came quite cheaply, as we used only two split panes to do the trick. The point here is in the *idea* of thinking of any of a GUI's window layouts as flexible ones.

Hence, thinking dynamically about the layout of windows is essential for quality design, and has a relatively low impact on their development. Considering the possible degrees of freedom of a GUI usually isn't a demanding operation.

Unfortunately, developers and designers tend to neglect this aspect, producing nice-looking but totally rigid windows that could be made much more usable with only a little additional effort. Systematically considering how to make your GUI flexible is essentially a change in design and implementation habits, but one that can greatly improve the quality of the resulting GUIs with only a little extra effort.

> It is usually a good idea to make all dialogs – not to mention frames – resizable by the user. Unforeseen combinations of local and language locale settings, monitor resolution, and other factors can make your GUI unusable, even if it looks neatly designed in the development environment.

4.8   Common dialogs

GUI designers often tend to find themselves dealing with the same problems, such as showing information about their product, or notifying something basic to novice users. Over the years some design solutions have become consolidated in the industry. This section describes a few of the best-known, as implemented for the Java platform.

The 'About' dialog

This is a very common feature of GUIs, where details of the application are shown. Such a facility isn't mere cosmetics, in that information such as the license data, the software version, or the list of the JAR files currently loaded, can be accessed by users. As prescribed by the Java Look and Feel design guidelines, this information is usually organized into two dialogs, one for the essential data, and a second with additional information.

Depending on the complexity of the application and – more importantly – the degree to which you want to make it visible to end-users, you may decide to show only a portion of such data in your 'About' dialog. Technologies like JNLP[6] solve many of the commonest debugging and deployment problems, so that showing too many details of your application in the 'About' dialog may not be really needed.

---

6.   See the example application in Chapter 14

Main panel

The organization of the main panel is discussed in the official Java Look and Feel design guidelines. Figure 4.27 shows an example of an 'About' dialog.

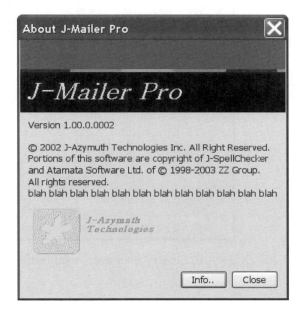

Figure 4.27   An About dialog example (Hillenbrand Windows)

Exploiting Web visual conventions, some areas of the 'About' dialog, such as manufacturer's information, may be made clickable like a link on a HTML page. The 'About' dialog in the example application in Chapter 15 shows such a technical trick at work. Here however we prefer a plain implementation to introduce the issue.

The visual organization of the main information panel, as prescribed in the Java Look and Feel design guidelines, is shown in Figure 4.28. The highlighted areas are: (1) product name, (2) dialog banner, (3) text information, (4) company logo, and (5) interaction buttons.

The way to reach the additional information dialog is suggested in the form of a single **Info...** button in Figure 4.27 and Figure 4.28.

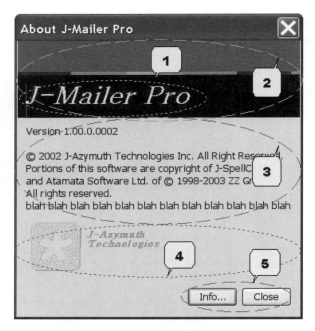

Figure 4.28   JL&F About dialog main panel organization (Hillenbrand Windows)

Additional info panel

A few words about the additional information panel, displayed prompted as a separated modal dialog when the **Info...** button is clicked, are relevant.

You aren't obliged to provide an additional information dialog in your 'About' dialog, as long as the data you need to show can be neatly accommodated in the main panel. If required, information stored in the additional information dialog can include:

- JAR files listing, each with its dimension and exact version.
- Java system properties, such as the current JRE used, the heap size, the locale, and so on.
- The version of the application.
- Some of the more important application-dependent configuration data.
- Other configuration data, such as the version and type of some of the Java extensions currently used.
- External modules, required applications, third-party libraries and the like.

This data is usually organized in tables and labels ordered by means of a JTabbedPane.

A general-purpose implementation of an 'About' dialog component that complies with the Java Look and Feel design guidelines is provided with the code bundle for this chapter. Our class implementation offers many constructors: you can specify the parent frame, the additional information dialog, the main image, and the company logos. When the empty constructor is used, the dialog is instantiated with a set of default values documented in the source code for that class.

Log-in dialog

Some applications need to identify specific users before they are granted access to the full functionalities of the GUI. This is usually done by means of an authentication phase, in which the user is requested to insert a log-in name and a password. An example might be a thick client application that needs to access sensitive data on the server, or a personalized application that has been tailored to a particular user.

In such cases a log-in dialog is shown. The Java Look and Feel design guidelines prescribe principles for the design of such dialogs. Figure 4.29 shows an example of a standard Java log-in dialog.

Figure 4.29   An example of a log-in dialog (Tonic)

Simpler dialogs, such as those without a product header at the top of the dialog, can also be provided, but it is always a good idea to make the identity and the purpose of the authentication phase explicit to the user, providing a recognizable indication of your application.

First-time message dialogs

The first time an operation is performed, inexperienced users might need to be reassured about the GUI's internal state, to answer the mental question 'what is going to happen now?' This can be done neatly by using message dialogs that describe the operation that is about to be performed, or that has just been performed. Allowing these dialogs to be shown only when required avoids annoying the user in subsequent sessions and makes the application more usable.

Figure 4.30, Figure 4.31, and Figure 4.32 show three examples of this kind of explanation dialog:

- The dialog in Figure 4.30 notifies the user of the consequences of an operation they have performed.

Figure 4.30   An example of a first-time only explanation dialog (Ocean1.5)

- The dialog in Figure 4.31 allows the application to both acquire an answer from the user and to avoiding asking the question again.

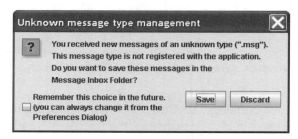

Figure 4.31   A first-time only explanation dialog (Ocean1.5)

In Figure 4.31 the dialog also explains where to find the option even when turned off. Sometimes insecure users avoid switching off a feature, fearing that they won't be able to restore it easily in the future. If wisely employed, such little details greatly increase the overall usability of a GUI.

- Finally, Figure 4.32 shows another example of a first-time dialog, in which such a facility is used to warn the user explicitly about the effect of the operation they have performed.

First-time dialogs can be implemented easily using simple memory components.

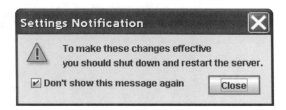

Figure 4.32   Another first-time only explanation dialog (Ocean1.5)

Splash window

Another commonly-used window in non-trivial GUIs is the screen that appears during application start-up. This window entertains the user during start-up and informs them of what is going on while waiting for the application. The Java Look and Feel design guidelines suggest a way to organize the visual appearance of a splash window.

A splash window is a good place to show an application's identity. A GUI compliant with the Java Look and Feel design guidelines doesn't loose its identity – rather, it becomes more usable and recognizable by users. The splash window is one of the correct places to put your application's 'personal' touch, so is important to not to waste such a chance.

An example is shown in Figure 4.33.

Figure 4.33   Splash window example

In this case you might find it interesting to look at the source code. This consists of a reusable yet simple class that provides all the functionality for a splash window. It provides a way to set up the static image shown in the window, the text in the message label at the bottom, and a mechanism to hide or show it as needed. The SplashWindow class is provided in the code bundle for this chapter.

4.9   *Command components*

This section discusses GUI components for managing user commands.

Menus, toolbar buttons and other means of asserting commands are an important part of a GUI. It is therefore no wonder that the Java Look and Feel design guidelines describe how such components should be organized in detail. We will give some examples here.

Figure 4.34 through Figure 4.38 show examples of a fictitious application that adopts the official guideline's suggestions for menu organization. As with all the other examples, you can run these on your own computer. Apart from menus, Figure 4.34 shows the use of command palette internal frames, which can be used in a multiple document interface (MDI) environment.

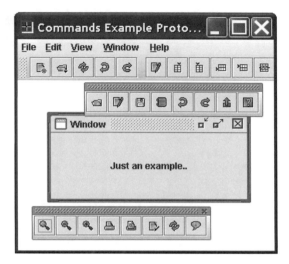

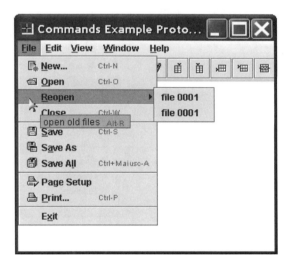

Figure 4.34   Examples of various command components (Ocean1.5)

Let's focus on menus first. The Java Look and Feel design guidelines prescribe a suggested structure for common menus, like **File**, **Edit**, and **Help**. Figure 4.35 shows the **File** menu. When the same commands are available through a toolbar, it is customary to associate a unique icon to the command to make it more recognizable by the user.

Figure 4.35   Eclipse menus

The standard **Edit** menu is illustrated in Figure 4.36 for both Swing and Eclipse.

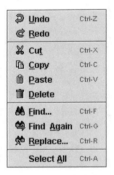

Figure 4.36   The suggested Edit menu organization for Swing (Metal) and Eclipse

Figure 4.37 illustrates an example of the **View** menu that employs radio button menu items for selecting the application's icon size.

> When information is accessed only infrequently, as in the case of the icon size for the application shown in Figure 4.37, the information can be put in a global configuration (preferences) dialog instead of directly in a menu.

Another example of menu organization is shown in Figure 4.38, which is taken from a fictitious graphics application.

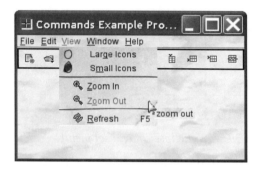

Figure 4.37   An example of view menu organization (Napkin)

Figure 4.38   Help menu suggested organization for Swing (OfficeXP) and Eclipse

Contextual menus are another important category of menu, one that should be made available for medium–large, non-form based applications, like that shown in Figure 4.39.

Figure 4.39   An Eclipse contextual menu

Expandable menus are a menu variant that is supported natively by SWT, as shown in Figure 4.40, which is also available for Swing through third-party libraries. Clicking on the title minimizes or expands the menu as required.

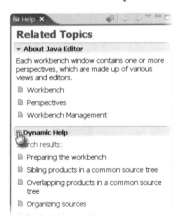

Figure 4.40   An expandable/collapsible menu

Graphic conventions

A number of conventions are adopted in SWT and the Java Look and Feel design guidelines. The latter provides four standard adornments for expressing common functionalities in button icons, as shown in Table 4.1.

Table 4.1   Graphic conventions for Java L&F button icons

Indicator name	Use	Example icon
Drop-down menu	A pop-up menu appears when clicking the button	
New object	A new object of the given type is created following the current GUI metaphor	
Add object	An object of the given type is added following the current GUI metaphor	
Properties	Prompt a property/setting window for that object	

The Java Look and Feel design guidelines describe the graphics for any of the adornments in Table 4.1 in full detail. The guidelines also warn designers about mixing two or more indicators in the same icon. Take the case of a 'new item' button that brings up a menu with a gallery of items available for creation. We should use both 'new object' and the 'drop down menu' indicators. We can slightly modify the button interaction to use only one indicator by resorting to an object gallery dialog that will work as the pop-up menu, leaving only the 'new item' adornment to the toolbar button. When the user clicks the button, a dialog appears that allows them to choose the type of new objects they want to create. In this way the button can be left only with the 'new' indicator.

An interactive example of the use of the button graphical indicators is provided with the code for this book, and shown in Figure 4.41.

Figure 4.41   Examples of button indicators at work for the Swing L & F

Apart from the standard adornments, there are a number of other common graphical designs for buttons. For example, customizing the main window areas is a common task. You can use a toggle button for collapsing unneeded window areas. For more details, see (Java L&F Design Guidelines 2001).

Toolbar composition

Toolbar creation is a topic necessarily involves implementation considerations. From a software design viewpoint, the toolbar composition is mainly a creational problem. The issues with which developers are often concerned are how toolbars are assembled, and from where the commands are obtained.

We provide various implementation strategies for command management throughout this book that can be employed in a wide range of situations. Problems arise when the application needs to support dynamic toolbar composition. There are of course several different levels of features that can be supported. Loading new commands when new modules are plugged into the application can be achieved via JNLP technology, and does not require any special programming such as reading commands from properties files and the like. As the JNLP protocol becomes more popular and widespread, its more advanced features, such as the JARDiff format, which allows downloading of only the portions of the JAR files that change from version to version, can ease the development of this kind of feature, not only for mounting new modules, but also for applications updates. The more popular solution, though, is to employ a plug-in architecture.

Another typical toolbar feature is enabling users to customize application toolbars. We briefly touched on the issue of user customization in the section about memory components. Conceptually, menus act as a predefined and logically-organized repository of the available commands for an application, while toolbars are often left to the user to customize: they may contain a subset of all possible commands, or can be even switched off completely by the user.

Some software designers like to use more sophisticated mechanisms for toolbar creation, based on negotiation protocols between the GUI builder and the objects that are publishing their functions via the GUI. We will not discuss such architectures here, especially because they tend to needlessly complicate the class architecture and weigh it down at application start-up – which, as we have seen, is a critical issue for Java applications. Usually a thoughtful and neat class design can provide many such features without sacrificing runtime performance.

Command composition

Several implementation considerations affect GUI design.

Contextual menus are a useful way of organizing user interaction. The underlying implementation should be taken into account for cost-aware, professional GUIs. One common issue is the gathering of commands from different GUI items into one menu. The user is not aware of such composition, but this mechanism has several benefits:

*   It organizes the menu commands in more rational groups or hierarchies.
*   It allows for an elegant mapping into an OOUI and the OO implementation of the designed GUI. Each item is mapped into an OOUI object, then into

several Java objects. The complexity of the GUI is divided into smaller, coherent pieces, each one exposing some specialized commands.

- The creation mechanism of complex menus is made systematic and general in order to be extensively adopted in a wide range of GUIs.

- It establishes a standard, general logical division between the responsibilities of complex commands, possibly involving several objects. Many commands, belonging to different objects, can be composed together in a unique menu. They are kept separated in compartments by separation lines within a menu for a clarity.

Command composition is not merely the gathering of available commands from each of the relevant GUI objects. The most general scenario involves the negotiation of commands among the classes involved. In fact, some commands may be not applicable in the given context – for example, an administrative user often has more commands available than normal users – and they may not even appear in the menus, or some commands may depend on the interaction of several objects, and so on.

An example of this latter case might be a list of items: depending on the current selection, the contextual menu can show selection-dependent commands. In a file listing window, for example, when selecting all image files, a **Create animation** menu item could be included in the pop-up contextual menu.

Figure 4.42 shows another example of this technique, in which the Eclipse GUI requests all its loaded plug-ins to provide their available views.

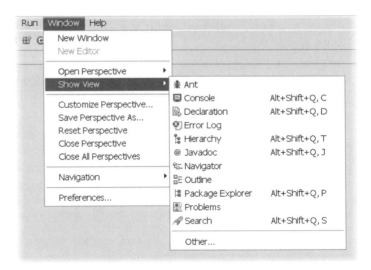

Figure 4.42   Eclipse 3.1 Example of command composition

From a programmer's viewpoint, in such complex cases it may be useful to employ a Java class devoted exclusively to negotiating the commands, populating the pop-up menu, and executing the more complex, cross-objects commands that are often needed.

4.10 Accessibility

Software accessibility is now legislated for in the USA and some other countries. It is an important commercial market, and supporting *assistive technologies* in Java is quite easy. When designing a GUI, the following four main disabilities should be taken in account as a minimum:

- Color blindness
- Partial or total deficit of vision
- Partial or complete lack of hearing
- Partial or total absence of mouse and keyboard use

> Other more complex disabilities (including cognitive ones) exist, but we do not cover them. The interested reader can refer to some of the URLs provided at the end of this section.

Designers should prepare their application for interaction with external assistive technology tools, such as screen magnifiers. This is only one side of the coin, however. The GUI should be made highly customizable for fonts, their size, colors, and so on. Color-blind users can need color combinations that may seem strange to others, while users with impaired vision might require unusually large fonts, and so on.

As a default, JFC applets and applications – and with some limitations, AWT ones as well – use the settings from the underlying environment. Fonts, their sizes, system colors, and other settings are therefore inherited automatically, as long as the application does not explicitly set them.

When implementing ad-hoc components[7], Swing developers implement the `Accessible` interface, which provides the core of accessible data that is used by assistive technologies. Naturally, Eclipse support for accessibility is provided as well.

---

7.   See Chapter 16.

Testing the final product for accessibility

No matter how diligently accessibility is designed into an application, the final test is its use by users with real disabilities. Although the next chapter covers GUI testing, there are some practical considerations worth mentioning here.

Firstly, we need to test the application for keyboard support without the mouse (you could even take it away). This allows an application to be tested entirely via keyboard: we need to verify that all the parts of the GUI remain accessible using only the keyboard. Usability should be verified as well – shortcuts, mnemonics, accelerators, and so on. Colors and fonts settings can be tested by choosing a large font size, say 24 points or more, and verifying what happens to each window in the application.

A special Look and Feel class is available from the Sun Web site for Swing that is designed for low-vision users. A GUI can also be tested with external assistive tools such as IBM's Self-Voicing Kit for Java.

Conclusions

This is only a brief discussion of accessibility in Java GUIs. There are many useful resources on the Web: IBM provides an excellent source of material on this issue, as does Sun's Web sites:

`http://www-3.ibm.com/able/guidelines/software/accesssoftware.html`

`http://www.sun.com/access/developers/developing-accessible-apps`

Many other resources on this important issue are available on the Internet.

4.11 Navigation and keyboard support

Navigation is the flow of control from one window to another. This section discusses navigation between elementary widgets. Navigation between screens has been touched on in various parts of this chapter, such as the discussion about wizard design, and will be discussed in depth in Chapter 9 in the section on Web user interfaces.

Keyboard support for command selection is essential in usable GUIs. Experienced users tend to use quicker ways of performing the same operation as they become knowledgeable with an application. The keyboard is a good way to shorten inter-action times for expert users, as it doesn't make the application more complicated for novices.

Keyboard shortcuts

The JFC library provides a complete set of tools for handling keyboard input at various levels of abstraction. We won't get into programming details here, but it is important to consider these features when designing a GUI.

A useful feature for enhancing the navigability of your dialogs is to provide a default button that is activated when the user hits the **Return** key. The Java Look and Feel will signal this special button, as shown for example by the **Close** button in Figure 4.30. Support for the **Escape** key is also widely used in dialogs, whenever appropriate.

Keyboard support should be designed while bearing in mind that it will often be the main support for repetitive users. As such, it should be employed to cover all the application's functionalities, even though critical ones where data can be lost, such as **Delete**, or closing a dialog, shouldn't provide keyboard shortcuts.

Tab traversal

The tab key is used for moving the focus between components in a window. By repeatedly pressing the tab key, users can navigate through all a window's components. Designing the correct traversal sequence enhances the usability of the GUI for those users that take advantage of keyboard support.

This feature is especially important for windows that are used frequently, such as data input forms. The default sequence is dictated by the order of component's addition into the window, as in the code listing, and can be modified explicitly by the focus framework provided in J2SE 1.4 and subsequent versions. An example of tab traversal in a simple dialog is shown in Figure 4.43 – the arrows indicate the movement of the focus for repeated presses of the tab key.

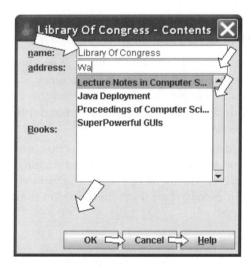

Figure 4.43   Tab traversal in a dialog

Tab traversal is a form of keyboard support, and as such it follows the general rules discussed here and in the Java Look and Feel design guidelines.

4.12 Internationalization

The design of applications suitable for a global marketplace, referred to as *internationalization*, and the related topic of customizing an existing application for a given locale, *localization*, are important issues in GUI design.

The cost of localizing an application can be roughly thought of as the sum of the development costs of the required infrastructure, plus the required messages translation. For this latter cost, (Maner 1997) indicates a sum of between $0.25 and $0.75 per word. For Java applications, however, such figures are usually an overestimate – thanks to the Java internationalization architecture, the translation process can be accomplished cheaply, for example by sending the relevant text files to be translated by a suitable localization company.

The key point is the provision of technical support for internationalization. Even if it is not planned to distribute the application in different countries, it is a good idea to consider the internationalization issue from the start of the GUI design process. Unfortunately, for effective localization, it is not enough to provide different translation files and a sound software design that supports external resource bundles. Apart from the software architecture, the following factors for international GUI design should be considered as a minimum:

- Translating messages and any other textual data, such as mnemonics, accelerators and help data, by means of properties or other support files.

- Other Java-specific technical facilities, such as input frameworks, good-quality font sets, and so on.

- Flexible layout, which is essential to accommodate labels, buttons and other text-based widgets in different languages.

- A thoughtful design of the general interaction style, to be as culture-neutral as possible – a loquacious GUI that displays many information messages can be viewed as polite in some cultures and arrogant in others.

- Specific cultural issues, such as:
  - Images, colors, sounds and other graphics conventions: icons, images and other locale-sensitive data references can be put in resource bundles so that they can be easily localized.
  - Currency, units of measurement, and any other number formats.
  - Various conventions such as date formats, phone numbers, salutations, and so on.

- Cultural issue in general. This is a complex problem, and involves the help of specialists in the target culture. A large number of 'cultural' accidents can be found in commercial GUIs. Some are unimportant, such as a progress bar that starts from the left in a country in which text is written from right to left, but others are more serious. Even some apparently neutral associations like using a Red Cross logo, for example, can be found offensive in some non-Western cultures.

Using resources bundles for all the relevant resources (icons, text messages, and the rest) can also be useful even if an application is not planned for internationalization, as it allows all messages, icons, and other resources such as audio clips to be polished more easily, by non-programmers if necessary.

A problem arises on platforms with different locales. From J2SE 1.4 onwards, multilingual support covers standard JFC components such as the file chooser dialog. This engenders the risk of providing users with fragmented multilingual GUIs, for example with the main frame in English and other standard dialogs in the application's current language. As a work-around, the locale can be over-written or labels can be set explicitly by developers, although this latter practice results in a hack rather than a disciplined design.

It is always good practice to consider internationalization issues in the first place when designing a GUI. This involves not only providing a flexible and dynamically-adjustable layout to handle text of unforeseen dimensions, or other technical tricks, but also to rethink icons, interactions, and even GUI concepts from a multi-culturally-aware perspective. Daunting as it may seem, such a task is well repaid in the long run. The cost of localizing an already-developed application from scratch is always much greater than the effort of designing it and testing it for usability with internationalization in mind. Even if internationalization is not foreseen in the near future, a preemptive minimal internationalization-aware design, for example implementing global icons, flexible layouts, and text files for messages, is always a wise choice.

4.13 *Help support*

J2SE ships with a library for full client-side help support. The JavaHelp library is an example of this kind of support, which provides context-sensitive help of two types: user-initiated and system-initiated. User-initiated help can be activated in four different ways:

- By pressing the **F1** key it is possible to display the help data about the container that currently has the focus. This is called *window-level help*, as it is recommended for use only in windows, frames and dialogs.

- After clicking the contextual help button, usually in the toolbar, or choosing it from the **Help** menu, the mouse cursor changes to a special contextual help cursor. This signals that the program is waiting for the selection of an item in the GUI, using the mouse or the keyboard, when the contextual help available for the selected object is displayed. This is referred to as *field-level help*.

- By using the standard **Help** menu in the menu bar. This can be used to provide help about specific tasks or objects. The **Help** menu contains a submenu of items that provide help about various tasks.

- In dialog boxes via a **Help** button. This provides help information about how to use the dialog. Clicking **Help** is usually equivalent to pressing the **F1** key while the dialog box has the focus.

System-initiated help is performed by the program itself reacting to some user action that is not explicitly related to help commands.

Help support can be useful both in prototype building and GUI extension. In a pre-release version for a selected user population, some of the functionalities to be added can be explained in the help system. By default, help information is displayed in the help viewer, but this can be customized as needed.

Other libraries also exist that provide help support, both for Swing and SWT applications, providing a different mix of runtime performances, simplicity, and range of available features.

4.14 Icons and images

A number of bitmap images are usually employed when creating a GUI with Java technology. Table 4.2 lists the most frequent ones. Designers should provide these images.

Table 4.2   Common images for swing applications

Description	Use	Size
Log-in app logo	Shown in log-in dialogs	~ 280 x 64
App icon	Shown in app frames and dialogs	small: 16 x 16 large: 24 x 24
'About' app logo	Used in the 'About' dialog	~ 280 x 64 or greater
Company logo	Appears in the 'About' dialog	
Splash window	Startup splash window	~ 392 x 412
Toolbar icons	Toolbar buttons	small: 16 x 16 large: 24 x 24
Other app-dependent graphics	Depends on the application	

The image sizes preceded by a '~' sign are merely illustrative.

> We will provide a number of practical examples throughout the book. Chapter 14 discusses a complete application where all these images are instantiated for a real case.

4.15 Leveraging object-oriented programming

Reusability of software components tends to produce better quality GUIs, because behavior and appearance are replicated in a coherent way throughout the whole interface, and coding effort is saved. OOP reusability is a key point for high-quality inexpensive Java GUIs.

A common, concrete case is provided by the fact that some dialogs are served in two main modalities that depend on how the user's actions are recorded by the application: *deferred* or *immediate* mode interactions. Some GUI design guidelines prescribe dialog appearance. It is possible therefore to envisage a small component that implements the area where buttons are displayed. Such a widget is shown in Figure 4.44 and Figure 4.45 for a typical deferred interaction dialog in which changes are committed using the **OK** button, or dismissed by means of the **Cancel** button.

Figure 4.44   The OKCancelPane component for Java L&F

Figure 4.45   The OKCancelPane component for Eclipse

A **Help** button could optionally be provided as well – in Swing GUIs this is officially mentioned, but not in the Eclipse guidelines.

The practice of adopting customized, reusable components is very useful. The next logical step is to provide a deferred-mode dialog that can be used every time you need to perform such an interaction in a GUI. A simple component might contain an OKCancelPane such as the one shown in Figure 4.44, as well as some other standard behavior, such as being sensitive to the **Escape** key to dismiss the dialog, or automatically visualizing the help data when the **Help** button is clicked. This is provided out of the box by the Eclipse GUI libraries.

No matter which mechanism you use to assemble GUI Content[8], the idea is to engineer this activity in a coherent way, so that the final user experience will be uniform and predictable throughout the whole GUI. A small investment in development time in implementing such basic facility will be repaid many times during software development and in the final, systematic aspect of the GUI.

One flaw in this approach of employing only few, highly customized components lies in visual components provided by someone else. This shouldn't be a problem, because GUI design guidelines nicely dictate all GUI details. Unfortunately third-party vendors sometimes tend to ignore such prescriptions, especially in older products. Such incompatibilities are being resolved over time with the Swing library – at least as long as the latest versions are used. For third-party GUI libraries, be careful to check out their design guideline compliance before adopting them in your project. All your development effort can be wasted if you provide your customers with an inconsistent user experience, no matter how elegant the underlying software implementation.

> The Swing implementation of the `OkCancelPanel` class is provided for readers that are interested. This provides global action buttons as prescribed by the Java Look and Feel design guidelines, and should be used extensively throughout the GUI, enforced by quality assurance if necessary. For usability reasons the appearance of the **OK** button may be changed in some cases. For example, in a **Print...** dialog it makes more sense to label the **OK** button with **Print** even if the underlying function remains the same. For the same reason the range of possible customization of this panel is limited. No icons should be used for the buttons, and the **Cancel** and **Help** buttons, although locale-dependent, cannot be arbitrarily labeled.

4.16 Summary

This chapter introduced some common design problems, together with their solutions for effective Java GUI design and subsequent development, and occasionally considered implementation issues. The approach was aimed at highlighting some often overlooked issues in GUI design, with particular relevance to the Java platform. Some of the issues were too broad to be addressed exhaustively in this chapter.

In particular, the chapter discussed:

* Window area organization, including some widely-accepted and used criteria for organizing the functional areas of a non-trivial GUI.

---

8. We discuss the main implementation alternatives available briefly in Chapter 6, in *Content assembly* on page 229.

- Choosers, including the preferred activation mechanism for choosers, and how to expand them to handle other features such as item creation. Choosers were also used for discussing the different types of dialog interaction: deferred, immediate, and mixed.

- Memory components, visual components that have a subset of their state made persistent.

- Lazy instantiation – complex Java applications can become excessively slow in some situations. Mixing design and implementation can substantially boost performance.

- The preference dialog, a common design: a centralized access point for configuration data is needed in all but the simplest applications.

- Command composition. Negotiating commands is a common practice in GUIs implemented with OOP, especially for OOUIs.

- Wizards. Although relatively easy to implement, wizards should be used only when needed, although they are a useful tool in a designer's toolbox.

- Waiting strategies, providing sound designs for situations in which the GUI is performing internal work and is currently unresponsive.

- Flexible layouts. It is not enough to provide scroll panes for the main components and a resizable window for the container of the dialogs or frames of your application.

- Common dialogs and windows – in current GUIs there are many de-facto standard windows and dialogs. We proposed only few of them with some examples, both to show their suggested design, and to provide a utility library that eases their development.

- Menu and toolbar organization, important and frequent design issues.

- Accessibility – it is always good practice to provide accessibility support in your GUI.

- Navigation and keyboard support – providing a planned keyboard support for any dialog or frame in your application is good design practice.

- Internationalization and localization, important aspects of modern GUIs that should be considered from the start of GUI design.

- Help support – integrating help support into an application using the Java-Help library.

- Common icons and images.

We also discussed proposed design solutions, providing some practical examples that highlighted the main advantages such architectures provide.

In the second part of the book we will leave GUI design and move to the implementation aspects of professional Java GUIs.

5 Iterative GUI Development with Java

No design is ever perfected at the first attempt. Instead, a professional design in many engineering fields is the result of several refinement cycles. This is true for software engineering in general, and is even more true for GUI development, where the presence of end users makes the engineering task highly unpredictable and dependant on subjective criteria. In this chapter we will examine the major approaches and the available techniques for building professional Java GUIs through iterative cycles of refinement.

The iterative GUI development approach consists of frequent product releases that continuously and smoothly expand the application by means of small additive changes, implementation refinements (such as refactorings) and continuous, pervasive testing. Testing 'in the large' is essential for achieving an effective iterative development. We will discuss GUI testing, usability testing and memory profiling, an often overlooked aspect of GUI development.

Readers are not forced to adopt an iterative development approach if they don't want to. Despite being a powerful development approach – see the discussion in Chapter 1 – it is labor-intensive, involves mastering many techniques, and ultimately leads to good and cost-effective results only when developers genuinely embrace its philosophy. Nevertheless, the techniques discussed in this chapter can be applied to a wide range of software engineering approaches, ranging from XP (Extreme Programming) to traditional waterfall development.

Iterating a GUI design that has already been exposed to end users is a delicate art, requiring skill, as well as a different attitude to that required for software refactoring. As we saw in Chapter 2, to a user the GUI *is* the application. As the most externally visible part of a system, the user interface tends to evoke strong feelings. Once a GUI design has been agreed, the process of changing it is often complex and politically charged. Evolving a GUI design from one iteration to the next can put a strain on end users. Users learn the application through the GUI, and even minor refinements can be unpopular once familiarity is established.

One of the advantages of iterative development is the possibility of constantly evaluating and changing the application using end users. Without end users and domain experts working with developers on a GUI there is little possibility of progress – at most we are developing a nice, abstract application that probably doesn't solve actual users' needs, just the needs of our fictitious idea of end users.

This chapter begins by introducing the fundamental strategy behind effective iterative development, followed by an introduction to Java GUI prototyping. Various aids to prototyping are introduced as well (GUI builders and some examples of utility prototyping classes). After an initial and inexpensive prototype has been assessed with users, iterative development will take care of evolving the application to meet user's needs. Common GUI-specific refactorings are discussed together with testing and runtime memory profiling. This chapter covers all these heterogeneous aspects, to provide a unique reference for iterative GUI development, spanning diverse topics such as prototyping, refactoring, testing, and profiling.

This chapter is structured as follows:

5.1, Iterating wisely discusses the strategies behind iterative GUI development.

5.2, Introduction to prototyping deals with the basic concepts for the design of effective GUI prototypes.

5.3, Prototyping alternatives discusses the various approaches to prototyping available, such as paper prototyping, storyboarding, and so on.

5.4, GUI builders introduces this kind of tool, useful for prototyping as well as for building final GUIs.

5.5, Reusable prototyping widgets discusses some widgets specialized for prototyping purposes, along with their implementation.

5.6, GUI refactoring illustrates the practice of refactoring GUI code, going into the details of GUI-specific refactorings.

5.7, Introduction to user interface testing introduces the general topic of GUI testing, focusing on some of its most controversial aspects.

5.8, Software testing of Java GUIs illustrates the role of software tests in producing professional Java GUIs.

5.9, Usability testing of Java GUIs briefly touches the main points related to usability testing of Java GUIs.

5.10, JRE runtime management discusses profiling of Java desktop GUIs.

5.1 *Iterating wisely*

Before introducing the various techniques and approaches for effective iterative development, it is important to discuss the overall strategy behind the assignment of priorities to development activities. This focuses on the development activities that need to be carried out, as opposed to use cases or user stories. The latter will depend upon the given project and customers, but will be influenced by the development process chosen.

We will focus on questions such as how much interaction and control behavior should be provided from one iteration to the next, the correct amount of GUI design to implement in the first release, or whether an explicit domain model should be implemented now or moved to a future release. We will use another incarnation of the cost-driven principle introduced for GUI design in Chapter 3 as the subject of this discussion, but this time apply it to an iterative style of software design and implementation for desktop application GUIs.

At first glance iterative GUI development seems a perfect candidate for the well-known 80:20 rule, or *Pareto Principle*[1]. This states that for many phenomena 80% of the consequences stem from 20% of the causes. This principle has been empirically validated on many software projects, in various forms[2]. GUI development is a circumscribed and well-known application domain in which experience can be reused fairly well. If we suppose that this rule roughly applies to GUI development, wouldn't it make a big difference to the way we plan our development activities? Such an 80:20 rule may not, however, apply to the design and development of top-quality professional GUIs – those with a sophisticated, innovative GUI design and substantial resources for their development – which is a fine art, the result of many tiny details carefully crafted together. Nevertheless, even a rough match with this rule would give us a very useful planning principle.

Clearly we will never be able to demonstrate empirically that the 80:20 law, or something similar, applies to GUI design projects. The main problem lies in assessing objectively the overall 'quality' of a GUI. How can we tell that a design is 80% done while also accounting for subjective and ephemeral aspects such as its usability and its overall appeal to users? Any developer who has built a number of desktop application GUIs can observe that there are common patterns of development activity that constitute the bulk of the job, in terms of an 'effective GUI' (a subjective definition, of course). What is invariably needed is a mixture of

---

1.   This principle can be seen as a special case of the Pareto Distribution, a power-law distribution found in various cases in nature, such as the frequency of words in long texts, the size of sand particles, the size of areas burnt in fires.
     See http://en.wikipedia.org/wiki/Pareto_distribution
2.   See for example: A. Ultsch, *Proof of Pareto's 80/20 Law and Precise Limits for ABC-Analysis*.

a 'minimum dose' of the various contributions: overall team attitude, testing, suitable software architecture, basic usability testing, and so on.

Apart from these abstract considerations, the *ranking* between development activities is important. Imagine having such a ranking documented neatly in the form of an ordered to-do list. Achieving cost-effective quality would then just be a matter of executing the items in the list using a 'greedy' style – starting from those activities that have the largest impact on the final result. Quality could be fine-tuned in this way depending on the budget, without risk of wasting precious resources in unproductive or counterproductive work.

> Scheduling development activities following such an 'optimum' list minimizes risk, by ensuring that roughly 80% of the required result is achieved before focusing on inessential requirements. We can maintain the project in good shape from early releases: customers gain confidence that the project is progressing well, developers are gratified by their work, the project manager enters the room whistling merrily, and so on. (Guess how often this happens...)

Unfortunately, such a ranking is almost impossible to calculate, because it is the final result of many intertwined factors – project details, business domain factors, project timeline, the people involved – that vary widely from project to project. Some rules of thumb can be given, but ultimately it is the developer, the team leader, or the application architect, that has the last word and should actively focus on cost-effectiveness when ranking development activities. A prioritized list of development activities can be sketched by leveraging past experience and the contents of this book, but an exact assessment is largely unattainable – a situation that applies to non-GUI development projects as well.

Here is an example of a mythical list of activities ordered by cost-driven criteria. The example list refers to a simple form-based rich client project, with no need for localization and with many simplifying assumption (people have been assigned already, preliminary analysis has been performed, etc.).

Set up a basic production environment, choosing simple and reliable technologies such as GUI and unit testing tools, version control tools, clear and simple look and feel or presentation technology, GUI toolkits and application platforms, deployment technology, and so on.

1. Determine the basic contents for use cases X and Y from customers and implement the control layer completely and without dynamic layout managers, validating it with end user representatives.

2. Define the data handled by the use case and implement it, whether it is part of the business domain or data IO.

3. Identify and implement the minimum set of commands that realizes the use case, given the data and the content from the previous steps. Provide a minimal implementation of client-side data validation.

4. Verify the GUI by software testing of critical points and a brief usability-testing session.

5. Provide extensive software testing and basic profiling, checking memory leaks and thread deadlocks.

6. Add additional control logic to ease interaction in the form of further validation behavior.

7. Provide basic help support and keyboard navigation.

8. Supply further content details for dynamic layout support.

9. Add a branded Look and Feel/presentation style, evaluated with end users and available client runtime resources (such as memory, CPU power, hard disk space, screen size).

10. Provide customized content widgets for easier interaction.

> This list implicitly assigns different weights to the quality of the final result, depending on the needs of the customers and the specifics of the project. It assumes that about the first five points in the list will deliver roughly 80% of the final result to users.

These assumptions are, of course, subjective and case-specific, yet intuitively appealing. For example, the choice to regard dynamic layout as optional, perhaps because localization is not needed, thereby ranking it ninth in the list, is debatable.

We are now ready to dip our toes into iterative GUI development with Java, starting with a well-known tactic: prototyping.

5.2   *Introduction to prototyping*

The development of a representation of a system for testing purposes is common practice in many engineering fields. It is an important method in GUI development as well. Design flaws or other incorrect assumptions can be individuated from the beginning, with resultant large savings in development costs. Prototypes can range from simple paper mock-ups to fully-functional products. Prototyping can be used not only for defining the GUI design, but also for eliciting requirements and as a mean of communication within the development team, with the customer, and with users. This chapter discusses the many different options available for prototyping Java GUIs.

Uses for prototyping

Prototyping is an essential aspect of any professional GUI development. During the analysis phase and later in the development lifecycle a prototype can be seen as another form of documentation. It can help the communication flow, both with the customer's organization and within the design and development team itself, and of course also with the final users of the product. Some of the most useful uses for prototypes are discussed below.

As a means of communication

Prototypes can convey a lot of information to people in a number of different roles within the development organization, as well as other stakeholders. A prototype can:

• Demonstrate to users and customers how the final GUI will look. This requires extra care, however, in order to avoid committing an early, sketchy design as the final one.

• Help to clarify the developer roles involved, especially on the client side – who is ultimately in charge of the GUI design, whether or not the representative users are the same as the end users, who has authority over the design of the GUI, and so on.

• Define detailed terminology, which can be used as the basis for building a *domain-driven ubiquitous language* for the project (see (Evans 2004)), as well as small details that would be tricky to guess from mere discussions.

• Document the GUI design: GUI prototypes are a powerful means of documenting a design, throughout the software lifecycle, especially for potentially risky aspect of the project.

Personally, and possibly unwisely, I love to amaze my clients. After a heavy analysis session in which they expect a recap document, I often release a functioning prototype instead, to much surprise. Pleasing clients early on in a project usually rebounds in the form of extra work and greater expectations, but I like to do so anyway. One of my favorite tricks is to add a general comment mechanism to the prototype application, so that end users can attach their own comments directly to specific areas of the prototype application. The comments they register in this way are precious, because they show how users think about the GUI in detail. They help to substantiate the A3GUI decomposition of screens, for analysis and design, and sometimes they even shape the final development.

Exploring the design space

Prototypes can also be used to explore the design space, especially for novel classes of systems for which no mature design has been established. Several parallel designs could be developed to try to generate as much diversity as possible, or just to focus on evaluating a few alternatives. A number of preliminary designs are created and the best ideas are used for the definitive design, as shown intuitively in Figure 5.1.

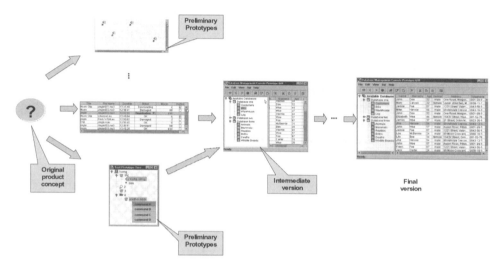

Figure 5.1   Exploring the design space with different prototypes

Developing parallel prototypes is clearly rather expensive because – to have the largest diversity possible – each prototype should ideally be developed by a separate team or individual, with little contact with other teams. However, in most actual cases, a single prototype is enough to produce a viable design.

> As suggested in (Hunt and Thomas 2000), when nervous or insecure about the beginning of a new project, or just about the design of specific screens, it is wise to break the ice with a prototype instead of committing unwillingly to a tentative solution.

A common risk is to close the design space prematurely, choosing as final a design solution that has not been thoroughly tested and validated with users. On the other hand, keeping too many design choices open is needlessly expensive and could lead to incoherent, 'stratified' designs, to which different and unrelated approaches were added over time.

> Some software development approaches like XP (see Chapter 1) push the prototyping approach outside the GUI domain, involving the whole software development at large (Beck and Andres 2004). XP projects can employ prototyping for exploring possible GUI solutions. These limited systems are called *spikes*. A spike solution is a very simple program built to explore potential solutions, addressing only the problem under examination and ignoring all other issues.

Capturing requirements

Prototypes are often used to elicit requirements for the system to be built. This is done both when building the prototype, and later when gathering feedback from the users on the prototype that has been built. Using prototypes in this way is a natural extension of the adoption of other functional requirement techniques such as use cases or XP's 'user stories.'

> Using prototypes as a mere form of requirements-gathering can lead to rather unusable GUIs. Usability and GUI design are different from functional requirement gathering, and should be handled in a different way, by using approaches focused on GUI design, such as user-centric design techniques, rather than system-centric ones like system requirements.

The two dimensions of prototyping

A prototype is a reduced version of the final system. Such a reduction can be achieved either by implementing less functionality, or by reducing the level of functionality of each feature. The former approach is called *vertical prototyping* – demonstrating few features, fully implemented – while the latter is called *horizontal prototyping*, demonstrating many features but with each shallowly implemented. These two dimensions of prototyping are shown graphically in Figure 5.2.

Horizontal prototypes are easier to build, as shown later in this chapter, because they focus mostly on GUI aspects, and can help to test the whole prototype and the full picture it produces. By reducing the number of features and their implementation level, we can obtain cheap 'subsets of use' of the final application, called *scenarios*. A scenario describes a single interaction session limited to few functionalities.

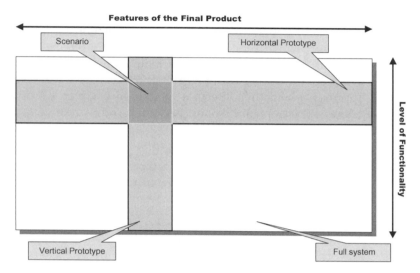

Figure 5.2   The two dimensions of prototyping (Nielsen 1993)

There are several different definitions of a scenario. We make the assumption that a scenario corresponds to the definition given in Section 1.4, when we introduced scenario use case diagrams.

Competitors' product as ready-made prototypes

A design approach known as *competitive analysis* considers similar products that are already available as a starting point for the design activity. A competing similar product is already fully implemented, and can be easily tested in detail. Even when we already have a prototype ready, we can compare concretely how well analogous tasks are implemented by the competing product and by our prototype application.

If several competing products are available, we can examine their differences and the way they approach the same abstract application using different GUI designs. This greatly helps the analysis and design phases – even if, as Nielsen points out, competitive analysis and design does not mean stealing other's hard-won designs, but rather taking them into consideration in your own design analysis, possibly to improve on them and overcome their weaknesses.

Prototyping as a philosophy for development

Evolutionary prototyping is a fully-fledged development philosophy in which the GUI development is just a part of the overall software lifecycle. Agile and other fully-iterative approaches are inspired by this type of highly iterative view of design and development. The prototype is constantly refined, expanded and validated with users until it becomes definitive, when the final product is released. This approach can be difficult to implement, due to the technical pitfalls involved in working with prototypes that constantly evolve. We mentioned such approaches and their lifecycle models in Chapter 1. For more details, see for example (McConnell 1996) or (Beck and Andres 2004).

In conclusion, prototyping deals with building a GUI incrementally and in a cost-effective way. The ability to state the quality of a given GUI is a key factor in driving the evolution of one or more prototypes into the final design correctly. In the next section we will see in detail the different kind of prototype presented above.

Prototypes and customers

Prototypes can have a significant impact on end users. Handling this aspect correctly is important in ensuring adoption of any prototype. Apart from the technicalities involved in creating prototypes, they also guide the perception of the product being developed by end users and customers. Customers often have a non-technical background, and a number of misunderstandings are possible:

- A bad GUI will impact negatively on the idea customers have of the product, irrespective of the fact that it is only a prototype. Customers often implicitly establish an emotional link with the software that will probably become part of their daily working life.

- Agreeing on a given prototype with customers is an important statement. From that moment on customers will be expecting that specific user interface, and anything different could be considered as a change in any agreement made with them.

- An overly-sophisticated prototype can convey to users the false idea that the product is almost complete. When presenting a prototype, it is essential to state the current state of development of the product, and not just focus on how the prototype is different from the final product. One can provide some graphical adornment such as watermarks to signal the fact that the prototype is just a prototype, no matter how good it might look. There is even a Swing Look and Feel that is expressly designed to provide this feeling of 'sketchiness,' as we will see later.

To recap, it's important to remember when dealing with customers that prototyping often represents their perceived image of the product you are building: special care is needed to deal with such a delicate issue.

5.3 Prototyping alternatives

There are a number of possible approaches to prototyping, depending on which aspects designers want to focus on.

Different types of prototypes

This section introduces the main types of prototyping discussed in this book: the subsections that follow describe them in detail.

Storyboard prototyping

Storyboard prototyping is a technique for representing parts of an interface in a way similar to the 'storyboard' used to represent and evaluate the script of a film before committing to the expensive process of shooting the final motion picture.

Storyboarding is a simple, informal way of representing a scenario associated with a given task in the user interface. It is mainly useful for the initial phases of the design process, where accurate feedback from users is still not needed.

Figure 5.3 shows a simple storyboard for the task of selecting a color from a form on screen. Storyboards usually comprise more GUI screens than is shown in this example, as we will see later.

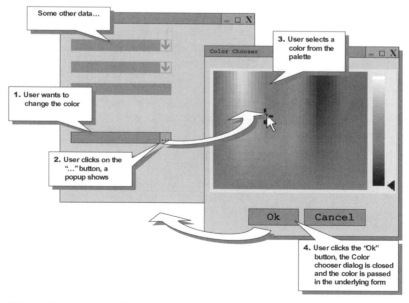

Figure 5.3   An example of a simple storyboard

The storyboard in Figure 5.3 has been designed using a computer graphics application. Storyboards are more often sketched informally, for example on paper, as can be seen in the examples in Figure 5.5 and Figure 5.6.

Paper-based prototyping

Paper-based prototyping needs as its technical support only a piece of paper and some pencils. Sketching out a GUI in this way usually produces rather coarse prototypes, but helps to make key ideas explicit quickly and cheaply. For a thorough discussion of this topic, see (Snyder 2003).

Several slightly different techniques are gathered under the term 'paper prototype.' In a later section of this chapter we will discuss in detail this family of techniques, maybe the most popular form of prototyping. Figure 5.4 shows an example of a paper prototype taken from the example in Chapter 14.

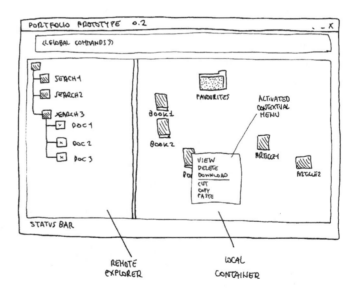

Figure 5.4   An example of a simple paper prototype

Paper prototypes can be used for usability testing with users (Snyder 2003). Following this approach, one or more paper prototypes are built to model the GUI and test it for usability. Testing for usability in this case means letting users try the prototype as if it was the real interface, and try to discover any difficulties and problems to which its design might give rise.

Rapid prototyping

Rapid prototyping (also known as *throw-it-away prototyping*) is the technique of building scaled-down applications, usually using the same technology as the final product. The prototype developed in this way is abandoned at some point in the development process, after it has accomplished its duty – for example in pinpointing defects in the design of the GUI with end users. The GUI prototype is cheap and serves as a first point for requirements gathering and defining the design space.

Rapid prototyping and GUI iterative development can complement each other. Iterative development focuses on building a working GUI starting from the most-needed and best-understood requirements, while rapid prototyping is usually employed to validate or elicit specific aspects, and focuses on those requirements that are poorly understood.

The different expressiveness of prototype techniques

The following table summarizes the different expressiveness properties of paper versus rapid prototyping.

Table 5.1   Expressiveness of prototyping techniques

Entity type	Category of entities that can be represented using the given type of prototype	Prototyping method	
		Paper	Rapid
Business	Main concepts	✓	✓
	Terminology	✓	✓
	Documentation, help	✓	✓
	Requirements, functionalities	✓	✓
	Data size, dimensions	-	✓
GUI	Navigation, work flow	✓	✓
	Appearance (Look and Feel)	-	✓
	Screen layout	✓	✓
	Response time	-	✓
	Keyboard, mouse, other input	-	✓

Clearly, paper prototyping has numerous disadvantages when compared with rapid prototyping. Nevertheless, given its cheapness and simplicity – even end users can come up with their own proposal – paper prototyping is widely used. Rapid prototyping can be used in cases in which specific development risks that need to be evaluated early in the development are not made explicit by a paper prototype. Consider for example an application that is required to be close to an existing application, with a high level of fidelity. Only a software prototype can fulfill this need.

Different types of prototypes can be used in combination to give the best of both approaches. Suppose we want to design the GUI for an application with a heavy data load – perhaps tens of thousands of items. This aspect is a potential risk that needs to be explicitly addressed as early as possible. The first informal prototypes are written on paper: when a suitable design emerges, it is rendered in a rapid prototype that simulates a large number of data items and their related latencies, so that the design can be validated and agreed with end users.

Prototyping technologies

Prototypes rely on specific technologies, whether the same technology as the final product (in our case Java) or another, for example using Web pages to sketch form-based screens. Comparing Java with other technologies:

- *Java technologies.* A number of visual tools that generate Java sources for GUI layouts and screens by direct manipulation are widely available. Open source software (OSS) tools such as NetBeans or Eclipse VE, as well as commercial products such as JBuilder and Idea, are commonly used in development. A number of stand-alone Java visual builders are available too – we discuss this in Chapter 11.

- *Non-Java technologies.* Prototyping technologies can be employed too: drawing or authoring tools such as Microsoft Powerpoint and Visio, CorelDraw, for sketching paper prototypes, or tools for building horizontal prototypes, such as Visual Basic or MacroMedia Flash. None of these tools effectively model the Java Look and Feel, however.

Storyboards

A storyboard documents how a part of a user interface is employed to accomplish a given task. A storyboard is a simplified representation of the GUI, usually drawn on paper, showing how a user interacts with the product to achieve a specific task. Storyboards usually represent the user interface at a higher level of abstraction than paper prototypes, allowing a wider perspective – storyboards are often drawn on large sheets and hung on the wall. They provide navigation, meaningful data, and all other details needed to represent the task performed in the GUI to a suitable level of detail. Figure 5.5 shows a storyboard for an example application.

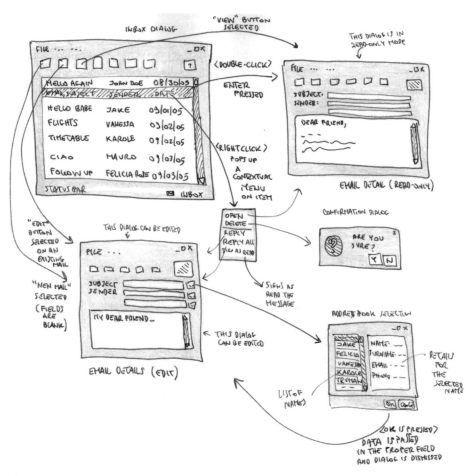

Figure 5.5   An example storyboard

This storyboard describes navigation details as well as UI details. Storyboards usually focus on navigation and on providing a wider picture of the GUI. The storyboard in Figure 5.6 shows an example of this latter approach for an account management user interface.

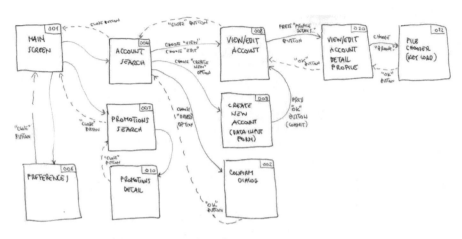

Figure 5.6   *Another example storyboard*

A number of details can be seen in Figure 5.6:

• Every screen is represented by a box showing a window title.

• Transitions from one window to another are shown by arrows labeled with the GUI action that triggers the transition.

• Dashed arrows represent the navigation when the current screen is dismissed.

• Windows are identified with a unique id number in their upper-right corners, for quick reference both during design and at runtime .

Storyboards are a valuable tool for describing GUI navigation and for sketching the GUI, especially at early stages of design.

5.4   *GUI builders*

GUI builders are another commonly-used aid for building prototypes, as well as entire simple GUIs. They consist of visual environments that ease the construction of GUIs by means of a user-friendly construction interface that creates the code behind the scenes. All major Java integrated development environments (IDEs) provide such a graphical UI editor. This section gives an example of the use of one such tool.

A screenshot of the JBuilder IDE visual designer is shown in Figure 5.7.

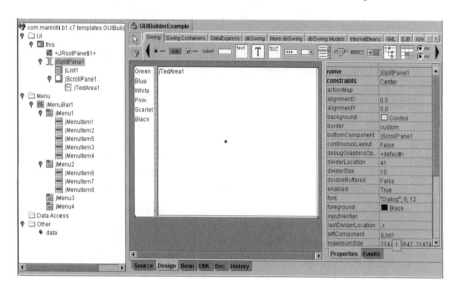

Figure 5.7   The JBuilder IDE designer

The final result of using the builder took less than ten minutes to create, and is shown in Figure 5.8. No extra-GUI, functional code was provided, to keep the resulting code as short as possible.

Figure 5.8   An example GUI

The JBuilder editor creates an auxiliary method (`jbInit`) that gathers all the GUI-related code. Code statements generated as commands are issued via the user interface shown in Figure 5.8. Widget visibility is provided for all components, which are created as instance variables of the visual container class. Instance variables are named automatically by the tool, but can be renamed manually.

Even in such a simple case we needed to modify/insert the generated code by hand. JBuilder is flexible enough to recognize lines of code added by hand. This is illustrated in the code example that is available on-line, in which the string array used for filling the list widget has been added in the source code. This is still successfully recognized by the tool, as can be seen in Figure 5.8.

Using a GUI builder tool

Whether code builders are used or not, achieving a professional GUI is always a matter of detail. You will therefore always need to dig into generated code to polish the details of even the simplest GUI. Visual editors do not simplify the overall coding effort if your GUI is complex enough to require massive extension or rewriting of the code automatically produced by the tool.

Visual editors can help quick development of content structure, such as widgets and their layout. They can be used as aids to create the structure of the required class quickly, which can be refined later manually. They can be useful for building rapid prototypes, or can be used by novice programmers for learning the basics of Java GUI libraries in a 'learning-by-doing' fashion.

Programmers tend to have their own opinions of these kinds of automatic tools. Some find them stimulating but limited, others are confident they can save a lot of time, while many simply hate them altogether. Clearly, the perception you have of a tool directly impacts your performance when using it: it's a matter of usability here as well, only here developers are the end users. The ultimate choice depends on your preferences.

Visual editors do have a number of practical shortcomings:

- It is cumbersome, if not impossible, to modify some parts of the generated code. For example, some editors allow only Java Beans – widgets with void constructors – to be created.

- Some editors, such as the one provided with Netbeans, rely on vendor-specific files as well as vendor-neutral comments in source code. This ultimately leads to a form of vendor lock-in. It also makes it harder to adapt the generated code to particular needs without breaking the compatibility between the tool and the edited GUI code.

- The general structure of the generated class is hard to tweak. Special methods can be hard or even impossible to circumvent. In some cases maintaining source code compatibility with the visual editor can become so complex that the simplest solution is to abandon the GUI editor tool altogether.

- Architectural issues are not supported by visual builders that tend to build weak and deeply-coupled code.

5.5 Reusable prototyping widgets

In this section we will examine practical applications of reusable classes to proto-typing. In particular, we will look at two classes that are specialized for building rapid prototypes inexpensively.

A tree prototype utility class

The reusable class introduced here simplifies the creation of complex Swing tree components. Such trees are limited to use as rapid prototypes. Despite that, their use could be quite helpful for producing medium- and even high-fidelity proto-types. The class we describe here is implemented as a specialized JTree that reads its configuration from a properties file. In this way it is easy to populate a tree, change its appearance and provide contextual menus, tooltips and drag and drop (dummy) support. We will introduce and discuss a sample properties file first, then present the class code, and conclude with another example of its use.

In our implementation, all the appearance is delegated to the properties file, though for specific features it may be necessary to add an external listener class, or to subclass the prototype class itself. For example, in Chapter 4 we saw a tree prototype that simulated a delay by attaching a tree expansion listener to a JProtoTree instance. The properties file used in the constructor dictates the appearance and behavior of the prototype tree. Listing 5.1 below shows an example of such a properties file. The resulting output is shown in Figure 5.9.

Listing 5.1 The Tree.properties file

```
00: root=home,a tooltip string,root.gif,command A%%command B%%--%%com-
mand C%%command D,a1,a2,a3,a4
01: a1=1,tt1,bit1.gif,command E%%command F%%command G,a11,a12
02: a2=2,tt2,light.gif,-
03: a3=3,tt3,bit1.gif,-
04: a4=4,tt4,-,-,a41
05: a41=another node, and its tooltip,bit1.gif,-
06: a11=aaa,-,-,-
07: a12=bbb,-,-,-
08:
09: # special properties
10: setShowsRootHandles=true
11: setScrollsOnExpand=true
12: setRootVisible=true
13: setDragEnabled=true
14: setClosedIcon=closed.gif
15: setOpenIcon=open.gif
16: setLeafIcon=dot.gif
17:
18:
19: # tree properties
20: JTree.lineStyle=Angled
```

The properties can be specified in any order. In Listing 7.1 above there are three main groups of properties:

- The first group dictates the structure of the tree. Line 0 says that the root node has a label 'home,' a tooltip 'a tooltip string' and should be rendered using the image 'root.gif.'
- The contextual menu is composed of four commands: string commands are separated by '%%' and the '- -' represents a menu separator.
- Finally, the root node has two children, identified by the labels a1, a2, a3 and a4 that in turn are defined in lines 01–04.

The final result. the JProtoTree instantiated with the properties file of Listing 7.1, is shown in Figure 5.9.

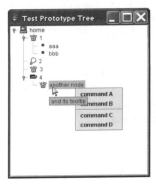

Figure 5.9   An example of a prototype tree

Each line is composed of a string id that is used by the tree to identify the given node. The special string 'root' is used to identify the root element, and is mandatory. There follow the appearance values for that node, separated by the '=' character used by default in Java properties files.

Such values are the ordered sequence of the following data:

1. The ext label. This can be a sentence or even an HTML fragment.
2. The icon used to render the node. When not used, the standard icons are used instead.
3. The contextual menu that is activated by right-clicking with the mouse on the given node. Note that contextual menus are inherited from a parent node by its children. If we have only one type of contextual menu for all the nodes, we therefore just specify the required menu in the root element, and this is then used by all its descendents. If another node needs to show a different contextual menu, we then have to declare it in the properties file for the given node, as node 'a1' does in Listing 7.1.

4. The list of child node ids that builds the tree structure recursively, or ' - ' if the node is a leaf.

In this way the nodes and their appearance are defined. There are other attributes that can be defined as well, to control the global tree appearance, These are specified in lines 10–16 in Listing 7.1. It is possible to define properties such as whether the root handles should be made visible, or whether the tree nodes should be draggable. Finally, Swing tree properties can be added to the file.

Whenever an item of information is missing – for example omitting to specify a particular icon, so that the node will be rendered using the standard icons for leaf, open and closed folder nodes – we use the '-' character.

For brevity, we don't show the implementation here. For readers interested in it, the `JProtoTree` class uses two inner classes: a custom tree cell renderer and a custom tree model.

The constructor simply instantiates a specialized tree model based on the input properties file, then queries it to change the tree's appearance. This use of the tree model is incorrect – the purpose of the Swing modified MVC architecture is primarily for separating appearance from data. Loading the model with appearance data is thus conceptually incorrect. The tree is created using default tree nodes that have an array of strings as the user object. Such an array contains the appearance information extracted from the properties file.

The `ProtoTreeModel` inner class reads the properties file and creates the related tree model, which will be used by the enclosing tree class. In particular, the `create-Node` method is used for populating the tree recursively using a deep-first strategy.

The inner class `ProtoCellRenderer` is a subclass of the `DefaultTreeCell-Renderer`, and is used to customize the node appearance as prescribed in the input properties file. The main method of the `JPro-toTree` class shows a sample use of the class, and requires a properties file named '`tree.properties.`'

Another example of the use of a properties file for defining tree appearance is shown in the sample code for this chapter, in the `DBTree.properties` file. The corresponding instantiated tree is shown in Figure 5.10.

Note that in this prototype we have modified the appearance of few special nodes only, while allowing all the remaining nodes to comply with the general tree rendering rules. These distinguish between open and closed folders – any node that has at least one child – and leaves, those nodes that have no children. We then modified the appearance of these three types of nodes in turn, allowing us to use a cheaper standard component for the working implementation.

> The sample syntax shown in the previous listing can be seen as a simple, although rough and very simplistic form of a Little Language specialized for rapid prototyping. Little Languages are described in Section 12.5.

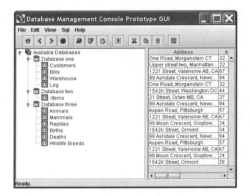

Figure 5.10   Another example of a prototype tree

We also supply a simplified version of this utility class for the SWT (Standard Windowing Toolkit) library in the source bundle for this chapter.

To recap, utility classes can be useful for quickly building tree samples from scratch for use in rapid prototypes, whether for Swing or SWT programs.

A visual container prototype utility class

This section introduces a reusable class for creating prototypes of directly-manipulatable, two-dimensional containers, such as file system folders in Windows or the Macintosh operating system. We will see these working in Chapter 15. Figure 5.11 shows an example of such a prototype component.

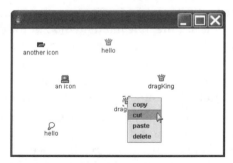

Figure 5.11   An example of a container prototype

Users can drag the icons within the container and right-click on them to show their contextual menus. This kind of component is not provided by the standard Sun libraries, but it can be employed usefully in GUIs, especially OOUIs. The `SandboxExample` class provided with the code for this chapter shows a sample use of this component for creating rapid prototypes.

5.6 GUI refactoring

Having explored the various options available to Java developers for building effective GUI prototypes, we now focus on iterative GUI development, in which the code is not meant to be thrown away, but instead is refined and improved continuously by means of small steps that do not alter its functional behavior. These are called *refactorings*.

Fowler's classic work on refactoring (Fowler et al. 2000) describes a set of changes that improve the internal structure of code without changing its external behavior. Refactoring is 'a disciplined way to clean up code that minimizes the chances of introducing bugs.' Refactoring changes the design of a system without modifying its observable behavior. We discuss refactoring in this chapter because it is instrumental to iterative GUI development. We refer to Fowler's refactorings as 'classic,' to differentiate them from the higher-level, GUI-specific refactorings introduced in this section.

The refactoring we introduce here is performed as a sequence of classic (low-level) refactorings that focus on enhancing the structure of GUI code while preserving its external behavior. Some of these GUI-specific refactorings might slightly modify the GUI's appearance, however. When this happens, the changes are always focused on standardizing the GUI design and making it systematic throughout the application.

One important point is *when* to refactor. (Fowler 2000) suggests refactoring *the third time* we happen to do something similar – this is called the 'rule of three' and is credited to D. Roberts. This means duplicating things at first and living with the duplication temporarily. For example:

- The first time we implement our panel.
- Later it happens that we find ourselves implementing a panel that is very similar to the one we have just implemented. The rule says we should leave the two panels separate.
- The third time we encounter the same situation we proceed to apply the required refactoring – see *Parameterize panel* on page 198.

Some classic refactorings

In this section we briefly introduce some classic refactorings commonly used in GUI development – for a complete discussion, refer to (Fowler et al. 2000). In the next section we discuss the most common GUI-specific refactorings.

The refactorings described here are simple and specifically concern GUI code restructuring. Refactoring techniques apply to any piece of code, of course, not just GUI code. We describe four refactoring techniques that can come to our rescue when restructuring GUI-oriented code. The first three, *Move Method*, *Duplicate*

Observed Data and *Extract Method*, are simpler and are all used in the final technique, *Separate Domain from Presentation*.

Move method

This is one of the most useful and frequent refactoring techniques, and consists simply of moving a method from one class to another. Of course you should check whether the method is declared in the superclass or in some subclasses of the current class.

After moving the method to the other class, the old method could be emptied and transformed into merely a delegating one – that is, one that invokes the corresponding new method in the other class – or it can be removed altogether. In the latter case all references are made directly to the new method in the other class.

There are no clear-cut criteria for applying this pattern – it depends on many factors, such as the semantic coherence of the code, its coupling with other classes, and so on. Move Method, and other refactoring techniques as well, are needed for example when enforcing a given structure in existing code by moving methods to different classes. This is discussed in Chapter 7.

Duplicate observed data

Business domain methods need to access business data hosted by GUI widgets – also referred to as *screen data state*, and discussed in Chapter 8. A solution is to duplicate the data, so that one representation lives in the content layer, and the other in the business domain[3], and keep them synchronized through an event-based mechanism. In the example in Figure 5.12 the latter mechanism is provided by means of the `java.util` implementation of the Observer design pattern (Gamma et al. 1994).

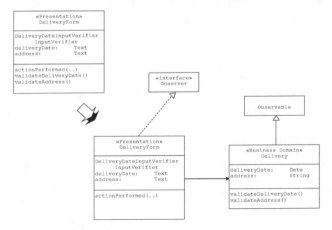

Figure 5.12   Duplicate observed data

---

3.   The layers' names may vary according to the architecture of choice.

There is a facility in the `java.util` package that helps with the implementation of such a pattern through the `Observer` interface and the `Observable` class, as used for example in the Sandbox application in Chapter 16.

As we saw at the beginning of this chapter, such an approach is employed in the MVC pattern and in its variant adopted in the Swing framework.

Extract method

This is another very common refactoring technique. It consists of grouping code statements into a new method, and is often used with GUI code. For example, in a frame or dialog initialization, when the visual container is filled with components and these are initialized, one can organize this code into a number of methods. This is shown in the following example, in which all initialization code of a `JFrame` subclass has been organized in few self-explanatory methods.

```
private void initGUI(){
  createToolbar();
  createMainPanel();
  populateDataTable();
}
```

This organization makes the same code more readable and easy to understand without modifying its externally-observable behavior. Clearly, new methods should be devised depending on the function the code performs, and not on how it is implemented. The objective is to clarify the code rather than make it more complicated with the addition of more methods.

Separate domain from presentation

This is perhaps the most obvious refactoring in the large for GUI code. It is a 'macro' refactoring technique, taking many small steps to be accomplished, and cannot be performed automatically, but is all-important in GUI development. Its result is to separate business logic and data from the presentation, as shown in Figure 5.13.

Figure 5.13   Separating domain from presentation

Figure 5.13 uses UML stereotypes to show the functional layer – related to the functional decomposition shown in Chapter 1 – to which the class belongs.

This technique deals with the guiding principle of separating presentation code from domain logic. We have already discussed this principle and its implications: here we present a refined version of the corresponding refactoring technique. In fact, the rules stated in (Fowler et al. 2000) are:

1. Create a domain class for every window
2. Study the data shown in the GUI windows. If there is any data that is used only in the window, leave it in the presentation layer. If some data is not shown, move it into the domain class for that window using Move Method refactoring. Finally, if any data is used both in the presentation and in the application layer, use Duplicate Observed Data refactoring to split them into two separate classes, as discussed earlier.
3. Separate the domain logic inside a presentation class using Extract Method refactoring. When the domain logic is clearly separated into one or more methods within the presentation class, move these methods to the corresponding domain object.
4. Finally, when all the code for the domain logic is separated from the presentation, 'polish' the resulting domain logic classes with further refactoring.

This approach can be further refined depending on the kind of libraries on which your application relies. For example, if your GUI uses the Swing framework, instead of relying on the first rule (create a domain class for every window) you can take advantage of the modified MVC model adopted in the Swing toolkit.

Some GUI-specific refactorings

Before introducing some of the most common refactorings used in iterative GUI development, we need to introduce the concepts of Composable Unit and Content Assembly, which we discuss in greater detail in Chapter 6.

In medium or large applications there could be a need to aggregate code following some defined abstractions. These 'units' are fully-fledged autonomous entities that handle their own data, control behavior, content, and so on. They are sort of 'mini-GUIs' within the GUI itself, aggregated following the Composite pattern. We call them *composable units*.

These aggregations can be useful for a number of reasons, such as code organization and code reusability. A composable unit is a formal building block of the GUI represented within our architecture. For example, if we adopted an MVC architecture for composable units – that is, an adoption of MVC in the large, different than using it at widget-level as in Swing or JFace – then an EmployeeMVC would be a triplet of a Model, View and Controller that together would form a single, formalized unit of reuse within our application. Following this architecture, whenever we need a panel that represents an employee, we just instantiate the related MVC triplet.

Many approaches are possible, apart from technical-oriented ones such as MVC, as we discuss in Chapter 6. The OOUI approach shown in Chapter 15 also illustrates this. Of course reuse and other functionalities can also be provided more informally, without resorting to a fully-fledged approach like an architecture based on composable units.

Content assembly is the procedure of assembling widgets using a given layout manager. The simplest way to compose widgets and composite aggregates of widgets into working panels and windows with OO technology is to use panel subclasses and put the assembly code into their constructor. This scheme works well in the majority of cases, but there could be situations in which this intuitive approach can be problematic. Other techniques are possible, and we discuss them in Chapter 6. Here, for ease of discussion, we refer to the case of content assembly implemented via subclassing. Nevertheless the following refactorings can be applied as well when other content assembly approaches are used, such as specialized factories or builders.

Extract explicit panel

We are now ready to discuss some explicit refactoring in the large for desktop application GUIs based on OO technology.

A common situation is that in which we design a panel for some purpose and then realize we may want to make a part of it an explicit, separated panel, perhaps because we may need it for reuse somewhere else in the class. This situation is shown in Figure 5.14, in which an explicit panel, `AddressPanel`, in extracted from the `PersonPanel` implementation.

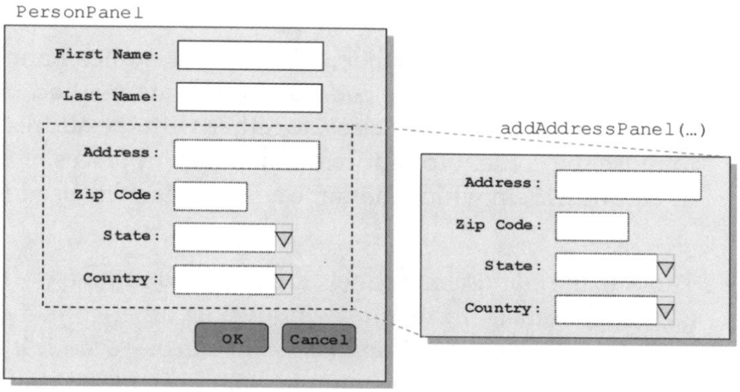

Figure 5.14   Extracting an explicit panel

After the refactoring, `PersonPanel` now invokes `AddressPanel`, while the GUI design remained unchanged. Usually an explicit panel is implemented as a private method within the same class as the container panel. Even this simple refactoring can be complicated to achieve in practice because of the intricacies of layout management.

Extracting a panel can be tricky, because we want to have a flexible panel that can adapt to different use scenarios – when it was implicit, there was no need to provide this flexibility. Let's consider visual composition, for example. We might in some cases want our extracted panel to align seamlessly with the containing panel *without knowing about it*. Think about the address panel in Figure 5.14. When we add it to another panel, we expect all its fields to be nicely and seamlessly aligned with the other fields in the containing panel.

We have two basic strategies for providing widget layout flexibility in our newly extracted panel:

- *Black box support.* The panel is provided as a unique visual container, and it is up to the layout manager to adapt it to the rest of the containing panel. In practice this might mean providing your own implementation of a layout manager that deals with this aspect.

- *White box support.* The explicit panel exposes its internal structure to the outside world so that its component pieces can be aligned with the widgets in the containing panel. An example of support for this kind of approach can be provided by means of attributes, as discussed in Chapter 12.

You can of course provide an approximated alignment without resorting to the complex mechanisms outlined above – for example alignment values for form-based GUIs, or even no alignment at all. This will result in slightly poorer visual symmetry, but it will simplify development.

Extract stand-alone panel

We might go one step further and make our explicit panel a stand-alone class. This encompasses moving the code of the private method implementing the explicit panel in a separate panel class, together with the address widgets. This allows us to reuse the content for addresses in different places of the application, as shown in Figure 5.15, in which the same address panel is used in two different contexts.

> Extracting stand-alone panels is performed routinely when implementing GUIs through panels, instead of windows or other containers. Focusing on panels promotes reuse and simplifies GUI changes, even if it may seem unnatural at first. It can be a needless complication in simple applications, however – see the discussion of the *Smart GUI Antipattern* in Chapter 7.

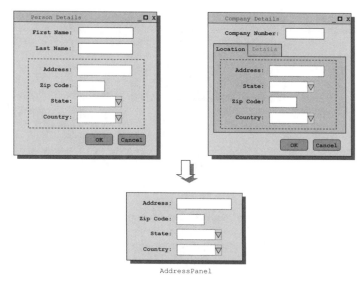

Figure 5.15   Extracting a standalone panel

Of course, extracting a stand-alone panel guarantees only content reuse – that is, the graphical aspects – and some simple, local kind of control and business code. For full reuse, we may need to escalate to a composable unit, as discussed in the next section.

Extract composable unit

Transforming a standalone panel into a composable unit means adding all the required code to make the new unit a coherent reusable block, comprising interaction and control, data IO, and domain code. Architectural behavior must also be provided – for example, composable units may be needed to implement some interfaces, or bind to a register facility. Figure 5.16 shows an example of the extraction of a composable unit from a stand-alone panel and its support code, scattered among other classes.

Merge panel

Refactorings of this type aim at visually merging a panel – either a stand-alone or an explicit panel – into another existing panel. Merge panel is the twin of the extract refactorings discussed previously.

Add parameter to panel

While building a GUI iteratively, we may find that we need to add a degree of flexibility to the code to avoid duplicating it. Suppose we implemented an address stand-alone panel that is embeddable in other panels or windows. In a new

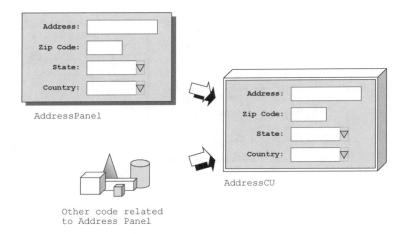

Figure 5.16   Extracting a composable unit

window we are coding, though, we then find that there is an address to display, but it should be laid out differently than would our reusable address panel.

This is a frequent problem in many places in a GUI. When new objects need to use our 'reusable' visual components, many unforeseen subtleties arise. Working in a continuous iterative way as we do, we don't worry too much about adding all the required behavior up-front, but instead add it as required, trying to keep our code as simple as possible.

We then:

1.   Decide on the abstractions to be provided by our parameterization.
2.   Implement these abstractions by means of a number of refactoring steps.

In our example, we may add to our address panel a `setVerticalLayout(boolean)` method that by default is false, to preserve backward compatibility with all existing clients, which accommodates this special case without revealing internal details of the address panel implementation.

Remove parameter from panel

As with methods, sometimes specific parameters are not used at all in a panel implementation. In this case it is good practice to remove them from the implementation.

Parameterize panel

Most of our development efforts focus on avoiding code duplication. Sometimes we end up having two slightly different panels that share a great deal of code, such as business logic, content, control, and so on, but that differ in detail. A simple solution is to extract a stand-alone panel and provide some means of configuration – usually using an accessory method – that implements the differences between the two approaches, as shown in Figure 5.17.

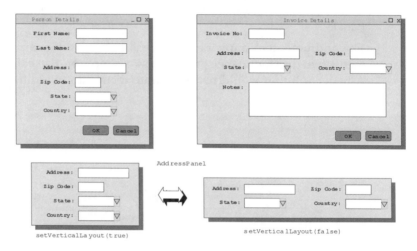

Figure 5.17   Parameterizing a panel

A trivial use of this refactoring is that in which you have the same panel duplicated in different parts of the GUI, and you want to extract a single implementation. In this case there is no need for parameters, because the designs are the same (although they might differ slightly in unimportant details).

This refactoring technique, like the similar Add Parameter to Panel, tends to create procedural code within panels to handle configuration behavior. This can be limited by using classic refactorings such as Replace Conditional with Polymorphism and Convert Procedural Design to Objects, as discussed in (Fowler et al. 2000).

Parameterize Panel and Add Parameter to Panel are similar in theory, but are used in different contexts in practice. You find yourself using this refactoring when developers were not able to exert tight control over GUI design, in cases in which GUI design was done by others – GUI designers, analysts, and so on – or when the initial design was implemented with a GUI builder that made panel extraction and reuse difficult. In these cases we would use Parameterize Panel for factoring out common panels into a single implementation.

Replace parameter with panel

The more parameters we add to a panel, the more complex it gets. We may end up with an overly intricate panel that would be better off split into two or even more separate panels. This is the dual of the Parameterize Panel refactoring technique. It should be used when a panel represents conceptually different aspects that would be more meaningfully represented with different stand-alone or explicit panels.

The address panel implementation has become too complex because it implements two different panels in one class: a simple and an extended address panel. A better solution would be to separate them into two different panels, as illustrated in Figure 5.18.

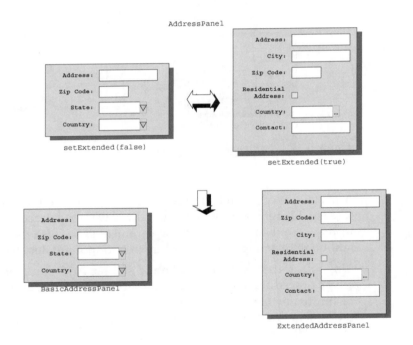

Figure 5.18   Replace parameter with panel

Here, as in all the refactoring techniques presented in this chapter, depending on the content assembly technique we use, panels will be implemented as visual panel subclasses, methods or builder strategies (see Chapter 6). Various classic refactorings can be applied to minimize code duplication between the two newly-created panels, depending on the implementation chosen.

Rename panel

Like methods or classes, the names of panels, as well as windows and other explicit visual composites, are of great importance in defining the specific conceptual identity of visual areas. If the A3GUI approach is used during analysis, then the identifiers of the areas found can be used to name the corresponding panels' implementations. Even more important than A3GUI, renaming should be done following domain-driven abstractions and a domain-driven Ubiquitous Language (Evans 2004).

Failing with style

We conclude this section with a discussion of general strategies for managing implementation errors – that is, software and systemic errors, not business-related ones. We include it here because it is an often-overlooked aspect of GUI development that should be tackled from early on in the development cycle.

Despite not being a refactoring technique, defining a clear, explicit failure strategy early in development is important for providing a coherent, usable GUI from the earliest iterations. By the term *failure*, we mean some software error or unexpected situation that hinders the execution of a program. We focus here on situations in which it is possible to continue execution, provided that the program is allowed to make some assumptions in order to proceed. That is, 'hopeless' situations for which we have no alternatives are not taken into account. Clearly, if an application is unable to find any resource bundle, messages cannot be shown at all and the GUI is unable to run. In these cases we have no option but to fail to provide the required amount of information – as described in the discussion that follows on security and error messages.

The chances are that any application will break one day, no matter how skillful we might be. This issue needs to be addressed explicitly, because providing a coherent failure strategy will affect not only the developers, but ultimately end users as well.

There are two broad strategies for dealing with failure:

- *Fail first.* As soon as there is an unexpected situation, we halt execution, providing a clear explanation of what happened. This makes it easier to detect the problem and fix it.

- *Fail later.* This approach tries to carry on program execution as far as possible. Suppose, for example, we detect that a required remote connection is down: we can signal this to the user, but still continue execution.

In practice, the problem is that the best strategies for failure are conflicting. For developers, a fail first strategy is advisable because the program does not enter into unforeseen behavior, and the problem is more easily detected. Filling code with default, specific behaviors degrades its readability, forcing us to constantly ask ourselves tortuous questions of the form 'Ok, if the program can't find the resource bundle, then it connects to the server, but if the server is down…' and so on.

On the other hand, end users don't want to be bothered by problems that might be handled without sacrificing the current session data. When driving I wouldn't like my car to stop because it is signaling something like 'Running out of air conditioning fluid. This might seriously damage the air conditioning system,' and refusing to start until a mechanic is provided.

Despite the fact that the optimum failure strategies for end users during runtime and the chosen failure strategy of developers during development are conceptually separate, it happens in practice that although maintaining two completely opposite strategies in the same application is hard, it is not impossible.

> When default behavior becomes non-trivial, it can be useful to resort to a specific class to represent it, to decouple it from the rest of the GUI, enhancing code readability and eliminating tangled conditionals dispersed in the code. This allows default strategies, spanning client to server and database tiers, to be represented at a high level of abstraction.

The nastiest situations arise in practice from the repercussions of unforeseen data such as null values or empty lists on the subsequent execution of the application. When encountering an unforeseen value such as a null query result, applications are usually programmed to make some assumptions in order to provide a minimum degree of ruggedness, for example by displaying an empty results table, instead of throwing an embarrassing `NullPointerException` in a pop-up message dialog.

The problem is that from that point on the application slips into uncharted waters, while still being fully responsive to the unwary user – that is, its actual behavior is no longer clearly defined. When an unrecoverable error happens five minutes later, it might be quite hard for developers to track down the sequence of events that led to it.

Extensive testing will hopefully catch most of these situations, but without an *a priori* strategy the code will contain a cluttered tangle of `if (a!=null){` statements and endless, convoluted chains of default behaviors.

A simple remedy to this is to provide a clear, global strategy for failure and its implementation with OO technology as early as possible, such as a set of instances of the Special Case pattern (Fowler et al. 2003) that explicitly represent special cases by defining subclasses for handling special cases only, such as `EmptySearchResults, UnspecifiedAddress, NullObject`. These classes will know what to show on the screen without forcing conditional control to be scattered throughout the GUI, will properly log themselves, and will prevent the application from being crippled unpleasantly in some unforeseen situation.

Error messages

Making an application fail is a well-known form of security threat. A surprisingly high number of Web sites are relatively weak in this respect, and can sometimes be made to fail by reusing the data obtained from empty or non-meaningful queries, for example. Web applications are supposed to be much simpler than fully-fledged GUIs, so the threat is even more serious for rich clients and other client applications. Alas, GUI developers usually overlook security threats, because they assume that a restricted end user population, as is often the case with Java GUIs, will shield them from malicious use.

Fortunately, client GUIs are less restricted than Web applications, and a local log file will be able to provide technical information to the developers, and not to the end user – who shouldn't be bothered by these details, or even worse, might potentially use them against the system. Separating technical error messages from end user messages in two different distribution channels (log files and the GUI) simplifies the error notification architecture, while ensuring higher levels of security.

> In some scenarios it could even be desirable to provide users with low-level technical details of errors, for example an application that is intended to be used by developers such as an Eclipse plug-in.

5.7   Introduction to user interface testing

When developing iteratively it is essential to maintain the code tested, launching unit tests after every change. More rarely, we might change the GUI design too, perhaps refining an existing feature or adding new ones. In this case we may want to test the application for usability as well as for technical soundness. While being two different practices involving different skills, both GUI test and usability testing are essential for an effective final result.

> Agile approaches offer a new and refreshing 'take' on testing. The approach of giving test responsibility to the developers themselves from the early stages of development is a radical departure from 'old school' QA approaches, in which an unspoken adversarial climate often arises between developers and testers, complete with different cultures and career paths and a perception of testing as an authoritarian practice that takes place after completion of development.

Testing can be seen as a long-term investment in code – the additional investment is repaid in the small cost of further code modifications in the medium to long term. Simple forms of testing can escalate into testing practices that influence the structure of production code heavily.

Tests should be written to cover newly-written code and existing code that has been modified. Unit testing is perhaps perceived by developers as the most valuable form of testing, because of its fine granularity that allows a high coverage of the code base. No matter which type of test you use, automatic tests should be launched as part of a continuous build environment.

Test-driven development

Perhaps the single most important advice about testing, which has been validated empirically by decades of development practice, is to *test early*. The sooner, the better. Taking this to the extreme, we have test-driven development, which prescribes that tests should be written even before the code itself. This strategy works well when developers are motivated to build effective tests, but can otherwise result in a development overhead that produce vapid, ineffective tests.

Test-driven development (TDD) focuses on developers writing unit tests before writing code. It improves the design by providing goals, guidance and early feedback to developers, reduces coupling, and improves cohesion. It may involve major use of refactoring and other practices such as specifications and testing by example, as well as Agile techniques such as providing automated regression tests written in collaboration with customers.

Tests also provide a measure of a project's success and a realistic indication of overall progress. All of this nice magic comes to a price, of course. The price is higher development costs, a change in mind-set requiring greater motivation from developers and managers, and a generally more labor-intensive, responsible development style.

It is common for developers to focus the implementation and even the architecture on easing testing or other implementation aspects. While this is common practice for software that does not interact with end users, for desktop application GUIs this practice needs deeper thought. The real question behind this approach is how much the development should influence the final product – in our case, the GUI design, its performance, and its overall usability.

What's first – GUI design or implementation?

In the early Middle Ages in Western Europe towers, a very important means of defense in those days, were built with an iterative process in which scaffolding was attached to the tower itself as construction progressed, greatly simplifying the building process. Traveling across Europe you can still see these old towers, which can be recognized by regular patterns of holes in their walls that were used to insert scaffolding logs.

A tourist might dislike this effect, as it is a temporary construction trick that affected the overall result right through to today. Moving from the building techniques of the past to current software engineering practice, a frequent question is how much a GUI design should be influenced by its implementation. We saw in Chapter 2 and at the beginning of this chapter that cost-driven design is an all-important practice, but even with this approach, usability and end user-centered considerations always have the last word over implementation details.

In real situations, especially with developers not familiar with GUI design issues and concerned mostly with implementation aspects, such as providing a robust, cost-effective and easily maintainable GUI, this might not be the case. To them, implementation is *the* priority, with GUI design considered a sort of a nice-to-have, slightly dangerous luxury.

Such developers would probably consider holes in medieval towers to be part of the design, not a side effect. Structural integrity is a quality achieved by means of the building technique employed, and not a spurious, secondary effect. Cost-effectiveness is an important part of a construction technique. Others may argue that GUI design is the final product, and development must serve the final result only, possibly constrained by cost-driven considerations. You can imagine how such topics were debated in past millennia for civil engineering and architecture.

Such considerations are also important in software engineering practice, because implicit assumptions made by developers can drive the project towards unforeseen and dangerous situations. Contrary to server-side development, GUI builders also face customers' judgment. Imagine that you are an architect and your client, a wealthy entrepreneur, is paying you a substantial sum to design and build his next factory, a place where people will spend most of their daytime and which should be optimized to provide the best possible working conditions. Now imagine your feelings when during a design review the top managers and the boss ask you about the weird holes into the walls shown the drawings of the new building… equally, you don't want any holes showing in your GUI.

These apparently abstract considerations boil down to very practical situations when developing real-world GUIs. Think for example of the habit of many developers of keeping the GUI layer as thin and simple as possible. This makes extensive unit testing much easier, bypassing the GUI 'skin,' and confines presentation details outside the 'real application' automatically. Unfortunately this approach becomes burdensome as the complexity of the GUI increases, especially with regard to complexity of interaction with end users – think for example of complex, extensive interaction and control behavior.

To use a metaphor, it's like trying to build an easy-to-maintain and robust Formula 1 race car. It is hard to design your car for other objectives than speed and performance. Providing additional equipment and mechanisms for easing car maintenance could decrease performance and, as the competition gets tougher, be a costly luxury.

The bottom line is to design and develop as much as possible focusing on implementation details, as long as this strategy doesn't clash with usability and the overall, *user-perceived* effectiveness of the final GUI.

5.8   Software testing of Java GUIs

This section describes details of GUI implementation testing, and some techniques that help to build a GUI that is easy to test.

Exhaustive software testing of a GUI can be complex and expensive. You can trade technical complexity for cost, and let human beings test your GUI, or you can automate part of the testing to save time and money, but this may prove to be complex and limited, at least with current technology, a problem not confined to Java. GUIs and their building blocks are built for users. Only as an afterthought are they made available for automatic manipulation, and even when they are, it is not easy to declare interactions and expected behavior.

Expressing interaction properties of any complexity in a formal language in a simple and widely-adoptable way is a long-held dream of the GUI engineering community that is yet to prove feasible in reality.

> This section provides a complete perspective of GUI testing. Practical examples are provided in some of the later chapters of the book.

How to test – GUI software test approaches

Referring to Figure 5.19, we divide our code into three broad categories for GUI software testing.

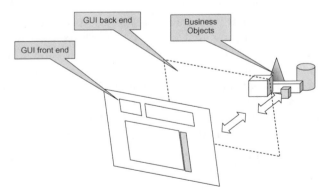

Figure 5.19   Partitioning code for software GUI testing

These are:

- *GUI front end code.* This is where widgets and all the graphics code lies, including the content layer. It is important to note that copies of the business data are stored within widgets as well, referred to as the *screen data state* – this is described in Chapter 8. We assume a general lifecycle as follows: some business objects' data is copied to widgets' data, and after specific user interactions via the GUI back end code, data is passed from or to the business objects.

- *GUI back end code.* This code oversees at the binding between GUI and data. In MVC terminology it is the controller code. This part of the code also contains the business rules and other control code. In the particular MVC flavor implemented in Swing, this code is contained within the widgets themselves.

- *Business objects.* These are the domain-dependent business data our GUI is representing, referred to here as the business domain layer. We assume that developers have tested these objects autonomously, using libraries such as JUnit, so we will not discuss their testing here, and take their integrity for granted.

   Some toolkits like Swing allow business objects to be used as GUI models directly, but for various reasons developers sometimes do not use this feature – that is, business objects are copied in and out of the MVC's model objects – so that we keep the MVC's controller and model explicitly separated for clarity.

The commonest way to test the implementation of a GUI is to get a person to test it. This is the kind of testing all of us have done many times in our lives. Figure 5.20 shows this situation.

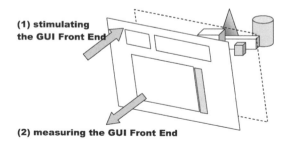

(1) stimulating the GUI Front End

(2) measuring the GUI Front End

Figure 5.20   Manually testing a GUI

The tester stimulates the GUI – pressing buttons in a certain order, typing in values, and so on – and sees whether the expected result is obtained. This kind of testing has all the problems we can imagine for testing:

- It is not repeatable. Even if a written test script is used, someone has to perform all the steps requested by the script.
- It is not 100% safe. Humans may make errors, both in manipulating the GUI and in interpreting the outcomes.
- It is expensive, because testers need a lot of time to perform extensive testing.

It has also some benefits, the major one being that unexpected problems can be found easily. Some tools allow the recording of test sessions and other limited forms of automation, as we will see, but for fully testing a real-world complex GUI, human beings are still necessary.

For effective automatic testing of a GUI, some form of modification of the implementation is needed. Special software access points must be added to the GUI code to allow it to be tested without (or with limited) human intervention, to allow the kind of interactions described above.

An example can help to explain this: think about a text field within a panel that a developer may want to manipulate and then make the resulting value available to the program. Access to the specific widget might require some form of OO visibility relaxation, such as making the field protected, for example, or some other form of runtime access.

A practical discussion of testing is provided in Chapter 8, focused on form-based rich client applications, although limited to a concrete case only.

Adding a layer of indirection between presentation and the rest of the GUI implementation works well for GUIs with a low level of interactivity. The higher the interactivity bandwidth with the user – that is, the more interaction and control behavior in our GUI – the more work is needed to maintain the additional decoupling. Ultimately, some form of testing through the GUI is always needed: for end-to-end tests, for testing interaction logic, or for (automated) acceptance tests.

Framework-dependent code in GUIs can be confined to the presentation and content layers – that is, the GUI toolkit in use. By adopting a Rich Client Platform, however, container-dependent code grows through the addition of business rule validation, data binding, multithreaded operations, and so on, and unit testing code needs to pass through this container-managed code. This situation resembles the testing of application-server contained Java server code.

The three most frequent approaches to GUI software testing are fully manual, semi-automatic and fully automatic. Each approach has its own benefits and drawbacks, and the best result is obtained when using two or all three approaches together:

- *Fully manual*. A test team ensures the robustness of the GUI by testing it directly. Documents such as refinements of analysis use cases describe detailed scenarios of use and their expected outcomes.

- *Semi-automatic*. Testers use some form of tool to automate some tests, usually lower-level ones. They launch scripts and inspect the results in the GUI.

- *Fully automatic*. Developers implement test cases provided by the test team. Such tests can be run together with the other unit tests as part of the code for the GUI.

The characteristics of these testing approaches are briefly summarized in the following table.

Table 5.2   The characteristics of testing techniques

Type	Initial setup cost	Run costs	Precision	GUI coverage
Fully manual	Medium / Low *(writing test cases in plain language)*	High	High	Low
Semi-automatic *(human tester with recording device)*	Medium /High *(learning/ purchasing tool, …)*	Low	Medium *(depends on tool)*	Medium/ High
Automatic	High / Very High *(tweak existing code, write code test cases)*	Low	High	Medium *(some GUI-only interactions cannot be tested fully)*

Designing for testing

A number of techniques can be employed to simplify automatic unit testing of GUI code. These techniques range from high-level design strategies to practical details. A number of design strategies can be employed to simplify API access to GUI code:

- Presentation Model is a design technique used in Smalltalk VisualWorks that aims to decouple toolkit-dependent code completely from the rest of the application. The data and the behavior of the GUI are isolated from the content. The class that represents the Presentation Model contains data that is displayed in a visual container such as a panel or a window and needs to be maintained in sync.

- Model-View-Presenter (MVP) is a variant of the Model-View-Controller (MVC) pattern discussed in the next chapter. This design pattern allows for a certain level of decoupling between the toolkit-dependent code and the rest of the application.
- Provide programmatic access. This approach aims to make as much as possible in a GUI reachable by API methods, so that automatic unit testing can be used to include behavior such as GUI events, interaction and control, and other parts of GUI implementation that are usually not accessible to unit tests. This is a fairly intrusive technique that requires many methods to be added to support automatic testing.

What to test – test coverage criteria

The following table shows the most useful types of tests available for 'unit'-testing widgets, that is, without interactions with other areas. For example, when ticking in a check box, are panels of related properties disabled? The italics show the tests than can only be run through the GUI back-end layer – that is, tests that are not available through GUI interaction.

Table 5.3   *Data-bound widgets 'unit' tests*

Data Type	Widgets	Typical Tests
List-Of	Combo box, table, List	0 elements, 1 elem., Random N elems., *Null value,* *1 Null elem.*
(Formatted) Field	Data formatted fields (Date, currency, etc.)	Empty value, Random valid* value, *Invalid* value, *Null value,*
Ad-hoc	Ad-hoc component (for example color chooser, and so on)	Ad-hoc property, Empty value, Random valid* value, *Invalid* value, *Null value*
Group of Boolean values	Check box, radio button	0 elements selected, *1 Null elem.,* *Null value*

(* Indicates values whose validity as defined by business rules, if any)

This type of testing can be extensively automated, including testing for special cases. We discuss some testing frameworks and tools that can be used for this purpose in Chapter 11.

> In my experience many of the problems with robust GUI development today are due to non-optimal use of testing tools. The market offerings for GUI testing tools for Java are still fragmented and oblige developers to use a careful tool selection process, often using more than one test tool, depending on need.

An ideal GUI testing tool for Java

Every test tool currently on the market has some nice, unique feature that would be good to have in a comprehensive product. Perhaps this will never happen, but the characteristics listed here may be useful when choosing an existing tool.

- The ideal tool should be simple and lightweight, built with customers as reference users for acceptance tests, thus ensuring usability, simplicity, and so on.

- It should use a high-level scripting language, easily embeddable and usable by developers and non-developers alike.

- It should have a basic set of elementary GUI test functions that apply equally to SWT or Swing GUIs, and specialized libraries that provide both higher-level and toolkit-dependent behavior.

- It should provide hooks to the JVMPI interface, so that stress tests can be automated, abstract-to-concrete pick-selection, allowing the use of a widget logical identifier to find a component, then use GUI low-level events to fully simulate human interaction and integration with unit testing libraries.

- Essential features should include: proved in large, complex projects, provided with some IDE support, well documented with non-developers in mind, possessing a recording/playback facility, a lively support forum, and so on.

- Most importantly, it should be designed with a testing philosophy in mind. Instead of being a set of loosely-assembled diverse features, it should support testers, developers and customers throughout the product lifecycle.

Is this asking too much?

5.9 Usability testing of Java GUIs

Usability testing is an all-important form of testing, related to the semantic and emotional impact the GUI has on end users, the consumers of the product and those for whom it was built.

Usability testing of user interfaces is very different than the GUI implementation testing described in the previous section. While the latter can be thought of as the equivalent of testing text for grammar and spelling errors, usability testing is the equivalent of testing for poetical resonance and pathos. It involves a completely different set of skills and is a subjective form of evaluation, because it depends on the user population that will use the application. Results obtained in this way should not be generalized to other situations and users outside those in the test population.

Usability testing is important. An application that is difficult or aesthetically unpleasant and punishing to use will frustrate end users and increase the proportion who will ask for support or who will fail to complete application tasks effectively. This can ultimately cost more than the software's development.

We do not discuss usability testing in detail here – many books on this subject exist, such as (Nielsen 1993), (Rubin 1994), or (Snyder 2003) for paper prototypes. We do briefly discuss a practical approach to usability testing, leaving the interested reader to more specialized resources.

Usability tests are carried out with real users and using a specific number of defined tasks. They comprise the following activities:

1. Determine the goal of the testing. Possible goals include:
   – Testing the ease of understanding and ease of use of certain features.
   – Verifying empirically the way real users perform specific tasks in particular situations .
   – Collecting some form of data for an empirical assessment of specific GUI aspects, such as the average time to accomplish a task, how often a critical operation is achieved successfully, and so on.
2. Defining the user population and the user profile for the intended tests.
3. Finding suitable users that correspond to the profile, or picking representative users from the client's organization.
4. Defining the tasks that users will perform in the testing environment.
5. Preparing the application, or the prototype that will cover the tasks, for usability testing, including data and other simulated support, such as remote communication delay times.
6. Defining the boundaries of the prototype (see Figure 5.2 on page 177) and testing the application or prototype internally before using it for usability testing with real users.

7. Conducting usability tests with users on given tasks:
   - Usability testing is a delicate form of testing. Giving guiding instructions or letting the tester struggle fruitlessly for half an hour with a particularly cumbersome feature can both make testing a waste of time.
   - A single test usually lasts half to one hour.
   - Testing consist of letting the user use the application to perform the planned task while recording details about their experience unobtrusively.
   - Special attention should be given during usability testing to issues such as choosing the most realistic test context.
8. Collecting results from the tests, prioritizing the issues found.
9. Applying the feedback obtained. This implies modification of the GUI design to address the most important issues discovered during testing.

> In the development of an experimental plug-in for Eclipse I created a special additional plug-in to observe the user at work, producing a sequence of screen shots that provided a record of the user's behavior while solving the proposed tasks. Such material, together with handwritten notes taken during the testing sessions, is extremely precious in understanding the usability shortcomings of the application with a specific user population.

Don't forget to use some form of 'informed consent' agreement signed by your users prior to testing, explaining the purpose of the tests, the amount and type of data being collected, and other privacy concerns, such as the fact that all user data is collected in an anonymous way.

Several different roles are involved in the creation and running of usability tests:

- Those who design the GUI, comprising some developers, and those who created the prototype.
- Usability testers, who conduct the tests and takes notes.
- End users, the subjects of the testing.

Many problems can be isolated by the use of simple prototypes. Once spotted during usability testing with a prototype, such problems can be tackled at an early development stage, saving money and time. The most frequent problems are:

- Navigation and ease of accessibility of features within the GUI.
- Lack or unsatisfactory implementation of business requirements.
- The terminology and concepts used in the application.
- Visual issues such as widget layout in form-based applications, and so on.

5.10 JRE runtime management

This section discusses the profiling and tuning of application runtime resources, which is an often overlooked aspect of GUI development. We discuss this topic in this chapter because a simplified, focused form of profiling can be carried out during iterative development, and this can save valuable time and energy in the medium to long term, much as can continuous testing.

Performance is a concern in any non-trivial Java application. Making a Java application perform well is a matter of design, implementation and profiling skills, as we will see.

Introduction to profiling

Profiling an application allows a developer to glean useful metrics, such as the memory use of a given object and the execution times of specific methods. This can provide detailed and valuable insights into how an application is performing. Even with a good design and the best developers, issues related to performance or memory management can be introduced, particularly in programs that consist of multiple layers and deep object graphs.

We introduce JRE profiling here in a general way, abstracting from the many tools that are available for it. The general concepts can be applied to any tool. It is important that every developer is confident with even a simple profiler, at least for detecting blocking runtime issues early in the development process. The good news is that profiling for desktop application GUIs is easier than profiling server applications, and after a little practice results will be easy to achieve.

There are two main approaches to profiling:

- *Preemptive.* Profiling is done to prevent problems occurring. We want to keep preemptive profiling as simple and cheap as possible, because if it becomes too difficult we will abandon it. For this reason preemptive profiling should be fully automated and as rapid as possible.

- *A posteriori.* This is done after something wrong is discovered in an application and we need to understand the problem. Usually it is a deeper and more comprehensive analysis than preemptive profiling, and it is performed manually by expert developers.

> The JRE provides a standard interface for profiling agents, JVMTI. The old profiling interface (JVMPI) is supported only in Java 1.5. Both these interfaces are native (through JNI) and provide a two-way interaction with the JRE.

Developers usually discover profiling when a problem is found in the application, and this often happens close to the release deadline – or even later – when integration tests are run extensively. This can result in quick and dirty solutions that might spoil an otherwise carefully thought-out design.

Systemic and application-level concerns

Measuring, inspecting, and acting on threads and JRE runtime memory allocation is different than working with GUI events and widgets' data models. Using a debugger and executing tests are application-level activities, while profiling operates at the 'systemic' level. Systemic is a concept borrowed from biology, and is used to indicate something relating to or affecting an entire living organism or one of its subsystems. To make an analogy with newspaper editing, when we perform tests of any type, it's similar to editing an article for grammar, while when we do profiling, it's like examining the paper on which the newspaper is printed.

It can be hard to track a problem from its systemic, low-level effects back to its application-level causes. For example, an improper use of the GUI event queue can cause unnecessary production of GUI events, which will in turn appear at a systemic level as an excessive thread overhead, or in some cases thread contention.

Luckily, Java technology allows for fairly transparent access to the JRE's inner workings, allowing developers to inspect the fine-grained detail of runtime objects, threads, and resources.

Profiling techniques

Two main techniques exist for inspecting runtime performance in Java code, which are often used together:

- *Bytecode instrumentation*, also known as 'bytecode injection' or 'bytecode insertion.' This technique transparently modifies the .class bytecode and inserts special code to capture events like method entry, method exit, object allocation, and object freeing, while the code is executing.

- *Profiling agent sampling*. The JRE-native interface to profiling agents allows for interactions with a running JRE. Examples of such interactions are querying for current threads and their status, obtaining a memory heap dump, or invoking the garbage collector.

At the application level we don't have to know how these features are accomplished when we use a profiling tool.

Profiling can also be used for understanding the working mechanism of portions of an application whose source code cannot be accessed, or that it is extremely hard to understand. This is often the case with third-party libraries or with large and tangled code bases. In this cases it can be useful to inject special data into the application that has a recognizable pattern, and track its transit inside the application at the systemic level, much as chemical or radioactive tracers are used in medicine. When code is truly obfuscated, however, even this technique can prove ineffective.

Common problems

A number of problems can be detected by profiling, discussed in the following subsections.

Memory leaks

Memory leaks are characterized by an unstable memory allocation that will eventually halt the JRE with a `OutOfMemoryException` error. Memory leaks are characterized by the following equivalent effects:

- The heap decreases after every garbage collector (GC) invocation: the average heap size appears graphically as a downward linear graph. The steepness of this graph reveals the rate of memory leaking after each GC invocation – see Figure 5.21 below.
- On average the GC successfully discards fewer and fewer objects at every invocation.

As Figure 5.21 shows, the free memory heap size in a Java application should oscillate around an average value, which can be roughly shown as a straight line. The application execution will create new objects, while the garbage collector will periodically remove those that are no longer referenced. In the case of a memory leak, the average heap size appears as rising graph.

The greater the slope of this graph, the easier it is to isolate the location of the problem at the application level. This happens both because it is easier to notice large changes in time, and also because for a developer it is easier to spot differences to other object allocation trends that remain roughly constant.

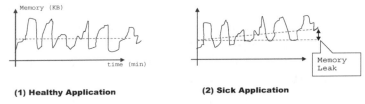

(1) Healthy Application   **(2) Sick Application**

Figure 5.21   JRE heap memory allocation profiles

The strategy for finding memory leaks is similar to the strategy used for finding other performance problems. Start from the effects and backtrack, from the invoked method to the method invoking it, and so on, until the source of the problem is detected. Most profiling tools have special performance data view to make problem detection easier.

> `OutOfMemoryException` errors can be thrown for reasons other than memory leaks. An infinite recursion loop, or just too small a heap size, can exhaust the JRE's available memory.

Typical occasions when memory leaks can occur in desktop application GUIs include screen disposal that is not performed thoroughly by means of an explicit `disposeResources()` method. This is specially true of Swing applications, as many developers refuse to write such methods, convinced that resource disposal is performed automatically by the library[4].

Consider the case in which you have an `Observer` instance registered to a `Subject`, for example a subclass of `Observable`. Now you dispose of the screen, which is perhaps implemented as an SWT `Dialog`. The `Observer` instance does not get disposed, because a reference to it is kept into the `Subject`'s list of listeners.

Another common situation is that in which some utility class such as the help manager is used, and we register an object contained in a screen to such a utility class – for example, through JavaHelp's `CSH.setHelpIDString(widget1, "widget id")`; method. This reference now keeps the object alive, as well as all other objects it refers to within the disposed screen.

> Sometimes it can be time-consuming to track down the location of a performance problem. It may be the case that a memory leak is so negligible that you would need hours of interaction to spot the cause of the problem. To speed up the detection process, you can artificially exaggerate the problem. In the case of memory leaks caused by an incorrect resource deallocation, for example, it might be useful when working with Swing to install a Look and Feel with very memory-expensive graphics and resource consumption, so that after just a few interactions you can spot easily where the problem lies.

CPU hot-spots

Profiling can help you to identify methods that consume the most CPU execution time[5]. This is achieved by isolating the points in the code where the program spends most time, starting from the effects – the location where the time hot-spot is detected – and backtracking from method to method, starting from the method

---

4. This is true only as far as graphics resources are concerned, and provided that developers follow common use patterns.
5. Generic execution time also includes other running threads and the time resources consumed by the profiler process itself. As a first approximation, they can be thought of as equal.

currently executing to the one that invoked it, and so on, to detect where the problem lies.

Threading issues

Threads that are competing for locks exhibit the phenomenon of thread contention. Luckily, a careful design and implementation will prevent this sort of issue in Java GUI code. Desktop application GUIs in Java are usually built on a simple single-thread scheme, as adopted by Swing and SWT. Simple design criteria ensure no threading issues as long as some basic rules are observed.

In Swing applications, for example, two main rules shape thread design:

- Manipulate Swing components – that is, invoke methods on Swing widgets – only from the event dispatch thread (EDT). This is because JFC/Swing is not thread safe, contrary to AWT.

- Lengthy tasks should not be performed on the event dispatch thread, because this will freeze the whole application. Instead, use the `SwingWorker` class to fork a new thread, allowing the application to remain responsive. Return to the EDT only when the results from longer processes are available.

Access to the EDT is achieved by means of the `SwingUtilities.invokeLater()` method. Too many such method invocations can hinder performance. The `Swing-Worker` class supports the coalescing of `Runnables` – that is, many small `Runnable` instances merged into one – to ease this problem. Simple test classes can verify automatically that all widget manipulation is performed within the EDT[6], and that the EDT is not clogged by too many `Runnables`. For example, you could periodically create a `Runnable` to be inserted in the EDT that measures the elapsed time for its execution since its insertion into the EDT.

Thread problems with SWT are immediately obvious – in contrast to Swing, SWT does not allow widget manipulation outside the EDT at all: instead, a runtime exception is thrown. In cases in which data from another thread needs to be provided to a SWT widget, the method `display.asyncExec()` provides a similar function to Swing's `invokeLater()`, allowing a separate thread to communicate with widgets.

Garbage collector activity

Excessive garbage collector (GC) activity should be a primary concern when optimizing performance. An application may exhibit excessive object creation or object retention due to bad design. This will cause the GC to be launched more

---

6.   See for example the Spin project at http://spin.sourceforge.net/.

frequently than it should, slowing the application's execution and thus its interaction with the user. The following situations can pose an excessive burden on the GC:

- *Excessive object turnaround.* Creating too many short-lived objects will cause the GC to be invoked more often than needed. This is the case in a loop that creates many temporary objects, for example.

- *Excessive object retention.* Storing objects that are no longer needed reduces the available memory and thus forces more GC invocations.

In interactive GUIs, excessive GC activity may affect the application's responsiveness. Imagine that you are using an application that occasionally and unpredictably freezes for few seconds, then returns to normal responsiveness. This is very frustrating. A reason for this bumpy type of interaction could be an excessive heap size, requiring much time to parse during GC activity, or some other form of poor GC tuning.

In tuning the GC for interactive GUIs, the focus is usually on minimizing *pauses* – the times when an application appears unresponsive because garbage collection is occurring – instead of maximizing *throughput* – the percentage of total time not spent in garbage collection, averaged over long periods.

J2SE 1.5, differently than 1.4, chooses the GC algorithm automatically depending on the type of machine on which the application will run. For more information about JRE's GC tuning, read the excellent Sun documentation for the J2SE version of interest.

> In enterprise applications and rich clients by far the predominant source of latency and lack of responsiveness is caused by remote communication and the way it is designed. No matter how well the work of the garbage collector is streamlined, or how well local threads handle complex operations on the client, the latency of remote communication is almost always orders of magnitude greater than these client-side enhancements.
>
> In this common case, optimizing data communication over the network will have an enormous impact over the overall performance perceived by the end user.

Continuous profiling

Continuous profiling is an automated, simplified version of application profiling that focuses on isolating the most serious systemic problems as early as possible, such as:

- Memory leaks
- Thread deadlocks and contentions

Continuous profiling doesn't reveal the exact line of code where the problem lies. Instead, it generates an alarm signal for developers to investigate a serious problem while an application is still in production, using a smaller and easier-to-examine application. Developers will have fresher knowledge of the implementation at this stage and will be able to spot the issue more quickly than they might a few months after product release. Finding the problem and solving it in parallel with on-going iterative development augments the chances of providing a good solution without a last-minute rush.

Continuous profiling demands automation, at least of input stimuli, to emulate end-user interaction. At least two main scenarios must be simulated in an automatic and repeatable fashion: stress and average use of the application. These tests are applied to the application and appropriate performance measurements – elapsed time, available memory after a GC invocation – are verified. When using JUnit, for example, JUnitPerf, a collection of specialized test decorators, can be used to measure performance automatically.

Premature optimization is the root of all evil[7]

Continuous profiling should focus only on isolating systemic problems that may seriously hinder the application, or stop its execution completely. Any further optimization should be postponed to *a posteriori* profiling sessions, if any. This ensures that the application will work well without last-minute nasty surprises, and without wasting precious time optimizing code that may later be heavily modified or discarded.

A posteriori profiling

This is the commonest form of profiling, performed when a serious, blocking problem is threatening development and it needs to be isolated and fixed, usually in a short time-frame. Common issues for this kind of profiling are:

- Finding the slowest methods. Optimizing performance is a frequent theme in Java GUIs, especially in cases of non-trivial tasks and limited memory resources. As with CPU hotspots, this is achieved by backtracking from invoked methods to the invoking ones to discover where the bottleneck lies.

- Detecting where most garbage collection activity is concentrated. Mysterious abnormal GC activity degrades the performance of an application, making it almost impossible to use on some machines. The culprit is usually an area in the code where there is excessive object creation and subsequent disposal, possibly within a loop.

---

7.   Despite being traditionally credited to Donald Knuth, this popular quote is of uncertain origin. Others credit it to Edsger Dijkstra.

Several other common profiling and optimization issues can be verified during *a posteriori* profiling. This is unfortunately the most common case in practice. We are pressurized to find memory leaks and thread contentions only after they bring the application to a halt, and in the worst possible time-frame: close to the product release date.

A posteriori profiling is also concerned with careful fine tuning of application performance, if necessary. This can be different than the profiling work we have discussed previously, which is only aimed at avoiding blocking problems during program execution.

> *A posteriori* profiling often needs the data from the particular context in which the problem surfaced in order to solve it. An interesting aspect of Java profiling and debugging technology is the ability to perform these operations remotely using a dedicated communication protocol. This allows developers to 'plug into' a client's JRE at a specific point during execution and inspect its current internal state, thus studying a problem within the actual scenario that caused it.

5.11 Summary

This chapter discussed the various techniques that are collectively used when developing desktop application GUIs iteratively using Java technology. Although we focused on J2SE and desktop GUIs, much of the advice provided here is applicable to J2ME applications as well, and, with some modifications, to Web GUIs too.

We discussed the important issue of ordering activities to provide a more practical approach to iterative development by focusing on the most important issues first. We then presented the different alternatives available for producing scaled-down, inexpensive representations of real GUIs using Java technology.

We also provided an introduction to refactoring practice and testing for software soundness and general usability, both much-needed techniques when developing iteratively. The chapter concluded with an introduction to the often overlooked practice of profiling for runtime resources, another useful tool for producing sound and usable GUIs.

The next chapter delves into software design details for building professional Java GUI applications.

6 Implementation Issues

As we saw in the first part of the book, user interface design is not a matter of taste, or at least, shouldn't be. On the contrary, while the exterior appearance of a GUI should adhere to standard design guidelines, in practice the inner software design is more or less left to the developer's goodwill, with the tacit assumption that the implementation is okay as long as it works.

This chapter discusses some of key issues in the implementation of Java GUIs, such as how many closely-intertwined objects can communicate in a modular fashion, which criteria are traditionally followed for organizing the code of complex GUIs at design time, and how user interactions and the way the GUI reacts to them are represented and managed. General problems are introduced and the most effective solutions to those problems proposed. Such solutions usually imply adopting one or more OOP design pattern and other techniques[1]. The chapter organization follows the functional decomposition of the general model introduced in Chapter 1. The chapter is structured as follows:

6.1, Revisiting the abstract model discusses various issues related to the implementation of GUIs and the abstract model presented in Chapter 1.

6.2, Content discusses common design solutions for implementing the content layer, such as content assembly and navigation.

6.3, Business domain illustrates the main issues related to representation of the business domain in GUIs.

6.4, Data input-output discusses general design issues concerning the data I/O layer, data communication and code security, and the Data Transfer Object (DTO) design pattern.

6.5, Making objects communicate introduces the Observer pattern and its variants, and discusses the pitfalls of event-based designs and other related issues.

6.6, Separating data from views discusses the main design strategies used for separating data from its visualization, discussing MVC and its various flavors.

---

1. Most of the patterns described here can be found in (Gamma et al. 1994). For a discussion that is more specific to Java (but with a smaller selection of patterns) see for example (Cooper 2000). GUI-specific and original patterns are also discussed.

6.7, Interaction and control introduces the three main design strategies for implementing this functional layer in Java – scattered, centralized, and explicit design.

6.8, Some design patterns for GUIs introduces other patterns and design strategies that are useful in more than one functional layer.

6.9, GUI complexity boosters lists some implementation issues that dramatically complicate software development for Java GUIs.

6.1 Revisiting the abstract model

Chapter 1 presented a generic, abstract GUI model, in which functionalities are decomposed in layers, as shown in Figure 6.1.

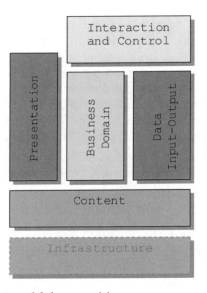

Figure 6.1   An abstract model decomposition

The functional layers in the figure are:

* *Business domain.* The representation of the domain of interest, without references to GUI details. This layer can be modeled using a domain-driven approach (Evans 2004).
* *Content.* The 'structure' of the GUI: widgets, panels, windows, and navigation among different windows. Layout is also included, to ease the understanding and manipulation of widgets.
* *Data IO.* The interface with the rest of the software that supports all interaction with the GUI other than the user's. This layer defines the

communication data in applications that need to exchange information with remote servers.

- *Infrastructure*. Low-level support, GUI frameworks, runtime environment, utilities.

- *Interaction and control*. Low-level events and control logic. This layer contains controls such as disabling the commit button in a form when a required field is empty. Despite being business-dependent (like any form of software) this type of control is also generic and can be factored out as a separate layer, leaving the domain model more focused on business logic and less on GUI details.

- *Presentation*. Graphical details dependent on the given presentation technology. Pixels, colors and the like are confined in this functional layer.

Functional organization – that is, storing and organizing things depending on their use – is a criterion we all use extensively in everyday life: for example, we don't look for our car keys into the fridge. This model suggests a comprehensive organization of GUI implementations based on function, together with a minimal organization of relationships in layers[2]. The main purpose of this model is to provide a useful trade-off between generality and practicality. For example, navigation is considered part of the content layer, and not of the presentation layer. This is because it is easier to define navigation during prototyping and early design, together with GUI content. As with any classification, the decomposition into layers proposed in this abstract model highlights some aspects and ignores others.

One of the most useful benefits of the model is in decoupling responsibilities. For example, having a clearly-separated business domain layer helps when applying all the experience and tools object-orientation has provided over the years. Analysis and design patterns, refactorings, Domain Driven Design and more become available for non-trivial GUIs. All of this power and its related complexity may not always be needed, of course. In such cases some of the layers can be merged, until a unique, comprehensive 'blob' of presentation, data and business logic is obtained, such as the one-layer architecture discussed in Chapter 7[3].

Having a general functional model also helps to move more easily between technologies. This is especially useful for the Java world, in which many competing technologies and tools can be used interchangeably. Several libraries exist for data binding, multithreading, or GUI testing. They can be mixed effectively as long as a sound decoupling between different functional aspects can be enforced.

---

2. See Chapter 7 for a definition of a software layer.
3. Also known as the 'Smart GUI antipattern' (Evans 2004).

Some issues are common to all the layers of the abstract model in Figure 6.1:

- *Adaptation*. Desktop application GUIs adjust themselves to context data such as the locale or the graphics resources available. From an implementation viewpoint, these external factors work like *parameters* to the GUI. There are many forms of adaptation that may affect some or all of the abstract layers in Figure 6.1, as we will see later.

- *Requirements*. Requirements may apply to any aspect of the GUI and need to be addressed explicitly throughout the software lifecycle. Some requirements may be specific to only one functional layer, such as for example a business rule, or cross several layers, such as details of the data handled in a given screen.

- *Testing*. The various kinds of testing discussed in Chapter 5 affect all the functional layers.

- *Preferences and configuration data*. GUIs need to accommodate a wide range of situations. Each layer may have a set of configuration data and user preferences. Preferences are set directly by users by means of a preference panel, as discussed in Chapter 4. An example of preference data, which mainly affects the presentation layer, might be selection of a special look and feel for visually-impaired users. Configuration data is more implementation-oriented, for example defining the time interval between which clients ping their server, or the JRE memory configuration, and is set manually by users, or in some circumstances by an administrator.

Testing the various layers

Testing follows the general model proposed in Figure 6.1. Because the content layer is the base for the other functional layers, testing it is also useful for testing all other layers. The infrastructure layer and its code – GUI toolkit, third-party libraries, and so on – usually don't need to be tested. A common approach to unit testing is to limit testing to a functional area of interest. Depending on the layers in Figure 6.1, different tests are possible:

- *Business logic tests*. Testing domain logic should be done in business logic terms, not through the GUI. It is pointless indirection to translate business logic tests into GUI interactions that in turn invoke business domain objects. Client business logic tests are usually a subset of the comprehensive test suites found on server software. Integration and acceptance tests will of course check all the functional layers in an application via the GUI.

- *Content tests*. To perform these tests, the content layer implementation should provide a means to access data and widget properties. As a basic facility, content units such as widgets, panel and windows should be made accessible, usually by means of a registry[4] and unique ids.

- *Data IO*. Data tests are predictable and can be largely automated or generated. Some possible tests are:
  - Data binding from data transfer objects (DTO) to widgets. Testing for null values, for empty collections, and so on.
  - Results of commands, especially from server to client. Client to server testing is performed as part of interaction testing.
  - Sequences of commands and other control data.

- *Infrastructure*. This layer is composed of support frameworks, GUI toolkits, and other third-party libraries outside the application developer's control. Although it should be possible to take the infrastructure's soundness for granted, sometime this may not be the case. When developing for a new release of a rich client platform, for example, or isolating the causes of some unexpected behavior, infrastructure testing can be useful.

- *Interaction and control*. Trigger interactions and assessment of the results can be performed thanks to facilities in Java GUI toolkits that simulate input and allow widget properties to be probed. Such tests are the cornerstone of automatic GUI testing. By building on them, it is possible to represent complex interactions and define GUI acceptance tests. This kind of testing is fundamental in agile methodologies such as XP.

- *Presentation*. Presentation testing is rarely done, because presentation is more closely related to general usability testing rather than to specific unit tests. If graphics plays an important role in the software (such as a GUI toolkit or some visual tool) it may make sense to provide presentation tests. Such tests might look for expected pixel patterns in the resulting GUI, or prescribed colors, and so on.

The principle of Single Functional Responsibility

The *Single Functional Responsibility* principle is a simple yet useful design technique, and its associated code documentation, that can be used in the development of any GUI. I derived this technique from my practical experience of applying R. Martin's principle to GUI development (Martin 2002). This is a formulation of the cohesion principle in designing classes, and states that a class should be designed to have only a single responsibility.

This principle can be mapped to the functional layers in Figure 6.1 by striving, when it is meaningful, to have classes that belong only to a single functional layer. When this is not possible, sometimes we might apply this approach to the

---

4. See for example (Fowler et al. 2003).

fine-grained level of methods as well. By designing fine-grained methods to belong to a single functional layer, code can be kept decoupled and different responsibilities organized by functional layer, additionally to domain-specific responsibilities (managed by the single functional responsibility principle). This can be seen as an addition to the general single functional responsibility principle.

A simple technique for applying this principle in code is to tag methods and classes with metadata. One simple tagging approach is to tag the method (or class) with the main functional layer from Figure 6.1 to which it is thought to belong.

Assigning a single functional responsibility to a method or class is a good discipline that tends to keep code more decoupled. This is less important when adopting a layering technique that is based on functional decomposition, as metadata tagging becomes redundant because the functional responsibility of the class is then defined by package or layer identity.

Suppose you are developing a widget library in which pixel spacing must comply with specific guidelines. To test this, you could prepare a `testPixelCompliance()` test fixture and tag it as `@Presentation`, meaning that you mean to test the presentation layer:

```
@Presentation Public void testPixelCompliance() {
```

The use of metadata could enable automatic processing and other features beyond mere code documentation, even though the main intent is to support a clean OOP design. It's possible to build on this approach, describing complex architecture information with metadata and their attributes. This is discussed in Chapter 7 in the context of evolving architectures.

Isolating presentation details

The presentation layer in the abstract model of Figure 6.1 is composed of those graphical details that are not strictly related to content functionality, data, and other non-graphical aspects. A common design strategy is to enforce the same type of separation as is provided in the reference model. This is often done at the level of infrastructure libraries and basic GUI toolkits, in that presentation details are intrinsically *extensive* values (that is, they are common to all widgets and screens in a GUI) and centralizing them in a separate implementation module eases their application throughout the whole GUI, transparently from application code.

In particular, it is useful to isolate the implementation of the following details from the rest of the implementation:

- High-level visual details such as graphics design (that is, the visual aspects in a look and feel).
- Interaction behavior. Some forms of user interaction styles can be separated from the implementation, such as whether a button is triggered by a single or

a double click. Although a powerful feature, it is one that is seldom used: achieving this kind of separation would provide a complex implementation structure that will complicate the overall implementation, providing little practical utility.

- Fonts are an example of a presentation detail whose management is usually defined separately from the rest of the GUI implementation, to provide separated management and centralized access.

- Colors and color themes are usually factored out in separate modules to provide easy customization of GUI appearance.

Separations of this type are achieved by Swing thanks to its pluggable Look and Feel design, but SWT, AWT, and many other modern GUI toolkits also enforce some variants of this modularization. It provides important advantages: for example, GUI appearance can be customized independently of the application, maybe by setting a large font in the current profile and so changing the font in all other applications. GUI can also be made 'skinnable' – different visual styles can be applied without modifying application executables, even by the user. User preferences can be adjusted transparently to application code, which is very useful for supporting visually- or kinetically-impaired users.

6.2 Content

This section discusses two key engineering issues for the content layer: content assembly and screen navigation.

Content assembly

A practice common to all desktop GUIs is to place a set of widgets on screen. The widget's layout depends strongly on the chosen layout manager, the object that is responsible for abstracting layout details. The positions of widgets are abstractions of real X, Y screen locations handled by the layout manager. We refer to the procedure of preparing widgets and assembling them in a visual container to be shown on screen as *content assembly*.

The simplest way to implement content assembly with OOP is to subclass a container class (that is, panels, or windows) and provide widget initialization and layout code in its constructor, or in another method, as in the following idiom:

```
panel.add(new OkCancelPanel());
```

An alternative way to implement content assembly is to provide factory methods that create the required, pre-assembled panels, as in the following code:

```
panel.add(Factory.createOkCancelPanel());
```

When there are many variants of panels, or when the application is extremely large and complex, one can resort to a 'little language[5]' to describe the layout and widgets involved:

```
panel.add(Builder.create("btn:ok, btn:cancel"));
```

Content assembly is almost always a statically-defined behavior (that is, content doesn't change at runtime). In a few cases content assembly can be adapted to external parameters – this is discussed in Section 6.8. For usability reasons content assembly should be made variable at runtime only in few situations, for example when changing the layout of widgets in reaction to some event, such as showing advanced search features in a search dialog.

Who assembles content?

From a pure OO approach, content should be created by objects that own the corresponded data and that represent the business domain. Such 'responsible' objects are in charge of representing domain knowledge and also of how such information should be represented on the screen. From a practical perspective, though, enforcing such an approach extensively can be complex, because in following it, it is easy to mix business logic with presentation details.

Assembler intermediaries can be called in to take care of the visual details needed to represent domain information objects. But such intermediary objects, such as a `BankAccountPanel` class that represents a `BankAccount` instance visually, should be treated with care by developers, in that they carry sensitive information and are not just a mere implementation requirement.

Content details are extremely important, because they convey essential semantic information to users. When this information is business domain-dependent, it should not be overlooked or, even worse, automated. Consider for example the position of an **Account number** field within a bank account form. While this is just another string in the class `BankAccount`, it may be the most frequently-accessed information within the account form, and as such deserves a prominent position within the form. It may also need some additional real-time searching facility, assuming that users search accounts usually by their number. Other content, conversely, obeys domain-independent rules, such as **Ok** and **Cancel** buttons at the bottom of a dialog. Such content can be assembled automatically, or, at least domain-independently of the rest of a screen. In this case content assembly can be implemented as support code, separately from domain-sensitive GUI design behavior.

---

5.   See *Domain-specific and Little languages* on page 466.

Explicit navigation

Navigation, the flow of control from one window to another, is a major part of the user experience in GUIs with many screens, such as form-based applications. It is usually hard-wired into the code, like content assembly. Navigation behavior is usually assigned to event listeners, which invoke methods such as `actionperformed()` and the like.

In a few cases, though, navigation need special attention. In cases in which user adaptation is needed, for example if screen navigation depends upon the current user's role, using the Adaptation pattern will suffice, as it leads to the implementation of a suitable `NavigationManager` class.

In other cases, when navigation changes often, for example during development, or in a complex navigational mapping scenario, a centralized, explicit navigation scheme can be useful. Such a mapping of event $\rightarrow$ screen transition can be implemented with a hash map, or with a more elaborate structure in which other support information is represented together with transition rules.

6.3   Business domain

Representing domain logic within a GUI is always a tricky engineering issue. In client–server applications, domain logic should be limited as much as possible to the server tier. 'Pollution' of the GUI implementation with business code brings classic problems such as duplication of code – the same business rule code duplicated on the client and on the server – and code rigidity. On the other hand, confining business logic to the server can transform a rich client into a dumb HTML-like application, degrading responsiveness and overall usability. It is still useful to isolate business-related code, because it is likely to be one of the most volatile parts of a GUI, even for applications that don't exhibit repetitive remote connections, or for very simple ones.

> In the following the term *business rule* is used to refer to a very specific form of domain-specific behavior in which domain logic is represented in the form of a declarative rule suitable to be handled by rule engines or an embeddable little language interpreter. By representing domain logic with business rules, developers can leverage the wide literature and tools available.

Many solutions have been considered for implementing a business domain effectively on a client application. Some of the possible strategies are:

- Including a rich domain model representation in the client application. Usually this is a subset of the wider domain model that resides on a server application, or is dispersed on various servers. This is the case for example when using Web services from multiple organizations.

- Adopting a software architecture for separating domain logic from the rest of the GUI implementation, as we will see in Chapter 7.

- Using an explicit representation of business rules that can interoperate with the rest of the GUI code and that can be deployed from a server at runtime as needed. This solution may involve the adoption of a little language, such as a script language specialized for business logic. This is a technically non-trivial solution that makes sense in large applications with many, mission-critical, and dynamic business rules.

  A cheaper alternative is to formalize business rules with a lightweight OOP framework that is embeddable into the rest of the client application and provides some form of 'zero-deployment[6]' mechanism.

- Separating business logic in packages or classes that are shared with the server code base. This eliminates code duplication, but necessitates a new application build and deployment to clients after changes in business rules.

- As a minimum solution, using the principle of single functional responsibility to identify explicitly portions of code that are intended to capture business behavior. This ensures simple traceability of business logic code within the application, but alone does not enforce decoupling and modularity.

Domain logic can creep into GUIs in unexpected ways. Suppose you have a form that shows customers loans. Your client wants customers with a debit rate higher than 10% of their annual income to be signaled by the GUI with a special warning icon, and to require extra confirmation when such customer's data is manipulated. A rule `isCautionCustomer()` is then clearly part of the business domain layer, even if it is used only on the client.

It is important to address explicitly the representation of business logic within the application design. Lack of awareness can easily lead to tangled code that becomes increasingly hard to maintain as the application evolves. For large applications it is also important to maintain common policies among developers to keep the code uniform and coherent.

In practical situations, some form of tolerance is often used to simplify the software design. Defining mandatory fields[7] directly in client code, for example, is a violation of the separation between presentation and business logic, because if such data should subsequently become no longer mandatory, the client code would need to be modified.

---

6. Zero deployment, also known as 'dynamic deployment,' is a general term for a number of techniques and technologies aimed at simplifying software installation and update, both for users and for developers (Marinilli 2001).
7. Mandatory fields are those widgets that must be filled in to complete data entry in a form.

6.4   Data input-output

Data IO is the conceptual layer that defines all possible interactions of an application with software external to the GUI. Depending on the application, interaction might be with a local database, with a remote server, or with a set of Web services. Figure 6.2 shows such a situation.

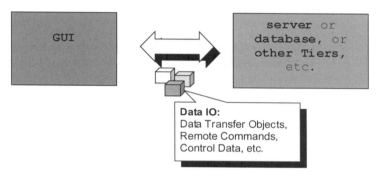

Figure 6.2   Interacting with external software

The main benefit of a well-thought-out data IO layer is the decoupling of the GUI from the rest of the system. This provides many benefits, such as clear conceptual and practical borders, technology independency, and greater flexibility, but also affect the whole application. Data IO is often overlooked as a detail, 'backyard' facility. But GUI performance, even GUI navigation and structure[8], depend directly on the data IO layer.

A good design for this layer should always consider a comprehensive data IO design strategy. For example, how will external communication evolve, and what will future requirements be? What's the driving force behind IO? Typical design criteria could be performance, flexibility, security, and interoperability.

A comprehensive data IO design strategy

While approaching the design of the data IO layer it is a good idea to work out an explicit design strategy. The main design criteria are:

*   *Performance.* If the runtime responsiveness of a client–server application is a requirement, then DTO structure and the serialization format must be chosen carefully.

*   *Flexibility.* Allow for ease of modification.

---

8.   For example, windows are often mapped directly to DTOs.

- *Technology independence*. If independence from technology is required, the data IO layer should be designed accordingly. A common case is the ability to provide different presentation technologies for the same application cost-effectively. Depending on the type of technology, this can be achieved with various levels of reuse. A Web application and a rich client, for example, can share DTO and service information, such as commands and responses, while such sharing may be less for a J2ME applet, which might need much custom DTO. Designing DTO explicitly with flexible reuse in mind may be worthwhile.

- *Security*. Even if communication protocols provide authentication and security, it is always important to think about security up-front for security-sensitive applications.

- *Network* topology. Particular network topologies might favor some form of DTO structure rather than others. As a basic example, for communication performed with network portions using unreliable protocols/connections, small and simple DTOs should be designed.

- *Scalability*. An application deployed on a large number of clients, or exhibiting peak-like use patterns – say several thousands of users submitting transactions at the same time – should have a specific DTO design.

- *Interoperability*. Will the application provide its communication format to others?

- *Infrastructure services* such as security and authentication. These services are provided 'for free' by the underlying technology and should be taken into consideration as part of a data IO design strategy. Is there really a need to provide a home-grown, custom 'ping' protocol facility when adopting HTTP, for example?

It is good practice to focus only one main criterion. This will drive a clearer design and avoid dangerously ambiguous statements such as 'our application will perform the fastest possible remote communication while ensuring maximum levels of independency from data formats.'

Some design patterns

A number of design patterns are commonly used when implementing the data IO layer. These patterns are used for designing distributed systems, such as Proxy, and Broker. This section discusses the Data Transfer Object pattern, because it is specific to GUIs.

Data Transfer Objects

A Data Transfer Object (DTO) is an object used for holding business data in transactions between client and server. A single method call is used to send and retrieve the DTO, which is passed by value. In this way DTOs are used to reduce bandwidth: by substituting them for a number of remote calls to exchange data between client and server, data is clustered in coarse-grained chunks. Needless to say, DTOs should be kept as simple as possible, to speed up their translation to other formats such as XML. For this reason, when remote communication can be a bottleneck in an application, DTOs should contain other objects only when strictly necessary.

Remote communication design

The way a client application communicates with the external world over the Internet affects its user interaction style and the overall user experience. When designing the details of communication between a client application and its server counterpart, a number of options are available:

- *Asynchronous/synchronous communication.* Asynchronous communication is preferable when the communication channel is intermittent or unreliable, as in wireless communications, and also when synchronous communication might take too long. Synchronous communication is used in desktop applications as well because of its familiar conceptual model, similar to method invocation: issuing a request to the server and waiting for the response.

- *Bandwidth constraints.* From a bandwidth consumption viewpoint, desktop application GUIs are a blessing when compared with Web applications, in which all the presentation information must be sent with the data. In some cases, however, such as for wireless devices, bandwidth can still be an important issue. In such cases a proprietary binary format, or some form of object serialization, can be a necessary choice over other more common protocols such as HTTP.

- *User population.* Users affect the way a client–server communication channel is designed. The number of users concurrently using the application, the nature of the transactions, user habits, and various other details all influence the choice of communication design.

- *Scalability.* If you plan to deploy a client over thousands of installations, communication protocol should be able to cope with the likely scenario of thousands of concurrent communications.

Multithreading issues aren't considered here, as they are taken for granted.

Most of the time client–server communication will take advantage of the HTTP protocol, especially for desktop applications. HTTP is extremely useful in that it shields developers from a whole array of network-related issues, such as avoiding additional communication ports, proxies, and firewall administration. Most important of all, though, is its ubiquity.

Seamless deployment

Some form of remote connection is needed to install an application and keep it up-to-date, as this feature is now expected. CD ROMs or other physical means are usually expensive to create and distribute when compared with on-line deployment, and in a world of continuous releases, are useful only for major installations.

Seamless deployment, the ability to install an application directly from the Internet and update it as required during its lifecycle, is a *must* for modern desktop applications. In this book we treat it as a basic infrastructure service, such as fresh water or electricity. Without powerful and seamless deployment support, modern client applications could not exist. Such a feature can be achieved with a variety of technologies:

- OS-dependent ones like those provided by Microsoft on Windows machines.
- Fully Java-based ones, such as Java Web Start and JNLP.
- The Eclipse deployment facility (with a different feature set).
- On-line installer files.

What is important is that the installation is as automated as possible, even though for first-time Java users this will mean downloading JRE's 7 MB-plus and that, after installation, the deployed clients can be controlled remotely for the provision of updates[9]. Java technology also provides remote debugging and profiling, so that the idea of 'standalone clients, remotely connectable' is now largely obsolete.

Familiarity with these new technologies is important, as they affect the way the application is built and conceived, and affect the user's perception of the software. For example, they allow business domain code on the client tier to be updated seamlessly and inexpensively as required, or additional functionalities installed while the application is running.

Security issues

Security is seldom considered at the start of design when developing desktop application GUIs. Usually there is more to security than a secure transmission channel. An important part of security for client applications is ensuring the authenticity of the other party – clients to trust their servers, servers to authenticate clients.

Desktop application GUIs need to add another link to this chain of authenticated transactions: the user. The mechanism of user name and password is a widely-used form of authentication. Authentication mechanisms are needed for applications

9.   See (Marinilli 2001) for a general discussion of Java deployment, even if slightly out of date for some technologies.

that transfer sensitive data to external entities, and also for accessing local resources. For example, a security XML file might be stored in one of the application's JAR files and used for collecting the addresses of trustworthy servers. Ensuring that it is never tampered with and fake (and dangerous) addresses inserted is vital.

Fortunately, security is addressed at various levels in all the technologies on which Java applications rely. HTTPS can be used to ensure secure communication channels, while fine-grained Java security policies or signed JAR files can be used for almost any aspect of the Java platform, or for local resources authentication.

Given the additional complexity that such technologies pose to development, developers often postpone these aspects to subsequent releases, even if the required details can be added relatively easily to the build environment, such as automatically signing sensitive files with certificates, and obfuscating executable code.

When using iterative development on a project on which security is a major issue, security should be implemented from the initial releases[10].

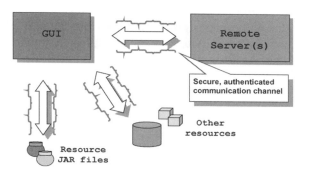

Figure 6.3   *Securing communication*

The following high-level steps are involved in securing desktop application GUIs:

1. Identify sensitive assets within the application.
2. Create a security architecture that considers security throughout the whole software lifecycle.
3. Detect and document possible vulnerabilities. This usually implies the entities shown in Figure 6.3.
4. Assess the risks and plan a risk strategy.

---

10. See Chapter 11, *Security tools* on page 412.

How users perceive security and privacy impacts their experience of an application as well. Such a perception is not limited to the GUI. This is a large topic that goes far beyond the scope of implementation issues.

One thing has been taken for granted so far – that the code base of the application, the `.class` binaries stuffed into the JAR files installed on the local machine, is safe. Unless you actively take care of this issue, the chances are that your executable code is absolutely open to all sort of attacks and malicious behavior. The very first step in securing an application at all levels therefore lies in securing its binaries first.

Securing the code base

Java code can be decompiled very easily. This exposes not only your intellectual property, algorithms, and architecture, but also the management of license keys, where an application is distributed with some form of license control, and virtually any other aspect of the application, including encrypted remote communication and authentication protocols.

Using a good code obfuscator[11] is not enough, because a good protection strategy begins with the design of the code itself. There might for example be situations in which you want to leave some classes open to your users, maybe because they are supposed to extend or interact with them, or times when you rely on class names for some reason, such as logging a class name along with an error message. In such common situations obfuscation cannot be a last-minute matter, but should be an integral part of the whole design.

Securing the code base goes beyond obfuscation to target the way an API can be exposed to malicious eyes, or unforeseen breaches left open through inattention. Imagine for example what could be extracted from a running application with a debugger.

In most cases, perhaps, nobody would be interested in your code, so a standard security policy would be fine – and *always* better than nothing. In cases in which security *is* an issue, because your code contains some secret algorithm, or just because competitors would love to see how you have implemented a specific feature, you need to resort to a thoughtful security strategy to protect your code base.

Such a strategy should focus on sensitive Java packages – those that need to be absolutely secure – and also on other code with a lesser security priority. The signature of methods and the structure of classes belonging to these sensitive

---

11.   Chapter 11 describes a selection of available tools.

packages need to be planned explicitly and carefully designed, to expose the least possible information to malicious eyes.

The default approach to security is to include obfuscation in the build environment as a routine task, even if it is limited only to some packages, together with unit testing and continuous profiling.

6.5   *Making objects communicate*

This section focuses on a foundational aspect of GUIs implemented with OOP: the basic communication infrastructure as implemented with event-based communication mechanisms.

The following sections discuss the various OOP implementations of event-based communication that are part of the Interaction layer in the abstract GUI model shown in Figure 6.1 on page 224. Such implementations are not perfect, as they suffer from typical OOP shortcomings, such as too low a level of representation and an excessive cognitive burden on developers[12]. They are nevertheless one of the most successful applications of OOP to practical software engineering.

The event-driven object communication mechanism is a cornerstone of modern OOP GUI implementations. We first introduce the Observer pattern, then, after looking at some uses of its concepts in Java GUI technology, conclude by discussing two conflicting forces in any software design, object communication and decoupling, from a software design viewpoint.

The following section refers to OOP design patterns. A design pattern describes a proven solution to a common design problem, emphasizing the context of the problem and the consequences of the proposed solution. OOP design patterns have a number of benefits:

i.   They are proven designs: they are the results of the experience, knowledge, and insights of developers who have successfully used these patterns in their own work.

ii. They are reusable: when a problem recurs, there is no need to invent a new solution.

iii. They are expressive: design patterns provide a common vocabulary of solutions that can be used to describe complex systems succinctly.

---

12. These shortcomings become significant in medium-sized and large systems with complex designs. A cognitive abstraction effort is often needed to mentally visualize and to correctly manipulate abstract concepts such as events from just reading the source code or the available documentation.

iv. Design patterns reduce the time for designing, describing, and understand-
      ing software. Clearly, wisely applying design patterns helps in writing better
      software, but it does not guarantee software quality.

The Observer pattern

GUI implementations typically suffer from the problem of trying to make many
loosely-coupled classes communicate. The Observer pattern defines a one-to-
many communication method by means of a publish-and-subscribe mechanism.
Objects that are interested in changes in a *source* object's state, referred to as
observers or *listeners*[13], register for later notification by *subscribing* to the source
object's changes. Later, when the source changes – for example, if a new item is
added to a collection – all its registered observers are notified. The source object
does this by invoking a conventional method on each of the observers, passing a
representation of the given event as a parameter.

Note that it is the source object that is responsible for triggering the notification
event, by scanning its list of registered observer instances and invoking the
method associated with the given event on each of them.

Although many possible variants of this pattern are possible, we will focus on the
scheme shown in Figure 6.4.

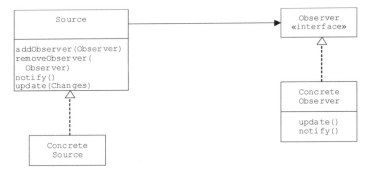

Figure 6.4   *The Observer design pattern*

---

13. Both terms are in common use, and we use them here as synonyms.

Figure 6.5 shows an example of the runtime behavior of an example of the Observer pattern represented as a sequence diagram.

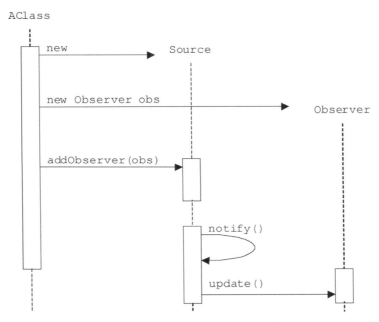

Figure 6.5   *An example of runtime execution of the Observer design pattern*

Each event can be described by an object that encapsulates useful information about what happened, typically the event source and other event-dependent data. Each source object can have multiple observers registered on it in a one-to-many communication mechanism that is defined at runtime by observers subscribing to the source object. Like any modern high-level GUI toolkit, the Swing library makes extensive use of specialized events – that is, specialized classes that handle particular kinds of events, such as `KeyEvent`, `ListSelectionEvent`, `CaretEvent`, and so on. SWT also uses an additional low-level simplified event representation.

The listener class needs to provide the related methods for handling the event, for example using Swing events:

```
public class ListenerClass implements ActionListener
```

Any instance `listenerClass1` of the listener class registers itself with the event source, for example:

```
eventSource1.addActionListener(listenerClass1);
```

This design is an example of another useful strategy in OOP design, that of favoring object composition over class inheritance. For example, compare the difference between using object composition instead of subclassing when defining the action triggered by a button widget. In the case of object composition, you will be setting an action listener object (that is, an Adapter object implementing the `ActionListener` interface) while in the other case you would be obliged to extend the `JButton` class. Clearly the first approach is much more versatile and flexible.

The event-based approach is widely used in GUIs, because it provides various benefits:

- It is simple to understand and use, while general enough to accommodate a large number of practical cases.

- It implements a mechanism of broadcast communication. Observer objects need to adopt the event description defined at design time (the classes defining the event), so that source objects don't have to know anything about their observers apart from a reference to each of them.

- Observers don't need to know anything about each other, and in practice they don't. This minimizes the visibility references among objects, although this could be a problem in some cases, because of reduced compile–time dependencies between different parts of a program.

- It increases extensibility and encourages code reuse, while easing the maintainability of code.

- It makes the coupling between source and observer object instances more abstract.

Perhaps the greatest shortcoming of event-based mechanisms regards the control flow indirection they bring to code. The Observer pattern can be thought of as a scheme in which control flow (procedural runtime execution) bounces back and forth from the source object to all its observers whenever they invoke methods. This implies that reading the source code alone is not enough to work out the actual flow of a chain of events. Developers need to run a sort of simulation of runtime execution in their heads to understand the control flow. The real situation can be determined only through careful, time-consuming debugging. Heavy reliance on event-based mechanisms makes the actual behavior of an application at runtime hard to understand.

Swing events

The Swing framework has adopted a variation of the Observer pattern since JDK 1.1 in which listeners listen for events using the same mechanism as for Java Beans – not surprisingly, as Swing widgets *are* Java Beans.

Figure 6.6 shows the classes involved in this approach. Compare this with Figure 6.4, which shows the classic Observer pattern.

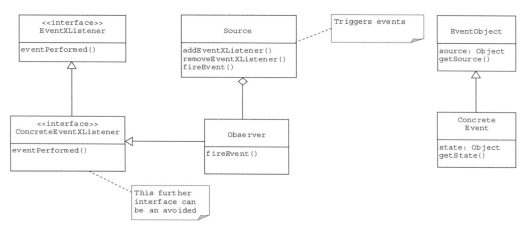

Figure 6.6   Swing events

Given the fact that Swing widgets are also Java Beans, they may use another event-based mechanism specific to Java Beans: `PropertyChangeListener`. We will see an example of the use of this variant of the Observe pattern later in this chapter.

SWT events

SWT's event architecture is similar to Swing's, although Swing-like high-level events are implemented as a convenience for the application developer. In fact, a low-level, simplified event mechanism is used by SWT classes for implementing the typed events SWT event mechanism. All subclasses of the `Widget` class can have an observer added to them by using the method: `void addListener(int, Listener)`, where the `int` parameter defines the event type. All available event types are supported by constants within the SWT class (such as `SWT.Selection`, `SWT.Collapse`, `SWT.Deiconify`, and the like).

Design-time class decoupling with events

Suppose you are going to develop a multi-player video game for the Java 2 Micro Edition. The video game will show a large 2D world in which a number of entities 'live' and interact. Players control one of the actors through a Java-enabled wireless device, while some entities are controlled by the game server. Figure 6.7 shows what this might look like.

Suppose one of the requirements of the implementation is that users should not be forced to download newer versions of the client software from time to time to play the game, as newer features or classes are added, as downloads might involve expensive communication apart from normal client–server data exchange. The code has to be designed to work with new classes added in newer versions of the game. Older versions of the game should work with newer ones as far as possible.

Figure 6.7   Using design-time class decoupling through events in a J2ME application

This is a situation similar to the design of an OOP library, for which you design utility classes that will be used by other programmers in the future. When you design a reusable library, you don't know which client class will use it, all you can do is to try to minimize the constraints imposed on clients that will use the code.

Suppose a player runs a teddy bear instance in the video game using Version 1.0 of the code, downloaded few months ago. When it encounters another game character released in Version 1.1 two weeks ago, the code in Version 1.0 of the game must be able to deal with it[14].

The simplest and most effective solution is to define an event-based decoupling mechanism among entities. When the teddy bear class is designed, all the possible entities it might encounter during its lifetime, and the possible reactions, are unknown, but what a teddy bear can ever do in the virtual world is known. By formally defining its possible interactions with the external world by means of Java code, you can make it available to future classes to interact with. For example,

---

14. This is a design issue: in fact, thanks to dynamic class loading, the J2ME client running Version 1.0 can load the new Version 1.1 class, but without proper software design they cannot interact.

you might decide that a teddy bear instance can sleep, run, and possibly do more in future releases. The class diagram would then be like that shown in Figure 6.8.

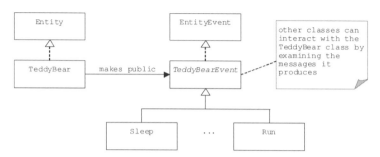

Figure 6.8　　Decoupling class interaction

When an entity wants to interact with the rest of the world it will prompt an event to interested parties – that is, it will issue a coded representation of a change in its internal state.

You could design one or more types of event for your video game, or even a fully-fledged hierarchy. The essential point here is about communication. Subjects make public predefined messages to whichever instance is interested, without having to know anything about the observers. Such event messages are published to the rest of the world, and interested classes know how to deal with them. This kind of communication mechanism guarantees a powerful, dynamic decoupling among interacting classes.

When developing ad-hoc components it is common to create new, specialized kinds of events. Extensive use of event-based communication mechanisms among classes is demonstrated in the examples in the chapters that follow. In this chapter the QuickText example application (Figure 6.18 on page 263) shows a simple example of the Observer pattern at work in detail.

Event Arbitrator

Events are so useful for implementing modern GUIs that they easily become one of the predominant aspects in the runtime execution of a Java GUI, and one of the main sources of difficulty in understanding the actual execution of the application. This provides an additional degree of complexity, especially for readability and extensibility – adding a new class implies adding extra code to connect the new class with the event mechanism.

An Event Arbitrator is a class that listens to a number of events and redirect or manipulates them according to some objective. It is used to simplify or provide structure to the software design, enhance performance by rationalizing event distribution instead of broadcasting to many listeners, and to centralize event flow. An Event Arbitrator can:

- Forward events, by shunting specific events to interested parties for some particular situation.
- Absorb events, for example for debugging purposes.
- Aggregate events, for example by aggregating low-level events into higher-level events.
- Manipulate events to provide some useful service.

An Event Arbitrator does three things:

1. Receives events it is in charge of, called *input events*. It needs to register as a observer to the objects that fire those events.
2. Arbitrates events, processing them to provide a specific feature.
3. Possibly transmit other events, or those it received, to interested parties, following some given organization criteria. In some cases it can also provide some collateral effect, such as modifying global variables, as well as issuing new events.

The most common form of Event Arbitrator works synchronously with its input events, so that the reaction to the received input event is performed sequentially to its reception. Other Event Arbitrators work with more sophisticated arbitration schemes and require extra care when handling threading issues.

The following subsections discuss the most common applications of this pattern in desktop application GUIs.

Aggregating events

A particular case of the Event Arbitrator strategy is for aggregating events from various sources, exposing them in a simplified, centralized fashion to interested parties[15]. In this case the Event Arbitrator acts as a single source of events, hiding other detail events fired by other objects. The Arbitrator class registers for all the detail events, so that clients need to register only with it.

Suppose we are designing an address composable unit (CU), that is, an assembly of simple widgets that act like a unique macro-component representing addresses, as shown in Figure 6.9. We want to hide detail events of the internal widgets and its clients. When using the `AddressCU` class, other client objects only need to register for `DataChangedEvent`s.

---

15. This case is also called Event Aggregator by Martin Fowler.

Figure 6.9   The SWT Address CU

Aggregated events can be of the same or different types as the detail events listened for by the Arbitrator. In this example the `AddressCU` works like an Event Arbitrator and fires new high-level events, as shown in Figure 6.10.

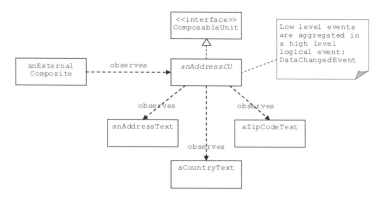

Figure 6.10   The SWT address CU as an event aggregator

Forwarding events over hierarchies of closely-related objects

It is often useful to organize event flow in hierarchical fashion, with a master event listener asnd many slave listeners that receive events forwarded by the master. This organization can be nested using the Composite pattern – that is, the master can contain other masters. This is the case with HMVC controllers, introduced in a later section, and with various other designs that we discuss below.

Sometimes many domain-specific objects enclosed in a container object must be handled in a GUI, possibly a subclass of a standard class such as a panel, or the root of a complex text document. The container forwards events to its contained objects, implementing a hierarchical Event Arbitrator.

The example ad-hoc component discussed in Chapter 16 implements a 2D desktop-like container into which items can be dragged, dropped, and manipulated by the user. In order to achieve maximum flexibility and decoupling, the container doesn't know anything about the nature of the contained items apart from their basic behavior, and forwards mouse events to them in a hierarchical fashion, thus implementing an Event Arbitrator. This might also be the case in a complex CAD GUI, in which a given scene is made up of a large number of small objects organized following a recursive Composite structure. Container objects will behave as Event Arbitrators on contained objects, enforcing some sort of domain-specific event-forwarding criteria.

An important property of Event Arbitrators, and especially for hierarchical Event Arbitrators, is that they should never allow loops in the graph induced by the event flow. The Composite structure of a hierarchical Event Arbitrator should form at least a direct acyclic graph (DAG), even if a simpler tree structure is much easier to manage and fits most practical cases. In the simple tree case it's sufficient to avoid any cross-references among objects in the Composite structure. Having cycles in the flow of events will of course lead to `StackOverflowExceptions`, as the same event is forwarded indefinitely.

Misuses of event-based messaging

Like every good thing, you can have too much of the Observer pattern. A common problem with the overuse of this pattern is Observer chains longer than one, for example when an Observer A observes another Observer B that in turn observes another object, and so on[16]. Control flow becomes very hard to figure out in such situations, and unforeseen behavior is likely. In some particularly unfortunate cases events can go into *resonance* – that is, an event X can cause a chain of events in which a new event X is triggered, causing another chain of events to be fired all over again, and so on.

In some case this incorrect behavior is not apparent from application execution, other than users noticing weird delays in particular circumstances, and log inspection or debugging are needed to work out what is really going on in the application. A possible solution is to use an Event Arbitrator, although this should be used carefully: adopting this pattern alone does not guarantee a cleaner design or a solution to unwanted event-based side effects.

Understating event-infested code

When inspecting someone else's code, it can be difficult to work out the actual chains of events. I personally remember a few cases in which there was such a

---

16. See for example a discussion on this aspect on Martin Fowler's Web site, http//:www.martinfowler.com.

massive use of events that fully understanding the runtime execution control flow was very hard. In one case an event-based composable unit strategy was adopted at a very fine level of granularity, making even the simplest local communication a matter of event messages. With time I resorted to a simple sketch diagram while inspecting code, and for the unfortunate reader who needs to decipher a tangled web of events, describe it here.

Depending on the situation, you might be interested either in who fires events, or in who is observing them. A simple variant of the standard UML sequence diagram can help to identify potential hot-spots in event chains. This diagram can be drawn by hand as you navigate the code, and can be applied to other event-based designs as well, such as those discussed in the next section.

Start by inspecting the code to see which objects register for changes in a source/subject. A simplified version of this diagram that takes into account only classes, and not objects, is much simpler to draw, but nevertheless useful. Whenever you find an object observing another object, draw an arrow from the subject to the observer representing the change propagation event, as shown in Figure 6.11.

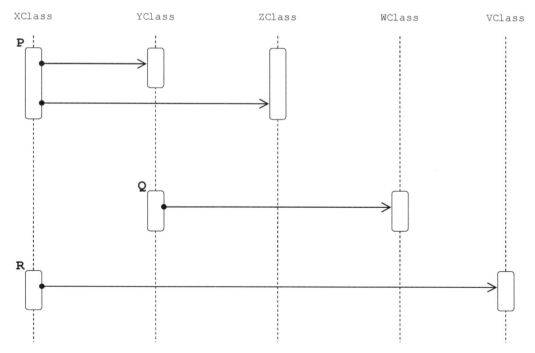

Figure 6.11   Informally describing events

This diagram[17] represents an object of class XClass that has two observers for a property P. Instances are invoked whenever P changes the listener methods in YClass and ZClass. An instance of YClass is also observed by an instance of WClass.

At the end of the code inspection this diagram will tell you roughly the possible chains of events in the code. The next step is to individuate those classes that have two or more boxes – for example, YClass and XClass in Figure 6.8. Focus your attention on these classes, for example adding debug breakpoints, because they are likely candidates for odd behavior.

You may think that problems arise only from combinations of ingoing events and outgoing events, such as YClass in Figure 6.8. This is not always the case, however – in some situations a subject that is common to more than one set of observers can create unexpected problems as well, like XClass in Figure 6.8. For example, this can arise when a change to a property A in a class also modifies another property B, and these properties are observed by two different sets of observers with a common class C. This could lead to unexpected side effects in C when the observer is notified.

A good guideline is to have chains of observers no longer than one, to avoid such possible problems and to keep runtime behavior easily understandable. For complex event schemes, consider using one or more Event Arbitrators to simplify and handle the resulting complexity, carefully designing the desired event flow.

Alternatives to event-based communication mechanisms

Message-oriented approaches are an alternative to event-based communication. Such approaches focus on sending messages asynchronously on a common message bus, where interested parties register to receive messages without any knowledge of who could be sending them. Event-based communication instead obliges the connection of the source – the object that fires the event – with the destination to be established explicitly.

How does this affect the design of client GUIs, with communications performed on the same machine and within the same JVM? Message-based communication for desktop application GUIs is most useful for interaction in-the-large, where the problem is to have an object X be visible to an object Y, rather than as a substitute for low-level interactions such as key presses and 'item selected' notifications. The easy solution to this, although not such a nice solution from an OOP design viewpoint, is to use some form of static visibility to access the required object references.

---

17. The diagram in Figure 6.8 is not a standard UML sequence diagram, nor does it have similar semantics. To avoid confusion, it uses different graphical details than UML sequence diagrams.

This might be done by implementing some form of object registry in which all required objects can be located by accessing a static service or Singleton class, or by making key objects available from a number of Singletons and then extracting the required references from them.

To avoid this drudgery you could resort to message-based communication, or, for the bravest, to a well thought-out OOP design – which is almost invariably the scarcest resource in real-world, deadline-tight, fast-paced production environments.

Message-based communication can be useful at an application level, in medium to large GUIs built by large teams for whom employing communication-specific infrastructure code makes sense. Outside such scenarios, message-based interaction is still attractive, because it provides a simple mechanism for communicating among different classes within the same application with a level of automated threading support. Queues usually run transparently in different threads, so that developers can focus on sending messages via specific queues to communicate with other classes and perform operations. The presence of a centralized bus also makes other automatic forms of control over the messages themselves possible, such as enabling or postponing actions. This approach appears natural to developers used to working with server-based messaging technologies.

Despite the possible benefits of message-based communication systems, they are not so popular among Java GUI developers. Technologies such as JMS[18] exist to enable message-based communication in distributed heterogeneous environments, but they are beyond the scope of this discussion.

As with any technology, message-based communication can be misused, bloating the volume of messages published on the message bus, or even worse, using it as a short-cut for serious design effort.

6.6 *Separating data from views*

GUI implementations usually need to define many classes and other support resources. As the complexity of the GUI increases, the code size increases dramatically. Therefore some code organization, usually at class or package level, is needed in all but the most trivial cases. The most common organizational criterion focuses on the separation between data and presentation.

This section introduces the Model-View-Controller (MVC) pattern (Buschmann et al. 1996), a popular design that enforces the separation of presentation and business code. In reality the MVC approach has proved far from perfect, as witnessed by the many variants that have been developed to try to cope with its shortcomings. Nevertheless, MVC still proves a popular design strategy for GUI code.

---

18. Java Message Service (JMS) API

Model-View-Controller

The MVC approach builds on the Observer pattern for connecting data *models* and their graphical representations (called *views*) by means of specialized entities called *controllers*. MVC was introduced and popularized by Smalltalk (Burbeck 1992) along with the Observer pattern. A variation of MVC has been adopted in the Swing library for separating business data from its GUI representations[19].

The model is the part that represents the state and the abstract data of the given component, separately from its visual representation. The model oversees the state and manipulates it as requested from outside. Following the Observer pattern, the model has no specific knowledge of either its controllers or its views. The view is thought of as being the graphical representation of the model's data. It handles the visual display of the state represented by the model. The controller manages user interaction with the model, providing the mechanism by which changes are made to the model.

> One of the critical points in the large-scale adoption of MVC derives from the deeply-coupled relationship of controllers with models and views. In non-trivial scenarios controllers tend to become deeply intertwined with models and views.

In the Swing implementation of MVC, both the controller and the view are gathered in the same class, the user interface component, while the model is implemented as a separate entity, thus enforcing the separation between presentation and business logic. Each controller–view pair is associated with only one model. However a particular model can have many controller–view pairs.

The MVC design is also widely used for Web-based architectures. A simpler and less sophisticated version of MVC is used for server-side Web GUIs, briefly mentioned in Chapter 9.

Adopting an MVC approach provides the following major benefits:

- *Design clarity.* The list of a model's public methods describes a model's behavior clearly. This trait makes the entire program easier to implement and maintain.

- *Design modularity.* New types of views and/or clients can be created and plugged into existing models at design time just by adding new view and controller classes. MVC works well even when only enhancing existing classes – that is, when supporting incremental development. Controller and view implementations can be modified independently from the model.

---

19. Following SWT's design philosophy of being lightweight and performance-driven, there is no built-in support for MVC, which is delegated to the JFace library.

Older versions of views and controllers can still be used as long as a common interface is maintained.

- *Multiple concurrent views on the same model.* The separation of model and view allows multiple views to use the same business data model. Views could be even different classes, for example a tree view and a table view on the same data model instance. Despite being one of the most interesting features of MVC, the possibility of many concurrent views on the same model is rarely used in common GUIs.

Hierarchical MVC (HMVC)

The HMVC pattern decomposes the client tier into a hierarchy of parent-child MVC layers. The repetitive application of this pattern allows for structured architecture, as shown in Figure 6.12.

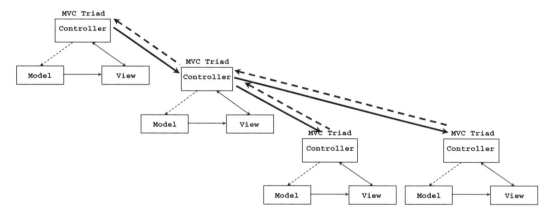

Figure 6.12   The HMVC pattern

Views hide the presentation technology from the model and the controller. GUI-related events are intercepted within the view, and eventually a request is made to the related controller in the form of an HMVC event. If the controller cannot handle the request on its own – each controller is responsible only for its own view and controller – it dispatches the request to its parent controller[20], and so on recursively.

---

20. Following the Chain of Responsibility design pattern.

This hierarchical structure relies on controllers, which are in charge of responding to HMVC events for navigation, such as changing screens and so on, and updating visual data.

HMVC, when applied to non-trivial applications, adds additional complexity to the implementation in the form of burdensome machinery – events and messages are exchanged through dispatchmethods that follow a hierarchical structure – and cognitive workload, as it can be hard to track down bugs and work out the current behavior of an application with many nested HMVC composable units. As a result, HMVC is not one of the most used variants of MVC for client desktop application GUIs.

Model View Presenter (MVP)

Model View Presenter (MVP) is a variant of MVC that attempts to loosen the coupling between the view and both the model and the controller in classic MVC. This tight relationship complicates MVC adoption and makes it hard to use in practice, resulting in MVC's various variants and workarounds.

In the MVP approach the actors have the following characteristics:

- The view in MVP is mainly responsible for graphical output. It also performs user-input gathering of low-level events like keystrokes and mouse events that are redirected to the presenter via events. Views communicate with their model via events. This limited responsibility of views in MVP makes this approach useful for reducing the amount of behavior to be tested without the view – and hence without testing through widgets and GUI toolkit classes. This in turn allows the testing to be accomplished without GUI testing tools, possibly using simpler unit testing tools.

- The presenter holds direct references to both the view and the model and is responsible for manipulating the view and the model to keep them in synch. The presenter does this by reacting to the events forwarded by the view itself.

- The model is similar to the classic MVC model. It is a business domain class that has no connection with GUI-related code, and also no connection with the presenter.

MVP experienced a new popularity with the advent of Test-driven development (TDD) and test-intensive practices, where the view is kept as simple as possible so that the application code can be tested, without full coverage, by writing standard unit tests focused only on the presenter and model.

Figure 6.13 shows the differences between MVC and MVP designs. Dashed lines represent event notifications, while solid lines denote object messaging (that is, direct method invocation).

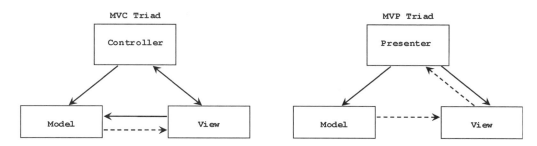

Figure 6.13   Differences between the MVC and MVP approaches

Concluding notes on MVC

The MVC design strategy enjoys a wide popularity among developers and in GUI-related frameworks, especially for Web user interfaces, where the level of interactivity and the overall complexity are lower than desktop application GUIs. One might wonder why it has been so successful, given that it produced a number of secondary issues that the various MVC variants have been created to solve. A simple answer is that MVC is an intuitive, practically-proven arrangement that works better than alternative solutions in real cases.

MVC, or one of its many variants, is already provided by all major presentation technologies and frameworks: adding another MVC layer on top of the one provided by the toolkit (as in Swing for example) usually adds complexity without providing any important benefit to the design[21].

In practical cases the MVC approach or one of its many variants, used alone, provides a minimal, localized decoupling between presentation and non-presentation code. The kind of decoupling provided by MVC may be improved by adopting some other complementary approach, such as a layering scheme[22] or a composable unit structure. This is especially true for non-trivial GUIs, when the implementation architecture is more important.

MVC is often used as a means of design, while it should always be treated as a *solution* to a given problem – it should be used as a design *means* rather than a design *end*. If there is no serious problem, perhaps there should be no need for its solution, and thus no need for MVC. In other cases MVC is used as a solution to a different problem, for example in an attempt to provide a structural organization to a design. This is not bad in itself, but should be achieved with a more comprehensive strategy, including layering, defining Java packages and so on, rather than just 'applying the MVC pattern' to a bunch of classes.

---

21. This is another example of the 'going against the flow' antipattern mentioned at the end of this chapter – in this case adding too much of a given solution to a design!
22. See Chapter 7.

For more information about MVC, see (Burbeck 1992), and as an example of its numerous variants (Potel 1996), while for some of the problems it raises and the possible remedies, see (Reichert 2000). See (Sundsten 1998) for an article introducing the Swing version of MVC, or (Fowler 2000b) for a comprehensive overview of Swing's MVC flavor.

Adapters

The flavors of MVC discussed so far employ the Observer pattern for synchronizing views, and models to provide the ease of use and flexibility modern GUIs need. This comes at the price of increased complexity, even for simple situations in which a fully-fledged MVC architecture is not really needed.

Building such a powerful, complex, and expensive design into a basic toolkit would force all users to employ it and to pay its price in terms of complexity and performance. This was the dilemma faced by Eclipse's architects when deciding how to provide data models on top of raw SWT widgets. To avoid over-engineering the JFace library, which provides utility features on top of SWT, including data support, Eclipse's architects employed a different design than MVC to separate data from presentation – they used Adapters.

The `org.eclipse.jface.viewers.Viewer` class implements a general Adapter for SWT widgets and handlers of data objects. A concrete example is the `Table-Viewer` class. This class adapts an SWT table widget with a *content provider* object. Such an object is responsible for providing content data, taken from a data object. The content provider therefore acts as a mediator between the viewer and the domain-specific data object itself.

This scheme is not a traditional MVC design as we discussed it, because it doesn't couple data with view – if you change the data model object, neither the viewer nor the content provider will automatically notice the change. It is nevertheless a simple and effective way to decouple data from presentation. It is even better than full MVC designs, such as Swing, in this respect. In a full MVC implementation, to have a table model for a `JTable` requires domain-specific data classes to extend a Swing class or interface such as `DefaultTableModel` or `TableModel`. With the SWT approach based on Adapters of content providers and raw widgets – called *viewers* in JFace – data can be provided by any Java class, without any constraint or dependency on SWT/JFace classes. A drawback of this simple design is that developers are in charge of managing coherence between data objects and views.

A traditional, event-powered MVC design is of course possible using SWT and JFace, and has been implemented in some of the standard libraries, such as the GEF[23] viewer classes.

---

23. The Graphical Editing Framework (GEF) is a Java library for creating ad-hoc components on top of SWT.

6.7 Interaction and control

One major source of complexity in modern GUIs is the high level of interactivity derived from sophisticated GUI designs. Features like undo/redo, or highly responsive GUI designs, need a sound implementation architecture.

Interaction here means the explicit representation of user interactions with an application, and the GUI's reactions to user interactions. A very simple GUI doesn't need to represent user interaction explicitly, it only needs to react to simple user input such as a button press by just executing the associated code. More elaborated GUIs can react in more sophisticated ways, for example by triggering a set of reactions throughout the user interface itself.

Control means an explicit form of management of interactions. Handling complex, changing interaction rules during the lifetime of an application can be a major source of architectural degradation if not addressed properly in the design from the beginning.

Representing user actions with the Command pattern

Handling user commands is a common problem when building GUIs. This book illustrates a number of solutions, most of them based on the Command design pattern. Such a pattern essentially transforms requests (commands) into objects: the request is contained within the object itself. This involves encapsulation of the code associated with the request or, more specifically, the code that actually performs the command.

Figure 6.14 shows the Command pattern directly instantiated for the Swing library.

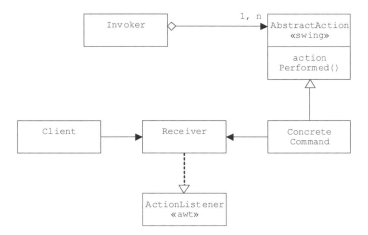

Figure 6.14   The Command design pattern

For the Swing library, the invoker can be a `JMenuItem`, a `JButton` instance, or similar. The `ConcreteCommand` is the command instance that is set up by the `Client` class, usually the main frame or the director. The `Receiver` is the class that actually carries out the action's execution. It implements the `ActionListener` interface for Swing and its analog for JFace's actions, implementations of `org.eclipse.jface.actions.Action`.

At the price of a little additional complexity, the main benefits of using actions are:

- The whole implementation is more natural than with command code centralization, taking advantage of OOP polymorphism over centralized, procedural mechanisms such as chains of conditions for executing commands.

- Behavior specific to a single command is kept logically localized within an `Action` subclass.

- Undo and redo features stem naturally from this approach.

- The class organization that derives from this approach is clearer and more systematic than that using a centralized mechanism for commands. This is especially true for large and complex applications.

- This pattern has been officially adopted in the Java API, in both Swing[24] and SWT.

Such an approach also has some drawbacks. It produces many small classes (the commands themselves), scattering command code among them. This implies additional complexity that must be addressed at design time, essentially in the form of communication between classes and overall management.

An unorthodox use of Swing actions

The Swing implementation of the Command pattern in this book make two different uses of Swing's `Action` subclasses. The difference lies in where the command code is located.

- Those `Action` instances that delegate command execution to an external class are referred to as *shallow* actions, acting as mere containers of data related to the given command, such as icon, mnemonic key, command name. These classes work like an expanded version of the action command string used in the AWT framework, holding GUI data passively, but not the command logic itself, which is stored somewhere else. Shallow actions do not therefore implement the Command pattern, even if they subclass the `Action` interface of the Swing library[25].

- In contrast, *deep* actions those classes that fully implement the Command pattern – that is, normal action classes. In this case the behavior of the

---

24. A brief introduction on the use of Swing actions can be found in (Davidson 2000).
25. See also the use of *retargetable* actions in the Eclipse framework.

given command is coded into the `Action` subclass, as the Command pattern suggests.

The shallow use of actions has been introduced in this book only for practical convenience. In simple GUIs, or where we don't want to use the Command pattern but still want to use a framework that adopts it, like Swing, it is handy to have `Action` subclasses delegating the execution of their command to a centralized point. This is shown in the sequence diagram in Figure 6.15.

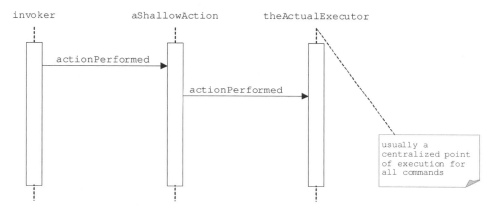

Figure 6.15   Shallow actions at work

Here the `actionPerformed()` method merely invokes the `actionPerformed()` method of the registered class. This simplistic delegation mechanism supports only one invoked class.

An example of fully-fledged 'deep' actions can be seen in Chapter 16. The code provided in Chapter 15 uses the unorthodox, shallow use of the `Action` class introduced here.

Command composition

A frequent solution for making command menus available to users is to aggregate commands hierarchically. Every object in the GUI is responsible for the commands it supports. In an iterative sequence similar to the Chain of Responsibility pattern (Gamma et al. 1994), commands are aggregated in pop-up menus suitable for use in menu bars or contextual menus.

Chapter 16 contains an example of such a behavior for container objects, which negotiate with their contained items the list of available commands to be incorporated in a common menu. This mechanism allows for maximum flexibility in an OO way, in that every object only knows its available commands, while keeping clearly-defined responsibilities among different classes.

Control issues

Some common issues arise when implementing control in professional GUIs. We have seen in the first part of the book how alert or error messages can disrupt the usability of an application. A good GUI provides coherent metaphors and low-level interaction rules that avoid the possibility of inconsistent interactions as far as possible. This translates into software that constantly manages parts of the GUI to enforce the abstract rules that govern it.

Depending on the complexity of the controls to be implemented, different design strategies are possible:

- *Scattered control.* Control is implemented on a local basis, attaching observers to the areas to control and executing reactive code as required. Control code is scattered throughout the GUI implementation and is thus hard to maintain. This approach is quite simple to adopt, but is useful only for limited control needs.

- *Centralized control: the Mediator design pattern.* As a rule of thumb, when more than three objects need to be controlled in a window, we need to escalate to another design strategy: centralizing the control behavior in one place. This has several benefits: tangled event listeners and references derived by the extensive adoption of the previous strategy are limited, and control is centralized in one place. This technique scales to a non-trivial number of controlled objects, even though references to controlled objects become a problem, together with handling the control logic code.

- *Explicit control state.* When things get really complicated even the Mediator pattern shows its limits. In these few cases, very articulated control logic can be represented in explicit classes. These classes represent the concepts behind the control logic and interact with the rest of the GUI. In this way screen control state is not represented within a Mediator class, but is shared among explicit objects.

While some control behavior strongly depends on business logic[26] other control logic is essentially domain-independent. This latter form of control can usefully be extracted in reusable, general-purpose code. We can tell whether specific control logic is business-dependent or not by answering the following question: if the business rule changes, would the given control logic on the GUI change?

Distinguishing between business and non-business control rules is also useful because it is frequently the case that changes in business rules also impact the GUI. Separating them from the rest of the code helps maintenance and implementation clarity. Non-business control behavior rarely changes after the initial design

26. Such as data validation – see Chapter 8, *Validation* on page 332.

phase, so it can be treated differently than business-dependent controls. An example of a non-business control might be the following: in a GUI in which users can inspect item properties, whenever they modify data for an item and close the property dialog, the application asks whether the modified data should be saved or discarded. Such control can be performed automatically for any kind of item, independently from the business domain.

When control layer behavior that comes from actuating a domain's business logic rule in the GUI is used extensively within an application, for example in a highly interactive application with a formalized business domain, it can make sense to capture this behavior in a domain-based interaction control framework.

Figure 6.16 shows examples of interaction control rules governing in an example GUI.

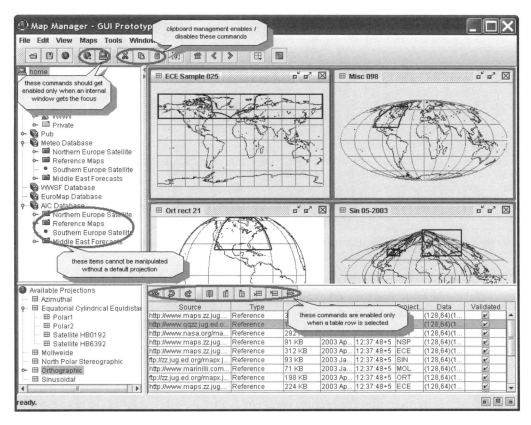

Figure 6.16   Examples of GUI control rules

Such a control behavior isss the essence of any credible user interface, one that presents sound metaphors, that needs minimal memory load on users, minimizes errors, and so on. The Mediator design pattern is commonly used in the implementation of this layer of control.

The Mediator pattern

A Mediator object (Gamma et al. 1994) provides a common connection point, centralizing the behavior of a number of disparate classes.

The use of the Mediator pattern in GUIs typically consists of the organization of relationships and interactions between visual components, their data models, and related events, all in one controller class. Such a class enforces a form of domain-dependent logic, so is specifically tailored for a given application – that is, it belongs to the Application layer. Figure 6.17 shows the Mediator pattern class diagram.

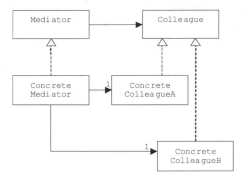

Figure 6.17   The Mediator design pattern

The Mediator pattern is useds in many of the examples in the third part of this book.

The `AbstractDirector` class represented in the UML diagram in Figure 6.18 is a simple and limited example implementation of the general behavior of a Mediator class used in some of the example applications.

Mediators can also work as Event Arbitrators, tidying event management for actions and other controlled objects. This is one of the advantages of centralized control over scattered.

Any director class manages a number of actions. Apart from keeping them coherent (enforcing business rules on them), other possible uses are to act as an Event Arbitrator, releasing actions to interested classes, and also possibly taking care of executing actions by funneling (aggregating) various `ActionPerformed` events in

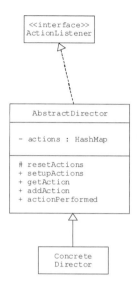

Figure 6.18   The AbstractDirector class

the director's `actionPerformed()` method. Such actions directly implemented by the director usually need many references to various objects and involve a complex web of references if they are to be executed outside the director class. This latter arrangement can prove useful:

* In architectures in which commands are centralized at a unique point, as could be the case when using shallow actions.

* When the nature of the action itself makes it simpler to handle this way – for example when one action needs to manipulate other actions or other classes that are already visible to the director.

Mediators can manage any class, not only actions. The example class in Figure 6.18 considers only actions, because in general they are the commonest case. Subclasses can add similar functionality for other classes as well.

Thread management

Apart from control design patterns, thread management can also be considered a form of dynamic runtime control.

Thread handling is essential for professional GUIs, and is the backbone of any interaction and control implementation. From Chapter 2 we know that response time is an important parameter for the user's perception of usability. GUIs that freeze while executing a command, or that have unexpected concurrency problems, are unusable no matter how well-designed they are. As we will see later, multithreading is necessary, but not sufficient in itself, to achieve a responsive GUI. Poor object life-cycle management, and the overhead it poses to the garbage collector, might also induce a 'jagged' user experience[27], even for a multithreaded GUI.

The basic issue with multithreading support in Java GUI derives from the fact that GUI toolkits are single-threaded. This applies equally to SWT and Swing toolkits. The underlying OS platform detects low-level GUI events and places them in the application event queue using the toolkit's event classes and other toolkit-specific formats. The toolkit is acting as an Event Arbitrator, isolating a platform-specific event model from a Java-specific one.

Multithreading is needed in several cases in GUIs:

• Most importantly, to keep the application responsive, a key characteristic from the users' viewpoint.

• By far I/O time is the commonest case of long-running task in client-server applications.

• Whenever an asynchronous task must be performed, for example when a background computation starts but the user must still be able to interact with the GUI.

• For faster initialization. Applications can resort to a separate thread to instantiate details asynchronously from the application's start-up process.

• To better take advantage of existing and future hardware power. People always faithfully hope that newer, more powerful hardware will magically and dramatically speed up their applications' performance. This is unlikely to be the case if their GUIs keep doing all their work sequentially. Employing multithreading wisely is an investment in higher performance on more powerful machines.

• For object creation. Creating expensive objects in parallel with other tasks whenever possible will enhance GUI performance and improve responsiveness. This use of multithreading couples with object lifecycle management, which is the subject of a later section.

• In the general case of multiple, concurrent tasks that need to be performed interactively, for example a memory manager thread that runs with a low priority.

From a usability viewpoint it is important to communicate what is going on inside the application during task execution. This is usually accomplished by displaying progress indicators coupled, via events, to the running task thread.

---

27. During garbage collector activity the application freezes.

Software bugs due to concurrency issues can be an annoying problem, because they are difficult to track down, in that they are not always repeatable. They can also occur in completely unexpected ways, as they depend on the particular user interaction with the GUI. So don't use threading differently than suggested for GUI applications (use threading for example by applying the Active Object pattern, or for performance optimization) or in situations where there is no apparent need for it.

A common way to organize threads on single-threaded architectures built using Swing and SWT is to use objects that represent tasks that are executed within a specialized support class or within a larger framework. This scheme is simple to use and accommodates a vast number of practical cases. When using the Eclipse RCP, it is straightforward to use the thread management provided by the framework, while for Swing one can use the `SwingWorker` class.

Chapter 5 contains a more technology-oriented discussion on threading in connection with profiling. Later in this chapter we introduce the Active Object design pattern that is the design approach used for multithreaded support in both Swing and Eclipse.

The next section discusses another approach to organizing design-time control issues in GUIs.

A state-oriented approach to GUI control

In some cases the level of complexity of control needed in a GUI justifies the adoption of some kind of formalized, explicit representation. Figure 6.16 shows the GUI of a fictitious MP3 player. Such a GUI enforces a non-trivial set of interaction control rules. A *mode* is maintained to represent the different operational states (playing, paused, stopped, and so on), and this information affects the functionalities available in the GUI – such as which buttons are enabled, what information is displayed. See the disabled buttons in the application toolbar in Figure 6.19, for example.

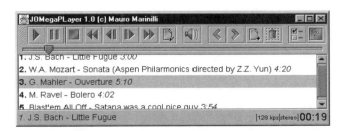

Figure 6.19   An application with an internal state representation

A useful common abstraction is the use of *states* to describe the GUI's internal situation. States are defined when designing the GUI, and can be organized temporally in a state transition diagram that shows how the GUI's state changes when specific events occur. The granularity of each state definition depends on the GUI design[28].

States are also useful for clarifying the implementation of an application in which states were not explicitly defined in the GUI's design. Most of the time software designers don't need to formalize the possible states of a GUI explicitly, either for a single window, a part of the GUI, or the whole system. There are cases, though, where they may be confused by the abstract working of the theoretical GUI design, or its equivalent analysis documents. In these cases it's a good idea to try to write down a list of the GUI's possible states at a suitable level of abstraction, as well as their possible transitions. This exercise will make analysis clearer, even if there is no need to represent states explicitly in the code.

These considerations bring us directly to the Memento pattern. After a brief introduction to this pattern, we will see it at work in a practical example that implements an explicit control state.

The Memento design pattern

Sometimes the state of an object needs to be manipulated as a whole. Doing this straightforwardly may disrupt OOP encapsulation, leading to weaker code.

In the Memento pattern one class, called the Originator, is made responsible for creating the Memento object, usually transferring a portion of its internal state into it. Another class, called the Caretaker, requests the Memento from the Originator and uses it. Figure 6.20 shows the class diagram for Memento.

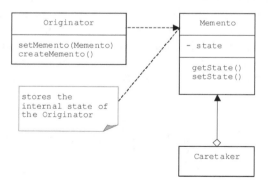

Figure 6.20   The Memento design pattern

---

28. The natural generalization of this approach – providing specialized classes for each meaningful state and a common interface for any generic state – leads directly to the State pattern (Gamma et al. 1994).

The Caretaker object is responsible for the memento's safekeeping, although it never examines the contents of a memento instance. Memento objects are inherently passive. They are used to encapsulate carefully-planned portions of the Originator's internal state for some specific purpose: a common case is to make it persistent.

The Memento design pattern can be used to represent and manipulate both the data state and control state[29] in a GUI. Consider for example a point of sale rich client application. In no case must the application lose data about a transaction, even when the connection is down and the user needs to close the application. In such cases the application can make the memento that represents transaction data persistent, so that it can be sent to the server as soon as the connection is restored.

We are now ready to see a practical application of these ideas to representing the control state of a GUI.

The QuickText application

This subsection describes an example application that uses several design strategies and some code tactics that are oriented towards simplicity and performance.

In any GUI there is usually a practical need to access data from different places. Such data can be variable over time, or needed just once in a session. An example of the former could be the row and line values of the caret cursor in a text editor, for example. We want to associate some control behavior to these values, for example to issue a beep when the end of text is reached, and to show them in a status bar component. This is a classic example of the use of an event-based mechanism – that is, some variant of the Observer pattern. In such cases it can be useful to adopt a mental habit of centralizing the required information in a meaningful way by providing abstractions over the current state of the GUI. Generalizing this idea, we might consider a class that represents the GUI's internal state, or at least what we need of it, which can be accessed by all interested classes. Some portions of the state could therefore be made observable.

In simple situations this approach can be pushed to the extreme, accommodating in a common class both dynamic information, requiring an event-like communication mechanism, and less variable data such as system properties and preferences. Such a class could also enforce business logic rules for the GUI state as a whole.

Here is an example that can be useful when a basic approach to modeling a GUI's state suffices. The idea is to model the dynamic part of a GUI's state as a set of `Boolean` flags. Changes in these values are of interest to other classes. Examples of state flags in a text editor application could be used to indicate things like

---

29. See Chapter 8 for more details about these definitions.

whether the current file is saved, or whether a spell checking error occurred. Here we are only interested in a proof of concept, so the implementation is minimal to just show the basic ideas at work. This model can be used with other more elaborate abstractions for handling more complex situations.

Figure 6.21 shows the QuickText application, a simple text editor for compiling and executing Java code that serves as a background for the implementation techniques introduced here. Java code is entered into a text area, below which there is a console showing the compiler/JRE command-line messages.

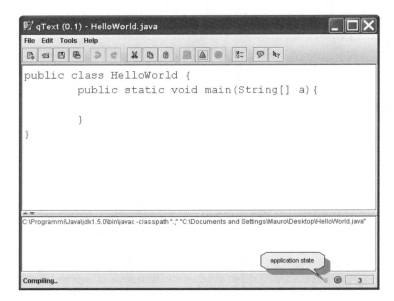

Figure 6.21   The QuickText application

A listener has been added to the text model (the document), so that whenever its content changes, the **Save** and **Save As** buttons are enabled. The status bar at the bottom of the main window reacts to this event as well as the commands, by showing an icon on the right-hand side of the state code[30]. A green icon signals correct compilation, while red means that errors occurred during compilation or execution. Finally, the current caret line number is shown at the bottom right-hand corner.

---

30. The state code is shown only for debugging – in a production application it would be invisible.

Whenever the text file is saved, the file is assumed to be unmodified and the application returns to its initial state. The set of GUI state flags are implemented as integer values, as you can see from the number shown in the status bar at the bottom-right in Figure 6.22, the decimal equivalent of binary 011.

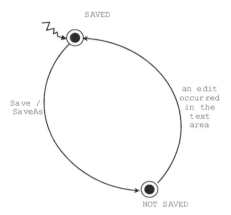

Figure 6.22   Text modifications as control state changes in the QuickText application

In this simple application only two classes are interested in state changes, as shown in the class diagram in Figure 6.23: the director, which coordinates all actions, and the status bar component. The director is in fact not really needed in this arrangement, as single actions can listen to state changes without passing through a common director class.

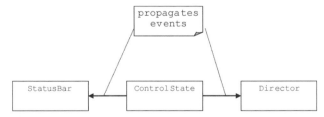

Figure 6.23   State changes

The `ControlState` class holds the current GUI state, and is responsible for exposing changes[31] to interested parties using the Observer pattern. This class implements a variant of the Memento pattern, shown in Figure 6.23 above.

---

31. Instead of writing an event class, the sample application uses the `PropertyChangeEvent` class from the `java.beans` package to represent state change events.

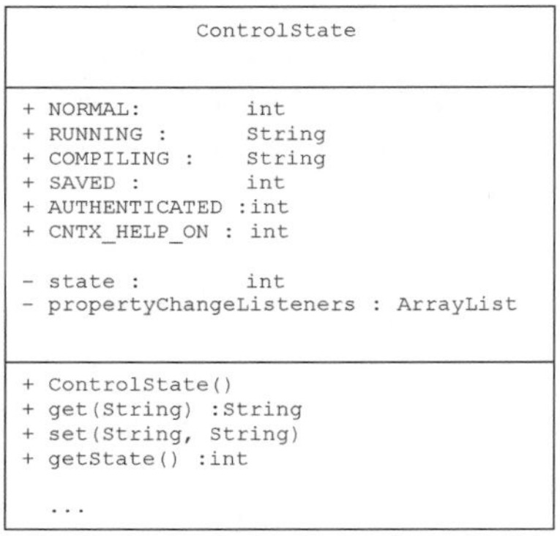

```
                    ControlState

  + NORMAL:          int
  + RUNNING :        String
  + COMPILING :      String
  + SAVED :          int
  + AUTHENTICATED :int
  + CNTX_HELP_ON : int

  - state :          int
  - propertyChangeListeners : ArrayList

  + ControlState()
  + get(String) :String
  + set(String, String)
  + getState() :int

  ...
```

Figure 6.24   The ControlState class

Only the required part of the control state has been made accessible through the event mechanism. Minimizing event coupling is important to avoid needless complexity and unforeseen behavior. Another class, `Props`, stores the application's properties, without using event notifications when a property changes. Application properties must be queried when required, such as the application name property used by the main window for its title.

For simplicity the event implementation does not use any event representation when triggering a change notification message. Swing events use specialized classes to represent event data that is sent with the event notification. In this example, listeners retrieve the state when receiving the change notification message, for example displaying the state value in the application's status bar whenever it changes.

The `ControlState` class implements the GUI state with one or more integers and a bit mask. Interested readers can see this in the implementation of methods `isState()`, which tests whether a given flag is true, `addState()`, which sets a given flag to true, and `subtractState()`, which sets a given flag to false. Flags are implemented as Java constants, powers of 2. Bit masks provide a simple and extensible data representation mechanism. For the QuickText application the possible control states are shown in Table 6.1.

> An example of bit mask use in GUIs is provided by the SWT library, in which component properties (called *styles*) are represented with sets of Boolean values.

The `Director` class implements the Mediator pattern in a very simple way. Whenever the application control state changes, the `Director` class is notified. The director then queries the GUI state and enables the **Save** and **Save As** actions according to the value of the STATE_MODIFIED flag. The Director class is also responsible for creating, managing and updating the internal state of all the actions used in the application and executing them using the 'shallow' action approach.

The status bar component is another listener to changes in control state flags – like the Director class, it implements the PropertyChangeListener interface. It registers itself for changes in the GUI state, and the method propertyChange() reacts to state flag changes.

Table 6.1   Possible control states in the QuickText application

Type	Data
RUNNING	An external JRE process is currently executing code
COMPILING	An external Javac process is currently compiling code
CNTX_HELP_ON	Contextual help is on
NORMAL	Start up, default value
SAVED	Current text has been saved

The QuickText example application also demonstrates an alternative solution for localization. Instead of using property files or other dynamic support for locale-sensitive data, it employs Java constants, for performance reasons. This is demonstrated in the Msgs interface provided with the source code of the application.

6.8   Some design patterns for GUIs

This section introduces designs typically used in OOP GUI implementations, some formulated explicitly for the first time, others well-known design strategies for desktop application GUIs.

Adaptation

Developing a professional GUI can be a complex task, with many requirements to be met. Adding some form of adaptation to GUI code can help to decouple different concerns and conceptually-separated responsibilities effectively. Typical of such requirements might be different behavior depending on runtime information such as different user roles or locale, or the resources available on the client machine.

These situations can be resolved in the same way:

i.   Clearly define the adaptation mechanism.

ii. Elicit the context data the adaptation mechanism will need.

iii. Assign the runtime-dependent behavior to a separate manager class.

Providing a separated implementation avoids cluttered code by decoupling extraneous issues from existing code, making the whole application more modular.

The design goal of Adaptation is to make the application absorb the additional complexity without degrading the quality of the final implementation. This general approach can be applied to any functional layer.

Some examples of adaptation

Suppose a program contains the following code:

```
textField.setText("controle el valor");
```

We can make this message text locale-parametric as follows:

```
textField.setText(ResourceManager.get("control.value"));
```

This confines the responsibility for locale-dependent messages to a specialized class, `ResourceManager`, and only the minimum amount of information must be provided for it to do its job of providing localized message strings.

Figure 6.25 shows an example of localization. Localization is not only a matter of locale-dependent text messages, but can imply a deep adaptation of the whole GUI, from widget layout, dimensions, and more, as discussed in Chapter 4.

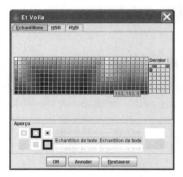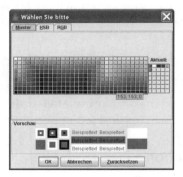

Figure 6.25   Examples of locale-based GUI adaptation

Another example of adaptation might be authorization code. Suppose one requirement in a GUI prescribes that sensitive information like employees' wage details must be available only to certain user roles. This rule could be added to every widget that required authorization. Suppose pressing a button in the GUI shows the salary for the selected employee:

```
if (RoleManager.getCurrentRole().equals(BossRole.class)){
    button.setEnabled(true);
} else
    button.setEnabled(false);
```

Everything works well until the management want to change the authorization policy because someone complained that they don't want anyone else to see their wage details. The new requirement now states that:

i.   Senior managers can still see other employees' wages.

ii. Middle managers can know that wage details are available to their superiors, but cannot actually see them.

iii. All other employees don't have to know that there is such a button in the GUI at all.

You could change the if–else code above to accommodate managers (button.setEnabled(false)) and all other employees (button.setVisible(false)). But what if managers complain and you have to change this authorization policy yet again? You would need to go into the code again and modify all this conditional behavior, which is likely to be scattered in many places throughout the GUI's screens. Authorization code shouldn't be intermingled with presentation code, and should be made more flexible to change. After all, these are business requirements, much as localization is a translator's job, and they should not burden programmers. It would be better if authorization could be handled to some administrator or customer representative rather than being relegated to developers.

This problem can be seen as an application of adaptation to runtime data. We want a GUI to adapt to the current user role. As the role is only available at runtime, a form of dynamic parameterization is required. The nice thing about adaptation is that it is somebody else's worry. Developers only need to enforce it, while decisions will be taken somewhere else, away from code.

You could provide the following implementation:

```
AuthorizationManager.prepare(button, this);
```

where authorization is relegated to a specialized manager, much like localization, and you provide the subject (the button) and the context (in the present example, the parameter this) where the subject appears. The authorization manager then retrieves the current user role and performs all the appropriate authorization policies on the subject.

Adaptation is common in any professional GUI. Some examples are:

- *Localization.* Here the context parameter is the current locale. This is a classic form of parameterization that is handled explicitly by the Java API.

- *Authorization and other role-based adaptations.* Here the context parameter is the current user role. Some commands, screens, or single widgets may depend upon the user role.

- *User profiling.* We may want to save preferences, customizations, and other information on a single-user basis, so that different users using the same application installation find their own settings and specific data.

- *Business-specific parameters.* Country, international branch, or some other domain-specific concept are examples of parameters for which adaptation rules might be dictated by specific requirements.

- *Resource-dependent constraints.* An example is a client application that runs in two different remote connectivity scenarios: modem lines and broadband connections. To provide a good GUI design, the commands available might need to be adapted to the remote connection type.

> Adaptation techniques make sense when the need for adaptation is common to a sizeable part of the GUI. If only one or two panels need a limited form of adaptation, and no extensions are planned in future, a simple local solution would be cheaper to implement yet still effective.

Building a comprehensive API for parameterization could be a complex task for most real-world applications, with few real benefits[32]. What is important though is to be aware of the problems adaptation may generate. Some guidelines for effective adaptation are:

- *Clearly define parameters and carefully separate them.* Define exactly what the parameters are in your application and their reason for existing. It is important to keep parameters conceptually separate. Implementing this conceptual separation involves enforcing orthogonality in code (Hunt and Thomas 2000). The effects of different adaptations should provide cumulative, predictable results. If for example an application already provides localization and role-based adaptation, and you add business rules parameterization, you expect these three aspects to coexist gracefully without unexpected side effects.

---

32. Common parameterizations such as localization are already provided by standard APIs. Other forms of adaptation can be achieved relatively easily without requiring a comprehensive, unique framework.

- *Avoid explicit parameters scattered in the code.* These are hard to modify and make code fragile. All context information should be sent to the manager object responsible for the parameterization, such as the following code example:

```
if (user.getRole().equals(ROLES.ADMIN)){
// admin users-only code here
...
}
```

- *Define a common strategy and enforce it.* If some aspect is parameterized using an XML file, for example, no code should deal with that parameter in a different way, for example by means of local conditional clauses.

Advanced adaptation

Adaptation is normally performed at runtime depending on context information. Other more complex forms of parameterization can exist, although these are needed only in special cases.

Adaptation may become a source of complexity if differences between individual adaptations are too wide to be housed in the same application. In such cases different code bases should be considered. This could be the case for example with the development of a single application that supports a multinational insurance company. Laws, cultures, practices, and other differences in each country could make it too complex to bundle such aspects into a single application code base. Shipping such a huge single application would make little practical sense. In such cases solutions other than dynamic adaptation should be considered, such as a software family-based approach – building a common framework that comprise all the common aspects, and creating the required adaptations using different custom builds of the application, or simply building different applications with a common organization, software reuse policy, development infrastructure, and so on.

Another example of non-dynamic adaptation is parameterization of an application at build time for security reasons. For example, you might want to generate an application installation on demand to work only with a given license key. In this case the license key is the parameter.

Using A3GUI for parameterization

A3GUI (Abstract-Augmented Area for GUIs) was introduced in Chapter 2 as a flexible approach for expressing generic information about a GUI. The idea is to identify areas of a GUI – a single widget, a panel, or a complex screen – and attach useful information to these abstractions. Augmented areas can also be used to express parameterization, even in cases in which there is no direct link with a screen area, such as business rules parameterization.

This approach lends to a declarative parameterization style in which localities in the GUI are identified by A3GUI identifiers, and their correct instantiation[33] is done somewhere else, as we saw before when discussing the `AuthorizationManager` example. Suppose you must implement the security of a very sensitive banking application. In certain parts of the GUI a number of controls are enforced in reaction to specific GUI events, such as modifying sensitive fields, pressing buttons, or displaying specific screens. Security practices may change over time – some parts of the GUI may become sensitive, while other areas may have existing checks loosened – so you need to make your implementation flexible.

Areas can occur in different places in the same application. Suppose the panel shown in Figure 6.26 is currently an extra-sensitive part of the GUI. Whenever such a panel appears in any part of the GUI, its behavior is dictated as follow:

- Depending on the current user and the current time of the day[34], it is possible to modify the **Amount** field. During holidays and at night, when there is no central human control, some potentially dangerous transactions are not allowed.

- In certain other circumstances, such as combinations of the context data mentioned above, other behavior is needed, such as making the panel invisible to the current user.

By providing a unique A3GUI id for the panel, you could associate the current security level, stored in a signed encrypted file for example, with that identifier, without scattering ad-hoc controls in the application's code. This would centralize the GUI's security implementation in a specialized and reusable manager. Such areas can be defined at analysis time, during GUI design, or later. A3GUI ids can be composed following the GUI containment hierarchy, to provide an exact identification for a given panel instance in a given screen, or used generically for all occurrences of relevant panels.

In cases in which a total A3GUI identification of the whole GUI is not needed, for example when parameterized properties don't change so often, ids for specific widgets or panels can be provided directly in the code. This keeps the application modular, but avoids the complications needed in the general case.

A useful technique for providing unambiguous context information for the adaptation design strategy is to take advantage of the visual composition of widgets into screens. This technique can also be used for requirements other than defining Adaptation contexts. It is discussed in the next section.

---

33. Here we mean the instantiation of an A3GUI area, that is, a portion of a screen that is adapted depending on specific parameters. Implementing this in Java implies instantiating a number of classes.
34. As measured on the server, for security reasons.

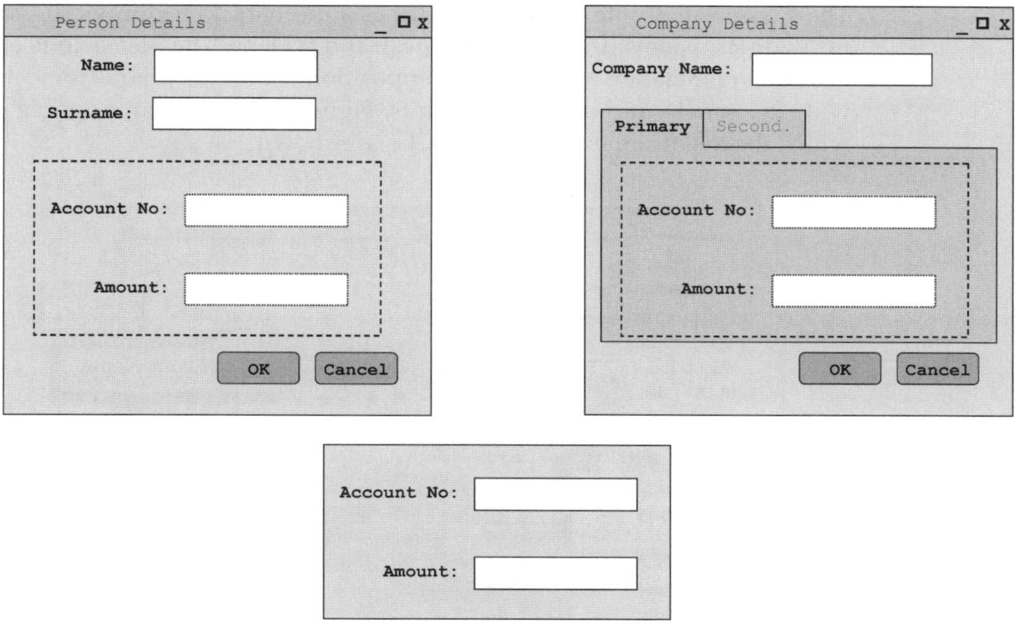

Figure 6.26   A sensitive panel

Composite Context

GUI content composition is heavily based on the Composite design pattern. In some cases it is necessary to identify specific areas of the screen. Identifying components, whether elementary widgets or composite aggregates, could be needed for various reasons:

- Suppose you want to provide every meaningful widget in a GUI with its own unique identifier, for testing, ease of look-up, and so on. The problem is that the widget may be nested in different panels, but you want it to have a unique id throughout the entire GUI. One possible solution is to use the Composite pattern for the ids as well, recursively attaching all components' ids to create a global, unique id for the widget, no matter how many instances there are of the same class.

- You used the Adaptation pattern, but you need a formal context id to represent the adaptation context in a simple way.

- You employed a composable unit strategy in your GUI in which all CUs are registered in a common registry for look-up. You need to provide an infrastructure service that will supply unique ids for CU instances automatically.

The Composite Context pattern describes a mechanism for providing identifiers for widgets, panels (that is, composites), and screens. The idea is to use the hierarchical organization of the visual composition to provide unique (or local) ids for widgets, panels, and composable units. Figure 6.27 shows an example dialog in which the ids of some widgets and CUs are shown.

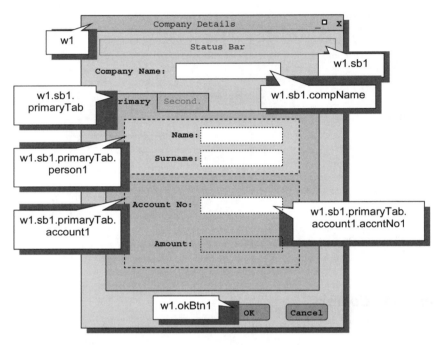

Figure 6.27   Composite Context at work

Referring to the figure, the screen w1 contains a status bar whose standalone id is sb1, and when composed within the screen as shown in the figure, has an identifier w1.sb1 that reflects the actual visual composition of the screen. The same widget composed in another screen would have a different identifier.

Composite Context can also be used to provide ids for A3GUI areas in analysis and design phases. In this case identifiers are simply applied by hand by analysts or developers, following the hierarchical approach proposed above.

The hierarchical mechanism provided by Composite Context can be used to provide information other than just identifiers. Support information, or an automatic mechanism for generalizing ids, can be provided as well – for example, for querying all items contained in a composite, or for simplifying the support XML files with inherited values.

Active Object

The Active Object design pattern[35] focuses on the creation of objects whose state develops asynchronously. As a consequence, the state, details about the operation in progress, or the final result, need to be shared among different threads. In the case of GUIs, the interested threads are the event dispatch thread and a worker thread that is executing a long-running task such as a remote transaction. Another thread is used by the scheduler object, which takes responsibility for executing tasks requested by clients transparently to them.

The Active Object pattern consists of three phases:

1. *Method request construction and scheduling.* In this phase, the client invokes a method on a proxy class, which in turn packages the task and forwards it to an executor in the form of a method request. This maintains references with the method itself, as well as any other data required to execute the method and return its results. A reference to a `Future`[36] instance is returned to the client that will provide the result when available.

2. *Method execution.* After the client requests the execution of a task, it continues its normal activity. Within its own execution thread, the scheduler determines which method request can be executed, depending on its synchronization constraints. When a method request becomes runnable, the scheduler executes it, usually passing responsibility for its execution to a servant instance.

3. *Completion.* In the final phase, the results are stored in the `Future` reference for the client to access them. The method request and the `Future` instance are no longer needed and are ready for garbage collection.

Both Swing and SWT toolkits provide framework support for this pattern. Given its importance in supporting smooth interaction with users, it is used in all the examples provided in the third part of the book.

A Swing example of Active Object

A simple implementation of a long-running task using the `SwingWorker` class is provided as an example of the Active Object pattern in the code bundle for this chapter. The task is activated by pressing the **Paint Nicely** button shown in

---

35. For more details, see http://www.cs.wustl.edu/~schmidt/PDF/Act-Obj.pdf, an updated version of the original chapter in (Vlissides et al. 1996).
36. The java.util.concurrent.Future interface represents the result of an asynchronous computation. Additional methods are provided to check whether the computation is complete, to wait for its completion, cancel the computation, to retrieve the final result, and more.

Figure 6.28. This starts an instance of the class `FancyPaintWorker`, which paints the area in the window without freezing the rest of the application.

Figure 6.28   An example of SwingWorker

Object lifecycle management – a general mindset

Any non-trivial Java desktop application GUI handles tens of thousands of objects, especially if implemented using Swing. Large applications might handle hundreds of thousands of objects or more. No matter how powerful and well-tuned the garbage collector, it will always have a lot of work to do. Taking care of the lifecycle of the objects we create is important for providing a simpler life for the garbage collector, and thus providing smoother interaction for the user. We don't want an application to freeze from time to time, out of the blue, while the hard disk whirs mysteriously. Neither do we want an application to take a long time to start or launch specific features because it needs to create many expensive objects at the same time.

From a GUI design viewpoint users generally prefer to have a partially-functional application that starts up quickly, even if some secondary portions of the application are initialized later, than wait longer to have the whole application up and running at once. This general design strategy is more important in medium to large applications that handle many objects, but the habit of taking care of the lifecycle of objects is nevertheless always a healthy one, even in small applications. To condense the experience of many projects into one line, *instantiate lazily and dispose eagerly.*

The many virtues of lazy instantiation of objects in desktop application GUIs have already been discussed. A less well-known strategy concerns object disposal. Disposing of objects as soon they are known to be no longer needed is important, in that it helps the work of the garbage collector and keeps the memory profile of an application trim. This is also true for Swing applications, where there is no need for explicit object-disposal policies, although disposing of particularly expensive objects manually helps garbage collection, thus smoothing GUI interaction.

An object's lifecycle can be optimized as follows:

- *Object creation.* When is an object needed, and is it possible to postpone its creation until required using lazy instantiation?

- *Object disposal.* As soon as it is known that an object is no longer needed, it can be disposed of explicitly, easing garbage collector work and enhancing the application's responsiveness. Object disposal in Java is achieved very easily by setting the variable that refers to (and holds) the object to null.

- *Multithreading support.* Sometimes the instantiation of many objects, or of a few expensive ones, can be performed in parallel with other tasks, thus speeding up performance.

Here are some common scenarios of object lifecycle management that can be used for enhancing application performance:

- *Application start-up.* Forking threads to allocate resources and the essential start-up configuration of an application as soon as possible is the best introduction an application can give to its users. As we know from Chapter 2, the overall user experience is often dictated by the first impression they have of an application.

- *Lazy instantiation of hidden panels in tabbed panes.* This is a relatively simple and useful optimization, especially on large forms with many complex tabs. Only the first tab is populated, and the others are created lazily when opened. For forms with mandatory tabs – that is, tabs that must be opened to complete a task – it is better to let them be populated asynchronously after the first tab is completed and is occupying the user's attention.

- *Partial initialization of widgets.* Some widgets can be shown empty to the user initially, and while they are interacting with the GUI, initialize themselves asynchronously. Examples might be a table that populates itself asynchronously, or an ad-hoc panel showing a graphic chart that requires a lot of data to be drawn, so is shown initially as a grayed-out area. In such cases it is important to exert robust control over any unintended interactions the user can cause on partially-instantiated widgets.

- *Dataset paging in large lists, trees, and tables.* For large data sets, paging is the only viable design solution for loading only visible data and discarding previously-seen values. This technique consists of fetching only a number of pages of data at any time. The minimum number of items fetched is usually 1.5 to 2 times the current visible view size, or a constant, reasonable value derived from that. Hence, if you have a table showing 100 rows, you would fetch 150 or 200 rows, to fill the view and allow for some leeway for scrolling. An efficient mechanism for coarse-grained scrolling is needed, so that it is possible to jump directly from, say, the 100th element to the 5000th. The topic is clearly more complex than this, and is a perfect fit for a utility library such as those available for Swing. An example of lifecycle management for large trees is described in Chapter 15.

Special care is needed over handling events and interactions on objects that are not yet instantiated, such as data models for expensive widgets, to preserve the robustness of the GUI.

Such techniques should be used conservatively and without over-doing it. Trying to optimize code preemptively is always asking for trouble, and ultimately needs extra care to avoid weaker implementations.

Value Model

The Value Model design pattern originated in Smalltalk to allow sharing values between different actors. It can also be used as a form of Adapter between an actor interested in a single value and a large object that stores the value along with other data.

Sometimes this design is used for coupling data models with widgets in Java applications. An Adapter class could be used to bridge the different method signatures of a widget with a data model, for example an SWT `Text` with the `street` string property in an `Address` class, and change property events used for notification when the value changes. This arrangement requires an Adapter for each widget – if another widget `PostalCode` needs to be synced or bound to another string property of the same instance of the `Address` class, a new Adapter is required. We can solve this by using a Value Model object that complies with a standard signature, using the value property of type `Object`. An Adapter object is still needed to convert widgets' method signatures to the `ValueModel`. Figure 6.29 illustrates this design.

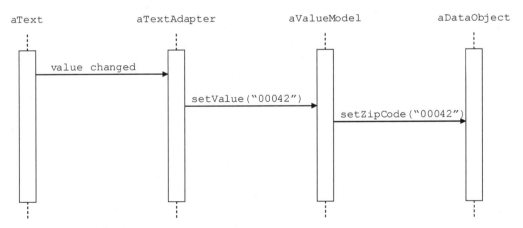

Figure 6.29   How Value Model works

This design can be thought of as an application of the Chain of Responsibility and Adapter design patterns. Communication the 'other way around,' that is, when a property value changes in a data object, is ensured by events. Note that this mechanism implements the binding between a widget and a generic data `Object`. When values are copied back and forth this binding can be made automatic on data changes, or it can be enforced explicitly. The latter choice eases debugging, because synchronization events are easier to track at runtime than data changes (see Figure 6.30).

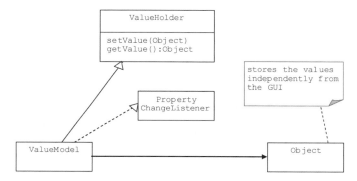

Figure 6.30   Value Model class diagram

An example of use of this design is discussed in Chapter 8 for binding widgets to data objects in form-based rich client applications.

6.9   GUI complexity boosters

This chapter concludes by discussing some issues in GUI development that significantly raise the level of complexity in an implementation.

J. Coldewey describes typical 'complexity boosters' in the development of distributed applications[37] as issues that dramatically complicate software development. More circumscribed, common sources of complexity can be found in GUI development as well. Even when such sources of complication cannot be avoided, as is unfortunately often the case when developing professional GUIs, being aware of them is nevertheless important. To use a colorful metaphor, you can imagine these issues as being like items on your workbench with a 'Danger!' label on them, to remind you to handle them with extra care.

---

37. These are distribution, multithreading, multi-platform, extreme performance, and paradigm gaps (such as Object-Relational Mapping), as mentioned in (Fowler et al. 2003).

The main sources of sharp increases of complexity in developing GUIs are:

- *Extensive control.* When you want to control explicitly a large and increasing number of disparate objects, such as a word processor with hundreds of commands that need to interact.

- *Going against the flow.* Some solutions are naturally supported by GUI tool-kits, while others are just unnatural. Deciding on a personal, arbitrary design approach may prove a useless and expensive choice. An example might be deciding to avoid the Command pattern for representing commands in favor of a homegrown approach. This is a general situation that can apply to GUI design as well as software architecture. It can be paraphrased as *avoid unnatural choices.*

- *Ad-hoc solutions.* This can be seen as a special case of the previous point. Creating alternative solutions to those provided in standard toolkits, such as developing special ad-hoc widgets, can be a necessity in certain situations, but it remains an expensive choice.

- *Flexible layouts.* Despite the fact that we take dynamic layout managers for granted (also known as 'liquid layouts'), these are an explicit cause of complexity in GUI development.

- *Internationalization and localization.* Providing a GUI ready for multiple languages is a common source of complexity. This in turn involves flexible layouts – fixed sized screens and widgets are a certain recipe for internationalization troubles, as we saw in the GUI design perspective in Chapter 4.

- *Multithreading.* This issue comes into play in different ways depending on the GUI toolkit and runtime platform of choice. Multithreading is also at the root of remote IO. Even the simplest communication in fact requires an explicit management of threading control. While standard IO needs are serviced with toolkit facilities, other specific threading issues must still be developed in-house.

- *Remote IO.* Everything works fine in a GUI until you start to interact with the rest of the world, either via a single remote server or several Web services. Suddenly your code gets messed up with try-catch clauses, multithreading, and remote connection code spread all over its once neat implementation. Note that multithreading is usually involved with interactive remote access, depending on the support provided by the underlying infrastructure, as mentioned in the point above.

- *Distribution of business domain code among client and server.* This is typically the case with rich client applications, in which business logic needs to reside on the client side as well as the server to allow the client to perform meaningful operations off line.

- *Runtime constrains.* Requirements like a maximum memory footprint of 128 MB, or a maximum limit of thirty seconds for obtaining the list of all registered passengers in a flight reservation application, will impact deeply on a GUI design and its subsequent development, constraining the possible choices of a Java application.

Issues such as these are often closely intertwined, so that they exhibit a 'burst-like' behavior. For example, suppose you decide to provide internationalization in an application, but also need to adopt flexible layouts throughout the GUI – for some locales, such as Asian ones, this might involve installing a custom input method implementation, which could in turn require multithreading support for better performance. I use to call these situations, in which a single feature prompted a domino-like effect, 'complexity bursts.' Good engineers should be aware of them, ideally before triggering the burst, and be daring in evaluating the real benefits of the features to be added.

6.10 Summary

This chapter introduced several techniques useful in the design of the implementation of professional GUIs using Java technology. We have seen how the main implementation issues, presented as the functional layers in the model in Figure 6.1, can be addressed, and how objects communicate by means of the Observer pattern and its various variants, as well as the main problems in over-use of event-based communication mechanisms. The chapter also discussed the three main strategies for implementing control: scattered, centralized, and explicit representation of screen control state information.

Other common design strategies for building professional user interfaces were discussed, such as Adaptation, Composite Context, Active Object, Objects Lifecycle Management, and Value Model. It is useful to recap the main design strategies discussed:

- The principle of Single Functional Responsibility for a clear definition of functional responsibilities.
- Content Assembly and its various implementation strategies for handling widgets' layout.
- Explicit Navigation for managing explicitly the navigation among the various screens in an application.
- Some issues for representing business domain logic effectively in an application.
- Devising a comprehensive data IO design strategy.
- Addressing security concerns in an application explicitly, and including them in the overall architecture.

- The Data Transfer Object (DTO) pattern for exchanging information remotely.
- Designing remote communication with server applications.
- The Observer design pattern, its various flavors, and the high-level designs built with it: MVC and its main variants, HMVC and MVP.
- Representing user commands, composing them, and taking advantage of existing support frameworks for your design needs.
- Representing reactive control behavior with implementations that depend on the complexity required by the GUI design.
- Other design strategies commonly used in GUI implementations, such as Adaptation, Composite Context Active Object, and Value Model.

Figure 6.31 recaps the main design strategies used specifically in GUI designs, represented by the functional layer on which they mainly focus. These are only the commonest solutions used in modern OO client software designs, and the techniques listed in the figure are not exhaustive.

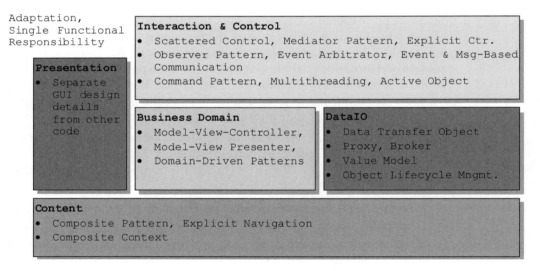

Figure 6.31   Common solutions by functional layer

The next chapter discusses the main issues involved in the definition of the overall software architecture for applications, covering the most popular solutions found in real-world GUIs.

7 Code Organization

This chapter discusses the main trade-offs and issues related to the organization of code and other implementation artifacts for application GUIs. Experimental or unproven approaches, or solutions that don't fit within existing Java GUI technologies, are not considered. The client tier – that is, the portion of software that is deployed on a client machine – is the principal focus. The chapter includes some implementation details for an example layering scheme. It focuses on J2SE/J2EE, but the design strategies discussed here can be applied to J2ME applets, as shown in Chapter 10, as long J2ME's resource constraints are observed.

The chapter is structured as follow:

7.1, Introducing software architectures discusses some general issues of software architectures and related software design strategies for GUI applications.

7.2, Some common GUI architectures introduces some of the most useful software architectures for GUIs.

7.3, A three-layer organization for GUI code goes into the details and the trade-offs of the layering scheme.

7.4, Two examples of a three-layer implementation shows examples of the application of the layering scheme, one to a simple project and one to a large one.

7.5, The service layer describes the details of the proposed implementation of the service layer for the three-layer architecture.

7.1 Introducing software architectures

Layering is a well-known technique for reducing dependencies between parts of a software system. An element in a particular layer is only permitted to access elements in the same layer or in layers below it. Strict layering, which is more laborious to enforce, prescribes communication only with the layer immediately beneath the current layer[1].

---

1. This induces a directed acyclic graph (DAG) structure in which nodes are layers, and arcs are dependencies, ensuring that, among other things, there are no circular dependencies.

Organizing implementation artifacts is a vast field for which a large amount of literature is available. It is also an important topic that will affect any project during its lifetime, even though it is not a guarantee of quality.

Layering is an attempt at structuring code by minimizing dependencies, removing duplication, and possibly attempting some form of reuse. The most important issue when deciding a strategy for organizing GUI implementation artifacts is the definition of clear responsibilities for each layer. That is, what is the main issue we want to address with our architecture? Some of the main practical strategies are:

- *Data flow.* This decomposes an application based on the flow of data within the application. The runtime data flow is a vivid concept, easily defined and shared. This strategy is used particularly in data-centric applications such as form-based GUIs. Chapter 8 has an example of a runtime data model in the context of rich client applications.

- *Domain-driven.* This strategy aims at enabling a portion of a rich (OO) domain model to operate on the client machine. To achieve this, a number of services and infrastructures are built to host the domain model as well as possible[2]. Developers focus on domain-driven issues first, carefully decoupling them from any technical 'plumbing' or graphical details. This strategy works well with GUIs for complex application domains, where non-trivial domain representation is needed on the client side and some form of a rich domain model is available (or planned) on the server side.

- *Functional.* This approach focuses on the function of each module, decoupling concerns on a functional basis. Business concepts usually drive the Composable Unit[3] strategy, if any. Instead of domain concepts, a commoner strategy for Java GUIs is to use implementation-driven concepts. An example could be using a variant of the functional decomposition proposed in Chapter 1 to define the layering scheme.

- *Reuse.* The main objective of this layering strategy is to simplify future reuse of software. 'Reuse' is a magical word that implies different things to different people. We could reuse concrete code, code patterns, or abstract approaches and skills – for example, we might want to use a full OO technology because we can then leverage our existing design patterns experience. This is one of the most often-used organizational strategies, even if the results are not always guaranteed to be fully reusable.

---

2. That is, leaving the domain model in its purest form, free of GUI or low-level details.
3. See Chapter 6.

These are just some of the strategies for breaking down GUI code: other are possible. Our underlying assumption is that there is no one single 'killer architecture,' not even in the relatively well-defined and circumscribed domain of Java GUIs. Instead, each implementation organization has its advantages and drawbacks, as we will see. Successful adoption of one architecture over another also depends upon the development team's skills, the problem at hand, the chosen technology, the timeline, and other non-technical factors.

Choosing the right strategy is the most difficult point in using a layering scheme (Fowler et al. 2003). Lack of deep knowledge, conservative attitudes, or just plain sloppiness are possible causes for naïve GUI architectures. This is often the case with Swing, due to its high-level feature-rich design. Imagine for example that you are called to help a project in trouble. Its developers show you a complex tabbed form, containing hundreds of Swing widgets, then explain that a PAC (Presentation-Abstraction-Controller[4]) variant was used as a layering on top of Swing widgets 'to make things clear.' The implicit underlying concept here is 'We don't care about that Swing mess.' The PACs are nested in reusable panels, so there are nearly thirty PAC triads in the form, plus all the associated specialized event machinery, all of this sitting on top of Swing widgets that add hundreds of other objects (Swing's MVC support, decorators, and so on). At that point you realize what causes the room's lights to dim every time the application is launched...

Taming references

Suppose our team has developed the application shown in Figure 7.1. We adopted a clean architecture, unit-tested all our code, and did everything we considered beneficial. Next week we are going to release the application – guess what... we are late with the planned schedule.

We then observe a strange problem in the data in the exploration tree on the left-hand side, and need more time to track the source of the problem. For some mysterious reason our caching mechanism, which we thoroughly tested, is not responding well. We run more unit tests, but the problem seems to be caused by the final integration with the server application. We don't want to spend time on an ad-hoc basis, such as profiling by hand, or spending too much time trying to

---

4.   The Presentation-Abstraction-Control (PAC) pattern was defined in (Buschmann et al. 1996). This pattern defines a hierarchy of cooperating agents for structuring interactive software systems. Each agent is responsible for an aspect of the application's functionality and consists of three components: presentation, abstraction, and control. These components separate the human and computer aspects of the agent from its business domain-dependent core and its communication with other agents.

replicate the problem, or involving time-consuming end-to-end test sessions. What we really want is a reusable, lightweight test that will also be useful in the future.

We think this is a great opportunity to set up some partial integration testing, even if we are late with the schedule. When we try to simulate data from the server to the client realistically, however, we stumble on a number of unforeseen issues. A number of services, both server-side and local facilities on the client application, need to be started up front to prepare the scene for even the simplest test. Testing the exploration tree in this way involves also starting the table component on the right-hand side, otherwise we would be obliged to step back to a previous CVS snapshot, and this in turn needs other parts as well. Ultimately we find we need to launch the whole application!

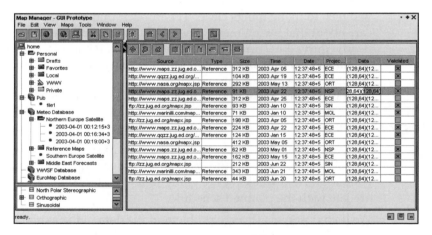

Figure 7.1   A buggy application (Squareness)

Although the previous situation is not such a nightmare, it is a common experience that at a late stage of development and without careful planning and continuos discipline, application modules start to look 'tangled' together, despite our initial commitment. What happens in reality is that dependencies are added very easily to code, so easily that you don't even realize, but are much harder to get rid of.

Application GUIs are composed of many interacting parts. Some of these parts are outside our control, such as GUI toolkits or third-party libraries. As the application grows and parts are added over time, such interactions tend to intensify, driving the implementation toward degradation of the decomposition strategies we initially devised. Intertwined references are not only a problem for testing, they are also a problem for the stability of the whole implementation – degrading the system's 'orthogonality' (Hunt and Thomas 2000), they hinder maintenance, parallel work, future reuse, and so on.

Layering helps to avoid mutual references, at least at the level of specific layers. Various solutions have been proposed for this: the well-known OO design principle of 'designing to abstractions' is one – abstraction being usually interfaces, but in some cases also abstract classes. A useful principle for untangling layer references is to use the 'dependency inversion principle' (DIP) discussed in (Martin 2002). Although there are many other principles around for clean OO structuring, we focus here only on the simplest and most useful.

The Dependency Inversion principle

The dependency inversion principle (DIP) (Martin 2002) states that:

- High-level modules should not depend on low level modules. Both should depend on abstractions.

- Abstractions should not depend on details. Details should depend on abstractions.

This principle suggests designing to interfaces rather than to concrete implementations. This newly-added layer of static indirection helps in the overall decoupling. 'Dependency inversion' refers to the effect that results from applying this principle to software layers, as shown in Figure 7.2.

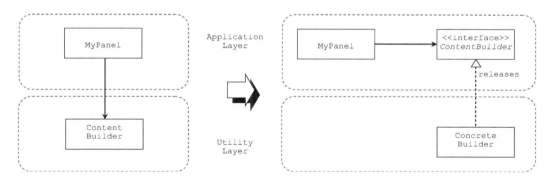

Figure 7.2   Inverted layers

A class `MyPanel` directly invokes a utility class `ContentBuilder` for content assembly of common widgets such as buttons, panel structure, and so on. This single invocation makes the whole application layer dependent on the utility layer. Whenever something is changed in the utility layer we need to modify all its clients.

A better solution would be to decouple the two layers by means of a Builder abstraction (usually an interface or an abstract class). This inverts the dependencies: the utility layer now depends on the application layer. `JLFBuilder`, a concrete `ContentBuilder` specialized for the Java Look and Feel design guidelines, will implement the details of building common widgets without strong dependency on its clients.

This technique does not protect designs from the annoying problem of modifying an interface that is already implemented by many clients, of course. This problem can disrupt a design if we are not in control of client code, for example when releasing a library to clients. A careful design of abstractions such as interfaces is extremely important in such cases.

> The Observer design pattern discussed in Chapter 6 uses DIP in separating `Subject` from `ConcreteSubject`.

As a variant of this technique, you can expose all your abstractions in a separate package, allowing implementation classes to extend them, so that violations of the DIP principle become evident as package dependencies.

Separated Interface

The Separated Interface pattern, as described in (Fowler et al. 2003), can be seen as a generalization of DIP for decoupling two packages by providing interfaces (or, when meaningful, abstract classes) in separate packages. The separate package can belong to the client package that uses the interfaces, or to a third separated package when more clients are possible. There are usually a set of 'concepts' – the interfaces – separated from their various concrete implementation classes. This in turn requires factories for generating concrete implementations of such interfaces, which might themselves require other separate interfaces. To provide the right implementation for separated interfaces, we can use static references (that is, at compile time) or adopt a more flexible form of code configuration, such as the plug-in approach discussed in Chapter 13.

Composable units

Disciplining references is just one aspect of organizing OO code for non-trivial GUIs. Another aspect concerns aggregation criteria, that is, principles for organizing an implementation into useful clusters.

A simple form of code organization is the notion of reusable stand-alone units, following the Composite design pattern. These 'composable units' can be thought of as micro-GUIs, because they encapsulate content, presentation, data IO, business domain, and interaction and control in a set of classes that are thought of as a single reusable unit that can be composed together with similar units to build user interfaces in a modular fashion. Clearly a support infrastructure needs to be provided to enable this approach.

> Composable units can either partially or fully coincide, or be orthogonal to the layer architecture of an application. For example, you can have a three-layer architecture and use MVP triads as composable units. That is, MVP triads form the autonomous macro components that compose the application: each triad spans the three layers into which the implementation is decomposed.

There are two common, practical main strategies for composable units:

- *Implementation-oriented abstractions,* such as MVC designs and their many variants. In these designs the focus is on implementation-oriented abstractions.

- *Domain-oriented abstractions.* These can be defined at various levels of formality. For example, we can define an Address composable unit as a set of classes responsible for rendering and managing data about addresses in a GUI. A design can range from simple, informal aggregations to fully-formalized component-based decompositions.

Composable units are useful for aggregating code in medium to large projects. They favor reuse, clean organization, and a systematic approach to decomposition. The drawback of endorsing a composable unit formal design is that the design process becomes more complex, and with a more formalized (that is, heavy) infrastructure. Therefore consider the use of a composable unit-based design only if the project is medium to large, or if many developers are involved, possibly in multiple locations, so that an objective, formal code aggregation criteria is needed.

> Composable units are *intensive* code aggregations, that is, they only focus on limited parts of the implementation. Layering architectures, in contrast, are *extensive* aggregations, in that every class in the application belongs to a layer, with no exceptions. These differences are important in practice, because a layering architecture always guarantees a total decomposition of the implementation code, while composable units, being specific to a time and location, do not enforce full code coverage and are consequently harder to put into effect[5].

Microsoft's Composite UI Application Blocks architecture is an example of a composable unit strategy. This approach uses the concept of a shell application,

---

5.   The concept of *intensive* and *extensive* entities is borrowed from physics. Intensive measurements are specific to some point in space, such as pressure. Extensive measurements tend to be constant in a whole environment, such as temperature.

for example a Windows form application that provides services to composable units, within which one or more composable units – called 'SmartParts' – can interact. Such units are the building blocks of rich client applications delivered as plug-ins, here referred to as 'Modules.'

Once a good architecture is devised for a GUI, and perhaps some form of clustering has been decided on, either extremely formal like a composable unit strategy, or a more informal approach such as panel reuse, we are still left with one last issue: facing the reality of development.

Evolving order and appropriate architectures

Changing an architecture during the implementation of a GUI is an apparently bizarre idea. However, client applications have common design aspects, and are usually smaller and more manageable than server-side applications. These aspects make architecture evolution more feasible for desktop application GUIs than for large server applications that have many external dependencies. Changing architectures is not a new idea – it occurs for example in Agile approaches, and also in the Evolving Order pattern for domain-driven designs (Evans 2004). But given the nature of desktop application GUIs, one could question the real effectiveness of such a potentially costly activity.

The Book of Five Rings contains all the art and science of the famed duellist and undefeated Japanese Samurai Miyamoto Musashi, who died in 1645[6]. Among the many insights in this book, one interesting thing concerns the acquisition of knowledge about an opponent. Musashi said that if you know your enemy, and you know yourself, you can't lose a duel – although that is clearly different from always winning. Transferring this idea to software engineering, we may say that if we know ourselves (our organization, people skills, technologies, and so on) and the problem to solve (the enemy) we cannot fail – at worse we can wisely give up a task that is too daunting. Then why do so many projects fail or produce poor results from so much effort?

Whole forests have been chopped down to explain this, and we don't want to event try here[7]. Luckily we can say something about architectures and the structuring of implementation artifacts, especially as regards desktop application GUIs.

The reality is that most of the time we don't know the problem exactly (including the domain, its context, technologies, the potential of our own organization). This is even truer when problems change over time, through relentless iterations, changing requirements, and so on. Our initial assumptions based on past

---

6. For an on-line version, see http://www.samurai.com/5rings/.
7. As the reader can see, I am following Musashi's advice here too.

experience and reasonable evidence might look completely misplaced after a few months in this challenging environment. To what extent will our old architecture design be able to copy effectively with the current problem?

If the architecture has to fit the given scenario (domain, extra-functional requirements, team composition, implementation technology) and the scenario is changing, the architecture should change as well. In order to have a 'fit' architecture – that is, one that matches the engineering task as a whole without uselessly wasting resources – we need to provide an architecture that, if necessary, can evolve smoothly.

Individuating patterns

It is possible to modify the structural configuration of an application using sequences of basic refactoring steps. The required input is a number of patterns that need to be present systematically in the code. It is possible to refactor GUI code at a macro level under limited circumstances, such as finding precise patterns in the code automatically, a simple transformation path to the new structure. This is normally possible only for rather specific scenarios within GUI implementations.

> Using this assumption, one could see some aspects of a software architecture as a set of systematic low-level patterns found in the code. It does not really matter which particular pattern is present, as long as it is used extensively and systematically throughout the whole application.

When a given architecture is applied systematically and extensively, it is possible to refactor GUI code at a macro level to modify existing patterns into new ones, thus evolving the software architecture. In fortunate cases these refactorings can be automated, for example perhaps factoring out all Command pattern instances from the view layer in a three-layer architecture, making them part of the Application Model in a four-layer architecture[8].

The ability to modify an architecture inexpensively and predictably during development makes the whole issue of guessing the perfect architecture at project start-up less crucial. This in turn allows for more flexibility and a greater degree of adaptation to the problem at hand as it evolves during development iterations.

7.2   Some common GUI architectures

Having discussed some of the main issues of software architectures for GUIs, we are now ready to see some of them in action. This section discusses some common architectures seen in real-world projects. It briefly reviews some of the most used

---

8.   See the next section for details about these architectures.

architectures for client applications in order of the complexity of the problem at hand. *A three-layer organization for GUI code* then discusses one particular architecture in detail, providing a practical implementation of it.

> On the principles of continuous architectural refactoring and iterative development, one could think of these architectures as various evolutionary stages of the same application in its lifecycle, even though refactoring of a working architecture should be done only when needed.

The smart GUI antipattern

The shame of every GUI book is the 'smart GUI antipattern' (Evans 2004). This consists of shoveling all implementation into one class and forgetting about sophisticated layering techniques or fine OO design. Building a GUI this way has a small start-up complexity, but one that tends to grow sharply. Nevertheless, this could be just what we need in some situations. Simple projects with form-based GUIs and with little business behavior are good candidates for this approach.

By adopting such an approach, developers don't have to worry about decoupling, reuse, and domain-driven wisdom. The approach is to provide a class for each dialog or screen, and incorporate all the business logic, interaction, control, threading, and client–server communication we may need into this class. The only thing to worry about is providing some form of defined protocol for:

* *Presentation*. No matter how we have built them, screens must comply with standard GUI guidelines and other constraints.

* *Data IO*. Having everything encapsulated in a single (possibly bloated) class, all we need to care about is data transfer with a remote server. By providing a data transfer protocol with the rest of the world[9], we ensure a minimal protocol that can be used to decouple the poorly-implemented client from the server.

This approach couples well with the many visual builder tools available, doesn't require sophisticated developers, and results are almost immediate. With this organization, GUI testing options are limited to testing through the GUI (both automatic and manual), and some limited unit testing.

> This architecture was the default choice in the early days of mainstream distributed computing (the early 1990s) when OO technology was still to become widespread and the server side of an application usually consisted of a relational database.

---

9. Perhaps using data transfer objects (DTOs), as discussed in Chapter 8 in the case of rich client applications.

A semi-smart GUI architecture

This approach is a slightly more structured variant of the previous architecture. A layering scheme attempts to factor out content – widgets and layout – and a data IO layer that defines the remote connection with a server. The rest of the application remains as a 'blob' of business rules, event listeners, and everything else that is needed.

In cases in which this scheme is just a temporary stage towards a more well thought-out architecture, the 'blob' layer will be thrown away and replaced by a more structured implementation. The important aspect of this layering approach is that the front-end interface (GUI) and the data transfer backend interface are implemented in separate, and therefore more easily evolvable and reusable, layers. This is as shown in Figure 7.3.

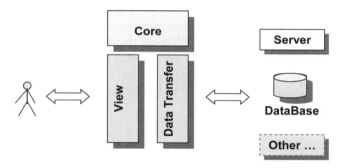

Figure 7.3   *A semi-smart application architecture*

This organization can be applied to cases that lie between the smart GUI antipattern and more demanding requirements that might await future iterations. Suppose for example that you are asked to port a Web application to a rich client, leveraging an existing J2EE server application. Suppose either that this is an exploratory project, or that you simply don't feel confident with a more complex architecture. You could then organize your GUI into three layers:

• The *presentation layer* is a passive container for widgets, layout, and other graphical details. No interaction or control is provided here. Widgets are manipulated passively by the core layer. Visibility is provided by package-level visibility or accessor methods. The responsibility of the presentation layer is only to contain widgets and organize their layout (for example content assembly). This allows panels to be assembled using visual builders, possibly by less skilled developers.

- The *data transfer* layer contains the POJO classes (or their XML equivalent, or the like) that enable communication with the external world.
- The *core* is the 'glue' layer that controls and drives the other two. This layer will be the most complex of the three, and potentially the least maintainable in the long term.

This approach has the same drawbacks and advantages of the semi-smart architecture, while providing a smoother curve regarding evolution costs.

> I like to call this approach the 'ice cream cookie sandwich architecture,' in which you are only concerned about the two 'cookies' – the end user interface and the server application – and not about the 'ice cream' – the business logic and control – which remains a fluid, monolithic implementation.

A three-layer architecture

Following this popular approach, code is organized into three layers: one for the presentation (the GUI code), another for the application (a suitable representation of the business domain), and one for common utility services, as shown in Figure 7.4. This layering scheme focuses on reuse. Factoring services into a common layer modularizes the rest of the implementation and enables the reuse of the service layer.

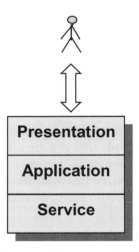

Figure 7.4   Three-layer application architecture overview

Some variants are possible, especially regarding the 'thickness' of the presentation layer. Some versions also have a quantity of control logic built into the presentation layer, while others prefer to maintain only simple control in the presentation as long as it is needed to spare the presentation layer from low-level GUI details.

Developers can use visual builders for defining content. Application layer code may contain some spurious reference to GUI classes, possibly concerning their higher-level aspects[10]. The service layer contains infrastructure code such as database connections, client server communication, and so on. Some layering strategies also put graphics utilities in the service layer, while others prefer to keep such toolkit-dependent code with the presentation layer.

The main differences between this approach and a semi-smart architecture are:

- In the semi-smart GUI approach, the view layer is thin and passive, while in three-layer architectures the presentation layer undertakes more responsibility, decoupling the application layer from widget details.

- The service layer gathers infrastructure behavior and works as a façade for a number of services, both in the presentation, such as providing the message localization service, and in the application, such as packaging a server request or handling a database connection. The service layer works also as a dynamic indirection facility at runtime.

- The purpose of this architecture is to provide a simple yet beneficial organization that allows for a robust application layer representing a business domain to operate within the application separately from presentation details, both statically, for example code references, and conceptually. For example, we might have exported existing business classes from a server application and want to reuse them in a client application.

- The 'glue' code is provided by the presentation layer. Most of the time this is just limited to a `main()` method that launches various components shared between the other layers.

A possible incarnation of this architecture is detailed later in this chapter.

A four-layer architecture

Four-layer architectures are a well-known extension to the three-layer approach, in which the application layer is split into an application model, responsible for decoupling the view layer from the domain model, and a domain model, in which view-independent domain representations manage information (see Figure 7.5).

This organization allows for better decoupling of the domain model from the rest of the view layer details. Depending on the variant chosen, the application model

---

10. This is the case with Swing applications in which model classes need to extend abstract toolkit classes, or interfaces where SWT+JFace domain classes don't have any dependency on GUI toolkits.

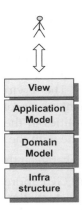

Figure 7.5   Four-layer application architecture overview

can factor out both commands and operations, not just GUI-related commands, so that the domain model remain a foundational layer for domain-specific knowledge (Evans 2004).

The application model layer will typically contain all the commands offered to users by the application: the Command pattern is used in both Swing and SWT for this. A 'thin' variant of the application model would typically contain no state apart from that needed by GUI commands.

> In cases in which a high level of sophistication is needed, the infrastructure layer can also handle the application's internal communication infrastructure, or other services typical of server-side applications, such as JMS support, advanced caching mechanisms, and the like.

As we are only discussing desktop application GUIs, we are implicitly assuming that all four layers will be deployed on the client side. This architecture can also be deployed with the upper two layers (the view and application models) on the client and the other two layers on the server. This latter scenario is more common for Web clients, in which there is no need for off-line capabilities and the whole domain model can comfortably operate on the server side.

7.3   *A three-layer organization for GUI code*

It is now possible to look at the details of a specific implementation of the three-layer architecture discussed in the previous section. This section discusses a reuse-based decomposition of a client implementation that is based on three parts:

presentation, application, and service. These three parts are composed mainly of Java classes, possibly with other resources such as images, support files, and so on.

This scheme has its strengths and weaknesses, as we will see. Our objective is to discuss this type of GUI architecture in some detail, rather than suggest that it is some sort of 'silver bullet' architecture.

Overview

The presentation layer is what we see on the screen. Users interacting with dialogs or watching a splash window at application start-up are dealing with presentation objects. The other two layers are the 'behind-the-scenes' of the software:

- The application layer is where the application domain's objects are gathered, the business objects or domain logic.
- The service layer provides a wide range of standardized utility services.

Figure 7.6 illustrates this.

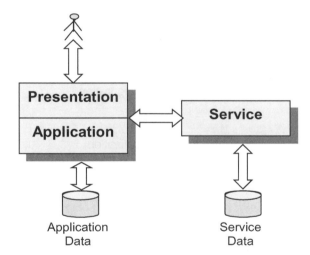

Figure 7.6   Three-layer GUI architecture overview

There is always a presentation layer in a user interface. It is made up of components that are usually inherited from `javax.swing.JComponent` (or, in SWT, from `org.eclipse.swt.widgets`), plus other classes that represent user input, or that are responsible for interaction and control. The user interacts with the presentation layer mostly with mouse and keyboard. This layer separates users from the application's logic.

The application layer lies immediately behind the presentation layer, tightly coupled to it. It is made up of Java classes that implement the logic and the business objects that are represented graphically in the presentation layer. If we have a clock window, for example, the application layer will contain a `Date` object that is tightly coupled with a `DateViewer` widget in a panel with some buttons, and so on, all of them in the presentation layer.

The third layer comes into play when we want to reuse some aspect of the code. Let's suppose we want to add more features to the clock. We want to offer international language support, with on-line help, and the option of customizing the clock's appearance depending on a user's tastes, and in such a way that users customizations are persistent across sessions. Thinking of these services as a separate layer helps in reusing them more systematically.

The following table shows how data is managed by the various layers:

Table 7.1   Relationship between layers and data

Type	Data
Presentation	Depends on the underlying GUI technology
Service	Authorization
	Configuration
	Help
	Localization
	Security
	User Profiles
	Etc.
Application	Application-dependent

This basic architecture is not intended to be all-encompassing, but rather to impart a minimum organizational infrastructure to GUI code, without being too pervasive. Developers can adapt it to their own production environments and needs.

Some of the benefits of this layering scheme are:

- *Division of work.* In the early stage of a development cycle, somebody will work on the GUI, designing and validating it with users, while perhaps someone else will take care of the business objects specific to the application domain, database issues, and so on. The two groups might even work in parallel after an initial period. This architecture helps to divide responsibilities neatly and so better organize the work.

- *Integration with existing toolkits.* This approach fits nicely with the Model-View-Controller (MVC) architecture and with similar object-oriented mechanisms that are in widespread use in Java programming, even though it can be used with simpler libraries such as SWT or AWT as well.

- *Flexibility.* One of the main practical advantages of such an architecture is its neutrality – it can be used for both medium-sized and small GUIs.

- *Common reference.* Like any kind of structured organization, this architecture is also useful for reference. Throughout the product lifecycle (and in this book as well) we can address functional parts with the same name. This helps developers working in teams to standardize their cooperative efforts. It also gives us an overview of all the challenges and problems designers and developers will face during the product lifecycle.

Some of this scheme's drawbacks are:

- *It needs a clearly-defined separation between presentation and application.* If this is not maintained, the architecture can easily degrade.

- *Extra care in testing is required.* The service layer can be a problem for testing. Mock-ups are needed for expensive services such as remote connections, databases, and so on, and special care is needed with Singletons that initialize statically.

- *It gives poor insulation for complex domain models.* The model doesn't scale well for projects with a complex domain model. In these cases a four-layer architecture is strongly recommended.

The following three sections look more closely at the three individual layers.

The presentation layer

The structure of the presentation layer is repetitive: the user interacts with some widgets, clicking with the mouse, filling up text fields, and so on. A control manager[11] is normally used to support the widgets, supervising all the widgetry and keeping it coherent – for example, disabling fields in a form until all required data is valid.

Figure 7.7 shows a high-level conceptual view of the presentation layer with a centralized control state that implements the Mediator design pattern.

---

11. See Chapter 6.

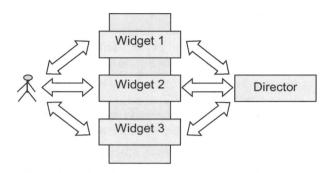

Figure 7.7   The presentation layer

In Swing this layer includes all the views in the MVC, plus related support classes such as table decorators, together with the objects that represent user input and control. In SWT it includes the content widgets.

The application layer

If we use Swing or other MVC-based frameworks, all the MVC models needed for the views in the presentation layer can be gathered here, as shown in Figure 7.8. As well as these, other objects are needed for the particular domain with which we are working. The application layer is the most variable of the three, because it implements the logic of the application domain (possibly accessing remote services) and also commands that use that logic. The application layer might also include other details apart from a representation of the business domain, such as commands, domain-specific support functions, and so on, and for this reason we prefer to call it the *application layer*.

MVC models can be used as the interface with the application layer. This is a simple choice and helps to decouple the two layers clearly – but 'pollutes' the application layer with classes that are needed to extend the GUI toolkit's interfaces for data models.

> Even if your GUI does not use the Swing library, or JFace on top of SWT, this architecture still turns out to be useful – as shown in Chapter 10 in the context of J2ME GUIs.

The application layer, also known as the 'business domain model,' is domain-specific. You can find a comprehensive and insightful discussion of its design in (Evans 2004).

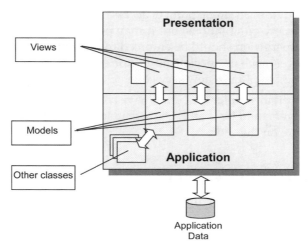

Figure 7.8   One flavor of application layer

The service layer

The service layer implementation described here has just one class, Service-Manager, as its interface with the other two layers. It usually performs all the initializations – loading configuration files, initializing external devices, and so on – and offers infrastructure services to the application and presentation layers. A common service offered to the presentation layer, for example, is localization support of widget appearance. Figure 7.9 illustrates a possible structure for this layer.

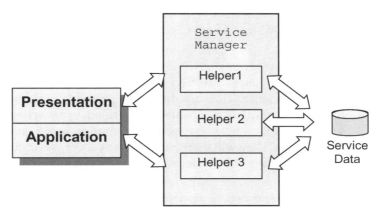

Figure 7.9   The service layer

Providing a single point of access is useful and intuitive, and can be used in a wide variety of situations, but it may pose problems in non-trivial applications. Code supervision should be enforced to prevent invalid services being moved into this layer, such as specialized Factories, for example. A configuration facility can be used to plug in new services, such as support for special hardware devices.

Even in simpler GUIs that have a minimal service layer implementation a service layer could be useful, because it enforces a standard, systematic yet simple structure on the code.

7.4   *Two examples of a three-layer implementation*

Two examples of the three-layer architecture serve to illustrate it:

- A simple example describes the architecture from a technical, programmer's viewpoint.
- The second example zooms out to see how the model can be used to organize a more complex and formal project.

These examples illustrate the practical application of the architectures described in the previous section, and will be discussed in detail in the following chapters.

We know from Chapter 3 that we can think of components – that is, subclasses of the `Component` class – as being divided into three groups, in order of complexity and development cost:

- Standard components, such as `Tree`, `Panel`.
- Custom components, such as `DataBaseTree`, `MyCoolButton`, obtained from the specializations of standard – Sun, Eclipse, or third-party – components.
- Ad-hoc components, such as the graphic equalizer in a music player, for example, that have no counterpart in standard components and must be developed from scratch.

An MP3 player

Kenrick and Rajeev are two friends in their first university year of study in computer science. They are developing some Java classes for playing MP3 files, for fun. One day Kenrick comes to his friend, very excited. He has found out from a Web site that a Java shareware distribution being launched on CD-ROM in a week's time. They will therefore have only a very short time to ship their product, and although their MP3 decoder classes work nicely, there is no GUI at all at the moment.

Rajeev has some experience with the Java Swing library, and decides to develop the GUI with the help of this book, while Kenrick will add the file streaming and other essential features to the Java audio subsystem classes they have already developed.

Rajeev is amazed by the possibilities Java can give their GUI, such as portability and a pluggable look and feel, but at present he has no time for advanced GUI features. He decides to build a simple GUI for the first release, leaving 'cool' features for future releases. The paper mock-up is straightforward, and the GUI design is inspired by similar products already on the market.

Rajeev gets into the implementation details of his GUI, devising the following top-level containers:

- A main frame.
- Four modal, unrelated dialogs, one for information about the current track, another for application settings, one for the help, and one for choosing files.
- Two accessory pop-ups – a pop-up window for the volume control, and a simple pop-up menu triggered by the right mouse-button on the track list.

Rajeev decides not to use any particular UI approach, mainly because he has never used one before and feels that he has no time to learn new material at present. He sketches the main window on paper, defining all its components, shown in Table 7.2, together with their development complexity.

Table 7.2   The main frame components for the MP3 player

Component name	Java class	Type
ToolBar	JtoolBar	Standard
TrackList	Jlist	Custom
TrackSlider	Jslider	Standard
StatusBar	JstatusBar	Ad-hoc

The next step – to define the required services – is straightforward: Rajeev decides not to use any standard service at all. He then defines the user interaction, basing it on the following commands.

- Track-related commands:
  - Play
  - Stop
  - Rewind
  - Fast forward
  - Pause
  - Show track properties, which displays the track properties dialog
  - Step back, which rewinds the current track by five seconds
  - Step forward, which steps the current track forward by five seconds

- General commands:
  - Preferences, which shows the dialog for changing the application's options
  - Help, which shows a simple dialog with a text area describing authors and product
  - Set volume, which shows the pop-up window with the volume slider control
- Track-list commands:
  - Next track
  - Previous track
  - Add to track list
  - Remove from track list
  - Select from track list, which plays the selected track in the list

The other user interactions are the right-click on the track list, which displays a menu with track list-related commands, the double-click that launches the 'Select from track list' command, and the keyboard accelerators.

A simple director class will manage all the GUI coherence – for example, the track list navigation arrows should be disabled when it is not possible to use them, such as at the beginning or the end of the list.

Once finished with the director class, the presentation layer and the service layer (here empty) are defined. The last step is to define the model classes in the application layer. There are three MVC models: the track list, the current track elapsed time, and the volume slider models. Another application class represents the tracks to be played.

Rajeev decides to incorporate the elapsed time model in the track class, because this simplifies the handling of the two views. The same object – the current elapsed time for the track – is observed by two views: the interactive slider and the read-only digital display at the bottom-right of the main frame. This type of model – the slider model and the ad-hoc digit display model within the status bar – is quite simple. The track list model is just an ordered collection of `Track` object specializations of the `ListModel` class.

Rajeev adds the other application classes that have been refined by Kenrick meanwhile, resulting in the GUI shown in Figure 7.10. Kenrick simply couldn't believe it.

With his remaining time, Rajeev refines the `StatusBar` component and tests the GUI with the help of their friends.

This example shows how a principled, top-down general implementation organization also helps in the development of small applications, not only at a technical level, but also in team organization.

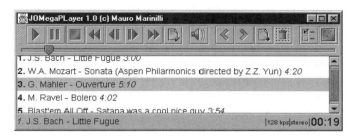

Figure 7.10   The MP3 player's GUI (Metal1.2)

An electronic circuit simulator and editor

In the next example we take another perspective, without going into technical details, to see how a three-layer architecture can be used for managing large projects.

A joint venture by a university and a private software firm is set up to develop a graphical electronic circuit simulator and editor in Java. The plan is to begin by wrapping an existing, reliable simulation tool that is based on a command-line user interface that has been developed by university researchers over the past ten years. In future releases the code will be ported entirely from C to Java, so that the application will become 100% pure Java and totally cross-platform.

This highlights an interesting and important aspect of the Java community – not only its end users, but also developers, architects and designers. Java technology is widely used by open source and not-for profit organizations, where the Java characteristics of portability, inexpensiveness, and inherent multi-vendor sourcing, make it the perfect development choice in these cases.

The goal for the first release is to lay out the GUI, while the backend will interface with the existing legacy command-line application. Users are both engineers and academics, and the software will be released in two versions:

- A basic one as freeware, which will provide the same functions as the existing command-line application.

- A 'professional' edition that will be the starting point for future enhancements.

The software company will hold the copyright for the source code, possibly expanding the software to handle more features in the professional edition. They will manage the overall development, while leaving the university partner to work with the legacy code they know well.

We won't discuss the management of the project here, although this can be handled within the three-layer architecture as well: we just focus on the code development effort.

After the development group is created, three teams are formed, one for each functional layer:

- The presentation team will interact with the other two teams and with end users.
- The application team will interact with the other two teams, and with the researchers who developed the command-line simulator for the domain analysis.
- Finally, the service team will interact with the other two internal teams.

Development begins with an estimation of key numbers, such as how many and which type of services the GUI will need. Then, after several meetings with users of the command-line version of the application, the presentation team proposes the first GUI mock-up. In the meantime the application team starts discussions with the developers of the command-line simulator, while trying to define the software architecture best suited for a graceful migration to Java in forthcoming releases.

The first version of the GUI is shown in Figure 7.11. It took less than half an hour for an expert developer to build the mock-up using a visual GUI builder[12].

The idea behind the proposed GUI is to centralize circuit building and manipulation in one ad-hoc component, the circuit editor, shown on the right-hand side of the figure, while the left-hand side provides a data navigation facility that allows circuit elements to be inspected. The designed interaction is from the data inspector to the circuit editor and back – that is, selecting an element in the circuit editor automatically selects the data in the inspector, and vice-versa. A palette of circuit elements is used to add items to the circuit editor and the underlying circuit model interactively.

The circuit editor is chosen as a key component in the whole design, so the presentation team divides its responsibilities in two sub-teams: one responsible for the circuit editor and its related classes, the other for the remaining classes in the presentation layer, together with the organization of the feedback interviews with users.

The second presentation sub-team plan thirty or so commands (action classes), with one director and two auxiliary classes, allowing an initial approximate cost

---

12. See Chapter 5.

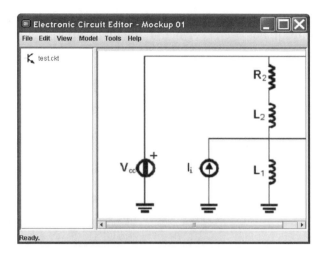

Figure 7.11   The first version of the mock-up

estimation for the whole development. The design of the exploration area requires an extra meeting with end users.

After a feedback session with users, it emerges that the command-line interface, which is provided as an on-demand pop-up dialog in the first version, is so important and frequently used that needs a more central place in the GUI. The presentation team therefore decides to incorporate it permanently in the GUI. This change won't affect the application team that is working on the business classes.

The project needs the following services: standard internationalization, interactive help, and basic persistence. The service team does not need to implement these functions immediately, but needs to publish the interfaces other teams have to use right from the beginning.

The two presentation teams continue the design phase. The first team has a somewhat easier job, in that they already have a clear idea of what to develop in the circuit editor component. The second team still has to define some design issues. For the data inspector, two hypotheses are viable:

- A table-like solution, possibly implemented with a specialized `JTable` component that adopts a high-density approach to data visualization[13].
- A hierarchical browser style using a specialized `JTree` and opting for a limited information layout strategy.

_____

13. See Chapter 2.

The former solution with a tabular inspector is shown in Figure 7.12, and the latter solution has been sketched in the mock-up in Figure 7.13.

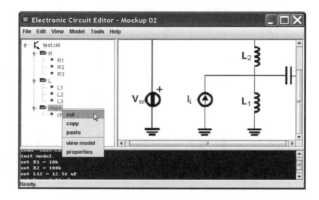

Figure 7.12   The second version of the mock-up

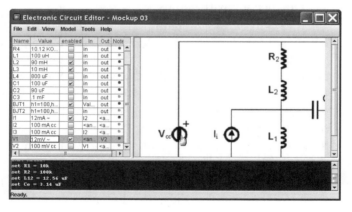

Figure 7.13   The third version of the mock-up

After some discussion within the development team and some brief usability testing with users, it becomes clear that the table-like solution is less usable and more difficult to manage, especially for large circuits with a greater number of elements. For budgetary reasons no other ad-hoc component will be implemented for this release, for example for the exploration area.

Meanwhile, the application team is working on the overall analysis, starting from the business classes and leaving the model classes, the part that is more changeable – at least at the beginning of the development cycle – to last.

The service team is working in parallel on the services the application needs: internationalization, persistence of the application settings, and help support. These features will be implemented using standard libraries (such as those provided with this book) so the implementation cost is almost zero.

After another meeting with users and university staff, it transpires that the GUI is mature enough to be considered definitive, at least for this release. An internal meeting is also held between the presentation and the application teams to define the interfaces (classes) that describe the boundaries across which the team's code will communicate. This is often just a matter of defining the models of the MVC architecture. In this version of the GUI there are three main models, corresponding to the three views used:

- A `DataTreeModel,` which subclasses the `TreeModel.`
- A `CircuitModel` that represents the electronic circuit managed by the circuit editor component.
- A `CommandLineModel,` for the command line component, which is a specialized `JTextArea` component.

While the `DataTreeModel` and the `CommandLineModel` are relatively easy to write, the first because it is just an implementation of the standard Swing tree model, and the second because of the intrinsic simplicity of the command line component, the `CircuitModel` is a new component, and hence needs more effort.

The interfaces required are agreed, and from now on the four groups have defined their responsibilities more clearly. The two presentation teams will use dummy model classes to refine the prototype, while the application team is still busy with domain analysis. The only possible problems could be in the definition of the `CircuitModel` class, which could change in the future. The service team finishes its job and its members join one of the three remaining teams. The two presentation teams work to refine the prototype, adding dummy delays and other real-world constraints, the second team constantly validating the user interface with end users.

In time the application team finishes the implementation of the three models, together with the remaining classes. After local tests, the three set of classes (application, presentation, and service) are merged in one application, while the three teams – the two presentation teams and the application team – continue to work separately. The end of the integration produces the first alpha release of the whole application.

This example shows a possible division of work for development teams on non-trivial GUIs and how this architecture can be applied on medium-scale projects.

7.5   *The service layer*

The service layer is essentially a reusable library that implements a number of services offered to both application and presentation classes. The key value of the service layer lies in its specialization. Centralizing general-purpose, service classes in a top-down manner provides a number of benefits. This section looks at the implementation details of the service layer, together with a simple implementation.

Overview

The services offered by the service layer are centralized in a `ServiceManager` class whenever this is meaningful. Expanding on Figure 7.6 on page 301 gives us the architecture details shown in Figure 7.14.

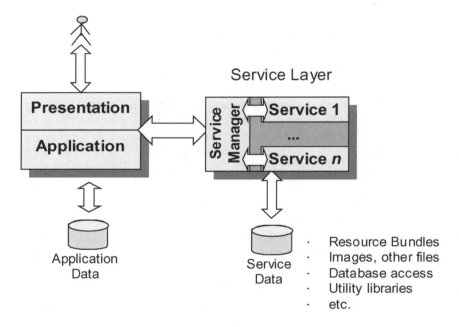

Figure 7.14   Architecture overview for the service layer

We keep the organization of the proposed service layer as simple as possible, providing a static structure with no dynamic discovery or plug-in of services. Figure 7.15 shows a possible set of services.

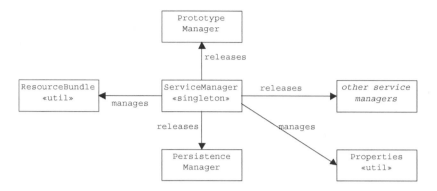

Figure 7.15   Service layer class diagram

The `ServiceManager` class is a Singleton that acts as a one-stop access point for many of the services provided in the service layer. From a software design perspective, such a class is a useful container for the many utility services needed by a graphical application.

The `ServiceManager` class also provides useful features at development and testing time. For example, when resources aren't found, a dummy (non-null) default resource is always supplied to keep the application running: a dummy image is built programmatically by the `initializeDefaultResources()` method. In this way a default image is always available, even when no resources are provided. For example, a picture (`EMPTY_ICON`) is returned by the `getImage-Icon` method whenever the requested image is not found. Similarly, the `getMsg` method doesn't abruptly break execution when a resource string is not found, returning an empty string instead.

The private constructor initializes each specialized service class by using lazy instantiation. Only when a particular service is needed is it instantiated on the fly. The same technique can be used during application shut-down.

Service interfaces should be kept as simple and homogeneous as possible, following the Segregation Interface Principle[14], especially when shared among diverse developer groups. General advice for developing public APIs should be

---

14. The Segregation Interface Principle states that clients should not be forced to depend on methods that do not pertain to them and that they won't use. Such external methods clutter the design and should be made available separately. For more details, see (Martin 2002).

used when designing the public interface of the service layer[15]. The enforcement of the principle of Single Functional Responsibility also helps to keep services 'fit' (that is, focused only on a well-defined, coherent responsibility) and more understandable.

Loading services

Loading external resources is a common functionality in an application. Images, property files, and other data should be loaded in a coherent way, because a Java application can be launched in different contexts.

More common situations could be:

- *Development time execution*. During development, testing or debugging, the application is in a protected environment in which some parts (resources or code) could be missing.

- *Standalone runtime execution*. This is the standard way to run a Java application.

- *Java Web Start runtime execution*. Given the particular implementation of Java Web Start technology, some mechanisms for loading resources cannot work.

- *Java programs run as applets*. In this case the loading mechanism is simplified by the applet container.

It is good practise to centralize external accesses to the local file system and the Internet. This strategy could prove useful also for security control and other issues. It will be far easier to change the loading mechanism used in the program if this is centralized in a service class. If the application is planned to be deployed in different scenarios, a pluggable specialized `ResourceLoader` could be provided. Nevertheless, in all common situations the loading mechanism provided by the `ServiceManager` implementation in the code bundle will suffice.

Localization services

Localization is essentially the loading of files that translate text messages or other resources shown in an application appropriately for different countries and cultures. These files can store references to the relevant resources, such as images and text strings, that need to be localized. For simplicity we will deal here only

---

15. Countless book discuss good OO design, such as (Martin 2002) mentioned above. For a more specific discussion, see for example 'Evolving Java-based APIs' by Jim des Rivières, available at http://eclipse.org/eclipse/development/java-api-evolution.html

with properties files, although more elaborate schema are possible, such as XML files.

Localization properties files are often edited and managed by different people, such as programmers or translators. To prevent problems, the development team can agree on simple guidelines for their format. The localization files provided here are compliant with a simple standard.

There are a few simple properties that should be enforced for localization files, as well as other configuration and development files:

- It should be possible to navigate back to the point in the source code where a text string in a resource bundle is used. *Traceability* is essential for maintaining the files in a complex development environment.

- The files should be owned by only one member of the development team. In this way responsibilities are clearly defined.

- The files should be kept to a reasonable size. Excessively large files are difficult to maintain and manage, while too many small files could be excessively resource-consuming at runtime.

We use a simple convention for resource files in this book that ensures these properties, and that has proved quite robust in large projects:

- Key strings are composed of tokens separated by a period. They begin with the fully-qualified class name, excluding common paths, and eventually include inner classes. A brief explicatory label is used.

- A two-character code is used for special-purpose labels, to distinguish the type of label. In this book we use the following suffixes:
  - 'tt' for tooltip text
  - 'ad' for accessible descriptions
  - 'mn' for mnemonics
  - 'im' for images
  - longer, ad-hoc suffixes such as 'title' where required

- Finally, some additional information can be inserted in the heading comments, such as the current version, the authors, and so on. This would typically follow your company standards.

You can adapt this type of convention to suit your project's needs and development organization as required. If the planned application is not complex, or the development team is limited in number and stable over time, you can consider dropping any convention on properties files altogether.

An example of a resource bundle file following this convention is provided in Listing 7.1 below.

Listing 7.1 the `message.properties` file.

```
00: #
01: # Naming convention adopted here:
02: # (especially useful for large projects)
03: #
04: # 1.package path (excluded common base like "com.marinilli.b1") to
the first class that uses it, then the classname followed by "." and
05: # 2.optionally 2-char code (tt=tooltip, mn=mnemonic, ad= accessi-
ble desc., im=image), followed by "." and
06: # 3.finally a short description of the string
07: # (in case of simple text label the 2-char code is omitted)
08: #
09: # (c) 2000-2006 Mauro Marinilli
10: #
11:
12: c6.util.ui.memory.MemoryCheckBox.label=Don't\ show\ this\ message\
again
13:
14: c4.common.LoginDialog.title=Log\ In
15: c4.common.LoginDialog.login=Login\ Name:
16: c4.common.LoginDialog.login.mn=l
17: c4.common.LoginDialog.login.tt=insert\ user\ name
18: c4.common.LoginDialog.pword=Password:
19: c4.common.LoginDialog.pword.mn=p
20: c4.common.LoginDialog.pword.tt=insert\password
21:
22: c4.common.AboutDialog.title=About\ J-Mailer\ Pro
23: c4.common.AboutDialog.close=Close
24: c4.common.AboutDialog.info=Info..
25: c4.common.AboutDialog.logos.im=CompanyLogo.gif
26: c4.common.AboutDialog.about.im=AboutLogo.jpg
27: c4.common.AboutDialog.version=Version\ 1.00.0.0002
28: c4.common.AboutDialog.text1=&copy;\ 2002\ All\ Right\ Reserved.
29: c4.common.AboutDialog.text2=blah\ blah\ blah\ blah\ blah
30:
```

This listing refers to the message labels in two classes:

- `com.marinilli.b1.c4.common.LoginDialog`
- `com.marinilli.b1.c4.common.AboutDialog`

Remember that once your application is deployed, zipped JAR files eliminate most of the redundancy seen in message keys, both in properties files and in compiled classes.

Note that the '\' character is needed to enable portability only when developing on multiple platforms, for example mixing Unix, Microsoft, or Apple Macintosh machines.

Resource bundles and other configuration files are also useful for non-technical staff that need access to messages and other GUI appearance material. For example, designers can use them to finely tune the final GUI.

Persistence services

Persistence services are provided as a way to save data persistently from session to session. Memory components[16], for example, are implemented by using persistence services. From J2SE 1.4, a limited form of persistence is provided by the library `java.util.prefs`. We will use such a library in the example application in Chapter 14 and its utility libraries. This example code is provided with the rest of the source code bundled with the book.

The `PersistenceManager` is organized as a Singleton, following the design of the other specialized service handlers. Its private constructor loads a specialized properties file from the local disk that stores class-persistent data in a text format. This method can be used for static variables and common object instances. Saving static fields requires you to serialize the whole instance. The `get()` and `put()` methods, and their various versions specialized for handling elementary types, work on the class-instance persistent cache. This is written and read as a properties (text) file. In contrast to binary serialized objects, text can be read and manipulated by humans easily.

Interested readers can experiment to see what is written in the `persistence.properties` file in the application directory, set to '`.app`' by default in the system root. This mechanism is quite useful for storing GUI options and other persistent data so that it can be manipulated with a text editor outside the application. For more details about class and instance persistence, see (Marinilli Persistence 2000).

For more details, see the implementation of the `PersistenceManager` class provided in the code bundle. Apart from class persistence, the proposed `PersistenceManager` class supports instance-level persistence by means of the `loadInstance` and `saveInstance` methods. This type of persistence is handled using normal serialized files, one for each object. The proposed implementation can be modified to use external libraries or other persistence means such as remote servers, databases, and so on.

Factory services

One example of an additional service that can be provided by a service layer is a facility for creating new objects from prototypes. This is an implementation of the classic Prototype software design pattern (Gamma et al. 1994). This service

---

16. See Chapter 4.

can be used by the application for creating new objects from templates, or directly by the user, as in the Library example application in Chapter 15. In this latter case, users can modify the templates themselves using the same GUI that is used to modify normal objects, so providing a handy reuse of an object's property screens for developers.

This general service can be employed in a variety of different contexts. The implementation of the `PrototypeManager` class supports a cache for storing class instances. Such a cache, implemented by the `repository` instance, is made persistent by means of the standard persistence services provided by the service layer.

To avoid unnecessary commits when the cache has not been modified, a 'dirty' bit is employed. The `firstTimeInitialization` method performs the initialization, building a number of default prototypes that are used when the program is first launched. These default prototypes can then be overwritten by new instances. The `PrototypeManager.defaultValues` property defines where the default values – used only at start up – are stored. The (private) constructor loads the array of default prototypes from disk. The static method `createNewFrom` creates a new instance, given the prototype object. It tries to fetch the prototype from the cache, and returns a new instance from it. In this way new types that are not provided at design time can be managed by the program at runtime. Finally, accessory methods like `remove`, `get`, and `put` can be used to manipulate the cache directly.

The `PrototypeManager` class is available in the code provided for this chapter.

Other services

Different kinds of services may be needed, depending on the application domain. Designers often include graphical utilities with the sort of general services discussed above, especially for medium to large projects. This approach can easily lead to a fully-fledged graphical-utility static class (that is, a collection of static methods) that solves common graphical problems such as component resizing, dynamic container introspection, and so on. A potential problem with this approach is that novice developers tend to reinvent the wheel, providing features that are already present in the standard GUI library, but often of a lower quality, because of a lack of knowledge of the technology used.

Common services are often those related to application IO, such as client–server communication or database connection management. A database manager can centralize connection pooling and other related features. Specialized managers providing adaptation can also be gathered here.

Providing new services

A few words about the boundary between the application domain classes and the service layer are relevant here.

Consider for example the domain of GIS applications, such as the Geopoint example in Chapter 3. In this context the API for geolocalization and managing physical values on the Earth's surface can be included as a general-purpose service within the service layer. Although wrong from a theoretical viewpoint (such an API is not a general-purpose one), it could be an appropriate decision if the company is specializing in geolocalization products and the API will be used in other applications as well.

The Swiss army knife syndrome

Improper design of the `ServiceManager` class can easily lead to a do-it-all service class with many disparate utility methods patched together. In (Brown et al. 1998) this scenario is called the *Swiss Army Knife Antipattern*.

A common solution to this problem is to differentiate the classes that provide the different services, eventually providing a more elaborated architecture within the service layer itself. This is another point of friction in the proposed implementation of the three-layer architecture in real-world scenarios.

7.6   Summary

This chapter presented advice about code organization, and proposed a three-layer architecture suitable for Java GUI development in detail. Such an architecture is composed of three layers, as follows:

- *Presentation*. This layer contains all the GUI-related classes and resources, essentially `Component` subclasses, and graphical resources such as images.

- *Application*. This layer gathers the business-specific classes and the remainder of the MVC classes whose view components were included in the presentation layer.

- *Service*. This layer consists of a standard reusable library of services that recur in all non-trivial GUIs. It can sometimes be expanded to handle special services typical of the current application.

We discussed the proposed architecture, providing two practical examples that highlighted the main advantages such an architecture provides.

Key ideas

Here are some of the more interesting ideas seen in this chapter:

- The main criteria and issues related to code organization for desktop application GUIs, especially for layering.

- Providing a code structure organized around service classes has a number of benefits, such as code reusability, a systematic software design, better communication among developers, and so on.

- Service classes can be reused easily to provide sophisticated services inexpensively. The factory services implemented by the `PrototypeManager` class is a good example of this.

- For simple applications the service layer approach can still be used, compacting the services offered to reduce the additional runtime overhead.

Aside from general discussion and practical examples of implementation organizations, we also have looked at the three layers of a proposed layering scheme in detail.

8 Form-Based Rich Clients

In this chapter we will explore a very popular class of GUI applications: rich clients (also known as 'smart' or 'fat' clients). While we focus our discussion on desktop applications, most of the concepts and approaches discussed here can be applied also to J2ME applications, as described in Chapter 10.

This chapter focuses on form-based GUIs, on their design, and on issues such as input validation, and distribution of code between client and server tiers, while other chapters complete the puzzle by providing related advice on this popular class of GUIs – Chapter 11 discusses various tools and technologies for Java GUIs, while Chapter 13 focuses on Java rich client platforms.

The chapter is organized as follows:

8.1, Introduction clarifies various details related to rich clients.

8.2, Reference functional model applies the abstract functional model discussed in Chapter 1 to rich clients.

8.3, Runtime data model introduces a general, simple, informal model for runtime data representation that is used in the example application.

8.4, The cake-ordering application, the XP way proposes an example form-based application created using this methodology.

8.1 Introduction

Figure 8.1 shows a screen shot of a fictitious application for Java-powered cell phones. This illustrates a type of Midlet[1] (see Chapter 10) that is provided by the central transportation authority of a major city to its clients. The user is admitted into the transportation system by means of an ingenious system – when requested by the user, the cell phone screen displays a special machine-readable pattern that is interpreted by fixed devices.

The application also works as an 'e-wallet' – the user can purchase transportation credits electronically – and receives broadcast messages about transit and other transport-related news. These messages are optional: the user needs to pay their

---

1. A small Java application that is intended to be executed within a managed container conforming with CLDC and MIDP profiles for mobile devices.

carrier provider for the cell phone traffic, so it can be disabled by users who do not wish for the service. This type of application works mostly off line – displaying the machine-readable pattern and thus allowing the cell phone owner to pay for the ticket – but needs some on-line type of connection from time to time, to update the user's credit and to show news messages.

Figure 8.1   *A J2ME rich client*

This type of application cannot be implemented as a WAP (or Web) page, because it needs to be able to function off site. At the same time, by working off site and using the same appearance as the cell phone's software environment, it can camouflage itself alongside the other cell phone applications, and so appear more natural to its users.

The application must be easy to download, for example from a Web page, and be easy to use, because repetitive users are going to use it more than once a day. Being written in Java allows it to be deployed inexpensively to a wide range of devices. This is an imaginative – and imaginary – example of a particular breed of client GUIs, straddling the ground between complex Web pages and lightweight traditional applications.

Defining rich clients

There are many definitions for rich and smart clients, some of them elegant and useful, but none yet suit the uniqueness of the Java platform. We will introduce Java rich clients (RC) gradually, starting from their differences from Web applications, and next from the other GUI client environments.

First of all, let's look at the properties that define a rich client for the purposes of this book:

- They offer richer user experience than other media. If rich clients are to be useful, they should be superior to existing alternatives, namely Web-based applications. This is true for both end users and developers.

- They offer a *network-centric* approach. The ability to connect to remote servers smoothly, also for first-time deployment, together with the ability to operate off line, are two important characteristics of rich clients.

- They are *local environment-savvy*. In contrast to Web applications, RCs might have access to local resources, and can fit into the overall GUI experience of existing applications and operating systems. Also in contrast to Web applications, rich clients have to be designed with a specific target environment in mind, both technically and as regards the user experience.

It's useful to briefly review the reasons why we might need to develop a rich client application:

- When the application is targeted at many different platforms, or when ease of deployment and administration is favored over end-user experience, Web-based applications should be preferred over other client strategies. In situations in which a computer is used by more than one user, by occasional users, or when users access the application from more than one machine, then Web applications are also preferable.

- When end user productivity and overall experience are important, or when off-line capabilities are needed, rich clients should be preferred over Web applications. This latter decision should be based on an assessment of the real need, however, rather than 'nice-to-have' features.

Java rich clients

A wide variety of rich client technologies exist, such as Microsoft client technologies, Macromedia Flash, and many others. There are at least three factors that make Java different: a fully-fledged object-oriented approach, multi-platform execution, and a lively, highly collaborative developer community. While the first two factors can be problematic if not mastered, these three aspects together offer a unique blend of features.

Before going further, it is important to highlight the fact that Java desktop clients suffer from one major drawback due to Java's multi-platform characteristics. The hurdle is the Java Runtime Environment, which requires at least 7.2 MB to run (J2SE 5.x, using special optimized installers). This can be a problem that should be considered in advance before opting for Java client technology.

On the other hand, OO technology has been around for decades, and developers can rely on a host of well-proven techniques and patterns, of which this book takes advantage heavily. As domain complexity rises and application scale grows, OO technology has proven a valuable although labor-intensive approach. In addition, thanks to the availability of SWT, the portability of pure Java GUIs can be sacrificed for tighter integration with the underlying OS environment on some platforms.

GUI design for rich clients: the Third Way

First came traditional desktop application GUIs, which thrived unchallenged for decades. Then came Web browser-based GUIs, with their document-like structure, hyperlinks, lots of scrolling, and so on. Now, an interesting design crossbreed is slowly making its way onto our desktops. Perhaps you have already noticed some desktop applications that have hyperlink-like buttons, panels that resemble Web pages, and other features. This convergence is taking place on the Web side as well – think of 'rich' Web applications such as Google's services, and those offered by similar Web sites.

Unfortunately, this middle ground is still largely uncharted territory, in which GUI design habits and conventions are not yet established. There are no GUI design guidelines, nor even established informal idioms, and this 'third way' of lightweight rich clients remains a wild land that GUI designers enter at their peril.

This is a pity, because Java rich clients have the potential to offer a unique end user experience that falls between traditional desktop applications and Web applications, by providing a unique, platform independent 'Web desktop' feeling, backed by traditional software engineering technology and libraries proven by decades of industrial development.

8.2   Reference functional model

Returning to the functional decomposition we presented in Chapter 1 and discussed in Chapter 6, in this section we will specialize it further for rich clients. Figure 8.2 repeats the model from Chapter 1.

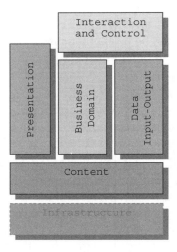

Figure 8.2   A functional decomposition for rich clients

It is worth reiterating that this is just one possible, general functional decomposition of a rich client application, merely a reference to theoretical concepts. On the other hand, when organized as a practical decomposition, rich client implementations help in the discussion of common issues at a higher level of abstraction.

> This discussion applies to all Java GUI technologies, libraries and toolkits – the model is even valid for Web applications and non-Java GUIs.

To recap briefly, the various functional layers possible in a rich client application, following the model in Figure 8.2, are:

- *Content*. This is the 'base' of the GUI, composed of widgets, screens, and navigation. For convenience we can also represent widget layout information here.

- *Presentation*. This is an orthogonal layer to the others, containing graphics appearance and low-level presentation details such as look and feel information, icons and the like.

- *Business domain*. This is the logic of our application. Very simple rich clients do need very little client logic, so this layer would be almost empty in their cases

- *Data IO*. This layer contains behavior and data needed for exchanging information with the outside world. It mainly gathers data related to client–server communication and data binding information.

- *Interaction and control*. This is the topmost layer and 'glues' the other layers together. It is responsible for enforcing data validation by invoking rules from the business domain's layer, together with low-level interaction and control, such as disabling buttons or executing commands.

- *Infrastructure*. This layer is the foundation of the entire application, and includes the Java platform, the GUI toolkit (such as Swing or SWT), and other infrastructure frameworks such as a rich client platform like Spring RCP or Eclipse RCP. We won't focus on this layer here.

This functional decomposition will be a guide when discussing the many details and issues related to rich client application development. It applies not only to code, data and resources, but also to testing and business analysis as well.

Distributing behavior between client and server

One of the most obvious bonuses of developing a Java rich client lies in the synergies possible with server-side Java code. One such advantage is the ability to use the same code on both client and server. Another advantage lies in using the same proprietary protocols between client and server, such as RMI. The latter situation is less often available and it is fairly straightforward to implement: a wide range of tutorials are available on the topic.

A less-discussed although important issue concerns the distribution of common code between client and server, from a client application perspective. (Although we are discussing it here for rich clients, this point is valid also for other applications that need to connect remotely with server-side applications.)

One of the achievements of multi-tier systems is the ability to keep business code away from clients. This was a major step in implementing business logic that is dispersed on remotely-installed clients. Changing deployed business logic with 1990s technology was about as hard as updating the firmware of a space probe that had already landed on Mars. With today's deployment technologies, it is possible to bring business code back to client machines while maintaining centralized control, allowing rich clients to work off line as well, and to provide a richer user experience with more natural and responsive GUIs. See for example the discussion about data validation later in this chapter.

The important point is to *control* business logic, not on which tier it is physically located. With technologies such as JNLP and Java Web Start, for example, it is possible to update business code seamlessly, and also to force clients to update to a specific required version of the business code before running the application.

Unfortunately, even today's technology is still far from perfect, and distributing code between client and server is still one of the 'complexity boosters' for GUI applications. Bringing business code to the client complicates design, because apart from deployment issues, we need to design remote communication, with coarse-grained interfaces, DTOs, and all the required machinery of its implementation[2].

Business logic on the client also generates a number of issues concerning caching of data and code. Code caching can be performed with deployment technologies, but data caching it is still up to the application developer. Considering the transportation Midlet example, we need to set up a mechanism for synchronizing the user's local e-wallet, contained in the application, with the account held on the central server. Client validation logic might also need to refresh some parameters periodically – for example, we might want to update the currency exchange rate used to give customers an approximate transaction value before issuing them.

Rich clients need business logic locally, usually for data validation and other calculations on user-input data. Suppose we implement a loan calculator screen as part of a larger financial application, for example. This could instantly calculate

---

2.   See for example the discussion on Data Transfer Objects in Chapter 6.

the market interest rate of financial data as soon as we insert some amounts, without incurring the overhead of time-consuming connections.

> For more details about designing client/server communication, read the technical discussion in Chapter 6, or one of the many sources available on line and in the literature, such as (Fowler et al. 2003).

Common problems

There are several common problems related to rich client development. The most common solutions, in the form of OOP design patterns or simple best practices, were briefly discussed in Chapter 6, and will be shown in the various examples in this book. Figure 8.3 shows the choices needed when developing rich clients, together with the functional layer to which they belong.

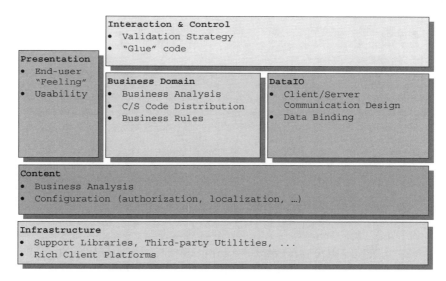

Figure 8.3   Common decisions for rich clients

The next section discusses a key aspect of rich client applications: the business domain data they handle.

8.3   Runtime data model

As well as the functional model discussed in the previous section, another useful model exists that is particularly apt for form-based, rich client applications. This model abstracts the data concepts that recur in all data-centric GUI applications. Data is the 'lymph' of rich client applications, and its management is essential for well-designed software.

We have data in a GUI that is first represented in a buffer within widgets, the *screen data state*. This data can be transferred in *business domain objects* (BDOs) for further processing, and eventually copied into other objects – or equivalent structures, such as XML files – for remote transfer as data transfer objects (DTOs).

Figure 8.4 shows this simple model of data representation within a GUI. Screen data state is the software interface to the user data with the remainder of the client application.

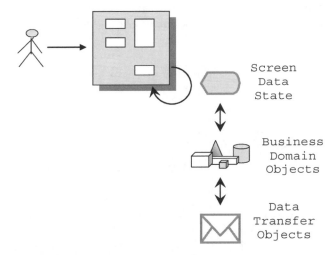

Screen
Data
State

Business
Domain
Objects

Data
Transfer
Objects

Figure 8.4   Runtime data model for rich clients

While they represent the same data for different functional purposes – end-user input-output, business processing, and remote communication respectively – these concepts help to clarify the implementation design.

> The concept of screen data state can lead directly to application of the Memento design pattern to the data backed by content widgets. This approach is useful in a number of cases. Suppose we are building a form in which a great deal of data needs to be input by users to complete a transaction. A requirement states that at any point users can close the screen, and all the data they input previously should reappear when they re-run the application in a new session to complete the transaction. A simple way to achieve this is to serialize the screen data state Java Bean locally and resume it as needed.

As shown in Figure 8.4, we refer to three different representations of the information manipulated by an application at runtime. These are essentially copies of the same data, represented in different parts of the implementation. The synchronization of these various representations is dictated by the GUI design between screen data state and business domain objects (for example at form commit) and by technical constraints over transferring information between BDO and DTO. For simple applications these three types of data can collapse into just one representation: you can use the same class as widgets' data state, domain data, and transfer object, all at the same time. Such a trick is quite limiting, though, and might work only on very simple implementations.

> Part of the J2EE community refers to DTO as *value objects*. This is misleading, because VOs have a different, more general meaning – their identity is based on their state, rather than on their usual object identity. VO examples are numbers, dates, strings, and currency values (Evans 2004).

(Fowler et al. 2003) distinguishes three types of data, depending on the runtime lifecycle. *Screen state* is the data that is deleted when a screen is disposed, so it chiefly corresponds to the screen data state. *Session data* lasts for a whole session, while *record state* is persistently recorded from session to session. Our approach here focuses on practical abstractions over implementation models, and not on the strict lifetime of data. Hence, for example, screen data state can survive even after the window is disposed – for example, because we dismissed a modal dialog, but we still have to access to its data – and business objects can be created for specific business logic computation, then dismissed along with a dialog.

> A common problem with data representation in Swing widgets comes from an incautious use of the default model classes. These models come with predefined data structures that may not adapt well to the given application needs. I am still amazed by how often I have seen the results of a database query copied into some form of default table model subclass, thus uselessly duplicating data and wasting precious client execution time. Developers doing this have applied the idioms learned in simple tutorial applications, in which a couple of rows are loaded into a dummy data collection, to real-world situations. They can be apprehensive of going outside what they learned in tutorials and tackling the complicated internals of Swing's widgets. This problem is less frequent with SWT and JFace, but it is still possible.

While SWT can be used without a predefined screen data state implementation – such as JFace – Swing can be used *only* with its MVC models. This means that

Swing models are the only available option for implementing the screen data state buffer.

Validation

We want to assess the validity of user input as soon as possible. From an implementation viewpoint, validating data early is good, because code can be more robust and simpler. From a usability viewpoint, the closer to its input invalid data is notified to users, the easier it will be for them to understand the problem.

The simple runtime data model introduced in the previous section is useful for discussing validation. Validation is basically a form of interaction and control based on user input and business logic. From an implementation viewpoint, it can be seen as defining *security perimeters* over the data within our application. When designing an application, we can:

- Decide to confine invalid data to screen data state only, so that business objects and DTO remain secure.
- Decide to evaluate some data as BDO.
- Delegate the evaluation directly to the server.

These security perimeters are enforced by means of widget interactions, data filters, notifications to users, and the like. If we adopt extensive testing, this security check becomes less critical, but validation and notification still remains important, because it has an impact on end users. If data has already been validated in the GUI, it relaxes the need to further validation later, for example on the server.

As with any design, the more quality we pour into it, the more it will cost. The cheapest form of validation is of course no validation. We offload all responsibility to the server, which eventually returns notification to the client, for example the list of fields that didn't match some business rule. This kind of interaction slows down a GUI terribly.

On the other hand, as soon as we start to perform non-trivial business validation on the client, we observe an increase in development complexity on the client side. This is because we now need business domain classes on the client side, causing a whole new host of implementation and design issues.

Let's expand the runtime data model in Figure 8.4 to better illustrate validation, to give that shown in Figure 8.5. This figure represents examples of different forms of validation that can occur during a rich client session.

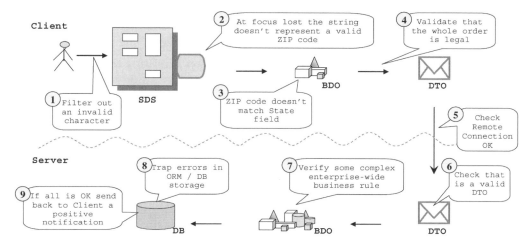

Figure 8.5   The journey of valid data from client to server

The figure shows the following examples of validations, in chronological order:

1.   The simplest validation – that with the narrowest data scope[3] – can be done on low-level events. For example, filtering out all invalid characters in a Zip code text field.

2.   Single values can be validated only when user data entry is completed. This is usually performed when the field loses the focus. Here the validation scope is a single field value.

3.   More complex or wide-ranging validations also need other values. For example, to assess if a Zip code matches a State field, even in an approximate way. This type of confirmation needs a number of values to be assessed.

4.   Before packaging data for transfer to the server, an overall validation can be performed, limited by the data and business logic available on the client.

5.   Further validation can be performed on the server connection, such as time out, reliability, and so on.

6.   When the DTO arrives at the server, a preliminary corroboration should always be performed, checking for (i) client authenticity, (ii) an eventual session consistency, and (iii) other forms of basic validation.

---

3.   Here scope does not refer to the lifecycle of objects, as in the EJB specification, but just to the amount of data needed to evaluate a specific business constraint.

7. After the DTO is transformed back in business domain objects, plus further data that is available only on the server, a complete business validation is possible – possibly repeating the evaluation of client-side business rules.

8. Another validation is performed when persisting the business data. Exceptions and errors are trapped and treated as a (non-business) negative validation result.

9. Finally, the validation result is returned to the client for notification to the user.

The situation in Figure 8.5 is only an example, of course. Real-world situations can be simpler or more complex. In some situations business validation is performed entirely on the server, while in other cases data is requested from other servers to perform some form of business validation on the client – consider for example a transaction that requires results from various Web services that we might want to validate on the client.

No matter how complex a validation rule may be, it is always composed of the following six elements:

- The triggering event: *when* a validation rule has to be started. Activation events could be:
  - A low-level GUI event, such as a selected checkbox, a keystroke, and so on.
  - Focus lost or other forms of entry field completion. In the good old days mainframes used the **Enter** key to validate user input data, and completion was so much simpler to detect as a result.
  - Screen completion. When committing a dialog, either for submission, disposal, and the like. This type is also referred to as 'deferred mode,' while the previous two are referred to as 'immediate mode.'
  - At client–server connection. Before connecting – usually an expensive operation – data can be safely assumed to be ready for evaluation.
  - Other events as well may trigger a validation process, depending on the given situation.

- The scope: *what* needs to be validated. That is, the data needed in order to assess the result. Scope can be:
  - Simple low-level interaction data. Imagine a function that takes as its input a single character and validates it against some built-in criteria.
  - A single field value. This usually needs a simple validation
  - Some values. This case is mostly handled in the business domain layer.
  - Internal and external data. For example, an application may need to invoke a remote Web service in order to retrieve data about a user's identity, to be used together with input data to validate the current operation.

- *Where* the rule is to be evaluated, whether on the client or on a remote server.

- The business rules that logically define the rationale behind the validation. Even a simple rule, like 'only digits,' is rooted in a business rule.

- The notification to the end user. This is an essential feedback that can take different forms, depending on the kind of conventions we have established:

    - If we establish the 'silent success' convention, nothing will be provided in the case of valid values.

    - In other designs we could provide feedback, such as a change in the value's formatting, to provide response to the user that the value was input correctly.

- Further reactions to the evaluation outcome. For example, other fields might change value, or other control rules could be triggered, enabling/disabling other widgets, and so on. Such forms of reactive validation have the purpose of ensuring a specific level of quality on the application data, hence defining the security perimeter.

Note how the data scope depends upon the domain situation at hand, while the 'when' of validation is decided by the designer.

> The distinction made in *Control issues* in Chapter 6 between business domain-dependent and non-business domain dependent logic also applies to validation.
>
> For example, disabling the **Submit** button in a form until at least one field has been modified – to save the bandwidth required to submit unchanged data to the server – is a form of validation that is not dependent on the given application domain, and can be implemented as part of a reusable, domain-independent infrastructure framework.

Figure 8.6 shows the interactions that occur among the various layers in the functional decomposition when a validation rule is triggered.

The interaction and control layer is notified by the triggering event, and assembles the scope data needed to evaluate business rules. The results are used to prepare notifications, depending on some reaction policy, for example 'always delete invalid data if focus lost.' Further reaction is still possible.

This is just a theoretical scenario. In real-world cases we would probably require validation at the business domain layer only for complex, abstract business rules. Trivial rules like 'field must be numeric-only' don't need such a complex organization.

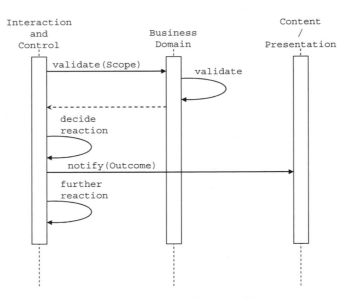

Figure 8.6   Sequence of interaction among functional layers

When seeking a validation framework to include in a project – to build, or to extend an existing one – we need to look for the following requirements in addition to the usual ones of good documentation, reliability, and so on:

- *Integration.* The framework should integrate well with other infrastructure code – data binding, and especially with business rules. Even if not mandatory, the ability to work with both Swing and SWT, for example through specialized presentation decorators for notification, would be an advantage.

- *Flexibility.* It should allow a wide range of validation strategies and designs. The ability to allow for a high-quality design of end-user notification is essential.

- *Extensibility.* It should be simple to extend, to provide unforeseen behavior or for handling particular cases (for example, validating JDNC components). For large projects, the ability to provide extensibility for higher-level validation behavior, within a more complex framework, is also important.

- *Non-intrusiveness.* The framework should not require special widget subclasses and other invasive design constraints. Ideally the framework should fit the interaction and control layer, as shown in Figure 8.2, without invading other functional areas.

- *Transparent remotization.* Whether we validate on the client or on the server shouldn't change the way the framework is used and the way in which it works. When validating remotely, latencies must be taken in account automatically. This feature allows for an easy distribution of business domain code along distribution tiers.

An important question is 'Do you really need explicit validation support?' In simple cases, and for early development iterations, we can provide a good GUI without extra machinery. Criteria for adopting explicit validation support in our implementation are:

- We already have a formalized representation of business rules, even if on a functional decomposition basis only. That is, business rules are still represented informally but systematically in our code, for example as a collection of static methods.

- We are going to build more than a few screens that need a non-trivial amount of control.

- The development team is not homogeneous and/or we need to enforce fine-grained systematic development patterns. We are outsourcing part of the development, or we want to impose uniform development in a large team.

The user side

Our discussion so far has been mostly technical. Unfortunately, the trickiest issues in validation lie in usability. To begin with, reactions should be designed uniformly. While an improvised implementation of validation (if thoroughly tested) may pass unnoticed by the end user, an improvised validation interaction design certainly won't.

In practice, we might be forced to validate some data entirely on the client, because we have all the required information there, while in other parts of the same application we may need to send it to the server and wait for the outcome. Our GUI design should manage this heterogeneous form of validation in such as way that it provides a predictable and reliable experience to end user. This implies, among other things, that we must provide a clear indication in the GUI of those areas where validation is going to be performed remotely. Notification plays an important role in ensuring a high-quality user experience. If the user doesn't know why the focus cannot leave a field, or why the filled-in values have errors, the whole experience can be frustrating.

Too high level of reactivity can be confusing, such as fields that change value in reaction to other events too often, and it may be expensive to provide uniformly throughout the whole application. Such details are never a purely technical decision. Customers are always eager to automate data entry as much as possible, even by devising less-than-usable GUI designs. Our job is also to say 'no' to customers when we have to.

Even little hints can make an enormous difference for the user. Figure 8.7 shows some hints that reveal the data affordances[4] allowed by two fields, a date and a currency field. This speeds up interaction by preventing users from making erroneous inputs.

Figure 8.7   Providing visual hints as a form of preemptive validation

> Visual or interaction clues help users to understand *why* data is not valid: they are part of the notification strategy. If the user knows that a given text control is a currency field and they entered an asterisk, they could probably figure out the reason for a validation error.

Another common example of signaling explicit validation constraints preemptively is the use of mandatory fields, which are illustrated by the dialog in Figure 8.9 on page 342.

Given the double nature of validation – the user side and the software side – its careful design is important from early development iterations. During development it is useful to think about intermediate validation strategies, and to evaluate them with users. Changing sensitive interaction issues such as validation from iteration to iteration can be frustrating for end users.

The overall validation policy should be defined in terms of a general objective. Completion time or data integrity could be possible objectives. In specific situations we might want the user to be able to work as smoothly as possible, always providing correct values when possible, while adjusting entries to match meaningful values, providing default values when possible, automatic completion with previous input, and so on.

In other cases the input data may be too important to make use of default values or automatic adjustments, and we might have to slow down the user's interaction, using an analog of speed bumps in the GUI, and implement a stricter validation policy. We might even want to be intentionally cryptic for security reasons. For example, while filling in a bank account transfer operation with codes that don't

---

4.   See Chapter 2.

match, we might want to issue a generic error instead of being more specific and by so doing, reveal sensitive data.

The general objective should be defined in terms of the user population. Most of the time Java rich clients are built mainly for repetitive users. In such cases visual and interaction smoothness must be balanced against the clarity and completeness of information.

We provided general advice for form-based GUIs in Chapter 2. Here we briefly recap the main points from a validation perspective, referring to Chapter 2 for more details.

- Provide clear, consistent, and visually non-intrusive validation signals:
  - Provide a hint to the data affordances allowed by a field, as shown in the example in Figure 8.7.
  - Signal mandatory fields, using an asterisk in the field label, a border decoration or the like. Don't provide signals for optional fields.
- Guide user input as much as possible, but without getting in the way of users' work. Consider the investment in creating your own widget support.
- Provide meaningful feedback. Validation errors, warnings and status should be devised early in the development process, so that inconsistencies across the application and costly modifications can be avoided. Enabling or disabling portions of the GUI can be a valuable form of interaction. Try to minimize the cognitive load on users by providing local feedback, instead of messages like:

```
Wrong value on <address> field
```

Don't forget that you have full control of the GUI in a rich client!

Validation should also harmonize with the local visual conventions. This will save development time and provide a uniform experience to end users. For example, when building an Eclipse plug-in, we should always use Eclipse's built-in validation design, as shown in Figure 8.8.

In the Eclipse GUI guidelines, validation is performed as much as possible in immediate mode, and feedback is provided at the top of the dialog. This notification mechanism, simple to implement for developers, is fine for repetitive users, the main target of the Eclipse user population, but can be a little uncomfortable for occasional users, who might have to scan the GUI to find the package field that happens to cause the problem.

When to validate and notify

Ideally data should be validated as early as possible, so that users have the lowest possible cognitive burden in associating notification with their input. Validating and notifying data as early as possible means that, when the data scope is limited to values already known, the best moment to validate a piece of information is immediately after the user has completed data input.

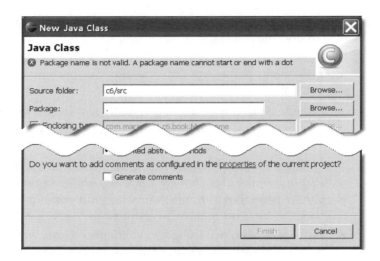

Figure 8.8   Eclipse GUI as an example of local validation style

Three strategies are usually used for starting validation and subsequent notification:

- *During user input.* As the user enters data, it is validated constantly, even if incorrect values are typed before completion of input. This is the strategy chosen by Eclipse – see the dialog in Figure 8.8, for example. This requires constant invocation of validation methods, which can be a costly overhead in complex Swing forms. If validation involves expensive calculations (in time or resources) this method should be avoided. From a GUI design perspective, immediate validation should be unintrusive as possible – we don't want to disturb the user with bells and whistles while they are entering data that is only temporarily invalid.

- *At user input termination.* This usually corresponds to the user leaving the field (on the 'focus lost' event). This is cheaper, but it might involve some subtleties, as explained in *The hidden pitfalls of validation* on page 342.

- *Deferred to a given event.* Examples might be form submission to the server, or when the user presses a button. The farther the notification from the input, both in time and space, the harder it is for the user to correctly interpret it. For this reason deferred notification is usually best performed with local, extensive clues.

How and where notify

A number of approaches can be used throughout a rich client application for notifying users of the outcome of input validation. Also in this case, consistency is a very important factor for an effective notification strategy. Some common forms of notification are:

- *Final summaries*. In deferred notification it can be useful to recap a form's data before submission. This approach is rarely used in rich client applications, however, as developers can use more powerful and direct communication.

- *A notification area*. This consists of a fixed area of the screen that is devoted to communicate with users, for example a status bar. This technique makes it possible to convey more information than with other approaches, and can be a good choice for applications designed for occasional users. In some cases navigation cues can be useful, for example signaling the notification information (text message plus icon) of the current focus. The major drawback of this approach is the load of keeping the notification area updated, and shortening the link between the focus and the notification area.

- *Local notifications*, done with:
  - *Icons*. Icons are a simple yet effective notification means that is better suited for repetitive users. Be aware that people with visual deficiencies may have problems with icons that are too small.
  - *Text messages*. Labels beside fields can convey notification information and constraints. The problem with this approach is that it can be expensive in terms of screen real estate.
  - *Colors and other adornments*. Special borders, background colors or other visual signals can notify the user of the outcome of input validation.

- *Control*. Disabling widgets after validation can be useful, but it needs an expressive notification support, otherwise occasional users can find it hard to understand the reasons for specific reactions to their input.

To simplify our discussion, we assume that validation and notification are close in time. In some cases this may not be the case.

Figure 8.9 shows some examples of local notifications.

For brevity Figure 8.9 shows various notification styles together, which explains its confusing and inelegant appearance. The figure shows examples of various local notification strategies:

- Providing an icon, in the case of the **Postal Code** field.
- Using label adornments such as color, or font style, to signal mandatory fields or invalid values, and so on.

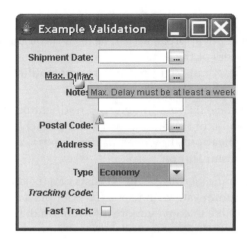

Figure 8.9   Local notification examples

- Using tooltips or hyperlink-like labels to provide more information to occasional users about why their input value is not valid.

- Supplying borders or background colors to communicate notification result, or that a given field is mandatory.

> Carry out at least a basic but effective usability test with your end users, even if you are adopting a supposedly harmless validation design, perhaps provided as the default by a third-party library. Colors or other adornments such as borders can be hard to notice – 1 in 12 people have some sort of color deficiency[5] – or be too visually overbearing for repetitive users.

The hidden pitfalls of validation

Just because a specific GUI technology allows a specific feature, it doesn't necessarily mean that it should be employed in a GUI design. This applies equally to validation. In this section we discuss a concrete case of misuse of technology in implementing validation in a rich client application.

There is an interesting quirk in Swing's validation support – one of several – that highlights some of the complexities involved in handling low-level events, specifically focus-lost events, and validation at the same time. Swing provides the class `InputVerifier` to allow developers to validate user input before the focus leaves a widget. Using this mechanism in the case of invalid data, we could restore an old value, or we could force the focus back to the field to allow valid

---

5.   Source http://www.iamcal.com/toys/colors/stats.php.

data to be input. When we choose this latter approach, though, we have an additional problem – users remain trapped in fields that have invalid values.

Suppose we have a date field that forces users to type in a valid date before leaving the field. In the case of an invalid date, users cannot leave the widget. Clearly this is clumsy GUI behavior. Users cannot close a dialog, as this would involve moving the focus from the date field to push the **Cancel** button, or to click on the **x** icon, or do almost anything else before entering a valid value.

To solve this problem in a general way, a specific method was added to the `JCom-ponent` class: `setVerifyInputWhenFocusTarget()` defines when a component can circumvent an `InputVerifer` block on focus. Thus, by setting the `verifyInputWhenFocusTarget` property of the **Cancel** button to `true`, users can close a dialog even when trapped in a field with an invalid date value.

Unfortunately, this still doesn't solve the issue, for a number of reasons. A particularly nasty one is the following. Imagine that an indecisive user clicks on the **Cancel** button without releasing the mouse button and moving the mouse pointer away from the **Cancel** button. The **Cancel** button will not be triggered and the dialog will not close. The focus is now transferred to the **Cancel** button, thus escaping the block on invalid values and crippling the entire validation schema.

The bottom line is to avoid being trapped in complex situations. If we observe a steady increase in complexity in our implementation without any real benefit, we should question our previous choices and be prepared to lose some work instead of heading towards an increasingly convoluted situation.

> In this example the mistake was to block user input of invalid values in the first place. Things can get even more complicated such an application is released without extensive testing. Users are now accustomed to a blocking validation approach, and it becomes a political issue to change the data validation interaction throughout the whole GUI. This is a typical case in which developers might blame perverse end users, or the toolkit, rather than themselves.

8.4 The cake-ordering application, the XP way

This section introduces an example of a simple rich client GUI developed with iterative design practices that follows the Extreme Programing (XP) methodology introduced in Chapter 1. Our intention is to illustrate common issues that arise when following an iterative development approach to GUI development.

Our customer is the Cake-o-Matic company. This company makes custom cakes to order that are then delivered to clients. They order their cakes through a call center. Phone operators use a rich client application to place orders with the factory and to organize delivery. The application's end users are call-center operators – frequent, but possibly unskilled, users – who will use the GUI while interacting by phone with Cake-o-Matic's clients.

Setting up the first Iteration

The first iteration will take two weeks and will implement the first story, the placement of a simplified delivery order on the server. In an Agile approach we focus constantly on the specific practises discussed in Chapter 1. Figure 8.10 shows the simple application decomposed in its functional parts. For the purposes of this example, we adopt the theoretical functional decomposition as the layering architecture for code and tests as well.

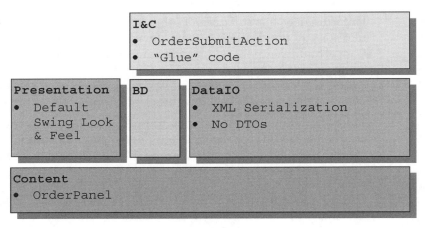

Figure 8.10   Functional parts for a first iteration

Following an XP approach, the first iteration of the application will be the simplest thing that could possibly work. There will be no business domain layer at all, we provide no custom presentation, and data IO will be limited to plain XML serialization. The runtime data model will be even simpler. There will be no DTO, nor a business domain model. We avoid all validation.

An occasional misunderstanding is that following an Agile approach means focusing on implementation, then deriving the GUI design accordingly. This is a completely wrong assumption. GUI design should always drive the implementation. Iterative development is just a mechanism for implementing GUI applications effectively. Considering development costs during design, as in the cost-driven design approach described in Chapter 3, is part of GUI design, not of its subsequent implementation.

Defining the testing strategy

It remains to define the overall test strategy for the project. We know from Chapter 5 that we need to find the best mix of two main options:

- Testing through the GUI (TTG). This is slow and somewhat coarse-grained when compared with traditional unit testing. We need TTG at least because it's needed for automated acceptance testing – another useful XP practice.

- Testing bypassing the GUI. This is faster than testing through the GUI, and we are going to adopt it extensively in our project.

As we pointed out in Chapter 5, TTG is useful for writing acceptance tests – ideally created by the customer, but we can provide them with some support – for testing interaction and control, although we won't have this at least until the second iteration, for end-to-end coarse testing, and for all those tests that necessarily involve the GUI. Non-GUI testing (such as plain unit testing à la xUnit) it is required for Agile approaches such as XP – continuous refactoring and integration, TDD, and so on.

> In a real world scenario, with such a simple application, manual TTG would probably make more sense than using the various testing tools we are going to use in our example. To illustrate the chosen development approach, we opt for a fully-automated testing strategy. Chapter 5 discusses more considerations for general cases.

To highlight the differences in the two approaches to testing:

- Unit testing can be performed thousands of times for each integration.

- TTG is much slower, running at users' speed – open a dialog, click here, insert text there, wait for the result to appear here, and so on.

The first approach would be much better than TTG, but unfortunately it is not exhaustive enough for GUI testing. We may want to use TTG selectively for automatic acceptance tests, interaction tests – for example testing our interaction and control rules with the most extreme data/interaction sequence we can think of. We may also want to use it for generic end-to-end testing, such as inserting some data, submitting to the server and check the final result, and profiling – an often overlooked aspect of GUI testing that can be fully assessed only with a TTG approach. (Imagine for example a GUI in which we want to perform hundreds of transactions and probe the inner state of the client JRE, for example to look at memory allocation or other properties on the server side.)

> To achieve a pervasive testing mechanism, one could resort to extending the underlying toolkit to provide automatic test behavior. Given its flexibility, Swing is particularly well-suited for this technique. For example, we could register a custom `ComponentUI` factory for testing presentation details, or extending one of the many default factories such as that for `Formatter` classes.

Content first

Content is the base of any rich client application. Beginning iterative development from content implementation is a simple approach – we just translate use story GUI prototypes directly into code, thereby lowering risk as long as we validate our work with the customer, and providing a basis for all subsequent work. Working with the customer results in the sketch GUI shown in Figure 8.11.

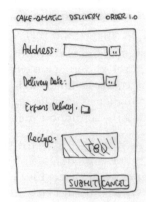

Figure 8.11   GUI prototype for the delivery order panel

Our first step is to implement it. Using a TDD approach, we start with our first test case[6]:

```
public void testWidgetsExists() throws Exception {
  DeliveryPanel dp = new DeliveryPanel();
  Assert.assertTrue(PrivateAccessor.getField(dp,"recipeDesc")instan-
ceof JTextField);
  Assert.assertTrue(PrivateAccessor.getField(dp,"deliveryDate")instan-
ceof JTextField);
  Assert.assertTrue(PrivateAccessor.getField(dp,"expressDelivery")
instanceof JCheckBox);
  Assert.assertTrue(PrivateAccessor.getField(dp,"pickUpDelivery")
instanceof JCheckBox);
  Assert.assertTrue(PrivateAccessor.getField(dp,"submitButton")
instanceof JButton);
  Assert.assertTrue(PrivateAccessor.getField(dp,"cancelButton")
instanceof JButton);
}
```

---

6. This first step is probably too big: our objective here is not to introduce XP practices (there are many books about that) but to show common issues when adopting XP practices for effective GUI development.

This test fixture was written with JUnit and the JUnit-Addons suite, which provides the `PrivateAccessor` class for testing private members and methods. Clearly this test fails, because class `DeliveryPanel` does not exist yet. Nevertheless, it is defining the content of the application, because it mentions the class `DeliveryPanel`, its intended widgets and their types. For brevity, we will skip testing the `DeliveryPanel` class.

After a brief discussion between our two programmers, they decide to go with private members for widgets. As with every beginning, we are full of good intentions and we definitely want to keep the widgets for our forms private.

> This choice gives us the chance to discuss the possibility of testing properties on private methods and members. This is not regarded as an orthodox approach, otherwise the class `PrivateAccessor` wouldn't be part of an optional package. From encapsulation and data hiding dogma, we know that modifying the inner (private) behavior of a class shouldn't necessitate rewriting its tests. On the contrary, if we need to access such private members only for testing, would it be wise to make them publicly available through accessors, thus cluttering `DeliveryPanel` without providing any real application-level behavior? The two programmers could go on discussing this issue in length: "Application and testing behavior are at the same level... this way production code can be in a separated package from tests... once you have the accessor methods you might want to use them for other purposes... but this violates Agile methods' simplicity principle..." and so on. This is important, because such a dilemma underlies implicitly the importance we want to give to unit testing within our GUI development. A whole school of thought asserts the need to make unit testing drive any implementation, especially complex ones like GUIs. We will return to this important and often overlooked aspect of GUI development later.

Our work now focuses in implementing the `DeliveryPanel` in order to make the test pass.

We quickly write the following class implementation:

```
public class DeliveryPanel extends JPanel {
    private JFormattedTextField deliveryDate;
    private JTextField recipeDesc;
    private JCheckBox expressDelivery;
    private JCheckBox pickUpDelivery;
    private JButton submitButton;
    private JButton cancelButton;
}
```

To our surprise, we still don't pass the test. Fields need to be instantiated. We therefore provide a constructor:

```
public DeliveryPanel() {
  deliveryDate = new JFormattedTextField();
  pickUpDelivery = new JCheckBox();
  recipeDesc = new JTextField();
  expressDelivery = new JCheckBox();
  submitButton = new JButton("Submit");
  cancelButton = new JButton("Cancel");
}
```

This time we get the green light. Now basic content is secured. What's next?

We would like to have some concrete, reassuring feedback – that is, we'd like to have something that we can see working and make us feel good. We want to put our widgets onto the panel. This will also serve as a basis for writing acceptance tests.

Laying out widgets is not that difficult, but how should we test it? The easy way would be to prepare a clever unit test fixture, but this cannot test our layout visually. Testing for properties within the layout class leads to brittle test code. If we change the layout class or some layout parameter, as is more than likely in future when we refine the details, we would need to change the test as well.

On the other hand, we can use a GUI testing framework to define an all-*visual* test. The developers opt for this choice. They use JFCUnit, an extension of JUnit – although in this example tools are not important, as we are focusing on concepts. We would like to express the visual properties of the widgets in Figure 8.11 in a form of automated test. We therefore define the following JFCUnit fixture:

```
public void testWidgetsVisible() throws Exception {
    NamedComponentFinder finder = new NamedComponentFinder(JCompo-
nent.class, "cancelButton");
    JButton cancelButton = ( JButton ) finder.find( dp, 0);
    assertNotNull( "Could not find cancel button", cancelButton);

    finder.setName( "submitButton" );
    JButton submitButton = ( JButton ) finder.find( dp, 0);
    assertNotNull( "Could not find Submit button", submitButton);

    finder.setName( "recipeDesc" );
    JTextField recipeDesc = ( JTextField ) finder.find( dp, 0 );
    assertNotNull( "Could not find the recipeDesc TextField", recipe-
Desc);
    assertEquals( "recipeDesc field is empty", "", recipeDesc.getText(
));
    ...
}
```

We can make a couple of observations from this. First of all, we are merely asserting that the widgets are found in the container panel, and that they are empty. Then, there is a lot of machinery for interfacing with the Swing toolkit. This time we went closer to reality, as this test is stronger than the previous ones. We observe that the previous test (JUnit) took 0.1 seconds to execute. This one takes 0.95 seconds. Clearly, we expect a proportional increase in time consumption as the number and the size of tests grows. But we can also observe that the tests are largely overlapping.

When we launch the test, it fails, complaining that it cannot find widgets, despite the fact that we created a frame in the fixture's `setup()` method and showed the panel properly.

The reason is that Swing requires widgets to be named, using the `setName()` method, for the finder facility to work.

So our `DeliveryPanel` constructor becomes:

```
public DeliveryPanel() {
   deliveryDate = new JFormattedTextField();
   deliveryDate.setName("deliveryDate");
   pickUpDelivery = new JCheckBox();
   pickUpDelivery.setName("pickUpDelivery");
   recipeDesc = new JTextField("");
   recipeDesc.setName("recipeDesc");
   expressDelivery = new JCheckBox();
   submitButton = new JButton("Submit");
   submitButton.setName("submitButton");
   cancelButton = new JButton("Cancel");
   cancelButton.setName("cancelButton");
}
```

The Model View Presenter (MVP) pattern is an approach to better decouple the view from the rest of the implementation. With the valuable advent of extensive, early testing, MVP also became useful as a way to test a GUI by bypassing its graphical 'skin.'

To build really effective testing tools and GUI technologies with TDD in mind, we wouldn't need systematically to adopt MVP as a workaround for easy testing: unfortunately this is not only the case with current GUI technologies. Decoupling and structuring GUIs is of course beneficial and a valuable best practice, apart perhaps from simple cases, and MVP can be very useful.

One question remains unanswered: how to balance the two types of testing approaches in the most effective way for Java applications?

Testing overhead can be seen as a long-term investment in code. Simple forms of testing can escalate into testing practices that influence the structure of production code heavily, but ultimately what makes things work well is a deep understanding and faith in the approach, rather than a list of 'gotchas' such as 'we need to do extensive testing in our project.'

Getting back to work

We need TTG only for interaction and control, and content and presentation – which rarely needs to be tested, as discussed in Chapter 5. Business domain, data IO and some parts of other layers can be tested with non-GUI practices.

Our team decide to continue using both approaches. Non-GUI testing will be used as much as possible, because it is much more fine-grained, faster to develop and run, and code coverage can be assessed easily. TTG, on the other hand, is needed for testing the whole application and for GUI-only details.

Now that we have tested our simple content, we can write the acceptance test for this simple user interface. To do so, we would like to have an easy-to-use tool, because writing acceptance tests is often done by the customer under the XP approach. For this simple example we can still use JFCUnit. We could arrange for the customer to record the acceptance tests, for example in an XML file, or we can record them in association with our customers.

JFCUnit shows its limits here. Acceptance tests don't look good as JUnit-like Java code, and they look even worse as bloated XML files. We need to resort to another tool, as discussed in Chapter 11 in the GUI test tools section.

Our next move in moving from the GUI to the server is to focus on data. Rich clients are discrete data-driven applications, so we now focus on designing the data structure.

Data second

The next step is creating the data that will back up our content. Here we have a number of choices available: we choose the one that seems the simplest and provides enough feedback. We define the data in a 1:1 fashion from the data we represented in the content layer, then we implement the server support for it, deliberately ignoring any additional behavior or data so far. Our objective is to demonstrate content data moving back and forth between the client and the server.

We want to define a plain Java Bean – sometimes called a Plain Old Java Object, or 'POJO' – that holds content data within the GUI. We can think of it as screen data state (SDS), thus replacing the default Swing models built into the panel so far, or as a data transfer object – it doesn't really make much difference at the moment. We opt for an SDS, part of the content layer. We define its structure by means of a test, and we work on creating the class to make this test pass. Speeding up our iterative development a little, we don't show these steps.

We are provided with the class in Figure 8.12.

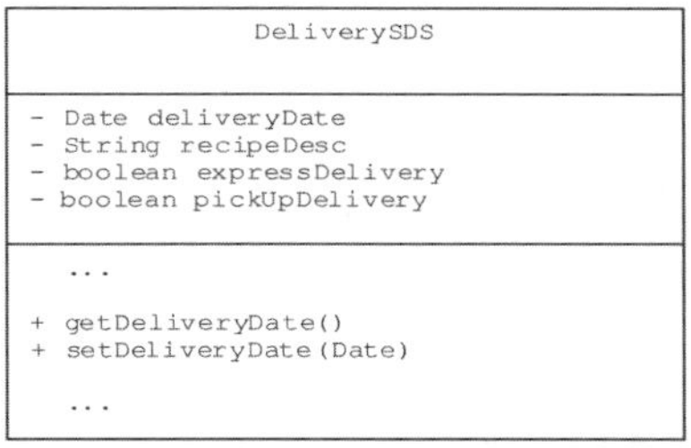

```
                       DeliverySDS

  - Date deliveryDate
  - String recipeDesc
  - boolean expressDelivery
  - boolean pickUpDelivery

    ...

  + getDeliveryDate()
  + setDeliveryDate(Date)

    ...
```

Figure 8.12   Delivery panel data transfer object

It's now time to bind the data to the content. We decide to use the JGoodies data binding framework, which is based on the MVP and Value Model patterns[7] and serves as a basis for the Spring RCP implementation.

Before we even think about the way to implement this binding, we should first focus on expressing it in a unit test. We want to bind the content to a POJO using a support library. Of course, we could write copy methods that copy values into the data holder and vice-versa, or even automate them in a general utility class that uses reflection, for example. We prefer to use this approach to show a more realistic but simple scenario.

No matter how we do it, we need some specialized behavior that performs the binding and some test on it. Let's work first on the route from user to data. This is a tentative test fixture:

```
DeliverySDS sds = new DeliverySDS();
DeliveryPanel dp = new DeliveryPanel();
dp.setDeliveryData(sds);
testWidgetsExists();
```

We can now work on the `setDeliveryData` method in `DeliveryPanel`.

Our idea is to bind the data holder object to the content while honoring the layered architecture in Figure 8.2, which we decided to use as the reference architecture for this example. For DTO, we will use the same SDS class. This separates the two layers (data IO depending upon content). We decide for simplicity to use a plain `Object` instead of the SDS class: this will ease subsequent refactorings, but we now lack compile-time checks, especially when field names are changed.

---

7.   See Chapter 6.

Anyway, we are confident in our tests for this kind of control – that's why we use them so extensively, after all. This results in the following code in the `Delivery-Panel` class:

```
public setDeliveryData(Object data) {
  this.deliveryData = data;
  PropertyAdapter pickupVM =
      new PropertyAdapter(deliveryData, "pickupDelivery", true);
  Bindings.bind(pickUpDelivery, pickupVM);
  ...
}
```

In the previous code we only provided one example of field binding, to keep the code short. The JGoodies binding framework needs an adapter object (which works as a Value Model) for adapting a given Swing widget's model to a generic POJO, the `deliveryData Object`. The `true` value as a parameter passed in the constructor of the `PropertyAdapter` object will make it actively reactive to change events. In this way we have bound the content panel to the related SDS class.

What are the implications of the fact that the data holder now *is* our SDS object? What happened to the default Swing models built in each widget we created with an empty constructor? Here is the implementation of the method `Bindings.bind()` for Boolean values in the JGoodies framework:

```
public static void bind(JCheckBox checkBox, ValueModel valueModel) {
  boolean enabled = checkBox.getModel().isEnabled();
  checkBox.setModel(new ToggleButtonAdapter(valueModel));
  checkBox.setEnabled(enabled);
}
```

That is – via a newly-created Swing model that is specialized for representing values as of the Value Model pattern – data is directly bound to the SDS. We still have Swing models, but they are connected dynamically to our data source. In order for this mechanism to work, though, we need some event-plumbing machinery in the data holder, such as methods for adding and removing listeners and firing events. The simplest way to achieve this is to make `DeliverySDS` extend the `Model` class provided by this data binding library.

Before moving on, one of the developers started discussing the use of the accessor method for setting the data holder. He found it disturbing, arguing that a `setScreenDataState()` method, used to substitute the model, was useless or even dangerous now that such an automatic binding is established, and that only the constructor method should be provided. After a brief discussion they refactored the panel class in order to have only a data constructor. This choice may turn out to be too inflexible, but they decide to provide the data class at construction time only.

The `DeliverySDS` class now serves as a screen data state via the Swing adapters provided by the JGoodies binding framework. We don't yet have a business domain class.

An alternative and simpler solution that avoids using third-party data binding libraries would be manually to synchronize the SDS and the panel, thus making the `DeliverySDS` class a plain POJO extending `Object`.

Commands third

In our use story, after users fill in the order form, they have to submit the order to the server. We need to add commands for this to our GUI. For content, we add the two standard buttons **Submit** and **Cancel**. We use a content factory, part of the content layer of a utility library, that provides standard buttons out of `AbstractActions`:

```
public static JButton[] createButtons(AbstractAction...
    action) {
```

It is responsibility of the interaction and control layers to integrate all the individual parts. In our case we bind the buttons to the related commands[8]. In the interaction and control layer we define the class `SubmitOrderAction` and the class `CancelOrderAction` for the commands.

For further details on the Command pattern, see *Representing user actions with the Command pattern* in Chapter 6.

A first version of the submit command is shown below, skipping TDD tests for brevity:

```
public static class SubmitOrderAction extends CtrAction<DeliveryPanel>
{
    public SubmitOrderAction(){
super("Submit");
    }
    public void actionPerformed(ActionEvent e) {
Application.server().submitOrder(panel.getData());
    }
}
```

This code assumes that we have a class `Application` that centralizes utility access – so far, only the remote access to the server application – and initializes the whole application. We also have the class `CtrAction` that subclassed `AbstractAction`, for generic support of commands that need to operate on

---

8.   The Command design pattern centralizes graphics and control together, which works against our extremely articulated layering scheme. See (Gamma et al. 1994) or (Buschmann et al. 1996).

content objects. For more details of this, see the source code provided with the book.

Clearly, being our first step, the naïve implementation of the **Submit** command shown in the code above is limited:

- Error handling is not defined – what happens, for example, if the server is down?

- The GUI doesn't support asynchronous submissions: the application will completely freeze until the results are available to the client. Despite the fact that we might want to enforce this behavior, because users could not do anything useful anyway in this interval, we always need to provide some basic form of asynchronous behavior for long operations, at least to allow the user to abort the process if desired.

- No feedback is provided to the user: the return value from the remote connection is not used. It is likely that a mere `boolean` value for success/ failure will not be enough to describe a remote operation outcome in the future, but we are working iteratively and we need to keep things simple at this stage!

- There is no basic low-level Control. If we have an asynchronous remote invocation, we need to disable the submit action, thus disabling all the bound widgets, otherwise the user could click the **Submit** button again, potentially invoking the same transaction many times.

Despite the fact that all these issues are important, perhaps the most delicate one regards multithreading. This aspect, specific to Control, needs to be addressed early in the implementation, because it can be costly to upgrade a non-trivial code base with some tens of remote commands or more.

We need a mock object[9] for the proxy server class that simulates latencies and server failures, plus some good tests that will assess whether our code is performing as expected with respect to multithreading.

Defining the tests is not difficult as long as we have a library for unit testing that support time constraint test decorators, provided that we expect the instruction after the command execution to be executed without any substantial delay. The interesting point arises when devising the simplest functional multithreading scheme.

---

9. Mock objects replace real objects with mock implementations that are used only for ease of testing. Mock objects are widely employed in unit testing, because they help to mask unnecessary factors during testing, helping developers to focus on the specific aspects to be tested.

We now change the natural order of iterative steps followed so far to get to this important issue quickly.

Implementing robust commands

Dealing effectively with time-consuming operations that might have non-predictable completion time, such as a remote request, requires some precautions when working with single-threaded toolkits like Swing and SWT. Here are the main issues:

- Operations that take more than a few seconds to complete should be handled in a separate thread, to maintain the GUI's responsiveness.

- Such threads should be handled judiciously. Most of the time we don't need to fork many new threads at once in a GUI, but simply to keep the main event dispatch thread (EDT) working while one or two other worker threads are performing some specialized task on behalf of the user.

  This seems to be a perfect scenario for the Executor pattern[10]. This technique essentially applies a simple indirection layer to shield the developer from thread execution details. This allows the developer to focus on writing the `Runnable` at hand (that is, the task) while leaving its execution details to a specialized class that can implement an optimized thread pool privately, a simple task queue, or a simple thread fork.

- Tasks have a common lifecycle:

  1. They are forked from the EDT on a separate thread.

  2. At a certain point in their execution they may produce intermediate results. The thread now needs to interact with the rest of the GUI. Because the task's code is currently executing on a thread different than the EDT, it needs to invoke the synchronizing utility methods: Swing's `invoke-Later()` or SWT's `asyncExec()`.

  3. Eventually the task concludes its work, producing a final result. This situation is similar to point 2. The task now interacts with the EDT via synchronous utility methods, `invokeandWait()` for Swing and SWT's `syncExec()` for SWT.

  4. The worker thread is no longer needed. All its resources are freed, and testing should ensure this. The thread might be recycled or garbage-collected, depending on the Executor's policy.

- During the whole of their lifecycle tasks can be interrupted at any moment. A server connection can time out, or a user can change their mind. Before or immediately after halting a task, we should take care to switch the GUI

---

10. See http://www.cse.buffalo.edu/~crahen/papers/Executor.Pattern.pdf

Control state from 'work in progress' to '[no] work done.' For example, in the delivery panel, when the **Cancel** button is pressed, the **Submit** button becomes re-enabled and the dialog's content becomes active again, as if nothing had ever happened.

This discussion applies equally to Swing and SWT applications.

In general we can think of the possible scenario:

1. A command object is invoked by user interaction.

2. The operation is started in a worker thread separated from the EDT so that the GUI remains responsive. From a GUI design viewpoint, we need to address the 'command in execution' Control state in our GUI.

3. The result is returned to the user, represented as an `OperationResult` object. Such instances are fed to a `VisualDecorator` instance, which notifies to the user of the outcome of the transaction in a meaningful way. The outcome could be nothing – in the case of success, we just dismiss the dialog – or some visual decorations, for example to notify validation errors, or some Control behavior (perhaps because we don't have enough credit in our bank account, so that a **Purchase** button – yet to be implemented – gets disabled). From a GUI design perspective, we are handling the 'command executed' state.

4. The application implementation usually returns to the state just before step 1. This is important from an implementation viewpoint. After a command is concluded, all involved objects should be released apart from notification graphics or other meaningful data. Testing should aim to check for a fully restored situation.

Handling the operation in progress

When the worker thread is ready to go we are left with the task of providing feed-back to the user. This can be done in several ways:

*   Enforce the 'work in progress' state of the dialog or the whole GUI by changing the mouse cursor and/or the state of the **Cancel** button.

*   Disable all the content in the dialog, or put a semi-transparent panel on it, or some other visual hint that signals to the user that the window is 'busy' at the moment[11].

*   Provide some simple means of controlling the time-consuming operation. Usually the same button that is used to dismiss a dialog can be used to stop its operation as well, but in this case the operation is interrupted and the

---

11. This solution applies to communications where the final result is needed to conclude the operation. Suppose you have a text chat application in which, once submitted, you don't need to know what happened to a message: in this case there is no need to freeze the GUI.

dialog is not dismissed. Clicking the **Cancel** button a second time would dispose the dialog[12]. Alternatively, the dismissing button in the dialog, shown in the top-right corner of Figure 8.13, will close the dialog and stop the task, possibly after a confirmation dialog.

Figure 8.13 shows these steps visually, and uses the solution of recursively disabling all the widgets within the content area of the dialog. This solution is visually less appealing that using a semi-transparent overlay panel.

Figure 8.13   Providing visual hints for remote communication

At this point our cake delivery GUI is roughly equivalent to a Web application, in that we have content, a limited form of command execution, and no business logic.

Closing the loop with the server

For the sake of this exercise, we assume that we already have a J2EE server where all domain logic is implemented: all we have to do is to connect to it. We assume that our client will interface with a Session Facade instance – that is, an application of the Facade design pattern for J2EE in which coarse-grained session beans hide server-side fine-grained business objects (Alur, Crupi and Malks 2001), (Marinescu 2002).

The next step would be to represent this behavior in our architecture, providing a stub implementation for the server application.

---

12. Note that this design slightly overloads the **Cancel** button's semantics, creating a potentially tricky state-dependent interaction (see Chapter 2) in the GUI's design.

8.5   Summary

This chapter discussed some details of the development of form-based rich client applications with Java. We focused on the following issues:

*   Common implementation challenges and software design choices for Java rich clients, discussed by means of the functional decomposition proposed in Chapter 1.

*   A simple runtime data model that applies well to form-based rich clients.

*   The design of an effective validation strategy for rich client applications.

*   An example iterative development that abstracted from the particular situation/technology to discuss general and common issues in rich client practical development, such as testing approaches, multithreading management, and so on.

9   Web-Based User Interfaces

This chapter introduces user interfaces delivered within a Web browser using Java technology. This covers a wide array of options, spanning classic server-side markup-based Java technologies such as JSP, JSF, Servlets, and so on, Java applets, and other Web-based GUI technologies. We will also consider technologies for Web GUIs that are not strictly Java, such as Javascript, XMLHttpRequest, and others, because they can be generated by a server-side Java application alone. In general Java can be used in a wide number of different combinations, both on the client and on the server, so covering all the possible alternatives would make the discussion needlessly detailed.

A brief discussion of Web GUI[1] design is provided for consistency with other chapters book that discuss analogous topics for different platforms, such as wireless devices and the desktop.

The chapter is structured as follows:

9.1, An overview of Web user interfaces briefly introduces the main characteristics of Web GUIs.

9.2, GUI design for the Web introduces some considerations for GUI design for Web user interfaces.

9.3, Implementing Web applications with Java provides an overview of the the technical details of implementing Web applications with Java.

9.4, From Web applications to rich clients discusses the common case of Web developers facing the task of building a rich client interface for an existing application that supports a Web client.

9.1   An overview of Web user interfaces

Web-based user interfaces are GUIs executed within a Web browser, usually rendered using a form of markup language such as HTML, XML, or XHTML. The richness and variety of the markup and scripting languages available allow for a great number of choices, ranging from pure HTML to the use of sophisticated

---

1.   This chapter uses the term 'Web GUI' to mean the client-side GUI application that runs within a Web browser, whether it is a Web page, Java applet, or some other technology. 'Desktop GUI' is used to refer to the user interface of applications.

frameworks based on scripting and forms of client-side control, or to code interpreted by separate plug-ins such as Flash or Java applets.

Web applications have a number of distinctive traits:

- The Web user experience[2] is hard to design down to the final pixel on the Web, given the wide differences in display size, connection types, hardware platforms, and software infrastructures of the various possible clients. This forces the designer to adopt a conservative approach and to give up the notion of cross-platform fidelity.

- Due to the nature of Web GUIs, designers have to limit their exploitation of Web technology to enforce fine-grained control, as the amount of control they can enforce is limited. Navigation buttons are always accessible to the user, and it is hard, if not impossible, to impose any form of flow control. Even browser configuration settings can limit the interactivity of a Web site, such as security options that block local storage of information. These shortcomings are an intrinsic part of the Web medium, and have the result that users expect a great deal of control when interacting with a Web application.

- GUI design coherence is usually limited to a single Web site – few GUI design guidelines apply across multiple Web sites. This is the opposite of OS GUI design guidelines, which apply to all applications executing on a client machine. This makes the Web GUI design process more delicate.

- The main reason for the rapid diffusion of Web applications lies in the ubiquitous presence of Web browsers on client machines. Among other things, this provides the ability to update and maintain Web applications without distributing and installing software on clients[3].

- Web applications are usually available only when the client is on line and the server is accessible and working[4]. That is, they cannot operate when disconnected from the server unless using an embedded client-side HTTP server or similar technique. Web clients that implement some form of active control

---

2. User experience denotes the overall experience perceived by a customer engaged with a product, a service, or some form of communication from a company. Such an experience includes feelings, observations, perceptions, and interactions. This definition aims to bring the concept of customer experience to the digital world.

3. Unfortunately this reason, as economically compelling and practical as it might seem, is inherently technical. It turns out in reality that porting complex applications to the Web makes economic sense, but, given the nature of Web technology when compared with conventional applications, ultimately results in greater difficulty in providing usable and compelling user interfaces.

4. Technologies like Macromedia Flash can be made to operate off line, and, using some form of local caching, it is possible to execute applets or other Web-based content while off line.

can run disconnected for some time, even though their initial deployment always requires download of the relevant page from the remote server.

9.2   GUI design for the Web

Every type of Web application domain has its own type of users and established GUI design idioms. The details of GUI design for the Web would take another book (or more) on its own. The general material in Chapters 2 and 3 applies to Web GUIs as well: this section introduces topics specific to Web GUI design.

Fine graphics details

The potential audience for Web applications is much wider than for desktop application GUIs. Appealing and creative graphical contents are more important than in classic desktop GUIs. When it comes to delivering 'rich' visual experiences, designers often resort to plug-ins. However, despite being a powerful tool in this respect, Java applets are not a popular choice among Web designers. This is essentially due to two reasons:

- The lack of pre-installed JRE support within the most widespread Web browser, Internet Explorer. Applets can also be created with the older Java 1.1, even though sophisticated GUI support is missing.
- The burden of using object-oriented technology for Web designers, graphic artists and other non-programmers.

Nevertheless, there are many examples of well-executed applets on the Web, and the sound OO framework provided by Java is well suited to tackling complex domains and implementing sophisticated user interactions.

Other technologies related to Java are also available for creating Web-based GUIs, such as specialized XML formats and other proprietary technologies.

Unexpected shortcomings

Even though graphic details in a Web GUI can be specified only at an approximate level of definition, in a few cases such low-level details can be handled better by the Web browser than by a desktop application GUI, potentially providing a greater level of control.

For example, aligning widgets along their text baseline provides a pleasant visual effect that enhances usability, as shown in Figure 9.1. Even a basic effect such as this is not available automatically in Swing (as of JSE 1.5), and developers wishing to fine-tune visual appearance must provide this kind of alignment explicitly in their code, consuming time that could have been spent on more business-critical issues.

Figure 9.1   Text baseline alignment in a Web GUI

Area organization

The organization of display area in Web applications strongly depends on the type of Web site and its intended audience. *Wireframe prototypes* are non-graphical layouts of a GUI design that are popular for the design of Web pages. Content-rich Web sites need a clear and well-defined organization of contents, layout, and control flow, and specialized prototypes can be used to evaluate such a critical aspect of their design.

Figure 9.2 shows an example of such a technique applied to a generic corporate home page.

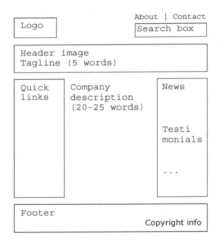

Figure 9.2   An example wire frame prototype for a Web GUI

Levels of client-side control

Current Web GUIs are starting to compete head-to-head with traditional desktop application GUIs in terms of graphics and interactive features, and also their ease of use for developers. This section briefly discusses the current landscape for Web-based GUIs, from a user interface design viewpoint, without going into details of the many available technologies. The technologies considered here work within the client browser, so that they can also be used together with server-side Java technology.

Web developers used to face the challenge of low bandwidth and control-free Web pages, which taken together provided a poor interaction experience for users. This problem is disappearing thanks to better connections – greater bandwidth, increased availability, and decreased cost – and better Web GUI technologies.

Bandwidth and interaction

A peculiar aspect of Web GUIs is the relationship between the available communications bandwidth and the perceived quality of interaction. We know from Chapter 2 that items remain in people's short-term memory for fifteen to thirty seconds at most. For computer interaction, most users tolerate long delays poorly, and become highly frustrated when interactions take more than, say, ten seconds. Connections are increasingly improving in this respect, but consuming bandwidth and time with glitzy graphics and presentations[5] never increased the usability of a Web site. A good means of providing more responsive Web applications lies in the use of client-side control technologies. These also impact on the server tier, in that a lesser number of interactions are required between client and server, allowing server code to be simplified to handle fewer and more specific requests.

More responsive Web GUIs such as this can be built using a number of technologies and approaches, ranging from plug-in-specific code such as Flash, OpenLazlo, or Java applets, to combinations of scripting and other recent technologies widely available in Web browsers.

> This type of highly interactive Web GUI should not be confused with rich clients, introduced in the previous chapter. Rich clients are client applications installed locally that don't need a Web browser, can operate off line, and allow for a certain level of integration within the host client machine.

In Web applications where there is little client-side control behavior, the application forwards all the requests to the server, as shown in Figure 9.3. This is the situation with older applications, or where development simplicity was preferred over a more sophisticated GUI.

---

5.   I am a great fan of the 'skip intro' link found in many home pages.

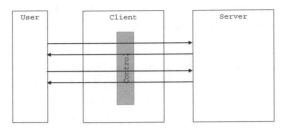

Figure 9.3   Web application with thin control

In Web applications with a control layer, requests are intercepted and processed on the client, and only in some cases are they forwarded to the server, as shown in Figure 9.4.

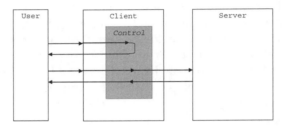

Figure 9.4   Advanced Web application with client-side control

Newer Web technologies such as XHTML, DOM scripting, XMLHttpRequest, and JavaScript, not to mention plug-ins such as Flash, and combinations of these technologies[6], can be used together to provide more responsive and interactive Web GUIs. For example, the use of XMLHttpRequest object support in all major browsers allows for background server connections without reloading a Web page, thus providing a more fluid and interactive experience than classic plain Web applications.

A substantial client-side control layer allows for some form of business logic to be hosted on the client, even if this incurs all the dangers discussed in Chapter 6, such as duplicating code for handling the same domain-specific representation, both in the client and on the server, establishing some form of control over deployed code for upgrading obsolete business logic, and so on.

---

6.   Various Web technologies used together and wrapped in a convenient framework are often dubbed with acronyms as if they were themselves fully-fledged new technologies, such as AJAX and its variants, or the new client scripting support from Microsoft, code-named ATLAS.

Navigation issues

Because of the many different screens involved in Web GUIs, well-designed navigation becomes essential in providing a usable Web GUI. This involves designing hyperlinks and connections within and between pages in a way that is both usable and that provides an effective means to access required information or perform the task in hand.

It is important to provide clear navigation aids, such as consistent and clear graphics, systematic organization, and so on, to provide support for access to information or to perform some operation via the Web site. A common form of support is to provide feedback about the location of the current page within the Web site. Figure 9.5 shows an example of use of 'breadcrumbs' to provide navigational feedback.

Figure 9.5   Providing feedback of Web site navigation

Basic navigation links, for example back to the home page and other navigation crossroads within the Web site, should be present in consistent locations on every page, to help users avoid dead-end pages, and to take account of users that jumped into the Web site without following a planned navigation path, for example through the use of a search engine. Ideally, all valuable content within a Web site should be one or two clicks away from the home page.

The following subsections provide some examples of various GUI design strategies, organized by the main layout strategy employed. Layout strategies were introduced in Chapter 2 in the section *Display Organization*. Various combinations of such strategies are often used in real-world Web sites. For a more comprehensive discussion about navigation, see for example (Fleming 1998).

High-density information strategy

This strategy is used to provide users with a quick and informative overview of the primary choices available. It is usually employed in home pages only, because it eats up precious screen estate and tends to clutter other content information in the page. An example of such an approach for a fictitious Web site is shown in Figure 9.6.

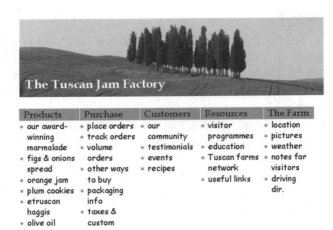

Figure 9.6   Example design of Web site navigation employing a high-density strategy

Another solution is to rely on Web page scrolling – another key difference between Web GUIs over traditional desktop application GUIs – and providing a scrollable navigation area on the left-hand side of the page, as shown in the example in Figure 9.7. Alternative solutions can be used, such as adopting hierarchical menus, or only showing the main categories.

*Figure 9.7   Design of Web site navigation arranged vertically employing a
                high-density strategy*

Limited information strategy

A dual strategy for high-density visualization consists of hiding unnecessary navigation information, and is frequently used in real cases. Figure 9.8 shows a navigation menu modeled on traditional desktop application GUI menu bars.

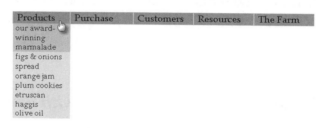

Figure 9.8   *Classic application menu-like navigation*

When only two levels of navigation are shown, a common design is that shown in Figure 9.9, in which the lower bar changes dynamically depending on the category activated by hovering the mouse in the upper row.

Products	Purchase	Customers	Resources	The Farm	
award-winning marmalade	figs & onions spread	orange jam	plum cookies	etruscan haggis	olive oil

Figure 9.9   *Showing navigation items on two levels*

Web sites are accessed and used differently than desktop application GUIs, and usability tests are crucial for ensuring that a pleasant-looking abstract idea is really working with target users. From various empirical evaluations conducted on Web GUIs, most users seem to adopt a very aggressive approach to information seeking within a Web page, focusing almost exclusively on their current goal. The very compact navigation design shown in Figure 9.10 certainly saves precious screen estate, but more than likely some of the menus are going to pass unnoticed by many users.

Other possible solutions can range from a combo box containing the most popular link destinations – a sort of a collection of navigation shortcuts – to combinations of graphics and interactive features. The important issue is still the same: devising the best GUI design for the given user audience.

Figure 9.10   Too compact a navigation design

9.3   *Implementing Web applications with Java*

This section discusses the main technologies available for implementing Web GUIs with Java. Before going into details, it briefly introduces the 'big picture' in current architectures for Web GUIs.

The typical architecture of a Web application

One of the most striking differences in building Web interfaces using Java technology, rather than applications, is the fact that Web pages are defined in non-object-oriented languages. This results in an 'impedance mismatch' between the presentation technology and the remainder of the code that is implemented with Java classes and other languages, similar to that created by relational databases.

Web presentation also impacts GUI interaction, which usually results in GUIs with a lower level of user interaction than for desktop application GUIs, such as lack of features like drag and drop, undo, and so on. In Web GUIs event-based communication is usually needed less, because Web clients usually provide less interactive features for users, which is reflected on the server-side implementation. Furthermore, additional care is devoted to simplifying the generation of the GUI in the markup language of choice, and the content assembly of different areas of the GUI.

A Web GUI typically communicates with a Web server, submitting HTTP requests that the Web server forwards to other parts of the Web application. Such requests contain the session state and the data related to the current request. Although many arrangements are possible, the Web server is usually part of a Web tier in a J2EE architecture, interacting with the business and enterprise information system tier.

Design details of Java Web applications can be found in countless books, such as (Alur, Crupi and Malks 2001) for J2EE patterns, (Fowler et al. 2003) for general enterprise patterns, (Marinescu 2002) for EJB-specific design patterns and (Johnson 2003) for a general introduction to J2EE applications.

Basic Java Web GUI technologies

Java Web technology can be seen historically as a stack of technologies that have grown by accretion over the years – that is, a higher-level layer on top of an existing, less powerful one – in an attempt to provide more powerful features with lower complexity for developers. This technology stack can be roughly described from the bottom as:

- Servlet technology (from the first half of 1997) accepts and processes Web requests using server-side Java code executed in a specialized container application, the servlet container.

- JSP (JavaServer Pages) technology (from the first half of 1999) builds on top of the Servlet technology to provide easier management of dynamic Web pages.

- JSF (JavaServer Faces) technology, whose first specification release was at the end of 2003, builds on JSP technology to provide higher-level specification for user interfaces.

Given its novelty, JSF deserves a brief introduction of its own. JavaServer Faces[7] is a framework for visual components for Web applications that allows the creation of Web GUIs that run on a Java server. The GUI's rendering is left to the browser. Components are rendered separately from their logical definition – different types of table widgets can be used, or the same command component can be rendered as a button or hyperlink as needed, for example.

JSF comprises a Java API and custom tag libraries. The API represents UI components, manages state, handles events, and validates input, as well as supporting internationalization and accessibility options. JSP custom tag libraries are provided for defining visual components within a JSP page, and for binding components to server-side objects. Tag libraries can be created using various disparate Web presentation technologies.

The stack of technologies for Web GUIs for server-side Java is shown in Figure 9.11.

---

7.   Defined in Java Specification Request (JSR) 127.

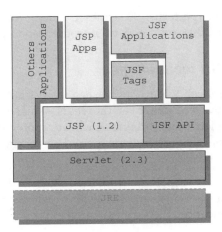

Figure 9.11   Basic technology stack for server-side Java Web GUIs

Java applets

Instead of adopting a markup-based technology to represent primary content within a browser, developers can use Java applets embedded in Web pages and interpreted by a dedicated browser plug-in that launches a JVM to execute them. Two main options are available:

- *Java 1.1 support.* This can be achieved by targeting the older JDK Version 1.1, does not require any additional installation, as JRE 1.1 comes pre-installed on all the main Web browsers, and can optionally take advantage of other libraries for more sophisticated services. Swing can also be loaded as a separate library, and a wide range of third-party libraries and client environments that support JDK 1.1 exist. For a discussion about such third-party technologies, see Chapter 11.

- *Targeting the Java 2 environment.* Writing code for the Java 2 platform makes it easier to achieve sophisticated graphical effects and in general to take advantage of its more powerful and up-to-date software runtime environment. The major drawback of this approach is the need to download and install the JRE plug-in.

Java applets are not straightforward mini-applications written in Java, as Java game developers know only too well. Code written for a general applet container must target a number of different environments – different applet containers built for different browsers all differ slightly from each other, even for different versions of the same browser – and must cope with their quirks uniformly.

Fortunately, Java applets have been available since late 1995, so a wide knowledge base is available to developers. Despite their demise in favor of more domain-specific technologies such as Flash, Java applets are still a viable and competitive choice in many scenarios. There are niches of application domains in which Java applet technology is widely used, such scientific simulation, didactic client-side Web applications in general, small applications, video games, and so on.

9.4 From Web applications to rich clients

The architectural discussion of Web applications mentioned code that resides on the server tier and provides Web content suitable for display on a client Web browser. From a technical viewpoint, Web applications with basic GUI design requirements are simpler to build than desktop applications, because of their more regular structure and the wide availability of mature support frameworks. On the other hand, the sheer range of possibilities available when building a desktop application GUI can confuse developers with a background solely of Web programming.

Accommodating a desktop application GUI as an additional client of an enterprise application poses the following challenges for Java developers whose programming background is mainly in Web technology:

- The intricacies of putting together a desktop GUI go far beyond laying out widgets on a screen, as this book demonstrates.

- Given the current stack of technologies available for building desktop application GUIs, developers are more involved in GUI design details when working on desktop applications than for Web-based ones. This poses a number of critical issues regarding usability, visual design, and others that only developers themselves can solve.

- Developers work in an environment in which the domain model and business logic is already built and working on the application's servers. Some parts of it might be able to be extended to accommodate specific needs of the desktop application GUI, but much of the domain is often given 'as is' to GUI developers. This poses problems if the business domain was weakly modeled on and/or influenced by the Web paradigm, or if details dependent on Web issues leaked into the model itself, such as a page-oriented API for obtaining query results.

- When it is not feasible to separate the Web-oriented user interface aspects fully from the business domain, the simplest solution may be to reuse some of the existing code for the rich client application. This will inevitably tend to create a Web-like GUI that costs as much as a full-blown desktop GUI, as well as being harder to maintain because of the common dependencies with the Web-specific code. Such an approach, although sometimes unavoidable, can lead to dangerous long-term maintenance scenarios, and impact the quality of the GUI design itself, which can have extensive ramifications on customers and the real value added to the whole application.

Different development habits

Web development and GUI development are slightly different animals, for a number of reasons:

- Development and installation brings a number of issues and technical decisions that Web GUIs don't have.
- User are always ready to judge the results of your work, and expect a more compelling experience from desktop application GUIs than from Web GUIs. Desktop applications are usually preferred over Web clients because of their better user experience, especially in specific areas, such as for repetitive users, or business-critical tasks, so developers must satisfy higher expectations than merely providing a 'Web interface.'
- Rich client platforms, although catching up, are still less refined and usable than their server-side counterparts, and a unifying standard is missing[8], something like EJB on the server side, for example. This confuses developers who are familiar with the Web technology landscape and who often prefer using raw GUI toolkits and few other support libraries even when developing mid-sized projects.

Deeper software design differences also exist when the same design strategies are applied to the two different scenarios. As an example of this, consider the differences between the MVC (Model-View-Controller) design introduced in Chapter 6 for desktop applications, and its corresponding version for the Web.

The classic MVC design for the Web[9] organizes an application into:

- A model with its data representation and business logic.
- A number of views for the model, providing data presentation and user input.
- A controller to dispatch requests and handle control flow.

This design works fine over the Web, where requests to the server comprise a small fraction of the total volume of user interactions in the client GUI. There is thus no need to add the Observer pattern to track changes among the various parts, and hundreds if not thousands of MVC instances may be active at the same

---

8. See the discussion in Chapter 13 about standard components for rich client applications.
9. See the Struts library or, for a general reference, (Alur, Crupi and Malks 2001).

time, all needing to interact with each other (at least when the Swing toolkit is used).

It is little wonder therefore that Web developers feel a bit lost when building complex desktop GUIs, and resort to vague concepts like the 'need to centralize controllers' or to set up some form of central command management. Despite being called by the same name, client-side and server-side MVCs are very different when it comes to their details.

9.5   *Summary*

This chapter discussed the scenario for Web GUIs using Java technology, covering some aspects of Web GUI design in relation to the general concepts introduced in Chapter 2.

We covered the implementation aspects of Java Web GUIs and the architecture of Java Web applications. Differences between desktop and Web GUIs were highlighted for the common case of adding a rich client to an existing server application. We also mentioned differences between client and server applications in the implementation of some common design strategies, such as MVC.

10 J2ME User Interfaces

This chapter introduces the user interfaces supported by the Java 2 Micro Edition (J2ME or JME) edition. Java platforms other than J2EE/J2SE, such as the JavaCard environment, which has no explicit GUI support, won't be covered. The practical examples in this chapter are based on the J2ME Mobile Information Device Profile (MIDP). However, most of the material in this chapter, whenever not explicitly expressed otherwise, applies to J2ME GUIs in general, not only MIDP GUIs.

J2ME is introduced briefly with a technical introduction of this programming environment, followed by some details about GUI design for this profile. Practical examples are given. A questionnaire for assessing the usability of J2ME applications can be found in Appendix B.

This chapter is structured as follows:

10.1, Introduction to the MID profile briefly introduces the J2ME MID profile.

10.2, The MIDP UI API introduces the details of the API for MIDP GUIs.

10.3, Designing MIDP GUIs provides an overview of GUI design for MIDP GUIs.

10.4, Designing navigation discusses the specific of navigation in a MIDP GUI.

10.5, An example custom item discusses the customization of a MIDP GUI component by means of a practical example.

10.6, An example ad-hoc item shows an example an ad-hoc item component for representing numeric data using pie charts.

10.7, An example application introduces the Park MIDP application, illustrating a GUI design and development approach to navigation.

10.1 Introduction to the MID profile

J2ME is targeted at embedded and consumer electronics devices. It has two primary types of component – *configurations* and *profiles*. The J2ME architecture is composed of a few configurations that define the common features for a class of devices. Two configurations are currently available:

- The Connected Limited Device Configuration (CLDC), designed for devices with constrained hardware resources. Such devices typically run on either a

16- or 32-bit CPU and have 512 Kilobytes or less of memory available for client applications and the Java platform itself.

• The Connected Device Configuration (CDC), aimed at next-generation devices with more robust resources than CLDC devices.

These configurations dictate the Java virtual machine, core libraries and some APIs, while leaving the differences between each device to be described by a profile. User interfaces are defined on a per-profile basis, allowing for maximum flexibility when taking advantage of device characteristics. Tailoring APIs to a particular profile allows for efficiency and accuracy, but results in several different class packages and slightly different vendor-specific API implementations.

This chapter concentrates on the MID profile, part of the CLDC configuration. The MID profile is aimed at modeling the large category of Java-enabled wireless handheld devices. Such profiles describe all issues, such as the user interface, the application model, networking, and persistence storage, that are related to Java-enabled mobile devices like two-way pagers and cellular phones. We focus on the UI API here.

An application running on this type of Java-enabled devices is referred to as a *MIDlet*, because it can be deployed seamlessly on a wide range of different MIDP-compliant devices, just as an applet is deployed in different Web browsers. This capability is one of the most important features of the J2ME initiative for wireless devices, and has the potential to create a completely new and huge market for such software applications. The MID profile has been designed both to abstract applications from the client hardware on which they run, and to ease the development of similar applications. The latter aspect arises when we discuss the UI API, which has been modeled around the typical UI seen in today's consumer cellular phones.

Both the terms *applet* and *application* are used to refer to MIDP programs.

For more information about the J2ME platform, visit:

`http://www.javasoft.com/products/j2me/`

The code suggested here was developed and executed using various development tools. The J2ME Wireless Toolkit from Sun, for MIDP 2.0, is available at `http://www.javasoft.com/products/j2mewtoolkit/`.

Main UI concepts

The J2ME MIDP GUI API has been designed for generic handheld devices with LCD screens of various sizes, a typical minimum being 96 x 96 pixels, and running on hardware with limited resources. The richness of concepts and software architectures employed in the AWT and Swing APIs in the desktop Java world is clearly out of reach here, even if the MID profile assumes quite powerful hardware – at least when compared with other embedded devices or the JavaCard specification.

The basic functionalities provided include the capability of manipulating the device's screen to show a top-level component, a widget that occupies the whole screen, that has been decorated previously with simpler UI components, referred to as *items*.

There is always only one screen object active at a time, representing the whole contents of the current device's display: the concept of multiple windows is absent. Applications simply switch from one screen to another.

No navigation semantics have been provided, both for generality and because applications are expected to be simple and not require many different screens and menus. One common navigation semantic seen on such devices, for example, is stack-like screen navigation, in which users find their way from one screen to another, closing the current one and redisplaying the previous one as screens are 'piled' to resemble a hierarchical organization. Navigation styles are left to the application developer's implementation.

Only basic widgets and a simple user input framework are provided. The Java classes provided are designed to reduce the need for subclassing by providing a comprehensive range of built-in options.

It is important to note that, given the nature of the platform, developers must always query the current screen size for all but the simplest UI screens: assuming a fixed screen size can produce unusable UIs on MIDP-enable devices.

The lifecycle of a MIDlet

The lifecycle of a MIDlet is important, because it involves the concept of screen management directly. The native module that handles MIDlets in the MIDP-enabled device is called the *application manager*.

A MIDlet can be in one of the following three states:

- *Paused.* The MIDlet is shallowly initialized – that is, it does not use or hold any resources. The instance is quiescent in device RAM and is waiting for the application manager to be activated. This state is reached every time the application management invokes the `pauseApp` method on the given MIDlet, not only after its creation. The MIDlet screen is removed from the device display.
- *Active.* The application manager has activated the MIDlet by invoking its `startApp` method. The MIDlet must explicitly assign the screen device.
- *Destroyed.* This state is entered only once, and instructs the MIDlet to release all its resources and terminate its execution.

All the UI initialization is performed in the `startApp` method.

User input management

User input is handled both at high level, using `Command` objects, and at low level using the device keys directly. Although the latter solution is available, it is discouraged, because it can hinder the portability of an application.

The `Canvas` class provides a general abstraction for input keys that is portable across all implementations, encompassing all the keys in the ITU-T standard telephone keypad – numbers from 0 to 9, the '*' and '#' keys – as well as a set of abstract input actions called *game actions* that include the four navigation keys (up, down, left, right), a 'fire' button, and four application-dependent keys.

Commands are the most important means of expressing user directions. Commands are managed by the underlying MIDP implementation, and can be rendered as soft buttons – text labels shown above special buttons near the device screen – voice commands, or in any other platform-specific way. To help the MIDP implementation interpret a given command correctly, commands have different types, each with a precise use:

- *Back*, used to return to the previous *logical* screen.
- *Cancel*, which cancels the current screen and all data previously set in it. Cancel is the standard negation command.
- *Screen*, reserved for application-specific commands related to the current screen.
- *OK*, the standard affirmative command.
- *Help*, used to show display content.
- *Item*, associated with a particular item on the current screen.
- *Stop*, which stops the current operation. This should be implemented, to allow users to stop lengthy operations.
- *Exit*, used for quitting the whole application.

The command type is used only as a rendering hint for the MIDP implementation: developers should always specify the corresponding action in their code by implementing the `CommandListener` interface. This is demonstrated in the example code provided for this chapter.

Two levels of API

While J2ME's UI API is oriented towards easing development in most common situations, some hooks have been left for implementing ad-hoc UIs as well. This allows developers to subclass low-level general classes such as `Canvas` and `Graphics`. This is however a complex procedure, and one that may ultimately produce non-portable MIDlets, for example by relying on a key present on a specific mobile phone model but not on other MIDP-compliant devices. Nevertheless, in some situations this is the only way to go.

Figure 10.1 on page 381 shows the relationship of the `Canvas` class to other classes of the package.

Main UI limitations

The J2ME API has several limitations, mostly dictated by hardware resource availability. First, whenever possible UI implementation details are left to the device vendor, to simplify the implementation of the MIDP for a given platform. This encourages implementation differences between one device and another, not only in the UI's look and feel. Developers are urged to consider the API as a high-level and not completely accurate specification. Furthermore, the absence of any guidelines for navigation semantics encourages different approaches that could confuse the user when moving from one application to another.

These and other similar considerations highlight the API 'shortcomings when used in non-trivial UIs – and such applications will be growing in number with the trend towards more powerful devices in this industry sector.

Cost-driven design for J2ME GUIs

Cost-driven design can also be applied to J2ME GUIs, as for all the general technique discussed so far, from iterative GUI development to Agile methodologies, test-driven development and the design patterns and architectures discussed in the previous chapters. The devil, as usual, is in the details. Aiming for professional user interfaces on constrained devices should involve a constant focus on usability rather than other, secondary, issues. This is not often the case: with tight deadlines and tough technical challenges to cope with, usability concerns often slip away.

10.2   The MIDP UI API

This section describes the practical UI component classes provided in the `javax.microediton.lcdui` package using a top-down UI design–oriented approach, rather than illustrating low-level API details. These can be found in the related literature[1].

UI widgets

This section describes the top-level components of the MIDP UI library.

Table 10.1 shows the built-in components provided for developing MIDP applets.

---

1.   See http://java.sun.com/products/midp/.

Table 10.1   MIDP UI Top-Level Components

Top-level component name	Description
Alert	Similar to a dialog box for showing read-only messages., composed of simple *items* (see Table 10.2).
Form	Shows a collection of *Items*.
List	Shows a list of homogeneous, selectable elements .
TextBox	Similar to a TextArea for editing multiline text.

In Table 10.1 the first two top-level containers, the Alert and Form classes, are visual containers of simpler UI widgets called *items*, which all extend the Item abstract class. The remaining two, List and TextBox, are specialized components that are designed to fill the device screen.

The standard items provided with the MID profile are listed in Table 10.2.

Table 10.2   MIDP UI Items

Component name	Description
Label	Shows a single line of read-only text.
DateField	Shows a calendar or other device-dependent date / time picker.
ChoiceGroup	Shows a set of boolean values.
ImageItem	Shows an image.
StringItem	Shows some text.
TextField	Shows some formatted text.

When creating data input screens or other GUIs, developers use a Form instance containing properly initialized Items. Menus are meant to be implemented through List instances, while Alerts are used for notification only. TextBoxes are used for displaying long text strings, such as SMS text messages, memos, and so on.

TextField and TextBox components provide built-in data input constraints. Developers can specify which of the following constraints the component will enforce when handling user input:

- *URL format* – only Web-compliant addresses will be accepted.
- *E-mail format* – only e-mail address will be accepted.
- *Phone number format.* This is implementation-dependent due to regional conventions for phone number formatting, network requirements – the GSM network, for example, may use '+' at the beginning of every number – and device implementations. Once a phone number format field is filled out, a device-dependent key can start a telephone call on a cellphone host device.
- *Integer value format.* In this case only digits can be entered, optionally prepended with a minus sign. Range constraints can be enforced by developers.
- *Password field format.* Inserted characters are masked as they are typed.
- *Free text.* Any character can be entered.

Other constraint types can be combined with the password constraint to create, for example, a numeric-only, password-like text field.

Figure 10.1 shows the basic static class diagram of the major classes in the `javax.microediton.lcdui` package: some classes, such as `Font` or `Graphics`, are omitted.

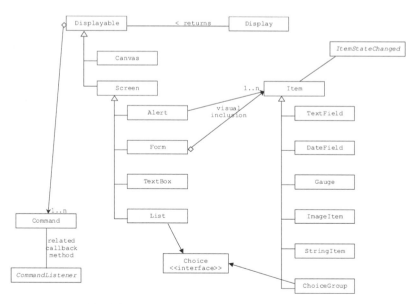

Figure 10.1   Simplified class diagram of the `lcdui` package

10.3   *Designing MIDP GUIs*

Today's J2ME GUIs range from basic cell phones to sophisticated personal assistants, and new devices are broadening the already wide choice constantly, such as WiFi-enabled 'smart' cell phones that can also be used as much cheaper, standard devices for a variety of computational tasks, ranging from work to personal entertainment.

The main difficulty in designing GUIs for such a diverse set of devices arises from the fact that J2ME technology provides only an approximate definition of the GUI's final details. Such details are rendered autonomously by the device on which the application is hosted. This point is discussed in more detail later.

The main characteristics of a MIDP application that impact on its design, both the GUI design and its implementation, are as follows:

- *Personal devices.* Differently than other computing means, wireless devices are inherently personal devices, and as such they are used differently than desktop PCs or other similar computing machines. Wireless devices are carried with the owners throughout the day, and applets can be used at any hour of the day or night.

- *Privacy concerns.* As an important detail of the previous point, users feel uneasy in allowing foreign code to execute on devices that contain as much private data as does a cellphone. This also applies to applications sharing data externally. Even if J2ME poses important limits on applet intrusiveness, users should not be expected to have to know the MIDP specification. GUI designers need to consider this aspect when designing privacy-sensitive applications.

- *Type of users.* Differently than desktop applications, mobile applications have a much wider range of possible user types. Households, retired people and teenagers can all be potential mobile users. Their education and levels of computer literacy can vary greatly, requiring more care than for desktop applications in the choice of language used in the application, and in general in the whole GUI design. Outside North America cellphones are more widespread than desktop computers.

- *Limited bandwidth and intermittent connection.* A wireless device typically has much less bandwidth available for transmitting and receiving data than a wired device. Furthermore, wireless connections are typically unreliable, so an intermittent connection should always be assumed.

- *Pay-per-use billing schemes on bandwidth/connection.* Most carrier operators charge for bandwidth consumption on a per-use basis. This is an additional psychological factor in shaping use patterns, because users might be uneasy about allowing applets to connect remotely.

- *Power consumption and related use patterns.* A wireless device is usually a mobile device as well, with batteries as its only means of power supply while on the move. Even the longest-lasting batteries offer a limited amount of power. This dictates use patterns for such devices that GUI designers must take into account.

- *Limited hardware resources on client devices.* Because of their mobile nature, the available power source, and sometimes also for economical reasons as low-end consumer devices – wireless devices have limited resources. The same reasons limit processing power.

- *Restricted input means.* Limited keyboards and compact pointing devices are available on only a small segment of devices. On others input is obtained via keypad and navigation keys.

- *Context of use.* Wireless devices can be used in the most diverse surroundings, such as in school classes, on a train, in a café. This obliges designers explicitly to study sets of use contexts for applications. Furthermore, the context can be an important input for the application, such as those making use of localization services such as the Global Positioning System, GPS[2].

- *Intermittently active sessions.* When interacting with mobile applications, users can be interrupted at any moment, either by an incoming call on the same device, or by some situation in the environment. This means that MIDP applets should be able to chunk both user attention and transactions in small quanta, and need to provide simple mechanisms for restoring session data.

- *Limited GUI output screen.* Typical displays are very small compared to other devices. This makes viewing more difficult. Combining this limitation with some classes of users, such as those with visual impairment, might transform a GUI design that seems brilliant when run in an emulator into a totally unusable and frustrating experience for some users.

- *Fragmented market for client devices.* This can result in a number of small incompatibilities in the way the J2ME MIDP specifications are implemented among different vendors, and even among different models of end device. Fortunately the industry has provided a thorough set of test criteria for a mobile device to be certified as 'Java compliant.' Vendors also tend to add proprietary APIs that are not widely portable, so that developers are often faced with choices about whether to restrict portability or simplify development[3].

---

2. Not to be confused with GPRS (General Packet Radio Service) a mobile telephone network standard that can be used by wireless J2ME devices for remote connection.
3. This is especially true for those market segments in which Java applets follow consumer-led paths – new devices are continuously released with a short time to market, shrunk budgets, and quick obsolescence.

- *GUI details are ultimately left to the actual client device implementation.* GUI design is ultimately dictated by the device that is executing the applet, and there might be discrepancies between different, supposedly compatible, devices. While this was a major problem with early versions of embedded JVMs, it is still a hindrance for developers.

General advice about multi-presentation applications was given in Chapter 9 in connection with Web GUIs, so won't be repeated here.

Abstract GUI designs

Accommodating a professional GUI design in a lowest-denominator platform like the J2ME MIDP is challenging. It should always involve thorough testing on the commonest target devices available on the market, not just on their software emulators used for early testing and development.

A simple solution to this challenge is to choose a target platform explicitly, usually from one of the major vendors for the target user population that has a wide choice of development resources, such as documentation, emulators, GUI design guidelines, and so on. This situation is similar to that of designing for the Web in the 'old days' when there was no single market-leading Web browser.

An incorrect solution to the problem is to try to bypass the JME (or J2ME) specification by rolling out a home-grown look and feel in an attempt to provide a consistent 'branded' user experience across various devices[4]. This usually results in a poor, possibly weird-looking, user interface that is expensive to build: low-level details need to be handled explicitly and cannot be left to the underlying device's implementation.

In cases in which the lowest common denominator is too problematic a solution to pursue – and only in these extreme cases – a better strategy is to segment the design in a divide-and-rule fashion. This is discussed in the next section.

Segmenting the GUI design

Some scenarios are clear-cut and allow two main segments to be easily identified. Consider for example a traffic congestion applet being developed for a major city traffic authority. The target user population is identified by means of preliminary questionnaires, and is roughly divided into two groups:

- Those that will access the application from the Web.
- Those that will use it from a Java-powered consumer wireless device.

---

4. Possible because MIDP 2.0 allows more low-level GUI details to be specified. This is especially true for those market segments in which Java applets follow consumer-led paths – new devices are continuously released with a short time to market, shrunk budgets, and quick obsolescence.

The latter group is better served by MIDP applets, because the user population will be made mostly of repetitive users that prefer to download the applet only once, instead of using other more expensive solutions. A WAP-based GUI, for example, would require city maps to be downloaded for every session, while with a rich client, only current traffic congestion data is needed.

Building a single GUI for these two group of users can prove tricky, as it is a situation in which designers cannot transfer complexity to end users, and one where usability is an essential requirement. Such a GUI would have to serve two distinct needs at once: that of satisfying both power-users and normal drivers, groups that have very different information needs. Splitting the design serves both segments better, greatly enhancing the usability of the overall application.

Two types of GUIs can therefore be designed:

• Using a high-density visual strategy. This version is aimed at expert users that need more data and a richer interaction, such as people that spend most of the day driving in the city – taxi drivers, delivery drivers, and so on.

• Leveraging a limited information style[5]. This type of user would prefer a mainly textual application, where details are limited and only basic congestion information is provided. This version will accommodate most users, so cheaper phone models can be used, leaving the 'power-user' version to deal with more powerful devices with larger screens.

For such an approach to be viable, however, requires thoughtful implementation, otherwise it can escalate into an expensive and risky development situation. Portions of code not common to the two GUI versions should be minimized, by providing a rich set of utilities and a supporting architecture implemented in a GUI-neutral way that factors out all commonalities among different GUI implementations. The objective of such a design is to minimize GUI-dependent code and maximize GUI-independent code. Building and deploying the two versions can be completely automated and a few classes can assemble the building blocks to ship the different versions of the same application that are geared towards different user segments. For larger application scenarios, this strategy leads to the Software Families software engineering approach.

10.4 Designing navigation

MIDP GUIs have to cope with small physical screens. One of the main consequences of this constraint is that GUIs will have to have more, and smaller, screens. Navigating between such screens therefore becomes all-important for the usability of all but the simplest applet.

---

5. See Chapter 2.

Finite State Automaton (FSA) is a formal model of computation for modeling UIs on simple devices such as wireless phones. FSA, which can also be represented as a finite state machine, consists of a set of states, with a special start state, an input alphabet, which defines the type of input to the FSA, and a transition function that maps input symbols and current state to the next state.

Given the simplicity of MIDP GUIs, the user interface structure can be expressed by means of simple diagrams like that shown in Figure 10.2.

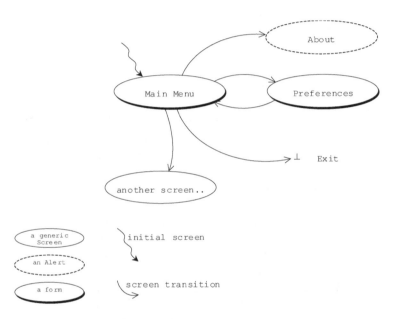

Figure 10.2   The structure of a typical MIDP GUI

The diagram describes the possible transitions among different MIDP screens in a typical mobile application. A later section shows an example of use of this diagram for the design of a simple GUI.

GUI design needs to match the limited client resources of J2ME clients – memory, processing power, screen real estate, and so on. From a usability perspective, this involves placing a lower cognitive burden on users. The widely-used strategy of localizing feedback[6], for example, becomes increasingly difficult to enforce on devices with limited screen space. Interaction design can then degenerate into a sort of long wizard with tiny pages. Consider data input in one screen that affects

6.   This was discussed in connection with validation in Chapter 8.

data in another screen, for example disabling some option. With limited screen estate it might not be possible to keep these related items close, presenting a puzzling experience to the user.

10.5 An example custom item

We are now ready to see some practical examples of J2ME MIDP applications. In contrast to desktop computers and other rich computing appliances, wireless devices have a limited set of features, and this influences their user interfaces. A common error when developing MIDP GUIs is to try and achieve a cross-device look and feel – that is, a look and feel that is the same on all supported platforms. This might initially seem highly desirable, because it is supposed to help users, while giving a strong brand identification to the product. However, such efforts sometimes end with incomplete, arbitrary GUIs that can confuse end users. Users become accustomed to a mobile device's look and feel, and may be uncomfortable with a downloaded applet that behaves 'weirdly.' Figure 10.3 shows a sample custom alert box that illustrates this[7].

Figure 10.3   An ad-hoc alert box developed for a specific task

It is interesting to see how easy is to manipulate the display area directly. In the MID profile there is no deep and complex class hierarchy like Swing's, and taking advantage of the `paint()` method is straightforward. The custom class that creates the alert box shown in Figure 10.3, whose source code is provided in the code bundle for this chapter, extends `Canvas` and draws directly on the display's `Graphics`.

---

7. Such a custom component is an extension to a standard visual component provided by a
reference toolkit, as discussed in Chapter 3.

10.6   *An example ad-hoc item*

Providing ad-hoc GUI solutions is a powerful feature of J2ME. It needs to be used with care, but can enhances an application's usability enormously.

This simple example of the correct use of ad-hoc components – from a GUI design viewpoint – takes advantage of a custom item component. The `Item` class represents the generic component that can be used in lists and forms. With MIDP 2.0 the `CustomItem` class is available for subclassing, which provides a simple way to create ad-hoc items.

Figure 10.4 shows a simple custom item for representing numeric data using pie charts. It consists of a form composed of custom items on the left, and the legend in the right-hand figure.

Figure 10.4   A form made of pie charts

Each element is itself a form item, so it can be manipulated with the same conventions, such as check boxes, text fields, and other standard items. This is a powerful way to employ ad-hoc designs without disrupting native platform usability. Figure 10.5 shows how users can move through items in the applet using the cell phone's navigational keys.

The implementation is organized around three classes[8]:

* The `PieItemTest` class, needed to launch the demo.
* The `PieItem` class, which implements the pie chart custom item.
* The `PieData` class, which represents all configuration data, such as colors.

The related classes are provided in the code bundle for this chapter. The `PieItemTest` class is a test MIDlet that creates a screen composed of custom pie chart items. The core of the example is the `PieItem` class. The `values` array stores

---

8.   This is a demo implementation that has been developed only to show the visual component customization features of standard J2ME MIDP widgets.

Figure 10.5   Navigating through specialized items

the data related to the current item. Whenever a non-empty string label is provided in the constructor, this is used as the item's caption (see Figure 10.4 and Figure 10.5).

The methods `getMinContentHeight()`, `getPrefContentHeight()` and `getPref-ContentWidth()` are needed by the `CustomItem` class. The `paint()` method draws the data as a pie chart.

The `PieData` class gathers all configuration data relevant to pie charts. It provides the chart legend shown in Figure 10.4. Such a screen itself employs another custom item implementation, an inner class of the `PieData` class. The `PieData` class manages configuration data for all pie chart items.

10.7   An example application

This section describes an example application that illustrates a simple mechanism for implementing Finite State Automaton (FSA).

The example application manages the billing of car parking in which users pay for parking via an applet. As only its user interface is of interest, the applet's other details are only sketched. For simplicity it use only few screens, as shown in Figure 10.6.

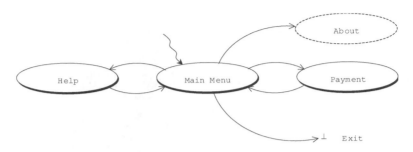

Figure 10.6   The Park applet's GUI structure

Figure 10.7 shows the main menu for the applet on the left, and the 'About' box on the right.

Figure 10.7   The Park applet's main menu

The most interesting screen in this applet is the Payment Details screen, which persists the user data from session to session. In the demo applet it is implemented very naïvely, as shown in Figure 10.7.

Figure 10.8   The payment details form

However, we are interested more in implementation solutions than the applet's realism.

The code

The MIDlet subclass (the `ParkMain` class) manages the overall UI, the user commands, and the transitions between screens. In the `ParkMain` class the `commandAction()` method handles all the applet's command management. Most of the code implements the transition diagram shown in Figure 10.6 – for example, when the user issues the HELP command from the main menu screen, the help screen is shown.

The `ParkMain` class implements the Explicit Navigation design strategy discussed in Chapter 6.

We diverged from the simplest implementation to deal with main menu commands more efficiently. More object-oriented mechanisms are possible, such as using specialized `CommandItem` events, but minimizing implementation complexity is a key objective when writing J2ME applications. The techniques shown here try to minimize the number of employed classes and objects – that is, static classes and their runtime instances – while maintaining a simple software design by minimizing the number of classes.

Following this approach, all the application's screens are gathered in the `Screens` class. This class is invoked by the `ParkMain` instance whenever a screen is needed. The `Screens` class lazily creates the required displays. Consider the help screen, for example. Such a screen is only needed a few times, and experienced users might never invoke it. Keeping it `null` until it is needed saves runtime space and initialization time. Lazy instantiation, used here for screens, which are created only when needed, is a key technique in the implementation of MIDP UIs.

There are cases in which keeping a reference to a screen that has already been created is counterproductive. This may happen for example when the screen needs to be created anew each time, or when it is accessed only once per session. This latter case is exemplified by the `About` screen, displayed by the `showAbout()` method. In this case it would be a waste of space to keep a reference to the screen throughout the whole life of the applet (assuming of course that the 'About' screen contains only standard product information, rather than data that needs to be frequently referenced). Some J2ME applications can run for weeks, so careful memory management is essential.

Separating screens from control code may be beneficial for non-trivial applets, in that it separates presentation from control and keeps the implementation organized coherently, even if it might favor closer coupling among classes. In this example, the MIDlet and the `Screens` instances are tightly coupled.

Finally, the `AppData` class contains all the business data required by the application. In the trivial implementation used here, `AppData` uses has only two attributes:

- The user's amount of parking credit – the `money` attribute.
- The user's name.

This class is also responsible for retrieving and saving data persistently, by means of the J2ME MIDP `RecordStore` mechanism, which is properly initialized in its constructor.

10.8   Summary

This chapter has discussed factors relevant to graphical user interfaces in Java 2 Micro Edition briefly, demonstrating the built-in support for GUIs in the J2ME MID profile. It also discussed some simple demonstration examples of the use of such libraries, together with some high-level strategies for organizing the user interface of a MIDP applet GUI.

11 Java Tools and Technologies

This chapter discusses an aspect that is critical for Java application development, and one that is often overlooked – the right mix of ingredient tools and technologies for a project. It focuses mostly on GUI development and is slightly biased towards open source software (OSS) over commercial products. It deals with Java GUI development tools and technologies only.

After introducing the practice of tool selection for Java technology and covering some aspect of OSS, we will focus on perhaps the most crucial, and often irreversible, choice in Java GUI tool selection: whether to opt for Swing or SWT. After discussing the various issues related to these two toolkits in detail, other tools and technologies available to Java GUI developers are outlined.

This chapter is structured as follows:

11.1, Introduction to tool selection discusses the general issues involved in selecting ingredient technologies and tools for building a Java GUI.

11.2, Evaluating open source software illustrates various aspects of OSS technology evaluation in more detail, introducing the OSS maturity model.

11.3, SWT or Swing? is dedicated to the differences in the two foundational technologies for Java desktop GUIs.

11.4, Other GUI technologies discusses some alternative technologies to SWT and Swing for Java GUIs.

11.5, Utility libraries lists various (mostly OSS) GUI utility libraries, including development, security and deployment tools, sets of specialized components, and utility libraries such as JGoodies, Glazed Lists and others.

11.6, Test tools discusses some GUI testing tools for Java.

11.7, Profiling tools illustrates some profiler tools for Java GUIs.

11.8, GUI builders discusses some visual editors for content assembly that are available for Java developers.

11.9, Presentation layer technologies demonstrates some Swing look and feels and presentation technologies for SWT.

11.10, Declarative GUIs with Java discusses the various alternatives for specifying GUIs declaratively for Java-based applications.

11.1   Introduction to tool selection

Literally hundreds of Java libraries, plug-ins, and tools for Java development are available on the market, with either OSS or commercial licenses. Not taking advantage of such a bounty would be a pity, given the maturity of many of these products, which have been built over years, and the added value they provide, often as OSS. Perhaps the strongest aspect of Java technology as a whole lies in its community of developers and its orientation towards open source and free collaboration: the OSS offering is just the final by-product of this active, open, collaborative climate.

Such an abundance of products poses problems over the best mix of libraries and tools. Many situations are possible, ranging from development teams tactically choosing libraries and tools for a single project, to a company selecting tools and libraries for a long-term strategic investment in personnel training and large-scale adoption for multiple projects.

Assuming that you have a development environment already set up, which hopefully provides modern comforts such as code editors, unit testing, refactoring tools, concurrent versioning, and continuous integration, to develop a decent GUI the following ingredients are usually required:

- Support libraries – specific layout managers, look and feel, favorite logging facility, XML parsing, and so on.
- A GUI testing tool of your choice. Such a tool would also be used for acceptance testing.
- Optionally, a visual GUI builder.
- A set of development tools specific to client application development, such as deployment support (either using JNLP or creating an installer package), code obfuscators, license management, and others.
- Domain-specific libraries, where required, such as a library for representation of currency and monetary values.

11.2   Evaluating open source software

Before reviewing the best OSS product currently available for Java GUI development, how should you evaluate the usefulness of an OSS technology, and how can you make an informed plan about the ingredient technologies that will be used in a project?

When evaluating the adoption of a tool or a library, some practical considerations apply:

- The type of product license, and whether it is compatible with other OSS you plan to use and with your overall business goal. For example, suppose you plan to build an application for playing music using the Eclipse RCP. You might find an OSS Java library that plays all sorts of popular music formats, released under the GPL license[1]. In such a scenario, it is not legally possible to combine such a library with the Eclipse RCP and obtain a commercial product.

- Satisfying your requirements. The most important point is how effective the OSS is for solving your problems. This is key. It doesn't matter how well documented, mature, and powerful a tool or a library is if it doesn't meet your needs.

- The community involved with the project – whether any active on-line forums or other means for useful exchange exist with people that already use and are knowledgeable with the technology or tool.

  One consequence of a vibrant user community can be a reduction in the cost of professional services.

- The availability of useful documentation. This can be easily checked with a Web search. The quality and coverage of the documentation required depends on the importance of the OSS in your application scenario. If you are looking for something useful but not critical to your development, such as, say, a GUI test tool for a small internal application, you may not be concerned if there is no documentation for advanced customization features. In contrast, if you are looking for a critical component of your GUI, you should be careful in assessing the availability of effective documentation for advanced users.

- How the tool or technology you are investigating integrates with your existing basket of technologies. For example, if you use the JBuilder IDE and you find an OSS layout manager library, you need to know how well it can be integrated with JBuilder's visual editor, and whether it is available as an IDE extension than can be added to your development environment.

  The only sure way to assess the compatibility of a new tool or library with an existing environment and your class path is by testing. Overlooking compatibility issues can lead to degradation of an implementation. For example, including a library that use an XML file for configuration, while your application is already using a preferences file, results in an application with configuration data scattered over two separate files.

- The current maturity level of the product and its evolution strategy. Some OSS libraries start off small and pretty but grow to be huge and ugly by trying to solve everybody's problems in the most comprehensive way. In such cases,

---

1. For more on OSS licenses, see the discussion about RCP licensing in Chapter 13.

you are either forced to fork[2] the code base, and thus take responsibility for the code, or put up with bloated installation JAR files and amend your code for newer features you might not actually need.

Open Source Maturity Model

This section discusses a specific, formal model for assessing the maturity of OSS. Despite being a general technique that can be applied to comprehensive scenarios, including hardware, infrastructure software and large applications, the main ideas can also be used for selecting the best tools for smaller projects and in daily work.

The Open-Source Maturity Model (OSMM) described in (Bernard 2004) proposes a model for assessing open source products for their readiness for use in an industrial production environment. It can be useful to companies that are evaluating how a given OSS technology can fit within a given software development organization. In many cases though, when limiting to consider only OSS Java development technologies and for small projects, there is little need to resort to a fully-fledged model.

Factors such as functionality, support, documentation, training, product integration, and professional services are considered in the OSMM. The model considers two types of users: *early adopters*, who are more keen to adopt new but unfinished OSS technology, and their counterparts, the *pragmatists*, as well as three levels of implementation of the OSS in a project: experimentation, pilot, production.

The OSMM assesses an OSS product's maturity in three steps:

1. Assessing product elements. The output of this phase is a set of scores for each of the key product elements. Sub-steps of this phase are:
   - Define requirements. Determine the required functionality for the current scenario.
   - Locate resources. Determine whether essential resources are available to assist your organization in implementing the open source software. Examples include specialized consultants, or an approved partner company.
   - Assess element maturity. Maturity levels range from *non-existent product* to *production-ready*.
   - Assign a final element score in the range 1–10.
2. Assign weights summing to 10 to each element's maturity score to reflect its importance. For example, in evaluating a GUI testing tool, good documentation could be more important to the product's overall maturity assessment than the availability of professional services. Default values are shown in Table 11.1.

---

2.   Some licenses don't allow modification of OSS source code that is to be used commercially.

3. Calculate overall product OSMM score.

OSMM ranking = (Element Score × Element Weightings)

The output of an OSMM assessment is a numeric score between 0 and 100 that is then compared with recommended values. Table 11.2 shows the minimum values suggested by default by the model.

Table 11.1   Table 1 OSMM default weights

Software	4
Support	2
Documentation	1
Training	1
Integration	1
Professional Services	1

Table 11.2   Table 2 OSMM recommended minimum scores

	Type of user	
Purpose of Use	**Early adopters**	**Pragmatist**
Experimentation	25	40
Pilot	40	60
Production	60	70

11.3   SWT or Swing?

After a general introduction to OSS evaluation comes perhaps the most critical choice in technology selection for a Java GUI project, one that will shape the development and dictate support and testing tools: the base GUI toolkit. Deciding which GUI toolkit to use for a GUI is extremely important, as this choice is hard to reverse. This section discusses and compares both toolkits thoroughly.

The toolkits

We assume readers are more experienced with Swing than SWT, so a quick introduction for readers not familiar with SWT is also provided.

Although it is a valid choice in various situations, for brevity AWT has only been considered briefly here.

The Swing toolkit and typical problems using it

Swing has been around since 1997, and a large number of resources such as documentation, code example, discussion forums, and so on, are available on line and in books. This also implies the existence of a large number of experienced developers proficient in Swing.

While Swing can be seen as a more conservative and less risky choice over SWT, it nevertheless suffers from a number of well-known issues that developers need to deal with:

* Swing applications need to be finely tuned, both as regards the final appearance of GUIs, by choosing or customizing an existing look and feel, adjusting pixels for baseline text alignment[3] and other fine details, and for the final implementation, which needs to be profiled and optimized for almost every non-trivial application.

  Worse, operating system vendors constantly update their platforms both for the appearance and richness of GUI components, involving Swing look and feel implementations in a never-ending chase in which native GUIs are constantly leading innovation and Swing is lagging behind[4].

* Swing is currently too basic a toolkit to support any but the most basic GUIs. In fast-paced production environments it therefore has to be complemented by other support libraries to provide cost-effective implementation and high-quality GUI detail. Producing good GUIs using the Swing toolkit alone is still too labor-intensive and needlessly hard.

* Swing's history lacks a complex project for effective testing, as Eclipse was for SWT, and is characterized by premature release and the commitment of Sun to diehard compatibility with legacy applications written as long ago as 1997. Because of this, it feels cumbersome and convoluted in some aspects. It is easy to criticize some of its architectural choices and implementation details, but nevertheless some parts of it are not of excellent quality.

* In the past Sun's support for Swing has been inadequate for its large developer base and its diffusion to the variety of applications built on top of Swing. Today there still are many bugs that have been open since the late

---

3.   See Chapter 9.
4.   This does not even consider the case of users personalizing their desktop environment: Swing Version 1.5 does not yet fully support native OS themes and some other customizations.

1990s[5], and the toolkit itself has been merely maintained in recent years. Sun's Swing development team has coped with these issues heroically, but perhaps only the advent of SWT and the jolt of fresh competition it brought to the scene has revived Sun's efforts with Swing.

Standard Windowing Toolkit

Readers familiar with Standard Windowing Toolkit (SWT) library can safely skip this section: the next section discusses the differences between SWT and the Swing toolkit.

Despite common folklore, SWT is not tied into Windows[6]. SWT runs on Apple Macintosh, Linux (using GTK or Motif), and a number of J2ME platforms. The design strategy of SWT focuses on building a simple, essential GUI toolkit that produces GUIs that are closely linked to the native environment, but abstract enoughs to be portable across supported platforms. SWT delegates common components such as labels, lists, tables and so on to native widgets, as AWT does, while emulating more sophisticated componesnts such as toolbars on Motif in Java, similar to Swing's strategy.

SWT has been designed to be as inexpensive as possible. One result of this is that it is native-oriented to the current platform: SWT provides different Java implementations for each platform, and each of these implementations makes native calls to the underlying platform implementation through the Java Native Interface, JNI. AWT is different, in that all platform-dependent details are hidden in native C code and the Java implementation is the same for all the platforms. This is illustrated in Figure 11.1.

Despite similarity in the features they provide, SWT and AWT have different design objectives:

- SWT explicitly aims at using native-driven widgets and being in control of the underlying OS GUI toolkit, while AWT attempts a simple form of cross-platform GUI support.

- AWT's overall philosophy is to provide a least-common- denominator across all platforms, while SWT also supports widgets by emulating them on platforms on which they are not supported natively.

- AWT hides the native layer from the Java programmer, while SWT make it available.

---

5. For example *'ButtonGroup-cannot reset the model to the initial unselected state'* or *'JMenuBar.setHelpMenu() not yet implemented'* are still open from 1997, as can be seen at http://bugs.sun.com/bugdatabase.
6. Even though its API has been designed in a very Windows-centric fashion.

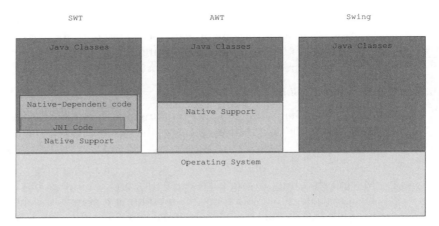

Figure 11.1   Java GUI toolkit architectures

- AWT employs different peers on different platforms, and exposes a common, cross-platform widget to the Java developer, while SWT provides less insulation from the native widgets.

The following table sketches the different widgets available for the main Java GUI toolkits.

Table 11.3   Comparison of visual components
in Standard toolkits

Component	SWT	Swing	AWT
Advanced button	✔	✔	
Advanced text area	✔	✔	
Button	✔	✔	✔
Internal windows		✔	
Label	✔	✔	✔
List	✔	✔	✔
Menu	✔	✔	
Progress bar	✔	✔	
Sash	✔	✔	

Table 11.3   Comparison of visual components in Standard toolkits (Continued)

Component	SWT	Swing	AWT
Scale	✔	✔	
Slider	✔	✔	
Spinner	✔	✔	
TabFolder	✔	✔	
Table	✔	✔	✔
Text area	✔	✔	✔
Toolbar	✔	✔	✔
Tree	✔	✔	

The following figure shows the main classes of the class hierarchy of the SWT toolkit.

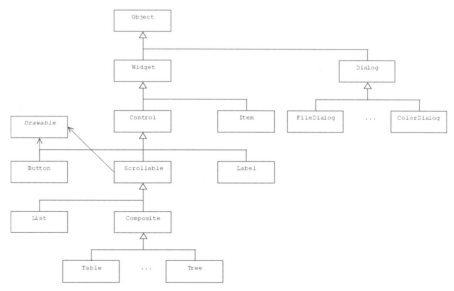

Figure 11.2   SWT widgets essential class hierarchy

Swing developers learning SWT might experience some difficulty in getting into its API style, which is more practical and simplified than Swing's. The main things that usually perplex Swing developers learning SWT are:

- The use of *styles* – bit masks represented as integers that customize the various aspects of a widget.

- The fact that when creating every widget, it is mandatory to specify the parent container as a parameter in the constructor.

For example, check box and button widgets are obtained using the same SWT widget (`org.eclipse.swt.Button`) with two different styles (respectively `SWT.PUSH` and `SWT.CHECK`).

After initial puzzlement, developers usually start to appreciate the coherence and predictability of the API and its good balance between the amount of control of low-level details and overall ease of use.

Native resource management with SWT

An important difference between SWT and Swing is in SWT's handling of native resources – platform resources that are allocated natively through the SWT API. Such resources must be explicitly released by the programmer through the `dispose()` method. The JVM's garbage collector finalizes unreferenced SWT objects, just as for any other object, but it does not dispose of the native resources used by them.

Native resources are represented in SWT by the following objects or their subclasses: `Color`, `Cursor`, `Display`, `Font`, `GC`, `Image`, `Printer`, `Region`, and `Widget`. Apart from the last, in the case of `Container` widgets, when disposing a parent container automatically disposes of all its contents, all other instances should be carefully disposed when no longer needed. The rule is that the object that created them is also responsible for disposing of them.

Typical problems when using SWT

SWT also has its own shortcomings, the main ones being:

- Developers cannot expect wide diffusion of SWT to less popular platforms. Porting the SWT toolkit to new platforms and maintaining existing ones is complex work that require a deep knowledge of the various GUI platforms and of SWT's inner workings, so it is hard for the open source initiative to successfully port SWT to minor platforms.

- SWT is a new API and as such requires costly learning. On the other hand, the greater spread of Swing means that it is widely taught in universities, and many organizations already have developers skilled in Swing who can mitigate the learning effort for novice programmers. The balance is changing, however, as SWT gains in popularity over Swing, at least for some application typologies.

- There is not yet a real market of SWT widgets and third-party libraries. This is not a serious hurdle in itself, as SWT will continue to thrive under the shadow of the Eclipse project, which today provides all reusable classes and utilities for SWT-powered applications. In some niche application domains, however, this could be a problem, such as the rich ad-hoc components or chart widgets that are available for the Swing toolkit.

- Some developers and managers feel that SWT and its related technologies (JFace, high-level utility classes, and the Eclipse RCP) have yet to prove their maturity and viability as a fully-fledged base toolkit, not just the GUI framework that powers Eclipse. Investing in learning and building a code base on such a stack of technologies is still seen as controversial by some. This perception may change with time and other factors, such as the evolution of competing technologies like AJAX[7].

JFace

A good design choice made by SWT's architects was to separate the low-level features (basic widgets, basic content handling, and events) clearly from the utility support built on top of widgets (data handling, commands, application windows, wizards, handy support for native resource disposal, and so on). The latter layer is provided by the JFace library. Developers normally use JFace support on top of SWT, and manipulate raw SWT widgets only when specifying content details or handling low-level events. All data handling and high-level control (commands) is processed by means of JFace.

One of the advantages of separating basic widget support from higher-level features is that SWT remains compact and self-contained. This in turn makes SWT easier to learn for a novice, and more straightforward to use also for experienced developers.

Choosing a toolkit

Since SWT was released there has been a lot of discussion in the Java GUI developer community over which toolkit is the best – of an unexpectedly exasperated tone. A sort of religious war has been raging among developers over such an apparently mundane topic.

Putting away any religious bias, the solution to this puzzle is clear: there is no single 'best' toolkit. Both SWT and Swing have their own strong points and weaknesses and are individually best suited for specific problems. This is actually great

---

7. A discussion of new Web-oriented GUI technologies (such as Ajax) is provided in *Bandwidth and interaction* in Chapter 9 – see page 363.

news for Java developers, because it widens the possibilities. Increased power comes at a price though – Java GUI developers need to stay up-to-date on more than a single library.

The hidden cost of learning

Learning the basics of SWT is not too difficult for a Swing developer, given the fact that both toolkits share the same architectural concepts (single event dispatch thread, event model, overall toolkit widgets). SWT and Swing result in two different programming experiences, however, Swing being higher-level and Smalltalk-like, while SWT feels more like C/C++. Indeed at times it feels pretty much like programming Windows MFC. These tactical differences in the API style can confuse inexperienced programmers and double the workload of learning and mastering both toolkits. This is the major drawback, and is the hidden cost of the coexistence of two independent toolkits for Java.

Apart from basic concepts, however, such as events, layout managers, and simple widget handling, the two toolkits are rather different, both in philosophy and practical features. Failing to acknowledge this and trying to use them without considering their specificity – for example, trying to customize the appearance of SWT widgets to the pixel, or avoiding fine-tuning the details of Swing GUIs – is another example of the 'going against the flow' complexity booster discussed in Chapter 6.

The speed myth

It is not normally possible to assess whether SWT is faster than Swing, because there are so many parameters to consider in a fair comparison, such as raw speed depending on a given port of SWT, the type of application, or the time spent profiling and optimizing the particular application. Such factors make a thorough assessment of the two technologies possible in only few cases.

The Swing team has worked hard to improve performance as much as possible in recent releases, so that the 'raw speed' issue – SWT uses native OS-specific resources, and thus faster than Swing – seems less important than in the past. In these circumstances runtime performance of all but trivial GUIs depends mainly on the overall design and amount of care spent in its optimization, rather than the GUI toolkit alone. Having said that, one would expect an SWT profiled[8] application to take less memory and run faster than an equally profiled Swing application, but this is more a personal expectation than a mathematical law.

---

8. An application whose runtime execution has been carefully examined by means of a profiler tool and optimized accordingly.

Heavily-loaded widgets

Another common assumption is that SWT supports situations in which components need to sustain large volumes of data or other non-trivial situations, such as very large trees, much better than Swing. While such differences still remain, they are smaller than one would expect.

Consider a directory with 10,000 files on the local file system. If you don't mind cluttering your own file system, you could create such a directory by executing the following raw lines of code:

```
public static void create10000Files(){
  File f = null;
  for (int i = 0; i < 10000; i++) {
      f = new File("C:/temp/testfiles/file"+i);
      try {
          f.createNewFile();
      } catch (IOException e) {
          e.printStackTrace();
      }
  }
}
```

Opening a Swing file chooser dialog on such a directory and waiting for it to populate takes roughly 2.1 seconds[9], shown on the left in Figure 11.3. The equivalent dialog in SWT takes 1.3 seconds to completely start up. When using 50,000 files instead, the Swing dialog takes roughly 4.9 seconds to fully start up, and its SWT counterpart needs 7.6 seconds.

Even though this is a simple example, it nevertheless shows a couple of things:

*   The power of competition. Swing performance used to be *much worse* than SWT in the past. In one project in 2000 we spent almost a month optimizing a Swing file chooser that was hanging when visualizing directories with thousands of files in a core part of the application. This was a substantial hindrance, and such accidents gave Swing a bad reputation among developers.

*   Using the underlying native widgets via SWT is more reassuring for developers than using Swing, especially if they know up front that an application risks a potential performance bottleneck.

*   Figure 11.3 shows how closely the Swing appearance in J2SE 1.5 using Windows look and feel matches the native operating system. Such a

---

9.   These measurements are indicative only and provide data useful for a first evaluation. They were performed on a 1.6 GHz Pentium M 725 with 512 MB running Windows XP Professional, with 90MB of available physical memory. The application was executed first without measurement, then the results of the next three executions were averaged. Data gathered in this way is by no means reliable or indicative of real performance.

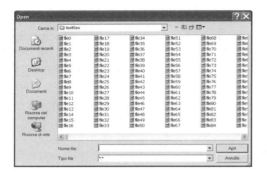

Figure 11.3   Swing (left) and SWT (right) file choosers

similarity is limited mostly to the presentation layer rather than effective interactions details, which still differ – for example, the native platform's contextual menus for files are not supported in the Swing dialog.

A similar comparison can be done for data tables with 10,0000 elements and a specific render, in this case a check box for Boolean values. No conspicuous differences emerge, although the SWT version seems slightly more responsive than the Swing case. Figure 11.4 shows this with Swing on the left and SWT on the right.

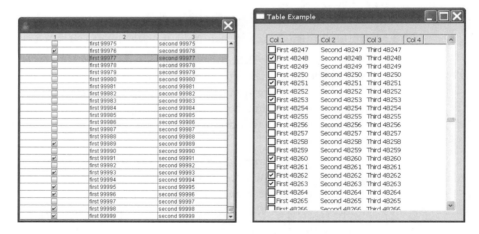

Figure 11.4   Swing (left) and SWT (right) large tables

In conclusion, data loads foreseen for an application can influence the choice of toolkit, but performance differences with JSE 1.5 are less dramatic than one might expect.

Scenarios to which SWT+JFace is better suited than Swing

Behind the IBM marketing talk and the implacable facade of the Eclipse Foundation there is real value in SWT (and JFace) that can support developers better than existing alternatives in many practical cases. The following list summarizes the main scenarios in which SWT is a good choice over Swing and other Java GUI technologies:

- Where the main target platforms are Windows, MacOS, Linux, and some J2ME profiles, SWT provides the many benefits discussed previously without limiting development – although admittedly at various levels of soundness.

- When the advantages of native widget support are important, SWT should be considered over Swing. These advantages are:
  - Different (that is, native) appearance and behavior on different platforms – SWT makes it is possible to completely mimic a native application.
  - A simpler API – all low-level details are left to the native GUI infrastructure.

- When the use of an RCP framework is advisable, such as for large projects, or applications with planned long-term maintenance, and it is viable to use SWT, using the Eclipse RCP[10] should be considered over similar technologies. The Eclipse RCP is in fact probably one of strongest points in favor of the adoption of SWT.

- Developers should be willing to embrace the technology, because effective use of it ultimately depends on them. This means that developers should be keen to learn the new API and deal with the typical problems SWT brings.

Scenarios in which Swing is a better choice than SWT

There are several cases in which Swing carries advantages over SWT:

- When maximum platform independence is needed Swing should be preferred. Platform independence should always be considered from a cost-driven perspective: vague long-term options should be examined very critically, as full platform independence is a costly and laborious feature to achieve.

- When providing the exact appearance and behavior of the GUI across a wide range of platforms is a requirement.

- For GUIs with particular graphics requirements (fancy, or extremely customized GUIs). Such developments should focus on Swing because of its greater rendering flexibility.

---

10. See Chapter 13.

- If developers already experienced in Swing and the wider diffusion of Swing skills are available. This means developers with a *deep* knowledge of Swing. Given the complexity of the toolkit, having just – say – delivered simple forms is not enough to be considered truly experienced with a complex framework such as Swing.

- When ad-hoc components are required. Using Swing to create a component such as the one discussed in the example application in Chapter 16 is straightforward, while with SWT the Draw2D library, part of the GEF library, must be used. There is no equivalent to Swing's `Graphics` and `Graphics2D` classes for accessing low-level raster rendering within standard widgets in SWT.

  Building ad-hoc components with SWT also renders one of its strong points useless – its support for native widgets. If ad-hoc components form the main parts of the GUI, some of the benefits of SWT, such as its native widgets, are lost, while you pay the price of its shortcomings, such as lack of availability on all Java-powered platforms.

From Swing to SWT

Some of the main differences between Swing and SWT are listed in the following table.

Table 11.4   Some of the differences between Swing and SWT

Concept	Swing	SWT+JFace
Data provider	MVC Models (that is, `TreeModel`, `TableModel`, and so on)	Implementations of IContentProvider
Data presentation	Cell renderers (that is, `CellRenderer`)	Implementations of ILabelProvider
Customization of data presentation in data-bound widgets (trees, tables, and so on)	Complete (every widget can be used)	Limited (for example, for tables, only images and check boxes can be embedded in table cells)
Main choosers (file, color, and so on)	Available as panels	Mostly available only as dialogs
Providing scroll behavior	Explicitly add `JScrollPane` instance	On main widgets use `SWT.*_SCROLL` style.

For more details, convenience wrapper classes, and a general discussion about Swing versus SWT, a thorough tutorial for migrating Swing code to SWT available on line[11].

Mix and match

It is of course possible to avoid the choice of one toolkit over the other by mixing them in the same application. Swing and SWT are increasingly being combined in a variety of development scenarios. There is often a need to employ legacy code in a newly-written SWT GUI, or to use a specialized third-party Swing widget in a SWT GUI, such as for example packaging an existing Swing GUI into an Eclipse plug-in, or to use some of the features of SWT from within a Swing GUI.

While mixing SWT and Swing widgets in the same application is technically feasible, there are a few design points that must be observed:

- Swing and SWT are different toolkits in appearance and behavior. Mixing them in the same GUI will confuse users. To avoid this, always try to follow the GUI guidelines and style of the embedding toolkit. For example, when developing an application using SWT and a third-party Swing widget, install the native look and feel for Swing. More generally, when embedding Swing widgets within SWT GUIs, always use the look and feel of the current platform.

- Following from the previous point, it is good plan never to mix the same type of widgets in the same application. For example, despite the fact that a Swing `JTree` and an SWT `Tree` can be made to look very similar, they have different behaviors and subtle interaction differences that will confuse users.

- From a visual viewpoint, carefully circumscribe the use of widgets from one toolkit in another to minimize user confusion. For example, limit to a single Swing ad-hoc component within an SWT application, or embed a whole Swing-powered panel into an Eclipse plug-in.

Here are the various possible technical combinations that allow a mix of the two GUI toolkit technologies.

- *Swing with SWT.* The most interesting situation is using Swing widgets from within an SWT application, often from within Eclipse. This is made straight-forward by using the SWT class `org.eclipse.swt.awt.SWT_AWT` and adding the Swing or AWT widgets to it. This is the most frequent solution in SWT applications that need to include a Swing GUI, chiefly because this

---

11. The *Migrate your Swing application to SWT* tutorial is available from IBM's developerWorks at: http://www-128.ibm.com/developerworks/edu/j-dw-java-swing2swt-i.html

approach works well in practice and it is well supported by the SWT toolkit on a variety of platforms.

- *Swing on top of SWT.* SwingWT[12] is an open source project that aims to build the Swing API on top of SWT instead of AWT. The project has already been adopted for some applications despite being currently still in beta.

- *SWT on top of Swing.* Some OSS projects focus on making SWT available on top of Swing. This is particularly useful for executing an SWT GUI on a platform that is not yet supported by the relative platform-dependent runtime. Some tools that adopt such an approach, all in the early stages of development, are SWTSwing and SWT on Swing[13]. At the time of writing, SWTSwing appears to have been discontinued.

SWT and Swing together: the Java GUI dream team?

It is possible that the apparent schism within Java GUI toolkit technology between SWT and Swing will be partially resolved with time. It is still unclear how, as various options are viable. Practically, it is possible to incorporate some of the SWT ideas or architecture into AWT, even though the two libraries are in reality totally independent. SWT technology was in fact built as a total replacement for Swing – there are no references to AWT and Swing from within SWT. Even simple classes such as `Point` and `Rectangle` were duplicated in SWT.

The inclusion of portions of SWT within the standard Java API would however pose some technical challenges, as SWT is not completely platform independent. It would also further Balkanize and clutter the Java GUI API, which has grown by accretion from AWT to Swing, and through the various API revisions and enhancements of Swing. Perhaps the biggest obstacles are political and organizational – SWT is maintained outside Sun's control and is constantly evolving alongside Eclipse. SWT also requires maintenance for its platform-dependent lower layer on a variety of machines.

The GUI technology landscape has never been so rich and promising for Java. By choosing between SWT and Swing, or a combination of both, developers can build sophisticated user interfaces that leverage the power of Java technology.

11.4   Other GUI technologies

By themselves, or as the foundation of an RCP application, Swing and SWT are not the only available base technologies for GUI development. This section reviews other GUI technologies that are related to Java, both open source and commercial. The list is partial and by no means complete.

---

12.   http://swingwt.sourceforge.net/
13.   Available at: http://www.3plus4.de/swt/

Table 11.5   GUI technologies related to Java

Name	Notes	URL
Remote SWT	Exports the graphic display of a Java SWT application running on one host on a remote host, also transmitting GUI events.	`http://rswt.sourceforge.net/`
Canoo ULC	Execute Java Swing application with domain logic running on the server. Requires a small-footprint client installation.	`http://www.canoo.com/`
Asperon	Combination of Java and XML running in a browser using JVM 1.1.	`http://www.asperon.com/`
Thinlets	Execute in browser using JVM 1.1.	`http://thinlet.sourceforge.net/home.html`
XUL	Content in XML, Control and Business Domain in Javascript, for Firefox/Mozilla browsers.	`http://www.mozilla.org/projects/xul`
OpenLazlo	XML and Javascript rendered in Flash, standalone client or with server support (J2EE)[a].	`http://www.laszlosystems.com/`

a. Despite not using the Java language on the client (as of Version 3.x) OpenLazlo's popularity is growing among Java developers.

Almost all the products listed in the table are bound to the Web browser, testifying to the enormous interest for empowering Web technology with the power of fully-fledged Java GUIs. The technologies in Table 11.5 that use declarative languages, such as XUL and Thinlets, are discussed later in this chapter.

11.5   Utility libraries

This section lists a number of well-known and useful libraries and frameworks available for creating Java GUIs. Most of them target the Swing toolkit, essentially for historical reasons that reflect its longer availability than SWT. Similar libraries for SWT are expected to appear with time.

The list provided here is not meant to be exhaustive or fully descriptive of the features and details of each library. Interested readers are encouraged to visit the related Web sites for more information.

Security tools

Before diving into widgets and components, let's present some useful tools and libraries for GUI development.

Note that source code obfuscation is always needed to secure a Java application. License keys and the inner workings of the application can be tracked and hacked easily when full decompilation of executables is possible. Effective code obfuscation also impacts class design. At design time it is important to individuate carefully the set of core classes and methods that will be made inaccessible by means of obfuscation. Discussing the important topic of code obfuscation in depth is beyond the scope of this section.

The following list illustrates some of the available tools and libraries useful for securing the investment and hard work needed to build a professional Java application. In addition, downloading a decompiler such as JAD, DJ or Cavaj will help in testing the robustness of the security strategy chosen.

- yGuard is an OSS Java obfuscator packaged as an Ant task, and thus can easily be integrated into many development environments.

  `http://www.yworks.com/en/products_yguard_about.htm`

- Zelix KlassMaster is a Java obfuscator that claims to provide an unmatched obfuscation technology while also attempting various optimizations to the final obfuscated code. It is licensed commercially.

  `http://www.zelix.com/klassmaster`

- JLicense is a library for managing, creating, and validating license keys, and also includes a simple GUI tool. Its use in binary format is free, but source code needs to be purchased separately.

  `http://www.websina.com/products/jlicense.html`

- TrueLicense is an OSS library for handling the creation and validation of licenses. It uses the Java Cryptography Extension library (JCE). A Swing-based wizard is provided for installing new licenses by users .

  `https://truelicense.dev.java.net`

Paradoxically, an OSS license tool can be more secure than a home-made or even a commercial one, because its architecture and implementation has been publicly exposed and all sorts of attacks and weak points have been studied as a result, allowing countermeasures to be added to the public code. If you feel current OSS license tools are not secure enough for your application, you can opt for a commercial solution or a custom one, possibly by modifying an existing OSS license library.

Deployment tools

An important part of concluding the development of a client application is being able to deploy it effectively on the target machine. A number of options are available:

- For Java Web Start technology, a number of OSS and commercial tools ease the generation of JNLP files and certificates, such as CSR Generator for creating certificate signing requests, or the Java Web Start tools that form part of JDK 5.0 and are available in various IDEs.

  `http://www.apgrid.org/csrgenerator`

- Advanced Installer for Java provides native support for the installation of Java code on Windows platforms. It allows also the creation of MSI (Microsoft Installer) files.

  `http://www.advancedinstaller.com/java.html`

- Install4J is a commercial multi-platform installer that provides native integration with the underlying platform.

  `http://www.ej-technologies.com/products/install4j/`
  `overview.html`

- IzPack is an OSS Java installer tested on Windows, MacOS X, Linux, and BSD platforms.

  `http://www.izforge.com/izpack`

- GCJ is an OSS compiler of Java to native code. Compilation can be done both directly on Java source code and also on `.class` files. The result is a native executable that is better performing and more secure, even if this approach loses platform independency. This approach also suffers from a major drawback: compilation of Swing and AWT applications is not yet fully supported, although that for SWT is working.

  `http://gcc.gnu.org/java/status.html`

Deployment also impacts users, and its design should therefore consider them. In some cases, such as shrink-wrapped products distributed on line as shareware, a technically simpler solution such as Java Web Start might prove unappealing for some users, as they might feel that accepting the certificate required to launch the application represented a security risk.

The remainder of this section discusses widgets and components available to Swing and SWT developers.

Glazed Lists

Glazed Lists is a library for handling GUI-savvy list collections. It provides a number of useful features, such as easy creation of table and list models, support for filtering and sorting (and their combinations), and a thread-safe architecture. The library supports both Swing and SWT toolkits. Performance on large lists has been considered, with optimized sorting and filtering algorithms. A number of non-GUI utility manipulations on lists are also provided. Figure 11.5 shows a screenshot of Glazed List at work.

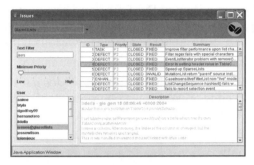

Figure 11.5   Screenshot of the Glazed List demo

Glazed Lists is provided with the LGPL OSS license. It is available at `http://publicobject.com/glazedlists/`.

JGoodies Swing Suite

JGoodies Swing Suite is a comprehensive, professional suite for easing the burden of writing Swing applications. It ranges from basic support (look and feel, data validation, factories, utility code for form-based GUIs, data binding) to reusable components such as wizards, splash windows, log-in, license, 'About' dialogs, and so on, and includes various utility classes (enhanced help, lazy loading support). While most packages are distributed under a commercial license, some of them are freely available.

The following useful parts of the JGoodies Swing suite are released as OSS:

- *Animation.* A compact library for creating real-time animations with Swing, using concepts and notions from the W3C specification for the Synchronized Multimedia Integration Language (SMIL).

- *Data binding.* A useful library for binding Swing widgets to data sources (data models) in various ways.

- *Forms.* An easy to use and effective layout manager and builder specialized for form-based GUIs.

- *Looks.* A set of professional look and feels. Looks is discussed in more detail on page 436.

- *Validation.* A library for performing data validation and notification.

A screenshot of the Looks demo is shown in Figure 11.6.

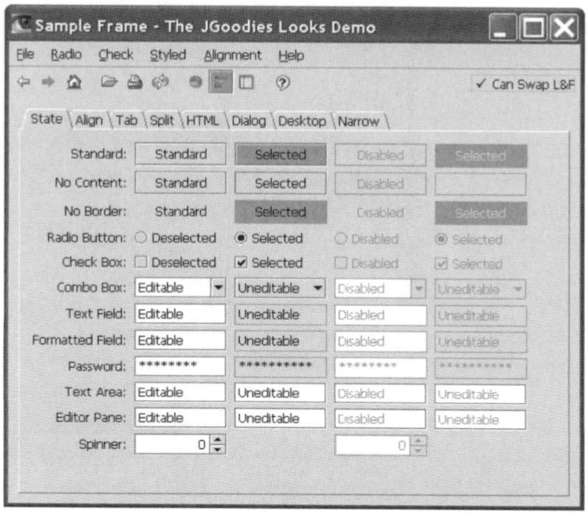

Figure 11.6   Demonstration screenshot of JGoodies Looks

Among the many things I personally appreciate most in the JGoodies libraries is the careful attention to detail they provide. For example, see the text baseline alignment in the form shown in Figure 11.6, where the text in the label is aligned with the text in the corresponding text field or combo box.

JGoodies is available at `http://www.jgoodies.com`.

L2FProd Common Components

L2FProd Common Components is a set of Swing components available as OSS. The list of Swing widgets includes 'tip of the day,' property sheets, expandable/ collapsible lists, and others. Figure 11.7 shows the L2FProd `JFontChooser` component, both as a panel contained in a tabbed pane, and as a pop-up dialog.

L2FProd Common Components is available at `http://www.l2fprod.com`.

Other OSS component libraries

Other OSS component libraries relevant to Java GUIs include:

*   Buoy is a set of widgets on top of the Swing library that aims to provide a simpler development environment at a higher level of abstraction than plain Swing, with a minimal footprint of less than 200KB. Buoy is released as OSS.

    `http://buoy.sourceforge.net/`

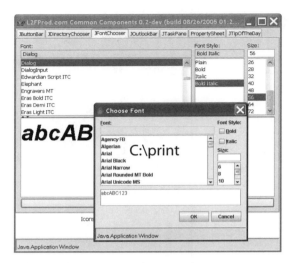

Figure 11.7   Demonstration screenshot of L2FProd Components

- The Java GUI Programming Extensions, Java-GPE, is an OSS library for developing Swing GUIs. Java-GPE includes some look and feels, some classes for preference dialogs, and other utility classes. See Figure 11.8 for a screenshot from the demo application.

  `http://www.markus-hillenbrand.de/javagpe`

- UICompiler is an OSS project that also provides a set of Swing widgets, ranging from a look and feel to various specialized choosers and general purpose components. A screenshot of the file chooser is shown in Figure 11.9 on page 418.

  `http://uic.sourceforge.net`

- Blazze provides a set of Swing components and utility classes specialized for business application GUIs. It is licensed as OSS.

  `http://blazze.sourceforge.net`

- JBalloon is a compact set of classes that provides balloon tooltips for Swing GUIs under the LGPL license.

  `http://www.allworldsoft.com/software/17-476-jballoontooltip.htm`

- Geosoft provides some utility classes under LGPL. Among them, the 2D graphics library provides a useful 2D graphics library and a rendering engine featuring layered hierarchical graphical objects, 3D world extents, style support, smart annotation, and image support.

  `http://geosoft.no`

- Batik is a Swing library for managing and rendering SVG[14] files licensed under the Apache OSS license. This library is used by many other products for managing and exporting data formats to SVG.

  `http://xml.apache.org/batik`

- JFreeChart is a library for generating charts licensed under LGPL. It can generate 2D and 3D pie charts, bar, line and area charts, scatter plots, Pareto, Gantt, and many other types of chart. It provides zooming, printing, and exporting to PDF, SVG, and bitmap formats.

  `http://www.jfree.org/jfreechart`

- Various OSS architectural frameworks for separating data from views are also available, such as TikeSwing or MVCMediator. For a critical discussion of the usefulness of such libraries in your application, see Chapter 6.

  TikeSwing: `http://sourceforge.net/projects/tikeswing`

  MVCMediator: `http://www.danmich.com/mvcmediator/1.0`

- CUF is a utility library and an application framework for building GUI applications in Swing that is also available for .NET. It provides callback handling close to .NET's delegates (Java CUF), a JTable extension, declarative state management of widgets, data binding, and more. Little documentation is currently available.

  `http://cuf.sourceforge.net`

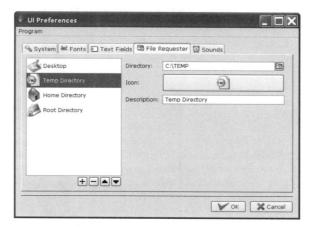

Figure 11.8   Demonstration of Java GPE preferences

---

14. SVG (Scalable Vector Graphics) is a language for describing two-dimensional graphics in XML.

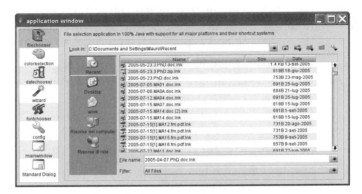

Figure 11.9   Demonstration of UI Compiler components

Some commercially-available Swing components

A great number of Swing-based widgets are available commercially from various vendors, some tens of libraries. Some of them are summarized here. The objective is not to promote one vendor over another, nor to provide an exhaustive and detailed list of the available features for each product, but just to highlight their existence. The list is not exhaustive and vendors were chosen without any prejudice towards their products.

- Eltima components provide a set of feature-rich widgets, although some of them might need some tweaking to fit into a standard Swing application coherently. Figure 11.10 shows a demo screenshot downloaded from the Eltima Web site.

    ```
    http://www.eltima.com
    ```

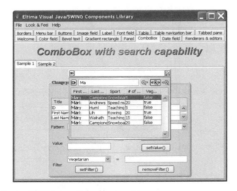

Figure 11.10   Screenshot of Eltima demonstration

- JAPI Libraries sports a set of specialized components (XML editor, and various browsers) and utility APIs.

  `http://www.japisoft.com`

- JSuite from Infragistics is a comprehensive although pricey set of components and utility classes for Swing: some AWT components are also supported. It includes Gantt charts, scheduling and calendar panels, advanced tables, navigation support, and more.

  `http://www.infragistics.com`

- ICESoft provides various browsers implemented in Swing, capable of rendering PDF, XML, XSL/XSLT, and many other formats and technologies.

  `http://www.icesoft.com`

- Javio provides a Web browser that supports HTML 4.0, CSS, and Javascript, plus other features, a graphic modeler component, and several widgets and tools for editing and viewing JavaHelp files, all implemented in Java.

  `http://www.javio.com`

- JGraph provides a range of specialized Swing ad-hoc graphic components that implement direct manipulation, in-place editing, zooming, pluggable routing algorithms, and more. Figure 11.11 shows the demo application of the Layout Pro component. JGraph also provides some general-purpose Swing components.

  `http://www.jgraph.com`

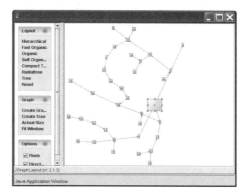

Figure 11.11   Screenshot of JGraph Layout Pro demonstration

- InfoNode provides a number of widgets, a dockable windows library for creating GUIs similar to the Eclipse IDE workbench, and a look and feel family. InfoNode products are available under a dual license: as a commercial product, or under the GPL license.

http://www.infonode.net

- ILOG's JViews library is a set of ad-hoc and custom components ranging from diagrams, maps, process control, Gantt diagrams, 2D and 3D charts, and others.

http://www.ilog.com

- Quest's JClass Desktopview library delivers a number of specialized widgets, including 2D and 3D chart components.

http://www.quest.com

- JProductivity Components! is a suite of calendars and date-oriented widgets that also includes a calculator and other components.

http://www.jproductivity.com

- JIDE provides a large set of components that include a dockable window framework, action support, extended tables, and other widgets. A number of look and feels are available as well that mimic Visual Studio and Eclipse appearances.

http://www.jidesoft.com

- ConfigureJ from JASE software is a Swing library for creating configurable menus, toolbars, and pop-ups that can be customized by the user.

http://www.configurej.com

- Webcharts3D from Greenpoint Inc. is a set of Swing components for rendering various types of chart.

http://www.gpoint.com

- I-net Crystal-Clear is not a component library, but is a report generator that can generate various types of report in many formats.

http://www.inetsoftware.de

- yWorks' yFiles is a library of ad-hoc components for visualizing, analyzing, and automatic layout of graphs and diagrams.

http://www.yworks.com

11.6 Test tools

This section lists only the most popular GUI testing tools specifically for Java desktop GUIs. Being written specifically for Swing/Java GUIs, these tools allow for a more robust widget location and other useful features tailored for Java GUIs. Unit test tools and general GUI test tools that can also test Java GUIs, such as

Eggplant, Rational Functional Tester, Xeus, and many others, are beyond the scope of this discussion.

- Abbot is a GUI testing framework that was initially available only for Swing, but has now also been ported to SWT – although its SWT support still needs improvement. Due to its API-centric nature, Abbot combines well with a unit test tool such as Junit. Costello is the companion tool for Abbot that enables recording and playback of Abbot GUI tests. Both Abbot and Costello are available as OSS.

  `http://abbot.sourceforge.net`

- Jacareto is a GUI testing tool released under the GPL. It performs recording and playback of GUI scripts, and can also be used for packaging animated demonstrations of existing Swing applications.

  `http://jacareto.sourceforge.net`

- Jemmy is an (OSS) module of the Netbeans IDE that can also be used without Netbeans. Like the other tools listed here, it can record and play test scripts and automatic demos of existing applications.

  `http://jemmy.netbeans.org`

- JFCunit is an extension to Junit for testing GUIs and is distributed as OSS. An example of use of JFCUnit is provided in Chapter 8.

  `http://jfcunit.sourceforge.net`

- Marathon is a GUI testing framework built with Swing. It supplies a test script recorder, a script player, and an editor to edit test scripts manually. Scripts are implemented in Python. Among other features, it provides useful support for writing acceptance tests.

  `http://marathonman.sourceforge.net`

- qftestJUI is a test tool for Swing GUIs that provides a number of interesting features such as record and playback of test scripts, including an integrated test and debugger, and others. It is distributed under a commercial license.

  `http://www.qfs.de`

11.7 Profiling tools

Profiling a Java application is an essential activity that is needed for refining the implementation of any complex GUI. This section lists only the major products, given the many OSS simple but effective Java profilers that are available.

- JProfiler is a commercial product featuring thread, memory, CPU profiling, and specialized views.

  `http://www.ej-technologies.com`

- Netbeans Profiler is the profiler part of Netbeans. Its functions include CPU, memory, and thread profiling, as well as basic JVM monitoring by means of dynamic bytecode instrumentation[15]. Note that, depending on the current license scheme of JFluid, a proprietary Sun technology used in the Netbeans profiler, the whole profiler is not licensed as OSS.

  `http://profiler.netbeans.org`

- Eclipse Profiler is currently still in beta, but is nevertheless interesting for its implementation built with SWT.

  `http://sourceforge.net/projects/eclipsecolorer`

- JProbe is a commercial profiler that provides various features such as thread, memory, CPU and heap profiling, and a number of task-oriented GUIs for solving common profiling issues such as memory leaks and performance bottlenecks.

  `http://www.quest.com/jprobe`

- OptimizeIt from Borland is a powerful profiling tool that integrates with various IDEs.

  `http://www.borland.com/us/products/optimizeit`

11.8 GUI builders

Visual builders are tools for visually composing GUIs that then generate the final Java code. They help to define widget layout and various components details visually by means of direct manipulation. They leverage the fact that both SWT and Swing-AWT have JavaBeans-compliant APIs, and as such can be processed by automatic tools.

The utility of such tools can be explained in terms of cognitive burden. Humans find it much easier to understand the map of a place as an image rather than as a textual description, no matter how clever the description may be.

The following partial list summarizes some visual editors for Java GUIs. It is not exhaustive – several tens of visual editors for Java GUI are currently in existence.

- JBuilder provides one of the first really complete GUI builders that remains a competitive and unintrusive tool (see item 1 of the list on page 423).

  `http://www.borland.com/jbuilder`

- Netbeans, with its much-trumpeted Matisse visual editor, was a leap beyond its old GUI builder, even if some issues remain unresolved.

  `http://www.netbeans.org/`

---

15. See *JRE runtime management* in Chapter 5, page 214.

- Eclipse, with its VE (Visual Editor) plug-in, has had to solve a couple of technical problems, that of integrating SWT and Swing, and building a powerful foundation visual environment that can be extended easily by third-party developers. Given these constraints design choices were made that currently hinder its use as of Version 1.1, such as using a whole JVM per screen. These issues will hopefully be optimized in forthcoming versions.

- Intellij Idea also provides its own GUI builder environment. This provides basic two-way support and a number of layout managers, and, most importantly, it integrates elegantly with the rest of the IDE platform.

Good visual builders speed up development time, despite what diehard coders such as the author might think about them. After all, there is little to be proud of in the ability to put together a complex form with a grid bag layout without touching a visual editor or the documentation, unless of course you don't have anything better to do with your time and mental energies. More importantly, the real world contains various types of developers, each with different skills and roles. Employing a good visual builder in your project can help less-skilled developers take charge of more mundane tasks.

Substandard GUI builders only decrease development time at first. Going beyond basic use and integrating the generated code into a larger code base, or tweaking it, often loses any time saved by consuming the precious time of (usually) skilled developers.

A GUI builder is itself a GUI, and as such its main purpose should be to simplify the work of its users. Assume that the objective of a GUI builder should be to lower the cognitive burden of developing real-world GUIs instead of using a text editor. A GUI builder should therefore affect only the visualization and manipulation of a GUI, not the way the generated code is structured, nor impose other hindrances like support files – such as the ghastly Netbeans' `.form` files – or any other by-product of the GUI builder tool.

Here is a checklist of desirable features for a GUI builder:

1. Integration with the application's existing code. The generated code should be exportable or importable into the GUI builder without any restrictions. This avoids vendor lock-in, and generally ensures higher code quality and productivity.

2. Modification and customization of every aspect of the generated code. Once imported, the code should be made available for modifications as required.

3. Architectural flexibility. This is the higher-level version of the external code integration property. Many GUI builders completely ignore the fact that Java is an OOP language, and that developers work using design patterns as well as their own frameworks and conventions. OOP-conscious developers are often faced with the dilemma of using GUI builders and then having to

tweak the resulting code heavily. With some weaker GUI builders, this means losing the possibility of importing the GUI into the visual editor, or initially writing everything by hand.

4. Layout manager support. Unfortunately, this is the weakest aspect of any GUI builder, in that they need some form of built-in support for a given layout manager to be able to lay out widgets in the visual environment. The newest or less-known layout managers are often unsupported in GUI builders.

5. Quality of the generated code. GUI builders often generate unreadable, lengthy, and structured code that is hard to understand. This is important for applications with many screens and where code maintenance is an important issue.

6. Real two-way support. 'Two-way support' is the term used to indicate the automatic alignment of the source file with the visual representation provided by the GUI builder. Ideally, whatever modification is done in either of these views should immediately be reflected in the other, and vice versa. If something is easier to do in the text editor, rather than opening up a couple of dialogs and clicking around in the visual builder view, then the tool should support editing from the source code to the visual environment in every respect.

7. Optimization. Like any good user interface, GUI builders should be optimized for common tasks. Developers often need to put together form-based GUIs with labels, fields, and buttons aligned on a grid basis managed in some form of dynamic layout.

The next section covers look and feels and visual customizations for Swing and SWT GUIs.

11.9 Presentation layer technologies

Customizing the visual appearance of a Java GUI can provide a strong branding for a product, or give it the final touch that will make users enthusiastic. This is the 'magical power' of professional GUI design, but as well as magic, graphical appearance can also spoil an otherwise well-designed product when badly employed. Fine-tuning the appearance of an application should be done very carefully and not as an afterthought. Developers, following their mental model, tend to think about a visual theme or a look and feel as very easily replaceable, and thus secondary to the rest of the GUI. This is wrong.

Assuming that the visual appearance of a GUI is not an important issue is very dangerous, a fact to which anybody who has ever chosen a look and feel in haste can testify. Customizing the visual appearance of a GUI can also have powerful political connotations. The author has personally witnessed the use of a new look and feel as a 'political' means of quickly and easily demonstrating a result – any result – in a troubled project.

This section deals with the practical choice of a look and feel or OS theme. Issues like how to properly customize the visual appearance, whether to allow users to change the installed look and feel, and similar GUI design concerns were discussed in Chapter 3. For brevity the term 'look and feel' is also used to refer to SWT presentation layer customizations.

Assessing a look and feel

Choosing the right look and feel (L&F) for an application requires many parameters to be considered and shouldn't be an oversight – the L&F is often selected as an afterthought on very ephemeral and subjective considerations, without considering users.

A Swing L&F is a Java library, and as such the general discussion for assessing OSS in Section 11.2 applies. Specifically, the main criteria for assessing the suitability of a L&F for a given application are:

- Fitness for purpose
- Usability testing
- Technical considerations
- Esthetic considerations

Fitness for purpose refers to the intended use of the presentation layer in an application. A GUI's visual appearance does not have to please developers or managers, but it should have a purpose that is coherent with the whole product experience. Simplifying things, a good criteria is to focus on the principal categories of users for an application. This is not an exact rule, but it will avoid gross mistakes.

What is going to be the main group of users? When a GUI should please occasional users, as in a kiosk GUI, for example, then an 'eye-candy' visually pleasant L&F is a perfect choice. When the GUI is geared towards repetitive users, too many bells and whistles get in the way of daily work, and usability-driven GUIs should be preferred over visually compelling ones. Of course, both a visually appealing and a usable L&F is possible at the same time for a given application. The best way to assess the right balance of simplicity and visual appearance in any scenario is to perform a usability test with users, covering the tasks that are more frequent in real use and more dependent on visual appearance.

Technically-dependent performance is the easiest parameter to assess with profiling, without the need to be exact or statistically meaningful. While some statistics are more significant for Swing than for SWT GUIs, measurements never hurt. The next subsection considers the following data for various L&Fs:

- *Memory consumption.* How much memory does the L&F alone consume to support the required visual tricks?

- *Time consumption.* How fast is the L&F to load and operate? As an extreme case, an 'eye-candy' and amateurish L&F could prove too slow to render critical components, making the whole user experience unacceptable.

Esthetic considerations are also important when choosing the best L&F for a given application. GUIs are mundane artifacts, and they are subject to all the same fashions, personal tastes and tiresomeness of this kind of thing. Think of the sort of GUIs software had back in 1997. Would you like your hard-built application look like one of those? How do you think your customers would react to it?

Swing look and feels

There are many L&F implementations around, so many that a comprehensive list would be too large and of little practical use[16]. To provide a fair evaluation, the same application was used to measure some performance data, a tweaked version of the SwingSet2 demo application that forms part of Sun's distribution of JDK 1.5.

Developers often stop bothering about L&F and visual details as soon as a good candidate is found that works well with their application. An extra step that most professional L&Fs support is customization of the L&F to optimize visual details and enrich the appeal of the GUI. More important than optimizing appearance details, most L&Fs support different color themes. Color themes, with their varying contrasts, are especially useful for visually-impaired or color-blind users[17].

Ocean 1.5

Ocean is the replacement for the glorious Steel L&F[18], the default cross-platform L&F for the Swing library. A cross-platform L&F should define behavior and appearance that are consistent between all the platforms on which Java can run. Despite Swing architecture making this technically simple[19], a number of other details are also required, such as pixel-level tuning of images, or smoothing the various differences between Java's and the native L&F. For example, MacOS Aqua users are used to certain conventions, while Windows users to others. Ocean uses

---

16. The L&Fs listed here were selected from http://javootoo.l2fprod.com/.
17. A starting point for color themes associated with color blindness can be found at http://www.visibone.com/colorblind/.
18. The Steel L&F is more commonly known as Metal. The name *Metal* is used to refer to the cross-platform Java L&F at large, of which Steel and Ocean are particular implementations.
19. The same Swing code runs on all the J2SE platforms.

graphics gradients to enhance the look of an application, and a caching mechanism for speeding up rendering.

In cases in which visual compatibility with existing applications running on JSE 1.5 or higher is needed, the old Steel L&F can still be obtained by setting the system property `swing.metalTheme=steel`. For compatibility with the older L&F, Ocean uses bold fonts for labels and text. This can be turned off with the system property: `swing.boldMetal=false`.

Table 11.6   Ocean 1.5 details

L&F name	Ocean
Time to load L&F at startup (seconds)	0
Time to launch application (seconds)	1.71
Free memory (KB) Initial - after startup	67.29
License	Sun's Binary Code License Agreement
Author / Company	Sun Microsystems Inc.
URL	`http://java.sun.com/products/jfc/`

The above data was measured over three runs, discarding first-time executions to avoid JIT compilation overhead and other initializations, and also spurious values, for example when a garbage collection occurred. These measurements depend heavily on the machine on which they are performed and are indicative only.

The time to load the L&F is the time measured between the moment the L&F loading is started and when it is completed. It is not rigorously determined: a L&F that forks a thread to complete its installation will show a shorter loading time. Clearly for Ocean, because it is the default option, the time to load is zero.

The time to launch figure is an indication of the time needed to launch the application after all initialization is done and the GUI is ready for user interaction. For the purpose of these benchmarks, a particularly crammed form was added to the standard demos to see the effect of the L&F for form-based GUIs.

Finally, free memory shows the total amount of free memory consumed by the application, that is, initial free memory minus the free memory remaining after start-up. This figure gives some indication of the L&F's memory footprint.

The larger these numbers – time to load, time to launch, and the memory occupied by the application – the more expensive it is to use the given L&F. Of course they only give an initial intuitive and non-rigorous evaluation of the L&F's performance. They are by no means substitutes for profiling and other measurements performed within the real context of a given application use domain. Figure 11.12 shows two screenshots of this L&F.

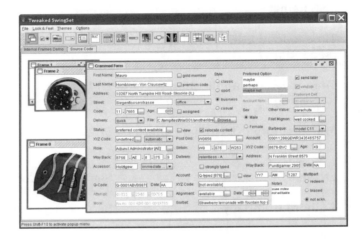

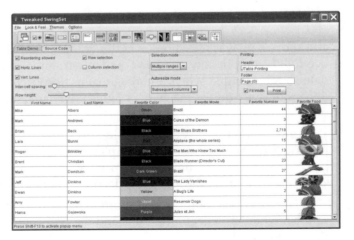

Figure 11.12   Ocean 1.5

Synthetica

Synthetica was one of the first professional L&Fs available on the market. Despite being based on Synth, which loads its data from external XML files, its performance isn't too bad, possibly because the example uses the default XML file contained in the JAR file along with the classes and loaded by the JRE at class loading time. Figure 11.13 shows two screenshots of this L&F.

Table 11.7   Synthetica details

L&F name	Synthetica 1.0.0
Time to load L&F at startup (seconds)	0.61
Time to launch application (seconds)	0.98
Free memory (KB) Initial - after startup	1527.18
License	Dual license: LGPL and commercial
Author / Company	Javasoft
URL	`www.javasoft.de/jsf/public/products/synthetica`

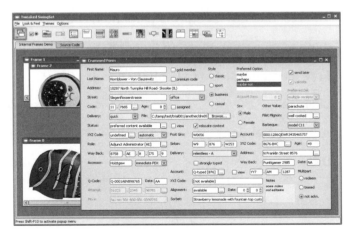

Figure 11.13   Synthetica 1.0.0

Figure 11.13   Synthetica 1.0.0 (Continued)

Alloy

The Alloy L&F is a commercial L&F that extends the standard cross-platform Java L&F. It has been around for many years, although it still lacks support for some of the latest features, such as scrollable tabs in tabbed panes. Figure 11.14 shows two screenshots of this L&F.

Table 11.8   Alloy details

L&F name	Alloy 1.4.4
Time to load L&F at startup (seconds)	0.06
Time to launch application (seconds)	1.15
Free memory (KB) Initial - after startup	650.93
License	Commercial
Author / Company	INCORS GmbH
URL	http://www.compiere.org/looks/

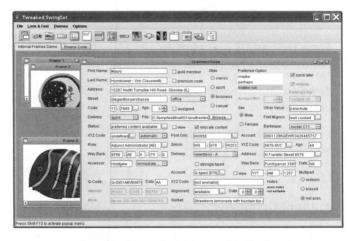

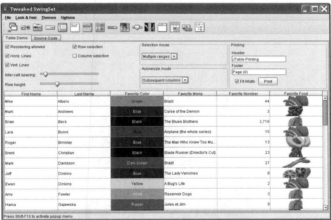

Figure 11.14   Alloy 1.4.4

Metal 3D

Despite being relatively lightweight on memory, this L&F has a rather outdated look that appears cluttered when used in crammed forms (see Figure 11.15).

Table 11.9   Metal 3D details

L&F name	Metal 3D
Time to load L&F at startup (seconds)	0.3
Time to launch application (seconds)	1.30
Free memory (KB) Initial - after startup	274.19
License	LGPL (OSS)
Author / Company	Marcus Hillenbrand
URL	`http://www.markus-hillenbrand.de/3dlf/index.shtml`

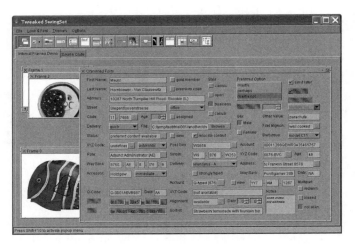

Figure 11.15   Metal 3D

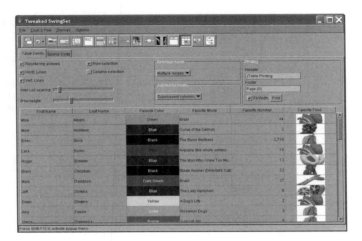

Figure 11.15   Metal 3D (Continued)

Hippo

The purpose of Hippo is to provide a simple, clean, and essential look and feel. It provides a clean result for complex form GUIs, although it is still not fully complete (see Figure 11.16).

Table 11.10   Hippo details

L&F name	Hippo 0.7.1
Time to load L&F at startup (seconds)	0.03
Time to launch application (seconds)	1.34
Free memory (KB) Initial - after startup	904.29
License	BSD (OSS)
Author / Company	Robert Blixt
URL	`http://www.diod.se/`

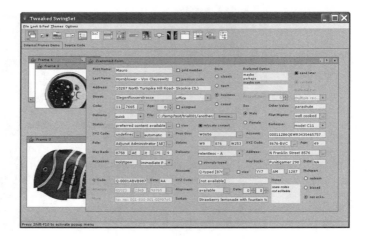

Figure 11.16   Hippo 0.7.1

Compiere

Compiere L&F is part of an OSS framework for building ERP applications. The Compiere L&F is geared towards form-based GUIs, is relatively fast to load, and can be customized through a dedicated GUI (see Figure 11.17).

Table 11.11   Compiere details

L&F name	Compiere Looks 1.2.0
Time to load L&F at startup (seconds)	0.01
Time to launch application (seconds)	1.40
Free memory (KB) Initial - after startup	1460.33
License	Variant of Mozilla Public License (OSS)
Author / Company	Compiere Inc.
URL	`http://www.compiere.org/looks/`

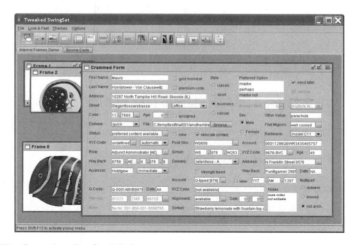

Figure 11.17   Compiere Looks 1.2.0

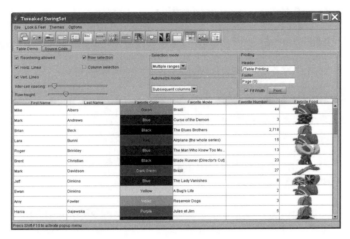

Figure 11.17   Compiere Looks 1.2.0 (Continued)

JGoodies Looks

JGoodies Looks is a family of look and feels that provides quality design to the pixel and multi-platform coherence. The Plastic L&F, for example, has been designed especially for Windows users (see Figure 11.18).

Table 11.12   JGoodies Looks details

L&F name	JGoodies Looks 1.3.1
Time to load L&F at startup (seconds)	0.05
Time to launch application (seconds)	1.37
Free memory (KB) Initial - after startup	1355.59
License	BSD (OSS)
Author / Company	Karsten Lentzsch
URL	http://www.jgoodies.com/

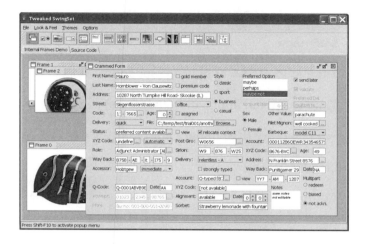

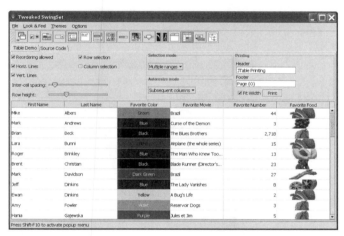

Figure 11.18   JGoodies Looks, Plastic L&F

Liquid

Liquid provides a Swing look and feel based on the Mosfet Liquid KDE 3.x theme (see Figure 11.19).

Table 11.13   Liquid details

L&F name	Liquid
Time to load L&F at startup (seconds)	0.13
Time to launch application (seconds)	1.11
Free memory (KB) Initial - after startup	617.76
License	(OSS)
Author / Company	M. Lazarevic and E. Vickroy
URL	`https://liquidlnf.dev.java.net/`

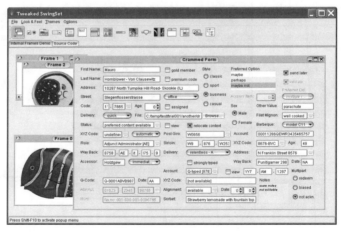

Figure 11.19   Liquid

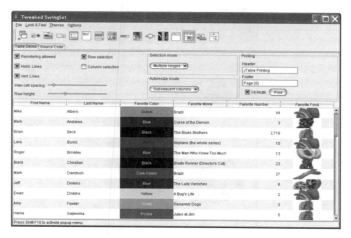

Figure 11.19   Liquid (Continued)

Oyoaha

Despite Oyoaha's coherent design, some visual details, particularly the 3D effect of buttons and text fields, result in a cluttered ensemble when the L&F is employed in non-trivial forms. For an example, see Figure 11.20.

Table 11.14   Oyoaha details

L&F name	Oyoaha 3.0
Time to load L&F at startup (seconds)	0.08
Time to launch application (seconds)	0.92
Free memory (KB) Initial - after startup	1017.26
License	(OSS)
Author / Company	Philippe Blanc
URL	http://www.oyoaha.com/ lookandfeel/

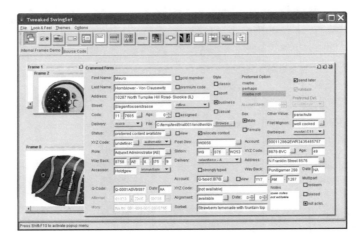

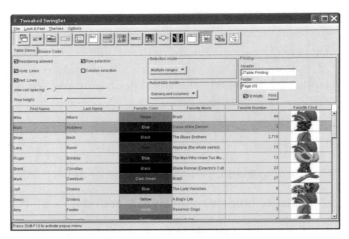

Figure 11.20   Oyoaha 3.0

Napkin

Napkin is a simple look and feel that provides an informal and provisional appearance to Swing GUIs. It is not intended to be used with a final product, but only in development and during demonstrations to users. This enables developers to avoid committing to a given L&F until needed by highlighting the fact that the GUI is not ready.

AS it is a L&F that is not used in production, Napkin's performances lags behind other L&Fs, with a relatively large memory occupancy due to the many bitmap it uses, as well as long time to load and launch values. Given the intended use of this L&F, these are not problems, especially if the application is executed on powerful development machines. Napkin is a good example of the many possible uses of Swing L&F technology. See Figure 11.21.

Table 11.15   Napkin details

L&F name	Napkin Beta 0.07
Time to load L&F at startup (seconds)	0.95
Time to launch application (seconds)	1.85
Free memory (KB) Initial - after startup	2394.29
License	BSD (OSS)
Author / Company	Ken Arnold
URL	`http://napkinlaf.sourceforge.net/`

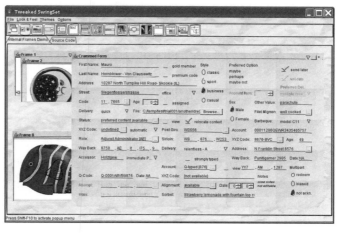

Figure 11.21   Napkin L&F

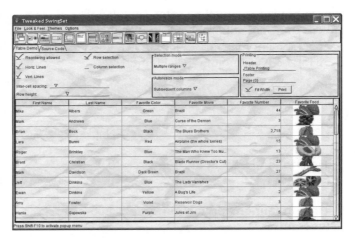

Figure 11.21   Napkin L&F (Continued)

SWT Presentation

Although less flexible than Swing's counterpart, SWT also allows for the customization of the toolkit's visual appearance via native OS themes. This option is still poorly supported as of Eclipse 3.0. To enable Windows XP themes in SWT, a special manifest file is included in the same directory that contains the JRE that launches the application.

Figure 11.22 shows Eclipse on Windows with two different themes: XP (above) and Windows classic (below).

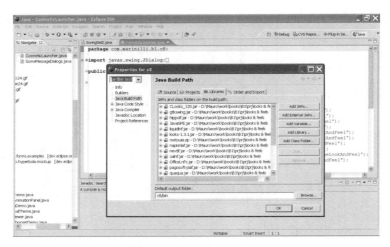

Figure 11.22   Eclipse 3.0 with different themes

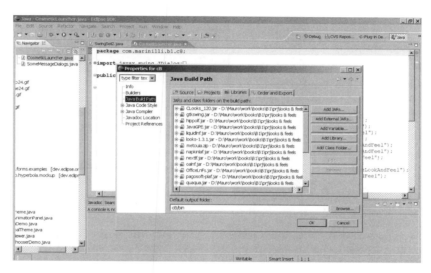

Figure 11.22   Eclipse 3.0 with different themes

11.10 Declarative GUIs with Java

Many projects aim to provide declarative capabilities to Java GUIs, mostly to express content, even if some projects also strive to provide a minimum amount of interaction and control behavior.

XML-based formats

Unsurprisingly, the largest family of declarative formats is based on XML. There are more than a dozen such XML schemas[20], with projects like JDNC[21], Mozilla XUL, Luxor, SwiXml, XUI, Beryl XML GUI, Purnama XUI, SwingML, Thinlet, jXUL, KoalaGML, WidgetServer, Gui4j, and XAMJ.

The Thinlet project is an example of this family of formats, a LGPL-licensed, tiny-footprint (39 KB) interpreter of Thinlet XML files. Thinlets can run in a Java 1 JVM, the default shipped with Microsoft Internet Explorer, and other J2ME profiles, and don't require Swing. Figure 11.23 shows a sample GUI demo using Thinlet.

---

20. For a quick comparison, can see: http://xul.sourceforge.net/counter.html.
21. JDNC is discussed briefly as an alternative implementation for the example application in Chapter 14.

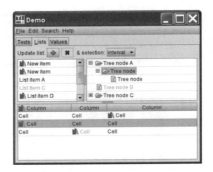

Figure 11.23   Thinlet demonstration

An extract of the source file that generates the GUI in Figure 11.23 is shown in Listing 11.1 below.

Listing 11.1 The `demo.xml` file

```xml
<?xml version="1.0" encoding="ISO-8859-1"?>
<panel columns="1" gap="4">
  <menubar weightx="1">
  <menu text="File" mnemonic="0">
   <menuitem text="New" icon="/icon/new.gif" mnemonic="0" />
   <menuitem text="Open..." icon="/icon/open.gif" />
   <menuitem text="Save" icon="/icon/save.gif" />
   <menuitem text="Save As..." icon="/icon/saveas.gif" />
   <separator />
   <menuitem text="Page Setup" icon="/icon/pagesetup.gif" />
   <menuitem text="Print" icon="/icon/print.gif" />
   <separator />
  ...
  </menubar>
  <tabbedpane selected="1" weightx="1" weighty="1">
    <tab text="Texts">
      <panel columns="5" top="4" left="4" bottom="4" right="4" gap="4">
        <label text="Find in the text:" mnemonic="10" />
  ...
    <tab text="Lists" mnemonic="0">
      <panel columns="1" top="4" left="4" bottom="4" right="4" gap="4">
        <panel gap="4">
          <label text="Update list:" />
  ...
```

Another approach that avoids the use of Java on the client altogether is to take advantage of other presentation technologies, such as Macromedia Flash, that are installed on clients as Web browser plug-ins. SWF bytecode can be generated dynamically on the server side by tools such as OpenLaszlo, using servlet technology, or Flex. Both these approaches make use of XML-based user interface languages in which the XML is generated and prepared on the server side, compiled, and send to the client's Flash player.

11.11 Summary

This chapter discussed some of the most popular technologies and products for developing Java GUIs. We introduced the issue of evaluating an OSS in general, and specifically for the purpose of creating Java GUIs. Major Java GUI technologies and tools currently available were discussed and compared, including development aids, third-party components, utility libraries, and presentation technologies.

12 Advanced Issues

This chapter deals with various issues that are encountered less often by developers. Rather that being classified as 'advanced,' these topics can be seen as solutions to specialized problems that seldom occur in average GUIs and would not be of interest for the average reader, but that are still useful to consider, as they apply to a wide range of real cases.

The chapter is organized as follows:

12.1, Building on top of existing libraries discusses some of the issues related to creating APIs and frameworks, also taking advantage of usability.

12.2, Memory management for complex GUIs illustrates problems and possible solutions with practical examples.

12.3, Restructuring existing GUI code discusses various issues related to renewing and restructuring existing Java GUI code.

12.4, Exploiting technology proposes alternative uses of some Java GUI technologies.

12.5, Domain-specific and Little languages discusses the use of this technique for Java GUIs.

12.6, The future of Java GUIs attempts to forecast the future of Java GUI technologies.

12.1 *Building on top of existing libraries*

A frequent habit of designers is to create reusable classes in order to save development time in future projects. Even if full reusability is often an unfulfilled dream, there are certain common patterns, as we have seen throughout this book. We have discussed some possible strategies, focusing mostly on more reusable patterns. Here we will explore another approach to code reuse for non-trivial GUIs: to formalize the support for higher-level attribute implementation into reusable classes.

We mentioned this issue when discussing OOUIs. Imagine that we have to develop a business application that needs many data structures that are in turn composed of simpler attribute data such as strings, integers, files, and so on. We could assign a great deal of common behavior to these attribute classes, sparing developers from writing many lines of service code, for example to implement persistence, or for sophisticated content assembly, and so on. Providing a high-level library for such utility functions will also help to speed up the software design process. This is not a new idea. Standard libraries and much corporate effort have devised this strategy to simplify GUI development, especially for predictable applications such as business management, database-oriented domains, and so on. We will explore this idea in the next section.

Attributes

A common solution for easing the implementation of non-trivial applications is to think of a given business class as a compound of high-level attributes. Such attributes can themselves be composed of other attributes, and so on, implementing a Composite pattern (Gamma et al. 1994). Basic attributes (which we will call *fields*) will wrap basic data types, such as strings, dates, and numerical intervals. Apart from wrapping business data at a higher abstraction level, attributes provide several useful services.

Usually attributes are responsible for handling the following services:

- Providing GUI interfaces for accessing the business data.
- Providing automatic mechanisms for default values, message bundles, preference storage, serialization, and so on
- Negotiating appearance and layout with their composite parents (similarly to Swing's and AWT's components).
- Providing a business logic layer for administering their data.

Many proprietary or publicly-available GUI frameworks exist, such as JFace for the Eclipse platform, that – with different degrees and perspectives – take advantage of the attribute concept.

By way of demonstration, will discuss a simple, lightweight example implementation of a possible attribute framework. The class diagram in Figure 12.1 shows the design of such a library.

Adopting the Composite pattern, we could have simple 'leaf' attributes, our fields, and compound attributes, represented by the abstract class `Composite-Attribute`. Fields are the basic building blocks we use to build complex data structures. Each field has a name and other common properties that are used for initialization, such as a default value, for example, or for GUI purposes, such as tooltip and a mnemonic key for example. Taking advantage of the `Viewable` interface[1], each attribute can provide different views of its data suitable for aggregation into a larger view in its parent's composite attribute.

---

1.   See Chapter 15, *The Viewable interface* on page 538.

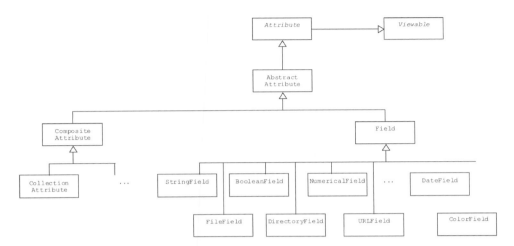

Figure 12.1   A complete framework for attribute management

Among developers, attribute frameworks are often seen as suspect, given the additional complexity they bring to a design and the subsequent application development. Usually such frameworks justify themselves in terms of future reusability (but we know how vague this can be) and faster development. But like any other class library, they need to be properly mastered.

This solution is needlessly powerful for simple GUIs in which there is no need for multiple views of the same attributes. In such cases the attribute framework can be greatly simplified. Avoiding the use of multiple views and a fully-fledged MVC architecture leads to the design shown in Figure 12.2 below.

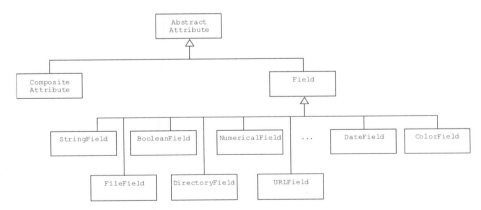

Figure 12.2   A slimmed-down class diagram for attribute management

Let's look at this second solution in detail, sketching out a skeleton of a basic attribute framework. Our attributes will provide the following services:

- Preferences persistence.
- Default values.
- Naming and other labeling facilities, such as tooltip, field name, and mnemonic key, obtained from the message bundle properties file.
- Simple graphical views, with basic commit/rollback behavior similar to the `Viewable` interface.

An implementation of the `AbstractAttribute` class is provided with the code bundle for the book.

Attributes can carry domain-dependent information that is needed in the content layer, such as validation constraints, or whether or not an attribute is mandatory, for example. This enables a clear and systematic separation between the business domain and the other functional layers to be obtained.

The `createLabelFor` method is a convenient method for obtaining a label component from the attribute. The `createComponent` method is implemented by `AbstractAttribute`'s subclasses.

The persistence mechanism, which is used mostly for user-customized data, has been implemented using the preferences mechanism present in J2SE from Version 1.4 onwards. The text messages have been managed using properties files directly, to ease localization, relying on the `ServiceManager` class.

Concrete subclasses of `AbstractField` (`BooleanField` and `StringField`) are provided with the code bundle for the book. The `Employee` class in the code bundle is an example of a composite attribute that represents data for an employee. In our simple implementation, an employee is composed of three elementary fields:

- `name` – the employee's first name, implemented with a `StringField` instance.
- `surname` – the employee's family name, implemented with a `StringField` instance.
- `senior` – whether or not the employee is a senior worker, implemented with a `BooleanField` instance.

The `Employee` class is itself an attribute, so it can be combined with other attributes to create bigger attributes, such as a `PayRoll` class, or standard compound attributes such as a `CollectionAttibute` for modeling sets of employees.

In our implementation we choose to adopt static encapsulation – that is, the attributes of a composite class are instances of variables of that class – instead of dynamic encapsulation, where a collection variable holds all the attributes. This means that a lower degree of automation is possible. Methods such as `doCommit()` or `doRollBack()` therefore do not need to invoke any sub-attribute. The `doLayout()` method is different, because a semantic notion of each sub-attribute is needed to achieve an effective layout.

> Static attribute encapsulation has its own advantages. The main ones are readability – inspecting the class source is enough to understand its attributes – and simplicity, as the attribute instances look like normal class members.

Finally, the `Example` class creates an `Employee` and requests it to show its contents on the screen in a test frame. The final result is shown in Figure 12.3.

Figure 12.3   The Example class shows an employee (PGS)

> The example implementation is very simplistic and lacks many useful features, for example the ability to open the attribute's visual component in read-only mode, better persistence support, localization, and so on.

Roll your own framework

Sometimes there is a need to extend an open source library that falls short in the features needed for the current project. At other times we might want to collect utilities and code we keep on writing over and over again for every GUI into a coherent API, or we are called on to provide some specialized framework for an organization, and so on. In all these situations, developers need to wear the API provider's hat rather than that of the client.

Java GUI developers are often faced with this kind of task for two main reasons. Reusable GUI libraries aren't so reusable in practice, given the sheer number of requirement our 'reusable' code should fulfill for real-world GUIs. For example, imagine that you have found the 'perfect' calendar widget for your applications, but that it unfortunately doesn't fit within your existing GUI design because it cannot be inserted in a lightweight pop-up window like all your other choosers.

Open source libraries *encourage* developers to tweak someone else's source code and enhance it, providing of course acknowledgements are given and license compliance is met.

Building GUI code for other developers instead of final users is a gratifying experience that need extra technical care in its details. Two very useful documents on this perspective are *Evolving Java-based APIs* (Des Rivières 2000) and, specifically on the client side, *How to Use the Eclipse API* (Des Rivières 2001). There is much more material available on this topic, but this is out of our scope.

Designing usable APIs and frameworks

This subsection discusses the idea of applying usability principles to general API and OOP framework design. This is of course not a new idea, but the original approach taken here is to leverage sound usability and HCI advice taken from the first part of the book to guide us through our revisit of API design as a product.

Unsurprisingly, GUI design and API design have many points in common. Both have users of many types and levels of experience, API users being mainly developers. Both design processes leverage devised metaphors and abstract concepts embodied in the design, be it a GUI design or an API, to solve user's needs effectively. On the other hand the user experience of the product – the new API to be designed – is shaped by many factors: class and method names, the design patterns employed, concepts and abstractions, documentation, and the general 'feeling' of its use, as perceived by the developer.

As examples of existing APIs we refer to the APIs and frameworks for GUIs such as Swing, Netbeans API, and Eclipse API, as the reader is likely to be more familiar with these. Nevertheless, the ideas discussed here apply to any kind of API and OOP framework, not only graphical ones.

Here is a list of the main GUI design concepts, which briefly discusses how they translate to API design. The term *user* and *developer* are used here as synonyms.

- Focus on your users:
  - Design for different types of users. Usually you'll have novice users, expert full-time developers, and possibly also knowledgeable, part-time developers as well. Each class of users has its own needs and priorities.
  - Provide a user-centered, task-oriented, and context-aware design. Performing a classic task analysis, adding context and user data, seems an almost trivial suggestion, but it will shape the final API design tremendously. Think about what the main tasks your API will solve are, with user goals, how developers carry out these task now without your API, their context of work, task breakdown decompositions, ethnographic study of developers in their work environment, and so on.

For example, a task could be to create and customize a data-bound table for expert SWT users, for adding to an existing panel. But beware – such an approach can bring a subtle but conceptually devastating consequence: API designs, just as GUI designs, depend heavily on their context of use and on their intended users. So there is no such a thing as perfect API for all seasons.

- Ensure consistency and predictability. This can be also understood in terms of lowering the use of long-term memory (LTM) and using short-term memory (STM) as much as possible. To ease management of STM, use no more than 7±2 items (that is, parameters in methods, methods in interfaces, and so on). Consistency involves the use of design guidelines, analogous to GUI design guidelines, that prescribe how errors should be handled, patterns to use and those to avoid, naming conventions, and so on.

- Design effective metaphors and concepts to:
  - Solve user problems. This is implicit, but is important to point out. Unless your API won't solve problems, it won't be worth developer's time using it.
  - Behave as expected by its intended users. For example, if you are designing a domain-specific language (a 'little language') don't use an exotic, fancy syntax with which Java developers are not familiar.
  - Keep close to the application domain. Don't use first-order logic for a dynamic layout API, even if it looks cool. Concepts too distant from the domain and users should be avoided. For example, even if quantum physics provides a wonderful and elegant metaphor for (say) a GUI toolkit, hide the internal details of the implementation, so that users don't need to study physics before putting together a form using your API.
  - Communicate the API effectively. Documentation, training, and other forms of learning are very important, but ultimately what makes an API (or a GUI design) usable are the concepts themselves.

- Test your API with user representatives not previously exposed to the design process for usability – classic usability testing – and effectiveness – productivity: how easy is to achieve the required goal with the API? You might want to test also for flexibility – can expert users tweak any aspect of the framework – and future modifications – what are the unforeseen needs of our users? Developers are like GUI users: putting them in control of the GUI will make them feel better. How can your API be modified to accommodate them without degrading its architecture? Releasing a badly-tested API implies many modifications on a tight schedule that will deteriorate the initial design.

- Make the API pleasant to use and easy to learn.
  - There is no need to torture developers, who are stressed enough already. Designing your API to provide early gratification is a good technique for keeping them interested and stimulated.
  - Hide unnecessary complexity, for example by separating interface from implementation[2] or by providing a carefully thought-out class hierarchy.
  - Provide default behavior, to employ it usefully with minimal effort, and ready-to-use, predefined behavior for common cases.
  - Provide informative feedback. Learning an API by trial and error is a common habit among developers. Providing useful feedback, such as the Amazon Web Service API feedback in the example application in Chapter 13, eases API comprehension and developer productivity.
- Design in error prevention and management. Many techniques can be used here:
  - Use immutable objects when possible, providing their mutable counterpart when performances or usability are a concern.
  - Decide what to do with null. Despite appearing a trivial suggestion, many 'home-grown' APIs fail to define such a basic issue consistently and effectively, causing a number of minor weaknesses, and opening the door to some annoying errors. By generalization, also consider using Special Case design (Fowler et al. 2003).
  - Design the API as you might design a GUI, to try and make errors impossible. For those errors that cannot be eliminated by clever design, provide both a 'baby-proof' path – safe objects that only allow a protected and safe subset of all possible data and behavior – and a 'pro' path, allowing for maximum freedom and customization power, but also allowing inconsistent and dangerous behavior.
  - Devise a comprehensive failure strategy, as discussed in Chapter 5.

12.2   Memory management for complex GUIs

A common problem with large Java applications is managing the memory needed during execution. The situation can be complicated when such applications need to run for a long time, requiring more sophisticated memory policies.

The simplest solution for such a class of Java applications is to provide a means for the end user to control the JRE's garbage collector directly. Clearly this is feasible only when the typical user population can be assumed to be knowledgeable enough to manipulate such a low-level feature like the garbage collector. This

---

2.   See Chapter 7.

is the case in all major development environments implemented in Java, such as JBuilder Eclipse or Idea.

When providing access to the garbage collector is not feasible, for application-dependent reasons, for end user characteristics, or whatever other reason, you have to employ some ad-hoc strategy. A common solution is to provide a low-priority thread that takes care of memory management, invoking the garbage collector when needed.

There is another reason for adopting such an ad-hoc approach. Usually the garbage collector takes some time to perform its operations, and this appears to the end user as if the application is freezing for a moment. This kind of pause, which can appear random, can be unacceptable. In such cases it's advisable to 'pilot' garbage collection at a specific time, such as just before a heavily interactive session. In general, there could be too many different situations in practice to discuss them all here, but we can suggest a simple test situation that can be adapted to manage a wide range of practical cases.

Some applications are required to handle vast amount of data, such as the large datasets shown in table components of database clients GUIs. The amount of data to be viewed is largely decided by the user. This poses some problems, because memory management should be adapted to the current user interaction.

A practical case

Imagine a tree component that is bound to a large data source that can grow almost infinitely. This could be the case for example with a client application that shows data from a remote source that can supply a very large amount of information. Clearly, some solution is needed to make this tree component manageable without compromising GUI interaction. A screenshot is shown in Figure 12.4.

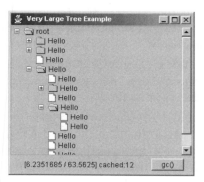

Figure 12.4   A very large and expensive tree (Tiny)

Below the tree widget the demo application, available in the source code bundle, shows the currently-available memory, overall memory, and the number of current cached nodes.

The `Node` class represents a single tree node that gobbles up a large quantity of memory (0.5 MB of dummy data), so a few new nodes can consume almost all available client memory.

The `VeryLargeTree` class is the cornerstone of the example. This class invokes the `setRowHeight()` method with a fixed size, and `setLargeModel()` with `true` on a Swing `JTree` instance, to prompt the object to use an alternative code path optimized for models with large data sets. One important consequence of this setting is that the model will be queried more often – clearly in order to reduce the tree's cache size.

An interesting method in the `VeryLargeTree` class is `treeWillExpand`, part of the `TreeListener` interface. This method is invoked whenever a folder node of the tree is going to be expanded. In our fictitious example, we simply fill the folder node with data obtained from the dummy server. Just before the tree expansion takes place, this method is invoked, and a new request is issued to the server by means of a queue of worker `Runnable` instances.

> The example uses a lazy instantiation mechanism for the tree nodes. Whenever the user expands a node, the branch is populated with fresh data from the server. This avoids useless memory allocation for those folders that the user will never explore, but we pay for it with a less interactive GUI.

Another section of code in the example is the `MemoryManager` class, which implements a simple caching mechanism, the `Cache` inner class. The method `removeEldestEntry()` removes the eldest entry in the cache. The `findAllChildren()` method recursively finds all the child nodes of a given element that are candidates for removal whenever the node is deleted by the tree. The `MemoryMonitor` class controls the `MemoryManager` instance, and shows the memory state through a status label. This class provides a way to activate the JRE's garbage collector explicitly.

Finally, the `DummyServer` class simulates a remote server that returns data nodes with an unpredictable latency, simulated by a pseudorandom delay via the `simulateIOLatency()` method.

A simpler and 'lighter' implementation, in that it takes advantage of special reference types, part of the J2SE standard API, is also possible. The `SimpleLargeTree` uses the `WeakReference` type, contained in `java.lang.ref`. This makes it possible to implement 'soft' reference types that are automatically cleared out when the JRE runs out of available memory. This means that programmers don't have to bother too much about cache maintenance, because reclaiming memory held by weak references will be done automatically by the JRE. This simplifies coding, but shields programmers from tight control over memory management.

Which of these strategies is best will depend on the situation. Other solutions are possible, using other special types of references provided in the `java.lang.ref` package that allow for more control over garbage collection.

12.3   *Restructuring existing GUI code*

We have discussed how to apply our basic reference architecture and other techniques to build high-quality GUI code from scratch. Sometimes, however, the opposite problem arises – existing GUI code must be restructured in a scenario that differs from development, for example code that was written elsewhere, that was written more than a few years ago, and so on. Sometimes it's cheaper to throw legacy GUI code away, using it only to capture requirements for a new implementation, while at other times this choice is quite hard to make in the general case – it could be wiser to keep it, even in the form of an unmaintainable patchwork of code.

Complex or large GUIs built over the years have usually absorbed so much change in their source code under the influence of tight deadlines, different developers, and so on, that they appear very hard to maintain, especially when the initial developers are no longer available. Despite that, building such GUIs from scratch can prove to be too dangerous an enterprise, and step-by-step refactoring could be the wiser approach to enhancing the quality of the code base while keeping the product 'alive' without incurring release delays.

Several reasons for modifying such sources can exist:

- It must be ported to newer technologies, such as porting an old AWT applet to Swing, or renewing an old open source library.

- The architecture and the overall software quality need to be enhanced, for example for performance optimization.

- Routine software maintenance is required, where the goal is to intervene in a specific portion of existing code.

- New features must be added to the application. This implies a deep understanding of at least some parts of the code, to modify it without disrupting the rest of the application.

Restructuring may range from applying general-purpose techniques, Java-specific manipulations, or other processes, such as applying coding guidelines. Nevertheless, some general principles apply – it's important to:

- Understand the legacy code, or at least enough of it to carry out what is required. Getting a 'grip' on old code may be hard, even for circumscribed and specific pieces of software like Java GUIs. No matter how deep your understanding of Java GUIs and your toolkit knowledge, understanding and modifying convoluted old code successfully is always time-consuming.

- Work with a clear objective in mind, such as enhancing performance, or porting the code to a newer technology or a different layering architecture, and so on.

- Develop a clear plan of what is going to be done, and deliver it one step at a time.

As any programmer knows, modifying existing code is a complex task, and an exhaustive discussion is out of scope here. One basic point, though, is the relationship between the overall restructuring cost and the fraction of modified code. Figure 12.5 shows data collected from NASA software projects (Selby and Porter 1998). Even if this data focuses on code reuse[3] rather than code restructuring, it still shows some interesting facts.

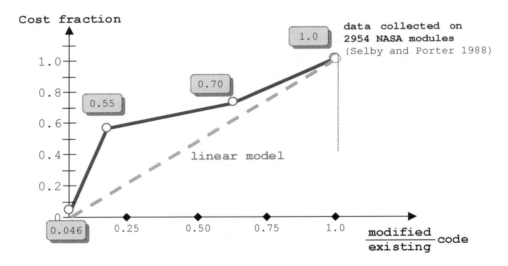

Figure 12.5   The cost of modifying existing code

---

3. Even if OOP was meant to cut down such high reuse costs, it cannot spare today's programmers from code restructuring. Writing poor code, or the need to renew code from time to time, is still an open problem in the software industry.

First, whenever we embark on a code restructuring project, we always pay a toll, even if we don't touch a line of code – see the first point on the left, which shows that preliminary costs amounted to 4.6% of the cost of initially building the code. Such costs comprise analysis, code comprehension, retrieving meaningful documentation, and so on.

Another interesting observation is that code modification has a nonlinear cost associated with it as the proportion of modified code grows. This is intuitive – if programmers don't know the code very well, even small modifications in the early phase may cause the whole application to behave unexpectedly. This is why the first segment of the graph is much steeper than the others, while the last part is less expensive (less steep) because by this stage developers are familiar with the code, allowing additional changes to be made more cheaply.

> This discussion of code modification costs doesn't take Agile coding approaches into account. Having a solid suite of tests for code that is to be modified, and proceeding in small iterative steps, as discussed in Chapter 5, ensures a cheaper and less risky restructuring process. Alas, such practices were not the norm even as recently as a few years ago.

Essentially, GUI code restructuring involves the following activities:

- Code analysis and comprehension, the necessary prerequisite for all other manipulations.
- Code refactoring, as we introduced in Chapter 5.
- Code porting to newer features, such as to new libraries, new deployment technologies, and so on. In general this kind of porting is not painless. and is hard to estimate for *a priori*.
- GUI-specific higher-level manipulations, such as introducing particular abstractions and architectural strategies.
- GUI-specific lower-level activities, such as providing internationalization support, or increasing the performance of some GUI code.

It is therefore important to tackle GUI code renewal and porting incrementally, especially complex GUI code. Once the process has been started, one should bear the high initial costs of modifying existing code effectively. A sound approach is to take advantage of the vast literature on the subject, and consolidate best practices about code enhancement.

Porting an old applet – a case study

A real case can help to illustrate some general issues about maintaining existing GUI code. The Rubik Cube applet shown in Figure 12.6 on page 461 was developed by two students of mine[4]. At one point the program was completed: it allowed users to play the Rubik's Cube puzzle by means of direct manipulation, rotating and manipulating the cube by mouse dragging in a virtual 3D space. It was implemented by interacting with low-level canvas and mouse events, pure AWT code, desirable for an applet that, as a result, doesn't need 7 MB additional downloads for the JRE.

A year or so later another group of students came with the idea of building a simple general framework for solving Rubik's Cube. Basically the idea was to provide heuristics, or even a small AI planner[5], to drive resolution, or at least some sort of tip for a player stuck at a difficult point. Clearly the old AWT applet was the perfect fit for the GUI of the new program. I handed the students all the documentation for the old applet and they started happily working on the project.

It turned out that the simplest and most effective GUI for representing moves in this domain was a tree widget. This posed some problems, though, because there are no native tree widgets for AWT. Instead of resorting to one of the various AWT trees available on the Internet, the idea of porting the old AWT applet to newer technologies, such as Swing, was becoming more compelling, which in turn would have fostered a whole host of new technologies, such as Java Web Start, standard help support, and others.

> From an implementation viewpoint, referring to the classification introduced in Chapter 3, the applet is made up of a custom component tree for the moves (on the left-hand side of the applet's display area) and an ad-hoc component for the cube representation on the right-hand side.

A screenshot of the port of the old code to a Swing applet is shown in Figure 12.6. The tree on the left-hand side represents the moves computed by a resolution algorithm that takes advantage of heuristics. By double-clicking on a move node in the tree, the move is directly performed on the 3D representation of the cube.

---

4. Various people were involved, at various levels of commitment – I am sorry if I can't cite their names.
5. An artificial intelligence planner is a tool that plans domain-dependent steps automatically in order to solve a problem using AI techniques.

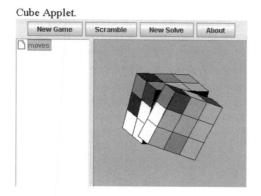

Figure 12.6   A Rubik's Cube applet (Ocean1.5)

The option of throwing everything away and rebuilding from scratch wasn't feasible because of the high cost of building the ad-hoc Cube component. In other situations, though, this could be the best choice (and not just because I was called in to consult on it). When old code is relatively easy to rebuild with a newer technology, the simplest way is just to use the running application as a black-box prototype embodying a given set of requirements for the new program, while throwing away its implementation.

We considered the available possibilities. Let's recap them, organized by deployment means:

- Java applet:
  - AWT applet, running in any browser. This is the simplest solution for deployment, and it is almost straightforward in this case, but has some drawbacks: AWT lacks a tree component, which would need to be created in-house or bought from a third-party vendor. In the long term, when expanding the applet further, we might be forced to switch to more powerful technologies, and forced to migrate an expanded code base.
  - Swing applet, running in any browser before Java plug-in installation. This solution provides more benefits in the long run. All major libraries and utilities are built for Swing rather than AWT (help support, layout manages, and so on).
- Java application:
  - Standalone AWT application. Similar to the case of the AWT applet configuration, even though it wastes the most important strong point of AWT: ease of deployment. For this reason it's less attractive than the AWT applet solution.

- Standalone Swing application. While a number of deployment means can be devised, we discuss JNLP here, mostly.
- Standalone SWT application. This is the same as the AWT case, although in this case SWT provides a standard tree component that works well with large tree models. On the other hand, developers not familiar with SWT need further study of the technology, and this can be an important practical hurdle. This is even truer for ad-hoc components such as the cube panel, which require deep knowledge of the underlying graphics libraries. Luckily, SWT's low-level graphics rendering model is close to AWT's.
- Native application created from pure Java code, for example using GCJ with SWT libraries. This could be an interesting possibility, but we should sacrifice pure Java deployment for a number of (limited) native executables. Given the current context – non-for-profit educational software – we abandon this choice, even if it would have been very interesting in its runtime performance for large puzzle solution plans.

As you can see, the array of possible configurations is complex even for such a simple case. One possible pitfall lies in the programmers' experience. Developers not familiar with the target technology can become unexpected and dangerous obstacles in a porting process.

We opted for the Swing applet solution, which appeared to provide the best cost/risks/results ratio, although with a subsequent porting to a JNLP application in the longer term.

We started from the first step, porting the old AWT applet to Swing. The idea was to solve the most basic problems first, lowering risks and fostering many other porting steps[6]. While porting graphics from AWT to Swing, essentially migrating from the old `Graphics` class to `Graphics2D`, was easy, some unexpected problems arose along the way, all related to incorrect assumptions made by the earlier developers, such as too low-level code. User interaction such as mouse dragging wasn't working as expected in the Swing porting, and in-depth corrections were needed to make things work. We will get back to this point in a later section that discusses tips for ensuring greater longevity for Java GUIs.

Applets are still among us. Even if they didn't fulfill the triumphant vision of Java's early days, there are still a lot of them around, ranging from sophisticated, commercial software to educational, scientific simulators, video games. and so on. In many companies it is not unusual to find bloated applets – all the rage at the end of '90s – still on duty in intranet business applications.

___

6.   See the ranking of such steps in Chapter 5.

When choosing the right client configuration, you should consider several factors:

- The intended user population and operating scenario. Will an Internet connection be needed? Is one available, and to what extent can it be relied on? Do the conditions and scenario prevalent when the code was first implemented still apply today? A new port of an old Java GUI is a perfect opportunity to consider such extra-functional issues.

- The cost of filling the gap between the old and the new technologies, including the porting of higher-level runtime models and all the work involved.

- Deployment means. This involves deciding between applet, JNLP or a 'plain' application, or even native executables (and their related family of installers), or other possible arrangements.

- The developer's skills. Obviously developers are more productive and effective when working with known technologies.

- The business model and other organizational constraints. In our previous example we were developing a non-for-profit applet with no demanding timeline, but in industrial scenarios the situation could be much more complex, and such constraints could impact heavily on the chosen porting strategy.

In conclusion, Java client technology is still evolving after more than ten years, and the many possible choices available on the market demand a clear view and a careful decision-making process by lead developers and architects.

Long-life GUIs

Despite the heroic commitment of Sun to supporting compatibility in the past, it is still possible to experience glitches and unforeseen changes in behavior when porting applications written for a given JRE to a newer version.

The problem is that compatibility can be ensured only at the API level. A performance enhancement in Swing's internals, such as resource loading, or small enhancements in the way some details of the low-level event pump are handled, *should* be transparent to client applications. This might not be case with software built without attention to long-term maintenance, however. We are not talking about good design and architectural details here, but about a clean separation from low-level behavior. The main source of incompatibility with a newer Java release lies in incorrect assumptions hard-wired into the code, making it dependent on obscure and undocumented implementation details in the technologies used in the application (for example the GUI toolkit). This is the case with the order of execution of some low-level operations, for example. These details are meant to be internal to the library used by an application, and relying on them will jeopardize the stability of code in the long term.

Even harmless code such as that for detecting specific mouse configurations, to support right-clicking on a tree for example, can work well with old JREs but start to behave bizarrely with newer versions. Other problems could arise as well, such as unfortunate variable naming – for example enum as a variable name plus a switch to JRE 1.5 or newer, or the like – but these are usually easily solved compared with the kind of low-level incompatibility often found in graphics-oriented code such as is used in video games or direct-manipulation GUIs.

Incorrect assumptions about specific thread timing combinations, and other incidental situations that make the application work but are not formally documented anywhere, can cripple code when executing it with a newer JRE. Unfortunately these sorts of issues are hard to detect at coding time, and developers are always uneasy about getting rid of hard-won code that works – perhaps a little murkily and with a couple of low-level hacks – but that works nevertheless.

As a rule of thumb, it is always better to resort to code that follows formally-documented features, to make a GUI independent of low-level, empirically-proven details.

Providing new deployment support

We discuss the issue of deployment separately because it is a common theme that can be handled easily by following some simple steps.

The JNLP protocol is suited to the deployment of Java applications via Web browsers. Rich Java clients usually take advantage of the Java Network Launching Protocol (JNLP) for launching and deploying Java application over the Web. This protocol works by means of special XML files (.jnlp files) that instruct the JRE how to deploy the application. This is done through a special launcher application on the client that is bundled with every JRE.

Once your Java application is ready for deployment, you publish its JAR files, together with the special JNLP file, on your Web server. Your customers only have to click on the link to the JNLP file to launch it automatically without any extra intervention. Actually JNLP does much more than this – interested readers can find more details on Sun's Java Web Start site or in (Marinilli 2001).

The specific case of porting to a newer deployment technology is interesting because it is a common situation that luckily is easy to manage in practice. The main point about porting applications to JNLP concerns external resource loading. The JNLP protocol works thanks to the J2SE class loader mechanism – application resources such as icons, property files and the like would not be accessible if loaded by any other mechanism. This can be easily demonstrated by substituting all external access with the following idiom:

```
URL res = this.getClassLoader().getResource(name);
    if (res!=null)
        // use the resource URL as needed
```

Remember that you should also fix your development environment, as it might now fail to load external resources if not properly set up. Here again a wise software architecture, one that gathers all external accesses into a minimum number of places, such as the Service layer implementation proposed in Chapter 7, can greatly ease the porting effort.

> There are basically three different ways to deploy and subsequently manage your software in J2SE: by using applets, taking advantage of the Java Plug-In facility, by using JNLP-deployed applications, as discussed above, or by simply providing your own deployment solution, for example supplying your customers with installation CD-ROMs.

It is worth making a final point about applet deployment porting, useful for the many corporate applet-deployed applications still around. Applets are container-managed programs, developed to run in an applet container. This means that they have an underlying lifecycle model that is too simple for any but limited application scenarios, covering only `init()`, `start()`, `paint()`, `stop()`, and `destroy()` methods.

Apart from most business applications, today's applets are usually strongly graphics- and interactivity-oriented, such as video games or simulators, and this in turn makes them lower-level oriented, employing low-level GUI events and making assumptions about them. When porting an applet to an application, usually a JNLP-powered one, one should always consider the hidden cost of porting the program model as well, that is, the cost of making the applet code work outside the applet container.

12.4 Exploiting technology

Java GUI technology is powerful, although its uses are still limited to the production of GUI code. The technology can be used in other ways, however, such as applying it to development phases other than production and execution. For example, in Chapter 11 we discussed a look and feel, Napkin, that is specifically targeted at prototypes and early GUI designs.

Figure 12.7 shows an example of an original use of Swing's flexibility in rendering presentation details and applied to analysis and early development iterations. The GUI in Figure 12.7 is a prototype in which various design choices are still to be validated and finalized with customers, and on which additional analysis is required. Blurred widgets have therefore been used to represent items that need further work. Comments can also be embedded in the GUI itself that can help to understand the final intended behavior of the application, even from this early, limited version.

Figure 12.7   An example of the use of presentation technology

Instead of communicating this information in a document, possibly bloated, costly to maintain, and ultimately unnatural when compared with the application in Figure 12.7, we embed it directly in the real thing, removing it as the application proceeds iteratively to its final refinement. After all, the GUI in Figure 12.7 *is* the application as we know it today. Such details could also be made visible or invisible under the control of a runtime flag.

12.5   *Domain-specific and Little languages*

Java is a general-purpose object-oriented programming language. It can represent and manipulate information in any domain of interest as long as it is represented using the particular flavor of the OO paradigm realized by the Java language. We can model business logic rules and weather forecast data, creating new specialized classes and intertwined relationships between them. The generality of Java has a drawback, however – its abstractness. For example, developers have experienced the complexity of specialized OOP frameworks in expressing domain-specific concepts, for example how cumbersome it is to use layout managers in non-trivial situations. This is because dynamic layout classes express what are essentially visual concepts using a text-based syntax optimized for general-purpose problems.

'Little languages,' or 'Mini-languages' (Hunt and Thomas 2000), are specialized, small languages that are created to fit a specific purpose and which are then 'embedded' into a more general-purpose language such as Java. This allows them to be more effective and simple to use than a fully-fledged specialized OO class framework. Little languages can grow out of the development environment and become full languages, although simple and extremely specialized, such as the Hibernate or Ant XML file formats, for example, which can be thought of as two little languages specialized respectively for Object–Relational Mapping and expressing tasks for driving the building process of Java programs.

On a more restricted level, the string format used by layout managers such as JGoodies's FormLayout, in which cell constraints are expressed compactly with strings like `right:pref:grow`, `left:max(50dlu;pref)`, `l:m:g` instead of dozens of lines of code, can be thought of as a little language specialized in the effective high-level definition of layouts. Even the rather crude properties file protocol shown for developing throw-it-away prototypes in Chapter 5 could be polished and to form a little language for customizing and populating widgets quickly.

The syntax of choice for little languages is usually a simple one-line text format or XML schema. In many cases, however, some form of more powerful language is needed to combine the required expressivity with ease of use. Scripting languages such as Groovy, Jython, Beanshell, and many others, provide a powerful environment that accommodates even the most complex problems. Escalating to such a powerful solution, though, can be costly.

One example of the use of such language support could be the representation of business domain logic, encoding business rules in a scripting language that can also be used by non-developers, and which can be treated explicitly by the application itself, easing deployment and perhaps providing features like a simple COTS[7] business rule editor.

---

7. COTS, 'Component Off the Shelf' are software components built by a third party organization and ready to be employed in software.

Deployment of business rules can also be achieved easily by means of JNLP technology. By using conventional OOP, instead of adding another level of complexity to a client application by introducing a script interpreter engine, it is possible to provide all the required features using the same technology that is used for initial deployment. Code updates can then be used to patch application JAR files with new business rules.

12.6 The future of Java GUIs

While authors should always avoid making risky forecasts in a book, some trends can be recognized in the medium term, at least as regards the technologies available for Java GUIs.

Infrastructure and utility platforms are expected to flourish, growing more powerful and providing sophisticated concepts and tools, such as high-level support, sophisticated composable unit mechanisms, aspect-oriented support, and the like. While it is unclear whether a fully-fledged market for 'macro components' will ever gain momentum – paralleling the enterprise world and the history of J2EE – more powerful application platforms and specialized frameworks are expected to ease the lives of developers, at least in common scenarios such as rich client development and form-based GUIs.

The evolution of declarative languages for GUIs discussed in Chapter 11, and other non-Java based languages such as XHTML 2.0 for form-based GUIs, and other competing languages, is also interesting. Declarative languages are already used in conventional Java GUIs, in the form of little languages of greater or lesser sophistication. The Adaptation pattern discussed in Chapter 6 lends itself naturally to the declarative definition of aspects of GUIs independently of the rest of the application. Declaring a GUI has several advantages over representing it procedurally, especially for medium to large applications: it is easier to separate the various issues and keep them more maintainable, in many cases the resulting representation is more natural and easier to understand, and reuse is made easier because of the clearer decomposition.

Perhaps the real issue of non-trivial GUIs built with Java technology lies in the *language* issue. OOP scales to very complex scenarios and applications, but at the price of complexity and manageability. Domain-specific languages and tools can relieve this burden for such a well-known and circumscribed class of software applications, but professional GUIs will always remain complex beasts that need dedicated, multidisciplinary developers when tackling complex application domains and providing usable, cost-effective software for their customers.

As a concrete example, imagine running a poll among developers: would they prefer to have an `XPanel` component that provides full XHTML 2.0 form support à la Eclipse Flat Look – that is, defining complex forms with validation and binding by means of a standard, XML-based declarative language – or would they prefer a comprehensive OOP framework that delivers the same high-level powerful functionality by means of subclassing, API support and the like? My personal choice would be to give both a try, but in the process the XML-based language would perhaps be easier to understand and to tweak than a fully-fledged OOP framework. But this is a personal choice – much lies in the quality of the implementation and how well it exploits the specific details of the domain.

12.7   *Summary*

In this chapter we discussed specific design problems and some possible solutions. We have seen the notion of specialized, high-level attributes for managing complex data. We discussed some of the issues and possible solutions to the problem of handling runtime memory in large Java applications. We presented a practical example of porting a Java program to a new Java configuration, and we also discussed the use of little languages in our applications. The chapter concluded with a brief discussion of upcoming innovations in Java GUI technology.

13 Rich Client Platforms

This chapter discusses the practical use of Java rich client platforms (RCPs) for developing desktop application GUIs. The trade-offs between adopting an RCP infrastructure instead of using a more lightweight infrastructure such as a plain GUI toolkit plus possibly some support libraries are also covered. An example RCP application for the Eclipse RCP is included, focusing on its architecture.

The chapter contains the following sections:

13.1, Introduction to Java rich client platforms discusses the main issues involved in employing an RCP framework to build an application GUI.

13.2, The NetBeans RCP briefly introduces this RCP.

13.3, The Spring RCP provides an overview of the Spring RCP.

13.4, The Eclipse RCP discusses the Eclipse RCP in detail, including its architecture, windowing infrastructure, and GUI design guidelines.

13.5, Choosing the best RCP for your needs helps in picking the RCP best suited for your application. A section discusses the general issue of when to adopt an RCP for a project.

13.6, Legal issues introduces the main license issues related to the adoption of an RCP.

13.7, An example Eclipse RCP application shows a practical implementation of an application based upon the Eclipse RCP.

13.1   Introduction to Java rich client platforms

An RCP is an infrastructure framework for building medium-to-large desktop applications. Basing an application on an RCP simplifies development in many ways, providing structured GUI window support – including high-level widgets such as dockable windows, utility dialogs, high-level integration for internationalization and accessibility – coherent GUI guidelines, a common application environment, and an abundance of utilities, including user preferences, configuration support, and data-driven editors. An RCP can be intuitively thought as of the analog of an application server for the client side, even if this analogy works only at a high level, the server side and GUI development being rather different worlds. Both aim at relieving developers of the responsibility of domain-independent development, leaving them free to focus on domain-specific development.

The slow evolution of RCPs in the Java world compared to application servers and middleware is due mainly to the unexpected explosive success of the Web, which has made RCPs appear as 'dinosaurs from the desktop era' (as they were dubbed a couple of years ago). This is no longer true: today's Java RCPs are modern, Web-aware platforms that perfectly fit the need for developing cost-effective, Internet-aware, medium to large desktop application GUIs in Java[1].

The case for RCP applications

RCPs are not a panacea, of course. They tend to be costly to learn and even more time-consuming to master in detail. Employing a RCP is not always a cost-effective solution. In small projects there is no need to resort to an RCP application, especially if the developers are not familiar with the technology and deadlines are tight. Learning an RCP is learning a complex OOP framework, with all the related issues. Learning an RCP can be seen as an investment for the future, meaningful in a large project, or over several small ones, that could take advantage of a RCP. RCPs do provide a number of benefits, such as proven solutions to common problems, and a higher-level framework than low-level GUI toolkits such as SWT+JFace or Swing, in which developers can focus on domain-specific code rather than reinventing the wheel. They also benefit users, because the risk of producing bizarre or clumsy GUI designs is much lower when using a RCP framework.

RCPs fit nicely into an iterative development scenario: given their modular structure, developers are forced to conceive their code in terms of loosely-coupled components that can be added or updated with newer releases,. This makes it easy to build an extensible application on top of an RCP, with all the benefits that this brings.

RCPs are in many ways still focused on their origins: the integrated development environment (IDE). General-purpose and useful components – referred to as 'modules' or 'plug-ins,' depending on the RCP, are not yet available, such as a general-purpose security model, or an administrative console and services for system administrators. However, there are plenty of well-executed CVS clients, Ant support tools, and sophisticated text-based source editors that are fine if something like a development environment is to be built, but of little use in the majority of applications. This is unlikely to be a long-term problem, as a market for RCP extensions is growing rapidly, along the same lines as the well-established 'ecosystem' for IDE extensions.

---

1.   Especially Eclipse RCP, with its native support for integrated browser and its Web-like form widgets.

What's in an RCP

RCP support ranges from high-level GUIs to data models, GUI design and presentation details or, put another way, everything but the domain. Figure 13.1 illustrates the services provided by RCPs using the same functional decomposition adopted in Chapter 1, in which grayed areas represent the degree of coverage of the features provided by RCPs. These areas represent what is already provided for solving most application problems in the specific functional area.

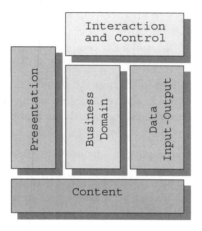

Figure 13.1   RCP support organized functionally

While RCPs provide many features 'out-of-the-box,' developers have a certain degree of freedom in customizing them – for example, presentation graphics are easier to modify in NetBeans RCP-powered applications than in a GUI built using the Eclipse RCP. For some domains, though, even the wide array of support libraries provided by RCPs is not enough, and developers have to resort to specific solutions, such as domains that require ad-hoc components.

From the diagram in Figure 13.1 it is clear that RCPs can be used as powerful tools for building client applications using the Domain-Driven Design approach[2], in which complex domains can be represented effectively by assigning all non-domain concerns to infrastructure components.

---

2.   See (Evans 2004).

GUI design guidelines and RCPs

Large IDEs built collaboratively by large teams, such as NetBeans and Eclipse, have precise guidelines for rationalizing their GUI design and smoothing user interaction. Strict GUI design guidelines become necessary for extensible applications that need to accommodate many third-party components seamlessly. While NetBeans fully adopted the Java Look and Feel design guidelines[3] (Java L&F Design Guidelines 2001), Eclipse created its own GUI design guidelines for effective use of the SWT toolkit.

Clearly, there are no strict rules regarding the adoption of the original platform's GUI guidelines in an application, even though all the GUI details and machinery used by the application will conform to these guidelines, and departing widely from them could make the overall GUI of an application look awkward.

Conversely, the GUI details of the various widgets and windowing support employed in large IDEs might not necessarily fit your own project: when in doubt, the wisest choice is always to avoid using such free solutions in a GUI and to limit an RCP-powered GUI for simplicity and usability.

SWT and the Eclipse RCP deserve a separate discussion, which is done in Section 13.4., while an example application based on the Eclipse RCP is discussed in Section 13.7.

13.2   The NetBeans RCP

The NetBeans RCP (NRCP) is a general-purpose platform for building desktop application GUIs with Java. It is the result of a refactoring of the code originated in NetBeans, the open source IDE provided by Sun.

NRCP provides roughly the same features as the Eclipse RCP, which is introduced in Section 13.4. Both RCPs provide a modular architecture for adding new components, and provide agile installation bundles, stripped of any unnecessary code[4]. The main difference between the two RCPs lies in the GUI toolkit employed: NRCP uses Swing and related technologies, such as JavaHelp for help support, while Eclipse RCP uses SWT and JFace, which were built expressly to support the IDE.

The learning curves differ too: there is a wealth of documentation (both in literature and on line) for Eclipse-related technologies, but little material regarding Netbeans RCP. Eclipse also provides many generated template applications that speed learning of the platform considerably. The NetBeans IDE does provide a wizard for creating an application based on NCRP.

---

3.   These guidelines were discussed in Chapter 3.
4.   The NRCP 4.1 download is 4.41 MB.

The most surprising thing about NRCP is its lack of popularity, despite the fact that it was around long before the Eclipse RCP. This is perhaps partly due to the current momentum of SWT technology over Swing. It is a pity, because the set of features NRCP offers to developers is quite impressive, ranging from window management, generic data access, scripting support, auto-update, and user settings management.

Figure 13.2 shows a screenshot of Version 4.1 of the NetBeans IDE, showing some of the windowing components that are available for NRCP applications. Note the sliding panel containing a tree on the right-hand side of the screen.

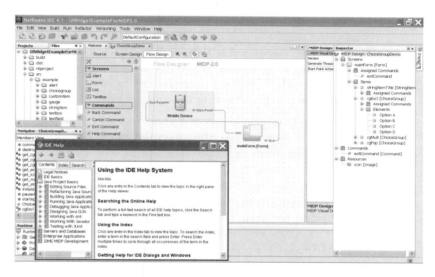

Figure 13.2   NetBeans 4.1 window support

NRCP architecture

NetBeans' modules, equivalent to Eclipse plug-ins, are components that provide various functionalities to the NetBeans platform. They are implemented following the Java standard for extensions that is built into the JAR file definition, as defined in the JAR MANIFEST.MF file. The modular architecture of NetBeans takes advantage of various Java standards, such the JavaBeans Activation Framework (JAF) for determining the type of arbitrary data and others.

Rather than a fully modular architecture, current NetBeans organization more closely resembles a sort of large API-centered ecosystem, in which several complex APIs interact at a fine level of detail. In the future the architecture of NetBeans will probably evolve towards a more componentized approach, following Eclipse's architecture.

The API for windowing support is based on the idea of supplying components to be displayed, which are positioned and rendered as decided by the platform's window management system. All components are subclasses of the `org.openide.windows.TopComponent` class, which provide methods for basic GUI management, such as activating the component view, opening it, and so on, in a high-level fashion.

13.3   *The Spring RCP*

The Spring RCP is a framework built on top of Swing to support the construction of medium to large client applications. The Spring RCP is still in its early stages of development[5] compared with both NetBeans and Eclipse RCPs. In contrast to the latter two RCPs, the Spring RCP is not the result of refactoring the implementation of an existing IDE, so its features don't include those typical of development-oriented tools, such as version control and advanced text editor support.

Perhaps the strongest point of the Spring RCP over the other RCPs lies in its coupling with server-side Spring applications, both in its coding approach and runtime object communication. The Spring RCP project focuses on providing 'an elegant way to build highly-configurable, GUI-standards-following Swing applications faster by leveraging the Spring Framework and a rich library of UI factories and support classes[6].' This means that developers familiar with the traditional Spring server application framework's 'elegant' implementation style (a popular mix of inversion of control[7] and aspect-oriented programming[8]) can apply the same approach to client applications.

It is too soon to say whether the independent efforts of both NetBeans and Eclipse RCPs will be able to provide the same level of quality over the same array of features that these two projects already provide. Nevertheless, the Spring RCP takes an interesting approach that has already proved popular among Java developers building server applications.

---

5.   At the time of writing (late 2005) the framework is still in alpha, so there is little practical utility in discussing such an early product in detail.
6.   Taken from the Spring RCP Web site, http://www.springframework.org/spring-rcp
7.   Inversion of control, or its Spring-specific variant known as 'dependency injection' are techniques for reversing the traditional flow of control in which client code invokes server code directly, by making server code invoke callback methods in client code. The dependency inversion principle is described in Chapter 7 – see page 358.
8.   Aspect-oriented programming (AOP) is an approach to programming (which happens to complement OOP nicely) to express different behaviors in a program in a more effective and modular way.

13.4   *The Eclipse RCP*

The Eclipse RCP (ERCP) grew out of the standard Eclipse project when it became clear that much of the work spent in building the various parts of Eclipse could also be used for building general applications, following the example of NetBeans. In fact, Eclipse itself can now be thought of as a specific application for software development built using the ERCP.

This apparently simple refactoring was due mainly to the high quality of Eclipse's design and plug-in architecture, which allows for a clear decomposition of code into separate units. Something described as 'applies to Eclipse' in this section means that is applicable to the ERCP as well.

Eclipse plug-in architecture

In Eclipse plug-ins are loaded in their own class loader. Given the rules of visibility for Java class loaders, plug-ins cannot access other classes or resources loaded from other plug-ins. The basic interoperability mechanism among plug-ins is provided by *extension points* that define how a given plug-in can be extended by other plug-ins and, symmetrically, by providing extensions to other plug-ins by extending their extension points. The details are declared in the plugin.xml manifest file for that plug-in.

Extension points can be used to override the default behavior of a plug-in, or for example to group related elements in the GUI, such as grouping commands in a common point in the GUI. Every component in an ERCP 'ecosystem' is defined in this way, apart from the importing of Java packages from another plug-in, achieved by means of the specific requires attribute in the plugin.xml file. At start-up the platform scans the plugin.xml declarations, creating an in-memory registry of all available plug-ins, although they are loaded only when needed by another plug-in.

The following (simplified) plugin.xml file defines an application launched through the class com.marinilli.Application, containing only one command:

```
<?xml version="1.0" encoding="UTF-8"?>
<?eclipse version="3.0"?>
<plugin>
   <extension
        id="application"
        point="org.eclipse.core.runtime.applications">
      <application>
         <run
               class="com.marinilli.Application">
         </run>
      </application>
   </extension>
   <extension
```

```
        point="org.eclipse.ui.commands">
    <category
        name="Save"
        id="app.category">
    </category>
  </extension>
</plugin>
```

From Eclipse 3.0 plug-ins can be added and removed (with certain restrictions) at runtime as well as at deployment time, the former being referred to as *dynamic* plug-ins. From Eclipse 3.1, some kernel support is factored out of the `plugin.xml` file into OSGI's `MANIFEST.MF`.

Eclipse RCP plug-ins

The Eclipse RCP can be defined as the minimum set of Eclipse plug-ins that can be used to build an application using the Eclipse 'bare-bones' infrastructure. Only two items are necessary:

- The Eclipse runtime plug-ins, which is comprised of three plug-ins, including the OSGI[9] kernel implementation.
- The GUI support, composed of three distinct layers: the SWT library, with some native auxiliary code at the lower level, the JFace library for data-driven support to SWT, and the workbench support for detachable windows, dialogs, and so on.

A downloaded RCP installation from the Eclipse Web also contains other auxiliary plug-ins that are needed for file-related chores such as XML and various other infrastructure support. Auxiliary plug-ins can be omitted to further decrease the installation bundle size.

This set of plug-ins is the minimum set. Clearly SWT can be used without any other plug-ins, so that GUIs can be built using this toolkit without using ERCP at all, as discussed in Chapter 11. The ERCP 3.1 bundle for Windows is 5.80 MB to downloaded and 8.38 MB unzipped, excluding JRE.

Figure 13.3 shows the main plug-ins organized in a layered fashion. Plug-ins shown with dashed borders are optional.

---

9. The Open Services Gateway Initiative (OSGI) is an industry group responsible for defining an open standard for component interoperability: see http://www.osgi.org for more details.

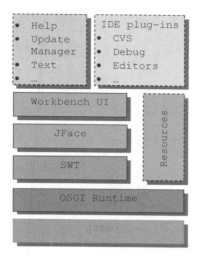

Figure 13.3   Eclipse layers

As the figure shows, the main plug-ins in ERCP are the OSGI Runtime and the user-interface support items – SWT, JFace, and the Workbench plug-in. All other plug-ins can be optionally used in building an application.

The plug-in component model in Eclipse 3.1 is powerful and effective, allowing the creation of very rich component 'ecosystems,' a thousand or more plug-ins in some installations. It does still lack the features mentioned previously, however: a sound security model that provides various levels of security, managing trusted and non-trusted plug-ins, sandboxing[10] non-signed plug-ins, and so on.

The workbench – the building blocks of ERCP GUIs

The Eclipse workbench, consisting of the Eclipse main window and its structure, can be reused in ECRP applications. Eclipse developers are familiar with its organization, shown in Figure 13.4.

---

10. Sandboxing is a technique for containing code execution within predefined rules. It is used for example in the code managed in the applet container, and also for Java Web Start applications. For example, an unsigned (untrusted) Java applet cannot access the local file system.

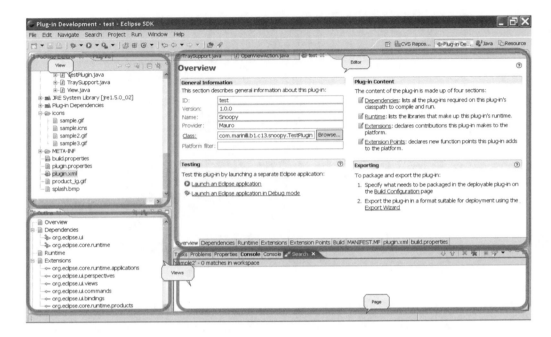

Figure 13.4   The Eclipse workbench

The term 'workbench' usually indicates the set of classes and visual components that implement the Eclipse GUI structure, and that are also used for ERCP applications.

The main parts of the workbench are:

- *Windows*. It is possible to open several windows on the same workbench.

- *Pages* are containers for the current *perspective*, and are used mainly for implementation purposes.

- *Perspectives* are organizations of views, editors, and actions within a window. By customizing views, editors, and actions using a perspective, GUI designers can optimize the same components and commands for different tasks, thus creating more productive and task-centered GUIs.

- *Editors* are areas of a window devoted to information manipulation. In complex GUIs, such as Eclipse itself, editors are the main focus of the user interaction after the data to work on has been selected using a suitable exploration view, so they occupy a central position within the window layout.

- *Views* are the window areas other than editors. Views are used for exploring and selecting data, for showing properties, or other auxiliary information. Depending on the kind of application you are building you will use one or more views to organize results, select data, and so on.

These entities are related as shown in the following UML class diagram, which represents relationships among concepts, rather than the real Java implementation in ERCP. See Figure 13.5.

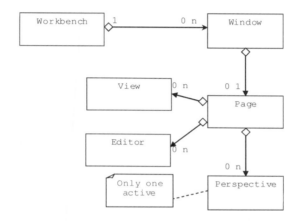

Figure 13.5   Eclipse workbench structure

The workbench's windowing organization, despite initially being intended for IDE applications only, is highly flexible and can be adapted to a wide range of different scenarios. Figure 13.6, for example, shows a workbench instance for the Azureus application, a client for the BitTorrent file sharing protocol, which was built with ERCP. The main window is implemented using only ERCP workbench views, organized in a fixed layout.

The ERCP plug-in architecture and the workbench support together provide a powerful mechanism for implementing composable units[11]. Despite the visual composition of loosely-coupled GUI-based components being supported only at the rather coarse-grained level of composing views and editors within a perspective, it is also possible to define plug-ins that participate in the composition of a single view or editor.

---

11. See Chapter 6.

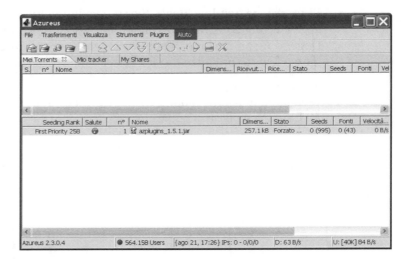

Figure 13.6   An ERCP-based workbench example

GUI design guidelines for ERCP applications

This section gives GUI design guidelines for the Eclipse IDE[12] annotated with the related rule numbers. Basically, these guidelines can be summarized as 'Follow what the Eclipse IDE does.'

Views, editors, and perspectives in Eclipse should conform to the following rules:

- Views are used to navigate a hierarchy of information, open an editor, or display the properties of an object (7.1). Commit in views must be done in immediate mode (7.2) while in editors commit is achieved in deferred mode – that is to say, data in views in saved immediately, while in editors it is saved only by means of an user action such as 'Save.'

- Editors are used to edit or browse a file, document, or other primary content. Only one instance of an editor may exist for each editor input within a perspective, but different input can be opened in separate editor instances.

- Perspectives should be created for long-lived tasks that involve the performance of smaller, non-modal tasks (8.1). When only one or two views need to be shown, it is suggested to extend an existing perspective type, rather than create a new one (8.2).

---

12. Available at http://www.eclipse.org/articles/Article-UI-Guidelines/Contents.html.

The following is a brief list of other details from the GUI design guidelines for Eclipse, with the relevant rule numbers in parenthesis:

- Use capitalization (1.5, 1.6) in text with headline style for menus, tooltips, titles of windows, dialogs, tabs, column headings, and push buttons. Capitalize the first and last words, and all nouns, pronouns, adjectives, verbs, and adverbs. Do not include ending punctuation. Use capitalization of the first word (and any proper names) only for all labels in dialogs or windows, including those for check boxes, radio buttons, group labels, and simple text fields.

- Error handling (1.8). When an error occurs that requires either an explicit user input or immediate attention from users, communicate the occurrence with a modal dialog.

- Icons. There are eight different types of icons used in Eclipse, and new icons should use the standard color palette provided by IBM (with a separate palette for wizard icons). The guidelines also prescribe file naming and directory structure for placing icons.

- Object properties should be placed in a view (the Properties view) when they can be calculated quickly, otherwise they should be placed in a dialog.

- Preferences. Global preferences are handled in a common Preferences dialog (15.1). Local preferences, such as those related to single views or editors, should be handled locally. Use the root page in the Preferences dialog for frequently-used preferences, or those preferences that have widespread effect. The root preference page should not be blank (15.4).

- Use Flat Look design for user scenarios that involve extensive property and configuration editing (16.1).

The native twist

As long as an application is close to the Eclipse IDE in concept (or ideally is one of its plug-ins) it is safe to follow the guidelines introduced above. Things start to become blurred when the GUI design of an application departs from the original IDE concept.

Because of SWT's 'native' nature, it is possible instead to use OS-specific guidelines, such as the Windows GUI design guidelines. While this limits cross-platform portability, it may make sense when there is only a need to target a single platform. In such cases working directly with the native platform GUI design style is the best solution.

13.5   Choosing the best RCP for your needs

So far we have described the three main open source RCPs available to Java developers for building medium- to large-scale applications. These provide roughly the same features – Netbeans and the Eclipse RCP, in particular, have very similar functionalities. What differs is the level of documentation and the community base supporting them, and perhaps more importantly, the underlying GUI toolkit used.

With the constant refinement of open source RCPs, GUI development for all but trivial Java GUIs has changed dramatically. Apart from specific application domains, RCPs can be used in a wide range of scenarios and business domains. Gone are the days when the knowledge of the GUI toolkit alone was enough to build GUIs – expensively, and sometimes with poor results. In the author's opinion, RCPs should be taught in university courses along with GUI toolkits, both as a practical means of building GUIs, and as an example of current industrial practice in constructing large applications[13].

A potential problem in adopting an RCP instead of a more lightweight solution such as the SWT/Swing toolkit and a GUI support library lies in the comprehensive nature of RCP frameworks. RCP frameworks tend to have an 'all-or-nothing' effect on development. Before attempting a solution to a given problem, developers using an RCP should first focus on the way the RCP handles that situation, and follow that design, instead of providing their own solution that might not work. This requires time-consuming learning that goes beyond a mere study of the documentation, otherwise problems could manifest themselves later in development.

Ultimately every RCP fits a specific purpose. Spring RCP is aimed at developers familiar with Swing and the Spring framework. NetBeans RCP addresses the needs of the Swing community at large, while applications based on the Eclipse RCP are shaped by the SWT toolkit[14].

When deciding which RCP to adopt in a new project, if any, perhaps the most important point lies in the choice of the GUI toolkit – that is, in the choice between Swing and SWT. Other details such as documentation and support, the availability of a strong developer community, and the other factors discussed for tool selection in Chapter 11, all shape a final decision. For general documentation and practical support for the generation of plug-ins, ERCP is currently preferable to the NRCP, but this may possibly change in future.

When to employ an RCP

When should one consider using an RCP for a small project? How small does a project have to be not to warrant an RCP?

---

13. The Eclipse RCP seems the best suited to this from an architectural viewpoint.
14. Although it is still possible to use Swing, as discussed in Chapter 11.

Answering these questions involves knowledge of many details, such as the developers' previous knowledge of the platform, the schedule for the planned releases, the future maintenance and extension plan for the application, and so on. As a rule of thumb, building more than eight screens, or the need to actively maintain an application for more than six months, justifies the adoption of an RCP, given that the time to learn it and the other constraints, such as the type of application and the domain fit with an RCP, are satisfied. These are just rough rules of thumb that should be customized to each case – each project has its own peculiarities, and a universal set of rules is not practical.

In conclusion, learning an RCP or adapting it in a medium to large project can be seen as a form of long-term investment. Even if both NetBeans or Eclipse disappear in the near future, their source code is public, so that they still remain a viable choice even for long-term projects. As regards cost and their competitiveness with other similar frameworks, much remains to be done in enhancing ease of use, documentation, code generation facilities, and other means of lowering the initial adoption cost. In this respect, NetBeans needs to catch up with Eclipse.

13.6   Legal issues

You might think that all this discussion of RCPs sounds interesting, and perhaps also useful, but what about the small print on the license page? What are the legal constraints over use of an RCP as part of a commercial product, or in some other form? Here is a brief overview, but for definitive information on such delicate issues, you should refer to the licenses themselves.

Eclipse

The Eclipse Public License (EPL) evolved from the Common Public License (CPL) created by IBM 'to encourage a model in which commercial products could be based on open-source efforts[15].' The EPL differs from the CPL in a few details, such as a specific, less restrictive treatment of software patents[16]. Here is a brief summary of the key points in the EPL: a *contributor* is a person or organization that creates the initial code under EPL, or who originates changes or additions, or who distributes the code under the EPL:

- Only mere distributors can be anonymous, all other contributors cannot.
- Contributors creating 'modules' that use or modify existing EPL code can distribute the final result under their own terms, as long as the portion of the

---

15.   From *A history of IBM's open-source involvement and strategy*, IBM Systems Journal, July 2005. Available on line.
16.   For more details, see http://www.eclipse.org/legal/index.php.

derivative work under the EPL license is still acknowledged under an EPL-compatible license. This clause causes incompatibility of EPL/CPL with a popular OSS license, GPL[17]. Contrary to the EPL, extending/modifying code licensed with the GPL forces the derivative product to be licensed under GPL.

- Contributors can compile code licensed under the EPL and distribute it commercially under EPL terms.

- Contributors that modify EPL code but don't distribute it, perhaps for internal use, are not obliged to make their modifications available to others.

Some problems might arise if for example you plan to use GPL-licensed code with code licensed under the EPL, because these licenses are incompatible. You can refer to the Free Software Foundation license page for more details[18].

Netbeans

NetBeans is covered by the Sun Public License[19] (SPL), which is a variant of the Mozilla Public License. Both of them are 'free software' licenses, in that they envisage software as a free artifact to which contributors are free to make modifications and use them privately, or distribute changes, without specific permissions apart from those prescribed in the license itself. This doesn't mean that versions of so-called 'free software' cannot be distributed commercially – license terms for 'free software' can still be enforced under copyright law.

Given its distribution philosophy, the SPL is not compatible with the GPL. For more details, the reader is urged to consult the SPL text.

In conclusion, ERCP, NRCP, and Spring RCP allow commercial products to be built on top of their platforms provided that legal information is provided when the application is downloaded, and that the legal requirements dictated by the various licenses are satisfied.

13.7 An example Eclipse RCP application

In this section we discuss a practical example of an application built on top of ERCP. Given the number of examples freely available on line or discussed in other books, we will focus on the architecture of the application and on its high-level GUI design aspects. You can download the code and try the application yourself.

---

17. The GNU General Public License (GPL). For details, see: http://www.gnu.org/licenses/gpl.html.

18. Available at: http://www.fsf.org/licensing/licenses/index_html.

19. Details available at: http://www.netbeans.org/about/legal/license.html.

To install the code of the example application, you need to:

i.   Download the freely-available RCP distribution from the Eclipse Web site.
ii. Download the bundle code for this chapter.
iii. Copy the contents of the `features` and `plugins` directories into the same directories as in the RCP directory (this procedure is also valid also for installing Eclipse plug-ins).
iv. Copy the `.ini` file of your platform (Windows, Mac, GTK), renamed as `config.ini` into the ERCP's `configuration` directory, to replace the existing file of that name.

The application

Snooper is a demo application for gathering data about people. You may have seen this kind of application at work in many movies or TV shows, where detectives or secret agents type in the name of some bad character and everything about him is magically discovered, from his driving license number to his favorite brand of shoe.

Despite the fact that such an application would be on the edge of legality on grounds of personal data management, privacy, national security, and so on, at least in some countries, our management has decided that this is the ultimate high-margin market, so we are asked to provide an initial release in three months time.

We decide to use ERCP because it provides us with a robust and powerful platform that can host future extensions, such as specialized searches, access to specific databases, facial image processing, and all that fancy spy story stuff, and it only needs to be available on the major OS platforms.

We would like to make the application available in a modular fashion, so that premium customers can buy extra modules for more sophisticated research.

You will be disappointed to hear that the implementation provided with this chapter doesn't connect to a Pentagon database – for security reasons – but, more humbly, to free resources available on the Web. Figure 13.7 shows the application with the Amazon search service loaded.

The main interaction we design for the application in Figure 13.7 is as follows:

1. The user selects an individual from a persistent list, or creates a new person as needed.
2. Selecting a person populates the other views with data about the selected individual. For search views, or other calculated views, if the search button is not used, nothing is displayed. When the button is clicked, the search process starts for all the registered search providers (that is, all plug-ins loaded at deployment time). For simplicity, no 'stop search' action has been provided.
3. Previously-launched searches, if not refreshed, show old data.

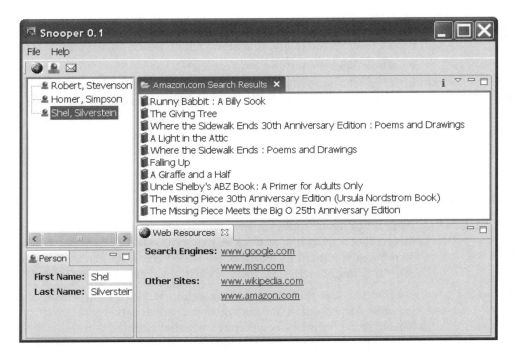

Figure 13.7   The Snooper application

The first release of the application is a little vapid, in that you only get material such as published books and data from standard Web sites, but it nevertheless provides an interesting example of a simple ERCP application.

The GUI design of the application is organized as follows:

- We use ERCP views to represent all data managed within the application. We don't need editors because of the nature of the application: all data input is performed in immediate mode – see *GUI design guidelines for ERCP applications* on page 482.

- Every module provides one or more views for user interaction.

- View capabilities are related to domain-specific issues, as will be shown later.

Building the application using modules provides many advantages, such as an easier iterative development environment – we can add more features later without modifying the core components – flexibility and extensibility, the possibility of more powerful billing and licensing schemes, and clearer organization of the development teams.

The code provided shows many useful tricks, such as splash screen, a localized 'About' dialog (Figure 13.8), OS-dependent system tray support (Figure 13.9), and others. See the code bundle for this chapter for more details.

The remainder of this section focuses on the architecture of ERCP applications, and how to employ its plug-in architecture usefully.

Figure 13.8   *Bells and whistles in Snooper*

Figure 13.9   *The system tray support for Windows*

Introducing client-side modular architectures

This section introduces general issues about the modular architecture of RCP applications that are based upon a plug-in architecture, whether the Eclipse RCP, NetBeans RCP, or other plug-in support frameworks. These general points are then illustrated in the context of the Snooper application in the next section.

Plug-ins and pomegranate seeds

Most people find pomegranates tedious to eat. One needs a lot of patience to deal with the inner intricacies of a pomegranate, so it comes as no surprise that such fruits are not as popular as, say, peaches. Working with ERCP is much like eating pomegranates. You have no choice but to deal with its 'seeds' one by one, because much like a pomegranate, the bulk of an ERCP application is all in the seeds themselves.

Learning to deal with plug-ins is tedious and time-consuming, despite what the IBM marketing department may claim. Mastering the subtleties of the OSGI manifest or the flow of control during the platform start-up[20] takes substantial time that detracts from that available for, say, a thoughtful componentization of the various plug-ins with which an application is to be implemented.

No wonder that few developers find the time, or are willing to see the ERCP plug-in architecture (or NetBeans') as an opportunity for fine, useful design, rather than as a necessary hindrance on the route to the next release of their application.

Packing everything into one or two big plug-ins and using the plug-in architecture only as a necessary means of integration of code with the rest of the ERCP framework is a valid strategy for delivering small applications quickly. Unfortunately, even for small- to medium-scale applications, the application's structure tends to degrade quickly as maintenance and code additions are performed during the application's lifecycle. A sound modular structure becomes a serious concern in medium to large RCP applications and where long-term maintenance is an issue.

The next section illustrates a simple approach to using the plug-in architecture in ERCP and in other frameworks for building modular RCP applications, but first, a brief introduction to software components.

Pomegranate seeds and software components

The use of the term 'software component' when talking about loosely-coupled modules that execute on a client-side application is a little misleading. The definition of a software component is still controversial: many different approaches at various levels of granularity, and focusing on different application scenarios and business domains, all define themselves as 'components,' such as J2EE EJB, .NET components, JavaBeans, CORBA, and COM components. All these approaches share two characteristics:

- They focus on writing software units that comply with a given specification.
- Such units may be reusable in other contexts[21].

Clearly we are interested in a smaller subset of the characteristics of enterprise and distributed software components. For example, GUI aspects are extremely important for us, while remoting capabilities are not, as our 'components' all reside in the same RCP instance. For these reasons, and also because we used the term 'component' throughout the book when referring to aggregates of basic

---

20. Sooner or later you need to face such details unless you can maintain your plug-in as a carbon copy of those automatically generated by Eclipse PDE (Plug-in Development Environment) wizards.
21. For more details. see for example: http://en.wikipedia.org/wiki/Software_component

widgets (that is, visual components), we will give our components the more specific term of *module*.

To the Java programmer, components tend to resemble Java packages, as they can be used to group elements into logical structures. Clearly components go beyond mere structuring of multiple classes, providing a semantically-rich grouping mechanism that discreetly takes advantage of the theoretical underpinnings of object orientation – encapsulation, self-containment, loose coupling, and so on.

Figure 13.10 introduces UML2 component diagrams, which we will use here even though we are not discussing fully-fledged software components. The diagram uses the UML2 feature of visual stereotypes to represent components.

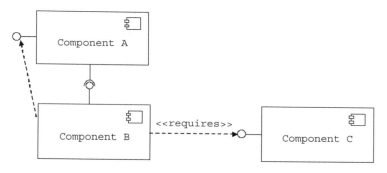

Figure 13.10 An example component diagram

In the diagram Component B exposes one interface to the outside, while using the interfaces provided by Component A and Component C. Component A requires an interface (a set of services) that is provided by B, so Component B provides the services Component A requires. The 'lollipop' icon expresses an interface a component is providing to other components, while the half circle represents a required interface.

A standard specification for a component model on the client side of Java applications would give a great boost to medium to large GUIs in Java, especially for enterprise-level GUIs such as business-critical applications, ERP, or financial software. Unfortunately, the availability of two major GUI toolkits, and specifications such as JSF, make things more difficult for the creation of an effective standard for client-side components. But a closer look suggests that such apparent difficulties in fact represent strengths that such a specification could leverage.

Designing modular RCP applications

Plug-ins therefore interact mainly by exposing interfaces to other plug-ins through extension points and by providing extensions to existing interfaces (that is, extension points from other plug-ins). In a modular mindset like that briefly introduced above, some guidelines can be defined:

- A module in a GUI-focused RCP should be fully self-contained: it has to include its own GUI, typically as a number of views or editors, as well as actions, help support, business domain classes, and so on, and it should also contain everything needed for its own build: sources, resource files, test cases, and the like.

- A module should be designed and made to interact with other modules only by means of the underlying RCP architecture. When using Eclipse this is accomplished by means of its plug-in architecture and, as a general design guideline, by providing one module per plug-in. Despite the fact that this 1:1 mapping could seem limiting in some situations (such as large modules) it provides a general, simple, and practical rule of thumb.

- Modules represent either business domain concepts or services. Two commonly-used service modules are the `Frame` module, a base infrastructure module providing framework support to all other modules, and optionally the `Main` module, which glues together all other modules and launches the application[22].

These guidelines build on the existing RCP infrastructure, and also apply to RCPs other than ERCP.

Here we take a more humble approach than that of designing general software components. For example, reuse is a secondary concern in our approach, which focuses on enhancing software design, development, and maintenance of medium and large RCP applications. Modules are a means of rationalizing and raising the abstraction level in the development of an RCP application.

The Snooper application architecture

The Snooper RCP application is designed around four modules:

- The `People` module handles:
  - The management of a collection of individuals, shown on the left-hand side of Figure 13.11.

---

22. In simple applications the one module that has the best fit semantically with the application's purpose can work as the main module, glue together all other modules, and launch the whole application.

 – The currently-selected person, shown in the **Person** view in Figure 13.11.

 – The list of specialized searches for the selected person on a set of search Web sites, the **Web Resources** view at the bottom right-hand side of Figure 13.11.

• The AmazonSearch module, which provides search management specialized for the Amazon site. This is shown in the **Amazon.com Search Results** view in Figure 13.11.

• The Main module, which glues together the other plug-ins in order to run the application.

• The Frame module, which provides common support services to all the plug-ins.

Figure 13.11 shows the ERCP views provided by the various plug-ins in the architecture. References to the underlying platform (org.eclipse.ui and org.eclipse.core.runtime plug-ins) are excluded for brevity.

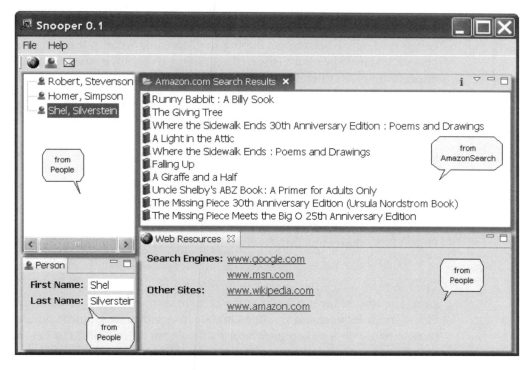

Figure 13.11   Component diagram of the Snooper application

The two business domain modules both extend the window support provided by ERCP and provide their own specific interfaces. More specifically:

- The `People` module provides three Eclipse views (**Person**, **People List**, and **Web Resources**) and an extension point useful for attaching customized searches. The `People` module depends only on the `Frame` module.

- The `AmazonSearch` module provides one Eclipse view, **Search Results**, and extends the `People` module's extension point for implementing searches on the selected person provided by the `People` plug-in.

For usability reasons the views are designed so that:

- The collection of people cannot be moved or closed, and its location is fixed on the left-hand side of the main window. This view works as the exploration area where the subject for searches is selected.

- The **Person** view cannot be closed, but it can be moved and docked as required within the main window.

- The other views can all be closed or docked as required in the main window.

This arrangement is just one possible solution: the same application could be partitioned into a different set of plug-ins. More importantly, the design is far from perfect. It should be seen as the first version in an iterative development, in which imperfections are tolerated for the sake of simplicity.

In this example, creating half a dozen almost-empty modules to anticipate their use in future releases could be a mistake, because it entails the costs of creating the modules without any functional added value. This design is also imperfect in that it centralizes too many responsibilities in the `People` module, which could well be split into two or three separate modules in a subsequent iteration. For example, the **Web Resources** view should be a separate search provider, while `People` will remain as a collection of `Person` instances, with `Person` possibly a separate module with its own view, and so on.

Figure 13.12 shows an UML2 component diagram that illustrates the organization of the plug-ins used in Snooper.

The modules in the figure are organized in a layered scheme to aid comprehension. The lowest layer, shown at the bottom of the diagram, is composed of the `Frame` module. Business modules are represented in the middle, while the topmost module depends implicitly or explicitly on all the modules below it. Note that `People` provides the extension point for the various search providers currently installed, currently extended only by the `AmazonSearch` module.

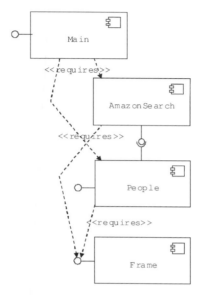

Figure 13.12   Component diagram of the Snooper application

The `People` plug-in exposes the extension point for registering external search providers, as shown in its `plugin.xml` file:

```
<?xml version="1.0" encoding="UTF-8"?>
<?eclipse version="3.0"?>
<plugin>
    <extension-point id="peopleSearch" name="peopleSearch"
schema="schema/people.exsd"/>
...
```

The `people.exsd` schema file describes the details of the extension point provided. The `AmazonSearch` plug-in extends such an extension point, declaring it in its `plugin.xml` file and implementing the corresponding interface shown in the following section of code:

```
package com.marinilli.b1.c13.snooper.search;
import com.marinilli.b1.c13.snooper.model.Person;
public interface ISearchProvider {
   public void launchSearch(Person p);
}
```

Whenever the **Search** button is clicked in the GUI, all the registered search plug-ins are requested to start a new search using the currently-selected person. This mechanism is implemented by the `People` plug-in, invoking the `launchSearch()` method on all registered plug-ins.

13.8   Summary

This chapter introduced the main RCPs currently available to Java developers, briefly discussing their characteristics. It then focused on the Eclipse RCP, providing an example application that illustrates the many options available to developers. The example is also useful to focus discussions of general design strategies for medium- to large-scale desktop application GUIs built on top of a Java RCP, using the Eclipse RCP as a practical example.

14 The Personal Portfolio Application

In this chapter we will look at a complete application that covers all the important issues in professional GUI design and subsequent development – or, better, two distinct designs and implementations that solve the same needs. The application has been developed from scratch for this chapter. Although the scenario for which it is designed is totally fictional, it was chosen for its resemblance to real-world situations, especially in the common problems it addresses. The demo applications are available for download together with the source code for the book. The scenario is introduced with the first implementation: an alternative approach is discussed later in the chapter.

14.1 The scenario

A publisher of scientific and technical material maintains a large document repository that is constantly growing with the addition of new documents from disparate authors – books, scientific papers, conference proceedings, technical articles, and so on. The repository is accessed by subscription via a Web interface, and is known as the Personal Portfolio application.

One category of users find the GUI rather poor. Librarians, who use the repository intensively, as well as editors and other frequent users, are unhappy with the current browser-based interface, in that it offers limited functionality, and performing advanced and repetitive searches on the repository is extremely time-consuming. Furthermore, the publishers are considering launching new advanced services such as specialized news streaming, personalized e-learning content, P2P-based information dissemination, and more.

An engineering task force has been set up to address the issue. The objective is to come up with an initial working prototype of a new GUI within three months. The whole project is focused on addressing power users and their needs, while creating a platform to which to add future advanced services.

After informal interviews with representative users and within the publisher's engineering branch, the landscape became clearer:

• The old Web-based GUI was adequate for average and non-repetitive users, while repetitive users – for example, those who access the system more than once in a day – need a 'geared-up' search facility.

- Despite the fact that the repository is accessed by thousands of subscribers world-wide, power users who demanded an advanced GUI were limited to roughly a hundred people scattered around the world.

- Repetitive, power users were generally enthusiastic about the project and willing to collaborate in its development. A group of such user representatives was formed to investigate the new GUI, together with people from the publisher's organization. Another, larger, group of expert users was formed for early testing of the prototype.

- The new GUI needs to be made expandable to handle sophisticated services, which will be tested within the power user community. This will give the publisher a privileged channel for testing new services, and in the medium to long term, an edge over their competitors.

- The whole project will not affect the existing GUI and the well-established Web repository site, but will instead be organized separately.

- After an initial start-up phase, during which a preliminary prototype with some limited functionality will be tested within the power user community, the project will eventually evolve into a new, stable service for advanced users. Such a service will provide early access to new features.

That is the setting. Unfortunately, nobody in the engineering team discovered this book, and this chapter in particular…

This development scenario is representative of a type of project that includes the following characteristics:

- A complex, professional GUI needs to be developed within a relatively tight timescale.

- Regardless of the inherently distributed nature of the problem, traditional HTML-base Web-based interfaces cannot satisfactorily be employed.

- The focus is on quality, even if constrained by time-to-market and development cost-effectiveness, just like any other real-world software project.

- Despite a small set of users being located geographically close enough for some preliminary meetings, the test group and the remaining user population is physically out of the reach of the development team. This poses some interesting organizational and technical problems.

A note on lifecycle models

This chapter follows the Rational Unified Process software lifecycle model and terminology. We introduced this model in Chapter 1: for convenience here we highlight the phases of the process only. For more details on UML and the Rational Unified Process, see for example (Fowler 2003) or (Rosenberg and Scott 1999).

The main phases of the software lifecycle according to the RUP model are illustrated in Figure 14.1.

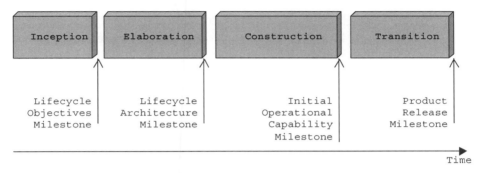

Figure 14.1   The phases and milestones of an RUP project

For brevity we will only briefly touch on all the details of each phase – see Figure 14.2: we discuss the software architecture in some detail, as well as the final source code. The deployment, an important part of the whole engineering scenario, is also briefly discussed.

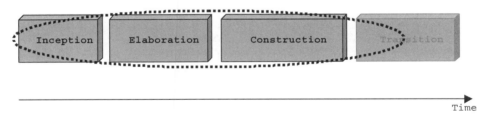

Figure 14.2   RUP phases covered in this example

Management and other issues, such as the business case, evaluation and change control are glossed over, the focus being only on technical details.

14.2 Analysis

The project team started the analysis activity, following the RUP approach.

Early analysis

The core design group of users was chosen from those geographically close to the development team, to speed up the initial design, while the test user group was set up to cover people from different countries to test the prototypes extensively.

These groups were formed taking care to select a representative set of the user population. Parameters like geography, culture, role in the end user population, background computing skills, platform used, and so on were all taken into account.

Figure 14.3 shows an initial use case diagram representing the use cases obtained from an initial analysis.

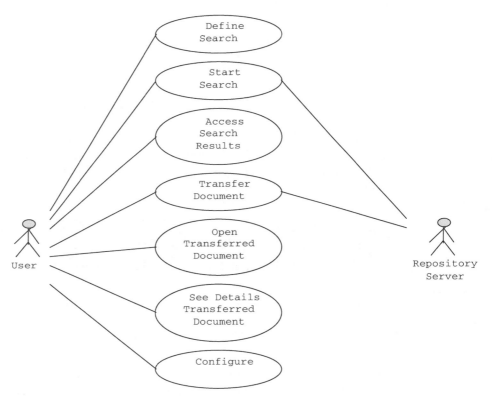

Figure 14.3   An initial use case diagram

Two actors were considered: the end user (a human) and the repository server (a server machine). From this early analysis seven use cases were elicited, as shown in Figure 14.3. Prior to refining the use case diagram, the intent needs to be better defined, by means of a vision document.

The vision

Before getting into the analysis phase in details, it's important to focus on the philosophy behind the product and its clear-cut definition. This focus is a typical RUP concept – that of a clear 'vision' of the product being developed that meets stakeholders' real needs.

In the publisher's situation, the vision is focused around the notion of a personal document portfolio that manages document searches and found documents on behalf of the user. More generally, however, the vision document should fulfill the following requirements:

- State the problem(s) that the application will solve.
- Define the stakeholders, including the end users of the product, and their needs.
- Identifying the product's required features.
- Characterize the functional requirements, which can later evolve into the use cases.
- Define non-functional requirements.
- Identify design constraints.
- Define a glossary of the key terms.

To fulfill these requirements requires a formal document, not just a mere list. This chapter briefly covers the vision for the following aspects:

- Stating the problems that the application will solve:
  - Managing personalized document searches for expert users.
  - Relieving the strain and unnecessary complication of repetitive and advanced searches performed with the existing Web-based GUI.
  - Enabling the creation of an access point for future services for expert users of the digital library.
- Identifying the stakeholders, among them the end users of the product, and their needs:
  - End users: expert, repetitive users of the old digital document repository system. Often such users perform their searches on behalf of others, as is the case with librarians.
  - Engineers and other developers within or external to the publisher.
  - The rest of the user population, even if they won't be affected by the new system.

- Defining the product features:
  - Providing an advanced user interface for the digital repository's repetitive users.
- Characterizing the functional requirements. The system will provide at least the following basic functionalities:
  - Authenticate the given user.
  - Create a new search.
  - Store and reuse/modify a search.
  - Submit the search to the server.
  - Managing billing, subscriptions and other related services.
- Identifying the non-functional requirements:
  - Usability requirements. The application's usability should be at least equal as that provided by the existing Web-based interface.
- Defining the design constraints. The main ones will be:
  - A user's searches should be located on the server to support future features such as collaborative working, and to improve reliability.
  - The software interface with the server should be the same as the old Web-based interface, to minimize risk.
  - In general, the new application should have a minimum impact on the existing server software.
- Eliciting a glossary of key terms. The main terms will be:
  - *Search*. A set of values that embody a query to the remote digital repository.
  - *Document*. A single item obtained by searching the remote digital repository. Documents are consumed by users.
  - *Search preferences*. The information that composes a search. A common set of properties, such as how often the search should be performed, keywords, and the like.
  - *Digital document repository system*. The existing, Web-based interface to the digital library service offered by the publisher.
  - *Personal portfolio*. This concept has been elicited from the early design meetings for capturing the application's basic approach, and subsumes the overall 'vision.' The application will provide a personal portfolio of documents taken from the digital repository on behalf of the user.

The main risks to the project are found to be bounded mainly by usability. Since the application will integrate with, rather than replace, the older digital document repository, it should be superior to the existing application in order to be successfully accepted by expert users.

A further risk is the economic impact of the project.

Some scenarios

The following scenarios emerge from a few interviews with users in the design group.

User search

Since the initial interviews, the focus has been on identifying the most typical interaction. This is illustrated by the following scenario, represented in natural language.

1. User accesses the application.
2. User logs in.
3. User creates a new search and enters the search details, then the search is launched on the server automatically.
4. Server gives a response to the query.
5. The application presents search results.
6. User chooses some documents from the search results and transfers them to their local machine.
7. The application handles requested documents, checking for permissions, security, and performs billing.
8. User opens the transferred documents in the relevant OS-specific tool, for example a PDF viewer.
9. The application automatically saves the user's search for future use if user doesn't explicitly delete it.

Some alternative paths could be:

*   Authentication failed.
*   2.1: the user is informed of the problem and a 'Retry Y/N' message is displayed. If the user chooses 'Y,' step 2 is repeated, otherwise the application exits.
*   Server or connection is currently unavailable.
*   1.1: the application signals the condition with some unobtrusive feedback. From now on certain functions (like creating a new search) are not available.

User manages search results

Another scenario could involve the following, a session in which the user's objective is to access retrieved documents.

1. User accesses the application.
2. User logs in.
3. User accesses a previous search by means of the GUI.

4. User changes search preferences (search name, search parameters, and so on) to modify the set of retrieved documents.

5. User commits the changes. The search is submitted to the server.

From this point on this scenario follows the preceding one. In a real-world use case document, more refined scenarios would follow.

A refined use case diagram

After further interviews with end users and more analysis activity, the following use case diagram is defined.

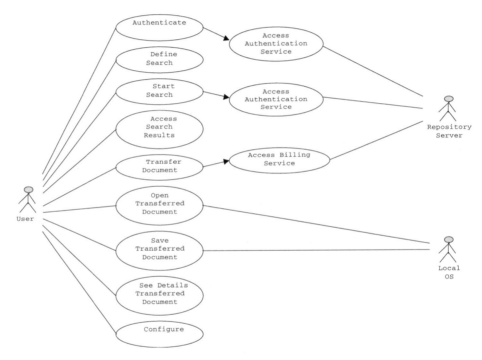

Figure 14.4   A refined use case diagram

Note that this refined diagram includes a new actor, the local operating system (OS), which is needed to store and view downloaded documents, together with a more structured use case organization. This diagram forms the input to the first GUI paper mock-up prototype.

The next step in following an RUP methodology is to elicit the actors-system boundary classes.

Individuating boundary classes

Boundary classes are those classes that lie at the boundary between the system and the external actors. Using the concept of a personal portfolio of documents, and studying the previous scenarios from the viewpoint of the end user actor, we could think of the main boundary class as a collection of search objects: search objects gather retrieved documents from the remote repository, and users will mainly deal with a collection of searches.

After initial interviews a partial conceptual model of the application domain is nailed down, as shown in Figure 14.5.

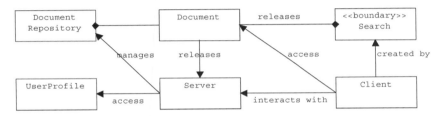

Figure 14.5   An initial conceptual class diagram

The class diagram in Figure 14.5 is related to the conceptual domain only, and shouldn't be confused with the implementation class diagram that we will consider in a later section.

Before proceeding to the design, we need to make some basic choices about the underlying technology. Clearly, our design will be radically affected by this strategic choice.

14.3   Choosing a technology

The choice of a suitable implementation technology is basically restricted to Web-based technology, essentially JSP, php, or other Web page–based technologies, and some form of client technology.

The choice of Java is driven by several cultural and practical issues:

- The repository server is implemented with J2EE technology.
- Developers feel more comfortable with Java rather than with other technologies.
- It takes advantage of existing development tools to minimize risk and additional cost, such as expensive licenses, the evaluation of and training for new software, and so on.

- The end user population relies on recent machines with a variety of OSs, and Java would be a cost-effective choice at least for the first generation of the application – the riskier one.

This scenario dictates that, among the various Java client options, the most useful deployment technology is the JNLP protocol, as it is available for all Java-enabled platforms. Deployment aspects are considered later in this chapter.

The choice of JNLP choice ensures the following benefits:

- A team of developers is available that is familiar with the implementation platform.
- Synergy between client and server technology is guaranteed.
- Ease of deployment and debugging facilities over the Web is supported. This is particularly useful for the frequent deployment of updated prototypes.

Now that a stable set of functional requirements for the application exists and the technology has been chosen, the GUI design phase can begin.

14.4   An initial GUI design

The main tasks that need to be addressed by the application are:

- Authenticate the user
- Create and manage repository searches
- Access documents retrieved by these searches
- Manipulate and modify the searches
- Store the searches

The preliminary design phase produces a number of documents that describe the basic functional requirements, the product vision, a number of use case diagrams and scenarios, plus some models that sketch the application domain, and other informal observations. All this information is ready for convergence into a tentative GUI prototype. The team follows a participatory design approach, in which users actively contribute to the GUI design. This method is chosen because of the nature of the current case – the intended user population, the focus on usability, and so on.

An initial GUI paper mock-up

From an informal meeting among designers, the first design proposal is sketched out.

The main window is composed of a toolbar, a list of all the active searches, and a status bar, as shown in Figure 14.6. Each item in the list represents a search, with a title and other useful data, such as the current status of the search, an is available for quick selection. The commands in the toolbar affect the currently-selected search item in the list.

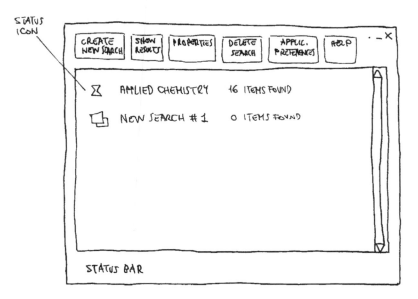

Figure 14.6   The first paper mock-up

By double–clicking on a search item, another window pops up that lists the documents retrieved by the search. This second window is sketched in the paper mock-up in Figure 14.7.

Double–clicking on a single document in the list starts the download process, following which the relevant viewer for the specific document type is opened. The buttons in the toolbar manipulate the currently-selected document in the list. The **Info** command pops up a dialog with the document's data, such as author, publication date, and so on, without downloading the document. The **View** command works like a double click: first the document is downloaded, then it is opened.

From a conceptual viewpoint, the prototype relies on the idea of a list of searches created and maintained by the user. Any of these searches can be opened to show all the retrieved documents and, in turn, the documents can be manipulated by the user.

This mock-up is used as a starting point for a subsequent discussion with representative users. The objective of this second meeting is to produce an early GUI prototype that is representative of user's needs, and which in turn will be validated with a larger user population.

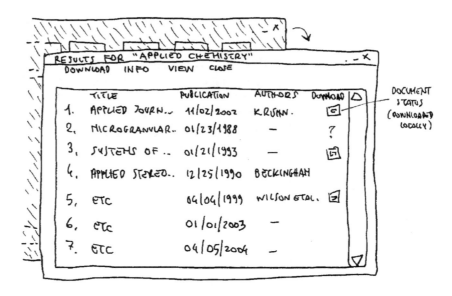

Figure 14.7   Another paper mock-up

A second GUI paper mock-up

The design team holds a second meeting, in which a selected group of users discussed the GUI design sketched in Figure 14.6. Their objective is to nail down an initial stable prototype that is validated by representative users.

This meeting results in a major redesign of the GUI: the users explain the most frequent tasks for which they intend the GUI to be suited, using the first prototype as a common discussion ground. A crucial aspect that emerges from this meeting is the desire of users to be able to fully customize their workspace. They see this as one of the major limitations of the existing Web interface.

Many different interaction strategies emerge from this second meeting. End users turn out to have radically different (and unexpected) approaches to solving the same tasks: for example, one uses several slightly different searches to explore the documents on a given topic, carefully recording the best searches on paper for future reference, while another is accustomed to launching broad queries and then scanning the large list that results.

Other important issues expressed by users were:

*   To be able to use more natural interaction styles, such as 'drag and drop' (there is a significant Apple Macintosh community among end users).

- The importance of having a lot of information in one screen, rather than continuously switching between different windows.
- Gearing up the GUI for repetitive users, providing powerful 'horizontal' features rather than complex specialized 'vertical' ones – continuously popping up windows to inspect search outcomes seemed too awkward.
- To focus the whole GUI on common tasks, or at least making them as easy as possible.
- The difficulty of making comparisons between two different searches.
- A bookmark concept, very useful in practice, is lacking.
- A properties panel beside the search lists, including some basic information about retrieved documents, would help the details of each search to be inspected more easily.

The designers gather all these suggestions, and after further interaction, worked out the prototype shown in Figure 14.8.

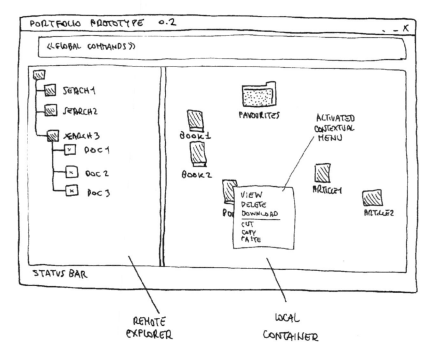

Figure 14.8   The revised paper mock-up

This GUI is substantially different than that shown in Figure 14.6 – 'drag and drop' and a more flexible interaction allow for a richer GUI experience and more intuitive interaction.

Lurking behind the GUI design sketched in Figure 14.8 are some interesting conceptual considerations. As often happens, limitations in a GUI design often derive from a poor conceptual model. As well as the concept of an *explorer* object that represents the searches performed by users, as previously implemented by the list in the prototype in Figure 14.6, the prototype in Figure 14.8 introduces a new and useful abstraction, the *local container*. This is an object that contains all the documents of interest to the current user, and follows the Desktop metaphor used by all modern OS GUIs. This container maintains an image of selected documents that can be manipulated by the user, and documents transferred in the container can later be downloaded to the user's local file system.

A typical interaction for creating a search object now leads to the creation of a new node in the tree on the left hand-side of the GUI, termed the *remote explorer* area. Retrieved documents are shown as subnodes of the search node, mimicking a file system hierarchy. Clicking twice on a document node, or dragging a node to the right-hand side of the screen, transfers the relevant document into the local container. Documents in the container can be managed just like documents in a desktop environment. In particular, by double-clicking on a container document, it is possible to view the document's contents, perform background user authentication, billing, and other operations, and finally download the document content to a local cache.

The 'drag and drop' metaphor is intended to be coherent outside the container as well – dragging a document out of the application window and onto the OS desktop area should cause the document to be downloaded to the desktop or to a target folder.

Locating the exploration task on the left-hand side of the screen and the manipulation area on the right follows a general and widely-accepted pattern in modern GUIs, as we saw in Chapter 4. Taking advantage of this kind of convention is usually a 'win-win' approach: on one hand designers get useful guidelines for limiting the initial design space to the promising avenues, while on the other users feel comfortable using a GUI that resembles software with which they are familiar.

Nailing down the logical model

This is an important and often overlooked aspect of GUI design. Designers may need to change their assumptions later in the development process, but a sound conceptual analysis is still indispensable at an early stage to achieve a professional GUI design. Designers should carefully refine the conceptual model behind the GUI, searching for inconsistencies and conceptual fallacies.

The two abstract concepts the new document repository client's GUI relies on so far are:

- *Remote explorer.* A collection of search objects defined by the user and the retrieved document metadata. The document metadata only contains sparse data, to avoid downloading useless information. The search objects reside on the server, allowing for collaborative features, and are updated when the application is started.

- *Local container.* This represents a collection of information about the documents transferred by the user as a result of document searches. Document transferred into this container are not yet downloaded. The final step in fully accessing a document – after initiating a search, selecting one or more retrieved documents, and transferring them into the local container – is by downloading the document and viewing it via a suitable OS-dependent viewer application. Document metadata stored in the local container is kept in a cache on the user's local file system, together with document content files.

Clearly, this is only the first refinement of the GUI's conceptual model, but it is important to define it a soon as possible, even if it may be changed in the future.

A throw-away GUI prototype

Having tested the mock-up with users, the designers are ready to implement it in order to build a more vivid representation of the final GUI that can be validated by a larger number of users. Technology now enters directly into the design process. The aim is not to produce a working GUI prototype, but rather to capture basic interactions (inexpensively), and hence requirements, in further interactions with users.

They produce the prototype shown in Figure 14.9.

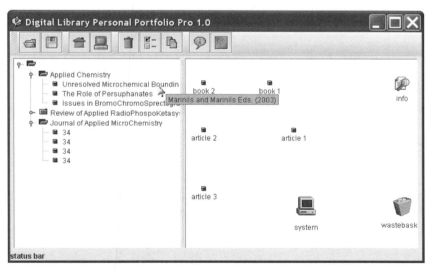

Figure 14.9   The throw-away prototype (Ocean1.5)

The GUI closely resembles the revised paper mock-up discussed in the previous section (Figure 14.8). Users can drag items from the tree on the left-hand side into the container on the right of the window, mimicking the transfer process.

Three system icons are placed in the virtual desktop container on the right-hand side, as shown in Figure 14.10. These icons are used for 'drag and drop' manipulation of documents . For example, dragging a document onto the wastebasket icon removes the document from the local container.

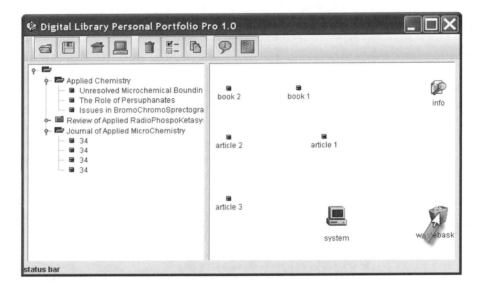

Figure 14.10   The throw-away prototype at work (Ocean1.5)

We will go into the implementation details of this prototype later.

Validating the throw-away prototype

Usability tests done on a larger user population reveal that some of the GUI assumptions were wrong. In particular, the system folders on the right-hand side in Figure 14.9 and Figure 14.10 are misunderstood by the vast majority of users – only few of them can correctly work out their use. Clearly, it seems that the design team, including the users who participated in the design, were biased in their preliminary assumptions.

In such cases – when the interaction needed to activate some functionality is not clear – the best solution is to rely on the underlying platform guidelines. Here the designers adopted the Java Look and Feel design guidelines[1], so in this case a typical interaction would follow a contextual menu style. By right-clicking on the chosen item, users could access all the available functionalities for the selected item.

A second version of the prototype is produced in which the system icons were removed. This second version, using contextual menus, was successfully validated with users.

Finally the design team came out with a reliable and detailed design, ready to be used as a specification for the first release of the Portfolio project.

14.5   *The final GUI*

Before getting into the details of the implementation, let's review the final GUI from an end user perspective. This will help to better clarify the interaction details while keeping the discussion at a intuitive and concrete level.

Figure 14.11 shows how the final application looks. Suppose we create a new search **My Search** using the toolbar button, or by right-clicking on a remote explorer folder via the contextual menu. The new search folder will appear in the remote explorer, as shown in Figure 14.11.

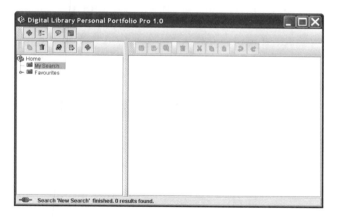

Figure 14.11   *Creating a new search (Ocean1.5)*

---

1.   See Chapter 2.

After a while the first results appear from the server. We can manipulate them via the contextual menu, as shown in Figure 14.12.

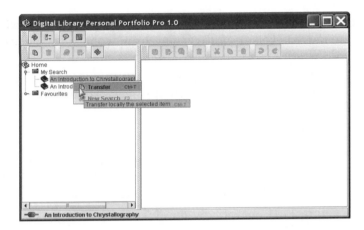

Figure 14.12   Manipulating search results (Ocean1.5)

A document can be transferred into the local container in several ways: by invoking the 'transfer' command, by dragging it into the local container, or simply by double-clicking on its tree icon. When the transfer process begins, the corresponding node in the remote explorer becomes disabled – see Figure 14.13.

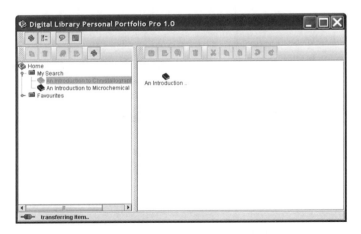

Figure 14.13   The GUI at work (Ocean1.5)

When the document is fully transferred into the local container, it can be manipulated with a richer set of commands, as shown in Figure 14.14. Double-clicking on documents in the local container opens them for viewing – the corresponding icon will change to signal this when implemented in the final version.

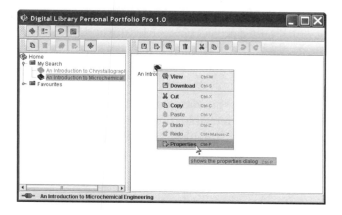

Figure 14.14   *Manipulating a document transferred locally (Ocean1.5)*

Apart from the usual operations, the GUI provide a configuration command, **Preferences**, that follows the standard Java Look and Feel design guidelines: icon size, the text used on buttons and other configuration details can be set from the preference dialog[2].

The best way to understand the various parts of the GUI is by launching the demo application and interacting directly with it. Let's now see how it was implemented.

14.6   Implementation

The project team is now ready to get into the implementation of their application. They proceed in a typical top-down manner, beginning from the software architecture and finishing with its final implementation. The description here focuses on architectural and reusable techniques rather than code-level aspects.

---

2.   Preference dialog design is discussed in Chapter 4.

Software requirements

An important step before proceeding with an implementation is eliciting its required properties. These properties can be seen as fine-grained design constraints, as describe in the vision document on page 501:

- Separation into different composable units. Separating the code into coherent parts is a highly desirable property, making the code easier to manage, and facilitating project team structure and possibly code reuse.

- Traceability of detailed software requirements to functional requirements, another desirable property for an implementation, and often mandatory in real-world projects.

- Maximizing software reuse. This could be a rather tough requirement to meet – fully reusable code tends to be more expensive to build and only pays back the investment in its creation in the future.

The team's software solution will be designed to satisfy these high-level requirements, but we don't have the space to discuss their list of detailed software requirements here.

The software architecture

The team begin from the boundary – conceptual – classes established during the analysis process.

Boundary classes

Their earlier analysis had the purpose of better identifying the boundary classes, at least as regards the end user. RUP methodology focuses on beginning the implementation phase from the boundary classes, which in turn are refined iteratively to obtain the final implementation class architecture. The class diagram in Figure 14.15 shows the two major classes with which the user interacts.

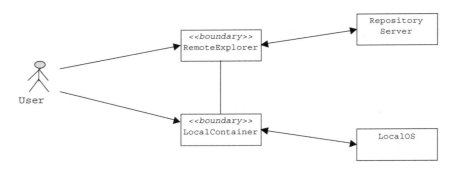

Figure 14.15   *Class diagram for main boundary classes*

These two classes correspond to the two specialized macro-level components:

- *The remote explorer,* a collection of searches defined by the user and their corresponding retrieved document images. The remote explorer is represented by a dynamic tree view loosely synchronized with the remote document repository.

- *The local container,* a collection of document information manually transferred by the user from the document searches. The local container is represented by a desktop-like container. An example of an implementation of such as container is given in Chapter 16.

In this version of the application the team adopt the OOUI (*Object-Oriented User Interface*) approach outlined in Chapter 2. Chapter 15 contains a practical implementation of such an interface.

The organization of code into packages can be naturally derived from the software requirements, and in particular, the identification of the two specialized components. Such an organization is detailed below.

Package organization

The team know from their analysis that their application will be essentially composed of three parts:

- The remote explorer component.
- The local container component.
- A global framework comprising all global-level functionalities and encapsulating the other two components.

They will then add a further set of logical classes to the latter package for gathering business objects. The package decomposition of the code is shown in the UML diagram Figure 14.16.

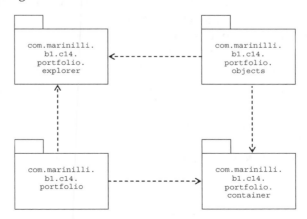

Figure 14.16   *Class diagram showing packages dependencies*

Note from the figure that the two visual components, which correspond to classes in the packages `explorer` and `container`, don't interact directly, as this would disrupt reusability and code separation, some of the concerns for the construction phase.

The other two packages are designed to allow for the integration of the two components as one coherent and reliable macro-component – that is, the whole application.

The team adopt a typical top-down approach that fits nicely both with the chosen implementation approach (OOUI) and with the RUP design philosophy. The next steps will be iteratively to refine the design to the final classes, then turning them into code. The only digression from this pure top-down approach will be to take the JFC classes that will constitute the basic building blocks into account.

Business objects

Eliciting the business classes involved is a key step in implementation analysis. For the first release of the Portfolio application, only three types of documents will be available through the system:

- *Articles*, both academic papers and technical articles published by some branch of the publishing group.
- *Books*. Book properties include titles, pages, authors, and so on. For simplicity the team assume that searches are done only on keywords, as for all other publication types.
- *Subscriptions*. These are special internal publications from the publishing house.

A `Publication` is the top-level type in the simple hierarchy used for handling published documents. A `Publication` object will follow the OOUI approach: it will be `Viewable` (in the sense of being able to provide graphical views of its content) and `Configurable` (that is, capable of providing special views for configuring itself)[3]. This results in the static class diagram of Figure 14.17.

Publications represent the document data types stored on the server, and are logically gathered in the `objects` package. As we will see, these documents can be alternatively seen as nodes in the remote explorer tree or icons in the local container.

The next step is to refine these two major components.

---

3.   See Chapter 15 for more details about these interfaces.

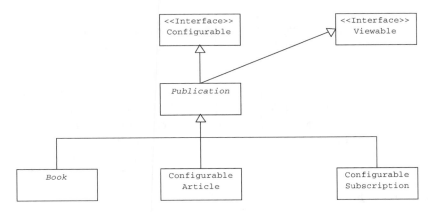

Figure 14.17   Class diagram for publications

The local container

This component is logically a folder of documents selected by the user. We implemented it as a sandbox instance – that is, following the 'desktop' metaphor. Icons in the sandbox all belong to the AbstractSymbol class type. Given the type of publications the system will handle, three different concrete subclasses are required for representing articles, books, and subscriptions. Note that in this first release folders are not supported.

The static class diagram is shown in Figure 14.18.

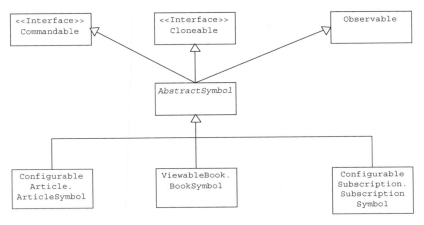

Figure 14.18   Class diagram for the local container's symbols

AbstractSymbols can issue their own commands within the sandbox container. This is modeled with the Commandable interface, and is discussed in Chapter 15.

There is an interesting point to notice at the code level. AbstractSymbol subclasses, one for each kind of document, are implemented as inner classes of their corresponding business objects. This implementation approach tends to minimize inter-class references and makes the code more readable, but at the price of a stronger binding among different code packages (here objects and container).

The remote explorer

The remote explorer component is a collection of remote searches. Each search in turn contains a set of publication nodes, each of which can be of the three different types discussed before, plus search nodes and special 'system' nodes. This is summarized in the static class diagram of Figure 14.19.

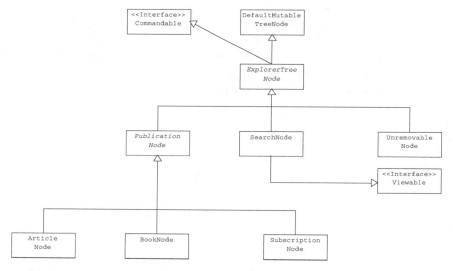

Figure 14.19   Class diagram for the remote explorer's nodes

The publication nodes – elements in the remote explorer tree – are conceptually different than publication instances[4], which in turn are different than publication symbols – that is, items contained in the local container.

---

4.   Document instances are application domain entities.

The retrieval process follows the following mechanism:

- When a search operation is performed, the server returns a set of suitable document metadata bundles to the client. The first release doesn't use any expiration or automatic refresh mechanism, users just have to refresh the search manually.

- This document metadata needs to be as compact as possible to speed up transfer time and ease the burden on the server. It therefore contains only a brief description of each document and the id needed to eventually access it. These lightweight document representations are rendered with nodes in the remote explorer tree.

- When the user selects one or more such document metadata bundles and drags them into the local container, the application queries the remote document repository with the corresponding document ids, and the related publication instances are downloaded. These in turn contain further details of the publication, but still no content data.

- Only when the user explicitly requests download or view of the publication's content, by manipulating the local container representation, is the document content downloaded.

Control

Control here refers to the functional layer introduced in Chapter 1. The GUI must always preserve its coherence when responding to external events, such as the Internet connection suddenly disappearing, or user–initiated events, such as clicking a toolbar button. Interactivity is all about maintaining this consistency, and you can judge professional GUIs by the way in which they ensure the correct behavior under all conditions.

One of the key problems with control code is that it generally needs to span many heterogeneous classes. This gives rise to a natural tendency for control code to be scattered among many different classes, resulting in a spaghetti-like web of class references. This Balkanization of control logic has many drawbacks. First of all, it lacks a clear and systematic software engineering approach – the arbitrary definition of control responsibilities tends to generate subjective code organization that is hard to understand, and even worse to maintain. Furthermore, the web of references among classes may disrupt code reusability and architecture modularity.

We have discussed the Mediator pattern and its variants previously in this book. Now we will see a hierarchical application of this pattern to a concrete, non-trivial case. In our implementation we will call instances of the mediator class *directors*.

We basically have two components in our software architecture. These two components (the remote explorer and the local container) should not interact directly, to promote their future reuse in different contexts. Each has its own

specialized director. The simplest integration approach is to provide a third
director that will take care of coordinating the other two, while also providing
control for global-level commands in the GUI. The class diagram in the following
figure shows this architecture.

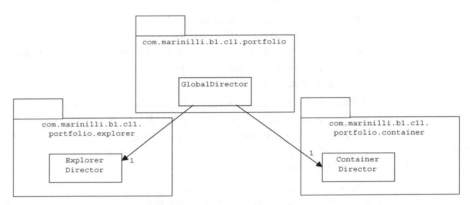

Figure 14.20   A hierarchical organization of directors

This makes both code modularity and a neat class architecture possible. The
`GlobalDirector` class is also useful for wrapping components' complexity by
providing a single interface to the rest of the world (that is, global-level classes)
for many different functionalities.

Looking at the details of the control code for the director classes results in the class
diagram in Figure 14.21.

Each director manages its own action classes, whether 'shallow' or 'deep[5].' Hence,
for example, the remote explorer director class manages the following actions:

- Delete a search.
- Refresh the current search.
- Issue a new search.
- Inspect a search's properties.
- Transfer a document metadata bundle (the outcome of a search) into the local
  container.

> Note that 'undo' features are only provided in the local container director. This
> is an accidental consequence of our GUI design.

---

5.   See Chapter 6.

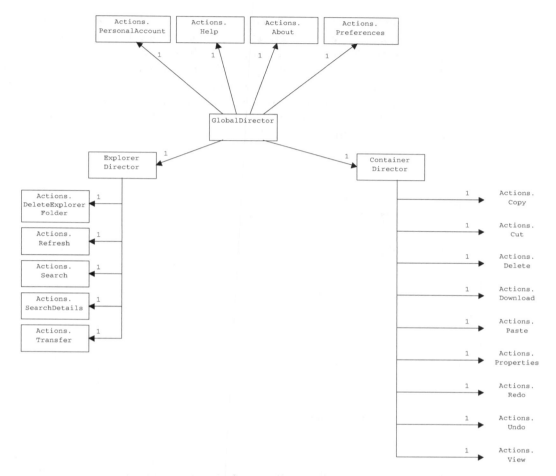

Figure 14.21   Class diagram for directors and their actions

This sketches enough of the static structure of the implementation – now for some runtime aspects.

Start-up

The start-up of a complex Java GUI is always a delicate phase that should be engineered carefully, as the initial impact of an application on its users is greatly influenced by the way it launches. Start-up time should always be minimized as much as possible. Fortunately, this kind of application can be optimized for this aspect.

We saw from Chapter 4 that the main technique for cutting start-up time relies on extensive use of lazy initialization technique and local caching. At start-up an application needs to restore its state, which was stored in an instance of the `Application` class. For simplicity in this implementation we only persistently store and retrieve a small amount of configuration data, but this doesn't hinder start-up efficiency in general for the complete implementation of the Portfolio application. The start-up phase for class creation and arrangement is shown in the sequence diagram in Figure 14.22.

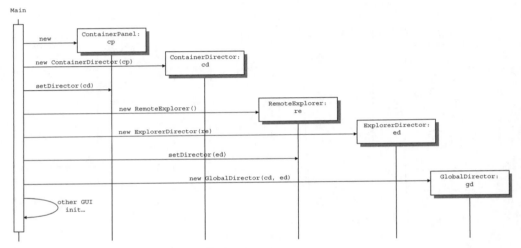

Figure 14.22   *Startup sequence diagram*

This sequence diagram refers to the activation procedure performed by the `Main` class, the main application class. After creating and properly setting all the three directors and their related visual counterparts, some GUI initialization is performed and the application is ready to take off.

14.7   Resources

Resource loading is an important part of any application start-up process. Professional GUIs tend to make extensive use of resources such as message bundles, help data, images, and so on.

Before getting into implementation code details, a few points about resources management are relevant. This is an important aspect for advanced GUIs, but if you are not interested in it, just skip this section.

The code for the Personal Portfolio application makes extensive use of a service layer library. This library provides code with service-layer features such as advanced resource retrieval to support issues such as localization, image management, and other resource-intensive aspects.

Localization bundles

Message bundles are organized on a per-package basis to support localization, as you can see in the sample code for this chapter. Any string and any image can be changed by modifying these text files, which can even be done by non-programmers. But this is not enough – professional resource management also requires the externalization of tooltips, accelerators, mnemonics, and any other locale-sensitive or important data.

Images

The team organize images on a two-level basis:

- When not specified, they are fetched directly by their identifying string as usual. The service library supports a distinction between 'small' and 'large' images.
- When explicitly stated, an image is treated by the service layer as 'large' or normal.

This distinction allows all button icons to be switched from small to large, for example. This kind of functionality is essential, for example for users with visual deficiencies. Apart from this, there are a large number of images that the GUI manages. The main types are:

- Icons, used for buttons and menu items.
- Deployment images, used for short-cuts, during download, and so on.
- Labeling images, used in the 'About' box, in the help data, and so on.

Note that a splash window and its related images has not been provided, to further speed up application start-up.

14.8 The code

This section goes into details of the code behind the Portfolio application. We don't have space to discuss the whole code of the application, so we will focus on a few classes that shed light on the underlying implementation, chosen for complexity and for the reusable high-level solutions they embody.

The remote explorer director

The logical organization of command and control management within the application has already been discussed, so it's time look at the details of a director. The remote explorer director is interesting because it is quite sophisticated, for example by comparison to the `GlobalDirector`, and helps to clarify its basic interaction within the remote explorer.

The basic structure of a director is dictated by its superclass, `AbstractDirector`. Among other things, this affects where actions are located, for example in a hash table for external access, and as instance variables for convenience of internal manipulation, and where their initialization takes place[6].

Actions managed by the remote explorer director are all of the 'shallow' type. That is, they delegate command execution – the code executed whenever the user activates them – to the director. The container director, in contrast, handles a number of 'deep' actions – those that fully implement the Command design pattern. No undoable actions need to be performed within the remote explorer, so deep actions aren't really needed.

A further duty of a director class in this architecture is to package the toolbar and other similar structures so that the external container can place them where needed. This is done by the `getActionToolBar()` method. The director class is also responsible for coordinating the GUI, especially for action enabling. This is performed by the `checkAction()` method that is invoked whenever the director's actions state needs to be updated.

The remote explorer component takes charge of listening for `DropTargetListener` events using the standard methods of this interface. This means that when the user drops something, the standard `drop` method is invoked. This will in turn invoke the `transfer()` method – which can also be invoked by activating the transfer action, or simply by double-clicking on a document metadata bundle in the remote explorer tree. Note that the transfer method essentially fires a `RemoteExplorerEvent` for initiating the transfer process.

The `getActionToolBar()` method is invoked on correct initialization of the remote explorer's content. In the current implementation search objects are not saved persistently and refreshed at start-up, but instead a random search only is added, for demonstration purpose.

Explorer events

The remote explorer director also acts as a source of `RemoteExplorerEvents`. As we know from Chapter 6, events offer one of the most effective techniques for decoupling groups of classes. This allows new code to take advantage of existing

---

6.   See the `setupActions()` method.

classes without modifying them. This technique is used in the `RemoteExplorer` component for interacting with other classes. The events thrown by this class are received by the `GlobalDirector`, which couples the remote explorer with the local container, as shown in the class diagram in Figure 14.23 below.

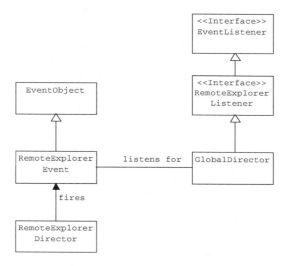

Figure 14.23   Class diagram for remote explorer events

The `RemoteExplorerEvent` class is shown in Figure 14.24.

Figure 14.24   Remote explorer event class

Listeners for `RemoteExplorerEvent` events react depending upon the type of event received. The current version supports only `ITEM_TRANSFERRED` events, listened for by the global director, which takes care of transferring the document into the local container, requesting the remote document repository for it using its id.

Representing application data

A common problem for non-trivial GUIs is storage of application preferences and other properties. The Portfolio application uses the Memento design pattern to encapsulate all meaningful data in a single class, the `Application` class, that can be made persistent through sessions.

The simplest way to view the role of the `Application` class is to see it as a simple Java Bean that stores useful application properties and is able to fire `Property-ChangeEvent` events[7] whenever some sensitive property is modified. But this Bean is also able to show its contents graphically for configuration purposes. In fact, thanks to the `Configurable` interface, the `Application` class can create `ConfigurableViews` of itself – that is, of the application's general preferences data – just like any other entity in the architecture[8]. The properties handled by the current implementation of this class are:

- `largeIcons`, a Boolean value representing whether the icons should be large or small.
- `textOnButtons`, which may have one of four possible values:
  - No text to be shown with button icons
  - Text shown on top of the command icon
  - Text shown to the left of the command icon
  - Text shown to the right of the command icon

Note that while the `textOnButtons` property is updated immediately at runtime, the icon size property needs the application to be restarted for changes to take effect.

Implementing searches

The `SearchNode` class helps to illustrate a solution to the common problem of interacting with remote hosts over unreliable and unpredictable connections. This class implements a remote explorer tree node type and contains two inner classes:

- The `ContentView` class supports inspection and modification of search properties such as keywords, text caption, and so on.
- The `ServerSearch` class implements a particular server request.

This simple framework implements a work queue that queues `Runnable` instances to be served by invoking their `run()` methods sequentially. The solution provided here shows an alternative, older design that provides the same functionality that is now provided by the standard `SwingWorker` class, which should be preferred in general.

---

7.   See for example the `setTextOnButtons()` method.
8.   See the `ConfigurableView` inner class.

Client–server communication is a common problem for thick client applications that need to connect to a remote computer network – connections delays, and the state of the connection itself, cannot be predicted. When accessing the network, therefore, the best solution is to fork a thread so that the user can perform other operations while the application is waiting for the server's response.

Depending on the design approach, this will be signaled to the user either by a status bar message, as in the Portfolio application, by a progress dialog that allows users to abort the process, or in other ways, for example by modifying the mouse cursor shape. The demonstration code employs a minimal notice strategy, using only the status bar and visually disabling the transferred/transferring node, because its GUI is intended for experienced, repetitive users.

The prototype

Throw-it-away prototypes are often neglected pieces of software, mistreated by programmers because they serve a limited function, restricted in time and in overall interactivity. A support library can ease the development of such software enormously. The source code for the `Prototype1` class can be found in the source bundle of this chapter – we are now left with the deployment aspects of the Portfolio application.

14.9   Deployment issues

Deployment is an often overlooked part of the software lifecycle. Professional products are characterized by the way they ship and how they can be managed remotely. Deployment services are essential to high-quality software (Marinilli 2001).

Server support

A fully-fledged implementation of Portfolio requires server-side code that responds to clients requests via HTTP. This would have required readers to install a servlet container in order to see the application working. To simplify the installation, the server side has been omitted and has been surrogated by the `ServerProxy` class. This class replaces a real server in many aspects. Although this class is not properly a part of the application, useful only for simulating a real remote server to understand how the application reacts, it is nevertheless necessary to look briefly at how the remote server is simulated.

Essentially, publications on the 'server' side are created randomly. The document repository is simulated by a simple hash table where publications are stored for future retrieval by the client. The process of creating publications is performed in the `getPublicationNode()` method. A pseudorandom number between 0 and

100 is created in this method. If the number is greater than 40, a new node for the current search is retrieved, otherwise the search is finished. In this way searches are filled with randomly-created documents. The retrieval time is also randomized to simulate connection delays, using the `simulateIOLatency()` method.

The server behavior affects the client's performance. When a new search is issued, the number of retrieved documents, and the duration of the retrieval process for each of them that is experienced whenever the user tries to transfer a document into the local container, are determined randomly. This behavior has been simulated to better imitate 'real' server connections.

14.10 An alternative, cost-driven implementation

The GUI design the team proposed, along with its implementation, were both nice and interesting, but expensive to build: the more GUI design involved, the more usability testing is required, and analogously, the more code that is written, the more tests must be created to validate it.

The first design proposed is expensive both because of the GUI interaction devised and because of the relatively large code base needed to implement it. The approach of domain-related composable units might also not be reusable other than in very similar projects, as well as being vulnerable to changes in business details. Focusing on more practical, industrial considerations, a more cost-driven design and implementation would be advisable. Following this approach doesn't sacrifice usability completely, just counters it with engineering constraints.

Here is a description of an alternative design that will solve the requirements outlined the *Analysis* section, but in a more cost-driven fashion.

Choosing a higher-level starting point

Optimal reuse of existing technology and design is key in a cost-driven approach. In the first design the team built a small composable unit framework from scratch and architected the Portfolio application around it. Here we focus on minimizing the amount of code and GUI design we provide, with the idea that 'less is better.' The adoption of effective practices and technologies is instrumental in this approach.

We choose JDNC (Java Desktop Network Components) as the basis of our cost-driven implementation, because it provides a proven, higher-level set of components that will minimize the code base. JDNC is a perfect example of what a high-level, specialized library can do for developers in terms of savings in development time. Many other third-party high-level toolkits exist, but we focus on JDNC because it represents the 'natural evolution' of the Swing library provided by Sun.

Choosing a more sophisticated technology is only one prerequisite for a cost-driven design – the other is its effective use. If I opt for an automatic excavator instead of a shovel to dig a hole, the real benefit will still depend upon my ability to use the tool!

To provide a truly cost-driven design, we need to focus on the GUI design first. By examining the set of requirements in the *Analysis* section, we note that 'drag and drop,' although nice to have, is not essential to a usable GUI, and could well be left for a future release. Further, the nature of the data provided by the server is inherently tabular, not hierarchical. A table widget would represent it in a more effective and inexpensive way. By using a high-level widget, features like search, ordering and filtering will be provided by the toolkit, enhancing the overall usability of the GUI even though using the (supposedly) less intuitive representation of a table, versus trees or other more domain-oriented designs.

A cost-driven prototype using JDNC

The prototype shown in Figure 14.25 was built by implementing only few classes, mostly for data support, with only one class for implementing content, but it nevertheless provides a wide array of GUI features not covered by the previous application, such as ordering, results filtering, and so on.

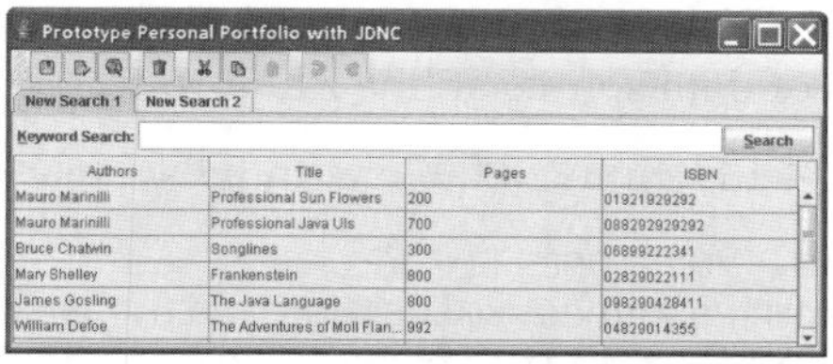

Figure 14.25   A cost-driven prototype built with JDNC

Clearly, JDNC components don't allow for the wide array of customizations and design freedom, both in implementation and in the GUI, that are provided by raw Swing widgets, as seen in the previous application. Despite that, they provide a cost-effective solution to most frequent implementation scenarios.

A brief introduction to JDNC

JDesktop Network Components are a family of GUI technologies based on J2SE (and Swing) that aim to reduce the complexity of GUI building in common scenarios, such as data-driven network-rich clients. They are organized into layers so that developers can use those parts that best fit their development needs.

The most basic JDNC layer is a set of Swing classes that extended basic Swing widgets to provide features like table sorting, better validation, and the like.

(These extensions are increasingly being absorbed into the standard Swing library.) A further layer built on top of the Swing extension classes is represented by classes that implement high-level, rich visual components that can easily be connected to data sources and which offer a simplified API for developers not familiar with Swing – although a deeper Swing knowledge is clearly needed for special customizations.

On top of this layer, a further set of classes implement a declarative markup language that can accommodate developers' needs very easily in a restricted, although quite large, number of practical cases.

JDNC and its various layers are a promising and much-awaited development of Swing which, with its basic palette of widgets, is still too labor-intensive to use in professional GUIs. It is yet to be seen whether the higher levels of the JDNC layering scheme, such as the markup language, will prove successful among developers. What JDNC does provide, though, is a very important refinement of basic Swing widgets for common practical cases.

An example of JDNC declarative language

The JDNC markup language allows developers to define most important properties for abstract components, which are then interpreted by the `org.jdesktop.jdnc.runner.Application` class. As a very basic example of this approach, Listing 14.1 shows the definition of a table widget with simple customizations of data source at line 7 and row colors at lines 15–18.

Listing 14.1 Defining a table with JDNC markup

```
00: <?xml version='1.0'?>
01:   <om:resource xmlns:om="http://www.openmarkup.net/2004/05/om"
02:     xmlns="http://www.jdesktop.org/2004/05/jdnc"
03:     xmlns:xsi="http://www.w3.org/2001/XMLSchema-instance"
04:     xsi:schemaLocation=
05:       "http://www.jdesktop.org/2004/05/jdnc schema/ jdnc-1_0.xsd">
06:     <table>
07:      <tabularData source="http://...">
08:         <metaData>
09:            <columnMetaData name="AUTHORS"/>
10:            <columnMetaData name="TITLE"/>
11:            <columnMetaData name="PAGES" type="integer"/>
12:            <columnMetaData name="ISBN" />
13:         </metaData>
14:       </tabularData>
15:       <highlighters>
16:          <alternateRowHighlighter oddRowBackground="white"
17:             evenRowBackground="light grey"/>
18:       </highlighters>
19:     </table>
20:   </om:resource>
```

The resulting table is shown in Figure 14.26. All these features are available programmatically using the `JNTable` class. Note the availability of automatic sorting on column headers and field type validation on columns. For example, non-integer values are not allowed in the Pages column, as defined by line 11 of Listing 14.1.

Figure 14.26   A simple table defined with JDNC content markup

14.11 Summary

In this chapter we have seen a complete yet simplified real-world example application. We discussed all its lifecycle phases, following the RUP terminology – inception, elaboration, construction, and transition – from a practical viewpoint, trying to highlight the interesting points while emphasizing more reusable ideas and solutions.

We discussed the Personal Portfolio application in two proposed incarnations. We have shown with a practical case study how object-oriented technology can play a critical role in developing quality GUIs. Leveraging existing technical skills and the set of simple approaches highlighted in previous discussions can produce top-quality software in a cost-effective way.

15 An Example OO User Interface

In this chapter we will explore some software design techniques for building professional user interfaces, demonstrating a way to implement GUIs with the Java programming language by taking advantage of the OOUI conceptual approach introduced in Chapter 1, within the reference architecture introduced in the previous chapter. As well as providing a set of Java classes that implement this approach, we will also see it at work in a complex example that uses several of the design patterns mentioned in Chapters 6 and 14, as well as a number of practical code tactics. All the ideas proposed here are illustrative and can be used separately in a wide range of contexts.

The chapter is structured as follows:

15.1, Introduction briefly discusses some general characteristics of the implementation solutions proposed in this chapter.

15.2, Implementing object-oriented user interfaces introduces a simple framework for implementing object-oriented user interfaces (OOUI).

15.3, Some utility classes extends the simple framework introduced previously with some useful classes.

15.4, Configuration views discusses the specifics of configuration views.

15.5, Interacting with the user discusses some general-purpose implementation strategies for representing user interactions within the proposed OOUI framework effectively.

15.6, Managing user commands clarifies how user commands are represented in the proposed framework.

15.7, An example application describes the implementation of the Library application using the proposed OOUI framework.

15.8, An alternative implementation using Naked Objects shows a different GUI design and implementation of the same problem using an existing OOUI framework, Naked Objects. It illustrates the great simplification that a specialized framework provides to development, although at the price of a much constrained GUI design.

The chapter concludes with a summary.

15.1   *Introduction*

As technology evolves, developers and designers can rely on more and more powerful computers, enabling them to afford more sophisticated designs, a trend that doesn't only apply to the user interface – the software architecture behind the UI has also been evolving. Nowadays, the creativity of software developers can rely on a wealth of computational resources – not a bad thing in itself, but one that inevitably adds a great deal of complexity that must be explicitly addressed.

> As in the rest of the book, we use the term 'GUI' as a synonym for any generic graphical user interface, OOUIs included.

A matter of style

This chapter illustrates a variety of design choices, so that the reader can grasp the benefits and weaknesses of each. Depending on your needs, you may prefer one solution over another. Personally, I still haven't found the UI software architecture 'silver bullet,' and I don't expect to find it in the near future.

As an example, let's take a classic UI software design approach. The top-level container (usually a `JFrame` instance) contains all the required widgets as instance variables, eventually using other GUI-related classes as needed, for example a subclass of `JTree`. Visibility and object communication is provided by the fact that 'everybody sees each other' thanks to the instance membership, so that, say, an `actionPerformed` method of such a class can manipulate all the widgets as it needs to.

This is not a bad approach per se – it works wonderfully for small GUIs, it's simple to understand and to master, it produces GUIs in a breeze – but unfortunately it has its drawbacks. Among these, it doesn't scale well – have you ever had two dozens or more buttons to cope with? It also tends not to produce readable code for large classes. This approach to GUI development is used by automatic GUI builders found in the most popular IDEs, such as JBuilder, Netbeans Matisse, and the like, and is also one followed by many programmers, especially novices. We will take advantage of it as well whenever it is suitable.

The purpose of this chapter is to explore several design approaches to the software architecture behind a GUI made with Java. The solutions proposed here are partial and not intended to be definitive, as the task of choosing the correct software architecture for a given GUI design is a complex one and involves many variables, such as the architect's preferences and habits, the GUI's inherent complexity, the project size, and so on.

The solutions proposed have several properties in common:

- They tend to be initially costly, both conceptually in understanding and practice, and as regards practical coding, as they usually involve a more elaborate code organization, but they will pay back in the long run.

- They tend to scale well – that is, to be more useful for large or complex GUIs designs. They can however be usefully employed for mid-sized or even simple projects.

- They were designed explicitly with priority given to the GUI design. Sometimes programmers tend to favor the software side of the development process, resulting in GUIs that are simpler to build, but which may ultimately be poorer.

- They are illustrative, rather than polished, commercial frameworks. The code proposed here is not intended as a final product ready to be employed in a production environment. However, all its flaws are highlighted.

- They are the result of many years of programming experience.

The code provided for this chapter, apart for the book package, which is related to the example application, is also intended to be reusable in other projects.

15.2 *Implementing object-oriented user interfaces*

Object-oriented programming (OOP) is a good match with Object-oriented User Interfaces (OOUI): although the two concepts are not strictly related, it is not by chance that GUI widgets model nicely as objects.

On the other hand, from an OOP purist's viewpoint, many of the GUI libraries provided with Java, such as Swing or SWT, are not perfectly object-oriented. This is because one of their goals is to enable the composition of a GUI by means of a rapid development tool (RAD), dictating the choice of the Java Beans mechanism. Such *accessory methods* – setter and getter methods, such as setTitle – are used liberally in GUI libraries, even if they break the pure OOP paradigm. Accessory methods are a necessary evil, and although they violate one of the main principles of object-oriented development, data hiding, they help developers in many ways if carefully used. Writing your code using accessory methods dovetails nicely with pre-existing standard libraries such as SWT or Swing[1].

Several existing OOUI implementations exist for Java, for example the Favabeans project. Compared with such frameworks, we adopt a more lightweight approach

---

1. For an alternative approach to these issues, see (Holub 1999).

when designing an OOUI implementation, favoring simplicity and clarity over advanced features and exhaustiveness.

In the following we indicate OOUI objects by capitalizing their names – the Book object – to distinguish them from their Java implementation, the `Book` class.

The Viewable interface

From a GUI design perspective, views are visual proxies of the data manipulated by users. How does one implement such a design paradigm? An object, among its many attributes, may be given the ability to provide a graphical representation of itself. This is not a violation of the data-hiding principle – it is in fact the proper way to build a GUI with an object-oriented language, especially when the GUI design is an OOUI.

Every suitable object should be able to provide a graphical representation of its own state, at least as far as it concerns the current user. We refer to this as a *view* of the object. Providing only one type of view is generally not enough, because we could require the same object to supply several different views depending on external situations. We can also imagine objects capable of providing their own help data, or perhaps providing several levels of detail for the same view, and so on.

As software designers we could provide a method `getView(parameterType)` that would return the proper view given the right type. For illustration, and to make this discussion easier to understand, we instead provide a static list of all possible views in our generic `Viewable` interface. Wherever a new view is required, this generic interface can be extended as required. This approach tends to produce more understandable code, even if its classes won't fully implement all the interface's methods. A specialization of the generic viewable interface that deals with object configuration is considered later.

We will use four different types of views:

- *Brief views* are those that should fit in a small display area, like a short text label defining the identity an object.
- *Content views* are the canonical views – those that show the object's full state, for editing or for inspection.
- *Help views* – it's handy to accommodate the help facility within this mechanism, as it makes every viewable object responsible for showing its own help data.
- *Partial views* are the 'wildcard' views. In some special situations objects need to offer different views, depending on some external parameter such as the current user's role. A partial view is provided by an Object to expose visually some particular aspect of its state. Usually some extra parameter is needed to

specify domain-specific details and a convention shared with the `Viewable` class to use it.

Listing 15.1 shows the `Viewable` interface. Every object that implements this interface provides one or more views of itself to the outside world.

Listing 15.1 The `Viewable` interface

```
00: package com.marinilli.b1.c15.util;
01:
02: /**
03:  * The Presentation Layer
04:  *
05:  * @author Mauro Marinilli
06:  * @version 1.0
07:  */
08:
09: public interface Viewable {
10:
11:    public View getBriefView(boolean editable);
12:
13:    public View getContentView(boolean editable);
14:
15:    public View getHelpView(boolean editable);
16:
17:    public View getPartialView(boolean editable, Object
argument);
18:
19: }
```

Although the method naming seems correct, it hides a pitfall. In most common cases objects are intended to create a new view whenever one of the methods in the `Viewable` interface is invoked. So, for example, `getBriefView` should be renamed `createNewBriefView`. Some objects may have the semantic constraint of always returning the same view instance, so that the view is *static* to the class and not dependent on the particular instance. For simplicity, to maintain the same signature for every `Viewable` class, we keep this potentially misleading naming convention.

Some simplifying assumptions

A general note is needed at this point. We are planning to build, bit by bit, a complete framework to address the most common issues of GUI software design. We need to make some choices and to decide the level of complexity and resulting sophistication of this framework. For example, I used to have an `EmptyView` Singleton object, a subclass of `View`, to neatly handle the case of a view type requested from an object that doesn't support it. This solution turns out to be especially useful during development – I even subclass it for more specialized behavior. To keep the discussion focused on general GUI software implementation patterns and to avoid getting bogged down in detail, we'll skip this kind of refinement and provide just the basic framework, stopping in the middle of the route towards a comprehensive, sophisticated GUI class framework. The set of classes proposed here, and the concept behind them, can nevertheless be adapted to manage complex GUIs.

A key factor in building professional GUIs is reliance on a set of utility classes that consistently and exhaustively adopt and enforce the use of a coherent set of GUI design guidelines – in our case, the standard Java Look and Feel design guidelines. It's also important to be able to build high-quality GUIs quickly and cheaply. These advantages can be obtained both with general-purpose reusable classes and with more abstract design patterns, focusing on GUI design as well as software design, as we saw in Chapter 4 and we will see in the remainder of the book.

> The OOUI approach can be employed with SWT and other GUI toolkits as well.

Implementing views

Viewable objects return views of themselves, but is a `View` class really necessary? Why not provide a `Component` – that is, a generically displayable object, both in Swing and AWT frameworks – directly, instead of yet another layer of indirection?

Having an explicit, general `View` type is handy in many situations. For completeness we want to implement both standard deferred and immediate mode interactions[2], so we need some form of control over the view object. Consider the common situation of modifying the widgets' state in a dialog and then saving the changes with the **OK** button. The consequence of this action should be to commit the changes to the view, which is in charge of keeping view's screen data state[3] aligned with the related domain data.

When working in deferred mode there should be a way to signal to the view the undo of any changes that have occurred so far, so a `doRollBack` method should be provided. It's possible to imagine several mechanisms to describe this behavior. We will choose the simplest: just one interface, `View`, that models both deferred mode and immediate mode behaviors. Usually only one of these two methods will be used. The `View` interface therefore has three methods: `doCommit()`, `doRollBack()`, and `getComponent()`.

---

2. See Chapter 4, *Waiting strategies* on page 141.
3. See Chapter 8, *Runtime data model* on page 329.

Conceptually, a view is responsible for coupling the widgets and the domain data. Widgets' data, such as the string manipulated by `setText/getText` in a `JTextField` component, is thought of as a kind of temporary buffer that exists as long as the corresponding GUI item exists. The domain data is the source and the possible destination of the widgets' data, following the MVC pattern.

The approach of using `View/Viewable` and other auxiliary classes can be extended to handle every GUI transaction, so that even the main application window could show itself via this mechanism, for example. We are not interested here in proof-of-concept of a pure OOUI implementation with Java – we are more interested in exploring some useful design solutions in order to apply them in common programming practice. We therefore limit the use of the `View/Viewable` mechanism to domain objects only, instead of applying it to every GUI object.

Let's recap on what usually happens. Figure 15.1 shows a typical `View/Viewable` interaction, in which a visual container, say a `JPanel` or a `JFrame`, asks `viewable-Object` for a given visual representation of itself. The graphical container extracts a visual component, say a `JLabel` instance, from the returned view and composes a larger view with it as required. The MVC pattern fits well with this approach: models are the responsibility of the `Viewable` object, while related Swing widgets are provided by `View` instances.

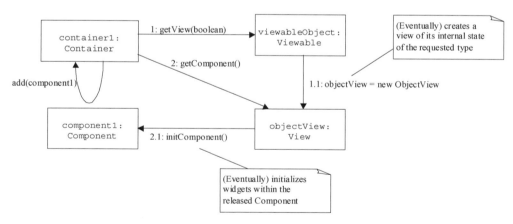

Figure 15.1   A typical interaction

The `View/Viewable` mechanism described here has several benefits for software developers:

- It tends to produce more reusable code. GUI code is encapsulated in the related class, so that whenever the class is reused in a new context, the chances are that its views will work in the new GUI as well.

- The mechanism works well with high-quality GUI projects. The extra care and discipline spent in the software design turns out to be paid back in terms of reliability and overall quality.

- It can be used in its broadest form as a common ground for discussions among development team members, either engineers or GUI designers.

- It creates a common ground that can be exploited to produce a number of reusable utility classes that turn out to be very useful in practice. This is essential for minimizing the cost of software development, especially in terms of time. We will not introduce such utility classes here because they would be of little conceptual interest, and because you are encouraged to develop your own. The more OOUI-aware reusable components are employed, the more this approach pays back.

The approach has also some potential drawbacks:

- It tends to produce more intricate code in which the same results are obtained in a more indirect way compared with more straightforward, simple software design strategies[4].

- It needs time to get used to, especially initially, making it hard for developers to get involved in the project, especially at later stages. Once this strategy is mastered, designers usually tend to develop frameworks on top of it, which in turn makes it hard for newcomers to pick up the details of a project.

15.3   Some utility classes

There are a number of refinements that could be added to the ideas exposed above. We will see just a few, to give an idea of the possibilities and of the most common issues they raise. Any class library should provide convenience classes to address the most frequent cases.

Brief views

Let's look at some default implementations. Given the ability to handle generic views, we could use default implementations to ease their creation.

A brief view can be implemented in a standard way, by means of a single `JLabel` paired with a 'More' button. If the view is editable, the button is enabled, allowing the user to modify the object's state – the implementation of the `More-Button` invokes the content view for editing. We can see an instance of this class at work in Figure 15.6 on page 548, where it is used to describe the book template currently used.

---

4.   The advantages of such an apparently convoluted approach depend on the nature of the project. Another example of this approach is shown in Chapter 14.

What we refer to as a 'More' button is a button with the conventional label '...' (ellipsis), indicating the generic behavior of opening another window for further interaction. An example is shown in Figure 15.2 on page 545 in the Book's brief view. For more details, see the use of this convention in (Java L&F Design Guidelines 2001).

The implementation of the `DefaultBriefView` class provided in the code bundle for this chapter illustrates some interesting points:

- It consists of a brief view, obtained by a viewable instance passed through its constructor, with a button placed beside it. Whenever the user clicks on the button, a content view of the same viewable object pops up automatically in a deferred mode standard dialog.

- The model behind `DefaultBriefViews` is a subclass of `PlainDocument`, the simplest text model provided by Swing. By taking advantage of Swing's data models, we are implicitly using the MVC pattern in our class framework and leveraging its advantages.

- We handle widgets within the class itself. This turns out to be by far the simplest and most effective approach in situations with specialized, reasonably short classes.

- The `DefaultBriefView` removes its visual components from the underlying model whenever they are removed from the container that held them. This greatly improves garbage collection, minimizing the risk of dangling pointers.

- For simplicity, we implemented the `View` interface in the widget class itself, a tactic that you will see often in the demonstration code. This minimizes the possible problems caused by the additional indirection layer introduced by the Viewable-View mechanism.

- Implementing the `View` interface on the visual component itself can give rise to unexpected problems, the commonest being name-space pollution. Widget classes usually come from deep hierarchies and have large signatures (many methods) that can conflict with domain-related names for methods or fields in the business classes, which belong in the application layer in our terminology.

Other reusable classes could be provided, for example for handling general collections of items.

Making collections viewable

The other general-purpose class presented in this chapter, `DefaultViewableList`, deserves comment. Being reusable, it can be used in many different contexts. It subclass the Swing default model class `DefaultListModel`, and provides content views in the form of `JList` instances, opportunely bounded to the origin's model. At runtime such views can be manipulated by the user with a contextual menu to provide the available commands.

> We adopt a fully-automated approach to list manipulation. Those operations that are allowed on the origin's collection instance (create a new element, remove a selected element, modify a selected element) are available to the user. This aspect crops up again in the discussion of command composition later in this chapter.

15.4   *Configuration views*

Interactions with a GUI can be thought of as being divided in two broad groups: operational and configurational. When you drive a car, you turn the steering wheel and operate the pedals to control the vehicle. This is a normal, operational interaction. If there is too little room, you can move the seat back and modify its geometry accordingly to your preferences. Here you are configuring the car, that is, modifying some parameters that are changed less often and that don't impact on normal operations.

Configuring GUI items is a common operation, and specialized facilities, often under the form of a configuration dialog, are found in many GUIs. The Java Look and Feel design guidelines terms such operations *preferences*.

A `Configurable` type that specializes `Viewable` for objects that can be configured is available with the source code bundle for this chapter. This interface is made up of two methods:

- The `getConfigurationView` is the straightforward specialization of the `View`/`Viewable` mechanism for configuration views.

- The other method, `getCategory`, is an auxiliary method used for tagging the configuration views, and is used in a specialized container.

We will see this interface at work in the following section.

A utility class

Designing OOUI objects requires a decision about whether to make them configurable – that is, to make them implement the `Configurable` interface. Although in theory a utility class can inspect the current namespace to discover all `Configurable` instances automatically, it is far simpler to embed in the code the list of configurable objects gathered in a specialized dialog. This list of configurable items changes only at design time. In the implementation proposed, we have designed a `ConfigurationDialog` class that gets an array of `Configurable` objects as a parameter for its constructor.

To see some real action, we have to anticipate this chapter's example application. Such an application offers two OOUI objects for user manipulation, books and libraries. That is enough to understand the next couple of figures, while we will see the details of the Library example application itself later in the chapter.

Figure 15.2 shows the structure of the Configuration dialog used by the example application. Within a deferred mode dialog, a `JSplitPane` divides the list of all available items on the left from the configurable data presented on the right. When the user selects **Books**, the book's `ConfigurationView` is shown on the right. This design avoids a confusing set of nested tabbed panes, while preserving the same data presentation[5].

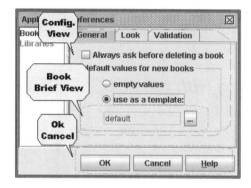

Figure 15.2   The configuration dialog

Note the following:

- The aspect of the item presented on the left – the categories into which the system configuration is organized – is not bound to a given class, but is obtained by querying the `getcategory` method in the `Configurable` interface.

- The `Configuration` view of the `Book` class uses a brief view of itself to describe the template book used for creating new book instances. More precisely, they are two different instances of the same class.

- This utility class can be used for *any* configurable set of classes. For enhanced usability, each of these classes should oblige their configuration views to use

---

5. Although with some limitations.

a deferred mode style of interaction, otherwise users could become confused. This constraint is not enforced in our class framework.

Figure 15.3 shows how the book OOUI object's appearance can be configured.

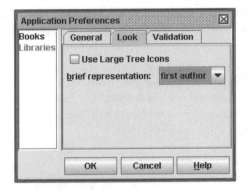

Figure 15.3   The book configuration panel -- book appearance

15.5   *Interacting with the user*

In the last section we discussed an approach to the task of building a configuration facility for GUIs. This section looks in some detail at the more general problem of setting out the software architecture for managing effectively GUI-user coordination.

The Commandable interface

We plan to make OOUI objects capable of releasing different visual representations of their internal state. What we need is a way to model the set of possible actions that each of them can support. Users are already familiar with contextual menus and with right-clicking on a GUI object to see what commands the object supports. The only method in the `Commandable` interface therefore returns an array of menu items suitable for attachment to a pop-up or drop-down menu. We use an array of `JMenuItems` instead of a generic collection make the code easier to understand.

Composing commands

A common approach is to compose commands from multiple OOUI objects at a centralized point in the GUI, to facilitate user access to specific actions, such as an object that returns menu items ready to be incorporated into a toolbar or a menu bar. This behavior also occurs in classes that are responsible for contained objects, in a conceptual hierarchy that is similar to the Facade design pattern.

Such behavior can be created using the `DefaultViewableList` component. Despite its long name, this is just a visual container of generic list objects. The container itself issues several collection-related commands, such as add and remove items. When the user selects a given object, the list of all available commands for the object is displayed in a pop-up menu, as shown in Figure 15.4.

Behind the scenes, the container negotiates with the selected `Commandable` object to acquire the list of available commands to be incorporated into the menu. In Figure 15.4 Library objects can be created and removed, commands that are the responsibility of the visual container, and offer two additional commands:

- **Properties**, to inspect an object's internal state.
- **Inventory**, which is a Library business-related command.

Note the separator in Figure 15.4 that divides the two command groups.

This mechanisms allows for maximum flexibility – every object knows which commands it supports and whether they are enabled or not at any specific moment, while maintaining clearly-defined responsibilities between different OOUI objects.

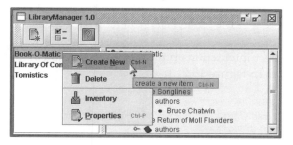

Figure 15.4   The contextual menu for libraries

Similar behavior is employed in the tree view for Libraries, where no object-dependent action is allowed, as shown in Figure 15.5.

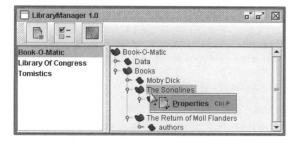

Figure 15.5   The contextual menu for books

The `DefaultViewableList` class goes a step further, adapting its menus dynamically to the kind of list in use. For a collection that cannot be expanded or shrunk, for example, only the **Properties** command is available, as shown in Figure 15.6.

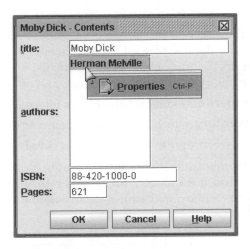

Figure 15.6   The contextual menu for a fixed-size list

The object interactions typical of this mechanism are illustrated by the sequence diagram in Figure 15.7.

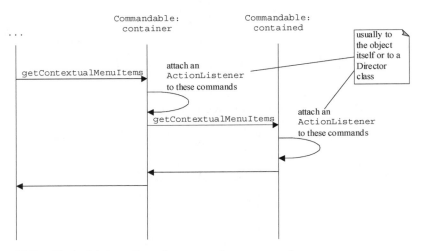

Figure 15.7   Typical interactions for composing commands

15.6 *Managing user commands*

So far we have looked at the Commandable interface and two different uses of the Action class. It's a good idea to take additional care when designing user commands. Apart from standard commands like **OK**, **Cancel**, **Help**, commands should be designed both from a GUI viewpoint and from an implementation viewpoint, because they will be the main interaction points with users. Whether you use shallow or deep actions in your programs, it's useful to keep them centralized in repository classes in your code.

The example implementation uses two classes:

- Commands, a factory class that creates all the actions used in the GUI, indexed by unique string identifier.
- ActionRepository, an interface that contains a version of ShallowAction, an implementation of the AbstractAction Swing class seen in Chapter 6.

The factory methods in the Commands class could have been implemented by cloning prototypes stored in a hash table and indexed by the command strings. Instead, the more hard-wired approach of a long chain of if statements is used here. As a rule of thumb, it's a good idea to consider the dynamic option (the hash table) when the number of actions is greater than about a dozen.

Indexing actions with a unique key string has several advantages:

- It keeps the action's creation centralized, for better code readability and maintenance.
- It allows for faster string comparison (the '==' operator can be used).
- It avoids any spurious operation with actions, such as a string mistyping, which could be hard to track down in large programs.

In the solution proposed here, such strings are treated as class tokens, in that they uniquely identify a class rather than a single action instance.

> The 'token' command strings in the Commands class are only used internally, and not for presentation, so they must not be localized.

To keep the example simple, actions are not localized. Chapter 8 contains examples of localized (locale-dependent) actions.

We are now ready to put all these pieces together in a concrete example application.

15.7   An example application

The task is to build a GUI that manages various libraries. Libraries have several attributes (such as name, address, and so on), and a collection of books that are publicly available.

We will build this application using the OOUI approach to drive the application implementation. The example was constructed with the idea of using an architecture of sufficient complexity to illustrate some of the main issues that can arise in a real-world software development environment following the OOUI approach. However, too complex an example would be confusing and distracting.

The example shows a GUI that serves merely as a showcase for the ideas presented earlier. Try it for yourself: compile the code provided and run the `com.marinilli.b1.c15.book.MainFrame` class, or more simply, just launch the `c15.jar` file provided for this chapter.

The main window in Figure 15.8 shows a list of libraries on the left and the currently-selected library on the right.

Figure 15.8   The library application GUI

Library objects can be manipulated by right-clicking on the list of the available libraries on the left-hand side. In particular, domain-dependent operations can be invoked, such as making an inventory of the selected library, or performing collection operations such as creating or deleting libraries. The implementations of these actions are all provided by the standard behavior of the `DefautViewableList` class.

A few sample commands have been implemented – the toolbar shows three. As well as library creation, there is a **Preferences** button, which displays the system configuration dialog, and a **Help** button.

The nice thing about the OOUI approach is that it spans naturally from the GUI design phase to the implementation details. Hence we focus our development effort at designing and building the OOUI objects employed in the GUI that will later be implemented as Java classes.

OOUI objects

Chapter 1 showed that OOUI objects are domain-related, conceptual objects that are offered to users for manipulation. When it comes to implementing such objects in practice, a single OOUI object is usually realized by several Java classes.

First we need to define carefully the OOUI objects needed in the GUI. We have only two OOUI objects in this simple example: Books and Libraries. Libraries are collections of Books, with some additional attributes. This situation is represented in the UML class diagram in Figure 15.9.

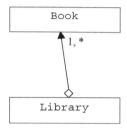

Figure 15.9   OOUI object relationships

> We indicate OOUI objects with capitalized names, such as 'Book' or 'Library.' Don't confuse these with the Java classes that are needed to implement them. In the end, the user's experience should be as close as possible to manipulating a unique OOUI object, no matter if trees or tables (Java classes) are used to represent its state and the intended interaction. Thus the class diagram in Figure 15.9 refers to 'abstract' OOUI objects, not to Java classes.

Book objects and their implementation

For brevity we concentrate only on the implementation of the Book object, leaving the classes that implement the Library object for interested readers.

We want the Book object to provide different views, depending on the part of the GUI where books appear. The three normal views (brief, content, and configuration) and a tree view are shown simultaneously in Figure 15.10.

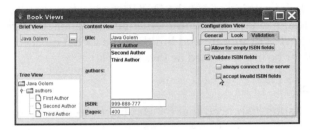

Figure 15.10   *Possible views of a Book object*

The Book object offers more views than OOUI objects normally do, but they will help us to better explore the proposed approach.

The interaction mechanism is as follows: the requester, usually a graphic container (a dialog or a panel) requests a view of itself from a viewable object. In practice only complex views are coded into specialized classes: default and standard views work well for simpler cases, such as brief views, or for content views of collections.

Suppose a brief view is requested of a Book instance. The Book UI is designed to provide default brief views, so it is enough to provide the Book's model for this kind of view to a specialized factory that creates a standard brief view ready to be used in the GUI container. This mechanism caters for views asking other for views, and so on – the Composite pattern.

The sequence diagram in Figure 15.11 shows this scenario: the `ViewableBook` uses a model – in the MVC meaning of 'model' – of its internal data for building its views. Models are essential because they allow for the creation of 'live' views that change as the model behind them changes, modifying the current view's appearance.

Taming complexity

When developing large and sophisticated GUIs, for example those in which the same classes provide different types of views, it is essential to tame the complexity of the resulting code.

Two problems always conflict:

* *Visibility.* Viewables and views need to be tightly coupled with their respective domain objects. This conflicts with the principle of separation of presentation from domain-related code. The three-layer architecture proposed in Chapter 7 dictates a separation of layers into presentation, application, and service layers, which helps to create high-quality code.

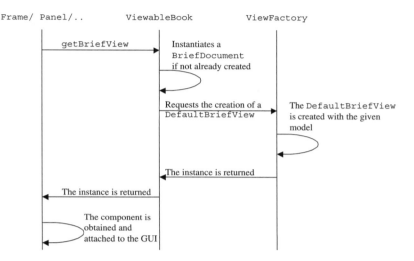

Figure 15.11   A Book object's views implementation

- *Code size*. Inevitably, sophisticated GUIs tend to need more code. One problem is that high-quality GUIs cannot rely on automatic, general-purpose widget layout, and have to be positioned manually by the GUI designer on a per-case basis. The OOUI mechanism described can lead to large class sizes if not properly handled.

There are several approaches to these problems. The right mix of visibility and class management is essential for long-term code maintenance. In the example here we use class inheritance to separate presentation code from domain code and to keep classes to a reasonable size. Inner classes are then used to keep view code logically organized but still visible within the class. This simplifies manipulation of domain-related fields by the presentation code.

Using inheritance is a less flexible solution than using object composition[6]. The use of inheritance depends on the particular business domain, because if presentation classes (here `ViewableBook` or `ConfigurableBook`) need to extend some other class, we cannot subclass the domain object (`Book`). Using inner classes solves many visibility problems, but tends to produce large files that could be difficult to maintain. With this approach, we need a new package to protect the domain class fields from outside, because we want only subclasses to be able to access them. This could conflict with the analysis phase, in which class packages should be designed, and on the fact that low-level implementation details should not affect the domain analysis.

---

6.   See Chapter 6.

The classes in the example are organized as follows:

- One application class, `Book`, containing only domain-related code.
- Two presentation classes, one for managing all non-configuration views, and one to produce configuration views as well. Throughout the GUI we will always use the `ConfigurableView` class.

With this code organization long-term code maintenance is greatly improved. The class hierarchy implementing the Book object is shown in Figure 15.12.

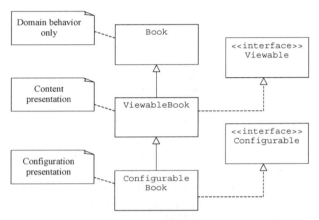

Figure 15.12   The implementation of the Book object

The following Java classes implement the Book object:

- `ViewableBook` contains the views the object releases to other classes, and the model used for the brief view. It has the following inner classes:
  - `ContentView` is the class that implements the content view for the object.
  - `TreeView` is the tree view.
  - `BriefDocument` relies on an adapter of the `PlainDocument` class, which in turn extends the `AbstractDocument` class, both provided by the Swing library.
- `ConfigurableBook` contains configuration-related code and has only one inner class:
  - `ConfigurationView` implements the book's configuration view. Given the many options available for books, we used a tabbed pane.

Unexpected views

We have added a twist to the example by providing an ad-hoc view, mainly to show the practical limits of the view/viewable framework.

Views, in the meaning of graphic representations of an OOUI object, can come in many flavors, and there is no standard, once-and-for-all way to implement them. As proof of this, the Book object releases views of itself as a tree. Using trees is quite useful, because they realize the Composite pattern (Gamma et al. 1994) nicely. For example, an object that is composed of instances of itself can be represented easily, although this is not done in this example.

From the developer's viewpoint, the general problem is that views can be implemented with classes other than `Components`, which makes our `View` interface unusable. There are a number of technical solutions to this problem, such as a `TreeView` interface that specializes `View`. In this example we choose a more straightforward solution, adding a `getTreeView` method to our `ViewableBook` class. In this way, tree views return Swing `TreeNode` instances, ready to be combined with other tree nodes to compose any hierarchical view we need.

Reducing development costs

The Book object, even if it implements more views than objects usually do, exhibits some common factors for reusability. While content and configuration views are often specialized GUIs tailored for their domain objects, brief views can be implemented using reusable components, as our example shows.

Taking advantage of the `View/Viewable` mechanism, a number of general-purpose classes can be used. For example, the `DefaultViewableList` class is used by the Book's content view to provide the representation of the Book's author list. The same component is used in other parts of the example GUI as well, such as in the `MainFrame` container. This programming style also has consequences for the GUI's usability.

The code

We are now ready to look at the final code. Listing 15.2 shows the `Book` class.

Listing 15.2. The `Book` class.

```
00: package com.marinilli.b1.c15.book;
01: import java.net.URL;
02: import java.io.Serializable;
03:
04: /**
05:  * The Presentation Layer
06:  *
07:  * @author Mauro Marinilli
08:  * @version 1.0
09:  */
10: public abstract class Book implements Serializable {
11:    String title;
12:    String[] authors;
13:    String isbn;
```

```
14:     int pages;
15:     URL homePage;
16:
17:     final static int BOOK_TITLE = 0;
18:     final static int FIRST_AUTHOR = 1;
19:     final static int ISBN = 2;
20:
21:
22:     public Book() {
23:     }
24:
25:     public Book(String t, String[] a, String i, int p, URL u) {
26:         title = t;
27:         authors = a;
28:         isbn = i;
29:         pages = p;
30:         homePage = u;
31:     }
32:
33:     public String toString() {
34:         return title;
35:     }
36:
37:
38:
39:
40: }
```

The Book class belongs the Application layer[7]. It embodies the domain-related data and behavior associated with the Book object: the separation of business code from its presentation is an essential benefit of such an architecture.

The business class is very simple: there are no methods, just a collection of fields. These are the book title, an array that represents the authors, and a few other data items. As we are primarily interested in the GUI-related code and its organization, we kept the domain classes as simple as possible. The Library class, whose implementation is not discussed here, is slightly more complex, in that it provides a business-related method for the inventory.

The ViewableBook class

The ViewableBook class is the main graphical class that represents Books in the GUI. Its source code can be found in the code bundle for this chapter. The class essentially implements a book suitable for display and manipulation on screen via

---

7.   See Chapter 7, *A three-layer architecture* on page 298.

the class framework. The class contains some configuration fields, such as currentBriefViewType, used to decide what book data to use for the brief views, and other GUI-related details.

The ViewableBook class contains the views it releases to other classes and the model used for the brief view. Recapping, it has the following inner classes:

- ContentView is the class that implements the content view for the Book object.

- TreeView is added for demonstration reasons and it is not fully implemented.

- BriefDocument relies on an adapter of the PlainDocument class, which in turn implements the model for DefaultBriefView instances. Note that instances of this class are created only when brief views are requested. When this is not the case, the related briefDocument field is kept null to minimize space.

ViewableBook adopts a solution that is repeatedly applied in the code described in this chapter: the main class extends a less-specialized version of the same OOUI object, and all the auxiliary code required (view classes, MVC models, and the like) is provided as inner classes. This guarantees high OOP cohesion among the Java classes involved in the implementation of the Book OOUI object. As a result, the visibility of the various instances involved is highly simplified. Whenever a coupling can be relaxed, for example for views in the MVC meaning of the term, there is no need to accommodate these code objects as inner classes, as is done for BriefDocument within ViewableBook, for example.

The Book object implemented by these three Java classes is serializable. This is required to allow Book instances to be made persistent. The book template is recorded persistently so that it can be used for the initialization of books created from scratch[8].

The ConfigurableBook class

The configuration view is separated from the other views. Although there is no precise conceptual reason for this, it is handy for practical code maintenance. The ConfigurableBook class is the extension of the ViewableBook class, providing configuration views in addition to all the other views the superclass provides.

The ConfigurableBook class provides two implementations of Configurable methods. The ConfigurationView inner class implements the preference

---

8.   See Chapter 7 for details of localization mechanisms and naming conventions.

setting facility for Book objects in the GUI. Physically, it is a `JTabbedPane` made up of three panels, built and added in the constructor, that correspond to the three categories into which Book object preferences were divided by the GUI designer:

- The **General** panel is created by the `createGeneralPanel()` method. It is initialized with the persistent values from the last time the application was run – see Figure 15.3 on page 546.
- The **Look** panel is created by the `createLookPanel()` method. Note that not all the widgets are actually used: the `treeLargeIconsCheckBox` is shown to the user but not bound to an actual use in the GUI, for simplicity.
- The **Validation** panel is created by the `createValidationPanel()` method – see the right-hand side of Figure 15.10 on page 552.

The `ConfigurationView` method `doCommit()` is different than usual `doCommit()` methods, because it doesn't only affect one class instance, but also persists the values through the persistence facility offered by the Service layer: when a user commits the book configuration view, its settings are intended to be used by all currently open books as well as those yet to be created. Configuration views are often a type of Singleton view, that is, only one instance is shown to the user at any one time.

Apart from the methods that take care of the GUI details, the `clone` method is employed here to support advanced object creation, as discussed in Chapter 7 in relation to the Service layer.

Libraries

We implement libraries following the same approach used for books, with some small differences, like using accessory methods (get and set) to interface with the application layer's class, `Library`.

The implementation of the Library domain object closely resembles that of Book, so we will illustrate only the essential details:

- `ConfigurableLibrary` has only one inner class:
  - `ConfigurationView`, the configuration view of Library objects.
- `ViewableLibrary` has only one inner class:
  - `ContentView`, the content view of Library objects.

Figure 15.13 shows the Library content view.

For brevity the Java code for the classes that implement Library objects is not listed here. Nevertheless, we hope that, apart from conceptual ideas, the example code can show you many useful, practical tactics.

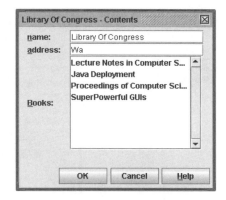

Figure 15.13   *The Library content view*

Some GUI design considerations

One question remains unanswered: what kind of GUI do we get with the design strategies described here?

Let's look at the Library manager application. Suppose you want to modify the author of one book in a given library. You right-click on the libraries in the main frame, selecting **Properties**, and do the same on the book list that pops up. In turn, you then select the author from the chosen book, and select the **Properties** command again, finally obtaining what you need. Figure 15.14 shows this path.

One of the reasons an example application that uses container-contained OOUI objects is chosen is to show some of the peculiarities of this kind of GUI. Using heavily OOUI-modeled relationships such as containment hierarchies in domain objects tends to produce highly 'vertical' GUI interactions, such as those shown in Figure 15.4 – many pop-up windows stacked one above the other.

This is not a bad design per se. It keeps the whole GUI highly focused by leveraging the context the user creates during an interaction – in the figure, the context of the **Herman Melville** string object is the **Moby Dick** Book object, that is in turn inherent in the **Tomistics** Library object. But precautions are needed, such as keeping the stacking level to a reasonable size, perhaps no more than three or four depending on the type of application windows and intended users, or maintaining a tight grip on the GUI by allowing only modal dialogs and hooking them to the proper container to avoid floating dialogs when users switch to another process window. Solutions to such problems are available in the literature and were also mentioned in Chapter 4.

Applying the methods described here doesn't guarantee a perfect GUI. Usability and guidelines compliance should always be kept in mind, no matter of how sophisticated an implementation may be.

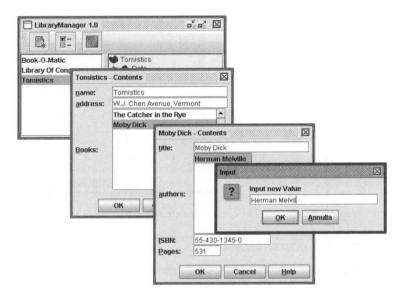

Figure 15.14   Using the LibraryManager GUI

Control issues

The example implementation follows both the centralized approach using the Mediator design pattern (Gamma et al. 1994), and scattered control, both discussed in Chapter 6.

Centralized control

The director class employed in the example application implementation supervises command management and other classes that need centralized control and have a web of visibility references. In the example we kept the director simple and straightforward: a more complex version of this pattern featured in Chapter 14.

The `BookDirector` class provides the following services:

*   Initialization of data.
*   Execution and management of application-wide commands.
*   Conceptual centralization of all GUI-related control code.

This book contains several examples of directors at work, from the simple one in the QuickText application (Chapter 7) to that presented in Chapter 16, as well as the flexible arrangement proposed in the example application in Chapter 14, with one global director coordinating two specialized ones.

Scattered control

This is related to a common situation in many GUIs. When an event takes place that is bound to some widget or domain data, something else should happen as a consequence. For example, whenever the user fills in a text field, a group of components are enabled, and vice-versa[9].

More complex interactions are possible in GUIs, making a standard and systematic approach highly desirable. This is where the Mediator design pattern comes into play: there is often no need for a fully-fledged director class. In the book's configuration dialog for the example application, some simple reactive behavior is effectively handled locally to the class, without the need for an external director.

From the book configuration dialog, users can specify how new books are created. They can decide whether empty values or template data should be used when a new book is created from scratch. In the latter case, they can inspect and modify the book template data, as shown in Figure 15.15.

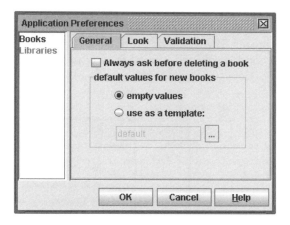

Figure 15.15   Book configuration panel, general panel

Whenever the user selects the **use as a template** option, the area corresponding to the book template is enabled, as in Figure 15.16. This area corresponds to a `DefaultBriefView` component.

---

9.   It is always best to keep such widgets – even if disabled – always on screen, rather than making them appear magically, thus modifying content dynamically at runtime, because this confuses the user.

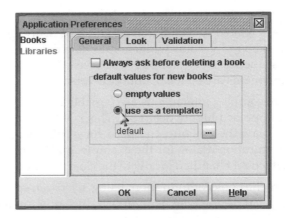

Figure 15.16   *Book configuration pane*

Another case in the same OOUI object's configuration panels is shown in the next two figures. The first two check boxes in Figure 15.17 are unrelated, but whenever the second is selected, the other two 'nested' checkboxes are enabled.

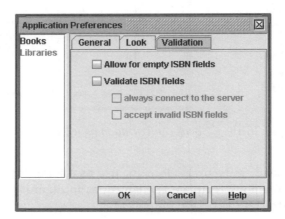

Figure 15.17   *Book configuration panel –book validation*

Figure 15.18 shows the situation in which the **Validate ISBN fields** option is selected.

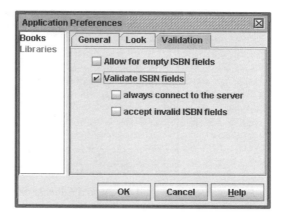

Figure 15.18   Book configuration panel – enabling fields

In these two cases, interaction is so simple and circumscribed that setting up two, or even one, separate directors would be a needless complication. In these specific cases, using an `ItemListener` to listen for checkbox (Figure 15.18) and radio button (Figure 15.16) events suffices These are examples of the scattered control design strategy discussed in Chapter 6.

15.8   *An alternative implementation using Naked Objects*

This chapter concludes with an alternative implementation of the Library application, built using a specialized framework, Naked Objects.

Naked Objects is a framework for building applications by defining the business objects and their relationships only – that is, focusing on the domain model alone – and letting the framework take care of GUI details. This is the main advantage provided by this approach, but also its biggest weakness: developers have little control over GUI design details. The framework (unsurprisingly) adopts a direct manipulation, OOUI-inspired GUI design to show business objects to users 'naked' of any presentation-specific code.

A screenshot of a simplified version of the Library application implemented with this framework is shown in Figure 15.19.

This version of the application was built with only three extremely simple classes (`Book`, `Author`, and `Library`) and a framework-dependent launching class, `LibraryExploration`. To give an idea of the simplicity of this version – although providing a smaller feature set compared with the previous version – the following listing shows the implementation of the `Book` class within the Naked Objects framework.

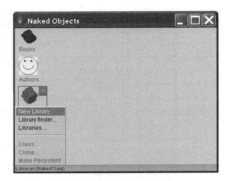

Figure 15.19   *The Library GUI – Naked Objects version*

Listing 15.3 The Book class

```
00: package com.marinilli.b1.c15.naked;
...
07:
08: public class Book extends AbstractNakedObject {
09:
10:    private final TextString isbn = new TextString();
11:    private final TextString title = new TextString();
12:    private final WholeNumber pages = new WholeNumber();
13:    private final InternalCollection authors =
14:                new InternalCollection(Author.class, this);
15:
16:    public TextString getTitle() {
17:       return title;
18:    }
19:    public TextString getIsbn() {
20:       return isbn;
21:    }
22:
23:    public Title title() {
24:       return title.title().append(",", pages);
25:    }
26:
27:    public InternalCollection getAuthors() {
28:       resolve(authors);
29:       return authors;
30:    }
31: }
```

Interested readers can look at the source code of the remaining classes provided with this chapter. For more details on Naked Objects, see http://www.nakedob-jects.org/.

Figure 15.20 shows the rather unusual GUI generated by the framework for business objects. It is possible to create new instances, assign them to their respective containers, and make them persistent, with many available alternatives. The icons on the left-hand side represent the classes, while their instances that are open for modification or inspection are represented by the various internal frames. To add an author to a book, for example, the user first has to create a new author instance by right-clicking on the **Authors** icon on the left-hand side of the window, selecting the **create new** command, filling in its data, then dragging it to the **Authors** area within a book instance.

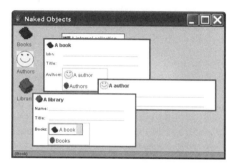

Figure 15.20   *Managing data the Naked Objects way*

In conclusion, it is interesting to note the amount of code employed in the first version of the Library application that is devoted purely to GUI details, compared with the second version, in which all GUI details are handled automatically by the framework. Unfortunately, GUI development is all about GUI details, and while frameworks such as Naked Objects are appealing to developers, they appear less effective to customers and GUI designers, no matter how well the GUI is automatically generated.

15.9   Summary

In this chapter we discussed the details of developing an application following an alternative approach, OOUI objects. We examined common situations that developers face when implementing non-trivial Java GUIs using the OOUI approach. We introduced several classes, some of them reusable in many different situations, and a complete example that leverages them to show how complex GUIs can be built following the OOUI approach. We also contrasted our application with a fully-fledged, OOUI-inspired framework, Naked Objects.

16 An Example Ad-Hoc Component

This chapter describes an example of the design and implementation of an *ad-hoc* component with the Java programming language, focusing on the J2SE and the Swing library only.

Chapter 2 stated that a GUI can be thought of as being composed of visual components and their auxiliary elements. From a developer's viewpoint, such components can be thought of as belonging to three main groups, depending on their development cost:

- *Standard components*, such as a 'plain' `JTree` instance.
- *Specialized components*, such as a complex `JTree` subclass that re-implements many of the `JTree` auxiliary classes.
- *Ad-hoc components*. These are visual components completely different than the standard ones provided by Swing or other GUI libraries. Ad-hoc components are much more expensive to develop, because their development effort comprises GUI design, testing, and coding.

If there were no reusable, standard libraries, we would develop components from scratch over and over, at enormous cost and without any coherence between different implementations of the same component. Luckily, the last twenty years of software engineering has provided today's developers with a wide range of tools for reusability and easy customization of their programs. See for example (McConnell 1993).

Unfortunately standard libraries don't cover all the possible components so that, although rarely, it is still possible to find yourself engaged in ad-hoc component building.

This chapter is structured as follows:

16.1, Introduction discusses the issues related to the GUI design and implementation of ad-hoc components.

16.2, The Drawing Sandbox application introduces an example ad-hoc component, showing an example of its use.

16.3, The Sandbox architecture discusses the overall architecture of the proposed component.

16.4, The Sandbox component discusses the top-down refinement of the design of the example application.

16.5, User interaction describes how user interactions are managed by the proposed implementation of the Sandbox ad-hoc component.

16.6, Control discusses how control is implemented in the proposed ad-hoc component.

16.7, The whole picture puts the various pieces together, showing a complete picture of the implementation design.

16.8, Stressing the software design discusses the proposed design critically, highlighting its strong points and its drawbacks.

16.9, Introducing JHotdraw contrasts the implementation provided so far with another implementation using the specialized library JHotdraw. After a brief introduction of the library, the alternative implementation is discussed and compared with the previous Sandbox implementation.

The chapter concludes with a summary.

16.1 Introduction

The design and development of high-quality ad-hoc components involves typical dangers that are accentuated for novice developers:

- The unnecessary effort of reinventing the wheel. When developers launch themselves into the process of creating ambitious ad-hoc components together with their support classes – thus creating a de-facto specialized small class framework – they tend to ignore the vast API that Java offers, re-implementing existing functionalities in their code.

- Given the difficulty of the implementation process, developers tend to favor coding aspects over the GUI design of the ad-hoc component being created. This is a classic problem, but it is accentuated for ad-hoc component development – the designer says: "We need drag and drop here," and the programmer replies "No way – it's too costly."

- Ad-hoc components tend to be domain-specific, so developers often overlook their development in favor of other parts of the system that are judged more 'important' and reusable in future applications.

- All the typical risks associated with the design and development of new and complex software artifacts, such as bad cost estimates.

- The risk of a bad design, originating not from technical deficiencies, but rather the fruit of GUI design inexperience and over-ambition.

While standard and specialized components have been properly designed and are thus harder to misuse, ad-hoc components are like a blank sheet in the hands of eager and sometimes inexperienced designers and developers.

Given the potentially large costs associated with ad-hoc component development, it's best to discourage their use in GUI design and favor wiser, less bold GUI design choices such as specialized components, as discussed in Chapter 14. Nevertheless, when one of the requirements is high GUI quality, or when the business domain dictates it, designers have to resort to ad-hoc components.

Essentially, ad-hoc components leave too much freedom to the designer. This can be a great thing, or a disastrous one, depending on the designers' experience and the context. Venturing into such a complex and time-consuming task is best avoided if it's not absolutely necessary. While it can relatively cheap in some cases, such as in the example presented here, in general it is a hazardous route rife with unforeseen problems and delays that slow down the whole development process. All the discussions in the first part of the book should be taken to heart when evaluating ad-hoc component development. When the ad-hoc component isn't a supplementary part of the GUI, but is its cornerstone, the risk is not only to at least double the development and design effort, but even to produce an unsuccessful GUI.

In the next section we look at an example of a relatively complex ad-hoc component implementation in some detail. The scenario is a familiar, interesting and intuitive domain, enhanced by some ambitious requirements that demand sound software design. Details have been reduced to a minimum to focus only on the essential aspects of the problem and produce a concrete, working example of a complex GUI cut down to its simplest implementation. The focus of this chapter is on object-oriented software design. This is often the weakest point of an ad-hoc component implementation – it is a less relatively visible aspect, but in the long term the most delicate.

16.2   The Drawing Sandbox application

Most computer users are familiar with using a graphic drawing editor into which you can drop graphic items, drag them, and modify them as you want. Commercial applications such as Adobe Illustrator, Corel Draw, or the drawing palette in Microsoft Word, provide such features.

We focus here on the mechanism of a graphic container that handles such items and provides basic operations for manipulating them – a kind of 'sandbox,' similar to Windows or MacOS folders, into which users can drop items and arrange them as desired. We will adopt something close to the direct manipulation approach in our GUI design. We are not however so much interested in GUI design issues as in the software design needed to implement them. The objective is to build just such a visual component together with all its support classes. This will be an ad-hoc component because such a visual container is not provided by the standard Java API.

The application

We'll begin with the user's experience of the final product, then explore the behind-the-scenes software design and discuss some of its aspects. Figure 16.1 shows the main application frame. For simplicity we have only one toolbar, which groups all the commands, and no menu bar.

Figure 16.1   The main application frame (Liquid)

Following the order of buttons in the toolbar in Figure 16.1, you can:

- Add graphical objects[1] to the Sandbox component.
- Cut, copy and paste an object as needed.
- Undo or redo previous operations.
- Move a selected graphical object to the front, so that it lies above all others.

---

1.   Referred to as 'symbols' in the Java code.

All other actions are object-dependent. Two graphical objects, the bitmap and the multiple-segment poly-line, have been implemented, to show how different interactions are accommodated within the same class framework. For example, the poly-line can be manipulated by mouse dragging and button combinations.

The interaction is rudimentary: you choose an object from the palette, then create it in the sandbox by clicking on it. The mouse cursor's shape changes to signal the drawing mode. Toggle buttons or more refined mechanisms like drag and drop to inform the user that the application is in 'adding' mode aren't used. In this simple implementation there is no way to exit object adding mode if you change your mind – the only way is to add the object to the sandbox and then remove it. Such niceties have been omitted to keep the code to a reasonable size for an example. In Figure 16.2 shows a bitmap object being manipulated.

Figure 16.2   Manipulating an object via its contextual menu (Liquid)

Each object independently provides its own commands, as shown in Figure 16.3 for the bitmap.

When interacting with the GUI, actions are automatically enabled or disabled depending on context. For example, if no object is currently selected, the actions appear as in Figure 16.3: note that the pop-up contextual menu, obtained by right-clicking on the object, is coherent with the toolbar buttons.

Try launching the executable `sandbox.jar` file, and have fun with the actual program.

An example interaction

Suppose the user has already performed some manipulations on the objects shown in Figure 16.2. First undo the rotation on the bitmap using the contextual menu, as in Figure 16.3.

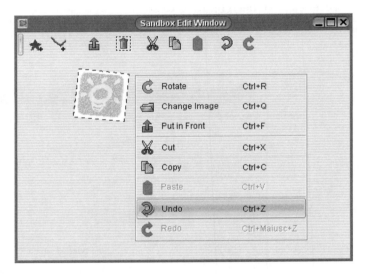

Figure 16.3   Undoing a rotation (Liquid)

Note that in the interaction example the clipboard is not used – that is, nothing was cut or copied, so the paste command remains disabled.

New lines are added just like objects of the type 'image,' by clicking on the relevant tool button, then clicking in the sandbox area where the new line is to be placed. Double-clicking on a line allows its control points to be edited, as shown in Figure 16.4. Control points are moved by dragging them with the mouse. Line editing mode is disabled by selecting another object, or by clicking somewhere else on the sandbox area. To add new control points to a line when in edit mode, the mouse right button and the control key are used together.

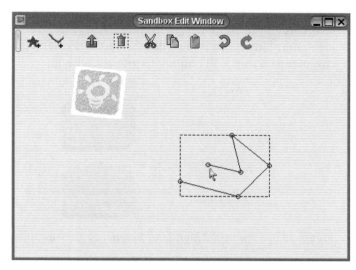

Figure 16.4   Modifying the control points of a poly-line (Liquid)

16.3   The Sandbox architecture

Now we can look at the implementation of the Sandbox component.

Chapter 2 introduced the OOUI approach, mentioning its usefulness both as a means for designing the GUI, as well as a way to organize the resulting implementation. The OOUI approach can be used as a fully-fledged composable unit strategy[2].

The software design discussed here is arranged around the development of the ad-hoc component using a top down, functional partition. Figure 16.5 shows an initial high-level division of the software design. A common approach in many architectures is to separate the domain definition from the application logic – that is, the functionalities made up of simpler, low-level features that expose the domain to users[3]. An e-mail inbox, for example, represents the generic domain of an archive of e-mails. Possible actions in such a domain depend on the purpose of the application. For example, an inbox component could be used in a customer-care application in which customer complaints are filed with e-mails that can sorted by specific heuristics to extract a tentative subject, category, urgency, and so on. By implication, we are differentiating our ad-hoc component and the set of elementary functions it provides for interaction with the rest of the world from the commands a user will employ to interact with it.

Figure 16.5   An initial high-level functional decomposition

Following this decomposition, we will build our component around a set of generic, low-level functionalities that in turn will be used by other specialized code that packs them into higher-level, useful commands for user interaction.

Figure 16.6 shows a possible refinement of the initial decomposition of Figure 16.5. The most important part is the ad-hoc component itself, which interacts with the control subsystem that is responsible for maintaining the coherency of the whole GUI. The third division accounts for the commands issued by the user, each part being composed from several Java classes. This high-level functional division focuses only on the more important portions of the implementation, and intentionally omits auxiliary code.

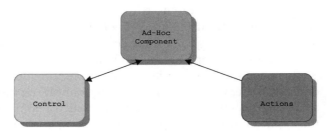

Figure 16.6   Refining the functional decomposition

The GUI will be designed by refining the simple functional organization shown in Figure 16.6 iteratively. This decomposition takes advantage of the peculiarity of the application, that of an ad-hoc component as the center of the application, but can be applied to the development of any GUI.

It would be nice to create a flexible, highly expandable framework, but the key issue here is to provide a simple, lightweight design. Features that are desirable, such as allowing for runtime palette loading – loading new graphical objects from a file and using them without having to reinstall a new version of the application – can be left for future versions.

16.4 The Sandbox component

First we concentrate on building the ad-hoc component, the core of the application, beginning software design refinement from the ad-hoc component.

Top-down refinement of functional organization

Conceptually the Sandbox component is a container of graphical objects. Both the objects and the container itself can issue commands by means of contextual menus. This functionality can be modeled using the `Commandable` interface from Chapter 15.

An initial refinement of the software design for the ad-hoc component in Figure 16.6 is shown in Figure 16.7.

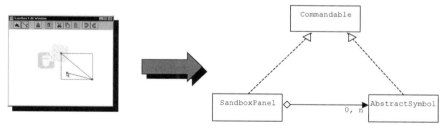

Figure 16.7   From the component to an initial high-level class diagram

So far there is the visual container, which we'll implement as a Java class called `SandboxPanel`, and the objects it contains that are manipulated by the user. Different objects will extend a base class, `AbstractSymbol`.

Organizing object communication

How should we organize the communication between the container and its objects?

One of our requirements is to guarantee flexibility to the ad-hoc component in terms of new object classes that can be used. A clean way to obtain this is to delegate responsibility to the objects themselves. The container merely holds objects and performs some common operations on them. Objects are responsible for drawing themselves on screen, for interacting with the user, and so on. This approach offers a great deal of flexibility, allowing for the use of different object types without impacting the container.

The container needs access to objects to draw them on the screen. Objects in turn now have many responsibilities delegated to them, rather than keeping them all centralized. Following this strategy, mouse input events, for example, need to be re-issued to the relevant objects, so that the objects themselves can consume the mouse event as required, transparently to the container and to other classes. Objects are black boxes as far as the other classes are concerned – the essence of object-oriented programming.

Suppose that an object is modified and the changes are committed. The container needs to be notified so that it can refresh the screen to show the changes. Decoupling responsibilities at design time is always a great idea, but generally it needs extra care when it comes to runtime object communication. One possible solution is to adopt the Observable pattern (Gamma et al. 1994). This makes the design more modular – components interested in object behavior just register themselves as observers – and allows for future expansion, with more sophisticated events being distributed by more complex objects, while keeping the overall design simple. When we need to make the director class communicate with objects, we can then just add it as another listener without making any change to the class structure. Figure 16.8 shows this arrangement.

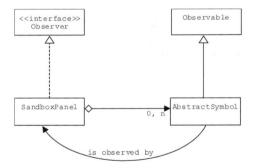

Figure 16.8   Making objects communicate with their container

Instead of creating our own event classes, we adopt the `Observer`/`Observable` mechanism implemented in the `java.util` package. This decision has the practical drawback that the `Observable` class must be extended, instead of an interface for objects to be observed, but this is not a problem.

Using the Observer design pattern simplifies class coupling enormously. A class interested in object behavior registers itself as an `Observer`. This application has two classes that are interested in monitoring object behavior:

- The graphic container – when an object changes, it is time to refresh the screen.

- The director, which manages the coordination among interacting objects.

We could have mimicked the Swing API, for example for screen area invalidation, but we prefer to explore and illustrate alternative mechanisms.

We avoid an MVC architecture for our ad-hoc component to show that similar designs can solve the same problems. We don't need the flexibility of multiple views of the same model, and such a complex arrangement might make it difficult to focus on the important ideas.

The SandboxPanel class

The `SandboxPanel` class is the graphical container of `AbstractSymbol` instances. It is implemented as a specialization of the `JPanel` class, as shown in Figure 16.9.

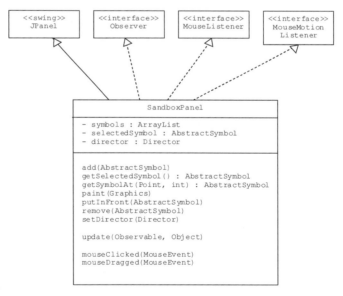

Figure 16.9   The SandboxPanel class

The `SandboxPanel` class is responsible for showing objects to the user and making them available for direct manipulation. Apart from this, the graphical container is essentially a passive object, manipulated by the director class. To ease the interaction between the two classes we allow the graphical container to invoke the director directly.

Objects are drawn on the screen by means of the `paint()` method, which has been customized to support our logical model. Interested users can find more information on the `paint()` method in (Fowler 2000).

The container scans the ordered list of objects, drawing each of them by invoking their `draw()` method. The order of the list defines the graphical layering of the objects, so that the method `putInFront()` simply moves the given object to the end of the ordered list, ensuring that it will be painted last and thus lie graphically 'above' all the others. The graphical container provides other methods for manipulating objects, such as `remove()` for eliminating an object.

Another duty of the container is to capture user input by means of mouse event listeners, decode it, and submit it to interested components.

The `mouseClicked()` method handles the following events:

- It adds new objects to the graphical container.
- It manages double clicks for placing objects into edit mode.
- It handles contextual menu pop-up.
- It selects objects.
- It issues events to the object itself.

The `mouseDragged` method simply reissues the event to the relevant object, so that the object can manage the event accordingly.

Following a top-down approach, we now turn to the objects themselves. At this level of detail we manage the `AbstractSymbol` class as the most general class representing any object able to be added to the container. Now we refine the part of the ad-hoc component that represents objects.

The features implemented in this example are chosen for illustrative reasons, and the application has been simplified in a variety of ways. Only single selection is available, for example, so its clipboard can contain only one object at a time. This avoids the implementation of multiple-selection interaction with the mouse, dragging a rectangle on the screen or holding the shift key while selecting more objects. This could be implemented easily using an array of objects in the clipboard. In addition, only two object types are implemented, but the design can allow for a much larger object palette. The number of different object classes is limited to focus on the more interesting aspects. There are no save or load features, although they could be added relatively easily by means of serialization extended to all the involved classes. There is no way to delete all the objects at once, or to create a new, blank sandbox.

Graphical objects

The `AbstractSymbol` class is the most generic object to be contained and manipulated by the Sandbox component. It represents the behavior of any object that can be added to the framework, and is shown in Figure 16.10.

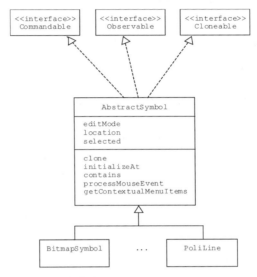

Figure 16.10 The AbstractSymbol class

Users can select an object, move it within the container, and open it for editing by double-clicking on it. These features translate into three properties of the `AbstractSymbol` class shown in Figure 16.10, respectively: `selected`, `editMode`, and `location`. There are a small number of methods that apply to any object, both for convenience:

- The `initializeAt()` method for creating an object at a given point
- The `contains()` method, which verifies whether a given point lies within that object area

and for interacting with the rest of the world:

- The `processMouseEvent()` method manages mouse input
- The `getContextualMenuItems()` method implements the `Commandable` interface for publishing user commands).

Finally, we need a `clone()` method for creating new objects.

From a practical viewpoint, the contains() method is used for picking an object, given its screen coordinates. This method in turn uses getRectBounds(), so that simple-shaped object classes don't have to implement the contains() method. This is helpful for objects that have a rectangular shape. For other objects types, it will be necessary to override the contains() method. When the user clicks on an object to select it, the container class scans the list of all objects to find the first one whose contains() method returns true. Note that the first one in the list will also appear to the user as the visually top-most one.

In real applications when several dozen or more different objects can be employed in the same palette, it is crucial to design the object class hierarchy carefully, both to maximize code reuse among different object classes, and to keep the design easy to maintain and expand in the future. Such considerations are out of our scope here, but (Marinilli 2000) gives more details.

The BitmapSymbol class implementation

The bitmap object represents an image in the container, as shown in Figure 16.1 on page 570. The BitmapSymbol class implements this simple type of object. The class is shown in Figure 16.11.

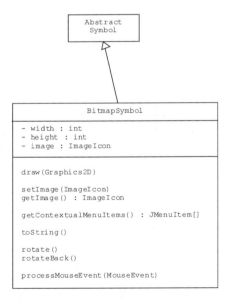

Figure 16.11 The BitmapSymbol class

The bitmap object exposes the following two commands to the user via the getContextualMenuItems() method of the Commandable interface:

- Rotate the object, performed by the rotate() method.
- Change the bitmap image, implemented by the ChangeImage action class. This is described in *The Actions class* on page 584.

A default image is used when creating a new bitmap object – see the related code in the BitmapSymbol class.

The draw method is invoked to paint an object onto the screen. The image is rotated at the current rotation angle, depending on the rotate commands previously performed on the object.

The setImage() accessory method implementation is worth mentioning. After updating the internal data with the new bitmap image, the method invokes the observer/observable mechanism. This will invoke all its listeners, giving them a chance to react to the event. The director checks for logical – business domain – coherence, while the graphical container repaints itself, refreshing the screen with the new object image.

Open-ended communication via events

The BitmapSymbol class is very simple and doesn't use all the flexibility the design allows. The sequence diagram in Figure 16.12 shows a representation of the PoliLine class' mouseEvent() implementation.

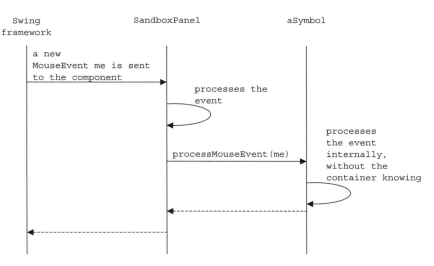

Figure 16.12   Objects independently process mouse events

The mouseEvent() method in the PoliLine class implements the GUI interaction style used by poly-line objects. By dragging the control points that appear when the line is being edited, the appearance of the poly-line changes. While standard dragging is implemented for all object classes, when moving them around in the container area, this class processes mouse events in a specialized way. Adding a new control point to the line is achieved through the same method as is used to process mouse events. We could also have used a custom action, such as those that are provided by the Commandable interface.

An abstract poly-line shape, composed of a sequence of lines, is represented as a sequence of control points – see the generalPath variable in the source code. Straight lines connecting pairs of control points are drawn directly in the sandbox graphical container by the draw method. If an object is selected, a bounding box is drawn around it.

16.5   User interaction

This section discusses how user interactions are handled by the example application.

Command composition

The creation of command menus uses a typical command-composition scheme[4]. The list of available commands for a given object is built by composing the commands available to the object container and to the object itself. We could equally have chosen a more general and powerful mechanism to implement contextual menus for objects.

The container forwards all mouse events to listening objects. Objects are themselves left with the responsibility of interpreting low-level mouse events, as well as the right-click for contextual menu pop-up. The code for commands common to all objects is kept in the root class of the object hierarchy, AbstractSymbol (see Figure 16.10). The approach of composing menus is chosen because it leads to a simpler class arrangement, especially as regards visibility. Note that our solution doesn't limit the freedom of AbstractSymbols to handle mouse events. Although programmatically feasible, it can be confusing for users to have the same input event (a mouse right-click) associated with context-dependent actions, such as for example both displaying a contextual menu and modifying control points in a curve.

Figure 16.13 shows the sequence diagram for contextual menu composition.

---

4.   See Chapter 4 for the GUI design for composing commands, and Chapter 6 for the software design.

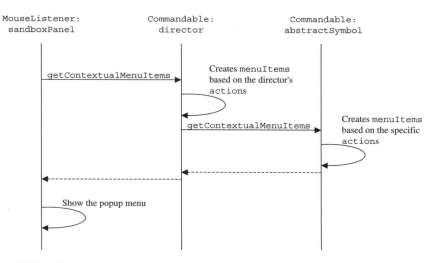

Figure 16.13   Creating the contextual menu for an AbstractSymbol instance.

The Action framework

The higher-level user commands are shown as one of the three main parts of our initial decomposition in Figure 16.6. We used 'shallow actions' in the Library application in Chapter 15 for handling user commands. The Sandbox application instead demonstrates the Command pattern at work, employing what we referred to as 'deep actions' in Chapter 6. We defined deep actions as the proper way to use Swing's Action class to implement the Command design pattern fully.

Figure 16.14 restates the Command design pattern from Chapter 6.

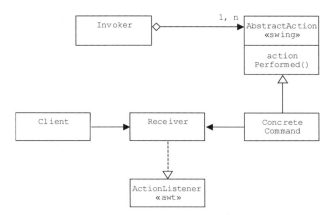

Figure 16.14   The Command design pattern

Using the Swing library, the `Invoker` is usually a `JMenuItem`, a `JButton` instance, or similar. The `ConcreteCommand` is the command instance that is set up by the `Client` class, usually the main frame or the director. The `Receiver` is the class that actually carries out the action execution. Following Java conventions, the latter class implements the `ActionListener` interface.

This approach enables several features, at the affordable price of a little additional complexity. The main benefits are:

- The whole implementation becomes closer to the domain representation than with command code centralization.

- Behavior specific to a single command is logically localized within an `Action` subclass.

- Undo and redo features stem naturally from this approach.

- The class organization that results is clearer and more systematic than that when using a centralized mechanism for commands. This is especially true for large and complex applications.

- This pattern has been adopted extensively in Java APIs, both in Swing and SWT and in other toolkits.

On the other hand, such an approach has some drawbacks, and these more evident in smaller projects. Mainly, it produces more and smaller classes, the commands themselves. This means additional complexity that has to be tamed with extra effort at design time, primarily with class interaction and management.

One solution is to use a static repository, a cluster of many, small classes obtained statically at design-time, or a dynamic one, using a runtime container such as a hash table, for example. The Sandbox application uses both strategies in the `Actions` class, which acts as a container class to rationalize action-related code maintenance. Action classes are grouped statically in the `Actions` class as inner classes, and held at runtime in a collection object managed by the `Actions` class itself. This is an implementation trick to avoid a proliferation of small classes. The `Actions` class is not a proper factory class because it doesn't create new actions, but merely provides the same action instances to interested clients.

The Actions class

The implementation of the `Actions` class is interesting for several reasons. It can be seen essentially as a static design-time container of actions. This arrangement has been adopted to ease code maintenance, as discussed in Chapter 15, where the analogous class was `ActionRepository`. Apart from grouping the code for the `Action` instances used in the application, the `Actions` class serves as a dynamic repository as well – that is, live instances are kept in memory at runtime. This is achieved using a hash map that stores the instances of the required actions.

The class name string is used to retrieve such instances when they are needed. This type of organization works nicely for this particular application, in which we need only one instance of each command. When new instances are needed, you can resort for example to the Prototype design pattern (Gamma et al. 1994), as we do for objects.

Within each `Action` subclass is the related `Edit` inner class, needed for supporting non-trivial undo/redo operations. The `Actions` class, and some of its inner command classes, is shown in Figure 16.15.

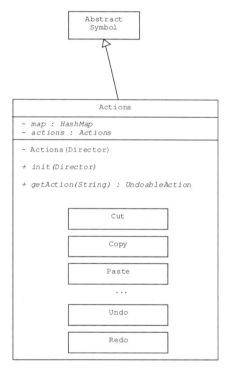

Figure 16.15   The Actions class

The constructor is kept private to avoid instantiation by other objects, which in turn is done through the `init` static method. The latter method is used to pass the `Director` instance needed for correct `Actions` initialization. The constructor initializes the dynamic repository (the static instance variable `map`) statically – that is, it is hardwired into the code. The `getAction()` method is used to query the dynamic repository.

This class is not a factory class, in that it doesn't create new object instances, but rather keeps a predefined set of them available to other classes as needed.

The `Action` subclasses used in the simple class framework are subclasses of the `UndoableAction` class, which in turn specializes `Action` for undo behavior. We adopt two slightly different designs for the Command pattern: the first one deals with classes such as `ChangeImage` or `Rotate`, while the second arrangement is a simplified version of the first and is discussed later.

The `ChangeImage` class implements the command for placing an image as a bitmap object. The implementation could have employed a content view of the bitmap object to gather all the properties of the object into one command with a single dialog, but such an arrangement has already been used in Chapter 6, so we've used a different approach here. All the details of the action, such as the icon, the tool-tip, the shortcut, and so on, are prepared in the constructor. The heart of this class is the `actionPerformed()` method, which executes the command, manipulating the rest of the application directly as needed.

This is a completely different approach than the 'shallow' actions illustrated in Chapter 6. Here the `actionPerformed()` method in the `Action` subclass takes charge of everything needed to carry out the command, in a distributed fashion – that is, the code related to commands is not centralized in one class, but is distributed throughout the related action classes. A file chooser dialog is displayed for selecting an image from the file system that is then substituted for the previous image. The old image is not lost, but is kept in the related `Edit` object in case it is needed for undoing the action. The proper `Edit` instance is created and stored in the history of executed commands, administered by the `Director` class. The `ChangeImage` class also employs an inner class, an `Edit` subclass, which is in turn an inner class of the `Action` class specialized for representing 'change image' commands.

Following the Command pattern, we define a class specialized in handling one particular command. To fully support undo and redo operations we need a further custom class that represents the 'edits' obtained by means of the command. Both the `Edit` and `Action` subclasses are tightly coupled, so the inner class implementation mechanism is ideal in this case. The `Edit0` inner class at lines 99–123 in the `ChangeImage` action stores all the information and the code for undoing the master class' command.

This elaborate design has several characteristics:

- From an OOP viewpoint it is natural – that is, it stems directly from the entities involved, so that even the resulting static class diagram is expressive, which could be useful if new developers are added to a team.

- It is easy to maintain, because the code is gathered systematically in well-defined areas.

- It is easy to expand without modifying the existing code.
- Drawbacks of static class clustering are scalability, the strain imposed on the runtime class loader when a lot of small objects are loaded, and the runtime occupancy when many such instances are kept in memory throughout an application's execution.

Our design is simplified by the double role we assigned to the `Director` class. The director works as a central access point for the manipulation of the Sandbox component. The use of fully-fledged `Action` classes poses the problem of the many objects that need to be visible to the action itself for 'doing' and 'undoing' its commands. This is why we pass the director to the `Action` class.

It is a coincidence that we have just one instance of each action class alive at any time in the application. We could equally have used just one `Add` class, for example, and slightly modified the dynamic repository by providing two methods, `getAction()` and `createNewAction()`, the latter employing the `clone()` method for creating new instances from those in the dynamic repository.

The design approach described above tends to produce many similar command classes. To reduce the number of classes, we employ a simplified version of the Command pattern. The simplest commands and their related specialized inner edit classes can be factored out into common classes. We adopt this tactic for the `AbstractUndoableEdit` subclasses, using the `Edit` class as the commonest edit instance that all other edit classes specialize. We are interested in its use for handling simple commands like cut, paste, and remove.

Take the `Cut` class. Here we have a different scheme than the `ChangeImage` action. The cut command passes the request for command execution to the director. We use a general-purpose edit class, `Edit`, that is manipulated by the `Cut` class' methods. This conservative design spares us code lines and unnecessary complexity. We can use it because of the nature of some of the commands employed – when there are many simple commands that resemble each other, this arrangement can make sense over the cleaner and more powerful one seen for the `ChangeImage` action class.

Undo-redo support

Another part of our command framework is undo/redo support. We need a class to store executed commands. In the swing `undo` package these are called *edits* – every action performed is stored in a new edit instance for future use[5].

---

5. We are only interested here in undo/redo implementation issues. For details about GUI design issues related to undo support, see (Cooper 2003).

When an object is rotated, for example, the application creates a new `Edit` object that stores the rotate action, together with its argument – the object that has been rotated. If the user asks for the operation to be undone, the `Edit` instance is picked up and the `undo` method of the `Rotate` action class is invoked, restoring the situation as it was before the command was issued.

This scenario is a simple one. In real-world cases more sophisticated mechanisms need to be employed, for example coalescing single small undos into larger ones, supporting undoable commands by means of specialized exceptions, and so on.

The Edit class

The `Edit` class represents the generic 'executed action' by the user on the system, and is recorded for future use in undo/redo operations. It is implemented as a subclass of the `AbstractUndoableEdit` class, part of the `swing` library for undo support. It is shown in Figure 16.16.

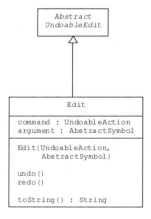

Figure 16.16 The Edit class

An `Edit` instance stores a command and its argument. Such a class can be used in two ways:

• For instantiating simpler edits, those that take only one object as an argument and that can be un/done by invoking the corresponding command class.

• As a base class for creating classes that are specialized for recording and handling more complex edits.

Recording edits

A few words about a data structure useful for managing undo and redo commands are appropriate here, but readers not interested in such implementation details can skip this section.

For simple undo support there is no problem, because a simple `Stack` instance could contain all the edits to be undone. When a redo command is to be supported, however, an additional stack can be used in which edits popped from the undo stack are pushed onto the redo stack, and vice-versa, or a specialized data structure could be used. The following shows a simple implementation of such a data structure.

Suppose the following user commands have been issued:

1. A new object `symb1` is added to the Sandbox.
2. The object is rotated.
3. A new object `symb2` is added to the Sandbox.
4. The first object is put in front of the others.
5. A new object `symb3` is added to the Sandbox.
6. The previous action (addition of `symb3`) is undone.
7. The previous action (`symb1` move front) is undone.
8. The redo command is issued, so that the `symb1` rotation is restored.

Figure 16.17 shows the state of the command history at the end of these interactions.

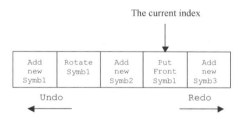

Figure 16.17 The CommandHistory implementation using an ordered list

If the user were to issue a new command, say 'add new `object4`,' it would be inserted to the right of the one pointed to by the index value, and the index incremented, moving right one position. For a redo command, the current index pointer would be moved to the right, so that it points to the next command to be undone. To keep the data structure to a manageable size and avoid expanding it indefinitely, a maximum size parameter can be enforced and the oldest edits discarded.

The source code for this chapter is available in the `sandbox` package.

Memory issues

Recording edits using strong references (that is, the usual normal Java references) can result in a naïve design – memory occupancy grows indefinitely with application use, so that sooner or later the heap memory is completely filled with undo records. This is especially true when working with large images. This is just the kind of situation we want to avoid.

Limiting the `CommandHistory` size to keep memory use under control circumvents this problem, but may limit the user experience – limiting the number of commands that can be undone can result in nasty surprises for users.

To provide a more flexible mechanism, we could release memory only when it is really needed. The simplest solution for this situation, from a technical viewpoint, is to use `WeakReferences`, special references that can be reclaimed by the garbage collector when the JVM is short of free heap memory. The net effect for the user is to experience a sudden reset of the undo history. Using a `ReferenceQueue` instance means that the application is notified when the most weakly referenced edits are about to be discarded. The user can then be informed about what is going on, for example by providing a pop-up message dialog like the one shown in Figure 16.18.

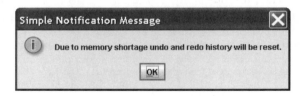

Figure 16.18   Notifying users of undo history (Ocean1.5)

From a technical perspective this solution is quite simple, as the garbage collector takes charge of all the work. From a usability viewpoint, though, this solution could cause problems, as the memory flushing happens unpredictably and ougtside of user control – and it often tends to happen during delicate, complex, and memory-consuming operations. It may therefore disrupt the user's work, and will certainly creates a vaguely unpleasant feeling.

A better solution from a usability viewpoint is to leave the user in control of the application. This can be done by checking memory occupancy before issuing an undoable command. This allows users to decide whether or not to continue with the operation, reducing the probability of their being trapped in harmful situations. In this approach the application might show a dialog like that shown in Figure 16.19 before executing the command.

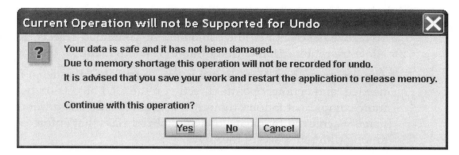

Figure 16.19   Preemptive control provides less intrusive notification (Ocean1.5)

Note that Figure 16.19 has a reassuring **Cancel** option – even though it is redundant, given the **No** option. This design choice is provided deliberately to ease user comprehension of the GUI in challenging situations when users are not used to this messages and become anxious about the security of their data. Look and feel design guidelines, for example those for Java and Apple Macintosh, explicitly dictate that every command has a 'cancel' option.

This type of preemptive control can be achieved as shown in the following simplified code extract:

```
if (Runtime.getRuntime().freeMemory()<MINIMUM_THRESHOLD){
    int userChoice = requirePermissionForCommand();
    if (userChoice==JOptionPane.OK_OPTION) {
        // execute command without undo support
    } else {
        // return without executing command
    }
} else {
    // execute command with undo support
}
```

Solutions that combine several techniques could of course be used. For example, we could use preemptive controls together with a policy of releasing the oldest edits explicitly, by setting their references to null and checking that they are no longer referenced using a memory profiler.

Which solution is best? It depends on the application. When developing a financial application in which the effect of every command must be tracked, the preemptive control shown in Figure 16.19 may be the simplest and most usable solution. In other cases there may be no need to record every operation exactly, and a less intrusive application could be used in which the oldest edits simply 'slip away' without users noticing.

16.6   Control

So far we have defined the container, the contained objects, and the actions that allow user interaction with the Sandbox component.

The design of the action control is left. In trivial GUIs such a feature is often not needed, and actions operate directly on the GUI objects on behalf of the user. In more complex situations, though, it is useful to add an additional layer of control, usually achieved by means of a specialized class that enforces the business logic among different parts of the GUI.

This is where the director class comes in, and has a twofold purpose. Its main duty is to implement the Mediator design pattern[6] for overseeing the interaction among different parts of the GUI. Such a class also turns out to be a good candidate for centralizing action-related code, which minimizes class coupling. Actions need only to see the director class, which in turn executes commands by manipulating the rest of the GUI. This ensures logical coherence, undo/redo support, and also rationalizes class communication. Intuitively, the director class represents the 'brains' of the application.

Figure 16.20 shows this connection scheme for the Cut action class.

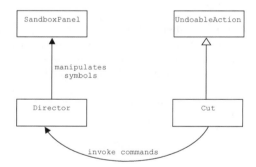

Figure 16.20   The Cut action executes the related command through the director class

---

6.   See Chapter 6.

In this example we are going to limit control logic to action coherence, as we will see later in the implementation details.

The director is coupled to the other classes by an event-based mechanism. The director listens to object events and acts directly on the container class, as shown in Figure 16.21.

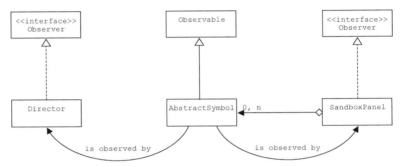

Figure 16.21   Making objects communicate with the rest of the world

The director also manages the undo/redo support by means of the `CommandHistory` class, as shown in Figure 16.22.

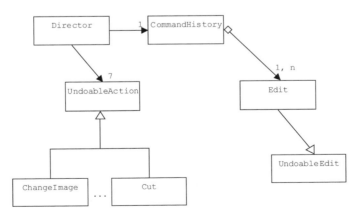

Figure 16.22   The control framework

The Director class

The `Director` class implements the Mediator design pattern, which was introduced in Chapter 6. It is shown in Figure 16.23 below.

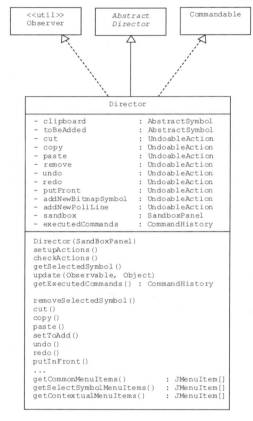

Figure 16.23   The Director class

To see how this works, suppose the user invokes the cut command:

1. The `cut` method is invoked.
2. The currently-selected object is stored to the clipboard, then removed from the graphical container.
3. The whole operation is recorded for undo support.
4. The graphical container is informed of the remove operation and updates itself, making the selected object disappear.
5. An event is issued to the director to refresh command coherence.

6. If the clipboard was previously empty, after the execution of this command the paste action is automatically enabled.

The sequence diagram in Figure 16.24 illustrates this operation.

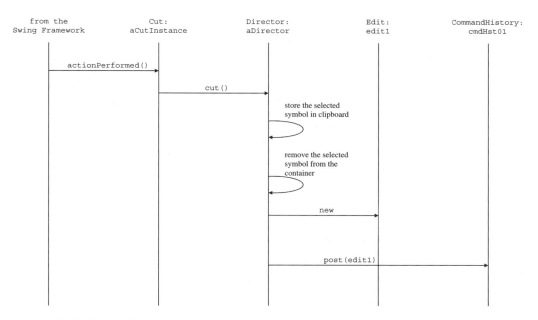

Figure 16.24 Executing the 'Cut' action

The director manages the following:

- A group of actions, described in *Managing actions* next.
- The graphical container, the `sandbox` instance variable.
- The internal clipboard, where copied or cut objects are stored.
- The set of already-performed actions, for undo/redo support.
- The object to be added to the graphical container, if any – when the user clicks the 'add new object' button, the director is informed and set to 'add' mode.

Managing actions

The director is responsible for a group of commands. These are initialized by the `setupActions()` method common to all directors, and is overridden from the `AbstractDirector` class. Such commands are packaged together for use via the `getActionToolBar()` method. Other commands are out of director's scope, such as those that are contextual to a specific object. Keeping a group of commands centralized in one class is useful in practice, because it minimizes class coupling and visibility. The latter is a classic OOP technique: lessening visibility helps to avoid cluttering the whole design and avoid misuses of public methods by other classes.

The command composition mechanism is implemented with the methods `getSelectedSymbolsMenuItems()` and `getContextualMenuItems()`. When the graphic container is queried by the user – when requesting a contextual menu – the director is invoked. The director merges the commands available from the currently-selected object, if any, with those provided by the container.

The director also takes care of the execution of some commands. Consider the `copy()` method invoked by the **Copy** action. The currently-selected object is cloned and stored in the clipboard. It is then deselected, because the standard `clone()` mechanism also copied the selected attribute value from the original, selected object, so it needs to be explicitly de-selected. Finally a check for logical coherence among actions is executed, as discussed in the next section[7].

Enforcing logical constraints on actions

The `checkActions()` method maintains coherence among all actions. This is a one of the key benefits of the Mediator pattern.

This application has three different kinds of constraints on actions:

*   A group of commands (**Move front**, **Cut**, **Copy**, and **Remove**) operates on selections: if no object is selected, these actions cannot be invoked and should be disabled.

*   Other action types need a non-empty clipboard: in the Sandbox application only the **Paste** action has this constraint.

*   Undo/redo commands are available only when an action has been performed (undo) or when at least one old action has been undone (redo).

Abstracting from this simple example, the task of centralizing action coherence is a common one in sophisticated GUIs. Enabling or disabling actions following the application domain logic is a feature that is often dictated directly by the GUI design. From an implementation viewpoint, when the number of actions to check at any one time is non-trivial – perhaps ten or more checks, with related method calls and the like – the design suggested in the director class used in the example

---

7.   The example code does not include undo support for copying objects.

component needs to be modified. One solution is to provide specialized events, and their related listeners, for the various types of constraint to be enforced. This avoids the frequent computation of a unique, catch-all, expensive, method. Instead, more specialized methods are invoked only when needed. This is the same idea that was used for enhancing the event delivery mechanism of the old AWT library.

As the size of applications grows, the use of a director class becomes more and more useful. You may even end up with one or more specialized classes that are solely responsible for keeping your many commands logically coherent. This reduces the maintenance costs associated with dispersing control code locally throughout the various widgets' listeners.

We are now ready to see all the different parts put together in the final application.

16.7   The whole picture

Figure 16.25 shows the overall static class diagram of the Sandbox application.

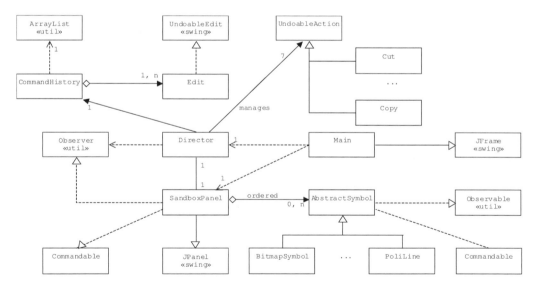

Figure 16.25   The static class diagram of the Sandbox application

We have finished the iterative refinement steps, and the application is ready to run. But what about the top-down approach initially adopted to organize the design? Figure 16.26 shows how the final classes match the initial functional partition.

Gray classes are not part of our framework. Note that the only class not contained in any of the three parts devised at the beginning is the `Main` class containing the window and the `main` method.

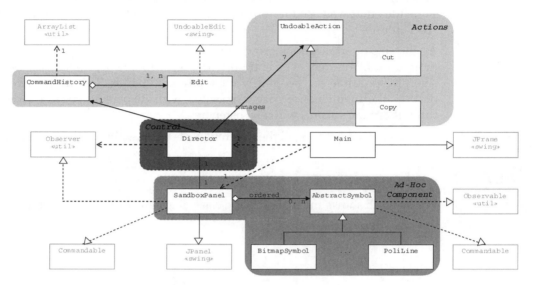

Figure 16.26   The static class diagram mapped to the functional partition

The preliminary high-level partition shown in Figure 16.6 on page 574 has been respected almost completely, apart from the communication flows among different functional parts.

16.8   Stressing the software design

At this point, some authors would hastily conclude the chapter, perhaps chanting the many virtues of design patterns, or exhorting readers to tweak the proposed source code. Instead, we take a different path, one rarely taken in technical publications in which only perfect – or supposedly perfect – solutions are presented. We already know that our design is too simple and limited to deal effectively with features like extensibility and flexibility. What we still don't know is *where* its major weak points are.

There is nothing wrong with code that works well. Code organization can of course be improved by refactoring, or by more painful design restructuring, but the real test of a design – the chances of making it better, or the risk of degradation – comes when changes are needed. Below we briefly analyze how our 'toy' Sandbox design reacts to change.

Adding objects and commands

The first experiment is to see what happens to the design when new commands such as **Print** or **Save** are added to the application. Given the design, the minimum set of steps needed to, say, add a new object class to the Sandbox application are:

1. Create a new action class, usually by extending `UndoableAction` containing the code for the relevant command.

2. Enlist the new action class in the dynamic repository held by the `Actions` class.

3. Register the new action class semantically within the Director instance. This in turn involves two steps: (i) Attaching the command to the toolbar, to make it available to users, and (ii) Writing the code that determines how the new command is going to interact with the rest of the application.

A further interesting expansion is the addition of new objects, such as text, box, or ellipse, for example. This involves defining a new object class, and the creation of an action for adding such objects to the drawing. The minimal steps we need to add a new object class to the Sandbox application are:

1. Create the new class that implements the object, extending `AbstractSymbol` or some of its subclasses.

2. Make a new action class for creating and adding objects of the new type to drawings.

3. Register the new action class in the dynamic repository held by the `Actions` class.

4. Make the director provide the new 'create object...' action to the rest of the application by attaching it to the toolbar.

5. Modify the Director class to handle the intended interactions and control for the new object.

The addition of a new object type to the design of the Sandbox application, excluding its special commands, therefore involves the creation of a new class, and adding code to other two classes, `Actions` (to add the 'create new object' command) and `Director`. The latter dependency is suspect, because the 'create new object' action doesn't involve any special control from the `Director`.

The point is that we gave the simple Director class the responsibility of creating *all* the commands, not only those that need centralized control, such as **Copy** or **Undo**. This may become a problem as the number of 'not controlled' actions outnumbers the controlled ones – the Director class may become cluttered with code unrelated to interaction control. Such code can be factored out in, for example into a `SymbolPalette` class, that is provided with mechanisms for semantic registration of specific actions with the director.

The design's weak points

Adding new objects or commands is relatively easy: the real trouble starts when we need to implement 'horizontal' features that might affect many existing classes in unforeseen ways. Adding zoom support, for example, could impact the whole design deeply. The effect of implementing other features might be more circumscribed, such as multiple views of the same drawing, for example, by adopting a fully-fledged MVC approach, or the ability to group and ungroup objects.

The relative complexity of just adding a new command to the application should ring alarms that suggest closer inspection.

Our director implementation seems to be centralizing some of other classes' responsibilities too much, such as command execution and command status (that is, whether a command should be enabled or disabled given specific external states). This stems directly from the limited use of events in our design – command classes delegate the execution of actions to the director. This simplifies many things initially, such as control: the director pulls together all the data needed to execute and control actions.

However, such a design is too tightly coupled to be maintainable in even a simple real-world situation in which tens of commands to be managed: following such a centralized design in the evolution of an application will lead to a large, convoluted Director class with a myriad of responsibility-free little classes delegating to it. To use a colorful metaphor, it's like feeding a baby monster, currently so small and cute that we don't realize its intrinsically evil nature that, once big enough to be out of control, will devour us.

Despite that it seems that sound design patterns were adopted, and what happened in reality was a misuse of them. For example, controlling whether the **Cut** action should be disabled could be done within the Command pattern approach in a decentralized fashion by letting the Cut action listen to clipboard events and enable or disable itself accordingly.

There is another, subtler issue with the proposed design. Commands in the design affect at least three classes: the Action subclass, the Actions repository that is queried for new commands, and the Director that executes the command itself and takes care of maintaining coherence among the actions and objects contained in the sandbox container. This can be seen as a simple, currently harmless lack of decoupling in the design. This is a well-known aspect of software. Orthogonal systems, using (Hunt and Thomas 2000) terminology, are those systems in which there are no 'effects between unrelated things.' Perhaps this is exaggerating a little, but if it is necessary to modify the implementation of the **Save** command to provide a new file format, for example, why should it also be necessary to study the implementation of three other unrelated classes as well?

16.9   *Introducing JHotdraw*

JHotDraw is a Java GUI framework for technical and structured graphics that is derived from an initial Smalltalk design by Ward Cunningham and Kent Beck. It has been developed as a 'design exercise' in Java by Erich Gamma and Thomas Eggenschwiler, and has a design that relies heavily on standard design patterns. It is freely available at `http://www.jhotdraw.org`.

We introduce this framework as a gallery of interesting design solutions to the problems found with our simple Sandbox application. It would make little sense to compare our toy application, with its ten classes, with such a framework, which has more than 180 classes, the many systems developed using it, and the many experienced designers who have worked on its design, but nevertheless its introduction may help further discussions.

> A framework is a reusable, 'semi-complete' application that can be specialized to produce custom applications (Johnson 1998).
>
> Frameworks are different than usual class libraries, even though sometimes the term is also used for complex class libraries. OOP frameworks usually represent a domain of interest (for example insurance) or application area (for example GUI toolkits) with OOP technology, with the explicit aim of being reused. Frameworks are intended to be reused, with client code extending them and make them concrete as required, and often define particular control flows such as inversion of control, and other devices for reuse such as hook methods, base types to be extended by client code, and so on.

The class diagram in Figure 16.27 shows only the interfaces for clarity, not the real implementations. The concrete class structure is made up of implementation classes for the interfaces shown in the following diagrams.

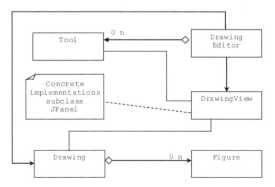

Figure 16.27   The main core class diagram of the main classes of the JHotDraw framework

The `DrawingView` implementation, such as `org.jhotdraw.standard.Standard-DrawingView`, for example, redirects user input to the installed `Tool` instances. `Drawing` implementations act as containers for `Figure` instances (the equivalent of `AbstractSymbol` in the Sandbox application) taking care of firing `DrawingChanged` events to registered `DrawingChangeListeners`. This type of listener is specialized for dealing with three types of occurrence:

- When an area of the `Drawing` instance is invalid.
- When the `Drawing` instance requests an update.
- When the title string changes.

Instances of the `DrawingEditor` interface coordinate the various parties involved in the editor interaction that realizes the Mediator design pattern, as does the `Director` class in the Sandbox application. To minimize decoupling with the rest of the interested classes, the main container implements the `DrawingEditor` interface, for example like `org.jhotdraw.application.DrawApplication`, a `JFrame` subclass.

It is interesting to contrast the concept of a JHotdraw tool with the way in which user input is handled in the Sandbox application. Basically, a tool defines a modality of the drawing view as perceived by the user. Tools are activated when the user clicks on a button in the palette, and deactivated when the user clicks on another button. While active, a tool consumes all input events captured by the drawing view instance and redirected to the currently-active tool. Tools inform their editor when they are finished with an interaction, for example after the creation of a new figure, by calling the editor's `toolDone()` method. Similarly to Sandbox's actions, tools are created once and then reused. Apart from this similarity, however, JHotdraw tools and Sandbox actions represent the functions available to the user in a different way. Specialized tools, subclasses of `org.jhotdraw.standard.CreationTool`, handle the creation of new figures, while in the much simpler Sandbox application, object creation is performed directly by the application.

(Christensen 2004) provides a more detailed static view of the core types of the JHotDraw framework, which still apply in Version 6.0.b1, and this is shown in Figure 16.28.

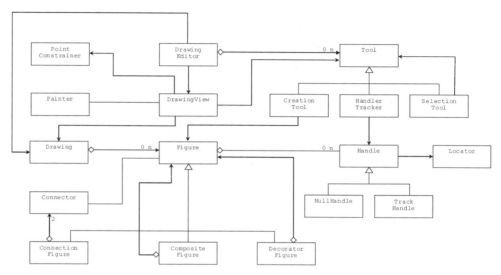

Figure 16.28   The static class diagram of the main classes of the JHotDraw framework

JHotDraw main classes can also be decomposed following the same simple decomposition that guided the development of our ad-hoc Sandbox component, as shown in Figure 16.29.

A functional decomposition like that shown in Figure 16.29 can be helpful in showing alternative organizations for the OOP implementation of our own ad-hoc component, but it might be more useful to show a decomposition based on a standard and not domain-dependent set of abstractions. The perfect candidates for these abstractions are the well-known OOP design patterns. Following (Christensen 2004) again, we have the decomposition in Figure 16.30.

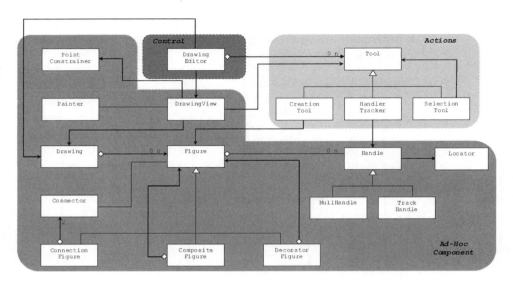

Figure 16.29   A functional decomposition of the main classes of the JHotDraw framework

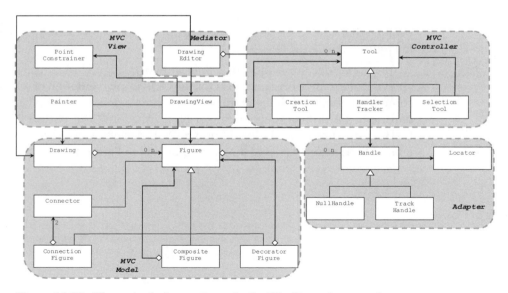

Figure 16.30   The main design patterns in the JHotDraw framework

It is easy to customize the JHotDraw framework to provide the same features as the Sandbox application. Figure 16.31 shows such a prototype.

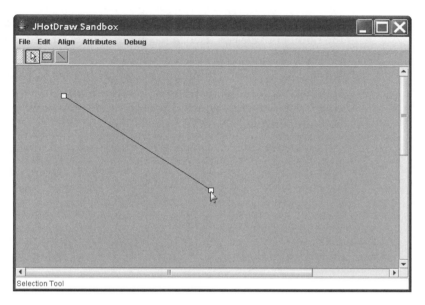

Figure 16.31   The Sandbox application with the JHotDraw framework (Ocean1.5)

16.10 Summary

In this chapter we have discussed an example of an ad-hoc component design. Such components can be quite expensive, both in terms of design and implementation, but in some cases they can make the difference between a great GUI and a mediocre product.

Key ideas

We saw many ideas at work that could also be useful in other contexts. Let's recap some of them:

*   Design and use ad-hoc components only when it is really necessary. Usually, this is the case only for domain-specific and/or high-quality GUIs.

*   Small classes can be gathered into container classes at compile-time, a technique that is referred to as 'static containment.' When the same arrangement is needed for runtime instances, a similar approach can be adopted,

employing a container class that releases instances as needed. Such instances can be released, or new ones created, by prototyping the stored instances.

- Adopting the fully-fledged Command pattern for handling GUI commands has many advantages, but can increase code complexity. Some remedies can be used, such as factoring out common commands or undo data to save on the number of classes used, a technique demonstrated in the Sandbox example.

- Ad-hoc components development can easily slide into the construction of specialized, fully-fledged, small class frameworks. Beware of the 'feature creep' phenomenon, which can be common among developers building ad-hoc components.

A   A Questionnaire for Evaluating Java User Interfaces

This questionnaire can be used as an acceptance test at the end of a test session with users, or for a first-cut usability evaluation. It should not be used as a substitute for usability tests.

Section A: Your experience with the program

How long have you worked with the program?

1 hour or less ☐

1 hour to 1 day ☐

1 day to 1 week ☐

1 week to 1 month ☐

1 to 6 months ☐

6 months to 1 year ☐

More than a year ☐

Section B: Overall reactions

Please rate your reactions to the program:

terrible – wonderful

☐ ☐ ☐ ☐ ☐

difficult – easy

☐ ☐ ☐ ☐ ☐

frustrating – satisfying

☐ ☐ ☐ ☐ ☐

boring – stimulating

☐ ☐ ☐ ☐ ☐

rigid – flexible

☐ ☐ ☐ ☐ ☐

unhelpful – productive

☐   ☐   ☐   ☐   ☐

extremely slow– very
responsive

☐   ☐   ☐   ☐   ☐

Section C: Past experience

How many other operating systems have you worked with?

1   ☐

2   ☐

3   ☐

4 or more   ☐

Please rate your familiarity with Java:

never used before – very high

☐   ☐   ☐   ☐   ☐

For the following items, tick those that you have personally used and are familiar
with:

PC	Cellphone	PDA	Eclipse
☐	☐	☐	☐
Flash drive	Web browser	CD-ROM drive	Database software
☐	☐	☐	☐
Java runtime software (JRE)	Java	J2ME applet	JavaCard
☐	☐	☐	☐

Section D: Terminology

How well does the program terminology relate to the work you are doing?

not at all – very well

☐   ☐   ☐   ☐   ☐

Program terminology is used:

too frequently – appropriately

☐ ☐ ☐ ☐ ☐

The terminology is:

ambiguous – precise

☐ ☐ ☐ ☐ ☐

Messages are:

confusing – clear

☐ ☐ ☐ ☐ ☐

Message positions on the screen are:

consistent – inconsistent

☐ ☐ ☐ ☐ ☐

How often do error messages clarify the problem?

never – always

☐ ☐ ☐ ☐ ☐

Error messages seem:

annoying – constructive

☐ ☐ ☐ ☐ ☐

How often do error messages help to solve the problem?

never – always

☐ ☐ ☐ ☐ ☐

Section E: Feedback

Does the program keep you informed about what it is doing?

never – always

☐ ☐ ☐ ☐ ☐

The mouse pointer shape help in showing the current software state:

never — always

☐ ☐ ☐ ☐ ☐

While performing a task, the program freezes without showing what it is doing:

never — always

☐ ☐ ☐ ☐ ☐

Is it possible to configure the feedback level?

impossible — easy

☐ ☐ ☐ ☐ ☐

Section F: Learning the application

Learning to use the software was:

difficult — easy

☐ ☐ ☐ ☐ ☐

Getting started with the software was:

difficult — easy

☐ ☐ ☐ ☐ ☐

Learning advanced features was:

difficult — easy

☐ ☐ ☐ ☐ ☐

Exploring the application by trial and error was:

risky — safe

☐ ☐ ☐ ☐ ☐

Discovering new features was:

difficult — easy

☐ ☐ ☐ ☐ ☐

Section G: Display organization

The display organization (windows, panels, etc.) was:

confusing – clear

☐　☐　☐　☐　☐

Characters and icons were:

hard to read – very readable

☐　☐　☐　☐　☐

The command icons were:

confusing – clear

☐　☐　☐　☐　☐

The overall graphic appearance was:

annoying – pleasing

☐　☐　☐　☐　☐

Section H: Help support

Technical manuals were:

confusing – clear

☐　☐　☐　☐　☐

On-line manuals were:

confusing – clear

☐　☐　☐　☐　☐

On-line manuals were meaningfully structured:

never – always

☐　☐　☐　☐　☐

Help material covers the program features:

inadequately – completely

☐　☐　☐　☐　☐

Help support activation was:

slow – quick

☐   ☐   ☐   ☐   ☐

Help material was concise and to the point:

never – always

☐   ☐   ☐   ☐   ☐

Learning to use the program by using the help was:

difficult – easy

☐   ☐   ☐   ☐   ☐

Section I: Deployment

Installation was:

difficult – easy

☐   ☐   ☐   ☐   ☐

Launching the program is:

tricky – straightforward

☐   ☐   ☐   ☐   ☐

Upgrading to a newer software version was:

difficult – easy

☐   ☐   ☐   ☐   ☐

B A Questionnaire for Evaluating J2ME Applications

This questionnaire can be used as an acceptance test at the end of a test session with users, or for a first-cut usability evaluation. It should not be used as a substitute of usability tests.

Section A: Your experience with the program

How long have you worked with the program?

1 hour or less ☐

1 hour to 1 day ☐

1 day to 1 week ☐

1 week to 1 month ☐

1 to 6 months ☐

more than 6 months ☐

Section B: Your overall reactions

Please quantify your reactions to the program:

terrible – wonderful

☐ ☐ ☐ ☐ ☐

difficult – easy

☐ ☐ ☐ ☐ ☐

frustrating – satisfying

☐ ☐ ☐ ☐ ☐

boring – stimulating

☐ ☐ ☐ ☐ ☐

rigid – flexible

☐ ☐ ☐ ☐ ☐

unhelpful – productive

☐ ☐ ☐ ☐ ☐

Section C: Your past experience

How many cell similar devices have you used before?

1 ☐

2 ☐

3 ☐

4 or more ☐

Rate your familiarity with Java applets: never used before – very high

In the following items check those that you have personally used and with which you are familiar:

PC	Smart phone	Handheld device	Portable Game Console
☐	☐	☐	☐

SMS	Web Browser	Portable MP3 Player	Digital Camera
☐	☐	☐	☐

Java	Java Virtual Machine (JVM)	J2ME applet	WiFi Network
☐	☐	☐	☐

Section D: Terminology

How close is the program's terminology to what you would expect?

not at all – very close

☐ ☐ ☐ ☐ ☐

The terminology is:

ambiguous – precise

☐ ☐ ☐ ☐ ☐

Technical terminology is used:

too frequently – appropriately

☐ ☐ ☐ ☐ ☐

Messages are:

confusing – clear

☐ ☐ ☐ ☐ ☐

Messages positions on the screen are:

consistent – inconsistent

☐ ☐ ☐ ☐ ☐

How often do error messages clarify the problem?

never – always

☐ ☐ ☐ ☐ ☐

Error messages seem:

annoying – pleasant

☐ ☐ ☐ ☐ ☐

Error messages help to solve the problem?

never – always

☐ ☐ ☐ ☐ ☐

Section E: Program feedback

The program keeps you informed about what it is doing?

never – always

☐ ☐ ☐ ☐ ☐

How frequently does the pointer shape (if any) help in showing the current application state?

never – always

☐ ☐ ☐ ☐ ☐

How often does the program freeze without showing what it is doing?

never – always

☐ ☐ ☐ ☐ ☐

Section F: Learning to use the application

Learning to use the application was:

difficult – easy

☐ ☐ ☐ ☐ ☐

Getting started with the application was:

difficult – easy

☐ ☐ ☐ ☐ ☐

Learning advanced features was:

difficult – easy

☐ ☐ ☐ ☐ ☐

Exploring the features by trial and error was:

risky – safe

☐ ☐ ☐ ☐ ☐

Discovering new features was:

difficult – easy

☐ ☐ ☐ ☐ ☐

Configuring the application's preferences was:

difficult – easy

☐ ☐ ☐ ☐ ☐

Section G: Display organization

The display organization (screens, forms, etc.) was:

confusing – clear

☐ ☐ ☐ ☐ ☐

Characters and icons were:

hard to read – very readable

☐ ☐ ☐ ☐ ☐

The command icons were:

confusing – clear

☐ ☐ ☐ ☐ ☐

The overall graphic appearance was:

annoying – pleasing

☐ ☐ ☐ ☐ ☐

The application had the same look as other programs:

totally different – exactly the same

☐ ☐ ☐ ☐ ☐

Section H: Navigation

It was possible to cancel an operation or navigate back to a previous screen:

never – always

☐ ☐ ☐ ☐ ☐

Navigation keys and navigation commands were:

confusing – clear

☐ ☐ ☐ ☐ ☐

confusing – clear

The number of screens was:

too many – about right

☐ ☐ ☐ ☐ ☐

Reaching a given screen was:

difficult – easy

☐ ☐ ☐ ☐ ☐

Section I: Help support

Help content was:

confusing – clear

☐ ☐ ☐ ☐ ☐

Other manuals (if any) were:

confusing – clear

☐   ☐   ☐   ☐   ☐

Help material covers the program features:

inadequately – completely

☐   ☐   ☐   ☐   ☐

Help activation was:

slow – quick

☐   ☐   ☐   ☐   ☐

Help material was easy to find:

never – always

☐   ☐   ☐   ☐   ☐

Learning to use the application by using the help support was:

difficult – easy

☐   ☐   ☐   ☐   ☐

Section J: Deployment

Installation was:

difficult – easy

☐   ☐   ☐   ☐   ☐

Launching the application the first time was:

confusing – clear

☐   ☐   ☐   ☐   ☐

Launching the application was:

tricky – straightforward

☐   ☐   ☐   ☐   ☐

The waiting time for launching the application was:

extremely long – reasonable

☐ ☐ ☐ ☐ ☐

Upgrading to a newer version was:

difficult – easy

☐ ☐ ☐ ☐ ☐

Section K: Mobile experience

Switching the application on or off (pausing and restoring it) was:

difficult – easy

☐ ☐ ☐ ☐ ☐

Operations required extra attention:

never – always

☐ ☐ ☐ ☐ ☐

How many times did you have to start an operation all over again?

never – more than three times

☐ ☐ ☐ ☐ ☐

The application respected my privacy:

never – always

☐ ☐ ☐ ☐ ☐

The application handled interruptions such as phone warnings, phone calls, other external situations:

badly – very well

☐ ☐ ☐ ☐ ☐

Remote connections were signaled:

confusingly – clearly

☐ ☐ ☐ ☐ ☐

The application asked permission before making remote connections:

never – always

☐   ☐   ☐   ☐   ☐

The application respected the current phone settings, such as ringer off:

never – always

☐   ☐   ☐   ☐   ☐

References

(Advanced Java L&F Design Guidelines 2001)	AA.VV. 2001. *Java Look And Feel Design Guidelines: Advanced Topics.* Reading, Massachusetts: Addison-Wesley.
(Alur, Crupi and Malks 2001)	Alur, Deepak, Crupi, John and Malks, Dan. 2001. *Core J2EE Patterns.* Englewood Cliffs, New Jersey: Prentice Hall.
(Beck and Andres 2004)	Beck, Kent, and Andres, Cynthia. 2004. *Extreme Programming Explained*: *Embrace Change.* Second Edition. Reading, Massachusetts: Addison-Wesley Professional.
(Bernard 2004)	Golden, Bernard. 2004. *Succeeding with Open Source.* Addison-Wesley.
(Brooks 1995)	Brooks, Frederick P Jr. 1996. *The Mythical Man-Month, Anniversary Edition.* Reading, Massachusetts: Addison-Wesley.
(Brown et al. 1998)	Brown, William H et al. 1998. *Anti Patterns. Refactoring Software, Architectures, and Projects in Crisis.* New York: John Wiley & Sons, Inc.
(Burbeck 1992)	Burbeck, Steve. 1992. *Application Programming in Smalltalk-80: How to Use the Model-View-Controller (MVC).* Technical Report.
	Available at: http://st-www.cs.uiuc.edu/users/smarch/st-docs/mvc.html
(Buschmann et al. 1996)	Buschmann, Frank et al. 1996. *Pattern-Oriented Software Architecture Volume 1: A System of Patterns.* New York: John Wiley & Sons, Inc.
(Buschmann et al. 2000)	Buschmann, Frank et al. 1996. *Pattern-Oriented Software Architecture Volume 2: Patterns for Concurrent and Networked Objects.* New York: John Wiley & Sons, Inc.
(Christensen 2004)	Christensen, Henrik B. 2004. *Frameworks: Putting Design Patterns into Perspective.* In Proceedings of ITiCSE'04, June 28–30, 2004, Leeds, United Kingdom.
(Conallen 2002)	Conallen, Jim. 2002. *Building Web Applications with UML*, Second Edition. Reading, Massachusetts: Addison-Wesley.
(Cooper 1995)	Cooper Alan. 1995. *The Myth of Metaphor.*
	http://www.cooper.com/articles/art_myth_of_metaphor.htm

(Cooper 1999)   Cooper, Alan. 1999. *The Inmates Are Running the Asylum: Why High Tech Products Drive Us Crazy and How To Restore The Sanity.* Sams Publishing.

(Cooper 2000)   Cooper James W. 2000. *Design Patterns in Java Technology.* Presentation at the JavaOne Conference. California.

(Cooper 2003)   Cooper, Alan, and Reimann, Robert. *About Face 2.0: The Essentials of Interaction Design.* New York: John Wiley & Sons, Inc.

(Davidson 2000)   Davidson, Mark. 2000. *Using the Swing Action Architecture.* Sun Technical Article. http://www.sun.java.com/

(Daconta et al. 2000)   Daconta, Michael C. et al. 2000. *Java Pitfalls. Time-Saving Solutions and Workarounds to Improve Programs.* New York: John Wiley & Sons, Inc.

(De Marco and Lister 1999) De Marco, Tom, and Lister, Timothy. 1999. *Peopleware. Productive Projects and Teams.* Second Edition. New York: Dorset House Publishing Co.

(Des Rivières 2000)   Des Rivières, J. *Evolving Java-based APIs* http://www.eclipse.org/eclipse/development/java-api-evolution.html

(Des Rivières 2001)   Des Rivières, J. *How to Use the Eclipse API.* http://www.eclipse.org/articles/Article-API%20use/eclipse-api-usage-rules.html

(Elkotoubi, Khriss and Keller 1999) Eloutbi, M, Khriss, I, and Keller, R. K. 1999. *User Interface Prototyping using UML Specifications.* Université de Montreal. Technical Report.

(Evans 2004)   Evans, Eric. 2004. *Domain Driven Design.* Reading, Massachusetts: Addison-Wesley.

(Fleming 1998)   Fleming, Jennifer. 1998. *Web Navigation: Designing the User Experience.* Sebastopol, California: O'Reilly & Associates Inc.

(Fowler 1997)   Fowler, Martin. 1999. *Analysis Patterns: Reusable Object Models.* Reading, Massachusetts: Addison-Wesley.

(Fowler 1999)   Fowler, Martin, et al. 1999. *Refactoring: Improving the Design of Existing Code.* First Edition. Addison-Wesley, Boston, Massachusetts.

(Fowler 2000)   Fowler, Amy. 2000. *Painting in AWT and Swing.* Technical Article. Available at: http://java.sun.com/products/jfc/tsc/articles/painting/index.html

(Fowler 2000b)   Fowler, Amy. *A Swing Architecture Overview. The Inside Story on JFC Component Design.* Technical Report. Available at http://java.sun.com/products/jfc/tsc/articles/architecture/

(Fowler 2003)	Fowler, Martin. 2003. *UML Distilled: A Brief Guide to the Standard Object Modeling Language,* Third Edition.
(Fowler et al. 2000)	Fowler, Martin et al. 2000. *Refactoring. Improving the Design of Existing Code.* Reading, Massachusetts: Addison-Wesley.
(Fowler et al. 2003)	Fowler, Martin et al. 2003. *Patterns of Enterprise Application Architecture.* Reading, Massachusetts: Addison-Wesley.
(Gamma et al. 1994)	Gamma, Erich et al. 1994. *Design Patterns.* Reading, Massachusetts: Addison-Wesley.
(Geary 1999)	Geary, David M. 1999. *Graphic Java 2. Mastering the JFC.* Third Edition. Englewood Cliffs, New Jersey: Prentice Hall.
(Holub 1999)	Holub, Allen. 1999. *Building Interfaces for Object Oriented Systems.* Java-World Article. http://www.javaworld.com/
(Hunt and Thomas 2000)	Hunt, Andrew and Thomas, David. 2000. *The Pragmatic Programmer. From Journeyman to Master.* Addison-Wesley.
(Hutchins et al. 1986)	Hutchins, Edwin, Hollan, James, and Donald Norman. *Direct Manipulation Interfaces,* in Norman, Donald, and Draper, Stephen, *User Centered System Design.* 1986. pp. 87–124.
(Java L&F Design Guidelines 2001)	AA.VV. 2001. *Java Look And Feel Design Guidelines,* Second Edition. Reading, Massachusetts: Addison-Wesley.
(Johnson 1998)	Johnson, Ralph and Foote, Brian. 1988. *Designing Reusable Classes.* Journal of Object-Oriented Programming. SIGS, 1, 5 (June/July. 1988), 22–35.
(Johnson 2003)	Johnson, Rod. 2003. *Expert One-on-One J2EE Design and Development.* Indianapolis: Wrox; John Wiley & Sons, Inc.
(Kerievsky 2004)	Kerievsky, Joshua. 2004. *Refactoring to Patterns.* Addison-Wesley Professional.
(Kruchten and Ahlqvist 2001)	Kruchten, Philippe and Ahlqvist, Stefan. *User Interface Design in the Rational Unified Process.* In M. van Harmelan, Ed., *Object Modeling and User Interface Design.* Addison-Wesley, 2001.
(Larman 2003)	Larman, Craig. 2003. *Agile and Iterative Development. A Manager's Guide.* Addison-Wesley Professional.
(Mandel 1997)	Mandel, Theo. 1997. *The Elements of User Interface Design.* New York: John Wiley & Sons, Inc.

(Maner 1997)   Maner, Walter. 1997. *Internationalization of User Interfaces.* Available at
                                http://web.cs.bgsu.edu/maner/uiguides/internat.htm

(Marinilli 2000)   Marinilli, Mauro. 2000. *A Java Drawing Editor.* Gamelan Article.
                                http://www.gamelan.com/

(Marinilli Persistence 2000)   Marinilli, Mauro. 2000. *Class Semipersistence and Instance Semipersistence:
                                Two Powerful tools in the Software Designer Toolbox.* Gamelan article.
                                http://www.gamelan.com/

(Marinilli 2001)   Marinilli, Mauro. 2001. *Java Deployment.* Indianapolis: Sams Publishing.

(Marinescu 2002)   Marinescu, Floyd et al. 2002. *EJB Design Patterns: Advanced Patterns,
                                Processes, and Idioms.* John Wiley & Sons, Inc.

(Martin 2002)   Martin, Robert C. 2002. *Agile Software Development. Principles Patterns,
                                and Practices.* Englewood Cliffs, New Jersey: Prentice Hall.

(McConnell 1993)   McConnell, Steve. 1993. *Code Complete. A Practical Handbook of Software
                                Construction.* Redmond, Washington: Microsoft Press.

(McConnell 1996)   McConnell, Steve. 1996. *Rapid Development. Taming Wild Software Sched-
                                ules.* Redmond, Washington: Microsoft Press.

(Mullet and Sano 1995)   Mullet, Kevin, and Sano, Darrel. 1995. *Designing Visual Interfaces. Commu-
                                nication Oriented Techniques.* Englewood Cliffs, New Jersey:
                                Prentice Hall.

(Nielsen 1993)   Nielsen, Jakob. 1993. *Usability Engineering.* San Diego: California
                                Academic Press.

(Norman 1990)   Norman, Donald A. 1990. *The Design of Everyday Things.* New York:
                                Doubleday.

(Norman 1993)   Norman, Donald A. 1993. *Things That Makes Us Smart. Defending Human
                                Attributes in the Age of the Machine.* Cambridge, Massachusetts:
                                Perseus Books.

(Norman 1998)   Norman, Donald A. 1998. *The Design of Everyday Things.* Bantam
                                Doubleday Dell Publishing.

(Potel 1996)   MVP: *Model-View-Presenter. The Taligent Programming Model for C++ and
                                Java.* Technical Report.
                                ftp://www6.software.ibm.com/software/developer/library/mvp.pdf

(Preece 1994)   Preece, Jenny. 1994. *Human Computer Interaction.* Reading, Massachu-
                                setts: Addison-Wesley.

(Reichert 2000)	Reichert, Raimond. 2000. *Interact with Garbage collector to avoid memory leaks. Use Reference Objects to Prevent Memory Leaks in Application Built on the MVC Pattern.* Javaworld article. http://www.javaworld.com/
(Rosenberg and Scott 1999)	Rosenber, Doug, and Scott, Kendall. 1999. *Use Case Driven Object Modeling with UML. A Practical Approach.* Reading, Massachusetts: Addison-Wesley.
(Rubin 1994)	Rubin, Jeffrey. 1994. *Handbook of Usability Testing. How to Plan, Design and Conduct Effective Tests.* Wiley Technical Communication Library. New York: John Wiley & Sons, Inc.
(Selby and Porter 1998)	Selby R. W. and Porter. A. A. 1988. *Learning from Examples: Generation and Evaluation of Decision Trees for Software Resource Analysis.* IEEE Trans. on Soft. Eng., 14(12), pp. 1743–1757.
(Shirazi 2000)	Shirazi, Jack. 2000. *Java Performance Tuning.* Sebastopol, California: O'Reilly & Associates Inc.
(Shirogane and Fukazawa 2002)	Shirogane, Junko and Fukazawa, Yoshiaki. 2002. *GUI Prototype Generation by Merging Use Cases.* Proceedings of the IUI Conference. San Francisco, California.
(Shneiderman 1998)	Shneiderman, Ben. 1998. *Designing the User Interface,* Third Edition. Reading, Massachusetts: Addison-Wesley.
(Snyder 2003)	Snyder, Carolyn. 2003. *Paper Prototyping: The Fast and Easy Way to Design and Refine User Interfaces.* Morgan Kaufmann.
(Sundsten 1998)	Sundsten, Todd. 1998. *MVC meets Swing. Explore the underpinnings of the JFC's Swing components Pattern.* Javaworld article. `http://www.javaworld.com/javaworld/jw-04-1998/jw-04-howto.html`
(Tidwell 1999)	Tidwell, Jenifer. 1999. *Common Ground.* `http://mit.edu/`
(Tufte 1990)	Tufte, Edward R. 1990. *Envisioning Information.* Cheshire, Connecticut: Graphic Press.
(Tufte 1997)	Tufte, Edward R. 1997. *Visual Explanations.* Cheshire, Connecticut: Graphic Press.
(Tufte 2001)	Tufte, Edward R. 2001. *The Visual Display of Quantitative Information.* Second Edition. Cheshire, Connecticut: Graphic Press.
(Vlissides et al. 1996)	Vlissides, John et al. (Eds.) 1996. *Pattern Languages of Program Design 2.* Reading, Massachusetts: Addison-Wesley.
(Vlissides 1998)	Vlissides, John. 1998. *Pattern Hatching. Design Patterns Applied.* Reading, Massachusetts: Addison-Wesley.

General advice on usability and GUI design

http://www.acm.org/sigchi/

CHI Conference proceedings abstracts and other academic research material.

http://www.acm.org/~perlman/readings.html

Suggested readings on HCI and UI development.

http://www.asktog.com

Bruce Tognazzini's Web site.

http://developer.apple.com/documentation/UserExperience/Conceptual/
OSXHIGuidelines/

Apple Macintosh design guidelines.

http://www.gui-designers.co.uk

Practical examples of GUI design.

http://www.ibm.com//ibm/hci/

IBM's human computer interaction Web site.

A couple of 'interface hall of shame' sites are available on line:

http://homepage.mac.com/bradster/iarchitect/shame.htm

This is the most interesting and complete one, although now a little dated.

Other Web sites on the same subject:

http://www.pixelcentric.net/x-shame/

http://www.frankmahler.de/mshame/index.html

http://www.rha.com/ui_hall_of_shame.htm

http://msdn.microsoft.com/ui

Microsoft MSDN user interface resources.

http://www.pegasus3d.com/apple_screens.html

The evolution of the Macintosh interface.

http://www.tworivers.com

General and practical discussion on GUI design.

http://www.usabilityfirst.com

General advice on usability and GUI design.

http://www.useit.com

Jakob Nielsen's Web site, with some useful articles.

Java-specific links

http://www.java.sun.com/products/jlf

Java look and feel design guidelines.

http://www.java.sun.com/products/jfc

The Java Foundation Classes (JFC) official home page.

http://www.java.sun.com/products/jfc/tsc

The Swing Connection official home page.

http://www.sun.com/access/articles/#articles

Discussion of the Multiplexing look and feel, providing accessibility features.

http://deyalexander.com/resources/design-guidelines.html

A list of resources about GUI Design guidelines.

http://www.cs.usm.maine.edu/~welty/

A comprehensive list of useful HCI/ UI design links.

Index

Cheat Sheet

An extremely simplified and by no means exhaustive basic reference to some of the topics discussed in the book.

GUI Design

- How do I signal to the user my GUI is busy?

  Change mouse pointer to hour glass for any operation that lasts more than two seconds, always use progress indicators, and update progress every five seconds.

- How do I validate my GUI?

  Involve users in design, use prototyping, software testing, memory profiling (Chapter 5), questionnaire evaluation (Appendices A and B), and usability testing.

- How do I organize the GUI window area?

  Use the *Area Organization* design strategy (120).

- How do I allow the user to select or create information in a GUI?

  Use the *Chooser* design strategy, 126.

- How do I deploy my GUI?

  Use Java Web Start when the user population is confident with approving certificates, as for internal software. Use installers in other cases, and for large installation bundles. Consider also using applets!

Software Design

- How do I keep my GUI responsive to user interaction during long-running operations?

  Use the *Active Object* pattern, 280 (for Swing, the `SwingWorker` class) for any operation that might last more than one second.

- How do I implement control (reaction to user interaction) in my GUI?

  Depending on the number of items to be controlled by control rules, use:
  - Scattered control (260) – few items, reactive-only control rules.
  - Centralized control, the Mediator pattern (263) – many items, any kind of control rule.
  - Explicit Control State (260) – complex control rules, need for flexibility.

- How do I implement undo/redo in a GUI?

  Build a queue or stack of edits (587), use the *Command* pattern (258) for user actions.

- How do I implement role-based authorization/security in my GUI?

  Build a dedicated authorization manager class using Adaptation (272).

Molecular Mechanism of
Steroid Hormone Action

Recent Advances

Molecular Mechanism of Steroid Hormone Action

Recent Advances

Editor
V. K. Moudgil

Walter de Gruyter · Berlin · New York 1985

Editor

Virinder K. Moudgil, Ph. D.
Department of Biological Sciences
Oakland University

Rochester, Michigan 48063
U.S.A.

Library of Congress Cataloging in Publication Data

> Molecular mechanism of steroid hormone action.
>   Includes bibliographies and indexes.
>   1. Steroid hormones--Receptors.   2. Hormones, Sex--Receptors.
>   3. Molecular biology.   I. Moudgil, Virinder K., 1945–
>   QP572.S7M65   1985   599'.0142   85-6787
>   ISBN 0-89925-032-7 (U.S.)

CIP-Kurztitelaufnahme der Deutschen Bibliothek

> **Molecular mechanism of steroid hormone action :**
> recent advances / ed. V. K. Moudgil. – Berlin ; New York :
> de Gruyter, 1985.
>   ISBN 3-11-010118-1 (Berlin)
>   ISBN 0-89925-032-7 (New York)
> NE: Moudgil, Virinder K. [Hrsg.]

3 11 010118 1   Walter de Gruyter · Berlin · New York
0-89925-032-7   Walter de Gruyter, Inc., New York

To dearest Bauji

FOREWORD

During the last two decades, progress in research on steroid hormone receptors has resulted in the development of new approaches for contraception and the diagnosis and treatment of endocrine-related disorders and cancers. Significant advancements also have been recorded in the purification, characterization and immunochemistry of steroid hormone receptors. However, despite such progress, understanding of the precise molecular mechanism of steroid hormone action has remained obscure. It is in the spirit of seeking a better understanding of the mode of action of steroid hormones that the idea of compiling such information was conceived. The chapters in this book represent invited contributions from the leading investigators engaged in research in the general area of steroid hormone receptors. The effort of comprising this volume has brought together the most significant and current work of prominent, world reknowned scientists. Each chapter has been written to provide the reader with an adequate background of the subject while, at the same time, introducing the state of the art and most current contributions of the investigator(s).

Although many excellent books, monographs and comprehensive reviews on the subject already exist, limitation of such works has often times rested in the inadequate interpretation and discussion of the information reviewed. This book provides a first-hand interaction with the various approaches and directions adopted by the authors in their quest for knowledge of the molecular mechanism of steroid hormone action. The need for a discussion on this subject cannot be overemphasized since, even after great strides and significant achievements in the molecular aspects of steroid receptors, the native structure of the receptor molecule still alludes investigators.

It is hoped that this book will provide a much needed and timely background for the cell, molecular and developmental biologist. Although the book was written with the scientist in mind, it should also provide an invaluable reference source for graduate students in biology and medicine.

VIII

I am indebted to Dr. David Toft, Mayo Clinic, for introducing me to this most exciting subject of steroid hormone receptors, and most certainly for his continued guidance and encouragement. I thank Ms. Cynthia Winston for her secretarial assistance and Walter de Gruyter for the rapid publication of this volume.

The effort invested in the organization and preparation of this book is dedicated to the living memory of my father, Pandit Harbhagwan Moudgil.

Rochester, January 1985   The Editor

CONTENTS

Phosphorylation

Regulation and Biological Responses

XII

MOLECULAR ORGANIZATION OF THE ESTROGEN RECEPTOR SYSTEM

Akira Murayama

Department of Physiological Chemistry, The Tokyo Metropolitan Institute of
Medical Science, Honkomagome, Bunkyoku, Tokyo 113, Japan

Introduction

Background

Method

Results

A. Estrogen receptor system of the cytosol of porcine uterus.

   a) Basic estrogen receptor molecule (vero-ER) and the proteolyzed
      estrogen receptor molecule (secto-ER).

   b) "8S" estrogen receptor-forming factor.

   c) Subunit structure of "8S" estrogen receptor-forming factor.

   d) Purification of basic estrogen receptor molecule (vero-ER) and
      estrogen receptor-binding factors.

B. Estrogen receptor system of the nuclei of porcine uterus.

C. Molecular mechanism of the translocation of estrogen receptor from
   the cytoplasm into the nucleus.

   a) Molecular mechanism of "5S" estrogen receptor formation.

   b) Mechanism of the nuclear translocation of estrogen receptor.

D. Regulation of the reactivity of basic estrogen receptor molecule
   (vero-ER) with estrogen receptor-binding factors.

   a) Strongly hydrophobic domain of basic estrogen receptor molecule
      (vero-ER).

   b) Regulation of association and dissociation of basic estrogen
      receptor molecule (vero-ER) with estrogen receptor-binding factors.

Discussion

References

Molecular Mechanism of Steroid Hormone Action
© 1985 Walter de Gruyter & Co., Berlin · New York – Printed in Germany

Introduction

Steroid hormone receptors are intracellular receptors, which recognize the
hormones not on the cellular membranes, but in the inside of the target
cells. Since steroid hormones labeled with tritium of high specific
activity became available in the early 1960s (1,2), intensive studies have
been made on steroid hormone receptors leading to many interesting
proposals on the mode of action of steroid hormones (see reviews 3-13).
However, there are as yet many discrepancies between the proposed molecular
models of steroid hormone receptors, and little is known on the reactions
of the receptors in the target cells to induce the hormonal responces.
Precise information of the molecular organization of the steroid hormone
receptor system is an important basis of the study of the action mechanism
of the hormones.

We presented recently a new molecular model of the structural constitution
of estrogen receptors (14-18) and progesterone receptors (19), which are

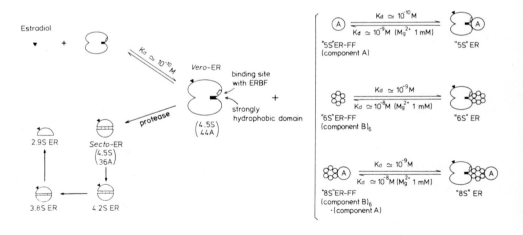

Fig. 1. Molecular constitution of the estrogen receptor system (17)

very similar to each other. We showed that there is one basic estrogen
receptor (ER) molecule (vero-ER) (sedimentation coefficient, 4.5S; Stokes
radius, 44 A) in the estrogen target tissues (14,18). Vero-ER interacted
specifically with the endogenous components designated as ER-binding factors
(ERBFs) ["5S" ER-forming factor ("5S" ER-FF), (component A); "6S" ER-FF,
(component B)$_6$; "7S" ER-FF, (component B)$_2$·(component A); "8S" ER-FF,
(component B)$_6$·(component A)] to form estrogen receptors ["5S" ER, (vero-
ER)·("5S" ER-FF); "6S" ER, (vero-ER)·("6S" ER-FF); "7S" ER, (vero-ER)·
(component B)$_2$·(component A); "8S" ER, (vero-ER)·(component B)$_6$·(component
A)] with various molecular constitutions (15-18). Vero-ER is proteolyzed
by the endogenous proteases (20) to form various receptor fragments [secto-
ER (sedimentation coefficient, 4.5S; Stokes radius, 35 A); "4.2S" ER;
"3.8S" ER; "2.9S" ER, etc.], which still bind with estradiol, but no
longer bind with ERBFs (14,18) (Fig. 1).

This chapter reviews the recent studies of our laboratory, and presents new
conceptions of the molecular organization of the estrogen receptor system.

Background

Steroid hormone receptors are extracted in the cytosol fractions with the
conventional buffers without utilizing detergents, in contrast to the
membrane-bound receptors. In spite of the facile extractability, study of
steroid hormone receptors on the molecular level is extremely troublesome.
Two majour obstacles seem to have been disregarded until now in the study
of steroid hormone receptors. First, steroid hormone receptors undergo
complicated association and dissociation with endogenous protein factors,
appropriate understanding of which is an important basis of the study of
the receptor phenomena. Second, steroid hormone receptors are extremely
susceptible to the modifications by the proteases coextracted with them.
Through the proteolytic modifications, the binding site of the receptors
to the hormones are slightly affected, while the capability of the receptors
to undergo specific reactions with the endogenous protein factors is lost.
The binding site to the hormone is only a part of the whole receptor molecule. It is important to protect the steroid hormone receptors from the

4

endogenous proteases, and to separate them from the protein factors which
associate with them with high affinities. The following studies on the
molecular organization of the estrogen receptor system were undertaken by
taking special care on these respects.

Methods

A. Buffer.
The following buffers were utilized. TEMA [10 mM Tris, 1.5 mM EDTA, 1.5 mM
2-mercaptoethanol, 0.25 mM antipain (21), pH 8.0] buffer. TEM (TEMA devoid
of antipain) buffer. TMA (TEMA devoid of EDTA) buffer. P_nEMA (n mM potassium phosphate, 1.5 mM EDTA, 1.5 mM 2-mercaptoethanol, 0.25 mM antipain,
pH 6.5) buffer. P_nEM (P_nEMA devoid of antipain) buffer.

B. Porcine (gilt) uteri (18).
Gilt (female pig before her first conception) uteri weighing less than 80
g/uterus were collected at the local slaughter house immediately after the
animals were killed. The uteri were removed of connective and adipose
tissues, and immediately used for the experiments.

C. Assay of estrogen receptor-binding factor (ERBF) activity (16).
The sample (0.1 ml in TEMA buffer) to be assayed was mixed with 2×10^{-13}
mol of basic estrogen receptor molecule (vero-ER) labeled with [^{3}H]estradiol
(assuming one molecule of vero-ER binds with one molecule of estradiol) in
0.1 ml of TEMA buffer, and then kept for 5 h at 1°C. The mixture was then
subjected to sucrose gradient (5-20%) centrifugation in TEMA buffer, and
ER activity appearing at 8S ("8S" ER), 6.5S ("6S" ER), 5.5S ("5S" ER), or
4.5S (vero-ER) was estimated. One unit of "8S" ER-forming factor ("8S"
ER-FF), "6S" ER-FF, or "5S" ER-FF activity was defined as the amount of the
respective factor to complex with 1×10^{-13} mol of vero-ER to form "8S" ER,
"6S" ER or "5S" ER under the assay condition.

D. Estimation of the equilibrium dissociation constants (Kd) of the basic
estrogen receptor molecule (vero-ER) for estrogen receptor-binding factors
(ERBFs) (22).
Aliquots of respective ERBF-preparations (0.5 units in 0.1 ml TEMA buffer)

were incubated with preparations of labeled vero-ER ranging from 1 x 10^{-10} M to 1 x 10^{-9} M at 1°C for 5 h. The complex, (vero-ER)·(ERBF), was separated from vero-ER by sucrose gradient (5-20%) centrifugation. It was assumed that the dissociation of the complex, (vero-ER)·(ERBF), into vero-ER and ERBF during the process of the centrifugation was negligible, since the obtained sedimentation patterns of the estrogen receptors were symmetrical. The equilibrium binding data obtained were plotted according to Scatchard (23) assuming that one molecule of estradiol binds to one molecule of vero-ER. Estimation of the apparent equilibrium dissociation constants in the presence of Mg^{2+} was carried out similarly in TMA buffer (24).

Results

A. Estrogen receptor system of the cytosol of porcine uterus.

a) Basic estrogen receptor molecule (vero-ER) and proteolyzed estrogen receptor molecule (secto-ER) (14,18). The estrogen receptor (ER) of the fresh cytosol sedimented at 8S ("8S" ER) in the low salt conditions, and at 4.5S in the presence of 0.4 M KCl or 0.4 M NaSCN (Fig. 2). Similar remarkable variation of the sedimentation pattern of steroid hormone receptors depending on the salt conditions have been widely reported. The molecular model of steroid hormone receptors is required to explain consistently the salt-dependent variation of the sedimentation pattern of the receptors. To solve this problem, it is necessary to separate the basic constituents of the receptor system from each other, and to reconstitute the association and dissociation.

When the cytosol was incubated in the presence of NaSCN for 12 h at 4°C and then analyzed, ER sedimented at 2.9S in the presence of 0.4 M NaSCN, and at 4.5S in the low salt conditions or in the presence of 0.4 M KCl (Fig. 2). However, when the incubation of the cytosol with NaSCN was carried out in the presence of antipain (0.25 mM), a protease inhibitor of microbial origin (21), the modification of the sedimentation pattern of ER through the incubation could be prevented (Fig. 2). These results indicated that the proteolytic modification of the cytosolic ER took place during the

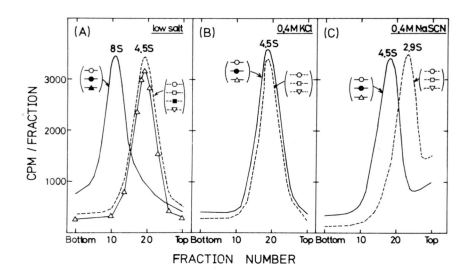

Fig. 2. Sedimentation analysis of native and proteolyzed estrogen receptors (18). Sucrose gradient centrifugation was carried out either in TEMA buffer (A), in TEMA buffer containing 0.4 M KCl (B), or in TEMA buffer containing 0.4 M NaSCN (C). Labeled cytosol (—○—). Labeled cytosol incubated in the presence of 0.4 M NaSCN for 12 h at 4°C (--○--). Labeled cytosol incubated in the presence of 0.4 M NaSCN and 0.25 mM antipain for 12 h at 4°C (—●—). Fraction III (Fig. 3B) (—△—). Fraction III + unlabeled cytosol (—▲—). Fraction II (Fig. 3A) (--□--). Fraction II + unlabeled cytosol (--■--). Fraction IV (Fig. 3B) (--▽--).

incubation with NaSCN in the absence of an appropriate protease inhibitor. We utilized antipain in the following study to prevent the eventual proteolytic modification of ER by the endogenous protease.

When the labeled cytosol prepared in TEMA (see method) buffer was subjected to a two-step gel filtration on a Sephadex G-150 column in TEMA buffer in the presence of 0.4 M KCl and in the presence of 0.4 M NaSCN, ER with a Stokes radius of 44 A (fraction III, Fig. 3B) and a sedimentation coefficient of 4.5S (Fig. 2) was obtained as a sole ER activity in the eluate. This indicated that there is one basic estrogen receptor molecule in the uterine cytosol. The basic receptor molecule with a Stokes radius of 44 A and a sedimentation coefficient of 4.5S was designated as vero-ER (vero, taken from the Latin verus). Vero-ER by itself did not undergo self-associ-

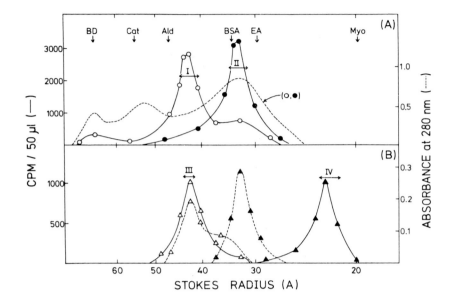

Fig. 3. Two-step gel filtration of the labeled cytosol (14). (A) Labeled cytosol was subjected to gel filtration on Sephadex G-150 in TEMA buffer containing 0.4 M KCl (O), or in TEM buffer containing 0.4 M KCl (●). (B) Fraction I (△) or fraction II (▲) was subjected to gel filtration on Sephadex G-150 in TEMA buffer containing 0.4 M NaSCN. ——— , [^{3}H]estradiol content; ------ , absorbance at 280 nm. The arrows indicate the peaks of elution for Blue Dextran (BD), catalase (Cat), aldolase (Ald), BSA, egg albumin (EA), and myoglobin (Myo).

ation and -dissociation depending on the salt conditions (Fig. 2). When the fraction of vero-ER was mixed with unlabeled cytosol, ER sedimented at 8S under the low salt conditions suggesting the presence of a component ("8S" ER-forming factor, "8S" ER-FF) which binds with vero-ER to form "8S" ER in the cytosol (Fig. 2).

When gel filtration of the labeled cytosol was carried out in TEM (TEMA devoid of antipain) buffer in the presence of 0.4 M KCl, ER eluted in the fractions (fraction II, Fig. 3A) with a smaller Stokes radius (35 A) as compared to vero-ER. This indicated that vero-ER was proteolyzed by a protease during the gel filtration in the absence of antipain. The proteolyzed receptor with a Stokes radius of 35 A and a sedimentation coefficient of 4.5S was designated as secto-ER (secto, taken from the Latin

8

secare). Secto-ER no longer possessed the capability to form "8S" ER when
mixed with unlabeled cytosol (Fig. 2). Secto-ER sedimented at 2.9S in the
presence of 0.4 M NaSCN (Fig. 2). When secto-ER was subjected to gel filtration in the presence of 0.4 M NaSCN, ER was eluted in the fractions with
a Stokes radius of 24 A (fraction IV, Fig. 3B). The ER of fraction IV
sedimented at 2.9S in the presence of 0.4 M NaSCN, and at 4.5S in the absence of NaSCN (Fig. 2). These results indicated that in the presence of
0.4 M NaSCN, secto-ER is dissociated into "2.9S" ER fragment (Stokes radius,
24 A) and a counterpart with a similar molecular size.

b) "8S" estrogen receptor-forming factor ("8S" ER-FF) (15,18). To analyze
the cytosolic factor ("8S" ER-forming factor, "8S" ER-FF) which binds with
vero-ER to form "8S" ER, the unlabeled cytosol was subjected to gel filtration on a Sephadex G-150 column under the low salt (TEMA) conditions, and
the eluate was divided into fractions as shown in Fig. 4. Each fraction

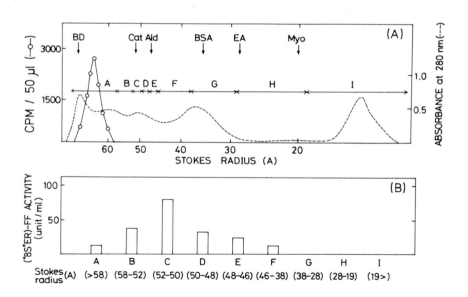

Fig. 4. Gel filtration of "8S" ER and "8S" ER-forming factor (15). Gel
filtration of the labeled and uniabeled cytosol was carried out on a Sephadex
G-150 column (1.6 x 96 cm) in TEMA buffer. —O—, [^{3}H]estradiol content;
-----, absorbance at 280 nm. The arrows indicate the elution peaks of the
standards (see the legend to Fig. 3).

was assayed for the activity [ER-binding factor (ERBF) activity] to bind
with vero-ER (sedimentation coefficient, 4.5S) to form ER with a higher
sedimentation coefficient. The main peak of "8S" ER-FF was eluted in the
fractions with a Stokes radius of approximately 51 A (fraction C in fig.
4B). Other ERBF activity was not detected in the eluate. "8S" ER-FF was
assumed to be a protein, since it was destroyed by trypsin, but not by
DNase and RNase. "8S" ER-FF did not bind with estradiol. When a mixture
of vero-ER and "8S" ER-FF was subjected to gel filtration under the low
salt (TEMA) conditions, ER eluted in the fractions with a Stokes radius
of 68 A similar to the cytosolic "8S" ER (Fig. 4A).

The levels of vero-ER and "8S" ER-FF of the cytosol preparations of various
specimens of gilt uteri are shown in Fig. 5. Variation of the level of
ER was relatively small. The ER-rich tissues contained approximately 2-
fold ER as compared to ER-poor tissues. In contrast, the content of "8S"
ER-FF varied over 50 times among the tissues. Positive correlation was

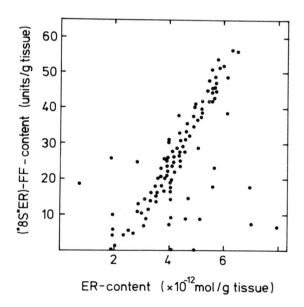

Fig. 5. Plot of uterine contents of "8S" ER-forming factor versus vero-ER
(18). The vertical axis represents the contents of "8S" ER-forming factor.
The horizontal axis represents the contents of vero-ER.

observed between the ER-level and the "8S" ER-FF level. The ER of the cytosol of poor "8S" ER-FF content sedimented at 8S indicating the presence of at least equimolar amount of "8S" ER-FF to vero-ER. This indicated that "8S" ER-FF is present in a larger molar excess to vero-ER in the normal gilt uteri.

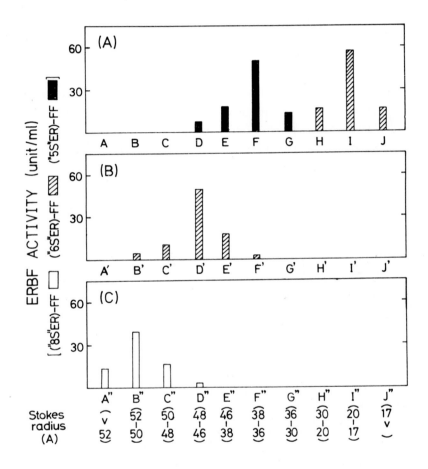

Fig. 6. Analysis of the subunit structure of "8S" ER-forming factor by gel filtration (16). Gel filtration was carried out on a Sephadex G-150 column (1.6 x 96 cm). (A) Gel filtration of "8S" ER-forming factor (fraction C in Fig. 4B) in TEM buffer containing 0.4 M NaSCN. (B) Gel filtration of component B (fraction I in Fig. 6A) in TEM buffer. (C) Gel filtration of the mixture of "5S" ER-forming factor (fraction F in Fig. 6A, 50 units) and "6S" ER-forming factor (fraction D' in Fig. 6C, 50 units) in TEM buffer.

c) Subunit structure of "8S" ER-forming factor ("8S" ER-FF) (16,18). The preparation of "8S" ER-FF was subjected to gel filtration on a Sephadex column in TEMA buffer containing 0.4 M NaSCN, and the eluate was fractionated, removed of NaSCN, and then assayed for the ERBF activity. Interestingly, "8S" ER-FF disappeared from the eluate, and instead, two new ERBF activities appeared (Fig. 6A). "5S" ER-forming factor ("5S" ER-FF) which binds with vero-ER to form ER sedimenting at 5.5S ("5S" ER) under both low salt and high salt (0.4 M KCl) conditions was eluted in the fractions with a Stokes radius of around 37 A (fraction F in Fig. 6A). "6S" ER-froming factor ("6S" ER-FF) which binds with vero-ER to form ER sedimenting at 6.5S ("6S" ER) under the low salt conditions was eluted in the fractions with a Stokes radius of around 18.5 A (fraction I in Fig. 6A). Other ERBF activity was not detected in the eluate. These results showed that "5S" ER-FF and "6S" ER-FF are subunits of "8S" ER-FF. The basic units of "5S" ER-FF and "6S" ER-FF were designated as component A and component B respectively.

When fraction I (component B) was subjected to gel filtration in the low salt conditions, "6S" ER-FF activity was eluted in the fractions with a Stokes radius of around 47 A (fraction D' in Fig. 6B). This indicated that component B (Stokes radius, 18.5 A) is present as monomer in the presence of 0.4 M NaSCN, and undergoes self-association under the low salt conditions to form "6S" ER-FF (Stokes radius, 47 A). In contrast, the elution profile of "5S" ER-FF (Stokes radius, 37 A) was not influenced by the salt condition. This showed that component A does not undergo self-association and -dissociation.

When component A and component B were mixed (1:1 in "5S" ER-FF and "6S" ER-FF activities) and then subjected to gel filtration in the low salt (TEMA) conditions, "5S" ER-FF and "6S" ER-FF disappeared, and "8S" ER-FF (Stokes radius, 51 A) emerged (fraction B" in Fig. 6C). The reconstructed "5S" ER did not bind with "6S" ER-FF. However, reconstructed "6S" ER bound with "5S" ER-FF to form "8S" ER. Accordingly, it was assumed that in "8S" ER, component A is bound to vero-ER not directly, but via component B.

The molecular parameters and the molecular constitutions of the various forms of estrogen receptors and ER-binding factors are summarized in Table 1.

Table I. Molecular parameters of estrogen receptors and estrogen receptor-binding factors (17).

		Sedimentation coefficient (S)	Stokes radius (A)	Molecular weight	Frictional ratio
Vero-ER	(R)	4.5	44	82,000	1.53
"5S" ER-FF (component A)	(A)	3.8	37	58,000	1.45
Component B	(B)	1.8	18.5	13,700	1.17
"6S" ER-FF (hexamer of component B)	(B_6)	4.1	47	80,000	1.65
"7S" ER-FF	$(A)(B_2)$	4.3	49	87,000	1.67
"8S" ER-FF	$(A)(B_6)$	6.9	51	145,000	1.47
"5S" ER	$(A)(R)$	5.5	60	136,000	1.77
"6S" ER	$(B_6)(R)$	6.5	60	162,000	1.67
"7S" ER	$(A)(B_2)(R)$	7.0	61	175,000	1.65
"8S" ER	$(A)(B_6)(R)$	8.0	68	225,000	1.69
Secto-ER		4.5	35	65,000	1.32
"2.9S"ER fragment		2.9	24	29,000	1.18

d) Purification of basic estrogen receptor molecule (vero-ER) and estrogen receptor-binding factors (ERBFs) (18,20). Basic estrogen receptor (vero-ER) of the cytosol of porcine uterus was purified after the procedures shown in Fig. 7. In the first step, we purified ER in the "8S" form by hydrophobic chromatography on phenyl-Sepharose, by taking advantage of the relatively strong hydrophobicity of "8S" ER (Fig. 7A). "8S" ER thus obtained was then subjected to hydroxylapatite chromatography (Fig. 7B). The obtained ER sedimented at 6.5S ("6S" ER) under the low salt conditions. "8S" ER is a complex between "6S" ER and component A. Accordingly, component A could be removed by the hydroxylapatite chromatography. The "6S" ER was further purified by DEAE-cellulose chromatography (Fig. 7C). Finally, vero-ER (Stokes radius, 44 A) was separated from component B (Stokes radius, 18.5 A) by gel filtration on a Sephadex G-150 column under the high salt (0.4 M KCl) conditions (Fig. 7D). The purification of vero-ER was about 1,200-fold starting from the cytosol with a yield of 5 - 10%.

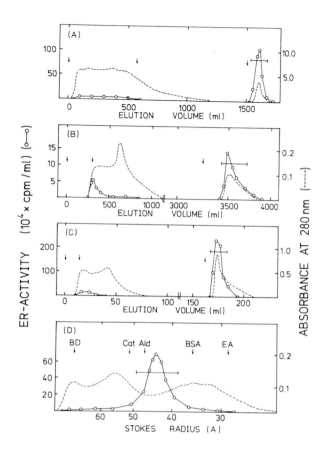

Fig. 7. Purification of vero-ER of the cytosol of porcine uterus (20).
(A) Phenyl-Sepharose column chromatography. Labeled cytosol was applied
(beginning at the first arrow) to the column, and then washed with P_{300}EMA
buffer containing 10% ethylene glycol (the second arrow). "8S" ER was
eluted with P_{50}EMA buffer containing 30% ethylene glycol (the third arrow).
Fractions pooled are indicated by the solid bar. (B) Hydroxylapatite column
chromatography. The "8S" ER fraction was applied to the column (the first
arrow), and then washed with P_{100}EMA buffer (the second arrow). "6S" ER was
eluted with P_{200}EMA buffer (the third arrow). Fractions pooled are indicated
by the solid bar. (C) DEAE-Cellulose column chromatography. The "6S" ER
fraction was applied to the column (the first arrow), and then washed with
P_{50}EMA buffer containing 0.1 M KCl (the second arrow). "6S" ER was eluted
with P_{50}EMA buffer containing 0.25 M KCl (the third arrow). Fractions
collected are indicated by the solid bar. (D) Gel filtration on Sephadex
G-150 column. The "6S" ER fraction from DEAE-cellulose was subjected to
gel filtration on Sephadex G-150 column. Fractions pooled are indicated by
the solid bar. The arrows indicate the elution peaks of the standards (see
the legend to Fig. 3).

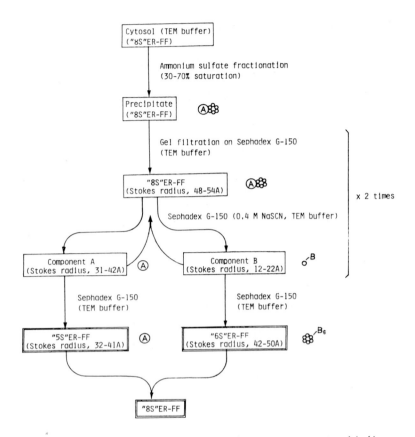

Fig. 8. The scheme for the purification of estrogen receptor-binding factors (18).

Estrogen receptor-binding factors (ERBFs) of the cytosol of porcine uterus were purified after the scheme shown in Fig. 8. The preparation of "8S" ER-FF obtained by the ammonium sulfate fractionation (30-70% saturation) of the cytosol was subjected to gel filtration on a Sephadex G-150 column in the low salt (TEM) buffer. "8S" ER-FF eluting in the fractions with a Stokes radius of around 51 A was collected. "8S" ER-FF was then subjected to gel filtration in the presence of 0.4 M NaSCN. Component A eluting in the fractions with a Stokes radius of around 37 A, and component B eluting in the fractions with a Stokes radius of around 18.5 A were collected. "8S" ER-FF was reconstructed from the obtained preparations of component A and component B. The gel filtrations in the form of "8S" ER-FF and in the dissociated forms of component A and component B were repeated again. Component A thus obtained was further purified by gel filtration in TEM buffer. The purification of component A was about 50-fold starting from the cytosol. Component B was further purified by taking advantage of the property to self-associate under the low salt conditions. The fraction of component B was subjected to gel filtration in the low salt (TEM) buffer. "6S" ER-FF [(component B)$_6$ (17)] eluted in the fractions with a Stokes radius of around 47 A was collected. The purification of component B was about 500-fold starting from the cytosol. "8S" ER-FF was reconstructed from the purified components A and B.

B. Estrogen receptor system of the nuclei of porcine uterus (25).

Steroid hormone receptors in the target cells are assumed to be translocated from the cytoplasm into the nucleus after binding with the hormones (see reviews 3-13). When the uterine slices were incubated with estradiol at elevated temperatures (37°C), cytosolic estrogen receptor (ER) declined with a concomitant increase in nuclear receptor (26-31). The cytosolic receptor and the nuclear receptor are assumed to be related to each other very closely. We then analyzed the ER system of the nuclei of porcine uterus based on the informations of the cytosolic receptor system. When the porcine uterine slices were incubated for 90 min at 37°C with [^{3}H]estradiol, approximately 10% of the cytosolic ER was translocated into the nucleus. About 60% of the ER translocated into the nuclei could be extracted with TEM buffer containing 0.4 M KCl. The extracted ER sedimented at 4.5S and 5.5S in the presence of 0.4 M KCl (Fig. 9A), and at 4.5S in the presence of 0.4 M NaSCN (Fig. 9B). When the nuclear extract was subjected to gel filtration in the presence of 0.4 M NaSCN, all of the ER activity was eluted in the fractions with a Stokes radius of 44 A. The molecular parameters of the nuclear ER in the presence of 0.4 M NaSCN coincided with those of vero-ER. These results suggested that vero-ER does not undergo proteolytic modification during the process of the translocation from the cytoplasm into the nucleus.

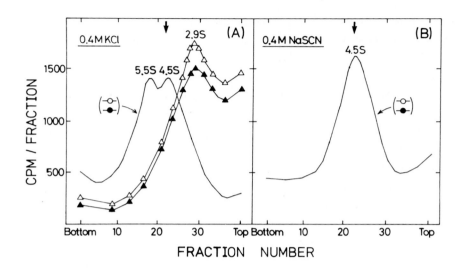

Fig. 9. Sedimentation analysis of the nuclear estrogen receptors (25). Sucrose gradient centrifugation was carried out either in TEM buffer containing 0.4 M KCl (A), or in TEM buffer containing 0.4 M NaSCN (B). The nuclear extract with 0.4 M KCl (—○—). The nuclear extract with 0.4 M KCl was incubated for 1 h at 25°C (—●—). The nuclear extract with 0.4 M NaSCN (—△—). The KCl-nuclear extract (6,000 cpm) was mixed with the NaSCN-nuclear extract (6,000 cpm), and then incubated for 1 h at 25°C (—▲—). The arrow marks the peak of ^{14}C-BSA (4.6S).

When the nuclear extract with 0.4 M KCl was incubated for 1 h at 25°C, the sedimentation pattern of ER did not change (Fig. 9). This showed that the nuclear extract with 0.4 M KCl was free from a protease which hydrolyzes vero-ER. When the nuclei of the uterine slices incubated with [^{3}H]estradiol as described above were extracted with 0.4 M NaSCN, all of the ER translocated into the nuclei through the incubation could be extracted. However, the extracted ER was not vero-ER, but "2.9S" ER fragment (Fig. 9A). When the nuclear extract with 0.4 M KCl (protease-free) was mixed with the NaSCN-extract, and incubated for 1 h at 25°C, all of the ER was proteolyzed into "2.9S" ER (Fig. 9A). These results showed that a nuclear protease which attacks vero-ER is extracted with 0.4 M NaSCN. In contrast to the cytosolic protease mentioned above, the nuclear protease was not inhibited by antipain.

The basic subunits of estrogen receptor-binding factors (ERBFs), component

A and component B, were further shown to be present also in the nuclei. The nuclei of fresh porcine uterus were extracted with TEM buffer containing 0.4 M NaSCN, and the extract was subjected to gel filtration on a Sephadex G-150 column in the presence of 0.4 M NaSCN (Fig. 10). The eluate was fractionated, removed of NaSCN, and assayed for ERBF activity. Fractions near the void volume (fraction A in Fig. 10B) contained a factor (aggregating factor, AF) which binds with vero-ER to form ER migrating to the bottom in the conventional sucrose gradient centrifugation under the low salt conditions. The AF activity was attributed to DNA, since it was destroyed by DNAse, but not by trypsin and RNase. Component A (Stokes radius, 37 A) and component B (Stokes radius, 18.5 A) were eluted in the respective fractions (fractions F and I in Fig. 10B) in accord with the results of the analysis of the cytosolic ERBFs. Component B underwent

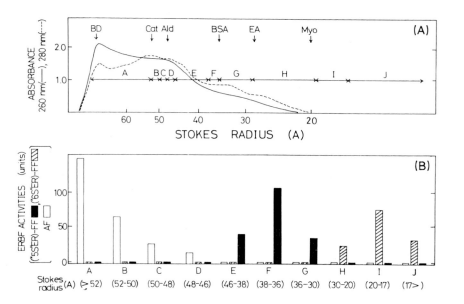

Fig. 10. Analysis of the nuclear estrogen receptor-binding factors (25). (A) The nuclei of fresh porcine uteri were extracted with 0.4 M NaSCN, and the nuclear extract was subjected to gel filtration on a Sephadex G-150 column (1.6 x 96 cm) in TEM buffer containing 0.4 M NaSCN. The eluate was devided into fractions A to J. Absorbance at 280 nm (-----) or at 260 nm (————). The arrows indicate the elution peaks of the standards (see the legend to Fig. 3). (B) Fractions A to J were concentrated to 0.5 ml, and then assayed for the estrogen receptor-binding factor activities.

self-association under the low salt conditions to give "6S" ER-FF. "6S"
ER-FF further formed complex with "5S" ER-FF to form "8S" ER-FF. "5S"
ER-FF and "6S" ER-FF form the nuclei cross-reacted with their counterparts
from the cytosol to form "8S" ER-FF. Components A and B extracted from the
nuclei amounted to approximately 25% of the level of these components in
the cytosol.

C. Molecular mechanism of the translocation of estrogen receptor from the
cytoplasm into the nucleus.

a) Molecular mechanism of "5S" estrogen receptor formation (17). Translocation of the receptor from the cytoplasm into the nucleus, as mentioned
above, did not take place when the incubation of the uterine slices with
[^{3}H]estradiol was carried out at 4°C instead of at 37°C (26-31). This
seemed to suggest the presence of a temperature-dependent step in the translocation of the receptor in the target cell (3,26,27,31). When the uterine
cytosol labeled with [^{3}H]estradiol was incubated at elevated temperatures
(25°C-30°C) in the high salt (0.4 M KCl) conditions, ER sedimented no
longer at 4.5S, but at 5.5S in the high salt (0.4 M KCl) conditions (3,26,
27,31). "5S" ER was also extracted from the uterine nuclei (32). Based
on these results, a two-step mechanism of the receptor translocation was
proposed (3,26,27,31). According to the proposal, cytoplasmic "4S" ER was
considered to be incapable to translocate into the nucleus. After binding
with the hormone, the cytoplasmic "4S" ER was assumed to undergo a temperature-dependent process (process of receptor activation) to be transformed
into "5S" ER. "5S" ER was assumed to be the activated receptor to translocate into the nucleus.

As mentioned above, vero-ER is bound to "8S" ER-FF via component B in the
fresh cytosol under the low salt conditions. "5S" ER was shown to be a
complex of vero-ER with component A. In the high salt (0.4 M KCl) conditions, "8S" ER dissociated into vero-ER and ERBF, while "5S" ER remained
stable. These results seemed to suggest that the liberation of component
A from binding with component B might be the rate-limiting step in the
process of "5S" ER formation. Accordingly, we compared the molecular forms

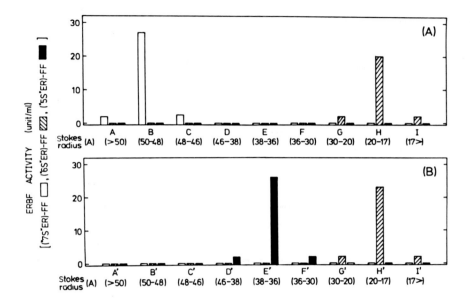

Fig. 11. Analysis of the molecular forms of the cytosolic estrogen receptor-binding factors in the presence of 0.4 M KCl at lower and higher temperatures (17). Gel filtration of the unlabeled cytosol was carried out on a Sephadex G-150 column in TEM buffer containing 0.4 M KCl at 4°C (A), and at 25°C (B).

of the cytosolic estrogen receptor-binding factors (ERBFs) in the high salt (0.4 M KCl) conditions at lower (4°C) and higher (25°C) temperatures. The unlabeled cytosol was subjected to gel filtration in TEM buffer containing 0.4 M KCl at 4°C and at 25°C respectively, and the eluates were assayed for ERBF activity. When the gel filtration was carried out at 4°C, "7S" ER-forming factor ("7S" ER-FF) which binds with vero-ER to form ER sedimenting at 7S ("7S" ER) under the low salt conditions was eluted in the fractions with a Stokes radius of around 49 Å (fraction B in Fig. 11A). Component B (basic unit of "6S" ER-FF) was further detected in the eluate (fraction H, in Fig. 11A). "7S" ER-FF was shown to be a 1:2 complex of component A and component B (17). These results showed that "8S" ER-FF is dissociated into "7S" ER-FF and component B in the high salt (0.4 M KCl) conditions at 4°C. As expected, when the gel filtration of the cytosol was carried out at 25°C (condition of activation of the cytosolic receptor), "7S" ER-FF disappeared, and component A and component B were eluted in the respective fractions (fractions E' and H', Fig. 11B). No other ERBF activity was observed in the eluate. These results supported strongly the assumption that under the activation conditions, component A is liberated from the binding with component B, and then forms stable complex with vero-ER to form "5S" ER during the subsequent process of cooling the cytosol (Fig. 12).

The sedimentation patterns of of the reconstructed estrogen receptors and the cytosolic estrogen receptors are shown in Fig. 13. "6S" ER, "7S" ER and "8S" ER are present only under the low salt conditions, and dissociated into vero-ER and ERBFs in the high salt (0.4 M KCl) conditions. "5S" ER is stable in the presence of 0.4 M KCl. Under the low salt conditions, reconstructed "5S" ER sedimented at 5.5S, however, the cytosolic "5S" ER migrated to the bottom fractions (Fig. 13A). When the reconstructed "5S" ER was mixed with the unlabeled cytosol and then analyzed by sucrose gradient centrifugation, ER migrated to the bottom fractions under the low salt conditions similar to the cytosolic "5S" ER (Fig. 13A). These results indi-

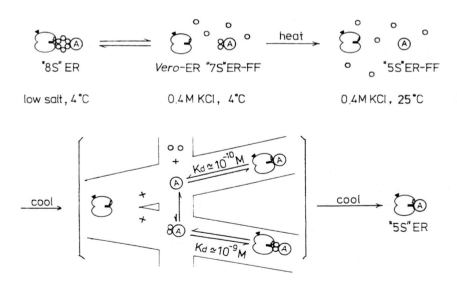

Fig. 12. Molecular mechanism of "5S" ER formation.

cated the presence of a cytosolic component (component C) which binds with "5S" ER under the low salt conditions.

b) <u>Mechanism of the nuclear translocation of estrogen receptor (33)</u>. It was expected that difference in the capabilities to translocate into the isolated nuclei might be observed among the various forms of estrogen receptor (ER) reflecting the regulating mechanism of the translocation of ER from the cytoplasm into the nucleus. Accordingly we compared the capabilities of various forms of ERs to translocate into the uterine nuclei in an <u>in vitro</u> system. The results are summarized in Table II. The amount of ER translocated into the nuclei was estimated by subtracting the amount of ER adsorbed on the nuclear envelopes from that of ER bound to the whole nuclei. Vero-ER·E (<u>vero</u>-ER bound with estradiol) possessed an outstandingly high capability to translocate into the nuclei as compared to the associated forms with ERBFs. This suggested strongly that ER is translocated from the

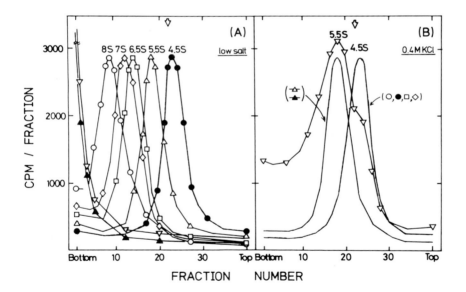

Fig. 13. Sedimentation analysis of cytosolic and reconstructed estrogen receptors (18). Sucrose gradient centrifugation was carried out in TEMA buffer (A), and in TEMA buffer containing 0.4 M KCl (B). <u>Vero</u>-ER (—●—). Reconstructed "8S" ER (—○—). Reconstructed "7S" ER (—◇—). Reconstructed "6S" ER (—□—). Reconstructed "5S" ER (—△—). Cytosolic "5S" ER (—▽—). Reconstructed "5S" ER + unlabeled cytosol (—▲—).

22

cytoplasm into the nucleus as vero-ER·E, and the translocation is suppressed through binding with ERBFs. Astonishingly, in contrast to the previous proposal (3,26,27,31), translocation of "5S" ER·E into the nuclei was nearly nil. We mentioned above that "5S" ER in the cytosol is complexed with component C under the low salt conditions. The complex, ("5S" ER·E)·(component C), possessed relatively high affinity for the nuclear envelopes, but did not translocate into the nuclei. The adsorption of the complex to the nuclear envelopes might have been taken as the translocation into the nuclei previously. The slight nuclear translocation of ER observed when "6S" ER·E and "8S" ER·E were incubated with the isolated nuclei is due to the liberation of vero-ER·E under the incubation condition caused by Mg^{2+} added to the incubation medium to protect the nuclei (34). The remarkable effect of Mg^{2+} on the dissociation of vero-ER from ERBFs is mentioned in the following section. The partially proteolyzed ERs (secto-ER·E and "3.8S" ER·E),

Table II. Capabilities of various forms of estrogen receptors to translocate into the porcine nuclei in an in vitro system (33).

$ER \cdot [^3H]E$	$ER \cdot [^3H]E$ bound to the nuclei	$ER \cdot [^3H]E$ adsorbed to the nuclear envelopes	$ER \cdot [^3H]E$ translocated into the nuclei	Translocation
	fmol	fmol	fmol	%
Vero-ER·$[^3H]E$	226	35	191	75
"5S" ER·$[^3H]E$	65	45	20	8
"6S" ER·$[^3H]E$	110	37	73	29
"8S" ER·$[^3H]E$	100	40	60	24
("5S" ER·$[^3H]E$)·(component C)	133	110	23	9
Secto-ER·$[^3H]E$	85	68	17	7
"3.8S" ER·$[^3H]E$	74	55	19	8

[a] ER·$[^3H]E$ (250 fmol) was incubated with the nuclei or nuclear envelopes in 0.32 M sucrose - 1 mM MgCl$_2$ - 10 mM Tris-HCl - 0.25 mM antipain, pH 8.0, for 3 h at 4°C.

[b] obtained by subtracting the amount of ER adsorbed to the nuclear envelopes from that of ER bound to the nuclei.

which no longer interact with ERBFs, did not translocate into the nuclei.
These results indicated that the binding site of vero-ER to ERBFs play
important roles in the regulation of the translocation of ER from the cytoplasm into the nucleus. It was assumed that the cytosolic protease might
reduce the hormone-sensitivity of the target cell through diminishing the
amount of ER capable to translocate into the nucleus.

D. Regulation of the reactivity of basic estrogen receptor molecule
(vero-ER) with estrogen receptor-binding factors.

a) Strongly hydrophobic domain of basic estrogen receptor molecule (vero-ER)
(35). Vero-ER was shown to possess an extremely strong hydrophobic domain,
which is concealed through binding with estrogen receptor-binding factors
(ERBFs). Vero-ER freed from ERBFs was bound to a phenyl-Sepharose column
under the low salt (TEMA) conditions, and could not be eluted even with
TEMA buffer containing 50% ethylene glycol (Fig. 14A). Most of the strongly
hydrophobic proteins of the cytosol are eluted from the column with the
low salt buffer in the presence of 50% ethylene glycol. To elute vero-ER
from the column, it was necessary to utilize ethanol as a polarity-reducing
agent. Vero-ER could be eluted quantitatively from the column with TEMA
buffer containing 30% ethanol (Fig. 14A). Dissociation of [^{3}H]estradiol
from the receptor was negligible during the process of the elution from
phenyl-Sepharose.

In contrast, reconstructed "5S" ER, "6S" ER and "8S" ER passed straight
through the phenyl-Sepharose column in TEMA buffer (Fig. 14B). This showed
that the strongly hydrophobic domain of vero-ER is concealed in the complexes of vero-ER with ERBFs. The association and dissociation of vero-ER
with ERBFs is regulated mainly by ionic forces. As mentioned above,
vero-ER is dissociated from ERBFs under the high salt (0.4 M KCl) conditions
favorable for the hydrophobic interactions. Accordingly, it is assumed
that the strong hydrophobic domain and the binding sites with ERBFs occupy
different positions on vero-ER molecule.

Both secto-ER and "3.8S" ER passed straight through the column under the

24

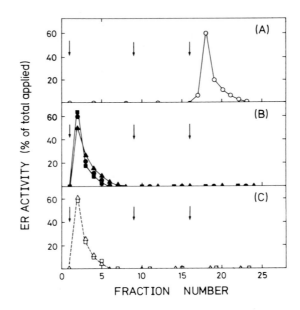

Fig. 14. Analysis of hydrophobicity of estrogen receptors with a phenyl-Sepharose column (35). 1.6 x 10^5 cpm of estrogen receptors in 1 ml of TEMA buffer were applied (beginning at the first arrow) to 0.2 ml columns equilibrated with TEMA buffer. The columns were washed 5-times with 1 ml TEMA buffer containing 50% ethylene glycol (the second arrow). The columns were finally washed 5-times with 1 ml of TEMA buffer containing 30% ethanol (the third arrow). (A) Vero-ER (—O—). (B) Reconstructed "5S" ER (—■—); reconstructed "6S" ER (—▲—); reconstructed "8S" ER (—●—). (C) Secto-ER (--△--); "3.8S" ER (--□--).

low salt conditions (Fig. 14C), indicating that the strong hydrophobic domain of vero-ER was totally destroyed by the endogenous protease. The concomitant removal of the strong hydrophobic domain and the binding sites with ERBFs suggested that they occupy each other close positions on vero-ER molecule.

b) Regulation of association and dissociation of basic estrogen receptor molecule (vero-ER) with estrogen receptor-binding factors (22,24). The affinity of vero-ER with ERBFs as estimated from the apparent dissociation constant (Kd) values [2.5 x 10^{-9} M ("8S" ER-FF); 3.0 x 10^{-9} M ("6S" ER-FF); 2.6 x 10^{-10} M ("5S" ER-FF)] is very high in TEMA buffer (Fig. 15). The affinity of "5S" ER-FF for vero-ER is one order higher than the affinity of

"6S" ER-FF or "8S" ER-FF. The stronger affinity of "5S" ER-FF to vero-ER is an important basis of "5S" ER formation from "8S" ER as mentioned in the previous section.

Astonishingly, Mg^{2+} at very low concentrations influenced significantly the interaction of vero-ER with ERBFs. The apparent Kd values of vero-ER for ERBFs [3.5 x 10^{-8} M ("8S" ER-FF); 6.0 x 10^{-8} M ("6S" ER-FF); 2.7 x 10^{-9} M ("5S" ER-FF)] observed in the presence of 1 mM Mg^{2+} were all increased over 10 times as compared with in the absence of Mg^{2+} (Fig. 15).

In Fig. 16 is shown the effect of Mg^{2+} on the translocation of vero-ER into the isolated nuclei. In the absence of ERBFs, vero-ER was translocated into the nuclei almost quantitatively independent of the concentration of Mg^{2+}. This indicated that the translocation of vero-ER dissociated from ERBFs is not influenced by Mg^{2+}. As mentioned above, ERBFs inhibited the nuclear translocation of vero-ER under the conventional assay conditions (containing 1 mM Mg^{2+} for the protection of the nuclei). The inhibitory effects of ERBFs on the nuclear translocation of vero-ER were reduced dras-

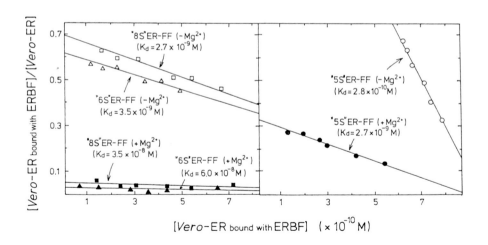

Fig. 15. Scatchard analysis of the affinity of vero-ER with estrogen receptor-binding factors in the absence or presence of 1 mM $MgCl_2$ (24).

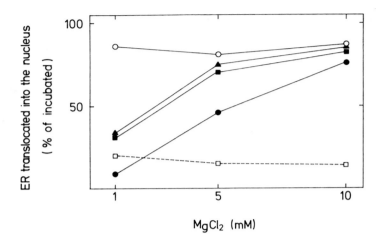

Fig. 16. Effect of Mg^{2+} on the nuclear translocation of vero-ER·E in the absence and presence of estrogen receptor-binding factors (24). Vero-ER·E (200 fmol) (—O—); vero-ER·E (200 fmol) + "5S" ER-forming factor (3 units) (—●—); vero-ER·E (200 fmol) + "6S" ER-forming factor (3 units) (—▲—); vero-ER·E (200 fmol) + "8S" ER-forming factor (3 units) (—■—); labeled cytosol (--□--).

tically by increasing the concentration of Mg^{2+} in the incubation medium. In the presence of 5 mM Mg^{2+}, the inhibitory effects of "8S" ER-FF and "6S" ER-FF on the translocation of vero-ER into the nuclei were nearly nil. The inhibitory effect of "5S" ER-FF on the nuclear translocation of vero-ER disappeared completely in the presence of 10 mM Mg^{2+}. These results showed that Mg^{2+} promoted the dissociation of vero-ER from ERBFs and restore the capability to translocate into the nuclei. As mentioned above, vero-ER in the uterine cytosol is complexed with "8S" ER-FF in the low salt conditions when Mg^{2+} is absent. In the presence of Mg^{2+} (10 mM), however, the cytosolic receptor sedimented not at 8S, but migrated to the bottom fractions (24). Purified vero-ER sedimented at 4.5S in the presence of Mg^{2+} (10 mM) (24). Accordingly it was assumed that, in the cytosol, vero-ER dissociated from "8S" ER-FF in the presence of Mg^{2+} is bound to other macromolecule under the low salt conditions. In accord with the assumption, the promoting effect of Mg^{2+} on the translocation of the cytosolic receptor into the nuclei was not evident (Fig. 16). Anyhow, Mg^{2+} is expected to play important roles in the action mechanism of estrogen.

Discussion

In this chapter, we presented new aspects on the molecular organization of the estrogen receptor system. In the early 1970s, Mueller et al. proposed presciently that "8S" ER is a complex of basic "4S" ER, which is common to different aggregates, and a subunit which does not bind estradiol (4,36-38). By incubating the labeled cytosol at higher temperatures they observed not "5S" ER formation, but formation of modified "4S" ER which no longer gives "8S" ER (4, 36-38). They considered that the basic "4S" ER interacts with a cytosolic factor which is dialyzable and ether soluble to form modified "4S" ER (4,37,38). The possibility of the interaction of lipophilic lower molecular components with the receptor remains, but the more frequently encountered modification of the basic "4S" ER into modified "4S" ER is caused by the endogenous protease.

Puca et al. reported for the first time the proteolytic modification of estrogen receptor by the endogenous Ca^{2+}-requiring protease (39). They further carried out detailed analysis of the estrogen receptor system by utilizing NaSCN to inhibit aggregation and dissociation of receptor (40). They proposed that "2.8S" ER is the basic subunit of estrogen receptor, and that "4S" ER (dimer), "5S" ER (tetramer), and "8S" ER (octamer) are formed through the self-association of the basic subunit (40). Modification of receptor by Ca^{2+}-not requiring protease takes place, however, in the presence of NaSCN. The disappearance of the property of the cytosolic receptor to aggregate and dissociate through the NaSCN-treatment (40) is attributed to the proteolytic destruction of the binding site of the native receptor with receptor-binding factors. The "2.8S" ER which they observed in the presence of NaSCN, and proposed to be the basic subunit of estrogen receptor (40) is obtained from the proteolyzed receptor through dissociating at the nick by the chaotropic salt.

Sherman et al. utilized antipain (21) for the first time to protect steroid hormone receptors from the endogenous proteases (41-43). They reported detailed analysis of the proteolyzed receptor (mero-receptor, "2-3S" receptor) and the relation to the native receptor (41-43). The concentration (50 mM) of the protease inhibitor utilized in their studies, however, might be too high to be applied widely for the analysis of the receptor system.

Molecular organization of steroid hormone receptor systems might be similar
to each other (44). We showed that the oviduct progesterone receptor system
is similar to the uterine estrogen receptor system (19). Colvard & Wilson
reported "8S" androgen receptor-promoting factor which binds with "4S"
receptor to form "8S" receptor (45). Joab et al. reported that "8S" progesterone receptor contains a non hormone binding protein component which is
common to "8S" receptors for other steroid hormones (46). Receptor-binding
factors might be common for the receptors of different steroid hormones.
It was proposed in various reports from O'Malley's laboratory that "6S"
progesterone receptor is a complex of two different basic "4S" receptors
(receptor A and receptor B) (7, 47, 48). It might be possible that receptor
A and receptor B suffered proteolytic modifications during the process of
the purification. Reconstruction of "6S" progesterone receptor from receptors A and B has not yet been accomplished.

The results presented in this chapter suggested strongly that vero-ER with
the free binding sites to ER-binding factors and open hydrophobic domain
is the activated receptor which translocates from the cytoplasm into the
nucleus. The temperature-dependent process for the activation of the receptor (3,26,27,31) is assumed to be necessary to dissociate vero-ER from
ER-binding factors. King & Greene reported the exclusive localization of
estrogen receptor by utilizing monoclonal antibodies generated against
estrogen receptor (49). It appeares that they utilized proteolyzed receptor
for   the production of the antibodies. The possibility remains that
their antibodies recognized proteolyzed receptors, but failed to recognize
native receptor. Proteolyzed receptor is easily detected in the uterine
nuclei (25), but not in the fresh cytosol (14,18,41). Further detailed
study would be needed to solve the problem.

References

1. Glascock, R.F., Hoekstra, W.G.: Biochem. J. 72, 673-682 (1959).
2. Jensen, E.V., Jacobson, H.I.: In: Biological Activities of Steroids in

Relation to Cancer. 161-178 (G. Pincus & E.P. Vollmer Eds.), Academic Press, New York 1960.

3. Jensen, E.V., DeSombre, E.R.: Ann. Rev. Biochem. 41, 203-230 (1972).

4. Mueller, G.C., Vonderhaar, B., Kim, U.H., Mahieu, L.M.: Rec. Prog. Horm. Res. 28, 1-49 (1972).

5. Gorski, J., Gannon, F.: Annu. Rev. Physiol. 38, 425-450 (1976).

6. Yamamoto, K.R., Alberts, B.M.: Annu. Rev. Biochem. 45, 721-746 (1976).

7. Schrader, W.T., O'Malley, B.W.: In: Receptors and Hormone Action. 189-224 (B.W. O'Malley & L. Birnbaumer Eds.), Academic Press, New York 1978.

8. Bualieu, E.E.: Klin. Wschr. 56, 683-695 (1978).

9. Clark, J.H., Peck, Jr.E.J.: Female Sex Steroids, Receptors and Function. Springer Verlag, Berlin 1979.

10. Baxter, J.D., Rousseau, G.G.: In: Glucocorticoid Hormone Action. 1-24 (J.D. Baxter & G.G. Rousseau Eds.), Springer Verlag, Berlin 1979.

11. Katzenellenbogen, B.S.: Ann. Rev. Physiol. 42, 17-35 (1980).

12. Kanazir, D.T.: In: Hormonally Active Brain Peptides. 181-214 (McKerns & Pantic Eds.), Plenum Publishing Corporation, New York 1982.

13. Moudgil, V.K.: In: Principles in Recepterology. 273-379 (M.K. Agarwal Ed.), Walter de Gruyter, Berlin 1983.

14. Murayama, A., Fukai, F., Hazato, T., Yamamoto, T.: J. Biochem. 88, 955-961 (1980).

15. Murayama, A., Fukai, F., Hazato, T., Yamamoto, T.: J. Biochem. 88, 963-968 (1980).

16. Murayama, A., Fukai, F., Yamamoto, T.: J. Biochem. 88, 969-976 (1980).

17. Murayama, A., Fukai, F., Yamamoto, T.: J. Biochem. 88, 1457-1466 (1980).

18. Murayama, A., Fukai, F.: J. Biochem. 89, 1829-1837 (1981).

19. Murayama, A., Fukai, F., Yamamoto, T.: J. Biochem. 88, 1305-1315 (1980).

20. Murayama, A., Fukai, F., Murachi, T.: J. Biochem. 95, 1697-1704 (1984).

21. Suda, H., Aoyagi, T., Hamada, M., Takeuchi, T., Umezawa, H.: J. Antibiotics 25, 263-266 (1972).

22. Murayama, A., Fukai, F.: J. Biochem. 92, 2039-2042 (1982).

23. Scatchard, G.: Ann. N.Y. Acad. Sci. 51, 660-672 (1949).

24. Fukai, F., Murayama, A.: J. Biochem. 95, 1227-1230 (1984).

25. Murayama, A., Fukai, F.: J. Biochem. 90, 823-832 (1981).

26. Jensen, E.V., Suzuki, T., Kawashima, T. Stumpf, W.E., Jungblut, P.W., DeSombre, E.R.: Proc. Natl. Acad. Sci. U.S. 59, 632-638 (1968).

27. Gorski, J., Toft, D., Shamala, G., Smith, D., Notides, A.: Rec. Prog. Horm. Res. 24, 45-80 (1968).

28. Giannopoulos, G., Gorski, J.: J. Biol. Chem. 246, 2530-2536 (1971).

29. Stancel, G.M., Leung, K.M.T., Gorski, J.: Biochemistry 12, 2137-2141 (1973).

30. Rochefort, H., Baulieu, E.E: Endocrinology <u>84</u>, 108-116 (1969).

31. Jensen, E.V., DeSombre, E.R.: Science 182, 126-134 (1973).

32. Puca, G.A., Bresciani, F.: Nature <u>218</u>, 967-969 (1968).

33. Murayama, A., Fukai, F.: J. Biochem. <u>94</u>, 511-519 (1983).

34. Tata, J.R.: In: Methods in Enzymology Vol. 31, 253-262 (S. Fleisher & L. Packer Eds.), Academic Press, New York 1974.

35. Murayama, A., Fukai, F.: FEBS Letters 158, 255-258 (1983).

36. Vonderhaar, B.K., Kim, U.H., Mueller, G.C.: Biochim. Biophys. Acta <u>208</u>, 517-527 (1970).

37. Vonderhaar, B.K., Kim, U.H., Mueller, G.C.: Biochim. Biophys. Acta <u>215</u>, 125-133 (1970).

38. Mueller, G.C., Cowan, R.A.: Adv. Biosciences <u>15</u>, 55-76 (1974).

39. Puca, G.A., Nola, E., Sica, V., Bresciani, F.: J. Biol. Chem. <u>252</u>, 1358-1366 (1977).

40. Sica, V., Nola, E., Puca, G.A., Bresciani, F.: Biochemistry <u>15</u>, 1915-1923 (1976).

41. Sherman, M.R., Pickerling, L.A., Rollwagen, F.M., Miller, L.K.: Fed. Proc. Fed. Am. Soc. Exp. Biol. <u>37</u>, 167-173 (1978).

42. Sherman, M.R., Berzilai, D., Pine, P.R., Tuazon, Fe.B.: In: Steroid Hormone Receptor Systems. 357-375 (W.W. Leavitt & J.H. Clark Eds.), Plenum Publishing Corporation, New York 1979.

43. Sherman, M.R., Tuazon, F.B., Miller, L.K.: Endocrinology <u>106</u>, 1715-1727 (1980).

44. Hazato, T., Murayama, A.: Biochem. Biophys. Res. Commun. <u>98</u>, 488-493 (1981).

45. Colvard, D.S., Wilson, E.M.: Endocrinology <u>109</u>, 496-504 (1981).

46. Joab, I., Radanyi, C., Renoir, M., Buchou, T., Catelli, M.G., Binart, N., Mester, J., Baulieu, E.E.: Nature <u>308</u>, 850-853 (1984).

47. Schrader, W.T., Kuhn, R.W., O'Malley, B.W.: J. Biol. Chem. <u>252</u>, 299-307 (1977).

48. Coty, W.A., Schrader, W.T., O'Malley, B.W.: J. Steroid Biochem. <u>10</u>, 1-12 (1979).

49. King, W.J., Greene, G.L.: Nature <u>307</u>, 745-747 (1984).

Acknowledgements

This review is dedicated to the memory of the late Prof. Tadashi Yamamoto (1917-1981) who inspired me with his profound insights.

I thank Dr. F. Fukai for his help in the preparation of this manusctipt.

STRUCTURE, PROPERTIES AND SUBCELLULAR LOCALIZATION OF THE CHICK OVIDUCT
PROGESTERONE RECEPTOR.

Jan Mester, Jean-Marie Gasc, Thierry Buchou, Jack-Michel Renoir, Irène
Joab, Christine Radanyi, Nadine Binart, Maria-Grazia Catelli, Etienne-Emile
Baulieu
INSERM U 33, Lab. Hormones, 94270 Bicêtre, France

I. Introduction

Although a considerable effort has been invested in the study of steroid
hormone receptors since their discovery in the early sixties, it is only
now that data concerning their primary structure as well as subunit
composition are becoming available. This breakthrough is to be thanked for
mainly to the progress that has been achieved in the techniques of
purification of these proteins which are not only relatively unstable, but
also present at low concentrations in target tissues and having a tendency
to aggregate under a variety of conditions. Stabilisation of the
non-activated receptor forms by molybdate has helped to surmount the
problem posed by tendency to form aggregates, and design of suitable
affinity derivatives makes it possible to obtain high purity preparations
of several kinds of steroid hormone receptors. Antibodies against such
purified receptor preparations have been raised and used in
immunohistological studies. In this chapter, we shall review our recent
results concerning the chick oviduct progesterone receptor.

II. Background

1)   Chick oviduct as a target tissue for progesterone.
     The term "progesterone" is in fact a misnomer insofar as the chicken

is concerned as there is no gestation to maintain. However, progesterone is secreted during the egg-laying cycle of the hen and is apparently important in its regulation. Their effects in the oviduct fall roughly into two categories. First progesterone is an inducer of synthesis of several of the egg white proteins. For this, the (immature) chick has to be first exposed to estrogen priming which leads to development of the tubular glands in the magnum portion of the oviduct. After withdrawal of estrogen, the tubular gland cells respond to progesterone by synthesis of large quantities of egg white proteins, mainly ovalbumin, conalbumin, ovomucoid and lysozyme. A secondary treatment of estrogen-primed, withdrawn chick with estrogen has a similar effect on the synthesis of these proteins in the tubular glands, and induces, in addition, tissue growth. The effects of progesterone and estrogen on the egg white protein synthesis are at least partly additive (see reviews 1, 2). Second, progesterone antagonizes certain of the estrogen effects, for instance tissue growth and differentiation of the immature oviduct (3, 4), as well as growth of the "withdrawn" oviduct tissue induced by estrogen treatment (5-7). In terms of specific protein synthesis, progesterone has often a transient "antiestrogen" effect : during a short period of time, for instance, it retards the estrogen-induced increase in the rate of conalbumin synthesis (6, 8). Similar observations hold also for the estrogen $\pm$ progesterone-induced changes in DNA-polymerase activity (6). Induction of ornithine decarboxylase, an enzyme implicated in polyamine synthesis and known to be active in growing tissues (9) is another estrogen effect (10) inhibited by progesterone (11). These observations are correlated with, and perhaps a consequence of, the decrease in the nuclear (and total cellular) estrogen receptor content of the oviduct cells after treatment with estrogen and progesterone as compared to estrogen alone. For more information on the effects of progesterone in the chicken oviduct, see the reviews cited above (1, 2) and references therein.

2)   Early studies on the chick oviduct progesterone receptor.

Since the first report of Sherman et al. (12) it is known that the
high affinity progesterone-binding protein of the chick oviduct is
recovered in the high-speed supernatant of the tissue homogenate.
Consequently, it has been assumed that, as the other steroid hormone
receptors, also this one is a cytoplasmic protein. (This assumption is
at present questioned : see section V).

Already in the immature chick oviduct, progesterone receptor is at
levels of the order of 10^3 molecules per cell as determined by
hormone binding (13), assuming one progesterone binding site/protein
molecule. Estrogen priming leads to tissue differentiation so that
eventually some 90 % of the cells become organized in tubular glands ;
at this stage, there are some $5-7.10^4$ progesterone binding
sites/cell. Estrogen withdrawal is followed by a progressive but not
rapid loss of the progesterone receptor : while the tissue regresses
from 1-2 g to about 100 mg after 2 weeks and remains without further
change, the progesterone receptor concentration is approximately
halved at 2 weeks of estrogen withdrawal and again after the following
2-3 weeks (13). Secondary estrogen administration induces again an
augmentation of the progesterone receptor level, probably by the novo
synthesis, after an   6 h lag (14).

Treatment in vivo with progesterone "translocates" only a relatively
small fraction of the total cellular progesterone receptor to the
nucleus. While this "translocation" may not imply a shift from the
cytoplasm to the nuclear compartment in the anatomical sense, the data
reflect the fact that a portion of the total receptor population has
become associated with the nucleus sufficiently tightly to resist
solubilisation by the (low-salt) homogenization buffer. The proportion
of the "nuclear" receptor decreases during the hours following
progesterone administration and by 6 h it differs little from that in
untreated controls).

Gel filtration studies suggested heterogeneitey of the chick oviduct
progesterone receptor : as many as five species differing by their

Stokes radii (R_s) were identified and numbered I – V, in decreasing order (15). The largest (form I) is probably a mixture of a "native" (non-activated ; see further) receptor and heterogeneous aggregates. The two following species, on the other hand, are authentic progestin-binding proteins in monomeric state. They can be easier resolved by ion-exchange chromatography and are now currently referred to a "subunit A" (= form III) and "subunit B" (= form II). Their identification was subsequently made possible by the use of a photolabile progestin R 5020, which can be covalently attached to the binding proteins by exposure to UV light (16). Their molecular weights were found to be 108K (B) and 79K (A), respectively, by SDS-PAGE analysis (see 17, 18 for review). Finally, the forms IV and V turned out to be fragments formed from the A and/or B subunits by action of an endogenous, Ca^{2+}-activated protease (19, 20).

II. Definition of "native" and "activated" ("transformed") receptors.

The ^{3}H-progesterone-receptor complexes formed in the soluble fraction of the homogenate of chick oviduct tissue, at low ionic strength and at low temperature, display the characteristics of what has been termed "native", i.e. non-activated form. This means that they do not bind to isolated nuclei or to their components (chromatin, DNA), nor to certain synthetic polyanions (phosphocellulose ; ATP-agarose). Within < 1 h at incubation at > 20°C or at high ionic strength (> 0.3) the receptor-hormone complexes acquire the capacity to bind to the above-mentioned solid supports or structures, although the binding is frequently incomplete (21, 22). This change of properties has been initially termed "activation" since it is presumed that binding to the nuclear components implies that the receptor is active in mediating hormonal effects on gene expression. Until present, no in vitro test of receptor "activity" is available and therefore "activation" remains a concept based on hypothesis rather than facts. It is also to be printed out that the binding of receptors to the cell nucleus does not always lead to hormonal effects (for ex. in the case of antiestrogen-estrogen receptor complexes of the chick oviduct, 23, 24).

As a result of "activation", physico-chemical properties of the progesterone receptor are altered : the hormone receptor complexes become smaller as reflected by a change of their sedimentation coefficient (from 8S to 4S) and R_s (from 7.7 nm to 5.2 nm) and the binding of the hormone is tightened, leading to a longer half-time of dissociation (25, 27). Acquisition of affinity for nuclei, chromatin, DNA and the change of physico-chemical properties of the chick oviduct progesterone receptor have always been observed to occur simultaneously. An alternative term, "transformation", is preferred by some authors (19) to cover the ensemble of the changes on receptor characteristics (see also section IV.4).

III. Methods

All methods are described in detail in the articles cited. The procedure we have developed for purification of the different forms of the progesterone receptor are schematically represented by a flowchart (Fig. 1). Affinity chromatography was performed by loading the high-speed supernatant of the homogenate of estrogen-stimulated (immature) chick oviducts onto a column of NADAC-Sepharose (28) ; the gel was washed sequentially with buffers containing KCl and urea and eluted with 2 μM ^{3}H-progestin (29, 31). The eluates were then subjected to fractionation on DEAE-cellulose where elution was carried out by applying a continuous or discontinuous KCl gradient.

The choice of buffers throughout purification was dictated by the forms of receptor desired to obtain. The non-activated form had to be protected by including 20 mM Na_2MoO_4 ; in addition, the concentration of urea had to be kept < 2.5 M during the affinity gel washing procedure since above this limit, a significant proportion of the receptor becomes transformed to 4S (32). To purify the "activated" receptor, KCl (0.3 M) was added to the cytosol > 1 h prior to loading onto the affinity native (26, 30). When the receptor was to be crosslinked with glutaraldehyde, phosphate buffers were used instead of Tris.

Antibodies raised against the progesterone receptor (polyclonal IgG-G, IgG-RB and monoclonal BF4) are characterized in Table I and references 33, 35.

Fig. 1 : Progesterone receptor purification flow-chart (refs. 28, 31).

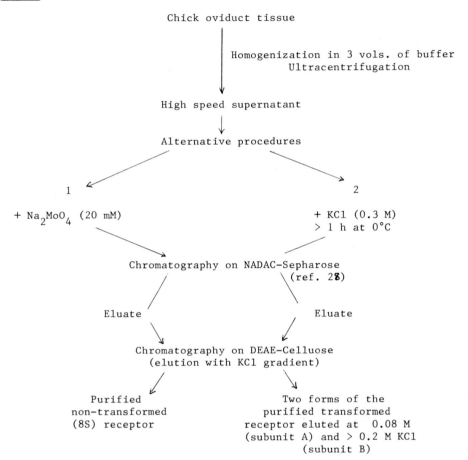

Chick oviduct tissue

Homogenization in 3 vols. of buffer
Ultracentrifugation

High speed supernatant

Alternative procedures

1

2

+ Na$_2$MoO$_4$ (20 mM)

+ KCl (0.3 M)
> 1 h at 0°C

Chromatography on NADAC-Sepharose
(ref. 28)

Eluate

Eluate

Chromatography on DEAE-Celluose
(elution with KCl gradient)

Purified
non-transformed
(8S) receptor

Two forms of the
purified transformed
receptor eluted at 0.08 M
(subunit A) and > 0.2 M KCl
(subunit B)

Immunohistological experiments were performed with paraffin sections of the tissue which had been fixed by one of the following procedures (36) :
- Bouin's fluid for 60 to 80 min, followed by several washes in 70 % ethanol.
- Carnoy's fluid for 60 to 80 min, followed by several washed in absolute ethanol.

- Glutaraldehyde (0,5 %) in 0,1 M Soerensen buffer pH 7.4 for 90 min, followed by several washed in either Soerensen buffer or PBS.
- Absolute ethanol + 1 % acetic acid for 60 to 80 min, followed by several washed in absolute ethanol.

Dehydration was made in graded ethanol when needed, and terminated in 1-butanol before embedding in paraffin. For antibody reactions, the sections were deparaffinized, rehydrated and rinsed with PBS. They were then incubated first in 3 % non-immune serum of the animal species in which the second antibody was raised. The excess of serum was removed and the sections were incubated with the first antibody (90 to 120 min).

After washing in PBS, sections received the second biotinylated antibody (dilution 1:400 ; 30 min). The second antibody was removed by washing with PBS and complexed with avidin-biotin-peroxidase (30 min). After washing, the peroxidase activity was revealed by 3-3'-diaminobenzidin tetrahydrochloride (DAB) (0.5 mg/ml) in presence of 0.01 % H_2O_2, in pH 7.6 Tris buffer. Sections were then rinsed, dehydrated and mounted.

TABLE I : Antibodies against the chick oviduct progesterone receptor (PR)

Antibody	Raised against	Non-denaturing conditions			Blots after SDS-PAGE		
		8S-PR	A subunit	B subunit	A subunit	B subunit	90kDa
IgG-G3 (polyclonal) (ref. 32)	8S-PR	+	+	+	+	+	+
IgG-RB (polyclonal) (ref. 33)	B subunit	+	+	+	+	+	-
BF4 (monoclonal) (ref. 34)	8S-PR	+	-	-	-	-	+

IV. Composition of the "native" and "activated" receptor forms.

1) Detection of receptor subunits.

The polypeptide chains present in the different forms of the chick
oviduct progesterone receptor were identified and their relative
proportions estimated. For the A and B subunits, this was a straightforward task, since these appear to be monomers as concluded from the
close agreement between the M_r values determined by SDS-PAGE and
those caculated from the hydrodynamic parameters measured under
non-denaturing conditions (Table II). In addition, the B subunit could
be obtained near to 100 % pure on the basis of its specific binding

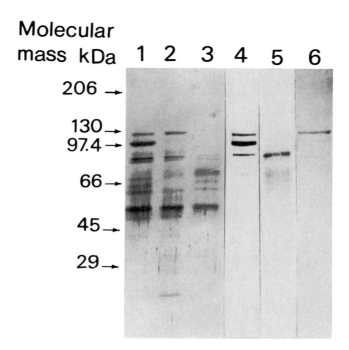

Fig. 2 : SDS-PAGE of purified progesterone receptor (18, 31). Lanes 1, 3
and 4 : molybdate-stabilized receptor ; lanes 2, 5 and 6 : KC1-"activated"
receptor. Samples in lanes 1-3 are eluates of affinity columns (in lanes 3,
"mock" purification in the presence of 2 μM unlabeled progesterone) ; lanes
4-6 show the composition respectively of the 8S, A and B receptor
containing fractions of DEAE-cellulose purified affinity column eluates.

TABLE II : Characteristics of the "native" and "activated" forms of the chick oviduct PR (18).

	Native PR	Activated PR	
		Subunit A	Subunit B
Sedimentation coefficient ($S_{20,w}$)	7.9S	3.6S	4.2S
Stokes radius (R_s)	7.1 nm (7.7 nm)[a]	4.6 nm	6.1 nm
Frictional ratio	1.55	1.5	1.77
M_r calculated from $s_{20,w}$ and R_s	245kDa (265kDa)	72kDa	111kDa
M_r calculated from SDS-PAGE data	270kDa[b]	79kDa	110kDa
Elution from DEAE-Sephacel (M KCl)	0.1 (form I) 0.16 (form II)	0.08	0.2
Binding to polyanions :[c]			
Phosphocellulose	−	+	+
DNA-cellulose	−	+	±
Heparin-agarose	+	+	±
ATP-sepharose	−	+	+
M_r of polypeptides detected in SDS-PAGE :			
(1) by antibodies :			
Polyclonal IgG-G3	110kDa ; 90kDa ; 79kDa	79kDa	110kDa
Polyclonal IgG-RB	110kDa ; 79kDa	79kDa	110kDa
Monoclonal BF4	90kDa	none	none
(2) by affinity labelling	110kDa ; 79kDa	79kDa	110kDa

[a] Found with PR in crude cytosol.
[b] PR cross-linked with glutaraldehyde.
[c] +, strong binding ; ±, weak binding ; −, very weak or no binding.

capacity assuming one hormone binding site per molecule. Such preparations contained a single protein detectable by staining in SDS-PAGE (30).

The situation is more complex as far as "native" progesterone receptor is concerned (18, 31, 37). In this case, purification by affinity chromatography followed by DEAE-cellulose yields preparations that are

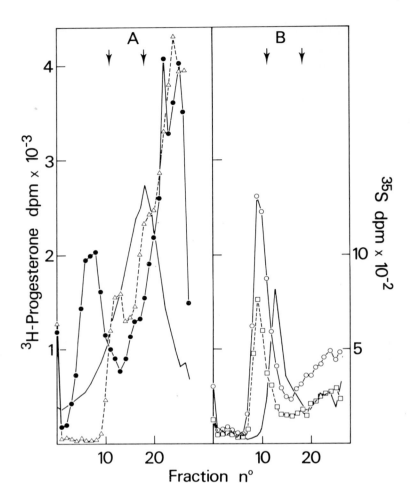

Fig. 3 : Interaction of the non-transformed progesterone receptor with the BF4 antibody (38). The molybdate-stabilized receptor purified by affinity chromatography was incubated either with BF4 (●), or with an equivalent fraction of the control myeloma culture medium (Δ) (panel A), or with ^{35}S-labeled BF4 (o) panel B). A portion of the affinity-purified, molybdate stabilized receptor was transformed by DEAE cellulose chromatography in the absence of molybdate. Fraction eluted with 0.25 M KCl was incubated with ^{35}S-BF4 (□; panel B), or with BF4 (—— ; identical with control 4S receptor ; panel A). ^{35}S-BF4 alone is also shown in panel B (——). All samples were analysed by density gradient ultracentrifugation ; arrows indicate marker proteins (peroxidase 3.6 S, and glucose oxidase, 7.9 S). Sedimentation is from right to left.

only < 30 % pure on the basis of specific hormone binding assuming one binding site/chain of 100K. Analysis by SDS PAGE revealed that such preparations contain both the A and B subunits and, in addition, a 90K band stained stronger than either of the former once (Fig. 2, lane 4). The purity we could reach by our procedure appears to be close to a "ceiling" : the specific hormone-binding capacity cannot be improved by additional operations tested, such as gel filtration. Several lines of evidence indicate that the non-activated ("native") receptor in fact cannot be purified more than to about 0.3 bound hormone molecules per polypeptide chain, and the reason for this is that such receptor molecules are oligomeric and contain non-hormone binding components, namely, molecules of the 90K protein. In particular, the 90K protein copurified with the progestin-binding A and B subunits only when the receptor has been stabilized in the (non-activated) 8S form but not when transformation to 4S forms has preceded the affinity chromatography step (Fig. 2, lanes 1 vs 2). The 90K protein as well as the A and B proteins, are all absent from the affinity gel eluate obtained in a "mock-purification" where specific binding of the receptor to the steroid residues on the resin has been prevented by prior preincubation of the cytosol with 1 μM unlabelled progesterone in order to saturate the hormone-binding sites (lane 3). Immunological evidence also indicates physical association between a non-hormone--binding protein of M_r ~ 90K and the progestin-binding components of the 8S oligomer (38). In these experiments we have studied the effects of incubation with a monoclonal antibody (BF4) raised against the 8S (non-transformed) receptor, on the size of ^{3}H-progesterone labeled receptor. This antibody reacted with the 8S receptor form which became ~ 11S ; the ~ 11S peak of ^{3}H-progesterone labeled receptor coincided with the peak of ^{35}S-labeled BF4 antibody, confirming the antigen recognition (Fig.3). In contrast, the BF4 antibody did not react with the 4S forms of the progesterone receptor : their sedimentation coefficient was not altered after incubation (Fig. 4). The antigen recognized by BF4 is however present in the (non-purified) transformed receptor preparations as documented by the fact that the sedimentation coefficient of ^{35}S-BF4 becomes greater (~ 9S instead of ~ 7S) during the incubation of the labeled antibody with the transformed receptor. No BF4-recognized antigen is present in the purified, transformed receptor preparations which do not contain the 90K protein. These observations are best explained by assuming that the 8S complex contains non-hormone-binding components, which are recognized by the monoclonal antibody BF4. In agreement with this

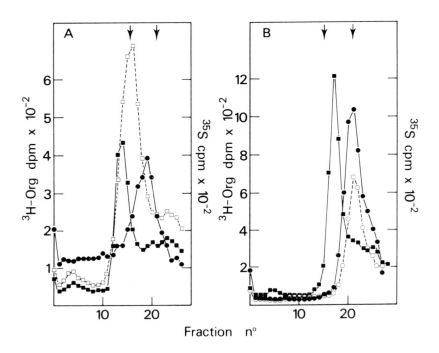

Fig. 4 : Density gradient sedimentation analysis of salt-transformed progesterone receptor after incubation with BF4 monoclonal antibody (38). Cytosol was prepared in the absence of molybdate. Panel A : the 30 % ammonium sulfate precipitate was labeled with ^{3}H-ORG 2058 and portions were incubated with BF4 crude ascitic fluid (●) or with control myeloma cell culture medium (not shown) : the two profiles were superimposable. Other portions were incubated with ^{35}S-BF4 in the absence (■) or presence (□) of ascitic fluid. Panel B : cytosol was treated with 0.3 M KCl and loaded onto NADAc-Sepharose column. Elution was performed with 2 M ^{3}H-ORG 2058. Affinity chromatography eluate was incubated with BF4 (●) or with control myeloma cell culture medium (o) ; ^{35}S-BF4 was centrifuged alone (not shown) or after incubation with the affinity chromatography eluate (■) ; identical profiles were obtained.

a   b   c

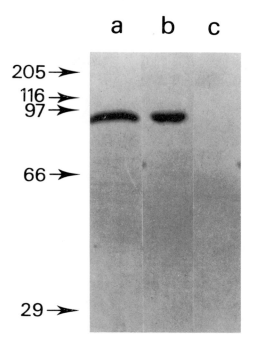

205 →
116 →
97 →

66 →

29 →

<u>Fig. 5</u> : Immunoblotting of progesterone receptor with BF4 monoclonal
antibody (38).
        a : Total cytosol (100 µg protein). b : Purified molybdate-
stabilized 8S-progesterone receptor (0.5 µg). c : Affinity chromatography
purified salt-transformed progesterone receptor (0.75 µg).

hypothesis and with the data obtained by analysis of the purified 8S
receptor, BF4 revealed a 90K band in immunoblots of total cytosol as
well as of the purified 8S receptor (Fig. 5) (38). The intensity of
the 90K band detected with the BF4 antibody indicates that the amount
of the corresponding protein in the cytosol is considerably greater
than that of the progesterone receptors. According to preliminary
estimations by radioimmunoassay (Binart, Catelli, Moncharmont,
unpublished), there is an 50-100 fold excess of the 90 protein over
the progesterone receptor in the oviduct cell (see also ref. 18, 37).

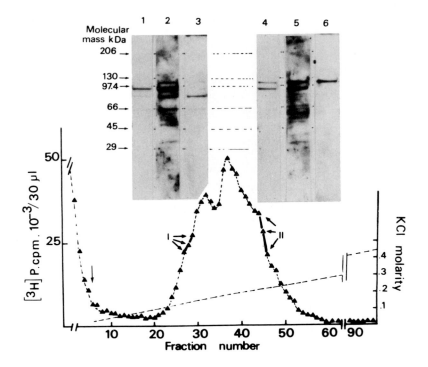

Fig. 6 : Polymorphism of the form of 8S progesterone receptor (31). The receptor eluted from affinity gel was chromatographed on DEAE-Sephacel in the presence of molybdate and eluted with a 0-0.5 M KCl gradient. Two overlapping radioactive peaks (forms I and II) were observed. Fractions of the ascending part and of the descending part of the radioactive were studied separately by SDS-PAGE and immunoblotting. Lanes 1 and 4 : silver staining performed after transfer onto two nitrocellulose papers. Lanes 2 and 5 : immunoblotting with IgG-G3. Lanes 3 and 6 : immunoblotting with IgG-RB.

2)   Heterogeneity of the "native" progesterone receptor.

In DEAE-cellulose chromatography, the non-transformed (molybdate--stabilized) progesterone receptor can be resolved into two peaks, one eluting at 0.1 M KCl (peak I), the other at 0.16 M KCl (peak II)(39). In our hands, the separation was not perfect (Fig. 6), and therefore we have taken samples from the ascending portion of the peak I and from the descending portion of the peak II for further analysis rather than pooling the peak fractions. It turned out that these samples contained different proportions of the hormone-binding subunits : in the peak I, predominantly the A subunit and in peak II predominantly the B subunit could be detected, by protein staining as well as by immunoblotting (Fig. 6). In both peaks, the 90K protein was present in greater amounts than the A or B subunits. These data are in agreement with those reported by Dougherty et al (40) who have separated the "form I" and "form II" of the progesterone receptor and have established that both sediment as 8S complexes in density gradients. When instead of the purified receptor, total oviduct cytosol is fractionated on DEAE cellulose in molybdate-containing buffers, a similar pattern of elution of receptor-^{3}H-progesterone complexes is observed, and again, immunoblotting reveals predominance of the A subunit in the peak I and of the B subunit in the peak II (not shown). The heterogeneity of the non-activated (8S) form of the progesterone receptor therefore does not seem to be an artefact introduced by the purification procedure.

3)   Stoichiometry of components of the non-activated receptor preparations.

Scanning of SDS-PAGE slabs after protein staining indicated that the content of the 90K protein was about twice the sum of the A and B subunits (Fig. 7) ; the mean ratio of experiments was 2.2 ± 0.3. The same stoichiometry of about 2.1 between the 90K protein and the hormone-binding subunits was observed when samples from the peaks I and II (resolved on DEAE-cellulose) were analysed separately by SDS-PAGE and scanning (not shown). This suggests that the purified "native" receptor is composed of three subunits, namely, two molecules of the 90K polypeptide and one hormone-binding subunit (A or B) (18, 31, 37).

Molecular weight estimation are compatible with this model. Calculated from the hydrodynamic parameters ($s_{20,w}$ and R_s) determined under non-denaturing conditions, M_r of the "native" form is approximately 265K on the basis of data obtained with total ("crude") cytosol, or 245K when taking the data found with purified

Molecular
Mass kDa

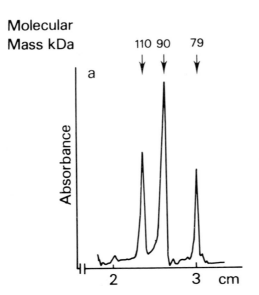

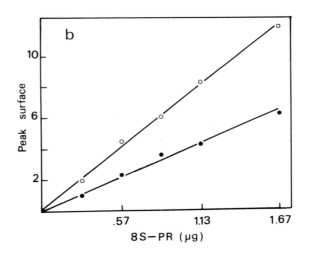

Fig. 7 : Determination of the relative amounts of components of the 8S form of progesterone receptor (31). Panel a : molybdate-stabilized receptor purified by affinity chromatography and DEAE-cellulose chromatography was analysed in 7-15 % polyacrylamide gradient SDS-PAGE and scanned by DU8 spectrofotometer. Panel b : Densitometric assay of the 90K protein (●) and of the sum of A and B proteins (o). Different amounts of the purified 8S receptor were analysed by SDS-PAGE, the lanes were scanned and the peak surfaces plotted against the amount of protein loaded.

preparations of the molybdate-stabilized receptor. The difference results from the lower Stokes radius (7.1 nM vs. 7.7 nm) determined for the latter. Whether this difference implies a real change of M_r during purification (i.e. loss of unidentified small component of the

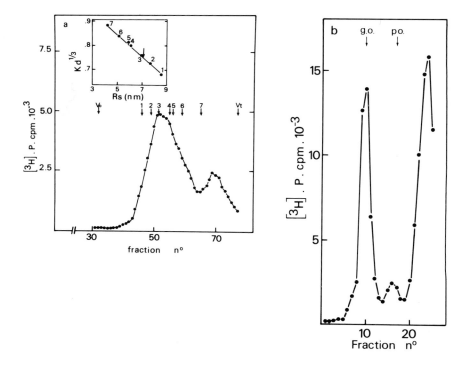

Fig. 8 : Stokes radius and sedimentation coefficient of cross-linked purified 8S-progesterone receptor. The receptor purified by affinity and ion exchange chromatography in molybdate-containing phosphate buffer was cross-linked with glutaraldehyde (31). Panel a : Stokes radius. An aliquot (1 ml) of cross-linked receptor was passed through the AcA 22 column. The standard proteins used were 1 : thyroglobulin, R_s = 8.6 nm ; 2 : crude 8S PR(I + II), R_s = 7.7 nm ; 3 : β-galactosidase, R_s = 6.9 nm ; 4 : ferritin, R_s = 6.14 nm ; 5 : pure B PR-subunit, R_s = 6.1 nm ; 6 : catalase, R_s = 5.22 nm ; 7 : yeast alcohol dehydrogenase, R_s = 4.55 nm. Insert : calibration curve in which the arrow indicates the position of the purified 8S-cross-linked progesterone receptor. Panel b : sedimentation coefficient. After 1 h incubation with glutaraldehyde, the cross-linked receptor 8S was analysed in a 10-35 % glycerol density gradient without molybdate.

native molecule), or only a change in conformation of the receptor during gel filtration possibly due to low protein concentration in the medium, remains uncertain. The forms I and II were indistinguishable by density gradient centrifugation as well as gel filtration techniques.

The M_r of the purified receptor (8S form) was also measured after crosslinking with glutaraldehyde (31). The crosslinked molecules have retained their hormone-binding capacity and could therefore be studied by both denaturing and non-denaturing techniques. Their hydrodynamic parameters were the same as those of the non-crosslinked molecules (Fig. 8). According to migration in SDS-PAGE (Fig. 9), the bulk of the crosslinked receptor had an M_r of about 260K, in good agreement with the value calculated from the $s_{20,w}$ and R_s determinations. A second, weak band was also seen in these gels at the position corresponding to $\sim$ 190K. Protein blotting of the crosslinked receptor was negative, probably due to loss of immunoreactivity after chemical alteration of the proteins.

The molecular weight estimations are compatible with proposed model according to which the non-transformed (8S) receptor is a mixture of molecules of the structure $A(90K)_2(I)$ and $B(90K)_2(II)$, (M_r's 260K and 290K, respectively) within the experimental precision of the 2 procedures employed. The very large molecules of crosslinked receptor were not resolved in SDS-PAGE and the stained bands were broad, indicating heterogeneity due also to the variable lenghts of glutaraldehyde polymers linked to the primary amine residues of the polypeptide chains (31, 37).

4)   Mechanism of activation.

It has been suggested previously (26) that activation of the chick oviduct progesterone receptor is a direct consequence of separation of the subunits forming the "native" oligomeric molecule. A change of primary structure(s) of the subunit(s) could however occur in the process, and participation of a cell component other than receptor itself could be required. Experiments with highly purified "native" receptor should bring about informations concerning the mechanism of activation. We have found that the purified 8S (molybdate-stabilized) receptor can be easily transformed to 4S forms as soon as molybdate is removed, and that the transformation is in fact spontaneous and fast unless carrier protein (such as BSA) is added to the medium (41). To examine the involvement of cell component(s) other than the receptor,

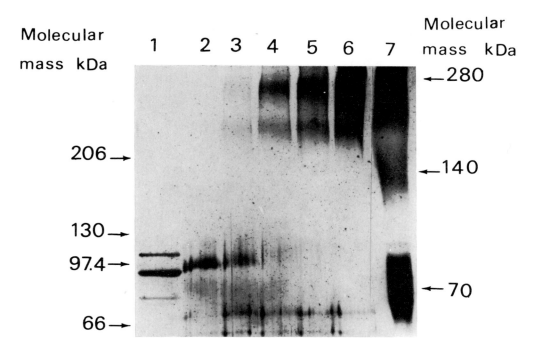

Fig. 9 : Analysis of cross-linked 8S-progesterone receptor by denaturing gel electrophoresis (31). The receptor purified by affinity and ion exchange chromatography in phosphate buffer containing molybdate was immediately treated with glutaraldehyde (0.4 % final concentration). After 0, 1, 5, 15, 30 and 60 min incubation at 0°C, cross-linked samples were analysed in 5-7 % polyacrylamide gradient SDS-PAGE (lanes 1-6). Lane 7 shows cross-linked hemocyanin used as marker for cross-linked samples (lanes 2-6). Non-cross-linked standard proteins are indicated by arrows on the left.

we have removed molybdate from the purified 8S preparations and supplemented them with either normal chick oviduct cytosol (preincubated with excess of unlabeled progesterone to saturate the endogenous receptor), or with cytosol preheated at 60°C for 30 min, prior to induction of transformation by incubation at 25°C or by high ionic strength. Under both conditions, the 8S to 4S transformation occurred at about the same rate, and in fact, the same result was obtained when BSA (10 mg/ml) was used instead of cytosol. The resulting 4S receptor displayed also a slower rate of dissociation of the bound steroid, and higher binding to phosphocellulose, like the activated receptor in total cytosol. It appears, therefore, that the activation process can be reproduced without participation of any cellular components other than those present within the native receptor structure.

Analysis in SDS-PAGE indicated the same M_r's of the receptor subunits (79K for A, 110K for B and 90K for the non-hormone binding protein) whether the material was activated or non-activated receptor, purified or crude. Immunodetection in nitrocellulose paper blots gave always results identical with protein staining. This does not, of course, exclude modifications such as phosphorylation in the course of receptor activation, and it is to be noted that at least certain of the subunits may be associated with, or possess, protein kinase activities (42). As mentioned above, properties of the activated A and B proteins suggest that they differ from their counterparts existing as subunits of the "native" oligomer at least by spatial conformation, if not by primary structure. While the 8S 4S transformation can be induced in the absence of ligand (26), the process is accelerated when the receptor is complexed with the steroid (18, 43). The steroid may also be necessary for the receptor to assume its biologically "active" configuration.

The striking stabilizing effect of molybdate, which inhibits the 8S to 4S transformation induced by all kinds of treatments, not only the "pseudo-physiological" incubation at 25°C but also exposure to high ionic strength (26), heparin (26), nucleotide triphosphates (43) or urea (32), can best be explained by assuming that bonds are introduced between the 90K protein and the hormone-binding subunit of the 8S molecule. These bonds are probably of the type

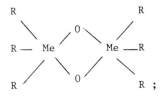

transition metals (Me) are in fact known to form this type of labile
coordination complexes with radicals (R) such as OH, SH, NH_2 which
can be supplied by water or by aminoacid side chains.

To summarize, activation of the chick oviduct progesterone receptor
may be seen as a two-step process. In the first step, the oligomeric
("native") molecule is dissociated. This step can occur in vitro in
the absence of hormone although it is facilitated by the presence of
the ligand ; in contrast, in the intact cell the presence of the
hormone seems to be indipensable (44). The second step involves any
changes in the receptor structure which result from binding of the
steroid to the receptor, leading to the formation of the "activated"
molecules. Evidently, the two steps may (and do, in vivo) occur in the
reverse order.

V. Subcellular distribution.

In the absence of progesterone (in vivo or in vitro), > 95 % of
progesterone-binding sites are recovered in the soluble fraction of the
oviduct tissue homogenate. This is independent of the buffer used
(hypotonic or isotonic, with or without ions stabilising nuclear membrane ;
13, and unpublished data). Homogenization under conditions protecting
cytoskeleton components did not either influence appreciably the extraction
of the progesterone receptor into the soluble fraction (unpublished data).
We have reexamined the subcellular localization of the progesterone
receptor by immunohistological methods using the antibodies raised in our
laboratory (see Table I). The crucial problem was that of fixation
technique such that the antigen-antibody reaction is not abolished (see
Methods and ref. 36 for details). The results obtained with the three
different antibodies do not support the notion that the receptor is a
cytoplasmic protein ; they can be summarized as follows :

1)   Studies with IgG-RB.
     In the oviduct tissue of estrogen-stimulated (immature) chicks, this
     antibody stained nuclei but not cytoplasm of cells in luminal
     epithelium, glands, stroma (Fig. 10a), mesothelium (Fig. 10b) and

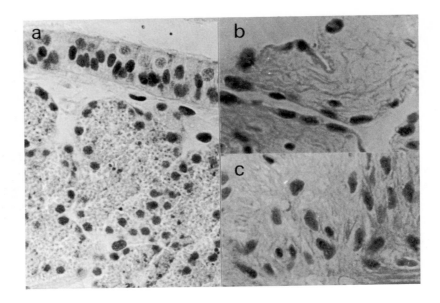

Fig. 10 : Immunodetection of progesterone receptor in estradiol treated chicken oviduct by an anti-B subunit antibody (36). The receptor is revealed exclusively in cell nuclei despite low levels of progesterone and in absence of exogenous ligand. Immunoreactive cells are observed in large number in the luminal epithelium, the stroma and the glandular epithelium (a), but also in the mesothelium surrounding the oviduct (b) and in the smooth muscle fibers (c). Glutaraldehyde fixation ; Magnification : x 550.

smooth muscle (Fig. 10c). Staining could be suppressed by presaturation of the antibody with purified subunits A or B but not with the purified 90K protein, in agreement with the antigen--specificity of this antibody.

Withdrawal of estrogen leads to oviduct regression, reduction of the proportion of tubular gland cells (1), and to an 4-fold decrease in the progesterone receptor content per cell (13). In such estrogen-withdrawn oviduct tissue, IgG-RB gave again a strong positive reaction in the cell nuclei of glands and of luminal epithelium, and a very weak reaction in the cytoplasm of epithelial cells (Fig. 11).

Oviducts of immature chicks which never received estrogen treatment have no tubular glands ; such tissues are composed of the so-called

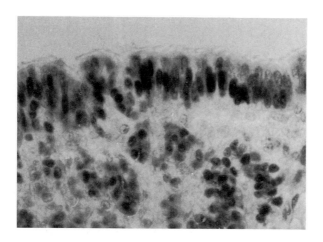

Fig. 11 : In oviduct of chickens withdrawn from estrogenic treatment for
several weeks progesterone receptor is still detected in cell nuclei by the
anti-B subunit antibody. The intensity of the reaction is strongest in the
luminal epithelium, weaker in the glands and faint in the stroma.
(Fixation : Bouin's fluid ; Magnification : x 550).

"progenitor cells" ready to enter the differentiation pathway upon
estrogen administration. They do contain progesterone receptor, at a
concentration of the order of 10^3 molecules per cell (i.e. about 10
times less than the estrogen-stimulated tissue) as shown by hormone
binding studies (13). In this "protodifferentiated" tissue, IgG-RB
still stained only nuclei of cells in the luminal epithelium
(Fig. 12), and occasionally of mesothelial cells (not shown).
Treatment of chicks with progesterone did not change the pattern of
staining with IgG-RB, irrespective of the estrogen exposure status of
the experimental animals (not shown).
All these experiments suggest that the progesterone receptor is in
fact a nuclear protein already before arrival of the hormone. They are

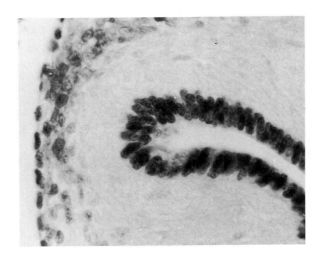

Fig. 12 : In absence of any hormonal treatment progesterone receptor is revealed in cell nuclei of the luminal epithelium and mesothelium of young, immature chicken oviduct, by the anti-B subunit antibody. Note the total absence of glands in the stroma. (Fixation : Bouin's fluid ; Magnification : x 550).

in contradiction with the evidence obtained earlier by measuring the progesterone-binding capacity of subcellular fractions after tissue homogenization. It may be that the native receptor is weakly associated with nucleus in the intact cell and "leaks out" rapidly once cell structure is destroyed ; only after binding the hormone, the (transformed) receptor-nuclear "acceptor" association becomes sufficiently tight to withstand tissue homogenization and fractionation. At present it is not possible to exclude formally the alternative that the nuclear localization observed in immunohistochemical experiments might be a "fixation artefact". In that case, one would have to assume that (a portion of) the receptor molecules have become associated with the nuclei during tissue fixation, possibly due to protein denaturation. These molecules may have been "cytoplasmic" in vivo, and present close to or within the nucleus only as a consequence of their free diffusion throughout the cell (cf. 45). However, it is important to note here that also in

certain biochemical studies (involving cell fractionation), steroid
hormone receptors have been detected in the nuclear compartment in the
absence of hormone (46-49). In the last of these (49), it has been
demonstrated that cytochalasin enucleation of GH3 cells yields a
predominantly nuclear association of the estrogen receptor, in
contrast with the usual (more disruptive) cell fractionation technique
(see 48). Nuclear localization of the estrogen receptor in the absence
of hormone has also been shown recently by immunological studies (50).
These facts favor the hypothesis that steroid hormone receptors are
localized predominantly in the nuclear compartment of the target
cells, irrespective of hormone exposure.

2)   Studies with BF4.

This antibody is specific for the 90K protein identified as a
component of the non-activated oligomeric progesterone receptor
molecule such as it exists in the soluble fraction of the oviduct
tissue homogenate. Immunochemical experiments demonstrated that the
subcellular distribution of the 90K protein is probably overlapping
but not identical with that of the hormone-binding subunits A and B of
the receptor recognized by the IgG-RB antibody.
Under appropriate staining and fixation conditions, BF4 strongly
stained the cytoplasm of all types of oviduct cells (Fig. 13).
Specificity of staining was confirmed by control experiments : the
reaction was abolished when BF4 was presaturated with the 8S purified
receptor preparations (or with the purified 90K protein but not with
the purified B subunit of the receptor. In estrogen-stimulated chick
oviduct, BF4 also gave a positive reaction in the nuclei of glandular
cells (Fig. 13) as well as of cells in the stroma, mesothelium and
muscle. In contrast, nuclear staining with BF4 could not be
definitively established in estrogen-withdrawn chicken oviduct tissue,
nor in the oviduct of chicks which never received estrogen.
These data could be taken to imply that the presence of the 90K
protein in the 8S form of the progesterone receptor is a consequence
of tissue homogenization. Alternatively, one may hypothesize that the
role of the 90K protein could be to ensure that the steroid-binding

56

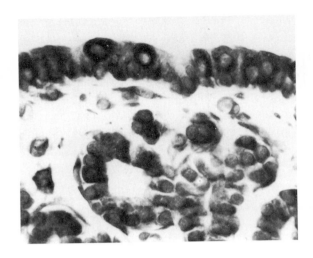

Fig. 13 : All cells, epithelial, glandular, stromal, muscular and mesothelial, are strongly stained after immunodetection of the 90K component by the BF4 antibody. Though the reaction appears stronger in cytoplasm the 90K protein is also revealed in the nucleus. In this picture a section of the oviduct of non estrogen primed chicken is represented. (Fixation : acidified alcohol ; Magnification : x 550).

proteins are maintained is non-activated (8S) complexes in the absence of hormone. All such complexes may be localized in the nucleus, while the excess of the "free" 90K protein is cytoplasmic ; this would facilitate formation of the 8S oligomers in the course of (or immediately after) synthesis of new A and B protein molecules. In this view, the amount of the nuclear 90K protein would be equivalent to the amount of the steroid-binding proteins in the cell. As mentioned above, the progesterone receptor levels in the oviduct of the estrogen-withdrawn and of the non-estrogen-treated (immature) chick are about 1 % and 1/10, respectively, of those in the estrogen--stimulated bird. Thus, the lack of clear nuclear staining with BF4 in the estrogen-withdrawn and non-estrogen-treated chick oviduct may be due to insufficient sensitivity of this antibody, or to inadequate fixation conditions. The problem of the intracellular localization and structure of the native receptor cannot yet be considered as definitively resolved.

References

1. Schimke, R.T., McKnight, G.S., Shapiro, D.J., Sullivan, D., Palacios, R.: Rec. Progr. Hormone Res. 31, 175-211 (1975).

2. Mester, J., Baulieu, E.E.: Trends in Biol. Sciences 9, 56-59 (1984).

3. Oka, T., Schimke, R.T.: J. Cell Biol. 41, 816-831 (1969).

4. Kohler, P.O., Grimley, P.M., O'Malley, B.W.: J. Cell Biol. 40, 8-27 (1969).

5. Palmiter, R.D.: J. Biol. Chem. 247, 6450-6461 (1972).

6. Sutherland, R.L., Geynet, C., Binart, N., Catelli, M.G., Schmelck, P.H., Mester, J., Lebeau, M.C., Baulieu, E.E.: Eur. J. Biochem. 107, 155-164 (1980).

7. Binart, N., Mester, J., Baulieu, E.E., Catelli, M.G.: Endocrinology 111, 7-16 (1982).

8. Palmiter, R.D., Mulvihill, E.R., McKnight, G.S., Senear, A.W.: Cold Spring Harbor Symp. Quant. Biol. 42, 639-647 (1977).

9. Tabor, C.W., Tabor, H.: Ann. Review Biochem. 45, 285-306 (1976).

10. Cohen, S., O'Malley, B.W., Stastny, M.: Science 170, 336-338 (1970).

11. Levy, C., Mester, J., Baulieu, E.E.: J. Endocrinol. 90, 1-7 (1981).

12. Sherman, M.R., Corvol, P., O'Malley, B.W.: J. Biol. Chem. 245, 6085-6096 (1970).

13. Mester, J., Baulieu, E.E.: Eur. J. Biochem. 72, 405-414 (1977).

14. Sutherland, R.L., Mester, J., Baulieu, E.E.: First European Symposium on Hormone and Cell Regulation edition J. Dumont, J. Nunez, Elsevier Amsterdam, Vol. 8, pp. 31-48 (1977).

15. Sherman, M.R., Atienza, S.B.P., Shausky, J.R., Hoffman, L.H.: J. Biol. Chem. 249, 5351-5359 (1974)

16. Dure, IV, L.S., Schrader, W.T., O'Malley, B.W.: Nature 283, 784-786 (1980).

17. Schrader, W.T., Birnbaumer, M.E., Hughes, M.R., Weigel, N.L., Grody, W.W., O'Malley, B.W.: Rec. Progr. Hormone Res. 37, 583-633 (1981).

18. Renoir, J.M., Mester, J.: Mol. Cell. Endocrinol. 37, 1-13 (1984).

19. Sherman, M.R.: Ann. Rev. Physiol. 46, 83-105 (1984).

20. Vedeckis, W.V., Freeman, M.R., Schrader, W.T., O'Malley, B.W.: Biochemistry 19, 343-349 (1980).

21. Jensen, E.W., DeSombre, E.R.: Ann. Rev. Biochem. 41, 203-230 (1972).

22. Milgrom, E.: In Biochemical Action of Hormones edition G. Litwack, Academic Press, New York, Vol. 8, pp. 466-491 (1981).

23. Sutherland, R.L., Mester, J., Baulieu, E.E. Nature 267, 434-435 (1977).

24. Binart, N., Catelli, M.G., Geynet, C., Puri, V., Hahnel, R., Mester, J., Baulieu, E.E.: Biochem. Biophys. Res. Commun. 91, 812-818 (1979).

25. Wolfson, A., Mester, J., Yang, C.R., Baulieu, E.E.: Biochem. Biophys. Res. Commun. 95, 1577-1584 (1980).

26. Yang, C.R., Mester, J., Wolfson, A., Renoir, J.M., Baulieu, E.E.: Biochem. J. 208, 399-406 (1982).

27. Yang, C.R., Seeley, D., Mester, J., Wolfson, A., Baulieu, E.E.: Biochim. Biophys. Acta 755, 428-433 (1983).

28. Renoir, J.M., Yang, C.R., Formstecher, P., Lustenberger, P., Wolfson, A., Redeuilh, G., Mester, J., Richard-Foy, H., Baulieu, E.E.: Eur. J. Biochem. 127, 71-79 (1982).

29. Mester, J., Redeuilh, G., Buchou, T., Renoir, J.M., Formstecher, P., Baulieu, E.E.: Proceedings of the 7th Inter. Congress of Endocrinology, Quebec, Canada, July 1-7 (1984) in press.

30. Renoir, J.M., Mester, J., Buchou, T., Catelli, M.G., Tuohimaa, P., Binart, N., Joab, I., Radanyi, C., Baulieu, E.E.: Biochem. J. 218, 685-692 (1984).

31. Renoir, J.M., Buchou, T., Mester, J., Radanyi, C., Baulieu, E.E.: Biochemistry (1984) in press.

32. Buchou, T., Mester, J., Renoir, J.M., Baulieu, E.E.: Biochem. Biophys. Res. Commun. 114, 479-487 (1983).

33. Renoir, J.M., Radanyi, C., Yang, C.R., Baulieu, E.E.: Eur. J. Biochem. 127, 81-87 (1982).

34. Tuohimaa, P., Renoir, J.M., Radanyi, C., Mester, J., Joab, I., Buchou, T., Baulieu, E.E.: Biochem. Biophys. Res. Commun. 119, 433-439 (1984).

35. Radanyi, C., Joab, I., Renoir, J.M., Richard-Foy, H., Baulieu, E.E.: Proc. Natl. Acad. Sci. USA 80, 2854-2858 (1983).

36. Gasc, J.M., Renoir, J.M., Radanyi, C., Joab, I., Tuohimaa, P., Baulieu, E.E.: J. Cell Biol. 99, 1193-1201 (1984).

37. Baulieu, E.E., Binart, N., Buchou, T., Catelli, M.G., Carcia, T., Gasc, J.M., Groyer, A., Joab, I., Moncharmont, B., Radanyi, C., Renoir, M., Tuohimaa, P., Mester, J.: In Steroid hormone receptors : structure and function. Nobel Symposium n°57 edition H. Eriksson, J.A. Gustafsson, Elsevier Amsterdam, pp. 45-72 (1983).

38. Joab, I., Radanyi, C., Renoir, J.M., Buchou, T., Catelli, M.G., Binart, N., Mester, J., Baulieu, E.E.: Nature 308, 850-853 (1984).

39. Dougherty, J.J., Toft, D.O.: J. Biol. Chem., 257, 3113-3120 (1982).

40. Dougherty, J.J., Puri, R.K., Toft, D.O.: J. Biol. Chem. 259, 8004-8009 (1984).

41. Yang, C.R., Renoir, J.M., Mester, J., Baulieu, E.E.: 64th Annual Meeting of the Endocrine Society. San Francisco, 16-18 June, abstract 251 (1982).

42. Garcia, T., Tuohimaa, P., Mester, J., Buchou, T., Renoir, J.M., Baulieu, E.E.: Biochem. Biophys. Res. Commun. 113, 960-967 (1983).

43. Moudgil, V.K., Eessalu, T.E., Buchou, T., Renoir, J.M., Mester, J., Baulieu, E.E. Endocrinology (1985) in press.

44. Wolfson, A., Mester, J., Yang, C.R., Baulieu, E.E.: In International cell biology edition H.G. Schweiger, SPringer-Verlag Berlin, pp. 861-871 (1981).

45. Sheridan, P.J., Buchanan, J.M., Anselmo, V.C., Martin, P.M.: Nature 282, 579-582 (1979).

60

46. Mester, J., Baulieu, E.E.: Biochim. Biophys. Acta 261, 236-244 (1972).

47. Lévy, C., Mortel, R., Eychenne, B., Robel, P., Baulieu, E.E.: Biochem. J., 185, 733-738 (1980).

48. Mester, J., Brunelle, R., Jung, I., Sonnenschein, C.: Exp. Cell Res. 81, 447-452 (1973).

49. Welshons, W.V., Lieberman, M.E., Gorski, J.: Nature 307, 747-749 (1984).

50. King, W.J., Greene, G.L.: Nature 307, 745-747 (1984).

STUDIES OF THE SUBUNIT COMPOSITION OF THE 8.5S RABBIT UTERINE PROGESTIN
RECEPTOR

LEE E. FABER; PING-K., K., TAI; YOSHIAKI MAEDA; JOHN E. MYERS

Departments of Obstetrics and Gynecology and Physiology, Medical College
of Ohio, Toledo, Ohio 43699.

KIYOHIDE NAKAO

Third Department of Internal Medicine, Toyama Medical and Pharmaceutical
University, Toyama, Japan.

ABSTRACT

      Several years ago we described the interconversions of the
nonactivated mammalian progestin receptor as a series of equilibria
(Equilibrium Model). For the most part this model was based on
sedimentation data and implied that the larger forms of the receptor may
have some unknown and unanticipated function. Data presented at that time
was based on work with the guinea pig uterine receptor. Here we wish to
discuss the confirmation of the basic tenets of the model with a second
species, the application of the concept to the isolation of the receptor,
the development of an anti progestin receptor secreting hybridoma and the
use of the monoclonal antibody to identify several components of the
receptor system.

INTRODUCTION

      Over the years the major thrust of our laboratory has been the
characterization of the 7S (and greater) forms of the mammalian uterine
progestin receptor. Our interest was piqued by the observation (1,2) that
estrogen was a necessary requirement for the detection of the 7S complex.
After estrogenization, not only does the 7S complex appear, but there is a
corresponding increase in 4S glucocorticoid binders. Saturation
experiments (2,3) suggested that the 4S binders were in great excess of
the 7S receptor.

      Scatchard analyses of cytosols rich in 7S material revealed fairly
high concentrations of progesterone receptor ("Ka" of 8×10^8 1/m). A
second class of sites with "Ka" an order of magnitude lower was also
present. These binders were similar to those of blood plasma. Extracts
of non-estrogen treated uteri contained little high affinity binding.
Potassium chloride has routinely been used to demonstrate the dissociation
of the receptors into basic components. In our hands not only did the

larger 7S progesterone receptor dissappear in the presence of KCl, but
this was accompanied by a pronounced depression of the "Ka" of the
cytosolic high affinity binder (2-4). The binding constants of the
resulting 4S material were indistinguishable from those calculated from
samples of blood plasma. Thus, the 7S to 4S conversion, noted under the
conditions of our early experiments appeared to be best explained by a
physical transfer of radioactive steroid from the receptor to plasma
proteins.

Unfortunately, in these experiments, the receptor was quite unstable.
The half life of the 7S rabbit uterine receptor in the commonly used
buffers was approximately 24 hr. In hopes of stabilizing the receptor we
studied the effects of various buffering media and salts on the complex.
As a result of these studies (4) we have adopted a phosphate buffering
system (see methods) in lieu of the more widely used TRIS·HCl solutions.

From these researches a pattern of receptor behavior became apparent.
The mammalian uterine receptor appeared to be a large molecule at the
onset of the experiment. Various manipulations resulted in the
dissociation of the complex. We could best describe our observations as a
series of chemical equilibria patterned after the gas laws. This concept
(The Equilibrium Model) is described in detail elsewhere (5). What is of
importance is that the basic concept appears to be sound, for we have
applied it to the study of the subunit composition of the nonactivated
rabbit uterine progestin receptor. This chapter is a summary of our
efforts in this direction.

MATERIALS AND METHODS

Tritiated Steroids

R5020 (dimethyl-19-norpregna-4,9-diene-3,20-dione,17α-methyl-^{3}H) 87
Ci/mmol; and 5α-pregnanedione, (1,2,^{3}H(N)-5α-pregnan-3,20-dione), 55.7
Ci/mmol were purchased from New England Nuclear.

Buffers

5 mM PGTA (5 mM potassium phosphate; 10% glycerol (v/v); 10 mM
monothioglycerol; 0.02% sodium azide, pH 7.4). 5 mM PGTMA (5 mM PGTA plus
10 mM sodium molybdate). 100 mM PGTA (100 mM potassium phosphate; 10%
glycerol (v/v); 10 mM monothioglycerol; 0.02% sodium azide, pH 7.4).
100 mM PGTMA (100 mM plus 10 mM sodium molybdate).

200 mM PGTMA (200 mM potassium phosphate; 10% glycerol (v/v); 10 mM
monothioglycerol; 10 mM sodium molybdate; 0.02% sodium azide, pH 7.4).
SDS sample preparation buffer (3% SDS; 3% merceptoethanol; 33% glycerol
(v/v); 0.167 M TRIS·HCl, pH 6.8). Citrate buffer (100 mM sodium citrate,
pH 5.8 or 5.95). 5 mM PGTMAP (5 mM PGTMA plus 0.5 mM phenylmethylsulfonyl
fluoride; 20 mM benzamidine; 2 ug/ml pepstatin A; 10 ug/ml leupeptin).

Animals and Cytosol Preparation

Ovariectomized virgin adult New Zealand white rabbits (4 to 6 kg)
were purchased from Dutchland Animal Laboratories (Denver, PA.), and
received a single injection of 250 ug of Depo®-Estradiol (Upjohn).
Cytosols were usually prepared by homogenization in phosphate buffers as
described (4). In the photoaffinity labeling experiments, uteri were
frozen on liquid N_2, pulverized on dry ice and homogenized in the presence
of protease inhibitors (5 mM PGTMAP buffer).

Sucrose Density Gradient Centrifugation

Samples of cytosol or 1:4 dilutions were placed in glass vials, containing
16 nM (^{3}H)-progestin, and incubated at 0°C for 1 hr. Some samples were
warmed to 20°C for 20 minutes. We employed two methods of centrifugation.
In the first method (SW 60Ti swinging bucket rotor) samples were layered
onto 5-20% sucrose gradients and centrifuged for 16 hr as described (4).
The second method utilized a vertical tube rotor (VTi 65). In these
experiments the 0.2 ml samples were layered onto 4 ml gradients (5-20%
sucrose in the corresponding buffer) in Quick-Seal® tubes. Centrifugation
time was reduced to 2.5 or 3 hr. Each sucrose gradient contained (^{14}C)-
labeled internal standards (ovalbumin, 3.6S; and ɣ-globulin, 7.0S)
purchased from New England Nuclear. Gradients were fractionated and
counted as described (4).

Purification of the Receptor

Cytosols (labeled with 80 nM [17α-methyl-^{3}H]-R5020, 10 Ci/mmol) were
applied to columns of spheroidal hydroxylapatite (HAP). After washing,
receptors were eluted by linear gradients of potassium phosphate.
Fractions comprising the peak of radioactivity, were pooled and
concentrated by means of Millipore® Immersible-CX Ultrafilters. The
samples were then diluted 1:4 with 5 mM PGTMA and applied to columns of
Whatman DE-52 (DEAE cellulose). Columns were eluted with linear gradients

of potassium phosphate. The radioactive peaks were concentrated to 1 ml in an Amicon® concentrator for immunization. Samples obtained after each step of the purification were analyzed for binding activity by Scatchard analyses as described (2,6).

Production of the Hybridoma KN 382/EC1

Enriched receptor preparations were emulsified in complete Freund's adjuvant. One third was injected I.P. into male BALB/c mice, the remainder into multiple subcutaneous sites. Booster immunizations, in incomplete Freund's adjuvant, were administered three weeks and eight weeks after the first injection. A final injection without adjuvant was given intravenously 4 days prior to fusion. The mice received approximately 1 mg of cytosol protein per injection.

Spleen cells from the immunized mice were fused with mouse myeloma cells (P3x63Ag8.653) according to the technique of Fazekas de St. Groth and Scheidegger (7). Cells were cultured in 240 wells and selected in HAT medium under standard conditions (6).

Screening of Colonies

We employed a three-step screening procedure. Initially, Ig secreting hybridomas were detected by an alkaline phosphatase "ELISA" assay (New England Nuclear Kit). Positive wells were then analyzed for binding to progestin receptor by solid phase radioimmunoassay (see Table 3) and sucrose gradient centrifugation (6).

Development of the Cell Line

One hybridoma colony gave positive results three times in all three of the assays. This colony, named KN382/EC1, has been cloned under conditions of limiting dilution. Subcolonies, were expanded and injected into BALB/c mice to produce ascites tumors.

Ascites fluid, (~10 ml) was precipitated by 50% saturated ammonium sulfate, and purified by affinity chromatography on Protein-A-Sepharose® CL-4B (Pharmacia) under standard conditions (6).

Specificity of the Antibody

Cytosols from MCF-7 cells, uteri of rabbit, rat, guinea pig, and chick oviducts, were incubated in 80 nM [17α-methyl-^{3}H]-R5020 or [2,4,6,7-^{3}H]-estradiol-17β and 1 uM cortisol for 1 h. Typically 10 ug of immune IgG$_1$ or nonimmune IgG$_1$ (Bionetics) were incubated for 3 h at 4°C with 125 ul of cytosol. Samples were sedimented through 5-20% sucrose gradients prepared in 100 mM PGTMA.

Immunoaffinity Chromatography of Rabbit Uterine Progestin Receptors

Purified immune IgG_1, (1 mg) or Bionetics nonimmune myeloma IgG_1 (1 mg) was coupled to 0.5 ml of Affigel-10® (BioRad) in 0.1 M $NaHCO_3$ (pH 8) according to the manufacturer's instructions. Uterine cytosol (0.9 ml to 1.25 ml) prepared in 5 mM PGTMA was incubated with 2 uM hydrocortisone, 2 uM dihydrotestosterone and 80 nM (17α-methyl-^{3}H)-R5020. Samples of uterine cytosol (0.9 ml) were incubated at 4°C for 4 hr with 200 ul of either the immune IgG_1 (IgGi) or the myeloma IgG_1 (IgGn) Affigel-10® preparations. Centrifugation was utilized to separate the protein bound Affigel-10® from the cytosol. The gels were successively washed with 4x1 ml of 5 mM PGTMA, 3x1 ml of 100 mM PGTMA and 2x1 ml of 200 mM PGTMA at 4°C. Sucrose (10%) was included in all the phosphate washings. Gels were then washed with 2 x 1 ml of Citrate buffer at 4°C. Protein tightly bound to the immunoadsorbent was eluted with 200 ul of SDS sample preparation buffer followed by 3 separate 150 ul volumes of the same media (8).

Various eluents were either pooled or directly dialyzed against distilled H_2O for 4 hr. Dialysis bags were placed in dry sucrose overnight to concentrate the solution. These samples and the material eluted by SDS sample preparation buffer were then subjected at SDS PAGE analysis.

Photoaffinity Labeling of the Receptor

Rabbit uterine cytosol (1 ml aliquots) was incubated with 80 nM (17α-methyl-^{3}H)-R5020, 2 uM hydrocortisone, and 2 uM dihydrotestosterone for 2 hr at 4°C. Control samples received a 100 fold excess of unlabeled R5020. Free R5020 was removed with dextran coated charcoal. A Mineralight lamp (UVM-57, 30 nM maximum, Ultraviolet Products) was placed 2 cm above the samples for 30 min at 4°C. Samples were gently mixed for 3 hr at 4°C with 100 ul of either immune IgG_1 (IgGi) or myeloma IgG_1 (IgGn) Affigel-10® adsorbents. Gels were washed successively with 3 x 1 ml of 5 mM PGTMA, 3 x 1 ml of 100 mM PGTMA, and 1 ml of Citrate buffer. Adsorbed material was eluted by SDS sample preparation buffer and subjected to SDS PAGE analysis.

Sodium dodecylsulfate polyacrylamide Gel Electrophoresis (SDS PAGE)

SDS-polyacrylamide gel electrophoresis with 7.5% or 10% acrylamide was carried out according to Laemmli (9). Protein bands were visualized by Coomassie Blue R-250 and some gels were restained with silver stain (BioRad Kit). Mr standards, (BioRad), included myosin (200,000); β-galactosidase (116,000); phosphorylase B (94,000); bovine serum albumin (67,000); ovalbumin (43,000); carbonic anhydrase (30,000); and soybean trypsin inhibitor (20,000).

Fluorography of SDS PAGE Gels

After destaining, gels containing the $(17\alpha-methyl-^3H)$-R5020 covalently bound protein were impregnated with 60 ml of Enlightening™ (New England Nuclear) for 30 min at room temperature. Kodak X-Omat film (Eastman Kodak, Rochester, New York) was placed next to the gels (dried under vacuum) at $-70°C$ for 14 days. Films were developed according to the manufacturer's instructions.

RESULTS

Effect of Centrifugation on the Sedimentation Coefficient of the Receptor

In the absence of Na_2MoO_4 the progestin receptor sedimented as an 8.5S complex, (Fig. 1A, 1B) when centrifuged in the vertical tube rotor. If, on the other hand, the receptor was centrifuged for 16 hours in the swinging bucket rotor, it sedimented as a 7S complex (Fig. 1CD). Dilution of the cytosol, prior to centrifugation in the vertical tube rotor also favored formation of the 7S complex (Fig. 1A,1B). Furthermore, R5020 was more effective than 5α-pregnanedione in maintaining the 7S complex after dilution and centrifugation in the swinging bucket rotor.

Warming the undiluted cytosol appeared to have little effect on the sedimentation coefficient (Table 1).

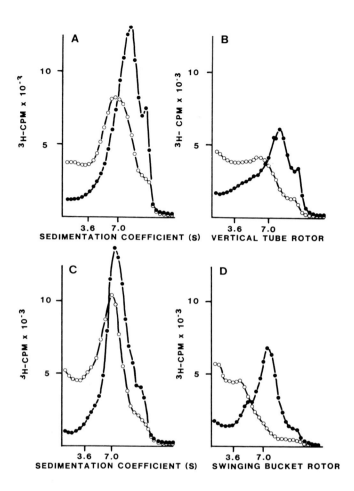

Fig. 1. Effect of Centrifugation time on the Sedimentation
Coefficient of the Rabbit Uterine Progestin Receptor
Cytosol was prepared in 5 mM PGT and incubated (either undiluted ●-●;
or diluted 1:4, O-O) with either 16 nM R5020 (panels A and C) or 16
nM 5∝-pregnanedione (panels B and D) for two hours at 4°C.
Sedimentation was for either three hours in the vertical tube rotor
(panels A and B) or for 20 hours in the swinging bucket rotor (panels
C and D). Internal standards, (^{14}C) ovalbumin, 3.6S and (^{14}C) gamma
globulin, 7.0S, are depicted on the abcissa.

TABLE 1 EFFECT OF CENTRIFUGATION AND LIGAND ON THE SEDIMENTATION
COEFFICIENT OF RABBIT UTERINE PROGESTIN RECEPTOR

LIGAND		R5020		5α-PREGNANEDIONE	
ROTOR		SW 60Ti	VTi 65	SW 60Ti	VTi 65
Undiluted Cytosol	5 mM PGT[1]	7.1$\pm$0.1(4)[2]	8.2$\pm$0.3(3)	6.7$\pm$0.7(3)	7.5$\pm$0.3(3)
	5 mM PGTM	8.8$\pm$0.1(3)	8.5$\pm$0.4(4)	8.7$\pm$0.7(4)	8.5$\pm$0.3(4)
Diluted Cytosol	5 mM PGT	7.0$\pm$0.3(3)	6.7$\pm$0.3(3)	4.0[3]	6.2$\pm$0.1(3)
	5 mM PGTM	8.5$\pm$0.4(4)	8.5$\pm$0.2(4)	NP[4]	8.3$\pm$0.4(4)

1. In this series of experiments the azide was left out of the buffers
2. Number of trials
3. In 2 of 3 experiments, no prominent peaks were detected
4. No prominent peaks were detected

Regardless of the progestin, the receptor sedimented as a relatively large complex when assayed with the vertical tube rotor. In paired experiments the receptor sedimented around 7S when centrifuged in the swinging bucket rotor.

The large complex noted in Na_2MoO4 free media (vertical tube rotor) disappeared upon dilution. In the case of R5020, the receptor was approximately 7S, while for 5α-pregnanedione the value was approximately 6.2S.

However, the method of centrifugation appeared to play a role with the less potent progestins. Extending the time of centrifugation to 16 hours (swinging bucket rotor) resulted in loss of discrete peaks. At best, we found a shoulder at 4S for 5α-pregnanedione (Table 1).

Addition of sodium molybdate (10mM) to the phosphate buffer (now 5mM PGTM) counteracted the effects of warming and prolonged centrifugation time. The 8.5S form was the preferred form in undiluted cytosol. We found a range of 8.5S to 8.8S independent of either progestin or method of centrifugation (Table 1). After dilution, however, sodium molybdate was not completely effective in maintaining the 8.5S complex. Although the R5020 receptor complex continued to sediment at 8.5S after dilution, deterioration of the 5α-pregnanedione complexes was noted after centrifugation in the swinging bucket rotor. Under these conditions the 8.5S 5α-pregnanedione complex was completely lost with no discernable peak being present. Appreciable amounts of 8.5S receptor were detected in paired experiments employing the vertical tube rotor.

Purification of the 8.5S Progestin Receptor Complex for Immunization of the Mice

From the previous series of experiments it became apparant that 5mM PGTMA was an appropriate buffer for isolation of the nonactivated receptor, and that a synthetic progestin of high biological potency (R5020) might be useful. Numerous isolation techniques were tested, including ammonium sulfate precipitation, DEAE chromatography (DEAE), hydroxylapatite chromatography (HAP), high performance liquid chromatography, preparative sucrose gradient centrifugation, polyamin precipitation, etc. In our hands, with the exception of the HAP and DEAE, most of these proved to be of little use. Each technique was usually accompanied by great losses of binding sites, with yields of receptor to low to be of use for the immunization of mice.

TABLE 2 TYPICAL YIELDS OF NON ACTIVATED RABBIT UTERINE PROGESTIN RECEPTOR

Rabbit uterine cytosols (20 ml prepared in 5 mM PGTMA) were incubated with 80 nM (17α-methyl-^{3}H) R5020 for 1 hour and applied to a 70 ml column of spheroidal hydroxylapatite. Receptor was eluted with a continuous gradient of 50 to 400 mM PGTMA[1]. Radioactive peaks were concentrated and applied to a 40 ml column of Whatman DE-52. Receptor was eluted by a 50 to 300 mM PGTMA gradient. Samples of material isolated after HAP and DEAE were analyzed by equilibrium dialysis. Each value is the mean of 3 trials $\pm$ SEM. Protein was determined by the Bio-Rad Protein Assay.

	HAP	DEAE
Receptor (ug)	60.3[2]	33.7
Protein (ug)	29,600	3900
Purity (%)	.2	.86

1. 50, 300, and 400 refer to the concentration of potassium phosphate.
2. Assuming a nominal molecular weight of 10[5] daltons.

We finally settled in a two step isolation of consisting successive chromatographies on HAP and DEAE. Typical results are presented in Table 2.

Production of Cell Line KN 382/EC1

Ten mice were immunized in this series of experiments. Receptor preparations utilized were typical of those reported in Table 2. Of the mice immunized, only one gave spleen cells that produced a useful hybridoma. Assuming that 1 mole of receptor binds 1 mole of progestin we estimate that the mouse received 1-3 x 10^{11} moles of receptor/mg protein (purity of about 0.9%).

After fusion, hybridomas were found in each of the 240 wells and multiple colonies appeared to be common. Upon assay, two colonies were positive three times in both the ELISA and solid phase RIA. They were tested by sucrose gradient analyses. Cell line KN 382/EC1 scored positive in the sucrose gradient assay for 3 consecutive weeks. KN 382/EC1 has been repeatedly cloned under conditions of limiting dilution, some cells have been frozen, and others pooled to produce ascites tumors. Antibody has been routinely purified from pooled ascites. Ouchterlony analysis revealed that the antibody was an IgG_1.

Sucrose density gradient centrifugation analyses revealed that the IgG_1 bound to nonactivated progestin receptors from rabbit uterus and the MCF-7 human breast cancer cells, however, it did not affect the sedimentation of estrogen receptors from either of these sources (Fig. 2 Table 3). The antibody did not change the sedimentation coefficient of uterine progestin receptor from either rat or the guinea pig. Likewise it did not affect the chick oviduct progestin receptor (Table 3). The antibody did not cross react with estrogen receptors derived from any of the sources we tested.

These results were confirmed by solid phase radioimmunoassay analyses. There appeared to be a small degree of cross-reactivity with estrogen receptors from rabbit and MCF-7 cytosol. However, presumptive estrogen receptor binding to the antibody was displaced by nonradioactive progestin.

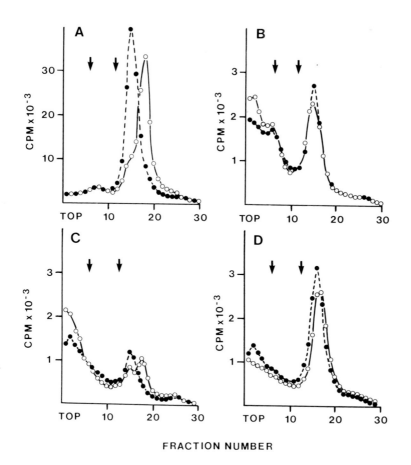

Fig. 2. Sucrose density gradient analyses of the specificity of the immune IgG_1. Purified immune IgG_1 (10 ug) and Bionetics nonimmune IgG_1 (10 ug) were incubated with 125 ul of cytosol labeled with 80 nM of either [17α-methyl-^{3}H]-R5020, or [2,4,6,7, ^{3}H]-estradiol-17-β. Receptor IgG_1 complexes were sedimented through 5 to 20% sucrose gradients containing 100 mM PGTMA. Arrows indicate the positions of the [^{14}C] ovalbumin and [^{14}C] gamma globulin internal standards. Panel A: rabbit uterine progestin receptor; O--O immune IgG_1, ●--● nonimmune IgG_1. Panel B: rabbit uterine estrogen receptor; O--O immune IgG_1, ●--● nonimmune IgG_1. Panel C: MCF-7 progestin receptor; O--O immune IgG_1, ●--● nonimmune IgG_1. Panel D: MCF-7 estrogen receptor, O--O immune IgG_1, ●--● nonimmune IgG_1.

TABLE 3 SPECIFICITY OF THE PURIFIED IMMUNE IgG$_1$ SECRETED BY CELL LINE KN 382/EC1

Highly purified immune IgG$_1$ (10ug) or Bionetics nonimmune IgG$_1$ (10ug) were incubated with 125 ul of cytosol containing either radiolabeled progestin or estrogen and subjected to sucrose density gradient ultracentrifugation. For assay of specificity by solid phase radioimmunoassay, 10, 5, 1, 0.5, and 0.1 ug of immune IgG$_1$ and nonimmune IgG$_1$ were incubated with 50 ul of Immunobeads® for 16 hours. Various cytosol preparations were added (20 ul) and allowed to incubate for 4 hours, whereupon the Immunobeads® were pelleted, washed, and the bound tritium measured (6).

SPECIES	PROGESTERONE RECEPTOR		ESTROGEN RECEPTOR	
	SUCROSE GRADIENT	SOLID PHASE RIA	SUCROSE GRADIENT	SOLID PHASE RIA
RABBIT	+	+	−	−
RAT	−	−	−	−
GUINEA PIG	−	−	−	−
MCF-7	+	−	−	−
CHICK OVIDUCT	−	−	N.A.	−

+ POSITIVE RESULT EITHER DISPLACED THE PEAK IN THE SUCROSE GRADIENT OR RESULTED IN A SIGNIFICANT NUMBER OF CPM TO THE PRECIPITATED BY IMMUNOBEADS®

− NEGATIVE RESULT

N.A. NOT AVAILABLE

Sucrose Gradient Analyses of Antibody Receptor Interaction

Our initial studies, indicated that the immune IgG$_1$ readily bound to the 8.5S sodium molybdate stabilized receptor. The antibody also bound to the molybdate free 8.5S receptor found after centrifugation with the vertical tube rotor (Fig. 3).

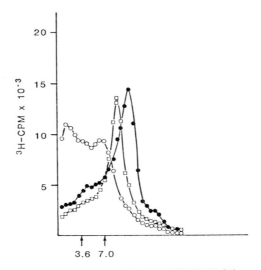

Fig. 3. Sucrose density gradient analysis of the binding of immune
IgG$_1$ to the rabbit uterine progestin receptor. 500 ul of cytosol
(5 mM PGTA) and 1:4 dilutions of cytosol (diluted with 5 mM PGTA)
were incubated in 16 nM (17α-methyl-^{3}H)-R5020 for 1 hr at 4°C.
Samples were warmed to 20°C for 20 min. Immune IgG$_1$ (40 ug in 2 ul
5 mM PGTMA) or buffer (2 ul 5 mM PGTMA) was added and incubated for
1 hr at 4°C. Approximately 250 ul samples were layered into 4.8 ml
5-20% sucrose gradients prepared in 5 mM PGTA. All gradients
received ^{14}C ovalbumin (3.6S) and ^{14}C globulin (7.0S) internal
standards. Centrifugation was for 3 hrs in a Beckman VTi 65 vertical
tube rotor at a maximum speed of 65,000 rpm. Undiluted cytosol plus
immune IgG$_1$ (●-●); undiluted cytosol plus buffer (□-□), cytosol
diluted 1:4 plus immune IgG$_1$, (O-O).

However, the antibody did not combine with 7S receptor, found under
conditions favoring formation of the 7S complex (Fig. 4B). Nor did the
antibody combine with 4 to 5S binders noted in molybdate free high ionic
strength gradients (Fig. 4C).

74

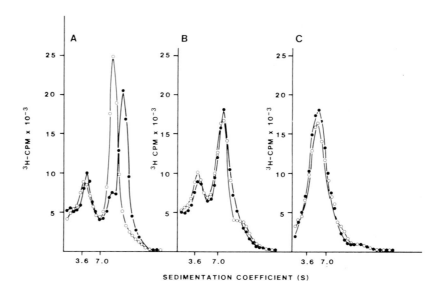

Fig. 4. Sucrose density gradient analysis of the binding of immune
IgG₁ to various forms of the rabbit uterine progestin receptor.
Cytosol (in either 5 mM PGTA or 5 mM PGTMA) was incubated with 80 nM
(17α-methyl-^{3}H)-R5020, 2 uM hydrocortisone and 2 uM dihydrotestosterone for 1 hr. Aliquots (200 ul) were incubated with 20 ug
immune IgG₁ (●-●) or 20 ug of the Bionetics nonimmune IgG₁
(0-0) at 4°C for 3 hr. Free steroid was removed by dextran coated
charcoal. Panel A, 5 mM PGTMA cytosol; 5mM PGTMA gradient. Panel B,
5 mM PGTA cytosol; 5 mM PGTA gradient. Panel C, 5 mM PGTA cytosol;
100 mM PGTA gradient. All gradients received ^{14}C ovalbumin (3.6S)
and ^{14}C ɣ-globulin (7.0S) internal standards. Centrifugation was for
16 hr at 50,000 rpm in a Beckman SW 60Ti swinging bucket rotor.

This suggested that the antibody either did not bind to the steroid
binding portions of the receptor or that the receptor was modified in the
absence of sodium molybdate as to prohibit binding of the immunoglobulin.
This question was resolved by sucrose gradient analysis of ^{125}I labeled
immunoglobulin receptor complexes. Sedimentation of ^{125}I-IgG₁ molybdate
stabilized receptor resulted in formation of 11S complexes (Fig. 5) not
unlike that noted earlier. However in the presence of high salt (no
molybdate) the ^{125}I-IgG₁ complex migrated at about 7.8 to 8.0S, as opposed
to a value of 7S for the ^{125}I-IgG₁ alone. The increase in sedimentation
coefficient suggested addition of a peptide from the dissociated receptor.

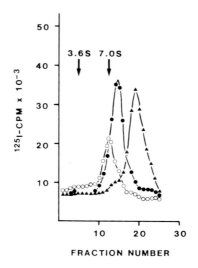

Fig. 5. Sucrose density gradient analysis of the interaction of the ^{125}I labeled monoclonal antibody and the rabbit uterine progestin receptor. ^{125}I-Immune IgG$_1$ (0.32 ug) was added to 500 ul of 5 mM PGTMA cytosol (16 nM [17$\propto$-methly-^{3}H]-R5020, or 5 mM PGTA cytosol (no steroid) and allowed to incubate 4 hours at 4°C. In control incubations (no cytosol) 0.16 ug of the ^{125}I-labeled antibody was incubated in 250 ul of 5 mM PGTA. After incubation, 200 ul of each were layered on 5-20% sucrose gradients and centrifuged at 50,000 rpm for 16 hr in a SW 60Ti rotor. Each gradient received ^{14}C-ovalbumin as an internal standard. ^{125}I-IgG$_1$, no cytosol; 100 mM PGTA gradient (O-O). ^{125}I-IgG$_1$, 5 mM PGTA cytosol; 100 mM PGTA gradient (●-●). ^{125}IgG$_1$, 5 mM PGTMA cytosol; 100 mM PGTMA gradient (▲-▲).

Immunoaffinity Purification of the Progestin Receptor

Immunoadsorbent, prepared from KN 382/EC1 IgG₁ Affigel-10®,
effectively extracted bound radioactivity from cytosol, while myeloma
immunoadsorbent did not (Fig. 6).

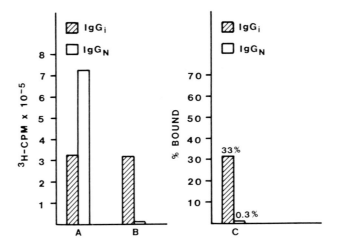

Fig. 6. Distribution of Radioactivity after immunoadsorption of
(17α-methyl-^{3}H)-R5020 labeled rabbit uterine progestin receptor.
Cytosol (0.9 ml) was incubated with 200 ul of Affigel-10® coupled
with either immune IgG₁ (IgGi) or myeloma IgG₁ (IgGn) for 4 hr at
4°C. A, ^{3}H cpm remaining in cytosol after removal of the gel.
B, ^{3}H cpm eluted from the immunoadsorbents by procedure A. C,
percent of total cytosol radioactivity precipitated by the two
immunoadsorbents.

SDS PAGE analysis of the adsorbed material (Fig. 7) revealed two bands, one with a Mr of 92,000, a second with a Mr of 59,000. These proteins were not adsorbed by control myeloma IgG_1-Affigel-10® (Fig. 7). Several minor bands of unknown origin and concentration appeared after silver staining.

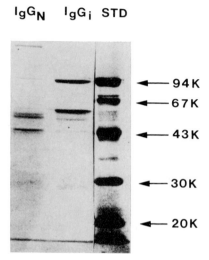

Fig. 7. SDS PAGE analysis of receptor immunoadsorbed from rabbit uterine cytosol. Cytosol (0.9 ml) was incubated with 200 ul of either immune or nonimmune IgG_1-Affigel-10®. After washing of the gels (Procedure A) bound protein was eluted with SDS sample preparation buffer and subjected to electrophoretic analysis. IgGn, nonimmune immunoadsorbent (Bionetics MOPC 21 myeloma IgG_1). IgGi, immune immunoadsorbent (IgG_1 from cell line KN 382/EC1). STD, Standards: Gel was stained with Coomassie Blue R-250.

Sequential washing of immunoadsorbed receptor leached the Mr = 92,000 protein which closely followed the loss of radioactivity. After exhaustive washing, the Mr = 92,000 peptide was almost completely cleared from the immunoadsorbent as was the $(17\alpha\text{-methyl-}^{3}H)\text{-R5020}$, leaving primarily the Mr = 59,000 material (Fig. 8). These data suggest that the immunoadsorbent bound to the Mr = 59,000 peptide, and that the Mr = 92,000 peptide is in turn bound to the Mr = 59.000 peptide.

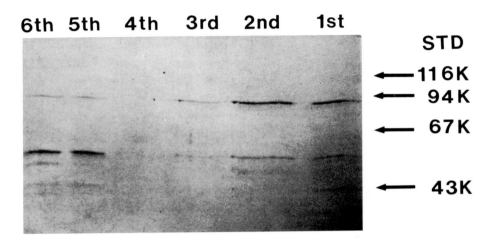

Fig. 8. SDS PAGE analysis of receptor immunoadsorbed from rabbit uterine cytosol (prepared in 5 mM PGTMA). Cytosol (1.25 ml) was incubated with 80 nM $(17\alpha\text{-methyl-}^{3}H)\text{-R5020}$ for 1 hr at 4°C, then incubated with 200 ul of immune-Affigel-10® for 3 hr at 4°C. Immobilized receptor was washed and eluted as described in Fig. 7. STD; standards. 1st; first citrate elution. 2nd; second citrate elution. 3rd; third citrate elution. 4th; fourth citrate elution. 5th; 1st SDS sample preparation buffer elution. 6th; 2nd SDS sample preparation buffer elution. Gel was stained with Coomassie Blue R-250.

Photoaffinity Labeling of the Progestin Receptor

Initial fluorographic analyses of immunoprecipitated receptor
revealed bands at molecular weights of 116,000, 90,000, 86,000 and 70,000
daltons (Fig. 9). Controls (lane 3) demonstrated that these proteins were
not precipitated by the nonimmune adsorbent.

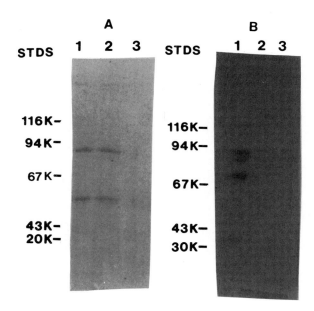

Fig. 9. SDS PAGE analysis of rabbit uterine cytosol after
photoaffinity labeling with 80 nM $(17\alpha\text{-methyl-}^3\text{H})$-R5020. Panel A:
Gel stained with Coomassie Blue R-250. Panel B: Radiofluorograph of
the gel of Panel A. Lane 1: Material precipitated from cytosol by
the immunoreactive Affigel-10® adsorbent. Lane 2: Material
precipitated by the immunoreactive Affigel-10® adsorbent from cytosol
receiving 8 uM unlabeled R-5020. Lane 3: Material precipitated
from cytosol by the nonimmunoreactive Affigel-10 adsorbent. STDS:
Standards.

When we improved our method of cytosol preparation to prevent proteolysis, no difference was noted in the Mr = 92,000 and Mr = 59,000 nonsteroid binding components (Fig. 10)). However, we found considerable enhancement of the Mr = 116,000 and Mr = 90,000 bands (Fig. 10).

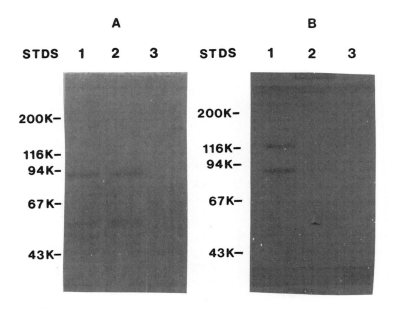

Fig. 10. SDS PAGE analysis of cytosol after photoaffinity labeling of rabbit uterine cytosol with 80 nM (17α-methyl-^{3}H)-R5020. Cytosol was prepared from frozen uteri in the presence of protease inhibitors. Panel A: Gel stained with Coomassie Blue R-250. Panel B: Radiofluorograph of the gel of Panel A. Lane 1: Material precipitated by 100 ul of immunoreactive Affigel-10® adsorbent. Lane 2: Same as Lane 1 except the cytosol received 8 uM unlabeled R-5020. Lane 3: Material precipitated by the nonimmune Affigel-10® adsorbent. STDS: Standards.

DISCUSSION

A pattern of receptor behavior is evident from Table 1 and Fig. 1. Experiments with the vertical tube rotor suggest the receptor may be a large molecule ($S^0_{20,w} \sim 8.5S$) at the onset of the experiment. Long term centrifugation and other in vitro manipulations result in disappearance of the 8.5S complex. Maintaining a fairly high concentration of receptor also serves to preserve the larger forms. This latter observation may have important consequences, for we do not know the intracellular concentration at which the receptor performs its biological chores. Intuitively, however, it is obvious that cytosol preparation subjects a functioning receptor to violent dilution. Furthermore, extraction of the receptor drastically alters its ionic environment, and the precise ionic and/or cofactor requirements for receptor activity remain a mystery. Assuredly a steroid receptor in situ does not labor as a dilute solution in 10 mM TRIS-HCl; 300 mM KCl, lacking divalent cations. A broad foundation of information defining the effects of the various in vitro techniques, including the effect of the steroid, upon the receptor has not been layed down. To help understand the behavior of the receptor after it is extracted from the cell, we have described the interconversions of the guinea pig uterine progestin receptor as a set of equilibria "Equilibrium Model" (5). Our work with the rabbit system leads to the following modification.

$$4.5S \rightleftharpoons 5.5S \rightleftharpoons 7.0S \rightleftharpoons 8.5S$$

Conditions for detecting each of these forms have been described (4,5,10) as has the reversibility of the 4.5S to 7S conversion (4). Data presented here, in addition to substantiating this basic concept, point out that the steroid stabilizes the 8.5S complex roughly in proportion to its biological activity.

The "Equilibrium Model" provided the theoretical base for our isolation of the nonactivated receptor. Our 5 mM PGTMA buffer, in concert with tritiated R5020 stabilized the complex sufficiently to allow isolation of the receptor. Our purification scheme was not designed to yield small samples of a highly purified material, rather it allowed a practical isolation of large amounts of unaltered receptor of sufficient mass to induce an immunological response in a mouse. Assuming a nominal molecular weight of 100,000 daltons, the receptor comprised 0.04% of the original cytosol protein. Thus our 25 fold purification yielded 25 to 50 ug of receptor at a purity of approximately 1%, near the purity of estrogen receptors reported by Green et. al (11) for production of hybridmas from rat spleen cells.

The antibody is an IgG_1 with a Kd of ~.86 nM for the rabbit receptor. It appears to be fairly specific, for of the receptors we tested, it recognized progestin receptors from rabbit and human. Similar results were noted by Feil (12) with his polyclonal antisera. Common antigenic determinants may be present in the human and rabbit system, but not in the rat and guinea pig systems.

Initial studies demonstrated that the monoclonal antibody bound only to the nonactivated 8.5S receptor. Dissociation of the receptor into basic components might have resulted in loss of the antibody effect if the antigenic determinants resided on a non-steroid binding subunit. In support of this, we found that ^{125}I labeled antibody bound to both the 8.5S form and a smaller dissociated component.

Under the conditions of these experiments (i.e. an excess of antibody) the antibody does not adhere to the smaller forms, hence there is no evidence of binding of the antibody to the steroid binding portions of the receptor complex. Washing of the immunoadsorbed receptor resulted in the loss of bound (17α-methyl-^3H)-R5020 (8) and the elution of the 92,000 Mr protein (Fig. 8). Under conditions where the subunits are dissociated from each other (i.e. in molybdate free sucrose gradients), we found only the 59,000 Mr peptide bound by the antibody. Thus the antibody appears to recognize the Mr = 59,000 protein.

Preferential binding of the monoclonal antibody to the 8.5S complex taken in concert with the inability to bind to more slowly sedimenting forms suggests that the Mr = 59,000 peptide dissociates from the complex during centrifugation. This implies that the 7S to 8.5S conversion of the receptor involves addition (or loss) of the Mr = 59,000 protein.

Initially we thought that the Mr = 92,000 peptide might be the steroid binding subunit. Photoaffinity labeling experiments have resolved the question. It appears that the nonactivated rabbit uterine progestin receptor system contains steroid binding proteins similar to that reported for the human progestin receptor (13) and chicken oviduct (14-16). Our work agrees with that of Jänne (17) and Lamb and Bullock (18) who detected photoaffinity labeled proteins at Mr 110,000, although we suggest that the smaller peptides may be derived from one of larger parent proteins as a result of proteolysis.

Inspection of the stained gels revealed that like the chicken oviduct system (14-16) the rabbit uterine system contains an excess of Mr = 92,000 nonsteroid binding protein. We can think of no reason why any of these components should be in perfect stoichiometry. Relative concentrations of each component may reflect various physiological states of the tissue. One has only to consider the case of calmodulin as an example. Calmodulin is in excess and provides a key intermediate for many rate limiting enzymatic functions (19). However, the stoichiometry and putative physiological function of receptor components are well beyond the scope of this discourse.

In conclusion, we have applied the concept of the equilibrium model to the isolation of the progestin receptor and the development of an anti-progestin receptor antibody. The antibody has been used as an immunoaffinity resin to isolate the receptor system. We have evidence that the 8.5S nonactivated rabbit uterine progestin receptor system contains both steroid binding and nonsteroid binding components. Thus, the nonactivated form of the receptor is a complex protein containing dissimilar components.

ACKNOWLEDGEMENTS

This work was supported by Grants HD-09367, AG/HD-02776 and BRS-5S01-RR-05700. We especially thank Ms. Shirley Doherty for preparation of the typescript.

REFERENCES

1. Faber, L.E., Sandmann, M.L. and Stavely, H.E.: J. Biol. Chem. 247, 5648-5649 (1972).

2. Faber, L.E., Sandmann, M.L. and Stavely, H.E.: J. Biol. Chem. 247, 8000-8004 (1972).

3. Faber, L.E., Sandmann, M.L. and Stavely, H.E.: Endo. 93, 74-80 (1973).

4. Faber, L.E., Sandmann, M.L. and Stavely, H.E.: Biochem. Med. 19, 78-89 (1978).

5. Faber, L.E.: Steroid Induced Uterine Proteins (M. Beato ed.) Elsevier North Holland p. 197-216 (1980).

6. Nakao, K., Myers, J.E., and Faber, L.E.: Can. J. Biochem. Cell Biol. in press (1984).

7. Fazekas de St. Groth, S., and Scheidegger, D.: J. of Immunological Methods 35, 1-21 (1980).

8. Tai, Ping-K., K., and Faber, L.E.: Can J. Biochem. Cell Biol. in press (1984).

9. Laemmli, V.K.: Nature (London) 227, 680-685 (1970).

10. Saffran, J., Loeser, B.K., Bohnett, S.A., and Faber, L.E.: J. Biol. Chem. 251, 5607-5613 (1976).

11. Greene, G.L., Nolan, C., Engler, J.P., and Jensen, E.V.: Proc. Nat'l Acad. Sci., U.S.A. 77, 5115-5119 (1980).

12. Feil, P.: Endo. 112, 396-398 (1983).

13. Horwitz, K.B., and Alexander, P.S.: Endo 113, 2195-2200 (1983).

14. Birnbaumer, M., Bell, R.C., Schrader, W.T., and O'Malley, B.W.: J. Biol Chem. 259, 1091-1098 (1984).

15. Dougherty, J.J., Puri, R.K., and Toft, D.O.: J. Biol. Chem. 259, 8004-8009 (1984).

16. Renoir, J.-M., Buchov, T., Mester, J., Radanyi, C., and Baulieu, E.-E.: Biochem. in press (1984).

17. Jänne, O.A.: Endo 110:A141 (1982).

18. Lamb, D.J., and Bullock, D.W.: Endo 114, 1833-1840 (1984).

19. Klee, T.H., Crouch, T.H., Richman, P.G.: Ann. Rev. Biochem. 49, 489-515 (1980).

ALTERATIONS IN MOUSE GLUCOCORTICOID RECEPTOR STRUCTURE: EFFECTS OF VARIOUS HYDROLYTIC ENZYMES

Wayne V. Vedeckis, Branka Kovačić-Milivojević, Margot C. LaPointe and Cheryl E. Reker

Department of Biochemistry, Louisiana State University Medical Center, New Orleans, Louisiana 70112, U.S.A.

Introduction

The structure of steroid hormone receptors has been the subject of intensive study for many years. It has recently been found that proteases, ribonucleases, and phosphatases can alter the structure and biochemical properties of steroid receptor proteins. This has allowed considerable insight into the structure of the hormone-binding, monomeric receptor protein, the organization of oligomeric receptor complexes, and the events leading to the conversion of the receptor into its gene regulatory form. Summarized below are our studies on the effects of hydrolytic enzymes on the structure of the glucocorticoid receptor obtained from mouse liver and the AtT-20 pituitary tumor cell line. A more general review on the structure of steroid receptors can be found elsewhere (1).

Background

Steroid receptors appear to exist as oligomeric proteins ($M_r \simeq 300,000$) which do not bind well to nuclei or DNA. These are referred to as untransformed receptors. After binding the steroid hormone, receptor transformation is facilitated by a wide variety of experimental manipulations (1,2). It is currently believed that receptor transformation

Molecular Mechanism of Steroid Hormone Action
© 1985 Walter de Gruyter & Co., Berlin · New York – Printed in Germany

involves subunit dissociation to yield the transformed species, which binds well to nuclei and DNA (1).

The oligomeric, untransformed AtT-20 cell glucocorticoid receptor (GC-R) has a sedimentation coefficient of 9.1S, a Stokes radius of 8.3 nm, and a calculated molecular weight of 319,000 (319K) (1,2,3). Two transformed GC-R species have been identified. One is an apparently oligomeric form with the following characteristics: 5.2S; R_s = 6-8.3 nm; M_r = 132-182K. The uncertainty of the actual Stokes radius (due to technical limitations) precludes a definitive assignment of a molecular weight to this form. Some of the studies described below are directed at this question. A monomeric, transformed, AtT-20 cell GC-R has also been identified (Table I). It has a sedimentation coefficient of 3.8S, a Stokes radius of 6 nm, and a molecular weight of 96K. This molecular weight has been independently confirmed by sodium dodecyl sulfate polyacrylamide gel electrophoresis (SDS-PAGE) of GC-R which is covalently affinity-labeled with dexamethasone-21-mesylate (Dex-M) (1,4,5).

A major goal of our laboratory is to determine the molecular composition and structure of these different GC-R forms, and the mechanisms involved in their interconversion. The use of proteases, ribonucleases, and phosphatases has been of significant value in this endeavor.

Results

1) Proteases. Perhaps the most fruitful utilization of hydrolases in receptor structure studies have been those involving various proteolytic enzymes. This stemmed from early observations that low molecular weight, hormone-binding receptor fragments are generated by various experimental treatments (reviewed in 1). These fragments are apparently produced by the action of certain endogenous cytosolic proteases on the receptor protein.

Table I. Properties of the monomeric, mouse glucocorticoid receptor and proteolytic receptor fragments.

	Monomer	Partially Proteolyzed	Mero-receptor
Size			
Sedimentation Coefficient	3.8S	3.2S	2.4S
Stokes Radius	6 nm	3.9 nm	2.4 nm
Molecular Weight	96K	53K	24K
Shape			
Frictional Ratio	1.82	1.45	1.15
Axial Ratio	16	8	3
Column Behavior [KCl]			
DEAE-Cellulose	0.08 M	0.03 M	DT
Phosphocellulose	0.17 M	0.30 M	DT
DNA-Cellulose	0.14 M	0.20 M	DT

Most tissues appear to contain significant levels of endogenous proteases, while receptor proteolysis occurs to a lesser extent in certain established cell lines. For the AtT-20 cell line, evidence suggests that this is due to a lower intracellular protease level (6,7), while a heat- and pH-stable macromolecular protease inhibitor appears to be responsible for lowered GC-R proteolysis in the mouse WEHI-7 lymphoma cell line (8). In either event, these cell lines are valuable sources of unproteolyzed receptors which can be used as substrates for receptor cleavage studies.

The endogenous proteases which cleave the calf-uterine estrogen (9) and chick oviduct progesterone (10,11,12) receptors have been partially purified and characterized. The properties of these enzymes are very similar to those of calpain, a ubiquitous, calcium-activated, neutral protease (13). That is, the uterine and oviduct enzymes are stimulated by calcium, and both are apparently sulfhydryl (cysteine) proteases, since their activities are eliminated by treatment with sulfhydryl-reactive reagents (9,11). No physiological role for these proteases has yet been demonstrated.

Initial studies seemed to indicate that the untransformed and transformed GC-R are equally susceptible to proteolytic cleavage (14), while others have suggested that the untransformed GC-R is a poorer substrate than the transformed species (7,15). This latter observation is consistent with the fact that the untransformed mouse liver GC-R does not undergo significant proteolysis when kept at 0°C, whereas all of the GC-R is proteolyzed 3 h after transformation by Sephadex G-25 filtration (7). Thus, it has been hypothesized that receptor transformation (subunit dissociation) is accompanied by the exposure of protease-sensitive regions of the receptor protein (7,15).

The cleavage of steroid receptors by proteases results in the production of discrete receptor fragments, and it is this property which has been of most value in receptor structure studies. Most remarkably, all classes of steroid receptors yield very similar cleavage products (reviewed in 1,7). Additionally, no absolute specificity is shown with respect to the protease utilized. This implies that the monomeric receptor protein is comprised of relatively discrete protease-resistant protein domains, separated by fairly extensive stretches of protease-sensitive sequence. It seems likely that these protease-sensitive regions contain the appropriate recognition sequence for a wide variety of proteases, but that non-denaturing techniques currently available cannot distinguish the small differences in the sizes of the proteolytic receptor fragments generated by the different enzymes. Better results showing differences in receptor fragment size with different proteases have been obtained using SDS-PAGE of covalently affinity-labeled receptors (16).

The 96K, monomeric, mouse GC-R can be cleaved into two discrete hormone-binding fragments. One of these, which has been designated the partially proteolyzed receptor (7), has the following characteristics: 3.2S; R_s = 3.9 nm; M_r = 53K. Additional properties of this proteolytic fragment are listed in Table I. When the mouse liver GC-R is transformed *in vitro*, the partially proteolyzed form is almost exclusively generated via cytosolic protease activity (Fig. 1) (7). In addition, this receptor fragment is readily produced by the addition of low levels of chymotrypsin. Importantly, this fragment retains its ability to bind the steroid hormone as well as to DNA-cellulose, although the latter property is not identical to that of the 96K monomer (see below). Thus, it can be concluded that the hormone-binding and DNA-binding sites of the mouse GC-R are probably linked contiguously on about one-half of the receptor polypeptide chain. The remaining half of the protein may not be involved in these receptor functions (see below).

It is important to note that the molecular weight for the partially proteolyzed GC-R was determined from hydrodynamic properties obtained under non-denaturing experimental conditions. However, when covalently affinity-labeled GC-R is treated with chymotrypsin and subjected to SDS-PAGE, the molecular weights obtained are smaller, that is, 39-40K (17,18). Thus, it is possible that the "native" partially proteolyzed GC-R (M_r = 53,000) contains two polypeptides, with molecular weights of 40K and 13K. It may be that proteolytic cleavage has occurred, but that these two polypeptides are held together by covalent (e.g., disulfide) or strong non-covalent bonds under non-denaturing conditions. Because of this complication (and the difficulty in analyzing the DNA-binding activities of these two putative fragments under denaturing conditions), it is not yet known if the DNA-binding activity of the partially proteolyzed GC-R resides in the 40K fragment alone, in the 13K fragment alone, or in both fragments in association. Western blot analyses of the binding activity of proteolyzed, purified glucocorticoid receptors to [32P]labeled cloned gene fragments [as has been done for the chick

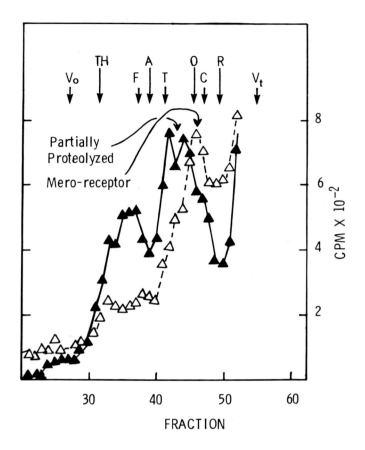

FIGURE 1: High-performance gel exclusion chromatography of glucocorticoid receptor proteolytic fragments. Mouse liver cytosol glucocorticoid receptor was labeled with [^{3}H]Dex and transformed by Sephadex G-25 gel filtration, followed by a 4 h incubation at 0°C (▲). An aliquot of the receptor-containing fractions was treated with 50 μg/ml trypsin for 1 h (0°C), followed by 500 μg/ml soybean trypsin inhibitor (30 min, 0°C) (△). Both samples were chromatographed on a TSK-4000SW (30 cm)/TSK-3000SW (30 cm) column combination at a flow rate of 1 ml/min. The first peak to elute (with ferritin) in the partially proteolyzed sample (▲) is unproteolyzed monomer (6 nm), while the partially proteolyzed receptor itself (3.9 nm) is indicated by an arrow. Mero-receptor (2.4 nm) is also indicated by an arrow. V_o = the excluded volume; V_t = the total volume. Protein standards used to calibrate the column are thyroglobulin (TH; 8.61 nm), ferritin (F; 6.15 nm), aldolase (A; 4.5 nm), iron-free human transferrin (T; 3.66 nm), ovalbumin (O; 2.86 nm), chymotrypsinogen A (C; 2.21 nm), and ribonuclease A (R; 1.64 nm).

oviduct progesterone receptor (19)] are required to answer this question.

The second discrete, hormone-binding, GC-R fragment which can be generated is called the mero-receptor (Table I). This form is observed when trypsin is added to cytosol (Fig. 1) (7). The salient physicochemical properties of the GC-R mero-receptor are as follows: 2.4S; R_s = 2.4 nm; M_r = 24K. Of great interest is the fact that this fragment retains its hormone-binding activity, but does not bind to DNA. This implies that the DNA-binding activity resides in a receptor fragment with a molecular weight of about 29K [53K (partially proteolyzed) minus 24K (mero-receptor)]. The mero-receptor has approximately the same molecular weight under denaturing conditions (SDS-PAGE) (18) as the native protein.

2) Receptor proteolysis and domain structure. The experiments described above, and others, have allowed a preliminary mapping of the structural (and, perhaps, functional) regions of the monomeric GC-R. Figure 2 is a tentative proteolytic map of the mouse GC-R. Under non-denaturing conditions the receptor appears to exist as three relatively protease-resistant protein domains, separated by protease-sensitive regions. The first, the hormone-binding domain, has been designated the mero-receptor, and it has a molecular weight of about 24K. The second (M_r = 29K) is apparently the DNA-binding domain since its presence imparts this property to the partially proteolyzed receptor. The last domain (M_r = 43K) has been designated the "modulating" domain (17,18). Although its function is unknown, its covalent attachment to the remainder of the receptor protein appears to be required for the hormonal regulation of gene transcription (see below). It is not yet known if the 43K modulating domain is removed from the 96K GC-R as a wholly intact fragment. However, when an antibody against this domain is used to analyze chymotrypsin-treated GC-R, an immunoreactive (but non-hormone-binding) 2.6 nm fragment is detected (20). Thus, the

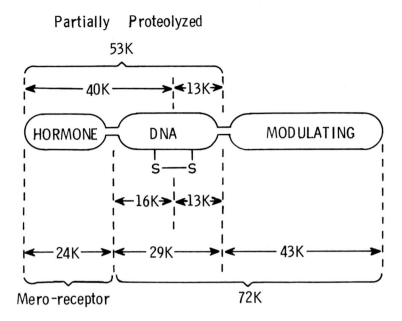

FIGURE 2: Hypothetical proteolytic map of the mouse glucocorticoid receptor monomer. The three protease-resistant protein domains (hormone-binding, DNA-binding, modulating) are separated by protease-sensitive regions. The disulfide bridge in the DNA-binding domain has not been demonstrated experimentally. Further details of the fragmentation pattern are discussed in the text.

modulating domain appears to be removed in a relatively intact (2.6 nm) state. A more extensive digestion of the receptor with chymotrypsin causes a decrease in size of the immunoreactive material to 1.4 nm (20).

Figure 3 depicts the various proteolytic pathways which the GC-R may follow. These are also reflected in the proteolytic fragmentation pattern postulated in Figure 2. It should be emphasized that these schemes are inferred, and have not yet been confirmed by rigorous experimentation. In Figure 3, those steps and receptor fragments which have not yet been convincingly demonstrated are indicated by question marks. Fragments which bind radioactive steroid are labeled with asterisks.

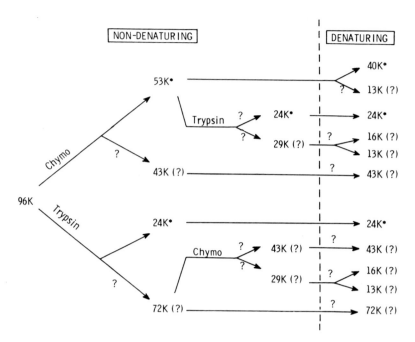

FIGURE 3: Hypothetical pathways for proteolysis of the glucocorticoid receptor monomer. Fragments which may be generated under non-denaturing conditions are depicted on the left of the vertical dotted line, while those which might be observed under denaturing conditions are shown on the right. Those steps and fragments which have not yet been empirically demonstrated are designated with question marks. Those fragments which bind hormone are labeled with an asterisk. Further details are discussed in the text. Chymo = chymotrypsin.

Chymotrypsin treatment of the GC-R results in the formation of a 53K hormone-binding fragment (partially proteolyzed GC-R) under non-denaturing conditions (Fig. 3, upper scheme). Since SDS-PAGE yields a hormone-binding fragment of 40K, we have suggested here that a 13K non-hormone-binding fragment is associated with the 40K hormone-binding fragment under non-denaturing conditions. This is depicted as being due to a disulfide linkage (Fig. 2), although no current evidence supports this. It is merely suggested due to the stability of 53K fragment under conditions using high salt. Additionally, this hypothesis can be tested by using disulfide reduction followed by alkylation with a radiolabeled sulfhydryl-attacking reagent (e.g., iodoacetamide). Naturally, this will require the use of highly purified receptor preparations.

If the GC-R is treated first with chymotrypsin and the 53K fragment then isolated, subsequent treatment with trypsin should yield the mero-receptor (24K) plus the DNA-binding domain (29K). If chymotrypsin has cleaved the DNA-binding domain as suggested above, the 29K fragment should contain two polypeptides, which are held together under non-denaturing conditions. Denaturation and reduction of the 29K fragment, therefore, should yield two fragments, with molecular weights of 16K and 13K.

As mentioned previously, trypsin treatment of the GC-R results in the generation of the mero-receptor (24K), that is, the hormone-binding domain (Fig. 3, lower scheme). Reduction and denaturation of the mero-receptor results in no alteration of its molecular weight (SDS-gels). This scheme implies that a 72K non-hormone-binding receptor fragment should also be generated by trypsin treatment of the 96K monomer. Although fragments of this size can be detected in purified GC-R preparations run on SDS gels (M.C. LaPointe and W.V. Vedeckis, unpublished), their identity as receptor fragments has not yet been accomplished. In a similar manner as has been proposed above, if this 72K fragment is treated with chymotrypsin, 43K (modulating) and 29K (DNA-binding) domain fragments should arise when analyzed under non-denaturing, non-reducing conditions, and three fragments (43K, 16K, 13K) should be generated under denaturing, reducing conditions.

The scenario presented here is not meant to necessarily indicate the actual state of affairs for GC-R structure. Rather, we wish to propose a framework which can be tested experimentally. These experiments will not be trivial. However, by using a combination of approaches the structure of the GC-R monomer can be investigated. These future studies will necessitate the use of purified receptor preparations, covalent affinity-labeled receptor, and antibodies against the receptor [utilized under both non-denaturing and denaturing (Western blot) conditions]. Experiments along these lines are already being conducted in a number of laboratories.

3) Functional significance of receptor domain structure. It is not
    possible to thoroughly discuss the implications of the domain
    structure of the GC-R here. A detailed treatment of this question
    can be found elsewhere (1). However, a few salient points deserve
    mention. First, physiological responses to glucocorticoids require
    the functional involvement of all three receptor domains. This has
    been shown most clearly using lymphoid cell lines which are killed
    by glucocorticoids (reviewed in 21,22,23). Thus, GC-resistant
    mutants exist in which mutations have apparently occurred in the
    GC-R gene. Mutations which affect either hormone-binding activity
    or the ability of the GC-R to interact with DNA can render cells
    GC-resistant. It is likely that the binding of hormone is required
    for efficient receptor transformation (conversion to its DNA-
    binding configuration). However, GC-R mutants exist in which
    hormone-binding is normal, but in which the interaction of the
    protein with DNA is either decreased or increased in intensity.
    Indeed, one class of mutants (nuclear transfer increased, nt^i) has
    properties quite similar to the partially proteolyzed receptor
    (reviewed in 1). That is, it binds more avidly to DNA-cellulose
    than the wild-type GC-R, in a manner similar to that of the
    partially proteolyzed GC-R (Table I). It has been suggested that
    the nt^i mutant lacks the modulating domain, since it is of a
    smaller size (40-53K) and since antibodies against this domain
    detect no cross-reacting material in nt^i mutant cytosol
    preparations (24). However, partially proteolyzed receptors can
    apparently interact with the same specific sequences in cloned DNA
    fragments to which the wild-type receptor specifically binds
    (25,26). Slight variations in the efficiency of GC-R binding to
    gene fragments (25) may explain the fact that the nt^i mutant does
    not respond to the hormone. Alternatively, rather than being
    involved in the DNA sequence-specific binding itself, it has been
    suggested that the modulating domain may be involved in an initial
    interaction of the receptor at the nuclear membrane or matrix,
    proximal to the location of hormonally-responsive genes (1). To
    further complicate matters, recent studies (27) using in situ

radiation inactivation of the GC-R in both wild-type and nt[i] mutant cells suggest that, in the intact cell, both receptor proteins are of the same size (rather than the nt[i] mutant GC-R being smaller). Further studies using a variety of techniques, especially those of molecular biology, will be required to address these questions. A combination of protease-mapping studies and the cloning and sequencing of the GC-R gene will also be required to determine the location of the hormone-binding, DNA-binding, and modulating domains in reference to the amino and carboxyl termini of the receptor monomer. Based on GC-R mutant studies it has been suggested that the hormone-binding domain is at the N-terminus while the modulating domain is at the C-terminus of the receptor monomer (1).

4) Ribonuclease. Ribonuclease treatment of steroid receptor proteins results in alterations in receptor structural features, most notably in their sedimentation coefficients (reviewed in 1). In our efforts to characterize the 5.2S, oligomeric, transformed and 9.1S, oligomeric, untransformed mouse GC-R, we discovered that a ribonuclease (RNase)-sensitive molecule may be involved in the structure of these forms (2,5).

Previous studies characterizing the 9.1S untransformed, 5.2S transformed, and 3.8S transformed glucocorticoid receptors suggested that these might be related via a homotetramer : homodimer : monomer scheme (3). At about the same time, a number of other laboratories suggested the same model for GC-R structure (28,29,30,31). We have attempted to study the interconversion of these receptor forms. When the 3.8S, monomeric GC-R is pooled from high salt sucrose gradients, desalted, and then rerun on low salt sucrose gradients containing 20 mM Na_2MoO_4, an increase in sedimentation rate to 5.2S is observed (2). Our initial thought regarding the 3.8S to 5.2S conversion was that the 3.8S monomers are dimerizing upon salt removal. However, if the 3.8S, monomeric GC-R is partially purified via DEAE-cellulose chromatography, desalted, and rerun on low salt, MoO_4^{2-}-containing sucrose gradients, it continues to sediment at about 3.8S. Thus, it appears that some component which cosediments on high salt sucrose gradients with the 3.8S GC-R is removed by DEAE-cellulose chromatography. Indeed, when a higher salt-eluting DEAE-cellulose fraction (which contains no hormone-binding activity) is added back to the 3.8S monomer, an increase in sedimentation rate to 5.2S is obtained (5).

These results were reminiscent of those obtained by others (reviewed in 1), which suggested that a non-hormone-binding receptor binding factor (RBF) is involved in the structure of oligomeric receptor species. Also based on these studies, we presumed that this factor would be proteinaceous. Indeed, we found that this factor is macromolecular (non-dialyzable). However, not only is it stable to freezing and lyophilization, it is also heat-stable (100°C, 20 min). Furthermore, if this factor is incubated with ribonuclease A either before or after addition to the 3.8S GC-R monomer no increase in receptor sedimentation rate is observed. Therefore, cellular RNA was purified using phenol/chloroform extraction. Addition of this purified RNA to the 3.8S GC-R monomer causes the receptor to shift to a discrete 5.2S form on MoO_4^{2-}-containing sucrose gradients (5). Thus, it appears that the 5.2S, oligomeric, transformed GC-R contains one monomeric receptor protein molecule plus RNA. If the Stokes radius of the 5.2S GC-R is 6 nm (as our most recent estimates seem to indicate), then the molecular weight of this receptor species is about 132K. This implies that the RNA component of the 5.2S GC-R has a molecular weight of approximately 36K [132K minus 96K (monomeric GC-R protein)].

These studies do not prove that the reconstituted 5.2S GC-R is the same as that obtained when the receptor is transformed in vitro (2,3,32). It likewise does not address the question of the possible role of RNA in the structure of the 9.1S, untransformed GC-R. Therefore, we prepared the 9.1S, untransformed GC-R, as well

98

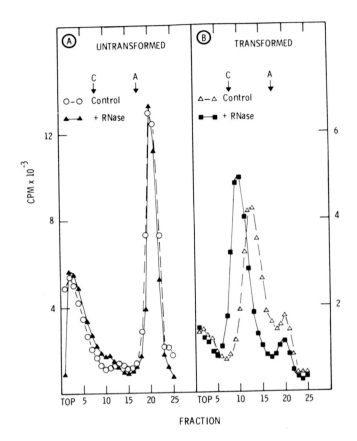

FIGURE 4: RNase sensitivity of the 9.1S, oligomeric, untransformed and
5.2S, oligomeric, transformed glucocorticoid receptor species. Panel
A - The untransformed, cytosolic GC-R from AtT-20 cells was either left
untreated (O) or was incubated with 90 U/ml of RNase A for 1 h at 0°C
(▲). After removal of the free hormone, aliquots were centrifuged on
vertical tube rotor 5-20% sucrose gradients in buffer containing 20 mM
sodium molybdate. Panel B - AtT-20 cell cytosol was passed over a
Sephadex G-25 column and then incubated for 4.5 h at 0°C (△). An
aliquot of this sample was also treated with RNase A as described above
(■). Both samples were then centrifuged in sucrose gradients as
described above. The results show that the 9.1S untransformed, GC-R is
unaffected when RNase treated, whereas the 5.2S, transformed GC-R is
converted to the 3.8S, transformed GC-R by RNase treatment. Protein
standards which were run in parallel tubes were chymotrypsinogen A (C;
2.6S) and aldolase (A; 7.9S).

as the 5.2S, transformed GC-R, from AtT-20 cell cytosol. The latter species was obtained by filtering the untransformed receptor over a Sephadex G-25 column, followed by a 4.5 h incubation at 0°C. Both the untransformed (9.1S) and transformed (5.2S) GC-R were left untreated or were incubated for 1 h at 0°C with 90 U/ml of bovine pancreatic ribonuclease A. These samples were then centrifuged on MoO_4^{2-}-containing vertical tube rotor sucrose gradients (2,5,32). These results are shown in Figure 4.

RNase treatment of the 9.1S, untransformed GC-R has no significant effect on its sedimentation rate, while the 5.2S, transformed receptor is converted to the 3.8S, monomeric receptor by the enzyme. No protease activity is detected in the RNase enzyme preparation when it is incubated with Dex-M affinity-labeled GC-R (5). A number of conclusions can be drawn from this experiment. First, RNA appears to be a component of the 5.2S GC-R which is generated after in vitro receptor transformation. In a separate study (2), we also showed that when the GC-R is transformed in the intact cell, the 5.2S species is obtained when cytosol is prepared. RNase treatment of this in vivo - transformed GC-R also decreases its sedimentation rate to 3.8S (2). Second, the reconstituted 5.2S GC-R which is obtained by the addition of purified RNA to the partially purified 3.8S GC-R monomer is indistinguishable from the 5.2S GC-R obtained after in vitro receptor transformation, at least in regard to sedimentation properties and ribonuclease sensitivity. Lastly, either RNA is not a component of the 9.1S, oligomeric untransformed GC-R, or it is inaccessible to ribonuclease hydrolysis.

Current studies are directed toward determining the physiological relevance of receptor-RNA interaction. The major question to be answered concerns the specificity of RNA-binding. For example, one possibility is that the 9.1S, untransformed receptor contains only protein subunits. Since transformation exposes the DNA-binding site it is conceivable that the untransformed receptor dissociates into 3.8S subunits, and that these (by virtue of their DNA-binding site) happen to bind to RNA molecules present in the cytosolic extract. However, this interaction is clearly not wholly non-specific, since the 5.2S GC-R species sediments as a discrete symmetrical peak. Also, titration of the 3.8S GC-R with crude or purified cellular RNA does not cause the receptor to aggregate to species with higher sedimentation coefficients. Thus, if the 3.8S monomer binds to cellular RNA after dissociation from the 9.1S untransformed species, some specificity of binding seems to exist. It is also not yet known if the RNA-binding site on the 3.8S GC-R monomer is equivalent to its DNA-binding site. However, mero-receptor does not interact with RNA and, thus, does not apparently contain the RNA-binding site (B. Kovačič-Milivojević and W.V. Vedeckis, unpublished).

A crucial question is whether RNA is a component of the 9.1S, untransformed complex, but is inaccessible to hydrolysis by added ribonuclease. At present our own studies do not answer this question. However, experiments performed by two other research groups provide some tantalizing information in this regard. When the untransformed rat liver GC-R is purified in the presence of Na_2MoO_4, two major macromolecular components are displayed upon SDS-PAGE (33,34). The larger component has a molecular weight of about 90K, and stains with both Coomassie Blue and silver stain. This appears to be the monomeric GC-R protein. A lower molecular weight component (24K) is also present, but it is revealed only upon silver staining of the gels. Both the 90K and 24K molecules are phosphorylated in vivo (34). Housley and Pratt (35) have also purified the untransformed GC-R after incubating mouse L cells with [^{32}P]orthophosphate. Upon SDS-PAGE four phosphorylated species are obtained, two of which have molecular weights of 92K and 21K. RNase treatment of the purified untransformed GC-R preparation results in the loss of the 21K band. Thus, the untransformed, oligomeric GC-R complex may be comprised of a number of 90-96K monomeric receptor proteins, plus a low molecular weight RNA (21-24K). Further studies, including a characterization of the RNA, are required to determine if this RNA species is an integral component of the 9.1S oligomeric, untransformed GC-R or if it merely copurifies with this species. Because of the

methods utilized in these purifications (steroid affinity chromatography, gel filtration), the former postulate seems more likely than the
latter.

5) Phosphatases. Perhaps one of the most active current areas in
   steroid receptor research involves receptor phosphorylation and its
   role in receptor structure and function. A number of laboratories
   have now shown that steroid receptors can be phosphorylated both in
   vivo (34,35,36) and in vitro (37,38,39). Furthermore, it has been
   suggested that the phosphorylated state of the receptor (or some
   other cytosolic component) may be important in controlling hormone-
   binding activity and receptor transformation state. Indeed, it has
   been postulated that the ability of various phosphatase inhibitors
   (most notably, molybdate ions) to both stabilize hormone-binding
   and inhibit transformation may be due to an inhibition of dephosphorylation (perhaps of the receptor itself).

   It has been shown that alkaline phosphatase addition to rat liver
   cytosol causes GC-R transformation, as assayed by the elution
   characteristics of the receptor from DEAE-cellulose and DNA-
   cellulose columns (40). We have recently embarked upon a study
   of the effects of calf intestinal alkaline phosphatase on the sedimentation properties of the mouse AtT-20 cell GC-R (4). When
   cytosol is incubated at 10°C for 2 h, most (75-90%) of the GC-R
   sediments as the 9.1S, oligomeric, untransformed species (Fig. 5).
   The addition of alkaline phosphatase causes a substantial decrease
   in the amount of 9.1S, untransformed receptor, with a concomitant
   increase in the amount of 5.2S, transformed GC-R (50-80% of the
   total receptor), while molybdate completely inhibits alkaline
   phosphatase-promoted receptor transformation (Fig. 5). These
   results suggest that dephosphorylation of some component in the
   cytosol allows GC-R transformation to occur.

   Additional experiments using a variety of phosphatase and protease
   inhibitors were conducted (4). We compared the ability of these

102

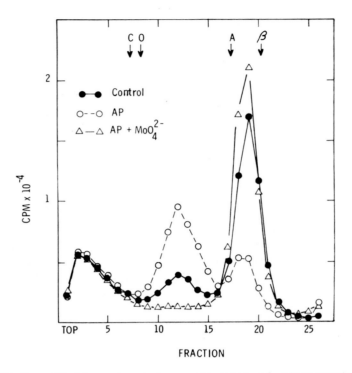

FIGURE 5: Alkaline phosphatase promotion of glucocorticoid receptor transformation. Mouse AtT-20 cell cytosol glucocorticoid receptor labeled with [³H]Dex was treated with buffer alone (●), 107 μg/ml bovine intestinal alkaline phosphatase (AP) (○), or alkaline phosphatase plus 20 mM sodium molybdate (△), for 2 h at 10°C. After removal of free hormone, the samples were centrifuged on vertical tube rotor 5-20% sucrose gradients in buffer containing 20 mM sodium molybdate. The results show that alkaline phosphatase promotes the 9.1S to 5.2S receptor transformation, while molybdate is effective in inhibiting this conversion. Protein standards which were run in parallel tubes were chymotrypsinogen A (C; 2.6S), ovalbumin (O; 3.5S), aldolase (A; 7.9S), and β-amylase (β; 9.4S).

inhibitors to block endogenous (dialysis-promoted) and alkaline phosphatase-promoted GC-R transformation to their potency in suppressing both cytosolic and alkaline phosphatase activity (paranitrophenyl phosphate hydrolysis). Very complex inhibitory profiles were obtained. In general, the ability of the inhibitors to suppress endogenous receptor transformation correlated fairly well with their ability to block cytosolic phosphatase activity. A much less satisfactory correlation was obtained with exogenously added alkaline phosphatase. The results obtained are somewhat difficult to interpret unequivocally. We attribute this to the following: the assay conditions varied significantly; the cytosol is a complex mixture of substances; substrate interactions with the inhibitors (e.g., molybdate) may be occurring, etc. Nonetheless, depending upon the specific assay used, a number of phosphatase inhibitors were effective in blocking GC-R transformation.

We have tried to determine if alkaline phosphatase-promoted receptor transformation might be caused by the addition of a contaminating protease activity in the enzyme preparation. A number of observations make this unlikely. First, certain phosphatase inhibitors which lack protease-inhibitory activity (such as levamisole, sodium fluoride, sodium arsenate, and glucose-1-phosphate) are effective inhibitors of GC-R transformation. Second, alkaline phosphatase treatment of the GC-R does not generate the 3.9 nm partially proteolyzed or the 2.4 nm meroreceptor fragments, when analyzed using high-performance, gel exclusion chromatography (data not shown). Third, when Dex-M affinity labeled GC-R is treated with alkaline phosphatase, no decrease in the labeling intensity or the size of the GC-R band is observed (4). Finally, neither antipain nor PMSF block alkaline phosphatase-promoted receptor transformation. However, one caveat must be mentioned. Leupeptin, a bacterial protease inhibitor, is effective in blocking alkaline phosphatase-promoted, as well as endogenous, GC-R transformation. This, therefore, indicates that it is still possible that proteolysis is involved when alkaline phosphatase is used to promote receptor transformation. An alternative hypothesis, that leupeptin is blocking receptor transformation by a previously unknown mechanism other than protease inhibition, is discussed elsewhere (4).

Although not proven, the preponderance of evidence suggests that dephosphorylation is somehow involved in steroid receptor transformation. Crucial future studies in this area will require an analysis of the cellular kinases and phosphatases which may regulate receptor transformation and the identification of the substrates which may be involved

in these reactions. Since steroid receptors are apparently phosphoproteins, it is tempting to speculate that they are the physiologically
relevant substrates for these reactions.

Discussion

Presented above are some of our recent studies on GC-R structure using
hydrolytic enzymes. The information gleaned from these studies, and
others, has led us to formulate a working model for GC-R structure and
its mechanism of transformation to its DNA-binding (gene regulatory)
form. This model is presented in Figure 6.

The 9.1S, untransformed GC-R is an oligomeric complex with a molecular
weight of about 319K. Its composition is unknown. One possibility is
that it is a homotetramer of 96K monomeric subunits. However, even
given experimental error, the discrepancy between the calculated molecular weight for a homotetramer (384K) and the experimentally determined
molecular weight (319K) is very large. Thus, a second possibility is
that the untransformed receptor is composed of an indeterminate number
of hormone binding monomers (one to three) plus non-hormone binding
receptor binding factors (RBFs). The putative RBFs may be proteinaceous
or RNA, and some evidence exists for both possibilities in various
receptor systems.

The steroid hormone ligand binds to the hormone-binding domain of the
receptor protein in the untransformed complex. This may destabilize the
subunit interactions, and may render a phosphate group on the receptor
accessible to hydrolysis by endogenous phosphatase activity. Receptor
dephosphorylation could conceivably further destabilize subunit interactions in the oligomeric complex. Finally, even further destabilization could occur after the dissociation of a low molecular weight
inhibitor of receptor transformation from the oligomeric complex
(reviewed in 41 and 42).

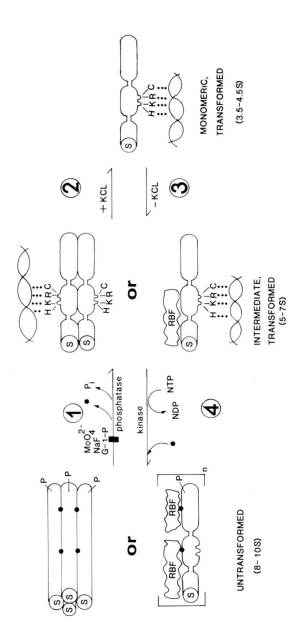

FIGURE 6: Hypothetical model for mouse glucocorticoid receptor structure and mechanism of transformation. The various aspects of this model are described in detail in the text. Symbols used are as follows: P, covalently-attached phosphate; S, steroid hormone; ●, low molecular weight inhibitor of transformation; H, histidine; K, lysine; R, arginine; C, cysteine; RBF, receptor binding factor; NTP, nucleoside triphosphate; NDP, nucleoside diphosphate. Chemical inactivation studies implicate the four amino acids shown in the DNA-binding activity of the receptor (reviewed in 1).

Subunit dissociation appears to be the actual molecular mechanism of receptor transformation. Two transformed GC-R species have been identified. One is a 5.2S oligomer with a molecular weight of 132-182K. This could be a dimer of identical hormone-binding subunits. Alternatively, one monomeric subunit may be associated with one or more RBFs. In our recent studies, it appears that a low molecular weight RNA ($M_r \simeq$ 36K) may be associated with a receptor monomer. The other transformed GC-R species appears to be the 3.8S monomeric, hormone-binding subunit itself (M_r = 96K).

Upon receptor transformation, two structural alterations can be detected besides the decrease in size of the complex. First, the DNA-binding site, which is apparently occluded in the untransformed oligomer, becomes exposed. This allows the receptor protein to interact with specific DNA sequences and regulate gene transcription. Second, the protease-sensitive regions appear to become more accessible to attack by endogenous cytosolic proteases. No physiological significance has yet been attributed to this latter occurrence.

The enzymatic dissection of steroid receptors is only beginning. For example, fine structural proteolytic mapping of steroid receptors, as suggested above, must be coupled to functional assays (e.g., in vitro transcription) to further elucidate structure-function relationships. Besides the crude uses of ribonucleases employed previously, more sophisticated utilization of this class of hydrolases will be forthcoming. Specifically, ribonucleases will undoubtedly be used to characterize and sequence the RNA which is found bound to receptors, with the ultimate purpose of determining if the RNA is homogeneous and specific. Phosphatases and kinases need to be purified from cells and their role in receptor regulation elucidated. The most immediate goal will be to isolate and characterize those enzymes which specifically phosphorylate and dephosphorylate steroid receptor proteins. Finally, the most exciting application for the use of hydrolases in analyzing receptor structure has not yet been mentioned here. That is, a very active current area of receptor research involves the use of DNA restriction endonucleases in attempts to clone steroid receptor genes. Once this is accomplished (certainly in the very near future) the entire polypeptide sequence of receptors will be revealed. Together with the analysis of mutant receptor genes, it will then be possible to identify those amino acid residues which are critical for steroid hormone receptor functions, such as their hormone and DNA-binding activity.

Summary and Conclusions

Various hydrolases have been used to characterize the mouse glucocorticoid receptor. Protease studies have revealed that the monomeric, 3.8S, transformed glucocorticoid receptor (M_r = 96K) is comprised of three protein domains, separated by protease-sensitive regions. These three domains have been designated the hormone-binding (M_r = 24K), DNA-binding (M_r = 29K), and modulating (M_r = 43K) domains. Ribonuclease studies indicate that the oligomeric, 5.2S, transformed glucocorticoid receptor (M_r = 132-182K) may contain RNA as a structural component. Phosphatase studies suggest that dephosphorylation of some cytosolic component (perhaps the receptor protein itself) may be involved in glucocorticoid receptor transformation. That is, the oligomeric, 9.1S, untransformed glucocorticoid receptor is converted to the oligomeric, 5.2S, transformed species by alkaline phosphatase treatment. Thus, the use of hydrolytic enzymes has contributed greatly to our understanding of the structure of the monomeric receptor protein, the structure of oligomeric receptor species, and the mechanism of glucocorticoid receptor transformation.

Acknowledgements

The research from our laboratory described here was supported by grants from the National Institutes of Health (AM-27038), the American Cancer Society (BC-436 and NP-422), the Cancer Association of Greater

New Orleans, and Cancer Crusaders of New Orleans. W.V.V. is the recipient of an NIH Research Career Development Award. B.K.-M. is a visiting scientist from the Faculty for Natural Sciences, Department of Biochemistry and Molecular Biology, University of Belgrade, Belgrade, Yugoslavia, and is partially supported by a Research Fellowship from the Yugoslav Government-Serbian Scientific Fund.

References

1. Vedeckis, W.V.: in "Hormonally Sensitive Tumors", V.P. Hollander, ed., Academic Press, New York, in press (1985).

2. Reker, C.E., Kovačić-Milivojević, B., Eastman-Reks, S.B., Vedeckis, W.V.: Biochemistry 24, in press (1985).

3. Vedeckis, W.V.: Biochemistry 22, 1983-1989 (1983).

4. Reker, C.E., Vedeckis, W.V.: Submitted for publication (1985).

5. Kovačić-Milivojević, B., Reker, C.E., Vedeckis, W.V.: Submitted for publication (1985).

6. Vedeckis, W.V.: Biochemistry 20, 7237-7245 (1981).

7. Vedeckis, W.V.: Biochemistry 22, 1975-1983 (1983).

8. Holbrook, N.J., Bodwell, J.E., Munck, A.: J. Steroid Biochem. 20, 245-250 (1984).

9. Puca, G.A., Nola, E., Sica, V., Bresciani, F.: J. Biol. Chem. 252, 1358-1366 (1977).

10. Vedeckis, W.V., Schrader, W.T., O'Malley, B.W.: in "Steroid Hormone Receptor Systems", W.W. Leavitt and J.H. Clark, eds., Plenum Press, New York, 309-327 (1979).

11. Vedeckis, W.V., Freeman, M.R., Schrader, W.T., O'Malley, B.W.: Biochemistry 19, 335-343 (1980).

12. Vedeckis, W.V., Schrader, W.T., O'Malley, B.W.: Biochemistry 19, 343-349 (1980).

13. Murachi, T.: Trends Biochem. Sci. 8, 167-169 (1983).

14. Wrange, Ö., Gustafsson, J.-Å.: J. Biol. Chem. 253, 856-865 (1978).

15. Mayer, M., Schmidt, T.J., Miller, A., Litwack, G.: J. Steroid Biochem. 19, 1719-1728 (1983).

16. Birnbaumer, M., Schrader, W.T., O'Malley, B.W.: J. Biol. Chem. 258, 7331-7337 (1983).

17. Dellweg, H.-G., Hotz, A., Mugele, K., Gehring, U.: EMBO J. 1, 285-289 (1982).

18. Gehring, U., Hotz, A.: Biochemistry 22, 4013-4018 (1983).

19. Schrader, W.T., Birnbaumer, M.E., Hughes, M.R., Weigel, N.L., Grody, W.W., O'Malley, B.W.: Rec. Prog. Horm. Res. 37, 583-633 (1981).

20. Carlstedt-Duke, J., Okret, S., Wrange, Ö., Gustafsson, J.-Å.: Proc. Natl. Acad. Sci. U.S.A. 79, 4260-4264 (1982).

21. Yamamoto, K.R., Gehring, U., Stampfer, M.R., Sibley, C.H.: Rec. Prog. Horm. Res. 32, 3-32 (1976).

22. Bourgeois, S.: J. Supramolec. Struct. 13, 401-410 (1980).

23. Gehring, U.: in "Biochemical Actions of Hormones", G. Litwack, ed., Vol. VII, Academic Press, New York, 205-232 (1980).

24. Okret, S., Stevens, Y.-W., Carlstedt-Duke, J., Wrange, Ö., Gustafsson, J.-Å., Stevens, J.: Cancer Res. 43, 3127-3131 (1983).

25. Geisse, S., Scheidereit, C., Westphal, H.M., Hynes, N.E., Groner, B., Beato, M.: EMBO J. 1, 1613-1619 (1982).

26. Scheidereit, C., Geisse, S., Westphal, H.M., Beato, M.: Nature (London) 304, 749-752 (1983).

27. Gruol, D.J., Kempner, E.S., Bourgeois, S.: J. Biol. Chem. 259, 4833-4839 (1984).

28. Raaka, B.M., Samuels, H.H.: J. Biol. Chem. 258, 417-425 (1983).

29. Norris, J.S., Kohler, P.O.: J. Biol. Chem. 258, 2350-2356 (1983).

30. Holbrook, N.J., Bodwell, J.E., Jeffries, M., Munck, A.: J. Biol. Chem. 258, 6477-6485 (1983).

31. Sherman, M.R., Moran, M.C., Tuazon, F.B., Stevens, Y.-W.: J. Biol. Chem. 258, 10366-10377 (1983).

32. Eastman-Reks, S.B., Reker, C.E., Vedeckis, W.V.: Arch. Biochem. Biophys. 230, 274-284 (1984).

33. Grandics, P., Miller, A., Schmidt, T.J., Mittman, D., Litwack, G.: J. Biol. Chem. 259, 3173-3180 (1984).

34. Grandics, P., Miller, A., Schmidt, T.J., Litwack, G.: Biochem. Biophys. Res. Commun. 120, 59-65 (1984).

35. Housley, P.R., Pratt, W.B.: Fed. Proc., Fed. Am. Soc. Exp. Biol. 43, Abst. no. 908, 1572 (1984).

36. Housley, P.R., Pratt, W.B.: J. Biol. Chem. 258, 4630-4635 (1983).

37. Weigel, N.L., Tash, J.S., Means, A.R., Schrader, W.T., O'Malley, B.W.: Biochem. Biophys. Res. Commun. 102, 513-519 (1983).

38. Garcia, T., Tuohimaa, P., Mester, J., Buchou, T., Renoir, J.-M., Baulieu, E.-E.: Biochem. Biophys. Res. Commun. 113, 960-966 (1983).

39. Kurl, R.N., Jacob, S.T.: Biochem. Biophys. Res. Commun. 119, 700-705 (1984).

40. Barnett, C.A., Schmidt, T.J., Litwack, G.: Biochemistry 19, 5446-5455 (1980).

41. Litwack, G.: Trends Biochem. Sci. 4, 217-220 (1979).

42. Schmidt, T.J., Litwack, G.: Physiol. Rev. 62, 1131-1192 (1982).

AFFINITY LABELING STEROIDS AS BIOLOGICALLY ACTIVE PROBES OF
GLUCOCORTICOID RECEPTOR STRUCTURE AND FUNCTION

S. Stoney Simons, Jr.
Laboratory of Chemistry, National Institute of Arthritis, Diabetes, and
Digestive and Kidney Diseases, Bld. 4, Room 132, National Institutes of
Health, Bethesda, Maryland 20205

I. Introduction

A major obstacle in elucidating the mechanism of glucocorticoid
hormone action has been the characterization and purification of the
glucocorticoid receptor. The only apparent activity of the free receptor
is its ability to bind steroid reversibly; and, denaturing conditions
cause essentially immediate dissociation of steroid from the receptor. The
availability of a stabilized, covalent receptor-steroid complex would
greatly facilitate chemical and biochemical studies of the receptor. This
chapter covers the design of affinity labels for glucocorticoid receptors,
the methods that have been used to identify affinity labeling steroids and
the covalently labeled receptor, and finally the applications of affinity
labeled receptors to yield information that is unattainable with conventional non-covalent receptor-steroid complexes. The data presented are
predominantly those from my laboratory; results from other laboratories
have been included when relevant.

A.) Theoretical considerations for affinity labeling of steroid receptors
Affinity labeling has been most commonly practiced with enzymes
(1-3). Dramatic success in achieving highly specific covalent labeling of
the active sites of enzymes has been obtained with "suicide inhibitors",
which are chemically inert molecules that, upon binding to an enzyme, are
converted by the action of the enzyme to affinity labeling compounds (3).
However, virtually all affinity labeled enzymes are biologically inactive.
In fact this loss of enzyme activity is commonly used as a criterion for
successful labeling of the active site of the enzyme (1; see

also 4). In contrast, steroid-free receptors do not appear to have any enzymic, or biological, activity and a "suicide inhibitor" can not be synthesized since the steroid itself is not altered as a consequence of binding to its specific site in the receptor. These two features make the design and assay of affinity labels for receptors more difficult than for enzymes. On the other hand, this also suggests that it should be possible to obtain non-dissociable, affinity labeled receptors that would still possess biological activity (i.e., agonist or antagonist activity).

In order to have an affinity labeling steroid possessing high affinity and specificity for the receptor, most people have chosen to modify a high affinity steroid with glucocorticoid activity. The affinity labeling functional group should be introduced without loss of the basic 11β-hydroxy-pregn-4-ene-3,20-dione structure I that is usually considered necessary for glucocorticoid activity (5). However, we have shown that some pyrazolosteroids (e.g., II) are the most potent glucocorticoids yet

described even though they lack a C-3 ketone and possess an extremely bulky substituent on the A-ring (6). Recently even steroids lacking the C-11 hydroxyl group and/or the C-20 ketone have been found to possess high affinity for glucocorticoid receptors (7-9).

A wide variety of functional groups can, in theory, be introduced into the glucocorticoid molecule to afford the prospective affinity labeling steroid (for recent reviews, see 10,11). The two most popular types of affinity labeling groups are 1.) photoaffinity labels, which will react with most amino acids but usually give low yields of covalent adduct containing a complex mixture of labeled amino acids, and 2.) electrophilic affinity labels, which react with a few amino acids but usually give high yields of covalent adduct containing a small number of labeled amino acids (1,10,11). Unfortunately it is not yet possible to predict which steroidal affinity labels will be successful in forming covalent complexes or whether they will possess agonist or antagonist activity.

Unlike the screening procedures for enzyme affinity labels which rely on the disappearance of enzyme activity, there is no simple technique to screen for steroid receptor affinity labels. The ability of a prospective affinity label to block subsequent [3H]steroid exchange binding to the receptor is a very useful assay but can give misleading results since destruction of the steroid binding site can occur without covalent attachment of the ligand (12,13). We have evaluated our potential affinity labels by using a combination of cell-free competition and exchange binding assays at 0°C along with whole cell assays at 37°C examining biological activity and the inhibition of glucocorticoid-induced biological activity (11). However these assays can only identify the most promising candidates; radioactively labeled compounds are required for more convincing evidence (See Section II B).

II. Formation, Identification, and Properties of Covalent Glucocorticoid Receptor-steroid Complexes

A.) Studies with non-radioactive steroids

Conversion of the C-21 -OH group of the naturally occuring glucocorticoid cortisol to the methanesulfonate ester also transforms the C-17 side chain into the reactive α-keto mesylate group. α-Keto mesylates react almost exclusively with thiols (14,15) and are thus excellent electrophilic affinity labeling functional groups.

Our initial studies revealed that cortisol mesylate 1.) displayed a low, but significant, affinity for cell-free rat hepatoma tissue culture (HTC) cell glucocorticoid receptors, 2.) bound to the cell-free receptors in a way that blocked the subsequent exchange binding with [3H]dexamethasone to an extent of about 75%, 3.) was a more potent antiglucocorticoid in its ability to block the whole cell induction of tyrosine aminotransferase (TAT) by dexamethasone than was expected on the basis of the cell-free affinity of cortisol mesylate for receptors, and 4.) continued to exhibit whole cell antiglucocorticoid activity under conditions that reversed the actions of progesterone, a known reversible antiglucocorticoid (16-18). These observations indicated that cortisol mesylate was an irreversible antiglucocorticoid, possibly due to the formation of a covalent receptor-steroid complex.

The 21-mesylate derivatives III and IV were synthesized to test the hypothesis that incorporation of the α-keto mesylate group into the more potent glucocorticoids dexamethasone and deacylcortivazol would yield steroid mesylates that would be even more potent irreversible antiglucocorticoids than cortisol mesylate (14,19). The apparent affinity of the mesylate derivatives for the cell-free HTC cell receptors decreased in the order IV > III > cortisol mesylate (17,19,20). This is the expected order based on the affinities of the parent steroids for the HTC cell receptor (6), which further suggests that these steroid mesylates are binding to the receptor in the steroid-specific binding cavity.

Dexamethasone 21-mesylate (Dex-Mes) was, as predicted, a more potent irreversible antiglucocorticoid than cortisol mesylate. In each of the above assays, 1/4 to 1/19 as much Dex-Mes was required to produce responses that were similar in magnitude to those observed with cortisol mesylate (20). Unlike cortisol mesylate, Dex-Mes did exhibit some agonist activity (30 ± 16% [mean ± S.D., n =9]) in HTC cells. This establishes that at least the agonist activity, and probably the antagonist activity, of Dex-Mes results from association with the receptor in the steroid-specific binding site. The antagonist activity of Dex-Mes was expressed at lower steroid concentrations than was the agonist activity. These data, coupled with Dex-Mes being a more potent receptor binder and irreversible antagonist than cortisol mesylate, strongly suggest that a covalent receptor--Dex-Mes complex is responsible for the antagonist activity while a non-covalent complex causes the glucocorticoid activity (20).

At this point, it should be emphasized that both cortisol mesylate and Dex-Mes display varying amounts of agonist activity in other cell lines including the FU5-5 rat hepatoma cells (21-24 and personal communications). In this respect, the variable activity of these mesylates is similar to that of the antiestrogen tamoxifen, which is a pure antagonist in chicks and a pure agonist in mice (24-26). Cortisol mesylate was a partial antagonist in rats (27).

Deacylcortivazol 21-mesylate (DAC-Mes) exhibited the highest apparent affinity for HTC cell receptors both in cell-free and whole cell systems but, in contrast to cortisol mesylate and Dex-Mes, DAC-Mes was a pure agonist (19). Furthermore, we could find no evidence for the formation of an irreversible receptor--DAC-Mes complex: 1.) pre-incubation of cell-free complexes with DAC-Mes did not prevent the subsequent exchange binding of [3H]dexamethasone, 2.) the apparent affinity of DAC-Mes for cell-free receptors did not increase with time (which was observed with Dex-Mes and which is consistent with the formation of a covalent complex), and 3.) deinduction of TAT in cells pre-treated with DAC-Mes or dexamethasone occurred at the same rate (19 and S. S. Simons, unpublished results). These data indicate that DAC-Mes fits into the steroid binding site of the receptor differently than do cortisol mesylate and Dex-Mes. It is not yet clear whether this "different fit" to give a non-covalent complex is a consequence of the agonist activity of DAC-Mes (it has been argued that the agonist activity of Dex-Mes is also due to a non-covalent complex [see above]) or of the unusual structure of DAC-Mes (IV)(19). Nevertheless, the results with the steroid mesylates demonstrate that the introduction of a single functional group into a glucocorticoid steroid is not always sufficient to convey antiglucocorticoid activity, irrespective of the potency of the parent steroid. We have therefore proposed that the expression of antiglucocorticoid vs glucocorticoid activity for a given receptor-steroid complex is determined by a balance of interactions between the receptor and several steroidal functional groups that are not located in a restricted portion of the steroid molecule. In particular, both A- and D-ring substituents were found to contribute to the observed biological activity (cf., 28). This conclusion was reinforced by the results with two other series of glucocorticoid derivatives (C-17 oxetan-3'-ones [29] and 17,21-acetonides [30]) which form reversible receptor-steroid complexes (19).

B.) Identification of [3H]Dex-Mes--labeled glucocorticoid receptors

Treatment of cell-free HTC cell receptors with [3H]Dex-Mes ± excess [1H]dexamethasone for 3.5 hr at 0°C followed by activated charcoal to re-

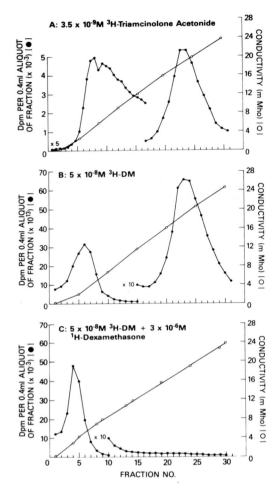

Figure 1. DEAE-cellulose chromatography of unactivated HTC cell receptors. Equal portions of HTC cell cytosol were labeled at 0°C with A.) [³H]triamcinolone acetonide, B.) [³H]Dex Mes, and C.) [³H]Dex-Mes plus excess [¹H]dexamethasone and then loaded onto and eluted from DEAE-cellulose columns with a phosphate buffer (pH 7.8 at 0°C) gradient (●——●,dpm; 0——0, conductivity of sample).

move the free steroid gave such high levels of non-specific binding of [³H]Dex-Mes that Scatchard plots gave meaningless results (S. S. Simons, unpublished results). In order to remove some of the non-specific binding, we employed DEAE-cellulose chromatography which has been shown to separate unactivated receptor-steroid complexes from activated complexes[1] and from many of the cytosolic proteins (32). As shown in Fig. 1, cell-free HTC

---

[1] We use the term "activation" to describe the process which converts the initially formed, "unactivated" receptor-steroid complex to a complex that will bind to DNA and/or nuclei (see also 31).

cell receptors that had been bound with [^{3}H]Dex-Mes gave a peak of radioactivity on DEAE-cellulose columns that eluted at the same position as
authentic [^{3}H]triamcinolone acetonide bound receptors. Furthermore,
all of the [^{3}H]Dex-Mes binding in this region was abolished by
co-incubation of the cell-free receptors with excess [^{1}H]dexamethasone
(Fig.1c), as is required if this peak is to represent receptor--[^{3}H]Dex-Mes
complexes. Analysis of this peak fraction on SDS-polyacrylamide tube
gels revealed the presence of one major, specific covalently labeled
species at $M_r \simeq 98,000$[2] (20).

Higher pHs are known to increase the yields in reactions of thiols
with α-keto mesylates (14). Increasing the pH of the cytosol plus
[^{3}H]Dex-Mes solution from 7.8 to 9.0 did increase the yields of the
covalently labeled species at $M_r \simeq 98,000$ but the levels of lower M_r,
non-specifically labeled materials were drastically elevated (S. S.
Simons, unpublished results). Sephadex G-100 chromatography at 0°C of
steroid-free HTC cell receptors in HEPES buffer ± 10 mM Na_2MoO_4 (10 mM
HEPES, 50 mM NaCl, 1 mM EDTA, 10% glycerol, pH 7.6 at r.t.), followed by
treatment with [^{3}H]Dex-Mes, increased the covalent labeling of the 98K
species and dramatically reduced the labeling of the low molecular weight
species. However the absolute yields of the labeled 98K species were
still low (S. S. Simons, unpublished results) (Note: all steroid binding
activity was lost during Sephadex G-100 chromatography in 20 mM Tricine, 2
mM $CaCl_2$, 1 mM $MgCl_2$ (pH 8.0 at 0°C) [6] without NaCl or Na_2MoO_4).
Scatchard analysis of the crude receptors before and after Sephadex G-100
chromatography in HEPES buffer revealed a 2-fold decrease in the affinity
of the receptors for [^{3}H]dexamethasone (Fig. 2). The data of Fig. 2 show
that the decreased affinity is due to the chromatographic step as
opposed to the presence of Na_2MoO_4 (cf., 34 vs 35). The cause of this
altered affinity is not known.

---

[2] The initially reported value for this species was $M_r \simeq 85,000$ (20). Subsequent analyses of this species on denaturing slab gels both by slice and
counting and by fluorography have yielded values of $M_r \simeq 90,000$ and, more
recently, 98,000 (31,33). These differences do not reflect changes in
receptor size (e.g., decreased proteolysis of the receptors); rather, they
are due to a reassignment of the M_r of the phosphorylase b standard and to
the use of a water-cooled slab gel apparatus. For consistency in this
review, we will use 98,000 as the mol. wt. of this species.

118

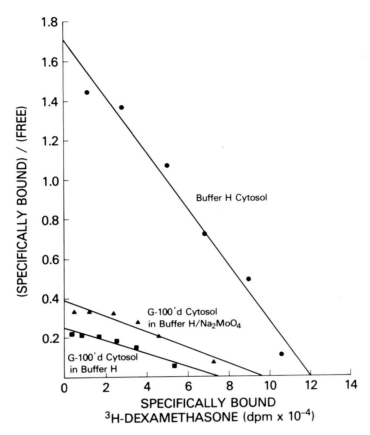

Figure 2. Scatchard analysis of [³H]dexamethasone binding to HTC cell receptors at 0°C. Steroid binding to receptor was determined in the unfractionated crude cytosol (●) and in the void volume fractions of crude cytosol chromatographed through Sephadex G-100 in HEPES Buffer H without (■) or with (▲) 10 mM Na_2MoO_4.

In crude rat liver cytosol, we could detect no inhibition of [³H]triamcinolone acetonide binding to receptors by [¹H]Dex-Mes and no covalent labeling of any proteins by [³H]Dex-Mes. This behavior was presumably due to the presence of high concentrations of low molecular weight thiols in the crude cytosol since Sepadex G-100 chromatography, or $(NH_4)_2SO_4$ precipitation in the presence of 20mM Na_2MoO_4, yielded receptor preparations in which competition binding by [¹H]Dex-Mes and covalent labeling by [³H]Dex-Mes were readily observed (15). Analysis of the [³H]Dex-Mes--labeled, fractionated cytosol on SDS-polyacrylamide slab gels revealed the presence of just one specifically labeled species at M_r ≃98,000, just as had been observed with HTC cell cytosolic receptors (see above). Using polyclonal antibodies that were raised against receptors that had been purified on the basis of a biological property (i.e., the ability to be activated to the DNA-binding state) (36), we found that anti-receptor antibodies immobilized on a protein A-Sepharose column selectively adsorbed a single covalent [^{3}H]Dex-Mes--labeled 98K species from $(NH_4)_2SO_4$ precipitated rat liver cytosol that subsequently had been treated with [^{3}H]Dex-Mes. This labeled 98K species was not obtained if the labeling with [^{3}H]Dex-Mes was conducted in the presence of 100 fold excess [^{1}H]dexamethasone or if the labeled cytosol was passed over a pre-immune IgG-protein A-Sepharose column. Furthermore, [^{3}H]Dex-Mes labeling of immunoadsorbed, steroid-free receptors from crude rat liver cytosol (i.e., not $(NH_4)_2SO_4$ precipitated) yielded the same labeled 98K species (15). Thus we have used affinity labeling and immunochemistry to provide a convergent identification of the [^{3}H]98K species as the [^{3}H]Dex-Mes--labeled glucocorticoid receptor.[3,4]

The fact that a 98K species can be specifically, covalently labeled by [^{3}H]Dex-Mes in whole HTC cells (31), where Dex-Mes is predominantly an irreversible antagonist (20; see also Section IIA), further indicates that this 98K species is the glucocorticoid receptor and strongly supports the above conclusion that the irreversible antiglucocorticoid activity of Dex-Mes is expressed through the covalent receptor--Dex-Mes complex. However we can not yet exclude the possibility that some antiglucocorticoid activity arises from a non-covalent complex since only a portion (i.e.,

---

[3] Reaction of [^{3}H]Dex-Mes with the receptor almost certainly involves the attack at C-21 of Dex-Mes by a nucleophilic group in the receptor to expel the methanesulfonate group as the anion and to produce a covalent receptor-steroid complex where the receptor protein is linked to the steroid at C-21 (see 11,20). In order to specify how the covalent complex was formed, and to avoid any confusion with the non-covalent receptor-dexamethasone complexes, we refer to the covalent complexes as Dex-Mes--labeled receptors or as covalent receptor--Dex-Mes complexes even though the mesylate group is no longer present.

[4] We refer to the monomeric steroid binding protein as the receptor; it remains to be shown that one of the larger molecular weight forms that have been described under non-denaturing conditions (37-41) represents the biologically active form of the receptor that is involved in the modulation of gene expression.

23-31%) of the available whole cell receptors can be covalently labeled
with [³H]Dex-Mes (20,31).

C.) Maximizing the yield of covalent [3H]Dex-Mes--labeled glucocorticoid
receptors

One of the advantages of an electrophilic affinity label is that, in
theory, quantitative yields of the covalently labeled binding
macromolecule can be obtained (11). Initially our yields of covalent
[³H]Dex-Mes--labeled HTC cell receptors were quite low (i.e., ≈13%) (20).
In studies with rat liver receptors, we were able to achieve a ≥ 90%
labeling efficiency of the receptors by removing low molecular weight
thiols and by adjusting the time and temperature of the reaction, the
concentration of receptor and [³H]Dex-Mes, and most importantly the pH of
the reaction solution (31). We had previously determined that α-keto
mesylates preferentially reacted with thiols and that virtually no
reaction occurred unless the thiol group was ionized (14). Accordingly,
when the pH of the reaction solution at 0°C was varied from 6.7 to 8.6,
the yield of [³H]Dex-Mes--labeled 98K receptors increased from ∿18% to
∿92% of the available receptors in $(NH_4)_2SO_4$ precipitated rat liver
cytosol (as determined by [³H]dexamethasone binding at the same pH) (31;
see also Section IIB). It could be calculated from these data that, if a
single amino acid was being labeled by Dex-Mes, that amino acid had a pK_a
of ∿7.4. While this appears low for the pK_a of a cysteine, the pK_a of the
-SH group in bovine serum albumin is <5 (42) and the [³H]Dex-Mes labeling
of rat serum albumin was found to decrease above pH 7.4 (31). At this
point it should be emphasized that, while the covalent labeling efficiency
of receptors increases with pH, the total yield of labeled receptors can
decrease since the steroid binding activity of some receptor preparations
(e.g., $(NH_4)_2SO_4$ precipitated rat liver receptors) is more pH sensitive
than others (31).

Steroid-free receptors can be degraded to lower M_r species (41,43),
some of which will no longer bind steroid; likewise, covalently labeled
receptors are sensitive to proteolysis (31,33). With HTC cell receptors,
simply changing the method of cytosol preparation from the usual
mechanical homogenization of cells (6) to a freeze-thaw procedure appeared
to dramatically reduce the efficacy of endogenous proteases. This one

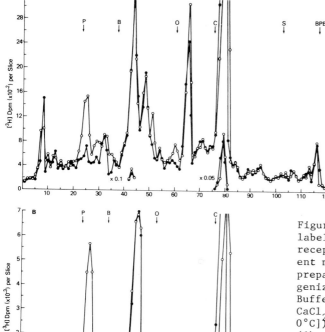

Figure 3. [^{3}H]Dex-Mes labeling of HTC cell cytosol receptors prepared by different methods. A. Cytosol was prepared by mechanical homogenization of frozen cells in Buffer A (20 mM Tricine, 2 mM CaCl$_2$, 1 mM MgCl$_2$ [pH 8.0 at 0°C]} as previously described (6). B.) Cytosol was prepared by freeze (-78°C)-thaw lysis of the cells in pH 9.5 TAPS buffer (25 mM TAPS, 1 mM EDTA, 10% glycerol [pH 9.5 at 0°C]) (33). For both cytosol preparations, covalent labeling of the receptors (i.e., 2 x 10^{-8} M [^{3}H]Dex-Mes without (O) and with (●) 1.6 x 10^{-6} [^{3}H]dexamethasone at 0°C, pH ~8.8, for 2-3 hr) and analysis of the solutions by SDS-polyacrylamide gel electrophoresis were conducted under similar conditions (see 31). P, phorphorylase b; B, bovine serum albumin; O, ovalbumin; C, carbonic anhydrase; S, soybean trypsin inhibitor; BPB, bromophenol blue. (From 33)

modification had the two-fold effect of virtually eliminating the presence of covalently labeled receptor fragments and of increasing the labeling efficiency of the 98K holo-receptors at pH 8.8 to ~90% (Fig. 3 and 33 vs 31).

In some situations, the yields of covalent labeling of the cell-free 98K receptors remained low even after maximizing all of the above parameters. Labeling the receptors in intact cells at 4 or 37°C followed by rupture of the cells and isolation of the labeled receptors can give reasonable yields of the intact [3H]Dex-Mes--labeled, 98K receptor with few receptor fragments and much less non-specific labeling (31,44).

III.   Applications of Affinity Labeled Glucocorticoid Receptors

Having learned how to obtain high yields of covalent [3H]Dex-Mes, affinity labeled glucocorticoid receptors, we were interested in exploiting the unique properties of covalent complexes to explore questions that could not be investigated with dissociable, non-covalent complexes. However, before using Dex-Mes--labeled receptors as a probe of glucocorticoid hormone action, we had to determine to what extent the covalent Dex-Mes--labeled receptors could be used as a model for the non-covalent receptor-glucocorticoid complexes (i.e., to what extent the biological properties of covalent and non-covalent complexes were identical). The data presented above in Sections IIA and B establish that cortisol mesylate and Dex-Mes are irreversible antiglucocorticoids in HTC cells and that at least part of the antagonist activity is due to the formation of a specific, covalent receptor-steroid complex. Therefore Dex-Mes--labeled receptors can be used as a model for non-covalent agonist complexes only up to that point where the pathways for agonist and antagonist activity diverge.   Analysis of the subsequent steps with Dex-Mes--labeled receptors should define one mechanism of antiglucocorticoid action.

A.)   Dex-Mes vs dexamethasone: mechanism of antiglucocorticoid action of Dex-Mes

One theory of anti-steroid action is that the antagonist must have a rapid rate of dissociation from the receptor (45).   Our findings are inconsistent with this theory and suggest that a covalent receptor-steroid complex can cause antiglucocorticoid activity since 1.) the more potent irreversible whole cell antiglucocorticoid activity of Dex-Mes vs cortisol mesylate parallels the higher apparent affinity of Dex-Mes for HTC cell receptors (17,20), 2.) the whole cell antagonist activity of Dex-Mes is expressed at a lower steroid concentration than is the agonist activity of Dex-Mes (20), and 3.) [3H]Dex-Mes can covalently label the intact 98K receptor in whole cells (31).

A second theory of antiglucocorticoid action is that antagonists bind to a form of the receptor that cannot be activated to a nuclear binding complex (46). Activation does occur in whole cells (47,48) and the cell-free binding of complexes to nuclei, chromatin, DNA, ATP-Sepharose, or DEAE-cellulose has been used to quantitate the amount of activated complexes (38, 49-53). We have used DNA-cellulose binding to detect activated complexes and have found that the efficiency of activation is the same (i.e., $\sim$36%) for both covalent [^{3}H]Dex-Mes--labeled and non-covalent [^{3}H]dexamethasone bound receptors from either HTC cells or rat liver. In these experiments, 50mM β-mercaptoethanol was added before the activation step in order to block further covalent labeling by [^{3}H]Dex-Mes during activation. The formation of a covalent receptor-steroid complex did not, per se, cause activation of the complex since covalent, unactivated complexes did not bind to DNA-cellulose columns (31). Thus the antagonist activity of Dex-Mes is not due to an inability of the covalent complexes to be activated.

Affinity labeled receptors could exert their irreversible antigluco-corticoid activity by undergoing activation in whole cells at a much slower rate than for non-covalent agonist complexes. However covalent, cell-free [^{3}H]Dex-Mes--labeled HTC cell complexes were activated at 0°C by dilution at high pH (8.8) at only a 2.6 fold slower rate than were non-co-valent [^{3}H]dexamethasone bound complexes (54). While this rate difference does not appear to be sufficient to account for the whole cell antagonist activity of Dex-Mes, the mechanism of whole cell activation could differ from that of our cell-free conditions. In fact, activation of [^{3}H]Dex-Mes--labeled complexes in whole HTC cells (37°C for 30 min) was less efficient than for non-covalent [^{3}H]dexamethasone bound complexes in that the ratio of nuclear:cytoplasmic complexes was 1:4 vs 1:1 respective-ly (31, P.A. Miller and S.S. Simons, unpublished). This reduced whole cell nuclear binding could reflect 1.) a greater difference in rates of activa-tion in whole cells, 2.) a difference in the mechanism of whole cell vs cell-free activation, 3.) the fact that whole cell activation is a multi-step process for which the acquisition of DNA-binding is an early step, or 4.) a difference in the affinity of the complexes for DNA and/or nuclei. Thus, in contrast to non-covalent receptor-antiestrogen and

-antiandrogen complexes (55-57), and to covalent receptor-antiestrogen complexes (58), all of which display normal nuclear binding, the "lesion" with the covalent receptor-antiglucocorticoid complex appears to be at some point proximal to the nuclear binding of the complexes.

The affinity of covalent Dex-Mes--labeled vs non-covalent dexamethasone bound receptors for DNA was examined to see if this could account for the above noted differences in nuclear binding. The affinity of receptor-steroid complex binding to DNA is often assessed from the salt concentration required for the elution of complexes from calf thymus DNA-cellulose columns (59-61). Using this criterion, we found no difference in the affinity of covalent and non-covalent complexes for DNA (31). However, using a more sensitive batch elution assay, we found that the concentration of added NaCl required to reduce the binding of covalent [³H]Dex-Mes--labeled complexes to DNA-cellulose pellets by 50% was 15 mM lower than that needed for non-covalent [³H]dexamethasone complexes (i.e., 70 vs 85 mM NaCl respectively, which includes the equivalent of 16 mM NaCl contributed by the cytosol) (54). An equilibrium double-reciprocal DNA-cellulose pellet binding assay (50) showed that the K_a of covalent [³H]Dex-Mes--labeled complexes was 2-fold lower than that of the non-covalent [³H]dexamethasone bound complexes (54). However, this difference does not appear to be enough lower to account for the reduced nuclear binding of [³H]Dex-Mes--labeled complexes in whole cells (cf., 31 vs 59, 60). These results further indicate that DNA- and nuclear-binding are not equivalent assays for activated receptor-glucocorticoid complexes (31,50,62). At this point, it should be noted that our data on the NaCl concentration required for 50% dissociation of DNA-bound [³H]dexamethasone labeled complexes is similar to that previously observed by Rousseau et al. (63) but significantly lower than what is found when complexes are eluted from a DNA-cellulose column (31,54,59,60), presumably due to weak DNA binding of the complexes on the column during the increasing NaCl gradient which artifactually retards the elution of the complexes (54).

Our pellet binding studies with added NaCl also failed to provide evidence that glucocorticoid receptor-steroid complex binding to calf thymus (i.e., non-specific) DNA is a multi-step process (cf., 64, 65) since the NaCl concentrations required for 50% inhibition of complex binding to DNA and for 50% dissociation of DNA-bound complexes were the

ceptors that were covalently labeled by [³H]tamoxifen aziridine (78). No major fragments of the labeled estrogen receptors were observed with time; rather the 69K receptor simply disappeared with a $T_{1/2}$ of 4 hr (58).

Munck and Holbrook (79) have recently proposed a kinetic model which simply and elegantly describes the whole cell distribution of non-covalent receptor-agonist complexes. Since the rate of dissociation of the activated receptor-steroid complex figures prominently into this model, the whole cell distribution of activated and non-activated, covalent, non-dissociable receptor--Dex-Mes complexes will provide a stringent test of this model.

C.) Analysis of receptor heterogeneity in the same tissue or cell line

Activation of the receptor-steroid complex to a form that will bind to DNA and DEAE-cellulose is thought to be one of the early steps in glucocorticoid hormone action (47,48). This step (but not the activation to a nuclear binding form of the complex) appears to be similar for covalent and non-covalent complexes (see Section IIIA). Thus affinity labeling of receptors, coupled with high resolution techniques such as SDS polyacrylamide gel electrophoresis (SDS-PAGE), represents a particularly powerful method for detecting possible receptor heterogeneity between unactivated and activated complexes.

Currently there are three general theories regarding the mechanism of activation (Fig. 5): 1.) dissociation of similar or dissimilar subunits (37-41), 2.) conformational change in the receptor molecule (51,80,81) and 3.) chemical modification of a small number of amino acids of the receptor (82-84). None of these theories predict a major change in the molecular weight of the denatured complex upon activation, which is precisely the result that we observed when unactivated and activated, covalent [³H]Dex-Mes--labeled receptors were analyzed on SDS-polyacrylamide slab gels (31,33). Limited proteolysis of unactivated and activated complexes should, however, provide a more sensitive probe for activation-induced changes in the complex, expecially since activated complexes may be more susceptible to proteolysis (85). As is depicted by the shaded areas of the receptor molecules in Fig. 5, there are portions of the surface of the unactivated complex that would be predicted to be inaccessible to proteases but which should be accessible in the activated complex and vice

1.) Oligomer dissociation

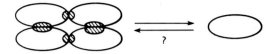

2.) Conformational change

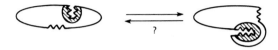

3.) Functional group modification

area not accessible to proteases

Figure 5. Models of activation of glucocorticoid receptor-steroid complex.

versa. Therefore sequence specific proteolysis of [^{3}H]Dex-Mes--labeled receptors followed by SDS-PAGE analysis of those fragments containing covalently attached [^{3}H]Dex-Mes would be expected to yield some fragments that were unique to unactivated and to activated complexes. To maximize our chances of detecting such differences, we employed three specific proteases (TPCK-treated trypsin, TLCK-treated chymotrypsin, and Staphylococcus aureus V8 protease); the digestion patterns of native and denatured receptors were also examined in order to detect chemical modifications that might be relatively buried in the native receptor.

Digestion of native and denatured activated [^{3}H]Dex-Mes--labeled HTC cell receptors, which had been partially purified by DNA-cellulose chromatography, gave unique ladders of labeled fragments for each protease that were consistent with precursor-product relationships (e.g., Fig. 6).

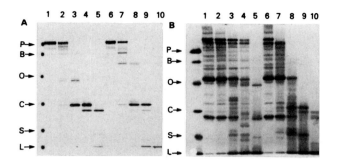

Figure 6. Digestion of activated, [³H]Dex-Mes labeled, HTC cell receptors by trypsin. Activated, covalently labeled receptors were treated with TPCK-trypsin in the native state (lanes 1-5; TPCK-trypsin concentrations were 0, 0.063, 0.5, 4 and 100 µg/ml respectively) or the denatured state (30 min/22°C/0.2% SDS/0.5 mM/DTT) (lanes 6-10; TPCK-trypsin concentrations were 0, 0.5, 4, 20, and 100 µg/ml respectively for 20 min at 10°C. These samples were treated at 100°C for 5 min with 2% SDS/0.1M DTT and then analyzed on SDS-polyacrylamide gels. The gels were subsequently stained with Coomassie Blue, impregnated with a fluorophor, and fluorographed. A.) Fluorograph of [³H]labeled, TPCK-trypsin digestion products. B.) Coomassie Blue stained TPCK-trypsin digestion products. Dots at edge of fluorographs indicate the positions of the molecular weight markers P, phorphorylase b; B, bovine serum albumin; O, ovalbumin; C, carbonic anhydrase; S, soybean trypsin inhibitor; L, lysozyme. (From 33)

Virtually identical results were obtained when the digestion patterns of native and denatured unactivated complexes (partially purified by $(NH_4)_2SO_4$ precipitation of unactivated complexes in the presence of 20 mM Na_2MoO_4) were examined (33). Therefore it is unlikely that the activation of HTC cell glucocorticoid receptor-steroid complexes involves a de-oligomerization of, or a major conformational change in, the unactivated complex. We can not yet rule out the possibility that such changes could occur in structurally "open" or "hinge" regions of the receptor that are far from the covalently bound steroid and are rapidly cleaved by proteases both in unactivated and activated complexes. Considering the very small area that would be affected if activation involved the covalent modification of a single amino acid, the absence of any differences in the protease digestion patterns of the two types of complexes can not be used to eliminate this model of activation (33).

Despite the very different specificities of the above three proteases, they each produced several similarly sized fragments of the native complexes (i.e., M_r ∿42,500, 30,500, and 27,000)(33). This result is consistent with the presence in the receptor of proteolytic "hot spots". In view of the increased proteolytic sensitivity of native receptors, compared to abundant cytosolic proteins (Fig. 6 and 31,33), these "hot spots" could be involved in the in vivo degradation of complexes. Furthermore, a single amino acid change in the appropriate "hot spot" may facilitate the generation of the smaller (i.e., ∿42K) receptor found in several lines of glucocorticoid resistant cells (59-61,86,87).

Cell-free analysis of receptors often reveals receptor heterogeneity that can be ascribed to digestion of the intact 98K receptor by endogenous proteases (31,33,41,43,87). The formation of two of these digestion products (a 28 Å and a 19 Å species) can be mimicked by controlled proteolysis with chymotrypsin and trypsin respectively (60,85,88,89). Under similar digestion conditions, [3H]Dex-Mes--labeled rat liver receptors yielded the DNA-binding 28 Å chymotrypsin fragment as a 42K species while the non-DNA-binding 19 Å trypsin fragment (or meroreceptor) was found to be two species of M_r ∿30,000 and 28,000 (33). Similar results have been observed with photoaffinity labeled rat liver (89) and mouse lymphoma (60) receptors.

Further heterogeneity in the form of receptor precursors, which may not bind steroid, would most easily be examined with anti-receptor antibodies. Nevertheless Housley and Pratt (90) have observed two [32P]-labeled L-cell proteins (M_r ∿92,000 and 100,000) on SDS-PAGE and 2D gels that co-migrated with specific [3H]Dex-Mes--labeled receptors. Both phosphoproteins were specifically eluted from a glucocorticoid steroid affinity column and were greatly reduced or absent in the cytosols of receptor-negative cells. An M_r = 104,000 phosphoprotein that was not labeled by [3H]Dex-Mes was often observed in these receptor-negative cells and could represent an initially synthesized receptor precursor (90). This type of analysis has also revealed charge heterogeneity among the [3H]Dex-Mes--labeled 98K receptors, which may be functionally significant (90 and J. M. Harmon, personal communication).

D.) Analysis of receptor heterogeneity among different tissues and cell lines

Conventional analysis of impure non-covalent receptor-steroid complexes has been confined to non-denaturing techniques such as sucrose gradients and column chromatography which have limited resolving power and are complicated by receptor aggregation, non-specific association with other cellular components, and proteolysis. Consequently it has been difficult to assess the question of conservation of glucocorticoid receptor structure during major biological changes such as evolution, cell differentiation, and the acquisition of glucocorticoid resistance. Affinity labeling with [^{3}H]Dex-Mes offers a means by which the M_r of the denatured receptor can be examined under powerful separating conditions such as 2D and SDS polyacrylamide gel electrophoresis.

Within the accuracy of SDS-PAGE, the molecular weights of [^{3}H]Dex-Mes--labeled receptors from rat liver and thymus, rat HTC and FU5-5 cells, and human IM9, CEM (sensitive and one resistant line), and lymphoid cells are all about the same as phosphorylase b (i.e., M_r ~97,400) (33,44,90,91, E. B. Thompson [personal communication], J. M. Harmon [personal communication], and P.A. Miller and S.S. Simons [unpublished]). A higher molecular weight precursor of the receptor that also binds steroid may exist (90) but it appears that the size of the glucocorticoid receptor has been highly conserved. Those [^{3}H]Dex-Mes-- labeled receptors whose molecular weight differs significantly from ~98K (e.g., HTC cell [87] and rat liver [92] receptors under particular conditions of preparation, and some resistant mouse S49 lymphocytes [60,87]) appear to be due to proteolysis of the intact 98K receptor and/or altered transcription of the receptor gene to yield a defective receptor.

Limited proteolysis of partially purified [^{3}H]Dex-Mes--labeled receptors produces progressively smaller fragments of the receptor where each [^{3}H]-labeled fragment contains at least a portion of the steroid binding site. This procedure offers a more stringent test of receptor homology since identical [^{3}H]Dex-Mes--labeled fragments will be obtained only if the steroid binding site and the protease cleavage sites are essentially identical. By this criterion, using trypsin and chymotrypsin, we have found that HTC cell and rat liver receptors are the same (33). A similar analysis indicated that the proteolytic fragments of the progesterone A and B subunits were identical (93,94). Unique proteolytic fragments for the smaller A subunit, indicating that the A and B subunits were products of two separate genes, were revealed only by tryptic peptide analysis of the [^{125}I]labeled subunits (94).

E.) Isolation and purification of the receptor

Perhaps the most obvious application of affinity labeled receptors is in the purification of receptors. The presence of a covalent bond between steroid and receptor permits the use of protein purification techniques that would cause the dissociation of non-covalent receptor-steroid complexes, in which case the receptor would be lost since the only distinguishing feature of receptors is their ability to specifically bind steroids with high affinity. [3H]Dex-Mes--labeled rat liver receptors have been purified to apparent homogeneity using denaturing conditions. Unfortunately, this purified receptor was found to have a blocked N-terminal amino acid (H. J. Eisen, personal communication), as has also been found by others for the progesterone receptor (W. T. Schrader, personal communication). Purification of a [3H]Dex-Mes--labeled receptor fragment could afford a polypeptide suitable for protein sequencing that contains at least part of the steroid binding site and does not have a blocked N-terminus.

F.) Identification of the steroid binding site of the glucocorticoid receptor

Several lines of evidence strongly suggest, but do not yet prove, that the covalent labeling of the receptor by Dex-Mes occurs in the steroid-specific binding site: 1.) [1H]Dex-Mes can inhibit 100% of the specific non-covalent binding of [3H]dexamethasone to receptors and [1H]dexamethasone can prevent virtually all of the covalent labeling of the 98K receptor protein by [3H]Dex-Mes (15,20,31), 2.) under conditions of maximal [3H]Dex-Mes--labeling of receptors, there is a 1 to 1 ratio of [3H]Dex-Mes--labeled 98K receptors to non-covalent [3H]dexamethasone bound receptors (31,54), 3.) intact -SH groups are absolutely required for steroid binding to the receptor (95,96) and this is the most likely functional group in the receptor to react with Dex-Mes (11,20) since the rate of reaction of Dex-Mes with -SH groups is at least 1000 times faster than with any of the other nucleophiles commonly encountered in biological systems (14,15), 4.) covalent Dex-Mes--labeled receptors can be activated to a DNA-binding complex with the same efficiency, and the activated covalent complexes exhibit the same DNA sequence specific binding with about the same absolute affinity, as do non-covalent dexamethasone bound receptors (31,54), and 5.) the smallest characterized fragments of the intact receptor (i.e., the 42K chymotrypsin fragment and the 30 and 28K trypsin fragments) display the same physical properties whether containing a covalently bound Dex-Mes or a non-covalently associated dexamethasone molecule (33). Therefore the Dex-Mes--labeled site of the receptor appears to be very close to, if not coincident with, the binding site of non-covalent glucocorticoid steroids. Unambiguous proof will require a demonstration that the biological activity of covalent and non-covalent receptor-antagonist complexes is the same. An x-ray determination of the three dimensional structure of covalent and non-covalent complexes would also help to resolve this question.

The formation of unique proteolytic fragments as small as ~15K from the [^{3}H]Dex-Mes--labeled 98K receptor is consistent with there being just one amino acid labeled by Dex-Mes (33; see also Fig. 6). Isolation of much smaller fragments (i.e., M_r ~2000) will be helpful in confirming this proposal and in sequencing a portion of the steroid binding site in receptor.

III. Conclusions

Studies of the receptor-steroid complexes of conventional glucocorticoid steroids are unavoidably restricted by dissociation of the non-covalent complexes. Affinity labeling of the receptor to give a non-dissociable, covalent receptor-steroid complex overcomes this problem. In many cases the covalent labeling of receptors is quite specific, despite the very low concentrations of receptors, so that it is fairly easy to obtain good yields of radiochemically pure, [^{3}H]-labeled complexes (albeit contaminated by other non-labeled proteins) for biochemical studies (15,31,33, 44,54,58,78,90). Many of these studies could also be performed with pure non-covalent receptor-steroid complexes but obtaining even ~50% pure complexes is a time consuming process that requires much larger amounts of starting material. Unlike most affinity labeled enzymes, affinity labeled receptors can still be biologically active in whole and broken cell systems. This additional property of affinity labeled receptors greatly expands the

potential uses of steroid affinity labels. The few, recently reported
applications of affinity labeled glucocorticoid receptors that are described in this chapter indicate that biologically active, affinity labeling
steroids should become powerful tools for investigating the mechanism of
action of glucocorticoid hormones and steroid hormones in general.

References

1. Jacoby, WB and Wilchek, M (eds.): Methods Enzymol.,46(1977).

2. Chowdhry, V and Westheimer, FH: Ann. Rev. Biochem.,48, 293-325(1979).

3. Walsh, CT: Ann. Rev. Biochem.,53, 493-536(1984).

4. Groman, EV, Schultz, RM, and Engel, LL: J. Biol. Chem.,250, 5450-5454(1975).

5. Williams, RH (ed.): Textbook of Endocrinology, Saunders(Phila.), p. 260(1981).

6. Simons, SS Jr., Thompson, EB, and Johnson, DF: Biochem. Biophys. Res. Comm.,86, 793-800(1979).

7. Giesen, EM, and Beck, G: Horm. Metabol. Res.,14, 252-256(1982).

8. Wojnar, RJ, Varma, RK, Free, CA, Millonig, RC, and Lutsky, BN: The Pharmacologist,25, 236(1983).

9. Bourgeois, S, Pfahl, M, and Baulieu, E-E: EMBO J.,3, 751-755(1984).

10. Katzenellenbogen, JA: Biochemical Actions of Hormones, vol. 4 (G Litwack, ed.) 1-84(1977).

11. Simons, SS Jr. and Thompson, EB: Biochemical Actions of Hormones, vol. 9 (G Litwack, ed.) 221-254(1982).

12. Payne, DW, Katzenellenbogen, JA, and Carlson, KE: J. Biol. Chem.,255, 10359-10367(1980).

13. Smith, SB and Benisek, WF: J. Biol. Chem.,255, 2690-2693(1980).

14. Simons, SS Jr., Pons, M, and Johnson, DF: J. Org. Chem.,45, 3084-3088(1980).

15. Eisen, HJ, Schleenbaker, RE, and Simons, SS Jr.: J. Biol. Chem.,256, 12920-12925(1981).

16. Simons, SS Jr., Thompson, EB, Merchlinsky, MJ, and Johnson, DF: J. Steroid Biochem.,13, 311-322(1980).

17. Simons, SS Jr., Thompson, EB, and Johnson, DF: Proc. Natl. Acad. Sci. USA,77, 5167-5171(1980).

18. Simons, SS Jr.: U.S. Patent no. 4,296,206(1981).

19. Lamontagne, N, Mercier, L, Pons, M, Thompson, EB, and Simons, SS Jr.: Endocrinol.,114, 2252-2263(1984).

20. Simons, SS Jr. and Thompson, EB: Proc. Natl. Acad. Sci.,78, 3541-3545(1981).

21. Simpson, ER, Ackerman, GE, Smith, ME, and Mendelson, CR: Proc. Natl. Acad. Sci. USA,78, 5690-5694(1981).

22. Mercier, L, Thompson, EB, and Simons, SS Jr.: Endocrinol.,112, 601-609(1983).

23. Terada, N and Oka, T: Horm. Metab. Res.,15, 508-512(1983).

24. Mercier, L and Simons, S. S. Jr.: Submitted for publication.

25. Sutherland, R, Mester, J, and Baulieu, E-E: Nature,267, 434-435(1977).

26. Sutherland, RL: Endocrinol.,109, 2061-2068(1981).

27. Chrousos, GP, Cutler, GB Jr., Simons, SS Jr., Pons, M, Moriarty, RM, and Loriaux, DL: Proceeding of the Sixth Annual Clinical Symposium, Tallahassee, on "Progress in Research and Clinical Applications of Corticosteroids" (Lee (HJ, and Fitzgerald, TJ, eds.) Heyden and Son, Inc., Phila., 152-176(1982).

28. Duax, WL, Griffin, JF, Rohrer, DC, Swenson, DC, and Weeks, CM: J. Steroid Biochem.,15, 41-47(1981).

29. Pons, M, and Simons, SS Jr.: J. Org. Chem.,46, 3262-3264(1981).

30. Rousseau, GG, Cambron, P, Brasseur, N, Marcotte, L, Matton, P, and Schmit, J-P: J. Steroid Biochem.,18, 237-244(1983).

31. Simons, SS Jr., Schleenbaker, RE, and Eisen, HJ: J. Biol. Chem.,258, 2229-2238(1983).

32. Sakaue, Y, and Thompson, EB: Biochem. Biophys. Res. Comm.,77, 533-541(1977).

33. Reichman, ME, Foster, CM, Eisen, LP, Eisen, HJ, Torain, BF, Simons, SS Jr.: Biochem., in press.

34. Cardo, PP, Gambetti, M, Vignale, B, and Divano, MC: Eur. J. Biochem., 137, 173-178(1983).

35. Noma, K, Nakao, K, Sato, B, Nishizawa, Y, Matsumoto, K, and Yamamura, Y: Endocrinol.,107, 1205-1211(1980).

36. Eisen, HJ: Proc. Natl. Acad. Sci. USA,77, 3893-3897(1980).

37. Vedeckis, WV: Biochem.,22, 1983-1989(1983).

38. Schmidt, TJ, and Litwack, G: Physiological Reviews,62, 1131-1192(1982).

39. Holbrook, NJ, Bodwell, JE, Jeffries, M, and Munck, A: J. Biol. Chem.,258, 6477-6485(1983).

40. Raaka, BM, and Samuels, HH: J. Biol. Chem.,258, 417-425(1983).

41. Sherman, MR, Moran, MC, Tuazon, FB, and Stevens, Y-W: J. Biol. Chem., 258, 10366-10377(1983).

42. Lewis, SD, Misra, DC, and Shafer, JA: Biochem.,19, 6129-6137(1980).

43. Carlstedt-Duke, J, Wrange, O, Dahlberg, E, Gustafsson, J-A, and Hogberg, B: J. Biol. Chem.,254, 1537-1539(1979).

44. Foster, CM, Eisen, HJ, and Bloomfield, CD: Cancer Research,43, 5273-5277(1983).

45. Raynaud, JP, Bouton, MM, Moguilewsky, M, Ojasoo, T, Philibert, D, Beck, G, Labrie, F, and Mornon, JP: J. Steroid Biochem.,12, 143-157(1980).

46. Samuels, HH, and Tomkins, GM: J. Mol. Biol.,52, 57-74(1970).

47. Munck, A, Foley, R: Nature,278, 752-754(1979).

48. Markovic, RD, and Litwack, G: Archives of Biochem. Biophys.,202, 374-379(1980).

49. Simons, SS Jr., Martinez, HM, Garcea, RL, Baxter, JD, and Tomkins, GM: J. Biol. Chem.,251, 334-343(1976).

50. Simons, SS Jr.: Biochim. Biophys. Acta,496, 339-348(1977).

51. McBlain, WA, Toft, DO, and Shyamala, G: Biochem.,20, 6790-6798(1981).

52. Redeuilh, G, Secco, C, Baulieu, E-E, and Richard-Foy, H: J. Biol. Chem.,256, 11496-11502(1981).

53. Murakami, N, and Moudgil, VK: Biochem. J.,198, 447-455(1981).

54. Simons, SS Jr. and Miller, PA: Biochem., in press.

55. Sutherland, RL and Murphy, LC: Mol. Cell. Endocrin.,25, 5-23(1982).

56. Rochefort, H, and Borgna, J-L: Nature,292, 257-259(1981).

57. Jänne, OA and Bardin, CW: Ann. Rev. Physiol.,46, 107-118(1984).

58. Monsma, FJ Jr., Katzenellenbogen, BS, Miller, MA, Ziegler, YS, and Katzenellenbogen, JA: Endocrinol.,115, 143-153(1984).

59. Yamamoto, KR, Stampfer, MR, and Tomkins, GM: Proc. Natl. Acad. Sci. USA,71, 3901-3905(1974).

60. Gehring, U, and Hotz, A: Biochem.,22, 4013-4018(1983).

61. Okret, S, Stevens, Y-W, Carlstedt-Duke, J, Wrange, O, Gustafsson, J-A, and Stevens, J: Cancer Res.,43, 3127-3131(1983).

62. Hirose, M, Ohshima, A, Maki, M, and Chiba, H: Biochim. Biophys. Acta,760, 84-91(1983).

63. Rousseau, GG, Higgins, SJ, Baxter, JD, Gelfand, D, and Tomkins, GM: J. Biol. Chem.,250, 6015-6021(1975).

64. Hunziker, W, Walters, MR, Bishop, JE, and Norman, AW: J. Biol. Chem.,258, 8642-8648(1983).

65. Svec, F and Williams, J: Endocrinol.,113, 1528-1530(1983).

66. Wu, FY-H, Nath, K, and Wu, C-W: Biochem.,13, 2567-2572(1974).

67. Scheidereit, C, Geisse, S, Westphal, HM, and Beato, M: Nature,304, 749-752 (1983).

68. Pfahl, M, McGinnis, D, Hendricks, M, Groner, B, and Hynes, NE: Science,222, 1341-1343(1983).

69. Payvar, F, DeFranco, D, Firestone, GL, Edgar, B, Wrange, O, Okret, S, Gustafsson, J-A, and Yamamoto, KR: Cell,35, 381-392(1983).

70. Scheidereit, C, and Beato, M: Proc. Natl. Acad. Sci. USA,81, 3029-3033(1984).

71. Miller, PA, Ostrowski, MC, Hager, GL, and Simons, SS Jr.: Biochem., in press.

72. Simons, SS Jr.: Biochem. Biophys. Acta,496, 349-358(1977).

73. Payvar, F, and Wrange, O: Steroid Hormone Receptors: Structure and Function, (H. Eriksson, and J-A. Gustafsson, eds.), 267-282(1983)

74. Govindan, MV, Spiess, E, and Majors, J: Proc. Natl. Acad. Sci. USA,79, 5157-5161(1982).

75. Ivarie, RD and O'Farrell, PH: Cell,13, 41-55(1978).

76. Spelsberg, TC: Biochemical Actions of Hormones, vol. 9 (G Litwack, ed.) 141-204(1982).

77. Kumar, SA, and Dickerman, HW: Biochemical Actions of Hormones,vol. 10, (G Litwack, ed.) 259-301(1983).

78. Katzenellenbogen, JA, Carlson, KE, Heiman, DF, Robertson, DW, Wei, LL, and Katzenellenbogen, BS: J. Biol. Chem.,258, 3487-3495(1983).

79. Munck, A, and Holbrook, NJ: J. Biol. Chem.,259, 820-831(1984).

80. Atger, M, and Milgrom, E: J. Biol. Chem.,251, 4758-4762(1976).

81. Bailly, A, Le Fevre, B, Savouret, J-F, and Milgrom, E: J. Biol. Chem.,255, 2729-2734(1980).

82. Sando, JJ, Hammond, ND, Stratford, CA, and Pratt, WB: J. Biol. Chem.,254, 4779-4789(1979).

83. Leach, KL, Dahmer, MK, Hammond, ND, Sando, JJ, and Pratt, WB: J. Biol. Chem.,254, 11884-11890(1979).

84. Barnett, CA, Schmidt, TJ, and Litwack, G: Biochem.,19, 5446-5455 (1980).

85. Vedeckis, WV: Biochem.,22, 1975-1983(1983).

86. Stevens, J and Stevens, Y-W: Cancer Research,41, 125-133(1981).
87. Nordeen, SK, Lan, NC, Showers, MO, and Baxter, JD: J. Biol. Chem.,256, 10503-10508(1981).

88. Wrange, O and Gustafsson, J-A: J. Biol. Chem.,253, 856-865(1978).

89. Wrange, O, Okret, S, Radojcic, M, Carlstedt-Duke, J, and Gustafsson, J-A: J. Biol. Chem.,259, 4534-4541(1984).

90. Housley, PR, and Pratt, WB: J. Biol. Chem.,258, 4630-4635(1983).

91. Harmon, JM, Eisen, HJ, Brower, ST, Simons, SS Jr., Langley, CL, and Thompson, EB: Cancer Research, in press.

92. Westphal, HM, Fleischmann, G, and Beato, M: Eur. J. Biochem.,119, 101-106(1981).

93. Gronemeyer, H, Harry, P, and Chambon, P: FEBS Letters,156, 287-292(1983).

94. Birnbaumer, M, Schrader, WT, and O'Malley, BW: J. Biol. Chem.,258, 7331-7337 (1983).

95. Baxter, JD, and Tomkins, GM: Proc. Natl. Acad. Sci. USA,68, 932-937(1971).

96. Kalimi, M and Love, K: J. Biol. Chem., 255, 4687-4690 (1980).

THE PHYSIOLOGICAL SIGNIFICANCE OF THE STRUCTURE OF GLUCOCORTICOID AND PROGRESTERONE RECEPTORS

Corinne M. Silva and John A. Cidlowski

Departments of Biochemistry and Physiology,
University of North Carolina
Chapel Hill, North Carolina

Introduction

Steroid receptors are responsible for binding the steroid hormone in target tissues and allowing the hormone to exert its physiological effects. The occupied receptor undergoes apparent change (activation) after the steroid binds which causes the steroid-receptor complex to interact with specific DNA regions. This interaction is reflected by increased mRNA levels presumably via initiation of transcription of steroid inducible genes. Additionally, steroid receptor complexes may act to stabilize mRNA via mechanisms currently not understood.

Although our knowledge of steroid hormone action has increased dramatically over the past years, many aspects of this complex problem remain poorly understood. Efforts in our laboratory have focussed on a comparative analysis of steroid receptor structure and hormonal responsiveness with the hope of gaining insights into the structure of biologically active receptors. In this review we will focus our attention on structure/function relationships of progesterone and glucocorticoid receptors. We utilize data from both systems interchangeably based on our preconceptions that all classes of steroid receptors share many common structural features.

We will first consider the recognized gross structural features of progesterone and glucocorticoid receptors. This work will be followed by an analysis of receptor structure during alterations in steroid responsiveness. Finally, we will touch upon some of the potential subtle post-transcriptional processes which may be involved in regulating receptor structure/function relationships.

Different Size Forms of the Steroid Receptor Complexes

A) Molybdate

Steroid receptors exist in a variety of size forms which depend on the preparative conditions. Of the factors which have been found to effect the molecular weight of the receptor molybdate is preeminent. It is well recognized that steroid receptors which are isolated in molybdate containing buffers have molecular weights of between 280 and 400 kilodaltons (1). This is the case for estrogen, progestin, androgen, mineralocorticoid, or glucocorticoid receptors. Isolation of these receptors in molybdate free buffers leads to a variety of molecular weight forms ranging from $\tilde{\ }$ 70-90 kilodaltons, depending on the class of receptor investigated. Molybdate seems to cause, therefore, either the formation of a macromolecular receptor complex or the stabilization of a complex which exists physiologically. Data on the physical characteristics (Rs, $S_{20,w}$, Mr, axial ratios) of the receptor in buffers containing or lacking molybdate led to the proposal of four monomer subunits of the receptor associating to form a molybdate stabilized tetramer (2). Whether each of these subunits represents a steroid binding moiety is currently unclear. Recent proposals (3) suggest that non-steroid binding proteins may be associated with macromolecular receptor complexes including those stabilized by molybdate. Since molybdate stabilization can be seen only in vitro, the physiological significance of its effect has been questioned. Certain evidence suggests that complexes similar to those stabilized by molybdate do exist in vivo. This evidence includes: (1) appearance of sharp receptor peaks in gel filtration and sucrose density gradient elution patterns; (2) existence of similar complexes in experiments done in 0.12M to 0.15M KCl; (3) appearance, on some occasions, of these 330kd complexes in experiments done with molybdate-free buffers; and (4) the presence of these large complexes in buffers containing the protease inhibitor, leupeptin (4). Although it was once thought that molybdate stabilized the receptor complex by inhibiting phosphatase, it is now known that the concentrations of molybdate used are far higher than necessary for inhibition of phosphatases. Concentrations of molybdate which inhibit phosphatases are ineffective on steroid receptor stabilization. Nevertheless, the mechanism by which molybdate works to stabilize the receptor complex is still unknown. Although it is apparent that molybdate stabilizes the interaction of receptor proteins with each other and/or with receptor-associated protein, the physical interactions responsible for this complex formation have not been defined. Molybdate, along with two other transition metals, tungstate and vanadate (5,6), can form weak bonds with certain protein groups. The ability of these three transition metals to stabilize receptor may occur by this mechanism. The question remains as to whether this occurs in vivo and what physiological conditions would bring about this effect.

B) Proteolysis

A variety of forms of steroid receptors which have molecular weights less than that of the 70-90kd monomer form have also been observed. Once again, these forms are highly dependent on experimental conditions and most probably reflect various states of receptor proteolysis. Evidence to support this notion comes from a variety of studies which show that exogenous proteases, Ca^{++}, prolonged incubation of cytosol in vitro, all stimulate the production of receptor forms smaller than 70-90kd (7,8,9,10). Many of these effects can be prevented by agents such as leupeptin, molydate or pyridoxal phosphate (8,9). The generation of

144

small receptor fragments does not appear to be a well defined process and
the nature of the fragments produced appears to be dependent on tissue
source and experimental conditions. Nevertheless, this proteolysis can be
controlled by: (1) using fresh tissue to make receptor preparations; (2)
using molybdate buffers; (3) using various protease inhibitors. Although
studying these effects may lead to an understanding of some of the
properties of the steroid receptor, it should be kept in mind that
neither the biological consequences of proteolysis nor whether the
process occurs in the living cell is known.

Table I summarizes the currently recognized forms of progesterone and
glucocorticoid receptors. While the majority of the data in the table
comes from the comprehensive review of Sherman et al.(8) and from
Vedeckis (11) it also contains our own estimates which are based on rat
thymocyte and HeLa S_3 cell glucocorticoid receptors (9,12,).

TABLE I: DIFFERENT SIZE FORMS OF STEROID RECEPTORS

		Mw	Rs	$S_{20,w}$
* + 1.	Macromolecular Forms	279–400K	80–95A	≅10S
+ 2.	Multimeric Forms	150–220K	60–70A	6–8S
3.	Monomeric Forms	70– 90K	52–60A	4–5S
4.	Intermediate Fragments	30–70K	25–40A	3–4S
° 5.	Mero-Receptors	17–25K	19–24A	2–3S

* Molybtate containing buffers
+ May contain non-steroid binding proteins
° Smallest form which binds to non affinity labeled receptors

Subunits of Steroid Receptors

In this section we will look in more detail at the composition of multimeric steroid receptor complexes (progesterone and glucocorticoid) which have recognized biological functions (i.e. DNA and chromatin binding capacities).

A) Progesterone receptors
The most complete picture regarding receptor subunits comes from studies on the chick oviduct progesterone receptor. In 1972 Schrader and O'Malley (13) first partially purified the chick oviduct progesterone receptor using (1) salt fractionation, (2) agarose gel filtration and (3) DEAE-cellulose chromatography. The last step of purification resolved the receptor into two components which were designated subunit A and subunit B. Gel filtration at high ionic strength (14) as well as more recent studies involving SDS-PAGE of photoaffinity labelled receptor (15) showed that the molecular weight of subunit A was 71kd and that of subunit B was 114kd. These investigations suggested, therefore, that native chick oviduct progesterone receptor consisted of A and B subunits which differed in molecular size. More recent work (16), along with observations made in other progesterone responsive cells (17), suggests that progesterone receptors from several species exist in two molecular weight forms.

The existence of the two size forms of the progesterone receptor (i.e. subunits) has led to a great deal of controversy over the past several years. Questions arose concerning what role, if any, proteolysis played in the generation of the smaller fragments. Similarly, the stoichiometry of the A and B subunits in the macromolecular and multimeric forms of the receptor which are seen in the presence of molybdate was investigated. The question of proteolysis and the potential precursor-product relationships of A and B subunits has recently been addressed by Birnbaumer et al. (15). Experiments using leupeptin and exogenous proteases showed that proteolytic degradation of receptor subunits occurred in a sequential manner. Certain domains appeared to be highly resistant to proteolysis while other domains were very sensitive. Once either subunit was degraded below a molecular weight of 60kd, however, the patterns of proteolysis from either were indistinguishable. Two-dimensional gel analysis of the proteolyzed subunits showed that there were both different and common peptides between subunits A and B. Furthermore, since some peptides appeared to be unique to the smaller subunit A, the relationship between subunit A and subunit B was obviously not a precursor product one. Rather, subunit A and subunit B seemed to have a similar conformational organization, resembling each other upon folding yet differing in their primary sequence.

Questions regarding the subunit composition of the 8 S molybdate stabilized receptor have been perhaps even more controversial. Analysis of the molybdate stabilized form of the receptor by ion-exchange chromatography in the presence of high salt resulted in two major peaks: (a) Peak 1 at 120 mM KCl and (b) Peak 2 at 170 mM KCl (18). A sedimentation coefficient of 7.8 S ± 0.1 for receptor in Peak 1 was comparable to values obtained by others (19) for the progesterone receptor from estrogen stimulated oviduct. Since 7.8 S is too big to be a single A or B subunit (which have sedimentation coefficients of 4 S), peak 1 must be comprised of more than one subunit. In order to study the composition of the 7.8 S form, pyridoxal phosphate was used. Pyridoxal phosphate not only causes the 8 S form of the receptor to dissociate into the 4 S form but also stabilizes the receptor and facilitates separation of the subunit on DEAE-cellulose. Cytosols were prepared in buffers with or without molybdate, dialyzed into a buffer containing pyridoxal phosphate and analyzed by DEAE-chomatography. Analysis of peak 2 by this method showed all the receptor from this peak eluting at the same place in the KCl gradient as subunit B elutes. There was no indication of subunit A being present in peak 2. Analysis of peak 1 by this same method did not give such conclusive results. Although receptor from this peak did not elute at the same KCl concentration from DEAE-cellulose as subunit B, neither did it elute at the same position as subunit A. However, because the elution position of receptor from Peak 1 was similar to that of subunit A and since Sephacryl S-300 chromatographic analysis showed that the 4 S component of Peak 1 was only 2-4°A larger than subunit A, a relationship between the two was suggested. It was speculated that Peak 1 was composed of a modified (i.e.phosphorylated) form of subunit A (20). Nevertheless, these results did suggest that subunits A and B do not exist together as a dimer, at least in the molybdate stabilized form. The question remains as to whether mixed dimers exist in vivo. Earlier studies (13) suggest that they do. In either case, it seems that the active form of the progesterone receptor exists as a dimer of A and/or B subunits.

B) Non-steroid binding subunits

In addition to receptor subunits which bind steroid (i.e. subunit A and subunit B) there is also recent evidence demonstrating the existence of a non-steroid binding subunit. In 1982 the nontransformed progesterone receptor from chick oviduct was purified by affinity chromatography on deoxycorticosterone-derivatized agarose (21). DEAE-Sephadex chromatography of partially purified receptor resulted in two peaks, as seen previously. SDS-PAGE showed that peak I contained a 90kd peptide and peak II contained 90kd and 104kd peptides. Receptor from both peak I and peak II sedimented at ≅8 S in glycerol gradients containing low salt and at 4 S in gradients containing high salt. The Stokes radius of receptor from each peak was determined by gel filtration and molecular weights were calculated. Peak I had a molecular weight of 228K and peak II of 254K. The combination of this data indicated the heterogeneity of the progesterone receptor. Furthermore, the identity of the 90kd and 104kd proteins was in question. Already, progesterone subunits A (71kd) and B (108kd) were known to exist. However, whether they were part of the nontransformed progesterone receptor was unknown. Studies based on the ability of the receptor to bind hormone began to shed some light on this matter (16). First, tryptic digest maps of ^{125}I-labelled proteins which had been eluted from SDS gels showed that the protein which banded at 90kd was distinct from either the A or B receptor subunits.

Furthermore, studies showed that the 90K protein eluted between the A and B subunits on DEAE-Sephadex. Attempts at labelling the 90K protein with [^{3}H]progesterone were unsuccessful. In addition, it was found that the 90K protein was weakly absorbed to the affinity column and could easily be washed off this affinity matrix. Evidently, the 90K protein is not a progesterone-binding subunit. Nevertheless, earlier experiments indicated that this protein was indeed associated with receptor. Further studies using a modified purification procedure were performed passing the receptor over a heparin-agarose column after eluting it from the steroid affinity column (22). The receptor eluted as a single peak from the heparin-sepharose column. Analysis of the eluate by SDS-PAGE showed that only a portion of the 90K material eluted with the hormone binding activity while most of the 90K material eluted before receptor binding activity. If the receptor which eluted from the heparin-sepharose column was fractionated on a DEAE-column it was fractionated into two peaks, Peak I and peak II, as demonstrated previously. Analysis by gel electrophoresis showed that a 90K band was associated with both [^{3}H]progesterone receptor peaks. Also, a 75K band was found from peak I and a 110K band from peak II. It was suggested that these proteins were subunit A (79K) and subunit B (108K). Sedimentation in buffer containing molybdate resulted in an 8 S peak which when analyzed by gel electrophoresis contained all three protein bands, 90K, 110K and 75K. However, receptor not stabilized by molybdate sedimented at 4 S in glycerol gradients containing high salt. When analyzed by gel electrophoresis, this peak was found to contain a 75K and 110K protein. The 90K protein, however, sedimented between 4 S and ≅8 S. In high salt the 90K protein was associated with the [^{3}H]-progesterone peak sedimenting at 8 S if molybdate was present but without molybdate, the 90K protein sedimented at 6-7S while the [^{3}H]-progesterone peak sedimented at 4 S. Therefore, all three peptides: 75K, 90K, 110K were influenced by the presence or absence of molybdate. To summarize: (1) Peak I (stabilized by molybdate) contained a 75K protein which binds hormone and a 90K which does not bind hormone; (2)

Peak II (in the presence of molybdate) contained a 110K protein which binds hormone and a 90K protein which does not bind hormone. Experiments using the covalent label [³H]R5020, a synthetic progestin, correlated with this summary. Fluorography of Peak I showed labelling at the position of subunit A but no labelling of the 90K protein. Peak II showed labelling at the position of subunit B but no labelling of a 90K protein. These results were confirmed by studies using the 8 S non-transformed form of the progesterone receptor which was purified and found to contain subunit A, subunit B, and a 90K protein (23). Furthermore, this complex is also resistant to dissociation in high ionic strength buffers which contain molybdate.

Use of a monoclonal antibody (BF4) to purified, molybdate-stabilized ≈8S progesterone receptor provided further evidence of a receptor associated 90K protein (3). If the receptor, purified by affinity chromatography, was incubated with BF4, in the presence of molybdate, the receptor peak was shifted from 8 S to 10 S on glycerol gradients. ³⁵S- labelled BF4 was also shifted to 9-10 S under these same conditions. However, in buffers lacking molybdate, there was no shift in the 4 S sedimentation coefficient of the receptor when it was incubated with antibody. Nevertheless, ³⁵S-BF4 shifted from its original 7 S to 10 S. These results are an indication of a non-ligand binding component of the non-transformed, 8 S progesterone receptor. Crude cytosol, prepared without molybdate was precipitated with ammonium sulphate and incubated with BF4. The ³⁵S-BF4 peak sedimented at 9 S but the [³H]progesterone peak sedimented at 4S. Addition of an excess of unlabelled BF4 did not effect the 4 S peak but caused the 9 S peak to disappear and the ³⁵S to be recovered at 7 S. These results are consistent with the presence of a non-hormone binding, receptor associated protein. Furthermore, salt-transformed cytosol preparation, labelled with [³H]-progesterone and put over an affinity column did not form an immune complex with BF4. The studies discussed in this section indicate that a non-steroid binding subunit is associated with the progesterone receptor, at least in the molybdate stabilized complex. The question remains, however, as to how molybdate stabilizes the complex and whether it represents the actual physiological subunit structure of the receptor. Perhaps this 90kd protein plays a role in the overall mechanism of steroid hormone action and is even associated with other steroid receptors. Since the BF4 monoclonal antibody has been found to specifically interact with estrogen, androgen, and glucocorticoid receptors (in the chicken) it seems this may be the case (3). Furthermore, since the 90kd protein seems to be associated with the non-transformed progesterone receptor and not the transformed receptor, it may act to bind to the receptor-hormone complex blocking DNA interaction. Upon transformation this 90K protein could leave the receptor-hormone complex, allowing it to bind to DNA and bring about the known physiological effects. If this protein is associated as closely with the receptor in the cell, as it is with the molybdate stabilized receptor, then it may play a role in steroid hormone action. Nevertheless, the controversy continues as to the exact composition of the macromolecular 7-8 S progesterone receptor complex.

B) Glucocorticoid receptors

The progesterone receptor appears to be composed, therefore, of two dissimilar subunits, A and B, with the association of at least one 90kd non-hormone binding protein. Experiments involving the glucocorticoid receptor demonstrate that its structure is in many ways similar to that proposed for the progesterone receptor. One major difference, however, is that the glucocorticoid receptor appears to contain similar subunits. In other words, subunit "A" is grossly indistinguishable from subunit "B". The receptor is not readily separated into two forms as the progesterone subunits are.

Evidence for the homogeneity of glucocorticoid receptor subunits came from work done with a mouse pituitary cell line, AtT-20 (24). [^{3}H]-triamcinolone-acetonide labelled cytosol, prepared at 0°C, was chromatographed on a DEAE-cellulose column. The elution profile showed two peaks: one major, relatively acidic peak, and one minor peak.

Cytosol which had been activated, either by Sephadex G-25 gel filtration or ammonium sulphate precipitation, and chromatographed on DEAE-cellulose showed one elution peak which corresponded to the minor peak seen with chromatography of unactivated receptor. Therefore, the minor peak seen from unactivated receptor seemed to be composed of activated receptor. Furthermore, addition of 20mM molybdate to the preparation buffer resulted in elution from the DEAE-column of only the one major acidic peak. Since molybdate is known to stabilize unactivated receptor, this was further evidence that the second minor peak was composed of receptor which had spontaneously activated during receptor preparation or during chromatography. The major peak eluting from DEAE-cellulose represented the only unactivated form of the receptor. Hydroxylapatite chromatography showed that both unactivated and activated receptor eluted as a symmetrical peak at the same potassium phosphate concentration. Also, activated receptor, which binds to both phosphocellulose and DNA-cellulose columns, eluted as a single peak from both. Therefore, the elution profiles of glucocorticoid receptor from DNA-cellulose, HAP, DEAE-cellulose, and phosphocellulose all show no evidence of dissimilar, heterogenous subunits as was seen for the progesterone receptor. Rather, the glucocorticoid receptor seems to consist of a single unactivated form which can convert to a single activated form.

In order to confirm the results obtained with the AtT-20 cell line, experiments were performed with mouse liver glucocorticoid receptor (25). Hydroxylapatite chromatography of this receptor resulted in an elution profile containing four peaks rather than the one elution peak seen with AtT-20 receptor. A combination of HAP, phosphocellulose, and gel filtration chromatography along with sucrose density gradients, molybdate stabilization, rechromatography, and mixing of cytosols from liver and AtT-20 cells, demonstrated that the heterogeneous forms resulted from proteolysis of the activated receptor. It was suggested that activation converts protease-sensitive regions of the receptor to a more susceptible state. Although definitive data on this point are still lacking. Molybdate, once again, was found to stabilize the receptor in a state which was protected from proteolysis. The native, activated receptor was found to have a molecular weight of 81kd. One form of partially proteolyzed receptor (53kd) contains both hormone and DNA-binding sites, while the mero-receptor (24kd) is the smallest form of the receptor which still contains the hormone-binding site. Experiments done with rat thymus cells supported the conclusions which resulted from the rat liver receptor work (7). Chromatography, along with agarose filtration showed that proteolysis of both the activated and unactivated receptor occurred in the absence of molybdate. Therefore, although the mouse pituitary line seemed to be relatively free of endogeneous proteases, receptor preparations from whole tissues contained very active proteolyzing enzymes. Even though proteolysis resulted in small receptor forms, the native, unproteolyzed glucocorticoid receptor, in contrast to the progesterone receptor, was found to consist of similar species. Although the species were not distinguishable by methods described here, this is not to say that dissimilar forms of glucocorticoid receptor subunits may not be present under certain conditions. In fact, there is evidence for the existence of charge variants of human glucocorticoid receptors (12). See Figure 1.

Experiments were then performed in order to investigate the structure of the activated versus unactivated receptor and the mechanism which leads to the conversion of one to the other. Data obtained from agarose filtration and sucrose density gradient ultra-centrifugation suggested that the unactivated receptor is a large 8.3nm, 9.0-9.5 S form and that the activated receptor is a smaller 5.0nm, 4.8 S form (7). This suggested that activation involved the conversion of large forms of the receptor to smaller forms. Since the dissociation of dissimilar subunits, A and B, was proposed as a mechanism of activation for the chick oviduct progesterone receptor,(14,26), an analogous mechanism involving dissociation of the similar subunits of the glucocorticoid receptor could be envisioned as the mechanism of activation in this

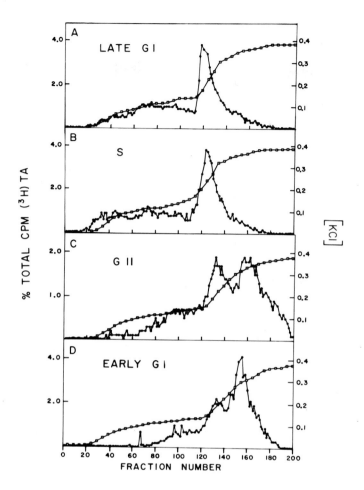

FIGURE 1. DEAE cellulose chromatography of cytoplasmic glucocorticoid receptor complexes. Analytical samples of cytoplasm (300ul; apprx. 8000 cpm) prepared in Buffer A (no salt) from each major cell cycle phase were applied to DEAE cellulose and eluted with a step KCl gradient. Data is expressed as a percentage of the total recovered radioactivity (●─●) vs. fraction number. The open squares (□─□) represent the measure of conductance (i.e., concentration) of the eluted Buffer A salt solution in every fifth fraction. Panel A (Late G_1/S phase); Panel B (S phase); Panel C (G_2 phase); Panel D (Early G_1 phase).

system. Experiments performed with the AtT-20 cell line indicated that this was the case (11). Analysis of activated and unactivated receptor by agarose gel filtration and by sucrose density gradient ultracentrifugation showed the presence of smaller forms when receptor was activated or treated with high salt. Unactivated, molybdate stabilized receptor, in either high or low salt concentrations, had a Stokes radius of 8.3 nm. On the other hand, activated receptor, stabilized by molybdate, had a radius of 6.0nm in high salt. Analysis of the activated receptor in buffers without molybdate, under the same high salt conditions, resulted in a 3.9 nm form. This is futher evidence of a decrease in size of the receptor upon activation. Experiments using sucrose density gradient ultracentrifugation also showed this decrease in receptor size. Intact, molybdate-stabilized, unactivated receptor sedimented at 9 S in low salt gradients. However, the same type of receptor had a sedimentation coefficient of 5 S in a high salt gradient. Furthermore, unactivated receptor that was not stabilized by molybdate, as well as the activated receptor, both had a sedimentation coefficient of 5 S in low salt gradients. The observation that the molybdate stabilized unactiviated receptor had a Stokes radius of 8.3nm in high salt but only a 5 S sedimentation coefficient (rather than 9 S), indicated that the 5 S form of the receptor may be an intermediate form in the mechanism of activation. Binding of the 5 S form to phosphocellulose showed that it was indeed an activated form. Nevertheless, activated receptor sedimentated at 3.2 S in sucrose gradients which contained high salt. It seems that activation proceeds through an intermediate 5 S form and then finally to the fully activated 3.2 S form having a radius of only 3.9nm.

Molecular weight calculations resulted in a value of 317kd for the unactivated, molybdate-stabilized receptor; 176kd for the high salt, molybdate-stabilized intermediate form; and 81kd for the fully activated species. These values, obtained from the sedimentation and filtration data discussed previously led to the proposal that subunit dissociation is the mechanism of receptor activation. This mechanism of dissociation

has been discussed previously for the chick oviduct progesterone receptor
(26, 27). The hypothesis is that, upon activation, a tetramer (317kd) of
similar hormone-binding subunits dissociates into a dimer (176K) and/or
monomer (81K) form (11). This model is completely analogous to the one
proposed for the progesterone receptor, differing only in that the
progesterone receptor subunits are dissimilar (A is different than B) and
the glucocorticoid receptor subunits are similar (A is the same as B).
See Figure 4. It was also hypothesized at the time that receptor complex
could contain not only the hormone binding moiety, but also
"receptor-binding factors" (11). In light of more recent evidence for
the existence of the 90kd receptor associated protein of the chick
oviduct progesterone receptor (22), there is a distinct possibility that
non-steroid binding proteins are associated with the glucocorticoid
receptor complex. Furthermore, subsequent experiments showed that a
monoclonal antibody (BF4) to the progesterone-receptor interacted with
this 90kd progesterone receptor associated protein (3). This antibody
also specifically interacted with the non-transformed 8 S forms of
estrogen, androgen, and glucocorticoid receptors. It seems, therefore,
that the glucocorticoid receptor complex does contain this 90kD protein,
or at least one closely related antigenically.

In conclusion, both progesterone and glucocorticoid receptor complexes
appear to consist of hormone binding subunits (either similar or
dissimilar) and a receptor associated (~90kd) protein. See Figure 4.
What this protein is and how it affects hormone action needs to be
elucidated. Nevertheless, dissociation of the various subunits of these
receptor complexes seem to play an important role in the mechanism of
receptor activation and consequently steroid hormone action.

Steroid Receptor Structure/Function Relationships: A Physiological
Approach

In this section we will review and compare two series of investigations,

156

those from Tom Spelsberg's laboratory concerning progesterone receptor, and those from our laboratory dealing with the glucocorticoid receptor. Although only limited analogy can be seen between the two systems, both sets of experiments point to the notion that changes in subunit composition and/or molecular charge of the steroid receptors without changes in receptor size (proteolysis or aggregation), leads to altered functional states of the receptor.

A) Physiological effects of progesterone receptor subunit structure

Over the past several years some interesting developments concerning the fluctuations in progesterone receptor binding capacity to nucleoacidic protein (NAP) have developed (28). It has been suggested that binding of the receptor to this nucleoacidic protein complex is a more physiological interaction than that of binding of receptor to pure DNA. It was observed that there was a seasonal variation in the capacity of the steroid-receptor to bind to NAP (28). Steroid receptor isolated in the summer showed a high level of binding to NAP whereas receptor isolated in the winter showed little binding to NAP. Since in vivo nuclear uptake of [^{3}H]progesterone reaches a maximum during the summer and lower levels in the winter, binding to NAP correlates well to the physiological response in the cell. Although this seasonal variation occurred with binding to chromatin, it did not occur with binding to DNA. Similarly, the effect progesterone has on RNA-polymerase activity was diminished in late winter/early spring. Despite these physiological differences in receptor action, physical characteristics of the receptor (sedimentation rates, elution profiles from molecular sieve columns, and binding affinity between steroid and receptor) were identical regardless of whether receptor was isolated in the summer or winter months. However, analysis by isoelectric focussing showed the presence of two receptor species. One species had a pI of 6 and the other had a pI of 7. These species were called subunit A and subunit B, respectively, since they correlated to the subunit species (A and B) discussed earlier(see Section III.A.). Most interestingly, it was observed that receptor isolated in the summer months had equivalent amounts of species

A and species B; whereas receptor isolated in the winter showed a decreased amount of subunit A. This suggested a correlation between progesterone receptor structure and physiological activity. More recent studies (29) showed that the amount of species A fluctuated in the same manner as in vivo and in vitro binding of progesterone receptor to NAP and chromatin. The decrease in subunit A explained earlier observations that cytosol levels of [^{3}H]progesterone receptor decreased in the winter months. As the season progresses and the biological activity returns, the concentration of subunit A increases. Therefore, biological activity, binding to NAP, seasonal variations, and amount of species A of the receptor all seem to be correlated.

This line of investigation was next extended to a developmental approach. Undeveloped chick oviducts were treated with estrogen in order to study the relationship between oviduct development and progesterone receptor subunit composition. These studies showed that the level of subunit B increased as estrogen-induced development proceeded. As the level of B increased so did the nuclear binding of the receptor and the resultant transcriptional response. Further experiments (30) examined progesterone receptor from estrogen withdrawn chicks. It was known that these chicks had oviducts that were smaller, and that receptor concentration was lower than that of estrogen treated chicks. Isoelectric focussing analysis of receptor from these chicks showed that there was a deficiency in the B receptor subunit. Furthermore, binding to NAP, in vivo and in vitro, was reduced. Thus, the properties of the progesterone receptor isolated from estrogen withdrawn chicks are similar to the properties of progesterone receptor isolated in the winter from estrogen treated chicks. The difference is that the former is deficient in subunit B, whereas the latter is deficient in subunit A.

In other studies, the relative amounts of receptor subunits have been examined in aged, non-laying hens(30). Once again, the oviduct size of these hens was much smaller than that of laying hens, and progesterone receptor concentration was one-fourth that of laying hens. Similarly, the receptor from these hens showed an isoelectric focussing pattern deficient in the B subunit and a total loss of progesterone receptor binding in vitro to NAP. Therefore, the conclusions from the previous two studies is that addition of estrogen (i.e. induction of oviduct development) results in an increase in the B subunit; whereas withdrawal of estrogen results in a decrease in the level of B subunit.

Time course studies were performed in order to investigate the appearance and disappearance of subunit species under various physiological conditions (19). In the first set of experiments chicks were treated with DES, the synthetic estrogen, for various times. It was found that receptors from more developed oviducts (12-24 days of treatment with DES) showed more in vitro binding to NAP than receptors from oviducts that received 0-8 days of treatment with DES. In vivo binding of [^{3}H]progesterone receptor to nuclear acceptor sites was lowest at day 6 of treatment and then rose continually. In addition, transcriptional activity (as measured by RNA polymerase II activity) increased after 8 days of treatment.

A study of the subunits of the receptor by isoelectric focussing analysis showed that oviducts at 0-6 days of development were deficient in subunit B, while developed oviducts had approximately equal amounts of subunits A and B. As development proceeded the B/A subunit ratio increased. The opposite was also true: a time course study of estrogen withdrawal showed a phasic loss in binding of [^{3}H]progesterone receptor to nuclear acceptor sites during estrogen withdrawal. As estrogen was withdrawn, the B/A ratio decreased. Upon restimulation with estrogen, there was an increase in [^{3}H]progesterone receptor binding to nuclear acceptor sites until on day 4 of restimulation there was a complete restoration of species B.

Based on these data, it seems that subunit A and subunit B are both essential for nuclear binding and physiological action of the progesterone receptor complex. Certain conditons cause the decrease of subunit A, while others cause the decrease of subunit B, but both result in decreased nuclear binding and consequently decreased transcription. This is consistent with a dimer model of the progesterone receptor, with both subunits being essential for physiological action.

Another possibility, rather than an actual decrease in the A and/or B subunit, is that [^{3}H]progesterone binding to the subunit decreases. Perhaps the circannual variation results from a fluctuation in binding of [^{3}H]progesterone to the A subunit. In the summer [^{3}H]progesterone binding to subunit A equals [^{3}H]progesterone binding to subunit B. Then in winter binding to A decreases. This could be due to a conformational change in subunit A which results in a loss of binding rather than the actual decrease in the amount of A subunit. If the A and B subunits do exist as a dimer, then subunit B, in addition to acting as a hormone binding subunit may bind DNA. Since binding to DNA is constant in summer and winter, then subunit B could contain the DNA-binding site. A conformational change in subunit A could cause not only a decrease in [^{3}H]progesterone binding to subunit A but also a decrease in binding of the A:B complex to proteins associated with chromatin and NAP. This would result in the seasonal fluctuation of receptor binding to chromatin and NAP.

Along the same lines, estrogen stimulation may cause an increase in the binding of [^{3}H]progesterone to subunit B rather than an increase in the synthesis of subunit B itself. A decrease in [^{3}H]progesterone binding could cause a decrease in binding to NAP and therefore a decrease in transcription and lowered biological response in estrogen withdrawn and non-laying hens. Perhaps with the development of monoclonal antibodies to chick oviduct progesterone receptor, this question can be addressed. Nevertheless, these studies clearly demonstrate that fluctuation in receptor subunit ratios or perhaps even selective post-transcriptional regulation of receptor subunits effects its function. It will be necessary in the future to characterize more than the binding capacity of the receptor in order to accurately understand this correlation.

B) Correlation between glucocorticoid receptor structure and physiological function

In addition to molecular weight forms, subunit composition, and non-steroid binding proteins, there are additional modifications of the receptor protein which can result in receptor heterogeneity and thereby alter function. For example, our own studies have shown that different charged forms of the glucocorticoid receptor have been found during the mammalian cell cycle (12). Early work with HeLa S3 cells demonstrated that alkaline phosphatase was induced by glucocorticoids. However, this induction took place only during late G_1 and S phases of the cell cycle, much in the same manner as ovalbumin induction by progesterone takes place only during summer months. In order to better understand this cell cycle dependent induction, the structure of the receptor from each stage of the cell cycle was studied. Using the double thymidine block method to synchronize cells, cytosols were prepared from cells at different stages of the cell cycle. Surface charge characteristics of the unactivated glucocorticoid receptors were determined by DEAE-cellulose chromatography and hydroxyl-apatite chromatography. As can be seen in Figure 1, it was found that receptor from late G_1/S phase eluted at 0.15M KCl. This was denoted Form I. Receptor isolated from S phase cells also eluted at 0.15M KCl (Form I). However, receptor from the G_2 phase of the cell cycle also eluted as a second more acidic form (at 0.25M KCl). This was called Form II. There was a further conversion of Form I to Form II in cells isolated from early G_1. Nevertheless, receptors isolated from each phase, late G_1, S, G_2, and early G_1, all sedimented as a 4S species in the presence of KCl and as an 8S species without KCl. Molybdate stabilized receptors from each cell cycle phase have sedimentation coefficients of 9-10S. See Figure 2. The Stokes radius of the receptor was found to be 65 angstroms, and the molecular weight was 123K regardless of the phase from which the receptor was isolated. These results are analogous to work discussed earlier on the progesterone receptor. Progesterone receptor isolated from different seasons of the year consisted of two subunits. These subunits, A and B, were regulated according to season. Here, two

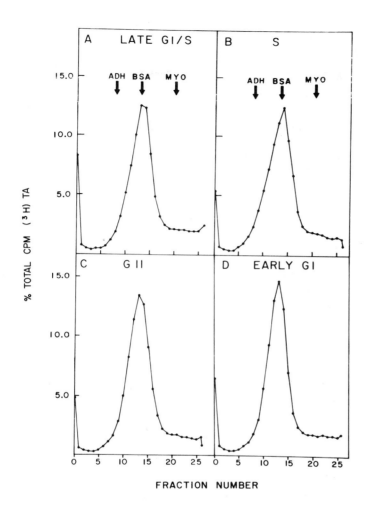

FIGURE 2. Sucrose density gradient analysis of cytoplasmic glucocorticoid receptors during the cell cycle. 0.3 ml aliquots of cytoplasm (approx. 8000–10000 cpm) were layered onto the top of a pre-cooled 5%–20% sucrose gradient and centrifuged at 190,000 x g for 16 h at 2–4°C in a Beckman SW 50.1 rotor. The data is expressed as a percentage of total recovered radioactivity (●—●) vs. fraction number. The heavy arrows denote the positions of the protein standards. Panel A (Late G_1/ S phase); Panel B (S phase); Panel C (G_2 phase); Panel D (Early G_1 phase).

glucocorticoid receptor forms were isolated during different phases of the cell cycle. In both cases, there are two species which appear during times of physiological response and decrease when the physiological response disappears. Although the molecular basis for this charge modification of the glucocorticoid receptor during the cell cycle has not been established, some recent observations suggest that the ability of receptor to become firmly associated with nuclei at 37°C in whole cells is highly dependent on the properties of the basic Form I receptor. Furthermore, the apparent transition from Form I to Form II of the receptor appears to be a reversible process with the majority of receptor reverting to Form I as cells reenter the mid-late G_1 phase of the cell cycle (31).

The apparent microheterogeneity of the glucocorticoid receptor was studied further using dexamethasone mesylate (DM) a synthetic glucocorticoid antagonist which can be covalently bound to the receptor at pH 8.3 (32). Cytosols were prepared from HeLa S3 cells that had been labelled with DM. Analysis of cytosolic proteins demonstrated saturable binding of a protein of 90kd molecular weight. Competition with a number of steroids shows specific glucocorticoid binding to this protein. It was found that the 90K protein labelled with [^{3}H]DM had physical properties similar to [^{3}H]dexamethasone labelled receptor complex. High resolution, two-dimensional gel analysis of the [^{3}H]DM labelled receptor showed a family of five discrete species with differing pI, but with a molecular weight of 90K. See Figure 3. Preliminary data on denaturing isoelectric focussing gels of [^{3}H]DM labelled glucocorticoid receptor from HeLa S3 cells also showed heterogeneously charged receptor species (33). Two-dimensional analysis on SDS-acrylamide, 5-12% gradient gels showed a family of at least five different spots. Furthermore, ^{35}S-labelled cytosol from HeLa S3 cells was reacted with a monoclonal antibody to the human glucocorticoid receptor (34). Two-dimensional gel analysis once again showed a family of spots differing in isoelectric point, although, there was an indication that many of the proteins had

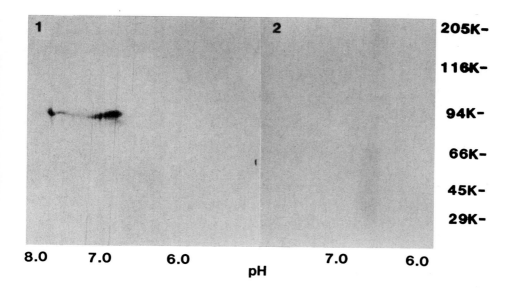

FIGURE 3. Two dimensional gel analysis of affinity labelled human glucocorticoid receptors.
Fractions of cytoplasmic receptors from HeLa S3 cells, incubated with 1×10^{-8} M [3H]dexamthasone mesylate alone (Panel 1) or [3H]dexamethasone mesylate plus 2×10^{-6} M unlabelled dexamthasone (Panel 2) were first subjected to isoelectric focussing and then to SDS polyacrylamide gel elecrtrophoresis. The polyacrylamide gels were transferred to BA84 nitrocellulose sheets electrophoretically, sprayed with [3H]enhance, and fluorographed for 5 days at −70°C. The molecular weights of the indicated proteins were determined from a companion gel. The pH ranges were estimated from companion wells in the original isoelectric focussing. The pattern shown is highly representative of eight experiments.

been proteolyzed to smaller forms (33). These experiments all indicate the heterogeneous nature of the glucocorticoid receptor and suggest that despite the overall gross similarity of the glucocorticoid receptor subunits (7,10), more subtle modifications in receptor are probably occuring. These charge changes in glucocorticoid receptor may result from posttranscriptional modifications and thereby provide mechanisms for a single receptor protein to carry out diverse functions within a given cell.

C) Steroid receptor modification

There are various biochemical processes which could account for a heterogeneous population of receptors. Phosphorylation is one of these processes which has been studied. There is evidence for in vivo phosphorylation of rat hepatic glucocorticoid receptor (35). Adrenalectomized rats were injected with ^{32}P-orthophosphate and hepatic receptor was prepared and purified using a deoxycorticosterone-derivatized agarose column. The receptor was then eluted, in the presence of 10mM molybdate, with a linear potassium phosphate gradient. ^{32}P containing material was found to coelute with peaks of [^{3}H]triamcinolone acetonide labelled receptor during both the intermediate and final purfication procedures. Receptor peaks from a DEAE column were precipitated with TCA and electrophoresed on SDS-gels. A 90K band was visualized by Coomassie Blue staining. The fact that this 90K protein can be seen by Coomassie Blue staining suggests that it it probably not the glucocorticoid receptor since receptor is not present in sufficient amounts in cytosol to be seen by this method of staining. It is possible that this 90K protein is the same one which associates with the progesterone receptor in the untransformed, molybdate stabilized state. This 90K protein, although it may not be receptor, is associated with receptor and autoradiography showed that it was phosphorylated. Earlier evidence also indicated that the 90K protein associated with the progesterone receptor was phosphorylated (21). If oviduct tissue mince was incubated with ^{32}P-orthophosphate, ^{32}P-containing material coeluted with both [^{3}H]progesterone binding peaks I and II. TCA precipitation of peaks I and II and subsequent analysis by slab gel electrophoresis showed Coomassie staining of a 90K band from peak I and 90K and 104K bands from peak II. Autoradiography showed that a 90K band from peak I and 90K and 109K bands from peak II contained ^{32}P. Although further experiments indicated that the 109K band was not the phosphorylated form of the 104K band, the 90K receptor protein appeared to be phosphorylated.

There is further evidence which suggests that the glucocorticoid receptor frm L-cells is phosphorylated (36). L-cells, a mouse fibroblast line, were grown in the presence of ^{32}P-orthophosphate. Glucocorticoid binding proteins were purified by deoxycorti-costerone-agarose chromatography, eluted, and electrophoresed on SDS-polyacrylamide gels. If the active glucocorticoid, 11β-cortisol was run through the column then a 92K phosphoprotein was eluted. Pre-incubation of the ^{32}P-cytosol with 50mM triamcinolone acetonide, resulted in much less of the 92K phosphoprotein staying on the column. Two-dimensional analysis of the ^{32}P-labelled 92K band showed two species, one at pH 6.0 (major), and one at pH 5.4 (minor). Comparatively, two dimensional gel electrophoresis of [^{3}H]DM labelled receptor resulted in a broad band between pH 5.3 and pH 6.2 with the most intense spot being at pH 6.0. Therefore, the ^{32}P and [^{3}H]DM-labelled species have similar characteristics indicating that both are at least associated with the glucocorticoid receptor. [^{3}H]DM labelling allowed gel analysis of the specific protein labelled by the hormone. An apparent 92K band was labelled by both [^{3}H]DM and ^{32}P. Experiments with L292 cells, which have only 5% of the glucocorticoid binding capacity of L cells, showed very little 92K phosphoprotein (36). This indicates a correlation between decrease in binding and decrease in phosphate incorporation into the 92K protein.Decreased binding would presumably be linked to a decrease in the active form of the receptor.This data suggests that the phosphorylated protein is the receptor.

Nevertheless, the possibility still exists that the phosphoprotein seen is the 90K receptor associated protein rather than the actual hormone binding 92K receptor subunit. Since the size of the glucocorticoid receptor (hormone binding) and the receptor associated protein discussed earlier (3) are so similar, gel analysis may not result in their separation. Therefore, although the phosphoprotein seen in these experiments does co-purify with [3H]DM labelled receptor, there is not definitive proof that the actual hormone binding subunit of the glucocorticoid receptor is a phosphoprotein. Furthermore, in addition to the 92K phosphoprotein, a phosphoprotein of 100,000 molecular weight was also found to specifically bind [3H]DM. The identity of this 100K protein is not known. This leads to further questioning of how these phosphoproteins are actually related to the glucocorticoid receptor subunits and whether they have a definite role in the physiological function of the glucocorticoid receptor.

Evidence, at least for glucocorticoid and progesterone receptors, suggests that they are phosphorylated. This phosphorylation may account for at least some of the heterogeneity found in receptor forms. The importance of phosphorylation as it relates to the mechanism of hormone action is still not fully elucidated, however.

D) Sulfhydryl groups associated with glucocortocoid receptor
In addition to the evidence that phosphate groups are associated with the receptor, there is also recent work dealing with sulfhydryl groups that are associated with the receptor. Glucocorticoid receptors isolated from rat thymus and liver cytosols are sensitive to sulfhydryl-modifying reagents. Treating receptor with these reagents will cause the inability of glucocorticoid to bind to the receptor. Barring one exception, these reagents have little effect once glucocorticoid is already bound to receptor. Preparation of reactive sulfhydryl matrices allowed for study of the importance of sulfhydryl groups in glucocorticoid receptor action (37). Agarose-diaminoethyl-succinyl-cysteinyl-2-thiobenzoid acid (DSCT) binds

mainly activated receptor. Whereas, agarose-diaminoethyl-succinyl-thioethylamine-2-thiopyridyl (DSTT) binds both activated and non-activated glucocorticoid receptor. Each matrix contains a thiodisulfide bond (-S-S-R). If the glucocorticoid receptor contains a thioanion (-S-GR) then a thio-disulfide interchange reaction will occur and the glucocorticoid receptor will become covalently attached to the matrix. The receptor complex can then be eluted with compounds containing a sulfhydryl group (i.e. mercaptoethylamine). Experiments showed that if [^{3}H]DM labelled receptor was treated with the sulfhydryl modifying reagent, binding to DSCT decreased by 52%. Binding to DNA-cellulose also decreased by 52%. Addition of calf thymus DNA to cytosols before putting then on DNA-cellulose or DSCT reduced complex binding. These data suggest that the activated complex may be interacting with the DSCT matrix through a sulfhydryl group located within the DNA-binding domain. It is known that dexamethasone-mesylate reacts with sulfhydryl groups to form a thioether bond. If most of the [^{3}H]DM labelled receptor is unactivated, there is little binding to DSCT (as would be expected since this column reacts with activated receptor). However, if the receptor is passed through a DNA-cellulose column in order to remove DNA-binding protein and then warmed to activate the receptor, there is substantial binding to DSCT. These studies indicate that the sulfhydryl which binds to the matrix is the same on associated with the DNA-binding domain. Furthermore, the glucocorticoid receptor obtained form these columns has a molecular weight of 87 ± 2Kd. This is consistent with work done in other labs on glucocorticoid receptor. These studies show, therefore, that the activated glucocorticoid receptor contains at least two sulfhydryl groups: one associated with the steroid binding site and one associated with the DNA-binding domain.

SUMMARY

It is evident that the physiological action of steroid hormones is closely linked to the structure of the steroid receptor. Figure 4 summarizes the structural characteristics of the progesterone and glucocorticoid receptors. This model encompasses data from both receptor systems. Two dissimilar progesterone subunits, A and B, are diagrammed. The glucocorticoid receptor would differ by containing two grossly similar subunits. Nevertheless, the structures would be analogous with respect to other modifying groups shown. In addition to the hormone binding subunits, the 90K protein which does not bind hormone is also shown. Modifications, i.e. phosphate groups and sulfhydryl groups, as discussed in the review, are also included. The presence or absence of these phosphate groups (and other modifications not yet studied) could account for the various forms of glucocorticoid and progesterone receptors which vary in charge.

The complex structure of the steroid receptor and its mode of action is not yet fully understood. The data reviewed here gives some indication of the many complexities of the structure. Although work on glucocorticoid and progesterone receptors has been reviewed here, there exists similarities between all steroid receptors. The similarities which do exist most likely will give us an insight into the way in which receptors perform their unique task.

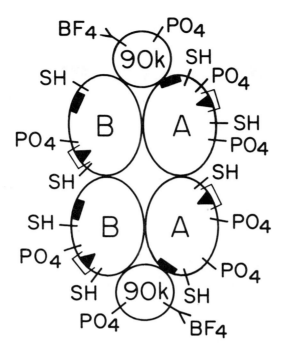

- ▬ chromatin binding site
- ▲ hormone binding site
- ⊓ hormone

SH   sulfhydryl group

PO_4 phosphate group

BF_4 monoclonal antibody

FIGURE 4. A model of steroid receptor structure.

170

References

1. Sherman, M.R., Moran, M.C., Tuazon, F.B., Stevens, Y.W.: JBC 258,
   10366-10377 (1983)

2. Sherman, M.R., Stevens,J.: Ann. Rev. Physiol. 46m 83-105 (1984).

3. Joab, I., Radanyi, C., Ranoir, M., Buchou, T., Catelli, M.G.,
   Binart, N., Mester, J., Baulieu, E.E.: Nature 308, 850-853 (1984).

4. Sherman, M.R., Tuazon, F.B., Miller, L.K.: Endo. 106, 1715-1727
   (1980).

5. Nigorishi, H., Toft, D.: Bioch. 19, 77-83 (1980).

6. Murakami, N., Quattrociocchi, T.M., Healy, S.P., Moudgil, V.K.:
   Arch. Bichem. Biophys. 214, 326-334 (1982).

7. Holbrook, N.J., Bodwell, J.E.,Jeffries, M., Munck, A.: JBC 258,
   6477-6485 (1983).

8. Sherman, M.R., Tuazon, F.B., Stevens,Y.W., Niu, E.M.: In: Steroid
   Hormone Receptors: Structure and Function. 3-24 (Eriksson, H and
   Gustafsson, J.A., (Eds), Elsevier Science Publishers, New York 1983.

9. Cidlowski, J.A.: Biochem. 19, 6162-6170 (1980).

10. Vedeckis, W.V., Freeman, M.R., Schrader, W.T., O'Malley, B.W.:
    Biochem. 19, 335-343 (1980).

11. Vedeckis, W.V.: Biochem. 22, 1983-1989 (1983).

12. Currie, R., Cidlowski, J.: Endo. 110, 2192-2194 (1982)/

13. Schrader, W.T., O'Malley, B.W.: JBC 24, 51-59 (1972).

14. Schrader, W.T., Birnbaumer, M.E., Hughes, M.R., Wiegel N.L., Gordy,
    W.W., O'Malley, B.W.: Rec. Prog. Horm. Res. 37, 583-633 (1981).

15. Birnbaumer,M., Schrader, W.T., O'Malley, B.W.: JBC 258, 7311-7337
    (1983).

16. Birnbaumer, M., Bell, R.C., Schrader, W.T., O'Malley, B.W.: JBC
    259, 1091-1098 (1984).

17. Horowitz, K.B., Alexander, P.S.: Endocrinology 113, 2195-2201
    (1983).

18. Dougherty, J.J., Toft, D.O.: JBC <u>257</u>, 3113-3119 (1982).

19. Boyd-Leinen, P.A., Gosse, B., Rasmussen, K., Martin-Dani, G.,
    Spelsberg, T.C.: JBC <u>259</u>, 2411-2421 (1984).

20. Dougherty, J.J., Puri, R.K., Toft, D.O.: JBC <u>257</u>, 1422-1423 (1982).

21. Puri, R.K., Grandics, P., Dougherty, J.J., Toft, D.O.: JBC <u>257</u>,
    10831-10837 (1982).

22. Dougherty, J.J., Puri, R.K., Toft, D.O.: JBC <u>259</u>, 8004 (1984).

23. Renoir, J.M., et al.: Biochem. J. <u>217</u>, 685-692 (1984).

24. Vedeckis, W.V.: Biochem. <u>20</u>, 7237-7245 (1981).

25. Vedeckis, W.V.: Bichem. <u>22</u>, 1976-1982 (1983).

26. Spelsberg, T.C., Boyd-Leinen, P.A.: Clinical Biochem. <u>13</u>, 198-203
    (1980).

27. Schrader, W.T., Heuer, S.S., O'Malley, B.W.: Biol. Reprod. <u>12</u>,
    134-142 (1975).

28. Boyd, P.A., Spelsberg, T.C.: Biochem. <u>18</u>, 3685-3690 (1979).

29. Spelsberg, T.C., Halberg, F.: Endocrinology <u>107</u>, 1234-1244 (1980).

30. Boyd-Leinen, P.A., Fournier, D., Spelsberg, T.C.: Endocrinology
    <u>111</u>, 30-36 (1982).

31. Fanger, B., Currie, R., Cidlowski, J.A. (submitted for publication).

32. Cidlowski, J.A., Richon, V.: Endocrinology (in press).

33. Silva, C.M. (unpublished results).

34. Cidlowski, J.A., Gillespie, G.Y. (unpublished observations).

35. Grandics, P., et al.: Biochem. Biophys. Res. Commun. <u>120</u>, 59-65
    (1984).

36. Housley, P.R., Grippo, J.F., Pratt, W.B.: In: Hormone Responsive
    Tumors. (Hollander, V.P., Ed.), Academic Press, (1984).

37. Bodwell, J.E., Holbrook, N.J., Munck, A.: Biochemistry, <u>23</u>,
    4237-4242   (1984).

ACKNOWLEDGEMENTS

We would like to acknowledge the support of National Institutes of Health grants AM32458, AM32459, and AM32460.

AN ALLOSTERIC REGULATORY MECHANISM FOR ESTROGEN RECEPTOR ACTIVATION

Angelo C. Notides, Shlomo Sasson*, and Steve Callison

Department of Radiation Biology and Biophysics
The University of Rochester School of Medicine and Dentistry
Rochester, New York 14642 (U.S.A.) and *Hebrew University
Hadassah Medical School, Jerusalem, Israel

Introduction

The role of the estrogen receptor, which is characteristic of all
receptors, is that of recognizing a hormonal signal and then transducing
this information, by means of a conformational change, into a functional
activity. It is generally accepted that the functional activity of the
estrogen receptor is to interact with specific DNA sequences of estrogen
responsive genes and thereby regulate gene transcription (1-4). The
selective binding of the glucocorticoid receptor to the mammary tumor
virus genome (5-7) and the progesterone receptor to the isolated avian
oviduct genes (8,9) has been demonstrated; however, the DNA sequence of
any estrogen-responsive gene with which the estrogen receptor selectively
interacts remains to be established. The nature of the molecular action
of any steroid hormone receptor at its chromatin binding site, the
functional activity, is also unknown.

Our studies of estrogen receptor activation focus on the molecular
mechanism by which estrogen-binding transforms the receptor from an
inactive to an active conformation, capable of modulating genetic
expression. An understanding of receptor activation should eventually
include an insight into the interaction of the active, in comparison
with, the nonactive conformation of the estrogen receptor with isolated
specific DNA sequences that respond to estrogen in vivo.

To obtain meaningful insight into the biochemistry of estrogen receptor
activation, it is important to specify the particular assay used. It
seems obligatory with the use of any assay of receptor activation that a

clear molecular mechanism and basis should be established, rather than using procedures that provide descriptive or operational data. This allows each study to be set in perspective to each other and more equitable comparisons to be made.

Some investigators use the increased capacity of the steroid hormone receptor to bind to isolated nuclei, DNA-cellulose, or phosphocellulose after dilution of the crude cytosol, heating, or exposure to high salt concentrations as an index of receptor activation (10-13). This operational definition of receptor activation should be reconsidered in the context of recent findings that show the steroid hormone receptors in the crude cytosol to be associated with macromolecules, particularly RNA (14,15). Feldman et al. (16), and Chong and Lippman (17) showed that merely the presence of the cellular or soluble RNA (even yeast RNA or synthetic polyribonucleotides) in buffers with low ionic strength was effective in blocking estrogen receptor binding to DNA-cellulose. We suggest that receptor-RNA association occurs during tissue homogenization with buffers of low ionic strength and results in blockage of the receptor's DNA binding site. The report of Tymoczko and Phillips (18) strongly suggests that the glucocorticoid receptor in crude cytosol was associated with RNA, contributing to the sedimentation of 8S in low salt sucrose gradients. Greene (19) similarly observed that the purified estrogen receptor sediments in low salt typically at 4.5S and when it sediments at 7-8S it does so only in the presence of receptor depleted cytosol, suggesting a nonspecific association of the other macromolecules with the receptor in low ionic strength buffers. Consequently, experimental procedures that remove this interfering association of RNA or proteins from the receptor will increase receptor binding to DNA cellulose without the receptor necessarily undergoing the hormone-induced conformational changes that are associated with receptor activation.

Our studies of the estrogen receptor define the molecular mechanism by which hormone-binding transforms the receptor from a nonactive into an active conformation. Our data support the concept that the estrogen receptor is an allosteric protein displaying the same unique kinetic and molecular characteristics common to all allosteric proteins (20-22).

These include: (1) a quaternary structure consisting of two or more
subunits or monomers, each containing a regulatory ligand binding site
(for example, a site that binds estradiol), and a functional or active
site (for example, a site that binds to DNA) that is nonoverlapping with
the ligand binding site; (2) complex equilibrium binding kinetics showing
a nonlinear Scatchard plot, indicating interaction between binding sites
of the protein; (3) complex association and/or dissociation kinetics; (4)
nonlinear dependence of ligand binding or enzyme activity upon the
concentration of the receptor or enzyme, indicating an ability of the
protein to either dissociate into subunits or associate into larger
units; and (5) the appearance of antagonist-effects when the antagonist
is present concurrently with the regulatory ligand, demonstrating the
presence of two binding sites on the protein that provoke opposing
site:site interactions. By analyzing the estrogen-binding
characteristics of the receptor, the ligand-induced conformational
changes of the estrogen receptor can be observed in a manner typical of
allosteric proteins. Complex estrogen-binding kinetics serve as a basis
for understanding the ligand-induced conformational changes of the
receptor, which in turn provide insight into the biochemical mechanism of
hormone binding and the relationship between hormone binding and the
functional activity of the receptor.

Re-examination of the intracellular distribution of the estrogen receptor
has extended and clarified our concepts of estrogen receptor activation
and function. The two-step model of Jensen et al. (23,24) and Gorski et
al. (25,26), based primarily upon subcellular fractionation studies of
estrogen receptor-containing tissue, showed that the unliganded,
nonactive form of the receptor was localized in the cytoplasmic fraction,
whereas the liganded receptor, in a hormone- and temperature-dependent
manner, was localized in the nucleus (23,25). This observation gave rise
to the concept that the receptor was cytoplasmic and that estradiol
binding induced the receptor's translocation to the nucleus. Recent
reports that the unliganded estrogen receptor can be isolated from nuclei
(27) and that the unliganded estrogen receptor exists in an equilibrium
between the cytoplasm and nucleus (28) are inconsistent with the two-step
model. Sheridan et al. reported (28) that tissue homogenized with

increasing volumes of buffer resulted in an increase in the fraction of the unliganded, but not liganded, estrogen receptor recovered in the cytosol. Similarly, the nuclear localization of the estrogen receptor is further supported by immunocytochemical staining of the estrogen receptor using specific monoclonal antibodies (29) and by cytochalasin B-induced enucleation studies (30). These studies lead to the realization that, in vivo, the estrogen receptor and possibly all steroid hormone receptors are nuclear proteins whose extractability depends upon ligation.

The current assessment that the estrogen receptor is a protein associated with the nucleus remains compatible with our concept that the estrogen receptor exists in two different forms or states (31-33). One state is the unliganded receptor, which because of its weak associations with nuclear sites is readily extracted by buffer without KCl, appears in the cytosolic fraction, and is commonly referred to as the nonactive or cytoplasmic form of the estrogen receptor. After extraction, the isolated nonactive form of the estrogen receptor dissociates into 4S subunits or monomers during sucrose gradient centrifugation analysis in buffers containing 0.15 M KCl or 0.4 M KCl, even though associated with estradiol, as long as the estradiol-receptor complex is maintained at 0°C so that hormone-induced conformation does not take place (32-34). Using the terminology applied to allosteric proteins, this nonactive state of the estrogen receptor can be viewed as the "relaxed" conformation (22). The other state is the liganded or activated estrogen receptor that is tightly associated with nuclear sites and only extracted with buffer containing 0.4 M KCl. The nuclear or activated estrogen receptor sediments at 5S in sucrose gradients with 0.4 M KCl and is a dimer of two 4S subunits of the receptor and is not dissociable under these experimental conditions (14,34). The activated estrogen receptor has properties that are characteristic of the "taut" or "constrained" state of an allosteric protein.

Purification and Structure of the Estrogen Receptor

The estrogen receptor from calf uteri was purified to near homogenity using a three-step procedure: ammonium sulfate fractionation of the calf

uterine cytosol was followed by estradiol affinity chromatography, and
then by heparin-Sepharose chromatography. The affinity absorbent
consisted of estradiol linked to Sepharose-6B via a substituted
di-n-propyl thioether linkage to the 17α position of estradiol according
to the method of Greene et al. (35). The overall purification of the
estrogen receptor was approximately 20,000-fold with a 10-22 percent
yield (Table 1). The specific activity of the purified estrogen receptor
was 14,760 p moles of [^{3}H]estradiol bound per mg of protein, which is
equivalent to one mole of estradiol bound per 67,800 gm of receptor or to
the gm molecular weight of each estradiol binding subunit.

Hydrodynamic measurements of the pure estrogen receptor in buffer with
0.4 M KCl at neutral pH show that the purified estrogen receptor
sediments at 5.4±0.02S, has a molecular Stokes radius of 60±0.5 Å, and a
molecular weight of 134,000. The molecular weight analysis of the
estrogen receptor by SDS gel electrophoresis shows a single protein with
a molecular weight of 68,000 (Fig. 1) in agreement with previous reports
(35-37). These values are similar to the estimates of the molecular
weight of the nonpurified estrogen receptor from the rat uterus, which
were 135,000 daltons for the 5S form of the receptor and 75,000 daltons
for the 4S form of the receptor (14,34). These observations (60) taken

Table 1. Purification of the Estrogen Receptor from Calf Uterus

Procedure	Protein	Receptor	Specific Activity	Yield	Purification
	mg	$\times 10^{12}$M	$\times 10^{12}$M/mg protein		-fold
Cytosol	2365	1650	0.69	100	1
30%, ammonium sulfate fraction	550	984	1.80	59	2.6
Estradiol-Sepharose chromatography	1.33	532	400.0	32	579
Heparin-Sepharose chromatography	0.025	369	14760.0	22	21,390

178

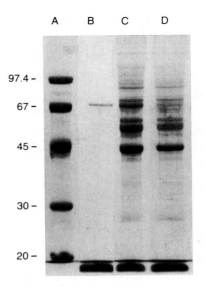

Fig. 1. The SDS-gel electrophoresis of the estrogen receptor from calf
uterus. Lane A contains the molecular weight standards. Lane B
contains 4 μg of the purified estrogen receptor after heparin-
Sepharose chromatography. Lane C contains the protein eluted from
the estradiol-Sepharose affinity chromatography step. Lane D is
identical with lane C, except that 1 μM of estradiol was added to the
30 percent ammonium sulfate fraction before the estradiol-Sepharose
affinity step; note that only the 68,000 molecular weight protein did
not adsorb to the estradiol affinity absorbent. The gel was stained
with Coomassie blue.

together suggest that the estrogen receptor is a homodimer of two

estrogen-binding 4S monomers.

Proteases have served as useful probes of the steroid hormone receptor's

binding domains. Studies of the glucocorticoid receptor (39),

progesterone receptor (40), and the estrogen receptor (32,41) demonstrate

that in each of these steroid hormone receptors there is a spatial

separation between the steroid-binding site and the DNA-binding site.

Accordingly, the trypsin- treated estrogen receptor retains its

estrogen-binding ability, but loses its capacity to form the 5S receptor

dimer as well as its ability to bind to DNA-cellulose or nuclei (32,41).

This separation of the DNA binding or functional site of the receptor from its steroid-binding or regulatory site is one of the distinguishing characteristics of an allosteric protein.

The composition of the 8S form of the estrogen receptor, the form that is observed in crude cytosol following sucrose gradient analysis in the absence of salt, remains an enigma. In sucrose gradients without KCl, the highly purified estrogen receptor not only adheres to the wall of the centrifuge tube, but sediments to the bottom of the tube as well, suggesting a tendency toward nonspecific binding and self-aggregation. Interestingly, upon the addition of crude cytosol from nonreceptor-containing tissues (for example, diaphragm), the highly purified receptor sediments at 8S in the absence of salt. These observations suggest that either the estrogen receptor is nonspecifically associating with other proteins, or RNA, and that these macromolecules are blocking binding sites on the wall of the centrifuge tube and thereby allowing the 5S estrogen receptor to form an 8S tetramer. Recently, some investigators (42,43) have suggested that the estrogen receptor and progesterone receptor are associated with a nonhormone-binding protein. Further study is necessary to determine whether the nonhormone-binding protein is a subunit of the receptor or a nonspecifically associated protein. Using a monoclonal antibody directed at a single antigenic determinant on the 4S estrogen receptor, Moncharmont et al. (44) concluded that the 5S estrogen receptor contained two antigenic determinants, which is consistent with a homodimer structure. They also found that the 8S contained only two such antigenic determinants, further supporting the presence of nonhormonal binding components. Overall, the biochemical significance of the estrogen receptor to produce an 8S sedimenting form, observed in the absence of KCl, is not evident.

Nevertheless, our analysis of the highly purified estrogen receptor has revealed a molecular structure characteristic of an allosteric regulatory protein. The receptor is a homodimer of two estrogen-binding subunits or monomers with binding domains for estrogens and DNA. Additional molecular study of the highly purified estrogen receptor may provide insight into the structure-function relationship of the receptor and the biochemical basis of the receptor's sedimentation at 8S in the absence of salt.

Cooperative Interactions of the Estrogen Receptor

Our investigation has established that the estrogen receptor exists in two discrete conformational states that are reversible and differ not only in their affinity for estradiol (31,32), but for other estrogenic ligands as well (45,46). In the presence of estradiol, the equilibrium between receptor conformational states is displaced toward the state that has the higher affinity for estradiol. The presence of more than one affinity state for ligand is a common hallmark of allosteric proteins and their site:site interactions (20-22). The analysis of the kinetics and equilibrium binding characteristics of the receptor is a particularly appropriate method for measuring the mechanism by which estradiol controls the conformational states (active vs. nonactive) of the receptor. Our equilibrium binding analyses of the interaction of estradiol with the estrogen receptor demonstrate that the receptor's binding is positively cooperative. The Scatchard plot of the [^{3}H]estradiol receptor equilibrium binding curve is convex at a receptor concentration of 1 to 20 nM at 0 to 30°C (Fig. 2). The Hill coefficient is 1.62 ± 0.02, a value consistent with a cooperative site:site interaction of a dimer. These data indicate that the receptor's affinity for estradiol increases with increasing occupancy of the receptor, which is consistent with the presence of two receptor states.

The molecular weight analysis, indicating that the 4S receptor monomer has only one estradiol-binding site, and the influence of salt concentration and receptor concentration, all strongly support the concept that the positive cooperativity of the estrogen receptor is inherently a property of the 5S receptor dimer. The cooperative characteristics of the receptor were present only at a receptor concentration above 1 nM and in buffers containing 0.15 M or 0.4 M KCl indicating that the site:site interactions are in the 5S dimer confirmed to be present under these conditions (34). Such interactions would not be seen in the salt-dissociable 8S oliogmeric form of the receptor. At a receptor concentration below 1 nM, there is a progressive decrease in the convexity of the Scatchard plot; at a receptor concentration of 0.2 to

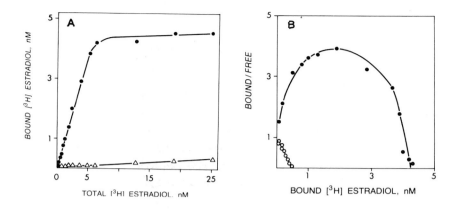

Fig. 2. Saturation binding analysis of the estrogen receptor after
purification by ammonium sulfate. Panel A is the titration of the
estrogen receptor with [^{3}H]estradiol at 25°C for 1 hr, the total
bound [^{3}H]estradiol is shown (●). The nonspecifically bound
[^{3}H]estradiol was measured by incubating [^{3}H]estradiol with an
additional 200-fold molar excess of unlabelled estradiol (Δ). Panel
B, Scatchard analysis of the [^{3}H]estradiol receptor saturation
binding at high receptor concentration, 3.6 nM, the Hill coefficient
was 1.67 (●) or at low receptor concentration, 0.3 nM, the Hill
coefficient was 1.2 (o).

0.3 nM (25°C) the Hill coefficient decreases to 1.10 ± 0.13. The
dependence of cooperative estradiol-binding upon the receptor
concentration strongly indicates that the binding sites are dissociated
and that each 4S monomer of the 5S estrogen receptor dimer has only one
estradiol-binding site. Site:site interactions of a 4S receptor with two
estradiol-binding sites or the presence of a nondissociable 5S receptor
dimer would both be independent of receptor concentration and hence the
Hill coefficient would have remained at 1.6.

Weaker estrogens such as estriol and estrone have a reduced capacity to
induce a maximal positive cooperativity when compared with estradiol.
Even at a receptor concentration of 20 nM, at 25°C, the Hill coefficient

182

of the estriol receptor interaction was 1.20±0.05, while the Hill
coefficient of estradiol interaction was 1.62±0.04 (Fig. 2,3). The
reduced cooperative interactions of the receptor suggest a relationship
between the extent of cooperativity and the estrogenic potency of the
ligand. The change in the degree of cooperativity observed is dependent
upon a number of kinetic and receptor conformational considerations,
including the intrinsic allosteric constant (i.e., the equilibrium
constant of the two states of the receptor in the absence of the ligand);
the ratio for the affinities of the ligand for the two states of the
receptor; and the apparent allosteric constant (i.e., the equilibrium
constant of the two states of the receptor in the presence of the
ligand). The reduced cooperativity observed with estriol or estrone is
probably due to their apparent allosteric constants--these ligands are
less efficient than estradiol in shifting the equilibrium existing
between the two affinity states of the receptor toward the higher
affinity or activated state. These binding mechanism studies suggest
that continuously high concentrations of these ligands would be necessary
to maintain the receptor at or near maximal activation. These
observations are consistent with in vivo findings (47) showing that a
weaker estrogenic response, compared with estradiol, results from a
single dose of estriol, whereas continuous administration of estriol
provokes a complete estrogenic response. Furthermore, we have shown that
estriol in the presence of estradiol will reduce estradiol's ability to
activate the receptor, indicating the presence of site:site interaction
of the receptor and the partial agonist/antagonist activity of estriol
(48,49).

When the binding mechanism of [^{3}H]estradiol is studied in the presence
of enclomiphene (Fig. 4), an estrogen antagonist, the estrogen receptor's
positive cooperativity is inhibited (50). Consequently, the mechanism of
enclomiphene antagonistic action does not operate merely as a simple
competitor of the estradiol, but likely binds to the receptor and
inhibits the transition from the low to higher affinity state. There is
evidently a relationship between the estrogen receptor's binding
mechanism and the biological activity of the ligand with which the
receptor interacts.

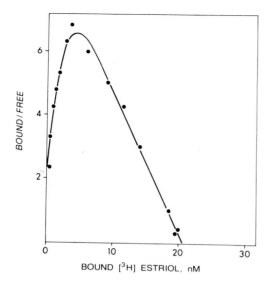

Fig. 3. The Scatchard plot of the positively cooperative binding of
[3H]estriol by the partially purified estrogen receptor
equilibrated at 25°C for 1 hr. The nonspecifically bound
[3H]estriol was less than 8 percent of the total bound
[3H]estriol. The Hill coefficient was 1.20.

Dissociation Kinetics of the Estrogen Receptor

The estradiol dissociation kinetics of the receptor are indicative of two
distinct affinity states in a manner consistent with the receptor's
equilibrium binding kinetics (31,32) and characteristic of an allosteric
protein having a positively cooperative binding mechanism (20). Weichman
and Notides reported (31,51) that the dissociation of [3H]estradiol
from the estrogen receptor is a complex process having two phases, a fast
dissociating phase (t 1/2 = 3 min at 28°C) and a slower phase (t 1/2 = 95
min at 28°C). The fast component of the biphasic dissociation curve is
proportional to the fraction of the receptor in the nonactive or 4S form,
while the second, slower phase is produced by the activated 5S form of
the receptor (51). Preincubation of the receptor for 15 to 45 min at
28°C decreases, proportionately, the magnitude of the fast component
until the receptor is completely activated (transformed into the 5S form)

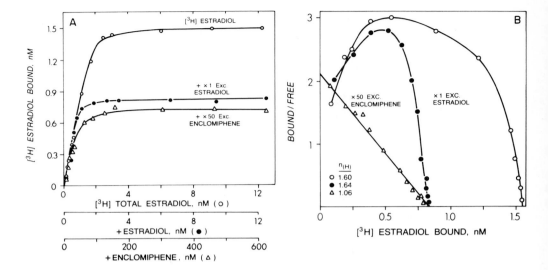

Fig. 4. The inhibition of cooperative [³H]estradiol binding of the estrogen receptor by enclomiphene. (A) The receptor is titrated with a 50-fold molar excess of enclomiphene or a 1-fold molar excess of estradiol over the [³H]estradiol concentration, so that the ratio of [³H]estradiol to the competitor is constant. (B) The Scatchard plot and Hill coefficient (n_H) indicate that enclomiphene inhibits the positive cooperativity of [³H]estradiol binding while estradiol does not, although both inhibit maximal [³H]estradiol binding by approximately 50 percent.

and only the slow monophasic component is present (compare curves B and C, Fig. 5).

The association rate constant of the estradiol receptor binding interaction is independent of both estradiol and receptor concentrations. In addition, the association rate constants are identical, whether measured in dilute Tris buffer with or without 0.4 M KCl or 0.4 M NaSCN, thereby indicating the presence of a simple second-order reaction (31). Thus, the receptor's estrogen-induced conformational changes can be analyzed by measurements of its dissociation rate constant, but not by its association rate constants. In addition, an estimation of the receptor's affinity, from the ratio of the rate constants, indicates that

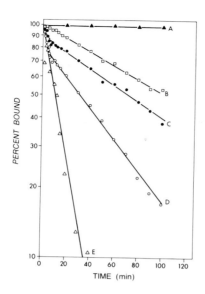

Fig. 5. The effect of receptor concentration on the dissociation of the
[³H]estradiol receptor complex. Calf uterine cytosol prepared in
buffer (40 mM Tris, 1 mM dithiothreitol, 0.5 mM leupeptin, pH 7.4)
was incubated with 10 nM [³H]estradiol at 0°C for 1 hr. The
receptor concentration was 2.7 nM (A,B,C). One aliquot (B) was
preincubated at 28°C for 45 min to activate the receptor, while
aliquots A and C were maintained at 0°C for 45 min. Two other
aliquots were diluted with buffer containing 4 mg diaphragm protein/ml
to a receptor concentration of 0.06 nM (D) or 0.01 nM (E) and
incubated at 0°C for 45 min. The dissociation of the [³H]-
estradiol-receptor complex was measured at 28°C after the addition of
1 μM estradiol to all aliquots except (A), which was used to measure
receptor stability at 28°C. Samples (0.5 ml) were removed at the
times cited and then incubated with hydroxylapatite for 30 min. at
0°C. The hydroxyl- apatite was washed with buffer and the bound
[³H]estradiol was extracted with ethanol and measured. The values
shown are corrected for nonspecific binding. The half-times of
[³H]estradiol dissociation were: 102 min for B; 3 min and 89 min
for C; 5 min and 45 min for D; and 20 min for E.

the affinity of the activated estrogen receptor is approximately 25- to
30-fold greater (at 25°C) than that of the nonactive state of the
receptor (31).

Our investigation of the estrogen receptor's dissociation kinetics has
demonstrated that the 4S monomeric form of the receptor cannot

simultaneously exist in two conformational states and display both the slow and rapid rates of [3H]estradiol dissociation and the corresponding active and nonactive conformations of the receptor (31-33,48,51). Sakai and Gorski (52,56) and Muller et al. (54,55) measured [3H]estradiol receptor dissociation kinetics while the receptor was adsorbed to hydroxylapatite and concluded that the 4S monomeric form displayed both the slow and fast [3H]estradiol dissociation kinetics (52-55). The estrogen receptor adsorbed to hydroxylapatite has served as a model for investigating estrogen receptor nuclear interactions (56,57). However, several considerations make the conclusions of these investigators (52-55) concerning the estrogen receptor's dissociation kinetics and structure unlikely. It remains to be demonstrated that adsorbing the 4S receptor monomer to hydroxylapatite does not mimic the receptors monomer:monomer interactions or conformational changes; that monomer:monomer interaction did not take place while bound to the hydroxylapatite, i.e., receptor dilution was sufficient to prevent site:site interaction; that the 0.4 M potassium phosphate used to desorb the receptor from the hydroxylapatite does not dissociate the receptor into a 4S form as reported by Miller et al. (58); and that the proteolytic activities present in crude cytosol, which accelerate in high salt containing buffers, did not produce a fragment of the receptor that sediments at 4S (59). Although it may seem reasonable to suppose that each 4S and 5S form of estrogen receptor exists in numerous conformations, several different experimental approaches indicate that the rapid dissociation kinetics of the estrogen receptor are an intrinsic property of only the nonactive, low affinity conformation of the receptor, i.e., the dissociated 4S form of the receptor, and that the active 5S form of the estrogen receptor displays the slower rate of [3H]estradiol dissociation. Specifically: 1) The magnitude of the fast [3H]estradiol dissociating component of the estrogen receptor's biphasic dissociation curve is dependent upon receptor concentration. As the receptor concentration decreases (i.e. increasing the fraction of the receptor in the monomeric form), the magnitude of the fast [3H]estradiol dissociating component increases, until only the fast monophasic component is observed at low receptor concentration (compare curves E and D with C, Fig. 5). If the biphasic dissociation kinetics of the receptor were an inherent property of the 4S monomer as proposed by Sakai and Gorski (52) and Muller et al. (54) then the magnitude of the two dissociation components would be independent of receptor concentration, whether the receptor were free in solution or bound to hydroxylapatite. In addition, sucrose gradient analysis of the estrogen receptor over a 200-fold concentration range shows that with dilution, the 5S receptor dimer dissociates to become the 4S monomer (60). 2) Furthermore, a detailed kinetic analysis (51) of the decrease in the magnitude of the fast component with time of incubation at 28°C demonstrates that the transition from a fast rate of [^{3}H]estradiol dissociation to a slow rate follows second-order kinetics, thereby supporting earlier findings (38) that estrogen activation, and/or transformation into the 5S form is a dimerization of the 4S monomeric receptor. 3) The positive cooperativity of the estrogen receptor is also dependent upon receptor concentration, indicating that the estrogen receptor is dissociated into subunits that display a single affinity state, the 4S monomer (32). At receptor concentrations greater than 1 nM (the intracellular receptor concentration is 10 to 40 nM), monomer:monomer interactions are facilitated and the positive cooperativity between receptor binding sites is observed (32,33). 4) The dissociation of [^{3}H]estradiol from the receptor in the presence of 0.4 M sodium thiocyanate is rapid and monophasic with a half-time of 4 min at 25°C. Sodium thiocyanate inhibits 5S estrogen receptor formation, but does not appear to influence the estrogen binding site directly since the association rate constant of the estradiol-receptor binding is not changed (31). 5) Sodium molybdate inhibits both receptor activation and the formation of the 5S receptor dimer, and also greatly increases the magnitude of the fast [^{3}H]estradiol dissociating component (61). 6) The dissociaton of a weaker estrogen, for example, estriol, shows a higher rate of dissociation and a larger magnitude of the fast [^{3}H]estriol dissociating component, which is consistent with the concept that estriol transforms a smaller fraction of the receptor from the lower affinity to a higher affinity conformation (62). 7) The [^{3}H]estradiol dissociation of the nuclear estrogen receptor measured while bound to nuclei shows only a slow monophasic dissociation rate and the 5S receptor conformation (56).

Biological Significance of Cooperativity, Intracellular Receptor
Concentration, and Hormone Retention

An allosteric protein is an multimeric protein that, as a consequence of
its monomer:monomer interactions, maintains a quaternary structure and
conformation(s) of its composite monomers that is not attained in the
isolated monomer (20-22). The estrogen receptor is a typical allosteric
protein. The positive cooperativity of the estrogen receptor indicates
that a conformational change induced by estradiol binding at one site,
also affects the spatially remote site occupied by another molecule of
estradiol, thereby causing a change in the affinity of the receptor for
the estradiol (32). Overall, estradiol shifts the conformation of the
receptor from having a lower affinity for estradiol, most clearly the
nonactive conformation of the estrogen receptor, to a conformation having
a higher affinity for estradiol, the activated state. A biological
advantage of the receptor utilizing a positively cooperative binding
mechanism is that the cooperativity enhances the receptor's responsiveness
to small variations in the concentration of circulating estradiol. When
the estradiol concentration falls below the biological optimal range, the
sensitivity of the receptor appears reduced in comparison with a receptor
having a noncooperative binding mechanism.

Insight into the exact molecular composition and behavior of the estrogen
receptor's subunits is important for understanding the kinetics and mode
of action of the receptor in vivo. For example, two molecular models can
be proposed. In the first model, the intracellular receptor concentration
may represent an important regulatory element of the receptor's functional
activity and may even be dependent upon the nature of the receptor's
monomer:monomer relationship. If the estrogen receptor in vivo were to
exist as free 4S monomers in an inactive comformation, then the
intracellular concentration of the 4S monomer could function as an
important regulatory mechanism that produces a differential response
between tissues containing different receptor concentrations, but the
same hormone concentrations. A tissue containing a relatively high
intracellular content of receptor such as uterine cells (approximately 10
to 40 nM, but which may be 4- to 5-fold higher if the receptor were

exclusively nuclear) may form a substantial amount of the active 5S
receptor dimer at a relatively low estrogen concentration. In contrast,
a tissue with a lower receptor concentration would not form a significant
amount of 5S receptor dimer until a greater fraction of the monomeric 4S
receptor were occupied. Hence, the overall activation of the receptor
would be characterized as a second-order reaction, controlled in part by
the concentration of the reactants; specifically, the 4S monomer
concentration would be important in determining the concentration of the
5S receptor dimer formed. In view of its high intracellular concentration
(10-40 nM), and in the presence of estradiol which promotes receptor
dimerization, the 5S dimer is clearly the preferred conformation of the
uterine estrogen receptor. The equilibrium constant of receptor
dimerization is approximately 0.3 nM at 30°C in 0.15 M KCl, as estimated
from measurements of the Hill coefficient under conditions of decreasing
receptor concentrations (32,33). Therefore, even at an intracellular
receptor concentration as low as 0.3 nM, which is approximately equal to
200 to 600 receptors per cell, and with a saturating concentration of
estradiol, 50 percent of the receptor would be in the 5S dimer
conformation. In the second model, if the estrogen receptor were to
exist in vivo as a dimer, but in two distinct conformations, one inactive
and the other active, the fraction of the receptor forming the active 5S
dimer would be dependent upon the estradiol concentration and independent
of the intracellular receptor concentration. The kinetics observed would
be similar to an isomerization or first-order reaction. Either of these
two molecular models of the estrogen receptor's properties in vivo are
consistent with the molecular properties of the estrogen receptor that
are observed in vitro, in which one conformation, an inactive dimer, is
readily extracted from the tissue with dilute buffers, and capable of
being dissociated into 4S monomers by 0.4 M KCl--whereas, the active 5S
dimer conformation cannot readily be extracted by dilute buffers nor
dissociated by the 0.4 M KCl. It is conceivable that some features of
both these models operate intracellularly. The mode of action, kinetics,
and contribution of the receptor's positive cooperativity on regulating
the receptor's functional activity may not be adequately addressed until
the purified receptor and its interactions with specific gene regulatory
sites are analyzed in vitro.

The high intracellular concentration of receptor, relative to the concentration of circulating estradiol (0.1 to 1 nM), produces a marked retention of intracellular estradiol which has a profound affect on the time course of the estrogen receptor's biological actions, as well as an affect on the analysis of the estrogen receptor's binding properties and kinetics using isolated cells. Originally, Jensen et al. (63) noted that uterine cells from estrogen-treated animals retained concentrations of [^{3}H]estradiol that were higher than the receptor concentration present. Although a portion of the intracellular estradiol concentration is due to estradiol nonspecifically bound by membranes, proteins, enzymes, etc., the studies of Silhavy et al. (64) provide a theoretical basis for understanding the effects of a high affinity receptor and the high intracellular retention of its ligand. Silhavy and co-workers demonstrated that the rate of diffusion of a ligand from a solution of the ligand-binding protein dialyzed against a ligand-free medium, is much slower than the dissociation rate of the protein-ligand complex, provided that the affinity of the protein or receptor is high and the receptor's concentration is higher than that of the ligand (i.e., significant rebinding of the ligand occurs under these conditions). The decrease in the total ligand concentration inside the cell or dialysis bag follows first-order kinetics, but the first-order rate constant is decreased by the factor (1 + [R]/Kd), so that the rate of disappearance is:

$$\frac{d[L]}{dt} = \frac{\alpha[L]}{1 + [R]/Kd}$$

where α is a constant depending upon the diffusional properties of the ligand (estradiol), the porosity of the membrane, and the geometry of the dialysis system; [L] is the total ligand concentration; [R] is the total concentration of binding sites; and Kd is the dissociation constant. Since the apparent Kd of the high affinity state of the estrogen receptor is in the range of 10^{-9} to 10^{-10} M (34) and the intracellular receptor concentration is approximately 10^{-8} M, then the factor [R]/Kd ranges from 10^2 to 10^3, suggesting that a significant retention of intracellular estradiol would be observed. This theoretical consideration is confirmed by in vivo observations. The long period of retention of [^{3}H]estradiol in uterus and other estrogen receptor containing tissues is well-documented; the half-time of the estradiol in the uterus is approximately 6-8 hrs (65). Nevertheless, the half-time of the dissociation of the [3H]estradiol receptor complex bound to chromatin is 20 min at 37°C (66) and for the dissociation of the activated [3H]estradiol-receptor complex from calf uterus is 23 min at 35°C (51).

Mulvihill and Palmiter (67) reported that the uptake of receptor into oviduct nuclei in estradiol-treated chicks is a positive cooperative process. Yet, some investigators (68-70) have used in vitro incubations of isolated uterine cells with variable concentrations of [3H]estradiol and incorrectly concluded that the estrogen receptor's mechanism of estrogen binding in intact cells is not positively cooperative, as observed with the isolated receptor (32). However, these studies are limited by their inability to measure an essential parameter for saturation binding analysis, the free intracellular [3H]estradiol concentrations. The retention phenomenon described by Silhavy et al. (64) only partially illustrates the experimental quandary. The assumption (68-70) that the intracellular free [3H]estradiol concentration is in rapid equilibrium and therefore equal to the extracellular [3H]estradiol concentration is incorrect. The retention phenomenon (64) indicates that establishing an equilibrium between the intracellular and extracellular estradiol concentrations would be very slow at high extracellular [3H]estradiol concentration. Yet, even more improbable would be attempting to measure the intracellular free [3H]estradiol concentration when the [3H]estradiol concentration in the medium is below the intracellular receptor concentration, particularly since the Kd is below the intracellular receptor concentration. In addition, the very high nonspecific binding in whole cell or isolated tissue studies presents technical difficulties in measuring the specifically bound and free [3H]estradiol concentrations.

Summary

The estrogen receptor is a homodimer of two identical monomers, each containing a single estrogen-binding site and having a molcular weight of 68,000. The receptor's estrogen binding site and the DNA-binding domain

are nonoverlapping. The conformation of the receptor is regulated by
hormone binding with a postively cooperative binding mechanism in a
manner characteristic of allosteric regulatory proteins. The estrogen
receptor exists in an equilibrium between two states of the receptor,
each with a different affinity for estradiol. Consequently, estradiol
binds preferentially to the receptor conformation that possesses the
higher affinity for the estradiol and thereby shifts the receptor from an
inactive into an active conformation, the 5S dimer. The nonactive
conformation of the receptor has a lower affinity for estradiol and is
dissociated by salt into the 4S monomer.

As the receptor's concentration is progressively decreased to below 1 nM,
the receptor's site:site cooperativity is reduced, indicating that the
receptor is dissociating. The [^{3}H]estradiol dissociation kinetics show
two phases, a rapid [^{3}H]estradiol dissociating phase produced by the
lower affinity nonactive conformation of the receptor and the slower
[^{3}H]estradiol dissociating phase characteristic of the high affinity,
active form of the receptor. The magnitudes of the two phases of
[^{3}H]estradiol dissociation are influenced by receptor concentration.
Reducing receptor concentration increases the magnitude of the rapidly
[^{3}H]estradiol dissociating phase, suggesting that site:site
interactions (i.e., formation of a 5S dimer) are therefore a necessary
prelude to observing the slower [^{3}H]estradiol dissociating component.
Estriol, a weaker estrogen than estradiol, induces a lower degree of
cooperativity than does estradiol. Enclomiphene, an estrogen antagonist,
inhibits the estradiol-induced cooperativity of the receptor, thereby
indicating an inhibition of the receptor's equilibrium between two
affinity states.

As a result of the estrogen receptor's high affinity and high
intracellular concentration, estradiol is retained intracellularly much
longer than can be accounted for by the estradiol-receptor dissociation
rate of the isolated receptor. The estrogen retention phenomenon
probably contributes to the long duration of estrogen action observed _in_
vivo. However, the retention phenomenon also prevents an accurate
assessment of the receptor's binding mechanism in whole cells as some

investigators have attempted, since intracellular concentrations of estradiol are not necessarily in rapid equilibrium with the extracellular estradiol concentration as assumed (68-70). A definitive understanding of the receptor's functional activity that is, its interaction with specific DNA sequences, remains to be described.

Acknowledgements

We gratefully acknowledge the assistance of Jane Notides in preparation of this manuscript. This research was supported by a National Institute of Health Grant HD06707 and a NIEHS Center Grant ES01247 has been assigned report No. DOE/EV/03490-2449.

References

1. Stone, R.T., Maurer, R.A., and Gorski, J.: Biochemistry 16, 4915-4921 (1977).
2. Maurer, R.A.: J. Biol. Chem. 257, 2133-2136 (1982).
3. Dean, D.C., Gope, R., Knoll, B.J., Riser, M.E., and O'Malley, B.W.: J. Biol. Chem. 259, 9967-9970 (1984).
4. Palmiter, R.D., Mulvihill, E.R., Shepherd, J.H., and McKnight, G.S.: J. Biol. Chem. 256, 7910-7916 (1981).
5. Payvar, F., Wrange, O., Carlsstedt-Duke, J., Okret, S., Gustafsson, J.-A., and Yamamoto, K.R.: Proc. Natl. Acad. Sci. USA 78, 6628-6632 (1981).
6. Pfahl, M.: Cell 31, 475-482 (1982).
7. Govindan, M.V., Spiess, E., and Majors, T.: Proc. Natl. Acad. Sci. USA 79, 5157-5161 (1982).
8. Mulvihill, E.R., Le Pennec, J.-P., and Chambon, P.: Cell 24, 621-632 (1982).
9. Compton, J.G., Schrader, W.T., and O'Malley, B.W.: Proc. Natl. Acad. Sci. USA 80, 16-20 (1983).
10. Le Fevre, D., Bailly, A., Sallas, N., and Milgrom, E.: Biochim. Biophys. Acta 585, 266-272 (1979).
11. Bailly, A., Le Fevre, B., Savouret, J.F., and Milgrom, E.: J. Biol. Chem. 255, 2729-2934 (1980).

194

12. Muller, R.E., Traish, A.M., and Wotiz, H.H.: J. Biol. Chem. 258, 9227-9236 (1983).

13. Muller, R.E., Mrabet, N.T., Traish, A.M., and Wotiz, H.H.: J. Biol. Chem. 258, 11582-11589 (1983).

14. Notides, A.C., and Nielsen, S.: J. Steroid Biochem. 6, 483-486 (1975).

15. Hutchens, T.W., Markland, F.S., and Hawkins, E.F.: Biochem. Biophys. Res. Comm. 105, 20-26 (1982).

16. Feldman, M., Kallos, J., and Hollander, V.P.: J. Biol. Chem. 256, 1145-1148 (1981).

17. Chong, M.T., and Lippman, M.E.: J. Biol. Chem. 257, 2996-3002 (1982).

18. Tymoczko, J.L., and Phillips, M.M.: Endocrinology 112, 142-149 (1983).

19. Greene, G.L.: in, Roy, A.K., and Clark, J.H. (eds.), Gene Regulation by Steroid Hormones II. Springer-Verlag, New York, pp. 191-200 (1983).

20. Kurganov, B.I.: Allosteric Enzymes, Kinetic Behaviour. John Wiley and Sons, New York, pp. 4-85 (1982).

21. Levitzki, A.: Quantitative Aspects of Allosteric Mechanisms. Springer-Verlag, Berlin, pp. 72-88 (1978).

22. Monod, J., Wyman, J., and Changeux, J.-P.: J. Mol. Biol. 12, 88-118 (1965).

23. Jensen, E.V., Suzuki, T., Kawashima, T., Stumpf, W.E., Jungblut, P.W. and DeSombre, E.R.: Proc. Natl. Acad. Sci. USA 58, 632-638 (1968).

24. Jensen, E.V., and DeSombre, E.R.: Science 182, 126-134 (1973).

25. Shyamala, G., and Gorski, J.: J. Biol. Chem. 244, 1097-1103 (1969).

26. Gorski, J., Toft, D., Shyamala, G., Smith, D., and Notides, A.: in, Astwood, E.B. (ed.), Recent Progress in Hormone Research, Vol. 24, Academic Press, New York, pp. 45-80 (1968).

27. Carlson, R., and Gorski, J.: Endocrinology 106, 1776-1785.

28. Sheridan, P.J., Buchanan, J.M., Anselmo, V.C., and Martin, P.M.: Nature 282, 579-582 (1979).

29. King, W.J., and Greene, G.L.: Nature 307, 745-747 (1984).

30. Welshons, W.V., Lieberman, M.E., and Gorski, J.: Nature 307, 747-749 (1984).

31. Weichman, B.M., and Notides, A.C.: J. Biol. Chem. 252, 8856-8862 (1977).

32. Notides, A.C., Lerner, N., and Hamilton, D.E.: Proc. Natl. Acad. Sci. USA 78, 4926-4930 (1981).

33. Notides, A.C., and Sasson, S.: in, Eriksson, H., and Gustafsson, J.-A. (eds.), Steroid Hormone Receptors: Structure and Function. Elsevier Science Publishers, Amsterdam, pp. 103-120 (1983).

34. Notides, A.C., and Nielsen, S.: J. Biol. Chem. 249, 1866-1873 (1974).

35. Greene, G.L., Nolan, C., Engler, J.P., and Jensen, E.V.: Proc. Natl. Acad. Sci. USA 77, 5115-5119 (1980).

36. Puca, G.A., Sica, V., Nola, E., and Bresciani, F.: J. Steroid Biochem. 11, 301-306 (1979).

37. Sica, V. and Bresciani, F.: Biochemistry 18, 2369-2378 (1979).

38. Notides, A.C., Hamilton, D.E., and Auer, H.E.: J. Biol. Chem. 250, 3945-3950 (1975).

39. Wrange, O., Okret, S., Radojcic, M., Carlstedt-Duke, J., and Gustaffson, J.-A.: in, Eriksson, H. and Gustaffson, J.-A. (eds.), Steroid Hormone Receptors: Structure and Function. Elsevier Science Publishers, Amsterdam, pp. 73-94 (1983).

40. Weigel, N.L., Minghetti, P.P., Stevens, B., Schrader, W.T., and O'Malley, B.W.: in, Eriksson, H., and Gustafsson, J.-A. (eds.), Steroid Hormone Receptors: Structure and Function. Elsevier Science Publishers, Amsterdam, pp. 25-42 (1983).

41. Notides, A.C., Hamilton, D.E., and Muechler, E.K.: J. Steroid Biochem. 7, 1025-1030 (1976).

42. Joab, I., Radonyi, C., Renoir, M., Buchou, T., Catelli, M.-G., Binart, N., Mester, J., and Baulieu, E.-E.: Nature 308, 850-853 (1984).

43. Dougherty, J.J., Puri, R.K., and Toft, D.O.: J. Biol. Chem. 259, 8004-8009 (1984).

44. Moncharmont, B., Anderson, W.L., Rosenberg, B., and Parikh, I.: Biochemistry 23, 3907-3912 (1984).

45. Sasson, S., and Notides, A.C.: J. Biol. Chem. 258, 8113-8117 (1983).

46. Sasson, S., and Notides, A.C.: J. Steroid Biochem. 20, 1027-1032 (1984).

47. Clark, J.H., Paszko, Z., and Peck, E.J., Jr.: Endocrinology 100, 91-96 (1977).
48. Sasson, S., and Notides, A.C.: J. Biol. Chem. 258, 8118-8122 (1983).
49. Sasson, S., and Notides, A.C.: J. Steroid Biochem. 20, 1021-1026 (1984).
50. Sasson, S., and Notides, A.C.: J. Biol. Chem. 257, 11540-11545 (1982).
51. Weichman, B.M., and Notides, A.C.: Biochemistry 18, 220-225 (1979).
52. Sakai, D., and Gorski, J.: Biochemistry 23, 3541-3547 (1984).
53. Gorski, J., Welshons, W., and Sakai, D.: Mol. Cell. Endocrinol. 36, 11-15 (1984).
54. Muller, R.E., Traish, A.M., Hirota, T., and Wotiz, H.H.: Excerpta Medica, 7th Internatl. Cong. Endocrinol. 652, 1061 (1984).
55. Muller, R.E., Beebe, D.M., Bercel, E., Traish, A.M., and Wotiz, H.H.: J. Steroid Biochem. 20, 1039-1046 (1984).
56. de Boer, W., and Notides, A.C.: Biochemistry 20, 1285-1289 (1981).
57. de Boer, W., and Notides, A.C.: Biochemistry 20, 1290-1294 (1981).
58. Miller, M.A., Greene, G.L., and Katzenellenbogen, B.S.: Endocrinology 114, 296-298 (1984).
59. Gregory, M.R. and Notides, A.C.: Biochemistry 24, 6452-6458 (1982).
60. Notides, A.C., and Callison, S. (submitted for publication).
61. Mauck, L.A., Day, R.N., and Notides, A.C.: Biochemistry 21, 1788-1793 (1982).
62. Weichman, B.M., and Notides, A.C.: Endocrinology 106, 434-439 (1980).
63. Jensen, E.V., and Jacobson, H.I.: Rec. Prog. Horm. Res. 18, 387-414 (1962).
64. Silhavy, T.J., Szmelcman, S., Boos, W., and Schwartz, M.: Proc. Natl. Acad. Sci. USA 72, 2120-2124 (1975).
65. Puca, G.A., and Bresciani, F.: Endocrinology 85, 1-10 (1969).
66. Sala-Trepat, J.M., and Reti, E.: Biochim. Biophys. Acta 338, 92-103 (1974).
67. Mulvihill, E.R. and Palmiter, R.D.: J. Biol. Chem. 252, 2060-2068 (1977).
68. Traish, A.M., Muller, R.E., and Wotiz, H.H.: J. Biol. Chem. 254, 6560-6563 (1979).

69. Williams, D., and Gorski, J.: Biochemistry 13, 5537-5542 (1974).
70. Muller, R.E., Traish, A.M., and Wotiz, H.H.: Excerpta Medica, 7th Internatl. Cong. Endocrinol. 652, 1870 (1984).

SPECIFIC EFFECTS OF MONOVALENT CATIONS AND OF ADENINE NUCLEO-
TIDES ON GLUCOCORTICOID RECEPTOR ACTIVATION, AS STUDIED BY
AQUEOUS TWO-PHASE PARTITIONING

P.A. Andreasen, Laboratory of Tumor Biology, Institute of
Pathology, University of Copenhagen, 11 Frederik V's Vej,
DK-2100 Copenhagen Ø, Denmark, and Finsen Laboratory, Finsen
Institute, 49 Strandboulevarden, DK-2100 Copenhagen Ø, Denmark

K. Junker, Department of Nuclear Medicine, Rigshospitalet,
9 Blegdamsvej, DK-2100 Copenhagen Ø, Denmark

Introduction

Glucocorticoid receptor "activation" or "transformation" was
detected by studies with reconstituted cell-free systems,
consisting of isolated nuclei and target cell cytosol. With
such systems, it was observed that the glucocorticoid-receptor
complexes had to undergo a temperature-sensitive modification,
before they could be accumulated in the nuclei. Besides the
acquisition of the ability to be accumulated in nuclei in
vitro, activation has also been found to alter the complex by
a variety of other criteria, such as increasing the affinity
for DNA and changing certain chromatographic properties (for
reviews, see 1, 2, 3, 4, 5). Furthermore, it has been shown
that glucocorticoid-receptor complexes, after their formation
in intact target cells at $37^{O}C$, are initially in the non-activated form, but within a few minutes, the activated form
becomes the predominant species (6, 7, 8). It, therefore,
appears that receptor activation is induced in vivo by the
binding of the steroid, although distinct from the binding as
such, and that it precedes the intranuclear action of steroid-
receptor complexes in the intact cell. Thus, receptor activation appears to be a key event in glucocorticoid action.

Accordingly, much effort has been put into characterizing the kinetics of glucocorticoid receptor activation, the molecular changes of the receptor molecule during activation, and the regulation of activation by compounds other than the steroid. Much of the interest in the regulation of the process stems from the finding that incubation under anaerobic conditions abolished the specific glucocorticoid binding in rat thymocytes and murine and human fibroblasts (9, 10, 11, 12). Parallel investigations showed that cyanide poisoning of mouse fibroblasts led to an increase in the nuclear-cytoplasmic distribution ratio of glucocorticoid-receptor complexes as measured by cell fractionation (10, 13). The latter observation is compatible with the view that energy deprivation changes the intracellular concentration of factors regulating the activation process.

We have utilized the method of partitioning in aqueous dextran-poly(ethylene glycol) two-phase systems for characterizing glucocorticoid-receptor complex activation. We here summarize this work, with special reference to studies of a specific adenine nucleotide effect on the complex, different from other reported nucleotide effects, and of differential effects of Li^+, Na^+ and K^+ on the activation process.

Background

The method of aqueous two-phase partitioning was originally introduced by P.-Å. Albertsson (14, 15). When aqueous solutions of dextran and poly(ethylene glycol) with concentrations above certain critical levels are brought together, two immiscible phases are formed. Because of the high water concentration in the phases (around 90%), proteins can be partitioned in such systems without denaturation. The partition behaviour of a protein is expressed by its partition coefficient, i.e. the ratio between its concentrations in the top and the bottom phase. The partition coefficient depends

both on the composition of the phase system and on the chemical properties of the protein, reflecting electrical, hydrophobic, hydrophilic and other types of interactions between
the protein and the phases. With salts present in the phase
systems, the slightly different affinities of different ions
for the two phases will create an electrical potential difference between them of a few millivolts (the "interfacial"
potential), its exact value depending on the nature of the
salts used (14, 15, 16, 17, 18). For instance, the interfacial
potential is different in phase systems with NaCl, Na_2SO_4 and
LiCl. Albertsson (14, 15) developed the following equation for
the partition coefficient K of a protein partitioned with an
excess of salt:

$$\ln K = \ln K_O + A_S \cdot Z \qquad (1)$$

All contributions to the partition coefficient from non-charge
interactions are here collected in the term K_O. Z is the net
charge of the protein. A_S is a constant, which is proportional
to the interfacial potential. Thus, A_S may be varied by
changing the salt composition of the two-phase system. Assuming that K_O does not depend on Z and the salt composition,
ln K will depend linearly on A_S and Z. Therefore, determinations of K in phase systems with different known A_S-values may
be used for determination of K_O and Z (14, 15, 17, 18).

On the other hand, when a certain treatment of a protein
results in a change in its partition coefficient under constant partitioning conditions, it is likely that the treatment
will have resulted in changes in net charge, surface hydrophobicity, aggregational state, etc.

The use of aqueous two-phase partitioning for studying
glucocorticoid-receptor complex activation originates from the
observation that incubation conditions favoring activation
resulted in a change in the partition coefficient of the
complexes (19). The method was therefore assumed to be able to
yield information about changes in the properties of the

complexes during activation. In addition, since the partitioning procedure can be performed very rapidly (~15 sec), the
method was assumed to be well suited for kinetic studies of
the activation.

Methods

Most of the receptor partitioning studies published to date
have been performed with cytosol preparations preincubated
with ^{3}H-triamcinolone acetonide in order to label the receptor. Excess of steroid was removed with dextran-coated charcoal. The labelled cytosols were then exposed to various incubation conditions. Cytosol samples were added to aliquots of
stock phase system at 0-4°C. The stock phase systems were
prepared by dissolving in buffer weighed amounts of Dextran
T500 (Pharmacia) and poly(ethylene glycol) 6000 (pro synthesis, Merck). The final composition of the phase systems was
6.25% or 5% (w/v) of each of the polymers in 10 mM potassium
phosphate, 6 mM Tris HCl (pH 8.1), 10% glycerol, 1 mM dithioerythritol, 1 mM EDTA, and various salts at different concentrations. The concentrations of salts, nucleotides etc. in the
stock phase systems were adjusted according to the concentrations of salts, nucleotides etc. in the cytosol samples, so
that the final concentration of these compounds in the phase
systems did not vary with the concentrations in the cytosol
samples. The final volume, after the addition of the cytosol
sample, was usually 1 ml. After the addition of the cytosol
samples, the aliquots of two-phase system were shaken for 15
sec and submitted to a brief low-speed centrifugation in order
to accelerate phase separation. The partition coefficient of
the glucocorticoid-receptor complex was assumed to be equal to
that of the tritium in charcoal-treated cytosol samples after
a correction was applied for the small amount of non-specifically bound tritiated steroid not removed by the charcoal (19,
20, 21, 22, 23, 24, 25, 26, 27).

Using this experimental design, it was important to ensure that the glucocorticoid-receptor complexes did not dissociate during incubations and partitionings, since this would preclude the use of tritiated steroid as a label for the complexes. This was accomplished by partitioning in phase systems, in which the tritium in charcoal-treated cytosol samples partitioned almost exclusively to one of the phases, while the free steroid had a partition coefficient near 1 (for instance systems with 3 M NaCl or with 0.1 M salt and DNA or dextran sulphate). Assuming that the receptor partitioned exclusively to one of the phases, it was possible to estimate a lower limit to the fraction of tritium bound to the receptor after the partitioning. Such control experiments showed that the ^{3}H-triamcinolone acetonide-receptor complexes survived most incubation and partitioning conditions, and that the variations in the partition coefficients of tritium in charcoal-treated cytosol samples represented variations in the partition coefficient of the receptor protein (20, 21, 22, 23, 25, 26).

Indications that the complexes themselves were not damaged during the partitioning were the facts that they retained their ability to bind to DNA (21), and that different receptor variants could be distinguished by partitioning (23).

The partition coefficient of the glucocorticoid-receptor complexes changed both with the partitioning conditions and with the incubation conditions, to which the cytosol preparations had been exposed prior to the partitionings. In contrast to the partition coefficient of other proteins investigated (14, 15, 17, 18), the partition coefficient of the complexes was found to vary with the cytosol concentration in the phase systems. This is indicative of aggregations or deaggregations of the complexes during the partitionings. This phenomenon was avoided by using high salt concentrations and cytosol concentrations of less than 100 µg protein per ml in the phase systems (25).

Activation during the partitioning was avoided by using

the short shaking time of only 15 sec. The amount of complexes
activated in 15 sec is insignificant, even in 1 M salt; in
addition, no conversion of nonactivated complexes changing
their partition coefficient took place after ending the
shaking, since the partition coefficients in 0.1-1 M ionic
strength systems were not changed by leaving the systems for up
to 1 min before centrifugation (unpublished).

Results and Discussion

Glucocorticoid-receptor complex activation, as studied by
aqueous two-phase partitioning

Based on the following criteria, the activated form of glucocorticoid-receptor complexes differed from the non-activated
form by having a higher partition coefficient in aqueous
dextran-poly(ethylene glycol) two-phase systems:

1) Incubation conditions resulting in a high fraction of complexes being activated also resulted in an increase in the
partition coefficient of the complex population as a whole
(19, 20, 21).

2) This increase of the partition coefficient of the complex
population as a whole occurred with a kinetics indistinguishable from that of the increase in the amount of
complexes able to bind to DNA-Sepharose (25).

3) Non-activated and activated complexes could be separated
by chromatography on DNA-Sepharose as clearly distinguishable peaks with different partition coefficients, and
a redistribution of complexes between the two peaks
occurred without changes of the partition coefficient of
each single peak (21).

4) Inhibitors of the activation process as measured by DNA-
binding were also inhibitors of the associated increase of
the partition coefficient. This was true for instance for
MoO_4^{2-} (26).

One particularly interesting use of aqueous two-phase partitioning is in investigations of the role of different domains of the receptor protein during activation. Different receptor domains have been defined by the use of partial proteolysis with chymotrypsin and trypsin. Hydrodynamic measurements of the M_r of glucocorticoid-receptor complexes under activating conditions showed that activated native complexes had an M_r of approximately 100,000, activated chymotrypsinized complexes one of approximately 45,000 and activated trypsinized complexes one of approximately 19,000; both of these partly proteolysed forms had intact glucocorticoid binding ability (28, 29). These M_r values are in agreement with those determined by photoaffinity labelling and SDS-polyacrylamide gel electrophoresis (30, 31, 32). The ability of activated complexes to bind to DNA was mapped to the domain cleaved from the steroid-binding domain by trypsin, but left by chymotrypsin (29). A crucial, but as yet unidentified receptor function is associated with the domain cleaved off by chymotrypsin, since this socalled "modulation" domain was also found to be absent in non-functional nt^i variant receptors (23, 31, 32, 33), defined by their abnormally high affinity for DNA (34). Aqueous two-phase partitioning allowed studies of the effect of partial proteolysis on nonactivated as well as activated complexes. Treatment of non-activated complexes with chymotrypsin led to either no change or a decrease in the partition coefficient, depending on the salt composition of the phase system (Table I; (23, 25)). In the activated state, chymotrypsinized complexes had partition properties at best slightly different from those of native complexes, but could be distinguished readily from those by their higher affinity for DNA (23, 29). The rates of activation of native receptors and receptors lacking the modulation domain are indistinguishable (23). A 10 min treatment of non-activated complexes with trypsin at 0°C initially resulted in the same change of the partition properties of the complexes as chymotrypsin treatment, but during incubations under

Table I. Partition coefficients of nonactivated and activated glucocorticoid-receptor complexes of cytosol from murine S49 lymphoma cells, with and without treatment with chymotrypsin.

Salts in phase system	Non-activated		Activated	
	Control	+Chymo-trypsin	Control	+Chymo-trypsin
0.1 M KCl+0.9M NaCl	0.323 ± 0.116 (18)	0.399 ± 0.011 (6)	3.14 ± 0.53 (14)	2.50 ± 0.16 (4)
0.22M KCl + 0.26M Li_2SO_4	2.41 ± 0.45 (16)	0.210 ± 0.013 (8)	7.58 ± 1.11 (12)	4.57 ± 0.40 (4)

[3]H-triamcinolone acetonide-labelled, charcoal-treated cytosol from murine S49.1 TB.4 lymphoma cells, containing approximately 7 mg protein per ml, was incubated with 10 µg α-chymotrypsin per ml for 10 min at 0^oC, or used without any protease treatment. Cytosol aliquots were partitioned before (non-activated) or after (activated) a 3 h incubation of the 10-fold diluted cytosols with 0.4 M KCl at 0^oC. The phase systems contained salts as indicated, 6.25% of poly(ethylene glycol) and dextran and approximately 140 µg of cytosolic protein per ml. Shown are the means, the standard deviations and the number of determinations of the partition coefficients. For further experimental details, see (23).

conditions with very slow activation of native and chymotrypsinized complexes, the trypsin-treated complexes were relatively rapidly converted to a form with partition properties indistinguishable from those of activated native and chymotrypsinized receptors (25). However, activated trypsinized complexes were readily distinguished from those by a lack of affinity for DNA (26, 29). Thus, partial proteolysis with chymotrypsin and trypsin resulted in changes in the partition coefficients of non-activated complexes, which could be distinguished clearly from those resulting from activation, and aqueous two-phase partitioning allowed the definition of non-activated and activated states of chymotrypsinized and of trypsinized as well as of native glucocorticoid-receptor complexes.

Interpretation of the differences in partition coefficients between non-activated and activated complexes in phase systems with different combinations of salts by the principles described above suggested that activation changed both net charge and non-charge surface properties of the receptor. A change in non-charge properties was found with native complexes as well as with complexes lacking the modulation domain (25). Since both M_r and surface hydrophobicity generally influence the partition coefficient of proteins (14, 15), this result is compatible with the dissociation of an oligomeric structure during the activation. Such a change has been inferred from hydrodynamic measurements of complexes stabilized in the non-activated state by MoO_4^{2-} (5, 33, 35, 36, 37, 38, 39, 40); the non-activated complexes were found to have an M_r of around 300,000 (5, 33, 36, 37, 39, 40). The difference in the hydrodynamically determined M_r of non-activated native complexes and complexes lacking the modulation domain was found to be only approximately 25,000 (33).

According to the same interpretation of the partition data, there were large differences in both net charge and non-charge surface properties between the non-activated forms of native complexes and complexes lacking the modulation domain. Non-activated native complexes appeared to be highly negatively charged, but non-activated complexes without the modulation domain to be only slightly negatively charged at neutral pH. In the activated state, both complex forms were only slightly negatively charged at neutral pH. Thus a large change in net charge during activation seemed mainly to be associated with the modulation domain. This finding seems to be in contrast to findings with DEAE-cellulose chromatography: the non-activated and activated forms of both native complexes and complexes lacking the modulation domain differed with respect to the salt concentration needed for their elution from DEAE-cellulose, but no differences in the elution pattern

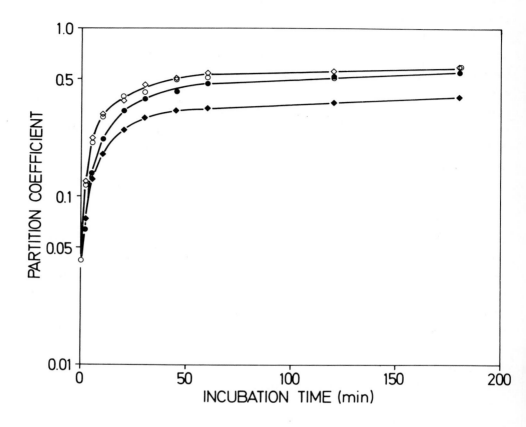

Fig. 1. Effects of ATP, theophylline and ATP plus theophylline on the time course of the partition coefficient of
glucocorticoid-receptor complexes of rat liver cytosol during
incubation with 0.4 M KCl at 0°C. ³H-triamcinolone acetonide-
labelled, charcoal-treated cytosol with approximately 25 mg
protein per ml was diluted 5-fold and incubated at 0°C with
0.4 M KCl, with 1.6 mM ATP (◆), 10 mM theophylline (o), 1.6 mM
ATP + 10 mM theophylline (◇) or without any nucleotide additions (●). At the indicated time points after the dilution,
cytosol samples were taken for partitioning in aqueous two-
phase systems with 0.1 M KCl, 5% of poly(ethylene glycol) and
dextran, and approximately 1 mg of cytosolic protein per ml.
Each symbol represents the mean of two determinations of the
partition coefficient; the standard deviations are smaller
than the symbols. For further experimental details, see (22).

resemblance between these compounds is their negative charge at neutral pH. This effect may involve the binding of these compounds to the DNA-binding area of the receptors, since it has been reported that ATP and pyrophosphate inhibit the binding of activated complexes to DNA (67).

Thus, the nucleotide/glucocorticoid-receptor complex interaction underlying the stimulation of the activation is by a number of criteria clearly different from that underlying the effect of adenine nucleotides on the complex partition coefficient in 0.4 M KCl at $0^{\circ}C$, most importantly by the specificity of the latter for adenine nucleotides and the antagonistic effect on the latter of theophylline. To our knowledge, the only other reports of specific adenine nucleotide effect on glucocorticoid receptors are those by Horiuchi et al. (69, 70, 71, 72), who described that MgATP, in milli-molar concentrations, stimulated the binding of activated glucocorticoid-receptor complexes to nuclei in vitro by relieving them from the inhibitory effect of cytosolic macro-molecular substances. With concentrations below 3 mM, there was no similar effect of other trinucleotides, ADP, AMP or pyrophosphate. This effect of MgATP may be related to the effects of ADP and ATP on the glucocorticoid-receptor complex partition coefficient in 0.4 M KCl at $0^{\circ}C$.

Much work has been done in order to elucidate the mecha-nism behind the effect of energy deprivation of cells on the glucocorticoid binding capability of the unoccupied receptor (9, 10, 11, 12). This work has led to the demonstration of a phosphoprotein co-migrating with the glucocorticoid receptor in SDS-polyacrylamide gel electrophoresis; this phosphoprotein is believed to be the receptor protein itself (73, 74, 75), and phosphorylation/dephosphorylation may be involved in the regulation of the steroid binding capability of the receptors (for a review, see (76)). Other workers, studying the effect on glucocorticoid-binding stability of adding various nucleo-tides to cytosol preparations or treating cytosol preparations with $(Na^+ + K^+)$-ATPase, have argued that nucleotides might

affect glucocorticoid binding by acting as allosteric modi-
fiers ((77, 78); see also (79)). Anyway, the relationship
between the effects of nucleotides and receptor phosphorylation on binding activity and the ATP/ADP-effect on the
partition coefficient of glucocorticoid-receptor complexes is
unknown.

Differential effects of Li^+, Na^+ and K^+ on the activation of
glucocorticoid-receptor complexes.

Li^+ inhibits the activation of cytosolic glucocorticoid-receptor complexes in vitro, as revealed by aqueous two-phase partitioning and DNA-Sepharose chromatography (Fig.3; (24, 26,
27)). During incubations with 0.4 M KCl at $0^\circ C$, a maximal
effect consisting in a partial inhibition of the activation
was attained with 5-10 mM LiCl. The half-maximal effect was
attained with approximately 1 mM LiCl. During incubations at
$25^\circ C$, higher Li^+-concentrations were needed to achieve this
effect. The effect was observed with rat liver cytosol (24),
rat thymocyte cytosol (26), and cytosol from the murine
lymphoma cell line S49 (27). The increase of the partition
coefficient of trypsinized glucocorticoid-receptor complexes
during incubation under activating conditions was much less
susceptible to the inhibitory action of Li^+ than that of
chymotrypsinized and native complexes (26). Unlike the inhibitory effect of ATP, the inhibitory effect of Li^+ was not
antagonized by theophylline (unpublished).
    One particularly interesting observation concerning the
Li^+-effect was that the substitution of 0.4 M KCl by 0.4 M
NaCl during incubations at $0^\circ C$ shifted the dose-response curve
towards higher Li^+-concentrations (24). We here report that
the activation rate, as measured by the rate of the change of
the partition coefficient, is different in 0.4 M KCl and 0.4 M
NaCl also in the absence of LiCl (Fig. 4).
    It is important to note that these effects of Li^+, Na^+ and

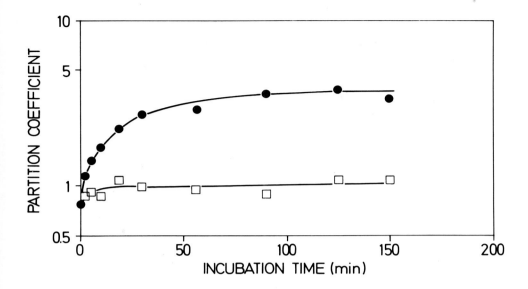

Fig. 3. Effect of Li$^+$ on the time course of the partition
coefficient of glucocorticoid-receptor complexes of cytosol
from murine S49 BrdUrd-40,3 lymphoma cells during incubation
with 0.4 M KCl at 0°C. ^{3}H-triamcinolone acetonide-labelled,
charcoal-treated cytosol with approximately 5 mg protein per
ml was diluted 10-fold and incubated at 0°C with 0.4 M KCl (●)
or 0.4 M KCl plus 5 mM LiCl (□). Aliquots were taken for phase
partitioning at the indicated time points after the dilution.
Phase partitionings were performed in phase systems with 0.1 M
KCl plus 0.9 M NaCl, 5% of dextran and poly(ethylene glycol),
and approximately 100 μg cytosolic protein per ml. Each symbol
represents the mean of two determinations. For further experimental details, see (27). Adapted from (27) with permission.

K$^+$ were exerted during the <u>incubations</u> with the salts. They
should not be confounded with the general effects on the partitioning of proteins of the salt composition of the phase
systems (as illustrated in Table I). In the experiments described here, the salt composition of the phase system was the
same whether the cytosol samples contained for instance 0.4 M
NaCl or 0.4 M KCl (see Methods).

Different effects on steroid receptors of Li$^+$, Na$^+$ and K$^+$
have never been described before, and the effects of mono-

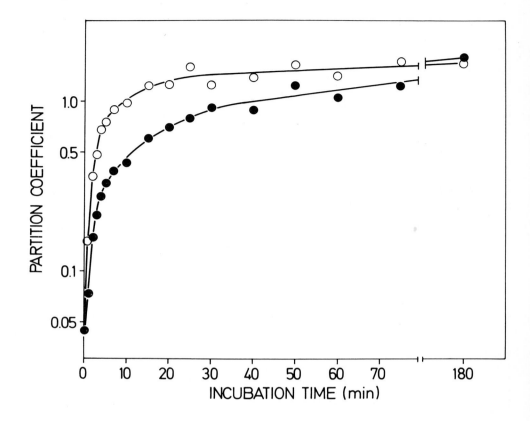

Fig. 4. Rate of activation of glucocorticoid-receptor complexes of cytosol from murine S49 BrdUrd-40.3 lymphoma cells in 0.4 M KCl and 0.4 M NaCl at 0°C. Cytosol was prepared by homogenizing cells in 10 mM K_2HPO_4 (pH 7.4), 50 mM KCl, 1 mM dithioerythritol, 1 mM EDTA and 10% (v/v) glycerol, and centrifuging at 100,000 × g for 60 min. The cytosol contained approximately 5 mg protein per ml. ^{3}H-triamcinolone acetonide-labelled, charcoal-treated cytosol was diluted 10-fold and incubated at 0°C with 0.4 M KCl (●) or 0.4 M NaCl (o). At the indicated time points, cytosol samples were taken for partitioning in aqueous two-phase systems with 0.2 M KCl plus 0.2 M NaCl, 6.25% of dextran and poly(ethylene glycol), and approximately 100 µg of cytosolic protein per ml. Each symbol represents the mean of two determinations of the partition coefficient. For further experimental details, see (27).

valent cations on steroid receptors have always previously been ascribed to nonspecific ionic strength-effects. It cannot be excluded that the different effects of Na^+ and K^+ described here is due to a differential effect of these ions on the overall physicochemical properties of the water/glycerol solvent of the cytosol preparations. However, the effect of the relatively low Li^+ concentrations favors the more attractive hypothesis that a specific ion binding site is involved. Li^+ is known to affect the activity of a variety of enzymes via competition for specific ion binding sites. These include enzymes, which are also affected by other monovalent cations, for instance $(Na^+ + K^+)$-ATPase (80) and $(Ca^{2+} + Mg^{2+})$-ATPase (81, 82, 83). But in other cases, Li^+ competes with divalent cations. This is for instance true for hormone-stimulated adenylate cyclases, whose inhibition by Li^+ is antagonized by Mg^{2+} (84, 85, 86), for glucose-1,6-diphosphate synthase, which Li^+ inhibits by a competition with the cofactors Zn^{2+} and Mg^{2+} (87), and for tryptophan hydroxylase, where the Li^+-effect is counteracted by Ca^{2+} (88). Analogously, K^+ competed with Ca^{2+} for binding to vitamin D-dependent Ca^{2+}-binding protein from pig duodenum, with an affinity approximately 10^6-fold lower than that of Ca^{2+} (89). As to the glucocorticoid-receptors, a variety of effects of the divalent cations Mg^{2+}, Ca^{2+}, Mn^{2+}, Zn^{2+}, Cu^{2+} and Hg^{2+} (90, 91, 92, 93, 94, 95) and of chelators of divalent cations (96, 97) have been reported. Ca^{2+}-activated proteases in cytosol preparations have been reported to degrade glucocorticoid-receptor complexes to forms with reduced M_r (98, 99, 100, 101). Although it is possible that also some of the other reported effects of divalent cations may consist in promotion or inhibition of Ca^{2+}-activated proteases in the cytosol preparations, it is also evident that not all of them are due to proteolytic activity. For instance, Ca^{2+} appears to protect against trypsin digestion of the glucocorticoid-receptor complex in rat liver cytosol (93). It therefore seems possible that the receptor itself or another polypeptide affecting the state of the receptor by a non-proteolytic mechanism may be a metalloprotein.

We have not yet investigated the relationship between the specific effects of monovalent cations and the effects of divalent cations. But it seems possible that the effects of monovalent and divalent cations may be due to the interaction of the various ions with a common metal ion binding site. The fact that the activation rate is different in Na^+ and K^+ in the presence as well as the absence of Li^+ may suggest the following hypothesis: Li^+ displaces, but at the same time mimicks the effect of a divalent cation, whose displacement from the receptor or an associated polypeptide is part of the activation, as brought about by treatment with high NaCl and KCl concentrations in vitro.

At present, it is unknown whether variations in cellular concentrations of monovalent cations would affect the gluco-corticoid receptor in vivo. No data are available as to whether the effects of energy deprivation of cells on the nuclear- cytoplasmic distribution of glucocorticoid-receptor complexes (10, 13) are correlated with changes in intracel-lular Na^+ and K^+ concentrations. The extent to which Li^+ would be expected to affect activation in vivo is not predictable from the presently available data, but Li^+ has been reported not to affect the steady state nuclear-cytoplasmic distribu-tion of complexes in S49.1 mouse lymphoma cells at 37^oC (27). However, it has been reported that Li^+ inhibits the cytolytic glucocorticoid effect on S49.1 cells independently of any effects on cellular cAMP levels (27). So Li^+ may somehow affect intracellular glucocorticoid receptor function. But any conclusions will have to await further studies of how general the Li^+-antagonism of glucocorticoid effects is.

Conclusions and Summary

Partitioning in aqueous dextran-poly(ethylene glycol) two-phase systems, a general technique for the characterization of proteins, has proved to be a powerful method for studying glucocorticoid-receptor complexes. It can be used for accurate measurements of activation kinetics and for studies of the activation of receptor forms which are unable to bind to DNA and nuclei, for instance receptors exposed to limited trypsination. When combined with limited proteolysis, it can also be used for studying how different domains of the receptor change during activation. In the present communication, emphasis has been put on the use of the method for studying effects on the complexes of nucleotides and monovalent cations. These studies led to the discovery of a previously unknown effect, specific for adenine nucleotides. The observed effect seemed to indicate that adenine nucleotides may be cofactors in and/or regulators of intracellular receptor action. Studies with aqueous two-phase partitioning also showed, that millimolar concentrations of Li^+ inhibit in vitro activation of the glucocorticoid-receptor complex, and that in vitro activation proceeds with different rates in buffers with K^+ and Na^+. However, with the effect of adenine nucleotides as well as that of monovalent cations, further studies are needed to reveal the relationship of these in vitro phenomena to events going on in the intact target cell.

Acknowledgement

Dr. U. Gehring is thanked for the gift of cells of the S49.1 TB 4.41 22R line. The work of the authors was supported financially by the Danish Cancer Society and the Danish Medical Research Council.

References

1 Higgins, S.J., Gehring, U.: Adv. Cancer Res. <u>28</u>, 313-397 (1978).

2 Higgins, S.J., Baxter, J.D., Rousseau, G.G.: in Glucocorticoid Hormone Action (Baxter, J.D., Rousseau, G.G., eds.) pp. 135-160, Springer-Verlag, Heidelberg (1979).

220

3 Simons, S.S.: in Glucocorticoid Hormone Action (Baxter, J.D., Rousseau, G.G., eds.) pp. 161-187, Springer-Verlag, Heidelberg (1979).

4 Schmidt, T.J., Litwack, G.: Physiol. Rev. 62, 1131-1192 (1982).

5 Sherman, M.R., Stevens, J.: Ann. Rev. Physiol. 46, 83-105 (1984).

6 Munck, A., Foley, R.: Nature 278, 752-754 (1979).

7 Markovic, R.D., Litwack, G.: Arch. Biochem. Biophys. 202, 374-379 (1980).

8 Miyabe, S., Harrison, R.W.: Endocrinology 112, 2174-2180 (1983).

9 Munck, A., Brinck-Johnsen, T.: J. Biol. Chem. 243, 5556-5565 (1968).

10 Ishii, D.N., Pratt, W.B., Aronow, L.: Biochemistry 11, 3896-3904 (1972).

11 Bell, P.A., Munck, A.: Biochem. J. 136, 97-107 (1973).

12 Wheeler, R.H., Leach, K.L., LaForest, A.C., O'Toole, T.E., Wagner, R., Pratt, W.B.: J. Biol. Chem. 256, 434-441 (1981).

13 Middlebrook, J.L., Wong, M.D., Ishii, D.N., Aronow, L.: Biochemistry 14, 180-186 (1975).

14 Albertsson, P.-Å.: Partition of Cell Particles and Macromolecules, Almquist and Wiksell, Stockholm (1971).

15 Albertsson, P.-Å.: J. Chromatogr. 159, 111-122 (1978).

16 Johansson, G.: Biochim. Biophys. Acta 221, 387-390 (1970).

17 Johansson, G.: Acta Chem. Scand. B28, 873-882 (1974).

18 Johansson, G.: Mol. Cell. Biochem. 4, 169-180 (1974).

19 Andreasen, P.A.: Biochim. Biophys. Acta 428, 792- 807 (1976).

20 Andreasen, P.A.: Biochim. Biophys. Acta 540, 484-499 (1978).

21 Andreasen, P.A., Mainwaring, W.I.P.: Biochim. Biophys. Acta 631, 334-349 (1980).

22 Andreasen, P.A.: Biochim. Biophys. Acta 676, 205-212 (1981).

23 Andreasen, P.A., Gehring, U.: Eur. J. Biochem. 120, 443-449 (1981).

24 Andreasen, P.A.: J. Steroid Biochem. 17, 577-579 (1982).

25 Andreasen, P.A.: Mol. Cell. Endocrinol. 28, 563-585 (1982).

26 Andreasen, P.A.: Mol. Cell. Endocrinol. 30, 229-239 (1983).

27 Junker, K., Svenson, M., Junker, S.: J. Steroid Biochem. 20, 725-731 (1984).

28 Carlstedt-Duke, J., Gustafsson, J.-Å., Wrange, Ö.: Bio-chim. Biophys. Acta 497, 507-524 (1977).

29 Wrange, Ö., Gustafsson, J.-Å.: J. Biol. Chem. 253, 856-865 (1978).

30 Nordeen, S.K., Lan, N.C., Showers, M.O., Baxter, J.D.: J. Biol. Chem. 256, 10503-10508 (1981).

31 Dellweg, H.-G., Hotz, A., Mugele, K., Gehring, U.: EMBO J. 1, 285-289 (1982).

32 Gehring, U., Hotz, A.: Biochemistry 22, 4013-4018 (1983).

33 Stevens, J., Stevens, Y.-W., Haubenstock, H.: Biochemical Actions of Hormones 10, 383-446 (1983).

34 Yamamoto, K.R., Gehring, U., Stampfer, M.R., Sibley, C.H.: Recent Prog. Horm. Res. 32, 3-32 (1976).

35 McBlain, W.A., Toft, D.O., Shyamala, G.: Biochemistry 20, 6790-6798 (1981).

36 Holbrook, N.J., Bodwell, J.E., Jeffries, M., Munck, A.: J. Biol. Chem. 258, 6477-6485 (1983).

37 Vedeckis, W.V.: Biochemistry 22, 1983-1989 (1983).

38 Eastman-Reks, S.B., Reker, C.E., Vedeckis, W.V.: Arch. Biochem. Biophys. 230, 274-284 (1984).

39 Grandics, P., Miller, A., Schmidt, T.J., Mittman, D., Lit-wack, G.: J. Biol. Chem. 259, 3173-3180 (1984).

40 Luttge, W.G., Gray, H.E., Densmore, C.L.: J. Steroid Biochem. 20, 545-553 (1984).

41 Westphal, H.M., Mugele, K., Beato, M., Gehring, U.: EMBO J. 3, 1493-1498 (1984).

42 Cake, M.H., Litwack, G.: Biochem. Biophys. Res. Commun. 66, 828-835 (1975).

43 Cake, M.H., Litwack, G.: Eur. J. Biochem. 82, 97-103 (1978).

44 Kato, K., Kobayashi, M., Sato, S.: J. Biochem. 77, 811-815 (1975).

45 Ullman, B., Perlman, R.L.: Biochim. Biophys. Acta 403, 393-411 (1975).

46 Li, H.-C., Hsiao, K.-J.: Eur. J. Biochem. 77, 383-391 (1977).

47 Titanji, V.P.K.: Biochim. Biophys. Acta 481, 140-151 (1977).

48 Hsiao, K.-J., Sandberg, A.R., Li, H.-C.: J. Biol. Chem. 253, 6901-6907 (1978).

49 Khatra, B.S., Söderling, T.R.: Biochem. Biophys. Res. Commun. 85, 647-654 (1978).

50 Khandelwal, R.L., Kamani, S.A.S.: Biochim. Biophys. Acta 613, 95-105 (1980).

51 Yan, S.C.B., Graves, D.J.: Mol. Cell. Biochem. 42, 21-29 (1982).

52 Robinson, G.A., Butcher, R.W., Sutherland, E.W.: Cyclic AMP, p. 84, Academic Press, New York (1971).

53 Clark, R.B., Seney, M.N.: J. Biol. Chem. 251, 4239-4346 (1976).

54 Buckley, J.T.: Biochim. Biophys. Acta 498, 1-9 (1977).

55 Kasvinsky, P.J., Madsen, N.B., Sygusch, J., Fletterick, R.J.: J. Biol. Chem. 253, 3343-3351 (1978).

56 Londos, C., Cooper, D.M.F., Schlegel, W., Rodbell, M.: Proc. Natl. Acad. Sci. USA 75, 5362-5366 (1978).

57 LeComte, M.-C., Galand, C., Boivin, P.: FEBS Lett. 116, 45-47 (1980).

58 Moss, J., Stanley, S.J., Watkins, P.A.: J. Biol. Chem. 255, 5838-5840 (1980).

59 Sandlie, I., Kleppe, K.: FEBS Lett. 110, 223-226 (1980).

60 Melchior, N.C., Melchior, J.B.: J. Biol. Chem. 231, 609-623 (1958).

61 Tobin, T., Akera, T., Brody, T.M.: Ann. N.Y. Acad. Sci. 242, 120-132 (1974).

62 Nørby, J.G., Jensen, J.: Ann. N.Y. Acad. Sci. 242, 158-167 (1974).

63 Skou, J.C.: Ann. N.Y. Acad. Sci. 242, 168-184 (1974).

64 Oriol-Audit, C., Lake, J.A., Reisler, E.: Biochemistry 20, 679-686 (1981).

65 Barnett, C.A., Schmidt, T.J., Litwack, G.: Biochemistry 19, 5446-5455 (1980).

66 Moudgil, V.K., John, J.K.: Biochem. J. 190, 799-808 (1980).

67 Holbrook, N.J., Bodwell, J.E., Munck, A.: J. Biol. Chem. 258, 14885-14894 (1983).

68 Hubbard, J., Kalimi, M.: Biochem. J. 210, 259-263 (1983).

69 Horiuchi, M., Isohashi, F., Terada, M., Okamoto, K., Sakamoto, Y.: Biochem. Biophys. Res. Commun. 98, 88-94 (1981)

70 Horiuchi, M., Isohashi, F., Okamoto, K., Matsunaga, T., Terada, M., Mitsui, Y., Sakamoto, Y.: Biochem. Biophys. Res. Commun. 105, 146-151 (1982).

71 Okamoto, K., Isohashi, F., Horiuchi, M., Sakamoto, Y.: Biochem. Biophys. Res. Commun. 108, 1655-1660 (1982).

72 Okamota, K., Isohashi, F., Horiuchi, M., Sakamoto Y.: Biochem. Biophys. Res. Commun. 121, 940-945 (1984).

73 Housley, P.R., Pratt, W.B.: J. Biol. Chem. 258, 4630-4635 (1983).

74 Grandics, P., Miller, A., Schmidt, T.J., Litwack, G.: Biochem. Biophys. Res. Commun. 120, 59-64 (1984).

75 Kurl, R.N., Jacob, S.T.: Biochem. Biphys. Res. Commun. 119, 700-705 (1984).

76 Housley, P.R., Grippo, J.F., Dahmer, M.K., Pratt, W.B.: Biochemical Actions of Hormones 11, 347-376 (1984).

77 Barnett, C.A., Palmour, R.M., Litwack, G., Seegmiller, J.E.: Endocrinology 112, 2059-2068 (1983).

78 Towle, A.C., Sze, P.Y.: Mol. Cell. Biochem. 52, 145-151 (1983).

79 Fleming, H., Blumenthal, R., Gurpide, E.: Proc. Natl. Acad. Sci. USA 80, 2486-2490 (1983).

80 Skou, J.C.: Biochim. Biophys. Acta 42, 6-23 (1960).

81 Shigekawa, M., Pearl, L.J.: J. Biol. Chem. 251, 6947-6952 (1976).

82 Duggan, P.F.: J. Biol. Chem. 252, 1620-1627 (1977).

83 Jones, L.R., Besch, H.R., Watanabe, A.M.: J. Biol. Chem. 252, 3315-3323 (1977).

84 Wolff, J., Berens, S.C., Jones, A.B.: Biochem. Biophys. Res. Commun. 39, 77-82 (1970).

85 Wang, Y.-C., Pandy, G.N., Mendels, J., Frazer, A.: Biochem. Pharmacol. 23, 845-855 (1974).

86 Blume, A.J., Lichtenstein, D., Bloom, G.: Proc. Natl. Acad. Sci. USA 76, 5626-5630 (1979).

87 Rose, I.A., Warms, J.V.B., Wong, L.J.: J. Biol. Chem. 252, 4262-4268 (1977).

88 Knapp, S., Mandel, A.J.: J. Neural Transm. 45, 1-15 (1979).

89 Bryant, D.T.W., Andrews, P.: Biochem. J. 219, 287- 292 (1984).

90 Milgrom, E., Atger, M., Baulieu, E.-E.: Biochemistry 12, 5198-5205 (1973).

91 Kalimi, M., Colman, P., Feigelson, P.: J. Biol. Chem. 250, 1080-1086 (1975).

92 Rousseau, G.G., van Bohemen, C.G., Lareau, S., Degelaen, J.: Biochem. Biophys. Res. Commun. 106, 16-22 (1982).

93 Kalimi, M., Hubbard, J., Ray, A.: J. Steroid Biochem. 18, 665-671 (1983).

94 van Bohemen, C.G., Eliard, P.H., Rousseau, G.G.: Mol. Physiol. 4, 95-110 (1983).

95 Rousseau, G.G., van Bohemen, C.G.: J. Steroid Biochem. 20, 37-41 (1984).

96 Schmidt, T.J., Sekula, B.C., Litwack, G.: Endocrinology 109, 803-812 (1981).

97 Hubbard, J., Kalimi, M.: Biochim. Biophys. Acta 755, 178-185 (1983).

98 Cidlowski, J.A., Thanassi, J.W.: Biochemistry 18, 2378-2384 (1979).

99 Arányi, P., Náray, A.: J. Steroid Biochem. 12, 267- 272 (1980).

100 Cidlowski, J.A.: Biochemistry 19, 6162-6170 (1980).

101 Náray, A.: J. Steroid Biochem. 14, 71-76 (1981).

LOW-MOLECULAR-WEIGHT AND MACROMOLECULAR TRANSLOCATION MODULATORS AFFECTING THE BINDING OF ACTIVATED RECEPTOR-GLUCOCORTICOID COMPLEX TO NUCLEI, CHROMATIN, AND DNA

Fumihide Isohashi and Yukiya Sakamoto
Department of Biochemistry, Institute for Cancer Research,
Osaka University Medical School
1-1-50, Fukushima, Fukushima-ku, Osaka, 553, Japan

Introduction

There is substantial evidence that specific cytoplasmic receptors mediate the modulation of gene expression by steroid hormones (for reviews, see 1, 2, 3, 4, 5) and that the occupancy and the level of receptors are correlated with the extents of cellular responses (6; for reviews, see 7, 8, 9). However, some steroid-resistant cells have been found to have normal receptors and a normal receptor level (10, 11, 12), suggesting that the action of steroid hormones is not regulated only by the receptor level and occupancy.

Steroid-receptor complexes, especially glucocorticoid-receptor complexes, are thought to be transferred from the cytoplasm to the nucleus through a two-step mechanism (for review, see 13). First they are activated (transformed) to a form with high affinity for nuclei, chromatin, and DNA, a step named activation (transformation). Then the activated complexes migrate into the nuclei and bind to chromatin. This step is called translocation. Activation (transformation) and translocation are suggested to be highly regulated processes.

This review is focused on the identification of possible substances regulating the translocation step and their regulatory mechanisms.

Molecular Mechanism of Steroid Hormone Action
© 1985 Walter de Gruyter & Co., Berlin · New York – Printed in Germany

Background

Many factors that affect the binding of various activated receptor steroid complexes to acceptors in vitro and in vivo have been reported as described below.

1) Macromolecular receptor translocation inhibitor(s). A putative translocation inhibitor was first observed by Chamness et al. (14) in the cytosol of rat uterus, spleen and MtTW5-pituitary tumor cells. This factor inhibited the binding of already activated estrogen-receptor complexes to isolated nuclei. In the presence, but not the absence, of this inhibitor, binding sites of estrogen receptor in isolated nuclei from several target and non-target tissues were shown to be saturable (14). Since heat-denatured MtTW5 cytosol (65°C for 10 min) or bovine serum albumin (10 mg) also had a similar effect, and since the inhibitory components of the cytosol were not limited to the cytosol from a particular tissue (14), they were considered to be nonspecific materials, and so were not characterized further by these investigators.

While studying the interaction of glucocorticoid ([^{3}H]dexamethasone)-receptor complexes with rat liver nuclear acceptor, Milgrom and Atger (15) observed apparent saturation of the acceptor (pseudo-saturation) that was probably due to the presence in the cytosol of an inhibitor of receptor translocation. This inhibitor was a macromolecule (possibly protein) and interacted in a concentration-dependent manner with the receptor steroid complex. Subsequently, these authors (16, 17) found that the presence of excess nuclei in the system for assay of binding of the activated form of glucocorticoid ([^{3}H]triamcinolone acetonide)-receptor complex to nuclei (excess nuclei assay method) overcame the interference of the macromolecular translocation inhibitor. By this method it is possible to test the activation (transformation) process in the presence of the translocation inhibitor, since in vitro experiments on either the activation or translocation step involved the determination of binding of the activated receptor complex to nuclei, chromatin and DNA (DNA-cellulose).

Under cell-free conditions with preparations from cultured rat
hepatoma cells (HTC cells), Simons et al. (18) found that the
cytosol translocation inhibitors were macromolecules, because
they were excluded by passage of the preparation through Sephadex G-25. Their effects could not be mimicked by albumin or
hemoglobin, in contrast to findings (14) in the estrogen receptor system. Simons et al. (18) also reported that either hen
egg white lysozyme or calf thymus histones caused a significant
reduction in the binding of activated glucocorticoid complex to
DNA-cellulose. Thus, these and perhaps other chromosomal proteins may be responsible for controlling the acceptor capacity
(18, 19). Simons et al. (18, 20) used computer simulation analysis to determine whether the macromolecular translocation inhibitor associates with the activated receptor-glucocorticoid
complex or with the nuclei, and concluded that it interacts directly with the complex to decrease the binding of the activated receptor complex to acceptors. Preincubated of nuclei with
high concentrations of the macromolecular translocation inhibit-
or, did not reduce the nuclear binding activity, supporting the
above conclusion and suggesting that the inhibitor does not destroy the acceptor sites (18). Experiments by the excess nuclei assay method also showed that the inhibitor does not destroy activated receptor steroid complexes (18). In a later paper, Simons (20) reported that the inhibitor in HTC cell cytosol inhibited the binding of the activated complexes to DNA by
the mechanism described above deduced from the results (18) of
nuclear binding experiments. Similar results were obtained by
Izawa (21), confirming the direct interaction of the macromolecular translocation inhibitor (probably protein) with the activated receptor glucocorticoid complex.
So far, all experiments on the effect of the macromolecular inhibitor on the translocation step have been carried out in
vitro. Liu and Webb (10) presented suggestive evidence that
the cytoplasmic macromolecular translocation inhibitor actually
functions in intact cells. They concluded (10) that this inhib-

itor does not prevent pharmacological (high) doses of glucocorticoids from blocking the proliferation of Novikoff hepatoma
cells, like regenerating liver cells, at the G1-S interphase,
but that it limits the amount of receptor entering the nucleus
when the glucocorticoid concentration is in the physiological
range. Recently, Munck and Foley (22) demonstrated the activation step in isolated rat thymus cells and showed that the process is time-dependent after glucocorticoid treatment. Similar
results were obtained by Markovic and Litwack (23) in the liver
and kidney from rats injected with [^{3}H]triamcinolone acetonide.
These studies (22, 23) are very important since they show the
physiological significance of not only an activation (transformation) process but also the subsequent, translocation step, because they showed that after treatment with glucocorticoid in
vivo, activated receptor-glucocorticoid complexes accumulate in
the cytosol of rat thymus cells (22), and rat liver (23) and
kidney (23) in a time-dependent fashion and then decrease significantly, presumably as a result of time-dependent nuclear
translocation of the activated complexes (23).
With respect to the possible physiological role of the putative
macromolecular translocation inhibitor, it is noteworthy that
glucocorticoid resistant cell lines, such as Novikoff hepatoma
cells (10), AH 130 ascites hepatoma cells (24, 25) and AH 7974
ascites hepatoma cells (24) have high concentrations of the inhibitors. Although the roles of these inhibitors in vivo are
difficult to assess and are still not clear, they are possibly
related with regulation of binding of the activated complex to
nuclei and influence subsequent modification of gene expression
by the activated receptor steroid complexes.
2) RNA and ribonucleases (RNase). Liao and his colleagues (26,
27, 28) and others (29, 30) reported that RNA can associate
with various steroid-hormone receptors and inhibit the binding
of activated receptor complexes to DNA-cellulose. RNase can also increase the binding of the activated receptor complex to
DNA-cellulose (29). More recently, Tymoczko and Phillips (31)
reported that the 7-8S form of the dexamethasone-receptor com-

plex is associated with RNA molecules that can be removed by RNase treatment or salt dissociation, and that this RNA inhibits the binding of the receptor to DNA. These results suggest that RNA may also be involved in the process of regulation of the action of steroid hormones.

3) Other macromolecules. Prostate α-protein, a major glycoprotein in the cytosol of rat ventral prostate (Mr$\cong$50,000), is known to interfere with the association of the androgen-receptor complex with isolated cell nuclei (32, 33, 34, 35).

In porcine uterus, Murayama and Fukai (36, 37) demonstrated estrogen receptor binding factors (ERBFs) which inhibit the translocation of the 4.5S estrogen receptor complex from the cytoplasm to the nucleus and bind directly to the estrogen receptor complex to form an 8S estrogen receptor complex (receptor complex in an unactivated or untransformed state that cannot bind to acceptor).

Colvard and Wilson (38) identified and partially purified a protein, referred to as 8S androgen receptor-promoting factor, that causes the 4.5S androgen receptor to sediment at 8S. Some of its physicochemical properties are remarkably similar to those of the androgen receptor.

More recently, Dougherty et al. (39) purified two 8S forms of progesterone receptor from chicken oviduct to near homogeneity and analyzed their peptide compositions. Both 8S forms contain 90,000 molecular weight peptides that do not bind to progesterone (39).

However, it is not clear whether there is any relation between various 8S forming factors including RNA molecules and putative macromolecular translocation inhibitors.

4) Low molecular weight translocation modulators (LTMs). Cake et al.(40) first demonstrated the involvement of an endogenous low molecular weight component(s) in the mechanism of action of the glucocorticoid receptor. It is unknown whether this endogenous factor in rat liver cytosol inhibits activation or the subsequent translocation process. In subsequent papers from the same laboratory (41; for reviews, see 13, 42), Sekula et al.

(41) reevaluated their earlier experiments (40) by DEAE-cellulose chromatography, on which the activated and unactivated receptor-steroid complexes are separated, and redefined a micromolecular inhibitor (modulator) as an inhibitor of the activation
step.

On the other hand, while studying the association of 3,000 to
5,000-fold purified activated receptor-glucocorticoid ([^{3}H]tri-
amcinolone acetonide) complex from rat liver cytosol with isolated rat liver nuclei (translocation step), Isohashi et al.
(43) found that dialyzed rat liver cytosol free of glucocorticoid receptors inhibited nuclear binding of the activated complexes to isolated rat liver nuclei much more effectively than
undialyzed receptor-free cytosol. This finding (43) suggests
the presence of a dialyzable substance(s) [low-molecular-weight
translocation modulator(s); LTM(s)] that decreases the inhibitory activity of the macromolecular receptor translocation inhib-
itor(s) [MTI(s)] in the binding of activated receptor complex
to nuclei. The MTI(s) was separated from the LTM(s) by gel filtration (Sephadex G-25 column), and the LTM(s) was shown to
have less inhibitory activity than the MTI(s) (43). Study of
the effect of mixing the two components separated by the gel
filtration showed that the inhibitory effect of the isolated
MTI(s) was decreased by LTM(s), suggesting that the LTM(s) by
interacting with the MTI(s) modulates the binding of already activated receptor-glucocorticoid complexes to nuclei. It is not
clear whether the LTM(s) is the same component as that reported
to inhibit the activation-process [a low molecular weight activation inhibitor (40, 41, 44, 45, 46) or factor f (47; for review, see 13)].

5) Nucleotides. There is increasing evidence that ATP is important in the action of steroid hormones with their receptors
by interacting with these receptors (48, 49, 50, 51, 52, 53, 54,
55), though the mechanism of its effect is unknown: ATP has
been reported to effect the stability of the unbound receptor
and to be involved in phosphorylation and dephosphorylation
mechanisms which influence the steroid binding activity of the

receptor (54). Furthermore, ATP is reported to stimulate the rate of activation of the rat liver glucocorticoid-receptor complex at low temperature (56). Moudgil and Toft (57, 58) using ATP-Sepharose first provided evidence for the interaction of partially purified activated progesterone-receptor complex from hen oviduct with ATP. Subsequently Moudgil and John (59) reported that the activated receptor-glucocorticoid complex of rat liver was also selectively adsorbed to a column of ATP-Sepharose (59). Binding of the activated receptor complex is reversible and ionic, but shows specificity over the bindings of other nucleoside triphosphates, AMP and cyclic AMP (57). Miller and Toft (60) obtained similar results on the estradiol receptor system of rat uterus and hen oviduct, suggesting that ATP binding might be a general property of activated steroid receptors. Moudgil and Toft reported that highly purified progesterone receptor preparations from avian oviduct catalyze an exchange reaction between ATP and PPi (61).

6) Pyridoxal 5'-phosphate. Pyridoxal 5'-phosphate, the active form of vitamin B_6, was reported by Litwack and colleagues (62, 63) to inhibit the binding of rat liver glucocorticoid receptor complexes to DNA-cellulose (native calf thymus DNA) and isolated rat liver nuclei. These workers further suggested that this compound interacted by forming a Shiff's base with the ε-amino group of a lysine residue that is one of the required basic residues for function of the DNA-binding site of the activated complex. This compound was also found to affect the binding of activated uterine estrogen-receptor complex to nuclei (64) and to DNA-cellulose (65), the binding of activated progesterone receptor complex to ATP-Sepharose (66), and the binding of activated androgen-receptor complex to DNA-cellulose (67). Pyridoxal 5'-phosphate affects not only the translocation step, but also the activation process: it enhances the conversion of the unactivated receptor glucocorticoid complex to the activated complex (68).

7) Other micromolecules. Rifamycin AF/013 (69, 70), a lipophilic derivative of the rifamycin class of antibiotics, and o-phenanthroline (69, 70), a metal chelator, which are both known

to inhibit the activity of RNA and DNA polymerase, also abolished the ability of [^{3}H]progesterone receptor to bind to purified oviduct nuclei. Furthermore, rifamycin AF/103 (71) and o-phenanthroline (72) both inhibited the binding of the activated glucocorticoid-receptor complex to DNA-cellulose.

Aurinticarboxylic acid, a triphenylmethane dye, which is also known to inhibit the activities of DNA and RNA polymerases, inhibits the nuclear binding of hen oviduct estradiol receptor (73), the bindings of the estradiol receptor from rat uterus to DNA-cellulose and ATP-Sepharose (74), the bindings of hen oviduct progesterone receptor to the nucleus, ATP and DNA (75) and the nuclear binding of glucocorticoid receptor (76).

Molybdate, tungstate and vanadate, which strongly inhibit phosphatase, were found to inhibit the activation (transformation) of cytosol steroid-receptor complexes to their activated acceptor binding form (for review see 13). Furthermore, reports from Moudgil's laboratory (77) showed that sodium molybdate blocks not only activation of the receptor complex but also the DNA and nuclear binding capacity of the activated rat liver glucocorticoid-receptor complex. Subsequent studies in this laboratory showed that tungstate at 1 mM completely blocked nuclear uptake of the heat-activated cytosol glucocorticoid-receptor complex (78, 79). The effects of tungstate are reported to be mediated via both the glucocorticoid-receptor and nuclear sites (79).

Methods

Our experimental procedures have been described (43, 80-92). But it should be emphasized that for studies on interaction of the activated complex with nuclear acceptors in the translocation step, it is important to use a homologous population of activated receptor-steroid complex uncontaminated by unactivated complex and receptor-translocation inhibitors or other endogenous factors. Thus, in all the experiments reviewed in this pa-

per (43, 86, 87, 88, 90, 91, 92), more than 3,000-fold purified
activated receptor-[^{3}H]triamcinolone acetonide complexes were
used. The concentrated preparations were stored at -80°C and
used within a month. These activated receptor complexes did not
contain any detectable putative translocation modulators (macromolecular and low-molecular weight translocation modulators) or
unactivated complexes. The molecular weight of the partially
purified activated sample was estimated by gel filtration
(Sephadex G-150) as about 98,000 and its sedimentation coefficient as about 4.2S.

The standard assay mixture (pH 7.4 at 4°C, in a final volume of
0.5 ml) consisted of 50 mM Tris-HCl, 250 mM sucrose, 4 mM MgCl$_2$,
25 mM KCl, 0.2 mM Na$_2$EDTA, 1 mM 2-mercaptoethanol, 2 mg of BSA,
2 x 10^6 nuclei [or DNA-cellulose (20 μg native DNA from calf
thymus)] and partially purified activated receptor-[^{3}H]triam-
cinolone acetonide complex (1.8-2.7 pmol) with or without various factors.

Results and Discussion

As already briefly mentioned under "Background", we found a low-
molecular-weight translocation modulator(s) [LTM(s)] in the
cytosol of rat liver (43). This dialyzable material(s) from rat
liver, which was a Sephadex G-25 included material(s), inhibited the binding of 3,000 to 5,000-fold purified activated receptor [^{3}H]-triamcinolone acetonide complex to isolated rat liver
nuclei (43). This LTM(s) appeared to differ from known cytosol
macromolecular receptor-translocation inhibitor(s) [MTI(s)] (10,
15, 17, 18). It was less inhibitory than the putative MTI(s) in
rat liver cytosol (43), but it had the remarkable property of
decreasing the inhibitory effect of cytosolic MTI(s) (43). This
effect was reversible: when the LTM(s) was removed, the MTI(s)
became much more inhibitory.

Pyridoxal 5'-phosphate in a mM order is reported to inhibit
binding of the activated receptor-steroid complex to nuclei

(see "Background" section). However, pyridoxal 5'-phosphate did not mimic the effect of cytosol LTM(s) in decreasing the inhibitory effects of MTI(s): pyridoxal 5'-phosphate and the MTI(s) had additive inhibitory effects (43). The molecular mechanism of the putative MTI(s) in the glucocorticoid receptor system was found by kinetic analysis by a computer simulation method to be its direct interaction with the activated-receptor glucocorticoid complex (18, 20). By this method, the inhibitory effect of LTM(s) was shown to be due to its direct interaction with the activated receptor complex, reducing the affinity of the latter for the nuclei (43). Our results, however, do not exclude the possibility of direct interaction of the LTM(s) with MTI(s) (43). Neither the acceptor site in nuclei nor the activated receptor complex was destroyed by this LTM(s) (43). We conclude from this work that rat liver cytosol contains at least two kinds of translocation modulators, the known MTI(s) and the LTM(s). As already mentioned under "Background", there is much evidence that a low-molecular weight inhibitor(s) acts in the process of conversion of the "unactivated" to the "activated" receptor-steroid complex (40, 44, 45). A factor f was found to stabilize unbound glucocorticoid receptor and inhibit activation of the glucocorticoid complex (47). However, the above factors probably differ from the LTM(s), because LTM(s) inhibits the binding of activated receptor-steroid complex to nuclei, although we could not exclude the possibility that we observed a different action of the low-molecular-weight activation inhibitor (modulator) reported previously (40, 44, 45) or factor f (47). Clarification of this point will require purification and identification of these endogenous components. Subsequently, we found that the LTM(s) consists of several components, judging from its elution pattern from a Sephadex G-10 column (93), and contains various nucleotides (86). Of the various nucleotides examined, ATP can partly mimic the properties of the LTM(s); that is, at up to 5 mM, it has a specific effect in decreasing the inhibitory effect of the putative MTI(s), but ATP itself at up to this concentration has no inhibitory effect

on nuclear binding of the partially purified activated complex
(86). Unlike ATP, ADP and AMP at concentrations of up to 5 mM
had no such effect (86). Furthermore, UTP, TTP, CTP and GTP,
and cyclic AMP at physiological concentrations had no detectable effect on nuclear binding (86). The mechanism of the effect of ATP is unknown. However, judging from the high affinity and specificity of the activated receptor-glucocorticoid complex for ATP (59), it seems probable that the ATP-bound activated receptor glucocorticoid complex is resistant to the inhibitory action of the MTI(s), although it is possible that ATP may
interact directly with the MTI(s). Irrespective of the mechanism involved, LTMs in rat liver cytosol and possibly ATP seem
to participate in regulation of the translocation or nuclear
binding step by interacting with putative MTI(s) in rat liver
cytosol.

We next tried to characterize the putative MTI(s). Okamoto et
al. (87) found that the MTI(s) in rat liver cytosol consists of
at least three components: when the rat liver cytosol was applied to a DEAE-cellulose column and material was eluted with a
linear gradient of 0 to 0.5 M NaCl, three peaks of MTI activity
were eluted from the column. The first peak (Peak I) (called
MTI-I) was eluted with about 0.1 M NaCl, the second (Peak II)
(called MTI-II) with about 0.2 M NaCl, and the third (Peak III)
(called MTI-III) with about 0.3 M NaCl. Before nuclear binding
assay, each fraction from the column was dialyzed to remove possible LTMs and salts and then heated (37°C, 30 min) to denature
possibly contaminating unbound receptor. Heat treatment at the
crude cytosol level (37°C, 30 min) gave vague peaks on DEAE-cellulose chromatography, presumably due to the effects of contaminated proteases or partial denaturation of the MTIs by this
treatment, or both (94).

In the presence of 5 mM ATP, the Peak I fraction enhanced nuclear binding of the activated complex about 1.9-fold, although in
the absence of ATP it inhibited nuclear binding, the Peak II
fraction showed no inhibitory effect, and the Peak III fraction
showed the same inhibitory effect as in the absence of ATP.

The behavior of Peak I with ATP was unexpected, since addition of ATP to liver cytosol only overcame its inhibitory activity, as described above (86). Furthermore, Isohashi et al. (90) reported subsequently that Peak I from the cytosol of AH-130 tumor cells (glucocorticoid resistant cells, originating from a hepatoma induced in a rat with ρ-dimethylaminoazobenzene (DAB)) does not enhance nuclear binding of the activated-receptor complexes in the presence of ATP, although the inhibitory effect of Peak I from AH-130 tumor cells is much stronger than that of rat liver (90). These results raised the further question of whether the material in Peak I from rat liver with ATP-sensitive enhancing activity is the same entity as the inhibitory material in Peak I. Okamoto et al. (91) purified the Peak I fraction further by DEAE-cellulose column chromatography and found that the enhancing activity of material that we named ATP-stimulated translocation promoter (ASTP) is different from the inhibitory material (MTI-I) in Peak I. We further characterized the ASTP in the presence of ATP: it is relatively heat stable (60°C for 15 min) (91), is eluted from DEAE-cellulose with about 0.025 M NaCl (91), and has a molecular weight of about 93,000 as determined by gel filtration (91).

Several reports (26, 27), suggest that the steroid-receptor complex can bind to certain RNA or ribonucleoprotein particles in the nuclei and cytoplasm of target tissues. Recently, Liao et al. (28) reported that polyribonucleotides with certain types of bases can compete effectively with DNA and promote the release of the receptor complex from DNA-cellulose. Furthermore, Chong and Lippman (29) reported that purified RNA from MCF-7 cells inhibits estrogen- and glucocorticoid-receptor binding to DNA-cellulose and that exogenous ribonucleases increase binding of the receptor complex of MCF-7 cells to DNA-cellulose. More recently, it was found that RNA induced reversal of glucocorticoid receptor activation (95) and that RNase A and RNase T1 induced the ability of the dexamethasone-receptor complex to bind to DNA-cellulose concomitantly with alteration of the sedimentation profile of the dexamethasone-receptor complex from the 7-8S

form to the 3-4S form in low salt-sucrose gradients (31). Therefore, we tested whether the ASTP in Peak I was RNase, but could
not detect RNase activity in the Peak I fraction (91). Moreover, addition of RNase A with 5 mM ATP in the nuclear binding
assay did not increase the binding of the 3,000-fold purified
activated complex to isolated nuclei from rat liver (91). Therefore, the results of our study do not support the possibility
that the enhancing activity of ASTP in Peak I in the presence
of ATP is due to RNase. This enhancing activity of ASTP again
shows specificity for ATP, and is not increased by ADP, AMP or
pyrophosphate (see below) (91). In this series of studies (86,
87, 90, 91), we demonstrated that the putative macromolecular
translocation inhibitor(s) is not a single molecule, but is composed of at least three macromolecular inhibitory components
(MTI-I, -II and -III) and that there is at least one ATP-sensitive macromolecular enhancing material (ASTP) other than Peak
II (MTI-II), the inhibitory activity of which is abolished by
ATP. We have been unable to separate the ATP-sensitive material and inhibitory material (MTI-II) in Peak II by DEAE-cellulose column chromatography or gel filtration. Therefore, MTI-II
itself may be ATP-sensitive (losing inhibitory activity in the
presence of ATP). Both MTI-II and ASTP are ATP-sensitive, but
they are apparently different molecules, judging from their different behaviors on DEAE-cellulose chromatography and differences in the effects of ATP on their actions: the former loses
inhibitory activity, whereas the latter promotes binding of the
activated complex to nuclei and chromatin.
While studying the effects of LTMs (43) and the various nucleotides on nuclear binding of the partially purified activated
complex to isolated nuclei, Horiuchi et al. (88) found that
pyrophosphate (PPi) greatly enhanced nuclear binding. This PPi
effect cannot be observed with a crude receptor-nuclear binding
system or even with more than 3,000-fold purified activated receptor complex and purified nuclei in the presence of receptor-
free cytosol as MTI(s) (88). The failure to observe this phenomenon in the crude system is presumably due to contamination

of the high activity of inorganic pyrophosphatase in the cytosol of rat liver (96), resulting in hydrolysis of added PPi to
phosphate. Purified nuclei of rat liver is known to have little activity of the enzyme (96). But it is possible that MTI(s)
interferes with the interaction of PPi with the receptor. Increase in concentration of PPi to $\geq$9 mM PPi gradually decreases
nuclear binding to below the control level (88). Addition of
phosphate has no detectable effect on nuclear binding either in
the absence or presence of MTI(s) (88). Recently, Horiuchi et
al. (92) characterized the PPi effects and the interactions of
ATP and PPi with the activated complex to elucidate the mechanism of the translocation or nuclear binding step. Although progressive addition of PPi up to 8 mM increased nuclear binding
of the activated receptor-[^{3}H]triamcinolone acetonide complex
and ATP at up to 5 mM did not affect nuclear binding, in the
presence of 5 mM ATP, nuclear binding of the activated complex
decreased steadily with increase in PPi concentration (92). ADP
also decreased the enhancing effect of PPi (92), though it was
less effective than ATP (92). AMP with PPi had little effect on
nuclear binding (92). ADP or AMP alone at up to 5 mM did not affect nuclear binding (86, 92). We analyzed the interaction between nucleotides and PPi on the activated receptor glucocorticoid complex by examining the effect of PPi on binding of the
activated complex to ATP-, ADP-, and AMP-agarose (92). If PPi
binds to the same site(s) as ATP, it should compete with binding of the activated complex to ATP-agarose. However, we observed that PPi enhances ATP-agarose binding of the activated
complex (92), suggesting that the binding site(s) for PPi on
the activated complex is different from the ATP-binding site(s).
Similar experiments demonstrated that PPi slightly enhanced ADP-
agarose binding (92), but did not affect AMP-agarose binding of
the activated complex (92). The bindings of the activated complex to ADP- and AMP-agarose were much lower than that to ATP-
agarose (about 12% and 16%, respectively) (92). Preincubation
with nuclei and PPi did not affect binding of the activated complex to PPi-pretreated nuclei that had been washed before nucle-

ar binding assay. These results suggest that PPi does not act
through acceptor sites in nuclei, or that it interacts only
very weakly with acceptors. Addition of ATP, or PPi, or a mixture of both to 3,000-fold purified activated receptor complex
(about 4.2S, Mr≅98,000) did not causes appreciably change in
its sedimentation coefficient or molecular weight (92). These
compounds greatly stabilized the 3,000-fold purified activated
receptor complex during gel filtration (92). However, the observed phenomena cannot be explained only by the stabilizing effects of these compounds, since PPi at up to 8 mM enhanced nuclear binding, ATP at up to 5 mM did not change nuclear binding
and a combination of ATP and PPi decreased nuclear binding (92).
Recently, Munck and his colleagues (97) reported that in addition of ATP, already known to promote activation at 0°C (98, 99,
100, 101, 102), PPi, ADP, and other triphosphates at millimolar
concentrations promoted activation of the unactivated complex
in a crude cytosol system from rat thymus cells (97), and that
ATP and PPi prevented formation of mero-receptor complexes (97),
a process which occurs relatively rapidly in thymus cytosol.
Furthermore, they reported that PPi and ATP weaken the binding
of activated complexes to DNA-cellulose (97) and concluded that
their results with PPi and ATP were probably due to the charge
properties of the DNA-binding domain on the receptor; this domain is thought to be positively charged (13, 103) and so
strongly negative PPi may unmask DNA-binding sites on the receptor and also weaken binding of these sites to DNA by competing
with negatively charged groups. Our results (88, 92) on the effects of ATP and PPi described above, however, cannot be explained only by the positive-negative charge relationship,
since PPi at up to 8 mM enhanced binding of the activated complex to nuclei but did not affect DNA-cellulose binding at up
to 10 mM PPi (92). However, a high concentration of PPi (≥ 9mM)
decreased nuclear binding of the activated complex and a combination of ATP and PPi decreased nuclear and DNA-cellulose binding. Thus, these phenomena might be correlated with the so-
called charge effect. We assume that the activated complex has

PPi and ATP binding sites. Binding of PPi may cause some allosteric conformational change of the receptor molecule resulting
in high affinity for nuclei and chromatin. However, this change
of the receptor caused by PPi does not alter the DNA-cellulose
binding, perhaps due to the existence of another DNA binding
site different form the chromosomal protein binding site(s) on
the receptor. Furthermore, PPi also causes conformation change
of the receptor favoring ATP binding. The simultaneous bindings
of ATP and PPi cause a change of chromatin and DNA-binding
sites on the receptor, which consequently become less accessible to chromatin and DNA-cellulose (92). Recent reports from
several laboratories (24, 104, 105, 106) have shown that the activated receptor glucocorticoid complex recognizes a specific
sequence in DNA. It is uncertain how ATP and PPi influence the
specific DNA binding site, since we used commercially available
DNA-cellulose prepared from native calf thymus DNA in our experiments.

Summary and Conclusions

In the series of studies reviewed in this paper, we demonstrated
that the process of binding of the already "activated" receptor-
glucocorticoid complex to nuclei (translocation step) may be
highly regulated. We tried to identify and characterize the putative macromolecular translocation inhibitor(s), MTI(s) involved in this step by studies with more than 3,000-fold purified activated glucocorticoid receptor complex and isolated nuclei, both from rat liver, and found that there are at least
three macromolecular inhibitors (MTI-I, MTI-II, and MTI-III)
and at least one ATP-stimulated macromolecular translocation
promoter (ASTP) that increase the nuclear binding of the activated complex in the presence of ATP. Of the inhibitory activities of these three MTIs, those of MTI-I and MTI-III were not
influenced by ATP, but that of MTI-II was overcome by 5 mM ATP.
We could not separate the inhibitory activity of MTI-II from

the ATP-sensitive activity by gel filtration or DEAE-cellulose chromatography. Thus we presume that these activities are due to the same component (MTI-II). Either MTI-II or ASTP is ATP-sensitive, but the two are apparently different macromolecules, since they show different behaviors on DEAE-cellulose column chromatography, and in the presence of ATP only MTI-II lost its inhibitory activity, whereas ASTP promoted binding of the activated complex to nuclei. Glucocorticoid-resistant tumor cells (AH-130 tumor cells, originating from a rat hepatoma) have a high concentration of the putative MTIs, in particular MTI-I, and a low concentration of the ATP-stimulated translocation promoter (presumably ASTP). These results suggest that these macromolecular inhibitors and modulators have a significant physiological role. However, their mechanisms of action are unknown. With respect to endogenous low-molecular weight materials that affect the translocation step, we found low-molecular-weight translocation modulators (LTMs) in the cytosol of rat liver. This type of modulator must be distinguished from a low-molecular weight activation inhibitor (modulator) that inhibits activation of the unactivated receptor-steroid complex to the activated receptor-steroid complex. Endogenous LTMs may consist of several components including various nucleotides. Of the various nucleotides tested at physiological concentrations, only ATP could mimic the properties of the endogenous LTMs [it overcame the inhibitory activity of crude MTI(s)]. Although ATP alone had no detectable effect on binding of the activated receptor complex to nuclei in the absence of endogenous MTIs (MTI-I, -II, and -III) and ASTP, we found that pyrophosphate (PPi) enhanced the nuclear binding of the activated complex in the absence of MTIs. A high concentration of PPi or ATP plus PPi decreased the nuclear binding. These results suggest that the binding of PPi and PPi plus ATP to the activated receptor complex caused some allosteric change of the acceptor binding sites of the receptor, resulting in increase or decrease in its binding to nuclei, chromatin or DNA.

We conclude from our work that the process of translocation or

binding of the activated complex to nuclei, chromatin, and DNA
is regulated by endogenous macromolecular translocation and low
molecular weight translocation modulators as well as PPi, ATP
and other compounds, and that such factors may in part influence modulation of gene expression by modifying the functions
of the activated receptor-steroid complex.

References

1. Schrader, W.T., Birnbaumer, M.E., Hughes, M.R., Weigel,
    N.L.,Grody, W.W., O'Malley, B.W.: Recent Progr. Hormone Res.
    37, 583-633 (1981).

2. Baxter, J.D., Rousseau, G.G.: Glucocorticoid Hormone Action
    (Ed. by J.D. Baxter and G.G. Rousseau). Springer-Verlag,
    Berlin, Heidelberg, New York 1979, pp. 1-24.

3. Lan, N.C., Karin, M., Nguyen, T., Weisz, A., Birnbaum, M.J.,
    Eberhardt, N.L., Baxter, J.D.: J. Steroid Biochem. 20, 77-
    88 (1984).

4. Isohashi, F., Sakamoto, Y.: Igaku no Ayumi 129, 908 (1984).

5. Jensen, E.V., DeSombre, E.R.: Endocrinology (Ed. by L.J.
    DeGroot, G.F. Cahill Jr., W.D. Odell, L. Martini, J.T. Potts
    Jr., D.H. Nelson, E. Steinberger and A.I. Winegrad). Grune
    and Stratton, New York, Vol 3, 1979, pp. 2055-2061.

6. Beato, M., Kalimi, M., Feigelson, P.: Biochem. Biophys. Res.
    Commun. 47, 1464-1472 (1972).

7. Feigelson, P., Beato, M., Colman, P., Kalimi, M., Killewich,
    L.A., Schutz, G.: Recent progr. Hormone Res. 31, 213-242
    (1975).

8. Sakamoto, Y., Isohashi, F.: Information on Receptors in
    Higher Animals (Ed. by M. Suda and H. Nakagawa). An Extra
    Edition of Protein, Nucleic Acid and Enzyme, Kyoritsu
    Shuppan, Tokyo 1977, pp. 181-189.

9. Sakamoto, Y., Nakata, Y., Isohashi, F.: Vitamins 51, 477-
    486 (1977).

10. Liu, S.H., Webb, T.E.: Cancer Res. 37, 1763-1767 (1977).

11. Zawydiwski, R., Harmon, J.M., Thompson, E.B.: Cancer Res.
    43, 3865-3873 (1983).

12. Sibley, C.H., Yamamoto, K.R.: Monogr. Endocrinol. 12, 357-
    376 (1979).

13. Schmidt, T.J., Litwack, G.: Physiol. Rev. 64, 1132-1192
    (1982).

14. Chamness, G.C., Jennings, A.W., McGuire, W.L.: Biochemistry 13, 327-331 (1974).

15. Milgrom, E., Atger, M.: J. Steroid Biochem. 6, 487-492 (1975).

16. Atger, M., Milgrom, E.: J. Biol. Chem. 251, 4758-4762 (1976).

17. Atger, M., Milgrom, E.: Biochim. Biophys. Acta 539, 41-53 (1978).

18. Simons, S.S.Jr., Martinez, H.M., Garcea, R.L., Baxter, J.D., Tomkins, G.M.: J. Biol. Chem. 251, 334-343 (1976).

19. Simons, S.S.Jr.: Glucocorticoid Hormone Action (Ed. by J.D. Baxter and G.G. Rousseau). Springer-Verlag, Berlin, Heidelberg, New York 1979, pp.161-187.

20. Simons, S.S.Jr.: Biochim. Biophys. Acta 496, 339-348 (1977).

21. Izawa, M: Endocinol. Japon 26, 431-437 (1979).

22. Munck, A., Foley, R.: Nature 278, 752-754 (1979).

23. Marković, R.D., Litwack, G.: Arch Biochem. Biophys. 202, 374-379 (1980).

24. Taira, M., Terayama, H.: Biochim. Biophys. Acta 541, 45-58 (1978).

25. Horiuchi, M., Isohashi, F., Okamoto, K., Matsunaga, T., Terada, M., Mitsui, Y., Nakanishi, Y., Tsukanaka, K., Sakamoto, Y.: Proc. 41st Annual Meeting of the Japanese Cancer Association, Osaka, Abstr. 267 (1982).

26. Liang, T., Liao, S.: J. Biol. Chem. 249, 4671-4678 (1974).

27. Liao, S., Hiipakka, R. A., Judge, S.M: Biochemical and Biophysical Studies of Proteins and Nucleic Acids. (Ed. by Lo, Liu and Li) Elsevier Science Publishing Co., Inc. North-Holland, 1984, pp 123-135.

28. Liao, S., Smythe, S., Tymoczko, J.L., Rossini, G.P., Chen, C., Hiipakka, R.A.: J. Biol. Chem. 255, 5545-5551 (1980).

29. Chong, M.T., Lippman, M.E.: J. Biol. Chem. 257, 2996-3002 (1982).

30. Feldman, M., Kallos, J., Hollander, V. P.: J. Biol. Chem. 256, 1145-1148 (1981).

31. Tymoczko, J.L., Phillips, M.M.: Endocrinology 112, 142-149 (1983).

32. Fang, S., and Liao, S.: J. Biol. Chem. 246, 16-24 (1971).

33. Shyr, C.-I., Liao, S.: Proc. Natl. Acad. Sci. USA 75, 5969-5973 (1978).

34. Chen, C., Schilling, K., Hiipakka, R.A., Huang, I-Y., Liao, S.: J. Biol. Chem. 257, 116-121 (1982).

244

35. Liao, S., Chen, C., Huang, I-Y.: J. Biol. Chem. 257, 122-125 (1982).

36. Murayama, A., Fukai, F.: J. Biochem. 92, 2039-2042 (1982).

37. Murayama, A., Fukai, F.: J. Biochem. 94, 511-519 (1983).

38. Colvard, D.S., Wilson, E.M.: Endocrinology 109, 496-504 (1981).

39. Duogherty, J.J., Puri, R.K., Toft, D.O.: J. Biol. Chem. 259, 8004-8009 (1984).

40. Cake, M.H., Goidl, J.A., Parchman, L.G., Litwack, G.: Biochem. Biophys. Res. Commun. 71, 45-52 (1976).

41. Sekula, B.C., Schmidt, T.J., Litwack, G.: J. Steroid Biochem. 14, 161-166 (1981).

42. Litwack, G., Schmidt, T.J., Sekula, B.C., DiSorbo, D.M., Ohl, V.S., Barnett, C.A., Phelps, D.S.: J. Molecular and Cellular Cardiology 14, 59-64 (1982).

43. Isohashi, F., Terada, M., Tsukanaka, K., Nakanishi, Y., Sakamoto, Y.: J. Biochem. 88, 775-781 (1980).

44. Bailly, A., Sallas, N., Milgrom, E.: J. Biol Chem. 252, 858-863 (1977).

45. Goidl, J.A., Cake, M.H., Dolan, K.P., Parchman, L.G., Litwack, G.: Biochemistry 16, 2125-2130 (1977).

46. Sato, B., Noma, K., Nishizawa, Y., Nakato, K., Matsumoto, K., Yamamura, Y.: Endocrinology 106, 1142-1148 (1980).

47. Leach, K.L., Grippo, J.F., Housley, P.R., Dahmer, M.K., Salive, M.E., Pratt, W.B.: J. Biol. Chem. 257, 381-388 (1982).

48. Munck, A., Brinck-Johnson, T.: J. Biol. Chem. 243, 5556-5565 (1968).

49. Ishii, D.N., Pratt, W.B., Aronow, L.: Biochemistry 11, 3896-3904 (1972).

50. Ishii, D.N., Aronow, L.: J. Steroid Biochem. 4, 593-603 (1973).

51. Nielsen, C.J., Sando, J.J., Pratt, W.B.: Proc. Natl. Acad. Sci. USA. 74, 1398-1402 (1977).

52. Nielsen, C.J., Sando, J.J., Vogel, W.M., Pratt, W.B.: J. Biol. Chem. 252, 7568-7578 (1977).

53. Sando, J.J., La Forest, A.C., Pratt, W.B.: J. Biol. Chem. 254, 4772-4778 (1979).

54. Sando, J.J, Hammond, N.D., Stratford, C.A., Pratt, W.B.: J. Biol. Chem. 254, 4779-4789 (1979).

55. Andreasen, P.A.: Biochim. Biophys. Acta 676, 205-212 (1981).

56. Moudgil, U.K., John, J.K.: Biochem. J. 190, 799-808 (1980).

57. Moudgil, V.K., Toft, D.O.: Proc. Natl. Acad. Sci. USA. 72, 901-905 (1975).

58. Moudgil, V.K., Toft, D.O.: Biochim. Biophys. Acta 490, 477-488 (1977).

59. Moudgil, V.K., John, J.K.: Biochem. J. 190, 809-818 (1980).

60. Miller, J.B., Toft, D.O.: Biochemistry 17, 173-177 (1978).

61. Moudgil, V.K., Toft, D.O.: Proc. Natl. Acad. Sci. USA 73, 3443-3447 (1976).

62. Litwack, G., Cake, M.H.: Federation Proc. 36, 911a (1977).

63. Cake, M.H., DiSorbo, D.M., Litwack, G.: J. Biol. Chem. 253, 4886-4891 (1978).

64. Müller, R.E., Traish, A., Wotiz, H.H.: J. Biol. Chem. 255, 4062-4067 (1980).

65. Muldoon, T.G., Cidlowski, J.A.: J. Biol. Chem. 255, 3100-3107 (1980).

66. Nishigori, H., Moudgil, V.K., Toft, D.: Biochem. Biophys. Res. Commun. 80, 112-118 (1978).

67. Hiipakka, R.A., Liao, S.: J. Steroid Biochem. 13, 841-846 (1980).

68. Sekula, B.C., Schmidt, T.J., Oxenham, E.A., DiSorbo, D.M., Litwack, G.: Biochemistry 21, 2915-2922 (1982).

69. Lohmar, P.H., Toft, D.O.: Biochem. Biophys. Res. Commun. 67, 8-15 (1975).

70. Toft, D., Lohmar, P., Miller, J., Moudgil, V.: J. Steroid Biochem. 7, 1053-1059 (1976).

71. Schmidt, T.J., Bollum, F.J., Litwack, G.: Proc. Natl. Acad. Sci. USA 79, 4555-4559 (1982).

72. Schmidt, T.J., Sekula, B.C., Litwack, G.: Endocrinology 109, 803-812 (1981).

73. Moudgil, V.K., Weekes, G.A.:FEBS Lett. 94, 324-326 (1978).

74. Moudgil, V.K., Eessalu, T.E.: Life Sci. 27, 1159-1167 (1980).

75. Moudgil, V.K., Eessalu, T.E.: Biochim. Biophys. Acta 627, 301-312 (1980).

76. Moudgil, V.K., Caradonna, V.M.: J. Steroid. Biochem. 17, 585-589 (1982).

77. Murakami, N., Moudgil, V.K.: Biochem. J. 198, 447-455 (1981).

78. Murakami, N., Moudgil, V. K.: Biochim. Biophys. Acta 676, 386-394 (1981).

79. Murakami, N., Quattrociocchi, T.M., Healy, S.P., Moudgil, V.K: Arch. Biochem. Biophys. 214, 326-334 (1982).

246

80. Isohashi, F., Terada, M., Nakanishi, Y., Sakamoto, Y.:
    Cancer Res. 36, 4382-4386 (1976).

81. Isohashi, F., Tsukanaka, K., Terada, M., Nakanishi, Y.,
    Tani, S., Sakamoto. Y.: Cancer Res. 38, 4243-4245 (1978).

82. Isohashi, F., Tsukanaka, K., Terada, M., Nakanishi, Y.,
    Fukushima, H., Sakamoto, Y.: Gann 70, 573-574 (1979).

83. Isohashi, F., Tsukanaka, K., Terada, M., Nakanishi, Y.,
    Fukushima, H., Sakamoto, Y.: Cancer Res. 39, 5132-5135
    (1979).

84. Isohashi, F., Tsukanaka, K., Terada, M., Nakanishi, Y.,
    Tani, S., Sakamoto, Y.: Cancer Res. 40, 877-881 (1980).

85. Tsukanaka, K., Isohashi, F., Sakamoto, Y.: Gann 72, 754-761
    (1981).

86. Horiuchi, M., Isohashi, F., Terada, M., Okamoto, K.,
    Sakamoto, Y.: Biochem. Biophys. Res. Commun. 98, 88-94
    (1981).

87. Okamoto, K., Isohashi, F., Horiuchi, M., Sakamoto, Y.:
    Biochem. Biophys. Res. Commun. 108, 1655-1660 (1982).

88. Horiuchi, M., Isohashi, F., Okamoto, K., Matsunaga, T.,
    Terada, M., Mitsui, Y., Sakamoto, Y.: Biochem. Biophys. Res.
    Commun. 105, 146-151 (1982).

89. Okamoto, K., Isohashi, F., Tsukanaka, K., Horiuchi, M.,
    Sakamoto, Y.: Endocrinology 112, 336-340 (1983).

90. Isohashi, F., Horiuchi, M., Okamoto, K., Sakamoto, Y.: J.
    Steroid Biochem. 20, 1117-1122 (1984).

91. Okamoto, K., Isohashi, F., Horiuchi, M., Sakamoto, Y.:
    Biochem. Biophys. Res. Commun. 121, 940-945 (1984).

92. Horiuchi, M., Isohashi, F., Okamoto, K., Sakamoto, Y.: J.
    Biochem. 96, 727-737 (1984).

93. Isohashi, F., Terada, M., Sakamoto, Y.: Seikagaku 52, 1009-
    1010 (1980).

94. Okamoto, K., Isohashi, F., Horiuchi, M., Sakamoto, Y.:
    Unpublished results.

95. Hutchens, T.W., Markland, F.S., Hawkins, E.F.: Biochem.
    Biophys. Res. Commun. 105, 20-27 (1982).

96. Irie, M., Yabuta, A., Kimura, K., Shindo, Y., Tomita, K.:
    J. Biochem. 67, 47-58 (1970).

97. Holbrook, N.J., Bodwell, J.E., Munck, A.: J. Biol. Chem.
    258, 14885-14894 (1983).

98. Toft, D., Moudgil, V., Lohmar, P., Miller, J.: Ann. N. Y.
    Acad. Sci. 286, 29-42 (1977).

99. John, J.K., Moudgil, V.K.: Biochem. Biophys. Res. Commun.
    90, 1242-1248 (1979).

100. Moudgil, V.K., John, J.K.: Biochem. J. 190, 799-808 (1980).

101. Moudgil, V.K., Eessalu, T.E.: FEBS Lett. 122, 189-192 (1980).

102. Moudgil, V.K., Kruczak, V., Eessalu, T., Paulose, C.S., Taylor, M., Hansen, J.: Eur. J. Biochem. 118, 547-555 (1981).

103. DiSorbo, D.M., Phelps, D.S., Litwack, G.: Endocrinology 106, 922-929 (1980).

104. Geisse, S., Scheidereit, C., Westphal, H.M., Hynes, N.E., Groner, B., Beato, M.: EMBO J. 1, 1613-1619 (1982).

105. Chandler, V.L., Maler, B.A., Yamamoto, K.R.: Cell 33, 489-499 (1983).

106. Scheidereit, C., Geisse, S., Westphal, H.M., Beato, M.: Nature 304, 749-752 (1983).

THE IMPORTANT ROLE OF CYTOPLASMIC MODULATORS IN THE PATHWAY FOR
STEROID RECEPTOR TO BE CONVERTED TO THE BIOLOGICALLY ACTIVE
FORM.

Bunzo Sato, Yasuko Nishizawa, Keizo Noma, Makoto Nakao,
Susumu Kishimoto

The Third Department of Internal Medicine, Osaka University
Hospital, Fukushima-ku, Osaka 553, Japan.

Keishi Matsumoto

The Second Department of Pathology, College of Medicine, Osaka
University, Kita-ku, Osaka 530, Japan.

Introduction

The intracellular transmission mechanism of some special signals to affect cellular functions has been the subject to be
most extensively studied in the cell biology. The ability of
cells to receive the extracellular signal would be primarily
dependent upon the presence of the special molecule interacting
with extracellular stimulants in a highly specific manner.
This specific molecule, so-called receptor, might be located on
plasma membrane or in intracellular compartments. Many peptide
hormones as well as amines have been well recognized to be associated with membrane receptors. Although these membrane receptor systems have been proved to be very attractive for elucidation of intramembraneous transduction mechanisms (1, 2),
the pathway for peptide hormones to affect gene activation after binding to receptor has been largely unknown. This is probably due to the lack of the sufficient information on intracellular machines to transmit from the membrane receptor to the
specific gene. On the other hand, the intracellular receptor
for hormonal steroids has been reported to translocate from the
cytoplasm into nuclei upon the binding to agonists and to act

as a direct gene stimulator (3, 4). Since the sophysticated
technology to identify the steroid receptor has been introduced
(5), this apparently simple system has been expected to provide
us with the impotant clue for elucidation of gene activation
mechanism in eukaryocyte. At the present moment, however, the
pathway for hormonal steroids to stimulate the specific gene
remains to be obscure. One of crucial but unresolved issues in
resolution of the mechanism of hormonal steroid is the structure of the receptor molecule. In addition, the alterations in
the size and shape of receptor molecules have been observed to
occur in the different environmental as well as hormonal conditions. Although experimental specifications may be altered to
produce a wide variety of receptor forms, their physiological
relevance may be inferred from the reported results showing a
marked alteration in physicochemical properties of the receptor
molecule upon its association with steroids (6, 7). It is of
considerable interest to speculate that the critical steps in
steroid hormone action mechanism, such as the binding of the
receptor to hormone, acquisition of increased affinity toward
nuclei or DNA (defined as "activation") and association with
the specific gene or its neighbouring site, is processed by alteration in the physicochemical characteristics of the receptor
molecules. The molecular basis for these alterations may involve either a conformational change or aggregation-deaggrega-
tion process. In this context, a number of recent studies have
suggested the existence of modulators affecting the structure
and function of steroid receptors in the target cell (7, 8, 9).
A pioneer study reported by Munck et al. indicated the involvement of energy-dependent process in maintenance of steroid
binding ability of glucocorticoid receptor (GR) (10). Thereafter, the modulator regulating receptor activation process has
been documented (7-11). In view of the cumulative evidence,
it seems to be reasonable to reconsider the molecular mechanism
of steroid hormone action on the hypothesis that the critical
steps in the pathway for receptor molecule reaching the specific site on chromatin are finely regulated by various kinds of

modulators. In this review article, we would like to try to
summarize experimental results reported from many laboratories
in an effort to emphasize the important role of these modulators for regulation of steroid receptor functions.

[1] Modulators Regulating Receptor-Ligand Interaction.

Steroid receptor has been defined as a proteinous molecule
which can bind to steroid with a high affinity in a specific
manner (12). These characteristic features were questioned by
the observation that an exposure of the rat uteri to the high
concentration of testosterone causes the nuclear translocation
of "estrogen receptor" (ER) with a resultant synthesis of the
so-called estrogen-induced protein (13). The possible cross-
reactivity of dexamethasone for the type 1 site (mineralocorticoid receptor) has also been reported (14). This ambiguity of
hormone specificity of steroid receptors would suggest that one
receptor is able to be associated with various kinds of hormonal steroids with the different affinity. Moreover, the affinity of the receptor toward ligands has been observed to be modulated by the cytoplasmic factor (15). On the basis of these
data, it is possible that hormone reactivity can be altered
quatitatively or qualitatively by the cytoplasmic modulator
which exerts its effects through changes in hormone specificity
and affinity toward ligands of receptor. The importance of the
affinity of the receptor in relation to hormone actions has recently been re-evaluated by the finding that a relatively small
decrease in the affinity produces glucocorticoid resistance in
man (16). A rapid fluctuation of the binding capacity of the
receptor without definite alteration in its affinity has also
published in the intact cell as well as cell-free conditions
(10, 17). In order to examine this fluctuation, we might consider two different processes: one is acquisition of the binding ability; another is stabilization of the receptor-ligand
complexes. In addition, its rapidity and reproducible affir-

mation under the cell-free condition would suggest the existence of the modulators affecting these processes. In the following part of this section, we will discuss these modulators
on the basis of our recent findings.

1)   The modulator altering the affinity of the receptor toward
     ligands.

The interesting observation that a removal of the dialyzable
compounds from the cytosol resulted in the increased affinity
of Progesterone receptor (PgR) toward the ligand promoted us to
study the estrogen binding system in mouse Leydig cell tumor
lines, since our initial study proved to be the presence of the
exceedingly low-affinity estrogen binder in estrogen-independent tumor lines using the conventional receptor assay condition (18). In the process of performing the studies on the
assay conditions, a removal of the dialyzable compounds from
the cytosol has been found to exert remarkable effects on the
estrogen binder with an apparent appearance of putative ER.
This conclusion was drawn from the following observations: i)
the affinity (Kd) for estradiol (E_2) was altered from ~10^{-7} M
to ~10^{-9} M; ii) diethylstilbestrol (DES), synthetic estrogen,
became an effective competitor in E_2-binder interaction upon a
dialysis of the cytosol, while the appreciable effect of DES on
the binding of E_2 to the whole cytosol was not detected; iii)
E_2-binding component in the dialyzed cytosol sedimented at 7-8
S in the low salt sucrose density gradient, patterns similar to
those for putative ER; iv) E_2-binding component in the dialyzed
cytosol was able to translocate into nuclei under the cell-free
condition (19). These observations would suggest the presence
of the dialyzable compound(s) which could regulate the steroid
specificity, the affinity and the nuclear binding ability of
E_2 binding component. The important role of the small molecular component was confirmed by the experiments involving the
gel-filtration and ultrafiltration techniques (20). In these
experiments, transformed Leydig cells were used. Therefore,

one might ask whether or not these unique estrogen binding systems are limited to the transformed cell. Turning to nontransformed testicular cells, ER has been identified in the whole cytosol from interstitial tissue of rats, using the conventional receptor assay procedures (21). With the development of cell separation techniques for testicular cells, it became possible to demonstrate that ER is present in Leydig cell (22, 23). These results would suggest that the modulator as descrived above is lacking in Leydig cell of rats. On the other hand, the relative low-affinity (Kd 5 x 10^{-9} M) E_2 binder has been identified in mouse cryptorchid testes, although its binding to [^{3}H] E_2 was effectively suppressed by unlabeled DES (24). The affinity toward E_2 of this binder, which might be definitely located in Leydig cell (25), was increased to ~5 x 10^{-10} M in response to a brief dialysis of the cytosol (24). Combined with these data, it can be reasonably concluded that the modulator regulating the affinity of ER toward estrogens is present in transformed as well as nontransformed mouse Leydig cell. The difference between transformed and nontransformed Leydig cell may be quantitative but not qualitative. The molecular mechanism of this modulator to lower the affinity of ER remains currently unknown mainly because of no available data concerning the molecular nature of this modulator. To gain some insight into this point, the effects of chaotropic salts on estrogen binding system in transformed Leydig cells were examined (20). These salts have been introduced in the area of steroid receptor research to prevent the aggregation of receptor molecule (26). Immediately after their introduction, these salts, particularly NaSCN, have been observed to lower the affinity of ER toward estrogen, leading a successful application of this salt for ER exchange assay at the low temperature (27). As opposed to this finding, an exposure of the cytosol from mouse Leydig cell tumors to NaSCN resulted in a marked increase in the affinity toward E_2 as well as DES (Kd 10^{-9} M) in a manner analogous to dialysis effects. Interestingly, this treatment with NaSCN caused an appearance of 2.8 S, but not 4 S, E_2 bind-

ing component in NaSCN (0.4 M) sucrose density gradient without concomitant acquisition of nuclear binding ability (20).
These were in contrast with those observed in dialysis experiments. However, dialysis of this tumor cytosol once exposed to
NaSCN could produce E_2 binding component indistinguishable from
putative ER. From these observations, we would speculate these
processes in such a way that NaSCN can facilitate the dissociation of the modulator from 2.8 S estrogen binding component,
resulting in its increased affinity toward estrogens. In order
to form ER-like molecule with nuclear binding ability, however,
the additional reaction of this "2.8 S" molecule to be associated with the other cytoplasmic component might be required.
This conversion of "2.8 S" component to ER-like molecule could
be inhibited by NaSCN, probably due to its fundamental nature
to disrupt the hydrophobic-hydrophobic interaction. The question might be raised whether or not there is the similar steroid binding systems in the other type of cells. To our knowledge, however, steroid binding systems analogous to those presented in estrogen-independent mouse Leydig cell tumor have not
been reported. An exposure of male rat liver cytosol to NaSCN
was observed to increase in the affinity of estrogen binder toward E_2 (28). However, any attempt to confer nuclear binding
ability on this estrogen binding component has been unsuccessful. Although the control mechanism of hormone responsiveness
by the cytoplasmic modulator lowering the affinity is quite interesting in understanding the structure and function of steroid receptor, this regulatory mechanism seems to be not universal but unique in our Leydig cell systems.

2)   Sulfhydryl bond-dependent reappearance of steroid binding
     ability of the receptor.

The extreme lability of the hormone binding ability of steroid
receptors has been well recognized. Many attempts have been
done in an effort to confer this ability to once destabilized
receptors. In this relation, two reagents, ATP and dithio-

threitol (DTT), have been successfully employed in glucocorticoid receptor (GR) systems (29, 30). Recently, the possible
role of phosphorylation-dephosphorylation reaction in the regulation of estrogen binding ability has been proposed also in ER
systems (31, 32). These interesting subjects will be fully
discussed elsewhere in this book. We would like to emphasize
only the fact that the binding capacity of the receptor, one of
the most important determinants for hormone responsiveness in
the target cell, is markedly influenced by the environmental
factors. Indeed, the addition of the sufficient amount of DTT
to cytosols from thymus or spleen resulted in more than 5-fold
increase in glucocorticoid binding capacity over that in cytosols lacking DTT (33).

3) Stabilization of the receptor by the cytoplasmic factor.

An exposure of cytosols containing unoccupied steroid receptors
to 30-37°C has been known to result in a rapid loss of their
steroid binding ability. The definite stabilization has been
observed upon its binding to agonists. Although the molecular
basis on this stabilization still remains unsettled, the important clue has been obtained from the experiments involving a
dialysis or gel filtration. In androgen receptor (AR) system,
a gel filtration of the rat prostate cytosol in the absence of
androgen has been reported to cause a loss of its hormone binding ability (34). A similar result has been observed in our
laboratory which shows that a dialysis of the rat liver cytosol
in the absence of glucocorticoid markedly destabilize the binding ability of GR (11). This dialysis-induced destabilization
of unoccupied GR was not able to be protected by the addition
of SH-reducing agent, suggesting that this destabilization
process is differently regulated from that for SH-dependent acquisition of hormone binding activity. This idea might be supported by the data that destabilized GR induced by a dialysis
does not revert to the steroid binding form. On the basis of
the experimental results cited above, we inferred that dialyza-

ble compounds in target cell cytosols are essential for the
molecular events that stabilize the receptor. This dialysis-
induced destabilization was receptor found to be able to be
protected by Na_2MoO_4 or its related oxyanions (35, 36). This
information in turn led us to study the mechanism of the dialyzable compounds and molybdate to stabilyze GR (36). The addition of molybdate to the rat liver cytosol previously gel-
filtered through a small sephadex G-50 column showed only partial stabilization effect. Inclusion of dialyzable compounds
obtained from the rat liver cytosol into this gel-filtered
cytosol was found to potentiate the stabilizing effect of molybdate. From these observations, we inferred that molybdate
produce its stabilizing effect through enhanced interaction of
receptor with dialyzable compounds, whose molecular nature remains entirely unknown. Another possibility is that dialysis
or gel filtration removes some protease inhibitor from the
cytosol, resulting in activation of proteases and proteolytic
degradation of hormone binding site of GR. However, the latter
possibility seems to be unlikely since partially purified GR,
which is separated from many proteases, can be stabilized moderately but definitely by molybdate (33). Despite these reservations, it is quite possible that steroid hormones act in
conjunction with dialyzable compounds to stabilize the hormone
binding ability of receptor.

[II]   How is Receptor Activation regulated by Environmental
       Factors?

The most important transformation of receptor molecule in the
pathway for steroid hormone to stimulate the specific gene resides in its activation process. In spite of considerable efforts, much uncertainty surrounds the molecular events by which
a receptor acquires high affinity for nuclei or DNA. The fundamental question concerning the kinetics of receptor activation still remains to be contraversial (37, 38). According to

original two-step theory proposed by Jensen, a 4 S to 5 S conversion of ER, when analyzed in high salt sucrose density gradient, was reported to be obligatory in receptor activation process (3). Thereafter, ER systems which can be activated without this conversion was found in various target tissues (18, 39), suggesting that this event is not essential for ER activation. Diverse proposed mechanisms of receptor activation seem to reflect the complicated situation. The majority of studies on receptor activation have employed various cell-free assay conditions. These nonphysiological assay methods may have contributed to the discrepancies among the molecular mechanisms proposed. With these problems in mind, an effort for establishment of the method which minimizes the artifactual results seems to be extremely important. In this section, we have attempted to summarize the methodological problems and to review the available data with reference to an important role of the so-called low molecular weight inhibitor for receptor activation. Some comments on the relevance of activation to receptor stabilization also will be provided.

1) Basic assay conditions for receptor activation.

The receptor properties have been expected to be influenced by the buffer compositions used for preparation of the cytosol. Using the rat uterine ER system as a model, we examined the effects of the buffer compositions on the receptor activation. As shown in Fig. 1, KCl concentrations in TM buffer (0.01 M Tris, 2 mM mercaptoethanol, pH 7.4) has been found to affect dialysis- or temperature-induced activation. Dialysis of the uterine cytosol containing [^{3}H] E_2-ER complexes against 0.03-0.1 M KCl for 3 hr resulted in a marked suppression of ER activation when compared with the data obtained by a dialysis against TM buffer (no KCl). This result seems to be in contrast with the well-known reported finding that an exposure to the high concentration of KCl facilitates ER activation (40). However, a prolonged dialysis (24 hr) reduced the inhibitory

258

activity of 0.03-0.1 M KCl against ER activation, reaching to the level seen in samples dialyzed against TM buffer. Moreover, temperature-induced ER activation was apparently suppressed by KCl. The molecular basis of KCl-induced inhibition of ER activation will be discussed in the following sections.

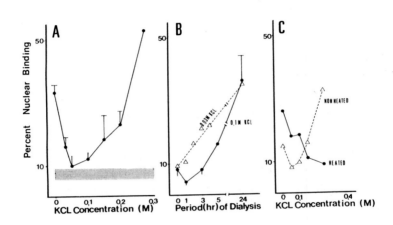

Fig. 1   Effects of KCl on ER activation.

The uterine cytosol was incubated with 4 nM [^{3}H] E_2 at 0°C for 1 hr and treated as indicated below. The aliquots (0.4 ml) of treated cytosols were incubated with the sufficient amount of nuclei at 0°C for 1 hr to measure the amount of nuclear binding of complexes. The nonspecific binding was corrected by the samples which were incubated with [^{3}H] E_2 in the presence of 100 fold excess of unlabeled E_2.

A.   The cytosol was dialyzed at 0-4°C for 3 hr against TM buffer containing various concentration of KCl. The dotted area showed the level of the nuclear binding ability of nondialyzed samples.

B.   The cytosol was dialyzed at 0-4°C for various periods of time against TM buffer containing 0.03 M (Δ----Δ) or 0.1 M KCl (●————●).

C.   The cytosol containing various concentrations of KCl was heated at 25°C (●————●) or kept at 0°C (Δ----Δ) for 30 min.

Nevertheless, these KCl effects on ER activation should be seriously taken into consideration since the cytosol prepared in 4 volumes of the buffer theoretically contains 0.03-0.05 M KCl. Next, the effects of various buffers (10 mM, pH 7.4) on ER activation were examined (Table 1). [³H] E_2-ER complexes in Tris (Tris(hydroxymethyl) aminomethane), the most commonly used buffer, did respond very well to activation procedures. The interesting results came from the experiments using Bis-Tris (2,2-Bis(hydroxymethyl)-2,2',2"-nitrilotriethanol) buffer. The conventional activation procedures, such as heating or dialysis, were not able to increase in the nuclear binding ability of [³H] E_2-ER complexes in Bis-Tris buffer without detectable effects on ligand binding ability. The relatively high nuclear binding of untreated complexes in Bis-Tris buffer does not support an idea that this buffer system destroys their nuclear binding site. Although clarification of the molecular mechanism explaining this difference will require further investigation, Tris buffer seems to be the suitable buffer system.

Table 1   Effects of buffers on ER activation

Buffer used (10 mM)	Percent nuclear binding		
	Heated	Dialyzed	nontreated
Bis-Tris	13.3 ± 0.6 [a]	15.4 ± 1.7	15.6 ± 0.4
Tris	23.7 ± 2.1	35.2 ± 2.5	8.2 ± 2.7
Phosphate	25.7 ± 10.4	19.2 ± 5.5	7.8 ± 2.8
Hepes	19.3 ± 0.6	26.6 ± 3.2	16.3 ± 1.1
Pipes	21.4 ± 6.6	19.1 ± 4.3	8.4 ± 0.8

The uterine cytosol was prepared in 4 volumes of indicated buffers at pH of 7.4, followed by complexing with 4 nM [³H] E_2 in the presence or the absence of 100 fold excess of unlabeled E_2 at 0°C for 1 hr. These complexes were heated at 25°C for 30 min or dialyzed against corresponding buffers for 3 hr at 0-4°C, and then subjected to measurement of their nuclear binding ability as described in the legend of Fig. 1.
    (a) mean ± S.E. obtained by three separate experiments.

2)   The important role of the low molecular weight inhibitor
     in receptor activation process.

As mentioned above, there are various procedures for receptor
to be activated. In the course of studies on ER systems in
mouse Leydig cell tumors, we realized that a dialysis is quite
suitable for investigation of receptor activation, since this
procedure is able to effectively activate ER even at low temperatures (0-4°C) which are expected to maintain various enzymes at the low activity state (41). These results prompted
us to investigate the hypothesis that the association of the
dialyzable compound (namely, low molecular weight inhibitor)
locks steroid receptor in the nonactivated form and its dissociation eventually evolves the receptor into the activated form.
In pursuing this possibility, we were confronted by various
difficulties such as purification of steroid receptor as the
nonactivated form. Knowing the importance of the dialyzable
compounds, we first examined the effect of the small molecules
on temperature-induced receptor activation. In the series of
these experiments, the rat liver cytosol was used to prepare
the dialysate or the ultrafiltrate through UM05 membrane, due
to its relatively high inhibitory activity. The addition of
the dialysate to uterine cytosols containing [^{3}H] E_2-ER complexes was found to require the higher temperatures for complexes to be activated (11), suggesting the possible involvement of the dialyzable compounds in temperature-induced ER activation. Conversely, activation was induced more easily by
heating at relatively low temperatures, when the concentration
of the small molecule (low molecular weight inhibitor) was decreased by a dialysis. Before going into further discussion on
the activation mechanism, the question arose as to whether or
not KCl itself is the low molecular weight inhibitor in view of
the data presented in Fig. 1. As shown in Fig. 2, the ultrafiltrate containing substances with the molecular weight of
less than 500 completely inhibited ER activation during 24 hr-
dialysis. This is in quite contrast with the results obtained

by a dialysis against 0.03-0.1 M KCl, in which delayed but definite activation of [^{3}H] E$_2$-ER complexes was observed. In addition to its prolonged activity, the low molecular weight inhibitor was found to be quite stable in both acidic and basic
conditions. Upon a re-dialysis of complexes pretreated with
the low molecular weight inhibitor against TM buffer, these
complexes were observed to become activated, excluding the

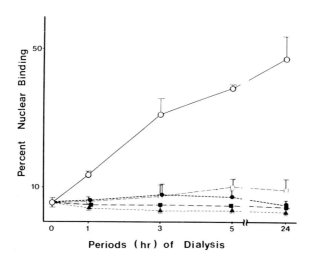

Fig. 2   Effect of UM 05 ultrafiltrate on ER activation

The rat liver cytosol prepared in 2 volumes of TM buffer was
ultrafiltrated through UM 05 membrane. This ultrafiltrate
was heated at 100°C for 30 min in 0.67 M NaOH or HCl. After
treated, pH of these ultrafiltrates was adjusted to 7.4.
The uterine cytosol containing [^{3}H] E$_2$-ER complexes was
dialyzed against these ultrafiltrates for the indicated periods of time, and then their nuclear binding ability was
measured as described in the legend of Fig. 1.

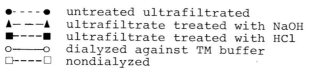

untreated ultrafiltrated
ultrafiltrate treated with NaOH
ultrafiltrate treated with HCl
dialyzed against TM buffer
nondialyzed

possibility that the low molecular weight inhibitor irreversibly destroys their nuclear binding site.

Although a removal of the low molecular weight inhibitor accelerated the activation of [^{3}H] E_2-ER complexes in the whole cytosol, it might be also possible that the low molecular weight inhibitor "indirectly" regulates ER activation. In this relation, purification of the steroid receptor as a nonactivated form seems to be quite desirable. For the sake of this purpose, Na_2MoO_4 was empolyed. Shortly after the discovery of molybdate effects on stabilization of ligand binding ability, several groups, including ours, observed that this anion is able to inhibit receptor activation and to maintain the receptor as a nonactivated form (36, 42, 43). In view of the alteration in the structure and function of the receptor molecule upon steroid binding as described above, the partially purified "unoccupied" form of the receptor was also required in order to investigate the molecular mechanism of the interaction of the low molecular weight inhibitor with the receptor molecule. Therefore, uterine ER of rats was attempted to be partially purified as a nonactivated as well as unoccupied form with a combination of DEAE cellulose chromatography, hyroxyl appatite chromatography and $(NH_4)_2SO_4$ fractionation in the presence of Na_2MoO_4 (44). These procedures gave us 20-fold purified unoccupied ER which was considered to be at the nonactivated state, judged by its nuclear binding ability and its rapid dissociation rate of E_2 from ER (45). After complexing with [^{3}H] E_2, these complexes were found to be readily activated by a removal of molybdate or heating at 25°C. This activation was markedly suppressed by the addition of the low molecular weight inhibitor partially purified by the methods as published before (44). With the reservation that the additional factors regulating ER activation were co-purified into the fractions containing ER, it seems to be highly possible that the low molecular weight inhibitor is able to directly control ER activation.

Some attempt has been invested in the application to GR and AR systems of concepts obtained in the studies on the mechanism of

ER activation. Several procedures have been known to activate
ER as well as GR and AR. These include an exposure to a relatively high temperature or to high concentrations of KCl.
These similarities would suggest that the common mechanism may
be involved in activation step(s) for all steroid receptors.
Recent observations on dilaysis-induced activation of GR and AR
which is inhibited by molybdate (36) would support the concept
as indicated above, although these data were obtained by using
the ligand-receptor complexes, but not unoccupied form (see below).

3) Is the hormone essentially required for receptor activation

The formation of agonist-receptor complexes has been believed
to be a prerequisite for steroid receptors to be activated,
since so-called two-step theory was proposed by Jensen (3).
However, some experiments casted some doubts against this central dogma. These include: the estrogen-independent stimulation of RNA polymerase by partially purified and unoccupied ER
under the cell-free conditions (46): a conversion of unoccupied
PgR into the activated form upon $(NH_4)_2SO_4$ fractionation (47).
Analyses of ER systems in human cultured breast cancer cell
line (MCF-7) gave us the additional data which showed that the
mechanism of steroid receptor activation is not necessarily
amenable to the original proposal (48). In the process of performing the studies on ER activation mechanism, we found that
the presence of estrogen is not essential for ER activation (7).
A brief dialysis of the uterine cytosol obtained from ovariectomized rats caused a conversion of the nonactivated ER into
unoccupied nuclear ER under the cell-free condition. In conjunction with the data cited in the previous section, we inferred that the low molecular weight inhibitor can be dissociated from ER even in the absence of estrogen. The biological
activity of this unoccupied nuclear ER should be seriously addressed. If this has some activity in elucidation of estrogen-
dependent biological responses, it can be concluded the hormone

actions are expressed without any aid of estrogenic compounds.
Two possible approaches to the investigation on this interesting possibility are; (i) stimulation of estrogen-specific genes
by unoccupied nuclear ER under the cell-free condition, and
(ii) identification of cells containing only unoccupied nuclear
ER without cytoplasmic ER. Despite significant methodological
progress on receptor-genome interaction (49, 50), the sophisticated and reliable method is not yet available in order to investigate the former possibility. Therefore, we have tried to
identify estrogen target cells where ER is exclusively located
in the nuclei even in the absence of estrogenic stimuli. One
of mouse Leydig cell tumor lines (T-124958) was found to contain the unoccupied nuclear ER without putative cytosolic ER.
This conclusion came from the careful experiments employing the
cell-free and the intact cell conditions (51). Using this cell,
estrogen effects on unoccupied nuclear ER were examined in relation to cell proliferation. Estrogenization of host mice
resulted in the significant enhancement of tumor growth in vivo.
This enhanced tumor growth could not be antagonized by simultaneous administration of ergocriptin, suggesting that this
tumor growth is affected by the direct estrogenic stimuli into
the tumor cell, but not mediated through pituitary hormones
such as prolactin. This consideration was supported by our recent observation that E_2 stimulates cell proliferation in the
culture condition in vitro (52). What emerges from these experiments is that the presence of unoccupied nuclear ER is not
enough for eliciting hormonal responses and the binding of estrogenic compounds to the nuclear ER is obligatory for triggering estrogen-dependent events. Although these findings re-
emphasized the important role of hormones, the additional step
in the process of estrogen action, namely a conversion from the
activated ER into the biologically active ER should be taken
into consideration. The conversion of ER from the nonactivated
form to the activated form is mainly regulated by the low molecular weight inhibitor. In order to promote this process,
estrogenic compounds play some role but is not essential. How-

ever, the additional conversion to the biologically active form is achieved only by complexing with estrogen. The molecular alteration in ER elicited by the association of estrogens with unoccupied nuclear ER is entirely unknown. This is partly due to resistance of this nuclear ER to various extraction procedures (51). Nevertheless, the specific molecular configulation of ER, the formation of which is achieved in the presence of estrogenic compounds, is needed to stimulate estrogen-dependent genes.

In order to obtain some clue for estrogen-dependent alteration in ER configulation, a brief survey of functional and structual analyses for activated ER would be valuable. Two distinct molecular events have been reported to be elicited in $[^3H]$ E_2-ER complexes by activation procedures: a conversion from a 4 S to 5 S form when analyzed in hypertonic (0.4 M KCl) sucrose density gradient (3): a shift from a fast dissociating to a slow dissociating state by measuring $[^3H]$ E_2-ER dissociation kinetics (45). The lack of a 4 S to 5 S conversion in dialysis-induced activated but unoccupied ER (7), which would be still biologically inactive, might suggest that this type of ER aggregation plays the important role in elucidation of ER-mediated biological responses. However, this concept seems to be not consistent with the finding that some target cells respond well to estrogenic stimuli without a 4 S to 5 S conversion of ER (18). A similar degree of uncertainty has also resided in the dissociation rate kinetic studies. Using weak estrogens and estrogen antagonists which were found to fail to produce a slow-dissociation state of ER (53), this shift to a high-affinity state has been proposed to reflect the conversion of ER into the biologically active form. Although this hypothesis is quite attractive, the well-known evidence has doubted its certainty that antiestrogen such as tamoxifen elicites definite estrogen responses especially at the early phase of treatment (54). In addition to these reported results, our recent observation has shown that agonistic and antagonistic responses produced by estrogenic compounds are not necessarily corelated

with the affinity state of ER (55). In view of these ambigui-
ties, the molecular structure of the biologically active ER remained entirely unknown.

Turning to the issue on the hormonal requirement for GR and AR
activation, their instability especially upon a removal of the
dialyzable compounds from the cytosol confronted us with difficulties in detailed studies on GR and AR activation. After a
brief dialysis of the rat liver cytosol in the absence of
glucocorticoid followed by complexing GR with [^{3}H] dexamethasone, the enhanced affinity of these complexes toward nuclei
was observed, suggesting the possibility that the dissociation
of the low molecular weight inhibitor from GR might occur even
in the absence of glucocorticoid (11). A simultaneous addition
of molybdate with [^{3}H] dexamethasone in the predialyzed cytosol
was found to effectively prevent GR activation (33). These results showed that GR activation can be facilitated by diminishing the concentration of the dialyzable compounds in the cytosol but complex formation with glucocorticoid is a prerequisite
for GR activation. These seem to be in conflict with those obtained from ER systems. This difference may be related to the
lack of reports showing the presence of unoccupied GR. However,
phytohemoagglutinin-stimulated translocation of unoccupied GR
into nuclei in human lymphocyte (56) reminded us of the recent
observation that the application of the technique using cyto-
kalasin-B resulted in the demonstration of the nuclear localization of unoccupied ER (57). This similarity suggests that
the difference between GR and ER may be quantitative, but not
qualitative.

[III] Intramolecular Signal Transmission from Ligand-Binding
       Site to Chromatin-Binding Site in Steroid Hormone Re-
       ceptor.

The limited proteolysis of the receptor molecule resulted in
the demonstration that there is some spacial distance between

two sites (58). On the basis of our recent studies that digested receptor has the altered affinity toward the modulator
(59), however, some caution should be paid for analyses of
these data. On the other hand, it has been widely accepted
that steroid binding site is functionally coupled with chromatin binding site. As described in the previous sections of
this review, several modulators were found to affect both ste-
roid- and chromatin-binding abilities. These include the dialyzable compounds and molybdate. A comprehensive survey of
this important issue is beyond the scope of this article. Considering the physiological conditions, we have decided to mention in some detail micromolecular modulators. Both stabilization and activation of steroid receptors have been realized to
be controled by the dialyzable compounds. The identity of
these small molecules should be seriously addressed. This
would be far from a final goal since their molecular nature is
not successfully identified. However, some experimental results provided us with some clue to discuss this important issue. For instance, a dialysis of the rat liver cytosol in the
absence of glucocorticoid induced destabilization of GR without concomitant GR activation. Formation of steroid-receptor
complexes enhanced stabilization of all steroid receptors with
accelerated response to activation procedures. These seem to
favor an idea that two distinct small molecules do separately
regulate activation and stabilization of steroid receptors
with the reservation that these molecules are directly interacted with the receptor molecules. As summarized in Fig. 3,
the association with the receptor of the small molecular stabilizing the ligand binding ability, desigated as the low molecular weight stabilizer, becomes tight upon hormone binding.
However, hormone binding also triggered the loosening of interaction of receptor with the small molecule inhibiting receptor
activation, designated as the low molecular weight inhibitor.
The complete dissociation of the this inhibitor from the receptor molecule resulted in receptor activation. This speculative
scheme would be worth performing further detailed studies.

268

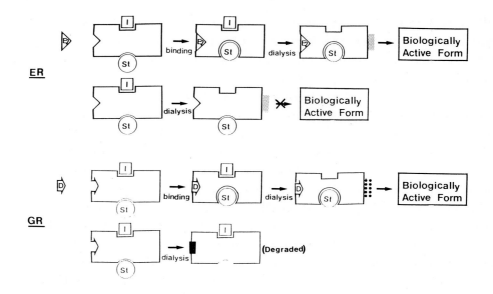

ER

GR

Fig. 3   Proposed interaction of steroid receptor with low
         molecular weight modulators.

Two different micromolecular modulators, namely low molecular weight stabilizer and low molecular weight inhibitor (see the text), are associated with ER or GR at the separate sites. Hormone binding loosens the binding of inhibitor but stabilize the binding of stabilizer. Activation procedures provoke the complete dissociation of inhibitor from receptor. The additional reaction may be required for activated receptor to be converted into the biologically active form. This process does not progress when activated receptor is not complexed with agonist. The reader should realize that discussion on monometric or polymetric structure of receptor is not incorporated in this speculative scheme.

(st) , low molecular weight stabilizer

[I] , low molecular weight inhibitor

▓ , chromatin binding site

E▷ , estradiol

D , dexamethasone

[VI]   Modulators Affecting Chromatin Binding Ability of
        Activated Steroid Receptors.

Incubation of activated receptor with a sufficient amount of
nuclei in the cell-free condition has been found to result in
the recovery of the relatively small amount of receptor from
nuclei. To explain this phenomenon, the presence of modulators
suppressing translocation of activated ER into nuclei has been
proposed. The relatively nonspecific and weak macromolecular
inhibitor has first been recognized by Chamness et al. (60).
Recent our investigation revealed the presence of macromolecular inhibitor specific for activated ER but not for GR (61).
This modulator inhibited nuclear translocation of activated ER
in a temperature- and KCl-dependent manner with concomitant
heavy aggregation of ER molecule. Its receptor specificity
raised the interesting possibility that the difference in the
molecular structure of chromatin binding site or its neighbouring site between ER and GR can be recognized by this modulator.
In addition, this modulator was identified in once-estrogenized
target tissue, but not in nontarget tissues or in target tissues from the immature rats, suggesting the possible role of
this modulator for protection against an over-exposure to estrogenic stimuli. Actualy, multiple administrations of a large
dose of E_2 caused a diminished nuclear translocation of ER in
the adult rat uteri in comparison with that provoked by single
injection (62). The other factors has been reported to affect
the nuclear binding ability. These include pyridoxal phosphate
(63), ATP (64) and micromolecular inhibitor identified in hepatoma cell cytosol (65). Some aspects related to these compounds will be discussed in detail elsewhere in this book.

Conclusion

The principal purpose of this review was to insist on the fact
that the critical steps for steroid receptors to be converted

into the biologically active form are in the stringent control
of various modulators. These modulators, including ones which
were not discussed in this article, were summarized in Table 2.
The concept of these modulators affecting steroid receptor
functions as the important biological regulator has been emphasized by recent observations. Nevertheless, significant gaps
remain in our knowledge of their molecular nature. In addition, the real molecular form of the biologically active receptor is far from a final goal. The recently-developed affinity
labeling technique as well as immunological technique might
contribute to resolution of these important issues.
In pursuing the final success, two undissolved problems should
be overcome. One is to identify the molecular nature of these
cytoplasmic modulators and the other is to purify steroid receptor as a nonactivated and unoccupied form. Although the
significant progress was made by the discovery that the non-
activated receptor can be stabilized by molybdate, this stabilizing effects are weakened in parallel with purification
fold. This indicates that further methodological progress is
required for purification of unoccupied as well as nonactivated
steroid receptors.

Acknowledgement

We are grateful to Dr. R.A.Huseby for providing us with mouse
Leydig cell tumors. We also acknowledge Drs. Y.Maeda, K.Maeda,
T.Honma and S.Kasayama for their valuable contributions to this
research. This study was partly supported by grants-in-aids
from the Ministry of Education, Tokyo, Japan, the grant from
the Cancer Research Foundation, the Hirai Cancer Research fund
and the Naito Research Grant for 1979.

Table 2   Brief summarization on exogenous and endogenous modulators affecting steroid receptors.

Modulator	Actions	
	Ligand binding and molecular form	Chromatin and DNA binding
ATP	increased binding capacity (GR,ER) (29,30)	block of temperature-induced activation at low concentration, but enhancement of activation at high concentration (PgR)(66,67) decreased DNA binding of activated GR (64)
ADP	increased binding capacity (GR)(68)	block of heat activation (PgR)(66) enhancement of activation (GR)(64)
2'.3'-dialdehyde derivative of ATP	decreased binding capacity (PgR)(69) conversion from 8S to 4-6S (PgR)(69)	inhibition of nuclear binding of activated PgR (69)
Dithiothreitol	increased binding capacity (GR)(30)	
N-ethylmaleimide (SH blocker)	decreased binding capacity (PgR,GR)(70,71)	block of heat activation (GR)(72)
Idoacetoamide (SH blocker)	decreased binding capacity (PgR,GR)(70,71)	block of heat activation (GR)(72)
Mersalyl (SH blocker)	decreased binding capacity (PgR,GR)(70,71) application to exchange assay (GR,AR) (73,74)	
Methylmethane-thiosulfonate (SH modifier)		decreased DNA binding (GR)(75)
5.5'-dithiobis (2-nitrobenzoic acid) (SH modifier)		decreased DNA binding (GR)(75)

continued

Molybdate	stabilization of ligand binding (GR, PgR,ER,AR) (35,36,42) formation of large receptor form (PgR, GR,ER) (76,77)	block of receptor activation (GR,PgR,ER) (36,42)
sodium fluride	stabilization of ligand binding (GR, PgR) (29,78)	
Glucose-1-phosphate	stabilization of ligand binding (GR) (43)	
Tungstate	stabilization of ligand binding (GR) (43)	block of receptor activation (GR,PgR) (43, 76), extraction of GR from nuclei (79)
Pyridoxal phosphate	conversion from 8S to 3-4S (ER,GR) (80, 81)	extraction of nuclear receptor (GR,ER,AR, PgR) (82,83,84,85) inhibition of nuclear binding of activated receptors (GR,ER,AR, PgR) (63,83,86,87)
5'-deoxypyridoxal	decreased binding capacity (GR) (88)	
Phenylglyoxal (Arginine specific reagent)	decreased binding capacity (GR) (89)	
1,2-cyclohexane-dione (Arginine specific reagent)	decreased binding capacity (GR) (90)	inhibition of heat activation (ER) (91)
Rose bengal (Histidine specific reagent)		inhibition of DNA binding (GR) (90)
Ethoxformic anhydride (Histidine specific reagent)		inhibition of DNA binding (GR) (70)
o-Phenanthroline		inhibition of nuclear binding (ER,PgR) (92,93)
Rifamycin AF/013		inhibition of nuclear binding (PgR) (93)
Aurintricarboxylic acid		inhibition of nuclear binding (ER,PgR,GR) (94)

continued

Cibacron blue F3GA		inhibition of DNA binding (ER,AR) (86,97)
Glycerol	increased affinity (PgR) (95)	
NaSCN	decreased affinity (ER) (27) inhibition of ER aggregation (26)	
Citrate	increased capacity (GR) (97)	
Alkaline phosphatase	decreased binding capacity (GR) (98)	
Phospholipase A$_2$	decreased binding capacity (GR) (99)	
Thioredoxin	increased binding capacity (GR) (100)	
Calcium-activated protease	fragmentation (PgR) (101,102)	decreased nuclear binding (PgR) (102)
Endoprotease	fragmentation of ER and PgR (59)	decreased binding to DNA (ER,PgR) (59)
Low molecular weight stabilizer	stabilization of ligand binding (GR) (11)	
Low molecular weight inhibitor		inhibition of receptor activation (ER, GR,AR) (11)
Small molecule in mouse Leydig cell	decrease affinity (ER) (19)	
RNA		inhibition of DNA binding (ER,GR) (103, 104), extraction of receptor from DNA (ER,GR)
RNase	increase in molecular size (ER) (105)	increased DNA binding (ER) (103,104)
Receptor transforming factor (RTF)	conversion from 5.3S to 4.5S (106)	
Macromolecular inhibitor		inhibition of nuclear binding of activated receptor (GR,ER,PgR) (60)
Aggregation factor		aggregation of activated ER (61)

References

1. Rodbell, M.: Nature 284, 17-21 (1980)
2. Nishizuka, Y.: Nature 308, 693-698 (1984)
3. Jensen, E.V., DeSombre, E.R.: Ann. Rev. Biochem. 41, 203-230 (1971)
4. O'Malley, B.W., Means, A.R.: Science 183, 610-620 (1974)
5. Gorski, J., Toft, D., Shyamala, G., Smith, D., Notides, A.: Recent Progr. Horm. Res. 24, 45-80 (1968)
6. Toft, D., Gorski, J.: Proc. Natl. Acad. Sci. U.S.A. 55, 1574-1581 (1966)
7. Sato, B., Nishizawa, Y., Noma, K., Matsumoto, K., Yamamura, Y.: Endocrinology 104, 1474-1479 (1979)
8. Cake, M.H., Goidl, J.A., Parchman, L.G., Litwack, G.: Biochem. Biophys. Res. Commun. 71, 45-52 (1976)
9. Bailly, A., Sallas, N., Milgrom, E.: J. Biol. Chem. 252, 858-863 (1977)
10. Munck, A., Brink-Johsen, T.: J. Biol. Chem. 243, 5556-5565 (1968)
11. Sato, B., Noma, K., Nishizawa, Y., Nakao, K., Matsumoto,K., Yamamura, Y.: Endocrinology 106, 1142-1148 (1980)
12. Baxter, J.D., Tomkins, G.M.: Proc. Natl. Acad. Sci. U.S.A. 68, 932-937 (1971)
13. Rochefort, H., Lignon, F., Capony, F.: Biochem. Biophys. Res. Commun. 47, 662-670 (1972)
14. Baxter, J.D., Schambelan, M., Matulich, D.T., Spindler,B.J. Taylor, A.A., Bartter, F.C.: J. Clin. Invest. 58, 579-589 (1976)
15. Feil, P.D., Bardin, W.: Endocrinology 97, 1398-1407 (1975)
16. Chrousos, G.P., Vingerhoeds, A., Brandon, D., Pugeot, M., DeVroede, M., Loriausc, D.L., Lipsett, M.B.: J. Clin. Invest. 69, 1261-1269 (1982)
17. Rees, A.M., Bell, P.A.: Biochim. Biophys. Acta 411, 121-132 (1975)
18. Sato, B., Huseby, R.A., Samuels, L.T.: Cancer Res. 38, 2842-2847 (1978)
19. Sato, B., Yamamura, Y., Huseby, R.A., Matsumoto, K.: Advances in Sex Hormone Research Vol.4 (ed. Thomas, L.A., Singhal, R.L.) Urban & Schwarzenberg, Baltimore-Munich p. 241-271 (1980)
20. Sato, B., Maeda, Y., Noma, K., Matsumoto, K., Yamamura, Y.: Endocrinology 108, 612-619 (1981)

21. Kato, J., Onouchi, T., Okinaga, S., Ito, N.: Endocrinology 94, 902-907 (1974)

22. Lin, T., Chen, G.C.C., Murono, E.P., Osterman, J., Nankin, H.R.: Steroids 40, 53-   (1982)

23. Nozu, K., Dufau, M.L., Catt, K.J.: J. Biol. Chem. 256, 1915-1922 (1981)

24. Sato, B., Spomer, W., Huseby, R.A., Samuels, L.T.: Endocrinology 104, 822-831 (1979)

25. Terakawa, N., Huseby, R.A., Fang, S-M., Samuels, L.T.: J. Steroid Biochem. 16, 643-652 (1982)

26. Sica, V., Nola, E., Puca, G.A., Bresciani, F.: Biochemistry 15, 1915-1923 (1976)

27. Sica, V., Puca, G.A., Molinari, A.M., Buonaguro, F.M., Bresciani, F.: Biochemistry 19, 83-88 (1980)

28. Sato, B., Nishizawa, Y., Maeda, Y., Noma, K., Matsumoto,K., Yamamura, Y.: J. Steroid Biochem. 14, 619-624 (1981)

29. Sando, J.J., LaForest, A.C., Pratt,W.:   J. Biol. Chem. 254, 4772-4778 (1979)

30. Grippo, J.F., Trienrungroj, W., Dahmer, M.K., Houseley,P.R. Pratt, W.B.: J. Biol. Chem. 258, 13658-13664 (1983)

31. Aurrichio, F., Migliaccio, A., Castoria, G., Lastoria, S., Schiavone, E.: Biochem. Biophys. Res. Commun. 101, 1171-1178 (1981)

32. Auricchio, F., Migliaccio, A., Castoria, G., Lastoria, S., Rotondi, A.: Biochem. Biophys. Res. Commun. 106, 149-157 (1982)

33. Noma, K., Sato, B., Nishizawa, Y., Kasayama, S., Kishimoto, S., Matsumoto, K.: Antagonists for gluco and mineralo corticoids (ed. Agarwal, M.K.) Walter de Gruyter Berlin-New York in press

34. Bruchovsky, N., Wilson, J.D.: J. Biol. Chem. 243, 5953-5960 (1968)

35. Hubbard, J., Kalimi, M.: J. Biol. Chem. 257, 14263-14270 (1982)

36. Noma, K., Nakao, K., Sato, B., Nishizawa, Y., Matsumoto,K., Yamamura, Y.: Endocrinology 107, 1205-1211 (1980)

37. Notides, A.C., Hamilton, D.E., Auer, H.E.: J. Biol. Chem. 250, 3945-3950 (1975)

38. Bailly, A., LeFerve, B., Savouret, J-F., Milgrom, E.: J. Biol. Chem. 255, 2729-2734 (1980)

39. Linkie, D.M.: Endocrinology 101, 1862-1870 (1977)

40. Milgrom, E., Atiger, M., Baulieu, E-E.: Biochemistry 12, 5198-5205 (1973)

41. Sato, B., Huseby, R.A., Samuels, L.T.: Endocrinology 102, 545-555 (1978)

42. Toft, D., Nishigori, H.: J. Steroid Biochem. 11, 413-416 (1979)

43. Leach, K.L., Dahmer, M.K., Hammond, N.D., Sando, J.J., Pratt, W.B.: J. Biol. Chem. 254, 11884-11890 (1979)

44. Sato, B., Nishizawa, Y., Maeda, Y., Noma, K., Honma, T., Matsumoto, K.: J. Steroid Biochem. 19, 315-321 (1983)

45. Weichman, B.W., Notides, A.C.: J. Biol. Chem. 252, 8856-8862 (1977)

46. DeSombre, E.R., Mohla, S., Jensen, E.V.: Biochem. Biophys. Res. Commun. 48, 1601-1608 (1972)

47. Buller, R.E., Toft, D.O., Schrader, W.L., O'Malley B.W.: J. Biol. Chem. 250, 801-808 (1975)

48. Zava, D.T., McGuire, W.L.: J. Biol. Chem. 252, 13703-13708 (1977)

49. Taylor, R.N., Smith, R.G.: Biochemistry 21, 1781-1787 (1982)

50. Payvar, F., DeFranco, D., Firestone, G.L., Edgar, B., Wrange, Ö., Okret, S., Gustafsson, J-A, Yamamoto, K.R.: Cell 35, 381-392 (1983)

51. Maeda, Y., Sato, B., Noma, K., Kishimoto, S., Koizumi, K., Aono, T., Matsumoto, K.: Cancer Res. 43, 4091-4097 (1983)

52. Sato, B., Maeda, Y., Nakao, M., Noma, K., Kishimoto, S., Matsumoto, K.: Eur. J. Cancer & Clin. Oncol. in press

53. Rochefort, H., Borgna, J.L.: Nature 292, 257-259 (1981)

54. Sutherland, R.L., Murphy, L.C.: Mol. Cell. Endocrinol. 25, 5-23 (1982)

55. Sato, B., Maeda, Y., Nishizawa, Y., Noma, K., Kishimoto,S., Matsumoto, K.: Cancer Res. in press

56. Papamichail, M., Ioannidis, C., Tsawdaroglow, N., Sekeris, C.E.: Exp. Cell. Res. 133, 461-465 (1981)

57. Welshons, W.V., Lieberman, M.E., Gorski, J.: Nature 307, 747-749 (1984)

58. Sala-Trepat, J.M., Vallet-Strouve, C.: Biochem. Biophys. Acta 371, 186-202 (1974)

59. Maeda, K., Tsuzimura, T., Nomura, Y., Sato, B., Matsumoto, K.: Cancer Res. 44, 996-1001 (1984)

60. Chamness, G.C., Jennings, A.W., McGuire, W.L.: Biochemistry 13, 327-331 (1974)

61. Nishizawa, Y., Maeda, Y., Noma, K., Sato, B., Matsumoto,K., Yamamura, Y.: Endocrinology 109, 1463-1472 (1981)

62. Sato, B., Nishizawa, Y., Noma, K., Kishimoto, S., Matsumoto, K.: Biochim. Biophys. Acta 755, 412-419 (1983)

63. Cake, M.H., DiSorbo, D.M., Litwack, G.: J. Biol. Chem. 253, 4886-4891 (1978)

64. Holbrook, N.J., Bodwell, J.E., Munck, A.: J. Biol. Chem. 258, 14885-14894 (1983)

65. Taira, M., Terayama, H.: Biochim. Biophys. Acta 541, 45-58 (1978)

66. Toft, D., Moudgil, V., Lohnar, P., Miller, J.: Ann. New York Acad. Sci. 286, 29-42 (1977)

67. Moudgil, V.K., Kruczak, V., Eessalu, T., Paulose, C.S., Taylor, M., Hansen, J.: Eur. J. Biochem. 118, 547-555(1981)

68. Barnett, C.A., Palmour, R.M., Litwack, G., Seegmiller,J.E., Endocrinology 112, 2059-2068 (1983)

69. McBlain, W.A., Lauquin, G.J-M., Vignais, P.V.: Biochemistry 22, 2202-2230 (1983)

70. Young, H.A., Parks, W.P., Scolnick, E.M.: Proc. Natl. Acad. Sci. U.S.A. 72, 3060-3064 (1975)

71. Coty, W.A.: J. Biol. Chem. 255, 8035-8037 (1980)

72. Kalimi, M., Love, K.: J. Biol. Chem. 255, 4687-4690 (1980)

73. Banerji, A., Kalimi, M.: Steroid 37, 409-421 (1981)

74. Traish, A.M., Muller, R.E., Wotiz, H.H.: J. Biol. Chem. 256, 12028-12033 (1981)

75. Bodwell, J.E., Holbrook, N.J., Munck, A.: Biochemistry 23, 1392-1398 (1984)

76. Nishigori, H., Toft, D.: Biochemistry 19, 77-83 (1980)

77. Sherman, M.R., Stevens, J.: Ann. Rev. Physiol. 46, 83-105 (1984)

78. Grody, W.W., Compton, J.G., Schrader, W.T., O'Malley,B.W.: J. Steroid Biochem. 12 115-120 (1980)

79. Murakami, N., Quattrociocchi, T.M., Healy, S.P., Moudgil, V.K.: Arch. Biochem. Biophys. 214, 326-334 (1982)

80. Cidlowski, J.A., Thanassi, J.W.: Biochemistry 18, 2378-2383 (1979)

81. Muldoon, T.G., Cildowski, J.A.: J. Biol. Chem. 255, 3100-3107 (1980)

82. Cidlowski, J.A., Thanassi, J.W.: Biochim. Biophys. Res. Commun. 82, 1140-1146 (1978)

83. Müller, R.E., Traish, A., Wotiz, H.H.: J. Biol. Chem. 255, 4062-4067 (1980)

84. Mulder, E.V., Vriz, L., Foekens, J.A.: Mol. Cell. Endcrinol. 23 283-296 (1981)

85. Chen, T.J., McDonald, R.G., Robidoux, Jr.W.F., Leavitt,W.W. J. Steroid Biochem. 14, 1023-1028 (1981)

278

86. Mulder, E., Vrig, L., Foekens, J.A.: Steroids **36**, 633-645 (1980)

37. Nishigori, H., Toft, D.: J. Biol. Chem. **254**, 9155-9161 (1979)

88. O'Brien, J.M., Thanassi, J.W., Cidlowski, J.A.: Biochem. Biophys. Res. Commun. **92**, 155-162 (1980)

89. Shyamala, G., Daveluy, A.: J. Biol. Chem. **257**, 11976-11981 (1982)

90. DiSorbo, D.M., Phelps, D.S., Litwack, G.: Endocrinology **106**, 922-929 (1980)

91. Müller, R.E., Traish, A., Wotiz, H.H.: J. Biol. Chem. **258**, 11582-11589 (1983)

92. Shyamala, G.: Biochim. Biophys. Res. Commun. **64**, 408-415 (1975)

93. Toft, D., Lohmar, P., Miller, J., Moudgil, V.: J. Steroid Biochem. **7**, 1053-1059 (1976)

94. Moudgil, V.K., Weekes, G.A.: FEBS Lett. **94**, 324-326 (1978)

95. Kumar, S.A., Beach, T.A., Dickerman, H.W.: Proc. Natl. Acad. Sci. U.S.A. **76**, 2199-2203 (1979)

96. Ogle, T.F.: Endocrinology **106**, 1861-1868 (1980)

97. Hubbard, J., Kalimi, M.: Biochem. J. **210**, 259-263 (1983)

98. Nielsen, C.J., Sando, J.J., Pratt, W.B.: Proc. Natl. Acad. Sci. U.S.A. **74**, 1398-1402 (1977)

99. Leach, K.L., Dahmer, M.K., Pratt, W.B.: J. Steroid Biochem. **18**, 105-107 (1983)

100. Grippo, J.F., Trienrungroj, W., Dahmer, M.K., Houseley,P.R. Pratt, W.B.: J. Biol. Chem. **258**, 13658-13664 (1983)

101. Sherman, M.R., Pickering, L.A., Rollwagen, F.M., Miller, L.K.: Fed. Roc. **37**, 167-173 (1978)

102. Vedeckis, W.V., Schrader, W.T., O'Malley, B.W.: Biochemistry **19**, 343-349 (1980)

103. Feldman, H., Kallos, J., Hollander, V.P.: J. Biol. Chem. **256**, 1145-1148 (1981)

104. Chong, M.T., Lippman, M.E.: J. Biol. Chem. **257**, 2996-3002 (1982)

105. Feldman, M., Burton, L.E., Hollander, V.P., Blackburn, P.: J. Biol. Chem. **258**, 5001-5004 (1983)

106. Puca, G.A., Nola, E., Sica, V., Bresiani, F.: Biochemistry **11**, 4157-4165 (1972)

PHOSPHORYLATION ON TYROSINE OF THE 17β-ESTRADIOL RECEPTOR

Ferdinando Auricchio, Antimo Migliaccio, Andrea Rotondi and
Gabriella Castoria

Institute of General Pathology and Oncology, Ist Medical School,
University of Naples
80138 Naples, Italy

Steroid receptors bind hormone with high affinity and strict
specificity. Other properties of receptors such as interaction with high
affinity with nuclear sites and modulation of the transcriptional
activity, although essential for steroid action, are secondary to
hormone binding to the receptor. Since hormone binding is preliminary to
all other activities of receptors we reserve the term "active receptor"
for receptor that binds hormone.

Phosphorylation-dephosphorylation is the reversible covalent
modification most frequently involved in the modulation of protein
activity (1,2). It has recently been reported that proteins are
phosphorylated on tyrosine and that this phosphorylation is apparently a
very early event in hormone-induced cell growth and retroviral
transformation of cells (3,4,5). Despite the surge of interest in
phosphorylation on tyrosine the relation between phosphorylation of
proteins on tyrosine and normal or neoplastic cell growth is not yet
understood.

In this Chapter we present recent data from our laboratory showing that calf uterus estradiol receptor is phosphorylated exclusively on tyrosine by an endogenous cytosol kinase and dephosphorylated by an endogenous nuclear phosphatase and that this phosphorylation-dephosphorylation process regulates the hormone binding of the receptor. We feel that this is a good example of how phosphorylation on tyrosine could be related to hormonal responses of cells, including cell growth.

Data relating to phosphorylation-dephosphorylation of 17 β-estradiol receptor with receptor recycling are also reviewed.

Inactivation of estrogen receptor by nuclear phosphatase

Estrogen receptor binding of mouse uterine cytosol is relatively stable during incubation at 25° C for 20 min. Addition of crude uterine nuclei (see Fig. 1), highly purified nuclei or nuclear extract (6) produces rapid inactivation of a significant amount (30-70%) of the initial receptor binding. However complete inactivation of the binding has never been observed. Data from our laboratory indicate that this is due to the production of inhibitor during incubation rather than to different types of binding sites (G. Castoria and F. Auricchio; unpublished data).

TABLE   1

TISSUE SPECIFICITY OF NUCLEAR PHOSPHATASE THAT INACTIVATES

THE HORMONE BINDING OF MOUSE UTERUS 17 β-ESTRADIOL RECEPTOR

TISSUE	Activity referred to an equal amount of DNA (% of uterus activity)
Uterus	100
Mammary Gland	88
Liver	9
Quadriceps Muscle	0

Nuclei from mammary gland also inactivate the uterus cytosol receptor whereas liver nuclei exert very little receptor inactivating activity and quadriceps muscle nuclei none at all (Table 1). Therefore the nuclear receptor inactivating activity is apparently present only in "classical" estrogen target tissues.

This enzyme can be only partially extracted by sonication of calf uterus nuclei in hypotonic buffer, which suggests a strong interaction with nuclear components (7). Phosphatase inhibitors prevent the nuclear activity whereas protease inhibitors do not (6).

A very simple and rapid method to purify the nuclear enzyme from uterus has been published: the nuclear extract is applied in the cold on a CM-cellulose column and the activity is eluted from the column by 0.2 M NaCl (8). The enzyme purified about 700-fold over the homogenate is very unstable (7), which prevents further purification.

The purified enzyme is stimulated by dithiothreitol and it is inhibited by several compounds that inhibit phosphatases (8). It shows a very high affinity for cytosolic estradiol filled binding sites (Km = 0.8×10^{-9} mol/l) as well as for the cytosolic unfilled binding sites (Km = 1.3×10^{-9} mol/l). This indicates that the receptor is the physiological substrate of this enzyme (8). It exerts no effect on tamoxifen- and nafoxidine-cytosolic receptor complexes (9). In analogy with these findings on cytosolic receptor, mouse uterus nuclear receptor translocated in vivo by 17 β-estradiol is extensively inactivated by this enzyme during incubation of nuclei at 25° C whereas receptor translocated by antiestrogens is refractory to it (9). This finding is in accordance with the observation that in intact cells receptor translocated into nuclei by antiestrogens is slowly lost (10), suggesting that in vivo the different half lives of nuclear estradiol- and antiestrogen- receptor complexes are due to different sensitivity of these complexes to the nuclear enzyme.

The purified enzyme inactivates not only crude but also pure receptor;

several phosphatase inhibitors prevent this inactivation (8). On this basis we postulated that the estradiol receptor is a phosphoprotein, that the inactivating enzyme is a receptor-phosphatase and that phosphorylation is required for hormone binding to the receptor (8). These hypotheses have been directly tested and found to be correct (see next sections).

Activation of estrogen receptor by cytosol kinase

Addition of ATP in the presence of $MgCl_2$ and Na_2MoO_4 to cytosol receptor partially preinactivated by incubation with nuclei (or nuclear extract) causes a complete recovery of the lost binding activity (Fig. 1). The same inactivation-reactivation process has been observed in vitro with calf uterus (11).

We have partially purified the enzyme responsible for the reactivation of the receptor (12). Cytosol was fractionated in the cold by ammonium sulphate. Proteins precipitated between 25-50% saturation were solubilized, and poured on a heparin-sepharose column which retains the receptor but not the enzyme. The flow-through was collected, diluted to decrease the ionic strength and poured on a DEAE-cellulose column. Saline gradient was applied on the column and the enzyme activating the receptor eluted at about 150 mM KCl. This enzyme sediments at ~6 S through sucrose gradient. It has a very high affinity for the inactive hormone binding sites (Km = 0.3×10^{-9} mol/l) in agreement with the affinity of the nuclear phosphatase for the active receptor, thus suggesting that both enzymes act on this receptor in vivo .

Using purified activating enzyme and pure estradiol receptor it has been observed that a combination of Ca^{2+} and calmodulin stimulates the activation of hormone binding sites (13,14). Singly neither substance produces a stimulatory effect. This finding suggests that Ca^{2+} acts through calmodulin. The effect of various concentrations of Ca^{2+} on the enzyme is shown in Fig. 2. Half maximal and maximal stimulation are

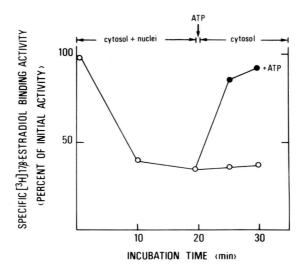

Fig. 1 – *Inactivation-Reactivation of hormone binding activity of estrogen receptor*

Mouse uterus cytosol was labelled in TED (50 mM Tris, 1 mM EDTA, 2 mM di-thiothreitol) buffer, pH 7.4, with 12 nM [³H]17β-estradiol in the absence and in the presence of a 100-fold excess of radioinert hormone, then incu-bated at 25° C with an equivalent amount of homologous nuclei. After 20 min, samples were centrifuged at 2° C to remove nuclei, supplemented with 10 mM Na₂MoO₄, and 10 mM MgCl₂, then incubated for further 10 min at 15° C in the absence (○) and in the presence (●) of 10 mM ATP. Specific [³H]17β-estradiol binding activity was measured at the indicated times. The initial binding activity was 1.2x10⁻¹² moles of 17β-estradiol binding sites (12).

observed with free concentrations of 0.8 μM and 1 μM, respectively. Intracellular concentration of Ca^{2+} is 0.1 μM. Upon stimulation of the cell, Ca^{2+} increases to 1 μM. Hence it appears that hormone binding of receptor increases with the increase in Ca^{2+} in stimulated cells. Trifluoperazine which inhibits calmodulin-sensitive enzymes completely prevents the Ca^{2+}-calmodulin stimulation of the enzyme, which confirms that calmodulin mediates the enzymic activation (13,14).

Evidences that the cytosol enzyme activating the hormone binding is a 17 β-estradiol receptor-kinase will be presented in the next section.

284

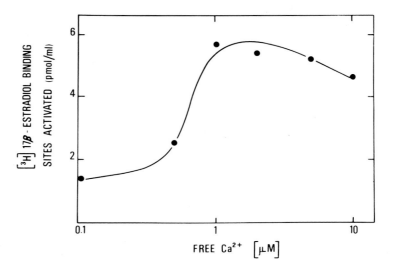

Fig. 2 - Dependence of Kinase Activating the hormone binding of 17β-estra-diol receptor on calcium
Pure calf uterus 17β-estradiol receptor binding 10×10^{-12} moles of hormone was partially inactivated by incubation with purified nuclear phosphatase, then incubated with purified cytosolic kinase in TGD (50 mM Tris, 0.2 mM EGTA, 2 mM dithiothreitol) buffer, pH 7.4, for 10 min at 15° C. The binding activation was followed in the presence of 5 mM $MgCl_2$, 10 mM Na_2MoO_4, 0.15 mM ATP, 0.6 μM calmodulin and the indicated amounts of free Ca^{2+} (14).

Phosphorylation-dephosphorylation of estradiol receptor

Although some investigations have suggested that steroid receptor are phosphoproteins, direct conclusive evidence was lacking until recently. Some reports suggested that the hormone binding activity of steroid receptors require phosphorylation: cortisol binding has been correlated to the level of ATP in thymocytes (15); and ATP enhances the hormone binding of crude androgen receptor (16). Observations in cell-free systems suggest that phosphorylation of glucocorticoid receptor may have a role in regulation of hormone binding (for a review see 17).

Glucocorticoid receptor phosphorylation in intact cells has recently been reported (18,19). Autophosphorylation of glucocorticoid receptor has also been demonstrated (20). Phosphorylation of progesterone

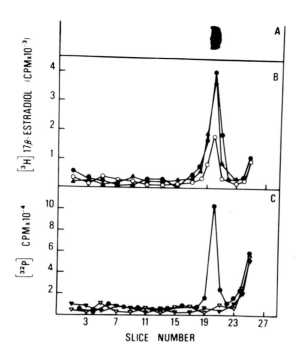

Fig. 3 - Phosphorylation of 17β-estradiol receptor: Polyacrylamide gel electrophoresis under non denaturating conditions.

Pure calf uterus 17β-estradiol receptor binding $32x10^{-12}$ moles of 17β-estradiol was partially inactivated by incubation with purified nuclear phosphatase at 25° C for 20 min (inactivated receptor) then reactivated by purified cytosol kinase in TED-buffer, pH 7.4, containing 5 mM $MgCl_2$, 10 mM Na_2MoO_4 in the presence of 0.15 mM $[\gamma-^{32}P]ATP$ (6 Ci/mmol) 1.050 mM $CaCl_2$ and 45 μg calmodulin for 10 min at 15° C (reactivated receptor). After incubation aliquots of each sample were submitted to slab gel electrophoresis under non denaturating conditions in TRISglycine buffer, pH 8.3, at 4° C after extensive dialysis against the same buffer. Panel A shows the silver stained gel lane loaded with the native (not inactivated) receptor, and Panel B the migration pattern of $[^3H]$17β-estradiol bound to native (▲—▲), inactivated (O—O) and reactivated (●—●) receptor. Panel C shows the migration pattern of $[^{32}P]$ of the reactivated receptor (●—●). Parallel samples incubated without kinase (▽—▽) and without receptor (▼—▼) are also shown (11).

receptor by exogenous cAMP-dependent kinase (21) and by epidermal growth factor receptor (22) suggests that this receptor could be a good substrate of kinases including kinases phosphorylating on tyrosine. This possibility has been confirmed by reports on phosphorylation (23) and autophosphorylation (24) of progesterone receptor from chicken. The function of all these phosphorylations has not yet been understood.

Findings reported in the previous sections of this Chapter strongly suggest that the estradiol receptor is a phosphoprotein and that phosphorylation-dephosphorylation of this protein is required for hormone binding to the receptor. We have obtained direct evidences of these important points. 17 β-estradiol receptor has been purified from calf uterus. The final preparation shows a single band of protein on PAGE, coincident with the hormone binding activity peak of the receptor.

Incubation with the nuclear enzyme that inactivates the hormone binding decreases this peak which can be restored by the cytosol activating enzyme. If this activation occurs in the presence of $[\gamma-^{32}P]$ ATP, a single $[^{32}P]$ peak on PAGE is observed in coincidence with the protein band and the peak of hormone binding. The results are presented in Fig. 3. For details see ref. (11).

Phosphorylation of a protein with the mol. wt. of the estradiol receptor was found when the sample of receptor reactivated with $[\gamma-^{32}P]$ ATP was submitted to SDS-PAGE (Fig. 4).

The use of monoclonal antibodies against the estrogen receptor has conclusively proved that the protein phosphorylated during the reactivation of hormone binding of the 17β-estradiol receptor is indeed the receptor. Purified ^{3}H-estradiol preinactivated by the phosphatase, was reactivated by the kinase in the presence of $[\gamma-^{32}P]$ ATP, and then divided into two aliquots. One was incubated with an excess of JS34/32 monoclonal antibodies against the estrogen receptor, and the other with an equal excess of control immunoglobulins (not reacting with the

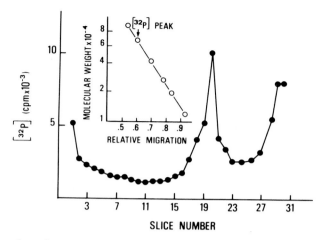

Fig. 4 - <u>Phosphorylation of 17β-estradiol receptor: SDS-polyacrylamide gel electrophoresis</u>.

Pure calf uterus estradiol receptor binding 7×10^{-12} moles of 17β-estradiol was partially inactivated by incubation with nuclear phosphatase and then reactivated with cytosol kinase under the same conditions reported in the legend to Fig. 3. The sample was extensively dialyzed against SDS-phosphate buffer, pH 7.2, and submitted to SDS-PAGE in the same buffer. The migration pattern of the $[^{32}P]$ peak of the reactivated receptor is shown. The insert shows the calibration plot obtained with reference proteins (Low Molecular Weight Calibration Kit, Pharmacia). The relative position of the $[^{32}P]$ peak is indicated by the arrow (11).

receptor). The two samples were analyzed by centrifugation on sucrose gradients prepared with buffer containing 0.4 M KCl. Figure 5 illustrates the results. The $[^{3}H]$ 17β-estradiol peak bound to the receptor incubated with control immunoglobulins sediments at 4.2 S, as expected from the high salt form of the receptor, and it coincides with a $[^{32}P]$ peak. Preincubation of the receptor with antibodies against receptor causes the $[^{3}H]$17β-estradiol peak to sediment at 7.5 S because the receptor with an excess of antibodies forms a 1:1 complex sedimenting in this region. This $[^{3}H]$hormone peak cosediments with a $[^{32}P]$peak. This experiment leaves no doubt that the receptor has been phosphorylated and that the enzyme activating the receptor is a receptor-kinase.

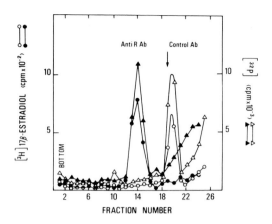

Fig. 5 – *Phosphorylation of 17β-estradiol receptor: Sucrose gradient centrifugation of receptor-antibody complexes*

Pure calf uterus receptor was partially inactivated by the nuclear phosphatase, then reactivated by the cytosol kinase under the conditions indicated in Fig. 3. Samples of reactivated receptor (0.3×10^{-12} moles of estradiol binding sites) were extensively dialyzed against 0.4 M KCl-TED buffer, pH 7.4 and incubated with control immunoglobulins (open symbols) and with JS 34/32 monoclonal antibodies to the receptor, (solid symbols) at a molar ratio of receptor/antibodies of 1/150. Samples were then centrifuged at 45,000 rpm for 14 h on 10-35% sucrose gradients containing 0.4 M KCl. The arrow indicates the position of the reference protein, bovine plasma albumin (11).

It has been found that Ca^{2+}-calmodulin stimulates binding activation and receptor phosphorylation to a similar extent (14). This finding together with the experiment reported in Fig. 3 shows that phosphorylation is required for hormone binding.

If the receptor phosphorylated with $[\gamma-^{32}P]$ ATP is incubated with the nuclear enzyme inactivating the receptor and submitted to SDS-PAGE, most of $[^{32}P]$ incorporated into the receptor is removed by the inactivating enzyme (Fig. 6) and a parallel decrease of hormone binding is observed. This is direct evidence that the enzyme inactivating the receptor is a receptor-phosphatase and it confirms that receptor phosphorylation is a prerequisite for hormone binding (13).

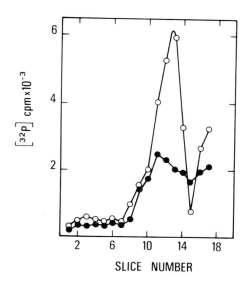

Fig. 6 - Dephosphorylation of [^{32}P] *receptor by the nuclear phosphatase: SDS-Polyacrylamide gel electrophoresis.*

Pure calf uterus 17β-estradiol receptor binding 8.71x10^{-12}moles of hormone was partially inactivated by incubation with the nuclear phosphatase at 25° C for 20 min and used as substrate of the kinase. The binding of the receptor was activated in TGD-buffer under the following conditions: the reaction temperature was 15° C; 5 mM MgCl$_2$, 10 mM Na$_2$MoO$_4$, 0.15 mM [γ-^{32}P] *ATP (6 Ci/mmol) and purified kinase were added to the incubation mixture together with 1 μM Ca^{2+} and 0.6 μM calmodulin. Two aliquots were incubated in the absence and in the presence of purified phosphatase for 20 min at 25° C. The samples were exhaustively dialyzed against SDS-phosphate buffer, pH 7.2, and submitted to SDS-gel electrophoresis. The gel lanes were sliced and counted for* [^{32}P] *radioactivity. Open symbols: receptor incubated in the absence of the phosphatase. Solid symbols: receptor incubated in the presence of the phosphatase (13).*

Phosphorylation of 17β-estradiol receptor on tyrosine

Less than 0.1% of the phosphate in proteins of normal cells is present as phosphotyrosine (25). Several oncogenes of retroviral origin produce tyrosine kinases (3).

Tyrosine kinases are also associated to growth factor receptors such as PDGF (26,27,28), EGF (29) and insulin (30,31). Therefore tyrosine kinases represent a functional linkage between oncogenes and growth factor receptors. The linkage between these two classes of proteins is confirmed by their structural analogies and by some similarities in substrate specificities. Structural analogies are shown by the finding that the kinase domain of the EGF receptor is strongly related to the erb B oncogene protein which resembles a tyrosine kinase (32). Biochemical relatedness is shown by the fact that the EGF receptor phosphorylates src peptides (33) and antibodies to the src kinase (34,35).

Although it is apparent that tyrosine kinase are involved in neoplastic and hormone-stimulated growth it is not known how phosphorylation on tyrosine of proteins can be related to cell growth. In this context the next finding is of particular interest.

We have found that phosphorylation of 17β-estradiol receptor which confers the hormone binding property to the estrogen receptor occurs exclusively on tyrosine (14): pure 17β-estradiol receptor was phosphorylated in vitro in the absence and in presence of Ca^{2+} -calmodulin. It was then submitted to SDS-PAGE, extracted from gel and submitted to partial acid hydrolysis. The samples were finally analyzed for phosphoaminoacids using mono- and bidimensional electrophoresis. The only phosphoaminoacid detectable by autoradiography was coincident with cold phosphotyrosine (Fig. 7).

We would like to point out that phosphorylation of the estrogen receptor that confers the hormone binding property to a target cell is an excellent example of how phosphorylation on tyrosine can be related to

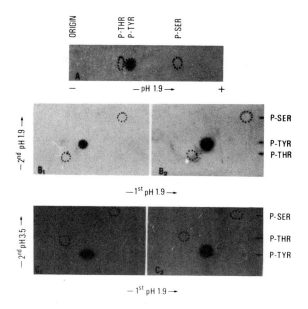

Fig. 7 - *Phosphoaminoacid analysis of the phosphorylated 17β-estradiol receptor.*

Pure calf uterus 17β-estradiol receptor binding $8.71x10^{-12}$ moles of 17β-estradiol was partially inactivated by incubation with the nuclear phosphatase. The binding of the receptor was reactivated by the kinase during 10 min incubation in TGD-buffer at 15° C with 5 mM $MgCl_2$, 10 mM Na_2MoO_4, 0.15 mM $[\gamma-^{32}P]$ATP (6 Ci/mmol) and with or without 1 μM free Ca^{2+} and 0.6 μM calmodulin in a final volume of 1.5 ml. The activated samples were exhaustively dialyzed against SDS-phosphate buffer, pH 7.2, and 150 μl aliquots were submitted to SDS-PAGE. Then the receptor was extracted from gel and finally subjected to acid hydrolysis, lyophilized and solubilized with 100 μl H_2O. 25 μl samples were applied on cellulose thin-layer plates. Electrophoresis was run at pH 1.9 in one direction (A), at pH 1.9 in two directions (B) and at pH 1.9 in the first direction and at pH 3.5 in the second direction (C). B_1 and C_1 show the electrophoresis of aminoacids from receptor activated in the absence, and A, B_2 and C_2, in the presence of Ca^{2+} and calmodulin. Samples of phosphoserine (P-SER) phosphothreonine (P-THR) and phosphotyrosine (P-TYR) were added to the radiaoctive samples analyzed. The dotted lines represent the ninhydrin stained standards superimposed on autoradiography.

hormone-induced effects including cell growth stimulation on target cells.

Experiments are under way in our laboratory to investigate whether the kinase phosphorylating the estradiol receptor shares other important features with kinases phosphorylating other growth factor receptors on tyrosine and kinases produced by retroviruses such as structural analogies and similarities in substrate specificities.

Evidences that phosphorylation-dephosphorylation is related to receptor recycling

The intracellular localization of the receptor-phosphatase and the receptor-kinase, the former in the nucleus, the latter in the cytosol, immediately suggests that the receptor acquires hormone binding in the cytoplasm and loses it in the nuclear compartment. According to the "classical" model of action of steroids the hormone binds to the receptor in cytoplasm, then the steroid-receptor complex is "transformed" to a nucleophilic form which tightly binds to specific nuclear sites.

In an attempt to integrate this model and our findings we have formulated the following hypothesis: in cytoplasm the kinase transforms the newly synthesized receptor from the inactive (not hormone binding) to active (hormone binding) form. The receptor-hormone complex thereafter migrates to the nucleus where it is dephosphorylated and inactivated by the phosphatase. The inactive dephosphorylated receptor loses the affinity for the nuclear sites and is released into the cytoplasm where it could be reactivated by the kinase and/or follow another fate (Fig. 8).

If this hypothesis is correct then nuclear translocation of receptor induced by estradiol should be followed by the appearance in the cytosol of target tissues of dephosphorylated receptor and later by a rephosphorylation of this inactive receptor. We have partially confirmed

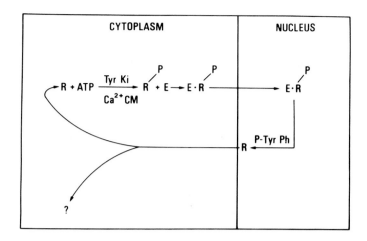

Fig. 8 – Hypothetical model of the mechanism of action of estradiol
Abbreviations: E = estradiol; R = dephosphorylated receptor;
R^{-P} *= phosphorylated receptor; Tyr Ki = tyrosyl receptor-kinase;*
P-Tyr Ph = phosphotyrosyl receptor-phosphatase; CM = calmodulin.

this hypothesis. Hormone injection in mice is followed by nuclear translocation of receptor and subsequently by the appearance in the cytosol of inactive receptor. This has been detected by incubation with ATP of uterus cytosol from estradiol injected mice, as well as incubation of receptor purified from uterus cytosol of 17β–estradiol injected mice with the purified kinase (36). These and other experiments suggest that in vivo nuclear receptor is inactivated by nuclear phosphatase, then released into the cytosol. These findings do not prove that in vivo the receptor inactivated by nuclei is recycled by the kinase but do show that at least in vitro this is possible.

Increase of specific 17β–estradiol binding after incubation with ATP of calf uterus cytosol which has not been pretreated with nuclear phosphatase has been frequently observed although at very different extent (unpublished experiments). This suggests that dephosphorylated not hormone binding receptor is present in the cytoplasm of intact cells. This could be due to recently synthesized, not yet phosphorylated receptor and/or to receptor released from nuclei after nuclear translocation.

It has recently been suggested that in addition to filled receptor also the unfilled receptor resides in the nucleus, and that cytosolic localization of the receptor represents an extraction artefact (37,38). According to these reports the different localization of estrogen receptor in disrupted cells is due to different affinities of filled and unfilled receptor for nuclear sites. If this is true, we could then expect that also the 17β-estradiol receptor-kinase is a nuclear protein with low affinity for nuclear sites similar to that of unoccupied or inactive receptor, whereas the phosphatase, like the filled receptor is bound to nuclear sites with high affinity. It then becomes feasible that the "recycling" of the receptor controlled by phosphorylation-dephosphorylation occurs between nuclear sites of low affinity and high affinity instead of occurring between cytosolic and nuclear compartment.

Summary

Mouse and calf uterus 17β-estradiol receptor is a phosphoprotein and a nuclear receptor-phosphatase inactivates and a cytosol receptor-kinase activates its hormone binding activity. Nuclear localization of the phosphatase, its high affinity for the receptor, its presence only in estrogen target tissues and its inability to inactivate the receptor complexed with antiestrogens suggest it is the enzyme responsible for the inactivation in intact cells of receptor translocated into nuclei by 17 β-estradiol. This possibility is confirmed by the finding that dephosphorylated, not hormone binding receptor appears in uterus cytosol of mice in vivo , after nuclear translocation of receptor.

The cytosol kinase is a tyrosyl receptor-kinase. Phosphorylation of 17 β-estradiol receptor on tyrosine as a prerequisite for receptor hormone binding is the first example of how phosphorylation on tyrosine can be related to hormone activity on target cells.

Acknowledgement

This research was financially supported by grant N. 84.00430.44 from "Progetto Finalizzato Controllo della Crescita Neoplastica", C.N.R., Italy and by a grant from M.P.I., Italy.

The Authors are indebted to Mr. Lucio Fusco for skillfull editorial assistance and to Mr. Domenico Piccolo for excellent technical assistance.

References

1. Krebs, E.G., Beavo, J.A.: Ann. Rev. Biochem. 48 , 923–959 (1979).

2. Cohen, P.: Nature 296 , 613–620 (1982).

3. Bishop, J.M.: Ann. Rev. Biochem. 52 , 301–354 (1983).

4. Heldin, C.H., Westermark, B.: Cell 37 , 9–20 (1984).

5. Carpenter, G.: Cell 37 , 357–358 (1984).

6. Auricchio, F., Migliaccio, A.: Febs. Lett. 117 , 224–226 (1980).

7. Auricchio, F., Migliaccio, A., Castoria, G., Rotondi, A.: in: Sex Steroid Receptors, ed. Auricchio F. (Field International Italia, Acta Medica, Rome) in press.

8. Auricchio, F., Migliaccio, A., Rotondi, A.: Biochem. J. 194 , 569–574 (1981).

9. Auricchio, F., Migliaccio, A., Castoria, G.: Biochem. J. 198 , 699–702 (1981).

10. Horwitz, K., Mc Guire, W.L.: J. Biol. Chem. 23 , 8185–8191 (1978).

11. Migliaccio, A., Lastoria, S., Moncharmont, B., Rotondi, A., Auricchio, F.: Biochem. Biophys. Res. Comm. 109 , 1002–1010 (1982).

12. Auricchio, F., Migliaccio, A., Castoria, G., Lastoria, S., Schiavone, E.: Biochem. Biophys. Res. Comm. 101 , 1171–1178 (1981).

13. Auricchio, F., Migliaccio, A., Castoria, G., Rotondi, A., Lastoria, S.: J. Steroid Biochem. 20 , 31–35 (1984).

14. Migliaccio, A., Rotondi, A., Auricchio, F.,: Proc. Natl. Acad. Sci. U.S.A. 81 , 5921–5925 (1984).

15. Munck, A., Brinck–Johnson, T.: J. Biol. Chem. 243 , 5556–5565 (1968).

16. Liao, S., Rossini, G.P., Hiipakka, R.A., Chen, C.: in: Perspectives in Steroid Receptor Research, ed. Bresciani F., New York, Academic Press, pp. 99–112, (1980).

17. Dahmer, M.K., Housley, P.R., Pratt, W.B.: Ann. Rev. Physiol. 46, 67–81 (1984).

18. Housley, P.R., Pratt, W.B.: J. Biol. Chem. 258, 4630–4635 (1983).

19. Grandics, P., Miller, A., Schmidt, T.J., Litwack, G.: Biochem. Biophys. Res. Comm. 120, 59–65 (1984).

20. Kurl, R.N., Jacob, S.T.: Biochem. Biophys. Res. Comm. 119, 700–705 (1984).

21. Weigel, N.L., Tash, J.S., Means, A.R., Schrader, W.T., O' Malley, B.W.: Biochem. Biophys. Res. Comm. 102, 513–519 (1981).

22. Ghosh-Datisbar, P., Coty, W.A., Griest, R.E., Woo, D.D.L., Fox, C.F.: Proc. Natl. Acad. Sci. U.S.A. 81, 1654–1658 (1984).

23. Dougherty, J.J., Puri, R.K., Toft, D.: J. Biol. Chem. 257, 14226–14230 (1980).

24. Garcia, T., Tuohimaa, P., Mester, J., Buchon, T., Renoir, J.M., Baulieu, E.E.: Biochem. Biophys. Res. Comm. 113, 960–966 (1983).

25. Hunter, T., Sefton, B.M.: Proc. Natl. Acad. Sci. U.S.A. 77, 1311–1315 (1980).

26. Ek, B., Westermark, B., Wasteson, A., Heldin, C.H.: Nature 295, 419–420 (1982).

27. Nishimura, J., Huang, J.S., Deuel, T.F.: Proc. Natl. Acad. Sci. U.S.A. 79, 4303–4307 (1982).

28. Pike, L.J., Bowen-Pope, D.F., Ross, R., Krebs, E.G.: J. Biol. Chem. 258, 9383–9390 (1983).

29. Ushiro, H., Cohen, S.: J. Biol. Chem. 255, 8363–8365 (1980).

30. Kasuga, M., Zick, Y., Blithe, D.L., Cretta, M., Kahn, C.R.: Nature 298, 667–669 (1982).

31. Roth, R.A., Cassel, D.J.: Science 219 299–301 (1983).

32. Dounward, J., Yarden, Y., Mayes, E., Scrace, G., Totty, N.,
    Stockwell, P., Ullrich, A., Schlessinger, J., Waterfield, M.D.:
    Nature 307 , 521-527 (1984).

33. Pike, L.J., Gallis, B., Casnellic, J.E., Bornstein, P., Krebs, E.G.:
    Proc. Natl. Acad. Sci. U.S.A. 79 , 1443-1447 (1982).

34. Chinnkers, M., Cohen, S.: Nature 290 , 516-519 (1981).

35. Kudlow, J.E., Buss, J.E., Gill, G.N.: Nature 290 , 519-521 (1981).

36. Auricchio, F., Migliaccio, A., Castoria, G., Lastoria, S., Rotondi,
    A.: Biochem. Biophys. Res. Comm. 106 , 149-157 (1982).

37. King, W.J., Greene, G.L.: Nature 307 , 745-747 (1984).

38. Welshons, W.V., Lieberman, M.E., Gorski, J.: Nature 307 , 747-749
    (1984).

PHOSPHORYLATION OF PROGESTERONE RECEPTOR

John J. Dougherty

Department of Biochemistry and Biophysics
University of Rhode Island
Kingston, Rhode Island U.S.A. 02881

Introduction

Two progesterone-binding components have been isolated from
chicken oviduct, and purified to near homogeneity. These were
designated type A and type B receptor according to the order
of their elution from DEAE-cellulose (1,2). Type A
receptor has a molecular weight of approximately 80,000 and
type B of approximately 110,000. It has been argued that
prior to transformation these two subunits form a dimer containing one type A subunit and one type B subunit (3). However, recent work has indicated that nontransformed progesterone receptors can be isolated as two 8S complexes which contain either type A receptor or type B receptor. In addition
to the steroid-binding components, each complex contains a
90,000 dalton peptide which does not bind progesterone. Recent investigations have shown that B and the 90,000 dalton
peptide are phosphorylated in vivo, and have suggested that A
is also. Furthermore, in vitro studies have shown these
polypeptides to be good substrates for a number of protein
kinases.

Components of the 8S Progesterone Receptor

Like other steroid receptors, progesterone receptor can be
found prior to transformation in a complex sedimenting at 8S
(3,4,5). Molybdate stabilizes the 8S complex and allows its

purification. In the presence of molybdate, two 8S forms can be separated on DEAE columns. Form I, which elutes first, contains the type A progesterone receptor. Form II contains the type B progesterone receptor (6). In addition, there is recent evidence that both 8S forms also contain a 90,000 dalton peptide which does not bind steroid. Workers in Baulieu's laboratory found evidence for such a component using an antibody against 8S progesterone receptor. They found that this antibody caused the 8S progesterone receptor and the 8S estrogen, androgen and glucocorticoid receptors to sediment at 10S. However it did not affect the sedimentation of 4S progesterone receptor. The antibody bound to a 90,000 dalton polypeptide in the progesterone receptor preparation which did not bind progesterone, so Joab and her colleagues proposed that this peptide was common to all these 8S forms (7).

Investigators in Toft's laboratory also found evidence for a 90,000 dalton component of 8S progesterone receptor which does not bind steroid. On glycerol gradients the 90,000 dalton polypeptide sedimented with [3H]progesterone binding at 8S, but it separated from the [3H]progesterone peak under conditions favoring the 4S receptor form. Receptor forms A and B were found with the [3H]progesterone binding at 4S (8). Additional evidence was found suggesting that the 90,000 dalton polypeptide forms 8S complexes with type A and type B receptor. Highly purified batches of 8S receptor can be separated on DEAE-Sephadex into two peaks of [3H]progesterone binding. When the proteins eluting from DEAE-Sephadex at different salt levels were examined by slab gel electrophoresis, the 90,000 dalton peptide showed two density peaks. The first coincided with receptor form A and with the first [3H]progesterone peak. The second coincided with receptor form B and with the second [3H]progesterone binding peak. A final proof that the 90,000 dalton peptide is complexed with the progesterone binding components made use of the fact that the purification of 8S forms

I and II involved steroid affinity chromatography. When cytosol was treated with progesterone prior to affinity chromatography and then taken through the standard purification procedure, no [^{3}H]progesterone peaks were seen on DEAE-Sephadex.
Slab gels of material eluting at the salt level where receptor
form I would elute showed that both receptor form A and the
90,000 dalton polypeptide were missing. Similarly, slab gels
of material eluting where form II would elute showed that both
B and the 90,000 dalton peptide were missing (8).

Phosphorylation In Vivo

Progesterone receptor form B and the 90,000 dalton polypeptide
are phosphoproteins, and for reasons described below it seems
probable that A is also a phosphoprotein. To examine progesterone receptor phosphorylation in vivo, oviduct tissue minces
were incubated with [^{32}P]orthophosphate, and receptor was
purified using deoxycorticosterone-agarose, heparin-agarose
and DEAE-Sephadex. Receptor form II was examined by slab gel
electrophoresis and by autoradiography. Two major bands of
phosphorylation were detected, coinciding with the positions
of B and of the 90,000 dalton polypeptide. Receptor form I
also showed two major bands of phosphorylation. One coincided
with the 90,000 dalton polypeptide. The second band of radioactivity from form I was located slightly above the position
of A on the slab gel (8). Phosphorylation can substantially
increase the apparent molecular weights of proteins on SDS-
slab gels (9,10). Both A and the phosphorylated material disappeared from "dummy" form I preparations treated with progesterone before exposure to the deoxycorticosterone-agarose
(8). Thus it seems likely that the phosphorylated material
may be a phosphorylated fraction of type A receptor. In addition to the tissue mince experiments, the labeling of these
receptor components with ^{32}P has been detected following in-

jection of chickens with [32P]orthophosphate (8,11). The labeled phosphoamino acids of the 90,000 dalton peptide and of receptor form B have been analyzed. Receptor was labeled by incubating an oviduct tissue mince with [32P]orthophosphate and purified as an 8S complex by a 3-step method including steroid affinity chromatography. The receptor components were separated by SDS-gel electrophoresis, eluted from the gels, hydrolyzed, and analyzed by thin layer electrophoresis and autoradiography. Phosphoserine was the only phosphoamino acid detected in the type B receptor, and the only phosphoamino acid detected in the 90,000 dalton peptide (11). In these experiments, the mince was exposed to [32P]orthophosphate for only one hour, and the incorporation of radioactivity into the receptor peptides was rather low. Thus phosphoamino acids whose phosphate groups turned over slowly might not have been detected.

The phosphorylation of receptor form B in vivo has also been examined by Weigel using a method which did not depend on 32PO4 incorporation. B was purified in the 4S form on a large scale and examined on an amino acid analyzer. Phosphoserine at 0.6 mol/mol peptide was the only detectable phosphoamino acid (12).

More recently receptor labeled with 32PO4 in tissue mince experiments has been examined by proteolytic cleavage and two dimensional peptide mapping. The 90,000 dalton peptide (Dougherty and Toft, unpublished) and receptor forms A and B (Puri and Toft, unpublished) all show multiple phosphorylation sites.

Phosphorylation In Vitro

Weigel et al. were the first to show that progesterone recep-

tor could be phosphorylated in vitro. They found that highly
purified type A and type B receptor both served as substrates
for cyclic AMP-dependent protein kinase from bovine heart.
Both receptor forms were rapidly phosphorylated by physiological concentrations of the kinase (13). Partial proteolytic cleavage and one dimensional peptide mapping were used
to locate the region of receptor B phosphorylated by the
cyclic AMP-dependent kinase. Using the one dimensional mapping
technique, progesterone binding was shown to occur on a 31,000
dalton peptide including the amino terminal end of B. This
steroid-binding region and regions close to it were not phosphorylated by the cyclic AMP-dependent kinase. Phosphorylation by the kinase was found on a 92,000 dalton peptide including the amino terminal end, but not on a 70,000 dalton
peptide including the amino terminal (12).

Recently, Weigel reported that partially purified preparations
of type A receptor contained a kinase which phosphorylated the
receptor more effectively than did the cyclic AMP-dependent
protein kinase. Partially purified preparations of B contained a second kinase which could phosphorylate the type B
receptor. In both cases, the kinase activity could be separated from the receptor subunits by additional chromatography
(14).

Both the A and B forms of progesterone receptor have been
found to be good substrates in vitro for the epidermal growth
factor receptor kinase (15). For these experiments A and B
were extensively purified in the 4S form by a procedure incor-
porating steroid affinity chromatography. Phosphorylation of
A and B occurred on tyrosine residues. No ^{32}P-labeled phosphoserine or phosphothreonine were detected. Approximately
1 mole phosphotyrosine per mole subunit could be incorporated
under optimal conditions. After in vitro labeling by epidermal growth factor kinase, receptor forms A and B were sub-

jected to extensive trypic digestion and analyzed by two dimensional mapping. Both forms showed similar patterns with two major and five minor labeled peptides (15). Phosphotyrosine was not detected during an investigation of progesterone receptor phosphorylation in vivo (11). However, the A and B receptor forms are high affinity substrates for the epidermal growth factor kinase in vitro (15). It is quite possible that the receptors are physiological substrates, but that the conditions for demonstrating phosphorylation in vivo have not yet been found.

The 90,000 dalton component of the 8S receptor form is a substrate in vitro for a nuclear kinase. This kinase has been partially purified by extracting nuclei with 0.3M KCl and by chromatography on phosphocellulose (16). When kinase activity eluting from the phosphocellulose was followed using phosvitin as a substrate, two major peaks were seen. The second peak contained a kinase which phosphorylated the 90,000 dalton polypeptide (Fig. 1). Treating the 90,000 dalton polypeptide with alkaline phosphatase prior to incubation with the kinase, increased the subsequent $^{32}PO_4$ incorporation six-fold (Dougherty and Toft, unpublished). Thus it seems probable that the 90,000 dalton peptide as isolated is substantially phosphorylated at the site or sites modified by this nuclear kinase. The present data suggest that the kinase is a type II nuclear kinase, an enzyme class which phosphorylates serine and threonine residues at acidic sites within proteins (17). However further purification and characterization of the enzyme will be required to establish definitely the identity of this kinase.

Recently Garcia et al. have suggested that both receptor form B and the 90,000 dalton polypeptide display protein kinase activity (18). In the presence of calcium but not magnesium, purified preparations of the 90,000 dalton peptide incor-

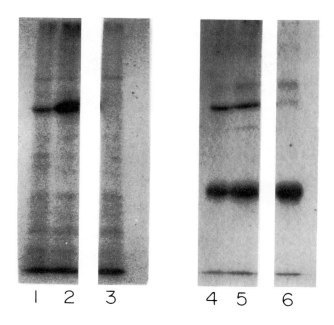

Figure 1. Phosphorylation of the 90,000 Dalton Component of
8S Progesterone Receptor by a Nuclear Kinase. Progesterone
receptor from chicken oviduct was purified in the presence of
molybdate using deoxycorticosterone-agarose, heparin-agarose
and DEAE-Sephadex. Peak I from the DEAE column was concentrated and dialyzed to remove molybdate. Aliquots were kept
on ice (1,4) or incubated for 1/2 hr at room temperature with
insoluble intestinal alkaline phosphatase (Sigma) (2,5).
After removal of the phosphatase, samples were incubated with
$[\gamma-^{32}P]ATP$ for 30 min at 30°C in pH 7.3 MOPS buffer containing
$MgCl_2$, spermine, spermidine and the nuclear kinase. Lanes 3
and 6 represent a sample containing kinase but no receptor.
Proteins were precipitated and separated by electrophoresis in
the presence of SDS. In the illustration above, lanes 1-3 are
autoradiograms of the proteins stained with Coomassie blue in
lanes 4-6. The primary high molecular weight bands in lanes
4 and 5 are the 90,000 dalton polypeptides. Ovalbumin was
added to all samples as carrier.

porated radioactivity from [γ-^{32}P]ATP into the 90,000 dalton
peptide. Highly purified preparations of type B receptor incorporated label from [γ-^{32}P]ATP into B on incubation with
magnesium but not with calcium. A key question with regard to
both of these observations is whether the phosphorylations
were catalyzed by the receptor components themselves or by
minor contaminants in the preparations. This question may be
particular pertinent to the kinase activity attributed to the
type B receptor. Weigel has reported a magnesium dependent
kinase activity associated with partially purified type B receptor which separated from receptor on further purification
(14). At present the possibility that a component of the 8S
progesterone receptor may be a protein kinase is a plausible
and intriguing one, but compelling evidence for hypothesis is
lacking.

Phosphorylation and Receptor Function

Puri et al. have shown that pre-treating chicken oviduct
cytosol with intestinal alkaline phosphatase abolished the
ability of that cytosol to bind [^{3}H]progesterone (19). Pre-
treatment with E. coli alkaline phosphatase or with potato
acid phosphatase had much less effect. This work showed that
intestinal alkaline phosphatase had an effect on cytosolic
preparations of progesterone receptor similar to that shown
earlier on cytosolic preparations of glucocorticoid receptor
(20). It is consistent with the hypothesis that phosphorylation regulates the ability of steroid receptors to bind
steroid, but in a system as complex as the cytosol one cannot
be confident that the phosphatase is acting directly on the
progesterone receptor. Working with purified estrogen receptor, Aurrichio's group has found a phosphatase which abolishes
steroid binding ability, and a kinase which restores it (21).
Thus far, no comparable effects have been demonstrated on
purified progesterone receptor.

Phosphorylation could also affect other receptor functions. Changes in receptor phosphorylation may affect the readiness of progesterone receptor subunits to undergo transformation to the forms which bind tightly to nuclei. In addition, the phosphorylation state of transformed receptor subunits could serve to regulate the binding of these subunits at the nuclear sites where they act to promote or inhibit the transcription of specific genes. Progesterone receptor components are phosphoproteins, and are good substrates in vitro for kinases involving in regulating cellular function. Thus studies on progesterone receptor phosphorylation promise to yield significant new insights about the regulation of steroid receptor function.

References

1. Schrader, W.T., Kuhn, R.W., O'Malley, B.W.: J. Biol. Chem. 252, 299-307 (1977).

2. Coty, W.A., Schrader, W.T., O'Malley, B.W.: J. Steroid Biochem. 10, 1-12 (1979).

3. Schrader, W.T., Heuer, S.S., O'Malley, B.W.: Biol. Reprod. 12, 134-142 (1975).

4. Toft, D.O., Shyamala, G., Gorski, J.: Proc. Natl. Acad. Sci. USA 57, 1740-1743 (1967).

5. Wolfson, A., Mester, J., Chang-Ren, Y., Baulieu, E-E.: Biochem. Biophys. Res. Comm. 95, 1577-1584 (1980).

6. Dougherty, J.J., Toft, D.O.: J. Biol. Chem. 257, 3113-3119 (1982).

7. Joab, I., Radanyi, C., Renoir, M., Buchou, T., Catelli, M-G., Binart, N., Mester, J., Baulieu, E-E.: Nature 308, 850-853 (1984).

8. Dougherty, J.J., Puri, R.K., Toft, D.O.: J. Biol. Chem. 259, 8004-8009 (1984).

9. Linne', T., Philipson, L.: Eur. J. Biochem. 103, 259-270 (1980).

308

10. Sy, J., Roselle, M.: Proc. Natl. Acad. Sci. USA 79, 2874-2877 (1982).

11. Dougherty, J.J., Puri, R.K., Toft, D.O.: J. Biol. Chem. 257, 14226-14230 (1982).

12. Weigel, N.L., Minghetti,P.P., Stevens, B., Schrader, W.T., O'Malley, B.W.: in Steroid Hormone Receptors: Structure and Function, H. Eriksson and L.-A. Gustafsson, eds., Elsevier Science Publishers, Amsterdam, pp 25-42 (1983).

13. Weigel, N.L., Tash, J.S., Means, A.R., Schrader, W.T., O'Malley, B.W.: Biochem. Biophys. Res. Comm. 102, 513-519 (1981).

14. Weigel, N.L.: Excerpta Medica, Abstracts, 7th International Congress of Endocrinology, Elsevier Science Publishers, Amsterdam, p 1615 (1984).

15. Ghosh-Dastidar, P., Coty, W.A., Griest, R.E., Woo, D.D.L., Fox, C.F.: Proc. Natl. Acad. Sci. USA 81, 1654-1658 (1984).

16. Keller, R.K., Chandra, T., Schrader, W.T., O'Malley, B.W.: Biochem. 15, 1958-1967 (1976).

17. Rose, K.M., Bell, L.E., Siefken, D.A., Jacob,S.T.: J. Biol. Chem. 256, 7468-7477 (1981).

18. Garcia, T., Tuohimaa, P., Mester, J., Buchou, T., Renoir, J.-M., Baulieu, E.-E.: Biochem. Biophys. Res. Comm. 113, 960-966 (1983).

19. Puri, R.K., Dougherty, J.J., Toft, D.O.: J. Steroid Biochem. 20, 23-29 (1984).

20. Nielsen, C.J., Sando, J.J., Pratt, W.B.: Proc. Natl. Acad. Sci. USA 74, 1398-1402 (1977).

21. Migliaccio, A., Lastoria, S., Moncharmont, B., Rotondi, A. and Aurrichio,F.: Biochem. Biophys. Res. Comm. 109, 1002-1010 (1982).

PURIFICATION, ACTIVATION, AND PHOSPHORYLATION OF THE GLUCOCOR-TICOID RECEPTOR

Thomas J. Schmidt

Department of Physiology and Biophysics
College of Medicine
The University of Iowa
Iowa City, Iowa 52242

Gerald Litwack

Fels Research Institute and Department of Biochemistry
Temple University School of Medicine
Philadelphia, Pennsylvania 19140

Introduction

During the past decade our understanding of how glucocorticoid hormones interact with their specific intracellular receptors and how these complexes subsequently interact with nuclear acceptor sites in such a way as to regulate the expression of specific genes has been greatly expanded. However, in order to further probe the structure of the receptor protein itself and to define the biochemical factors which regulate or mediate the various functions of these receptors, it was clear that highly purified glucocorticoid receptors would ultimately be required. Therefore, during the past several years research in our laboratories has focussed on the development of a scheme suitable for the purification of unactivated (untransformed) glucocorticoid-receptor complexes. We have felt that such a purification scheme would facilitate a number of crucial and potentially exciting experiments dealing with several aspects of the receptor. First, such a scheme would enable us to biochemically characterize the purified, molybdate-stabilized, unactivated glucocorticoid receptor and probe its

possible subunit structure. Secondly, the availability of
highly purified, unactivated complexes would allow us to directly test the various theories which have been proposed concerning the mechanism(s) by which these complexes acquire the
capacity to bind to DNA, a process which we refer to as
"activation." Reconstitution experiments with the purified,
unactivated glucocorticoid-receptor complexes would also facilitate evaluation of the possible role of cytoplasmic factors in mediating this physiologically relevant conformational
change. Finally, this purification scheme would hopefully
allow us to test whether the glucocorticoid receptor is a
phosphoprotein, and if so, what biochemical factors and experimental conditions regulate or influence the appropriate
kinase reaction. In this chapter we will review the recent
progress we have made in these specific areas of research and,
where appropriate, will attempt to relate our experimental results to those published by other laboratories studying the
glucocorticoid receptor.

Background

Glucocorticoids influence the growth, differentiation, and
function of a wide variety of tissues and cell types. These
responses vary dramatically and include catabolic effects,
such as lysis and death of lymphoid cells (1,2,3), as well as
anabolic effects, including induction of a limited number of
enzymes in hepatoma cells (4,5,6). A large volume of experimental data supports the concept that, as with other steroid
hormones, most of these effects of glucocorticoids are mediated through intracellular receptor proteins which bind this
steroid molecule with high affinity and specificity (7). Published studies have clearly suggested that this binding requires phosphorylation as well as reduction of the receptor
protein itself or some other cytosolic component required for
the steroid-binding reaction (8,9). If these criteria are

met and the glucocorticoid molecule has bound to its cytoplasmic receptor, the complex must then undergo a two-step
process in order to bind to nuclei and ultimately affect gene
expression. The first temperature-dependent step, termed
"activation" or "transformation", is thought to involve a conformational change in the steroid-receptor complex resulting
in the exposure of positively charged amino acid residues
(consisting minimally of arginine, histidine, and lysine) on
the surface of the protein (10,11) and hence an increased
affinity for nuclei and polyanions such as purified DNA and
DNA-cellulose (10,12,13,14). This conformational change is
also reflected in an altered elution profile of the activated
glucocorticoid-receptor complexes from anion exchange resins
such as DEAE-Sephadex (15) and DEAE-cellulose (16). The
second temperature-independent step which follows activation
is termed "translocation" and involves the movement of the
previously activated complexes into the nucleus where they
bind to acceptor sites within the chromatin (17) and, more
precisely, to DNA sequences which flank specific genes whose
expression is regulated by glucocorticoids (18,19,20). The
net results of this nuclear binding are the initiation of
transcription of these glucocorticoid-responsive genes and
the ultimate translation of mRNAs into specific proteins
whose activities contribute to the phenotypic response.

Maximal in vitro activation of glucocorticoid-receptor complexes in crude cytosolic extracts can be achieved by a number
of manipulations including elevated temperature, increased
ionic strength, elevated pH or gel filtration (10,11,22).
However the precise biochemical mechanism(s) underlying this
crucial step remains to be elucidated. Numerous enzymatic and
non-enzymatic theories including dephosphorylation of the receptor itself or an accessory protein (23,24), glucocorticoid-
receptor phosphorylation (25), limited proteolysis (26), dis-

sociation of a low molecular weight inhibitor or "modulator" (21,27,28) and simple subunit dissociation (29) have all been proposed as possible mechanisms involved in activation. However, rigorous testing of these theories, which have been evaluated in several published reviews (30,31,32), requires purification of unactivated glucocorticoid-receptor complexes and re-evaluation of the in vitro regulation of activation and the potential role of cytoplasmic factors in mediating this conformational change. Since activation of glucocorticoid-receptor complexes occurs in vitro under physiological conditions and is rate limiting for nuclear binding (33,34,35), insight with respect to the biochemical mechanism underlying this obligatory step would contribute to our understanding of how hormonal signals are transmitted within the target cell.

Data concerning both the structure of the receptor as well as the mechanism of activation, which have been generated with crude cytoplasmic extracts, are subject to multiple interpretations. Several laboratories have therefore attempted to develop a suitable purification scheme for this protein. Early attempts to purify the glucocorticoid-receptor complex in its unactivated form were relatively unsuccessful for several reasons. The steroid binding site of this protein, which is present at very low concentrations, is relatively unstable and most of the techniques used to purify proteins, including ammonium sulfate precipitation and gel filtration, quickly lead to activation of the glucocorticoid-receptor complexes. However, one of the first successful attempts at purifying unactivated complexes utilized affinity chromatography. Failla et al. (36) reported the partial purification (approximately 2000-fold) of unactivated glucocorticoid-receptor complexes from hepatoma tissue culture cells using a two-step procedure involving biospecific adsorption of the receptors to deoxy-corticosterone derivatized agarose, elution with [3H]triamcinolone acetonide and subsequent gel filtration on Bio-Gel A-

0.5m. These partially purified complexes were judged to be unactivated because subsequent warming (20°C for 30 mins) enhanced their nuclear binding capacity by approximately 2.6-fold. In these experiments the pH was maintained at 6.5, which probably minimized spontaneous activation which could occur during the purification procedure. Although additional reports of purification of unactivated glucocorticoid receptors appeared (37,38), neither the physicochemical characteristics of the receptors or the mechanism of activation were thoroughly investigated. After Leach et al. (23) demonstrated that sodium molybdate blocks both the inactivation (loss of steroid binding capacity) of unbound receptors as well as the activation of crude glucocorticoid-receptor complexes, the technical problem concerning spontaneous activation during purification was subsequently overcome by including this inhibitor in all the purification buffers. Most recently a three-step purification scheme, which includes affinity chromatography, gel filtration and DEAE-cellulose chromatography (39), has been employed successfully in our laboratories to yield highly purified, molybdate-stabilized, unactivated glucocorticoid-receptor complexes. This purification scheme also involves the initial adsorption of unbound cytoplasmic receptors to a deoxycorticosterone-derivatized agarose developed by Grandics (40,41). This affinity resin offers specific advantages over similar resins utilized previously. These advantages as well as the details of the purification scheme itself will be discussed in the Methods section.

Experimental data generated in several laboratories have suggested that phosphorylation/dephosphorylation reactions may regulate receptor functions including both glucocorticoid binding activity as well as the subsequent activation step (31). However, since unpurified glucocorticoid receptors were used in these studies it has not been possible to distinguish between phosphorylation/dephosphorylation of the receptor protein itself and similar modifications of other cellular components which influence receptor functions. It is a well established fact that the glucocorticoid-binding ability of cells can be correlated with ATP levels. In 1968 Munck and Brinck-Johnson (42) demonstrated that ATP levels and glucocorticoid binding ability decrease in thymocytes incubated briefly under nitrogen but that binding ability is restored as ATP levels increase in cells shifted back to aerobic conditions. Importantly, cycloheximide did not block the recovery of specific binding after restoration of oxygen (43), suggesting that new synthesis of receptor proteins was not required. A similar relationship between glucocortiocid receptors and ATP levels has also been observed in cultured human lymphocytes (44). The specific binding of glucocorticoids in cytosols from mouse fibroblasts that decreases during in vitro incubation can also be partially restored by added ATP (9). Similarly the estrogen-binding capacity of thermally inactivated rat and mouse uterine cytosols can be restored by an ATP-dependent activity (45,46). Although these data are consistent with regenerated steroid binding resulting as a consequence of phosphorylation, Barnett et al. (47) have subsequently demonstrated that ATP stabilization of the glucocorticoid binding site is due to ADP generated from the triphosphate by endogenous enzymes and is not due to phosphorylation or adenylation of the receptor by ATP. These investigators postulated that ADP may interact with a receptor nucleotide binding site and stabilize the glucocorticoid binding site by an allosteric mechanism.

The hypothesis that dephosphorylation resulting as a consequence of low ATP levels might control glucocorticoid binding is supported by the fact that incubation of crude cytosol with exogenous alkaline phosphatase greatly diminishes its capacity to bind glucocorticoids (48). In addition, the phosphatase inhibitors, sodium molybdate and sodium fluoride, have both been reported to stabilize the binding capacity of cytosolic glucocorticoid receptors (9,23). More recently Housley et al. (49) have demonstrated that inactivation of the unoccupied glucocorticoid receptor from mouse L-cells is stimulated by highly purified rabbit muscle protein phosphatase to a greater extent than by calf intestinal alkaline phosphatase. They also reported that this inactivation could be reversed by dithiothreitol if sodium molybdate was added to the cytosol at the time of enzyme addition. Based on these experimental results they proposed that phosphorylation of the receptor insures a conformation that prevents oxidation of sulfhydryl groups which are essential for steroid binding. The greater effectiveness of the muscle protein phosphatase, which demonstrates preferential activity toward phosphoserine residues, when compared to alkaline phosphatase, which shows preferential activity for phosphotyrosine residues (50), is also consistent with the observation that the mouse L-cell glucocorticoid receptor is phosphorylated in vitro on serine residues (51).

Just as there are indirect data which suggest a critical role for receptor phosphorylation in stabilization of the steroid binding site, there are also indirect data which suggest that dephosphorylation may be required during subsequent activation of glucocorticoid-receptor complexes. Barnett et al. (24) reported that exogenous alkaline phosphatase, which is known to secondarily dephosphorylate phosphoproteins, stimulates the rate of activation of rat hepatic glucocorticoid-receptor complexes. However, since unfractionated cytosols were employed in this series of experiments, it was again not possible to differentiate between dephosphorylation of the receptor protein itself and dephosphorylation of another protein which in turn stimulates or facilitates activation.

Also, as previously mentioned, the phosphatase inhibitor, sodium molybdate, has been shown to inhibit activation of glucocorticoid-receptor complexes (23,24). It is tempting to speculate that sodium molybdate, by inhibiting dephosphorylation, blocks inactivation of the steroid binding site and also blocks activation of glucocorticoid-receptor complexes. Although this hypothesis is consistent with the experimental data which have been presented, it may clearly represent an oversimplification. Harmon et al. (52) have reported that although sodium molybdate blocks inactivation of unbound receptors in an "activation labile", glucocorticoid resistant, lymphoid mutant it does not apparently inhibit activation of glucocorticoid-receptor complexes in this same mutant. Thus inactivation of unbound receptors and activation of bound complexes may not both involve simple dephosphorylation by a common phosphatase.

In light of this growing body of evidence which suggests that phosphorylation may significantly affect the functioning of steroid receptors, it is not surprising that several laboratories have demonstrated that steroid receptors are in fact phosphoproteins. Weigel et al. (53) first reported that the purified progesterone receptor A and B subunits can be phosphorylated in vitro using cAMP-dependent protein kinase. Direct evidence that the progesterone receptor is phosphorylated in vivo on serine residues has been reported by Dougherty et al. (54), who purified [^{32}P]-labeled progesterone receptors from the oviducts of chickens injected with [^{32}P]-orthophosphate. Subsequently it was reported that the purified subunits of chicken progesterone receptors demonstrate protein kinase activity (55). The experimental data suggested that although phosphorylation of the 90K component (subunit A) in the presence of Ca^{2+} may represent a very selective protein kinase activity, the phosphorylating activity of the 110K component (subunit B) in the presence of Mg^{2+} was less specific and resembles that described for most protein kinases. Recently, however, Weigel (56) has succeeded in separating the partially purified A and B subunits of the chicken oviduct progesterone receptor from the distinct kinases which co-purify with and mediate phosphorylation of these subunits. Thus it would appear that the A and B subunits are not themselves kinases which mediate autophorphorylation. Although less thoroughly described, the uterine estradiol receptor has also been reported to be phosphorylated in vitro by a cytosolic Ca^{2+}-calmodulin stimulated kinase (57).

Finally, several laboratories, including our own, have published data which demonstrate that the glucocorticoid receptor is also a phosphoprotein. Housley and Pratt (51) have reported that receptors in glucocorticoid-sensitive mouse fibroblasts (L929) are phosphorylated in vivo on serine residues. As will be discussed later in this chapter, our laboratory has also demonstrated that rat hepatic glucocorticoid-receptors are labeled in vivo with $[^{32}P]$-orthophosphate (58). Kurl and Jacob (59) have also presented preliminary data which suggest that the purified rat hepatic glucocorticoid-receptor contains protein kinase activity which is capable of phosphorylating the receptor. The purity of the receptor utilized for these experiments was based solely on staining with Coomassie Blue and hence minor contamination by a kinase which might co-purify with the receptor could not be totally excluded. Neither the potential dependency of the kinase activity on cyclic nucleotides or on ligand binding to the receptor were investigated. Before these data were published our laboratory had already initiated a thorough biochemical characterization of the kinase activity associated with the highly purified rat hepatic glucocorticoid-receptor and that data will also be reviewed in this chapter.

Methods

Receptor purification

The three-step scheme (affinity chromatography, gel filtration, DEAE-cellulose chromatography) which our laboratory has
developed for purification of unactivated rat hepatic glucocorticoid receptors has been described in detail elsewhere
(39) and hence will only be briefly outlined here. The livers
of adrenalectomized male Wistar rats (150-200 gm) are first
perfused in situ via the portal vein with cold 0.9% NaCl and
then with homogenization buffer A (50mM potassium phosphate,
10 mM sodium molybdate, and 10 mM thioglycerol, pH 7.0 at 4°C).
The excised and minced livers are then weighed and homogenized
with a motor driven Teflon-glass Potter-Elvehjem apparatus in
1 volume of buffer A. After the crude homogenate is centrifuged at 4000xg for 10 minutes and the upper lipid layer is
carefully aspirated, the supernatant fraction is centrifuged
at 105,000xg for 1 hour to obtain the cytosol. All of these
procedures are performed at 0-4°C and the final cytosol is
stored at -70°C until further use. To initiate the purification procedure, approximately 10 ml of thawed, molybdate-
containing cytosol is mixed with 5 ml of a deoxycorticosterone-
derivatized agarose synthesized by Grandics (40,41) and depicted in Figure 1.

Because of the steps employed in its preparation, this resin
offers several advantages for the purification of cytoplasmic

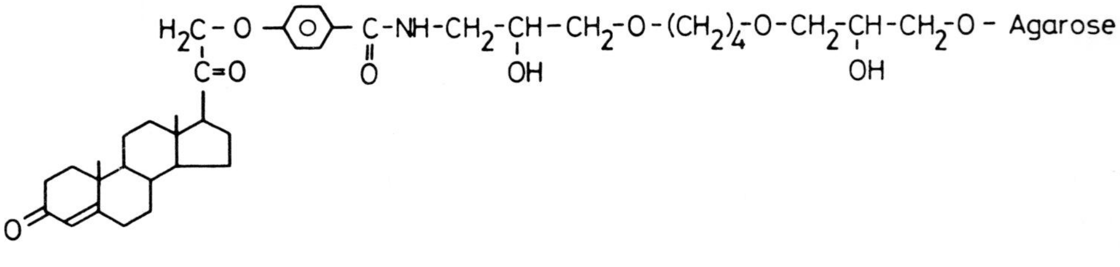

Figure 1   Structure of affinity resin.

glucocorticoid receptors (40). Although the cyanogen bromide technique (60,61) has frequently been used to attach various ligands to polysaccharides, this procedure often introduces anion exchange groups on the support (62) and hence enhances nonspecific protein adsorption. In addition, the immobilized ligand often leaks from the matrix due to the lability of the isourea bond formed during the introduction of the spacer (63). In contrast, adsorbents such as the present affinity resin, which have been prepared by the epoxide technique (64), usually exhibit much higher stability and lower nonspecific adsorption (65). In addition to these obvious advantages, other modifications were introduced during synthesis of the deoxy-corticosterone-derivatized agarose (40). The reactive groups which are introduced into the polysaccharide support by the initial epoxidation step were converted into non-reactive amino groups and the epoxidation step itself was modified to prevent formation of extended crosslinks on the carrier (64).

After crude cytosol is stirred with this affinity resin at 0-$4^{\circ}C$ for a minimum of 2 hours, the supernatant fraction (referred to as the affinity gel supernatant) is collected by centrifugation and assayed for specific binding of $[6,7^{-3}H]$ triamcinolone acetonide (TA) (32-37 Ci/mmole; New England Nuclear) by the hydroxylapatite technique (66,67). The resin is then washed batchwise eight times with 10 ml of buffer A to remove nonspecifically adsorbed proteins. The receptors are then eluted from the resin by adding 5-10 ml of buffer B (10mM potassium phosphate, 10mM sodium molybdate, 10mM thioglycerol, and 10% glycerol, pH 7.0 at $4^{\circ}C$) containing 2uM $[^{3}H]$TA and incubating the mixture at 0-$4^{\circ}C$ for 16 hours. The eluted $[^{3}H]$TA-receptor complexes are then collected by centrifugation or by filtering the slurry on a Teflon filter. The resin is then washed with an additional 4 ml of buffer B and the combined affinity gel eluate is assayed for bound $[^{3}H]$TA. The

320

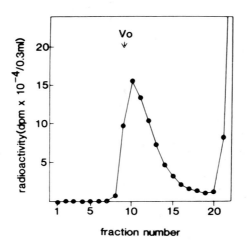

<u>Figure 2</u>   Bio-Gel A-1.5m column chromatography of affinity
            gel eluted [^{3}H]triamcinolone acetonide-receptor
            complexes. Reproduced with permission from J.
            Biol. Chem. (39).

used affinity resin is then regenerated as previously described (41) and is transferred into buffer A and stored at 0-
4°C. The affinity gel eluate is then filtered on a Bio-Gel
A-1.5m column (220 ml bed volume; inner diameter 2.5 cm)
equilibrated with buffer A at 0-4°C. Eight-ml fractions are
collected and aliquots are counted for radioactivity. The
[^{3}H]TA-receptor fractions elute as a single peak of bound radioactivity as seen in Fig. 2. The receptor peak fractions
are then combined and applied via a peristaltic pump to a
DEAE-cellulose column (3-ml bed volume) and the unactivated
[^{3}H]TA-receptor complexes are then eluted with a linear salt
gradient (50-500mM potassium phosphate) containing 10mM sodium
molybdate and 10mM thioglycerol, pH 7.0. Thirty 1-ml fractions are collected and 50ul aliquots are assayed for determination of radioactivity. As seen in Fig. 3, the unactivated
[^{3}H]TA-receptor complexes are eluted as a single peak at

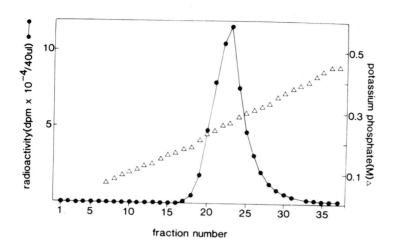

<u>Figure 3</u> DEAE-cellulose chromatography of purified [³H]tri-
          amcinolone acetonide-receptor complexes. Repro-
          duced with permission from J. Biol. Chem. (39).

approximately 280mM potassium phosphate. The unactivated
[³H]TA-receptor peak fractions are then pooled and either utilized immediately for experimentation or frozen under liquid
nitrogen for use at a later date. Prior to freezing, however,
the pooled peak is filtered through a Sephadex G-25 column
equilibrated with buffer C (10mM MES, 0.5mM EDTA, 0.5mM
dithiothreitol and 5mg/ml of bovine serum albumin, pH 7.0 at
4°C) containing 10mM MoO_4 to remove the high salt (unactivated
complexes eluted from DEAE-cellulose at 200-300nM potassium
phosphate). The eluate is adjusted to 10% glycerol and 60nM
[³H]TA is added to facilitate rebinding during the thawing
process. After thawing the purified, unactivated [³H]TA-
receptor complexes are again filtered through a Sephadex G-25
column to facilitate removal of sodium molybdate, glycerol and
free [³H]TA prior to activation studies.

SDS-polyacrylamide gel electrophoresis

Electrophoresis of the purified glucocorticoid receptors is accomplished in 10% linear polyacrylamide slab gels according to O'Farrell (68). The receptor samples are concentrated by precipitation with trichloroacetic acid (10% final) together with 10ul of 2% (w/v) sodium deoxycholate/ml of sample at 0°C for 30 minutes. The pellets obtained after centrifugation are washed once with 1 ml of 10% trichloroacetic acid and then with 1 ml of ether/acetone (1:1). Finally the precipitated proteins are redissolved in sample buffer (68) by boiling for 3 minutes. To ensure complete solubilization of the acid-precipitated material, 1 ul of 1M NaOH is added to every ul of sample buffer prior to boiling. Protein standards (Pharmacia Fine Chemicals) are processed in a similar manner. In order to detect proteins on the gels, a highly sensitive double stain procedure with Coomassie Blue R-250 and silver (69) is employed with minor modifications. After electrophoresis the proteins were fixed and stained in 45% ethanol, 10% acetic acid, and 0.24% Coomassie Blue R-250 (w/v) in distilled water. Destaining is achieved by washing the gel several times with this fixative mixture (devoid of Coomassie Blue) until the background is clear and the gel is further stained by an improved silver method (70). In the experiments designed to investigate the in vivo incorporation of [^{32}P] into the purified receptor the gels were stained only with Coomaisse Blue and after appropriate destaining were impregnated with EN^{3}HANCE, dried, and autoradiographed at -70°C using regular enhancing screens.

Quantitation of activation

The activation of partially and highly purified [^{3}H]TA-receptor complexes is quantitated by assaying the ability of these complexes to bind to DNA-cellulose according to the procedure of Kalimi et al. (13). Briefly, 100 ul aliquots of purified receptor are added in triplicate to 50 ul of packed DNA-cellulose and are then incubated at 0-5°C for 45 minutes. Two ml of cold TE buffer (10 mM Tris-HCl and 1mM EDTA, pH 8.0 at 0-4°C) are subsequently added to each tube and the suspensions are mixed. After centrifugation the supernatants are aspirated and the DNA-cellulose pellets are resuspended in 0.8 ml of TE buffer and 0.5 ml are subsequently counted for radioactivity. The [3H]TA bound to DNA-cellulose after a given treatment is then expressed as a percentage of the receptor bound [3H]TA following the same treatment (DNA-cellulose binding/hydroxylapatite binding x 100). Activation is both visualized and quantitated by the chromatographic separation of unactivated and activated [3H]TA-receptor complexes on DEAE-cellulose with a linear 5-400mM potassium phosphate elution gradient (16). The [3H]TA-receptor complexes eluted in the activated position (approximately 60-80mM potassium phosphate) were then expressed as a percentage of the [3H]TA-receptor complexes eluted in both the activated and unactivated positions.

Kinase assay

The highly purified, unactivated [3H]TA-receptor complexes are first filtered through a Sephadex G-75 column to remove sodium molybdate. The molybdate-free [3H]TA-receptor complexes are then incubated with approximately 10nM adenosine 5'-[γ-^{32}P]triphosphate ([γ-^{32}P]ATP) (2000 Ci/mmole; New England Nuclear) for 30 minutes at 25°C in the presence of 1mM Ca^{2+}. In experiments designed to test the potential requirement of bound steroid for kinase activity the [3H]TA was first stripped from the unactivated receptor complexes by a brief exposure to dextran-coated charcoal. The kinase assay is terminated by the addition of sample buffer and boiling for 5 minutes. The samples are then electrophoresed and the gels are either stained with Coomaisse Blue and silver or immediately dried and subjected to autoradiography as previously described.

Results and Discussion

Characterization of purified, unactivated receptor complexes

The unactivated, molybdate-stabilized rat hepatic glucocorticoid receptor has been purified approximately 4000-fold, as calculated by specific radioactivity, by the three-step procedure described (39). The average percent yield and the fold purification after the affinity gel, gel filtration and DEAE-cellulose chromatography steps are listed in Table 1. The purity of the receptor peak fractions eluted from DEAE-cellulose (Figure 3) was analyzed by SDS-polyacrylamide gel electrophoresis and the gels were subsequently subjected to the sensitive double staining procedure (69) with Coomassie Blue R-250 followed by silver. The protein pattern revealed a major $M_r = 90,000$ band in each fraction and the occurrence of this band closely paralleled the distribution of bound radioactivity seen in Figure 3. This observation is consistent with the fact that a number of photoaffinity and electrophilic affinity labeling as well as immunological studies have identified a $M_r = 90,000$ protein as the glucocorticoid receptor in a variety of tissues (51,76,77,78,79). The receptor peak fraction eluted from DEAE-cellulose was similarly electrophoresed and the gel was subjected to the double staining procedure, destained with Kodak Rapid Fix (80) and then restained by the double staining procedure. A scan of this gel in a

Table 1   Three-step purification of unactivated rat hepatic glucocorticoid receptors

Fraction	% Yield	Fold Purification[a]
Crude cytosol	100	1
Affinity gel eluate	60	144
Bio-Gel filtrate	50	566
DEAE-cellulose eluate	34	4295

a. Average data for three separate experiments (39).

Zeineh soft laser scanning densitometer revealed the presence
of two other protein bands corresponding to apparent Mr =
41,000 and 40,000. A Mr = 24,000 band, which appeared to be
present at very low concentrations in the receptor peak
fraction, was also eluted from DEAE-cellulose at a salt concentration higher than that required for the elution of purified, unactivated [³H]TA-receptor complexes. The relationship
of these three components (Mr = 41,000, 40,000, and 24,000)
to the Mr = 90,000 receptor was investigated by presaturating
liver cytosol with nonradioactive TA prior to proceeding with
the purification procedure. When the appropriate fractions
eluted from the final DEAE-cellulose column were analyzed,
the Mr = 90,000 component was very faint and the other three
components were totally undetectable. These data suggested
that these lower molecular weight components may either be
constituents of the purified, molybdate-stabilized, unactivated glucocorticoid-receptor complex or may represent proteolytic fragments of the Mr = 90,000 protein. However, as will
be discussed later in this chapter, the lack of incorporation
of [³²P] into either the Mr = 41,000 or 40,000 component
suggests that they are not proteolytic fragments of the [³²P]-
labeled Mr = 90,000 receptor (58).

As seen in Figure 4, the highly purified unactivated [³H]TA-
receptor complexes eluted from DEAE-cellulose sedimented at
9-10S in low salt (40mM KCl) linear (10-35%) glycerol gradients containing 10mM molybdate, and this sedimentation coefficient is similar to that reported for crude hepatic
glucocorticoid receptors (71). However, when the salt concentration was increased to 1M KCl the sedimentation coefficient of the purified [³H]TA-receptor complexes was only
slightly reduced to 8-9S. Thus, unlike crude cytosolic receptors (71), the purified receptor complexes appear to be
more resistant to a salt-induced conversion to an 8S form.
Elevation of the salt concentration of the purified prepara-

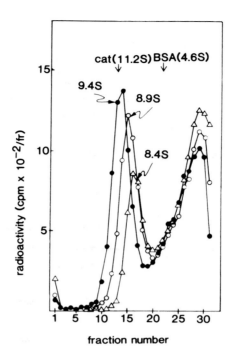

Figure 4   Glycerol gradient ultracentrifugation of purified
            [³H]triamcinolone acetonide-receptor complexes
            eluted from DEAE-cellulose in the presence of 40mM
            (●), 400mM (○) and 1M (Δ) KCl. Arrows indicate the
            presence of protein standards (catalase and bovine
            serum albumin). Reproduced with permission from J.
            Biol. Chem. (39).

tions also did not result in the appearance of 4-5S forms as
previously detected with other molybdate-stabilized, crude
cytosolic glucocorticoid receptors (72,73). These results
suggest that the salt-induced conversion of the large (9-10S)
receptor into smaller forms may not simply involve dissociation of subunits. As will be discussed shortly, a heat-stable
cytosolic protein appears to facilitate maximal DNA-cellulose
binding of thermally activated, purified [³H]TA-receptor complexes. It will be interesting to test whether this same
factor might also play a role in generating the 4-5S form of
the purified receptor.

The Stokes radius of the purified, unactivated [3H]TA-receptor complexes was estimated by filtration through a standardized column of Bio-Gel A-1.5m agarose. The initial Stokes radius which was obtained was approximately 6.0nm, but subsequent analyses suggested that dissociation of receptor complexes has occurred even in the presence of molybdate. This conclusion was consistent with the fact that multimeric proteins of extremely low concentration can dissociate upon gel filtration in a concentration-dependent manner (74,75) and the protein concentration in the purified receptor preparation is in the microgram/ml range. When a smaller gel filtration column equilibrated with 50ug/ml of albumin was utilized, a Stokes radius of 7.3nm was calculated and this value is again similar to that of crude hepatic receptors (71). From the sedimentation coefficient and the Stokes radius an apparent $Mr = 303,000$ was calculated for the purified receptor. A calculated frictional ratio of 1.64 and an axial ratio for a prolate ellipsoid of approximately 12 suggested that the purified receptor is highly asymmetric. Taken collectively these data suggested that the hydrodynamic properties and molecular parameters of the highly purified complexes resemble those of molybdate-stabilized, crude hepatic glucocorticoid-receptor complexes (71).

Activation of purified [3H]TA-receptor complexes

It was clear that the [3H]TA-receptor complexes which were purified by this three-step procedure were in the unactivated form because they could subsequently be heat activated and demonstrated enhanced binding to DNA-cellulose (39). In order to perform these activation experiments, however, the purified complexes were first filtered through Sephadex G-25 to remove molybdate which was present throughout the purification procedure. As seen in Table 2, this procedure alone resulted in increased binding of the purified [3H]TA-receptor complexes to DNA-cellulose, which agrees with the known activating

Table 2   In Vitro activation of purified [³H]triamcinolone
acetonide-receptor complexes eluted from DEAE-cellulose. Reproduced with permission from J. Biol.
Chem. (39).

Treatment	Number of experiments	[³H]Triam-cinolone acetonide-receptor dpm added	DNA-cellulose bound dpm	% of total bound to DNA-cellulose
Gel filtration in	1	111,600	1,000	0.9
the presence of	2	29,700	270	0.9
10 mM Na₂MoO₄				
Gel filtration	1	86,900	6,200	7.2
	2	28,600	1,320	4.6
Gel filtration +	1	84,000	15,200	18.1
heat (25 °C, 30	2	24,100	4,470	18.5
min)				
Gel filtration + 10	1	86,500	7,100	8.2
mM Na₂MoO₄ +	2	25,000	2,300	9.2
heat (25 °C, 30				
min)				
Gel filtration + cy-	1	85,400	39,000	45.6
tosol + heat	2	24,900	10,700	42.8
(25 °C, 30 min)				
Gel filtration + cy-	1	69,500	9,800	14.1
tosol + 10 mM	2	25,500	2,960	11.6
Na₂MoO₄ + heat				
(25 °C, 30 min)				

effect of gel filtration (21,22). What was clear from these
experiments was that although heating (25°C for 30 minutes)
enhanced the binding of purified [³H]TA-receptor complexes to
DNA-cellulose, this binding was significantly less than that
previously observed for receptors in crude cytosols (14,16).
In our laboratory generally 35-45% of the [³H]TA-receptor complexes in crude cytosols bind to DNA-cellulose after heating
at this temperature (24,81). This observation prompted us to
attempt thermal activation of purified complexes in a reconstituted system in which crude hepatic cytosol presaturated
with nonradioactive TA is mixed with the purified, unactivated [³H]TA-receptor complexes. As seen in Table 2, readdi-
tion of crude hepatic cytosol enhanced the DNA-cellulose

binding of the purified [³H]TA-receptor complexes to a level similar to that detected with complexes in crude cytosols. These data clearly suggested that a cytoplasmic factor(s) may stimulate activation of [³H]TA-receptor complexes purified from rat liver. This same factor(s) appears to be present in rat kidney cortex cytosol and enhances the DNA-cellulose binding of [³H]TA-receptor complexes purified from that tissue (M. Webb and G. Litwack, manuscript in preparation). Since the publication of these data we have attempted to further characterize this hepatic cytosolic "stimulator" and determine the mechanism(s) by which it apparently affects the conformation of the purified receptor. These more recent experiments (T. Schmidt, A. Miller-Diener, M. Webb and G. Litwack, manuscript in preparation) will now be summarized and the conclusions drawn from these data will be briefly discussed.

The cytoplasmic "activating factor" or "stimulator" which enhances DNA-cellulose binding of the [³H]TA-receptor complexes does not appear to co-purify with the glucocorticoid receptors even through the affinity chromatography step. This is suggested by the fact that heating of the partially purified [³H]TA-receptor complexes in the affinity gel eluate results in a minimal increase (1.5-3.0 fold) in activation as quantitated by DNA-cellulose binding, while heating in a reconstituted system in the presence of unfractionated cytosol facilitates maximal activation (9-10 fold increase when compared to the unactivated control which was not heated). The apparent separation of receptors from the active cytoplasmic "stimulator" at the initial purification step is also confirmed by the fact that the affinity gel supernatant (cytosol remaining after receptors have been adsorbed to affinity resin) is as effective as crude cytosol in stimulating activation in a reconstituted system. The cytoplasmic factor(s) in either crude cytosol or the affinity gel supernatant also appears to stimulate the fold activation of partially purified [³H]TA-receptor complexes in a dose-dependent manner. Although we originally reported that the cytoplasmic "stimulator" was stable when incubated at 60°C for 30 minutes (39), we have subsequently demonstrated that it is also stable after heating at 90°C for 30 minutes. This heat-stable factor is clearly a macromolecule since it is excluded from Sephadex G-25. We have also demonstrated that this factor is sensitive to trypsin and hence is a heat-stable protein.

These preliminary reconstitution data suggested that a heat-stable cytoplasmic protein stimulates activation of partially or highly purified [³H]TA-receptor complexes based on their ability to bind to DNA-cellulose. We subsequently wanted to demonstrate that this stimulation would be reflected in the expected shift in the elution profile of the activated [³H]TA-receptor complexes on DEAE-cellulose (16). When the purified [³H]TA-receptor complexes were thermally activated in the presence of the heat-stable protein, the expected 2-fold increase in DNA-cellulose binding was detected when compared to the heated control. However, despite this 2-fold difference in DNA-cellulose binding, we failed to detect any difference in the percentage of [³H]TA-receptor complexes eluted in the typical activated position. This somewhat paradoxical result lead us to suspect that the heat-stable cytoplasmic protein may not in fact stimulate the conformational change associated with activation which is reflected in the shift in the elution profile of the [³H]TA-receptor complexes from DEAE-cellulose, but rather stimulates or enhances the binding of the thermally activated (low salt eluting) complexes to DNA-cellulose. Appropriate experiments were therefore conducted to test this two-step model. Purified [³H]TA-receptor complexes were thermally activated at 25°C for 30 minutes. Following this first incubation (Step 1) the sample was adjusted to 10mM MoO_4 to block any further activation (shift to low salt eluting form on DEAE-cellulose). At the conclusion of Step 1 the DNA-cellulose binding of the purified [3H]TA-receptor complexes was assayed and activation was also quantitated by DEAE-cellulose chromatography. During Step 2 the thermally activated complexes were incubated for an additional 30 min- utes at 25°C in the presence or absence of the cytoplasmic "stimulator". The data generated from experiments such as the one described are consistent with the proposed model. They suggest that during the first molybdate-sensitive step, elevated temperature results in the appropriate shift in the elution profile of purified [3H]TA-receptor complexes on DEAE- cellulose but only in a 1.5 to 3.0 fold increase in the bind- ing of these complexes to DNA-cellulose. During the second molybdate-insensitive step, a heat-stable cytoplasmic protein interacts with these thermally activated [3H]TA-receptor com- plexes and enhances their binding to DNA-cellulose. In crude cytosol these two steps would presumably occur simultaneously and addition of molybdate prior to heating would block the first step and hence the substrate ([3H]TA-receptor complexes eluting at low salt from DEAE-cellulose) for the second step would not be generated.

Recently we have attempted to tentatively identify the active cytoplasmic "stimulator". Several lines of evidence, which will not be presently discussed, indicate that this "stimula- tor" is not a heat-stable protease or phosphatase. This "stimulator" is clearly distinct from other heat-stable acti- vities in rat liver cytosol which have been reported to affect glucocorticoid receptors (82,83). The stabil- ity of the "stimulator" at elevated temperature (90°C for 30 minutes) suggested that this endogenous protein may be ribo- nuclease (RNase), an enzyme which is known to be heat stable

(84). We have therefore tested the effects of exogenous pancreatic RNase A on the DNA-cellulose binding of thermally
activated, purified [^{3}H]TA-receptor complexes and have found
that it mimicks the effects of the heat-stable cytoplasmic
"stimulator". Additionally, the 90°C-treated cytosol contains significant RNase activity and when analyzed by SDS-
polyacrylamide gel electrophoresis contains a major protein
of the same molecular weight as exogenous RNase A. We have
therefore tentatively identified the heat-stable "stimulator"
as RNase and are currently designing experiments to confirm
this prediction.

This possible association of RNA with the purified, unactivated [^{3}H]TA-receptor complexes and the potential role of
endogenous RNase in enhancing the DNA-cellulose binding of
the activated complexes raise questions concerning the role
of RNA in steroid hormone action. Numerous published reports
demonstrate that RNA may play a specific role in the nuclear
retention of various steroid-hormone receptors (85,86). Likewise it has been reported that the interaction of a variety
of steroid-receptor complexes with DNA-cellulose is inhibited
by RNA and that this inhibition is specific with respect to
the base composition of the RNA (87,88,89). Several investigators have also reported that exogenous RNase affects
unpurified, activated glucocorticoid receptors (90,91,92,93).
More recently Tymoczko and Phillips (94) have reported that
both RNase A and RNase T$_1$ can stimulate the binding of activated rat hepatic dexamethasone-receptor complexes to DNA-
cellulose and also shift the sedimentation profile from the
7-8S form to the 3-4S form. The ability of MoO$_4$, when added
prior to heating at 20°C for 15 minutes, to block the RNase
mediated increase in DNA-cellulose binding in those published
experiments is consistent with our hypothesis that MoO$_4$
blocks the first step in activation. The possible physio-

logical role of an RNA species associated with the unactivated glucocorticoid-receptor complexes is unclear. Our data
suggest that this association is not artifactual and that this
RNA must be hydrolyzed, presumably by endogenous RNase, before
the activated [^{3}H]TA-receptor complexes can bind maximally to
DNA-cellulose. We are currently investigating the possibility
that this represents a unique species of RNA which is inaccessible to endogenous RNase in the unactivated glucocorticoid-receptor complexes but becomes accessible only after
the first step of activation has been completed.

Phosphorylation of the glucocorticoid receptor in vivo

In order to label the glucocorticoid receptor in vivo, adrenalectomized male rats were each injected with 10mCi [^{32}P]-
orthophosphate and 18 hours later their livers were perfused
and hepatic cytosol was prepared. The [^{3}H]TA-receptor complexes were then purified by the three-step procedure (39)
which has already been described. [^{32}P]-Containing material
was found to co-elute with the peaks of [^{3}H]TA from both the
Bio Gel A-1.5m column and the subsequent DEAE-cellulose
column. Aliquots of the receptor peak fractions eluted from
DEAE-cellulose were subsequently subjected to SDS-polyacrylamide gel electrophoresis and staining with Coomassie Blue.
As expected, the stained gel again displayed a single
$M_r = 90,000$ band in the receptor-peak fractions and the intensity of this band paralleled the distribution of bound
[^{3}H]TA. The autoradiogram of this gel also displayed a
pattern of the [^{32}P]-labeled $M_r = 90,000$ protein identical to
the Coomassie Blue staining pattern. These data thus demonstrated that the glucocorticoid-receptor ($M_r = 90,000$) in-
corporates [^{32}P] in vivo and they confirmed the results obtained earlier with mouse L cell receptors (51). Singh et al.
(95), who have incubated a rat liver mince with [^{32}P]-ortho-
phosphate, have also confirmed that the hepatic glucocorticoid receptor is a phosphoprotein.

334

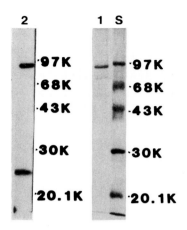

<u>Figure 5</u>   SDS-polyacrylamide gel electrophoresis of [^{32}P]-
labeled receptors of the pooled DEAE-fractions.
S, standard proteins; lane 1, Coomassie Blue
stained final receptor; lane 2, autoradiograph of
lane 1. Reproduced with permission from Biochem.
Biophys. Res. Commun. (58).

When the [^{3}H]TA-receptor complexes eluted from DEAE-cellulose
were pooled and subsequently electrophoresed and autoradiographed, another [^{32}P] component, which was undetected on the
Coomassie Blue stained gel, was visualized (Figure 5). This
phosphorylated component was subsequently shown to be primarily eluted from DEAE-cellulose at a salt concentration much
higher than that required for the elution of the purified, unactivated [^{3}H]TA-receptor complexes. This band also appeared
to be identical to the Mr = 24,000 component which we had previously shown to be related to the purified [^{3}H]TA-receptor
complex and detectable with the more sensitive double staining
procedure (39). Based on protein staining this Mr = 24,000
component appeared to be much more heavily phosphorylated than
the Mr = 90,000 receptor protein itself, and we speculated
that it may actually represent a polynucleotide which is
tightly associated with the purified, unactivated [^{3}H]TA-re-
ceptor complexes. In light of the more recent data, which has
already been discussed, which suggest that an RNA species may

be associated with the unactivated complexes, this speculation
appears warranted. We have not, however, repeated these in
vivo phosphorylation experiments and tested the effects of
exogenous RNase, or the heat-stable cytoplasmic "stimulator"
which we believe is RNase, on the appearance of this phosphorylated Mr = 24,000 component. In a related study Housley and
Pratt (96) have demonstrated that when mouse L cells are incubated in the presence of [^{32}P]-orthophosphate, several
[^{32}P]-labeled components including the 92K receptor protein
itself, a doublet at 37K, a heavily phosphorylated species at
21K and a band at 12K are detected in the final DEAE-cellulose
eluate. However, they found that treatment with exogenous
RNase eliminated the [^{32}P] detected at the 21K position. This
21K phosphorylated component, which may be identical to the
24K phosphorylated component which we have described, may
thus be an RNA species which co-purifies with the unactivated
[^{3}H]TA-receptor complexes from these cultured mouse fibroblasts. With regard to the phosphorylation data generated in
our laboratory, it is important to note that the Mr = 41,000
and 40,000 proteins, which we have previously shown to also be
related to the highly purified, unactivated [^{3}H]TA-receptor
complexes (39), are not phosphorylated in vivo. If these two
components represent proteolytic fragments generated during
purification of the unactivated receptor protein (Mr = 90,000)
then it seems reasonable to expect that they would also contain some [^{32}P]-labeled residues. Although these two components have not been further characterized, it presently appears
rather unlikely that they are generated artifactually from the
intact Mr = 90,000 receptor protein. Finally, in preliminary
experiments we have thermally activated the purified, unactivated [^{3}H]TA receptor complexes which had incorporated [^{32}P]
in vivo. The activated complexes were then visualized by
DEAE-cellulose chromatography and appeared to contain both
[^{3}H] and [^{32}P]. These preliminary, unpublished data suggest
that if receptor dephosphorylation occurs during activation

then it clearly does not involve complete dephosphorylation of the Mr = 90,000 receptor protein.

Protein kinase activity of purified glucocorticoid receptors

Subsequent to demonstrating that the glucocorticoid receptor is phosphorylated in vivo (58), and intrigued by the preliminary report that the purified subunits of the chicken progesterone receptor demonstrate protein kinase activity (55), we initiated a series of experiments to determine if the purified glucocorticoid receptor is capable of mediating autophosphorylation. In these experiments the purified [^{3}H]TA-receptor complexes eluted from DEAE-cellulose were incubated with [γ-^{32}P]ATP for 30 minutes at 25°C and then the various samples were electrophoresed and the gels were stained, dried, and subjected to autoradiography. The preliminary data which were generated clearly demonstrated that protein kinase activity is associated with the purified rat hepatic glucocorticoid receptor (97). These data also demonstrated that incorporation of [^{32}P] into the purified Mr = 90,000 receptor (and not into the Mr = 24,000 component which is phosphorylated in vivo) was Ca^{2+} dependent and that Mg^{2+} could not substitute for Ca^{2+} in the kinase reaction. Although we have no explanation for the discrepancy, Kurl and Jacob (59) reported that in their hands the kinase activity associated with the purified rat hepatic glucocorticoid receptor is Mg^{2+}-dependent. As seen in Table 3, neither exogenous cyclic nucleotides (cAMP or cGMP) or exogenous calmodulin promoted phosphorylation in our experiments in the absence of Ca^{2+}. Also, addition of the chelator, EGTA, in the presence of Ca^{2+} blocked the phosphorylation reaction. Histones (calf thymus Type III) appeared to be phosphorylated when incubated with the purified [^{3}H]TA-receptor complexes and [γ-^{32}P]ATP in the absence of CA^{2+}, but when Ca^{2+} was present the Mr = 90,000 receptor protein was preferentially phosphorylated. Finally, these preliminary experiments suggested that the Ca^{2+}-dependent autophosphor-

Table 3   Summary of the effects of exogenous reagents on
kinase activity associated with purified [^{3}H]TA-
receptor complexes

Reagents Tested	Effect on Kinase Activity
Tested Individually	
Ca^{2+}	stimulation
Mg^{2+}	no effect
cAMP	no effect
cGMP	no effect
calmodulin	no effect
Tested in presence of Ca^{2+}	
EGTA	inhibition
molybdate	inhibition
trifluoperazine	inhibition
chlorpromazine	inhibition
calmidazolium	no effect
calmodulin	no effect
fluorosulfonylbenzoyl adenosine	inhibition
8-azido ATP	inhibition

ylation of the purified receptor does not occur in the absence of bound ligand.

We have now analyzed this autophosphorylation in much greater
detail and in so doing have generated new information concerning the preferential ability of the activated receptor complexes to display kinase activity (A. Miller-Diener,
T. Schmidt and G. Litwack, manuscript in preparation). Our
preliminary observation that the autophosphorylation of the
purified [^{3}H]TA-receptor complexes was Ca^{2+} dependent prompted
us to investigate the potential role of calmodulin more thoroughly. As previously mentioned, in the absence of Ca^{2+} exogenous calmodulin failed to stimulate kinase activity. Subsequently we noted that exogenous calmodulin did not potentiate

the autophosphorylation even in the presence of Ca^{2+}. These data suggested that this is not a calmodulin-dependent reaction. However, the possibility existed that enough endogenous calmodulin co-purified with the [^{3}H]TA-receptor complexes to support maximal autophosphorylation when exogenous Ca^{2+} was added. It should be noted that when the gels were stained with Coomassie Blue and silver, endogenous calmodulin was not detected. However, exogenous calmodulin was easily detected using this sensitive staining procedure. In order to rule out the potential involvement of endogenous calmodulin a number of inhibitors were tested. As seen in Table 3, both trifluoperazine (TFP) and chlorpromazine (CPZ), which are relatively nonspecific calmodulin inhibitors, inhibited phosphorylation in the presence of Ca^{2+}. In contrast, calmidazolium, which is a very specific and potent inhibitor of Ca^{2+} calmodulin-dependent enzymes (98), did not affect autophosphorylation of the purified receptor. This latter result clearly demonstrates that the Ca^{2+}-dependent kinase activity associated with the purified [^{3}H]TA-receptor complexes is not calmodulin dependent. Phenothiazines such as TFP and CPZ are known to intercalate in the lipid-rich portions of membranes and nonspecifically inhibit membrane bound protein kinases and receptors (98). It is therefore possible that a lipid is associated with the purified receptor which might account for the effects of these nonspecific inhibitors on the kinase activity. Several published studies (99,100) indicate that Ca^{2+} may interact directly with the glucocorticoid-receptor. For instance, Van Bohemen et al. have demonstrated that Ca^{2+} decreases the affinity of crude receptors for synthetic glucocorticoids such as dexamethasone and that this effect can not be blocked by calmidazolium (100). In contrast, TFP competitively inhibits the binding of dexamethasone, not via calmodulin inhibition, but apparently through a direct interaction with the unpurified glucocorticoid-receptor (101).

The dependency of the kinase activity associated with the purified [3H]TA-receptor complexes on an ATP-binding site has also been demonstrated. Both fluorosulfonylbenzoyl 5'-adenosine and 8-azido-ATP, ATP analogues which inhibit a number of protein kinases (102,103,104), completely block phosphorylation of the purified receptors incubated with $[\gamma-^{32}P]ATP$ and Ca^{2+} (Table 3). Although these data demonstrate the requirements for an ATP binding site, they obviously do not identify the moiety which contains that site. Future experiments involving affinity labeling with fluorosulfonyl[14C]-benzoyl 5'-adenosine or photoaffinity labeling with 8-azido $[\alpha-^{32}P]ATP$ should facilitate identification of the ATP-binding site (hence kinase) as an integral part of the purified ($Mr = 90,000$) glucocorticoid-receptor.

As previously mentioned, the Ca^{2+}-dependent autophosphorylation of the purified receptor appears to require bound ligand. When the [3H]TA bound to the purified receptors was stripped by treatment with dextran-coated charcoal, [32P] labeling of the receptor protein was no longer detected. If the purified, unbound receptors were reincubated with [3H]TA for several hours, binding of [3H]TA and autophosphorylation were again detected. If the stripped, unactivated receptors were incubated with glucocorticoid antagonists such as [3H] progesterone or [3H] cortexolone, or with β-lapachone, a nonsteroidal compound which interacts competitively with the ligand binding site (105), no subsequent kinase activity was detected despite the fact that these ligands did bind to the receptor. Thus it appeared that only ligands which are glucocorticoid agonists and hence facilitate activation of the receptor (10, 12) will mediate or potentiate the kinase reaction. Numerous experiments also demonstrated that if 10mM MoO_4, which we had previously shown inhibits activation of purified receptor complexes (39), was added prior to the kinase reaction, no auto-

phosphorylation was detected. What is important to note is
that the kinase incubation is performed at 25°C for 30 minutes, which are conditions which will result in thermal activation of the purified [^{3}H]TA-receptor complexes (39).
Taken collectively these data suggested to us that perhaps
only the activated complexes demonstrate kinase activity.
Several subsequent experiments have in fact proven that this
theory is correct.

If purified, unactivated complexes were first thermally activated at 25°C for 30 minutes and then incubated with Ca^{2+} and
[γ-^{32}P]ATP in the presence of molybdate, significant incorporation of [^{32}P] into the receptor was detected. In the unactivated control, which was also incubated with Ca^{2+} and
[γ-^{32}P]ATP in the presence of molybdate, no incorporation of
[^{32}P] was detected. The inability of the purified receptors
which were rebound with [^{3}H] progesterone, [^{3}H] cortexolone
or β-lapachone to demonstrate kinase activity in the earlier
experiments probably reflects the fact that these ligands did
not facilitate activation during the kinase incubation.

Although the data thus support a model in which the purified
activated, but not the unactivated, glucocorticoid-receptor
complexes incorporate [^{32}P], they do not conclusively identify
the kinase molecule itself. One possibility is that the
Mr = 90,000 receptor protein itself is a kinase and mediates
its own phosphorylation. A second possibility is that a distinct Ca^{2+}-dependent kinase co-purifies with the unactivated
[^{3}H]TA-receptor complexes on DEAE-cellulose and, although undetected using a sensitive double staining procedure, is
present during the kinase incubation. Knowing that only the
activated complexes demonstrate kinase activity, we have performed the following experiment to address this second possibility. Purified, unactivated [^{3}H]TA-receptor complexes

were first thermally activated (25°C for 30 minutes) and then rechromatographed on DEAE-cellulose. The low salt-eluting, activated [^{3}H]TA-receptor complexes were then incubated with Ca^{2+} and [γ-^{32}P]ATP and phosphorylation of the receptor protein was detected. We feel that it is highly unlikely that the elution pattern of a contaminating kinase would shift to the exact same position as the activated [^{3}H]TA-receptor complexes unless that kinase is an integral part of the receptor. In contrast to the situation with the purified subunits of the progesterone receptor (56), DEAE-cellulose chromatography does not appear to facilitate separation of a contaminating kinase from the highly purified glucocorticoid receptor. Additional experiments are currently being planned to generate additional proof that the purified, activated receptor is in fact a Ca^{2+} dependent kinase.

Finally, recent data have indicated that during this kinase reaction primarily threonine and some serine residues in the receptor protein become phosphorylated. Based on a rough calculation of the ^{32}P:^{3}H ratio of the purified receptors, a maximum of ten sites appear to be phosphorylated per receptor molecule. The precise function of these phosphorylated residues and the kinase reaction itself is obviously unknown, despite the fact that phosphorylation/dephosphorylation have been speculated to regulate numerous receptor functions. Since histones can be phosphorylated by the activated glucocorticoid receptor it is premature, but tempting, to speculate that receptor mediated phosphorylation of nuclear proteins may play a role in gene activation by glucocorticoids. In this same vein it is conceivable that dephosphorylation of the receptor may "turn off" its interaction with specific genomic acceptor sites. Subsequent rephosphorylation, perhaps mediated by the receptor itself, may also play a role in the recycling of the receptor from the nucleus to the cytoplasm where it then rebinds another glucocrticoid molecule.

Summary

A three-step scheme (affinity chromatography, gel filtration, DEAE-cellulose chromatography) for the purification (approximately 4000-fold) of unactivated rat hepatic glucocorticoid receptors has been developed in our laboratory. The purified receptor (Mr = 90,000) sediments as a 9-10S complex in low salt glycerol gradients, exhibits a Stokes radius of 7.3nm and displays other hydrodynamic properties characteristic of molybdate-stabilized, crude hepatic glucocorticoid-receptor complexes. The purified, unactivated glucocorticoid-receptors can be partially thermally activated as evidenced by their increased affinity for DNA-cellulose. However, maximal activation can only be achieved in a reconstituted system which includes a heat-stable cytoplasmic protein or "stimulator". Exogenous pancreatic RNase mimicks the stimulatory effects of this heat-stable protein in terms of its ability to enhance the DNA-cellulose binding of purified glucocorticoid-receptor complexes. Taken collectively these and other data are consistent with a two step model for activation. During the first molybdate-sensitive step, elevated temperature results in the appropriate shift in the elution profile of purified, activated glucocorticoid-receptor complexes on DEAE-cellulose but only in a minimal increase in the binding of these complexes to DNA-cellulose. During the second molybdate-insensitive step, a heat-stable cytoplasmic protein, which may be endogenous RNase, enhances the binding of these thermally activated complexes to DNA-cellulose.

Additional data demonstrate that the unactivated glucocorticoid-receptor complexes are phosphorylated in vivo following injection of [^{32}P]-orthophosphate into adrenalectomized rats. Subsequent autoradiographic analysis of the highly purified receptors eluted from DEAE-cellulose demonstrates that in ad-

dition to the Mr = 90,000 receptor protein itself, a
Mr = 24,000 component also becomes heavily phosphorylated.
These data are consistent with this component representing a
polynucleotide, perhaps RNA, which is tighly associated with
the purified, unactivated glucocorticoid-receptor complexes.
Finally, recent experiments show that protein kinase activity
is associated with the purified glucocorticoid-receptor complexes. When the thermally activated, but not unactivated,
purified receptor complexes are subsequently incubated in the
presence of molybdate at 25°C for 30 minutes with $[\gamma-^{32}P]ATP$
and Ca^{2+}, the Mr = 90,000 receptor protein becomes phophor-
ylated. This kinase activity is not dependent or cyclic nucleotides (cAMP or cGMP) or calmodulin, as evidenced by the
fact that the specific inhibitor, calmidizolium, does not inhibit the Ca^{2+}-dependent enzymatic activity. This phosphorylation reaction can be blocked by the addition of sodium
molybdate or by stripping the ligand form the purified receptors, both of which block subsequent activation during the
kinase assay. The crucial role of an ATP-binding site in
mediating this kinase activity is evidenced by the fact that
non-hydrolyzable ATP analogues block incorporation of $[^{32}P]$.
ALthough there is a remote possibility that a contaminating
kinase co-purifies with the glucocorticoid-receptor complexes,
additional data strongly suggest that the activated rat
hepatic Mr = 90,000 receptor protein, in addition to containing the ligand binding site, also functions as a Ca^{2+}-depend-
ent kinase which mediates autophosphorylation.

Acknowledgements

First the authors would like to express their gratitude and
appreciation to those collegues, particularly Dr. P. Grandics,
Dr. M. Webb, and Mrs. A. Miller-Diener, whose research efforts
have contributed significantly to the experiments discussed in
this chapter. Secondly, the authors wish to acknowledge the

344

technical assistance of Mr. Melvin Paden and Mr. Vincient
Pearson of the Fels Research Institute and Mr. Timothy Volm
and Mr. Michael Puk of The University of Iowa. Finally, they
would like to thank Mrs. Carol Johnson for her excellent
typing of this chapter. The research discussed in this chapter was supported at the Temple University School of Medicine
by Research Grants AM 13531 and AM 32870 from the National
Institute of Arthritis, Metabolism, and Digestive Diseases,
NIH; by PCM 8215844 from the National Science Foundation; by
BC 361B from the American Cancer Society and by Core Grant
CA 12227 from the National Cancer Institute to the Fels Re-
search Institute. At The University of Iowa this work was
supported by Institutional Research Grant IN-122E from the
American Cancer Society to the University of Iowa; by a
Helmar Maage Memorial Grant for Cancer Research from the
American Cancer Society (BC 464); and by research grant 1
RO1 AM 34490-01 PC from the National Institute of Arthritis,
Metabolism, and Digestive Diseases, NIH. T. Schmidt is a
Scholar of the Leukemia Society of America, Inc.

References

1.   Claman, H.N.: New Eng. J. Med. 287, 388-397 (1972).

2.   Rosen, J.M., Rosen, F., Milholland, R.J., Nichol, C.A.:
     Cancer Res. 30, 1129-1136 (1970).

3.   Norman, M.R., Thompson, E.B.: Cancer Res. 37, 3785-3791
     (1975).

4.   Tomkins, G.M., Gelehrter, T.D., Granner, D.K., Martin,
     D.W., Samuels, H.S., Thompson, E.B.: Science 166, 1474-
     1480 (1969).

5.   Barnett, C.A., Wicks, W.D.: J. Biol. Chem. 246, 7201-
     7206 (1971).

6.   Thompson, E.B., Lippman, M.E.: Metabolism 23, 159-202
     (1974).

7.   Munck, A., Leung, K.: Receptors and Mechanism of Action
     of Steroid Hormones, Dekker, New York 1981.

8. Sando, J.J., Hammond, N.D., Stratford, C.A., Pratt, W.B.: J. Biol. Chem. 254, 4779-4789 (1979).

9. Sando, J.J., LaForest, A.C., Pratt, W.B.: J. Biol. Chem. 254, 4772-4778 (1979).

10. Milgrom, E., Atger, M., Baulieu, E.-E.: Biochemistry 12, 5198-5205 (1973).

11. DiSorbo, D.M., Phelps, D.S., Litwack, G.: Endocrinology 106, 922-929 (1980).

12. Baxter, J.D., Rousseau, G.G., Benson, M.C., Garcea, R.L., Ito, J., Tomkins, G.M.: Proc. Natl. Acad. Sci. U.S.A. 69, 1892-1896 (1972).

13. Kalimi, M., Colman, P., Feigelson, P.: J. Biol. Chem. 250, 1080-1086 (1975).

14. LeFevre, B., Bailly, A., Sallas,N., Milgrom, E.: Biochim. Biophys. Acta 585, 266-272 (1979).

15. Parchman, L.G., Litwack, G.: Arch. Biochem. Biophys. 183, 374-382 (1977).

16. Sakaue, Y., Thompson. E.B.: Biochem. Biophys. Res. Commun. 77, 533-541 (1977).

17. Beato, M., Kalimi, M., Feigelson, P.: Biochemistry 12, 3372-3379 (1973).

18. Govindan, M.V., Speiss, E., Majors, J.: Proc. Natl. Acad. Sci. U.S.A. 79, 5157-5161 (1982).

19. Robins, D.M., Paek, I., Seeburg, P.H., Axel, R.: Cell 29, 623-631 (1982).

20. Scheidereit, C., Geisse, S., Westphal, H.M., Beato, M.: Nature 304, 749-752 (1983).

21. Goidl, J.A., Cake, M.H., Dolan, K.P., Parchman, L.G., Litwack, G.: Biochemistry 16, 2125-2130 (1977).

22. Bailly, A., Savouret, J.-F., Sallas, N., Milgrom, E.: Eur. J. Biochem. 88, 623-632 (1978).

23. Leach, K.L., Dahmer, M.K., Hammond, N.D., Sando, J.J., Pratt, W.B.: J. Biol. Chem. 254, 11884-11890 (1979).

24. Barnett, C.A., Schmidt, T.J., Litwack, G.: Biochemistry 19, 5446-5455 (1980).

25. John, J., and Moudgil, V.: Biochem. Biophys. Res. Commun. 90, 1242-1248 (1979).

26. Miller, L.K., Tuazon, F.B., Niu E.-M., Sherman, M.R.: Endocrinology 108, 1369-1378 (1981).

27. Bailly, A., Sallas, N., Milgrom, E.: J. Biol. Chem. 252, 858-863, (1977).

28. Sekula, B.C., Schmidt, T.J., Litwack, G.: J. Steroid Biochem. 14, 161-166 (1981).

29. Vedeckis, W.V.: Biochemistry 22, 1983-1989 (1983).

30. Milgrom, E.: Biochemical Actions of Hormones, Volume 13, p. 465-492, Litwack, G., ed., Academic Press, New York 1981.

31. Schmidt, T.J., Litwack, G.: Phys. Rev. 62, 1131-1192 (1982).

32. Grody, W.W., Schrader, W.T., O'Malley, B.W.: End. Rev. 3, 141-163 (1982).

33. Munck, A., Foley, R.: Nature 278, 752-754 (1979).

34. Markovic, R.D., Litwack, G.: Arch. Biochem. Biophys. 202, 374-379 (1980).

35. Miyabe, S., Harrison, R.W.: Endocrinology 112, 2174-2180 (1983).

36. Failla, D., Tomkins, G.M., Santi, D.V.: Proc. Natl. Acad. Sci. U.S.A. 72, 3849-3852 (1975).

37. Govindan, M.V., Manz, B.: Eur. J. Biochem. 108, 47-53 (1980).

38. Lustenberg, P., Formstecher, P., Dautrevaux, M.: J. Steroid Biochem. 14, 697-703 (1981).

39. Grandics, P., Miller, A., Schmidt, T.J., Mittman, D., Litwack, G.: J. Biol. Chem. 259, 3173-3180 (1984).

40. Grandics, P.: Acta Biochim. Biophys. Acad. Sci. Hung. 16, 51-55 (1981).

41. Grandics, P., Gasser, D.L., Litwack, G.: Endocrinology 111, 1731-1733 (1982).

42. Munck, A., Brinck-Johnsen, T.: J. Biol. Chem. 243, 5556-5565 (1968).

43. Bell, P.A., Munck, A.: Biochem. J. 136, 97-107 (1973).

44. Wheeler, R.H., Leach, K.L., LaForest, A.C., O'Toole, T.E., Wagner, R., Pratt, W.B.: J. Biol. Chem. 256, 434-441 (1981).

45. Abou-Issa, H., Foeckling, M.K., Minton, J.F.: Fed. Proc. 41, 1164 (1982).

46. Aurrichio, F., Migliaccio, A., Castoria, G., Lastoria, S., Schiavone, E.: Biochem. Biophys. Res. Commun. 101, 1171-1178 (1981).

47. Barnett, C.A., Palmour, R.M., Litwack, G., Seegmiller, J.E.: Endocrinology 112, 2059-2068 (1983).

48. Nielsen, C.J., Sando, J.J., Pratt, W.B.: Proc. Natl. Acad. Sci. U.S.A. 74, 1398-1402 (1977).

49. Housley, P.R., Dahmer, M.K., Pratt, W.B.: J. Biol. Chem. 257, 8615-8618 (1982).

50. Swarup, G., Cohen, S., Garbers, D.L.: J. Biol. Chem. 256, 8197-8201 (1981).

51. Housley, P.R., Pratt, W.B.: J. Biol. Chem. 258, 4630-4635 (1983).

52. Harmon, J.M., Schmidt, T.J., Thompson, E.B.: J. Steroid Biochem. (1984) In Press.

53. Weigel, N.L., Tash, J.S., Means, A.R., Schrader, W.T., O'Malley, B.W.: Biochem. Biophys. Res. Commun. 102, 513-519 (1981).

54. Dougherty, J.J., Puri, R.K., Toft, D.O.: J. Biol. Chem. 257, 14226-14230 (1982).

55. Garcia, T., Tuohimaa, P., Mester, J., Buchou, T., Renoir, J.-M., Baulieu, E.-E.: Biochem. Biophys. Res. Commun. 113, 960-966 (1983).

56. Weigel, N.L.: Excerpta Medica, Abstracts of the 7th International Congress of Endocrinology, abt. 2710, Elsevier Science Publishers Co., Inc., New York (1984).

57. Migliaccio, A., Lastoria, S., Moncharmont, B., Rotondi, A., Auricchio, F.: Biochem. Biophys. Res. Commun. 109, 1002-1010 (1982).

58. Grandics, P., Miller, A., Schmidt, T.J., Litwack, G.: Biochem. Biophys. Res. Commun. 120, 59-65 (1984).

59. Kurl, R.N., Jacob, S.T.: Biochem. Biophys. Res. Commun. 119, 700-705 (1984).

60. Axén, R., Porath, J., Ernbäck, S.: Nature, London 214, 1302-1304 (1967).

61. March, S.C., Parikh, I., Cuatrecasas, P.: Anal. Biochem. 60, 149-152 (1974).

62. Wilchek, M., Oka, T., Topper, Y.J.: Proc. Natl. Acad. Sci. U.S.A. 72, 1055-1058 (1975).

63. Parikh, I., March, S.C., Cuatrecasas, P.: Methods in Enzymology, Volume 34, p. 77-102, Jakoby, W.B., Wilchek, M., eds., Academic Press, New York 1974.

64. Sundberg, L., Porath, J.: J. Chromatogr. 90, 87-98 (1974).

65. Murphy, R.F., Conlon, J.M., Inman, A., Kelly, G.J.C.: J. Chromatogr. 135, 427-433 (1977).

66. Erdos, T., Best-Belpomme, M., Bessada, R.: Anal. Biochem. 37, 244-252 (1970).

67. Grandics, P., Puri, R.K., Toft, D.D.: Endocrinology 110, 1055-1057 (1982).

68. O'Farrell, P.H.: J. Biol. Chem. <u>250</u>, 4007-4021 (1975).

69. Irie, S., Sezaki, M., Kato, Y.: Anal. Biochem. <u>126</u>, 350-354 (1982).

70. Morrissey, J.H.: Anal. Biochem. <u>117</u>, 307-310 (1981).

71. Sherman, M.R., Moran, M.C., Neal, R.M., Niu, E.-M., Tuazon, F.B.: Progress in Research and Clinical Applications of Corticosteroids, p. 45-66, Lee, H.J., Fitzgerald, T.J., eds., Heyden and Son, Phila. 1982.

72. Weatherill, P.J., Bell, P.A.: Biochem. J. <u>206</u>, 633-640 (1982).

73. Vedeckis, W.V.: Biochemistry <u>22</u>, 1983-1989 (1983).

74. Andrews, P.: Biochem. J. <u>91</u>, 222-233 (1964).

75. Andrews, P.: Biochem. J. <u>96</u>, 595-606 (1965).

76. Simons, S.S., Jr., Thompson, E.B.: Proc. Natl. Acad. Sci. U.S.A. <u>78</u>, 3541-3545 (1981).

77. Eisen, H.J., Schleenbaker, R.E., Simons, S.S., Jr.: J. Biol. Chem. <u>256</u>, 12920-12925 (1981).

78. Cidlowski, J.A., Richon, V.: Proceedings of the 64th Annual Meeting of the Endocrine Society, abst. 588 (1983).

79. Harmon, J.M., Eisen, H.J., Simons, S.S., Thompson, E.B.: Proceedings of the 64th Annual Meeting of the Endocrine Society, abst. 456 (1982).

80. Wray, W., Boulikas, T., Wray, V.P., Hancock, R.: Anal. Biochem. <u>118</u>, 197-203 (1981).

81. Schmidt, T.J., Sekula, B.C., Litwack, G.: Endocrinology <u>109</u>, 803-812 (1981).

82. Leach, K.L., Grippo, J.F., Housley, P.R., Dahmer, M.K., Salive, M.E., Pratt, W.B.: J. Biol. Chem. <u>257</u>, 381-388 (1982).

83. Grippo, J.F., Tienrungroj, W., Dahmer, M.K., Housley, P.R., Pratt, W.B.: J. Biol. Chem. <u>258</u>, 13658-13664 (1983).

84. Dubos, R.J., Thompson, R.H.S.: J. Biol. Chem. <u>124</u>, 501-510 (1938).

85. Liang, T., Liao, S.: J. Biol. Chem. <u>249</u>, 4671-4678 (1974).

86. Barrack, E.R., Coffey, D.S.: J. Biol. Chem. <u>255</u>, 7265-7275 (1980).

87. Feldman, M., Kallos, J., Hollander, V.P.: J. Biol. Chem. <u>256</u>, 1145-1148 (1981).

88. Liao, S., Smythe, S., Tymoczko, J.L., Rossini, G.P., Chen, C., Hiipakka, R.A.: J. Biol. Chem. 255, 5545-5551 (1980).

89. Tymoczko, J.L., Shapiro, J., Simenstad, D.J., Nish, A.D.: J. Steroid Biochem. 16, 595-598 (1982).

90. Chong, M.T., Lippman, M.E.: J. Biol. Chem. 257, 2996-3002 (1982).

91. Rossini, G.P., Barbiroli, B.: Biochem. Biophys. Res. Commun. 113, 876-882 (1983).

92. Hutchens, T.W., Markland, F.S., Hawkins, E.F.: Proceedings of the 64th Annual Meeting of the Endocrine Society, abst. 568, (1982).

93. Hutchens, T.W., Markland, F.S., Hawkins, E.F.: Biochem. Biophys. Res. Commun. 105, 20-27 (1982).

94. Tymoczko, J.L., Phillips, M.M.: Endocrinology 112, 142-149 (1983).

95. Singh, V., Eessalu, T., Ghag, S., Moudgil, V.: Excerpta Medica, Abstracts of the 7th International Congress of Endocrinology, abst. 2095, Elsevier Science Publishers Co., Inc., New York (1984).

96. Housley, P.R., Pratt, W.B.: Fed. Proc. 43, abst. 908(1984)

97. Miller, A.S., Schmidt, T.J., Litwack, G.: Excerpta Medica, Abstracts of the 7th International Congress of Endocrinology, abst. 1056, Elsevier Science Publishers Co., Inc. New York (1984).

98. Van Belle, H.: Cell Calcium 2, 483-494 (1981).

99. Aranyi, P., Naray, A.: J. Steroid Biochem. 12, 267-272 (1980).

100. Van Bohemen, C.G., Eliard, P.H., Rousseau, G.G.: Mol. Physiol. 4. 95-110 (1983).

102. Zoller, M.J., Taylor, S.S.: J. Biol. Chem. 254, 8363-8368 (1979).

103. Hathaway, G.M., Zoller, M.J., Traugh, J.A.: J. Biol. Chem. 256, 11442-11446 (1981).

104. Hoppe, J., Friest, W.: Eur. J. Biochem. 93, 141-146 (1979).

105. Schmidt, T.J., Miller-Diener, A., Litwack, G.: J. Biol. Chem. 259, 9536-9543 (1984).

INTERACTION OF NUCLEOTIDES WITH STEROID HORMONE RECEPTORS

Virinder K. Moudgil
Biochemical Endocrinology Lab., Department of Biological
Sciences, Oakland University, Rochester, Michigan 48063

Introduction

Under physiological conditions, steroid hormones are believed
to enter their target cells and interact with specific receptor proteins to form hormone-receptor complexes. The steroid-
receptor complex is thought to undergo a temperature-dependent
alteration called 'activation' or 'transformation' prior to
its interaction with certain, as yet undefined, nuclear chromatin sites (1). The interaction of receptors with nuclear
chromatin appears to be essential for eliciting a hormonal response (2,3). The complete sequence of events in the hormonal
regulation of gene expression has not yet been established,
but receptors seem to play a key role both in hormone binding
and in triggering a hormonal response. Steroid hormone receptors have generally been studied by histochemical and biochemical techniques using radiolabeled hormonal ligands. The
data which resulted from studies that employed such approaches
aided in the formulation of a two-step mechanism for the interaction of estradiol with the rat uterus (4). Accordingly,
in the absence of hormones, steroid receptors have been reported to be predominantly localized in the target-cell cytoplasm. Upon availability of hormones, the receptor-hormone
complexes are believed to relocate into the nucleus under
physiologic conditions.

Recently, nuclear localization of unoccupied receptors for estrogen and progesterone has been demonstrated in the target

cells by use of immunohistochemical and other approaches (5-8). The receptor recovered in the cytosol fraction of a homogenate may, therefore, represent receptor that is loosely associated with the nucleus, and its binding with the hormone may lead to a tighter association of the steroid-receptor complex with the nuclear sites. Should these postulations prove to be correct, the activation of the steroid receptors could be thought of as a process representing intranuclear event(s).

In cell-free systems, upon their extraction from the target tissue cytosols at low temperature, the steroid receptors can be complexed with hormones to form nonactivated complexes that do not bind to isolated nuclei (9,10). The nuclear binding capacity can be acquired in vitro under high ionic conditions, at elevated temperature in the presence of hormone, by dilution of the cytosol, by gel filtration and by other treatments (see review ref. 1). The steroid-receptor complexes activated by such treatments develop increased affinity for isolated nuclei, DNA-cellulose and phosphocellulose, and have altered dissociation kinetics and mobility on ion-exchange resins (2, 10-18). Since steroid-receptor complexes are unstable in the nonactivated form and the lengthy purification procedures promote activation (1), previous studies on receptor activation had been performed only in crude receptor preparations. This problem has now been overcome, and receptors can be maintained in their nonactivated form in the presence of sodium molybdate, an agent which stabilizes steroid receptors against thermal inactivation (loss of steroid binding capacity) and blocks their activation (19). Thus, preliminary results on heat activation of purified progesterone- and glucocorticoid receptors have been reported recently (20,21).

A number of cellular factors have been reported which are believed to influence the process of receptor activation. While no factor appeared to be necessary for heat-activation of

purified chicken oviduct progesterone receptor (20), a DNA-
cellulose binding capacity could only be conferred on the
purified nonactivated glucocorticoid-receptor complexes in a
reconstituted system (21). Furthermore, many cellular factors
have been reported to influence the activation of steroid receptors (22,23). An estrogen receptor activator protein,
which forms a complex with the 4S form of estrogen receptor to
produce the 5S activated form, has been reported in rat uterine
cytosol (24). Colvard and Wilson have reported that Zn^{++} 'po-
tentiates' binding of androgen receptor to nuclei in vitro
(25-27). They have also identified a factor that converts the
activated 4.5S form of the androgen receptor to the nonactivated 8S form which shows reduced affinity towards nuclear matrix in vitro. Although most studies on receptor activation
have been performed under cell-free conditions, activation of
glucocorticoid receptors has also been shown in intact cells
and appears to be an obligatory step in the response of normal
cells to glucocorticoids (28-30). A glucocorticoid resistant
mutant of CEM-7 cells has been reported to be activation defective (31). The exact role of cellular factors, if any, in
the process of activation of steroid receptors remains to be
established.

Mechanism of activation of steroid hormone receptors

A number of hypotheses have been proposed to explain the mechanism of activation of steroid receptors (1,13,32-34). Activation has been explained by the dimerization model based on
the 4S to 5S transformation of rat uterine estrogen receptor
monomers or the addition of a non-steroid binding subunit (35).
This is consistent with the kinetic studies of Notides and
Nielsen (36) which showed a second order reaction. It has
been suggested that activation and the accompanying changes in
the sedimentation properties of steroid receptors are two dif-

ferent processes (37,38). Sakai and Gorski (39) have recently
shown that estrogen induces a conformational change in the
monomeric receptor and that dimerization follows as a subsequent and separate event. The dissociation of receptor subunits (7-9S to 3.4S) concurrently with, or as a consequence of
receptor activation, has been widely accepted for progesterone
(5,20,40,41) and glucocorticoid receptors (42). Sherman et al.
(43,44) have postulated that in their native form the steroid
receptors are oligomers and may contain RNA associated with
the receptor, and that dissociation and proteolysis of steroid
receptors may be involved in the activation process. It is
difficult to explain the process of activation by one hypothesis since activation of only some of the studied steroid
receptor systems requires the presence of hormone (34). The
transformation of steroid receptors by ATP reported from this
laboratory (to be described later) appears to favour an allosteric mechanism which may consequently result in the dissociation of receptor subunits (1,41,43-45).

Measurement of receptor activation

The extent of receptor activation is generally determined by
measuring the binding of steroid-receptor complexes to target
cell nuclei and DNA-cellulose or phosphocellulose. Miller and
Toft (46) and Moudgil and John (47) have introduced another
method that involves measurement of activation by determining
receptor binding to ATP-Sepharose. All three methods appear
to be qualitatively comparable, although a greater portion of
activated receptor can be detected using ATP-Sepharose.
Weichman and Notides (16) have demonstrated that the dissociation of [^{3}H]estradiol from estrogen receptor follows a two-
component exponential process. The fast component results
from the dissociation of [^{3}H]estradiol from the nonactivated
receptor; the slow component from the activated one. The kinetics of [^{3}H]estradiol dissociation, therefore, provide a

sensitive criterion for distinguishing the two states of receptor in general (48,49).

The monitoring of receptor transformation by sedimentation analysis has been widely used. The nonactivated steroid-receptor complexes sediment as 7-9S molecules in salt-free glycerol or sucrose gradients and are converted to 3-5S moieties upon treatment with the transforming agents described earlier. This criterion of measuring receptor activation is more direct and it is possible to observe a gradual, complete change from one molecular form of receptor to another following activation.

Influence of nucleotides on steroid hormone receptors

Munck and Brink-Johnsen (50) had initially reported that specific binding of glucocorticoids is an energy dependent process. Subsequently, it was proposed (51) that receptor exists in two forms, and that ATP may be required to generate the steroid binding form from a non-steroid-binding percursor. It was suggested that following its release from the nucleus, the receptor was incompetent to rebind steroid, and that its conversion to a steroid binding from was an ATP-dependent process. In other studies, it was subsequently demonstrated that the loss of glucocorticoid binding by mouse fibroblast (L-cells) cytosol during an incubation at 25°C can be slowed by the addition of ATP (52). Additionally, the binding capacity of heat-treated cytosol from mouse L-cells and rat thymocytes can be partially restored by incubation with ATP-Mg in the presence of phosphatase inhibitors (52,53). Moudgil and John (44) reported an increased glucocorticoid binding in cytosol aliquots incubated with ATP. A role of nucleotides in generating active forms of steroid receptors (capable of binding hormone) remains to be established for other receptor systems. Although it is

356

apparant that either the receptor protein itself or some regulatory component(s) may be phosphorylated to facilitate steroid binding, information that provides direct evidence that
steroid binding occurs as a result of phosphorylation of receptor is lacking.

Interaction of ATP with steroid receptors

Preliminary observations made in Dr. Toft's laboratory (Moudgil and Toft, unpublished) showed that addition of ATP to
crude cytosol from cow uterus enhanced progesterone binding.
These observations led to investigations as to whether this
enhancement could be attributed to a direct effect of the
added ATP or to its metabolism. ATP was covalently linked
with Sepharose 4B through its ribose via a 6-carbon spacer to
yield an affinity resin. When progesterone-receptor complexes
from hen oviduct cytosol were fractionated with $(NH_4)_2SO_4$ and
passed over an ATP-Sepharose column, a majority of the complexes were adsorbed by the affinity resin and could be eluted
with buffers containing high salt or the free ligand (54,55).
This interaction was found to be reversible, ionic in nature,
and to have a preference for ATP over other nucleoside triphosphates, cAMP and AMP. The main features of this interaction are summarized in Table I.

Originally reported for avian progesterone receptor, the nu-
cleotide-receptor interaction has now been observed in many
other systems indicating that ATP binding by steroid receptors
is a general phenomenon (Table II).

Table I. Properties of the Interaction Between
ATP-Sepharose and Steroid-Hormone Receptors

1.	Ionic Nature	High salt disrupts the interaction
2.	Ligand Specificity	ATP is a necessary constituent
3.	Binding Specificity	ATP is preferred over other nucleotides
4.	Selective	Yields purification of 100 X-fold or higher
5.	Divalent Cations Not Required	
6.	Reversible	
7.	Steroid-Receptor Complex Remains Intact	

Reproduced with permission from reference 1

Table II. Interaction of Steroid Receptors with ATP-Sepharose

Receptor	Tissue	Animal	Reference
Progesterone	Oviduct	Chick, hen	Moudgil & Toft (54,55)
	Uterus	Hamster	Leavitt et al. (56)
	Brain	Rat	Moudgil et al. (47)
Estrogen	Uterus	Rat	Miller & Toft (46)
			Moudgil & Eessalu (58)
			Katzenellenbogen et al. (59)
	Oviduct	Hen	Moudgil & Weekes (60)
Glucocorti-coid	Liver	Rat	Moudgil & John (47)
	Mammary Gland	Mouse	McBlain et al. (61)
	Oviduct	Chick, hen	Moudgil et al. (62)
Androgen	Prostate	Rat	Mulder et al. (63)
Vitamin-D_3	Intestine	Chick	Haussler & Pike (64)

Reproduced with permission from reference 1

Requirement of Receptor Activation for ATP-Sepharose Binding

In previous studies (54,55), $(NH_4)_2SO_4$-precipitated receptor preparations were utilized to study the interaction between ATP-Sepharose and the chick progesterone receptor. It was soon discovered that the receptor in the freshly prepared cytosol had little or no affinity for ATP-Sepharose and that an activation step is required before binding to ATP-Sepharose could occur (46). The requirement of activation for receptor-hormone complex binding to immobilized ATP was subsequently shown for the rat liver glucocorticoid receptor (47). Cytosol that had been incubated with [^{3}H]triamcinolone acetonide at 0°C showed no retention on ATP-Sepharose. However, subsequent incubation at 23°C for various time periods enhanced receptor binding to the affinity resin (Fig. 1). The activated receptor was quantitatively adsorbed to ATP-Sepharose and could be eluted with 1M KCl. Employing this method of receptor activation, the maximum extent of receptor binding to ATP-Sepharose

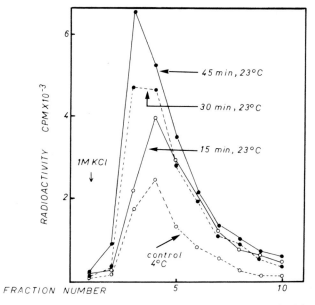

FIG. 1. Effect of heat-activation on the binding of glucocorticoid-receptor complex to ATP-Sepharose. Rat liver cytosol was incubated [^{3}H]triamcinolone acetonide for 4 h at 0°C. Aliquots (0.5ml) containing [^{3}H]triamcinolone acetonide-receptor complex were incubated at 23°C for times shown, cooled on ice and chromatographed on identical 2-ml columns of ATP-Sepharose. The columns were washed with 10mM Tris-HCl buffer, 20% glycerol, 10mM KCl, pH 8 and the adsorbed complexes were recovered with the same buffer containing 1M KCl. Taken with permission from ref. 47.

ranged between 50-70% of the total cytosol receptor. The
binding of receptor-hormone complexes (activated by salt or
heat treatment) to ATP-Sepharose has been shown to parallel
the nuclear uptake of the receptor (46). ATP-Sepharose chromatography, therefore, has application in the measurement of
activation of steroid hormone receptors. The resin can also
be conveniently used in batch assays for multiple sample measurements.

Inhibitors of ATP binding

The functional significance of ATP binding has not been established with certainty and will be discussed later in this
chapter. The nucleotide binding may represent an important
step in the mechanism of steroid hormone action. In an effort
to provide additional definition to the receptor-ATP interaction, inhibitors of this process have been sought. Several
compounds have been identified which appear to interfere with
the receptor binding to ATP-Sepharose (1,65,66). These compounds include o-phenanthroline (o-phe.), rifamycin AF/013
(Rif.), aurintricarboxylic acid (ATA), pyridoxal 5'-phosphate
(PLP) and sodium molybdate. These agents do not interfere
with the steroid binding process, but block the cell-free interaction of receptor with isolated nuclei, DNA-cellulose and
ATP-Sepharose (19,65-70).

The inhibitory action of o-phenanthroline, a metal chelator,
suggests that steroids receptors may be metalloproteins. Rifamycin AF/013 is an antibiotic derivative that has been shown
to interfere with the activities of DNA and RNA polymerases;
the latter have also been demonstrated to be metal-containing
enzymes. Aurintricarboxylic acid is a triphenylmethane dye,
with known inhibitory effects on the activities of nucleotidyl
transferases, that also blocks binding of steroid receptors to

ATP-Sepharose (58,60,71,72). Pyridoxal 5'-phosphate appears to block ATP binding due to the formation of a Schiff base between the inhibitor and a critical lysine of the receptor molecule which may be necessary for ATP and the DNA binding of the receptor (65,69,70). Although the exact modes of action of these inhibitors are not clear at present, their use in the characterization and identification of various acceptor sites on the steroid receptors should prove valuable. The effects of these inhibitors are applicable generally to different steroid-receptor systems and are summarized in Table III for rat liver glucocorticoid receptor.

Table III. Effects of Various Inhibitors on the Binding of [^{3}H]dexamethasone-Receptor Complex to DNA-Cellulose and ATP-Sepharose

Compound	Concentration Used	% Specific [^{3}H]dexamethasone binding DNA-Cellulose	ATP-Sepharose
Control (no inhibitor)	—	100	100
NaVO$_3$	10mM	75	74
Na$_2$WO$_4$	10mM	3	0
Na$_2$MoO$_4$	10mM	0	0
PLP	5mM	17	60
ATA	0.01mM	14	34
Heparin	300ug/ml	0	0
o-Phe.	3mM	0	7
Rif.	175ug/ml	0	0

Freshly excised livers from bilaterally adrenalectomized adult male rats were homogenized at 0°C in 2 volumes (V/w) of Tris-buffer (20mM Tris-HCl, 12mM thioglycerol, 10% glycerol and 0.3mM phenylmethylsulfonyl fluoride, pH 7.5). The homogenate was cleared by centrifugation at 150,000xg for 60 min. The resulting cytosol was complexed with 20nM [^{3}H]dexamethasone for 2 h at 0°C. The excess steroid was removed by treatment with a charcoal suspension and aliquots of cytosol were incubated with the compounds listed in the table and were heat-activated (23°C, 1 h). Portions (0.5ml) were used to measure DNA-cellulose and ATP-Sepharose binding. Taken with permission from reference 66.

A number of compounds have been identified over the years
which interfere with the ability of ATP to transform the cytosol receptor to an acceptor (nuclei, DNA-cellulose and ATP-
Sepharose) binding state. Effects of some of these inhibitors
are summarized in Table V. The mode of action of these compounds, which is not fully understood at present, has been
discussed earlier.

Table V.   Chemical inhibitors of the process of progesterone-
           receptor activation by ATP.

Inhibitor	Concentration	$[^3H]$R5020-receptor complex bound to ATP-Sepharose
	mM (ug/ml)	%
Control	--	100
PLP	5	84
o-Phenanthroline	3	83
Sodium levamisole	10	84
Sodium tungstate	10	59
Sodium molybdate	10	19
Rifamycin AF/013	(175)	11
Heparin	(300)	0
ATA	0.02	0

Freshly prepared hen oviduct cytosol was complexed with 10 nM
$[^3H]$R5020 for 2 h at 4°C. A series of tubes was set up (in
duplicate) in a final volume of 0.5 ml and contained 0.15 ml
of receptor complex, 20% glycerol, 10 mM ATP and different inhibitors at concentrations shown in the table. The contents
of tubes were mixed and incubated for 1 h at 4°C. Following
this, 0.5ml Dextran-coated charcoal suspension was added to
each tube to remove free nucleotides and inhibitors. After
centrifugation at 1000xg for 5 min, portions (0.7ml) of supernatant were used to measure the extent of receptor activation
by using ATP-Sepharose batch assays. Taken with permission
from reference 41.

Significance of the interaction between ATP and steroid
receptors

Several lines of evidence suggest a role for ATP in steroid
receptor function. Addition of ATP to target cell cytosol increases the extent of steroid binding by glucocorticoid receptor (44,80). The steroid-receptor complexes are activated

upon incubation at 0°C with 10mM ATP (pH 8). This activation can also be achieved by substituting a non-hydrolizable analog of ATP, adenosine 5'-[β,γ-imido] triphosphate (41). Although effects of ATP on the hormone binding capacity of receptor may possibly involve its metabolism, its influence on the process of activation appears to be direct. The latter view is supported by the numerous reports demonstrating interaction between steroid receptors and immobilized ATP (Table II). Additional clues to the existence of an ATP-binding site on steroid receptors come from studies of McBlain and Toft (81) who have demonstrated that an aldehyde derivative of ATP, 2'-3'-dialdehyde, can be irreversibly linked to avian progesterone receptor. Based on this and other available information, it has been proposed that some, if not all, of the ATP effects are mediated via nucleotide binding site(s) on the steroid receptors (1,41,43-47,54,55,73).

The mechanism by which ATP transforms the steroid-receptor complex is not completely understood. Binding to ATP-Sepharose requires an activated form of receptor. However, the cytosol receptor is in the nonactivated from and transforms into an activated state in the presence of free ATP. This would mean that ATP influences both activated and nonactivated receptor forms. ATP may bind to a nonactivated receptor and shift the equilbrium in favour of an activated receptor form which then binds to the polyanion resins and ATP-Sepharose more readily.

The present knowledge favours the hypothesis that the activation of chick oviduct progesterone receptor (and perhaps of receptor for other steroid hormones) is a direct consequence of the dissociation of the oligomeric native molecule, without involvement of enzyme-catalyzed steps (5,82). The nonactivated 8S oligomeric 'native' molecule behaves in vitro as a metastable structure, easily disrupted. ATP may bind with receptor and disrupt the 8S oligomeric structure (perhaps by

competing for certain bonds required to keep the subunits organized in the native structure)(82).

In recent years, phosphatase inhibitors like sodium molybdate
have been shown to inhibit temperature-dependent inactivation
of steroid receptors, and block transformation of cytosol receptor to nuclear, DNA-cellulose or ATP-Sepharose binding
forms (19,65,75). It has also been suggested that the steroid
binding as well as the transformation of steroid receptors are
influenced by phosphorylation-dephosphorylation processes (75,
83). Auricchio et al. (84) have reported partial purification
of an enzyme which apparently utilizes ATP to restore the estrogen-binding ability of mouse uterine cytosol. Whether the
ATP effects discussed in this chapter are related to the phosphorylation of the receptor or the two processes are unrelated, is not clear at present. A hypothetical model representing the sequence of events in a target cell for steroid
hormone is shown in Fig. 6 with particular emphasis on the
role speculated for ATP.

Phosphorylation of steroid receptors

It is becoming evident that steroid receptors are good substrates for phosphorylation. The physiologic significance of
phosphorylation of receptor remains to be established. Phosphorylation of receptors for progesterone (84,85), estrogen
(86) and glucocorticoid (87,88) has been demonstrated. Results of preliminary studies from this laboratory have shown
that the rat liver glucocorticoid receptor is a phosphoprotein
(88)(Fig. 7). To perform phosphorylation of glucocorticoid
receptor in the intact hepatic tissue, a liver mince was incubated with [^{32}P]orthophosphate and the tissue was used to
prepare cytosol. The cytosol was treated with 40% $(NH_4)_2SO_4$
and complexed with 40 nM [^{3}H]dexamethasone mesylate for 3 h at
0°C.

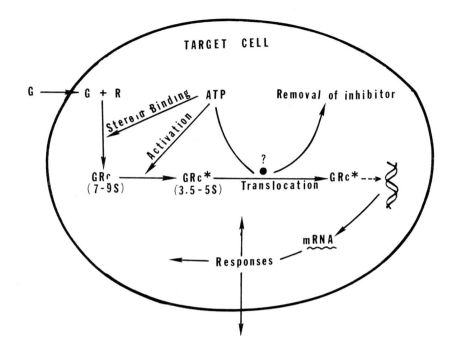

FIG. 6. A hypothetical model of glucocorticoid action in a target cell showing possible involvement of ATP. G, glucocorticoid; R, receptor; GRc, glucocorticoid-receptor complex. Taken with permission from ref. 75.

The glucocorticoid-receptor complex was purified by chromatography over DEAE-Sephacel and DNA-cellulose. SDS-polyacrylamide gel (7%) electrophoresis of the partially purified receptor revealed the presence of several ^{32}P-containing bands which depended on the availability of added $MgCl_2$ (Fig. 7).

Many questions about a specific function of ATP binding by steroid receptors remain unanswered. Whereas, under certain conditions, metabolism of ATP may result in effects on the receptors, under other circumstances the nucleotide may be meta-

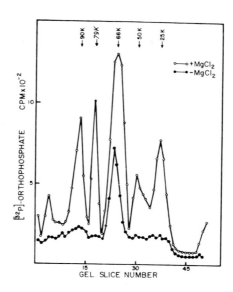

FIG. 7. Phosphorylation of rat liver glucocorticoid receptor by incubation of [^{32}P]-orthophosphate with liver tissue mince. The liver mince was suspended in a phosphate-free Joklik medium plus MgCl$_2$ and incubated for 3-4 h at 37°C. The mince was washed with cold homogenization buffer containing 25mM NaF and homogenized. The cytosol was fractionated with saturated ammonium sulfate, desalted on Sephadex G-75 column and was incubated with 50nM unlabeled dexamethasone mesylate for 3 h. Under identical conditions, liver mince was incubated with unlabeled phosphate and the receptor was fractionated and desalted as above but incubated with 50nM [^{3}H]dexamethasone mesylate for 3 h at 0°C. The preparations were then subjected to SDS-electrophoresis analysis on 10% acrylamide gels. Gels were sliced into 2-3mm pieces, digested with protosol and were mixed with scintillation cocktail (67:3:30; toluene:protosol: Triton X-100) containing 0.5g Omnifluor. Phosphorylation performed in presence (o——o) and absence (●——●) of MgCl$_2$.

bolized by the receptor. Although no studied have been performed or reported suggesting these views, the enzymic potential of steroid receptors has been explored recently.

370

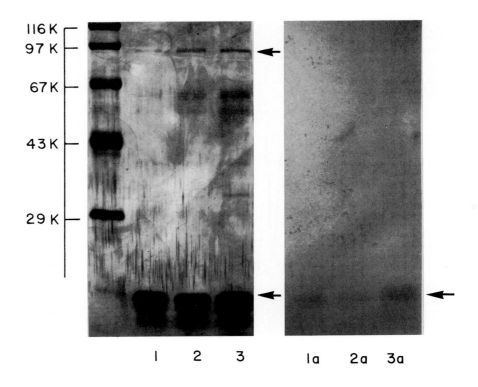

FIG. 8. Phosphorylation of calf thymus histones using purified GR as a protein kinase. Purified GR was dialyzed and incubated with histones, Mg^{2+} and/or Ca^{2+} and $[\gamma-^{32}P]ATP$. After
completion of the reaction, the TCA precipitated samples were
applied to 10% polyacrylamide slab gels and electrophoresis
was performed as detailed in ref. 90. Far left, mol. wt. markers; lane 1, histones with 5mM $MgCl_2$; lane 2, histones with
5mM $CaCl_2$; lane 3, histones and 5mM $MgCl_2$ + 50nM unlabeled TA.
Lanes 1a-3a are an autoradiograph of lanes 1-3. Arrows indicate the positions of receptor and phosphorylated histones.
Taken with permission from ref. 90.

Protein kinase activity of steroid receptors

The postulation that a steroid receptor may itself possess protein kinase activity was provided by Garcia et al. (89). These investigators reported that 110,000 and 90,000 dalton peptides of chick oviduct progesterone receptor exhibited protein kinase activity. In this laboratory, molybdate-stabilized non-activated rat liver glucocorticoid receptor was purified to near homogeneity and was incubated with different protein substrates in the presence of 50 μM [γ-^{32}P]ATP and divalent cations. The radioactive phosphate from [γ-^{32}P]ATP was incorporated into calf thymus histones, turkey gizzard myosin light chain kinase and rabbit skeletal muscle kinase in the presence of Mg^{2+} and Ca^{2+} ions (90). The addition of steroid ligand to the reaction mixture appeared to increase the extent of protein phosphorylation. Phosphorylation of calf thymus histones (H3, H4) by purified glucocorticoid receptor is shown in Figure 8. Our results agree well with the preliminary observations of Miller et al. (91) who have also reported phosphorylation of histones by purified glucocorticoid receptor.

The biological significance of the protein kinase activity of steroid receptors cannot be accurately assessed at this time, but an enzymatic role of receptors may be of critical importance for steroid hormone action. Since the regulation of gene expression by steroid hormones is well recognized, phosphorylation of chromatin proteins may be involved in the alteration in the transcription of specific genes (89). Other processes which might be influenced by phosphorylation of receptor or of other related proteins include steroid binding and activation of receptor, all of which have been shown to be affected by ATP and other nucleotides.

Acknowledgements: This work was supported by N.I.H. Grant AM-20893. Reading of the manuscript by Dr. N. Eliezer is thankfully acknowledged.

References

1. Moudgil, V.K.: In: Principles of Recepterology, 273-379 (M.K. Agarwal, Ed.) Walter de Gruyter, Berlin 1983.

2. Spelsberg, T.C., Steggles, A.W., O'Malley, B.W.: J. Biol. Chem. 246, 4188-4197 (1971).

3. Steggles, A.W., Spelsberg, T.C., Glasser, S.R., O'Malley, B.W.: Proc. Natl. Acad. Sci., U.S.A. 68, 1479-1482 (1971).

4. Jensen, E.V., Suzuki, T., Kawashima, T., Stumpf, W.E., Jungblut, P.W., DeSombre, E.R.: Proc. Natl. Acad. Sci., U.S.A. 59, 632-638 (1968).

5. Baulieu, E-E., Binart, N., Buchou, T., Catelli, M.G., Garcia, T., Gasc, J.M., Groyer, A., Joab, I., Moncharmont, B., Radanyi, C., Renoir, M.J., Tuohimaa, P., Mester, J. In: Steroid Hormone Receptors: Structure and function, 45-72 (H. Ericksson and J-A., Gustafsson, Eds.) Elsevier Science Publishers, Amsterdam 1983.

6. King, W.J., Greene, G.L.: Nature (London) 307, 745-747 (1984).

7. Welshons, W.V., Lieberman, M.E., Gorski, J.: Nature (London) 307, 747-749 (1984).

8. Gasc, J.M., Renoir, J.M., Radanyi, C., Joab, I., Tuohimaa, P., Baulieu, E-E.: J. Cell Biol. 99, 1193-1201 (1984).

9. Munck, A., Wira, C., Young, D.A., Mosher, K.M., Hallahan, C., Bell, P.A.: J. Steroid Biochem. 3, 567-578 (1972).

10. Buller, R.E., Toft, D.O., Schrader, W.T., O'Malley, B.W.: J. Biol. Chem. 250, 801-808 (1975).

11. Schrader, W.T., Toft, D.O., O'Malley, B.W.: J. Biol. Chem 247, 2401-2407 (1972).

12. Baxter, J.D., Rousseau, G.G., Benson, M.C., Garcea, R.L., Ito, J., Tomkins, G.M.: Proc. Natl. Acad. Sci., U.S.A. 69, 1892-1896 (1972).

13. Milgrom, E., Atger, M., Baulieu, E-E.: Biochemistry 12, 5198-5205 (1973).

14. Goidl, J.A., Cake, M.H., Dolan, K.P., Parchman, L.G., Litwack, G.: Biochemistry 16, 2125-2130 (1977).

15. Atger, M., Milgrom, E.: Biochemistry 15, 4298-4304 (1976).

16. Weichman, B.M., Notides, A.C.: Biochemistry 18, 220-225 (1979).

17. Sakaue, Y., Thompson, E.B.: Biochem. Biophys. Res. Commun. 77, 533-541 (1977).

18. Parchman, L.G., Litwack, G.: Arch. Biochem. Biophys. 183, 374-382 (1977).

19. Nishigori, H., Toft, D.O.: Biochemistry 19, 77-83 (1980).

20. Yang, C.R., Renoir, J-M., Mester, J., Baulieu, E-E.: Proc. Meet. Endo. Soc. Abstract 251 (1982).

21. Grandics, P., Miller, A., Schmidt, T.J., Mittman, D., Litwack, G.: J. Biol. Chem. 259, 3173-3180 (1984).

22. Sato, B., Huseby, R.A., Samuels, L.T.: Endocrinology 102, 545-555 (1978).

23. Okamoto, K., Isohashi, F., Horiuchi, M., Sakamoto, Y.: Biochem. Biophys. Res. Commun. 121, 940-945 (1984).

24. Thampan, T.N.R.V., Clark, J.H.: Nature (London) 290, 152-154 (1981).

25. Colvard, D.S., Wilson, E.M.: Endocrinology 109, 496-504 (1981).

26. Colvard, D.S., Wilson, E.M.: Biochemistry 23, 3471-3478 (1984).

27. Colvard, D.S., Wilson, E.M.: Biochemistry 23, 3479-3486 (1984).

28. Munck, A., Foley, R.: Nature (London) 278, 752-754 (1979).

29. Markovic, R.D., Litwack, G.: Arch. Biochem. Biophys. 202, 374-379 (1980).

30. Holbrook, N.J., Bodwell, J.E., Jeffries, M., Munck, A.: J. Biol. Chem. 258, 6477-6485 (1983).

31. Schmidt, T.J., Harmon, J.M., Thompson, E.B.: Nature (London) 286, 507-510 (1980).

32. Milgrom, E.: In: Biochemical Actions of Hormones (G. Litwack, Ed.) Academic Press, New York, 13, 465-492 (1981).

33. Schmidt, T.J., Litwack, G.: Physiol. Rev. 62, 1131-1192 (1982).

34. Grody, W.W., Schrader, W.T., O'Malley, B.W.: Endocrine Rev. 3, 141-163 (1982).

35. Notides, A.C., Nielsen, S.: J. Biol. Chem. 249, 1866-1873 (1974).

36. Notides, A.C., Nielsen, S.: J. Steroid Biochem. 6, 483-486 (1975).

37. Bailly, A., LeFevre, B., Savouret, J.F., Milgrom, E.: J. Biol. Chem. 255, 2729-2734 (1980).

38. Muller, R.E., Traish, A.M., Wotiz, H.H.: J. Biol. Chem. 258, 9227-9236 (1983).

39. Sakai, D., Gorski, J.: Biochemistry 23, 3541-3547 (1984).

40. Schrader, W.T., Heuer, S.S., O'Malley, B.W.: Biol. Reproduction 12,. 134-142 (1975).

41. Moudgil, V.K., Kruczak, V.H., Eessalu, T.E., Paulose, C.S., Taylor, M.G., Hansen, J.C.: Eur. J. Biochem. 118, 547-555 (1981).

42. Vedeckis, W.V.: Biochemistry 22, 1983-1989 (1983).

43. John, J.K., Moudgil, V.K.: Biochem. Biophys. Res. Commun. 90, 1242-1248 (1979).

44. Moudgil, V.K., John, J.K.: Biochem. J. 190, 799-808 (1980).

45. Moudgil, V.K., Eessalu, T.E.: FEBS Lett. 122, 189-192 (1980).

46. Miller, J.B., Toft, D.O.: Biochemistry 17, 173-177 (1978).

374

47. Moudgil, V.K., John, J.K.: Biochem. J. 190, 809-818 (1980).

48. Wolfson, A., Mester, J., Yang, C.R., Baulieu, E-E.: Biochem. Biophys. Res. Commun. 95, 1577-1584 (1980).

49. McBlain, W.A., Toft, D.O., Shyamala, G.: Biochemistry 20, 6790-6798 (1981).

50. Munck, A., Johnsen, T.B.: J. Biol. Chem. 243, 5556-5565 (1968).

51. Munck, A., Wira, C., Young, D.A., Mosher, K.M., Hallahan, C., Bell, P.A.: J. Steroid Biochem. 3, 567-578 (1972).

52. Sando, J.J., LaForest, A.C., Pratt, W.B.: J. Biol. Chem. 254, 4772-4778 (1979).

53. Sando, J.J., Hammond, N.D., Stratford, C.A., Pratt, W.B.: J. Biol. Chem. 254, 4779-4789 (1979).

54. Moudgil, V.K., Toft, D.O.: Proc. Natl. Acad. Sci. U.S.A. 72, 901-905 (1975).

55. Moudgil, V.K., Toft, D.O.: Biochim. Biophys. Acta 490, 477-488 (1977).

56. Leavitt, W.W., Chen, T.J., Evans, R.W.: In: Steroid Hormone Receptor System (W.W. Leavitt, J.H. Clark, Eds.) Plenum Press, New York 1979.

57. Moudgil, V.K., Prass, W.A., Kruczak, V.H.: Life Sci. 25, 1335-1342 (1979).

58. Moudgil, V.K., Eessalu, T.E.: Life Sci. 27, 1159-1167 (1980).

59. Katzenellenbogen, B.S., Pavlik, E.J., Robertson, D.W., Katzenellen-bogen, J.A.: J. Biol. Chem. 256, 2908-2915 (1981).

60. Moudgil, V.K., Weekes, G.A.: FEBS Lett. 94, 324-326 (1978).

61. McBlain, W.A., Toft, D.O., Shyamala, G.: Biochemistry 20, 6790-6798 (1981).

62. Moudgil, V.K., Healy, S.P., Shaffer, T.L., Szocik, J.F.: Biochem. J. 198, 91-99 (1981).

63. Mulder, E., Vrij, L., Foekens, J.A.: Steroids 36, 633-645 (1980).

64. Haussler, M.R., Pike, J.W.: Proc. 5th Workshop on Vit. D. Feb. 14-19, 1982, Williamsburg, Va., p. 36.

65. Moudgil, V.K., Nishigori, H., Eessalu, T.E., Toft, D.O.: In: Gene Regulation by Steroid Hormones (A.K. Roy, J.H. Clark, Eds.) 106-119, Springer-Verlag, Inc., New York 1980.

66. Moudgil, V.K., Murakami, N., Eessalu, T.E., Caradonna, V.M., Singh, V.B., Healy, S.P., Quattrociocchi, T.: In: Adrenal Steroid Antagonism (M.K. Agarwal, Ed.) 131-168, Walter de Gruyter, Berlin, New York 1984.

67. Lohmar, P.H., Toft, D.O.: Biochem. Biophys. Res. Commun. 67, 8-15 (1975).

68. Toft, D., Lohmar, P., Miller, J., Moudgil, V.: J. Steroid Biochem. 7, 1053-1059 (1976).

69. Nishigori, H., Moudgil, V.K., Toft, D.O.: Biochem. Biophys. Res. Commun. 80, 112-118 (1978).

70. Toft, D.O., Roberts, P.E., Nishigori, H., Moudgil, V.K.: In: Steroid Hormone Receptor Systems (W.W. Leavitt, J.H., Clark, Eds.) 329-342 Plenum Press, New York 1979.

71. Moudgil, V.K., Eessalu, T.E.: Biochim. Biophys. Acta 627, 301-312 (1980).

72. Moudgil, V.K., Eessalu, T.E.: Arch. Biochem. Biophys. 213, 98-108 (1982).

73. Moudgil, V.K., John, J.K., Eessalu, T.E., Fisher, V.K., Murakami, N., Healy, S.P., Quattrociocchi, T.M., Singh, V.B., Eliezer, N.: In: Mineralo- and Gluco-Corticoid Receptors (M.K. Agarwal, C.E. Sekeris, Eds.) Acta Medica, Rome (in press) 1985.

74. Andreasen, P.A.: Biochim. Biophys. Acta 676, 205-212 (1981).

75. Barnett, C.A., Schmidt, T.J., Litwack, G.: Biochemistry 19, 5446-5455 (1980).

76. Chong, M.T., Lippman, M.E.: J. Biol. Chem. 257, 2996-3002 (1982).

77. Holbrook, N.J., Bodwell, J.E., Munck, A.: J. Biol. Chem. 258, 14885-14894 (1983).

78. Nawata, H., Bronzert, D., Lippman, M.E.: J. Biol. Chem. 256, 5016-5021 (1981).

79. Nawata, H., Chong, M.T., Bronzert, D., Lippman, M.E.: J. Biol. Chem. 256, 6895-6902 (1981).

80. Barnett, C.A., Palmour, R.M., Litwack, G., Seegmiller, J.E.: Endocrinology 112, 2059-2068 (1983).

81. McBlain, W.A., Toft, D.O.: Biochemistry 22, 2262-2270 (1983).

82. Moudgil, V.K., Eessalu, T.E., Buchou, T., Renoir, J-M., Mester, J., Baulieu, E-E.: Endocrinology (submitted).

83. Leach, K.L., Dahmer, M.K., Hammond, N.D., Sando, J.J., Pratt, W.B.: J. Biol. Chem. 254, 11884-11890 (1979).

84. Weigel, N.L., Tash, J.S., Means, A.R., Schrader, W.T., O'Malley, B.W.: Biochem. Biophys. Res. Commun. 102, 513-519 (1981).

85. Dougherty, J.J., Puri, R.K., Toft, D.O.: J. Biol. Chem. 257, 14226-14230 (1982).

86. Migliaccio, A., Lastoria, S., Moncharmont, B., Rotondi, A., Auricchio, F.: Biochem. Biophys. Res. Commun. 109, 1002-1010 (1982).

87. Housley, P.R., Pratt, W.B.: J. Biol. Chem 258, 4630-4635 (1983).

88. Singh, V.B., Eessalu, T.E., Ghag, S., Moudgil, V.K.: Proc. VII Internatl. Cong. Endocrinol, Abstract 2095 (1984).

89. Garcia, T., Tuohimaa, P., Mester, J., Buchou, T., Renoir, J-M., Baulieu, E-E.: Biochem. Biophys. Res. Commun. 113, 960-966 (1983).

90. Singh, V.B., Moudgil, V.K.: Biochem. Biophys. Res. Commun. (in press).

91. Miller, A.S., Schmidt, T.J., Litwack, G. (1984) Proc. VII Internatl. Cong. Endo., Abstract 1056 (1984).

STEROID HORMONE RECEPTOR DYNAMICS: THE KEY TO TISSUE RESPONSIVENESS

Thomas G. Muldoon

Department of Endocrinology
Medical College of Georgia
Augusta, Georgia 30912

Introduction

By definition, steroid hormone receptors are the subcellular components which, to the best of our current knowledge, single-handedly dictate qualitative responsiveness of the cell to the respective hormone. Tissue specificity of receptor localization to responsive cells was established in the pioneering studies from Jensen's laboratory (1,2) and confirmed by an extensive series of autoradiographic analyses (3). Impetus into investigations of receptor nature and function was afforded by critical demonstrations of the biochemistry of these molecules by a number of groups (4-7), defining their proteinaceous nature and various physicochemical means of detecting and quantifying them. This early work set the stage for extrapolation from the qualitative role of receptors as effectors of intracellular retention to quantitative assessment of their function as determinants of specific hormonal responsiveness. A number of the chapters in this book are devoted to various aspects of such studies; the aim of this presentation is to focus on several areas of receptor regulation and localization which have represented a central thrust of the research in our laboratory within recent years. In terms of intracellular receptor distribution, our studies of the significance of microsomal components will be presented. Receptor level and functionality in relation to differential gene expression will be addressed by summarizing our studies on androgen receptors of the rat ventral prostate. Regulation of a specific sub-population of steroid hormone receptors within a responsive tissue will be exemplified by addressing our observations in the estrogen-LHRH-LH response system. Finally, the complex regulation of the estrogen and progesterone receptors

Molecular Mechanism of Steroid Hormone Action
© 1985 Walter de Gruyter & Co., Berlin · New York – Printed in Germany

by both steroidal and proteinaceous hormones in mammary tissue will be presented as representative of the diverse and divers ways in which responsiveness is subservient to regulators of steroid hormone receptor activity.

Intracellular Receptor Distribution

The steroid receptor literature is replete with measurements of specific
binding activity in cytoplasmic and nuclear compartments of hormonally-
responsive cells. This approach has been useful toward understanding actions and interactions of assorted natural and synthetic hormonal agents,
and for elucidating the gross features of the steroid-receptor complex
association with chromatinic components of the nucleus, generally considered to be a critical element of the mechanism whereby genetic expression
is altered by the hormone. Of recent vintage are a series of studies from
several laboratories (8-11) which present a strong case for intranuclear
localization of most, if not all, steroid hormone receptors within intact
cells. These findings indicate that receptors designated as cytoplasmic
are actually those which are not strongly bound to chromatin and are
leached out into the cytosolic fraction under homogenization and ultracen-
trifugational conditions. It is important to note that this change in our
manner of visualizing intracellular receptor distribution does not compromise the validity of the multitude of studies performed to determine relationships between receptor binding and functional response.

In an analysis of subcellular distribution of estradiol in castrate rat
uterine cells at intervals after administration of radiolabeled estradiol
(12), we observed that nuclear estrogen receptor content diminished sharply
between 3-5 hours without a concomitant rise in cytoplasmic receptor content (Figure 1); this was the first demonstration in a normal tissue of a
phenomenon subsequently to be referred to as receptor "processing" (13).
Strikingly, we were able to show that the complexes lost from the nucleus
at this time became associated with the *microsomal* fraction of the cell.
Between 5-10 hours after estradiol exposure, these microsome-associated
complexes re-entered the nucleus (Figure 1), leading to a second nuclear

peak which was also observed later in mouse uterus (14,15). The transient residence of the nuclear receptors on the microsomes was unexpected and suggested a role for the vacuolar membrane system as a conduit, shuttling steroid-receptor complexes to and from nuclear sites; this phenomenon is clearly distinct from the microsomal-associated receptor forms described by Jungblut and his co-workers (16-18), which appear to be biosynthetically developing species of the mature receptor molecule.

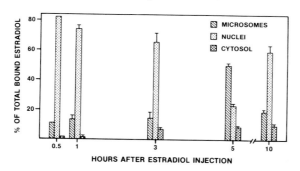

FIGURE 1. Subcellular distribution of estradiol in uteri of 2-weeks'-ovariectomized rats following estradiol injection. Animals were administered 0.25 μCi (1.25 μg) of estradiol at time zero and killed in groups at the specified intervals. The designated fractions were separated by differential centrifugation of the uterine homogenate. The data represent compartmental binding as a function of total specifically-bound estradiol recovered at each time point.

In a separate series of experiments, we obtained further evidence for a functional role of the microsomes in receptor-mediated events. Assessment of 4-mercuriestradiol as an affinity-labeling agent for the estrogen receptor revealed that this compound was possessed of robust inherent estrogenicity, but no detectable interaction with or effects upon the nuclear genetic material of the cell (19,20). This seemed to defy classical concepts of the mechanism of steroid hormone action, but in fact only strengthened a growing body of evidence that extranuclear sites of action, particularly those areas associated with translational processes (21-26), are involved in the response of the cell to steroid hormones. When we investigated the subcellular distribution of radiolabeled 4-mercuriestradiol following administration in vivo (20), we observed a rapid, elevated and prolonged association of this compound with the microsomes, relative to the interaction of estradiol with this fraction (Figure 2; compare with the estradiol data of Figure 1). The slow and gradual accumulation of small amounts of the mercury derivative within nuclei is also in contrast to the pattern of estradiol uptake by nuclei and reflects the lack of specific interactions in this organelle.

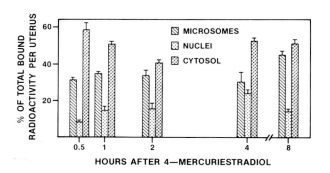

FIGURE 2. Subcellular distribution of 4-mercuriestradiol in uteri of 2-weeks' ovariectomized rats following 4-mercuriestradiol injection. Animals received 1.0 μCi of [^{3}H]4-mercuriestradiol intraluminally at time zero. Groups were killed at the intervals shown and the subcellular distribution of specifically-bound steroid in each fraction was determined. Results are expressed as the percentage of total recovery in each fraction.

At longer intervals after introduction of the mercury derivative, we have found that nuclear levels decline concomitantly with a second increase in microsomal content. Schematically, the interactions are described in Figure 3.

In recent investigations, we have quantified a population of microsomal estrogen receptors which are distinct from the cytosol receptors and can be solubilized in hypotonic buffer. This latter property distinguishes these binders from calf uterine microsomal receptors described by Parikh et al. (27), which are not readily solubilized. The concentration of these binding sites fluctuates in response to estrogen treatment and at various intervals of the estrous cycle in much the same fashion as do cytosol receptors. A salient difference from the cytosol form of the receptor is the inability of the microsomal receptor complexes to transform upon heating to a moiety which is capable of translocating into isolated nuclei. As shown in Figure 4, conditions which are conducive to transformation of 8S cytosol receptors to the 5S nuclear form simply lead to dissociation of the more labile microsomal estradiol-receptor complexes.

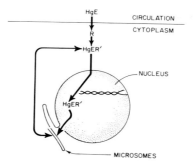

FIGURE 3. A mechanism of action consistent with the activity of 4-mercuri-estradiol (HgE). Initial interaction with the estrogen receptor causes transformation to a 5S complex (HgER') which accumulates rapidly and exten-sively in the microsomes. Small amounts slowly enter the nucleus, but do not interact with chromatin in a specific manner. These complexes are sub-sequently found in association with the microsomes.

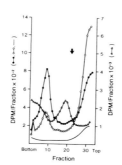

FIGURE 4. Failure of microsomal estrogen receptors to undergo transforma-tion to a nuclear form. Extracted microsomal receptors were incubated with [^{3}H]estradiol for 2 hrs at 4°C in the presence (---) or absence (●-●; o-o) of excess unlabeled estradiol. One sample (o-o) was further incubated for 30 min at 24°C, and a sample of uterine cytosol (△-△) was treated identi-cally. Sucrose gradient centrifugational analysis (15.5 hrs, 350,000 x g) was performed with ^{14}C-labeled BSA as an external marker (4.4S, arrow). Note difference in scale between cytosolic and microsomal samples.

An intriguing feature of the microsomal receptor system is that detachment of the receptors from the membranes by solubilization imparts to the re-ceptor-exhausted microsomes a newly-acquired acceptor capability for cytosol

382

estradiol-receptor complexes. As shown in Table 1, the capacity of this acceptor activity parallels rather closely the level of depleted microsomal receptors.

TABLE 1. Acceptor capability of microsomes for cytosol receptors following removal of microsomal estrophiles

Group	K_A $(10^{10}M^{-1})$	Concentration of specific binding sites (fmoles/mg protein)
Experiment I		
Control	1.31	126.7
Exhausted	4.12	16.9
Reconstituted	1.01	156.8
Experiment II		
Control	2.04	111.5
Exhausted	2.01	37.3
Reconstituted	2.04	87.4
Experiment III		
Control	3.10	114.7
Exhausted	2.16	63.8
Reconstituted	3.14	132.9

Uterine microsomes were prepared and suspended in buffer. One-third was taken to measure the Control binding level by saturation analysis. The remainder was extracted into steroid-free buffer and the pellet, representing Exhausted microsomes, was re-isolated by centrifugation. Half of these resuspended pellets were submitted to saturation analyses, and the other half was mixed with either an equivalent volume (Experiment I), 3 volumes (Experiment II) or 4 volumes (Experiment III) of original cytosol; these samples represented the Reconstituted microsomal preparations. Following mixing, the cytosol-microsome samples were submitted to saturation binding analysis, using the pelleted, resuspended material as source.

The perinuclear situation of microsomal components suggests that they may be included in the newly-described intact cell "nuclear" localization of the vast majority of cellular receptors. Our findings indicate a functional role for these very active protein-synthesizing organelles as both primary sites of steroid hormone action (through receptor interactions) and as regulators of access of hormone-receptor complexes to functional nuclear sites (through their role as acceptors for these complexes).

Receptors and Differential Gene Expression

Repercussions of the eruption of molecular genetics in recent years have
been felt in the area of steroid hormone action. Regulation of specific
transcriptional events in the chick oviduct by estrogen and progesterone
(28-30) was exploited as a working system for investigation of hormonal
control of gene expression, and progress in this area was swift and revealing. Work has advanced to the stage where hormonal loci of action are beginning to be mapped to specific DNA sequences in the vicinity of inducible
genes (for recent work, see 31), but the mechanism whereby the interaction
between steroid-receptor complexes and chromatin components alters specific
transcription is still not understood.

In recent studies performed in collaboration with Professor W.I.P. Mainwaring, we have undertaken an analysis of changes in androgen receptors of
the castrate male rat ventral prostate during the course of constant exposure to testosterone by silastic implant. Our observations have been compared with patterns of androgen-induced protein synthesis during this period. We have presented our data in preliminary form (32). Enzyme induction in this model system occurs in a distinct biphasic manner. Those enzymes involved in cell growth and normal functioning (including aldolase,
glucose-6-phosphate dehydrogenase, acid phosphatase and alkaline phosphatase) are maximally stimulated within 1.5 days of androgen exposure, and
their levels are dramatically reduced by 2 days. Enzymes involved in DNA
replication (thymidine kinase, thymidylate synthetase, DNA polymerase α
and DNA unwinding protein), on the other hand, are present in very small
amounts at 2 days, but the levels rise synchronously to a peak at 3 days
and then slowly recede. Our studies indicate that control is at the transcriptional level. The mechanism whereby nuclear acceptor activity changes
over the course of this constant hormonal stimulation, allowing temporally
differential expression of specific genes, will be the focus of our con-
tinuing investigations into this phenomenon.

In attempting to define a molecular basis for the observed effects on selective genetic triggering, we have studied ventral prostate androgen receptor dynamics during an identical testosterone-replacement regimen. The

results (Figure 5) revealed two distinct peaks of nuclear androgen receptor binding activity, mirroring the respective patterns of the two sets of enzymes induced. The initial nuclear retention phase appeared to involve the traditional steroid-stimulated association with specific nuclear chromatinic components, since it was operationally concomitant with cytosol receptor depletion. Extensive processing of these receptors followed their nuclear accumulation. At 2.5-3 days into testosterone treatment, the nuclear levels again began to rise, but, in this case, the increase was not at the expense of cytosol receptors, which showed only moderate and gradual decreases in levels during this period.

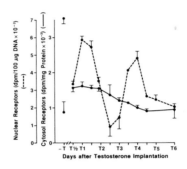

FIGURE 5. Fluctuations in ventral prostate androgen receptor levels following testosterone implantation into 7-day castrate rats. Cytosolic (—) and nuclear (---) receptor concentrations were measured as a function of days (½-6) after implantation of a testosterone pellet. The castrate levels (-T group) are presented for comparison.

In a previous study (33), we found differences in the androgen-binding properties of the two interconvertible forms of cytosol ventral prostate androgen receptors observed by Wilson and French (34,35) and not attributable to endogenous protease activity. The larger (8S on glycerol gradients) of the two forms has a 10-fold higher association rate constant for 5α-dihydrotestosterone than does the smaller 4S form. Thus, the receptivity and the responsiveness of the cell to androgen can be expected to be high when the 8S:4S ratio is high. Glycerol gradient analyses of the receptor forms at selected intervals of androgen exposure in our model system are shown in Figure 6. In the absence of androgen replacement, the cytosol androgen receptors of the castrate rat tissue are predominantly 8S in nature, indicating that the cells are highly responsive to androgen, as judged by their receptiveness. The distribution shifts during the first phase of nuclear binding, such that the 4S form of cytosol receptor is prevalent during the processing wave of this event. Between days 2 and 3 of androgen stimulation (the interval during which the second nuclear surge is occurring), the form of the cytosol receptor reverts back to the 8S and remains thus for the duration of this second stage of response. These findings have been substantiated by measurements of association rate kinetics for the interaction between androgen and the cytosol receptors from tissue at the selected intervals of stimulation.

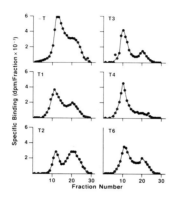

FIGURE 6. Glycerol gradient centrifugation of rat prostate cytosol from castrate animals subjected to testosterone replacement for various intervals (in days). Samples containing 6 mg protein/ml were incubated with [^{3}H]mibolerone. Sedimentation patterns were developed in 10-35% glycerol gradients at 365,000 x g for 75 min in a vertical rotor. The top of the gradient is to the right of each figure. Bovine γ-globulin (6.6S) sedimented at fraction #14 and BSA (4.4S) at fraction #21 under these conditions.

The second wave of androgen-induced transcription of DNA-replicating enzymes occurs as the cells pass into the replicative phase of their cycles; this does not, however, begin to explain the mechanism whereby these genes are selectively activated at this time, as opposed to earlier intervals of identical androgen stimulation (particularly those times during which the first wave of protein synthesis is occurring). The harmonious synchrony between the two stages of this overall response and the changes in nature and amount of androgen receptor activity suggest a functional correlation which should become clearer with our projected refinements of the experimental protocol.

Direct Regulation of Nuclear Receptors

In most instances where steroid hormone receptor regulation has been studied,
the regulator has been shown to initially alter the subcellular distribution of the receptors, which is probably largely a reflection of a change
in the affinity or extent of interaction of the receptor with genetic material in the nucleus (for review, see 36). Occasionally, however, a curious
situation is encountered wherein levels of nuclear receptor are altered in
the absence of any accompanying effect on cytosol receptor content. An interesting example is the action of progesterone on estrogen receptors of
the hamster uterus. In this system, progesterone selectively depresses
nuclear estrogen receptor binding (37) by a mechanism which requires intact
transcriptional and translational circuitry (38), and appears to be mediated by acid phosphatase (39). We have reported a similar effect in the rat
anterior pituitary, and have shown tissue specificity, since progesterone
has no effect on the hypothalamic estrogen receptors of the same animals
(40). The mechanism appears to be different from that of the hamster uterus since nuclear localization of the progesterone is not required even
though cytosol progesterone receptor does seem to be involved.

Along these lines, our curiosity was piqued by our observation that LHRH
administration in vivo caused nuclear estrogen receptors of the rat anterior
pituitary to increase without any concomitant decrease in cytosol estrogen
receptor level. In contrast to the progesterone studies mentioned above,
this study involved the action of a peptide hormone known to interact with
cell membrane receptors on a species of protein localized within the nucleus. Conditions were established for investigating this phenomenon in
vitro, using incubation of dispersed anterior pituitary cells in the presence of LHRH (41), and we were able to show the effect on whole cells
(Figure 7). The highly active LHRH analog, (D-Ala^6, des-Gly^{10})LHRH-N-
ethylamide (designated LHRH-A), had a greater intrinsic activity in elevating nuclear estrogen receptor than did LHRH, and was maximally effective
at a 10-fold lower concentration (Figure 8). TRH, on the other hand, was
totally devoid of such activity over a wide concentration range (Figure 9)
(42).

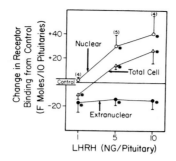

FIGURE 7. Estrogen receptor levels following incubation of intact cells with LHRH for 30 min. Whole anterior pituitary cells were incubated with 1,5 or 10 ng of LHRH per pituitary for 30 min at 37°C, and estrogen receptor binding was estimated in the nuclear and extranuclear compartments of the cells. The receptor level observed in control groups of cells was arbitrarily assigned a value of zero, and the positive or negative differences in the levels observed in treated cells was plotted at each dose level. Values represent triplicate determinations of the number of experiments shown in parentheses. Asterisk: $P < 0.05$. [Reprinted, with permission, from Singh and Muldoon (41)].

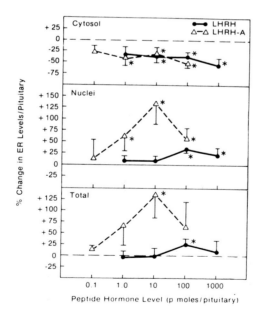

FIGURE 8. Response of estradiol receptor to LHRH and LHRH-A in intact pituitary cells. Enzymatically dispersed pituitary cells from castrated, low-dose estrogen primed rats were incubated with increasing concentrations of either LHRH or LHRH-A for 30 min at 37°C, followed by estimation of cytosol (A), nuclear (B) and the sum total (C) receptors. Values represent 10-24 observations in 6-18 separate experiments. Asterisk: $P < 0.05$, compared with control. [Reprinted, with permission, from Singh and Muldoon (42)].

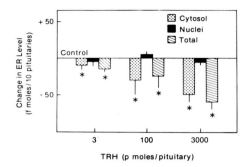

FIGURE 9. Effects of TRH on estrogen receptor populations in intact pituitary cells. Increase (+) or decrease (-) in femtomoles of cytosol, nuclear and total estrogen receptors per 10 pituitary equivalents is compared
to control values (assigned value of zero), resulting from incubation of
pituitary cells from castrated, low-dose estrogen primed rats with TRH for
30 min at 37°C. Each value is a mean ± SEM of 3 separate experiments.
Asterisk: P < 0.05, as compared with control. [Reprinted, with permission,
from Singh and Muldoon (42)].

Of significant mechanistic importance was the observation that LHRH was
capable of altering nuclear estrogen receptor when incubated with isolated
nuclei (Figure 10). In attempting to explain this unexpected finding, we
are forced to entertain the possibility that internalization of LHRH precedes an intracellular mechanism of direct action of this hormone.

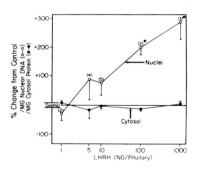

FIGURE 10. Effect of LHRH on estrogen receptors of isolated anterior pituitary cytosol or nuclei. Cytosol and nuclei were prepared and incubated
separately with 1-1000 ng of LHRH per pituitary for 30 min at 37°C. Estrogen receptor activity was then determined in each fraction. Values are
means ± SEM of (n) experiments. Asterisk: P < 0.05, compared with controls
incubated in the absence of LHRH. [Reprinted, with permission, from Singh
and Muldoon (41)].

The concept that internalization of peptide hormones represents exclusively the cellular mechanism for degradative elimination of the hormone (43,44) has been questioned (45) on the basis of a number of studies in which intranuclear localization of protein hormones has been observed at extra-lysosomal loci. A possible direct action of LHRH on cell nuclei is brought into the realm of feasibility by the report of specific receptor-like binding sites for LHRH on nuclear membranes (46).

In considering the mechanism whereby LHRH enhances nuclear estrogen receptor activity, it therefore becomes important to determine whether cAMP functions as a mediator of this action, under the presumption that such mediation should not be required if the action of the hormone is indeed directly intracellular. Of great significance to such studies is the observation that cAMP is not involved in the mechanism by which LHRH induces LH release from the anterior pituitary (47-50), in spite of the fact that LHRH does cause increased intracellular cAMP accumulation (51). In Figure 11 is presented evidence that LHRH is capable, at 100 pmoles/pituitary, of significantly elevating cAMP levels in anterior pituitary cells. The level of LHRH required was an order of magnitude higher than that which causes maximal nuclear estrogen receptor stimulation. The action of the above-mentioned hyperactive analog of LHRH was less pronounced than that of LHRH, in contrast to the opposite pattern in stimulating nuclear estrogen receptor (see Figure 8).

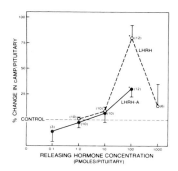

FIGURE 11. The influence of LHRH and LHRH-A on cyclic AMP production in anterior pituitary cells in suspension. Cells were incubated for 30 min at 37°C with the indicated levels of LHRH or LHRH-A. Concentrations of cAMP in the cells and released into the medium were measured by radioimmunoassay. Numbers in parentheses are separate experiments at each dosage.

When we attempted to reproduce with dibutyryl cAMP the effects of LHRH on nuclear estrogen receptors, we were unable to do so, using either intact cells (Table 2) or isolated nuclei (Table 3), and amounts of cAMP orders of magnitude greater than the maximally-LHRH-stimulated level.

TABLE 2. Effects of LHRH or DBcAMP on cytosol and nuclear estrogen receptor levels in whole cells under suspension or culture conditions

Agent	% of control			
	nuclear ER		cytosol ER	
	suspension	culture	suspension	culture
LHRH (pmoles per pituitary)				
1.0	102 ± 0.3	112 ± 1.6	76 ± 3.4	70 ± 1.8
10	166 ± 5.3	256 ± 8.5	62 ± 2.1	50 ± 6.5
100	192 ± 6.1	256 ± 5.9	56 ± 3.2	82 ± 0.7
DBcAMP (nM)				
0.1	95 ± 1.1	104 ± 0.5	66 ± 2.6	80 ± 1.5
10	98 ± 4.0	-	34 ± 2.0	-
100	116 ± 1.7	168 ± 3.3	20 ± 2.8	9 ± 4.1
1000	97 ± 6.4	95 ± 7.7	30 ± 5.4	20 ± 10.1
10,000	112 ± 2.2	88 ± 3.0	26 ± 2.6	23 ± 8.8

Fresh anterior pituitary cells in suspension or from 3-day culture were incubated at 37°C for 30 min in the absence (control) or presence of the indicated levels of LHRH or DBcAMP. Cells were collected and subfractionated into cytosol and nuclear fractions for determination of estrogen receptor content. Each value is the mean ± SEM of triplicate determinations, using groups of 20 animals per experiment.

We conclude from these studies that LHRH has a direct specific stimulatory effect on nuclear anterior pituitary estrogen receptors, independent of involvement of cAMP. This action of LHRH enhances the sensitivity of the cells to estrogen, precipitating the documented estrogen enhancement of responsiveness to LHRH (52,53) and providing an explanation for the phenomenon of LHRH self-priming, whereby one exposure to LHRH sensitizes cells to a second LHRH stimulus (54,55).

391

TABLE 3. Effect of varying levels of DBcAMP or LHRH on estrogen receptor binding in isolated cytosol and nuclear fractions from anterior pituitary homogenates

Agent	% of control	
	cytosol	nuclei
LHRH (pmoles per pituitary)		
1.0	112.0 ± 1.5 (4)	92.2 ± 3.5 (4)
10	121.1 ± 4.0 (4)*	221 ± 18 (4)*
100	110.5 ± 7.2 (4)	385 ± 36 (4)
1000	95.2 ± 3.1 (4)	590 ± 70 (4)*
DBcAMP (nM)		
0.1	92.4 ± 5.9 (4)	89.0 ± 6.0 (4)
1.0	95.6 ±11.8 (8)	136.1 ± 23.0 (8)
10	77.5 ± 4.2 (8)*	83.6 ± 15.3 (8)
100	73.9 ± 2.5 (12)*	79.7 ± 10.7 (8)
1000	62.5 ± 5.2 (12)*	139.4 ± 21.8 (8)
5000	67.7 ±11.0 (6)*	83.6 ± 20.9 (4)
10,000	33.0 ± 3.7 (2)*	87.3 ± 8.6 (2)

Cytosol and nuclei were prepared and incubated for 30 min at 37°C with the level of effector indicated. The samples were then cooled to 4°C and the nuclei were washed with buffer. Estrogen receptor content was assessed in each fraction and expressed as the percentage of that present in samples incubated without added agent. Asterisk: $P < 0.05$, as compared with controls. Values are mean ± SEM for the number of experiments shown in parentheses.

Diversity of Receptor Regulation

Numerous examples appear in the literature for regulation of steroid hormone receptor nature, level and functionality as a function of a wide array of effectors, hormonal and otherwise. As a representative of the complexity which can be involved, we will outline some of our observations on normal mouse mammary gland estrogen receptor control.

Estrogen receptors of the mouse uterus are maintained and regulated by estrogen in much the same manner as in the rat uterus (12,56). Prolactin has
no effect on these receptors of the uterus. In marked contrast, prolactin
is the most potent factor yet detected for controlling the level of estrogen receptors in mouse mammary tissue (57,58). Administration of prolactin
to virgin mice results in dramatic stimulation of cytosol estrogen receptor
activity (Figure 12). The receptor in the stimulated state exists as a
more highly-aggregated form than in the virgin animal and, of probably
greater physiological importance, has a diminished rate of interaction with
estradiol. We have recently described an analogous situation for androgen
receptors of the rat ventral prostate (33); in this system, we also find
two molecular forms of the receptor which differ with respect to their avidity for androgens. In Figure 12 is also presented a pattern of responsiveness of the mouse mammary estrogen receptors to prolactin in the thyroidectomized animal. We have previously observed an involvement of thyroid hormones in regulation of estrogen receptors in another tissue, the
rat anterior pituitary (59). Comparison of the two panels of Figure 12
demonstrates that thyroidectomy enhances the sensitivity of the mammary
estrogen receptor response to prolactin, since it has been shown that removal of the thyroid does not result in increased prolactin secretion (60).
Moreover, it has been reported that endogenous thyroid hormones inhibit
the mammotropic actions of prolactin.

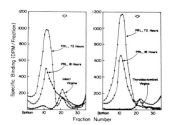

FIGURE 12. Effect of prolactin (PRL) on mouse mammary gland estrogen receptor level and nature. Intact (left panel) or thyroidectomized (right
panel) virgin mice were injected with prolactin and killed 18 hours later
(o), or injected daily with prolactin for 3 days and killed 1 hour after
the final injection (▲). Equivalent amounts of cytosol protein were incubated with [^{3}H]estradiol and applied to sucrose gradients prepared in low
ionic strength buffer. The arrow represents bovine serum albumin at a
value of 4.4S.

The effect of prolactin on mammary tissue estrogen receptors is seen when the animals are treated with estradiol (Table 4). It was originally thought that the estradiol directly regulated its receptor levels in this tissue as it does in the uterus; however, the data of Table 4, in which bromocryptine suppression of prolactin eradicates the possibility of estradiol enhancing estrogen receptor activity, demonstrate that the estradiol action is indirect and mediated through stimulation of prolactin secretion.

TABLE 4. Influence of prolactin on mouse mammary gland estrogen receptors

Treatment	Estrogen receptor levels as % of control	
	Cytosolic	Nuclear
Control[a]	100 ± 9	100 ± 7
Estradiol, 0.5 µg/day x 30, sc in oil	61 ± 5	500 ± 43
CB-154*, 100 µg/day x 30, ip in saline	87 ± 8	111 ± 17
Estradiol + CB-154	59 ± 5	133 ± 8
Rat prolactin, 50 µg/day, twice daily x 5, sc in oil	386 ± 38	273 ± 26

[a]Untreated, 58-day old virgin mice
*CB-154 = bromocryptine

It can also be seen from Table 4 that prolactin-induced estrogen receptor is heavily concentrated in the cytosol. When estradiol is subsequently administered, nuclear translocation occurs and progesterone receptor is induced (58). Thus, the primary control of estrogen receptors in this tissue is bimodal. Prolactin regulates the level of estrogen receptors and estradiol regulates their functionality. Neither hormone, in the absence of the other, is capable of eliciting maximal estrogenic response. This isolated instance of multifaceted regulation of a single receptor system in a tissue-specific manner exemplifies the complexity with which multiple homeostatic hormonal environments are regulated and maintained.

Concluding Remarks

In this presentation, work from my laboratory has been discussed, dealing with several specific studies chosen to exemplify different aspects of the ways in which regulation of steroid hormone receptor turnover occurs and is related to hormonal responsiveness. To adequately portray the paradoxical features of both uniqueness and universal commonness of steroidal receptor systems, I have deliberately selected four different tissue systems, i.e., uterus, prostate, hypothalamus-adenohypophysis, and mammary gland. While the quantitative features of control and function are variable, the basic denominator remains constant. For instance, the estrogen receptors of the uterus and mammary gland are principally regulated by estradiol and prolactin, respectively, whereas the fundamental processes of control of receptor dynamics and concentration appear to be common to both tissues. The overall process of receptor regulation, just as the mechanism of steroid hormone action, appears to be a highly-conserved evolutionary trait. However, the development of tissue and cellular differentiation which has evolved with time has given rise to both subtle and profound changes in the control of responsiveness to a given hormone or group of hormones. This chapter is designed as a mere introduction to this subject, directing the attention of the reader to an area of active current research in our quest for a better understanding of the molecular basis of reproductive physiology and pathology.

References

1. Jensen, E.V., Jacobson, H.I.: Rec. Progr. Horm. Res. 18, 387-414 (1962).
2. Jensen, E.V., DeSombre, E.R.: Annu. Rev. Biochem. 41, 203-230 (1972).
3. Stumpf, W.E., Sar, M.: In: Receptors and Mechanism of Action of Steroid Hormones, Part 1. Pasqualini, J.R. (Ed.), Marcel Dekker, New York, 1977, p. 41.
4. Gorski, J., Toft, D.O., Shyamala, G., Smith, D., Notides, A.C.: Rec. Progr. Horm. Res. 24, 45-80 (1968).
5. Liao, S.: Intl. Rev. Cytology 41, 87-172 (1975).
6. O'Malley, B.W., Schrader, W.T.: J. Steroid Biochem. 3, 617-629 (1972).

7. Rousseau, G.G., Baxter, J.D., Tomkins, G.M.: J. Mol. Biol. <u>67</u>, 99-115 (1972).

8. Linkie, D.M., Siiteri, P.K.: J. Steroid Biochem. <u>9</u>, 1071-1078 (1978).

9. Sheridan, P.J., Buchanan, J.M., Anselmo, V.C.: Nature <u>282</u>, 579-582 (1979).

10. King, W.J., Greene, G.L.: Nature <u>307</u>, 745-747 (1984).

11. Welshons, W.V., Lieberman, M.E., Gorski, J.: Nature <u>307</u>, 747-749 (1984).

12. Cidlowski, J.A., Muldoon, T.G.: Biol. Reprod. <u>18</u>, 234-246 (1978).

13. Horwitz, K.B., McGuire, W.L.: J. Biol. Chem. <u>253</u>, 8185-8191 (1978).

14. Korach, K.S., Ford, E.B.: Biochem. Biophys. Res. Commun. <u>83</u>, 327-333 (1978).

15. Korach, K.S.: Endocrinology <u>104</u>, 1324-1332 (1979).

16. Little, M., Rosenfeld, G.C., Jungblut, P.W.: Z. Physiol. Chem. <u>353</u>, 231-242 (1972).

17. Little, M., Szendro, P., Teran, C., Hughes, A., Jungblut, P.W.: J. Steroid Biochem. <u>6</u>, 493-500 (1975).

18. Szendro, P.I., Sierralta, W.D., Jungblut, P.W.: Z. Physiol. Chem. <u>364</u>, 1337-1344 (1983).

19. Muldoon, T.G.: Biochemistry <u>10</u>, 3780-3784 (1971).

20. Muldoon, T.G.: J. Biol. Chem. <u>255</u>, 1358-1366 (1980).

21. Talwar, G.P., Modi, S., Rao, K.N.: Science <u>150</u>, 1315-1316 (1965).

22. Berg, A., Gustafsson, J-A.: J. Biol. Chem. <u>248</u>, 6559-6567 (1973).

23. Sunshine, G.H., Williams, D.J., Rabin, B.R.: Nature (New Biology) <u>230</u>, 133-136 (1971).

24. Blyth, C.A., Cooper, M.B., Roobel, A., Rabin, B.R.: Eur. J. Biochem. <u>29</u>, 293-300 (1972).

25. Liang, T., Liao, S.: J. Biol. Chem. <u>249</u>, 4671-4678 (1974).

26. Liang, T., Castaneda, E., Liao, S.: J. Biol. Chem. <u>252</u>, 5692-5700 (1977).

27. Parikh, I., Anderson, W.L., Neame, P.: J. Biol. Chem. <u>255</u>, 10266-10270 (1980).

28. McKnight, G.S., Palmiter, R.D.: J. Biol. Chem. <u>254</u>, 9050-9058 (1979).

29. O'Malley, B.W., Woo, S.L., Tsai, M.J.: Curr. Topics Cell. Regul. <u>18</u>, 437-453 (1981).

30. Breathnach, R., Chambon, P.: Annu. Rev. Biochem. <u>50</u>, 349-383 (1981).

31. O'Malley, B.W. (Ed.): Gene Regulation. Academic Press, New York, 1982.

32. Muldoon, T.G., Mainwaring, W.I.P.: 7th Intl. Congr. of Endocrinology, Quebec City, 1984. Excerpta Medica, Amsterdam, p. 1061.

33. Feit, E.I., Muldoon, T.G.: Endocrinology <u>112</u>, 592-600 (1983).

34. Wilson, E.M., French, F.S.: J. Biol. Chem. 251, 5620-5629 (1976).

35. Wilson, E.M., French, F.S.: J. Biol. Chem. 254, 6310-6319 (1979).

36. Muldoon, T.G.: Endocrine Rev. 1, 339-364 (1980).

37. Evans, R.W., Chen, T.J., Hendry, W.J., Leavitt, W.W.: Endocrinology 107, 383-390 (1980).

38. Evans, R.W., Leavitt, W.W.: Proc. Natl. Acad. Sci. (USA) 77, 5856-5860 (1980).

39. MacDonald, R.G., Okulicz, W.C., Leavitt, W.W.: Biochem. Biophys. Res. Commun. 104, 570-576 (1982).

40. Smanik, E.J., Young, H.K., Muldoon, T.G., Mahesh, V.B.: Endocrinology 113, 15-22 (1983).

41. Singh, P., Muldoon, T.G.: J. Steroid Biochem. 16, 31-37 (1982).

42. Singh, P., Muldoon, T.G.: Neuroendocrinology 37, 98-105 (1983).

43. Amsterdam, A., Berkowitz, A., Nimrod, A., Kohen, F.: Proc. Natl. Acad. Sci. (USA) 77, 3440-3444 (1980).

44. Hizuka, N., Gorden, P., Lesniak, M.A., Van Obberghen, E., Carpentier, J-L., Orci, L.: J. Biol. Chem. 256, 4591-4597 (1981).

45. Posner, B.I., Bergeron, J.J.M., Josefsberg, Z., Khan, M.N., Khan, R.J., Patel, B.A., Sikstrom, R.A., Verma, A.K.: Rec. Progr. Horm. Res. 37, 539-582 (1983).

46. Millar, R.P., Rosen, H., Badminton, M., Pasqualini, C., Kerdelhue, B.: FEBS Letters 153, 382-386 (1983).

47. Naor, Z., Koch, Y., Chobsieng, P., Zor, U.: FEBS Letters 58, 318-321 (1975).

48. Tang, L.K.L., Spies, H.G.: Endocrinology 94, 1016-1021 (1974).

49. Clayton, R.N., Shakespear, R.A., Marshall, J.C.: Mol. Cell. Endocrinol. 11, 63-78 (1978).

50. Conn, P.M., Morrell, D.V., Dufau, M.L., Catt, K.J.: Endocrinology 104, 448-453 (1979).

51. Deery, D.J., Howell, S.L.: Biochim. Biophys. Acta 329, 17-22 (1973).

52. Drouin, J., Lagace, L., Labrie, F.: Endocrinology 99, 1477-1481 (1976).

53. Speight, A., Popkin, R., Watts, A.G., Fink, G.: J. Endocrinol. 88, 301-308 (1981).

54. Aiyer, M.S., Chiappa, S.A., Fink, G.: J. Endocrinol. 62, 573-588 (1974).

55. Castro-Vasquez, A., McCann, S.M.: Endocrinology 97, 13-19 (1975).

56. Cidlowski, J.A., Muldoon, T.G.: Endocrinology 95, 1621-1629 (1974).

57. Muldoon, T.G.: In: Ontogeny of Receptors and Reproductive Hormone Action. Hamilton, T.H., Clark, J.H., Sadler, W.A. (Eds.), Raven Press, New York, 1979, p. 225.

58. Muldoon, T.G.: Endocrinology 109, 1339-1346 (1981).

59. Cidlowski, J.A., Muldoon, T.G.: Endocrinology 97, 59-67 (1975).

60. Peake, G.I., Birge, C.A., Daughaday, W.H.: Endocrinology 92, 487-493 (1973).

61. Mittra, I.: Nature 248, 525-526 (1974).

AN ENDOGENOUS LIGAND FOR TYPE II BINDING SITES
IN NORMAL AND NEOPLASTIC TISSUES

Barry M. Markaverich and James H. Clark

Department of Cell Biology
Baylor College of Medicine
Houston, Texas   77030

Abstract

The rat uterus contains two classes of specific nuclear estrogen binding
sites which may be involved in estrogen action. Type I sites represent
the classical estrogen receptor (Kd 1nM) and type II sites (Kd 10-20nM)
are stimulated in the nucleus by estrogen under conditions which cause
uterine hyperplasia. Dilution of uterine nuclear fractions from estrogen treated rats prior to quantitation of estrogen binding sites by
[3H]-estradiol exchange results in an increase (3-4 fold) in the
measurable quantities of the type II site. Estimates of type I sites
are not affected by dilution. These increases in type II sites following nuclear dilution occur independently of protein concentration and
result from the dilution of a specific endogenous inhibitor of [3H]-
estradiol binding to these sites. The inhibitor activity is present in
cytosol preparations from rat uterus, spleen, diaphragm, skeletal muscle
and serum. Preliminary characterization of the inhibitor activity by
Sephadex G-25 chromatography shows two distinct peaks which are similar
in molecular weight (300). These components (α and β) can be separated
on LH-20 chromatography since the β-peak component is preferentially
retained on this lipophilic resin. Partial purification of the LH-20-β
inhibitor component by high performance liquid chromatography and
gas-liquid chromatography-mass spectrometric analysis suggest the putative inhibitor activity is not steroidal in nature and consists of two
very similar phenanthrene-like molecules (molecular weights 302 and
304). Analysis of cytosol preparations on LH-20 chromatography shows

that non-neoplastic tissues (uterus, liver, lactating mammary gland) contain both α and β inhibitor components whereas estrogen-induced rat mammary tumors contain very low to non-measurable quantities of the β-peak inhibitor activity.

INTRODUCTION

Estrogen administration to immature or mature ovariectomized rats sets in motion a number of biochemical events associated with the stimulation of true uterine growth. These events include hormone binding to the estrogen receptor (type I sites), translocation of receptor-estrogen complexes to the nucleus (1,2), and the stimulation or activation of nuclear type II sites (3-5). The precise role of type I or type II sites in estrogen action is unknown. However, we have demonstrated that antagonism of uterotropic responses to estrogen is associated with the inhibition of the nuclear type II sites. This is the case for steroid antagonists such as dexamethasone and progesterone (4) and triphenyl-ethylene derivatives such as nafoxidine and clomiphene (5).

In this paper we summarize our recent work (6) which demonstrates the presence of an endogenous inhibitor of [3H]-estradiol binding to nuclear type II sites. We will show that this inhibitor is specific for nuclear type II sites and does not interfere with [3H]-estradiol binding to cytoplasmic or nuclear estrogen receptors. This material has been purified by high performance liquid chromatography and analyzed by gas-liquid chromatography-mass spectrometry. On the basis of two derivatization procedures, we feel the activity is phenanthrene-like in nature with a molecular weight of approximately 300.

Detection and Measurement of Inhibitory Activity
The presence of an inhibitor for the binding of [3H]-estradiol to type II sites was first considered when we observed that the quantity of type II sites increased as uterine nuclear fractions were diluted (Figure 1 and ref 6. These data show that with dilution, (40 mg/ml-10 mg/ml) specific [3H]-estradiol binding to nuclear type II sites increases even

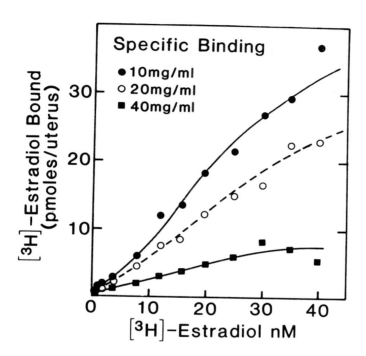

Fig. 1.   Effect of dilution on [³H]-estradiol binding in uterine nuclear fractions from adult ovariectomized rats implanted with an estradiol pellet for 4 days.

though the quantity of nuclei in the incubation mixture is decreased 2 to 4-fold. Expression of the data on a per uterine basis demonstrates that the quantities of nuclear type II sites measured at the lower nuclear concentrations (10 and 20 mg/ml) are at least 3- to 4-fold greater than levels measured at 40 mg/ml. Although these binding curves appear to show that type I sites (0.4-8.0 nm [³H]-estradiol) are also increased concurrently with dilution, we will show later that this is not the case. These apparent increases in receptor estimates are due only to an increasing influence of the type II site on the assay of type I sites as we have described previously (7).

These results suggest that the increased quantities of type II sites measured in more dilute nuclear fractions may result from dilution of a specific inhibitor of binding of [³H]-estradiol to nuclear type II sites. To examine this possibility further, various dilutions of cytosol or equivalent concentrations of BSA were incubated with uterine nuclei from estradiol-implanted rats which contain large quantities of type II sites. The results of these experiments demonstrate that the addition of increasing concentrations of cytosol to the nuclear suspension decreases the specific binding of [³H]-estradiol to nuclear type II sites (6). The inhibition was not directly related to protein concentration which decreased linearly with dilution as would be expected. In addition, concentrations of BSA which were identical to the protein concentration measured in cytosol (200 µg/ml) did not inhibit [³H]-estradiol binding to nuclear type II sites. These results suggest uterine cytosol contains a specific inhibitor of [³H]-estradiol binding to nuclear type II sites. The inhibitor appears to be a competitive inhibitor of the binding of [³H]-estradiol to type II sites yet does not inhibit the binding of [³H]-estradiol to either the cytosol or nuclear receptor (6).

GEL FILTRATION CHROMATOGRAPHY OF UTERINE CYTOSOL INHIBITOR ACTIVITY
Chromatography of boiled-acid precipitated cytosol from adult ovariectomized rat uteri on Sephadex G-25 revealed two major peaks of inhibitor activity which we designated α and β (Figure 2). This activity was

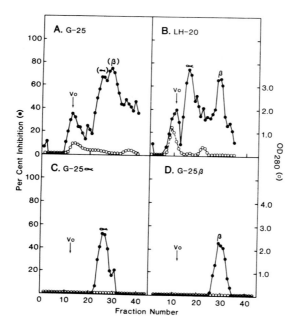

Fig. 2.   Chromatography of rat uterine cytosol inhibitor prepara-
           tions on Sephadex G-25 (A,C, and D) or LH-20 columns (B).

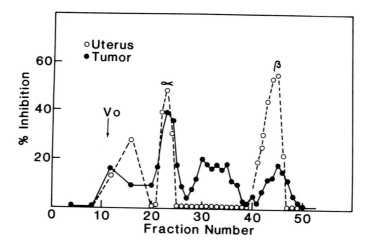

Fig. 3.   Comparison of LH-20 elution profiles from acid-
            precipitated-boiled cytosol preparations (100 mg fresh
            tissue equivalents/ml) from rat uterus (o) or an estrogen-
            induced rat mammary tumor (●).

measured in the column fractions by their ability to inhibit the binding [^{3}H]-estradiol to nuclear type II. A minor peak of activity was also seen in the void volume of the column, which is apparently associated with protein since there was a significant OD_{280} reading in these fractions. In addition, incubation of the cytosol inhibitor preparation with 0.4 M KCL for 60 minutes at 4° prior to chromatography on Sephadex G-25 (TE buffer containing 0.4 M KCL) dissociated the inhibitor activity from the void volume fractions (data not shown).

On the basis of sizing experiments using tryptophan (mw 204.2) and ATP (mw 507.2) as markers, we estimated that the molecular weight of the α and β inhibitor components is in the range of 300-400. Surprisingly, chromatography of an aliquot of this same cytosol preparation on LH-20 (Figure 2B) shows that the two components are more clearly resolved. To determine if the order of elution of the α and β peaks on LH-20 chromatography was analagous to their behavior on Sephadex G-25, we collected the individual α and β peak fraction from LH-20 and rechromatographed these fractions on the Sephadex G-25 column (Figure 2C and D). The results demonstrate that the β peaks from LH-20 columns correspond to the elution of this material on Sephadex G-25. Chromatography of cytosol preparations on larger preparative LH-20 columns facilitates complete separation of the α and β peak fraction due to the selective retention of the β material and has greatly facilitated purification of this inhibitor activity (see below).

COMPARISON OF LH-20 ELUTION PROFILES OF CYTOSOL OBTAINED FROM RAT UTERUS, NORMAL LACTATING RAT MAMMARY GLAND AND ESTROGEN-INDUCED RAT MAMMARY TUMORS

Since nuclear type II sites may be involved in the mechanisms by which estrogens cause cell growth (3, 4) we reasoned that perhaps this inhibitor may play a role in modulating these cellular responses. If this were the case, then rapidly proliferating neoplastic tissues which respond to estrogen might show deficiencies in inhibitor activity. To examine this possibility we prepared boiled-acid precipitated cytosol from rat uterus, normal lactating rat mammary gland and estrogen-induced rat mammary tumors, and chromatographed aliquots of these cytosols on LH-20. Individual fractions were assayed for inhibitor activity. These data show that the larger LH-20 column (1.0 x 50 cm: 75 ml bed volume) used for these experiments clearly separated the α and β inhibitor peaks (Figure 3) in rat uterine cytosol. Furthermore, although rat mammary tumor cytosol contained approximately equivalent quantities of the α peak material, the tumors contained little of the β component and in some cases the β-inhibitor component was nonmeasurable.

This observation has also been extended to mouse mammary tumors and human breast cancer (15). Detailed studies by dilution analysis and LH-20 chromatography showed that mouse mammary gland contained 20-fold more inhibitor activity than mammary tumors in the same strain of animals. This difference in activity appears to result from a primary deficiency in the β-inhibitor peak material (Fig. 4, ref 15). In addition, we have completed a series of mixing experiments where cytosol inhibitor preparations from uterus and tumor were mixed prior to LH-20 chromatography. The results of these experiments demonstrated that the β-inhibitor component in uterine cytosol was quantitatively recovered following chromatography. These results suggest that the tumor cytosol is indeed deficient in the β-inhibitor component, and the low levels of this molecule in tumor cytosol (as compared to uterus) is not due to some intrinsic degradation during the preparation. At present we do not know whether there is a precursor-product relationship between α and β inhibitor peaks (since they are of very similar molecular weight) and the tumor cannot readily form the β-material, or if perhaps the tumors metabolize this β-inhibitor component. Certainly the inhibitor activity in fractions 28-38 (Figure 3) suggests there is an altered form of inhibitor in tumors which is not observed in the uterus. Whether this activity (fractions 28-38) represents an altered or metabolized form of the β-peak material in tumors (Figure 3) remains to be resolved. However, preliminary experiments indicate that the presence of the β-peak material in crude inhibitor preparations is associated with biological activity. Acid-Precipitated-Boiled cytosol inhibitor preparations from rat uterus of liver (containing α and β inhibitor

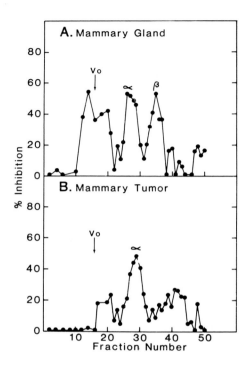

Fig. 4.   LH-20 chromatography of mouse mammary gland (A) and mouse mammary tumor (B) cytosol. Aliquots (1 ml) of the cytosol preparations (80 mg fresh tissue equivalents/ml) were loaded on an LH-20 column and the columns eluted with TE (10 mM Tris; 1.5 mM EDTA) buffer. Fractions (0.5 ml) were collected and assayed for inhibitor activity as described in methods. Results are plotted as [^{3}H]-estradiol binding to nuclear type II sites (% inhibition) were buffer controls (0% inhibition) contained approximately 45,000 cpm bound. The results were obtained from a single experiment. However, we have analyzed 15-20 separate tumor cytosol preparations and very similar results were obtained.

components) inhibit the growth of rat mammary tumor cells in culture by approximately 80–90% in 4–7 days. Conversely, preparations from rat mammary tumors (containing α, but lacking the β–inhibitor component) had no significant effect on cell growth in identical experiments continued for 3–4 weeks. These results suggest that the absence of the β–inhibitor peak material in tumors is correlated with rapid cell proliferation in these populations.

PURIFICATION AND PARTIAL CHARACTERIZATION OF INHIBITOR ACTIVITY

As stated earlier, positive structural identification of the inhibitor activity (LH–20 β–peak component) remains to be established. However, HPLC analysis showed a major peak of inhibitor activity can be eluted from the silica column. This experiment has been repeated a number of times on 3–4 separate liver preparations and the activity consistently elutes 5–6 minutes following injection. The samples at this point are very clean since we observe a single peak of uv absorbance at 254 nM which is coincident with the inhibitor activity. The peak is somewhat broad and appears to have shoulders, suggesting multiple inhibitor components which are not separated. To date we have tried a number of HPLC procedures to separate these components (various elution conditions; reinjection of peak fractions) and we cannot further separate these components on a straight phase column.

This heterogeneity of putative inhibitor molecules was supported by GC–MS analysis. The GC–MS analysis of the pooled HPLC fractions (5.4–5.8 minutes) positively identified a number of fatty acids as major components in the sample inhibitor preparations. However, these are unlikely candidates for the inhibitor since the authentic compounds did not inhibit [3H]–estradiol binding to type II sites over a wide range of concentrations (0.001 nM – 100 µM). The putative inhibitor activity appears to be associated with two remaining components in the sample which have a molecular weight of 302 and 304. Comparison of sample spectra to those of known compounds in the NIH bureau of standards library suggests the inhibitor is very similar to phenanthrene-like molecules.

DISCUSSION AND CONCLUSIONS

These experiments demonstrate that the adult ovariectomized rat uterus
and a variety of rat tissues contain an inhibitor which interferes with
[^{3}H]-estradiol binding to type II sites in uterine nuclei. This
inhibitor is specific for nuclear type II sites and does not interfere
with estrogen binding to cytoplasmic or nuclear estrogen receptor (6).
Consequently, if this inhibitor is involved in the modulation of
estrogenic response in target tissues, its effects are expressed through
an interaction with nuclear type II sites. We currently feel that this
molecule represents an endogenous ligand for type II sites (6).
Preliminary characterization of this inhibitor in rat uterine cytosol
demonstrates this molecule(s) is stable to heat (100° x 60'), and 0.1 N
HCL, and therefore it is unlikely to be protein in nature. In addition,
trypsin and proteinase K do not destroy its activity (data not shown),
and the inhibitor activity chromatographs on Sephadex G-25 or LH-20
(Figure 2) as two major peaks with an estimated molecular weight of
350. We have purified the β peak material from rat liver (which
appears identical to that seen in the uterus) by thin layer
chromatography and HPLC and it appears to consist of two nearly
identical phenanthrene-like compounds with molecular weights on the
basis of mass spectrometry of 302 and 304. Proof that these are in fact
the inhibitor molecules awaits purification to homogeneity, structural
identification and demonstration that the "identified" material has
equivalent biological activity. At the present time we feel these
phenanthrene derivatives are good candidates for the inhibitor activity
since the only other measureable compounds in the sample preparation
(free fatty acids) did not inhibit [^{3}H]-estradiol binding to nuclear
type II sites. Although one could argue that if the putative inhibitor
competes for [^{3}H]-estradiol binding to nuclear type II sites it should
also compete for [^{3}H]-estradiol binding to the estrogen receptor, this
is not necessarily the case. Nuclear type II do not bind
triphenylethylene derivatives (anti-estrogens) even though these
compounds bind to the estrogen receptor (7). Likewise, nuclear type II
sites also appear to bind this inhibitor with amazing specifity, whereas

we have been unable to show this inhibitor interacts with the estrogen receptor (6). Certainly, if the inhibitor were associated with the estrogen receptor in vivo we would have observed a dilution effect on binding (Figure 1) or direct inhibition of [^{3}H]-estradiol binding to type I sites in the direct competition experiments (6). It is also possible that if we were able to obtain milligram amounts of the inhibitor, competition for [^{3}H]-estradiol binding to type I sites would be observed with pharmacological concentrations (mM). Our data demonstrate that at physiological concentrations this interaction is unlikely.

Since we have not been able to directly assess the effects of this inhibitor activity in vivo it is very difficult at this early time to describe any direct role for this compound in estrogen action. These experiments await chemical identification of the inhibitor. Once a positive identification has been made, determination of its biological significance in vivo should be straightfoward. Preliminary in vitro experiments, however, are very promising. It appears that there is a deficiency in the β-inhibitor component in rat mammary tumor cytosol as compared to normal uterus (Figure 3), and lactating mammary gland (Figure 4). We have observed that inhibitor preparations from rat mammary tumors which were deficient in the β peak material did not inhibit growth of uterine stromal and myometrial cells, or rat mammary tumor cells in culture. In contrast, inhibitor preparations from uterus or liver which contain the β material reduced cell numbers by approximately 80% following 4-7 days of treatment. Whether or not this inhibition of cell growth in culture results from an acceleration of cell death, or an inhibition of cell division or both remains to be resolved.

Although the physiological significance of this inhibitor remains to be resolved, we speculate at this time that the inhibitor may act to modify or regulate uterotropic responses to estrogen or perhaps act in a "protective" capacity in cases of hyperestrogenization. Such hypothesis are consistent with our current knowledge concerning a possible role for nuclear type II sites in estrogen action. We have shown that these secondary nuclear estrogen binding sites are only activated or stimulated in the nucleus under conditions which cause uterine hypertrophy, hyperplasia and DNA synthesis (3-5). Furthermore, dexamethasone and progesterone antagonism of uterine growth in the rat is associated with an inhibition of estrogen stimulation of nuclear type II sites (4) and these antagonists do not affect the normal functions of the estrogen receptor. On the basis of these experiments we have suggested that nuclear type II sites may be involved in estrogen action. Since nuclear type II estrogen binding sites appear to be localized on the nuclear matrix (8) which has been implicated in DNA replication (9), we feel this inhibitor activity may modulate or block estrogen induced DNA synthesis by inhibiting estrogen stimulation of these secondary nuclear estrogen binding sites.

Perhaps the failure of estrogen to stimulate cell growth (hyperplasia; DNA synthesis) in estrogen target tissues such as the pituitary and hypothalmus (10) is related to the inability of estrogen to modulate the activity of this inhibitor in these tissues. Certainly, the failure of estrogen to stimulate nuclear type II sites in these estrogen target organs makes this a tenable hypothesis. Our findings that rat and mouse mammary tumors and human breast cancer (15) contain significantly lower levels (~ 15-20 fold) of this inhibitor activity which is correlated with a deficiency in the β-peak component is consistent with this hypothesis. Likewise, nuclear type II sites appear to be permanently activated in ovarian dependent (11) or independent (12) mouse mammary tumors and human breast cancer (13, 14) regardless of the endocrine status. Therefore these higher levels of nuclear type II sites in malignant tissues are correlated with this inhibitor deficiency. Likewise, we have measured basal levels of nuclear type II sites in a variety of tissues which do not normally respond to estrogen via hypertrophy and hyperplasia (diaphragm, spleen, liver) and these tissues do contain significant quantities of inhibitor activity (6). Therefore our hypothesis is that this inhibitor may be a component of all tissues as are nuclear type II sites. In tissues which do not normally respond to estrogen in a proliferative manner, type II sites are complexed with this inhibitor and consequently the functions of these sites are not expressed. Conversely, in tissues which do respond to estrogens, the association of the receptor-estrogen complex with target cell nuclei may result in a dissociation of the inhibitor from nuclear type II sites. Under these conditions cellular hypertrophy and hyperplasia is observed. Consistent with this hypothesis is our observation that in estrogen treated nuclei (Figure 1) additional nuclear type II sites are observed following dilution. Since this effect is not observed in uterine nuclei from ovariectomized animals (controls; not shown), we feel that this dissociation of the inhibitor from nuclear type II sites is estrogen dependent. Obviously, the lower levels of inhibitor activity in neoplastic tissues is consistent with the elevated levels of type II sites measured in tumors and the rapid proliferation rate in these cell populations. Although only tentative at this point in time, we feel that this is a reasonable model for potential regulation of cell proliferation by type II binding inhibitor.

ACKNOWLEDGEMENTS

The authors would like to thank Rebbecca Roberts and M.A. Alejandro for technical assistance, Georgietta Brown for typing the manuscript, and David Scarff for the illustrations. Supported by NIH grants HD-08436.

REFERENCES

1. Jensen, E.V., Numata, M., Brecher, P.I., DeSombre, E.R.: In The Biochemistry of Steroid Hormone Action (Smellie, R.M.S., ed.) Academic Press, London 133-159 (1971)

2. Shyamala, G. Gorski, J.: J. Biol. Chem. 244, 1097-1103 (1967).

3. Markaverich, B.M., Clark, J.H.: Endocrinology 105, 1458-1462 (1979).

4. Markaverich, B.M., Upchurch, S., Clark, J.H.: J. Steroid Biochem. 14, 125-132 (1981).

5. Markaverich, B.M., Upchurch, S., McCormack, S., Glasser, S.R., Clark, J.H.: Biol. Reprod. 24, 171-181 (1981).

6. Markaverich, B.M., Roberts, R.R., Finney, R.W. Clark, J.H.: J. Biol. Chem. 258, 11663-11671 (1983).

7. Markaverich, B.M., Williams, M., Upchurch, S., Clark J.H.: Endocrinology 62-69 (1981).

8. Clark, J.H. Markaverich, B.M.: In The Nuclear Envelope and the Nuclear Matrix, Alan R. Liss, Inc., New York 260-269 (1982).

9. Pardoll, D.M., Vogelstein, B. Coffey: Cell 19, 527-536 (1980).

10. Kelner, K.L.Peck, E.J., Jr.: J. Receptor Res. 2, 47-62 (1981).

11. Watson, C.S. Clark, J.H.: J. Receptor Res. 1, 91-111 (1980).

12. Watson, C.S., Medina, D. Clark, J.H.: Endocrinology 107, 1432-1437 (1980).

13. Syne, J.S., Markaverich, B.M., Clark, J.H., Panko, W.B.: Cancer Research 42, 4443-4448 (1982).

14. Syne, J.S., Markaverich, B.M., Clark, J.H. Panko, W.B.: Cancer Research 42, 4449-4454 (1982).

15. Markaverich, B.M., Roberts R.R., Alejandro, M.A. Clark, J.H.: Cancer Res. 44, 1575-1579 (1984).

REGULATION OF MAMMARY RESPONSIVENESS TO ESTROGEN: AN ANALYSIS OF DIFFERENCES BETWEEN MAMMARY GLAND AND THE UTERUS

Gopalan Shyamala

Lady Davis Institute for Medical Research, Sir Mortimer B. Davis - Jewish General Hospital and Department of Medicine, McGill University, Montreal, Quebec, Canada

I) Introduction

The mammary gland is a compound tubuloalveolar gland composed of adipose, connective and epithelial tissue elements. At birth the gland is still rudimentary which remains in a quiescent state until puberty at which time there is a limited development. In the adult female during each menstrual cycle, cyclic proliferative changes and active growth of the ductal tissue occurs but the full development and differentiation of the gland occurs only during pregnancy and lactation. Almost all aspects of mammary development and differentiation are under complex hormonal control and there are some apparent differences among various species with regard to hormonal regulation of mammary development and differentiation. Most of the classic studies on the developmental biology of the gland have been done with rodents and the conclusions derived from these experiments have been frequently applied to many species including humans.

Estrogens have been reported to have a variety of effects on various cell types of mammary glands and are believed to be important for both mammary development and differentiation (1). However, as yet the mechanism(s) underlying the actions of estrogens in mammary tissues is poorly understood. In fact there are even some doubts as to whether estrogens exert their effects on mammary glands directly (2), despite the wide documentation of the presence of estrogen receptors in this tissue.

A detailed discussion of various estrogenic responses occurring in mammary glands, their relationship to estrogen receptors, and their relative importance in the overall biology of the tissues is beyond the scope of this article. Therefore this chapter will focus only on certain selected aspects of estrogenic influences occurring during mammary development and differentiation and the possible mechanisms underlying these estrogenic responses in this tissue. The data used to illustrate various aspects of estrogen action are from our own laboratory using mouse as the experimental animal.

At present, the major body of literature pertaining to the mechanism of estrogen action has been obtained with rodent uterus. It is conceivable that estrogens may have different effects on different target tissues of the same animal both from a qualitative and a quantitative aspect, and these differences may bear a relationship to certain unique functions characteristic to a particular target tissue. As shown in this article in the same animal under identical physiological conditions there are differences in responsiveness to estrogen by mammary glands and uterus. Therefore an attempt has also been made to discuss certain aspects of mammary responsiveness to estrogens which appear to differ from those observed in the uterus. It is hoped that such a discussion will prove useful in the ultimate resolution of the mechanism of estrogen action in mammary gland.

II) Estrogenic Responses in Mammary Glands

A. Characterization of early and late responses

A characteristic feature of all hormones including estrogens is their ability to elicit a variety of biochemical responses in their target tissues, which may be roughly catalogued into early and late responses. The three well known responses to estrogens in most target tissues for estrogen are changes in

glucose metabolism, progesterone receptor synthesis and DNA
synthesis and these responses to estrogen also manifest in
the mammary glands. Based on the relative time required to
elicit each of these responses, the first wave of increase in
glucose oxidation occurring between 1-2 hours after estradiol
administration (Fig. 1) and progesterone receptor synthesis
(Fig. 2) may be termed as early responses while the increase
in DNA synthesis (Fig. 3) and the second wave of increase in
glucose oxidation occurring between 18-21 hours after estradiol
administration (Fig. 1) are classified as late responses.   It

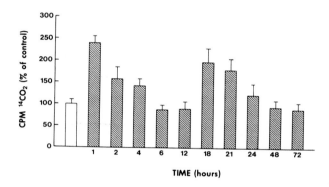

Fig. 1. Effect of estradiol on glucose oxidation in mammary
glands of castrated mice. A single injection of either saline
(□) or estradiol (▨) was given to castrated virgin mice prior
to killing at indicated times. The ability of the tissues to
oxidize glucose was estimated according to procedures previously described (3). The data represent mean ± SEM of three
experiments with duplicate determinations in each. The 100%
value corresponding to saline treated animals was 44.4 ± 4.4
$^{14}CO_2$/mg mammary tissue.

is, however, to be noted that while the overall pattern and
time scales for initiation of the three estrogenic responses
in mammary glands are similar to that previously observed in
the uterus (6), there are some differences between the two
tissues. In the case of uterus, both the early and late waves
of glucose oxidation are also associated with increases in the
phosphorylation of glucose as measured by the conversion of
2-deoxyglucose to 2-deoxyglucose phosphate (7). However, as

416

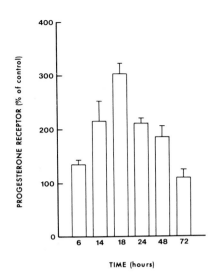

Fig. 2. Temporal relationship between estradiol administration and increase in cytoplasmic mammary progesterone receptor level. Castrated virgin mice were given a single injection of 1 μg of estradiol prior to sacrifice at times indicated. The progesterone receptor levels were assayed by measuring the specific binding of (^{3}H)R5020 in cytoplasmic extracts. Each bar represents the mean ± SEM of three to five experiments. Control values for saline injected animals were: 467 fmoles/mg DNA. [From Shyamala, 1984 (4)]

shown in Table 1, in mammary glands estradiol does not cause an increase in the metabolic conversion of 2-deoxyglucose to 2-deoxyglucose phosphate. Thus the conversion of 2-deoxyglucose to 2-deoxyglucose phosphate, an easy parameter used for detecting the estrogenicity of a compound in the uterus (7) cannot be used for assessing estrogenic responsiveness in mammary glands. Another striking difference between the mammary glands and the uterus is the temporal relationship between estrogen administration and estrogen mediated increase in DNA synthesis as shown in Fig. 3. Although in both tissues the increase in DNA synthesis due to estrogen becomes apparent at approximately 12 hr, in the uterus the maximal increase is observed around 24 hr which returns to control value by 48 hr; however, in the

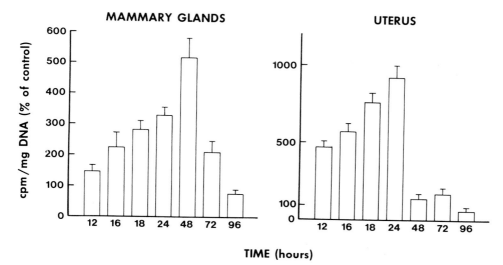

Fig. 3. Effect of estradiol on the in vitro incorporation of (^{3}H)thymidine into DNA in the mammary glands and uteri of castrated mice. A single injection of saline (control) or 1 μg E$_2$ was given to castrated virgin mice before killing at the indicated times. The data represent mean ± SEM for three to five experiments. The control values represent the data obtained at 24 hours after injection and were: mammary glands, 2989 ± 558 cpm/mg DNA; uterus, 3834 ± 403 cpm/mg DNA. [From Shyamala and Ferenczy, 1984 (5)]

case of mammary glands the maximal increase in DNA synthesis occurs at approximately 48 hr after estrogen administration returning to control values only at about 96 hr. Thus the duration in DNA synthesis due to a single administration of estradiol is greater in mammary gland than in the uterus. However, the magnitude of response to estradiol with respect to DNA synthesis is larger in the case of uterus when compared to the mammary glands. These relative differences in the degree of mammary and uterine responsiveness to estradiol is most likely related to the differences in the estrogen receptor content of these tissues (as shown later) since it manifests regardless of the dose of estradiol administered to the tissue (Table II). The possible importance of this difference in the pattern of DNA synthesis due to estrogen in mammary glands and uterus is discussed later in this article.

TABLE I. Effect of estradiol on 2-deoxyglucose metabolism in mammary glands and uterus of castrated mice.

Treatment	Dose	2-deoxyglucose phosphate (cpm)	
	µg	mammary glands	uterus
Saline	-	14.0 ± 0.45	1875 ± 274
Estradiol	1	14.9 ± 2.3	3233 ± 311
Estradiol	3	16.4 ± 1.9	4438 ± 344

Three groups of ovariectomized virgin mice were given a single injection of either saline or indicated dose of estradiol for two hours prior to sacrifice. The conversion of 2-deoxyglucose to 2-deoxyglucose phosphate by the tissues was assayed exactly according to the procedure described by Gorski and Raker (8). The data represent mean ± SEM of three experiments with duplicate determinations in each experiment.

TABLE II. Effect of estradiol on the in vitro incorporation of (^{3}H)thymidine into mammary and uterine DNA in castrated mice.

Dose of estradiol	cpm/mg DNA (% of control)	
µg	mammary glands	uterus
0.25	279 ± 36	912 ± 120
1.0	292 ± 49	921 ± 79
3.0	395 ± 107	656 ± 61

Three groups of castrated mice were injected with indicated doses of estradiol for 24 hours prior to killing. The tissues were processed for the in vitro incorporation of (^{3}H)thymidine into DNA according to procedures previously described (5). The data represent mean ± SEM of three to five experiments.

B. Effect of prolactin on mammary responsiveness to estrogen

It is known that the influence of estrogen on mammary development may be modified by virtue of its interplay with other hormones (1). More importantly, similar to estradiol prolactin is also required for mammary development and differentiation (1). Therefore, any precise understanding of the role of estrogens in mammary biology have to take into consideration the

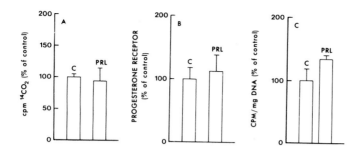

Fig. 4. Effect of prolactin on the estrogenic responses in castrated virgin mice. A single injection of either saline (C) or 1 mg of ovine prolactin (PRL) was administered prior to processing the mammary tissues at indicated times. (A) Glucose oxidation at 1 hr. (B) Progesterone receptor level at 24 hr. (C) Rate of DNA synthesis as measured by in vitro incorporation of labelled thymidine into DNA at 24 hr. [Adapted from Shyamala, 1984 (4)]

influence of prolactin on estrogenic responses.

In castrated virgin mice, exogenous prolactin has no effect on either mammary glucose oxidation (Fig. 4A) or progesterone receptor level (Fig. 4B) or DNA synthesis (Fig. 4C). If estradiol and prolactin are administered together, there is an increase in mammary response to estradiol as measured by all the three criteria but this increase is not significantly greater than that seem with estradiol alone (data not shown). Thus these data reveal that by the three criteria chosen for mammary responsiveness to estrogen, prolactin has no influence on estrogen action in mammary glands. However, since the animals used in these studies had not been hypophysectomized, the possibility that prolactin might be necessary for the expression of mammary estrogenic responses could not be ruled out. For instance it has been reported that the augmentation of both casein synthesis and lactose synthetase activity by estradiol in explants from pregnant mice depends on the presence of both prolactin and thyroid hormone (9). It has also been reported that prolactin may increase the level of mammary estrogen receptors in mice (10). Therefore it is possible that at least some of the estrogenic responses in the mammary glands is influenced indirectly by prolactin.

C. Loss of estrogenic sensitivity during lactation in mammary glands

Extensive studies from several laboratories have revealed that the sensitivity of normal mammary tissue to both protein and steroid hormonal stimuli may be profoundly altered in relation-ship to the ontogeny of mammary epithelium, i.e. the mammary glands can modulate their sensitivity to hormones as a function of various physiological states (1). This also appears to be true for estrogenic sensitivity of mammary glands since while the glands from castrated virgin mice are responsive to estra-diol as shown previously, by the same criteria for responsive-ness to estrogen the mammary glands of castrated lactating mice are nonresponsive to estradiol (Fig. 5). It is, however, to be noted that while estradiol does not stimulate glucose oxidation in mammary glands of lactating mice, the glucose oxidation in the mammary gland of saline-treated, ovariectomized, lactating mice is, in fact, approximately 8-fold higher than that seen in the mammary gland of saline-treated, ovariectomized, virgin mice. Thus, it appears that while estradiol can stimulate mammary glucose oxidation, this tissue is not necessarily de-pendent on this hormone to accelerate its metabolism of glucose. This is not surprising since it has been well established that pituitary (13), adrenal (14), and thyroid (15) hormones can influence several enzymatic reactions associated with glucose metabolism in the lactating mammary gland. As with the mammary gland, estradiol also did not stimulate significantly uterine glucose oxidation in lactating mice (Fig. 5A) although it was capable of stimulating the rate of glucose phosphorylation in the same tissue (Table III). Estradiol was also effective in increasing the level of progesterone receptor (12) and rate of DNA synthesis in uteri of lactating mice (11). Thus, these data indicate that while estradiol can accelerate several bio-synthetic pathways in its target tissues, the mechanisms by

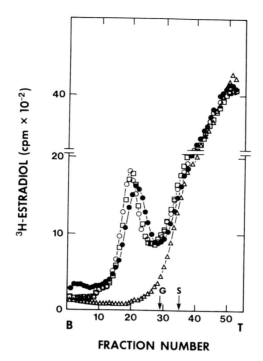

FRACTION NUMBER

<u>Fig. 8</u>. Cytosol from lactating mice either as is (●,△) or exposed to 10 mM molybdate (O,□) was incubated with 10 nM of (³H)estradiol either alone (O,□,●) or also with a 100-fold excess of unlabelled estradiol (△) prior to layering on gradients in phosphate buffer only (O,△) or on gradients also containing 10 mM molybdate (●,□). [From Gaubert et al, 1982 (21)]

to high ionic strength does vary between the mammary tissues of virgin and lactating mice. The estrogen receptor from lactating mammary glands are relatively less susceptible to dissociation and this in turn is reflected in their relative inability to undergo in vitro activation due to salt. Although these findings are consistent with the nonresponsiveness of lactating mammary glands to estradiol, it is to be noted that if estradiol is administered to lactating mice, estrogen receptor is found associated with the nuclear fraction (22). The precise relationship between estrogen receptor status and mammary responsiveness is therefore not clear at present. It is

426

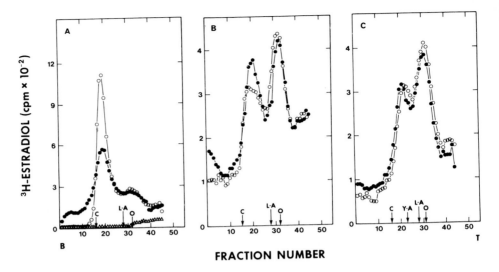

Fig. 9.   Sedimentation profiles of mammary ER from virgin C₃H
mice.   Cytoplasmic extracts were prepared either in phosphate
buffer (A) or in Tris buffer (B and C).   Other experimental
details were exactly as for Fig. 7.   (A) Cytosol from ovariectomized mice was incubated with 2 nM (³H)estradiol either
alone (●,O) or also with a 100-fold excess of unlabelled
estradiol (△) prior to layering on gradients in phosphate
buffer with (O) or without (●,△) 10 mM molybdate. (B) Cytosol from ovariectomized mice was incubated with 2 nM (³H)estra-
diol prior to layering on gradients in phosphate buffer with
(O) or without (●) 10 mM molybdate.   (C) Cytosol from ovariectomized mice was incubated with 2 nM of (³H)estradiol prior
to layering on gradients in Tris buffer with (O) or without
(●) 10 mM molybdate. [From Gaubert et al, 1982 (21)]

possible that in lactating mammary glands the nuclear estrogen
receptor is unable to undergo processing, a prerequisite believed to be necessary for estrogen responsiveness.

C. Relative distribution of estrogen receptor in the various
cell types of mammary gland

The mammary gland is composed of epithelial, adipose and connective tissues and the relative proportion of each cell type
varies according to the developmental state of the gland (1).
In the female mouse, the mammary epithelium is embedded in a

TABLE IV. Molecular properties of estrogen receptors isolated
from cytoplasmic fraction of virgin and lactating mice

Type of mammary tissue	Sedimentation coefficient $(S_{20,w})$*	Molecular Stokes radius $(Å)$**	Molecular weight
Virgin	9.5 ± 0.2	85 ± 2	340,000
Lactating	9.1 ± 0.5	78 ± 5	300,000

All assays were done in buffers containing 20 mM sodium molybdate. *Obtained by sucrose gradient centrifugation in hypotonic buffers. **Obtained by gel filtration. Molecular weight
was estimated by calculations using the sedimentation coefficient and molecular Stokes radius.

pad of adipose and connective tissue commonly known as mammary
fat pad; moreover it is the adipose tissue that occupies most
of the mass of the mammary gland in a non-pregnant female mouse.
However, it is possible to separate the mammary epithelium from
adipose and connective tissue in the inguinal mammary glands
of 21 day old mice according to the technique described by
DeOme et al (23). This mammary fat pad devoid of epithelium
is often referred to as the cleared fat pad or de-epithelialized fat pad. As shown in Fig. 10, the cleared fat pad contains
estrogen receptors. The concentration of the receptor in the
de-epithelialized gland was estimated to be about 330 ± 22
fmoles/mg DNA while in the intact gland it was found at
720 ± 314 fmoles/mg DNA. However, these figures do not necessarily indicate that in the intact gland of the virgin mouse
the estrogen receptors are equally distributed between the fat
pad and epithelium. It is known that there is metabolic cooperativity between epithelial cell and adipocytes in mammary
tissue and also local glandular factors may influence mammary
adipocyte activity (24,25,26); therefore the metabolism of fat
pad free of epithelium may be quite different from that containing the epithelium. Regardless, these data reveal that in
addition to the mammary epithelium, the mammary fat pad is
also a target site for estrogen action.

428

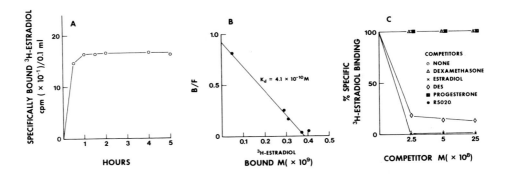

Fig. 10. (A) The time course of the specific binding of (^{3}H)-estradiol in cytoplasmic extracts of de-epithelialized mammary fat pad. (B) Saturation analysis of (^{3}H)estradiol binding in cytoplasmic extracts of de-epithelialized mammary fat pad. The data represents the Scatchard plot of specific binding only. (C) The relative effectiveness of various unlabelled steroids to compete for specific (^{3}H)estradiol binding in cytoplasmic extracts of de-epithelialized mammary fat pad. [Haslam and Shyamala, 1981 (24)]

IV. An Evaluation of Mammary Fat Pad as a Potential Site for Initiation of Estrogen Action

Beginning with the pioneering studies by DeOme and his colleagues it has been shown that the transplanted mammary epithelium can grow only in the mammary fat pad (23,28,29,30). In fact, Faulkin and DeOme (28,31) have suggested that fat cells may regulate the growth of mammary ductal epithelium in a sexually mature mouse. Since a principal effect of estrogen on the mammary gland is its impact on growth, it is conceivable that estrogen may initiate mammary epithelial growth through processes associated with the mammary adipose and connective tissue. Accordingly, studies were initiated to examine whether in addition to the epithelium the mammary fat pad can also respond to estradiol with increase in DNA synthesis. The incorporation of labelled thymidine into DNA in mammary gland of virgin mice as examined by in vivo DNA histoautoradiography is shown in Fig. 11. In mammary glands while there was an increase in the uptake of labelled thymidine into DNA at 24 hr after estradiol administration, there was virtually no labelling in the epithelial cells; the labelling seen at this time was mostly confined to the adipose and connective tissue elements. In contrast to the data obtained at 24 hr after estradiol administration, at 48 and 72 hr after estradiol administration, there was a significant labelling of mammary epithelium. A quantitative analysis of the labelling index of various tissue components is shown in Table V.

The data obtained for uterus in parallel analyses are also shown in Fig. 11. In contrast to the mammary glands, the increase in the incorporation of thymidine into DNA due to estradiol at 24 hr was confined predominantly to the epithelial cells. It is to be noted that as with the mammary glands, uterine connective tissues also responded to estradiol with an increase in the incorporation of thymidine into DNA.

TABLE V. Labelling index of the various tissue components in mammary glands of castrated virgin mice [From Shyamala and Ferenczy, 1984 (5)]

Tissue Components	Labelling index			
	Saline	(E_2)		
		24 h	48 h	72 h
Adipose tissue	0.37 ± 0.05	1.42 ± 0.22	3.30 ± 0.39	2.26 ± 0.35
Stromal fibroblasts	0.19 ± 0.03	1.08 ± 0.12	6.08 ± 0.63	3.63 ± 0.81
Epithelium	0.18 ± 0.03	0.34 ± 0.09	8.65 ± 1.07	7.43 ± 1.00
Vascular endothelium	0.17 ± 0.04	0.66 ± 0.16	1.85 ± 0.49	1.17 ± 0.40

A single injection of saline or 1 µg E_2 was given to castrated virgin mice before killing at indicated times. The labelling index in various cell types was estimated by in vivo DNA histoautoradiography.

430

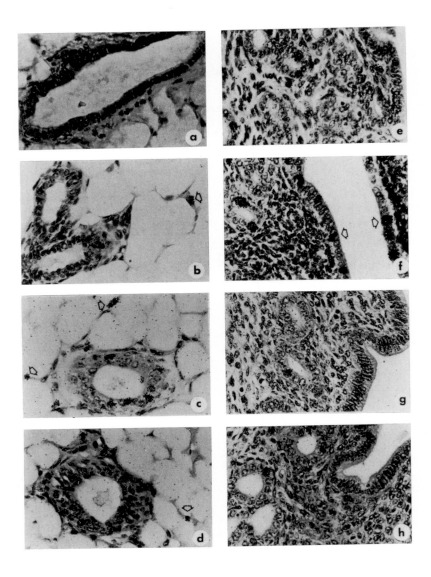

Fig. 11. DNA histoautoradiographs of mammary glands and uteri
from castrated virgin mice. a, Mammary gland of saline-
treated animal. There is no appreciable labelling in the
various tissue compartments [hematoxylin and eosin (H & E),
X500]. b, Mammary gland of animal 24 h after E_2 injection.
The epithelium lacks nuclear radiothymidine, whereas a neighboring adipocyte's nucleus is labelled (arrow) (H & E, X500).
c, Mammary gland of animal 48 h after E_2 injection. There is
marked incorporation of radiothymidine into the nuclei of epi-

thelial cells and neighboring adipocytes (arrows) (H & E, X500).
d, Mammary gland of animal 72 h after E_2 injection. Incorporation of radiothymidine into nuclei of epithelial cells and a
neighboring adipocyte (arrow) is still apparent (H & E, X500).
e, Endometrium of saline-treated animal (H & E, X500). f, Endometrium of animal 24 h after E_2 injection. Radiothymidine
labelling is conspicuous in the surface (arrows) and glandular
epithelium as well as in stromal fibroblasts (H & E, X500).
g, Endometrium of animal 48 h after E_2 injection (H & E, X500).
h, Endometrium of animal 72 h after E_2 injection. Isotope
labelling is confined to occasional glandular epithelial cells
and stromal fibroblasts. The number of cells labelled and intensity of labelling is comparable to that of saline control
(e) (H & E, X500). [From Shyamala and Ferenczy, 1984 (5)]

V. Mechanisms of Estrogen Action in Mammary Glands

In attempting to formulate a working hypothesis for the mechanism of estrogen action in mammary glands, certain general but
fundamental features concerning hormone action need to be considered. These are that while all hormones may give rise to a
multiplicity of biochemical responses in their target tissues,
also called pleiotypic responses (32), many of these
responses may occur in the tissue also independently of hormones (33). As discussed in this article, although in the
non-lactating female mouse, estradiol causes an increase in
certain aspects of glucose metabolism, increases in glucose
metabolism occur independently of estradiol during lactation.
The most likely explanation of this observation is that during
lactation, in response to the nutritional demands of the young,
the overall metabolic activity of the animal is elevated which
in turn leads to an increase in food intake. Thus the increase in mammary glucose metabolism during lactation is perhaps really associated with the nutritional adaptation of the
animal. It has been suggested by Tata (33) that many of the
multiple or pleiotypic responses to hormones represent primitive reflexes of cells when called upon to alter their activity. Accordingly the increase in mammary glucose metabolism
due to estradiol probably represents one such primitive reflex.

Mammary gland is also a target tissue for progesterone whereby progesterone is believed to be mainly responsible for the alveolar growth occurring during pregnancy (1). Thus the synthesis of progesterone receptors in the mammary glands of nonpregnant females by estrogen is critical for the mammogenic action of progesterone at the onset of pregnancy. In this regard, in contrast to glucose metabolism, the increase in progesterone receptor content due to estradiol probably represents a more specialized response to estrogen and also implies that this particular response to estradiol is related to the developmental program of the mammary cell. And this may be the underlying reason for the suppression of this particular estrogenic response in the mammary gland during lactation for reasons as follows: (a) during lactation the animal is in a pseudopregnant state with a high level of circulating progesterone (34) and as such if progesterone receptors are present in the lactating mammary tissue, it can lead to growth, and (b) since the principal function of mammary gland during lactation is to produce milk, it may not be advantageous for the cell to direct its metabolic activity towards growth. Thus it is possible that the estrogenic regulation of progesterone receptor synthesis has certain regulatory features unique for the mammary glands not present in other target tissues for estrogen such as the uterus which does respond to estradiol during lactation.

The estrogenic regulation of mammary DNA synthesis reveals that the mammary fat pad may be the site of initiation of estrogen action in this tissue. We have demonstrated the presence of estrogen receptors in de-epithelialized mammary fat pad and as such it does have the competence to respond to estradiol. There is sufficient documentation in the literature to suggest that estrogen may not exert their mitogenic effects directly on their target cells but that they may promote growth through endocrine, autocrine and paracrine control mechanisms (35). An observation on estrogen mediated mammary DNA synthesis suggests

that the estrogenic regulation of this responsiveness may involve a paracrine control. If this were so, the loss of
responsiveness to estrogen during lactation may really have its
basis on the altered sensitivity of the mammary fat pad to
estrogen.

VI. Summary

The mammary responsiveness to estradiol involves a variety of
biochemical responses which may be classified as slow and late
pleiotypic responses. The early pleiotypic response such as
an increase in glucose metabolism appears to represent a non-
specialized response by the tissue and as such its overall
significance to some of the specialized estrogenic responses
is not clear. The pattern of mammary responsiveness to estrogen with regard to progesterone receptor synthesis appears to
be connected to the developmental programme of the mammary
epithelial cell. Thus while this particular response to estradiol may represent a highly specialized response by all target
tissues for estrogen, the expression of this response may
nevertheless be dictated by a predetermined set of tissue specific physiological processes associated with differentiation.
In the case of mammary responsiveness to estradiol with regard
to DNA synthesis it is important to note that the major impact
of estradiol is on the epithelial cells. Yet, the regulation
of this estrogenic response appears to involve initially the
adipose and connective tissue elements. Thus this particular
estrogenic response may be regulated by processes associated
with cell-cell interactions. Thus overall, the studies described in this report on mammary responsiveness to estradiol
reveal that there may be more than one regulatory pathway by
which estrogens control mammary functions. Thus a precise de-
lineation of estrogen action in mammary glands integrating many
of the cellular responses to estradiol may be possible only
after a detailed analysis of individual responses. And finally

when the mechanism of estrogen action in mammary glands is resolved it may aid us in our understanding of not only the
developmental biology of this tissue, but also contribute to
our overall understanding of hormonal influences which impinge
upon mammalian cell growth and differentiation.

Acknowledgements

These studies were supported by a grant from the National
Cancer Institute of Canada. Ms. S. Fraiberg, Ms. C. Lalonde
and Mr. D. Saxe assisted in the preparation of the manuscript.

References

1. Topper, Y.J., Freeman, C.S.: Physiol. Rev. 60, 1049-1106
   (1980).
2. Sirbasku, D.A.: Proc. Natl. Acad. Sci. USA 75, 3786-3790
   (1978).
3. Cuppy, D., Crevasse, L.: Anal. Biochem. 5, 462-463 (1963).
4. Shyamala, G.: Prog. Cancer Res. Ther. 31, 293-308 (1984).
5. Shyamala, G., Ferenczy, A.: Endocrinology 115, 1078-1081
   (1984).
6. Katzenellenbogen, B.S., Gorski, J.: In: Litwack, G. (ed)
   Biochemical Actions of Hormones, Academic Press, New York
   Vol. 5, 187-243 (1975).
7. Lan, N.C., Katzenellenbogen, B.S.: Endocrinology 98, 220-
   337 (1976).
8. Gorski, J., Raker, B.: Endocrinology 93, 1212-1216 (1973).
9. Bolander, F.F., Jr., Topper, Y.J.: Endocrinology 106, 490-
   495 (1979).
10. Sheth, N.A., Tickekon, S.S., Ranadive, R.J., Sheth, A.R.:
    Mol. Cell. Endocrinol. 12, 167-176 (1978).
11. Shyamala, G., Ferenczy, A.: Endocrinology 110, 1249-1256
    (1982).
12. Haslam, S.Z., Shyamala, G.: Biochem. J. 182, 127-131 (1979).
13. Abraham, S., Cody, P., Chaikoff, I.L.: Endocrinology 66,
    280-288 (1960).

14. Greenbaum, A.L., Darby, F.J.: Biochem. J. 91, 307-317 (1964).

15. Walters, E., McLean, P.: Biochem. J. 105, 615-623 (1967).

16. Hseuh, A.J.W., Peck, E.J., Jr., Clark, J.H.: J. Endocrinol. 58, 1-9 (1973).

17. Gardner, D.G., Wittliff, J.L.: Biochemistry 12, 3090-3096 (1973).

18. Leung, B.S., Jack, W.M., Reiney, C.C.: J. Steroid Biochem. 7, 89-95 (1976).

19. Hunt, M.E., Muldoon, T.G.: J. Steroid Biochem. 8, 181-186 (1977).

20. Muldoon, T.G.: In: Hamilton, T.H., Clark, J.H., Sadler, W.S. (eds). Ontogeny of Receptors and Reproductive Hormone Action, Raven Press, New York, pp 225-247, 1979.

21. Gaubert, C-M., Biancucci, S., Shyamala, G.: Endocrinology 110, 683-685 (1982).

22. Shyamala, G., Nandi, S.: Endocrinology 91, 861-867 (1972).

23. DeOme, K.B., Faulkin, L.J., Bern, H.A., Blair, P.B.: Cancer Res. 19, 515-520 (1959).

24. Haslam, S.Z., Shyamala, G.: Endocrinology 108, 825-830 (1981).

25. Bartley, J.C., Emerman, J.T., Bissell, M.: Am. J. Physiol. 24 (Cell. Physiol.), C204-208 (1981).

26. Elias, J.J., Pitelka, D.R., Armstrong, R.C.: Anat. Rec. 177, 533-548 (1973).

27. Lucas, A., Scopas, C., Bartley, J.C.: J. Cell Biol. 70, 335a (1976).

28. Faulkin, L.J., DeOme, K.B.: J. Natl. Cancer Inst. 24, 953-969 (1960).

29. Hoshino, K.: J. Natl. Cancer Inst. 29, 835-851 (1962).

30. Slavin, B.: Anat. Rec. 154, 423 (1966).

31. Faulkin, L.J., DeOme, K.B.: Cancer Res. 18, 51-56 (1958).

32. Tomkins, G.M.: Science 189, 760-763 (1975).

33. Tata, J.R.: Mol. Cell. Endocrinol. 36, 17-27 (1984).

34. Smith, M.S., Neill, J.D.: Biol. Reprod. 17, 255-261 (1977).

35. Sirbasku, D.A., Lalond, F.E.: In: Litwack, G. (ed). Biochemical Actions of Hormones, Vol. 9, Academic Press, New York, pp 115-140, 1982.

PROGESTERONE REGULATION OF NUCLEAR ESTROGEN RECEPTORS: EVIDENCE FOR A RECEPTOR REGULATORY FACTOR

Wendell W. Leavitt
Texas Tech University Health Sciences Center
Lubbock, Texas   79430

Introduction

Steroid hormones influence gene transcription in target cells through a process involving hormone binding to specific intracellular receptor proteins (1,2). Much has been learned about the macromolecular events regulated by steroid hormones in target cells which synthesize and secrete hormone-specific protein products, and we understand some of the details about the hormonal regulation of egg white proteins in the avian oviduct and uteroglobin in the mammalian uterus. Estrogen and progesterone action can be attributed to the regulation of gene expression and the formation of specific messenger RNA molecules for these export proteins (3). However, the nature of the interaction between the receptor-hormone complex and the acceptor (effector) sites in the target cell nucleus which control gene expression remains largely unknown (Fig. 1). It is generally believed that a relationship must exist between the number of nuclear receptor sites and hormone-dependent gene transcription (4). However, evidence is needed to verify that such a relationship actually exists, and in the case of estrogen it is not certain whether hormone action is the result of receptor binding and retention by nuclear acceptor sites (3,4), receptor "processing" in the nucleus (5,6), or other events (7) (Fig. 1). Thus, we need to learn more about nuclear receptor retention and processing in order to learn how hormone action is mediated at the level of gene expression.

One hormone may act to alter the expression of a second

response to secondary estradiol stimulation (13). A mechanism was proposed for progesterone antagonism of estrogen action based on the premise that inhibition of cytosol Re replenishment would limit the quantity of Re available for binding with hormone, and thus blunt the uterine response to estrogen stimulation (13). We now know this is probably not true (8), and recent studies we have done with the hamster have provided further insight about the mechanism of progesterone regulation of the Re system. In a variety of experimental designs, we discovered that the primary site of progesterone action occurs in the target cell nucleus where progesterone mediates a selective loss of the occupied form of Re (8). Our studies with the estrogen-primed rodent uterus indicated that progestin promotes nuclear Re turnover by a process involving a receptor regulatory factor (ReRF) which appears to cause release of Re from nuclear acceptor sites thereby modifying estrogen-dependent gene expression (Fig. 2).

In this chapter, we will review recent studies aimed at a) the elucidation of the chemical nature of ReRF and b) how it functions in the progesterone-dominated uterus. Our results support the hypothesis that ReRF activity may be responsible for down regulation of Re and inhibition of estrogen-dependent responses during pregnancy. Information is available on the cyclic variation of uterine receptor levels in several species, but less is known about uterine receptor patterns during pregnancy and parturition. While it has been informative to correlate serum steroid and uterine receptor levels during the cycle and pregnancy, in fact such correlations fail to establish cause and effect relationships (8). Experimental approaches are needed to determine what happens to the number and subcellular distribution of receptors when serum steroids are varied within physiological limits, but unfortunately few laboratories have taken this approach. We have developed and validated new assay methods

(500 µg/h) is begun. This infusion rate produces plasma
levels of progesterone approximating those found during the
luteal phase of the ovine estrous cycle (21), and different
infusion rates can be used to provide different hormone
levels. Plasma estradiol and progesterone levels are
confirmed by specific RIA (10,19,20). After various periods
of infusion, the animal is anesthetized with fluothane/O$_2$,
and uterine samples are taken 1 h before and at various times
(eg., 3 h, 6 h and 12 h) after termination of progesterone
infusion. Uterine tissue samples are removed starting at the
tubal end of the uterine horn, and serial samples are
obtained from each horn taking care to avoid interruption of
blood supply to the remaining uterine tissue. Tissues are
chilled on ice immediately after excision, and the
endometrium is dissected away from myometrium in preparation
for receptor analysis.

Receptor Assays: Although several methods have been
developed for the study of uterine steroid receptors, few of
these procedures permit the simultaneous analysis of Re and
Rp in cell nucleus and cytosol. The original assay developed
for Re utilized a Tris-EDTA (TE) buffer which does not permit
adequate Rp recovery. Rp stability is improved by addition
of glycerol and monothioglycerol to the TE buffer system (10).
In addition, the nuclear exchange procedure developed for the
assay of total Re is performed with nuclear suspensions (22),
and this approach is not suitable for the assay of nuclear Rp
because hormone-receptor complex is lost from nuclei even at
low temperature (23). Nuclear Re can be measured after KCl
extraction from the nuclear fraction (24), and this procedure
gives good receptor recovery and assay precision.
Furthermore, good recovery of nuclear Rp can be achieved by
extraction from nuclei with Tris buffer containing glycerol
and 0.5 M KCl (25). Based on these considerations, we
developed and validated an assay which is appropriate for
studying the subcellular distribution of Re and Rp in uterine

tissues during the estrous cycle and pregnancy (20). Cytosol and nuclear KCl extract are prepared from a fresh tissue homogenate. Cytosol receptors are assayed at 0° C for 16-18h which provides the total Rp (10) and the unoccupied Re (26). Total Re can be determined by exchange assay at 30° C for 1h, and occupied Re is estimated from the difference between total and unoccupied receptor (27). The solubilized nuclear receptors are measured by exchange assay performed at 30° C for 1 h in the case of Re (20) and at 0° C for 16-18 h for Rp (25). The nuclear exchange assays determine total receptor and also permit estimation of unlabeled steroid in the nuclear KCl extract. The slope of the Scatchard relationship varies as a function of the unlabeled steroid content of the nuclear extract (25). The true K_A can be derived from the equation for slope when steroid content is known (8). In practical terms, this means that the true K_A can only be derived from the slope after correction for the influence of endogenous steroid.

New assay methods were needed for the study of occupied and unoccupied forms of nuclear Re. A significant problem with the KCl procedure was that it underestimated occupied Re because this form of Re is temperature sensitive and unstable during the exchange incubation done at elevated temperature (30° C for 1 h). Recently, we have succeeded in developing conditions for the low temperature exchange assay of nuclear Re using 10 mM pyridoxal phosphate (PLP) (15). Greater recovery of occupied Re can be achieved with the PLP assay done at low temperature as compared to the KCl procedure. Total Re is measured by [^{3}H]-E exchange in 10 mM PLP at 0° C for 18 h (15). Unoccupied Re is determined at 0° C for 2 h in the presence of glycerol which blocks dissociation of occupied Re (28). Occupied Re = total Re minus unoccupied sites. We had previously shown that PLP could be used to extract and measure nuclear Rp (30). Thus, the PLP assay permits the simultaneous measurement of total Rp as well as occupied and unoccupied forms of Re (Table 1).

Routinely, receptor assays are conducted using myometrial, endometrial, or other tissues which are minced and homogenized in the appropriate buffer with a Polytron Pt-10 (Brinkman Instruments, Westbury, NY). Care is taken to maintain the samples at 0-4° C at all times. Cytoplasmic and nuclear fractions are separated by centrifugation of the homogenate at 800 xg for 10 min. The low-speed cytoplasmic fraction is centrifuged at high-speed (170,000 xg) for 30 min to prepare cytosol and a high-speed pellet. The high-speed pellet containing the membrane fraction is homogenized in TMG (50 mM Tris-maleate, 5 mM $MnCl_2$, 1% gelatin, pH 7.6) buffer for R_{OT} assay as described by Soloff (31) and modified by Pearlmutter and Soloff (32). Cytosol and nuclear receptor extract are prepared for Re and Rp assay as described elsewhere (8,15).

RESULTS
1. Objectives and Background

Our laboratory discovered a new mechanism for progesterone down regulation of the Re system in the mammalian uterus (19). We established that preovulatory progesterone caused the loss of nuclear Re in the cyclic hamster uterus (20). Using subcutaneous estradiol implants and progesterone injections given to the ovariectomized animal, we were able to mimic the fluctuations in serum estradiol (E_2) and progesterone observed during the preovulatory period of the hamster estrous cycle, and cause and effect relationships were established between estrogen withdrawal and progesterone action in the control of cytosolic and nuclear Re levels. The down regulation of nuclear Re was found to be progestin specific and progesterone dose-dependent. However, cytosol Re depletion was controlled primarily by the serum estrogen titer, i.e., Re depletion was dependent on the availability

Table 1. COMPARISON OF ASSAYS FOR Re AND Rp

	KCl (0.5M)[1]	NASCN (0.5M)[3]	PLP (10mM)[3]
Total Re	30°C, 1h	0°C, 24h	0°C, 24h
Unoccupied Re	0°C, 24h	No	0°C, 2h[4] (+glycerol)
Occupied Re	Yes[2]	No	Yes
Total Rp	0°C, 24h	No	0°C, 24h[5]

1. Evans et al. (1980). Endocrinology 107, 383-390.
2. Okulicz et al. (1981). Science 213, 1503-1505.
3. Okulicz et al. (1983). Biochem. Biophys. Acta 757, 128-136.
4. Okulicz and Leavitt. Endocrinology Submitted for publication.
5. Chen et al. (1981). J. Steroid Biochem. 14, 1023-1028.

of circulating estrogen. Experiments with [^{3}H]-E$_2$ injections revealed that estrogen uptake and retention in the nucleus were not impaired during the first 2 h of progesterone action, but nuclear retention of hormone-Re complex was reduced after 4 h of progesterone treatment (33). Studies done with an in vitro uterine strip system indicated that progesterone-induced loss of nuclear Re was dependent on RNA and protein synthesis (34). These results supported the hypothesis that progesterone induced an activity, termed the Re regulatory factor (ReRF) which was responsible for the down regulation of nuclear Re. Thus, our objective has been to study ReRF and its mechanism of action in different physiological conditions.

2. Progesterone Action in the Rat

Whereas our previous studies of progesterone action in hamster uterus revealed a rapid and selective reduction of nuclear Re by a mechanism unrelated to cytosol Re depletion (20,33), we wanted to explore the generality of this phenomenon in another species. Therefore, we tested the short-term effects of progesterone on Re levels in the rat uterus employing the same experimental paradigm used for the hamster uterus, and in agreement with our previous observations, progesterone decreased nuclear Re in rat uterus by a process that was independent of cytosol Re or serum E$_2$ levels (35).

3. Type I vs type II sites

Two types of estrogen-binding sites have been described in the nuclear fraction of rat uterus using the [^{3}H]-E$_2$ exchange assay (36). The type I binding site exhibits properties of the classical estrogen receptor, i.e., limited binding capacity, high affinity, and estrogen-binding specificity. In contrast, the type II site has a greater binding capacity and a lower affinity than type I sites. Since the specificity of type II sites had been measured in the presence of type I (36), we decided to study the specificity of type II sites in the absence of nuclear Re. The type I site (Re) was extracted with 0.5 M KCl, and the estrogen specificity of type II sites could be assessed after removal of type I sites by KCl extraction. It is significant that type II sites lacked estrogen-binding specificity indicating that they do not mediate estrogen action. In addition, we tested the effect of acute progesterone treatment on type II sites in the estrogen-primed hamster uterus and found no response at 4 h when type I sites decreased markedly (unpublished data). From these results, we conclude that progesterone down regulates type I sites (Re) but not type II sites in the estrogen-primed uterus. This conclusion is somewhat different than interpretations from Clark's laboratory (36) for reasons that are not clear at the present time.

4. Occupied vs. unoccupied nuclear Re

According to current models of steroid hormone action, the binding of the receptor-hormone complex to nuclear acceptor sites causes changes in gene expression that lead ultimately to the biological response characteristic of the hormone (Fig. 1). Thus, the estrogen-Re complex is viewed as the transducer of the hormonal signal. Unoccupied nuclear Re is known to occur in significant amounts in both normal and abnormal target tissues (7), but a functional role for this Re form has not been established. We were interested in the possibility that progesterone might selectively modulate one form of nuclear Re. Total Re was measured by $[^3H]-E_2$ exchange assay performed at 30° C, and unoccupied Re was assayed at 0° C where dissociation of occupied sites is negligible (26). Occupied Re was determined by subtracting unoccupied sites from the total Re. Of considerable interest was the observation that progesterone caused a dramatic fall in the occupied form of nuclear Re at 4 h with no change in the unoccupied form (27). The discovery that progesterone induces the preferential loss of estrogen-Re complex from the target cell nucleus indicates that progesterone has a selective effect on the biologically active form of the nuclear Re. Therefore, we proposed that the progesterone-induced modulator, ReRF, acts selectively on the occupied form of nuclear Re (38).

5. Evidence for ReRF activity

In order to test the hypothesis that progesterone induces an ReRF, we reasoned that this factor (or its activity) should appear in the nuclear fraction during early stages of progesterone action. Therefore, we attempted a functional cell-free assay based on the ability of ReRF preparations to cause the loss of nuclear Re, especially the occupied form of nuclear Re. We decided to study early times when nuclear substrate (occupied Re) would not be limiting and ReRF activity might become associated with the nucleus. Thus, uterine nuclei were obtained at 0 time (control), 30 min, and 2 h after progesterone treatment of proestrous hamsters, and the loss of nuclear Re was determined during incubation of nuclei at 37° C for 30 min in 50 mM Tris buffer containing 1 mM EDTA, 12 mM monothioglycerol and 30% glycerol, pH 7.5 (39). Total nuclear Re decreased more rapidly in nuclei obtained at 2 h after progesterone injection than at 30 min or 0 time, and occupied nuclear Re followed the same pattern. To determine if ReRF activity could be extracted from the nucleus, a 0.5 M KCl extract was prepared and tested in the same manner as nuclei. Again, total Re was lost to a greater extent during incubation at 37° C in nuclear KCl extract obtained at 2 h after progesterone, and this was due to the preferential loss of occupied Re (39). Thus, these results provided support for the existence of an ReRF and showed that ReRF activity could be demonstrated in a cell-free system. However, since our previous studies employed crude uterine nuclei prepared in hypotonic buffer containing glycerol, it was not clear whether ReRF activity was actually a nuclear component or a cytoplasmic contaminant taken up during

450

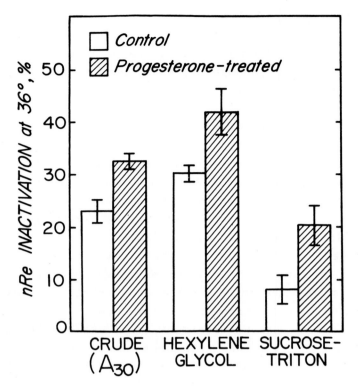

Fig. 3. Effect of 2-h progesterone treatment of the proestrous hamster on nuclear (n)Re inactivation in KCl extracts made from three different uterine nuclear preparations. Uterine nuclei from vehicle control (open bars) and progesterone-treated (hatched bars) animals were prepared by each of the three different methods. Then, the nuclear pellets were extracted with buffer A_{30} plus KCl and ReRF activity was measured in each nuclear extract. The amount of Re inactivated at 36° C is expressed as a percent of that measured in parallel samples incubated at 0° C. ReRF activity is the difference between control and progesterone-treated samples. A_{30}, $p < 0.02$, n=5; hexylene glycol, $p < 0.05$, n=3; sucrose/Triton, $p < 0.05$, n=4. From MacDonald et al. (40).

isolation of the nuclear fraction. Therefore, it was of interest to determine if ReRF activity is found in highly-purified and extensively-washed nuclei. Crude nuclei were purified by either the hexylene glycol method or an isotonic sucrose-Triton X-100 procedure (40), and both preparations of purified nuclei from progesterone-treated uteri contained ReRF activity which was KCl extractable (Fig. 3). Extensive washing of nuclei caused a progressive decline of ReRF activity in parallel with the washout of nuclear proteins and nuclear Re (40). Thus, these results establish that ReRF is contained within uterine nuclei. Although ReRF (or an activator) may enter the nucleus from the cytoplasm as a result of progesterone action, these studies (40) show that ReRF is not the product of general cytoplasmic contamination occurring during the nuclear fractionation procedure.

6. Properties of ReRF

Using cell-free assay conditions, we have begun to characterize the biochemical properties of ReRF. Protease inhibitors were tested using a standard ReRF preparation, i.e. uterine nuclear KCl extract derived from progesterone-treated proestrous hamsters. It appears unlikely that ReRF is a protease because different protease inhibitors (including 2 mM TAME (p-tosyl-L-arginine methyl ester), 0.5 mM PMSF (phenyl-methylsulfonyl fluoride), 0.5 mM leupeptin and 0.2 IU/ml trasylol) failed to block ReRF activity in this assay system (unpublished results).

Another mechanism by which progesterone might alter estrogen action in the uterus is by stimulating the metabolism of estradiol (E_2) to the less potent estrogen, estrone (E_1). Such a mechanism may operate in epithelial cells of human endometrium where progesterone enhances E_2 conversion to E_1 by increasing 17β-hydroxysteroid dehydrogenase (17β-HSD) activity (41). We tested the possibility that progesterone down regulates nuclear Re in the hamster uterus via stimulation of 17β-HSD activity, and there was no progesterone-induced change in uterine 17β-HSD activity during the 2-4 h interval required for induction of ReRF activity (42).

It is pertinent that ReRF activity was absent when nuclear extract was prepared in phosphate buffer or when ReRF preparations in Tris buffer were incubated with the phosphatase inhibitors, molybdate or vanadate, at 10 mM (39). Since high concentrations (10 mM) of molybdate and vanadate may directly stabilize Re protein, it was possible that these agents did not act by way of phosphatase inhibition. Therefore, we measured the concentration-dependence of vanadate and molybdate inhibition of ReRF activity and found that the concentration of inhibitor (0.1 mM) needed to block ReRF activity was two orders of magnitude lower than that (10 mM) needed to stabilize Re (43). Thus, these results support the idea that ReRF is a phosphatase, but not an alkaline phosphatase because ReRF activity was very sensitive to molybdate inhibition whereas nuclear alkaline phosphatase activity was not (43). However, ReRF could be an acid phosphatase or a modulator of acid phosphatase activity in as much as the inhibition curves for ReRF activity and acid phosphatase activity are in reasonable agreement (43). Furthermore, an increase in acid phosphatase activity was detected upon agarose-acrylamide gel electrophoresis comparing nuclear extracts from progesterone-treated and control animals (43). These results demonstrate a unique progesterone-induced activity (ReRF) which acts on the occupied form of nuclear Re. Inhibitor studies suggest that ReRF may be an acid phosphatase (or enzyme modulator) which if substantiated by purification and identification (Fig. 4), would indicate that progesterone regulation of nuclear Re retention and estrogen action may be controlled by a dephosphorylation step.

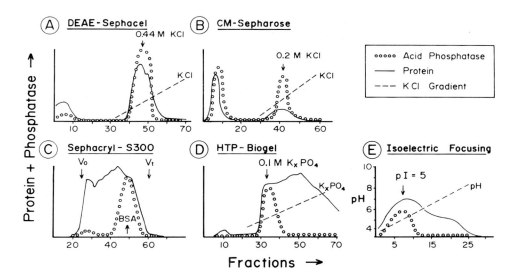

Fig. 4. Purification of acid phosphatase from nuclear KCl extract obtained from progesterone-treated hamster uterus. Nuclear extract was subjected to ion exchange chromatography (panel A, DEAE-Sephacel; panel B, CM-Sepharose): gel filtration (panel C, Sephacryl S300): adsorption chromatography on hydroxylapatite (HAP) (panel D, HTP-Biogel); and isoelectric focusing (IEF) using an LKB model 2117-301 flat bed system with a 4-10 pH gradient on Sephadex G75 (panel E). Each fraction was assayed for acid phosphatase activity and pooled fractions were assayed for ReRF activity at 36° C as described previously (40,43). ReRF activity co-eluted with acid phosphatase at the positions designated by the arrows in each of the above procedures, suggesting that ReRF may be an acid phosphatase. These results indicate that ReRF in nuclear KCl extract may be a macromolecule with MW~68,000, pI~5, affinity for HAP (phosphate) and anion exchanger (DEAE).

7. ReRF and nuclear Re assays

In order to proceed with ReRF purification (Fig. 4), a reliable assay was needed to monitor ReRF activity. In our previous studies, the cell-free system used for demonstrating ReRF activity relied on the coextraction of endogenous substrate (occupied nuclear Re) and ReRF activity from uterine nuclei obtained at 2 h after progesterone treatment in vivo. Therefore, we needed to establish conditions where exogenous substrate could be used to detect ReRF activity during purification. Mixing experiments were performed using a crude ReRF preparation (nuclear KCl extract at 2 h after progesterone treatment) and various Re preparations including nuclear Re and cytosol Re derived from progesterone-treated and untreated proestrous animals. Two significant procedural problems were encountered in these studies: 1) it was not possible to distinguish between the loss of endogenous and exogenous (added) Re substrate; and 2) Re loss occurred during the exchange assay for total Re (1 h incubation at 30° C) which was run subsequent to the ReRF incubation (30 min at 37° C). From these and other studies, it became clear that ReRF preparations have to be partially purified to remove endogenous substrate (occupied Re) prior to the ReRF assay. Secondly, new methods were needed to measure substrate (occupied Re) at low temperature following the incubation for ReRF activity at elevated temperature. Recently, we have succeeded in developing conditions for the low temperature exchange assay of nuclear Re using either PLP or NaSCN (15) (See Table 1). A significant finding in these studies was that the exchange procedure used previously underestimated occupied Re levels in nuclear KCl extract apparently because this form of nuclear Re is temperature sensitive and unstable during the exchange incubation conducted at elevated temperature (1 h at 30° C). Thus, maximum recovery of occupied Re can be achieved with the PLP assay done at low temperature. Total Re is measured by $[^3H]$-E_2 exchange in 10 mM PLP at 0° C for 18-24 h (15). Unoccupied Re can be determined by $[^3H]$-E_2 binding at 0° C for 2 h in the presence of 10% glycerol (28). Occupied Re = total - unoccupied sites.

We have compared the new PLP assay for Re with the KCl and NaSCN procedures in studies performed with the cyclic and

pseudopregnant hamster (28,29) (Fig. 5), and we have
demonstrated that the PLP assay can be used to monitor
occupied and unoccupied forms of Re in uterine cytosol and
nuclear fractions during the estrous cycle and pregnancy
(Figs. 6-7). The PLP assay provides greater recovery of
occupied Re as compared to the NaSCN and KCl procedures (Fig.
5). Thus, we now have a reliable Re assay that can be
applied to monitor the loss of occupied Re during ReRF
incubations or other experimental conditions (28,29).

8. Re recovery in the progesterone-dominated uterus
Progesterone is known to inhibit uterine Re levels during
pregnancy and pseudopregnancy (8). We reasoned that
information pertinent to the mechanism of ReRF action might
be obtained by studying the recovery of the Re system
following progesterone withdrawal. Our rational was that if
progesterone down regulates nuclear Re in the estrogen-primed
uterus by induction of an ReRF activity, then such a factor
may be present during pregnancy in the progesterone-dominated
uterus. Of interest are recent results obtained with the
pseudopregnant-decidualized hamster which demonstrate a rapid
recovery of nuclear Re in myometrium within 4 h to 8 h after
progesterone withdrawal (8). Animals were ovariectomized,
and constant serum hormone levels were maintained by
subcutaneous implants of estradiol and progesterone until the
time of progesterone withdrawal. Serum estradiol was
maintained at 100 pg/ml by an E_2 implant while serum
progesterone fell rapidly after removal of the progesterone
implant (Fig. 8). It is noteworthy that nuclear Re increased
within 4 h and cytosol Re rose substantially at 8 h following
progesterone withdrawal despite the fact that serum estradiol
remained at a steady state (Fig. 8). Since estrogen action
stimulates the synthesis of Rp and oxytocin receptor (R_{OT}) in
myometrium, it was of interest to correlate changes in these
estrogen-dependent proteins with the recovery of the Re
system. R_{OT} concentration in the myometrial membrane

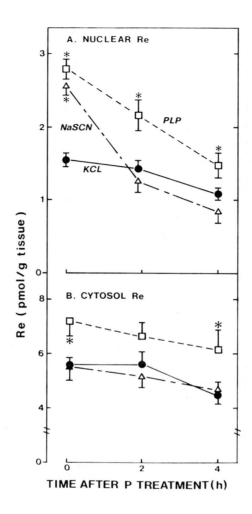

Fig. 5. The time course of uterine nuclear Re response to progesterone (P) action. Proestrous hamsters were treated with P (5 mg/100 g BW) and sacrificed 2 h or 4 h after treatment. Control animals (Oh) received oil vehicle. Cytosol and nuclear Re were assayed in individual uteri by three methods: KCl (●); PLP (□); and NaSCN (△). Each point represents the mean ± SEM (N=6). *Significantly different (p<.05) vs. result from KCl method. From Leavitt and Okulicz (29).

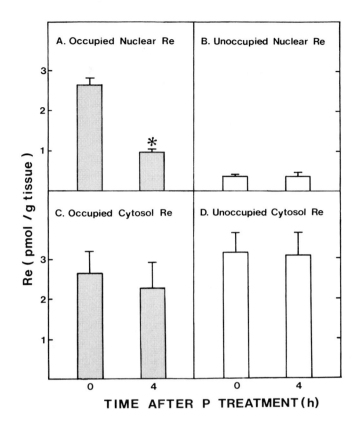

Fig. 6. Selective effect of progesterone (P) action on occupied Re in the nuclear fraction of the proestrous hamster uterus. P (5 mg/100 g BW) was injected at 0900 h on cycle Day 4. Controls (0 time) were injected with 0.3 cc oil vehicle. Re was measured by the PLP assay as described in the Methods. *$p<0.05$. From Okulicz and Leavitt (28).

fraction began to increase at 8 h and rose dramatically by 16h of progesterone withdrawal (Fig. 8). Although cytosol Rp could be influenced by the early fall in serum progesterone in addition to later estrogen stimulation, cytosol Rp did not increase until 8 h. Thus, this experiment demonstrates that one of the earliest responses detected upon progesterone withdrawal is the recovery of nuclear Re. Cytosol Re also recovers, but the cytosol Re replenishment response appears

458

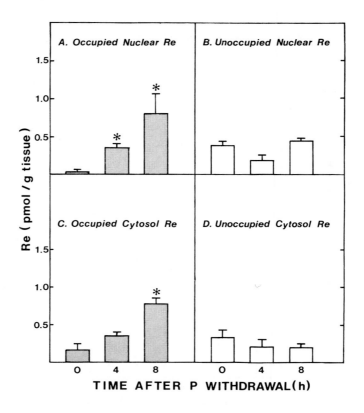

Fig. 7. Effect of progesterone (P) withdrawal on the recovery of Re in the myometrium of the decidualized hamster uterus. Pseudopregnant (PS) hamsters were ovariectomized and given Silastic implants of estradiol and P. Decidualization was induced on PS Day 4 and P withdrawal was initiated in the morning of PS Day 7 at time 0. Myometrial Re was measured by the PLP assay. Each bar represents the mean $\pm$ SEM for 3-6 assays. *Significantly different from 0 time, $p < 0.05$. From Okulicz and Leavitt (28).

to lag temporally the recovery of nuclear Re (8). Furthermore, other estrogen-responsive proteins such as R_{OT} and Rp respond after nuclear Re has increased. These results suggest that progesterone action inhibits nuclear Re levels leading to suppression of estrogen-dependent protein synthesis including production of R_{OT}, Rp and Re itself. This hypothesis is supported by an experiment in which

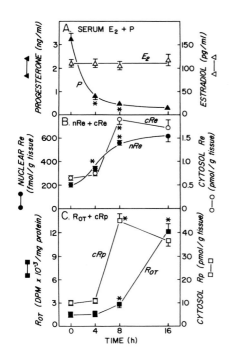

Fig. 8. Myometrial receptor responses to progesterone withdrawal in the pseudopregnant decidualized hamster. Pseudopregnant hamsters were ovariectomized at the time of deciduomal induction (day 4), and Silastic estradiol and progesterone implants were placed subcutaneously. Progesterone implants were removed on day 8, and receptor responses were measured at the indicated times thereafter. Abbreviations are: E_2, estradiol; P, progesterone; Re, estrogen receptor; R_{OT}, oxytocin receptor; Rp, progesterone receptor; c, cytosol; n, nuclear. *$p < 0.05$. From Leavitt et al. (8).

protein synthesis was inhibited by cycloheximide given from 4 h to 8 h after progesterone withdrawal. R_{OT}, Rp and Re responses at 8 h were all blocked by cycloheximide treatment at 4 h (8). Thus, it appears that the recovery of the Re system from progesterone suppression is dependent on protein synthesis and may involve the sequential production of Re followed by R_{OT} and Rp.

9. Re recovery in the progesterone-dominated sheep uterus
In order to determine whether the receptor recovery responses of hamster uterus could be observed in another mammalian species, similar studies were conducted with the sheep uterus (44). Ovariectomized ewes were estrogen-primed and then exposed to steady-state intravenous infusions of E_2 and progesterone for 5 days. With this large animal, we were able to obtain multiple uterine samples from individual animals

460

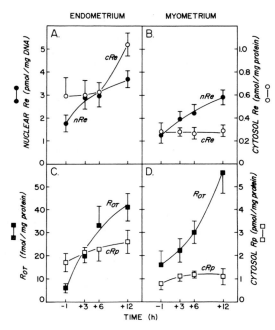

ENDOMETRIUM   MYOMETRIUM

Fig. 9. Recovery of uterine receptors in the sheep uterus following progesterone withdrawal. Ovariectomized ewes were primed with estradiol and infused intravenously with estradiol plus progesterone for 5 days. The progesterone infusion was terminated at time 0 and uterine tissue samples were removed for receptor analysis at -1h, 3h, 6h, and 12 h. Abbreviations are as in Fig. 8. Results are the mean + SEM. Adapted from Leavitt et al. (44).

and to compare receptor responses in endometrium and myometrium with time after progesterone withdrawal (Fig. 9). Nuclear Re rose progressively in both uterine compartments with time after interruption of progesterone infusion, but cytosol Re increased only in endometrium between 6 h and 12 h (Fig. 9). Similarly, the R_{OT} content of endometrial and myometrial membrane fractions increased in response to progesterone withdrawal, and there was a significant correlation between nuclear Re and R_{OT} concentrations in both uterine compartments (44). An unexpected finding was that cytosol Rp levels did not change appreciably within 12 h of progesterone withdrawal in the sheep uterus (44). Thus, these results demonstrate a rapid recovery of nuclear Re in sheep myometrium and endometrium at 6 h to 12 h after progesterone withdrawal that is associated with R_{OT} production. However, there appears to be an important species difference between the sheep and hamster in terms of uterine Rp responsiveness. Rp levels recover dramatically in hamster uterus (Fig. 8), but not in sheep uterus (Fig. 9) during the first 12 h of progesterone withdrawal.

DISCUSSION

These results indicate that the mechanism responsible for progesterone-induced changes in estrogen action is significantly related to the down regulation of the Re system. We discovered that the primary early site of progesterone action occurs in the target cell nucleus where progesterone mediates a selective loss of the occupied form of Re (8). Studies with the estrogen-primed rodent uterus suggest that progesterone promotes nuclear Re turnover by a process involving a receptor regulatory factor (ReRF) which appears to cause release of Re from nuclear acceptor sites thereby modifying estrogen-dependent gene expression (Figs. 1 & 2). The nature and subcellular distribution of the proposed uterine ReRF is not known. However, our hypothesis based on the results to date is that ReRF may be a phosphatase. Molybdate and vanadate inhibition studies suggest ReRF is an acid phosphatase (43) and fractionation and purification results are consistent with this idea (Fig. 4). Therefore, assay conditions for ReRF employ an approach generally patterned after established procedures for phosphatase detection.

A primary criterion used for the identification of ReRF is its induction by progesterone action. Total and occupied Re are measured after the ReRF incubation by PLP assay (15,28). Units of ReRF activity are defined as the quantity of Re lost per unit time per mg protein. Incubation conditions (temperature and time) are chosen which optimize the resolution of Re loss associated with progesterone action (the difference between Re loss of progesterone-treated fractions versus control) (Fig. 3). Ideally, the assay is conducted under conditions that reduce the contribution of "nonspecific" protease activity to Re loss, and thus maximize Re loss attributable specifically to ReRF action. For example a calcium-activated receptor protease (45-47) and an Re endopeptidase (48) have been isolated and characterized from chick oviduct and mammalian uterus, respectively. The contribution of these enzymes to Re degradation in ReRF assays is tested using conditions which stimulate or inhibit protease action, i.e., Ca^{++}, EGTA, leupeptin, dipyridyl disulfide (45-48).

It is possible that ReRF may be elevated in the absence of progesterone and that progesterone action may cause the activation of ReRF. Estrogen could stimulate ReRF production, and progesterone induce the synthesis of an ReRF activator. Progesterone might activate a temperature-independent process that degrades nuclear Re. This would be consistent with a mechanism in which an enzyme in one conformation requires elevated temperature for activation, and progesterone action may change ReRF such that the temperature threshold is lowered (49). This possibility can be approached by measuring ReRF activity at different temperatures. Thus, at 37° C, ReRF activity may be modest comparing progesterone-treated and control preparations, but at another temperature, ReRF activity would be greater.

Receptor proteins can be phosphorylated by various kinases (50-54) and both serine and tyrosine residues are phosphorylated (52,53). Cyclic nucleotides have been shown to influence Re levels in endometrial cancer cells (55) and this could be due to an effect on kinase activity and receptor phosphorylation. Although the evidence to date is scant, we must consider the possibility that progesterone action on Re may involve an effect on receptor phosphorylation perhaps via regulation of kinase activity. However, most evidence to date points to dephosphorylation as a more likely site of progesterone action. Dephosphorylation of Re could be mediated by either a specific or a nonspecific phosphatase. Thus, ReRF could be a receptor-specific phosphoprotein phosphatase composed of a nonspecific catalytic subunit (multifunctional phosphatase) that exists in combination with one or more regulatory subunits that in some manner dictate specificity (56). The existence of heat stable phosphatase inhibitors and activators need to be explored in this regard (57). Alternatively, ReRF could be a "nonspecific" acid phosphatase released from lysosomes in response to hormone action. In this case, treatment with the lysosomotropic agent, chloroquine (58,59), would be expected to attenuate progesterone-induced ReRF response. This latter possibility needs to be examined.

Models for the molecular structure and function of steroid hormone receptors have been proposed indicating the presence of spatially separate binding domains for hormone and components of the nucleus (i.e., acceptor sites) (1). The existence of specific receptor proteases further suggests binding domains or active sites on the receptors for specific enzymes (45-48). The enzyme may become bound in an inactive form to the receptor either in the cytoplasm or in the nucleus. In the case of ReRF, progesterone action may result in the activation of ReRF activity, thus triggering dephosphorylation and Re cleavage at the level of the nuclear acceptor site. Such a mechanism would represent an "off" signal for estrogen action so long as progesterone maintains ReRF activity. To address this possibility, ReRF binding studies need to be performed to determine the affinity of ReRF for:1) soluble Re in unactivated and active (nuclear E-Re complex) conformations, 2) E-Re complex bound to uterine nuclei, and 3) E-Re complex bound to chromatin, reconstituted chromatin, and DNA. Alternatively, ReRF may act on the nuclear acceptor site, i.e., chromosomal protein or DNA. Procedures developed by Spelsberg's group (4,60) can be used to test this possibility using chromatin-cellulose preparations containing crude chromatin, dehistonized chromatin, partially-purified chromosomal protein, DNA, etc.

Our previous studies with the hamster and sheep (8,44) demonstrate that recovery of nuclear Re is one of the earliest responses that can be detected upon progesterone withdrawal (Figs. 7-9). Cytosol Re also increases, but it appears to be the nuclear Re response that is required for the subsequent recovery of estrogen-dependent proteins such as Rp and R_{OT}. From this, it appears that progesterone action inhibits nuclear Re levels, and the down regulation of nuclear Re leads to the suppression of estrogen-dependent protein synthesis including the production of Rp, R_{OT} and perhaps Re itself. That protein synthesis is required for the recovery of myometrial receptors after progesterone withdrawal is indicated by the ability of cycloheximide to block the recovery of all receptors between 4 h and 8 h (8). This indicates that the recovery of the Re system from suppression by progesterone may be dependent on protein synthesis. However, it remains to be determined whether there is a sequential recovery of nuclear Re followed by Rp and R_{OT} synthesis or a simultaneous recovery of all receptors.

It is conceivable that ReRF or its function changes during pregnancy, and such an alteration might relate to the action of other hormones at term. For example, oxytocin and prostaglandins are two important myometrial stimulators which may be involved in triggering parturition in certain species such as the human (61). Since serum estrogen and progesterone levels don't change before parturition in the human, it is possible that a decline in ReRF activity could be involved in the up regulation of R_{OT} in the uterus at term. Thus, in the progesterone-dominated uterus, we found that progesterone withdrawal under steady-state estrogen exposure leads to a rapid recovery of nuclear Re and estrogen-dependent proteins such as R_{OT} in the hamster and sheep (8,44). Our results support the hypothesis that ReRF activity may be responsible for the down regulation of Re during pregnancy in different mammalian species. In future studies, it will be important to determine how long progesterone supports the production of ReRF and what happens to ReRF activity during hormone withdrawal at various stages of pregnancy in different species. Such information is pertinent to the understanding of the basic mechanisms responsible for controlling pregnancy and parturition.

It has not escaped our attention that receptor regulation may play an important role in the control of corpus luteum function during the sheep estrous cycle. Oxytocin-induced secretion of prostaglandin $F_{2\alpha}$ from the ovine endometrium is believed to be a significant event leading to luteolysis in this species (62), and a potential explanation for oxytocin action in this regard may be related to R_{OT} recovery at the end of the luteal phase (44). Such a mechanism would involve an increase in endometrial sensitivity to oxytocin action based on the recovery of nuclear Re and an attendant increase in endometrial R_{OT} levels. Recent findings with the human (63) demonstrate that progesterone secretion becomes pulsatile during the luteal phase of the menstrual cycle with a decrease in the frequency of pulses as the luteal phase progresses. We propose that an increase in the interval between progesterone pulses might account for Re and R_{OT} recovery and the secretion of prostaglandins. Additional study is needed to test this novel hypothesis.

ACKNOWLEDGMENTS

This work was supported by NIH grants HD18711 and HD18712. I thank Ann Laros and Rebecca Reeves for preparation of the manuscript.

REFERENCES

1. Grody, W.W., Schrader, W.T., O'Malley, B.W., Endocrine
    Rev. 3, 141-163 (1982).

2. Jensen, E.V., Pharmacol. Rev. 30, 477-491 (1979).

3. Mester, J., Baulieu, E.E., Trends Biochem. Sci. 9,
    56-59 (1984).

4. Spelsberg, T.C., In: Chromosomal Nonhistone Proteins,
    ed. L.S. Hnilica, CRC Press, Boca Raton, FL, pp. 47-69
    (1983).

5. Horwitz, K.B., McGuire, W.L., J. Biol. Chem. 253,
    6319-6322 (1978).

6. Horwitz, K.B., McGuire, W.L., J. Biol. Chem. 253,
    8185-8191 (1978).

7. Gorski, J., Welshons, W., Sakai, D., Mol. Cell.
    Endocrinol. 36, 11-15 (1984).

8. Leavitt, W.W., MacDonald, R.G., Okulicz, W.C., In:
    Biochemical Actions of Hormones, vol. 10, ed., G.
    Litwack, Academic Press, New York, pp. 324-356 (1983).

9. Milgrom, E., LuuThi, M.T., Atger, M., Baulieu, E.E., J.
    Biol. Chem. 248, 63656-6374 (1973).

10. Leavitt, W.W., Toft, D.O., Strott, C.A., O'Malley, B.W.,
    Endocrinology 94, 1041-1050 (1974).

11. Brenner, R.M., West, N.B., Ann. Rev. Physiol. 37,
    273-292 (1975).

12. Hseuh, A.J.W., Peck, E.J., Jr., Clark, J.H., Nature 254,
    337-345 (1975).

13. Clark, J.H., Hseuh, A.J.W., Peck, E.J., Jr., Annals N.Y.
    Acad. Sci. 286, 161-178 (1977).

14. Bhakoo, H., Katzenellenbogen, B.S., Mol. Cell.
    Endocrinol. 8, 121-134 (1977).

15. Okulicz, W.C., Boomsma, R.A., MacDonald, R.G., Leavitt, W.W., Biochem. Biophys. Acta 757, 128-136 (1983).

16. Leavitt, W.W., Blaha, G.C., Biol. Reprod. 3, 353-361 (1970).

17. Baranczuk, R., Greenwald, G.S., J. Endocrinol. 63, 125-131 (1974).

18. MacDonald, R.G., Morency, K.O., Leavitt, W.W., Biol. Reprod. 28, 753-766 (1982).

19. Leavitt, W.W., Chen, T.J., Evans, R.W., In: Steroid Hormone Receptor Systems, eds. W.W. Leavitt and J.H. Clark, Plenum Press, New York, pp. 197-222 (1979).

20. Evans, R.W., Chen, T.J., Hendry, W.J., Jr., Leavitt, W.W., Endocrinology 107, 383-390. (1980).

21. Hauger, R.L., Karsch, F.J., Forster, D.L., Endocrinology 101, 807-817 (1977).

22. Anderson, J., Clark, J.H., Peck, E.J., Jr., Biochem. J. 126, 561-567 (1972).

23. Walters, M.R., Clark, J.H., Endocrinology 103, 152-155 (1978).

24. Zava, D.T., Harrington, N.Y., McGuire, W.L., Biochemistry 15, 4292-4297 (1976).

25. Chen, T.J., Leavitt, W.W., Endocrinology 104, 1588-1597 (1979).

26. Katzenellenbogen, J., Johnson, H.J., Jr., Carlson, K.E., Biochemistry 12, 4092-4099 (1973).

27. Okulicz, W.C., Evans, R.W., Leavitt, W.W., Science 213, 1503-1505 (1981).

28. Okulicz, W.C., Leavitt, W.W., Endocrinology, MS submitted.

29. Leavitt, W.W., Okulicz, W.C., Biol. Reprod., MS submitted.

468

30. Chen, T.J., MacDonald, R.G., Robidoux, W.F., Jr., Leavitt, W.W., J. Steroid Biochem. 14, 1023-1028 (1981).

31. Soloff, M.S., Biochem. Biophys. Res. Commun. 65, 205-212 (1975).

32. Pearlmutter, A.F., Soloff, M.S., J. Biol. Chem. 254, 3899-3906 (1979).

33. Evans, R.W., Leavitt, W.W., Endocrinology 107, 1261-1263 (1980).

34. Evans, R.W., Leavitt, W.W., Proc. Natl. Acad. Sci. U.S.A. 77, 5856-5860 (1980).

35. Okulicz, W.C., Evans, R.W., Leavitt, W.W., Steroids 37, 463-470 (1981).

36. Clark, J.H., Markavarich, B., Upchurch, S., Eriksson, H., Hardin, J.W., Peck, E.J., Jr., Rec. Prog. Horm. Res. 36, 89-134 (1980).

37. Okulicz, W.C., Evans, R.W., Leavitt, W.W., Biochem. Biophys. Acta 677, 253-256 (1981).

38. Leavitt, W.W., Evans, R.W., Okulicz, W.C., MacDonald, R.G., Hendry, W.J., III, Robidoux, W.F., Jr., In: Hormone Antagonists-Antihormones, ed., M.K. Agarwal, Walter deGruyter Co., Berlin, pp. 213-232 (1982).

39. Okulicz, W.C., MacDonald, R.G., Leavitt, W.W., Endocrinology 109, 2273-2275 (1981).

40. MacDonald, R.G., Rosenberg, S.P., Leavitt, W.W., Mol. Cell. Endocrinol. 32, 301-313 (1983).

41. Tseng, L., Gurpide, E., Endocrinology 104, 1745-1751 (1979).

42. MacDonald, R.G., Gianferrari, E.A., Leavitt, W.W., Steroids 40, 465-473 (1982).

43. MacDonald, R.G., Okulicz, W.C., Leavitt, W.W., Biochem. Biophys. Res. Commun. 104, 570-576 (1982).

44. Leavitt, W.W., Okulicz, W.C., McCracken, J.A., Schramm, W., Robidoux, W.F., J. Steroid Biochem., MS submitted.

45. Puca, G.A., Nola, E., Sica, V., Bresciani, F., J. Biol. Chem. 252, 1358-1366 (1977).

46. Vedeckis, W.V., Freeman, M.R., Schrader, W.T., O'Malley, B.W., Biochemistry 19, 335-343 (1980).

47. Vedeckis, W.V., Schrader, W.T., O'Malley, B.W., Biochemistry 19, 343-349 (1980).

48. Gregory, M.R., Notides, A., Biochemistry 21, 6452-6458 (1982).

49. Neurath, H., Science 224, 350-357 (1984).

50. Weigel, N.L., Tash, J.S., Means, A.R., Schrader, W.T., O'Malley, B.W., Biochem. Biophys. Res. Commun. 102, 513-519 (1981).

51. Migliaccio, A., Lastoria, S., Moncharmont, B., Rotondi, A., Auricchio, F., Biochem. Biophys. Res. Commun. 109, 1002-1010 (1982).

52. Ghosh-Dastidar, P., Coty, W.A., Griest, R.E., Woo, D.D.L., Fox, C.F., Proc. Natl. Acad. Sci. U.S.A. 81, 1654-1658 (1984).

53. Dougherty, J.J., Puri, R.K., Toft, D.O., J. Biol. Chem. 257, 14226-14230 (1982).

54. Ibid., J. Biol. Chem. 259, 8004-8009 (1984).

55. Gurpide, E., Blumenthal, R., Fleming, H., In: Hormones and Cancer, Alan R. Liss Inc., New York, pp. 145-165 (1984).

56. Krebs, E.G., Beavo, J.A., Ann. Rev. Biochem. 48, 923-259 (1979).

57. Li, H.C., Current Topics Cell Reg. 21, 129-174 (1982).

58. Kalimi, M., Hubbard, J.R., Gaut, J.R., Lord, A., Biochem. Biophys. Res. Commun. 112, 488-495 (1983).

470

59. Moore, H.P., Gumbiner, B., Kelly, R.B., Nature 302, 434-436 (1983).

60. Ruh, T.S., Spelsberg, T.C., Biochem. J. 210, 905-912 (1983).

61. Fuchs, A.-R., Fuchs, F., Husslein, P., Soloff, M.S., Fernstrom, M.J., Science 215, 1396-1398 (1982).

62. Roberts, J.S., McCracken, J.A., Gavagan, J.E., Soloff, M.S., Endocrinology 99, 1107-1114 (1976).

63. Filicori, M., Butler, J.P., Crowley, W.F., Jr., J. Clin. Invest. 73, 1638-1647 (1984).

RECEPTORS AND BIOLOGICAL RESPONSES OF ESTROGENS, ANTIESTROGENS
AND PROGESTERONE IN THE FETAL AND NEWBORN UTERUS

Charlotte Sumida, Jorge Raul Pasqualini
C.N.R.S. Steroid Hormone Research Unit
Foundation for Hormone Research
26 Bd Brune, 75014 Paris, France

I. Introduction

It is well established that estrogens and progesterone are
steroid hormones which are essential for conception and gestation and that the biological action of progesterone is significantly increased by the influence of estrogens. Furthermore, the production rates and plasma concentrations of these
hormones increase very significantly during pregnancy in the
human and in some other mammalian species.

The endocrine control of the beginning of pregnancy is the result of the biological synchronization of hormones from the
hypothalamus, the pituitary, the ovary and the placenta and,
in late pregnancy, hormones produced by the fetus itself also
become involved.

At present, only limited information is available on the biological role of these hormones in the fetus and their effect
on the maturation of the different fetal tissues. In 1971,
steroid hormone receptors were found to be present in the
fetal compartment : aldosterone was found in the fetal kidney
of guinea pig (1), and estradiol in the fetal brain (2) ;
later, estrogen receptors were also found in the fetal uterus,
lung, kidney and testes of the same animal species (3, 4). In
subsequent years, cortisol receptors were detected in the

Molecular Mechanism of Steroid Hormone Action
© 1985 Walter de Gruyter & Co., Berlin · New York – Printed in Germany

fetal lung of rabbit (5) and androgen receptors in reproductive tracts of fetal rat (6). This chapter summarizes different aspects of cytosol and nuclear receptors of estrogens,
progestagens and antiestrogens, and their correlation with
biological responses in fetal and newborn guinea pigs.

II. Physico-chemical characteristics of the specific binding
    of Estrogen and Progesterone in the Fetal Compartment and
    in the Newborn

Table 1 gives the physico-chemical properties of the interaction of estradiol with the receptor protein in the fetal (end
of gestation) and newborn uteri of guinea pig. The data indicate that the physico-chemical characteristics of the estrogen
receptor in the fetal uterus are similar to those found in the
uterus and other target tissues during extrauterine life in
different mammalian species (7).

Studies of fetal and newborn uterine estrogen receptor using
monoclonal antibody

It was recently demonstrated that estrogen receptors of the
fetal uterus of guinea pig are recognized by a specific monoclonal antibody to the human estrogen receptor (D 547 Spγ) (8)
prepared using a partially purified estrogen receptor from the
cytosol fraction of MCF-7 human breast cancer cells (9, 10)
according to the method of Kohler and Milstein (11).

The interaction of the monoclonal antibody with the receptor
was shown by a shift in the sedimentation coefficient in high
ionic strength sucrose gradients from 4.5S to 7.4S (8). It was
also observed that only a part (∿ 40-60%) of the total estrogen
receptors) (α-form) was bound to the monoclonal antibody. The
remaining part of the receptor which does not bind the mono-

Table 1. Physico-chemical Characteristics of Estradiol Binding
          in the Cytosol of Fetal and Newborn Uteri of Guinea
          pigs

	Fetus (end of gestation)	Newborn (3-6 days)
Number of specific binding sites (pmoles/mg DNA)	12 - 19	4 - 6
Association rate constant k_{+1} ($\times 10^5$ mol^{-1}L^{-1}sec^{-1}), 4°C	0.5	0.6
Dissociation rate constant k_{-1} ($\times 10^{-6}$sec^{-1}), 4°C	2.2	-
Dissociation constant K_d ($\times 10^{-9}$M), 4°C	0.2 - 0.4	0.3
Sedimentation coefficient (S)	8 and 4	8 and 4
Isoelectric point (pI)	6.1 - 6.2	-

clonal antibody was denominated β-form (8).

On the other hand, in the nucleus all the receptors are bound
to the monoclonal antibody. Figures 1 and 2 show dynamic studies of the translocation in vitro of the cytosol receptor to the
nucleus as a function of time. It is observed that the α-form
decreases sharply while the β-form is only slightly affected
when the cytosol is incubated with the nuclei. On the other
hand, at the different periods studied only one form is found
in the nuclear fraction and in this fraction all the estrogen
receptor is bound to the monoclonal antibody (12). The presence of these two forms of the cytosol estrogen receptor was
also found in the uteri of newborn and immature animals (12).

Figure 1. Sucrose density gradients of the cytosol of fetal
guinea pig uterus after different times of incubation with the nuclear fraction

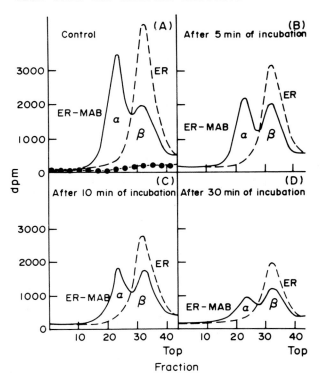

Aliquots of fetal uterine cytosol (containing 2 mg protein/ml
and prepared in TEDS buffer) were incubated with $10^{-8}M[^3H]E_2$
for 2h at 0-4°C, then added to the suspension of the nuclei and
reincubated for different times at 25°C (A: 0 min; B: 5 min;
C: 10 min; D: 30 min). The tubes were centrifuged and aliquots
of the cytosol supernatant were incubated with (——) or without (---) the monoclonal antibody D 547 Spγ (10 µg/100 µl cytosol) for 18h at 0-4°C. Unbound radioactivity was adsorbed
with dextran-coated charcoal and 100 µl of the supernatant
were layered onto sucrose gradients (10-30% w/v, 0.4M KCl).
Centrifugation was carried out for 105 min at 400,000 g using
a vertical rotor VTi65. Non specific binding (●-●-●) was determined in parallel by adding a 100-fold excess of unlabelled
estradiol.

Figure 2. Sucrose density gradients of the nuclear fraction of
fetal guinea pig uterus after different times of incubation with the cytosol

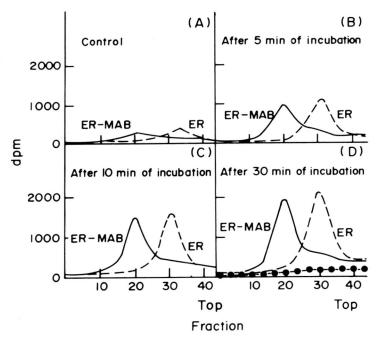

Nuclei of fetal guinea pig uterus were incubated with the cytosol fraction in $10^{-8}M[^3H]E_2$ at 25°C for different times (A:
0 min; B: 5 min; C: 10 min; D: 30 min). After centrifugation
the nuclear pellet was extracted as indicated in the text and
aliquots were incubated with (——) or without (---) the monoclonal antibody D 547 Spγ (10 µg/100 µl nuclear extract) for
18h at 0-4°C, then layered onto the sucrose gradients (10-30%
w/v, 0.4M KCl) and centrifuged for 105 min at 400,000 g using
a vertical rotor VTi65. Non specific binding was determined by
adding a 100-fold excess of unlabelled estradiol (●-●-●).

Progesterone receptor and progesterone binding globulin (PBG)
in the fetal compartment

Specific progesterone binding sites were found in the fetal
uterus and ovary of the guinea pig at the end of gestation (13).

In 1969, Diamond et al. (14) found in the maternal plasma of pregnant guinea pigs a protein which bound progesterone with high affinity (Progesterone Binding Globulin : PBG). As this protein was also found in the fetal plasma of the same animal species (15, 16), it was of interest to compare the physico-chemical characteristics of the interaction of progesterone or the synthetic progestagen R-5020 (17α,21-dimethyl-19-nor-pregnane-4,9-diene-3,20-dione) with this plasma protein and with the progesterone receptor of the fetal uterus. Table 2 indicates that the fetal PBG and the progesterone receptor are different proteins. In addition PBG is not detectable in the fetal uterus or ovary.

Table 2. Comparative physico-chemical properties of the specific binding of ^{3}H-progesterone (^{3}H-P) and ^{3}H-R-5020 in fetal uterine cytosol and plasma of guinea pig (13, 16)

	Fetal uterus		Fetal plasma	
	^{3}H-P	^{3}H-R-5020	^{3}H-P	^{3}H-R-5020
Dissociation constant K_D 4°C (x10^{-9}M)	3.3 ± 1.7	0.7 ± 0.3	0.88 ± 0.35	No specific binding
Coefficient of sedimentation (S)	6-7 ; 4	6-7 ; 4	4.6	–
Isoelectric point (pI)	5 – 5.5	–	< 3	–
Temperature* effect	Thermo labile	Thermo labile	Thermo-resistant	No specific binding

*Aliquots of fetal uterine cytosol fraction or diluted fetal plasma (1/10 - 1/50 v/v) were pre-heated for 1h at 37°C in the absence of the hormone and then reincubated with ^{3}H-progesterone or ^{3}H-R-5020 (4 x 10^{-9}M) with or without a 100-fold excess of the unlabelled steroids to measure the number of specific binding sites after adsorbing the unbound radioactive steroids with dextran charcoal.

III. Estrogen and Progesterone Receptors in Fetal Tissues

Estrogen receptors are found in high concentrations in the
fetal guinea pig uterus, an organ which is the typical target
organ for the action of estrogens in the adult animal, but besides the uterus, several other fetal organs also contain specific estrogen binding components which thus make these fetal
organs potential estrogen target organs although this has not
yet been clearly demonstrated for all tissues. Table 3 indicates the fetal organs for which quantitative data on specific
"receptor-like" estrogen binding exist in the literature. It
can be readily remarked that the fetal uterus contains the
highest concentration of estrogen receptors, but it is possible
that the estrogen responsive cell types of the various tissues
may represent only a small and variable fraction of the whole
organ. More information is needed on the precise location of
estrogen receptors and estrogenic responsiveness within these
fetal tissues. This table does not include publications on
qualitative observations of estrogen binding in fetal and neonatal tissues such as 8S binding of ^{3}H-diethylstilbestrol in
cytosol of Müllerian ducts of 20-day-old rat fetuses (25), a
4.5S protein in lung cytosol of 20 day fetal rats (26), the
localization by autoradiography of ^{3}H-diethylstilbestrol in
many fetal tissues of the mouse (particularly those considered
to be estrogen target tissues such as primordia of male and
female reproductive organs, brain, pituitary, mammary glands)
(27, 28) and high affinity binding of ^{3}H-estradiol in human
fetal brain (29). Estrogen receptors are distributed in many
fetal tissues but the estrogen response elicited and its degree may depend on the tissue.

Similar observations have been made of progesterone receptor
concentrations in tissues of fetuses which have not been
treated previously with estrogens (Table 4). Fetal guinea pig
reproductive organs contain the highest amount of progesterone
receptors (13) but fetal rabbit lung (31) is also important

478

Table 3. Concentrations of Cytosol Estrogen Receptors in Various Fetal Tissues

Organ	Animal species	Estrogen receptor fmol/mg protein	fmol/mg DNA	Reference
Uterus	Guinea pig	1,000 – 2,000	10,000 – 20,000	17,18,19
Brain	Guinea pig	14 – 16	100 – 200	4,20
HPOA	Rat	2.5 – 6	–	21,22
	Mouse	7 – 8	38 – 40	23
Cortex	Rat	2 – 3	–	22
	Mouse	3 – 4	11 – 12	23
Lung	Guinea pig	121 – 434	210 – 754	3,4
Kidney	Guinea pig	19 – 35	53 – 98	3,4
Testis	Guinea pig	30 – 56	–	3
Thymus	Guinea pig	22 – 31	40 – 57	24

Estrogen receptor binding was determined by incubations of cytosol with either ^{3}H-estradiol or ^{3}H-moxestrol (11β-methoxy, 17α-ethynyl estradiol-17β).
HPOA = hypothalamus-preoptic area

compared to the other fetal tissues examined in the same study. In fetal rat brain, progesterone receptors were not detectable until the day of birth (in the cortex) (30).

IV. Ontogeny of Estrogen and Progesterone Receptors in the Guinea pig Uterus

Estrogen receptors are already detectable in the cytosol fraction of the fetal uterus at a very early stage of development in the guinea pig (Figure 3) (3). Their concentrations rise until about 50 days of gestation. Progesterone receptors only appear 10 to 15 days after the estrogen receptor and they rise until after birth, parallel with the decline in estrogen receptor. The delay in development of the progesterone receptor

Table 4. Concentrations of Cytosol Progesterone Receptors in
Various Fetal Tissues

Organ	Animal species	Progesterone Receptor fmol/mg protein	Reference
Uterus	Guinea pig	136 + 35 (S.D.)	13
Ovary	Guinea pig	72 + 12	13
Brain	Rat	Non-detectable	30
Lung	Rabbit	31.8 + 1.6 (S.E.)	31
Kidney	Rabbit	9.7 + 1.6	31
Small Intestine	Rabbit	9.8 + 3.4	31
Brain	Rabbit	5.7 + 1.5	31
Muscle	Rabbit	5.0 + 0.3	31
Heart	Rabbit	3.8 + 0.9	31
Skin	Rabbit	2.4 + 0.4	31
Liver	Rabbit	2.0 + 1.1	31

Specific binding of ^{3}H-R-5020 was determined in cytosols of
fetuses which were not treated with estrogens.

would suggest that under normal physiological conditions, its
synthesis depends on the adequate functioning of the estrogen
receptor system and endogenous estrogens since it is well
known that progesterone receptor is induced by estrogens in
the uterus of the adult, ovariectomized guinea pig (32) as
well as in other adult animals (33). Since the circulating
levels of estrogens are relatively low and remain constant in
fetal guinea pig plasma (34), the increase in estrogen receptors and the appearance of progesterone receptor appear to be
independent of abrupt changes in endogenous estrogens. It is
possible that before 50 days of gestation, the estrogen receptor levels are not sufficient to induce progesterone receptor
synthesis in the face of such low levels of circulating estrogens. Furthermore, radioimmunoassay of the tissue concentration
of estrogens has shown that, at the end of gestation, the fetal

Figure 3. Ontogeny of Estrogen (ER) and Progesterone (PR) Receptors in Fetal and Neonatal Guinea pig Uterus

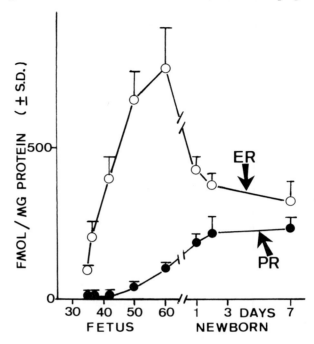

Receptor binding was measured by incubating uterine cytosol with 4×10^{-9}M ^{3}H-estradiol or ^{3}H-progesterone ($\pm$ a 100-fold molar excess of unlabelled steroid) at 4°C for 4h. Bound radio-activity was separated with dextran-coated charcoal.

uterus contains about 2800 pg of estradiol plus estrone per g tissue (34) which corresponds to the concentration of estrogen receptor binding sites occupied by endogenous estrogens in the fetal uterus (17), suggesting that a sufficiently high concentration of estrogen receptors may be a prerequisite for the action of endogenous estrogens in the fetal guinea pig uterus. Whether the acquisition of an adequate estrogen receptor concentration is a constitutive property of the developing uterine cells or influenced by other factors remains to be elucidated.

Figure 4. Uterotrophic Response to Estradiol in Fetal and Neo-
         natal Guinea pig Uterus

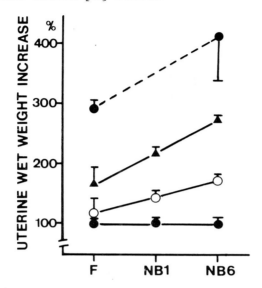

Pregnant guinea pigs (52-65 days of gestation) were injected
subcutaneously with 1 mg estradiol/kg body weight and 1 day
after the last injection, the fetuses were removed and fetal
uteri excised and weighed (F). One-day-old (NB1) or 6-day-old
newborns (NB6) were injected with 1-3 µg of estradiol and sacrificed 1 day after the last injection. Uterine weight gain is
expressed as a percent of weights of untreated animals assigned the value of 100%.
●——● = untreated animals; ○——○ = single injection;
▲——▲ = 3 daily injections; ●---● = 6 daily injections.

V. Estrogen Responses in the Fetus and Newborn

Since indirect correlations suggested that endogenous estrogens

are physiologically active in the fetal guinea pig uterus, a

range of responses to exogenously administered estrogens was

studied to demonstrate the precocious development of these

hormonal responses and the involvement of the estrogen receptor

system.

Uterotrophic effect

The growth of the uterus is one of the principal effects of
estrogens. To study the effects of estradiol on growth of the
fetal uterus, estradiol was administered to the maternal guinea pig (1 mg/kg body weight) which leads to a concentration
of about 3 to 4 μg of unmetabolized estradiol per fetus 30 min
after the injection (18). As seen in Figure 4, a single administration of estradiol 1 day before sacrifice leads to only
a 20% increase in wet weight of the fetal uterus but daily
injections for 3 consecutive days provoke a 70% increase and a
similar increase in dry weight (18). This increase can also be
elicited 2 or 3 days after a single injection (19). However,
prolonging the treatment to 6 daily injections leads to as
much as a 3-fold increase in wet weight (Figure 4). The uterotrophic effect is associated with a decrease in the concentration of DNA (mg per g tissue) (19) and the DNA content (mg per
uterus) increases only after 6 consecutive days of treatment
(35).

The effect of estrogens on fetal uterine wet weight does not
evolve as gestation progresses since 46-day-old fetuses (20 g
body weight) respond as well as the fetuses at term (19) but
the uterotrophic effect develops further after birth. In a 1-
day-old newborn (age at time of treatment), 1 μg of estradiol
increases uterine wet weight by 45% after only 1 day (Figure 4)
but 100 μg leads to an even larger increase (79%) (36). By 6
days after birth, the uterus responds with a 76% increase to
even a single injection of 1 μg of estradiol 1 day before sacrifice, with no further increase with higher doses (36) but 3
daily injections provoke a further 2.75-fold increase in weight
(Figure 4) and an increase in DNA content (35).

Histologically, estradiol treatment increases the height of
the uterine luminal epithelial cells by 95% in the fetus and
by 286% in the 6-day-old newborns with also greater increases

Figure 5.   Ontogeny of the Progesterone Receptor Response to
             Estradiol in the Fetal and Neonatal Guinea pig
             Uterus

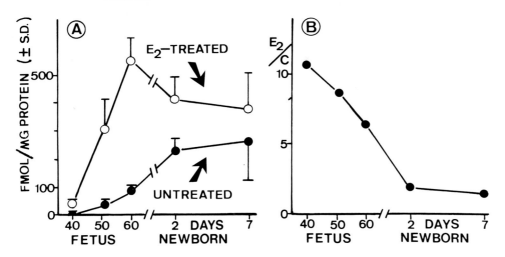

Pregnant guinea pigs were injected with 1 mg estradiol/kg body
weight daily for 3 days. After birth, animals received a single
injection of 1-100 µg estradiol. Animals were sacrificed one
day after the last injection. A: progesterone receptor binding
was measured in the cytosol fraction by incubation with 4×10^{-9}M
^{3}H-progesterone ($\pm$ a 100-fold molar excess of unlabelled progesterone) at 4°C for 18h. Bound steroid was separated by dextran-coated charcoal adsorption. B: The ratio of progesterone
receptor concentrations in estradiol-treated (E_2) over untreated (C) animals.

in the areas of the stroma and myometrium in the newborns (35).

These observations show that although the fetal uterus is capable of an estrogen-inducible growth response, this occurs
more slowly than in newborns, suggesting a progressive development of the uterotrophic effect of estrogens pre- and postnatally. The developing uterus intrinsically acquires increasing sensitivity to estrogens with age.

Progesterone receptor stimulation

Progesterone receptor concentrations are stimulated by estradiol in the fetal uterus but in contrast to the uterotrophic response, the increase is greater in the fetal uterus than during postnatal development as seen in Figure 5. Progesterone receptor can be induced by estradiol at a fetal age when its concentration is negligible (~40 days of gestation) and the highest values are attained at the end of gestation while basal levels are increasing during this time (Figure 5A) (13, 37). Proportionally, the degree of sensitivity declines prenatally with age until the immediate postnatal period (Figure 5B) (19, 36). It seems that, unlike the uterotrophic response, the progesterone receptor response either decreases in sensitivity or depends on factors extrinsic to the developing uterus, some of which are peculiar to the fetus.

In an attempt to study the control of progesterone receptor synthesis in an in vitro system, explants of fetal uteri were placed in organ culture for as long as 9 days. Surprisingly enough, as seen in Figure 6, progesterone receptor increased even in the absence of any addition to the M199 synthetic culture medium (estradiol or diethylstilbestrol had no additive effect) (38). This induction can be blocked by the protein synthesis inhibitors, actinomycin D and cycloheximide, during the initial period but gradually becomes less dependent on DNA transcription and more dependent on translation of already transcribed message until 3 days in culture when progesterone receptor protein is no longer being synthesized (38). Progestins and triphenylethylene antiestrogens inhibit the rise in progesterone receptor but dexamethasone has no effect (38). Unexpectedly, the observed rise in progesterone receptor occurred in the virtual absence of estrogen receptor in the cytosol fraction and the nucleus (Figure 6) although the concentration of estrogen receptor in the fetal uteri before explanting was 12.81 ± 0.51 (S.E.) pmol/mg DNA. In contrast, explants

Figure 6. Progesterone (PR) and Estrogen (ER) Receptor Con-
           centrations in Fetal Uterine Explants in Organ
           Culture

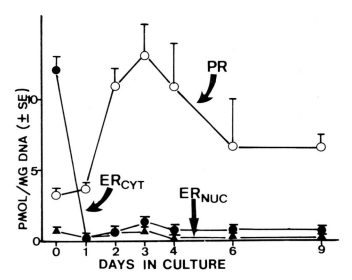

Explants of fetal uteri (50-65 days of gestation) were cultured
in Medium 199. Progesterone receptor binding was measured in
the cytosol fraction and 0.6M KCl nuclear extracts by incubation with 5×10^{-9}M ^{3}H-R-5020 ($\pm$ 100-fold molar excess of nonradioactive R-5020) at 4°C for 16h. Estrogen receptor binding
was determined in protamine sulfate precipitates in the same
fractions by incubation with 1×10^{-8}M ^{3}H-estradiol ($\pm$ 100-fold
excess of non-radioactive estradiol) under exchange conditions.

of neonatal uteri do not show a net increase in progesterone
receptor when placed in culture, even when exposed to estradiol
(38), suggesting a qualitative difference in the regulation of
progesterone receptor concentrations between the pre- and postnatal periods.

Histone acetylation, RNA polymerase activity, and protein
synthesis

The acetylation of nuclear histones leads to conformational changes in chromatin which are correlated with increased DNA template activity and transcription (39). Estradiol rapidly augments the acetylation of histones in the rat uterus (40). The uterus of the guinea pig fetus also responds very rapidly to estradiol treatment by increased acetylation of nuclear histones. Only 10 min after injection of 10 µg of estradiol directly to the female fetuses, a 7- to 10-fold increase in the acetylation of histones $H_2 + H_3$ and H_4 was observed (41). Very limited or no effect was found in fetal brain, kidney or liver, and testosterone did not elicit a response in the fetal uterus (41). It is very interesting to note that like the estrogen-induced progesterone receptor response, the degree of estradiol stimulation of nuclear histone acetylation in the uterus decreases postnatally to only 1.5 - 2 times the values of the untreated newborns (42).

Postnatally, estrogens are known to provoke increases in RNA polymerase I (ribosomal RNA synthesis) and II (messenger RNA synthesis) activities before increased protein synthesis occurs (43). In the fetal guinea pig uterus, RNA polymerase II activity increases rapidly in response to estradiol treatment, 2.5 times the control levels at 30 min and 4 times by 2h (44). RNA polymerase I activity also attained a 4-fold increase by 2h (44).

It has also been demonstrated that the incorporation of ^{3}H-leucine into acid-insoluble uterine proteins is increased by estrogen treatment of guinea pig fetuses. By 8h after administration of estradiol to the maternal guinea pig, amino acid incorporation is increased 10 times and by 24h there is a 20-fold increase (45).

Since the fetal uterus responds to estradiol by a very rapid increase in histone acetylation and, in view of the correlation between acetylation of the nucleosomal core histones and increased DNA template activity (39), it is possible that this rapid effect is associated with increased RNA polymerase activities which would be implicated in increased protein synthesis which is seen either by increased incorporation of amino acid into proteins or by higher concentrations of a specific protein such as the progesterone receptor.

Effects of estradiol in other fetal tissues

The presence of estrogen receptors in the fetal hypothalamus would suggest that the mechanism by which estrogen defeminization of the brain occurs by the aromatization of testosterone to estradiol (46, 47) is functional before birth in this animal species. Complementary autoradiographic studies have confirmed that in the fetal guinea pig brain, at the end of gestation, after administration of ^{3}H-estradiol to the fetus, radioactivity is localized in the nucleus arcuatus and preoptic area of the hypothalamus (48). Moreover, autoradiography combined with immunohistochemistry has demonstrated the simultaneous presence of ^{3}H-estradiol and GnRH (gonadotropin releasing hormone) in the cell body of neurons of the nucleus arcuatus and preoptic area (48), areas known to be implicated in the estradiol modulation of the release of GnRH (49, 50). The presence of estrogen receptors in fetal guinea pig brain would thus suggest their role in sexual differentiation of the brain whose critical period occurs prenatally in this animal species (51, 52, 53) and the possible functioning of the hypothalamo-pituitary-gonadal axis in the guinea pig fetus.

Estrogen receptors could possibly be mediators in the action of estrogens on the maturation of the fetal lung. A relationship has been observed between low levels of neonatal urinary estrogens and the incidence of respiratory distress syndrome (54) and estrogens increase surfactant biosynthesis in fetal lungs of rabbits (55, 56) and rats (57).

The fetal guinea pig thymus is a potential estrogen target organ as seen by the presence of estrogen receptors and by responses to exogenous estrogen treatment (24, 58). Administration of estradiol to the maternal guinea pig elicits a 50% decrease in weight of the fetal thymus, a reduction in size of thymic lobules and a decrease in width of the cortical lymphoid area. By 24h after the injection of estradiol, a selective decrease in the number of the large lymphoid cells (the more highly proliferating lymphocytes) in the subcapsular cortex occurs with reduced incorporation of ^{3}H-thymidine into DNA (24, 58). The response of the thymus to estrogens parallels the progressive increase in estrogen receptor concentrations in the cytosol fraction (58). The fetal thymus acquires increasing estrogen sensitivity apparently by the availability and development of the cytoplasmic estrogen receptor.

VI.   Estrogen Receptors : Mediators of Estrogen Responses in
      the Fetus and Newborn

In order to better understand the role of estrogen receptors in the biological responses observed in the fetus, the kinetics of the changes in subcellular distribution of receptor and responses in reaction to a single dose of estradiol were followed and compared with those of estriol whose complex with estrogen receptor has a shorter retention time in the uterine nuclei in immature rats (59). After a single injection of estradiol to the maternal guinea pig, an initial rise in fetal uterine weight is observed at 6h (Figure 7A), at which time the progesterone receptor also begins to increase (Figure 7B). During this time estrogen receptor translocates from the cytoplasm to the nucleus where levels are maximal after 6h (Figure 7C). If estriol is administered, a more rapid uterotrophic response is already observed by 1h (Figure 7A) accompanied by a small but

Figure 7. Comparative Kinetics of Responses to Estradiol (E_2)
and Estriol (E_3) in the Fetal Guinea pig Uterus

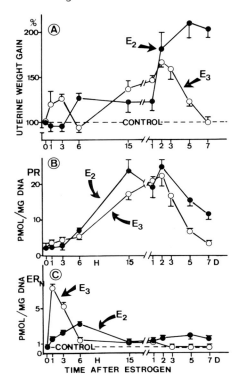

Pregnant guinea pigs were injected subcutaneously with 1 mg of
estradiol or estriol and animals were sacrificed at the indicated times. Uterine wet weight gain is expressed as a percent
of weights of untreated animals assigned the value of 100%.
Concentrations of progesterone (PR) and nuclear estrogen (ER_N)
receptors were measured as indicated in Figure 6. Means ± S.E.

significant increase in progesterone receptor as early as 3h
after injection (Figure 7B). The rapidity of the responses as
compared to estradiol appears to be related to the faster rise
in levels of estriol-receptor complexes in the nucleus (by 1h)
(Figure 7C). However, at long-term, the uterotrophic response
to estradiol persists for as long as 7 days after a single

injection while fetal uterine weight regresses 3 days after
administration of estriol, which correlates with long-term retention of estradiol-receptor complexes in the nucleus (as long
as 7 days) and more rapid clearance of estriol-receptor complexes. The differences between the kinetics of the estradiol-
and estriol- receptor complexes in the fetal uterus are due to
differences in the pharmaco-dynamic and receptor binding characteristics between the two estrogens. When injected in equal
doses to the maternal guinea pig, 2 times more estriol enters
the fetal compartment and 5 times more estriol appears in
fetal plasma than unconjugated, unmetabolized estradiol, but
estriol has a faster clearance rate so that 2 to 7 days later
more estradiol circulates than estriol (18). Moreover, the
estrogen receptor in the fetal uterus binds estriol with lower
affinity and a faster dissociation rate than estradiol (18,
60). However, when present in high enough concentrations,
estriol can be a potent estrogen in the fetus especially since
estriol is quantitatively the most important estrogen circulating during human pregnancy (61).

In contrast, the progesterone receptor response does not correlate as well with the changes in intracellular distribution
of the estrogen receptor. After both estradiol and estriol injections, progesterone receptor concentrations are not maintained for more than 2 days (Figure 7B) despite the retention
of estradiol-receptor complexes in the nucleus and the duration of the uterine weight gain. Although the uterotrophic
effect shows a correlation with estrogen receptor kinetics,
progesterone receptor stimulation seems to be estrogen sensitive but not directly dependent on the estrogen receptor system.

Estrogen receptor translocation and retention in the nucleus
have also been demonstrated to take place in the fetal guinea
pig thymus, which has been shown to be estrogen responsive
(24, 58) and in the fetal kidney and lung (62, 63).

Figure 8. Effect of Seven Different Estrogen Sulfates, as well
          as Unconjugated Estrone and Estradiol on the Weight
          of the Fetal Uterus of Guinea pig (64)

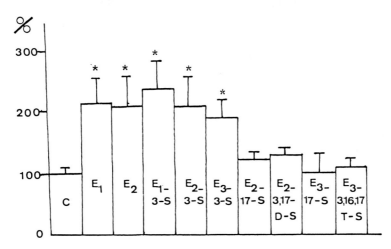

Pregnant guinea pigs (55-65 days of gestation) were injected
subcutaneously with 1 mg/kg/day of estrone (E$_1$), estradiol (E$_2$)
or with 1.4-2.1 mg/kg/day of the following sulfates : estrone-
3-sulfate (E$_1$-3-S), estradiol-3-sulfate (E$_2$-3-S), estriol-3-
sulfate (E$_3$-3-S), estradiol-17-sulfate (E$_2$-17-S), estriol-17-
sulfate (E$_3$-17-S), estradiol-3,17-disulfate (E$_2$-3,17-DS),
estriol-3,16,17-trisulfate (E$_3$-3,16,17-TS) (dissolved in 20%
v/v ethanol-saline solution) for 3 days and sacrificed on day
4. Uteri were excised, stripped of adhering fat and weighed.
Control (C) animals received the vehicle alone. Values represent the mean $\pm$ S.D. of 5-21 determinations. *$p < 0.001$
(p calculated versus non-treated animals).

VII. Biological Responses to Estrogen Sulfates in the Fetal
     and Newborn Uteri

It is well established that in human and in different mammalian
species (cow, sheep, guinea pig, Rhesus monkey) most of the
estrogens circulate in the fetal compartment as sulfates. In
guinea pigs, it was observed that 30 min after s.c. injection
of ^{3}H-estradiol in vivo and in situ to the fetus, most of the

radioactivity (50-70%) circulates in the fetal plasma as estrone and estradiol sulfates. An attractive hypothesis has been
put forward whereby these sulfates serve to protect the fetus
from the biological action of the hormone or that they can act
as a pre-hormone which becomes active after hydrolysis.

Figure 8 shows that after administration of different estrogen
sulfates (sulfates in C_3 and in C_{17}) to the pregnant guinea
pig only the C_3-sulfates (estrone-3-sulfate, estradiol-3-
sulfate and estriol-3-sulfate) provoke a significant uterotrophic effect in the fetal uterus. Similarly, this type of
sulfate stimulates (7-10 times) the number of specific progesterone binding sites (Table 5). The analysis of the concentration of the unconjugated and conjugated estrogens showed that
the estrogens with the sulfate in the C_3 position are partially
hydrolysed, while very little or no hydrolysis occurs with the
sulfates at the C_{17} position (64). Consequently, estrogen-3-
sulfates can act as pre-hormones which become active after hydrolysis or they can serve as protective and/or reserve material for the active hormones. On the other hand, sulfates in
C_{17} are end products of estrogen metabolism and are not involved in the biological modulation of the hormone.

VIII. Receptors and Biological Responses of Antiestrogens

Different triphenylethylene derivatives (e.g. : nafoxidine,
tamoxifen, chlomiphene) are extensively used in the treatment
of estrogen-dependent breast cancer, particularly during the
post-menopausal period (65, 66). It was also demonstrated that
these compounds antagonize estrogen action in different mammary cancer cell lines (67). However, in other estrogen target
tissues (e.g. the uterus of young animals) these derivatives
can act with a real estrogenic potency (68, 69).

Table 5. Effect of Seven Different Sulfates, as well as of Un-
         conjugated Estradiol and Estrone on the Concentration
         of the Specific Binding Sites of Progesterone in the
         Fetal Uterus of Guinea pig (64)

	pmoles/mg DNA		pmoles/mg protein	
	Cytosol	Nucleus	Cytosol	Nucleus
Control (non-treated)	1.97±0.67	0.10±0.07	0.30±0.05	0.04±0.01
Estrone-3-Sulfate	15.2±2.9*	0.71±0.25*	1.75±0.32*	0.42±0.10*
Estradiol-3-Sulfate	16.5±7.0*	1.39±0.60*	1.99±0.41*	0.69±0.29*
Estriol-3-Sulfate	18.4±3.34*	1.64±0.56*	2.02±0.28*	0.80±0.28*
Estradiol-17-Sulfate	1.45±0.60	0.09±0.05	0.22±0.07	0.03±0.01
Estriol-17-Sulfate	2.27±0.18	0.19±0.08	0.27±0.04	0.09±0.04
Estradiol-3,17-Disulfate	1.96±0.91	0.03±0.01	0.23±0.10	0.02±0.01
Estriol-3,16,17-Trisulfate	1.85±0.60	N.D.	0.21±0.09	N.D.
Estrone	18.1±3.5*	0.75±0.22*	2.71±0.71*	0.45±0.12*
Estradiol	18.9±2.5*	1.00±0.14*	3.10±0.80*	0.63±0.15*

Pregnant guinea pigs (55-65 days of gestation) were injected
with 1.4-2.1 mg/kg/day of the different estrogen-sulfates or
with 1 mg/kg/day of unconjugated estrone or estradiol for 3
consecutive days and sacrificed on day 4. Fetal uteri were separated and progesterone receptors were measured in the cytosol and 0.6M KCl nuclear fractions. Aliquots of these fractions
were incubated with ^{3}H-R-5020 (5 x 10^{-9}M) with or without a 100-
fold molar excess of unlabelled R-5020 for 14h at 4°C. Bound
and unbound steroids were separated with dextran-charcoal mixture and specific ^{3}H-R-5020 binding was calculated by the difference between the total and non-saturable binding. The values
represent the mean ± S.D. of 5-11 determinations. *p <0.001
(p calculated versus non-treated animals).

Heterogeneity of binding sites of ^{3}H-tamoxifen in the fetal
uterus of guinea pig

Figure 9 shows that tamoxifen competes with ^{3}H-estradiol for
the cytoplasmic estrogen receptors, but the relative binding
affinity is 10% that of estradiol (K_d = 1.3 x 10^{-9}M). On the
other hand, estradiol only partially displaces ^{3}H-tamoxifen

494

Figure 9. Interaction of Tamoxifen with Binding Sites in the
Fetal Uterus of Guinea pig (70, 71)

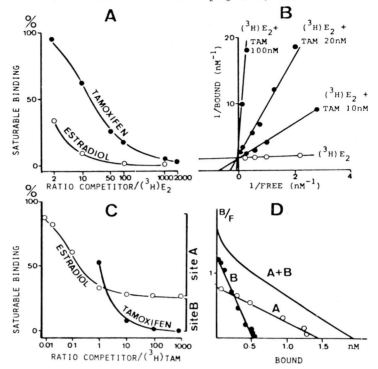

A) Effect of tamoxifen on the binding of ^{3}H-estradiol (E_2)
(4 nM) to fetal uterine estrogen receptor in the guinea pig.
B) Lineweaver-Burk plot of the specific binding of ^{3}H-E_2 to
cytoplasmic receptor in the presence of tamoxifen. C) Effect
of estradiol and tamoxifen on the binding of ^{3}H-tamoxifen
(15 nM) in the cytosol of fetal guinea pig uterus.
D) Scatchard analysis of the binding of ^{3}H-tamoxifen to
site A (O-O), and to site B (●-●).

from its binding to the cytoplasmic proteins (Fig. 9C). The
data suggest the presence of two different binding sites for
estradiol : Site A which corresponds to the estrogen receptor
and Site B which is specific for triphenylethylene derivatives
(70, 71). Table 6 gives the physicochemical characteristics
of the two sites (72).

Table 6. Physicochemical Characteristics of ^{3}H-Tamoxifen
Binding in the Cytosol of the Fetal Guinea pig Uterus
(72)

	Estrogen Receptor	Site B
K_d at 4°C ($\times 10^{-9}$)	1.8 ± 0.4	0.39 ± 0.04
Number of sites (pmol/mg DNA)	12 ± 1.8	5.5 ± 0.1
k_{-1} at 4°C ($\times 10^{-4}$ sec^{-1})	8.3 ± 2	0.81 ± 0.14
Binding specificity	Natural and synthetic estrogens	Triphenylethylene derivatives
Temperature effect	Themolabile	Thermoresistant
Precipitation by ammonium sulfate (%)	36	36
Effect of proteolytic treatment	Destroyed	Destroyed
Nuclear transfer	Yes	No

Biological responses to antiestrogens in the fetus and newborn

Uterotrophic effect. After treatment of pregnant guinea pigs
with two different triphenylethylene derivatives (tamoxifen
and nafoxidine), a significant uterotrophic effect was observed in the fetal uterus. The response is similar to that obtained with equimolecular quantities of estradiol (Figure 10)
(37). Histological studies showed that the action of these
antiestrogens is mainly on the epithelium of the endometrium
(35). Treatment of newborns indicated that after a short treatment (2-3 days), the uterotrophic effect is more intense with
the estrogens than with tamoxifen or nafoxidine, but after a
long treatment (12 days), the effects are similar for both
estradiol and tamoxifen and the effect is much more intense
when the two compounds are administered together (73). In
conclusion, the triphenylethylene-derived "antiestrogen"

Figure 10. Uterotrophic Effect of Estradiol (E) and Tamoxifen
(Tam) Administration in Fetal and Newborn Guinea
pig (37)

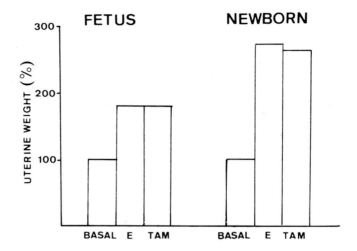

Tamoxifen and estradiol (1 mg/kg body weight) were injected
for 3 consecutive days to pregnant animals (55-65 days of gestation) and the uterotrophic response in fetuses was evaluated
on the fourth day. Estradiol (30 ng/g body weight) and tamoxifen (0.6 µg/g body weight) were injected daily for 3 days to
6-day-old newborn guinea pigs, and the uterotrophic effect was
determined 24h after the last administration. The results are
expressed as a percentage of basal values (assigned the value
of 100%).

tamoxifen acts in both the fetal and newborn uteri as a real
agonist.

Stimulation of progesterone receptors. In the fetal uterus,
the action of nafoxidine or tamoxifen on the stimulation of
the progesterone receptor is limited to only 1/4 - 1/2 the effect provoked by different estrogens (70, 74, 75), but in newborns the effect is similar (Figure 11) (74). It is to be remarked that progesterone receptor stimulation by estradiol,

Figure 11. Effect of Estradiol (E) and Tamoxifen (T) on Progesterone Receptor Synthesis in the Fetal and Neonatal
uterus (74)

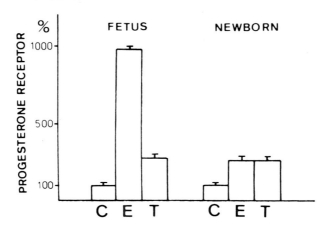

Estradiol or tamoxifen (1 mg/kg/body weight/day) were injected
to pregnant guinea pigs for 3 consecutive days. Newborn guinea
pigs (6 days old) were injected with 30 ng/g body weight of
estradiol or 0.6 g/g body weight of tamoxifen. 24h after the
last injection the fetal and neonatal uteri were separated and
processed for progesterone receptor assay, by incubating the
cytoplasmic fraction with ^{3}H-R-5020 (4 nM) $\pm$ a 100-fold excess
of unlabelled R-5020. Unbound steroid was removed by dextran-
coated (0.05% w/v) charcoal (0.5% w/v) 10 min at 4°C. The results are expressed as percent above control values (C) in untreated animals. Control values were 2.4 $\pm$ 0.7 pmol/mg DNA in
the fetal uterus, and 5.6 $\pm$ 0.8 pmol/mg DNA in the neonatal
uterus. The results represent the mean $\pm$ S.D. from 3-9 experiments.

estrone or estriol is significantly less intense in the newborn uterus than in the fetal uterus.

IX. Modulation of Estrogen Responses by Progesterone in the
Fetus and Newborn

In the immature or adult animal, progesterone antagonizes estrogenic activity, and it has been proposed that progesterone

Figure 12. Antagonistic Effects of Progesterone in the Uterus
of the Estradiol-primed Fetal Guinea pig

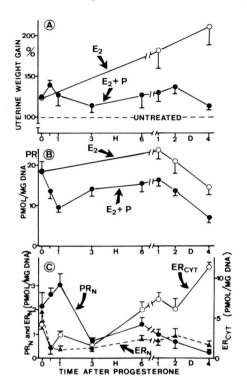

Pregnant guinea pigs were injected subcutaneously with 1 mg of
estradiol (E_2) and 1 day later half of the group received 5 mg
of progesterone ($E_2 + P$). Animals were sacrificed at the indicated times. Receptors were measured as indicated in Figure 6.
Means $\pm$ S.E.

acts by inhibiting the synthesis of the cytosol estrogen receptor and decreasing the concentration of its own receptor (76).
In the fetal guinea pig uterus, progesterone is also capable
of modulating estrogen responses as seen in Figure 12. When
administered to estrogen-primed fetuses, progesterone has no
effect on the initial 21% increase in fetal uterine wet weight
which occurs 1 day after estrogen treatment but it inhibits

any further increase (Figure 12A). Progesterone significantly
diminishes the concentration of its own receptor (Figure 12B)
(77). The mechanism by which progesterone acts in the fetus
appears to involve the nuclear estrogen receptor since progesterone treatment rapidly reduces the concentration of nuclear
estrogen receptor along with the translocation of progesterone
receptor into the nucleus, but has no effect on the replenishment of cytosol estrogen receptor (Figure 12C) (77, 78). The
neonatal guinea pig uterus also responds to progesterone by a
decrease in the estrogen-induced uterotrophic and progesterone
receptor responses but unlike the fetal uterus, cytosol estrogen receptor replenishment is impaired (79, 80).

Progesterone retains its capacity to down-regulate its own
receptor, even under organ culture conditions. The spontaneous
increase in progesterone receptor is completely inhibited by
the addition of progesterone to the medium and reappears upon
its removal (38).

Progesterone is also able to antagonize the estradiol-stimulated
acetylation of histones $H_2 + H_3$ and H_4 (81).

These data show that progesterone modulation of several estrogen responses is already functional in the fetal uterus and involves both the progesterone and the estrogen receptor systems.
In the fetus, progesterone leads to a rapid clearance of estrogen receptor from the nucleus while in the newborn its action
may be directed toward inhibition of cytosol estrogen receptor
synthesis and recycling which also evolves between the pre-
and postnatal ages (79).

X. Conclusions

The experimental data accumulated over the last decade of work
prove the existence of steroid hormone receptors in various

organs of the fetus and also show the evolution in the concentration of receptor during fetal and postnatal development. Further evidence also shows that a good correlation exists between receptor binding nuclear translocation and biological responses elicited by the hormone in the fetus and newborn. The biological responses themselves are sometimes much more intense during fetal life than after birth (e.g. : stimulation of progesterone receptor by estrogens). The fact that gonadal hormone receptors and responses are present during fetal life suggests that many of the processes of the maturation of the reproductive organs are very active during fetal life. Also, since estrogen receptors are present in the fetal hypothalamus and hypophysis, it is possible that the hypothalamo-hypophyseal-gonadal axis is already operational during fetal life. However, the physiological impact of these biological responses during fetal life on puberty or on the reproductive period remains to be explored. "Antiestrogens" are very active estrogen agonists during fetal life, particularly in their uterotrophic action. Concerning the stimulation of the progesterone receptor, antiestrogens are less active than estrogens in the fetus but their effect becomes similar after birth. Finally, after prolonged treatment of newborn animals with either antiestrogens or estrogens, the uterotrophic effect or the stimulation of progesterone receptor observed is similar, thus posing the question of the use of "antiestrogens" during the reproductively active period of life in the case of the treatment of breast cancer.

XI. References

1. Pasqualini, J.R., Sumida, C.: C.R. Acad. Sci. Paris 273, 1061-1063 (1971).
2. Pasqualini, J.R., Palmada, M.: Endocrinology Supp. Vol. 88, A242 (1971).
3. Pasqualini, J.R., Sumida, C., Gelly, C., Nguyen, B.-L.: J. steroid Biochem. 7, 1031-1038 (1976).

4. Pasqualini, J.R., Sumida, C., Gelly, C., Nguyen, B.-L.: J. steroid Biochem. 8, 445-451 (1977).

5. Giannopoulos, G., Mulay, S., Solomon, S.: Biochem. biophys. Res. Commun. 47, 411-418 (1972).

6. Gupta, C., Bloch, E.: Endocrinology 99, 389-399 (1976).

7. King, R.J.B., Mainwaring, W.I.P.:Steroid-Cell Interactions, Butterworth and Co., London, 1974, pp. 210-213.

8. Giambiagi, N., Pasqualini, J.R.: Endocrinology 110, 1067-1069 (1982).

9. Greene, G.L., Closs, L.E., DeSombre, E.R., Jensen, E.V.: J. steroid Biochem. 12, 159-167 (1980).

10. Greene, G.L., Nolan, C., Engler, J.P., Jensen, E.V.: Proc. Natn. Acad. Sci., U.S.A. 77, 5115-5119 (1980).

11. Köhler, G., Milstein, C.: Nature 256, 495-497 (1975).

12. Giambiagi, N., Pasqualini, J.R., Greene, G., Jensen, E.V.: J. steroid Biochem. 20, 397-400 (1984).

13. Pasqualini, J.R., Nguyen, B.-L.: Endocrinology 106, 1160-1165 (1980).

14. Diamond, M., Rust, N., Westphal, U.: Endocrinology 84, 1143-1151 (1969).

15. Castellet, R., Pasqualini, J.R.: C.R. Acad. Sci. Paris 276, 1205-1208 (1973).

16. Millet, A., Pasqualini, J.R.: C.R. Acad. Sci. Paris 287, 1429-1432 (1978).

17. Sumida, C., Pasqualini, J.R.: Endocrinology 105, 406-413 (1979).

18. Gulino, A., Sumida, C., Gelly, C., Giambiagi, N., Pasqualini, J.R.: Endocrinology 109, 748-756 (1981).

19. Sumida, C., Pasqualini, J.R.: J. Receptor Res. 1, 439-457 (1980).

20. Pasqualini, J.R., Sumida, C., Nguyen, B.-L., Gelly, C.: J. steroid Biochem. 9, 443-447 (1978).

21. Vito, C.C., Fox, T.O.: Devel. Brain Res. 2, 97-110 (1982).

22. MacLusky, N.J., Lieberburg, I., McEwen, B.S.: Brain Res. 178, 129-142 (1979).

23. Friedman, W.J., McEwen, B.S., Toran-Allerand, C.D., Gerlach, J.L.: Devel. Brain Res. 11, 19-28 (1983).

24. Screpanti, I., Gulino, A., Pasqualini, J.R.: Endocrinology 111, 1552-1561 (1982).

25. Sömjen, G.J., Kaye, A.M., Lindner, H.R.: Biochim. biophys. Acta 428, 787-791 (1976).

26. Mendelson, C.R., Brown, P.K., MacDonald, P.C., Johnston, J.M.: Endocrinology 109, 210-217 (1981).

27. Stumpf, W.E., Narbaitz, R., Sar, M.: J. steroid Biochem. 12, 55-64 (1980).

28. Narbaitz, R., Stumpf, W.E., Sar, M.: Anat. Embryol. 158, 161-166 (1980).

29. Davies, J., Naftolin, F., Ryan, K.J., Siu, J.: J. clin. Endocr. Metab. 40, 909-912 (1975).

30. Kato, J., Onouchi, T.: Endocrinology 113, 29-36 (1983).

31. Giannopoulos, G., Phelps, D.S., Munowitz, P.: J. steroid Biochem. 17, 503-510 (1982).

32. Corvol, P., Falk, R., Freifeld, M., Bardin, C.W.: Endocrinology 90, 1464-1469 (1972).

33. Feil, P.D., Glasser, S.R., Toft, D.O., O'Malley, B.W.: Endocrinology 91, 738-746 (1972).

34. Gelly, C., Sumida, C., Gulino, A., Pasqualini, J.R.: J. Endocr. 89, 71-77 (1981).

35. Gulino, A., Screpanti, I., Pasqualini, J.R.: Biol. Reprod. 31, 371-381 (1984).

36. Sumida, C., Gelly, C., Pasqualini, J.R.: J. Endocr. 85, 429-434 (1980).

37. Pasqualini, J.R., Sumida, C., Gulino, A.: In, Reproductive Physiology IV, International Review of Physiology, Vol. 27 (R.O. Greep, ed.), University Park Press, Baltimore (1983) pp. 225-273.

38. Sumida, C., Gelly, C., Pasqualini, J.R.: Biochim. biophys. Acta 755, 488-496 (1983).

39. Allfrey, V.G.: In, Cell Biology, Vol. 3 (L. Goldstein and D.M. Prescott, eds.), Academic Press, New York (1980) pp. 347-437.

40 Libby, P.R.: Biochem. J. 130, 663-669 (1972).

41. Pasqualini, J.R., Cosquer-Clavreul, C., Vidali, G., Allfrey, V.G.: Biol. Reprod. 25, 1035-1039 (1981).

42. Cosquer-Clavreul, C., Pasqualini, J.R.: J. steroid Biochem. Abstracts of the VI Intl Congr. Hormonal Steroids, Abst. 21 (1982) vii.

43. Katzenellenbogen, B.S., Gorski, J.: In, Biochemical Actions of Hormones, Vol. III (G. Litwack, ed.), Academic Press, New York (1975) pp. 187-243.

44. Lauré, F., Pasqualini, J.R.: Experientia 39, 209-210 (1983).

45. Sumida, C., Pasqualini, J.R.: Experientia 37, 782-783 (1981).

46. Baum, M.J.: Neurosci. Biobehav. Rev. 3, 265-284 (1979).

47. McEwen, B.S., Biegon, A., Davis, P.G., Krey, L.C., Luine, V.N., McGinnis,M.Y., Paden, C.M., Parsons, B., Rainbow, T.C.: Recent Prog. Hormone Res. 38, 41-92 (1982).

48. Tardy, J., Pasqualini, J.R.: Exp. Brain Res. 49, 77-83 (1983).

49. Knobil, E.: Recent Prog. Hormone Res. 30, 1-46 (1974).

50. Goodman, R.L.: Endocrinology 102, 151-159 (1978).

51. Brown-Grant, K., Sherwood, M.R.: J. Endocr. 49, 277-291 (1971).

52. Goy, R.W., Phoenix, C.H., Meidinger, R.: Anat. Rec. 157, 87-96 (1967).

53. Phoenix, C.H., Goy, R.W., Gerall, A.A., Young, W.C.: Endocrinology 65, 369-382 (1959).

54. Dickey, R.P., Robertson, A.F.: Am. J. Obstet. Gynecol. 104, 551-555 (1969).

55. Khosla, S.S., Gobran, L.I., Rooney, S.A.: Biochim. biophys. Acta 617, 282-290 (1980).

56. Khosla, S.S., Rooney, S.A.: Am. J. Obstet. Gynecol. 133, 213-216 (1979).

57. Gross, I., Wilson, C.M., Ingleson, L.D., Brehier, A., Rooney, S.A.: Biochim. biophys. Acta 575, 375-383 (1979).

58. Gulino, A., Screpanti, I., Pasqualini, J.R.: Endocrinology 113, 1754-1762 (1983).

59. Anderson, J.N., Peck, E.J. Jr., Clark, J.H.: Endocrinology 96, 160-167 (1975).

60. Pasqualini, J.R., Gulino, A., Nguyen, B.-L., Portois, M.C.: J. Receptor Res. 1, 261-275 (1980).

61. Oakey, R.E.: J. steroid Biochem. 11, 1057-1064 (1979).

62. Pasqualini, J.R., Sumida, C., Gelly, C.: Acta Endocr., Copenh. 83, 811-828 (1976).

63. Sumida, C., Gelly, C., Pasqualini, J.R.: Biol. Reprod. 19, 338-345 (1978).

64. Pasqualini, J.R., Lanzone, A., Tahri-Joutei, A., Nguyen, B.-L.: Acta Endocr., Copenh. 101, 630-635 (1982).

65. Ward, H.W.C.: Brit. Med. 1, 13-14 (1973).

66. Mouridsen, H., Palshof, T., Patterson, J., Battersby, L.: Cancer Treat. Rev. 5, 131-141 (1978).

67. Lippman, M., Bolan, G., Huff, K.: Cancer Res. 36, 4595-4601 (1976).

68. Terenius, L.: Acta Endocr., Copenh. 66, 431-447 (1971).

69. Jordan, V.C., Prestwich G.: J. Endocr. 76, 363-364 (1978).

70. Gulino, A., Pasqualini, J.R.: Cancer Res. 40, 3821-3826 (1980).

504

71. Gulino, A., Pasqualini, J.R.: Cancer Res. 42, 1913-1921 (1982).

72. Gulino, A., Pasqualini, J.R.: J. steroid Biochem. 15, 361-367 (1981).

73. Pasqualini, J.R., Nguyen, B.-L.: (unpublished data).

74. Pasqualini, J.R., Sumida, C., Gulino, A., Tardy, J., Nguyen, B.-L., Gelly, C., Cosquer-Clavreul, C.: In, Progesterone and Progestins (C.W. Bardin, E. Milgrom, P. Mauvais-Jarvis, eds.) Raven Press, New York, 1983, pp. 77-90.

75. Pasqualini, J.R., Sumida, C., Gulino, A., Nguyen, B.-L., Tardy, J., Gelly, C.: In, Hormones and Cancer. Progress in Cancer Research and Therapy, Vol. 14 (S. Iacobelli, R.J.B. King, H.R. Lindner, M.E. Lippman, eds.) Raven Press, New York, 1980, pp. 53-64.

76. Clark, J.H., Peck, E.J. Jr.: Female Sex Steroids. Receptors and Function. Monographs on Endocrinology, Vol. 14 (F. Gross, M.M. Grumbach, A. Labhart, M.B. Lipsett, T. Mann, L.T. Samuels, J. Zander, eds.) Springer-Verlag, Berlin, 1979, pp. 99-134.

77. Sumida, C., Gelly, C., Pasqualini, J.R.: J. Receptor Res. 2, 221-232 (1981).

78. Sumida, C., Gelly, C., Pasqualini, J.R.: Steroids 39, 431-444 (1982).

79. Gulino, A., Pasqualini, J.R.: Endocrinology 112, 1871-1873 (1983).

80. Pasqualini, J.R., Gulino, A., Sumida, C., Screpanti, I.: J. steroid Biochem. 20, 121-128 (1984).

81. Pasqualini, J.R., Cosquer-Clavreul, C., Gelly, C.: Biochim. biophys. Acta 739, 137-140 (1983).

Acknowledgements

Part of the expenses of this work was defrayed by the "Centre National de la Recherche Scientifique", France (Equipe de Recherche N° 187) and by grants from C.N.R.S. (ATP N° 955157) and the Fondation pour la Recherche Médicale Française.

STEROID RECEPTOR-DNA INTERACTIONS

S. Anand Kumar, Herbert W. Dickerman
Wadsworth Center for Laboratories and Research

New York State Department of Health
Empire State Plaza
Albany, NY   12201   USA

Introduction

Central to an understanding of the mechanism of action of
steroid hormones is the fact that they are components of
regulatory elements which alter the expression of genes
within target cells. To account for the experimental data, a
pathway of steroid migration evolved which included diffusion
across the cell membrane, binding to high affinity aporecep-
tors in the cytoplasm, translocation following activation of
the steroid holoreceptor to the nucleus and association of
the holoreceptor to effector sites within chromatin of the
target cell. Recently a modification of this scheme emerged,
at least, in the case of estrogen receptors. Unoccupied as
well as occupied receptors were identified in the nuclei of
target cells (1,2). However, this does not alter the fundamental question of steroid hormone modulation of gene expression. Namely, what defines nuclear effector sites as opposed
to those which are ineffective or abortive? Among the potential sites, DNA, alone or in concert with specific chromosomal proteins is of prime importance.

Molecular Mechanism of Steroid Hormone Action
© 1985 Walter de Gruyter & Co., Berlin · New York – Printed in Germany

Steroid hormone receptors were identified as DNA binding
proteins very soon after their identification as key molecules in hormone localization within target cells. This
characteristic led to facile analogies to the prokaryotic
gene regulatory proteins i.e. lac repressor and cAMP binding
protein of Escherichia coli. But receptor binding to DNA was
not saturable nor specific (3-6). Furthermore, experimental
evidence was obtained indicating that chromosomal nonhistone
proteins were the nuclear acceptor sites for chick oviduct
progesterone and uterine estrogen receptors (7-9). This led
to a prevailing concept that the DNA binding property of
receptors was nonselective and could not account for the
specific interactions necessary for the observed alterations
seen in stimulated target cells.

Yet the suspicion persisted that recognition of specific DNA
base sequences was a necessary factor in steroid hormone
action. Fundamental recognition was given to the property
that specific DNA binding proteins bound to all DNA, but to
the "operator" sequences with greater affinity and that the
prevelance of nonspecific binding could obscure the presence
of as many as 10^3 specific sequences using assays containing
unfractionated DNA (4). Subsequently other studies indicated
that estrogen, androgen and glucocorticoid receptors distinguished between polymers of different nucleotide composition
(10-14). If a holoreceptor could distinguish on its binding
between the four composite deoxynucleotide bases of DNA, then
it was possible for the receptor to recognize specific
defined sequences of chromosomal DNA. This culminated in the
important results of Payvar, et al. (15) that purified glucocorticoid holoreceptor bound with increased avidity to
selected sequences of the mouse mammary tumor virus (MMTV)
proviral DNA and these regions were coincident with areas of
the genome essential for hormone regulation of viral gene
expression.

These studies renew the interest in the characteristics of steroid hormone receptors as DNA binding proteins, selective and nonselective.

Non-specific Binding to DNA

Binding to DNA is an intrinsic property of all steroid receptors (16). Several lines of evidence have clearly demonstrated that steroid receptors have distinct domains for steroid and DNA binding. Analogous to prokaryotic gene regulatory proteins, the DNA binding domain becomes function-al as a consequence of the steroid ligand binding to its cognitive site. An allosteric structural transition is postulated to account for the dependence of DNA binding on the prior binding of steroid to its specific site on the receptor (17-19). By partial digestion of the ligand-bound steroid receptors, with proteolytic enzymes, it was demon-strated with estrogen (17,20), progesterone (21,22), and glucocorticoid (23-25) receptors, that the DNA binding property can be selectively destroyed while retaining all the properties of the steroid binding site. DNA-binding and steroid-binding peptides have been also obtained for pro-gesterone receptor by controlled proteolytic digestion (26). The DNA-reactive fragment represented at most ∿20% of the receptor monomer. The spatial arrangement of DNA binding and steroid binding sites is very similar and analogous to the gene regulatory proteins (e.g. cAMP receptor protein) of the prokaryotes.

Although, DNA binding was easily demonstrated, evidence for specificity and relevance to the mode of action, eluded the investigation for a long time. Steroid receptors bind to a variety of DNAs, RNAs, polynucleotides and polyanions. The kinetics of binding is non-saturable (3,6,11) indicating a lack of specificity. Yamamoto and Alberts (5) argued that binding to specific sequences could be masked from detection due to the preponderance of nonspecific interactions. Thus, estrogen receptor was found to bind with equal affinity to rat uterine DNA, E. coli DNA and the synthetic copolymer poly d(A-T). A molar dissociation constant of 0.5 mM DNA sites was calculated from the poly d(A-T) binding data as all the binding sites were equivalent and the concentration of binding sites corresponded to that of base pairs. Similarly, the binding of glucocorticoid receptors to DNA showed no differences in affinity for DNAs from rat hepatoma cells, calf thymus and E. coli (25). However, several investigations have demonstrated that steroid receptors prefer double stranded DNA over single stranded DNA and DNA over RNA (4,9,27-33). In addition there was no binding of estradiol receptor to double stranded reovirus RNA (4) and negligible binding of glucocorticoid receptors to E. coli rRNA (33). These results were interpreted as indications of steroid receptors' selectivity for specific secondary structures of DNA. Support for this interpretation came largely from the studies on the effect of compounds which alter the secondary structures of DNA on steroid receptor binding. The intercalative drugs, ethidium bromide, 9 hydroxyellipticine and actinomycin D, inhibited the binding of estrogen receptor to DNA cellulose. These drugs did not affect the binding of the receptor to other polyanions such as phosphocellulose (10,30). Equilibrium competition and dissociation rate studies showed that estrogen receptor bound bromodeoxyuridine substituted DNA tighter than native DNA (34). Using the rate of transfer of estrogen receptor bound to halogen substituted DNA to native DNA cellulose, as a measure, Kallos et al. (35) demonstrated that the transfer followed an order: unsubstituted DNA > chlorodeoxyuridine- > bromodeoxyuridine- >

iododeoxyuridine-substituted DNA. A correlation between estrogen binding and decreasing electronegativity accompanied by an increase in hydrophobicity was used to indicate that DNA binding of steroid receptors is not due solely to electrostatic interaction with polyanions. Halogen substitution of DNA is known to enhance base stacking and hence a recognition of specific secondary structures of DNA by the steroid receptor was implied by these studies.

Probes for Nucleotide Base Recognition by Steroid Receptors

Although there is a lack of specificity for homologous DNA, it is apparent that the steroid receptor binding to DNA involves a combination of electrostatic, hydrophobic and secondary structure interactions. All gene regulatory proteins bind unproductively to general sites on DNA with a lower affinity than they do for productive binding to sequence specific regulatory sites. The difference between these two binding affinities varies from 2 to 8 or 10 orders of magnitude. Binding to specific sequences on DNA, must be dependent on the intrinsic property of the binding protein to recognize the structures of the component bases of DNA. Synthetic polydeoxyribonucleotides of known base composition and sequence have been used to study this property of a number of prokaryotic gene regulatory proteins. Such studies have also been carried out for steroid receptors. Sluyser et al. (36) studied the binding of estrogen receptors (5s) of calf uterus cytosol to poly dT, poly dA:dT and poly dG:dC. Exclusion from Sepharose 2B was used as an assay for monitoring the formation of the polynucleotide steroid receptor complex. Poly dA:dT, poly dT and poly dG:dC bound significantly more receptor than calf thymus DNA. A more recent study (37) examined the binding of partially purified gluco-

corticoid receptors to natural and synthetic polynucleotides.
The binding was strongly base composition dependent, with
double stranded or denatured DNA$_s$ > E. coli rRNA > poly
d(A):dT $\geq$ poly d (A, T, G)$_7$ $\geq$ poly U > poly A:U > poly A >
poly C as determined by competition between the formation of
complexes with synthetic polynucleotides and binding to DNA
cellulose. Using the same competition assay, Kallos &
Hollander (10) showed that the copolymers, poly (dA-dT) and
poly (dG-dC), were better competitors than single stranded
homopolymers or homopolymer duplexes. In this assay, poly
d(A-T) was the most effective competitor for binding of
estrogen receptor to DNA cellulose. Similar studies with
androgen receptors indicated that dihydrotestosterone
receptor bound more to poly d(G-C) than poly d(A-T) (38).

Although these studies indicated that steroid receptors have
preferences for binding to synthetic polymers, their ability
to recognize nucleotide base structures could not be
inferred. The polynucleotides employed were heterogeneous
with respect to their size and secondary structure. A method
for analyzing the base recognition characteristics of steroid
receptors was developed (11) based on a report by Thrower et
al. (39) who showed that estradiol receptor complexes bound
to oligo (dT) cellulose in a manner analogous to their interaction with DNA-cellulose. While estradiol receptor could
bind to oligo (dT) cellulose, neither the high affinity-low
capacity estrogen binding α-fetoprotein nor the low affinity-
high capacity serum albumin (11) did, indicating a characteristic property of the steroid receptors. Oligodeoxynucleotide celluloses offer several advantages for use as affinity
matrixes. They are relatively homogeneous in length and are
attached to cellulose through their 5' termini, giving the
oligonucleotides a directional polarity. The covalent
attachment to cellulose overcomes the problem of dissociation

of ligand from the cellulose under experimental conditions.
The interference of secondary structure differences is
minimal because of the short length of oligonucleotides and
their attachment to cellulose.

Effect of Salt Concentration on Steroid Receptor Binding to
Oligonucleotide Celluloses

Binding of steroid receptors to oligodeoxynucleotide celluloses showed a typical bell-shaped dependence on salt concentration. The salt dependency of binding varied significantly
among the steroid receptors. While estradiol receptors bound
optimally in a broad range of monovalent cation concentrations (0.05 to 0.15 M KCl), the activated dexamethasone
receptors showed a sharp optimum at 0.1 M KCl and with testosterone receptors, binding was maximal at low concentrations (< 0.05 M) of KCl. (10,14). However, the binding of
all steroid receptors to oligonucleotide celluloses decreased
at salt concentrations higher than 0.2 M. Salt-dependence is
a characteristic property of protein : DNA interactions
including the cAMP receptor protein (40), lac repressor and
other gene regulatory proteins (41). The salt dependence is
indicative of large electrostatic interactions between the
binding domains of DNA and protein. The binding is presumed
to be entropically driven by the counterion diffusion potential. The binding of estrogen receptor to the oligodeoxynucleotide celluloses was sensitive to the type of monovalent
anions. Anions which promoted the order structure of water
were favorable for binding while those which disrupted this
structure were unfavorable. Significant differences were
observed in the binding of estradiol receptor to oligo (dT)-
and oligo (dG)- celluloses in the presence of various anions.
The binding of estradiol receptor to oligo (dG) cellulose was

less sensitive to I^-, ClO_4^- and SCN^- than to oligo (dT) cellulose. The sensitivity of _lac_ repressor to chaotropic anions for binding to DNA is believed to be due to conformational changes in the DNA binding domain of the repressor protein. The differences in the sensitivity of estradiol receptor to chaotropic anions for binding to oligo (dT) and oligo (dG) celluloses may represent the variations in the conformational changes induced by the anions in subsites of the DNA binding domain of the steroid receptors.

Preferences of Steroid Receptors for Binding to Oligonucleotides

A comparison of estradiol receptor binding to homologous oligodeoxynucleotides of equal average length attached to cellulose, showed that the order of affinity was oligo (dG) > oligo (dT) > oligo (dC) >> oligo (dA) > oligo (dI) (13,42) (Fig. 1). Androgen and glucocorticoid receptors also showed similar binding preferences although there were significant quantitative differences (14). Temperature-activated glucocorticoid receptor binding to oligo (dT) cellulose was markedly greater than to oligo (dC), while testosterone receptors showed no differences between oligo (dT) and oligo (dC). Binding of testosterone receptors to oligo (dA) cellulose was relatively better than that of estradiol or dexamethasone receptor (14). Association constants for estradiol receptor-oligodeoxynucleotide cellulose complexes were determined by the technique described by de Haseth et al. (43). The method employed a small column of the oligodeoxynucleotide cellulose (1 ml) to which was applied a sample of the cytosol estradiol receptor complexes. The protein was eluted from the column by passage of a buffer of constant salt concentration (0.15 M NaCl). Association constants were

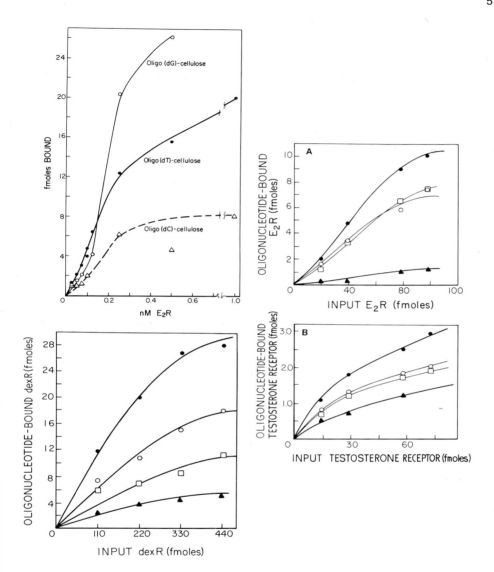

Figure 1. Binding of Steroid receptors to oligonucleotide
celluloses: (Top left), mouse uterine estrogen receptor
(46); (Top right), mouse kidney estrogen receptor (14);
(Bottom left), activated dexamethosone receptor (14);
(Bottom right) mouse kidney testosterone receptor (14).

calculated from the elution data by using the equation K^{RD}_{Obsd} = $V_f/_kD_t$ where V_f is the volume of the fraction and D_t is the total molar amount of nucleotides on the column. k was obtained from the slope of the semilogarithmic plot of the receptor protein remaining on the column after fraction i (P_{ci}) versus the fraction number. The association constants reflect the relative affinities of estradiol receptors for the oligonucleotide celluloses (Table 1). The observed

---

Table 1

Apparent association constants for mouse uterine

estradiol receptor . oligodeoxynucleotide complexes

Oligodeoxynucleotide	Apparent $K^{RD}_{0.15}$ M NaCl
oligo(dG)	$3.7 \times 10^4 M^{-1}$
oligo(dT)	$1.75 \times 10^4 M^{-1}$
oligo(dC)	$1.49 \times 10^4 M^{-1}$

---

values are comparable to the constant determined by Yamamoto and Alberts (4) for estradiol receptor binding to DNA. The binding pattern of estrogen receptor protein labeled with steroid or nonsteroid estrogens or antiestrogens, also showed the same selectivity (42).

The subsites of the polynucleotide binding domain of estrogen receptors were further characterized. Exposure of estrogen holoreceptor to elevated temperatures (37° for 10-30 min.) caused a rapid loss of binding to oligo (dT)- and oligo (dC)-, without affecting the binding to oligo (dG)- cellulose (13). Dissociation of the bound estrogen receptor from

oligodeoxynucleotide celluloses, by increasing concentrations
of KCl, or by cibacron blue F3GA showed that oligo (dG) bound
estrogen receptor was more stable than the receptor bound to
oligo (dC)- and (dT)-celluloses. The formation of the oligodeoxynucleotide cellulose - estrogen receptor complexes was
inhibited by cibacron blue F3GA, pyridoxal phosphate, and
diethyl pyrocarbonate. These studies showed that higher
concentrations of the compounds were necessary to inhibit the
formation of receptor-oligo (dG) cellulose complexes, than
for complexes with other oligodeoxynucleotide celluloses
(44,45). Competition for receptor binding to the insoluble
oligo (dT) cellulose matrix by the soluble oligomer was
efficient if the soluble oligomer contained 8 or more
nucleotides and was more pronounced with the homologous oligo
(dT) than with the heterologous oligo (dG). These observations led to the suggestion that the polynucleotide binding
domain of estrogen receptor is composed of two classes of
subsites: stable sites which bind to deoxyguanylate (G
sites) and relatively labile sites which interact with other
nucleotides (N sites) (19,46).

Activation of Steroid Receptors to Bind Oligodeoxynucleotide
Celluloses

It is generally believed that cytosol steroid receptors
undergo a temperature or high salt-mediated change in conformation which facilitates their migration to the nucleus
and binding to the nuclear acceptor sites. This generalization is not applicable to DNA and oligodeoxynucleotide
binding properties. While the glucocorticoid receptors
require activation to bind in vitro to DNA, other steroid
receptors do not (4). Studies on oligodeoxynucleotide
cellulose binding properties of steroid receptors clearly

showed that no significant increase in binding was observed due to preincubation of the estrogen and testosterone receptors at temperatures 18-37°C or with high salt concentrations. However glucocorticoid receptors without activation were minimally bound to oligodeoxynucleotide celluloses. Exposure to 0.5 M KCl for 30 min or preincubation at 22° for 30 min resulted in a 6 to 12 fold increase over the unactivated controls (14) (Fig. 2). The binding of glucocorticoid receptors to oligodeoxynucleotides following an activation process is consistent with the activation of these receptors for binding to nuclear acceptor sites or to DNA. The absence of such an activation step for other steroid receptors to bind either DNA or polynucleotides or oligodeoxynucleotides was reported by a number of laboratories (4,39,42,47).

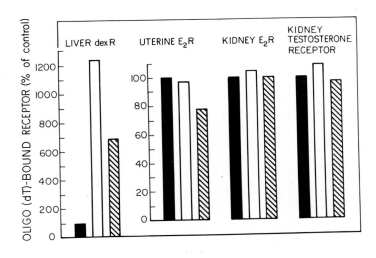

Figure 2. Activation requirements of steroid receptors for binding to oligodeoxynucleotide celluloses (14).

Binding of Steroid Receptors to Polyribonucleotides

Although steroid receptors bind preferentially to DNA, significant binding to RNA and polyribonucleotides can be demonstrated. King (48) showed that uterine estrogen receptor
bound to polynucleotides with an order of preference where
poly (rG) >> poly (rC) > poly (rA) > poly (rI). Liao et al.
(12) determined the relative affinities of steroid receptors
for the polyribonucleotides by their effectiveness in
releasing the steroid receptors bound to DNA-cellulose. Poly
(rG) was the most effective polynucleotide in this assay for
androgen, estrogen, glucocorticoid and progesterone receptors. Poly (rU) was about half as effective as poly (rG),
but poly (rC) and poly (rA) were almost ineffective. More
recently Feldman et al. (49) confirmed these studies and
demonstrated that in inhibiting the binding of estrogen
receptor to DNA the order of affinity was, poly (rG) > poly
(rU) >> poly (rA) = poly (rC).

It is, thus, evident that steroid receptors recognize different nucleotide base structures. All steroid receptors
have the highest affinity for guanine, the lowest for adenine
and intermediate affinities for pyrimidines.

Role of Accessory Proteins

Although many lines of evidence have clearly demonstrated
that steroid receptors bind to specific sites on the DNA, the
available evidence has not established that this binding is
solely responsible for the regulation of expression of
specific genes. The kinetics of binding is not consistent
with the proposed regulatory role. There are several reports
supporting the concept that functional binding of steroid

receptors to genomic DNA requires additional nuclear proteins [see review by Spelsberg et al.(50)]. Complete removal of histones and the bulk of nonhistone proteins from chick oviduct chromatin resulted in a fraction containing a few tightly bound proteins. This structure designated NAP was a more physiologic template for P-R binding than native chromatin or deproteinized DNA (51) in that receptor binding followed saturation kinetics and reflected the specificity of origin of the chromatin from target and nontarget tissues. Examination of progesterone receptor (P-R) binding following sequential removal of proteins from chromatin revealed that removal of histones and bulk of nonhistone proteins, which yielded a fraction (CP-3) containing nucleoacidic proteins (NAP) tightly bound to DNA with enhanced P-R binding. Similar findings were also reported for androgen receptor-rat prostate chromatin (52) and for estrogen receptors in the calf-uterine chromatin (53). In non-target tissues such as the spleen and the erythrocyte which show little P-R binding, removal of histones and the bulk of nonhistone proteins, increased binding indicating that may be involved in masking acceptor sites in non-target tissues. The proteins of CP-3 fraction did not bind to P-R directly. However, the reconstituted complex of CP-3 proteins with DNA showed marked binding of P-R (50,54,55). Further fractionation of the CP-3 proteins by molecular sieve chromatography using 6M guanidine hydrochloride buffered at pH 6, resulted in two fractions which promoted enhanced binding of P-R to DNA. These proteins were characterized as small molecular weight (13-18 k Da) and hydrophobic in nature (50). Monoclonal antibodies raised against these proteins blocked progesterone receptor binding to chromatin or to the NAP-DNA complex (56). DNA sequences which are tightly bound to the CP-3 proteins are a class of intermediate repetitive DNA (Spelsberg, personal communication). The significance of these sites in the productive binding of P-R remains to be elucidated.

In addition to the nuclear proteins, which upon binding to
specific sites on genomic DNA enhance steroid receptor binding to such sites, there are cytosol proteins which also
stimulate steroid binding to immobilized DNA or synthetic
nucleotide polymers. Thrower et al. (39) showed that addition of uterine cytosol to Sephadex gel filtered uterine
cytosolic estrogen receptors stimulated binding of the receptors to oligo (dT) cellulose. Thanki et al. (57) detected a
need for cytosol factors for mouse kidney estrogen receptor
eluted from oligo (dT) cellulose column, to rebind fresh
oligo (dT) cellulose. It appeared that during the adsorption
and desorption of estrogen receptor(s) from oligo (dT) cellulose, an accessory factor or factors remained bound to the
affinity matrix. One factor was shown to be heat-stable,
nondialyzable, sensitive to pronase, proteinase K, pepsin and
Staph.aureus protease V, but resistant to trypsin or chymo-
trpysin. Such factors were present in cytosols from kidney
uterus and lung but not in brain and skeletal muscle cytosols. The heat-stable factor was effective with all oligonucleotide celluloses as binding matrices. Prior incubation
with the matrices also stimulated receptor binding and there
was no indication that the factors directly reacted with the
holoreceptor. The role of such factors in specific binding
to DNA is unknown at this time.

During our studies on the accessory proteins for the binding
of estrogen receptor to oligodeoxynucleotide celluloses, it
was observed that basic proteins such as lysozyme and calf
thymus histones increased the rebinding of partially purified
holoreceptor to oligo(dT) cellulose. Fox et al. (58) also
found that estrogen and androgen receptors bound more strongly to DNA cellulose in the presence of lysozymes. Thanki et
al. (57) demonstrated that H2A, H2B and H3 were most effective while the lysine-rich H1 was inactive. Polylysine and

520

γ-globulin were ineffective. Addition of individual histones to a 200-fold purified mouse kidney estrogen receptor complex resulted in the stabilization of the steroid bound to the receptor. H2A and H2B were most effective, H1 and H3 were less effective while lysozyme and γ-globulin were ineffective. Histone H2B was cleaved by cyanogen bromide into a N-terminal half containing 32% of the residues as basic amino acids and the C-terminal half which contained 20% of its residues as basic amino acids. Both N-terminal and C-terminal half molecules were tested for their ability to stimulate the oligo (dT)-cellulose binding of estrogen holo-receptor. The N-terminal half was more active than the C-terminal half, while the mixture of N- and C-terminal half produced an intermediate effect (Fig. 3).

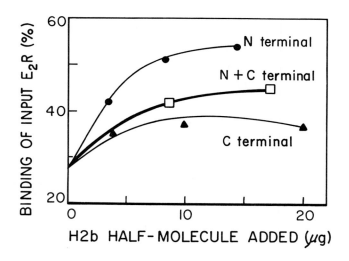

Figure 3. Effect of N- and C-terminal half molecules of H2B on oligo (dT) cellulose binding of estradiol receptor (57).

The N-terminal half of H2B stabilized the 4S species of the holoreceptor while addition of the C-terminal half led to the marked aggregation of receptor protein (Fig. 4). Kallos et al. (59) observed that rabbit uterine cytosol receptors bound to the immobilized histones with the affinity order; H2B > H2A >> H4 >H3 >>> H1. Formation of a complex between estrogen receptors and histones was shown by a shift in the isoelectric point to higher pH values. The presence of a distinct binding site, separate from estrogen and polynucleotide binding domains, was detected by limited proteolysis. In the partially digested estrogen receptor DNA binding of the receptor was markedly reduced while steroid and histone binding were unaffected. Thus, it appears that estrogen receptors have a site(s) for selective binding of nucleosomal histones or similar cationic proteins. Digestion of nuclei containing radio-labeled estrogen receptors, followed by density gradient centrifugation indicated that the radio-activity was primarily associated with the mononucleosomal fractions which contained H2A, H2B, H3 and H4 histones but not H1 (60,61). These observations may indicate a specific role for the histones in the nuclear positioning of the receptor molecules.

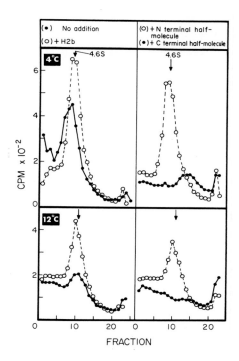

Figure 4. Stabilization of estrogen holoreceptor by the N- and C-terminal half molecules of H2B (57).

The effect of histone H2B on oligodeoxynucleotide binding properties of estrogen receptors also indicated another interesting feature. When uterine cytosolic estrogen receptor complexes were bound to the immobilized oligodeoxynucleotides and subsequently eluted with 0.5 M KCl, the receptor complexes obtained were incapable of binding to oligo (dT), oligo (dC) and oligo (dA), while retaining the binding to oligo (dG) at reduced levels. Addition of H2B to this preparation fully restored the binding to all the oligonucleotide celluloses in the order seen with crude estrogen receptors (Table 2). This property may reflect the ability of histones or histone-like cationic proteins to modulate the recognition capabilities of the DNA-binding domain of steriod receptors in general, and estrogen receptors in particular.

Table 2

Rebinding of E_2R eluted from oligo(dT)- and oligo(dG)-cellulose complexes to oligodeoxynucleotide-celluloses

	% bound of input E_2R			
	E_2R off oligo(dT)-cellulose		E_2R off oligo(dG)-cellulose	
Cellulose	-H2B	+H2B	-H2B	+H2B
Oligo(dG)	18	33	21	32
Oligo(dA)	0	6	0	6
Oligo(dC)	0	12	0	14
Oligo(dT)	0	22	1	23

E_2R oligo(dG)- or oligo(dT)-cellulose complexes were formed under standard binding assay conditions. Elution of Bound E_2R was achieved by using 0.5 M KCl. Samples (0.2 ml) of the eluates were used in the rebinding assay with fresh oligodeoxynucleotide-celluloses in a total volume of 0.6 ml so that the final concentration of KCl was 0.15 M. H2B was added to the rebinding assay at 50 µg where indicated.

Steroid Receptor Recognition of Specific DNA Sequences

The demonstration that steroid hormone receptors could discriminate between nucleotide bases indicated that specific
DNA base sequence recognition was a possible step in hormone
action. However, it remained for the tumultuous developments
in the role of glucocorticoids as inducers of mouse mammary
tumor virus (MMTV) transcription before a detailed analysis
of this interaction was forthcoming. Studies indicated that
addition of glucocorticoid to proviral containing cells
increased the rate of MMTV DNA transcription after short
periods of exposure (62). Furthermore, specific fractions of
MMTV DNA were enough to mediate a glucocorticoid hormone
response when transformed into glucocorticoid receptor containing cells (63). Exogenous MMTV DNA not integrated into
the host cell chromosome also was capable of response to the
hormone. These experiments indicated that the viral DNA was
sufficient for hormone responsiveness and that host DNA was
not involved (65,66).

These findings set the stage for a detailed search for the
glucocorticoid receptor effector region within the proviral
DNA. Fasel et al. (65) cleaved the MMTV genome with restriction endonucleases and recovered a 1.45 kb segment containing
the long terminal repeat region (LTR) and a small coding
region. They transfected this cloned product along with a
plasmid containing the herpes simplex virus gene for thymidine kinase (tk) into mouse L cells which were tk$^-$. The
recipient transformants were tk$^+$ when grown in the presence
of glucocorticoids. An in vivo assay is now available for
determining what part of the MMTV genome contained the hormone responsive region.

Hynes and her coworkers (66) constructed chimera of the MMTV
LTR and a HSV tk coding segment. They were able to produce

nucleotide deletions at defined distances 5' to the RNA
synthesis initiation or CAP site (penultimate 5' end of mRNA
at which methylguanosine residue is attached). In the transformed cells, RNA synthesis was correctly initiated from the
LTR promoter termination in the rightward tk coding region.
Among the deletions, those with the sequences from -137 to
-202 were responsive to glucocorticoids while those whose LTR
segments ended at -50 or -37 relative to the LTR CAP site
were not. This indicated that a limited region of the LTR
sequence was sufficient for response. Similar experiments by
Buetti and Diggelmann(67) indicated that the sequence from
-105 to -204 was necessary for the hormone response.
Although the correct truncated LTR was sufficient, these
investigators found that sequences between -204 to -600
increased the amplitude of response suggesting multiple
weaker sites of control, upstream of the primary response
site. When the -105 mutant was used in the transfection, the
basal level of correctly initiated transcripts was nearly the
same as that seen with the entire MMTV DNA. The glucocorticoid receptor effector region of DNA was clearly separate
from those nucleotides comprising the LTR transcriptional
promoter. Further alterations of the chimeric clone (68)
including addition of 4 exogenous base pairs or deletion of
20 base pairs at position -107 or substitution of the rat
sarcoma virus LTR for that of MMTV at position -59 to +100
had no effect on glucocortocoid responsiveness.

Analysis of the above studies indicated that a limited
sequence within the MMTV LTR was necessary for glucocorticoid
responsiveness but the position of this segment had no fixed
spatial distance from the transcriptional promoter and the
response region could be dissociated from a weak but functional promotor, suggesting that a specific protein-protein
contact with RNA polymerase II was not an essential ingredient for the receptor effect. The immediate consequence of

526

receptor interaction was proposed to be a local change in chromatin configuration and/or production of a facile entry site for RNA polymerase II or accessory transcriptional factors.

A complementary line of research was initiated by the finding of Payvar and his coworkers (15). They found selective binding of rat liver glucocorticoid holoreceptor, purified 10^4 fold, to be restricted to selected regions of the pro-viral DNA, some within the LTR region and some in coding regions of the viral genome. Scheidereit et al. (70) using the defined LTR deletion constructs of the LTR ∿ HSV Tk chimera introduced by Hynes et al. (66) studied the binding of 2 species of rat glucocorticoid holoreceptor, a 90 K and a 40 K molecule. Both species were alike in their preferential binding to MMTV DNA. If the chimeric DNA contained segments including nucleotide -202 relative to the CAP site or more sequences 5' upstream from that position, there was selective binding. If they included sequences -50 or less, there was no binding. Complexes of the 90 K receptor: DNA were recovered by immunoprecipitation using monoclonal antibodies directed against the non-DNA binding portions of the receptor and it did not matter whether purified receptor or a crude cytosol preparation was used.

These data suggested that non-receptor cytosol components were not essential for selective receptor binding but acti-vation of the glucocorticoid receptor was necessary, as $NaMoO_4$ prevented the interaction. Of paramount importance was the determination that a region of the MMTV LTR from -50 to -202 was the binding site which was the same area defined as the hormone response region in transformation experiments.

Having established a segment of the LTR DNA as a preferential binding target for glucocorticoid holoreceptor, it remained for Scheidereit and Beato (70) to pinpoint the contact points for the receptor within this segment. Using a combination of chemical and enzymatic probes, they established that there were four binding sites in a sequence from -72 to -192 nucleotides 5' to the CAP site. At these sites they found:

a) In the receptor: DNA complex, several guanine residues were protected against methylation by dimethyl sulfate. At the 4 sites, the protected residues were found in a common sequence:

$$5' \ T \ G \ T \quad T \ C \ T \ 3'$$
$$3' \ A \ C \ A \quad A \ G \ A \ 5'$$

The protection at the 4 sites increased with rising receptor concentrations. Hypermethylation of other bases also occured within the complex.

b) Binding to the sites occured independently but cooperative amplification was possible.

c) Methylation of a limited number of guanine residues abolished glucocorticoid holoreceptor binding. In the sense strand the guanine residue at -174 and in the antisense strand those at -171 and -180 were the bases most protected against methylation in the receptor: DNA complex.

d) No clear cut effects of protection or inhibition were observed in adenine residues.

e) Among the four sites, that at the most upstream position demonstrated greater avidity for the holoreceptor than the others. But at the lowest receptor concentrations, all sites bound receptor.

f) The protected guanine residues within the complex were separated from each other by 10 $\pm$ 1 nucleotide pairs. Since it is the N7 position of guanine which is methylated and it is exposed in G:C pairs of the major groove of the helix, the investigators concluded that points of maximal contact of the receptor were on the same face of

the helix at two guanine residues in the major groove
separated by 2 full consecutive turns.

A comparison of other glucocorticoid regulated genes 5'
flanking sequence indicated either similar binding specificity or sequence homologies. In the cloned gene of h
metallothionein II under regulation by the hormone as well as
cadmium, there was one strong binding site; located at -245
to -265 from the CAP site. Sequence analysis of those
regions protected against DNase I digestion by bound glucocorticoid holoreceptor (footprinting) yielded a sequence
containing 5' TGTTCT 3' common in digestion patterns of the
protected MMTV LTR region at two strong binding sites. The
5' flanking regions of tryptophan oxygenase and tyrosine
transaminase (73,74) have also been sequenced yielding the
homologous areas at positions relatively equivalent to the
transcriptional initiation of MMTV i.e. 5' TXAGTTCT 3'. The
near identical sequence in four glucocorticoid regulated
genes strongly suggest a primary recognition template for the
binding of the holoreceptor. Yet differences in the kinetics
of induction, multiplicity of sites, etc. indicate that additional factors may be important in each case.

Other steroid regulated genes studied at the level of holoreceptor interaction with control regions of defined DNA
sequences are those of the chick oviduct egg white proteins.
Compton and his coworkers (74) found purified progesterone
receptor subunit A, derived from mature hen oviducts, preferentially bound to cloned fragments of the ovalbumin gene.
They used the retention of receptor bound DNA on nitrocellulose filters as a measure of binding with subsequent elution
and electrophoresis as a means of identification of the DNA
fragment. An interesting detail of their work was that the
receptor did not distinguish between specific and nonspecific

DNA at low temperatures; following incubation at 37°C, the A subunit bound selectively to a small fragment of the ovalbumin gene compared to a larger plasmid fragment or a 6 molar excess of chicken α globin gene sequences. The ovalbumin fragment used was OV 1.7 which contained 1,338 nucleotides of the 5' flanking region and 589 nucleotides of coding sections. These authors estimated that there was a 10 fold difference in affinity of binding to specific as opposed to nonspecific sequences.

Using an alternative means of assay, Mulvihill and her coworkers (75) found selective binding of progesterone receptor to several cloned segments of the egg white proteins including ovalbumin, conalbumin, ovomucoid, the X and Y pseudogenes. These workers measured the displacement of holoreceptor from nonspecific calf thymus DNA cellulose by effective gene segment competitors. Crude or partially purified progesterone receptor, subunit A, were about the same in their binding descrimination with maximal interaction occuring at 0.05 - 0.08 M KCl or NaCl. At lower ionic strengths, the receptors aggregated and at higher ionic strengths, they dissociated from the DNA. The DNA cellulose assay is a measure of equillibrium binding while the nitrocellulose filter assay determines the rate of association of the holoreceptor to DNA. Deletion mutants were constructed from a 1.7 kb cloned segment including the 5' flanking region of the ovalbumin gene by successive digestions with exonuclease III and S1 nuclease or Bal 31 exonuclease. These deletions demonstrated 3 binding regions existing with a 40 fold increase in relative binding affinity. When a computer analysis, set at a cut off of 60% homology, was made of the 14 kb known sequences of egg white proteins a consensus 19 base pair sequence was identified 42 times in the overall group of genes. The sequence is:

$$A\ T\ C\ {C \atop T}\ {C \atop T}\ A\ T\ T\ {A \atop T}\ T\ C\ T\ G\ {G \atop T}\ T\ T\ G\ T\ A$$

Of the segments containing the homologous sequence, 41 of 42 were selective binding templates. The fidelity of the putative binding sequence is however a matter of current research.

In another study (77) the purified A subunit of oviduct progesterone receptor was found preferentially complexed to a segment of the 5' flanking region of the ovalbumin gene -135 to -247 relative to the transcriptional initiation site. The elucidation of steroid control of ovalbumin expression suffered because a lack of an in vivo transfection assay of biological responsiveness similar to the MMTV LTR-HSV tk chimeric transformants in tk -L cells. Recently, Dean et al. (78,79) linked the 5' flanking region of the ovalbumin including the transcriptional start site to a segment of the β-globin gene and an SV40 early gene under its own control (pSV-OG). In transfected primary oviduct cells, they found that the 5' flanking region -95 to -221 was needed for steroid enhancement but not for basal levels of synthesis. Again deletion mutants of the construct were used to define the effector region. Estrogen and progesterone were effective in increasing transcription of these chimeras. They concluded on the basis of individual hormone effects on a series of deletions that progesterone and estrogen had overlapping effector sites or they were in close proximity. However, this may be more complex as the authors state in a preliminary note that when the 5' flanking region of ovalbumin is spliced to a heterologous promoter and the chimera is transfected, it is progesterone sensitive and estrogen insensitive.

Finally, other genomic segments have been used to transform recipient cells and have maintained hormonal response -- these include $\alpha_2\mu$ globulin (80), growth hormone (81,82), lysozyme gene (83), tryptophan oxygenase (84) and prostatic steroid binding protein (85) segments. The structural determinants of receptor binding and hormone response should be forthcoming in the near future.

Conclusion

This chapter has recounted the shift of the pendulum regarding steroid hormone receptors interaction with DNA. From a questionable importance because of the nonspecific and nonsaturable character of the binding to the determination that receptor binding and hormone response is based on the presence of a limited, defined sequence present in the 5' flanking region of numerous steriod regulated genes. Our focus has been on the role of steroid hormone receptors as DNA nucleotide sequence recognition proteins, analogous to the myriad of prokaryotic genomic regulatory proteins i.e. lac repressor, cAMP binding protein. The analogy is compounded by the evidence that:

1. The steroid- and DNA binding sites of steroid receptors are spatially separated.
2. Binding of the receptor to DNA is modulated by their binding of small ligand molecules.
3. Steroid hormone receptor action is sensitive to inhibitors which modify cationic amino acids at the putative DNA binding sites.
4. Steroid hormone receptor binding to DNA is sensitive to agents which restructure the secondary structure at the template binding site.

Underlying the biological importance of interaction with a
particular sequence heterogeneity is the ability of the steroid holoreceptor to discriminate among the nucleotide bases
within the helix. Numerous studies using homologous or
heterologous polyribonucleotides, polydeoxyribonucleotides
and oligodeoxynucleotides indicating that steroid holorecep-
tors have common nucleotide base preferences for binding.
These are dG or G > dT or U > dC or C >, dA or A. Perhaps
the real meaning of all the nucleic acid, native and
synthetic, binding studies are that receptors possess
capabilities of interacting in particular ways with each of
these bases in a distinct manner. An indication of the
potential biological meaning of these affinities is the
critical role that the three dG base residues play in the
binding of glucocorticoid receptors to sequences flanking the
promoters of MMTV and h metallothionein II transcription.
Obviously, this clone is insufficient to explain the
specificity of interaction for there are numerous regions
containing dG residues on the same face of helix at two
consecutive turns. But it does underlie the anchoring role
that dG residues play in the receptor:specific sequence
interaction.

Two other aspects of DNA interaction may come to the fore as
purified participants are studied. First that the DNA
binding site of steroid receptors contain subsites - some
stable and others malleable. The latter probably are of
critical importance in deciphering the specific binding/
effector sequence. Secondly, the latter malleable sites are
subject to allosteric modulation by neighboring chromosomal
proteins. The pendulum has swung very far from the time when
chromosomal proteins were considered the nuclear acceptor
sites for steroid receptors but the protein composition
surrounding the DNA binding sequence is probably of crucial
importance -- in defining permissive or nonpermissive

chromatin targets, stabilizing or destabilizing steroid receptor:specific nucleotide sequence interactions, blocking access to binding sites within the genome or modulating regulatory areas near the genome, i.e. enhancer-like elements, independent of the receptor binding sites which are sensitive to receptor : DNA complexation. In this regard, the evidence that tightly bound nonhistone proteins of chick oviduct chromatin are required for the saturation kinetics and target cell specificity of progesterone receptor binding.

Chromatin alteration is currently visualized as an important early consequence of steroid receptor : DNA interaction. Zaret and Yamamoto (85) found that a single DNase 1 site was hypersensitive within a chimeric construct of MMTV LTR-HSV tk transfected into tk⁻ L cells. The sensitivity of the site to nuclease increased with exposure of the recipient cells to dexamethasone and rescinded with withdrawal of the hormone. Other sites were more modestly sensitive to DNase 1 digestion with hormone addition but remained so despite hormone depletion. These authors defined three classes of chimera chromatin structure a constitutive hypersensitive site, as well as irreversible and reversible inducible hypersensitive sites. The latter coincide closely with the region of receptor binding and hormone responsiveness in transformed cells. The importance of chromatin structure, as a determinent or consequence of hormone action, may be more approachable with the finding of Ostrowski and his coworkers (86) that chimeric plasmids of MMTV LTR and the transforming fragment of bovine papiloma virus type 1 can transform cells with as many as 200 copies of the chimeric molecules per diploid genomes. These are unintegrated, extrachromosomal episomes which are sensitive to glucocorticoid hormone regulation through sites in the MMTV LTR segment. Of most importance, they exist as mini-chromosomes which putatively contain the accessory

534

chromosomal proteins with a role in hormone receptor nuclear action. This probably represents an important step forward to the ultimate goal of a complete in vitro transcriptional system under steroid hormone control.

Research work in the authors' laboratories has been supported by grants from the New York State Health Research, Inc. (BRS 35074), National Institutes of Health (AM 23075; HD 18406) and National Science Foundation (PCM 7825517).

References

1. King, W.J., Greene, G.L.: Nature 307, 745-747 (1984).
2. Welshons, W.V., Lieberman, M.E., Gorski, J.: Nature 307, 747-749 (1984).
3. Chamness, G.C., Jennings, A.W., McGuire, W.L.: Biochemistry 13, 327-331 (1974).
4. Yamamoto, K.R., Alberts, B.M.: J. Biol. Chem. 249, 7076-7077 (1974).
5. Yamamoto, K.R., Alberts, B.M.: Cell 4, 301-310 (1975).
6. Andre, J., Rochefort, H.: FEBS Lett. 50, 319-323 (1975).
7. O'Malley, B.W., Spelsberg, T.C., Schrader, W.T., Chytel, F., Steggles, A.W.: Nature 235, 141-145 (1972).
8. Puca, G.A., Sica, V., Nola, E.: Proc. Natl. Acad. Sci., U.S.A. 71, 979-983 (1974).
9. Spelsberg, T.C., Webster, R.A., Pikler, G.M.: Nature 262, 65-67 (1976).
10. Kallos, J., Hollander, V.P.: Nature 272, 177-179 (1978).
11. Thanki, K.H., Beach, T.A., Dickerman, H.W.: J. Biol. Chem. 253, 7744-7750 (1978).
12. Liao, S., Smythe, S., Tymoczko, J.L., Rossini, G.P., Chen, C., Hiipakka, R.A.: J. Biol. Chem. 255, 5545-5551 (1980).

13. Kumar, S.A., Beach, T.A., Dickerman, H.W.: Proc. Natl. Acad. U.S.A. 77, 3341-3345 (1980).

14. Gross, S., Kumar, S.A., Dickerman, H.W.: J. Biol. Chem. 257, 4738 (1982).

15. Payvar, F., Wränge, O., Carlstedt-Duke, J., Okret, S., Gustafsson, J.A., Yamamoto, K.: Proc. Natl. Acad. Sci. U.S.A. 78, 6628-6632 (1981).

16. Yamamoto, K.R., Alberts, B.: Ann. Rev. Biochem. 45, 721-746 (1976).

17. Andre, J., Rochefort, H.: FEBS Lett. 29, 135-140 (1973).

18. Turnell, R.W., Kaiser, N., Milholland, R.J., Rosen, F.: J. Biol. Chem. 249, 1133-1138 (1974).

19. Kumar, S.A., Dickerman, H.W.: Biochemical Actions of Hormones, Ed. G. Litwack, Vol. 10, 259-301. Acad. Press, New York 1983.

20. Sala-Trepat, J.M., Vallet-Strové, C.: Biochim. Biophys. Acta. 371, 186-202 (1974).

21. Sherman, M.R., Pickering, L.A., Rollwagen, F.M., Miller, L.K.: Fed. Proc. 37, 167 (1978).

22. Vedeckis, W.V., Schrader, W.T., O'Malley, B.W.: in "Steroid Hormone Receptor Systems," Eds. Leavitt and J.H. Clark, 309-327, Plenum, New York 1979.

23. Wränge, O., Gustafsson, J.-A.: J. Biol. Chem. 253, 856-865 (1978).

24. Sherman, M.R., Berzilai, D., Pine, P.R., Tuazon, F.B.: Adv. Exp. Med. Biol. 117, 357-375 (1979).

25. Naray, A.: J. Steroid. Biochem. 14, 71-76 (1981).

26. Minghetti, P.P., Wiegel, N.L., Schrader, W.T., O'Malley, B.W.: Personal Communication (1983).

27. Simmons, S.S.: Biochim. Biophys. Acta. 496, 349-358 (1977).

28. Rousseau, G.G., Higgins, S.J., Baxter, J.D., Gelfand, D., Tomkins, G.M.: J. Biol. Chem. 250, 6015-6021 (1975).

29. Romanov, G.A., Sokolova, N.A., Rozen, V.B., Varryushin, B.F.: Biokhimiya 41, 2140-2141 (1976).

30. Andre, J., Pfeiffer, A., Rochefort, H.: Biochemistry 15, 2964-2969 (1976).

31. Thrall, C.L., Spelsberg, T.C.: Biochemistry 19, 4130-4138 (1980).

32. Milgrom, E., Atger, M., Baulieu, E.E.: Biochemistry 12, 5198-5205 (1973).

33. Romanov, G.A., Vanyushin, B.F.: Biochim. Biophys. Acta. 699, 53-59 (1982).

34. Kallos, J., Fasy, T.M., Hollander, V.P., Bick, M.D.: Proc. Natl. Acad. Sci. USA 75, 4896-4900 (1978).

35. Kallos, J., Fasy, T.M., Hollander, V.P., Bick, M.D.: FEBS. Lett. 98, 347-349 (1979).

36. Sluyser, M., Evers, S.G., Nijsen, T.: Biochem. Biophys. Res. Comm. 61, 380-388 (1974).

37. Romanov, G.A., Romanova, N.A., Rozen, V.B., Vanyushin, B.F.: Biochem. Intl. 6, 339-348 (1983).

38. Lin, S., Ohno, S.: Biochim. Biophys. Acta. 654, 181-186 (1981).

39. Thrower, S., Hall, C., Lin, L., Davidson, A.N.: Biochem. J. 160, 271-280 (1976).

40. Takahashi, M., Blazy, B., Baudras, A.: Nucleic Acid Res. 7, 1699-1712 (1979).

41. Record, M.T., Jr., Mazur, S.J., Melancon, P., Roe, J.-H., Shaner, S.L., Unger, L.: Ann. Rev. Biochem. 50, 997-1024 (1981).

42. Murphy, L.C., Sutherland, R.L.: Endocrinology 112, 707-714 (1983).

43. de Haseth, P.L., Lohman, T.M., Record, M.T., Jr.: Biochemistry 16, 4783-4790 (1977).

44. Henrikson, K.P., Gross, S.C., Dickerman, H.W.: Endocrinology 109, 1196-1202 (1981).

45. Gross, S.C., Kumar, S.A., Dickerman, H.W.: Mol. Cell. Endocrinol. 22, 371-384 (1981).

46. Dickerman, H.W., Kumar, S.A.: Adv. Exp. Med. Biol. 138, 1-18 (1981).

47. Yamamoto, K.R.: J. Biol. Chem. 249, 7068 (1974).

48. King, R.J.B.: in "Effects of Drugs on Cellular Control Mechanisms," Eds. B.R. Rabin and R.B. Freedman, 11-26. Univ. Park Press, Baltimore 1972.

49. Feldman, M., Kallos, J., Hollander, V.P.: J. Biol. Chem. 256, 1145-1148 (1981).

50. Spelsberg, T.C., Littlefield, B.A., Seelke, R., Dani, G.M., Toyoda, H., Boyd-Leinen, P., Thrall, C., Kon, O.L.: Recent Prog. Hormone Res. 39, 463-517 (1983).

51. Webster, R.A., Pikler, G.M., Spelsberg, T.C.: Biochem. J. 156, 409-419 (1976).

52. Perry, B.N., Lopez, A.: Biochem. J. 176, 873-883 (1978).

53. Ruh, T.S., Ross, P., Wood, P.M., Keene, J.L.: Biochem. J. 200, 133-142 (1981).

54. Spelsberg, T.C.: Biochemistry 22,13-21 (1983).

55. Spelsberg, T.C., Goose, B.J., Littlefield, B.A., Toyoda, H., Seelke, R.: Biochemistry in press (1984).

56. Spelsberg, T.C.: Personal Communication (1984).

57. Thanki, K.H., Beach, T.A., Dickerman, H.W.: Nucleic Acid Res. 6, 3859-3877 (1979).

58. Fox, T.O., Bates, S.E., Vito, C.C., Wieland, S.J.: J. Biol. Chem. 254, 4963-4966 (1979).

59. Kallos, J., Fasy, T.M., Hollander, V.P.: Proc. Natl. Acad. Sci. USA 78, 2874-2878 (1981).

60. Massol, N., Lebeau, M.-C., Balieu, E.-E.: Nucleic Acid Res. 5, 723-738 (1978).

61. Senior, M.B., Frankel, F.R.: Cell 13, 629-642 (1978).

62. Ringold, G.M., Yamamoto, K.R., Tomkins, G.M., Bishop, J.M., Varmus, H.E.: Cell 6, 299-305 (1975).

63. Yamamoto, K.R., Chandler, V.L., Ross, S.R., Ucker, D.S., Ring, J.C., Feinstein, S.C.: Cold Spring Harbor Symp. Quant. Biol. 45, 681-705 (1981).

64. Buetti, E., Diggelmann, H.: Cell 23, 335-345 (1981).

65. Fasel, N., Pearson, K., Buetti, E., Diggelmann, H.: EMBO J. 1, 3-7 (1982).

66. Hynes, N., van Ooyen, A.J.J., Kennedy, N., Herrlich, P., Ponta, H., Groner, B.: Proc. Natl. Acad. Sci. USA 80, 3637-3641 (1983).

67. Buetti, E., Diggelmann, H.: EMBO J. 2, 1423-1429 (1983).

68. Majors, J., Varmus, H.E.: Proc. Natl. Acad. Sci. USA 80, 5866-5870 (1983).

69. Scheidereit, C., Geisse, S., Westphal, H.M., Beato, M.: Nature, 304, 749-752 (1983).

70. Scheidereit, C., Beato, M.: Proc. Natl. Acad. Sci. 81, 3029-3033 (1984).

71. Karin, M., Haslinger, A., Holtgreve, H., Richards, R.I., Krauter, P., Westphal, H., Beato, M.: Nature 308, 513-519 (1984).

72. Schmid, W., Scherer, G., Danesch, U., Zentgraf, H., Matthias, P., Strange, C.M., Röwekamp, W., Schutz, G.: EMBO J. 1, 1287-1293 (1982).

538

73. Shinomaya, T., Scherer, G., Schmid, W., Zentgraf, H.,
    Schütz, G.: Proc. Natl. Acad. Sci. USA 81, 1346-1350
    (1984).

74. Compton, J.G., Schrader, W.T., O'Malley, B.W.: Biochem.
    Biophys. Res. Commun. 105, 96-104 (1982).

75. Mulvihill, E.R., LePennec, J.-P., Chambon, P.: Cell 28,
    621-632 (1982).

76. Compton, J.G., Schrader, W.T., O'Malley, B.W.: Proc.
    Natl. Acad. Sci. USA 80, 16-20 (1983).

77. Dean, D.C., Knoll, B.J., Riser, M.E., O'Malley, B.W.:
    Nature (Lond.) 305, 551-554 (1983).

78. Dean, D.C., Gope, R., Knoll, B.J., Riser, M.E., O'Malley,
    B.W.: J. Biol. Chem. 259, 9967-9970 (1984).

79. Kunz, D.T.: Nature (Lond.) 291, 629-631 (1981).

80. Robins, D.M., Paek, I., Seeburg, P.H., Axel, R.: Cell 29,
    623-631 (1982).

81. Doehmer, J., Barinaga, M., Vale, W., Rosenfeld, M.G.,
    Verma, I.M., Evans, R.M.: Proc. Natl. Acad. Sci. USA 79,
    2268-2272 (1982).

82. Renkawitz, R., Berg, H., Graf, T., Matthias, P., Grez,
    M., Schütz, G.: Cell 31, 167-176 (1982).

83. Renkawitz, R., Danesch, U., Matthias, P., Schütz, G.: J.
    Steroid Biochem. 20, 99-104 (1984).

84. Page, M.J., Parker, M.G.: Cell 32, 495-502 (1983).

85. Zaret, K.S., Yamamoto, K.R.: Cell 38, 29-38 (1984).

86. Ostrowski, M.C., Richard-Foy, H., Wolford, R.G., Berard,
    D.S., Hager, G.L.: Mol. Cell Biol. 3, 2045-2057 (1983).

THE RAT PITUITARY ESTROGEN RECEPTOR: ROLE OF THE NUCLEAR RECEPTOR IN THE REGULATION OF TRANSCRIPTION OF THE PROLACTIN GENE AND THE NUCLEAR LOCALIZATION OF THE UNOCCUPIED RECEPTOR

James D. Shull, Wade V. Welshons, Mara E. Lieberman, Jack Gorski

Departments of Biochemistry and Animal Science
University of Wisconsin, Madison, WI 53706

Introduction

We have recently examined the effects of administered estrogen on the synthesis of prolactin (Prl) messenger RNA by nuclei which are isolated from the anterior pituitary glands of intact male rats or from cultured anterior pituitary cells. Our results illustrate that estrogen stimulates the transcription of the rat Prl gene in vivo through at least two independent mechanisms (1-4). We have also used a cell enucleation procedure based on equilibrium density centrifugation of cytochalasin B-treated GH_3 cells in Percoll gradients to reexamine the subcellular distribution of the unoccupied estrogen receptor. In these studies we observed that most of the unoccupied estrogen receptor was associated with the fraction that contained nuclei (5). This and other observations have led to the revision of the classical model of estrogen action (6).

Molecular Mechanism of Steroid Hormone Action

Estrogen Regulation of Prolactin Gene Transcription

Estrogen has been shown to stimulate the synthesis of the
pituitary hormone Prl _in vivo_ (7-9) and _in vitro_ (10)
through a mechanism which results in increased levels of
Prl messenger RNA (11-14). It has more recently been shown
that this increase in Prl mRNA is due at least in part to
an increase in the transcription of the rat Prl gene (1-4,
15, 18).

Figure 1 illustrates that 17ß-estradiol, when administered

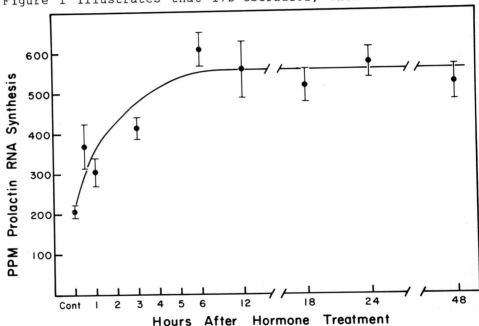

From Shull and Gorski, Endocrinology, 1984

Figure 1. Stimulatory effect of 17ß-estradiol on prolactin
gene transcription. Male rats were injected (10 µg, IP) at
the indicated times prior to sacrifice. Anterior pituitary
nuclei were then prepared and prolactin gene transcription
was assayed (3). Each data point represents the mean and
SEM (n=3) for the assay of prolactin RNA synthesized by
nuclei prepared from 8-10 animals.

to male rats (6 weeks of age) as a single injection (10 μg, IP), results in a rapid (within 30 minutes) and prolonged (48 to 72 hours) stimulation of Prl gene transcription. Similar results were observed by Maurer when he examined

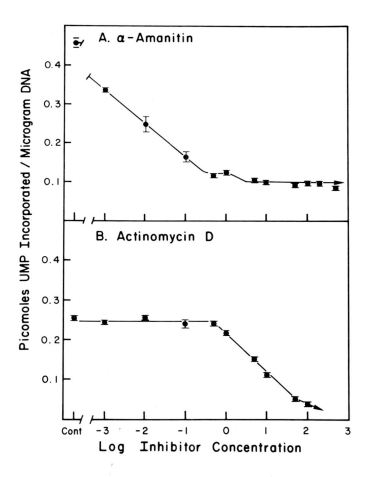

From Shull and Gorski, Endocrinology, 1984

Figure 2. Concentration effects of transcriptional inhibitors on RNA synthesis by isolated pituitary nuclei. Anterior pituitary nuclei were prepared, and the inhibitory effects of increasing concentrations of α-amanitin (A) and actinomycin D (B) on RNA synthesis were determined. Each data point represents the mean and SEM (n=3).

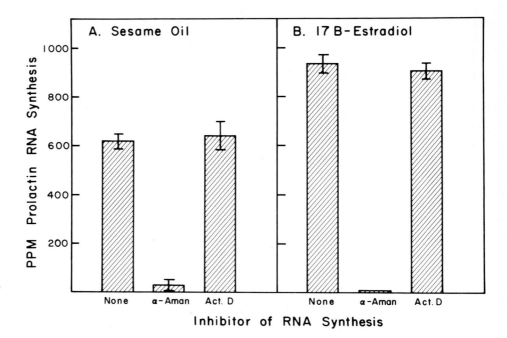

From Shull and Gorski, Endocrinology, 1984

Figure 3. Effects of transcriptional inhibitors on Prl RNA synthesis by isolated pituitary nuclei. Anterior pituitary nuclei were isolated 24 hours after injection of the sesame oil vehicle (A) or 10 μg 17β-estradiol (B) and were incubated under normal conditions or in the presence of α-amanitin (α-Aman; 1 μg/ml) or actinomycin D (Act. D; 10 μg/ml). Each bar represents the mean and SEM (n=3) of Prl RNA synthesis in nuclei pooled from 8-10 animals.

the effect of a single injection (20 μg) of 17β-estradiol into ovariectomized female rats (15). The stimulatory effects of 17β-estradiol are specific: no effects of this estrogen on the transcription of the evolutionarily related growth hormone gene were observed (1-3). In these experiments, Prl gene transcription was assayed by quantitating, by hybridization to immobilized cDNA probe, the level of radiolabeled precursor incorporated into Prl-specific mRNA sequences by anterior pituitary nuclei

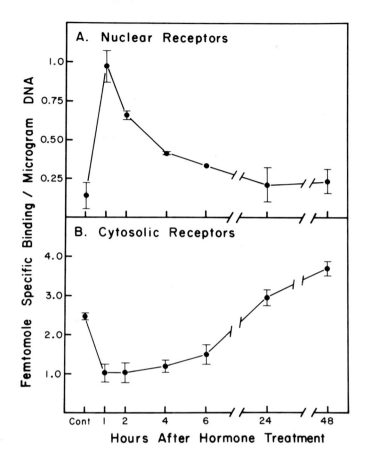

From Shull and Gorski, Endocrinology, 1984

Figure 4. Time course of the levels of the nuclear and cytosol forms of the pituitary estrogen receptor following a single injection (10 µg, IP) of 17ß-estradiol. Nuclear (A) and cytosol (B) receptors were assayed as described (3). Each data point represents the mean and SEM of specific binding measurements in individual anterior pituitaries (n=3).

isolated at the indicated times following estrogen treatment (3). This nuclear transcription assay has been well characterized and appears to reflect accurately the level of Prl gene transcription occurring at the time the nuclei are prepared (3). Briefly, these Prl-specific mRNA sequences are synthesized from a DNA template by RNA polymerase II. Alpha-amanitin at 1 µg/ml, a concentration which specifically inhibits RNA polymerase II, inhibits total nuclear RNA synthesis by 65 to 75% (Fig. 2A) while the synthesis of Prl mRNA sequences is inhibited by greater than 95% (Fig. 3). Actinomycin D at 10 µg/ml inhibits by 50 to 60% total nuclear RNA synthesis (Fig. 2B) and the synthesis of Prl mRNA sequences. Thus Prl mRNA synthesis when expressed as parts per million total RNA synthesis is uneffected (Fig. 3).

The prolonged stimulation of Prl gene transcription by 17ß-estradiol (Fig. 1) does not require a continuous elevation in the level of the nuclear form of the pituitary estrogen receptor (Fig. 4). Figure 4A illustrates that the level of nuclear-form receptor peaked within approximately 1 hour of 17ß-estradiol injection, decreased approximately 70% from this peak value within 6 hours and returned to its control value within 24 hours. These data suggest that 17ß-estradiol regulates Prl gene transcription through a stable mechanism which perhaps involves a modification of chromatin proteins or DNA sequences within or surrounding the Prl gene (3).

To investigate the possible requirement for the synthesis of intermediary proteins in the induction of Prl gene transcription by 17ß-estradiol, we examined this induction in cycloheximide-pretreated animals (3). When examined 3 hours following a single injection of 17ß-estradiol, Prl gene transcription was stimulated nearly 2-fold in both saline-treated (Fig. 5A) and cycloheximide-treated animals (Fig. 5B). Similar results were observed 8 hours following 17ß-estradiol injection (Fig. 6). In these experiments, cycloheximide inhibited by greater than 80% the incorporation of [^{3}H]leucine into acid-precipitable

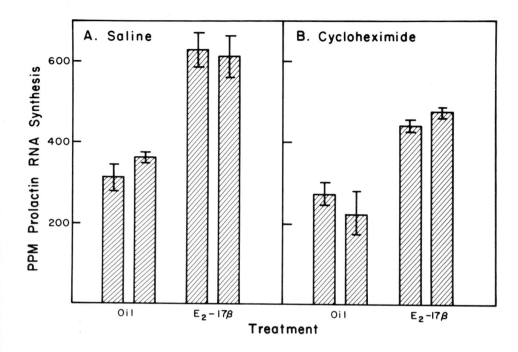

From Shull and Gorski, Endocrinology, 1984

Figure 5. The induction of prolactin gene transcription by 17ß-estradiol (10 μg, IP) under conditions of inhibited pituitary protein synthesis: an examination at 3 hours. Sterile saline (A) or cycloheximide (B) was injected 10 minutes before 17ß-estradiol or its sesame oil vehicle. The animals were killed 3 hours after hormone treatment and prolactin gene transcription was assayed as described (3). Each bar represents the mean and SEM (n=3) for the assay of prolactin RNA synthesized by nuclei prepared from 8-10 animals.

material by the anterior pituitary gland (Fig. 7). To eliminate the possibility that a protein (or proteins) required for the induction of Prl gene transcription by 17ß-estradiol may have been synthesized in a reduced but sufficient quantity in the cycloheximide-treated animals, we examined this induction in primary cultures of rat anterior pituitary cells in which cycloheximide had

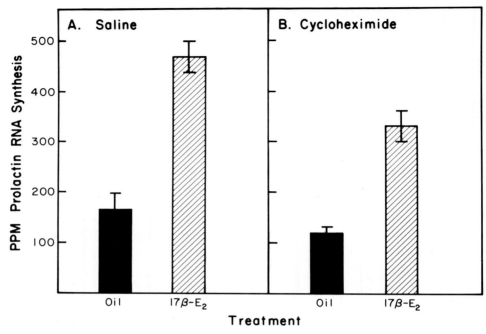

From Shull and Gorski, 1984

Figure 6. The induction of prolactin gene transcription by 17β-estradiol (10 µg, IP) under conditions of inhibited pituitary protein synthesis; an examination at 8 hours. Sterile saline (A) or cycloheximide (B) was injected 10 minutes prior to and again 4 hours following 17β-estradiol or its sesame oil vehicle. The animals were killed 8 hours after hormone treatment and prolactin gene transcription was assayed as described (3). Each bar represents the mean and SEM (n=3) for the assay of prolactin RNA synthesized by nuclei prepared from 8-10 animals.

inhibited the incorporation of [^{3}H]leucine by nearly 100%. We have observed that 17β-estradiol stimulates the transcription of the Prl gene within 8 hours of its addition to either untreated or cycloheximide-treated cultures (manuscript submitted). These observations demonstrate that at least part of the stimulatory effects of 17β-estradiol on Prl gene transcription are mediated through a mechanism which is independent of pituitary protein synthesis.

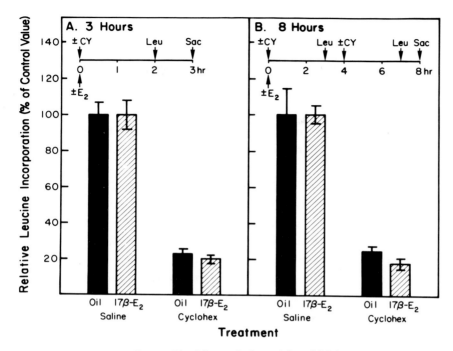

From Shull and Gorski, 1984

Figure 7. Inhibitory effects of cycloheximide on pituitary protein synthesis. Injections are as illustrated and described in Figures 5 and 6. Each bar represents the mean and SEM of the relative level of leucine incorporation in individual pituitaries from a total of five to eight animals.

The synthetic estrogen, 16α-estradiol, has been characterized as being "short acting" as a single injection of this hormone into immature female rats stimulates the early estrogenic responses, such as water imbibition and induced protein synthesis by the uterus, but not the late estrogenic responses such as uterine DNA synthesis (16). The rat uterine estrogen receptor has a lesser affinity for 16α-estradiol than for 17ß-estradiol (16). This results in a more rapid decline in the level of the nuclear form of the uterine estrogen receptor following a single injection of 16α-estradiol than is observed following an injection of

17β-estradiol (17). When the levels of the nuclear and cytosol forms of the pituitary estrogen receptor were examined following an injection of 16α-estradiol, they had returned to their control values within 4 hours (4, 18). In contrast, the level of nuclear-form receptor remained significantly elevated for at least 6 hours following an equivalent injection of 17β-estradiol while the level of cytosol-form receptor remained diminished (4, 18).

A single injection of 16α-estradiol stimulates the transcription of the rat Prl gene in a biphasic manner (2, 4, 18). The initial phase was observed within 30 minutes of injection and continued through at least 2 hours, thus paralleling in duration the elevation in the level of the nuclear form of the pituitary estrogen receptor. The second phase of stimulated Prl gene transcription was first observed approximately 6 hours following injection, after the level of nuclear-form receptor had returned to its control value (4, 18). The induction of the initial phase of stimulated Prl gene transcription by 16α-estradiol was observed in animals pretreated with either cycloheximide or puromycin indicating that this phase is mediated through a mechanism which is independent of pituitary protein synthesis. In contrast, cycloheximide pretreatment blocked the induction by 16α-estradiol of the second phase of stimulated transcription (4, 18). This effect of cycloheximide was not simply due to the prolonged treatment (6 hours versus 1 hour) as no such effect was observed following 8 hours of cycloheximide treatment when the induction of Prl gene transcription by 17β-estradiol was examined (Fig. 6). These data suggest the possibility that the induction of the second phase of stimulated Prl gene transcription by 16α-estradiol requires the synthesis of an intermediary protein although other unknown effects of cycloheximide cannot be ruled out.

Our observations that 16α-estradiol stimulates the transcription of the Prl gene in a biphasic manner and that the induction of the two phases differs in sensitivity to cycloheximide suggest that this hormone regulates Prl gene transcription through at least two independent mechanisms. One mechansim appears to involve the nuclear form of the pituitary estrogen receptor. It is attractive to hypothesize that this mechanism includes an interaction of the estrogen-receptor complex with regulatory regions of the Prl gene. Durrin and Gorski have localized regions near the 5-prime terminus of the Prl gene, which exist in a chromatin structure which is hypersensitive to nicking during a limited DNAse digestion of isolated pituitary nuclei (manuscript submitted). It is possible that these hypersensitive sites correspond to regulatory domains. We have hypothesized that the induction of the second phase of stimulated Prl gene transcription is the result of either an estrogen-induced alteration in the level of a second regulator of Prl gene transcription or to an alteration in the responsiveness of the cells of the anterior pituitary to a second regulator (3, 4). These hypotheses are currently being tested (18).

It seems likely that these same mechanisms function in the induction of Prl gene transcription by 17β-estradiol; the difference between 17β-estradiol and 16α-estradiol being that 16α-estradiol, with its lesser affinity to the estrogen receptor and its lesser ability to maintain elevated levels of the nuclear-form receptor, induces an initial phase of stimulated Prl gene transcription which is of shorter duration than following 17β-estradiol injection. This allows the two phases to be resolved in animals injected with 16α-estradiol while the two phases would overlap in animals treated with 17β-estradiol.

Intracellular Location of the Estrogen Receptor

Since the direct effects of estrogen involve the regulation of transcription in the nucleus of the cell, it is not surprising that after administering estrogen, the receptor-steroid complex is recovered in the nucleus of the cell after homogenization of the tissue. However, the location of the unoccupied receptor has been assigned to the cytoplasm of the cell. This was based on the appearance of most unfilled receptors in cytosol extracts of cells (19) and on autoradiography of cells labeled briefly at 0-4° C (20). Translocation of the receptor-steroid complex from the cytoplasm to the nucleus was proposed to account for the subsequent recovery of receptor-steroid complex in the nucleus (21, 22). This interpretation received wide acceptance for both the estrogen receptor and the other steroid hormones.

Some data suggest, however, that the unfilled receptor may also be found in the nucleus, and that the cytosolic localization represents an extraction artifact. The data include the appearance using autoradiography of a large fraction of receptor in the nucleus under nontranslocating conditions (23) and other observations (see below).

In order to avoid possible extraction artifacts, we used cytochalasin B-induced enucleation of cells (24, 25) to remove cytoplasm (as cytoplasts) from receptor-containing cells, without breaking open the cells. Both the cytoplast and the cell fragment containing the nucleus (nucleoplast) have an intact plasma membrane and are still alive, since they can be fused to reform a viable cell (26). Enucleation has been used to show that a cytosolic DNA polymerase, extracted when the cell is homogenized, is not cytoplasmic in the intact cell, but is instead nuclear (27).

Not all cells will enucleate well, and if enucleated, cytoplast and nucleoplast fractions are not always separated. Freshly dispersed pituitary cells and primary cultures of the cells were not enucleated satisfactorily, so we turned to the GH_3 cell line, derived from a rat pituitary tumor (28). The cells contain estrogen receptor that is found in the cytosol after the usual cell fractionation (29), and the cells respond to estrogen with increased prolactin synthesis (30). The cells therefore exhibit the usual characteristics of an estrogen-responsive tissue, even though the cells are tumor-derived.

We were able to partially enucleate 85% of the GH_3 cells, forming cytoplasts that averaged 1/5 of the size of the

PREPARATION OF CYTOPLASTS

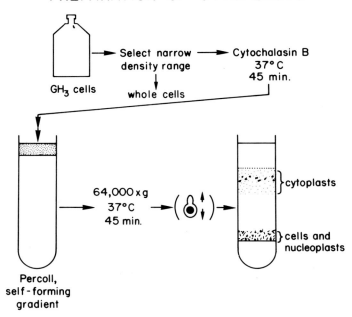

Welshons, Lieberman and Gorski, unpublished.

Figure 8. Preparation of cytoplasts from GH_3 cells.

original whole cells. Importantly, we were able to obtain a purified preparation of these cytoplasts, that sometimes contained less than 1% contaminating whole cells. The fraction from which the cytoplasts had been removed was more heterogeneous, containing some whole cells as well as the cells from which varying proportions of cytoplasm had been removed. We called this the cell + nucleoplast fraction.

If the unoccupied estrogen receptor is cytoplasmic then its concentration in cytoplasts should be as high or higher than the concentration in the whole cells. However, when we enucleated GH_3 cells using cytochalasin B and centrifugation (Fig. 8), we found the opposite

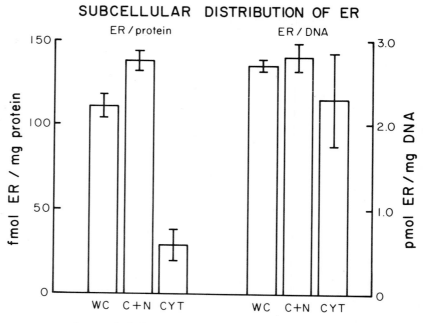

SUBCELLULAR DISTRIBUTION OF ER

From Welshons et al., Nature, 1984

Figure 9. Estrogen receptor (ER) concentration in whole cells (WC), in cells + nucleoplasts (C + N) and in cytoplasts (Cyt).

distribution (5). The concentration of estrogen receptor
per protein was low in cytoplasts and slightly higher in
the cells + nucleoplasts, compared to whole cells (Fig.
9). The concentration of receptor per DNA on the other
hand was similar in all fractions (Fig. 9), suggesting that
the receptor was following the DNA content of the cell. In
the experiment detailed in Table 1 (from ref. 5), the
receptor per protein was less than 10% of the concentration
in the whole cells. The recovery of protein, DNA and
estrogen receptor after enucleation was essentially
complete (Table 2), indicating that receptor was not
selectively lost from the cytoplasts.

The cell + nucleoplast fraction averaged approximately 1/5
less protein than the original whole cells, so that a
fraction average of only 20% of the cytoplasm had been

TABLE 1.   ESTROGEN RECEPTOR IN ENUCLEATED CELLS

	ER/ Prot.	ER/ DNA	Prot./ Cell	DNA/ Prot.	ER/Cell Equivalent
	fmol/mg	pmol/mg	pg	µg/mg	molecules
Whole cells	113	2.7	363	42	25,000
Cells + nucleoplasts	146	2.9	336	50	30,000
Cytoplasts	10	1.4	69	7.5	2,100*

Estrogen receptor per protein, per DNA and per cell (by
hemocytometer) in whole cells and enucleated cells. The
cytoplast fraction contained fewer than 1% whole cells.

*Number of molecules per 5 cytoplasts, since cytoplasts are
approximately 1/5 the size of whole cells.

Welshons et al., Nature, 1984.

TABLE 2. RECOVERY OF ESTROGEN BINDING,
PROTEIN AND DNA AFTER ENUCLEATION

	Total Applied or Recovered		
	Estrogen Binding pmol	Protein mg	DNA µg
Before enucleation:			
Whole cells	2.10	18.5	785
After enucleation:			
Cells + nucleoplasts	2.26	15.5	777
Cytoplasts	0.024	2.3	18
Recovery	109%	96%	101%

Welshons, Lieberman and Gorski, unpublished.

removed.   But microscopically, it could be seen that the
fraction contained some cells from which much more of the
cytoplasm had been removed.   To see if the cells lacking
most of the cytoplasm still contained the full estrogen
receptor content, the cell + nucleoplast fraction was
further fractionated on a density step gradient.   Cells
that contained less cytoplasm were found at the higher
densities.   When   the   estrogen   receptor   content   was
measured in these fractions, it was found that, while the
receptor per protein more than doubled, the receptor content per DNA (per cell) was constant (Fig. 10, ref. 5).
There was no evidence that removing most of the cytoplasm
of the cell removed any of the unoccupied receptor.

The enucleation procedure did not seem to damage the
cells.   Dye exclusion continued high from just after
enucleation throughout measuring the receptor content by
whole cell uptake of estradiol (Table 3).   The fractions
incorporated [^{3}H]leucine and synthesized prolactin after
enucleation (Table 4).   In addition, incubation in the
enucleation medium had no apparent effect on the receptor
content (Table 5), and the steroid receptor in the cell +

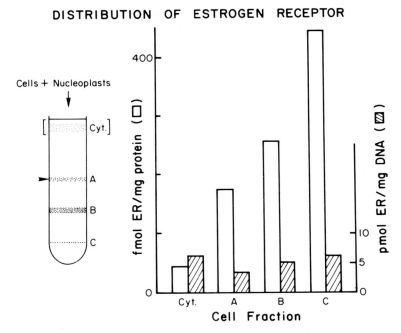

DISTRIBUTION OF ESTROGEN RECEPTOR

Welshons et al., Nature, 1984

Figure 10. The cell + nucleoplast fraction was further fractionated on a density step gradient. The (intact) cells at higher density steps have had more cytoplasm removed. Arrowhead indicates density of cells before enucleation, and the position cytoplasts would have occupied is indicated in brackets.

TABLE 3. DYE EXCLUSION OF CELLS AND FRACTIONS

	% Excluding Dye	
	Initial	Final
Whole cells	97 ± 1	95 ± 1
Cells + nucleoplasts	98 ± 1	93 ± 1
Cytoplasts	98 ± 1	73 ± 4

Mean ± standard error, n's of 6 to 9.

Trypan blue exclusion just after enucleation (Initial) and after measuring the receptor content by whole cell uptake at 37° C (Final). Welshons, Lieberman and Gorski, unpublished.

nucleoplast fraction just after enucleation was still extracted into the cytosol when the cells were homogenized (31). Therefore, the enucleation procedure had no apparent effect on the estrogen receptor that would indicate that redistribution of the receptor had occurred.

TABLE 4. PROLACTIN SYNTHESIS BY GH_3 CELLS AND FRACTIONS

	Leucine Incorporation: 10^{-6} x DPM Per 10^6 Cells or Equivalent	Prolactin Synthesis: % of Total Protein Synthesis
Whole cells	6.2	1.2 ± 0.02
Cells + nucleoplasts	5.7	1.3 ± 0.06
Cytoplasts	3.0*	3.4 ± 0.2

Cells, cells plus nucleoplasts, or cytoplasts were incubated with [^{3}H]leucine to measure general protein synthesis by TCA-precipitable leucine incorporation, and to measure prolactin synthesis using precipitation with antiprolactin antibody. *Assuming 5 cytoplasts per whole cell equivalent. Welshons, Lieberman and Gorski, unpublished.

TABLE 5. EFFECT OF INCUBATION OF CELLS IN ENUCLEATION MEDIUM ON RECEPTOR CONTENT

	Untreated	After Incubation
Whole cell uptake, fmol/mg prot.	102 ± 2	98 ± 1

Mean ± standard error, n=2

Estrogen receptor content was measured in untreated cells and in cells incubated at 37° C for 2 hours in cytochalasin B plus solvent DMSO in Percoll. Receptor content was not significantly affected. Welshons, Lieberman and Gorski, unpublished.

The estrogen receptor was measured in these experiments by using whole cell (or whole cytoplast or nucleoplast) uptake of [³H]estradiol at 37° C into the intact, live fractions. Specific uptake was calculated by subtracting uptake in the presence of 100-fold excess of unlabeled hormone. Whole cell uptake was used to avoid any losses of receptor that would have been encountered had we homogenized cells or cytoplasts in the 1 or 2 mg quantities that we used in assays. The specific uptake was more than 90% inhibited when the cells or fractions were incubated at 0° C instead of 37° C (Table 6) verifying that the receptors were inside the intact cells.

TABLE 6. TEMPERATURE-DEPENDENT UPTAKE OF ESTRADIOL BY INTACT CELLS OR CYTOPLASTS

	Specific Uptake, DPM	
	37° C	0° C
Whole cells	855	39
Cells + nucleoplasts	3,570	120
Cytoplasts	143	13

Welshons, Lieberman and Gorski, unpublished.

The specific uptake of estradiol was saturable, and by Scatchard analysis showed an affinity of 0.34 nM (Figure 11). There were approximately 25,000 binding sites per cell. The linearity of the Scatchard plot in intact cells contrasts with the cooperative binding (32, 33) that is observed in extracts when the receptor concentration is above 1 nM, as it is in the intact cell. We have interpreted this to suggest that the receptor is bound in the nucleus, not free in solution (6), since a soluble

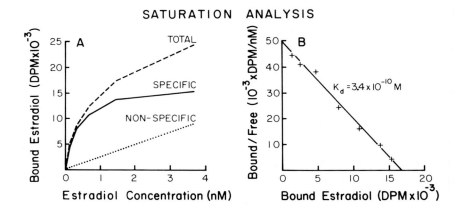

Welshons, Lieberman and Gorski, unpublished

Figure 11. Saturation analysis of the whole cell uptake of [^{3}H] estradiol at 37° C by GH$_3$ cells.

receptor would be expected to show the cooperative hormone binding, while immobilized estrogen receptor (on hydroxylapatite), like the receptor in intact cells, does not show this cooperativity (33).

While our finding that the unoccupied estrogen receptor is nuclear contradicts a large body of evidence that has been interpreted to indicate cytoplasmic location, several recent lines of evidence are in fact consistent with a nuclear receptor that is extractable during homogenization. 1. Sheridan et al. (23) found by autoradiography under "nontranslocating" conditions that most of the estrogen binding was already in the nucleus. 2. Recent immunohistochemical studies with the best-characterized set of monoclonal antibodies to the receptor have detected antibody binding in the nucleus, not the cytoplasm (34, 35), even though preliminary localization was reported in the cytoplasm (but without nuclear translocation (36)). 3. Extraction of the receptor would also explain the action of estrogenic compounds that seem to bind to the receptor and stimulate the full range of estrogenic (nuclear) responses, yet are found bound to the receptor in the cytosol when the cell is homogenized (37). The interpretation is that upon homogenization of the cell, the receptor- estrogenic compound complex, like the unoccupied receptor, is extracted from its nuclear locus of action. 4. In addition, the unfilled receptors for vitamin D and the unfilled receptors for thyroid hormone and dioxin (similar to steroid receptors) have been reported to be nuclear (38, 39, 40, 41).

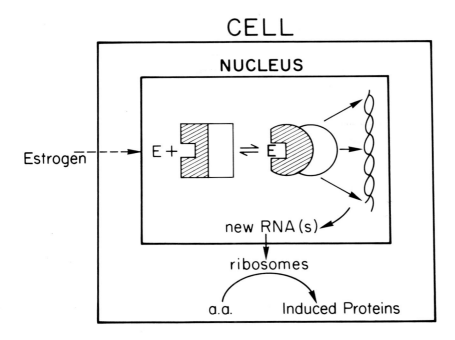

Figure 12. Diagram of interaction of estrogen with its receptor.

Our data in the context of the literature cited above suggest that the unoccupied estrogen receptor is mostly nuclear in the intact cell (Fig. 12). This places the receptor near the site of action at all times. In the absence of hormone, the receptor is only loosely associated with nuclear elements and is usually extracted from the nucleus when the cell is homogenized. After binding the hormone the receptor develops a stronger affinity for nuclear elements and resists extraction. The kinetic data suggest that the receptor may be bound at all times to its site of action, and is not a soluble protein within the nucleus. Although our data may apply only to the receptor in the GH_3 cell, the similarity of the steroid receptor mechanisms makes it tempting to speculate that all steroid receptors are located in the nucleus.

References

1. Shull, J. D., Gorski, J.: Endocrinology $\underline{110}$ (supplement), 292 (1982).
2. Shull, J. D., Gorski, J.: Fed. Proc. $\underline{42}$, 206 (1983).
3. Shull, J. D., Gorski, J.: Endocrinology $\underline{114}$, 1550-1557 (1984).
4. Shull, J. D., Gorski, J.: manuscript submitted for publication.
5. Welshons, W. V., Lieberman, M. E., Gorski, J.: Nature $\underline{307}$, 747-749 (1984).
6. Gorski, J., Welshons, W., Sakai, D.: Mol. Cell. Endo. $\underline{36}$, 11-15 (1984).
7. Yamamoto, K., Kasai, K., Ieiri, T.: Jap. J. Physiol. $\underline{25}$, 645-658 (1975).
8. MacLeod, R. M., Abad, A., Eidson, L. L.: Endocrinology $\underline{84}$, 1475-1483 (1969).
9. Maurer, R. A., Gorski, J.: Endocrinology 101, 76-84 (1977).

10. Lieberman, M. E., Maurer, R. A., Gorski, J.: Proc. Nat. Acad. Sci. 75, 5946-5949 (1978).

11. Stone, R. T., Maurer, R. A., Gorski, J.: Biochemistry 16, 4915-4921 (1977).

12. Ryan, R., Shupnik, M. A., Gorski, J.: Biochemistry 18, 2044-2048 (1979).

13. Seo, H., Refetoff, S., Vassart, G., Brocas, H.: Proc. Natl. Acad. Sci. 76, 824-828 (1979).

14. Lieberman, M. E., Maurer, R. A., Claude, P., Gorski, J.: Mol. Cell. Endo. 25, 277-294 (1982).

15. Maurer, R. A.: J. Biol. Chem. 257, 2133-2136 (1982).

16. Stack, G.: U.W. Ph.D. Thesis (1983).

17. Kassis, J. A., Gorski, J.: J. Biol. Chem. 256, 7378-7382 (1981).

18. Shull, J. D., Mellon, S. R., Gorski, J.: Proceedings Seventh International Congress of Endocrinology Abstract 2140 (1984).

19. Toft, D., Shyamla, G., Gorski, J.: Proc. Nat. Acad. Sci. 57, 1740-1743 (1967).

20. Stumpf, W. E.: Endocrinology 83, 777-782 (1968).

21. Gorski, J., Toft, D., Shyamala, G., Smith, D., Notides, A.: Rec. Prog. Horm. Rec. 24, 45-80 (1968).

22. Jensen, E. V., Suzuki, T., Kawashima, T., Stumpf, W. E., Jungblut, P. W., DeSombre, E. R.: Proc. Nat. Acad. Sci. 59, 632-638 (1968).

23. Sheridan, P. J., Buchanen, J. M., Anselmo, V. C.: Nature 282, 579-582 (1979).

24. Poste, G.: Methods in Cell Biology 7, 211-249 (1973).

25. Bossart, W., Loeffler, H., Bienz, K.: Exp. Cell Res. 96, 360-366 (1975).

26. Veomett, G., Prescott, D. M., Shay, J., Porter, K. R.: Proc. Nat. Acad. Sci. 71, 1999-2002 (1974).

27. Herrick, G., Spear, B. P., Veomett, G.: Proc. Nat. Acad. Sci. 73, 1136-1139 (1976).

28. Tashjian, A., Bancroft, F., Levine, L.: J. Cell Biol. 47, 61-70 (1970).

562

29. Haug, E., Naess, O., Gautvik, K. M.: Molec. Cell. Endocr. <u>12</u>, 81-95 (1978).
30. Haug, E., Gautvik, K. M.: Endocrinology <u>99</u>, 1482-1489 (1976).
31. Welshons, W. V., Gorski, J.: in preparation.
32. Notides, A. C., Lerner, N., Hamilton, D. E.: Proc. Nat. Acad. Sci. <u>78</u>, 4926-4430 (1981).
33. Sakai, D., Gorski, J.: Biochemistry <u>23</u>, 3541-3547 (1984).
34. King, W. J., Greene, G. L.: Nature <u>307</u>, 745-747 (1984).
35. McClellan, M. C., West, N. B., Tacha, D. E., Greene, G. L., Brenner, R. M.: Endocrinology <u>114</u>, 2002-2014 (1984).
36. Jensen, E. V., Greene, G. L., Closs, L. E., DeSombre, E. R., Nadji, M.: Rec. Prog. Horm. Res. <u>38</u>, 1-40 (1982).
37. Jordan, V. C., Tate, A. C., Lyman, S. D., Gosden, B., Wolf, M. F., Welshons, W. V.: in preparation.
38. Walters, M., Hunziker, W., Norman, A.: J. Biol. Chem. <u>255</u>, 6799-6805 (1980).
39. Samuels, H., Tsai, J.: Proc. Nat. Acad. Sci. <u>70</u>, 3488-3492 (1973).
40. Oppenheimer, J. H., Schwartz, H. L., Surks, M. I., Koerner, D., Dillman, W. H.: Rec. Prog. Horm. Res. <u>32</u>, 529-565 (1976).
41. Whitlock, J. P., Galeazzi, D. R.: J. Biol. Chem. <u>259</u>, 980-985 (1984).

CHARACTERIZATION OF DIFFERENT FORMS OF THE ANDROGEN RECEPTOR AND THEIR INTERACTION WITH CONSTITUENTS OF CELL NUCLEI

Eppo Mulder and Albert O. Brinkmann
Department of Biochemistry, Erasmus University Rotterdam, 3000
DR Rotterdam, The Netherlands

Introduction

It is now generally accepted that most, if not all, actions of steroid hormones are mediated by an effect of a steroid receptor complex on the transcription of specific parts of the genome in the nucleus (1). In this process the receptor most likely interacts with chromatin or DNA to modulate the transcription of specific genes (2, 3, 4).

Androgen receptors are characterized by a dipolar charge distribution. They are acidic proteins with an IEP of 5.8 (5) and with a net negative charge at neutral or slightly alkaline pH. Once the steroid has bound to its intracellular receptor protein, the resulting complex undergoes further changes, termed activation, that increases its affinity for specific acceptor sites within the cell nucleus. Whether this process occurs exclusively at the nuclear level is still a matter of debate but recently strong evidence has been presented for a nuclear locus of this important step in estrogen hormone action (6, 7). Activation of androgen receptors is supposed to be accompanied by a change in the ionic properties of the complex resulting in a higher isoelectric point (5). The dipolar behavior may represent an important characteristic in relation to nuclear interaction. Activated androgen receptors are reported to bind to positively charged chromatin histones and nonhistone basic proteins and to negatively charged

Molecular Mechanism of Steroid Hormone Action

ribonucleic acids and nonhistone nuclear proteins (8, 9).
Several forms of androgen receptors have been extracted from
nuclei but little is known about the physiological
significance of these forms (10, 11, 12). Alternatively the
occurrence of these different nuclear forms might reflect
partial degradation of the native form during isolation as has
been found for androgen receptors present in cytosol fractions
of rat prostates (13). This chapter deals with different
aspects of the transformation process (activation) of androgen
receptors to the nuclear binding state and the forms of the
receptor involved in this process. Furthermore both
characteristics of the interaction of the receptor with
nuclear acceptor sites and in vitro interaction of different
receptor forms with DNA, RNA and polynucleotides are
described.

Results and discussion

I   Characterization of the activation process of androgen
    receptors

Activation of receptors can be accomplished by a variety of in
vitro manipulations, such as heating, salt treatment, dilution
or aging of the receptor preparations (14). We have studied
this process for androgen receptors and have characterized the
different changes that occur in the properties of the receptor
during this process with respect to sedimentation rate,
interaction with polyanions, dissociation rate and charge
distribution.

Interaction of androgen receptors from seminal vesicles of the
ram with phosphocellulose. Cytosols containing two distinct
[^{3}H]-methyltrienolone binding proteins (8S and 4S) were

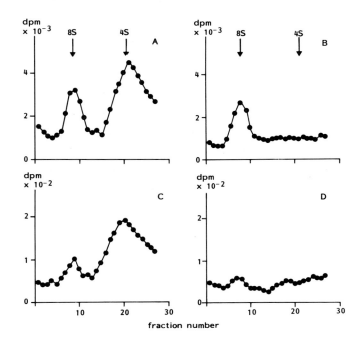

<u>Figure 1</u>
Binding of androgen receptors to phosphocellulose: analysis by
sucrose gradient centrifugation. The labelled cytosol obtained
from seminal vesicles of the ram was subjected to sucrose
gradient centrifugation (for 210 min at 1°C in a Beckman VTi-
65 rotor at 370,000 x g) either directly (A), or after
filtration over phosphocellulose (B). The receptors in the
residual fraction prepared as for panel B were activated and
again subjected to sucrose gradient centrifugation before (C)
and after (D) filtration over phosphocellulose.

incubated with phosphocellulose (fig. 1A). (Methyltrienolone,
R1881, is a synthetic, non-metabolizable androgen with high
affinity for the androgen receptor.)   Only the slower
sedimenting 3-4S form was retained by phosphocellulose (fig.
1B), probably representing the activated steroid-receptor
complex.   The 8S sedimenting form was almost completely
converted to a 3-4S sedimenting form after incubation with 0.4
M KCl., Sephadex G-25 gelfiltration and dilution (fig. 1C).

This fraction containing activated androgen receptor complexes, originating from the non-activated 8S form, was again incubated with phosphocellulose. This resulted in a complete retention of the 3-4S sedimenting form by the phosphocellulose (fig. 1D). The receptor could be recovered from phosphocellulose by salt extraction. From these results it can be concluded that the non-activated 8S sedimenting form of the androgen receptor can be converted into an activated, faster sedimenting form with a higher affinity for polyanions.

Dissociation rate of androgen receptors obtained from calf uterine tissue. For the estrogen receptor in calf uterine cytosol a temperature induced change of the steroid-receptor complex from a low affinity state to a high affinity state, measurable as a decrease in hormone dissociation rate, is accompanied by the formation of the DNA-binding form sedimenting at 5S (15, 16). Androgen receptors are also present in calf uterine tissue, a tissue with relatively low endogenous proteolytic enzyme activity. These receptors can be measured independently from the estradiol and progesterone receptor, when binding of androgens to these receptors is properly suppressed (e.g. with a 500-fold excess triamcinolone acetonide).

In fig. 2 the effect of molybdate (20 mM) on the hormone-dissociation kinetics at $25^{\circ}C$ of these androgen receptor complexes is shown. In the absence of molybdate most of the receptor is present as a high affinity state complex (slow dissociation) which binds to DNA- or phosphocellulose. After precipitation with ammonium sulphate of the receptor in cytosol in the presence of 20 mM molybdate the DNA-binding capacity increases from 5 to 65% and concomittantly an increase of the amount of slowly dissociating steroid receptor complex is observed. This indicates that molybdate prevents transformation at low ionic strengths, but does not inhibit

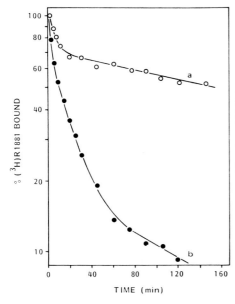

Figure 2
Dissociation rate at 25°C of R1881-androgen receptor complex from calf uterus.
a) Activated form, in the absence of molybdate.
b) Non activated form stabilized with 20 mM molybdate.

transformation by high salt concentration. Similar findings have been described for the androgen receptor from human foreskin fibroblasts (17). In sucrose gradients (0.4 M KCl) all forms of the uterine androgen receptor sediment at 4.5S. A change in sedimentation value comparable to the 4 to 5S transformation as shown for estradiol receptors after receptor activation is not observed for the androgen receptor.

These observations demonstrate that transformation of the androgen receptor to a form with a high affinity for polyanions and nuclear chromatin is accompanied by a 30-fold increase in affinity for the steroid.

Anti-androgens and the activation of androgen receptors.
Because the role of the ligand in the transformation step of androgen receptors to the activated (i.e. DNA binding) state is hardly known the effect of androgens and the anti-androgen

cyproterone acetate on the activation process of the androgen receptor in the rat prostate was studied.

In order to exclude any rapid degradation in vivo of the anti-androgen, experiments were performed with minced prostatic tissue obtained from castrated animals and incubated at 37°C with [^{3}H]-R1881 (20 nM) and [^{3}H]-cyproterone acetate (20 nM). After 1 h incubation nuclei were isolated as described previously (18) and bound radioactive ligand was measured. Metabolic degradation of [^{3}H]-cyproterone acetate and of [^{3}H]-R1881 during the incubation with minced prostatic tissue did not occur, as was checked by thin layer chromatography.

The results in fig. 3B show that only in the [^{3}H]-R1881 incubation a nuclear association of radioactivity could be measured. Radioactivity in a salt extract of these nuclei sedimented as 3.6S peak on sucrose gradients (not shown). Hardly any radioactive cyproterone acetate could be localized in nuclei after incubation of the prostatic tissue with the tritiated anti-androgen. Analogous results were obtained with unlabelled ligands (testosterone 40 nM or cyproterone acetate 4 μM) followed by estimation of nuclear receptor levels using an exchange assay. Under these conditions androgen receptors were measurable only when testosterone was incubated with the minced prostates (18).

The interaction of cyproterone acetate with prostatic androgen receptors was further investigated in vitro in order to establish the stability of the anti-androgen receptor complex in comparison with that of the R1881-receptor complex. For this purpose dissociation kinetics were studied of the radioactive ligand receptor complexes at 10°C. As shown in fig. 3A the R1881-receptor complex dissociated at this temperature with a dissociation rate constant of approximately 2.5×10^{-3} min^{-1}. The anti-androgen receptor complex dissociated at a much faster rate with a dissociate rate constant of 1×10^{-2} min^{-1}.

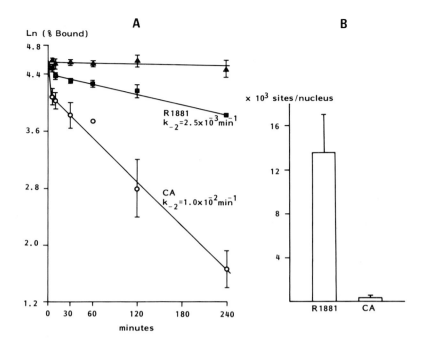

Figure 3

A. Dissociation kinetics at 10°C of androgen cytosol receptor complexes from rat prostate ligated either with [³H]-R1881 or with [³H]-cyproterone acetate. ▲ represents the stability of the R1881-androgen receptor complex under the incubation conditions.

B. Androgen receptor levels in prostate nuclei 1 h after in vitro incubation at 30°C of minced prostates obtained from castrated rats with 20 nM [³H]-R1881 or [³H]-cyproterone acetate (CA).

The present results demonstrate that activation of androgen receptors to a DNA-binding state is impaired in prostates from castrated rats after in vitro incubation with cyproterone acetate. A possible explanation for the mode of action of cyproterone acetate might be found in the instability of the anti-androgen-receptor complex. Although it has been shown in several studies that cyproterone acetate can compete for specific R1881 or dihydrotestosterone receptor binding sites

purification of the androgen receptor was achieved in fraction 28 with a recovery of 71%. On sucrose gradients (high ionic strength) the FPLC peak sedimented as 3.6S entity, while a molecular weight of 48,000 was found after ACA-44 gel chromatography. The molybdate-stabilized form of the androgen receptor in cytosols prepared from rat epididymis and calf uterus were eluted from the Mono Q column with a recovery of 85% and at the same ionic strength (0.32 M) as the prostatic androgen receptor. Further analysis of the eluted receptors on sucrose gradients and by ACA-44 gelchromatography resulted in

Figure 4
FPLC chromatography of androgen receptor complexes from the cytosol of rat prostates in the presence (A) or absence (B) of 20 mM sodium molybdate. 500 l cytosol samples were applied on a Mono Q column. Elution was accomplished with a linear salt gradient (0-0.35 M NaCl). Each l ml fraction was assayed for total radioactivity. In figure B only specific binding is represented.

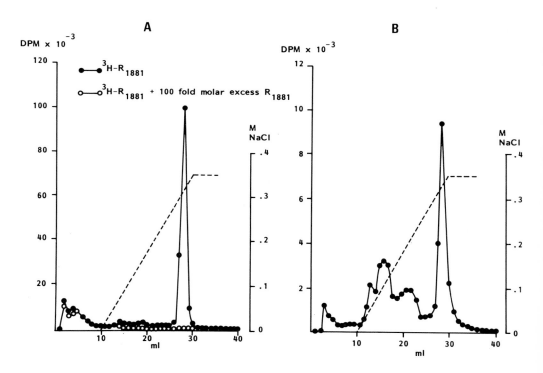

sedimentation coefficients of 4-5S and molecular weights of 90,000 (see also table I). These results indicate that androgen receptors prepared in the presence of molybdate show a strong interaction with anionexchange resins, indicating a net negative surface charge of the molybdate stabilized form. Furthermore, a substantial purification of the androgen receptor could be obtained within a reasonable short time (40 min).

Prostate cytosol, prepared in molybdate-free buffer, was also analyzed on FPLC. The elution profile is shown in fig. 4B. A three-fold reduction of the peak eluted at 0.32 M NaCl was observed (recovery 35%). In addition three other peaks of receptor-like androgen binding were found, indicating the presence of multiple forms of the androgen receptor in the absence of molybdate. These multiple forms eluted at a lower ionic strength might represent androgen receptor complexes which became activated either during the homogenization procedure or during the ionexchange chromatography. In addition the high proteolytic enzyme activity present in prostate cytosol might have caused further degradation of the androgen receptor due to the relative instability of the activated complex. Even generation of a mero-type receptor cannot be excluded (27; see table I, small receptor form).

It is concluded that the FPLC-anion exchange system is a powerful, fast tool for characterization and partial purification of steroid receptors. In addition this technique could be applied as a rapid procedure for the quantitative estimation of androgen receptors in small biological samples.

Estimation of molecular mass of androgen receptors. By defining the molecular properties of the activated form of androgen receptors, several investigators have used the elution volume during gelchromatography and the sedimentation coefficients in sucrose gradients for receptor sizes and the

ability to bind to DNA for receptor activation. Because
androgen receptor proteins are extremely labile, often
denaturation of the binding site occurs, which causes the loss
of the (radioactive) ligand and makes detection of the
receptor impossible. In addition androgen receptor levels in
cytosol preparations of androgen target tissues are 10 to 20
times lower than those generally found for oestrogen and
progesterone receptors. With respect to the estimation of
molecular mass of the receptors recently also SDS-PAGE
electrophoresis has been successfully applied. A prerequisite
for the application of this technique is the covalent
attachment of the ligand to the steroid binding domain of the
receptor molecule (affinity labelling). Several procedures
have been published in which the steroid can be covalently
attached to proteins e.g. via photoactivation of highly
conjugated synthetic ligands and of ligands containing groups
which become highly reactive upon irradiation with U.V. light.
Chemical linkages with protein might be obtained through
acetylation with bromo- or chloro-acetoxy derivatives of
steroids. Affinity labelling not only permits the
identification of proteins present at very low abundancy in
cytosolic preparations of high complexity, but also the
unequivocal identification of steroid binding proteins at any
stage of a purification procedure.
We have studied the molecular properties of a DNA-binding form
of the androgen receptor from calf uterine cytosol after
affinity labelling. A partial purified (approx. 40 times)
DNA-binding androgen receptor preparation ligated with the
synthetic androgen ligand [^{3}H]-R1881 was photolysed and
subsequently precipitated with trichloroacetic acid. After
extraction with ethylacetate the precipitate was solubilized
in SDS-sample buffer and applied on a 8% polyacrylamide gel.
After electrophoresis the gel was sliced and each gel slice
was counted for radioactivity. The SDS-PAGE profile of

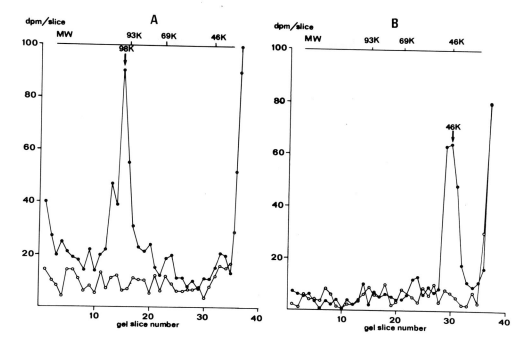

Figure 5
A. SDS-PAGE profiles of photolysed [^{3}H]-R1881-cytosol preparations from calf uterus in the presence of 2.5 μM triamcinolone acetonide. Irradiation of cytosol was performed after partial purification with ammonium sulphate precipitation (40%) and DNA-cellulose chromatography.
●: DNA-cellulose bound fraction irradiated in the presence of 15 nM [^{3}H]-R1881;
o: DNA-cellulose bound fraction irradiated in the presence of 15 nM [^{3}H]-R1881 + 3 μM dihydrotestosterone.
B. SDS-PAGE profiles of photolysed [^{3}H]-R1881 cytosol preparations from (Wistar) rat prostate after partial purification with FPLC anionexchange chromatography.
●: cytosol + 5 nM [^{3}H]-R1881
o: cytosol + 5 nM [^{3}H]-R1881 + 500 nM R1881.

photolysed [^{3}H]-R1881-androgen receptor complexes from calf uterus is shown in fig. 5A. One major peak of radioactivity could be detected associated with a protein of approximately 98,000 D molecular weight. The radioactive peak could be completely suppressed in a cytosol preparation where an additional 200-fold molar excess of dihydrotestosterone was present. This finding indicates that the sites to which the ligand is attached are saturable. Since in calf uterine cytosol 20 times higher progesterone receptor levels were found and the synthetic ligand R1881 has a high affinity for progesterone receptors, it is very important to establish that the observed peak does represent the androgen receptor and not the progesterone receptor. Two arguments favor the presence of a 98,000 D androgen receptor in calf uterine cytosol, first a 500-fold molar excess of triamcinoloneacetonide was added to the cytosol together with the $[^3H]$-R1881 in order to block $[^3H]$-R1881 binding to the progesterone receptor; second: photoaffinity labelling of progesterone receptors either with $[^3H]$-R5020 (a synthetic progestagen) or with $[^3H]$-R1881 resulted in two specifically labelled protein bands appearing at 110,000 D and 81,000 D respectively. It is concluded that the DNA-binding form of the androgen receptor from calf uterine tissue is a protein with a MW of 98,000 D.

Similar studies were performed with rat prostate cytosol. After irradiation, the molybdate stabilized cytosol of castrated rats was fractionated on a Mono Q column during FPLC as described in the previous section (see fig. 4A). The peak fractions 27-29 were further processed as described for the DNA-binding form of the calf uterine androgen receptor. In figure 5B the SDS-PAGE profile is shown. One major peak was detected at 46,000 D, which could be suppressed by a 100-fold molar excess of dihydrotestosterone. Whether the size of the photoaffinity labelled androgen receptor of the prostate represents the native form remains unanswered. The high proteolytic enzyme activities present in prostate cytosol might have influenced the molecular weight, despite the presence of molybdate (20 mM), PMSF (0.6 mM) and leupeptin (0.25 mM). A molecular weight of 86 kD for the prostate androgen receptor obtained from a different strain of rats has been reported recently (28). The receptor preparation used in that study for affinity labelling was more purified and the ligand used was bromoacetoxydihydrotestosterone. These methodological differences might probably explain to a certain extent the discrepancies observed.

However, the observed molecular weights for the androgen receptor of 98 kD in a tissue with low endogenic proteolytic activity and of 46 kD in a tissue with considerable proteolytic activity might indicate that for the activated androgen receptor a similar structure can be postulated as for the corticoid receptor (29): a receptor molecule with three different regions, one region showing steroid binding affinity, one region with DNA-binding affinity and a third region that is most prone to degradation by proteolytic enzymes. Further evidence for such a structure is given in the next sections and summarized in fig. 9.

III   Characteristics of the interaction of the receptor with nuclear acceptor sites

The activated androgen receptor displays an affinity not only for DNA, but for several natural and synthetic polyanions including chromatin, nucleosomes, RNA, phosphocellulose, heparin sepharose and 2'5'-ADP sepharose (10, 13, 30-35). Interactions with these polyanions is disrupted by high salt concentrations and in addition by various other inhibitors, which interact with the receptor. Pyridoxal phosphate, cibacron blue and heparin, added to low ionic strengths buffers were shown to be very effective for the extraction of androgen receptors from nuclei, DNA cellulose and ADP-sepharose. Under the influence of these reagents the steroid does not dissociate from the receptor, an indication for the presence of a separate chromatin binding region in the receptor molecule apart from the androgen binding site. Data obtained for extraction of androgen receptors from nuclei of rat prostates are summarized in table II.

Table II
Extraction of labelled androgen receptors from nuclear pellets
obtained from rat prostates incubated in vitro with
testosterone.

extraction medium	fmoles receptor/100 mg tissue
buffer	8
KCl, 0.4 M	53
cibacron blue, 0.4 mM	45
heparin, 0.2 mg/ml	60
pyridoxal phosphate, 10 mM	53

Prostates obtained from one day castrated rats were incubated
with 2.10^{-8} M [^{3}H]-testosterone and in a parallel experiment
with an additional amount of 2.10^{-6} M non-radioactive
testosterone. A thoroughly washed nucler pellet was prepared
and extracted for 1 h at 4°C. The amount of radioactive
steroid extracted was estimated and corrected for nonspecifically bound steroid with the values obtained from the
parallel incubation.

Cibacron blue probably acts as a substance showing both
localized cation exchange properties and some hydrophobic
interactions. The lower optimal concentrations of heparin and
Cibacron blue compared to pyridoxal phosphate required for
interference with receptor binding to nuclear chromatin might
indicate the involvement of a spatial arrangement of more than
one negatively charged group separated by a less polar region.
The effect of pyridoxal phosphate might primarily involve
binding of this molecule to an essential ε-amino group of the
receptor as was first shown for the corticoid receptor by
Litwack and co-workers (36).
The similarities in the effects of the various reagents used
for the extraction of receptors from nuclei and for the
elution of receptors from DNA-cellulose and related matrices
suggests that DNA-binding is involved in receptor binding in
the nucleus, but do not necessarily imply that DNA is the sole
molecular structure responsible for binding of the androgen

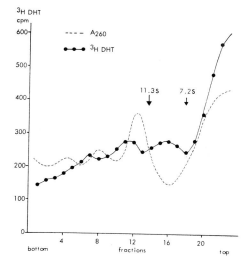

Figure 6
Digestion with micrococcal nuclease of nuclear chromatin obtained from rat prostate nuclei with [3H]-DHT labelled androgen receptors. The sucrose density gradient profiles show both distribution of [3H]-DHT labelled receptors and different nucleosome fractions (the peak in the dotted line indicates the position of the mononucleosomes, sedimenting slightly faster than the marker with a sedimentation value of 11.2 S).

receptor to chromatin.

In studies with nucleases Rennie (30) observed that the integrity of the linker regions of the nucleosomes in chromatin is necessary for steroid binding and that most of the androgen receptor is associated with fractions containing large oligomers of nucleosomes. In addition we observed small amounts of androgen-receptor complex sedimenting between 9-10S, suggesting release of androgen receptors partly coupled to a chromatin fragment (fig. 6).

Recent studies of Davies and Thomas (37) showed tissue specific binding by prostate chromatin of partially purified androgen receptors. The highest binding capacity was observed for oligonucleosome aggregates of up to twelve nucleosomes obtained from the fraction enriched in transcriptionally active genes.

IV Interaction of androgen receptors with DNA, RNA and polyribonucleotides

In our studies we have compared two different forms of the androgen receptor obtained from rat prostates, i.e. the small ("3S", from non-castrated rats) and intermediate ("4S", from castrated rats) forms as described in table I, with respect to their ability to interact with different polyanions. Both forms interacted strongly with ADP-sepharose (fig. 7). On the other hand binding to DNA-sepharose (containing mainly single stranded DNA) was reduced for the "3S" receptor form when compared with the "4S" receptor. This effect was particularly significant when small amounts of immobilized DNA were used and was not due to degradation of DNA, because the "3S" receptor preparation was free of DNAse activity (38). The specificity of the interaction of the androgen receptor preparations with nucleotides was investigated in a competitive binding assay, using inhibition of binding of the steroid receptor complex to ADP-sepharose (fig. 8). RNA and poly(UG) are potent competitors for the binding to ADP-sepharose of both "4S" and "3S" forms of the receptor. Fig. 8 illustrates the significant difference in DNA-binding for the two receptor forms. Double-stranded calf thymus DNA hardly inhibits binding of the "3S" form, but competes well for the binding sites on the "4S" receptor.

The "3S" form of the receptor obtained from rat prostates could be prepared in sufficient quantities in a partially purified form to perform a series of competition experiments (39). The high affinity of the "3S" receptor for certain polyribonucleotides e.g.: poly(UG), poly(AU), poly(I), poly(G) and poly(U), was striking and contrasted with the low affinity for restriction fragments of genomic clones from genes which code for prostatic binding protein (39). These gene fragments were obtained from regions of the genes which contain the

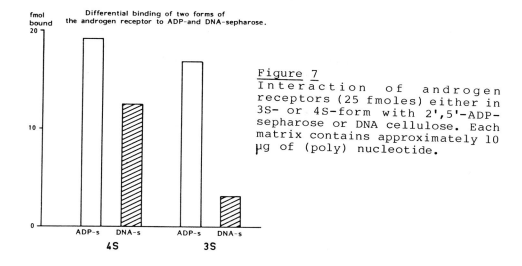

fmol bound

Differential binding of two forms of the androgen receptor to ADP-and DNA-sepharose.

Figure 7
Interaction of androgen receptors (25 fmoles) either in 3S- or 4S-form with 2',5'-ADP-sepharose or DNA cellulose. Each matrix contains approximately 10 μg of (poly) nucleotide.

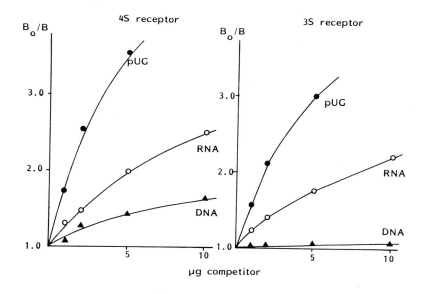

Figure 8
Competition experiments with two different forms of the androgen receptor. (from 38). B_o/B represents the ratio of androgen receptor complex bound to ADP-sepharose in the absence (Bo) and presence (B) of a competitor.

presumed hormone receptor binding site, located 5'-upstream from the transcription initiation site (40). Our data suggest that the "3S" form of the androgen receptor lacks the specific domain or conformation necessary for interaction with DNA, but retains a high affinity for certain forms of RNA.

As discussed in the section on multiple receptor forms, the small (3S) and intermediate (4S) receptor forms might be fragments of the transformed 4.5S receptor. It is tempting to speculate that in vivo transformation of the receptor to its DNA-binding form is followed by processing to a form that has lost the ability to recognize specific binding sites on double stranded DNA and is transported away from the chromatin binding site through its binding to RNA. In tissues of normal, mature animals the receptor would then be present for a substantial part in the intermediate (4S) and small (3S) form. In this respect it is interesting to note that for rat prostate nuclear receptors both a 3S form (11, 12, 21) as well as a 4S form (10, 12) have been reported.

Summary and conclusions

Androgen receptors isolated in a non-activated (i.e. non-DNA-binding) state can be converted in vitro to an activated (DNA-binding) state by treatment with concentrated salt solutions. Activation of androgen receptors is accompanied by a 30-fold increase in affinity for the androgen ligand and by a high affinity of the complex for polyanions and nuclear chromatin. Mainly three different forms of androgen receptors could be isolated, which could be distinguished on basis of their sedimentation coefficients, of their binding to DNA, RNA and certain polyribonucleotides, and of their molecular mass estimated by gelchromatography and electrophoresis under denaturating conditions after affinity labelling. It is

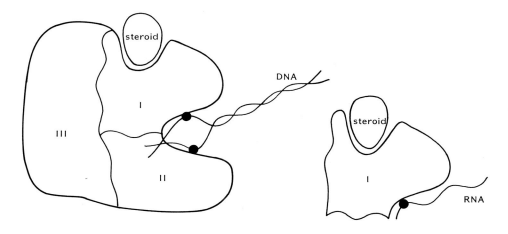

TRANSFORMED ANDROGEN RECEPTOR

Figure 9

I	25 kDa (3 S)
I + II	45 kDa (4 S)
I + II + III	80–120 kDa (4.6S)

hypothesized that the monomeric androgen receptor molecule consists of three different regions of which the smallest in size (region I) contains the steroid binding site and has a high affinity for RNA. Together with region II a larger fragment is formed with a molecular weight of approx. 45,000 and which contains the DNA-binding domain. Finally, the combination of region I, II and III results in the monomeric, largest formof the androgen receptor. A model relating the different regions of the androgen receptor is shown infig. 9.

Acknowledgements

We thank Drs. W. de Boer and J.A. Foekens for their

contributions to this study and Dr. H.J. van der Molen for his many helpful discussions. We are indebted to Schering AG (Berlin, FRG) for the supply of radioactive and radioinert cyproterone acetate.

References

1. Yamamoto, K.R., Alberts, B.M.: Ann. Rev. Biochem. 45, 721-746 (1976).
2. O'Malley, B.W., Means, A.R.: Science 183, 610-620 (1974).
3. Davison, B.L., Mulvihill, E.R., Egly, J.M., Chambon, P.: Cold Spring Harbor Symp. Quant. Biol. 47, 965-976.
4. Yamamoto, K.R., Payvar, F., Firestone, G.L., Maler, B.A., Wrange, O, Carlstedt-Duke, J., Gustafsson, J.-A^O., Chandler, V.L.: Cold Spring Harbor Symp. Quant. Biol. 47, 977-985 (1983).
5. Mainwaring, W.I.P., Irving, R.: Biochem. J. 134, 113-127 (1973).
6. King, W.J., Greene, G.L.: Nature 307, 745-747 (1984).
7. Welshons, W.V., Lieberman, M.E., Gorski, J.: Nature 307, 747-749 (1984).
8. Mainwaring, W.I.P., Symes, E.K., Higgins, S.J.: Biochem. J. 156, 129-141 (1976).
9. Tymoczko, J.L., Liang, T., Liao, S.: In: O'Malley, B.W., Birnbaumer, L. (eds) Receptors and Hormone Action, Vol. 2, Academic Press, New York, pp. 121-156, 1978.
10. Mainwaring, W.I.P.: The Mechanism of Action of Androgens, Springer-Verlag, New York 1977.
11. Liao, S., Tymoczko, J.L., Castaneda, E., Liang, T: Vitamins and Hormones vol. 33, Academic Press, New York, pp. 297-317, 1975.
12. Mulder, E., Vrij, A., Foekens, J.A.: Molec. Cell. Endocrin. 23, 283-296 (1981).
13. Wilson, E.M., French, F.S.: J. Biol. Chem. 254, 6310-6319 (1979).
14. Grody, W.W., Schrader, W.T., O'Malley, B.W.: Endocr. Rev. 3, 141-163 (1982).
15. Weichman, B.M., Notides, A.C.: J. Biol. Chem. 252, 8856-8862 (1977).
16. Bailly, A., Le Fevre, B., Savouret, J.F., Milgrom, E.: J. Biol. Chem. 255, 2729-2734 (1980).
17. Kovacs, W.J., Griffin, J.E., Wilson, J.D.: Endocrinology 113, 1574-1581 (1983).
18. Brinkmann, A.O., Lindh, L.M., Breedveld, D.I., Mulder, E., Van der Molen, H.J.: Mol. Cell. Endocrinol. 32, 117-129 (1983).
19. Raynaud, J.P., Bouton, M.M., Moguilewsky, M., Ojasoo, T. Philibert, D., Beck, G., Labrie, F., Mornon, J.P.: J. Steroid Biochem. 12, 143-157 (1980).

20. Zakar, T., Toth, M.: J. Steroid Biochem. 17, 287-293 (1982).
21. Rennie, P.S., Van Doorn, E., Bruchovsky, N.: Molec. Cell. Endocr. 9, 145-157 (1977).
22. Holbrook, N.J., Bodwell, J.E., Jeffries, M., Munck, A.: J. Biol. Chem. 258, 6477-6485 (1983).
23. Brinkmann, A.O., Bolt-de Vries, J., De Boer, W., Lindh, L.M., Mulder E., Van der Molen, H.J.: J. Steroid. Biochem., in press (1985).
24. Pavlik, E.J. Van Nagel jr. J.R., Muncey, M., Donaldson, E.S., Hanson, M., Kenady, D., Rees, E.D., Talwalkar, V.R.: Biochemistry 21, 139-145 (1982).
25. Hutchens, T.W., Wiehle, R.D., Shahabi, N.A., Wittliff, J.L.: J. Chromatogr. 266, 115-128 (1983).
26. Soderberg, L., Bergstrom, J., Andersson, K.: Protides Biol. Fluids Proc. Colloq. 30, 629-634 (1983).
27. Sherman, M.R., Pickering, L.A., Rollwagen, F.M., Miller, L.K.: Fed. Proc. 37, 167-173 (1978).
28. Chang, C.H., Lobl, T.J., Rowley, D.R., Tindall, D.J.: Biochemistry 23, 2527-2533 (1984).
29. Carlstedt-Duke, J., Okret, S., Wrange, O, Gustafsson, J.A^O.: Proc. Natl. Acad. Sci. USA 79, 4260-4264 (1982).
30. Rennie, P.S.: J. Biol. Chem. 254, 3947-3952 (1979).
31. Davies, P., Thomas, P., Borthwick, N.M., Giles, M.G.: J. Endocr. 87, 225-240 (1980).
32. Liao, S., Smythe, S., Tymoczko, J.L., Rossini, G.P., Chen, C., Hiipakka, R.A.: J. Biol. Chem. 255, 5541-5551 (1980).
33. Mulder, E., Foekens, J.A., Peters, M.J., Van der Molen, H.J.: FEBS Letters 97, 260-264 (1979).
34. Mulder, E., Vrij, L., Foekens, J.A.: Steroids 36, 633-645 (1980).
35. Lin, S., Ohno, S.: Eur. J. Biochem. 124, 283-287 (1982).
36. Cake, M.H., DiSorbo, D.M., Litwack, G.: J. Biol. Chem. 253, 4886-4891 (1978).
37. Davies, P., Thomas, P.: J. Steroid Biochem. 20, 57-65 (1984).
38. Mulder, E., Vrij, A.A., Brinkmann, A.O.: Biochem. Biophys. Res. Commun. 114, 1147-1153 (1983).
39. Mulder, E., Vrij, A.A., Brinkmann, A.O., Van der Molen, H.J., Parker, M.G.: Biochim. Biophys. Acta 781, 121-129 (1984).
40. Parker, M., Hurst, H., Page, M.: J. Steroid. Biochem. 20, 67-71 (1984).

DIFFERENTIAL SENSITIVITY OF SPECIFIC GENES IN MOUSE KIDNEY TO ANDROGENS AND ANTIANDROGENS

James F. Catterall, Cheryl S. Watson, Kimmo K. Kontula, Olli A. Jänne, and C. Wayne Bardin

The Population Council and The Rockefeller University, 1230 York Avenue, New York, N.Y. 10021

Introduction

Early studies on the action of testosterone emphasized that this steroid has a variety of actions on almost every organ in the body. Those on the reproductive tract were called androgenic while those on other organs were called anabolic actions. Androgen receptors were first identified in reproductive tissues such as prostate and seminal vesicle, and studies which showed that antiandrogens could compete with testosterone or its metabolite, 5α–dihydrotestosterone (DHT), for receptor binding sites were the first to clearly associate androgen receptors with the action of testosterone and DHT. The ultimate proof, however, that androgen receptors were an essential link between testosterone and the androgen-induced phenotype was the identification of receptor mutants in the rat and mouse which were insensitive to many of the effects of testosterone and other androgens (1-4). Studies on these animals also emphasized that both the androgenic and the anabolic effects of testosterone were mediated via androgen receptors (5).

Molecular Mechanism of Steroid Hormone Action
© 1985 Walter de Gruyter & Co., Berlin · New York – Printed in Germany

The general concept of androgen action that has evolved holds that interaction of testosterone or DHT with the androgen receptor changes its conformation which allows it to bind to an "acceptor site." In this manuscript the term acceptor is used to describe a functional site in chromatin to which the steroid-receptor complex binds. Current studies suggest that a portion of the acceptor site is formed by a unique segment of DNA at the 5'-end of hormonally responsive genes (6,7). Since the same gene is not responsive in all tissues, formation of acceptor sites is dependent upon organ specific differentiation. This implies that there are specific factors which are necessary for steroid-induced gene expression in some tissues. Interaction of the steroid-receptor complex with the acceptor site results in the expression of genes which ultimately determines the hormone-induced phenotype. Since the overall male phenotype for a given species is relatively uniform, it was assumed that androgen receptor interaction with acceptors resulted in the synthesis of a relatively uniform and characteristic group of mRNAs and proteins for a given organ, and that number of steroid receptor complexes on chromatin would determine the amount of each mRNA and protein produced. It was not known, however, how androgen receptor complexes were partitioned between the individual acceptor sites of different genes. One possibility was that the receptor had the same affinity for each acceptor in the same way that each molecule of testosterone had equal access to activate each receptor binding site. If this were the case, then one might predict that the dose of testosterone (which ultimately relates to the number of receptors bound to chromatin in a given organ) required both to initiate and to produce maximal responses would be similar for most genes. Alternatively, androgen receptor complexes might exhibit differential affinities for several acceptor sites. If this were the case, then the number of receptors required to initiate and to produce maximal activity would vary between different genes in the same cell. This latter possibility also predicts that the potency of a given androgen might not be strictly related to its affinity for a given receptor (5).

Much of the work on androgen induced gene expression has involved analysis of the abundant gene products stimulated by androgens in the rat prostate (8,9) and seminal vesicle (10-12). However, no attempts were made in these studies to correlate specific gene expression with androgen receptor dynamics or to compare the androgen sensitivity of these different genes. The mouse kidney has become an important system for the study of the androgenic control of individual gene expression. Gene-specific complementary DNA (cDNA) probes are now available for four mouse kidney mRNAs: two abundant species, kidney androgen-regulated protein (KAP) (13,14), an mRNA designated MK908 (15) and the non-abundant mRNAs for ornithine decarboxylase (ODC) (16,17) and β-glucuronidase (β-GLUC) (18,19).

In the present review, we summarize studies in which we used cDNA probes for KAP, ODC and β-GLUC in establishing the patterns of gene-specific responses to testosterone in the mouse kidney. The availability of these cDNAs to one group of investigators permitted the simultaneous measurement of the mRNA accumulation in the kidneys in response to a variety of stimuli. In addition, nuclear androgen receptor concentration has been correlated with the expression of each individual gene (20). The results reveal distinct responses of the three genes to physiological levels of testosterone, variations in nuclear receptor concentration, duration of hormone treatment, and to antiandrogens. The results are consistent with the hypothesis that androgen-responsive genes have differential sensitivities to the testosterone-androgen receptor complex.

Recent Advances in the Measurement of Bound Nuclear Androgen Receptor

Recent studies suggested that steroid receptors are nuclear proteins (21). However, in the absence of specific hormone, they are rapidly lost from nuclei and are found in cytosol when cells are disrupted in hypotonic buffers. When the appropriate steroid ligand is bound to the receptor, the conformation of this protein changes so that it will bind to nuclear constituents. In this state, receptors are not readily lost into cytosol when cells are broken. In this review these receptors are referred to as "bound nuclear receptors." It is these receptors that are believed to be bound to acceptor sites and are correlated with hormone action.

The concentration of bound androgen receptor in renal nuclei of the mouse following testosterone treatment _in vivo_ is low relative to other androgen-responsive tissues such as the prostate. In addition, apparent receptor concentrations have varied under different conditions for preparation and extraction of nuclei. For this reason, a rigorous analysis of the various components of the nuclear receptor assay was undertaken in order to maximize its specificity and sensitivity (20). The assay conditions that evolved for these studies were based upon the observations that a large fraction of bound nuclear androgen receptors was lost when nuclei were isolated in aqueous buffers and that another fraction of the bound receptors was excluded from the final assay since it could not be extracted by KCl.

To overcome these difficulties, nuclei were isolated in the presence of hexylene glycol (22) and bound nuclear receptor extracted with 5 mM pyridoxal 5'-phosphate (20,23,24). Nuclear receptor concentration was determined by incubating extracts, in triplicate, with a saturating concentration (22.5 nM) of [^{3}H]methyltrienolone for 18 hrs at 4°C. Non-specific and total binding were determined in the presence and absence of a 1000-fold molar excess of testosterone, respectively. Bound ligands were separated from those unbound by adsorption to hydroxylapatite. Using these assay conditions, 3-4 times more bound nuclear receptors are measured than when aqueous buffers are used for nuclear isolation and KCl is used for extraction.

Cloned cDNA Probes for mRNAs that Exhibit Unique Responses to Androgens

For studies of differential gene expression in response to androgens in mouse kidney, we have measured concentrations of three mRNAs with gene specific hybridization probes. The KAP mRNA is an abundant gene product which codes for a protein (Mr=20,000) of unknown function. The other two are low abundance mRNAs which code for the androgen-induced renal enzymes, β-GLUC and ODC.

Complementary DNA plasmids were prepared for each mRNA using two different approaches. Since KAP mRNA was shown to be approximately 100-fold more abundant than ODC or β-GLUC mRNA, KAP mRNA was purified by extraction of total mRNA from kidneys of androgen-treated female mice followed by sucrose density gradient centrifugation and oligo(dT)-cellulose chromatography (14). ODC and β-GLUC mRNAs, which represent approximately 0.05% and 0.02%, respectively, of the cell's mRNA after androgen treatment, were purified from renal polysomes by immunoadsorption to specific antibodies followed by chromatography on protein A-Sepharose (16,18). This was a modification of the immunoadsorbent chromatographic method of Shapiro and Young and resulted in a 300-fold purification of the ODC and β-GLUC mRNAs. The additional steps introduced into the procedure (16,18) (including passing of polysomes through protein A-Sepharose prior to antibody addition, use of the ribonuclease inhibitor, RNasin, and inclusion of a high concentration of heparin in the buffers) increased the purity of the two mRNAs.

Purified mRNAs were assayed by translation _in vitro_ and used as templates for preparation of cDNA plasmid libraries. These were screened by differential colony hybridization. In the case of KAP cDNA clones, the "plus" and "minus" probes were prepared from KAP mRNA-enriched gradient fractions and mRNA from female mouse kidney, respectively. A similar assay for ODC and β-GLUC cDNA clones was devised using probes prepared from protein A-Sepharose-bound ("plus") and drop-through ("minus") polysomal RNA fractions. In each case, colonies that preferentially bound the plus probe over the minus probe were selected for further analysis. Final identification of the cDNA clones was made by hybridization-selected translation _in vitro_, which correlated individual cDNA plasmids with each specific mRNA activity.

Acute Response to Testosterone

Following a single injection of a large dose of testosterone (10 mg), bound nuclear androgen receptor concentration increased to reach a maximum at one hr. By 2 hrs the receptor level was still seven times the control level or

182 fmoles/mg DNA (Fig. 1). The receptor concentration in the nuclei then decreased by approximately 50% over the next 48 hrs. The measurements of specific mRNAs indicated that there was no change at or before 2 hrs when receptor levels were highest. Thereafter, the response of these three mRNAs to a single dose of testosterone varied greatly, emphasizing the differential effect of the hormone on genes in the same tissue. ODC and KAP mRNAs responded rapidly, increasing 2.1- and 1.6-fold in 6 hrs, respectively. However, KAP mRNA was almost maximally stimulated at this interval in that it increased to only 2-fold by 48 hrs while ODC mRNA continued to accumulate to over eight times the untreated level by 24 hrs. β-GLUC mRNA remained unaffected until between 12 and 24 hrs of treatment when the first increase was detected; thereafter, it rose to 1.7 times the control value at 48 hrs. In another study, β-GLUC mRNA concentration reached maximal levels after 14 days of continuous androgen administration. These results indicated that for β-GLUC the lag before the first detectable response was evident and the time to reach the maximal response were strikingly different from those of the other two genes. The magnitude of the increases in mRNA concentrations in these studies was determined by densitometric scans of autoadiograms of transfer blot hybridizations. This semiquantitative method revealed relative increases, rather than absolute values. However, this type of analysis is valid when comparing the proportional responses of several genes in the same tissue to hormones and/or drugs (Fig. 1).

The results shown in Figure 1 indicate a differential responsiveness among the three genes in the presence of maximal levels of nuclear androgen receptors after a single dose of testosterone. Previous studies suggested that, in addition to the initial receptor concentration, the androgen response is in part dependent on the length of time that the androgen receptor complex remain tightly bound in nuclei (24). It was, therefore, of interest to determine the relative expression of the three genes in the presence of constant submaximal nuclear receptor levels. To do this we determined the response of each mRNA to the physiological testosterone concentration present in normal male mice.

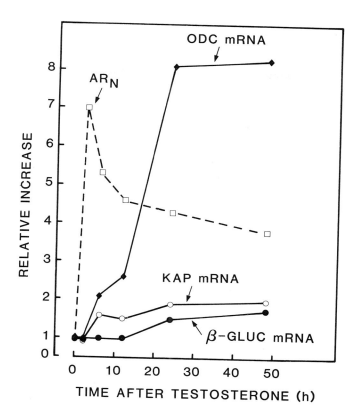

Figure 1: Changes in mRNA accumulation and nuclear androgen receptor concentration after a single dose of testosterone. Testosterone (10 mg) was administered by intraperitoneal injection of 0.2 ml of ethanol/sesame oil (1/9; v/v) to female NCS mice. At the indicated times poly(A)-mRNA was prepared from kidney extracts and analyzed by electrophoresis and blot transfer hybridization. Autoradiographs of each transfer filter were scanned with a densitometer (Shimadzu model CS-910). The untreated female level was assigned the value of 1. Androgen receptor measurements were made by an exchange assay on nuclear extracts prepared from identically treated animals. Nuclear androgen receptor, (AR_N) values represent the mean of 3 experiments. Kidneys from four animals were pooled at each time point in all experiments. Abbreviations: KAP, kidney androgen-induced protein; ODC, ornithine decarboxylase; β-GLUC, β-glucuronidase.

The Effects of Endogenous Testosterone

The relative differences in mRNA concentrations in intact females and intact males are shown in Table I. In each case, physiological amounts of testosterone secreted by the testes of the male mice were sufficient to cause an increase in mRNA concentration over the values in female animals. However, there was a major difference among the three genes as measured by the abundance of their mRNAs. The autoradiograms of the Northern blots from which the data were derived were exposed to achieve comparable signals; this required 24- and 13-fold longer exposure times for β-GLUC and ODC mRNAs, respectively, than for KAP mRNA.

Table I

Relative concentration of three mRNAs in intact female and male mice. Each mRNA concentration is expressed as a percent of that obtained after maximal stimulation with testosterone for 7 days.

	Relative mRNA Concentration	
Gene	Female %	Male %
KAP	35	100
ODC	10	30
β-GLUC	5	35

Table I also indicates the extent to which the individual RNAs could be increased with a maximal dose of exogenous hormone. Once again, variation among the gene products was evident. While β-GLUC and ODC mRNA concentrations were further increased by exogenous testosterone administration, KAP mRNA was unaffected. The concentrations of androgen receptor in the nuclei of female, male and testosterone-treated male mice are shown in Table II. The receptor level in females was approximately 50% of that of intact males, whereas chronic testosterone treatment increased the level in males five-fold. These latter nuclear receptor values represent the maximal concentrations attainable in mouse kidney and are associated with full expression of ODC and β-GLUC genes. It remains to be elucidated, however, whether maximal accumulation of these two mRNAs indeed requires this high nuclear receptor concentration. Taken together, these data suggest differential sensitivity of the three genes to low nuclear androgen receptor concentrations. Maximal expression of the KAP gene appears to occur at a low concentration of nuclear androgen receptors, as it cannot be further stimulated by pharmacological steroid concentrations above that achieved with physiological hormone levels. By contrast the same concentration of bound nuclear receptors resulted in ODC and β-GLUC mRNA concentrations which were only 30 and 35 percent of maximal.

Table II

Concentrations of bound androgen receptors in renal nuclei from intact female, intact male, and testosterone-implanted male mice.

Animal group	Androgen receptor concentration[a]	
Intact females	150 + 60	(13)[c]
Intact males	280 + 100	(6)
Testosterone-implanted males[b]	1,540 + 390	(5)

[a] The receptor concentrations (mean + SD) are expressed as molecules/cell assuming that receptors are evenly distributed within the kidney with 6 pg DNA/cell.

[b] The animals were treated with testosterone-containing implants (release rate, 200 μg steroid/day) for 7 days.

[c] Animals per group are shown in parenthesis.

KAP mRNA is Induced by Testosterone in Androgen Insensitive Tfm/Y Mice

The androgen insensitive Tfm/Y mouse is resistant to almost all of the actions of testosterone even when high doses are administered (25,26). In this respect, it differs from the Tfm rat which has a reduced quantity of presumably normal androgen receptors and responds in a dose-dependent manner to a 200-fold higher amounts of testosterone than normal rats (27-

29). The Tfm/Y mouse also has a low concentration of androgen receptor but it is disputed whether these are normal or mutant receptors (30-32).

The relative concentrations of the three mRNAs were determined before and after testosterone treatment of Tfm/Y mice. Unexpectedly, testosterone treatment increased the KAP mRNA concentration approximately 2-fold over that found in the kidneys of untreated animals. Neither ODC nor β-GLUC mRNA concentrations were significantly affected by testosterone in these animals. These observations suggested that the KAP gene was able to respond to the low concentration of androgen receptor in Tfm/Y mice, whereas the ODC and β-GLUC genes were not.

These results do not resolve the issue as to whether the receptors in Tfm/Y mice are normal. If the receptors in these animals are the same as wild-type, the results could be interpreted as indicating that the KAP gene responds to a lower concentration of bound nuclear receptors than almost any other gene in the mouse genome. Alternatively, if the receptors in Tfm/Y mice are abnormal, then the acceptor for KAP must be sufficiently different from that of other genes to accommodate the mutant receptor.

Differential Inhibition of Individual mRNAs by Flutamide

The results reported above indicate that testosterone-androgen receptor complex interacts with dissimilar genes to produce unique patterns of mRNA accumulation. These results also suggest that this variation in gene expression is due to the different responsiveness of each gene to a given amount of androgen-receptor complexes. If this is the case, then one would expect differential gene responses when the availability of receptor complexes is changed in the presence of an antiandrogen. That is, a gene that is very sensitive to low concentrations of androgen-receptor complexes should be more resistant to antiandrogens since there would always be a few receptors occupied by testosterone even in the presence of large doses of antagonist. Accordingly, female animals were treated with flutamide-containing Silastic rods (releasing either 150 μg/day or 650 μg/day) with

Table III
Inhibition of testosterone-induced mRNA accumulation by flutamide

Treatment group	Relative mRNA Concentration[a]		
	KAP	ODC	β-GLUC
T[b]	4.5	5.0	11.6
T + F1	3.7	2.9	5.1
T + F2	3.4	0.7	1.0

[a]The mRNA concentration is expressed relative to the untreated female level (1.0) of each group.

[b]Female NCS mice were implanted with Silastic rods containing testosterone (T, release rate: 40 μg/day) alone or in combination with similar implants of flutamide (F1, 150 μg/day; F2, 650 μg/day). Renal poly(A)-mRNA was prepared after 8 days of treatment.

Table IV.
Summary of Relative Gene-Specific Responses in Mouse Kidney[a]

Animal/treatment group	Relative mRNA Accumulation		
	KAP	ODC	β-GLUC
Female	++	+	+
Male	++++	++	++
Male + T	++++	++++	++++
Duration of Treatment			
12-24 hrs	++++	+++	+
2 days	++++	++++	++
14 days	++++	++++	++++
Tfm/Y	±	±	−
Tfm/Y + T	+	±	−
Female + T	++++	++++	++++
Female + T + F1	+++	++	++
Female + T + F2	+++	+	+

[a]This table is presented as a brief summary of the qualitative differences in sensitivity of the three gene markers to various conditions of androgen exposure. The symbols do not represent quantitative changes. T, testosterone; F1, F2, flutamide, 150 and 650 μg/day, respectively.

and without testosterone-containing rods (releasing 40 μg/day). The results shown in Table III suggest that the sensitivity of the three mRNAs to flutamide was essentially the inverse of their sensitivity to testosterone. KAP mRNA, which was shown to be unusually responsive to testosterone, was least affected by the non-steroidal antagonist. ODC and β-GLUC mRNAs were both much more sensitive to flutamide inhibition in that less than 10-15% of the testosterone-induced mRNA concentrations remained after treatment with the higher dose of antiandrogen. Flutamide alone resulted in no significant variation in the concentrations of any mRNA (data not shown).

Summary and Conclusions

1. Androgens stimulate the epithelium of the proximal tubule cells of the mouse kidney to increase the synthesis of several proteins (5). Cloned complementary DNA probes have recently been prepared and characterized for the mRNAs for three of these proteins: β-GLUC (18,19), ODC (16,17), and KAP (14). Previous studies had shown that β-GLUC and ODC enzyme activities were regulated differently by testosterone in this tissue (24,33) in that ODC responded to testosterone with more rapid kinetics than β-GLUC. KAP induction kinetics have not been demonstrated as the protein has been identified only by translation in vitro (13). KAP mRNA is a relatively abundant species while those of β-GLUC and ODC were of the non-abundant mRNA class. The availability of these three gene-specific probes allowed us to measure a unique spectrum of responses to testosterone.

2. In order to fully characterize the regulation of renal gene expression by testosterone, it was necessary to measure the concentration of the bound androgen receptor in nuclei under the same conditions as the gene expression studies. A reliable method for the measurement of bound androgen receptor in mouse renal nuclei was established (20).

3. In this study a general trend of androgen sensitivity was established with the following ranking: KAP mRNA >> ODC mRNA > β-GLUC mRNA. The results suggest gene-specific variations in response were related to duration of exposure to testosterone, physiological levels of testosterone,

concentration of bound nuclear androgen receptors, and treatment by antian-drogens (Table IV).

4. As the bound androgen receptor concentration in kidney nuclei was maxi-mal by 1 hr after a single steroid dose, it is clear that subsequent bio-logical responses which occurred over the next 4-48 hrs were determined in part by factors other than the initial receptor concentration. Indeed, our previous studies have suggested that, under these conditions, it is the product of nuclear receptor concentration and the residence time of the receptor that predicts the biological response (24). This product appears to be, however, dissimilar for the three mRNAs studied. In accordance with this notion, Watson et al. (34) hypothesized that a minimum number of receptor molecules must bind in the region of the [Gus] genetic complex in chromatin in order to achieve an induction response. This hypothesis is now extended to include differential kinetics of interaction between andro-gen receptors and chromatin binding sites on separate genes consistent with the data presented here. Furthermore, it has been suggested that effector molecules such as steroid hormone receptors bind to nuclease sensitive domains in chromatin (35,36). Differential responsiveness of individual genes to a hormone may reside in the size and/or complexity of the "active" domain with which the receptor must interact.

5. A related hypothesis was developed in order to explain the differences in expression of the conalbumin and ovalbumin genes in response to steroid hormones (37). In this case, multiple binding sites for the steroid recep-tor were postulated for the less sensitive gene which thus requires longer duration of treatment or higher receptor concentration to become fully induced. The same differential responsiveness could also be explained if the acceptor of various genes bound receptor complexes with different effectiveness. The results reviewed here provide evidence in support of such a hypothesis based on gene-specific sensitivity to the androgen-receptor complex. The KAP gene, which is the most hormonally "sensitive" gene studied, is maximally induced in males by physiological testosterone levels. Thus, the KAP gene may require the fewest number of bound receptor-androgen complexes for activation because its acceptor has either multiple binding sites or a high affinity for receptors.

6. The results reviewed here show that androgen-resistant Tfm/Y animals exhibit a condition in which receptor concentration appears adequate with respect to the KAP gene, but too low to have effects on ODC or β-GLUC mRNA, even with pharmacological doses of androgens. The induction of KAP mRNA in Tfm/Y animals suggests that all or part of the androgen receptor in this variant (30-32) is biologically active. The results do not exclude the possibility that these androgen receptors may be qualitatively different from wild-type receptors (38), but still capable of effecting the response of KAP mRNA. Further experiments will be required to distinguish this from other possibilities.

7. The antiandrogen flutamide was also used to evaluate the dissimilar androgen sensitivities of the three gene products in mouse kidney. We reasoned that expression of the most sensitive gene should be affected to a lesser extent than those requiring higher concentrations of nuclear androgen receptors for full expression. On the basis of differential androgen sensitivity of the three genes observed in other experiments, the KAP gene was predicted to exhibit the least inhibition by flutamide, while the ODC gene was expected to be less affected than that of β-GLUC. These predictions were verified providing further evidence that the KAP gene can be stimulated at very low functional receptor levels, consistent with a lower required threshold of androgen receptor binding to chromatin site(s) associated with this gene.

Acknowledgement

This work was supported by NIH grants HD-13541 and 3 F05 TW3192-0151. We wish to thank Ms. Susan Richman for preparing the manuscript.

References

1. Lyon, M.F. and Hawkes, S.G.: Nature Lond. 227,1217-1219 (1970).

2. Bardin, C.W., Bullock, L., Schneider, G., Allison, J.E., and Stanley, A.J.: Science 167,1136-1137 (1970).

3. Bullock, L. and Bardin, C.W.: J. Clin. Endocrinol. Metab. 31,113-115 (1970).

4. Bullock, L.P., Bardin, C.W., and Ohno, S.: Biochem. Biophys. Res. Commun. 44,1537-1543 (1971).

5. Bardin, C.W. and Catterall, J.F.: Science 211,1285-1294 (1981).

6. Compton, J.G., Schrader, W.T., and O'Malley, B.W.: Proc. Natl. Acad. Sci. USA 80,16-20 (1983).

7. Gustafsson, J.A., Carlstedt-Duke, J., Okret, S., Wikstrom, A.C., Wrange, O., Payvar, F., and Yamamoto, K.: J. Steroid Biochem. 20,1-4 (1984).

8. Page, M.J. and Parker, M.G.: Cell 32,495-502 (1983).

9. Dodd, J.G., Sheppard, P.C., and Matusik, R.J.: J. Biol. Chem. 258,10731-10737 (1983).

10. Mansson, P.-E., Sugino, E., and Harris, S.E.: Nucleic Acids Res. 9,935-946 (1981).

11. Kandala, J.C., Kistler, M.K., Lawther, R.P., and Kistler, W.S.: Nucleic Acids Res. 11,3169-3186 (1983).

12. McDonald, C., Williams, L., McTurk, P., Fuller, F., McIntosh, E., and Higgins, S.: Nucleic Acids Res. 11,917-930 (1983).

13. Toole, J.J., Hastie, N.D., and Held, W.A.: Cell 17,441-448 (1979).

14. Watson, C.S., Salomon, D., and Catterall, J.F.: Ann. NY Acad. Sci. (in press) (1984).

15. Berger, F.G., Gross, K.W., and Watson, G.: J. Biol. Chem. 256,7006-7013 (1981).

16. Kontula, K.K., Torkkeli, T.K., Bardin, C.W., and Janne, O.A.: Proc. Natl. Acad. Sci. USA 81,731-735 (1984).

17. McConlogue, L., Gupta, M., Wu, L., and Coffino, P.: Proc. Natl. Acad. Sci. USA 81,540-544 (1984).

18. Catterall, J.F. and Leary, S.L.: Biochemistry 22,6049-6053 (1983).

19. Palmer, R., Gallagher, P.M., Boyko, W.L., and Ganschow, R.E.: Proc. Natl. Acad. Sci. USA 80,7596-7600 (1983).

20. Isomaa, V., Pajunen, A.E.I., Bardin, C.W., and Janne, O.A.: Endocrinology 111,833-843 (1982).

21. Greene, G.L., Sobel, N.B., King, W.J., and Jensen, E.V.: J. Steroid Biochem. $\underline{20}$,51-56 (1984).

22. Wray, W., Conn, P.M., and Wray, V.P.: Meths. Cell Biol. $\underline{14}$,69 (1977).

23. Cidlowski, J.A. and Thanassi, J.W.: Biochem. Biophys. Res. Comm. $\underline{82}$,1140-1146 (1978).

24. Pajunen, A.E.I., Isomaa, V.V., Janne, O.A., and Bardin, C.W.: J. Biol. Chem. $\underline{257}$,8190-8198 (1982).

25. Bardin, C.W., Bullock, L.P., Sherins, R.J., Mowszowicz, I., and Blackburn, W.R.: Rec. Prog. Hormone Res. $\underline{29}$,65-109 (1973).

26. Schenkein, I., Levy, M., Bueker, E.D., and Wilson, J.D.: Endocrinology $\underline{94}$,840-844 (1974).

27. Sherins, R.J., Bullock, L., Gay, V.L., Vanha-Perttula, T., and Bardin, C.W.: Endocrinology $\underline{88}$,763-770 (1971).

28. Grossman, S.H., Axelrod, B., and Bardin, C.W.: Life Sci. $\underline{10}$,175-180 (1971).

29. Sherins, R.J. and Bardin, C.W.: Endocrinology $\underline{89}$,835-841 (1971).

30. Attardi, B. and Ohno, S.: Cell $\underline{2}$,205-215 (1974).

31. Gehring, U. and Tomkins, G.M.: Cell $\underline{3}$,59-64 (1974).

32. Fox, T.O.: Proc. Natl. Acad. Sci. USA $\underline{72}$,4303-4307 (1975).

33. Swank, R.T., Paigen, K., Davey, R., Chapman, V., Labarca, C., Watson, G., Ganschow, R., Brandt, E.J., and Novak, E.: Recent Prog. Horm. Res. $\underline{34}$,401-436 (1978).

34. Watson, G., Davey, R.A., Labarca, C., and Paigen, K.: J. Biol. Chem. $\underline{256}$,3005-3011 (1981).

35. Lawson, G.M., Knoll, B.J., March, C.J., Woo, S.L.C., Tsai, M-J, and O'Malley, B.W.: J. Biol. Chem. $\underline{257}$,1501-1507 (1982).

36. Bloom, K.S. and Anderson, J.N.: J. Biol. Chem. $\underline{257}$,13018-13027 (1982).

37. Palmiter, R.D., Mulvihill, E.R., Shephard, J.H., and McKnight, G.S.: J. Biol. Chem. $\underline{256}$,7910-7916 (1981).

38. Fox, T.O. and Wieland, S.J.: Endocrinology $\underline{109}$,790-791 (1981).

MOLECULAR PHARMACOLOGY OF TAMOXIFEN; AN ANTIESTROGEN WITH ANTITUMOR PROPERTIES IN ANIMALS AND MAN

V. Craig Jordan

Department of Human Oncology, Wisconsin Clinical Cancer Center, University of Wisconsin, Madison, WI USA 53792

Introduction

In 1958, Lerner and coworkers (1) described the pharmacological properties of MER 25, the first non-steroidal antiestrogen (Fig. 1). The compound is antiestrogenic in all species tested and also has antifertility properties in laboratory animals (1-3). Clinical trials with MER 25 confirmed its antiestrogenic activity in patients, however, the low potency and the occurrence of CNS side effects (4) caused a search for alternatives. Clomiphene (MRL 41) is more potent than MER 25, but unlike MER 25 has some estrogenic properties in animals (5). Although clomiphene has antifertility properties in animals, the drug induces ovulation in subfertile women (6). The commercial preparation Clomid®, a mixture of estrogenic (zuclomiphene) and antiestrogenic (enclomiphene) geometric isomers, is now routinely used for the induction of ovulation in annovulatory women (7).

Many structural derivatives of triphenylethylene have been synthesized and tested for antiestrogenic/antifertility activity, however, in the early 1970's investigators shifted the focus of research from contraception to hormone-dependent breast cancer. Nafoxidine (U-11,100A) (8,9) and tamoxifen (ICI 46,474) (10,11) were both shown to have a beneficial effect upon the clinical course of advanced breast cancer, however, only tamoxifen is available for breast cancer therapy because of the low reported incidence of side effects (12).

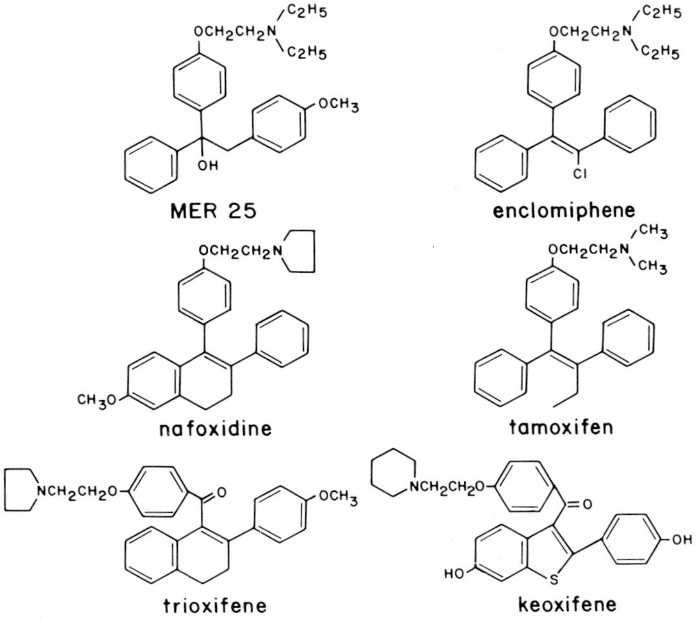

604

Fig. 1.   Structure of non-steroidal antiestrogens described in
the text.

Tamoxifen (Nolvadex®) is available for the treatment of breast
cancer in more than 70 countries throughout the world; in
dollar sales alone, it is one of the most important drugs used
in cancer therapy.   This fact has stimulated interest in the
discovery of new, and perhaps more specific, antitumor
agents.   Trioxifene is antiestrogenic in laboratory animals
(13,14) and possesses antitumor activity in animals (15) and
man (16), but the drug is not available for general clinical
use.   Keoxifene (LY 156758) and the related compound LY 117018
have weak estrogenic activity in laboratory animals and a high
binding affinity for the estrogen receptor (17-19).   These
drugs have a short duration action because of their polar

nature, which may facilitate their rapid conjugation and excretion (20). This property may explain the low potency of the LY-compounds as antitumor agents in animals (21).

In this chapter I will review the studies undertaken in my laboratory during the past decade, to describe the molecular pharmacology of tamoxifen and to support the use of the drug as an antitumor agent.

General pharmacology

Tamoxifen has a particularly interesting, and often per-plexing, pharmacology in laboratory animals. Tamoxifen exhib-its predominantly estrogenic properties in mouse uterine and vaginal assays (22-24). It is possible, however, to induce a refractoriness in the ovariectomized mouse vagina such that it cannot respond to exogenous estrogen stimulation for many weeks following a large subcutaneous injection of tamoxifen (25). During this period uterine growth is fully stimulated, and there is an increase in vaginal wet and dry weight. The vagina, however, is unable to cornify fully in response to estradiol and the smear remains leukocytic for 3-4 weeks. In contrast tamoxifen is a partial agonist with antiestrogenic properties in rat uterine weight assays and Allen-Doisy vaginal cornification assays (22,26,27).

The rat uterus is a complex organ and tamoxifen produces a differential stimulation of the cell types. Tamoxifen causes an increase in the size of the luminal epithelial cells but very little increase in mitotic activity or whole uterine DNA levels (14,27-29). Stromal and myometrial cells are apparently not affected by tamoxifen. Tamoxifen and its hydroxylated metabolite, 4-hydroxytamoxifen (Fig. 2) also increase the uterine level of progesterone receptors in vivo (30-32). Paradoxically, tamoxifen and 4-hydroxytamoxifen do

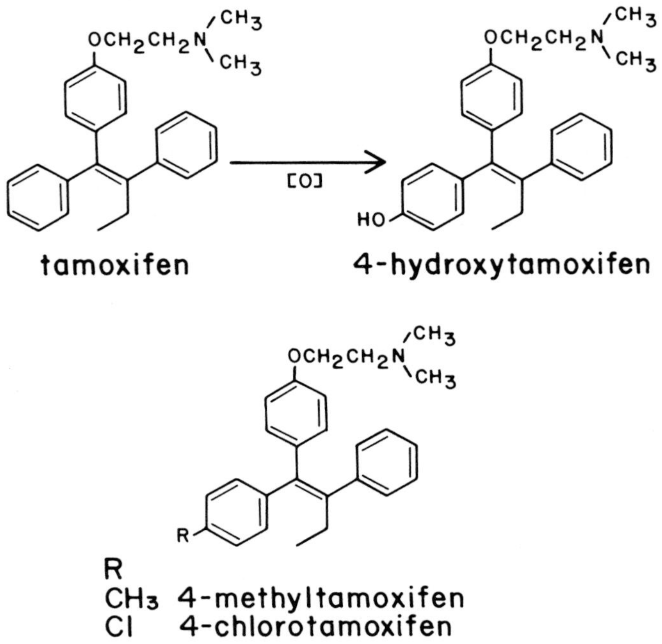

606

Fig. 2.   The metabolic activation of tamoxifen to 4-hydroxy-
tamoxifen and the formulae of the tamoxifen derivatives
resistant to hydroxylation.

not increase progesterone receptor induction by rat uterine
cells in culture, but both compounds reversibly inhibit
estradiol-stimulated progesterone receptor induction (33).

Metabolism

It is possible that the species differences in the pharmacology of tamoxifen are the result of differences in the metabolic transformation of the drug. As yet, no qualitative differences have been found between the metabolism of tamoxifen

in rats, mice and chickens (34). The principal metabolite of
tamoxifen in all three species is 4-hydroxytamoxifen. Indeed
the administration of 4-hydroxytamoxifen does not result in
the appearance of additional major metabolites (34). The
metabolic activation of tamoxifen to 4-hydroxytamoxifen occurs
in the rat and mouse so that the final expression of the
pharmacology of the parent is the result of the individual
actions of 4-hydroxytamoxifen and tamoxifen (and any other
metabolites not yet described). However, the potency of 4-
hydroxytamoxifen is greater than tamoxifen because 4-hy-
droxytamoxifen has a binding affinity for the estrogen receptor approximately 50 times greater than that of tamoxifen
(35). Studies with derivatives of tamoxifen substituted with
methyl or halogen in the 4 (para) position of tamoxifen (Fig.
2) which are unable to be metabolically activated, show a
lower potency in uterine weight tests in vivo than tamoxifen
although the relative binding affinities in vitro are
equivalent (36).

The known metabolites of tamoxifen in animals and man are
shown in Fig. 3. The high affinity metabolite 4-hydroxy-
tamoxifen is a minor metabolite of tamoxifen in patients (37),
whereas the major metabolite is N-desmethyltamoxifen (38,39).
Metabolite Y is a minor metabolite of tamoxifen in patients
(40,41) and this is believed to be formed from N-desmethyltamoxifen via an intermediate Metabolite Z (didemethylated
tamoxifen) (39). Metabolite D, Metabolite E and tamoxifen N-
oxide have only been described in vitro or in laboratory
animals (42,43). Metabolite D expresses little or no estrogenic activity in rat (35) or mouse (44) uterine weight tests
and is a weak antiestrogen. This catechol derivative of
tamoxifen has, however, been shown to be unstable in vitro
because it is readily oxidized (45). The binding affinity of
Metabolite D for the estrogen receptor is equivalent to that
of estradiol. Metabolite E, tamoxifen without the dimethyl-

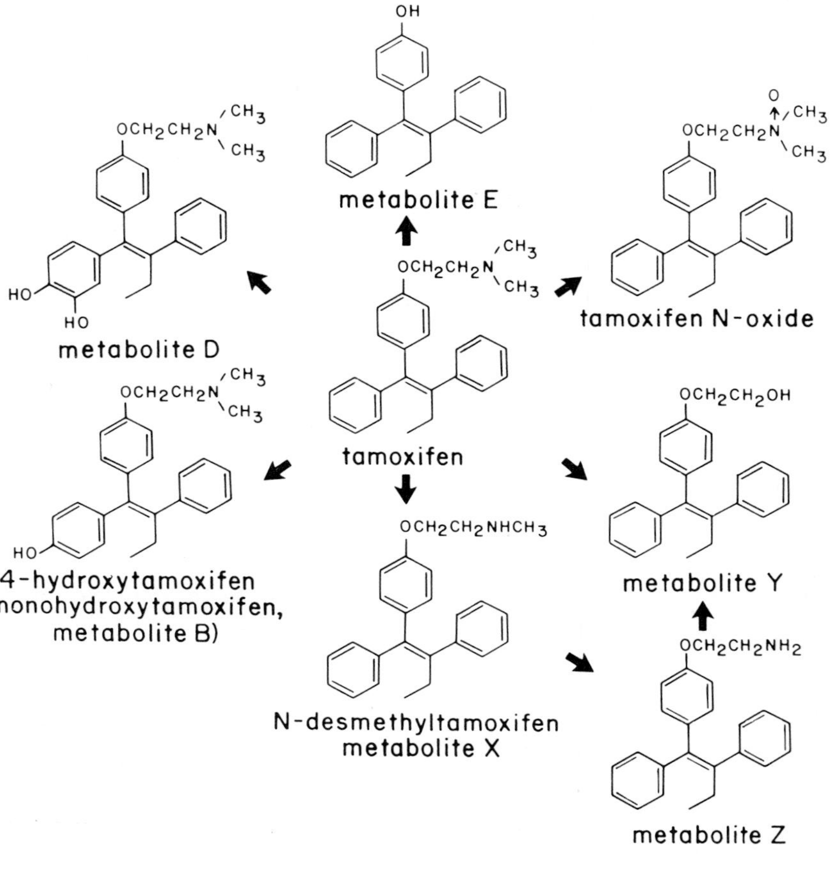

Fig. 3. The metabolites of tamoxifen in animals and man.

aminoethyl side chain, is fully estrogenic _in vivo_ (14) and _in vitro_ (45,46).

Mechanisms of action *in vivo*

The fact that non-steroidal antiestrogens will competitively
inhibit the binding of [3H]estradiol to estrogen receptors
derived from rat uteri (47) focused attention upon estrogen
receptor mediated mechanisms. The antiestrogens LY 117018 and
4-hydroxytamoxifen inhibit estradiol-stimulated increases in
immature rat uterine wet weight but the inhibition can be
reversed by increasing doses of estradiol (48). Similarly the
uterotrophic activity of tamoxifen in the mouse uterus can be
reversibly inhibited by MER 25 (49). These results indicate a
predominantly estrogen receptor mechanism for the expression
of both the antiestrogen and estrogenic action of tamoxifen.
Tamoxifen (27,50) and 4-hydroxytamoxifen (31,50) cause a
localization of occupied estrogen receptor complexes within
the nuclear compartment of rat uterine cells. Antiestrogenic
properties are probably expressed through a competitive balance of agonist and antagonist receptor complexes interacting
at sites within the nucleus (27,50). It is, however, not necessary (though probably an advantage) to occupy the cytosolic
estrogen receptor pool completely to produce antiestrogenic
effects. Apparent differences in the nuclear occupancy times
of estrogens and antiestrogens are reflected by differences in
the levels of available cytosolic estrogen receptors following
administration of compounds (51,52). Estradiol rapidly complexes with estrogen receptors in the nucleus but these are
lost over the next few hours as the steroid is cleared from
the blood. Antiestrogens have a long biological half life and
as such continue to maintain low levels of available cytosolic
receptors. This effect has been shown to be a property of
their duration of action and not their mechanism of action
(53).

The synthesis of radiolabelled 4-hydroxytamoxifen has permitted the direct study of the distribution and target tissue
location of an antiestrogen. [3H]4-hydroxytamoxifen binds to

estrogen receptors in the uterus, but also to antiestrogen specific sites in the uterus and liver (54). Antiestrogen binding sites were first described by Sutherland and coworkers (55) and have been shown to be located in the microsomal fraction of rat tissues (56). Many different classes of drugs bind to the antiestrogen binding site therefore, their precise role in the molecular mechanism of action of antiestrogens is controversial. Indeed, compounds can be identified that bind to the antiestrogen binding site in vitro but do not exhibit either estrogenic or antiestrogenic properties (49).

Recently we have observed some intriguing effects in vivo with antiestrogens and estrogens that are unlikely to be metabolically activated to compounds with a high affinity for the estrogen receptor (e.g., tamoxifen converted to 4-hydroxytamoxifen). The compounds (4-methyltamoxifen, Metabolite E and ICI 47,699) all stimulate rat uterine growth and progesterone receptor synthesis but the cytosolic estrogen receptors are apparently not "translocated" to the nuclear compartment. We have interpreted these data to support an estrogen receptor model for the uterine cell that has the unoccupied receptor already in the nuclear compartment. In the model (Fig. 4) ligands with either high or low affinity for the receptor can form a complex in the nucleus to produce biological effects. When the tissue is disrupted and fractionated, the high affinity ligand receptor complex remains with the nuclear fraction whereas the low affinity ligand dissociates from the receptor during homogenization. The unoccupied receptor thus is leached out into the cytosol. We have recently suggested that these observations are inconsistent with a cytoplasmic location for the estrogen receptor with a requirement for translocation to produce a biological response in the nucleus. We have argued that if the receptor can be leached out of the nucleus when a low affinity ligand dissociates then perhaps the unoccupied receptor is initially located in the nucleus and is

only extracted into cytosol during homogenization of the
tissue (57,58).

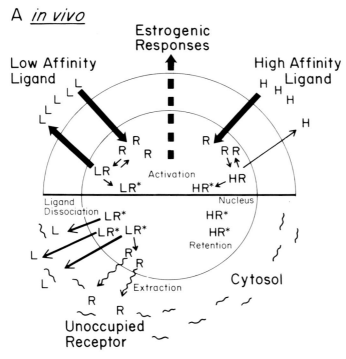

Fig. 4.   A functional model for estrogen action.   High
affinity ligand (H) enters the cell and binds to the estrogen
receptor (R) in the nucleus to produce an activated complex
HR* and estrogenic responses.   During cell disruption, this
complex is retained in the nucleus.   Low affinity ligands (L)
enter the cell and bind to nuclear receptor to produce an
activated complex LR*.   During homogenization in vitro, the
LR* complex dissociates and unoccupied R, and presumably
ligand, leaks out of the nucleus into the cytosolic fraction.

612

Mechanism of action studies in vitro

The potential mechanisms of action of antiestrogens are illustrated in Fig. 5.   In general, antiestrogens have been found
to inhibit the synthesis of estrogen regulated proteins (46,
59-62) and alter the rate of proliferation of hormone responsive cells (63-65).   Antiestrogens apparently induce a G_1
block in the cell cycle (65,66).   In this regard, it is

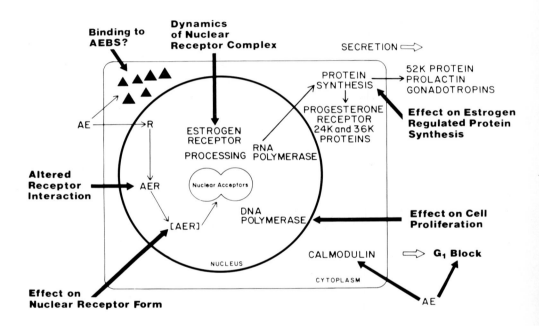

Fig. 5.   Potential mechanisms of action of antiestrogens (AE)
in vitro.

interesting to note that tamoxifen has been found to be one of
the most potent inhibitors of calmodulin mediated enzyme
systems (67).

Studies with [^{3}H]antiestrogen have resulted in the identification of a binding component located in the microsomal fraction
of cells (56). The component is generally referred to as the
antiestrogen binding site (AEBS) (65) but this is somewhat of
a misnomer as some potent antiestrogens like LY 117018 have a
low affinity interaction (49,56) and the estrogenic cis geometric isomer of tamoxifen has a high affinity for the AEBS
(49). The structural specificity of ligands has been determined; an alkylaminoethoxy side chain is very important for
binding to the AEBS (68). The role of binding sites in the
mechanism of action of antiestrogens in controversial and no
convincing evidence has been presented that they are involved
in either agonist or antagonist actions.

Most studies have focused upon the interaction of antiestrogens with the estrogen receptor in order to determine whether
any differences between estradiol- and antiestrogen receptor
complexes can be observed to account for the action of the
estrogen antagonists. The availability of tritiated antiestrogens has focused attention upon a search for physicochemical differences between estrogen and antiestrogen receptor
complexes. Similarly, precise assay systems in vitro to
describe the structure-activity relationships of estrogens and
antiestrogens has enabled the development of a map of the
estrogen receptor binding site. Each of these areas of
research will be briefly reviewed.

Studies with radiolabelled antiestrogens

[^{3}H]Tamoxifen binds directly to the 8S estrogen receptor of
the rat uterus (69,70), however, the interaction is weak
compared with [^{3}H]estradiol. Since tamoxifen can be metabolized in vivo to the antiestrogenic ligand 4-hydroxytamoxifen
which has a high affinity interaction with the estrogen recep-

tor, it is only natural that studies should have focused upon this superior research probe.

Monoclonal antibodies raised to the estrogen receptor are known to interact at different sites on the protein. Antibody D547 (raised to the extranuclear receptor from MCF-7 cells) which apparently interacts at a site far removed from the ligand binding site, binds equally with estradiol and 4-hydroxy-tamoxifen receptor complexes from human breast tumor cytosols (71). There are no differences whether D547 is pre-incubated with the receptor before the ligand or incubated with the receptor complex. In contrast a polyclonal antibody raised to the calf uterine estrogen receptor in the goat appears to be able to discriminate between the conformational shapes induced in the receptor by estrogens and antiestrogens (72). Based upon the structures of estrogens and antiestrogens we have proposed the following hypothetical model to describe the observed experimental results (Fig. 6).

Estradiol first binds with the resting receptor in the nucleus by an interaction of the C_3 phenolic group with a phenolic acceptor site on the protein. The initial binding step is followed by a change in the tertiary structure of the protein that locks the steroid into the receptor and as a result develops the intrinsic estrogenic activity of the complex. These changes in the interaction of the steroid and receptor have been described experimentally by alterations in the dissociation rate of the steroid following activation (transformation) i.e., untransformed receptors have a rapid dissociation of the ligand compared with transformed complexes (73,74). The antiestrogen 4-hydroxytamoxifen (monohydroxy-tamoxifen) binds with high affinity via the interaction of the phenolic group with the phenolic site on the receptor. However, the tertiary changes in the receptor that are necessary to develop intrinsic activity in the complex, are prevented by the alkylaminoethoxy side chain.

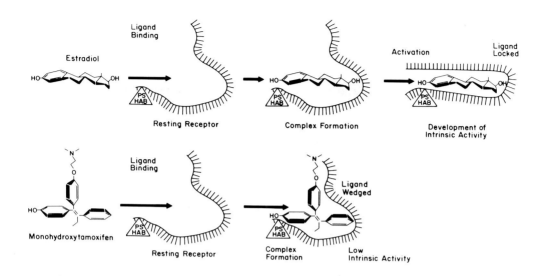

Fig. 6. Hypothetic models to describe the binding of
estradiol or 4-hydroxytamoxifen with the ligand binding site
on the estrogen. Estrogen can induce a conformational change
in the receptor to lock the ligand into the receptor whereas
the antiestrogen prevents these changes from occurring.

Studies with the polyclonal antibody raised to the estrogen
receptor tend to support the tertiary change model (72). Preincubation of antibody with cytosolic estrogen receptors from
human breast tumors impairs the subsequent binding of [^{3}H]-
estradiol and reduces the affinity of the ligand-receptor protein interaction. However, the binding of 4-hydroxytamoxifen
to the receptor is unimpaired by equivalent concentrations of
the antibody. Similarly, the interaction of the antibody with
preformed estradiol- and 4-hydroxytamoxifen-estrogen receptor
complexes does not affect the binding of the ligands. The
proposed model to explain these observations is illustrated in
Fig. 7. The polyclonal antibody may interact with the unfilled or resting receptor to present the conformational

616

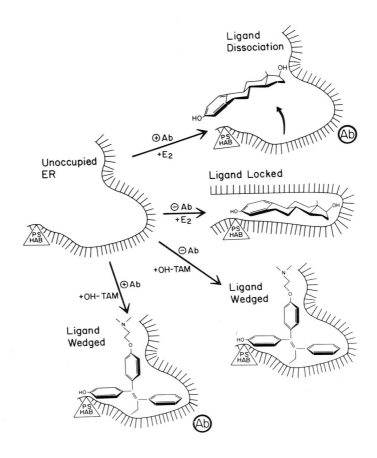

Fig. 7. Hypothetical model to describe the binding of estradiol or 4-hydroxytamoxifen to the estrogen receptor. The interaction of the phenolic site (PS) on the receptor protein induces a high affinity binding (HAB) to situate the ligand in the correct position. The interaction of the polyclonal antibody with the estrogen receptor is indicated by Ab. The antibody(ies) interacts with an unknown site to affect the conformational changes that occur at the ligand binding site.

changes that subsequently occur to lock estradiol into the receptor. Thus, the steroid falls out of the binding site. However, the antiestrogen can still wedge into the exposed binding site because it does not require further conformational changes to produce high affinity binding. We further suggest that once the conformation change does occur to lock the steroid into its binding site, the antibody is unable to reverse the process.

The ultimate fate of estrogen and antiestrogen receptor complexes within the nucleus of cancer cells is unknown, however, studies with radiolabelled ligands have provided some provocative results. Horwitz and McGuire (75) proposed that nuclear estradiol-estrogen receptor complexes are destroyed (or processed) during the first few hours of nuclear occupancy. In contrast, antiestrogen-estrogen receptor complexes apparently do not process but accumulate. The difference in the nuclear biochemistry of the receptor complexes is emphasized by the observation that antiestrogen-receptor complexes have a different sedimentation coefficient that estradiol-receptor complexes (76). We have recently confirmed (77) these original reports by comparing the nuclear receptor of [^{3}H]estradiol and [^{3}H]4-hydroxytamoxifen in MCF-7 breast cancer and GH$_3$ rat pituitary tumor cells. There is certainly a decrease in the salt extractable nuclear estradiol-estrogen receptor complexes during the first few (1 to 6 hr) hours and the 4-hydroxytamoxifen-estrogen receptor complexes accumulate and are readily extracted. Further work is required to determine whether this result reflects differential salt extraction or true loss of receptor. Nevertheless, there are differences in the sedimentation coefficients of estradiol- and 4-hydroxytamoxifen-estrogen receptor complexes from MCF-7 cells that do not alter during a 24 hr period. Although the results observed in MCF-7 cells may be related to the experimental conditions used, these differences are not observed in the GH$_3$ pituitary tumor cell line (77,78).

Structure-activity relationships

Primary cultures of rat pituitary cells respond to physiological concentrations of estradiol by a specific increase in
prolactin synthesis (79). This model system for estrogen
action has been validated for the study of structure activity
relationships within groups of non-steroidal estrogens and
antiestrogens. Tamoxifen and 4-hydroxytamoxifen inhibit
estradiol-stimulated prolactin synthesis, with potency related
to the binding affinity for the estrogen receptor. 4-Hydroxy-
tamoxifen is 30 times more potent than tamoxifen, however, to
ensure that tamoxifen is not metabolically activated to
4-hydroxytamoxifen in vitro, several para substituted derivatives of tamoxifen (4-methyl, 4-chloro, Fig. 2) have been
tested (59). The substitution does not affect binding affinity for the estrogen receptor and the derivatives of tamoxifen
inhibit estradiol-stimulated prolactin synthesis in a concen-
tration-related manner. Although it is an advantage for
tamoxifen to be metabolized to 4-hydroxytamoxifen, it is
clearly not a requirement for antiestrogen activity. Antiestrogen action in the pituitary cells is, however, both competitive and reversible with the addition of excess estradiol
(59).

A series of known estrogens and antiestrogens has been tested
to establish structure-activity relationships. The relative
potency of estrogens to stimulate prolactin synthesis was
diethylstilbestrol ≡ estradiol > ICI 77,949 (tamoxifen without
the dimethylaminoethane side chain) > ICI 47,699 (cis geometric isomer of tamoxifen) ≡ zuclomiphene (cis geometric
isomer of enclomiphene). The relative potencies of antiestrogens to inhibit estradiol-stimulated prolactin synthesis
was 4-hydroxytamoxifen ≡ LY 117018 > trioxifene > enclomiphene
≡ tamoxifen. The compound LY 126412 (trioxifene without the
side chain) does not interact with estrogen receptors up to

test concentrations of 10^{-6}M or exhibit estrogenic or anti-estrogenic properties using the prolactin synthesis assay.

Among the triphenylethylenes, compounds that have cis and trans geometric isomers are extremely important for the development of a ligand-receptor model because the isomeric molecules encompass estrogenic and antiestrogenic actions. The trans isomers (tamoxifen and enclomiphene) are antiestrogens with zero intrinsic activity whereas the cis isomers (ICI 47,699 and zuclomiphene) are estrogens with an intrinsic activity of 1.

To describe the interaction of the geometric isomers with the estrogen receptor, the trans stilbene-like structure of tamoxifen and enclomiphene could sit loosely at the binding site with low affinity binding so that the phenyl ring substituted with the p-alkylaminoethoxy side chain is projected away from the binding site (Fig. 8). The estrogenic ligands, zuclomiphene and ICI 47,699 with their low affinity for the estrogen receptor can create a trans stilbene-like structure with the para substituted phenyl ring. In this binding state, the aminoethoxy side chain would lie next to the phenolic site on the receptor, with a weak interaction through the ether oxygen (Fig. 8). There would be no interaction of the side chain with a hypothetical antiestrogen region of the receptor and, as a result, no inhibition of estrogen action. The tertiary changes that are necessary to develop a high intrinsic activity for the complex can occur unimpeded.

Overall compounds can be classified into three categories based upon their structure (80). Antiestrogens have a side chain extending away from the binding site, partial agonists have a bis phenolic structure and agonists have an unsubstituted phenyl ring (or no phenyl ring at all).

620

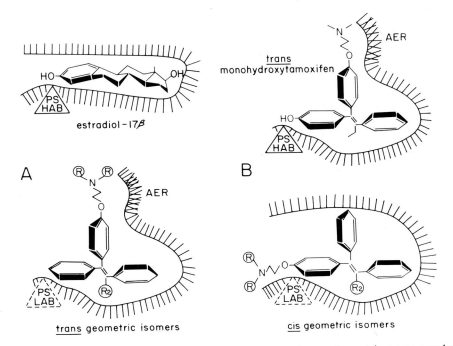

estradiol-17β

A

trans geometric isomers

trans monohydroxytamoxifen

B

cis geometric isomers

Fig. 8. Hypothetical models for estrogenic and antiestrogenic ligand binding to the estrogen receptor. Estradiol-17β is anchored at a phenolic site (PS) with high affinity binding (HAB). trans Monohydroxytamoxifen has the same high affinity binding but this antiestrogenic ligand binds to the receptor site so that the alkylaminoethoxy side chain can interact with a hypothetical antiestrogen region (AER) on the protein. Compounds without a phenolic hydroxyl have low affinity binding (LAB). The trans and cis geometric isomers refer to A) tamoxifen (R=CH₃, R₂=C₂H₅) and enclomiphene (R=C₂H₅, R=Cl); B) ICI 47,699 (R=CH₃, R=C₂H₅) and zuclomiphene (R=C₂H₅, R₂=Cl).

The geminal bis para hydroxy phenyl compounds (e.g., bisphenol) that are partial agonists in vitro are particularly interesting. Belleau's macromolecular perturbation theory (45), which was originally proposed to explain agonist, partial agonist and antagonist activity of drugs at the muscarinic cholinergic receptor, may be used to explain partial agonists in terms of the estrogen receptor model. According to Belleau's hypothesis, an agonist binds to the receptor and induces a specific conformational perturbation (SCP). An antagonist binds to the receptor and produces a non-specific conformational perturbation (NSCP) but the complex has zero intrinsic activity. Between these extremes a partial agonist binds to the receptor and produces an equilibrium mixture of agonist and antagonist receptor complexes. Applying these definitions to the estrogen receptor (Fig. 9), estradiol binds with high affinity to the resting receptor and induces a SCP which results in the ligand being locked into the binding site. 4-Hydroxytamoxifen (antagonist) wedges into the resting receptor and produces a NSCP. Bisphenol (partial agonist) interacts at the ligand binding site but while some of the receptors can be induced to lock the ligand into the protein, other ligand interactions are only able to induce a NSCP in the complex.

The study of the structure-activity relationships has provided an understanding of several features that are dominant and predict pharmacological activity (Fig. 10).

1. A phenolic hydroxyl equivalent to the C_3 phenol of estradiol is extremely important for high affinity binding to the estrogen receptor. This structural feature permits a variety of "spacing groups" to occupy the receptor binding site.

2. Alkylethers have a decreased affinity for the receptor (but an increased duration of action in vivo).

3. Substitution of the phenyl ring extending away from the binding site governs pharmacological activity. Compounds without substitution are estrogens but a para hydroxyl predicts partial agonist activity in vivo. Extension of a side chain predicts antagonist activity in vitro.

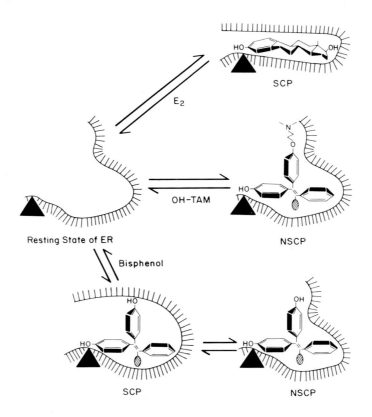

Fig. 9. Adaptation of Belleau's macromolecular perturbation theory to describe the interaction of agonist, antagonists and partial agonists with the estrogen receptor (ER). The phenol group on the ligand interacts with the phenolic site on the ER (closed triangle) and produce a high affinity interaction if the geometry of the ligand is correct. Estradiol (E_2), on agonist, induces a specific conformational perturbation (SCP) whereas 4-hydroxytamoxifen (OHTAM), antagonist, only induces a non-specific conformational perturbation (NSCP). Bisphenol (partial agonist) produces a mixture of SCP and NSCP in the ER.

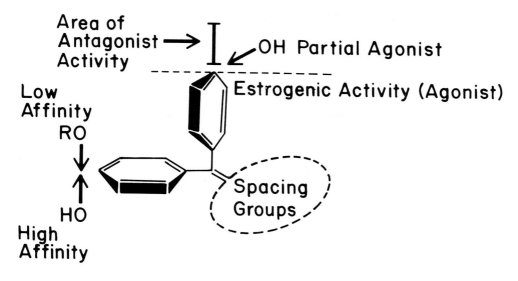

Fig. 10. A general ligand model to describe the structural requirement to control biological activity in vitro.

Antitumor actions in animals

The dimethylbenz(a)anthracene (DMBA)-induced rat mammary carcinoma model first described by Huggins et al. (81) has been used extensively to study hormone-dependent cancer and to evaluate potential therapies for breast cancer.

The early definition of hormone dependency was based on regression of tumors after ovariectomy and hypophysectomy (81). Since estrogen stimulates tumor regrowth in ovariectomized rats but not in animals which are also hypophysectomized (82), the pituitary gland clearly plays a central role in the growth and homoestasis of DMBA-induced tumors. Since 'hormone-responsive' DMBA-induced tumors have cytosol estrogen receptors a direct stimulation of tumor growth by estrogen is possible. However, the interesting observations that prolactin administration or increases in serum prolactin caused by perphenazine stimulate increases in estrogen receptor concentrations as well as tumor growth (83) may indicate that estrogen receptors in this model are a marker of hormone responsiveness rather than a mediator of hormone action.

Tamoxifen inhibits the growth of established DMBA-induced tumors (84-88). To explain the mechanism of action of tamoxifen in this model most investigators have considered an interaction with tumor estrogen receptors to be of fundamental importance. Terenius (89) first proposed that antiestrogens directly block the binding of estrogen to human and DMBA-induced rat tumors and that this might be their primary mechanism of action. Many studies have subsequently confirmed that antiestrogens inhibit the binding of [^{3}H]estradiol to DMBA-induced tumor tissues determined both in vivo and in vitro (85,90,91). At the subcellular level, tamoxifen inhibits the binding of [^{3}H]estradiol to the 8S estrogen receptor obtained from DMBA-induced tumors (90). The interaction of tamoxifen with the estrogen receptor system of DMBA-induced tumors has been studied extensively in vivo.

In addition to a direct action on the DMBA-induced tumor, tamoxifen may inhibit tumor growth by a number of other mechanisms as shown in Fig. 11. The ability of tamoxifen to affect the pituitary gland has been considered earlier. It is concluded, therefore, that tamoxifen causes tumor regression by multiple mechanisms; alterations in the hormonal milieu and direct biochemical effects within the tumor cell are both important. However, there is little doubt that the pituitary gland can have an overriding effect since administration of the dopamine antagonist, perphenazine, which stimulates prolactin secretion, will reverse tumor regression induced by tamoxifen.

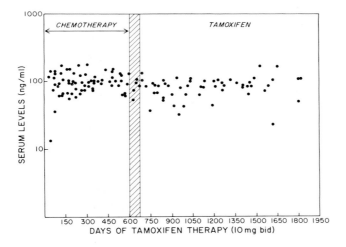

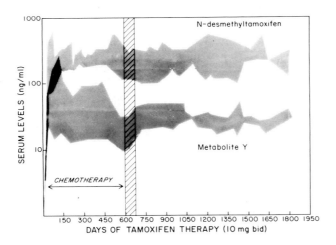

Fig. 12. The level of tamoxifen and its metabolites N-desmethyltamoxifen and Metabolite Y during long-term adjuvant therapy with tamoxifen (10 mg bid).

Acknowledgements

The studies described in this chapter were supported during the past 12 years by ICI Plc (Pharmaceuticals Division), England; the Yorkshire Cancer Research Campaign, England; Stuart Pharmaceuticals, Wilmington, Delaware; and National Institutes of Health (USA) grants P30-CA-14520, P01-CA-20432 and R01-CA-32713.

References

1. Lerner, L.J., Holthaus, J.F., Thompson, C.R.: Endocrinology 63, 295-318 (1958).

2. Segal, J.S., Nelson, W.L.: Proc. Soc. Exp. Biol. Med. 98, 431-436 (1958).

3. Chang, M.C.: Endocrinology 65, 339-342 (1959).

4. Kistner, R.W., Smith, O.W.: Fert. Steril. 12, 121-141 (1961).

5. Holtkamp, D.E., Greslin, S.C., Root, C.A., Lerner, L.J.: Proc. Soc. Exp. Biol. Med. 105, 197-201 (1960).

6. Greenblatt, R.B., Roy, S., Mahesh, V.B., Barfield, W.E., Jungck, E.C.: Am. J. Obstet. Gynec. 84, 900-912 (1962).

7. Huppert, L.C.: Fert. Steril. 31, 1-8 (1979).

8. Bloom, H.J.G., Boesen, E.: Br. Med. J. 2, 7-10 (1974).

9. Heuson, J.C., Engelsman, E., Blank-van der Wijst, J., Maas, H., Drochmans, A., Michel, J., Nowakowski, M., Garins, A.: Br. Med. J. 2, 711-713 (1975).

10. Cole, M.P., Jones, C.T.A., Todd, I.D.H.: Br. J. Cancer 25, 270-275 (1971).

11. Ward, H.W.C.: Br. Med. J. 1, 13-14 (1973).

12. Legha, S.S., Carter, S.K.: Cancer Treat Rev. 3, 205-216 (1976).

13. Jones, C.D., Suarez, T., Massey, E.H., Black, L.J., Tinsley, F.C.: J. Med. Chem. 22, 962-966 (1979).

14. Jordan, V.C., Gosden, B.: Mol. Cell. Endocrinol. 27, 291-306 (1982).

15. Rose, D.P., Fischer, A.H., Jordan, V.C.: Europ. J. Cancer Clin. Oncol. 17, 893-898 (1981).

16. Manni, A., Arafah, B., Pearson, O.H.: In, Non-steroidal Antioestrogens. (R.L. Sutherland, V.C. Jordan, Eds.), pp. 435-452. Academic Press, Sydney (1981).

17. Black, L.J., Goode, R.L.: Life Sci. 26, 1453-1458 (1980).

18. Black, L.J., Goode, R.L.: Endocrinology 109, 987-989 (1981).

19. Black, L.J., Jones, C.D., Goode, R.L. Mol. Cell. Endocr. 22, 95-103 (1981).

20. Jordan, V.C., Gosden, B.: Endocrinology 113, 463-468 (1983).

21. Clemens, J.A., Bennett, D.R., Black, L.J., Jones, C.D.: Life Sci. 32, 2869-2875 (1983).

22. Harper, M.J.K., Walpole, A.L.: Nature (Lond) 212, 87 (1966).

23. Terenius, L.: Acta. Endocr. (Copenh) 64, 47-58 (1970).

24. Martin, L., Middleton, E.: J. Endocr. 78, 125-129 (1978).

25. Jordan, V.C.: J. Reprod. Fert. 52, 251-258 (1975).

26. Harper, M.J.K., Walpole, A.L.: J. Reprod. Fert. 13, 101-119 (1967).

27. Jordan, V.C., Dix, C.J., Rowsby, L., Prestwich, G.: Mol. Cell Endocrinol. 7, 177-192 (1977).

28. Clark, E.R., Dix, C.J., Jordan, V.C., Prestwich, G., Sexton, S.: Br. J. Pharmacol. 62, 442P-443P (1978).

29. Furr, B.J.A., Jordan, V.C.: Pharmacol. Ther. (in press) (1984).

30. Jordan, V.C., Prestwich, G.: J. Endocr. 76, 363-364 (1978).

31. Dix, C.J., Jordan, V.C.: J. Endocr. 85, 393-404 (1980).

32. Dix, C.J., Jordan, V.C.: Endocrinology 107, 2011-2020 (1980).

33. Campen, C.A., Jordan, V.C., Gorski, J.: Endocrinology (in press).

34. Lyman, S.D., Jordan, V.C.: Biochem. Pharm. (in press).

35. Jordan, V.C., Collins, M.M., Rowsby, L., Prestwich, G.: J. Endocr. 75, 305-316 (1977).

36. Allen, K.E., Clark, E.R., Jordan, V.C.: Br. J. Pharmac. 71, 83-91 (1980).

37. Daniel, C.P., Gaskell, S.J., Bishop, H., Nicholson, R.I.: J. Endocr. 83, 401-408 (1979).

632

38. Adam, H.K., Douglas, E.J., Kemp, J.V.: Biochem. Pharmacol. 27, 145-147 (1979).

39. Kemp, J.V., Adam, H.K., Wakeling, A.E., Slater, R.: Biochem. Pharmacol. 32, 2045-2052 (1983).

40. Bain, R.R., Jordan, V.C.: Biochem. Pharmacol. 32, 373-375 (1983).

41. Jordan, V.C., Bain, R.R., Brown, R.R., Gosden, B., Santos, M.A.: Cancer Res. 43, 1446-1450 (1983).

42. Fromson, J.M., Pearson, S., Bramah, S.: Xenobiotica 3, 693-709 (1973).

43. Foster, A.B., Griggs, L.J., Jarman, M., van Maanen, J.M.S., Schulten, H.R.: Biochem. Pharmacol. 29, 1977-1979 (1980).

44. Jordan, V.C., Dix, C.J., Naylor, K.E., Prestwich, G., Rowsby, L.: J. Toxicol. Environ. Health 4, 364-390 (1978).

45. Jordan, V.C., Lieberman, M.E., Koch, R., Cormier, E.M., Bagley, J., Ruenitz, P.: Mol. Pharmacol. 26, 272-278 (1984).

46. Lieberman, M.E., Gorski, J., Jordan, V.C.: J. Biol. Chem. 258, 4741-4745 (1983).

47. Skidmore, J.R., Walpole, A.L., Woodburn, J.: J. Endocr. 52, 289-298 (1972).

48. Jordan, V.C., Gosden, B.: J. Steroid Biochem. 19, 1249-1258 (1983).

49. Lyman, S.D., Jordan, V.C.: Biochem. Pharmacol. (in press).

50. Jordan, V.C., Naylor, K.E.: Br. J. Pharmac. 65, 167-173 (1979).

51. Clark, J.H., Anderson, J., Peck, E.J.: Steroids 22, 707-718 (1973).

52. Clark, J.H., Peck, E.J., Anderson, J.L.: Nature (Lond) 251, 446-448 (1974).

53. Jordan, V.C., Rowsby, L., Dix, C.J., Prestwich, G.: J. Endocr. 78, 71-81 (1978).

54. Jordan, V.C., Bowser-Finn, R.A.: Endocrinology 110, 1281-1291 (1982).

55. Sutherland, R.L., Murphy, L.C., Foo, M.S., Green, M.D., Whybourne, A.M., Krozowski, Z.S.: Nature (Lond) 288, 273-275 (1980).

56. Sudo, K., Monsma, F.J., Katzenellenbogen, B.S.: Endocrinology 112, 425-434 (1983).

57. Jordan, V.C., Gosden, B., Tate, A.C.: Endocrin. Soc. Proc. (San Antonio) Abstract 1049 (1983).

58. Jordan, V.C., Tate, A.C., Lyman, S.D., Gosden, B., Wolf, M., Welshons, W.V.: Endocrinology (submitted).

59. Lieberman, M.E., Jordan, V.C., Fritsch, M., Santos, M.A., Gorski, J.: J. Biol. Chem. 258, 4734-4740 (1983).

60. Westley, B., Rochefort, H.: Cell 20, 353-362 (1980).

61. Edwards, D.P., Adams, D.J., Savage, N., McGuire, W.L.: Biochem. Biophys. Res. Commun. 93, 804-809 (1980).

62. Miller, W.L., Huang, E.S.R.: Endocrinology 108, 96-102 (1981).

63. Lippman, M.E., Bolan, G.: Nature (Lond) 256, 592-595 (1975).

64. Edwards, D.P., Murthy, S.R., McGuire, W.L.: Cancer Res. 40, 1722-1726 (1980).

65. Sutherland, R.L., Green, M.D., Hall, R.E., Reddel, R.R., Taylor I.W.: Europ. J. Cancer Clin. Oncol. 19, 615-621 (1983).

66. Osborne, C.K., Boldt, D.H., Clark, G.M., Trent, J.M.: Cancer Res. 43, 3583-3585 (1983).

67. Lam, D.H.Y.: Biochem. Biophys. Res. Comm. 118, 27-32 (1984).

68. Murphy, L.C., Sutherland, R.L.: Biochem. Biophys. Res. Comm. 100, 1353-1360 (1981).

69. Jordan, V.C., Prestwich, G.: Mol. Cell. Endocrinol. 8, 179-188 (1977).

70. Capony, F., Rochefort, H.: Mol. Cell. Endocrinol. 11, 181-198 (1978).

71. Tate, A.C., DeSombre, E.R., Greene, G.L., Jensen, E.V., Jordan, V.C.: Breast Cancer Res. Treat. 3, 267-277 (1983).

72. Tate, A.C., Greene, G.L., DeSombre, E.R., Jensen, E.V., Jordan, V.C.: Cancer Res. 44, 1012-1018 (1984).

73. Notides, A.C., Hamilton, D.E., Auer, H.E.: J. Biol. Chem. 250, 3945-3950 (1975).

74. Rochefort, H., Borgna, J.L.: Nature (Lond) 292, 257-259 (1981).

75. Horwitz, K.B., McGuire, W.L.: J. Biol. Chem. 253, 8185-8191 (1978).

76. Eckert, R.L., Katzenellenbogen, B.S.: J. Biol. Chem. 257, 8840-8846 (1982).

77. Tate, A.C., Jordan, V.C.: Mol. Cell. Endocrinol. 36, 211-219 (1984).

78. Tate, A.C., Lieberman, M.E., Jordan, V.C.: J. Steroid Biochem. 20, 391-395 (1984).

634

79. Lieberman, M.E., Maurer, R.A., Gorski, J.: Proc. Natl. Acad. Sci. USA 75, 5946-5949 (1978).

80. Jordan, V.C., Lieberman, M.E.: Mol. Pharmacol. 26, 279-285 (1984).

81. Huggins, C., Briziarelli, G., Sutton, H.: J. Exp. Med. 104, 25-41 (1959).

82. Sterental, A., Dominguez, J.M., Weissman, C., Pearson, O.H.: Cancer Res. 23, 481-484 (1963).

83. Sasaki, G.H., Leung, B.S.: Cancer 35, 645-651 (1975).

84. Jordan, V.C.: J. Steroid Biochem. 5, 354 (1974).

85. Nicholson, R.I., Golder, M.P.: Eur. J. Cancer 11, 571-579 (1975).

86. Jordan, V.C.: Europ. J. Cancer 12, 419-424 (1976)

87. Jordan, V.C.: Cancer Treat. Rep. 60, 1409-1419 (1976).

88. Jordan, V.C., Koerner, S.: J. Endocr. 68, 305-310 (1976).

89. Terenius, L.: Eur. J. Cancer 7, 57-64 (1971).

90. Jordan, V.C., Dowse, L.J.: J. Endocr. 68, 297-303 (1976).

91. Jordan, V.C., Jaspan, T.: J. Endocr. 68, 453-460 (1976).

92. Emmens, C.W.: J. Reprod. Fert. 26, 175-182 (1971).

93. Jordan, V.C.: Rev. on Endocrine-Related Cancer, Oct. Suppl. 49-55 (1978).

94. Jordan, V.C., Dix, C.J., Allen, K.E.: In, Adjuvant Therapy of Cancer II, eds. S.E. Salmon, S.E. Jones, 19-26 (1979).

95. Jordan, V.C., Allen, K.E., Dix, C.J.: Cancer Treat. Rep. 64, 745-759 (1980).

96. Jordan, V.C., Allen, K.E.: Eur. J. Cancer 16, 239-251 (1980).

97. Jordan, V.C., Dix, C.J., Allen, K.E.: In, Nonsteroidal Antioestrogens, eds. R.L. Sutherland, V.C. Jordan, 261-280 (1981).

98. Gullino, P.W., Pettigrew, H.M., Grantham, F.H.: J. Natl. Cancer Inst. 54, 401-404 (1975).

99. Rose, D.P., Pruitt, B., Stauber, P., Ertürk, E., Bryan, G.T.: Cancer Res. 40, 235-239 (1980).

100. Rose, D.P., Fischer, A.H., Jordan, V.C.: Eur. J. Cancer 17, 893-898 (1981).

101.   Jordan, V.C., Mirecki, D., Gottardis, M.M.: In,
        Adjuvant Therapy of Cancer IV, eds. S.E. Salmon, S.E.
        Jones. Grune & Stratton (in press).

102.   Jordan, V.C., Koerner, S.: Eur. J. Cancer <u>11</u>, 205-206
        (1975).

103.   Patterson, J.S., Edwards, D.G., Battersby, L.A.:
        Japanese J. Cancer Clinics. Suppl. 157-183 (1981).

104.   Fisher, B., Redmond, C., Brown, A., Wolmark, N. and
        other members of NSABP. New Engl. J. Med. <u>305</u>, 1-6
        (1981).

105.   Baum, M. and other members of the 'Nolvadex' Adjuvant
        Trial Organization. Lancet <u>1</u>, 251-261 (1983).

106.   Tormey, D.C., Jordan, V.C.: Breast Cancer Res. Treat.
        <u>4</u>, 297-302 (1984).

107.   Brown, R.R., Bain, R.R., Jordan, V.C.: J. Chromat. <u>272</u>,
        351-358 (1983).

STUDIES ON GLUCOCORTICOID RECEPTORS IN NORMAL AND NEOPLASTIC
RODENT AND HUMAN LEUKOCYTES: STRUCTURE, DEGRADATION,
KINETICS OF FORMATION AND ACTIVATION

Nikki J. Holbrook[*], Jack E. Bodwell, Dirk B. Mendel, Allan
Munck

Department of Physiology, Dartmouth Medical School, Hanover,
NH, USA

[*] Present address: Laboratory of Pathology, National Cancer
Institute, Bethesda, MD, USA

Introduction

Over the past several years a major goal of our laboratory
has been to characterize the various forms of the glucocorticoid-receptor complex which exist within the intact
cell under physiological conditions, and to define their
functional and kinetic relationships. Central to such
studies was the development of a rapid minicolumn
chromatographic procedure for analyzing glucocorticoid-
receptor complexes in cytosols. This procedure has enabled
us to perform studies which would otherwise be impossible.
In this review we will attempt to summarize findings from
several of our recent studies aimed at characterizing
glucocorticoid-receptor complexes in normal and neoplastic
cells both biochemically and functionally.

Results

Characterization of rat thymus glucocortioid receptor
complexes. As a prelude to more detailed studies of the

cytoplasmic glucocorticoid-receptor complexes we first characterized by standard physicochemical procedures the nonactivated (non-DNA-binding) and activated or transformed (DNA-binding) complexes formed in rat thymus cells (1). For this purpose we used buffers containing sodium molybdate (2, 3) to block activation and stabilize the complexes.

In rat thymus cells incubated with [³H]-triamcinolone acetonide (TA) at 0°C, the cytosolic complexes consist almost entirely of a non-activated species. At 37°C, both activated and nonactivated complexes are present with the activated species predominating. However, the ratio of activated to nonactivated complexes varies with different steroids as will be discussed below. Traces of mero-receptor and related complexes (small proteolytic cleavage products of the native receptor complex which retain the steroid binding site) are also found, but these complexes may have been formed rapidly after the cells are broken.

TABLE 1

CHARACTERISTICS OF GLUCOCORTICOID-RECEPTOR COMPLEXES FROM RAT THYMUS CELLS

PROPERTIES	COMPLEX		
	NONACTIVATED	ACTIVATED	MERO-RECEPTOR
BINDS TO DNA	NO	YES	NO
ELUTION FROM DEAE CELLULOSE (mM KCl)	200	50	DOES NOT BIND
STOKES RADIUS (nm)	8.3	5.0	2.3
SEDIMENTATION COEFFICIENT	9.2	4.8	2.9
MOLECULAR WEIGHT (Mr)	330,000	100,000	27,000
MOLECULAR WEIGHT BY SDS-PAGE	90,000	90,000	-

RAT THYMUS CELLS WERE INCUBATED AT EITHER 0°C FOR 2 HOURS OR 37°C FOR 30 MIN WITH [³H]-TRIAMCINOLONE ACETONIDE. CYTOSOLS PREPARED FROM THESE CELLS WERE SUBJECTED TO VARIOUS ANALYTICAL PROCEDURES (1).

The properties of these three cytosolic complexes are summarized in Table 1. In agreement with results of others (3, 4, 5), under non-denaturing conditions the nonactivated complex from rat thymus cells has an apparent molecular weight of around 330,000 and Stokes radius of about 8 nm; activation is accompanied by a reduction to a molecular weight of about 100,000 and Stokes radius of 5 nm. However, when analyzed by polyacrylamide gel electrophoresis in the presence of sodium dodecylsulfate (SDS-PAGE), both activated and nonactivated complexes appear as approximately 90,000 species (6; Mendel, unpublished results). Because of this, a question of some concern to us has been whether molybdate might cause the complexes to aggregate, and thus give a spuriously large apparent molecular weight for the nonactivated complex. At least two pieces of evidence argue against this. First, Sherman et al. (7) and we (unpublished results) have observed similar large complexes using the protease inhibitor leupeptin as a stabilizing agent. Second, we have observed that cytosols from WEHI-7 rat thymoma cells show clear indications of 8 nm nonactivated complexes even in the absence of molybdate or other stabilizing agents (8). Thus, the reduction in size associated with activation may represent dissociation of an oligomeric molecule, as we (1) and others (4, 5, 9) have suggested.

Proteolytic degradation of the molybdate-stabilized nonactivated receptor complex. The ability of molybdate to stabilize the 8 nm form of the nonactivated complex led us (1) and others (3, 10, 11) to conclude that molybdate, in addition to blocking activation, protects the nonactivated complex against proteolysis by endogenous enzymes. Subsequent results, however, have caused us to re-examine this conclusion.

By using cytosol generated from thymocytes incubated for 2 h at 3°C with [³H]dexamethasone 21-mesylate (DM), an affinity label for the glucocorticoid receptor (12), we have been able to examine the stability of the cytosolic nonactivated complexes under denaturing conditions (by SDS-PAGE) as well as under non-denaturing conditions (by gel filtration). Our results demonstrate that nonactivated complexes, generated and analyzed in the presence of molybdate, elute from a gel filtration column as the 8 nm complex even when the cytosol had been left at 3°C for 2 h before being analyzed. In marked contrast, however, analysis by SDS-PAGE shows that over the 2 h period under cell-free conditions the intact M_r = 90,000 receptor has been degraded to a M_r = 50,000 fragment. Nonactivated receptor complexes prepared in the absence of molybdate and left for 2 h migrate on SDS-PAGE in a manner which is identical to that of complexes which were prepared in the presence of molybdate.

TABLE 2

PROTECTION OF THE INTACT Mr = 90,000 RECEPTOR IN RAT THYMUS CYTOSOL
UNDER CELL-FREE CONDITIONS.

TREATMENT	% OF RECEPTOR COMPLEXES PRESENT AS THE INTACT Mr = 90,000 RECEPTOR
CONTROL	3.2 ± 2.8
+ EGTA	97.4 ± 1.4
+ LEUPEPTIN	95.7 ± 0.8
+ WEHI FACTOR	79.6 ± 1.7
+ LIVER FACTOR	87.3 ± 1.2

RAT THYMUS CELLS, INCUBATED WITH ABOUT 50 nM [³H]DM FOR 2 HOURS AT 3°C, WERE LYSED IN 5 VOLUMES OF HYPOTONIC BREAK BUFFER (1.5 mM MgCl₂, 20 mM MOLYBDATE, 1% DEXTRAN-COATED CHAR-COAL, 10 mM HEPES, pH 8.2 at 0°C) CONTAINING NO ADDITIVES (CONTROL); 5 mM EGTA (+ EGTA); 20 mM LEUPEPTIN (+ LEUPEPTIN); 100% (v/v) WEHI FACTOR (+ WEHI FACTOR); OR 20% (v/v) LIVER FACTOR (+ LIVER FACTOR). AFTER 2 HOURS AT 3°C, CYTOSOL SAMPLES WERE ANALYZED BY SDS-PAGE. SAMPLES LANES WERE CUT INTO 2 mM SLICES AND THE SLICES ANALYZED FOR RADIOACTIVITY.

VALUES ARE GIVEN AS THE AVERAGE PERCENT OF TOTAL RECEPTOR COMPLEXES PRESENT AS THE Mr = 90,000 RECEPTOR, ± RANGE/2. FROM 2 to 5 SEPARATE DETERMINATIONS WERE MADE FOR EACH TREATMENT.

As shown in Table 2, proteolysis of the receptor under these conditions could be blocked by breaking the cells in buffer containing EGTA (5 mM), leupeptin (20 mM), or the calpastatin-like heat-stable factor present in the cytosol of WEHI-7 cells and rat liver (see below). Proteolysis could not be attributed to the method used to prepare the samples for SDS-PAGE, since addition of any or all of these protecting agents after the 2 h incubation under cell-free conditions did not prevent formation of the M_r = 50,000 receptor fragment.

From these results we now conclude that molybdate does not protect the nonactivated glucocorticoid-receptor complex from being degraded to a 50,000 fragment under cell-free conditions in rat thymus cytosol. We can also conclude that the stability of the 8 nm nonactivated complex in the presence of molybdate is only apparent, and that a Stokes radius of about 8 nm measured by gel filtration is not sufficient evidence to indicate that the receptor-complex is present in its intact form.

Minicolumn analysis of cytoplasmic glucocorticoid-receptor complexes. Taking advantage of the differential DNA and DEAE binding properties of the complexes found in rat cytosols (see Table 1), we have developed a minicolumn method by which nonactivated, activated and other complexes, particularly mero-receptors, can be separated rapidly (1). The minicolumn, depicted in Figure 1, is composed of three small columns in 1-ml syringes connected in series. The top one consists of DNA-cellulose, the middle one of DEAE-cellu- lose, and the bottom one of hydroxylapatite (HAP). When a cytosol is passed through the columns, activated complexes are retained with high efficiency by the DNA column, nonactivated complexes by the DEAE column, and mero-receptor and other complexes that do not bind to DNA or DEAE are retained on the HAP column. Each column bed is then assayed for radioactivity as a single sample.

Minicolumns offer three major advantages over the conventional chromatographic methods from which they were derived. First, the speed of the minicolumn separation procedure (5-10 min, compared to hours by conventional DNA and DEAE gradient methods) reduces the time during which degradation and/or dissociation of complexes can take place.

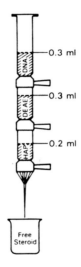

FIG. 1.   DIAGRAM OF MINICOLUMN USED FOR RAPID SEPARATION OF GLUCOCORTIOID-RECEPTOR COMPLEXES.   SEE TEXT FOR DESCRIPTION.

Second, the columns can be prepared and run simultaneously in large numbers, thereby affording the opportunity for experiments requiring analysis of many samples such as our kinetic studies described below. Finally, much smaller samples are needed for the minicolumn procedure than for conventional chromatographic procedures, an especially advantageous feature when the tissue source is limited.

Kinetics of glucocorticoid-receptor complexes in rat thymus
cells. Using the minicolumns along with techniques
developed earlier for assaying nuclear binding we have
measured rates of formation, activation and nuclear binding
of glucocorticoid-receptor complexes in rat thymus cells at
37°C, as well as steady state levels of these complexes with
various glucocorticoids. As shown in Figure 2 (13), when
radiolabeled TA is added to cells at 37°C, there is rapid
formation of nonactivated hormone receptor complexes (HR),
followed by increases in activated complexes (HR') and
nuclear complexes (HR'n) after a delay of 0.5 to 1.0 min.
In earlier studies we noted the delay at 37°C in the
appearance of HR'n compared to total cytosolic complexes
(14).

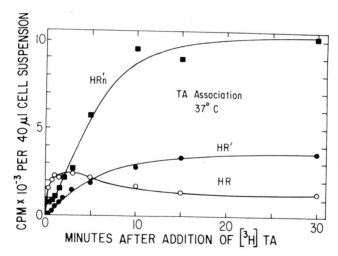

FIG. 2.   TIME COURSE OF FORMATION BY TRIAMCINOLONE ACETONIDE (TA) OF HR, HR', AND HR'n IN
RAT THYMUS CELLS AT 37°C (13). [³H]-TA AT 10 TIMES FINAL CONCENTRATION IN
KRBg-HEPES AT 37°C WAS ADDED AT TIME 0 TO A THYMUS CELL SUSPENSION IN KRBg-HEPES
AT 37°C, TO GIVE A FINAL CONCENTRATION OF ABOUT 15 nM. AT THE INDICATED TIMES,
ALIQUOTS OF CELL SUSPENSION WERE REMOVED FOR ASSAY OF HR, HR', AND HR'n. NON-
SATURABLE BINDING, DETERMINED FROM A PARALLEL INCUBATION WITH 1 µM TA, GAVE
CORRECTIONS (INDEPENDENT OF TIME) OF 1280 CPM FOR HR'n AND OF LESS THAN 2% FOR
HR AND HR'.

With the results in Figure 2, we can ascribe most of this
delay to the time required for generation of of HR', the

presumed intermediate between HR and HR'n, rather than to the time required for translocation and binding of HR' to the nucleus: while the formation of HR' clearly lags behind that of HR, no obvious delay is detectable in formation of HR'n relative to HR'.

To further distinguish the rates of activation and nuclear binding we performed 'temperature jump experiments'. In these experiments, a cell suspension which had been incubated for several hours at 0-3°C with labeled glucocorticoid to form HR was warmed rapidly to a given temperature by dilution with 10 volumes of warmed buffer, left for the desired amount of time, then cooled, lysed rapidly by further dilution with cold $MgCl_2$ and assayed for HR, HR' and HR'n. Such experiments were done with the warming step at 37°, 25°, and 15°C. Though the rate of formation of complexes decreased significantly with lower temperatures, no delay in formation of HR'n from HR' was discernible at any temperature. Thus, we concluded that nuclear binding is much faster than activation, with a time constant of less than 10 sec.

Our results with minicolumns also provided convincing support for our earlier suggestions (14) that triamcinolone acetonide and dexamethasone give higher steady state ratios of HR' to HR than cortisol and corticosterone.

Cyclic model of receptor kinetics and agonist-antagonist relationships. To account for the results just outlined we devised a cyclic model of receptor kinetics that accounts quantitatively for most of our own results and for results of others. The model (Fig. 3) assumes (i) a reversible reaction with rate constants k_1 and k_{-1} for formation of nonactivated complex HR from hormone H and receptor R; (ii) an irreversible reaction with rate constant k_2 for activation of HR to HR'; (iii) a rapid reversible reaction (essentially an equilibrium) between HR' and its nuclear-bound form HR'n; (iv) an irreversible reaction with rate constant k_{-1} (the same as that for dissociation of HR) for regeneration of R from HR' and HR'n. Different glucocorticoids are assumed to differ only in k_{-1}. All constants required for predicting kinetic behavious can be measured experimentally, so that the model can be tested without ad hoc assumptions.

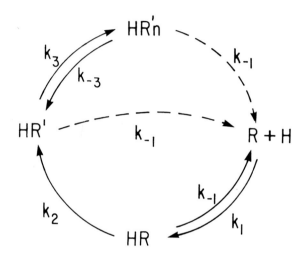

FIG. 3.   CYCLIC MODEL OF RECEPTOR KINETICS (13). HORMONE, H, IS ASSUMED TO REACT REVERSIBLY WITH FREE RECEPTOR, R, TO FORM A NONACTIVATED COMPLEX, HR, THAT THROUGH AN IRREVERSIBLE REACTION PRODUCES THE ACTIVATED COMPLEX HR'. HR' RAPIDLY EQUILIBRATES WITH THE NUCLEAR-BOUND COMPLEX, HR'n. HR' AND HR'n BOTH REGENERATE R THROUGH IRREVERSIBLE REACTIONS.

With measured values for TA and cortisol the model not only predicts accurately the kinetic results in Fig. 2, but gives steady-state ratios of HR' to HR for the two steroids in quantitative agreement with those found experimentally even though the activation reaction has no provision for steroid-specific control of activation. The different ratios turn out to be dynamic consequences of the choice of k_{-1} for the rate of the regeneration reactions.

The cyclic model predicts that steroids with high k_{-1} should be partial antagonists. Mathematically it can be shown (unpublished) that the cyclic model gives biological agonist-antagonist relations essentially indistinguishable from those of the steric-allosteric model (15). According to the cyclic model, antagonism should be predictable from k_{-1} alone. However, the model does not exclude other mechanisms of antagonism, such as allosteric equilibria or formation of covalent complexes; it provides an additional mechanism.

Since the model includes irreversible steps, it also predicts that normal receptor function requires energy. That prediction is consistent with earlier studies in which we found metabolic evidence for an energy requirement, and proposed a receptor cycle with an ATP-dependent step (possibly phosphorylation) for regenerating R (16).

Effects of ATP and pyrophosphate (PP_i) on activation and stability of cytosolic glucocorticoid-receptor complexes. A number of studies have suggested a possible role for ATP in the activation of steroid-receptor complexes or in the function (i.e. translocation or nuclear binding) of the activated complexes. In particular, Moudgil and John (17) reported that ATP at 5-10 mM promotes activation of rat liver cytosolic complexes at 4°C. In agreement with that observation we have found that ATP promotes activation of rat thymus complexes at 4°C (18). Somewhat surprisingly, however, our findings indicate that this effect is not limited to ATP, as other nucleoside triphosphates and PP_i at the same concentrations are similarly effective. Thus it is unlikely that the activation seen in vitro is related to the

energy dependence of glucocorticoid-receptor complex formation seen in vivo (16).

Two additional findings of interest were noted when we
looked further into the effects of PP_i and ATP on rat thymus
receptor complexes (18). We were initially surprised to
find that if we used these compounds to activate cytosolic
complexes we achieved much higher levels of DNA binding than
by warming cytosols to 25°C, with virtually no mero-receptor
formation. In fact, more than 95% of the total complexes
were converted to the DNA binding form, and that level was
maintained for up to 24 hours. This is in marked contrast
to warmed cytosols, in which by 24 hours more than 80% of
total complexes are converted to mero-receptor forms.
Further analysis by gel filtration in the presence of ATP or
PP_i revealed that these compounds do indeed prevent
conversion to mero-receptor. However, the DNA-binding
complex was not the 5.6 nm native form but had a Stokes
radius of 3.1 nm.

While the 5.6 and 3.1 nm DNA-binding complexes could not be
distinguished by our standard minicolumn procedure, they
could be separated using minicolumns in which the order of
the DEAE and DNA columns were reversed, as the intact 5.6 nm
DNA-binding complex binds to DEAE while the 3.1 nm complex
does not. The 3.1 nm complex was subsequently shown to be
formed in a time-dependent manner from the 5.6 nm form. It
accumulates in ATP-treated cytosols because its conversion
to meroreceptor is prevented.

The protection against mero-receptor formation is dose-dependent and requires concentrations similar to those that activate complexes. We also found that ATP and PP_i in the same
dose range interfere with binding of activated complexes to
DNA-cellulose.

The ability of ATP and PP_i to activate glucocorticoid-receptor complexes and weaken binding of activated complexes to DNA-cellulose is most likely due to the charge properties of the DNA-binding domain of the receptor. Since the DNA-binding domain appears to be positively charged (19, 20) it is reasonable to suppose that the strongly negative PP_i and ATP can both unmask DNA-binding sites on the receptor and weaken binding of those sites to DNA, by competing with negatively charged groups. The ability of ATP and PP_i to prevent formation of mero-receptor can probably also be accounted for by the same properties. This hypothesis is supported by the fact that the DNA-binding site appears to contain lysine residues (19) and lysine seems to be present at the sites for enzymatic cleavage that yields mero-receptor (21).

Sulfhydryl groups on the thymus glucocorticoid receptor complex. Glucocorticoid receptors in rat thymus and liver cytosols are sensitive to sulfhydryl-modifying reagents. Treatment of unbound receptors with such reagents prevents binding of glucocorticoid to form glucocorticoid-receptor complexes (22-24). However, once the glucocorticoid has bound to the receptor, these reagents usually have little effect on the integrity of the complex (25-27). We have suggested that there is a sulfhydryl group in or near the DNA-binding domain of the activated thymic complex that must remain reduced for the complex to bind to DNA. This suggestion originated from the observations that: i) the highly specific sulfhydryl-modifying reagent methyl methanethiosulfonate (MMTS) and 5,5'dithiobis(2-nitrobenzoic acid) (DTNB) substantially inhibit binding of the activated complex to DNA-cellulose (27); ii) when these sulfhydryl-modifying reagents are removed from the complex with reducing agents such as dithioerythritol, the complex regains the ability to bind DNA (27). Not all sulfhydryl modifying reagents produce these results. The commonly used reagents iodoacetamide and N-ethylmaleimide are ineffective at inhibiting DNA binding (27) and preventing activated liver complexes from binding to nuclei (26).

A central question that has concerned us is whether the sulfhydryl group involved with the inhibition of DNA binding after modification by MMTS and DTNB is the same sulfhydryl group whose modification prevents the glucocorticoid from binding to the receptor. In other words, is there a sulf-hydryl group common to both the DNA- and steroid-binding domains, or is there a separate group for each domain? Evidence for the latter situation has come from our studies involving chromatography of receptor complexes on reactive sulfhydryl matrices.

Reactive sulfhydryl columns (28) function as shown in Figure 4A. A thioanion on the glucocorticoid-receptor complex (GRC) undergoes a thio-disulfide interchange reaction with the disulfide of the matrix, thereby covalently attaching the complex to the matrix (I).

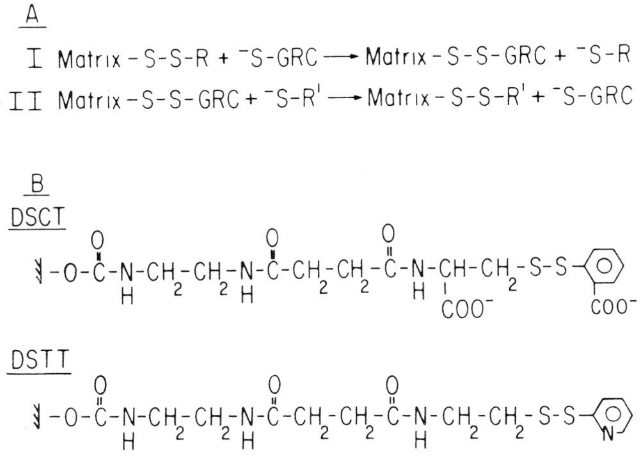

A

I   Matrix – S–S–R + $^-$S–GRC ⟶ Matrix – S–S–GRC + $^-$S–R

II Matrix – S–S–GRC + $^-$S–R' ⟶ Matrix – S–S–R' + $^-$S–GRC

B

DSCT

$\text{-O-C(=O)-N(H)-CH}_2\text{-CH}_2\text{-N(H)-C(=O)-CH}_2\text{-CH}_2\text{-C(=O)-N(H)-CH(COO}^-)\text{-CH}_2\text{-S-S-}\langle\bigcirc\text{-COO}^-\rangle$

DSTT

$\text{-O-C(=O)-N(H)-CH}_2\text{-CH}_2\text{-N(H)-C(=O)-CH}_2\text{-CH}_2\text{-C(=O)-N(H)-CH}_2\text{-CH}_2\text{-S-S-}\langle\bigcirc_N\rangle$

FIG. 4.   SEE TEXT FOR DETAILS.

This process can be reversed and the complex eluted from the column by the addition of compounds containing a sulfhydryl group (II).

We have synthesized over 20 reactive sulfhydryl matrices with different spacer arms and leaving groups. Of these, the matrices designated as DSCT and DSTT (Figure 4B) have proved to be the most useful. The DSTT matrix reacts equally well with both the activated and non-activated form of the complex while the DSCT matrix is able to distinguish between the 2 forms, reacting with the activated but not the non-activated complex (Table 3; 29).

TABLE 3

BINDING OF ACTIVATED AND NONACTIVATED GLUCOCORTICOID-RECEPTOR COMPLEXES TO DNA-CELLULOSE, DSTT AND DSCT[*]

TREATMENT OF CYTOSOL	RECEPTOR BOUND [3H] STEROID APPLIED TO COLUMNS	H[3] STEROID (CPM) RETAINED ON COLUMNS		
		DNA-CELLULOSE	DSTT	DSCT
[3H]TA LABELED CYTOSOLS				
UNWARMED	4796	162	-	133
WARMED	3698	2359	-	2334
UNWARMED	4941	327	4938	
WARMED	4807	2717	4940	
[3H]DM LABELED CYTOSOLS				
UNWARMED	1412	76	1334	0
WARMED	3890	3611	3880	3307

[*] GLUCOCORTICOID RECEPTORS WERE LABELED IN INTACT THYMUS CELLS WITH EITHER 20 nM [3H]TRIAMCINOLONE ACETONIDE (TA) OR 50 nM [3H]DEXAMETHASONE 21 MESYLATE (DM) for 2 HOURS AT 0°C AND THE RESULTANT CYTOSOL EITHER WARMED FOR 15 MIN AT 25°C OR KEPT ON ICE. CYTOSOLS WERE THEN BOUND TO DNA CELLULOSE, DSTT, OR DSCT (29).

Two pieces of evidence suggest that the interaction of the complex with the DSCT matrix is through a sulfhydryl group in or near the DNA-binding domain. First, soluble DNA inhibits the binding of the activated complex to both the DSCT matrix and DNA-cellulose by a similar amount (29);

second, treating purified complexes with sulfhydryl modifying reagents inhibits binding to DNA cellulose to the same
extent that DSCT-binding is inhibited (29).

Evidence to support the idea that these are separate sulfhydryl groups associated with the two domains comes from
experiments in which the sulfhydryl group in the steroid
binding domain was covalently blocked by labeling the
receptor with dexamethasone 21-mesylate, and the complex
then allowed to react with the DSCT matrix. If a common
sulfhydryl existed between the two domains, the complex
should not bind to the DSCT matrix, but if there were 2
separate sulfhydryls it should bind. As shown in Table 3,
the complex did react with the DSCT matrix, indicating the
probable existence of a sulfhydryl group located near the
DNA-binding domain.

The sulfhydryl group associated with the DNA-binding domain
appears to be located in a portion of the complex resistant
to degradation. We have digested the activated complex with
immobilized trypsin, thermolysin, subtillisin and endogenous
thymic protease (29) to a point where DNA cellulose binding
was lost, but there was only a moderate decrease in binding
to the DSCT matrix. Thus, this sulfhydryl groups appears to
be retained on mero-receptor and related complexes, even
though the DNA binding function is lost. Using similar
types of experiments Harrison et al. (30) also demonstrated
the existance of more than one sulfhydryl group on both
activated and trypsin digested complexes. However, they
were unable to associate these sulfhydryls with functional
areas of the complex.

Stability of cytosolic glucocorticoid complexes in leukemic
cells. Glucocortiocids have been used in the treatment of
leukemia for over 30 years. The benefit derived from

steroid therapy, however, varies widely within the particular subtype of disease. It is possible that in some cases lack of glucocorticoid responsiveness is the result of subtle alterations either in the properties of the receptor itself or in its regulation. In support of this notion McCaffrey et al. (31) reported that receptors from some leukemia subtypes, particularly acute nonlymphocytic leukemia (ANLL), appear to have altered characteristics compared to those from normal lymphoid tissues when analyzed by DNA and DEAE chromatography. They hypothesized that these abnormal characteristics would correlate with lack of patient response to therapy.

We have surveyed a number of leukemia specimens using the minicolumn procedure to determine the relative proportion of activated and nonactivated complexes in cytosols before and after warming cytosols to 25°C (cell-free activation) (32). What we found was that cytosols of chronic lymphocytic leukemia cells (CLL) contained glucocorticoid receptor complexes in proportions similar to those seen with normal lymphoid tissue. At 0°C, most complexes were in the non-activated state, with little evidence for activated or mero-receptor forms. In contrast, specimens of ANLL classification displayed a much higher proportion of mero-receptor complexes and much lower proportion of DNA-binding complexes than CLL or normal specimens. Of particular interest was the question of whether these differences were due to degradation taking place after the cells were broken, or reflected intrinsic differences in receptors from ANLL cells.

We undertook extensive studies to determine the cause of the lability of glucocorticoid receptor complexes in cytosols from ANLL cells (33). We found that mero-receptor accumulated rapidly in ANLL cytosols after cells were broken. The accumulation was most rapid in cytosols which contained activated complexes or under conditions used to produce activated complexes, but also occurred in cytosols containing only nonactivated forms. It was of interest that the lability of cytosolic receptors within the ANLL specimens were related to the differentiation state of the cells. That is, cytosols of ANLL specimens with properties of monocytoid differentiation [M_4 French-American-British (FAB) class] in general contained more stable complexes than specimens primarily of myelocytic differentiation patterns (M_1 - M_3 FAB classes). Consistent with this observation, cytosols of polymorphonuclear cells isolated from normal blood were much more labile than those of monocytes.

Most important, if cells were first incubated at 37°C with radiolabeled steroid to form activated complexes in vivo, then broken and analysed on minicolumns, there was in all cases clear evidence for activated or DNA binding complexes. From no experiments did we obtain evidence to suggest any difference in the native receptors of ANLL and CLL cells. We have concluded that the high proportion of mero-receptor in ANLL specimens was due to in vitro proteolysis of other- wise normal receptor complexes. Further support for this conclusion is given by the studies below.

We first hypothesized that the differences in lability of cytosolic preparations were due to the relative amounts of proteolytic enzymes capable of degrading the receptors. If so, then mixing labile and stable cell preparations prior to lysis should allow us to demonstrate the presence of such receptor-degrading enzymes. In other words, complexes from stable preparations in mixed cytosols should no longer appear stable, but should be converted to mero-receptor by the proteolytic enzymes from the labile cell preparations.

Unexpectedly, what the mixing experiments showed was that rather than the labile cytosols causing degradation of complexes from stable cytosols, the reverse was true; the stable cytosols stabilized receptor complexes in labile cytosols (Figure 5). Further experiments showed that the stabilizing effect was dose-dependent with respect to the proportion of stable cytosol used. Further attempts to characterize the stabilizing factor from human leukemic cells were hampered by the lack of availability of tissue. For this reason we looked for such a factor in other cell types. These studies are discussed below.

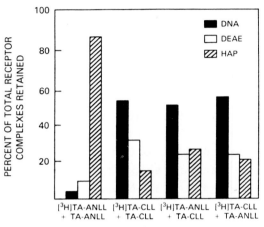

FIG. 5. DISTRIBUTION OF GLUCOCORTICOID-RECEPTOR COMPLEXES IN WARMED CYTOSOLS OF MIXED ANLL AND CLL CELL PREPARATIONS. CELLS OF ANLL AND CLL SPECIMENS WERE INCUBATED WITH [³H]TRIAMCINOLONE ACETONIDE ([³H]TA) OR UNLABELED TRIAMCINOLONE ACETONIDE (TA) FOR 2 HOURS AT 0°C. EQUAL ALIQUOTS OF SUSPENSIONS WERE MIXED AT A RATIO OF 1:1 IN VARIOUS COMBINATIONS; FROM THESE MIXTURES, CYTOSOLS WERE PREPARED. THE CYTOSOLS WERE WARMED TO 25°C FOR 15 MIN AND ANALYZED ON MINICOLUMNS.

Calpastatin, a stabilizer of glucocorticoid-receptor complexes. In addition to human CLL cells the stabilizing factor is also present in many tissues including WEHI-7 mouse thymoma cells and rat liver and spleen cells (34). Interestingly, it is not present in rat thymus cells which contain relatively labile cytosolic complexes (8,34). Table 4 summarizes the properties of stabilizing factor partially purified from rat liver cytosol. As shown in the table, it appears to be very similar to calpastatin, a naturally occurring inhibitor of a family of neutral calcium-activated proteases called calpains (35-37). Whether or not there is a physiological relationship between the calpains, calpastatin and glucocorticoid-receptor complexes must await further investigations. An important practical consequence of our findings however, is that the addition of calpastatin to thymus cytosols and to cytosols such as those from cells of patients with ANLL greatly enhances the stability of complexes.

TABLE 4

PROPERTIES OF THE GLUCOCORTICOID-RECEPTOR STABILIZING FACTOR (GRSF) AND CALPASTATIN

PROPERTY	GRSF	CALPASTATIN
HEAT STABLE (100°C, 30 MIN)	YES	YES
ELUTION FROM DEAE CELLULOSE (mM NaCl)	110	110 (100)
APPROXIMATE MOLECULAR WEIGHT OF NATIVE AGGREGATE	280,000	280,000 (280-300,000)
ISOELECTRIC pH	5.1	5.1 (4.55)
EFFECTS ON ACTIVATION OF GLUCOCORTICOID RECEPTOR COMPLEXES	NONE	NONE

VALUES ARE FROM BODWELL, J.E., HOLBROOK, N.J. AND MUNCK, A. (UNPUBLISHED) FOR RAT LIVER CALPASTATIN. VALUES IN PARENTHESIS FOR NaCl CONCENTRATION AND MOLECULAR WEIGHT ARE FROM MURACHI ET AL. (36), AND FOR ISOELECTRIC pH ARE FROM TAKANO AND MURACHI (37) FOR HUMAN ERYTHROCYTE CALPASTATIN.

Acknowledgements

This research was supported by research grants AM03535 and CA17323 from the National Institutes of Health, and by the Norris Cotton Cancer Center Core Grant (CA23108) from the U. S. Public Health Service. D.B.M. is a fellow of the

Albert J. Ryan Foundation. N.J.H. was supported by a fellowship from the Leukemia Society of America.

References

1. Holbrook, N.J., Bodwell, J.E., Jeffries, M.R., Munck, A.: J. Biol. Chem. 258, 6477 (1983).

2. Nielsen, C.J., Sando, J.J., Vogel, W.M., Pratt, W.B.: J. Biol. Chem. 252, 7568 (1977).

3. Sherman, M.R., Moran, M.C., Neal, R.M., Niu, E.-M., Tuazon, F.B.: In Lee, H.J., Fitzgerald, T.J. (eds.): Progress in Research and Clinical Applications of Corticosteroids, Philadelphia:Heyden, p. 45 (1982).

4. Raaka, B.M., Samuels, H.H.: J. Biol. Chem. 258, 417 (1983).

5. Vedeckis, W.V.: Biochemistry 22: 1983 (1983).

6. Simons, S.S., Jr., Schleenbaker, R.E., Eisen, H.J.: J. Biol. Chem. 258, 2229 (1983).

7. Sherman, M.R., Tuazon, F.B., Somjen, G.J.: In Soto, R.J., DeNicola, A., Blaquier, J. (eds.): Physiopathology of Endocrine Diseases and Mechanisms of Hormone Action, New York:Liss, p. 321 (1981).

8. Holbrook, N.J., Bodwell, J.E., Munck, A.: J. Steroid Biochem. 20, 19 (1984).

9. Weatherill, P.J., Bell, P.A.: Biochem. J. 206, 633 (1982).

10. Vedekis, W.V.: Biochemistry 22, 1975 (1983).

11. Sherman, M.R., Moran, M.C., Tuazon, F.B., Stevens, Y.-W.: J. Biol. Chem. 258, 10366 (1983).

12. Simons, S.S. Jr., Thompson, E.B.: Proc. Natl. Acad. Sci. USA 78, 3541 (1981).

13. Munck, A., Holbrook, N.J.: J. Biol. Chem. 259, 820 (1984).

14. Munck, A., Foley, R.: J. Steroid Biochem. 12: 225 (1980).

15. Sherman, M.R.: In Baxter, J.D., Rousseau, G.G. (eds): Glucocorticoid Hormone Action, Berlin:Springer, p. 123 (1979).

16. Munck, A., Wira, C.H., Young, D.A., Mosher, K.M., Hallahan, C., Bell, P.A.: J. Steroid Biochem. $\underline{3}$, 567 (1972).

17. Moudgil, V.K., John, J.K.: Biochem. J. $\underline{190}$, 799 (1980).

18. Holbrook, N.J., Bodwell, J.E., Munck, A.: J. Biol. Chem. $\underline{258}$, 14885 (1983).

19. DiSorbo, D.M., Phelps, D.S., Litwack, G.: Endocrinology $\underline{106}$, 922 (1980).

20. Schmidt, T.J., Litwack, G.: Phys. Rev. $\underline{62}$, 1131 (1982).

21. Moran, M.C., Tuazon, F.B., Stevens, Y.-W., Sherman, M.R.: Fed. Proc. $\underline{41}$, 1161 (1982).

22. Schaumburg, B.P.: Biochim. Biophys. Acta $\underline{261}$, 219 (1972).

23. Kobolinski, M., Beato, M., Kalimi, M., Feigelson, P.: J. Biol. Chem. $\underline{247}$, 7897 (1972).

24. Rees, A.M., Bell, P.A.: Biochim. Biophys. Acta $\underline{411}$:121 (1975).

25. Young, H.A., Parks, W.P., Scolnick, E.M.: Proc. Natl. Acad. Sci., USA $\underline{72}$, 3060 (1975).

26. Kalimi, M., Love, K.: J. Biol. Chem. $\underline{255}$, 4687 (1980).

27. Bodwell, J.E., Holbrook, N.J., Munck, A.: Biochemistry $\underline{23}$, 1392 (1984).

28. Brocklehurst, K.: Int. J. Biochem. $\underline{10}$, 259 (1979).

29. Bodwell, J.E., Holbrook, N.J., Munck, A.: Biochemistry $\underline{23}$, 4237 (1984).

30. Harrison, R.W., Woodward, C., Thompsom, E.: Biochim. Biophys. Acta $\underline{759}$, 1 (1983).

31. McCaffrey, R., Lillquist, A., Bell, R.: Blood $\underline{59}$:393 (1982).

32. Holbrook, N.J., Bloomfield, C.D., Munck, A.: Cancer Res., $\underline{43}$, 4478 (1983).

33. Holbrook, N.J., Bloomfield, C.D., Munck, A.: Cancer Res., $\underline{44}$, 407 (1984).

34. Holbrook, N.J., Bodwell, J.E., Munck, A.: J. Steroid Biochem. $\underline{20}$, 245 (1984).

35. Murachi, T.: In Cheung, W.Y. (ed.): Calcium and Cell Function, New York:Academic Press, Vol 4, p. 388 (1981).

36. Murachi, T., Tanaka, K., Hatanaka, M., Murakami, T.: Adv. Enzyme Regul. $\underline{19}$, 407 (1981).

37. Takano, E., Murachi, T.: J. Biochem. $\underline{92}$, 2021 (1982).

PROGESTIN TREATMENT, PROGESTERONE RECEPTORS, AND BREAST CANCER

Kathryn B. Horwitz, Scot M. Sedlacek, Carolyn d'Arville, and Lisa L. Wei
Department of Medicine, University of Colorado Health Sciences Center, Denver, CO 80262, USA

Introduction

In 1975 we showed that human breast tumors have progesterone receptors (PR), and suggested that these proteins would serve as markers of hormone dependence (1,2). This idea has been confirmed by extensive clinical trials which show, not only that PR-rich tumors are highly likely to respond to endocrine therapies, but also, that patients with such tumors have longer disease-free periods and a better prognosis than patients whose tumors are PR-poor (3). While the status of PR as predictive markers is firm, the functional significance of PR is unknown. The relationship between PR content and response to progestin treatment has also not been properly explored, even though there is increasing evidence that progestins are effective and well tolerated drugs for treatment of the disseminated disease. That the crucial role of progestins and PR in the biology of human breast cancer has not been precisely defined has been due to lack of experimental models. The measurement and structural analyses of mammalian PR have been difficult because the receptors are extremely labile, low in abundance, and require estrogen priming. The biological actions of progestins have not been adequately studied since even PR-positive human tumor cells have failed to respond to progestins in vitro and hormone antagonists have been unavailable. Here we review recent data from our laboratory, in which a progestin-responsive human breast cancer cell line

Molecular Mechanism of Steroid Hormone Action
© 1985 Walter de Gruyter & Co., Berlin · New York – Printed in Germany

has been used to circumvent these problems, permitting us to study the biochemical mechanisms involved in progesterone action. We also review the use of progestins in the therapy of advanced breast cancer and outline some treatment strategies combining progestins and antiestrogens.

Progesterone Receptors and Progestin Action In T47D$_{co}$ Human Breast Cancer Cells

A. The model

It is generally agreed that in appropriate target cells, PR are synthesized in response to estrogens acting through estrogen receptors (ER). This relationship has been demonstrated in a variety of experimental systems, including human breast cancer cells in culture, and led us to suggest several years ago that the presence of PR in human breast tumor biopsies could be used to deduce the integrity of ER and of the estrogen-response system, and would serve as markers of hormone-dependent tumors (1,2).

It was therefore of considerable interest to us that while measuring the steroid receptor content of a series of cultured human breast cancer cells, one cell line, T47D, had no cytoplasmic ER by sucrose density gradient analysis, yet had the highest PR levels of any breast cancer cell line we surveyed (4). We decided to characterize these receptors in 1981 and established a line from frozen stocks that initially had very low plating efficiency (<5%). However, the cells proliferated, and were passaged 20 to 30 times in medium that differed slightly from that recommended by the cell bank. It had lower serum and insulin concentrations, and no hydrocortisone. Figure 1 shows that after 30 passages the cells had less than 3 fmole/mg protein (<0.04 pmole/mg DNA) of specific, unfilled ER in cytosols and none in nuclear extracts (5). Human breast tumor biopsies with these levels of ER are

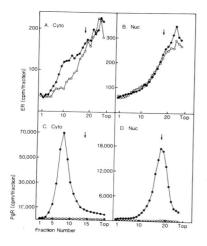

Figure 1. Cytoplasmic and Nuclear Estrogen and Progesterone Receptors in Untreated T47D$_{co}$ Human Breast Cancer Cells. Cells were homogenized, and a cytosol and 0.6 M KCl extract of nuclei were obtained by centrifugation. They were incubated with [^{3}H]estradiol (4 nM) with (o) or without (o) a 100-fold excess of unlabeled diethylstibestrol (A and B), or they were incubated with [^{3}H]R5020 (20 nM) with (o) or without (o) a 100-fold excess of unlabeled R5020 (C and D). Charcoal-resistant supernatants were layered on linear sucrose gradients and centrifuged. Fractions were collected from the bottom and counted. Cytoplasmic (Cyto) ER, 0.037 pmol/mg DNA; nuclear (Nuc) ER, O; cytoplasmic PR, 16.5 pmole/mg DNA; nuclear PR, 14.6 pmole/mg DNA. Arrow: [^{14}C]labeled bovine serum albumin (4.6S).

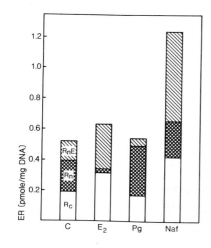

Figure 2. Effect of estrogen, progesterone and nafoxidine on ER distribution showing "processing reversal" by the antiestrogen. Triplicate flasks were treated with growth medium only (C), or with medium containing 10 nM estradiol (E$_2$), 0.1 μM progesterone (Pg), or 1 μM nafoxidine. Cell cytosols and nuclear extracts were incubated with [^{3}H]estradiol only, or together with a 100-fold excess of diethylstibestrol. Binding was measured by the protamine sulfate exchange assay after a 0°C or a 30°C incubation. R$_c$: unfilled cytoplasmic sites. R$_n$: unfilled nuclear sites. R$_n$E: filled nuclear sites.

classified as ER-negative. However, not only did the cells have large amounts of cytoplasmic PR (2.7 pmole/mg cytosol protein; 16.5 pmole/mg DNA), but a KCl extract of the nuclear pellet, showed that a considerable number of PR sites were associated with the crude nuclei (Figure 1). This compartment contained an additional 2.3 pmol of receptor per mg of extracted protein (14.6 pmol of PR per mg of DNA). Thus, under the culture conditions described, T47D cells have more than 300,000 total PR sites per cell. This is five to ten fold greater than is usually seen, even in estradiol-stimulated tissues.

T47D cells were established from the pleural effusion of a patient with breast cancer; they have mammary epithelial characteristics and synthesize casein (6). Various sublines have now been established with different ER content and estrogen responsiveness. We have therefore designated ours as T47D$_{co}$. It is likely that these are epigenetic variants rather than true mutations of the parental cells.

T47D estrogen receptors and "processing reversal". Are these really ER negative cells? Figure 2 shows that these cells are not entirely devoid of ER. With protamine sulfate precipitation we find some cytoplasmic ER, but these sites cannot be depleted by estradiol (Rc, figure 2) and are therefore a basal, nontranslocatable, possibly non-functional, receptor fraction. We see approximately the same irreduceable minimum cytoplasmic ER in MCF-7 cells after 90-95% of sites have been translocated by estradiol. Protamine sulfate also precipitates some (0.5 to 1 pmol/mg DNA) hormone filled (RnE) and unfilled (Rn) nuclear ER. These values approximate the steady state levels of nuclear ER seen after receptor translocation and down-regulation following chronic estrogen treatment of MCF-7 cells. This "processed" level is an activated state; continuous protein synthesis is required for its maintenance and PR are induced (7,8).

We therefore postulate that in T47D$_{co}$ cells, ER are in a persistent activated state in the nucleus. We have several indications that this is the case. First, when protein synthesis is inhibited, 65% of nuclear ER are lost in 18 h. Thus, continuous protein synthesis may be required to keep ER in the nucleus. Second, the antiestrogen, nafoxidine has an unusual effect: it doubles ER levels in 6 h (Figure 2), and the new sites are virtually all intranuclear. The rate of this increase is similar to the rate of nuclear ER processing. We believe this increase represents a reversal of some step involved in ER processing. Such a reversal can be brought about in MCF-7 cells when estrogen treatment is followed by antiestrogen treatment, and is too rapid to be explained by new receptor synthesis. Third, processing reversal, like processing, is independent of protein synthesis and cannot be blocked by cycloheximide (5). It would seem that the nafoxidine-induced increase in ER represents recruitment of preformed receptor protein from a previously unmeasured receptor pool.

These ER require further study using the new probes now available--electroaffinity labeling and immunochemical analysis. It would not be surprising if these receptors contain a mutant chromatin binding domain, analogous to domain C of GR in nti lymphoma cells (9,10), that accounts for chronic nuclear binding and chronic PR gene activation. These receptors may be estrogen insensitive because the mutation has dispensed with the only step that requires estrogen -- the initial receptor transformation step.

Biological actions of ER. To show whether the ER can mediate estrogenic or antiestrogenic effects we measured cell growth and PR levels after hormone treatment. First, the growth of T47D$_{co}$ was unaffected by the presence of estradiol (10 nM), or by concentrations of nafoxidine that are cytotoxic in ER-positive breast cancer cells (7). Insensitivity to the killing effects of antiestrogens is characteristic of cell lines that have no ER (11). Second, prolonged treatment (5 to 7 days) of the cells with estradiol, with nafoxidine or with steroid-depleted serum had little appreciable effect on the very high PR levels. Thus we conclude that the nuclear ER in these cells cannot respond to exogenously added estrogens in the usual way.

The progesterone receptors. The PR appear to be normal by
several criteria: the receptors are heat-labile, they sediment
at 7-8S on sucrose gradients, they bind only progestins
specifically and with high affinity (5,12) and they can only be
translocated by progestins (13). If the cells are treated with
progesterone for 5 min, the PR acquire tight nuclear binding
capacity. With longer progesterone treatment (10 min) nuclear
receptor levels begin to fall and as many as 85% of the sites
are lost in 1 hr in a step analogous to ER processing. Removal
of progesterone leads to new receptor synthesis, that includes a
cycloheximide sensitive step; total replenishment requires about
24 hrs (14). Replenishment is neither stimulated by estradiol
nor inhibited by antiestrogens, showing that these PR are
completely estrogen-independent (Figure 3). Some of these steps
are characterized further below.

We have indirect evidence that PR synthesis remains under
some regulation and is not simply constitutive, based on studies
with BUdR (5-bromodeoxyuridine) and sodium butyrate. The
thymidine analog BUdR selectively inhibits the expression of
some specialized functions in differentiated cells, but has
relatively little effect on proteins of more general use and
distribution (15). The ER from rabbit uterus have an enhanced
affinity for BUdR-substituted DNA (16), and in human breast tumor
cells this compound inhibits the synthesis of estrogen-induced
PR and of an estrogen-induced 46 kilodalton protein (17). Butyrate
preferentially inhibits the steroid-inducible component of
transferring and ovalbumin transcription, while only moderately
inhibiting the constitutive synthesis of these mRNAs (18). This
compound alters the level of histone acetylation (19) and has
stimulating (20) as well as inhibitory (18) effects on gene
induction.

We therefore used BUdR and butyrate to distinguish between
constitutive transcription and an inductive process involving
the PR gene. Both compounds suppress PR extensively, even though
at early time points they have little effect on overall DNA and
protein synthesis. After 96 hrs of 20 μg/ml BUdR, PR fell from

19.5 to 5.6 pmole/mg DNA, or approximately 70%. During this time, total protein levels fell only 10%, and growth as measured by DNA levels, was unchanged compared to controls. Similarly, 36 hrs of 10 mM sodium butyrate caused a 65% loss of PR while inhibiting total proteins by 20% and having no effect on DNA replication. We conclude that in T47D$_{co}$ PR retain characteristics of inducible proteins, and it is tempting to speculate that the persistent nuclear ER chronically stimulate transcription of the PR gene, even in the absence of exogenous estrogen.

B.   Regulation of PR levels by progestins

Ligand exchange. To study the kinetics of PR translocation, nuclear turnover, and replenishment, we needed to establish that the receptors could be assayed quantitatively in both cytoplasm and nucleus and when hormone filled or unfilled, and that receptors could be measured equally well whether they are occupied by progesterone or by a synthetic progestin.

To quickly assess exchange, we devised a "mixing" assay in which half of a cytosol is incubated with unlabeled ligand to fill the receptors, and the other half is left untreated. After adsorption of both cytosols with charcoal, the two preparations are mixed in different proportions and then assayed for [^{3}H]R5020 binding at either 0° or 10° C, with incubation times ranging from 4 to 24 hrs. Under conditions of complete exchange, we would expect to see similar [^{3}H]R5020 binding whether or not sites were previously hormone filled. Under conditions in which no exchange occurs, we would expect to see no binding of [^{3}H]R5020 to previously hormone-filled sites, and progressively more binding as the number of unfilled sites increase. Partial exchange would fall between these two extremes.

We have tested progesterone, and several synthetic progestins including R5020, medroxyprogesterone acetate, megestrol acetate, and the synthetic antiprogestin RU38 486. Progesterone-occupied sites exchange completely for [^{3}H]R5020 under all conditions. In contrast the synthetic progestins

666

exchange only 50%, regardless of the conditions used. In practice this means that progesterone-occupied sites can always be accurately measured, but that only half of all sites can be measured when PR are occupied by synthetic progestins. Clinically this suggests that PR are especially difficult to measure in patients that are using synthetic progestins like those found in oral contraceptives.

Translocation and Nuclear Processing. If translocation is a specific response to the action of one class of steroid hormones, then only those hormones should decrease soluble cytoplasmic receptors. To measure the specificity of PR translocation, T47D$_{CO}$ cells were treated for 5 min at 37°C with a variety of steroids, and residual soluble PR were measured in cytosols. Progesterone and synthetic progestins cause rapid decreases in PR; 65-70% of sites are depleted by progesterone and 90% to 95% by all synthetic progestins. At ten-fold higher concentrations androgens and estrogens have little effect. The glucocorticoids, hydrocortisone and dexamethasone also have no effect, but triamcinolone acetonide depleted 55% of PR, consistent with its known progestational properties (21,22). These and similar data prompt us to recommend strongly that PR be masked by an unlabeled progestin when [3H]triamcinolone is used to measure GR. In our opinion [3H]dexamethasone is a far superior ligand for GR determinations.

Although nuclear accumulation of PR is stoichiometric, an unusual and very rapid nuclear turnover, or processing step, characterizes the high affinity binding of nuclear PR when they are occupied by progesterone (Figure 4). After PR are translocated by 0.1 μM progesterone, they can be quantitatively recovered from nuclei only in the first few minutes. Thereafter, nuclear processing results in loss of 50-80% of the newly translocated sites. Rapid processing may be inherent to PR; it also occurs in PR of MCF-7 cells. The extent of receptor translocation and of nuclear receptor processing is increased at higher progesterone concentrations (13).

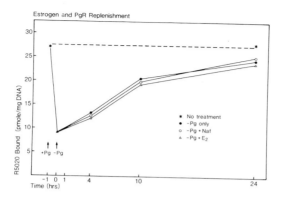

Figure 3. **Replenishment of Cytoplasmic PRs following Their Depletion by 1 hr of Progesterone Treatment: Effects of Nafoxidine and Estradiol.** Triplicate T75 flasks for each point were treated with growth medium only for 1 or 24 hr (*). Others were treated for 1 hr with 0.1 µM progesterone ( ), the growth medium was then removed, the cell surface was washed once with 10 ml of medium, which was discarded, and 15 ml of fresh medium containing no additions (o), nafoxidine (1 µM; o) or estradiol (10 nM:) were added to the cells. Cells were harvested at the times shown and assayed for cytoplasmic PRs by charcoal adsorption.

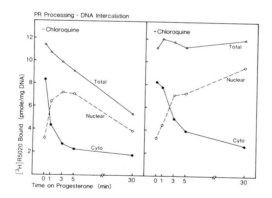

Figure 4. **Effect of chloroquine on the processing of nuclear PR.** Cells were pretreated with chloroquine (100 µM) for 30 minutes at 37°C before 0.1 µM progesterone was added for 1 to 30 minutes. Cells were cooled and homogenized and cytoplasmic and nuclear PR were measured by [³H]R5020 exchange and charcoal adsorption. Total receptors are the sum of sites in the two compartments.

Nuclear PR turnover is more difficult to study if cells are treated with synthetic progestins, because the exchange assay underestimates PR. However, we can measure nuclear PR labeled with [^{3}H]R5020 that have been covalently photolinked in situ with ultraviolet light at the end of the incubations. Under these conditions labeled nuclear receptors persist for several hours before they disappear from all cellular compartments, suggesting that nuclear PR processing is slowed when receptors are occupied by this synthetic hormone. A similar result is seen in time-course studies of subcellular [^{3}H]R5020 distribution(14).

Interestingly, covalently labeled PR subunits A and B (see further below) disappear from nuclei simultaneously and no small molecular weight fragments replace them, which means either 1) that during processing the receptors are clipped close to or at the hormone binding site, leaving a large receptor fragment that cannot bind hormone, or 2) that receptors are degraded into fragments smaller than the resolving capacity of 7.5 to 19% gradient gels (~10,000 daltons). With anti-PR antibodies we should be able to distinguish between these alternatives.

Inhibition of nuclear PR processing. We have previously shown that processing of nuclear ER can be entirely blocked by the G-C specific DNA intercalators, chromomycin A$_3$ and actinomycin D, but not by many other DNA binding agents including chloroquine, and that the inhibitory effects of actinomycin probably result from a direct disturbance of estrogen receptor-DNA interactions (4). To see if nuclear PR "loss" and ER processing are analogous, we tested a variety of DNA intercalators for their ability to interfere with the changes in nuclear PR levels. Ethidium bromide and chromomycin A$_3$ did not significantly prevent this loss (only 26-30% of translocated PR remain) and actinomycin is only minimally effective (40% of translocated PR remain). The most effective inhibitor is chloroquine (Figure 4), which prevents the loss of 70 to 100% of nuclear PR (13).

Since chloroquine is both a DNA intercalator and an inhibitor of lysosomal enzymes, it raised the possibility that inhibition of PR turnover by chloroquine was due to an effect of proteolytic

enzymes and not due to interference with receptor-DNA interactions. We therefore tested other enzyme inhibitors and
chloroquine analogs. Leupeptin and antipain, which prevent the
proteolytic breakdown of PR to meroreceptors (25), were
ineffective inhibitors of nuclear PR processing, as was
carbobenzoxy-L-phenylalanine, a chymotrypsin-like enzyme inhibitor that stabilizes glucocorticoid receptors (26). However,
primaquine and quinacrine were as effective as cholorquine in
preventing PR loss. These compounds are A-T specific
intercalators that yield characteristic banding patterns on
chromosomes (27,28). However, primaquine, unlike quinacrine and
chloroquine, is a poor (one-fifth as potent) lysosomotropic
agent. These experiments suggest that the actions of these three
agents on PR turnover result from their DNA-binding properties
and that it is PR interactions at A-T containing DNA regions
that are involved. Recently two groups (29-31) have provided
direct evidence for an interaction of PR with A-T rich sequences
upstream from PR-inducible genes. It would be interesting to
see if their in vitro receptor-DNA interactions are blocked by
the addition of chloroquine.

The mechanisms involved in processing of steroid-receptor
complexes in the nucleus are unknown. However, its course is
not inexorable, because processing can be rapidly and entirely
(13,23,24) prevented by agents which intercalate into and modify
the structure of DNA. Since some gene-regulatory proteins slide
from nonspecific to specific DNA target sites and undergo
conformational changes in the process (32), it is possible that
the intercalators prevent the movement of receptors from one
intranuclear binding site to another. In the end, a critical
step in steroid-receptor processing involves recognition of base
specific sites, since PR processing appears to be inhibited by A-
T specific intercalators, while ER processing is only inhibited
by G-C intercalators, and intercalators that have no base-sequence
specificity have no inhibitory effects on either PR or ER.

Progesterone receptor replenishment. Current mechanisms
of steroid receptor action postulate that receptors are site-

specific gene regulatory proteins that are transformed to high affinity chromatin-binding molecules by the hormone. It is further assumed, though no direct evidence exists, that after the transcriptional effects are elicited, the nuclear signal shuts off. How receptors are then reactivated is also unknown, but replenishment of hormone-free sites resulting from receptor recycling, from covalent modifications, or from new protein synthesis, probably restores cellular sensitivity to hormone. Thus, in progesterone target cells, the replenishment of PR following their transformation, nuclear binding and nuclear processing may be essential if the cells are to regain responsiveness to progesterone. We have studied the replenishment of PR in T47D$_{CO}$ cells to determine both the rate and the extent of this process (14).

If T47D$_{CO}$ cells are treated for 1 hour with progesterone, after which the hormone is removed and the cells are washed and reincubated in hormone-free medium, then receptors are down-regulated and one can measure the restoration rate of "cytoplasmic" untransformed PR. Under these circumstances, complete replenishment occurs in 24-36 hours (Figure 3). In contrast, if cells are treated for 1 hour with the synthetic progestin R5020, PR replenishment is suppressed even 96 hours after its removal from the medium, and an additional 6 days are required to restore PR to control values despite the transfer of cells to fresh flasks. This property is not restricted to R5020; every synthetic progestin that we have tested, including RU38 486, medroxyprogesterone acetate, and megestrol acetate, gives similar results. In fact, the block to replenishment cannot be prevented even in cells replated immediately after the 1 hr pulse, or in cells flooded with progesterone in an attempt to displace the intracellular synthetic progestin. Replenishment failure must be due, either to true inhibition of new receptor synthesis, or to the presence of a long-acting, tightly bound, intracellular pool of hormone that chronically retranslocates newly replenished receptors. Unlike progesterone, which is very rapidly metabolized (t$\frac{1}{2}$ 2-4 hrs) and ultimately converted to

5α-Pregnan-3,6α-diol-20-one by these cells (unpublished) the synthetic progestins are not degraded. This may account for their long-acting effects. If metabolism of progesterone is prevented by providing an alternative enzyme substrate (ie. androgens) or with enzyme inhibitors, then replenishment is also slowed.

It has been known for several years that demonstration of PR in breast tumor biopsies is often difficult in premenopausal women with normal circulating progesterone levels. Our data provide a molecular explanation for these clinical findings by showing that under continuous progesterone stimulation, total cell PR levels can be chronically suppressed, because progesterone sequesters receptors in nuclear compartments, where they are not measured by current assay procedures or because receptors are down-regulated or "processed". This can result in false-negative assays. The data also suggest that in women treated with synthetic progestins (for example women taking oral contraceptives), accurate measurement of available PR may be especially difficult, because the receptors may be chronically down-regulated. Finally, it is possible that some synthetic progestins have a much longer intracellular duration of action, than simple blood hormone clearance measurements indicate.

C.   The structure of PR in human breast cancer cells

Chromatography and DNA binding.   T47D$_{co}$ cells are the best available source from which to purify and characterize human PR. First, the receptors are present in relatively high abundance (2 to 5 pmole/mg protein), and constitute 0.05% of total cellular proteins. Second, the receptors are unusually resistant to degradation in cell-free extracts because endogenous protease activity is low. One can therefore eliminate some chromatographic steps designed specifically to remove proteases, and still obtain intact proteins.

When [^{3}H]R5020 photolabeled cytosol is applied to DEAE, a characteristic elution pattern is seen. A broad peak of specific binding (peak 1) elutes between 0.1 and 0.2 M KCl, and is followed by a second smaller peak eluting at 0.3 M KCl (peak 2). The average concentration of KCl required to elute these peaks in six separate experiments is 0.17 and 0.27 M. The smaller trailing peak 2 is not seen if the cytosol is precipitated with ammonium sulfate, resuspended, and diluted before DEAE chromatography and probably consists of a small percentage of receptors that either did not dissociate into monomers or dissociated late. Monomer separation is completed after fractions are eluted and pooled, since samples from both peaks sediment at about 4.1S on sucrose density gradients. When aliquots from peaks 1 and 2 are concentrated and subjected to SDS-PAGE, equimolar amounts of A and B proteins are found in each peak.

To assess the ability of PR to bind DNA, pooled fractions from peak 1 were ammonium sulfate precipitated, and the redissolved concentrate was applied to DNA-cellulose in 0.05 M salt. After extensive washing the column was eluted with a gradient of 0.05 to 0.4 M salt, and sequential fractions were collected, concentrated and analyzed by SDS-PAGE. We find that both subunits A and B bind to DNA-cellulose, albeit with different affinity. The B protein elutes from the column at a salt concentration of 0.08 M, while the A protein is retained on the column until the salt concentration reaches 0.15 M. This differs somewhat from recent findings with rabbit uterine PR in which two major PR proteins analogous to the A and B proteins of chick oviduct, could not be distinguished on the basis of their DNA-binding characteristics (33).

In situ photoaffinity labeling of PR. Although we were able to show, by in vitro photoaffinity labeling (34,35) that human breast cancer PR consist of at least two hormone-binding proteins of dissimilar size, it was possible that they were formed in vitro by proteolytic cleavage of a larger protein, or that A is a break-down product of B. We showed that A and B are always present in equimolar amounts, and that treatment of cytosols with a variety of thiol, serine, and metallopeptidase inhibitors [iodoacetamide (5 mM), PMSF (2 mM), o-phenanthroline

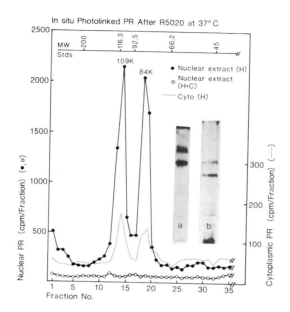

Figure 5. **The subunits of nuclear PR identified by <u>in situ</u> photoaffinity labeling.** <u>Main Figure</u>: SDS-PAGE and Scintillation Counting of Nuclear Salt Extract. Intact cells grown in petri dishes were incubated 5 min at 37°C with 40 nM [^{3}H]R5020 (H) or together with 100-fold excess unlabeled R5020 (H+C). Cells were cooled to 0°C and irradiated for 2 min with UV at 300 nm. Cells were harvested, homogenized, nuclei were sedimented and the receptors extracted with 0.4 M KCl. Cytosol was prepared from the postnuclear supernatant. Ammonium sulfate precipitated cytosol and nuclear receptors were redissolved, solubilized, and subjected to SDS-PAGE. Gel lanes were sliced and counted. Standard proteins of known molecular weight were electrophoresed in parallel lanes and stained. <u>Inset a</u>: The same as main figure, but fluorographed. <u>Inset b</u>: SDS-PAGE and flurography of nuclear PR subunits photolinked in situ and solubilized directly from intact nuclei. Nuclei prepared as in main figure, were incubated 30 min at room temperature in 1% SDS, and PMSF. Debris was pelleted and the proteins released into the supernatant were electrophoresed. The stained gel containing nuclear PR was then impregnated with PPO:DMSO. The PPO was crystallized with water, the gel was dried and used to expose Kodak X-Omat AR-5 film at -70°C for 10 days.

(5 mM), 1-chloro-3-tosylamido-7-amino-L-2-heptanone (200 µM), N-ethyl-maleimide (500 µM), ovomucoid trypsin inhibitor (100 µg/ml), and leupeptin (20 mM)] does not alter this stoichiometry (34).

Since such studies are still not conclusive, we developed an in situ photoaffinity labeling method for PR that permits study of their subunits with minimal in vitro incubations. The strategy is to use [^{3}H]R5020, a synthetic photoactive progestin (36), and suitable incubation temperatures, to place receptors into their precise intracellular sites in intact cells. The cells, still intact, are then irradiated with UV at 300 nm for 2 min. A spectrophotometric scan of R5020 had shown that it maximally absorbs UV at 304 nm. We therefore used a 300 nm output UV lamp, rather than one emitting 360 nm radiation described by Dure et al (36). With this lamp we increased the yield of specifically photolabeled receptors 10-fold, and decreased the irradiation time at least 15-fold (from 30-120 min irradiation, to 2 min irradiation). This method efficiently (-15%) yields covalently linked hormone-receptor complexes at any intracellular location, in the unbroken cells.

Cells are then rapidly ruptured, nuclei are separated, and receptors are extracted with salt, and/or solubilized with detergents before the subunits are displayed on denaturing gels. The time and temperature at which [^{3}H]R5020 is incubated with the cells determines the intracellular location of the receptors: if incubation is at 0°C (2 hrs) 80-90% of receptors are recovered in the cytosol; if incubation is at 37°C (5 min), more than 90% of receptors are transformed and recovered in a salt extract of nuclei (Figure 5 and inset a). Clearly, activated and translocated nuclear PR consist of two subunits present in equimolar amounts. Their mass equals that of holoreceptor subunits from untreated cells and equals the mass of the small fraction (7%) of residual receptors that fail to translocate. From these and time-course studies, we conclude that A and B are synchronously translocated by R5020.

675

To completely eliminate even the short in vitro incubation required by salt extraction of in situ photolinked nuclear PR, the nuclear pellets from a low speed 5-min centrifugation were immediately solubilized with detergent. The extracts were then separated on SDS-PAGE, and the radioactive bands were visualized by fluorography (Figure 5, inset b). Again, only two, specifically labeled bands (mol wt, 116,000 and 85,000 daltons) were present. Other solubilized minor R5020-binding proteins were nonspecifically labeled.

The data from a series of experiments are summarized in Table 5, and show 1) that the subunit molecular weights of cytoplasmic and nuclear PR are identical, and 2) that the subunits are present in both compartments in equimolar amounts, so that only their intracellular compartmentalization is altered by progestin treatment, and no other detectable modification occurs. We conclude that major subunit proteolysis does not accompany the acquisition of nuclear binding capacity.

In order to entirely avoid exposure of the receptors to cell-free conditions, even those created by homogenization, an experiment was performed in which [3H]R5020-treated and irradiated cells were solubilized directly with detergent while still intact. This lysate was then analyzed by SDS-PAGE. Both subunits can still be demonstrated by this method, and they are identical to those extracted from nuclei by the more conventional method. We conclude that the A and B proteins are integral intracellular proteins and that they are not artifactually formed in vitro. The peptide mapping studies of chick oviduct PR show that endogenous proteases cannot generate A from B intracellularly. It remains possible that A and B form part of a larger pro-receptor protein that is processed post-translationally to generate the 2 subunits, or alternatively, that they are the products of two genes. This question will be answered rapidly since the mRNA for the B protein has now been isolated.

Figure 6 shows that the nuclear receptors retain the hormone specificity expected of authentic PR. They bind R5020 (and all other synthetic progestins) and progesterone, but not estradiol,

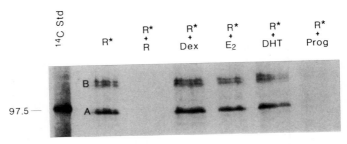

Figure 6. **Binding specificity of nuclear subunits A and B demonstrated by <u>in situ</u> photoaffinity labeling.** T47D$_{CO}$ cells were incubated 5 minutes at 37°C with 40 nM [^{3}H]R5020 only (R*) or with [^{3}H]R5020 plus a 100-fold excess of unlabeled R5020 (R), dexamethasone (Dex), estradiol (E$_{2}$), dihydrotestosterone (DHT) or progesterone (Prog). The cells were then cooled and irradiated, harvested, homogenized, nuclei were precipitated, washed and extracted with KCl-containing buffer. Extracted proteins were concentrated, solubilized in detergent, resolved on SDS-PAGE gels, and fluorographed. [^{14}C]standards were run in parallel lanes and the position of the Mr 97,500 phosphorylase B standard is shown.

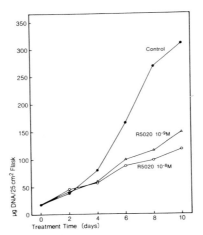

Figure 7. **Antiproliferative effect of the synthetic progestin R5020 in cultured T47D$_{CO}$ human breast cancer cells.** Cells were plated at a 1:7 split ratio. Eighteen hr later (Time 0), the medium was replaced with medium containing 5% charcoal-stripped fetal calf serum only (o) or with 1 nM (o) or 10 nM (o) R5020 added. At the indicated time-points, the cells from triplicate flasks were well suspended, and triplicate 1-ml aliquots/flask were taken for DNA analyses. Each point represents the average of 9 measurements.

dihydrotestosterone, dexamethasone, or (not shown) hydrocortisone. They do bind triamcinolone acetonide which, as we discussed above, is known to be progestational. The data in figure 6 address the frequently asked question, whether PR and GR share a common subunit. This is raised by studies with R5020 for example, since this compound is used to measure PR, but can also interact with GR (37), and has been used to photoaffinity label both classes of receptors (36,37). When used as a marker for GR in hepatoma or lymphoma cells, R5020 covalently labels a single protein of Mr 87,000-90,000. As a marker for PR in human breast cancer cells, R5020 covalently labels two other proteins of Mr 115,000 and 83,000. Presumably R5020 labels either the receptor class that is present, or if both are present, the more abundant class. In T47D$_{CO}$ cells, the levels of PR exceed GR by more than 100-fold, and addition of unlabeled glucocorticoid to the cells has no effect on R5020 binding, or on PR transformation. The failure of dexamethasone to compete for binding of R5020 to PR subunit A (the Mr 83,000 dalton protein), strongly suggests that the A subunit of PR and the Mr 90,000 subunit of GR, are two different proteins. The B subunit of PR is also not bound by dexamethasone, and is probably too large to be the common protein.

Figure 6 also shows the characteristic "doublet" structure of the B subunit following 5 min of R5020 treatment. This structural heterogeneity is still under investigation. However, we believe that it represents an intranuclear covalent modification of the protein that results from hormone binding, which increases the apparent mol wt of the B protein by 2000 to 3000 daltons. If hormone treatment is extended for longer periods before UV irradiation, the B protein is entirely converted to the heavy form. The nuclear A protein becomes similarly modified about 30 minutes after B. Such shifts in denaturing gels have been described when proteins become phosphorylated, and we are examining this, as well as other protein modifying reactions. It is interesting to note that such chemical modifications usually serve to regulate the biological activity of proteins, and that

678

in the case of PR, the changes occur after the proteins have acquired tight nuclear binding capacity.

A new, nuclear, progestin-binding molecule? Following [^{3}H]R5020 treatment and UV irradiation, the two PR subunits are extracted from nuclei with 0.4M KCl-containing buffer. If the residual, salt-resistant pellet is then solubilized with SDS, analyzed by PAGE, and the gels are fluorographed, a heavily labeled specific [^{3}H]R5020 binder is seen that has a mass of 28,000 daltons. This molecule has several interesting properties: 1) It is not solubilized by 2M salt and resists proteolytic digestion under conditions that destroy PR. It is, however, digested by exhaustive protease treatment, and we speculate that it is either a tight DNA-binding protein or a nuclear matrix protein. 2) The molecule can be [^{3}H]R5020-labeled by direct incubation of purified nuclei from untreated cells. Under these conditions there are few PR in nuclei and the 28K molecule is apparently not formed from them. This is also suggested by the fact, 3) that the 28K molecule is not "processed" by prolonged R5020 treatment, as are the PR. 4) The 28K molecule binds [^{3}H]R5020 with 10-fold lower affinity than do PR, but the binding is entirely competed by excess unlabeled R5020 and by certain other synthetic progestins; however, it does not bind progesterone, or any non-progestational steroid. It is possible that the natural endogenous ligand for this molecule is yet to be discovered, and tempting to speculate that 28K is analogous to the nuclear type II estrogen binding sites, whose natural ligand should soon be described (39).

D.   Biological actions of progestins in T47D$_{co}$

As reviewed below, there is renewed interest in the use of synthetic progestins to treat men and women who have advanced breast cancer. First, clinical results using pharmacologic progestin concentrations have been very encouraging. However, it is not known whether progestins act directly on the regressing tumors, or indirectly through other hormones. Second, PR are the single best marker for predicting both the hormone dependence of tumors, and the disease-free survival of patients. This has led to speculation that PR-rich tumors would be especially sensitive to progestin treatment. Third, in small series of studies, positive responses to progestins have been obtained in tumors that have failed to respond to, or have become resistant to antiestrogens or other endocrine therapies, or in tumors lacking ER. This suggests that some of the mechanisms responsible for the antitumor effects of progestins and antiestrogens must differ.

There is little experimental evidence underlying any of these assumptions. It has been difficult to study the direct biological actions of progestins separate from those of estrogens, because estrogen priming is required to maintain elevated -- and presumably functional -- levels of PR. Thus, the contaminating presence of estradiol in the system under study has precluded accurate assessment of true progestin effects _in vivo_, and prevented separation of the progestational from the anti-estrogenic properties of these hormones. Furthermore, for reasons that are not clear, progesterone action has been difficult to study _in vitro_, where conditions can usually be more carefully controlled. As a result, there are several established cell lines that contain estrogen-inducible PR, but in which direct responses to progesterone have not been demonstrable.

Since $T47D_{co}$ contain high levels of PR that are independent of estrogen controls, lack ER, and are antiestrogen resistant, they can be used in estrogen-free conditions, to assess the direct biological actions of progestins, distinct from their antiestrogenic ones. We find that progestins have multiple effects on these cells.

Lipid accumulation and ultrastructural changes. R5020 stimulates lipid accumulation as shown by staining of cells with Oil Red 0. The effect is extremely heterogenous, with some cells showing extensive lipid droplet formation and others showing no change when compared to untreated controls. Whether this heterogeneity reflects the PR distribution in these cells is not known.   Judge and Chatterton had previously reported that progesterone stimulates incorporation of [^{14}C]acetate into triglycerides in T47D cells (40). Interestingly, the same effect occurs when the cells are treated with prolactin or growth hormone (41), suggesting that all these hormones influence a common pathway involved in lipid biosynthesis.

Electron micrographs show that R5020-treated cells contain large numbers of lipid droplets and other inclusions, which are not found in the control cells. In addition, many R5020-treated cells are entirely filled with cytoskeletal elements, particularly bundles of tonofilaments. We do not know the significance of this, although filamentous accumulation may be a sign of regressive and degenerative changes in amitotic or terminally differentiated cells. This may be the morphological reflection of the cytostatic or antipromotional effects of progestins described further below. It would be interesting to see if similar ultrastructural changes are seen in tumors regressing after progestin therapy.

Growth inhibition of T47D$_{co}$ cells. We have shown that, in the absence of estradiol or ER, physiologic concentrations of progestins directly inhibit proliferation of these antiestrogen resistant cells (Figure 7). Ten days of treatment with 1 or 10 nM R5020 suppresses cell growth approximately 50 to 60%, consistent with the concentrations that either partially (approximately 10%), or more extensively (>60%), translocate cytoplasmic PR (42). Even a brief 1 hr pulse of R5020 inhibits cell growth for at least 4 days which coincides with the time that PR replenishment is blocked. Other synthetic progestins also inhibit cell growth, as does progesterone, whose effects are attenuated because, unlike the synthetic progestins, it is rapidly metabolized in the medium. At physiological concentrations (0.1 μM), estradiol, androgens, glucocorticoids, and 1,25-dihydroxyvitamin D$_3$ have no effect on cell growth. Our data indicate that the effects of progestins on mammary tumor cell proliferation can be direct, and independent of estrogen, and that antiestrogens and progestins can target different cell populations. This may explain the clinical efficacy of progestins in otherwise hormone-resistant tumors; the implications for endocrine therapy are outlined below.

Progestins and insulin receptors. Cell proliferation in culture is under complex regulation involving not only exogenous factors added to the growth medium, but growth stimulatory and inhibitory factors that can be synthesized by the cells themselves. Insulin is a common medium supplement and is required for the continuous serum-free growth of all human breast cancer cell lines in which it has been tested (43-45). Moreover, insulin and steroid hormones can reciprocally regulate each others actions (46-49). We have shown that in T47D$_{co}$ cells, progestins are among the heterologous hormones that regulate insulin receptor levels, an effect that seems to be closely related to the simultaneous cell-growth inhibition (42). In untreated cells, the number of insulin binding sites/cell increase slightly during the first round of cell division (Days 1 to 3) then settle down to control levels. In contrast, during the first 3 days, when little if any growth is demonstrable in R5020-treated sets, the number of insulin binding sites/cell increase 4 to 5-fold and peak on days 2 to 3. Thereafter, slow cell proliferation is paralleled by a fall in insulin receptor levels to about twice control values, where a new steady state is established.

Scatchard analysis shows that the increased binding is due to a real increase in the number of insulin binding sites/cell and not due to a change in binding affinity. At steady state (days 5 to 9) there are 18,000 insulin-binding sites/cell compared to 8000 in untreated cells (42).

To determine the hormone specificity of the increase in insulin receptors, cells were incubated for 5 days with several classes of steroid hormones or analogs, at concentrations sufficient to bind and translocate their respective receptors, but below pharmacological levels. The increase in insulin receptors was specific to R5020; neither estradiol nor dihydrotestosterone had any effect, consistent with reports in other systems. The synthetic glucocorticoid dexamethasone, decreased the number of insulin binding sites by 50%. Glucocorticoids are known to modulate insulin receptor levels, and their effects are variable depending on the cell type and the conditions used in the studies. RU38 486, a synthetic steroid with antigluco-corticoid and antiprogestin actions (see below), had no effect on insulin receptor levels when it was added to the cells alone; together with R5020, it partially blocked receptor induction by R5020. We are testing the possibility that regulation of insulin receptors (or any other inducible protein) may be a useful marker to distinguish progestins from antiprogestins in T47D$_{co}$. Other hormones that had no effect on insulin receptors were 1,25-dihy-droxyvitamin D$_3$ (0.1µM): testosterone (10nM), 21-hydroxyproges-terone (10nM); and the antiestrogen nafoxidine (1µM).

The antiprogestin, RU38 486. Despite the theoretical promise of synthetic antiprogestational agents -- as anticancer agents, as experimental tools, as mid-cycle contraceptives and implan-tation inhibitors -- none have been available for either basic or clinical studies. However, a candidate antiprogestin, RU38 486 [17ß-hydroxy-11ß(4-dimethylaminophenyl)-17 α-(1-propynl)-estra-4,9-dien-3-one] has recently been described that has antiprogestational and antiglucocorticoid activity in early clinical trials (50,51). Its mechanisms of action are unclear. Furthermore, development of this drug underscores an old bioassay problem: that biological screening of progestins and anti-progestins is complex because of the physiological requirement that progestational effects must be superimposed upon an estrogenized system. This has made it difficult to distinguish among progestational, antiprogestational, and antiestrogenic properties of unknown agents, a problem that can be entirely circumvented when T47D$_{co}$ are used for screening. These cells have therefore been used to contrast the agonist and antagonist actions of this interesting drug (52).

We find that like R5020, RU38 486 absorbs UV at approximately 300 nm, and this wavelength can be used to covalently photolink the drug to PR in situ. Like the synthetic progestin, low concentrations (10 nM) of [^{3}H]RU38 486 bind two PR subunits in nuclei of T47D$_{CO}$; glucocorticoid receptors are not bound. In competition studies, unlabeled RU38 486 is a potent inhibitor for in situ [^{3}H]R5020 binding to both nuclear subunits A and B. RU38 486 has a high affinity for PR in vitro (K$_d$ approximately 2 nM at 0-4°C) and in intact cells, low concentrations (6 to 8 nM) transform more than 95% of PR to a high affinity nuclear binding state. Like the other synthetic progestins, the compound is not metabolized, so that it chronically (3 to 6 days) suppresses PR replenishment. These biochemical properties of RU38 486 are typical of synthetic progestins, and distinguish it from pure glucocorticoids. To bioassay RU 38 486 both growth and insulin receptors were measured, with interesting results. RU38 486 is as potent as the other synthetic progestins in growth inhibition; as little as 1 nM concentration suppresses growth by 55%. When R5020 and RU38 486 are combined, cell growth remains inhibited. Since a 1 hour pulse of RU38 486 blocks receptor replenishment, we asked whether this would have a long-term effect on cell growth. Compared to hormone-free controls, the growth of 1 hour RU38 486-pulsed cells is suppressed for at least 4 days, after which the cells resumed growth at a rate similar to that of the controls. Other synthetic progestins are similarly long-acting, as shown here for R5020.

Thus, using cell growth as a biological marker, we would conclude that RU38 486 has agonist progestin-like properties, with no evidence of antagonist effects. This is, however, not the case when the biological end-point measured is the level of insulin receptors. T47D$_{CO}$ were incubated 60 hrs with medium containing R5020 alone, RU38 486 alone, or the two hormones together. R5020 increased the number of insulin binding sites as expected, but RU38 486 at concentrations sufficient to translocate PR and alter cell growth rate, had no effect on these proteins. When the two hormones were added to cells together, RU 38 486 blocked 20 to 50% of the R5020-induced increase, depending on the concentration of each hormone. Thus, if insulin receptor levels are used as a biological marker, RU38 486 displays some of the properties expected of an antagonist (52).

The dual action of RU38 486 is a classic property of synthetic steroid antagonists, and it is likely that <u>in vivo</u> RU38 486 will prove to have similar biphasic effects. Its actions as an antiglucocorticoid in some systems may well prove to be due to its progestational nature since pharmacologic levels of progestins have been known for more than a decade to antagonize glucocorticoid action by binding to GR.

Undoubtedly, RU38 486 is only the first in a long line of steroidal analogs that, in the next few years, will be synthesized and found to have clinically useful antiprogestational activity. The problems with past biological screening methods have been two-fold. First, it has been difficult to find markers that distinguish between progestin and antiprogestin actions; and second, it has been impossible to demonstrate pure and direct progestin and/or antiprogestin effects in systems that, of necessity, also contain estradiol. We propose that $T47D_{co}$ may be used to circumvent both problems.

The Role of Progestins and Progesterone Receptors in the Treatment of Breast Cancer

A. Use of progestins to treat advanced breast cancer

In 1895, Beatson reported the positive results of ovariectomy in a patient with advanced breast cancer (53). Since that time, the hormone dependence of breast cancer has been exploited in the treatment of patients with inoperable and/or disseminated disease. The first reported use of progesterone in advanced breast cancer involved 18 patients (54). Three (17%) showed an objective response to the treatment thus adding another agent to the armentarium of the cancer therapist.

Five different progestins have been used historically: progesterone, 17 α-hydroxyprogesterone, norethisterone acetate,

Table 1. Standard Dose Progestin Therapy

<u>Objective Response</u>

29 series $\frac{338}{1252}$ 27%
(1951-1984)   (range 0-56%)

References 54-81

Table 2. Treatment Response to High Dose Progestins
References 83 to 93

	<u>Objective Response</u>		<u>Drug and Dose</u>
Mattsson, 1978	7/25	(28%)	MPA 1000mg im QD
DeLena, 1979	6/28	(21%)	MPA 1000mg im QD
	17/53	(32%)	MPA 1000mg im QD
Castiglione, 1980	6/19	(32%)	MPA 1000mg im QD
Mattsson, 1980	14/26	(54%)	MPA 1000mg im QD
Madrigal, 1980	9/21	(43%)	MPA 1000mg im QD
Izuo, 1981	7/20	(35%)	MPA 400mg po TID
Morgan, 1983	15/25	(60%)	MA 80-200mg po QID
Pannuti, 1983	19/47	(40%)	MPA 500mg im QD
	41/97	(42%)	MPA 1500mg im QD
	7/17	(41%)	MPA 2000mg im QD
	15/44	(34%)	MPA 2000mg po QD
	15/32	(47%)	MPA 3000-5000mg po QD
Funes, 1983	13/46	(28%)	MPA 500mg im QD
	15/43	(35%)	MPA 1000mg im QD
Cavalli, 1983	9/73	(12%)	MPA 500mg im QD
	27/76	(36%)	MPA 1000mg im QD
DiCarlo, 1983	38/97	(39%)	MPA 500mg im QD

TOTAL   280/789   (35%)
Duration 5 - 13.1 mos
(7.0 median)

MPA = medroxyprogesterone acetate
MA = megestrol acetate
im, intramuscular; po, oral; QD, one a day; TID, 3 times a
day; QID, 4 times a day.

medroxyprogesterone acetate (MPA), and megestrol acetate (MA), in a variety of concentrations, routes of administration, schedules, and lengths of treatment. Criteria for responses cite World Health Organization, Eastern Cooperative Oncology Group, EORTC Clinical Screening Cooperative Group, or Cooperative Breast Cancer Group standards. A positive response includes either a complete response regarded as total disappearance of all known disease and/or a partial response which is at least a 50% reduction in tumor size, or a 50% decrease in the sum of the products of the perpendicular diameters of all measurable lesions.

A review of the clinical use of progestins in the treatment of advanced breast disease suggests that the data should be subclassified into studies using low doses versus those using high doses of progestins. We have arbitrarily chosen >500 mg/day of progestins as "high dose" therapy.

Using low dose progestins in 29 studies (Table 1), 1252 patients have accrued, and the total objective positive response rate is 27% (54-81). Survival ranges from 2 to 23+ months with a median of 7.0 months.

Pannuti et al. in 1978 (82) reported results of a study using high-dose MPA to treat metastatic breast cancer which was prompted by a pilot study in 17 patients, showing that intramuscular injection of 1500 mg/day was well tolerated. We have compiled the results of 11 centers (Table 2), with 789 patients, showing that the overall objective response rate to high dose progestins is 35% (83-93). With MPA given intramuscularly, patients have developed induration and sterile abscesses at the sites of injection thus limiting the duration and ultimately the amount of drug administered. However, the oral route has proven to be equally effective and as much as 5,000 mg per day (90) has been given with apparently no greater side effects than found with low dose therapy. At high concentrations, progestins are well tolerated, have no serious side effects (90), and their efficacy compares favorably with antiestrogens, the hormones currently in widest use (93).

Table 3. Responses to Tamoxifen vs. Progestins in Same
Clinical Centers

	Tamoxifen		Progestin		
Mattsson, 1980	15/32	(47%)	14/26	(54%)	MPA
Morgan, 1982	17/48	(36%)	14/46	(30%)	MA
Ingle, 1982	7/27	(26%)	4/28	(14%)	MA*
Pannuti, 1982	7/26	(27%)	10/27	(37%)	MPA
Johnson, 1983	14/49	(28%)	20/49	(41%)	MA
Van Veelen, 1983	17/58	(29%)	18/45	(40%)	MPA*
Alexieva-Figusch, 1983	17/80	(21%)	31/136	(23%)	MA*
TOTAL	**94/320**	**(29%)**	**111/357**	**(31%)**	

---

*low dose progestin
MPA = medroxyprogesterone acetate
MA = megestrol acetate
References 86, 94-99

Table 4. Response to Combination Tamoxifen/Progestin Therapy
References 103 to 108

Mouridsen, 1979	14/55	(25%)	concurrent
von Maillot, 1980	4/4	(100%)	concurrent
Forestiere, 1981	4/23	(17%)	concurrent
Trodella, 1982	8/18	(44%)	concurrent
Bruno, 1983	19/36	(53%)	sequential
	17/33	(52%)	concurrent
Garcia-Giralt, 1984	21/35	(60%)	sequential
TOTAL	**87/204**	**(43%)**	

That antiestrogens and progestins may be equally useful for the treatment of breast cancer is suggested not only from separate clinical trials reporting similar response data for each, but also from a number of studies in which progestin therapy has been directly compared with tamoxifen in the same clinical trial. The combined results of 7 studies in which 357 patients were treated with progestins and 320 were treated with tamoxifen show 31% responding to the progestins and 29% responding to tamoxifen (Table 3)(86,94-99). All of these women were postmenopausal. In many of these studies, the patients had been previously treated with cytotoxic chemotherapy (86,94,95) yet this did not preclude response to subsequent progestins or tamoxifen.

This brings us to a consideration of combination antiestrogen/progestin therapy, and the role of progestins in the treatment of antiestrogen-resistant tumors. Our studies (described further below) with antiestrogen-resistant and ER negative cultured human breast tumor cells (T47D$_{co}$), show that progestins can still inhibit growth in this setting. Similarly, there are clinical data showing that progestins can be of benefit in patients who fail to respond to, or become resistant to other hormonal agents including antiestrogens, or whose tumors are estrogen-receptor negative. Several studies report that 34% of patients responded to high dose progestins whose tumors had been antiestrogen resistant, or had failed or relapsed from previous hormonal therapy (83,84,88,90-92).

Based on these clinical, as well as our experimental data, we propose that antiestrogens and progestins act by different mechanisms to promote remission. Therefore, two treatment strategies using progestins are conceivable. Antiestrogens are successful in estrogen-receptor positive tumors. In addition, due to the estrogenic properties of antiestrogens, tumors treated for short periods with these agents, have increased PR levels (100-102). Thus simultaneous or brief pre-treatment with antiestrogens may increase the sensitivity of ER-positive tumors to subsequent progestins; the latter should then promote regression by other pathways thereby conferring synergistic therapeutic effects. There are some clinical data to support this model: a total of 204 postmenopausal women with advanced breast cancer have been treated with a combination of tamoxifen and progestins, (103-108) given either simultaneously or sequentially (Table 4). The response rate was 11% complete and 34% partial remissions or a total objective response of 43%. This level of response is as good as, if not better, than the response rates for tamoxifen or progestins when used singly; 29% and 31% respectively. Of note was the study by Trodella et al. (106) whose patient population was heavily pretreated with chemotherapy and/or hormonal therapy (61% and 83% respectively). They still found a 44% objective response rate with combined tamoxifen/progestin, which included 22% complete remissions.

These results using combination therapy warrant further study in an attempt to increase the response rates of present day conventional hormonal therapy. Though the two hormones can probably be administered together, theoretically, the anti-estrogen should precede the progestin by one to two weeks in order to maximally induce PR. Excessively prolonging the interval between the antiestrogen and the progestin could result in loss of PR altogether, leaving a hormone-insensitive cell population (102). Only one study has explored the value of repeatedly alternating the two hormones (108). Clearly, more extensive clinical trials of these well-tolerated hormonal agents are warranted.

2) The second strategy for use of progestins is based on our studies with ER negative, PR positive, antiestrogen resistant T47D$_{co}$ cells, which show that progestins can inhibit growth of such cells. Small clinical studies using high doses of MPA or MA, support the idea that a similar set of patients, whose tumors have become resistant to antiestrogen treatment, or whose tumors have no ER but are PR positive, may achieve further benefit from progestin therapy. Such patients are usually not considered to be candidates for endocrine therapies, but four trials based on 123 patients show that 22% respond to progestins after relapse from tamoxifen (86,95,98,99). In contrast, tumors rarely respond to tamoxifen (8%) if they have failed to respond to progestins (Table 5).

Table 5. Tamoxifen vs. Progestin Cross-Over: Same Center Studies

			Objective Response	
Mattsson, 1980	Tam→fail	MPA	6/10	(60%)
	MPA→fail	TAM	0/10	(0%)
Ingle, 1982	Tam→fail	MA*	2/16	(12%)
	MA*→fail	Tam	2/18	(11%)
Van Veelen, 1983	Tam→fail	MPA	5/14	(36%)
	MPA→fail	Tam	0/14	(0%)
Alexieva-Figusch, 1983	Tam→fail	MA*	14/83	(17%)
	MA*→fail	Tam	12/132	(9%)
TOTAL	**Tam→fail**	**Prog**	**27/123**	**(22%)**
	Prog→fail	**Tam**	**14/174**	**(8%)**

*low dose progestin
MPA = medroxyprogesterone acetate
MA = megestrol acetate
Prog = progestin
References 86,95,98,99

Table 6. Receptor Content and Response to Endocrine Therapies

		Objective Response	
ER+		312/586	(53%)
ER-		33/264	(13%)
PR+		240/352	(68%)
PR-		108/498	(22%)
ER+	PR+	230/323	(71%)
ER+	PR-	85/263	(32%)
ER-	PR+	10/29	(34%)
ER-	PR-	23/235	(10%)

Cumulative data 14 series 1978-1983
References 1,2,16,78,124-135

That progestins and antiestrogens inhibit the growth of breast tumor cells by different paths has important clinical implications, and we propose that, by targeting different cell populations, the complementary therapeutic actions of these two agents can be used to advantage in the design of treatment protocols.

Finally, an area in which progestins have also been used is in combination with cytotoxic chemotherapy. Similar studies have been performed comparing chemotherapy vs. chemotherapy combined with tamoxifen. Four recent randomized studies (109-112) have been reported, with two studies showing no benefit after tamoxifen addition and two showing a significant benefit of combination chemotherapy/tamoxifen.

The use of progestins in conjunction with chemotherapy was first reported by Stott et al. in 1973 (113). Since then randomized and non-randomized studies have been performed with response rates varying from 27% to 75% (114-118). In 6 studies, 218 of 402 (54%) patients on combined progestin/chemotherapy obtained an objective response. However, the 3 studies (114,116,117) that compared chemotherapy alone, with chemo-progestin therapy, were unable to show a statistically significant difference between treatment arms. Nevertheless, the patients treated with the progestin seemed to have an increased performance status, increased sense of well being, less pain, weight gain, and a protective effect on the bone marrow (116,118-120). Since MPA has been shown to protect patients against the neutropenia induced by vincristine, adriamycin and cyclophosphamide (121), it is possible that with reduced marrow toxicity due to the presence of a progestin, patients could receive more intensive chemotherapy, and be more likely to stay on the planned schedule of therapy.

B. Progesterone receptors as markers of hormone-dependent tumors

Estrogen receptors (ER) have been used since 1971 (122) as a guide to therapy, and they correctly predict a positive response in 50-55% of patients (123). However, assessment of tumor PR (1,2,26,28,124-135) is even more useful as table 6 shows, improving predictive accuracy by an additional 15-20%. In contrast, receptor-negative tumors rarely respond to endocrine therapies and such patients should be considered candidates for alternate treatments. Not surprisingly, few tumors are ER-, PR+ though some of these may be falsely negative due to methodological reasons (136). Others may have ER that are either sequestered in an unmeasured compartment or nonfunctional, and may resemble the variant $T47D_{co}$ subline that is antiestrogen resistant but progestin sensitive. Such tumors should be considered candidates for progestin therapy (see above).

Progesterone receptors have also proven to be more accurate than ER in predicting prognosis of limited stage (I and II) breast cancer (3,137-140); patients with PR+ tumors are 3 to 4 times less likely to develop metastases than those with PR- ones (137). In more advanced grade III disease, PR are an independent prognostic variable, and more useful for predicting disease-free survival than either clinical or pathological staging (138). Clark et al (3) reported similar results in patients with stage II breast cancer who were undergoing adjuvant therapy. An earlier study (141) had failed to detect these relationships, perhaps due to the small number of patients evaluated.

References

1. Horwitz KB, McGuire WL, Pearson OH and Segaloff A 1975 Science 189:726-727.
2. Horwitz KB and McGuire WL 1975 Steroids 25:497-505.
3. Clark GM, McGuire WL, Hubay CA, Pearson OH and Marshall JS 1983 New Eng J Med 309:1343-1347.

4.   Horwitz KB, Zava DT, Thilagar AK, Jensen EM and McGuire WL 1978   Cancer Res 38:2434-2437.

5.   Horwitz KB, Mockus MB and Lessey BA 1982 Cell 28:633-642.

6.   Keydar I, Chen L, Karbey S, Weiss FR, Delarea J, Radu M, Chaitcik S and Brenner HJ 1979 Eur J Cancer 15:659-670.

7.   Horwitz KB and McGuire WL 1978 J Biol Chem 253:2223-2228.

8.   Horwitz KB and McGuire WL 1978 J Biol Chem 253:8185-8191.

9.   Yamamoto KR, Stampfer MR and Tomkins GM 1974   Proc Natl Acad Sci 71:3901-3905.

10.   Gruol DJ, Kempner ES and Bourgeois S 1984   J Biol Chem 259:4833-4839.

11.   Lippman M, Bolan K and Huff K 1976 Cancer Res 36:4595-4601.

12.   Mockus MB, Lessey BA, Bower MA and Horwitz KB 1982 Endocrinology 110:1564-1571.

13.   Mockus MB and Horwitz KB 1983 J Biol Chemistry 258:4778-4783.

14.   Horwitz KB, Mockus MB, Pike AW, Fennessey PV and Sheridan RL 1983   J Biol Chem 258:7603-7610.

15.   Stellwagen RH and Tomkins GM 1971 J Mol Biol 56:167-182.

16.   Kallos J, Fasy TM, Hollander BP and Bick MD 1978 Proc Nat Acad Sci 75:4896-4900.

17.   Garcia M, Westley B and Rochefort H 1981 Eur J Biochem 116:297-301.

18.   McKnight GS, Hager L and Palmiter RD 1980 Cell 22:469-477.

19.   Samuels HH, Stanley F, Casanova J and Shao TC 1980 J Biol Chem 255:2499-2508.

20.   Leder A and Leder P 1975 Cell 5:319-322.

21.   Hagino N 1972 J Clin Endocrinol Metab 35:716-721.

22.   Zava DT, Landrum B, Horwitz KB and McGuire WL 1979 Endocrinology 104:1007-1012

23.   Horwitz KB and McGuire WL 1978 J Biol Chem 253:6319-6322.

24.   Horwitz KB and McGuire WL 1980 J Biol CHem 255:9699-9705.

25.   Sherman MR, Pickering LA, Rollwagen FM and Miller LK 1978 Fed Proc 37:167-173.

26.   Stevens J, Stevens YW, Rhodes J and Steiner G 1978 J Natl Cancer Inst 61:1477-1485.

694

27. Lurquin PF 1974 Chem Biol Interact 8:303-313.

28. Packman V and Rigler R 1972 Exp Cell Res 72:602-608.

29. Compton JG, Schrader WT and O'Malley BW 1982 Biochem Biophys Res Commun 105:96-104.

30. Compton JG, Schrader WT and O'Malley BW 1983 Proc Natl Acad Sci 80:16-20.

31. Mulvihill ER, LePennec J-P and Chambon ER 1982 Cell 24:621-632.

32. Berg OG, Winter RB and Von Hippel PH 1982 Trends Biochem Sci 7:52-55.

33. Lamb DJ and Bullock DW 1984 Endocrinology 114:1833-1840.

34. Horwitz KB and Alexander PS 1983 Endocrinology 113:2195-2201.

35. Raam S, Nemeth E, Tamura H, O'Brian DS and Cohen JL 1982 Eur J Cancer Clin Oncol 18:1-12.

36. Dure LS, Schrader WT and O'Malley BW 1980 Nature 283:784-785.

37. Nordeen SK, Lan NC, Showers MO and Baxter JD 1981 J Biol Chem 256:10503-10508.

38. Wegener AD and Jones LR 1984 J Biol Chem 259:1834-1841.

39. Markaverich BM, Roberts RR, Alejandro MA and Clark JH 1984 Cancer Res 44:1575-1579.

40. Judge SM and Chatterton RT 1983 Cancer Res 43:4407-4412.

41. Shiu RPC and Paterson JA 1984 Cancer Res 44:1178-1186.

42. Horwitz KB and Freidenberg GR 1985 Cancer Res In Press.

43. Allegra JC and Lippman ME 1978 Cancer Res 38:3823-3829.

44. Barnes D and Sato G 1979 Nature 281:388-389.

45. Barnes D and Sato G 1980 Cell 22:649-655.

46. Butler W, Kelsey WH and Green N 1981 Cancer Res 41:82-88.

47. Knutson VP, Ronnett GV and Lane MD 1982 Proc Natl Acad Sci 79:2822-2826.

48. Moore MR 1981 J Biol Chem 256:3637-3640.

49. Osborne CK, Monaco ME, Kahn R, Huff K, Bronzert D and Lippman ME 1979 Cancer Res 39:2422-2428.

50. Herrmann W, Wyss R, Riondel A, Philibert D, Teutsch G, Sakiz E and Baulieu EE 1983 CR Acad Sci (Paris) 294:933-938.

51. Jung-Testas I and Baulieu EE 1983 Exp Cell Res 147:177-182.

52. Horwitz KB 1985 Endocrinology In Press.

53. Beatson GT 1896 Lancet ii:104-107.

54. Escher GC, Heber JM, Woodard HQ, Farrow JH and Adair FE 1951 IN Symposium of steroids in experimental and clinical practice. White A P. Blukiston, Philadelphia pp 375-402.

55. Taylor SG III and Morris RS. 1951 Med Clin N Amer 35:51-61.

56. Gordon D, Horwitt BN, Segaloff A, Murison PJ and Schlosser JV. 1951 Hormonal therapy in cancer of the breast III. Cancer 5:275-277.

57. Jonsson U, Colsky J, Lessner HE, Roath OS, Alper RG and Jones R Jr. 1959 Cancer 12:509-520.

58. Lewin I, Spencer H and Herrmann J. 1959 Proc Am Assoc Cancer Res 3:37 Abst.

59. Douglas M, Loraine JA and Strong JA. 1960 Proc Roy Soc Med 53:427-431.

60. Baker WH, Kelley RM and Sohier WD. 1960 Am J Surg 99:538-543.

61. Jolles B. 1961 Brit J Cancer 16:209-221.

62. Bucalossi P, Dipietros J and Genneri L. 1963 Practitioner 191:702 Abst.

63. Curwen J. 1963 Clin Rad 14:445-446.

64. Stoll BA. 1965 IN Recent advances in ovarian and synthetic steroids. RP Shearman (Ed.) Globe, Sydney pp 147-155.

64a. Stoll BA. 1967 Brit Med J 3:338-341.

65. Segaloff A, Cunningham M, Rice BF and Weeth JB. 1967 Cancer 20:1673-1678.

66. Muggia FM, Cassileth PA, Ochoa M Jr, M, Flatow FA, Gellhorn A and Hyman GA. 1968 Ann Int Med 68:328-337.

67. Goldenberg IS 1969 Cancer 23:109-112.

68. Jones V, Joslin CAF, Jones RE, Davies DKL, Roberts MM, Gleave EN and Campbell HF, Forrest APM 1971 Lancet i:1049-1050.

69. Edelstyn GA 1973 Cancer 32:1317-1320.

70. Weeth JB. 1975 Proc Am Assoc Cancer Res 16:38 Abst 150.

696

71. Rubens RD, Knight RK and Hayward JL 1976 Europ J Cancer 12:563-565.

72. Klaassen DJ, Rapp EF and Histe WE 1976 Cancer Treat Rep 60:251-253.

73. Teulings FAG, vanGilse HA, Henkelman MS, Portengen H and Alexieva-Figusch J 1980 Cancer Res 40:2557-2561.

74. Alexieva-Figusch J, vanGilse HA, Hop WCJ, Phoa CH, Blonk-van der Wijst J and Treurniet RE 1980 Cancer 46:2369-2372.

75. Ross MB, Buzdar AU and Blumenschein GR 1982 Cancer 49:413-417.

76. Clavel B, Pichon MF, Pallud C and Milgrom E 1982 Eur J Cancer Clin Oncol 18:821-826.

77. Ansfield FJ, Kallas GJ and Singson JP. 1982 Surg Gyne Obst 155:888-890.

78. Johnson PA, Bonomi PD, Anderson KM, Wolter JM, Bacon LD, Rossof AH and Economou SG 1983 Cancer Treat Rep 67:717-720.

79. Haller DG, Glick JH and Ettinger NA. 1983 J Steroid Biochem 19 (suppl): 86s Abst 257.

80. Alexieva-Figusch J, Blankenstein MA, Hop WCJ, Klijn JGM, Lamberts SWJ, DeJong FH, Docter R, Adlercreutz H and VanGilse HA 1984 Eur J Cancer Clin Oncol 20:33-40.

81. DeLena M, Villa S and DiFronzo G. 1984 Recent Results Cancer Res 91:243-247.

82. Pannuti F, Martoni A, Lenaz GR, Diana E and Nanni P 1978 Cancer Treat Reports 62:499-504.

83. Mattsson W 1978 Acta Radiologica Oncology 17:387-400.

84. DeLena M, Brambilla C, Valagussa P and Bonadonna G 1979 Cancer Chemotherapy Pharmacology 2:175-180.

85. Castiglione M and Cavalli F. 1980 Schweiz Med Wschr 110:1073-1076.

86. Mattsson W 1980 IN Role of Medroxyprogesterone in Endocrine-related tumors. Iacobelli S and DiMarco A (Eds) Raven Press, New York pp 65-71.

87. Madrigal PL, Alonso A, Manga GP and Modrego SP 1980 IN Role of Medroxyprogesterone in Endocrine-related Tumors. Iacobelli S and DiMarco A (Eds) Raven Press, New York pp 93-96.

88. Izuo M, Iino Y and Endo K 1981 Breast Cancer Research Treatment 1:125-130.

89. Morgan LR, Donley PJ and Savage J 1983 Proc Am Assoc Cancer Res 24:134 Abst 529.

90. Pannuti F, Gentili MRA, DiMarco AR, Martoni A, Giambiasi ME, Battistoni R, Camaggi CM, Burroni P, Strocchi E, Iafelice G, Piana E, and Murari G 1983 IN Role of Medroxyprogesterone in Endocrine-Related Tumors Volume II. Campio L, Robustelli Della Cuna G and Taylor RW (Eds) Raven Press, New York pp 95-104.

91. Funes HC, Madrigal PL, Mangas GP and Mendiola G IN Role of Medroxyprogesterone in Endocrine-Related Tumors Volume II. 1983 Campio L, Robustelli Della Cuna G and Taylor RW (Eds) Raven Press, New York pp 77-83.

92. Cavalli F, Goldhirsch A, Jungi F, Martz G, Alberto P, for the Swiss group for clinical cancer research (SAKK) 1983 IN Role of Medroxyprogesterone in Endocrine-related Tumors Volume II. Campio L, Robustelli Della Cuna G and Taylor RW Raven Press, New York pp 69-75.

93. DiCarlo F, Bumma C and Gallo E. 1983 J Steroid Biochem 19 (suppl): 85s Abst 255.

93a. Horwitz KB and McGuire WL 1978 IN Breast cancer: modern approaches to therapy and research Volume II. McGuire WL (Ed) Plenum Press, New York pp 155-204.

94. Morgan LR and Donley PJ 1982 IN Review of Endocrine-Related Cancer. Supplement 9 pp 301-310.

95. Ingle JN, Ahmann DL, Green SJ, Edmonson JH, Creagan ET, Hahn RG and Rubin J 1982 Am J Clin Oncol 5:155-160.

96. Pannuti F, Martoni A, Fruet F, Burroni P, Canova N and Hall S 1982 IN The Role of Tamoxifen in Breast Cancer. Iacobelli S (Ed) Raven Press, New York pp 85-92.

97. Johnson PA, Bonomi PD, Wolter JM, Anderson KM, Economou SG and DePeyster FA 1983 Proc Am Assoc Cancer Res 24:172 Abst 680.

98. vanVeelen H, Roding TJ, Schweitzer MJH, Sleijfer DT, Tjabbes T and Willemse PHB 1983 J Steroid Biochem 19 (suppl) 86s Abst 259.

698

99. Alexieva-Figusch J, Klijn JGM, Blonk-van der Wijst J and van Putten WLJ 1983 J Steroid Biochem 19 (suppl) 87s Abst 260.

100. Horwitz KB, Koseki Y and McGuire WL 1978 Endocrinology 103:1742-1751.

101. Namer M, Lalanne C and Baulieu EE 1980 Cancer Res 40:1750-1752.

102. Waseda N, Kato Y, Imura H and Kurata M 1981 Cancer Res 41:1984-1988.

103. Mouridsen HT, Ellemann K, Mattsson W, Palshof T, Daehnfeldt JL and Rose C 1979 Cancer Treat Reports 63:171-175.

104. Von Maillot K, Gentsch HH, Gunselmann W. 1980 J Cancer Res Clin Oncol 98:301-313.

105. Forastier AA, Braun TJ, Wittes RE, Hakes TB and Kaufman RJ. 1981 12th Int Congress Chemotherapy Florence, Italy Abst 265.

106. Trodella L, Ausilli-Cefaro GP, Turriziani A, Saccheri S, Venturo I and Minotti G 1982 Am J Clin Oncol 5:495-499.

107. Bruno M, Roldan E and Diaz B 1983 J Steroid Biochem 19 (suppl):87s Abst 261.

108. Garcia-Giralt E, Jouve M, Palangie T, Bretandeau B, Magdelenat H, Asselain B and Pouillart P 1984 Proc Am Soc Clin Oncol 3:129 Abst C-504.

109. Link H, Ruckle H, Waller HD and Wilms K 1981 Dtsch Med Wochenschr 106:1260-1262.

110. Tormey DC, Falkston G, Crowley J, Falkson HC, Voelkel J and Davis TE 1982 Am J Clin Oncol 5:33-39.

111. Krook JE, Ingle JN, Green SJ and Bowman WD Jr 1983 Proc Am Soc Clin Oncol 2:106.

112. Cocconi G, DeLisi V, Boni C, Mori P, Malacarne P, Amadori D and Giovanelli E 1983 Cancer 51:581-588.

113. Stott PB, Zelkowitz L and Tucker WG 1973 Cancer Chemotherapy Reports 57:106 Abst 66.

114. Brunner KW, Sonntag RW, Alberto P, Senn HJ, Martz G, Obrecht P and Maurice P 1977 Cancer 39:2923-2933.

115. Buzdar AU, Tashima CK, Blumenschein GR, Hortobagyi GN, Yap HY, Krutchik AN, Bodey GP and Livingston RB 1978 Cancer 41:392-395.

116. Rubens RD, Begent RHJ, Knight RK, Sexton SA, Hayward JL 1978 Cancer 42:1680-1686.

117. Robustelli Della Cuna G and Bernardo-Strada MR 1980 IN Role of Medroxyprogesterone in Endocrine-Related Tumors. Iacobelli S and DiMarco A (Eds) Raven Press, New York pp 53-64.

118. Wander HE, Bartsch HH, Blossey HC and Nagel GA 1983 IN Role of Medroxyprogesterone in Endocrine-Related Tumors, Volume II. Campio L, Robustelli Della Cuna G and Taylor RW Raven Press, New York pp 85-93.

119. Pellegrini A, Massidda B, Mascia V, Lippi MG, Ionta MT, Muggiano A and Carboni-Boi E 1980 IN Role of Medroxy-progesterone in Endocrine-Related Tumors. Iacobelli S and DiMarco A (Eds) Raven Press, New York pp 29-51.

120. Robustelli Della Cuna G, Cuzzoni Q, Preti P and Bernardo G 1983 IN Role of Medroxyprogesterone in Endocrine-related Tumors Volume II. Campio L, Robustelli Della Cuna G and Taylor RW (Eds) Raven Press, New York pp 131-140.

121. Wils J, Borst A, Bron H and Scheerder H 1983 J Steroid Biochem 19 (suppl):85s.

122. Jensen EV, Block GE, Smith S, Kyser K and DeSombre ER 1971 Nat Cancer Inst Monog 34:55-70.

123. McGuire WL 1980 IN Hormone and Cancer. Iacobelli S et al. (Eds) Raven Press, New York pp 337-343.

124. Matsumoto K, Ochi H, Nomura Y, Takatani O, Izuo M, Okamoto R and Sugano H 1978 IN Hormones, Receptors and Breast Cancer. McGuire WL (Ed) Raven Press, New York pp 43-58.

125. Bloom ND, Tobin E, Schreibman B and Degenshein GA 1980 Cancer 45:2992-2997.

126. von Maillot K, Gentsch HH and Gunselmann W 1980 J Cancer Res Clin Oncol 98:301-313.

127. Degenshein GA, Bloom N, Tobin E 1980 Cancer 46:2789-2793.

128. Manni A, Arafah B and Pearson OH 1980 Cancer 46:2838-2841.

129. Osborne CK, Yochmowitz MG, Knight WA III, McGuire WL 1980 Cancer 46:2884-2888.

130. King RJB 1980 Cancer 46:2818-2821.

131. McCarty KS Jr, Cox C, Silva JS, Woodard BH, Mossler JA, Haagensen DE Jr, Barton TK, McCarty KS Sr and Wells SA Jr 1980 Cancer 46:2846-2850.

132. Nomura Y, Takatani O, Sugano H and Matsumoto K 1980 J Steroid Biochem 13:565-566.

133. Skinner LG, Barnes DM and Ribeiro GG 1980 Cancer 46:2939-2945.

134. Young PCM, Ehrlich CE and Einhorn LH 1980 Cancer 46:2961-2963.

135. Holdaway IM and Skinner SJM 1981 Eur J Cancer Clin Oncol 17:1295-1300.

136. Sarrif AM and Durant JR 1981 Cancer 48:1215-1220.

137. Pichon MF, Pallud C, Brunet M and Milgrom E 1980 Cancer Res 40:3357-3360.

138. Saez S, Pichon MF, Cheix F, Mayer M, Pallud C, Brunet M and Milgrom E 1983 IN Progesterone and Progestins. Bardin CW, Milgrom E and Mauvais-Jarvis P (Eds) Raven Press, New York pp 355-366.

139. Saez S, Cheix F and Asselain B 1983 Breast Cancer Research Treatment 3:345-354.

140. Schuchter L, Bitran J, Rochman H, Desser RK, Michael A and Recant W 1984 Proc Am Soc Clin Oncol 3:111 Abst 432.

141. Stewart JF, Rubens RD, Millis RR, King RJB and Hayward JL 1983 Eur J Cancer Clin Oncol 19:1381-1387.

STEROID HORMONES, RECEPTORS AND NEUROTRANSMITTERS

Gary Dohanich, Bruce Nock and Bruce S. McEwen
Laboratory of Neuroendocrinology, The Rockefeller University
New York, NY 10021

Introduction

The brain is characterized by its diversity of chemical signals and modes of communication, just as it is also known for
its incredible anatomical complexity. The two features are,
of course, closely linked, for it is one group of neuronal
products which direct nerve cells to form specific contacts
and then hold them together during development and another
category of diverse cellular products which allows mature
neurons to communicate with each other. It is now recognized
that besides the traditional neurotransmitter substances
released from synapses to act upon defined postsynaptic junc-
tions to trigger electrical activity, there are other neuroactive substances with a less precisely-defined mode of
action. These substances, sometimes called "neuromodulators",
show their effects by modifying what other neuroactive chemicals do rather than by acting on their own to excite neurons
(1). Neuromodulators may have other, more-or-less "silent"
effects to influence energy metabolism or the capacity of
cells to make, break down or respond to neurotransmitters
or other neuromodulators - such modulatory effects may only
show themselves under times of stress or prolonged activity.

Among the "neuromodulators" are hormones arising from outside
of the brain which gain access to the CNS from the cir -

culation or through the cerebral ventricles. Protein and peptide hormones such as prolactin (2) and ACTH (3-5) or TRH (6-8) are reported to alter nerve cell function and influence behavior. Steroid hormones are also important regulators of brain structure and function and produce effects during early development and in adult life which alter chemical transmission and neuromodulation and influence behavior and affective state. Steroid hormones gain access to the brain from the circulation and interact with receptors in certain groups of target neurons; mapping these receptor sites has occupied the efforts of a number of laboratories over the past 16 years (9-13). Recently, emphasis has shifted from locating receptor sites to how steroids affect brain function (eg. 14). In these studies the effects of steroid hormone exposure on neurochemical parameters has revealed a large variety of effects, ranging from direct interactions of certain estrogens with neurotransmitter receptors and metabolizing enzymes to more long-term actions to increase neurotransmitter receptor number or enzyme amount. In addition, a new facet has been added by the observation that neural activity, and in particular certain neurotransmitters, may influence how steroid hormones act. This review will summarize selected aspects of these studies to provide a picture of the diversity of steroid hormone interactions with neural tissue.

Steroid hormone receptors and actions in the brain

The brain is responsive to estrogens, androgens, progestins, glucocorticoids and mineralocorticoids (15), and the actions of these hormones in neural tissue follow the general pattern of steroid hormone action throughout the body, which involves intracellular receptors that bind the hormone to the cell nucleus. However, there are three special features of steroid action in brain which deserve emphasis and will be described below.

Localization of receptors and effects

Steroid receptors are not uniformly distributed throughout
the brain but are discretely localized to groups of nerve
cells in some brain areas (9-13). In addition, glial cells
have receptors for at least one class of steroids, namely,
glucocorticoids (16). Each class of steroid receptor has its
own pattern of distribution. For example, glucocorticoid
receptors are concentrated in hippocampus, septum and amygdala (13), whereas estrogen receptors are found predominantly
in hypothalamus, preoptic area and amygdala (9-12).

Steroid effects on these receptor-containing neural cells are
highly diversified. In many cases, this is a reflection of
the neurotransmitter phenotype of the cells in question:
eg., estrogens regulate cholinergic enzymes in some neurons
of the basal forebrain (see below) and tyrosine hydroxylase
in some neurons of the arcuate nucleus (17-19). There are
many cholinergic and catecholaminergic neurons throughout the
nervous system which are not apparently regulated by estrogens, and this is presumably due to the absence of estrogen
receptors in these cells. Sometimes, however, the regulatory
effects are not so clearly delineated according to neurotransmitter phenotype or presence or absence of hormone receptor.
For example, estrogens regulate serotonin-1 and alpha-2 adre-
nergic receptors in some, but not all, estrogen-sensitive
cell groupings where these neurotransmitter receptor types
are also found (20-22). And estrogen-sensitive neurons of
hypothalamus, preoptic area and amygdala may also be cate-
gorized on the basis of whether they show aromatase activity
(conversion of testosterone to estradiol), progestin receptor induction, or both (23).

Besides regional differences in hormone response, there are
also sex differences in response to hormone which do not

coincide with obvious differences in hormone receptor level:
eg., estrogenic regulation of cholinergic receptors and enzymes (see below), progestin receptors (24) and serotonin-1
receptors (21). In such cases as these, there may be additional regulatory factors besides presence or absence of
hormone receptor which determine the response of hormone-
sensitive cells to hormone (25).

Developmental versus activational effects of hormones on
neural tissue

Receptors for gonadal and adrenal steroids appear early in
development. In the rat, this occurs just prior to or immediately after birth (26). In neurons, the elaboration of
receptors appears to follow the final cell division and coincides with the beginning of neuronal differentiation (26).

The effects mediated by these receptors in early development
are often qualitatively different from the effects which are
mediated by the same receptors in mature neurons. For
example, glucocorticoids promote the expression of the catecholaminergic phenotype in cells of the autonomic nervous
system (27) and promote the development of the serotonergic
phenotype in the CNS (28); once these phenotypes are established, they are not so susceptible to hormonal influence.
Estrogens, on the other hand, promote neurite outgrowth in
groups of neurons of the hypothalamus and preoptic area (29).
Such growth is believed to form part of the process of sexual
differentiation of the brain, whereby male and female brains
become structurally and functionally somewhat different from
each other (26). During this period of morphogenesis and
synaptogenesis, estrogens do not have effects as they do in
mature neurons, such as the induction of progestin receptors
(30).

Direct versus genomic effects of steroids

Besides affecting gene expression via interactions with receptors in the cell nucleus, steroid hormones have direct effects on membrane-mediated processes and enzyme reactions. For example, glucocorticoids facilitate serotonin formation throughout the forebrain via a rapid action at nerve endings (31); and estrogens alter electrical activity of preoptic area and hypothalamus neurons within milliseconds after local application (32). Moreover, the 2-hydroxylated metabolite of estradiol interacts with enzymes such as tyrosine hydroxylase and catechol-O-methyl transferase and with receptors for noradrenaline, dopamine and serotonin, albeit at supraphysiological concentrations (33).

It is frequently difficult to assess the contribution which such direct effects make to overall physiological regulation. On the basis of latency of effect, many steroid actions require minutes to hours (34); furthermore, they are often susceptible to interruption following treatment with RNA or protein synthesis inhibitors (12) leading to the conclusion that genomic actions are involved. Nevertheless, non-genomic direct effects of steroids may be superimposed upon genomic actions, as is apparently the case for progesterone facilitation of monoamine oxidase (MAO) activity in estrogen-primed hypothalamus (35). Whereas the ability of progesterone to increase MAO activity is not blocked by protein synthesis inhibitors, it is dependent on prior estrogen priming in vivo over several days which involves, presumably, a genomic action.

In the remainder of the chapter we shall examine in some detail other examples of gonadal hormone-neurotransmitter interactions, which may represent both direct and genomic effects. We shall, however, be looking at them from the standpoint of their relevance to the mechanism of hormone action in regulating sexual behavior and neuroendocrine function related to reproduction.

Gonadal steroids and the cholinergic system of the brain

Overview

Steroid hormones are known to exert prominent effects on many complex physiological functions. These actions can range from a discrete fine-tuning of a particular function to the full activation of a system. Research on peripheral target structures indicates that one mechanism by which steroids may influence cellular activity is through the regulation of protein synthesis (36). Clearly, if central neurons that concentrate steroid hormones behave in a similar fashion, the consequences for neuronal activity could be profound. Although classical neurotransmitters are not proteins, their synthesis, degradation, and uptake involves enzymes, carriers, and receptors, all of which are proteins. Consequently, one way that steroids might regulate neurotransmitter activity is by altering the concentrations of proteins associated with these transmitters. Conceptually, this capacity to regulate neurotransmitter activity provides a mechanism by which steroids can activate intricate physiological and behavioral responses.

In this section, we review evidence pertaining to steroid effects on one neurotransmitter system - acetylcholine. Within this framework, we attempt to implicate the hormonal regulation of the cholinergic system in the mediation of a specific reproductive behavior. It is now clear that gonadal steroids such as estradiol, testosterone, and progesterone

have the capability of altering the concentrations and activities of the various neurochemicals involved in cholinergic
transmission. Furthermore, sexually-dimorphic functional
responses to gonadal hormones may arise, in part, from the
existence of sex differences in the hormonal regulation of
cholinergic neurochemistry. The exact manner in which these
hormone-induced changes in cholinergic activity might be
translated into biological function remains speculative.
However, available evidence suggests that certain biological
systems which are controlled by steroid hormones have a cholinergic component that is itself regulated by these hormones.

One system that is clearly dependent upon the action of gonadal steroids is reproductive behavior. Lordosis is a posture
assumed by the female rat when mounted by the male during the
period of sexual receptivity. Removal of the ovaries abolishes the capacity for lordosis in female rats while systemic
administration of estrogen (estradiol) for several days followed by progesterone restores lordosis in ovariectomized
females 4-8 hr after progesterone injection (37).

It has been demonstrated that intracerebral administration of
agents which elevate cholinergic activity stimulate the occurrence of this behavior in ovariectomized female rats (38-42).
In addition, if ovariectomized females are primed with low
doses of estradiol which are behaviorally inactive, the stimulatory effect of cholinergic agonists on lordosis is dramatically enhanced (41). This facilitation of lordosis by
cholinergic agonists is prevented if females are pretreated
with cholinergic receptor blockers. Conversely, agents that
antagonize cholinergic activity within the central nervous
system have been found to reduce the incidence of lordosis
in sexually-receptive female rats (39, 41, 43).

708

The minimum physiological dose of estradiol required to activate lordosis is also capable of inducing cholinergic receptors in the hypothalamus (44) and elevating cholinergic
enzyme activity in the basal forebrain (45). In addition,
both of these cholinergic changes are evident within 24 hr
after estradiol treatment, the precise time at which the onset of sexual receptivity occurs (44). These data indicate
that the regulation of cholinergic neurochemicals by estradiol may be one mechanism by which this gonadal steroid controls sexual behavior in the female rat. The following sections review some of the effects of gonadal hormones on cholinergic neurochemistry within the brain.

Muscarinic receptors

Cholinergic muscarinic binding is influenced by estrogen in
brain regions that mediate female sexual behavior. Estradiol
increases the number of muscarinic binding sites in the medial basal hypothalamus of ovariectomized female rats (44,
46-49). In microdissected samples, discrete subregions of
the hypothalamus that heavily concentrate estradiol such as
the ventromedial hypothalamus and anterior hypothalamus display similar estrogen-induced increases in muscarinic binding
(46). These increases are dependent upon protein synthesis
since they are not observed when a protein-synthesis inhibitor is administered in conjunction with estradiol (44). Male
rats, which are capable of only low levels of lordosis behavior, fail to display changes in muscarinic binding in the
hypothalamus following estrogen treatment (44, 47-49).

Olsen et al have suggested that this regulation of muscarinic
binding by estrogen in the medial basal hypothalamus is not
relevant physiologically since they have detected significant
changes in muscarinic binding over the estrous cycle only in

the medial preoptic region (48). However, available data are inconsistent in the medial preoptic region of ovariectomized female rats where estrogen has been reported to increase (48), decrease (47), or not alter (49) muscarinic binding. A variety of dissection procedures and estradiol regimens might explain these discrepancies. Reliable changes in muscarinic binding induced by estrogen have not been observed in other brain regions, including the arcuate nucleus, cerebral cortex, striatum, and amygdala (46, 47, 49).

Using a novel tritiated muscarinic antagonist, N-methyl-4-piperidyl benzilate, Sokolovsky and coworkers (50) reported that ovariectomy increased muscarinic binding in the median hypothalamus of rats and estradiol replacement returned binding to intact estrous levels. In an earlier study, these investigators failed to find differences in total muscarinic binding between males and females at three stages of the estrous cycle (51). However, a competition analysis of high and low affinity subtypes of the receptor revealed that the percentage of the high affinity subtype was significantly greater in the preoptic area of proestrous females compared to estrous and diestrous females and males. Furthermore, when preoptic homogenates from proestrous females were preincubated with estradiol, the percentage of high affinity sites was substantially reduced (52). These results suggest that estrogen may have important membrane-mediated effects on muscarinic receptor subtypes, in addition to those effects mediated by intracellular receptors.

Consequently, the medial basal hypothalamus and the medial preoptic area appear to exhibit alterations in muscarinic receptor density following estrogen treatment. Since both of these brain regions have been implicated in the control of lordosis by a variety of techniques, it is likely that this hormonal regulation of muscarinic receptors contributes to the expression of this behavior.

Cholinergic enzymes

<u>Choline acetyltransferase</u>. Anatomically the origin of choli-
nergic fibers that innervate the preoptic and hypothalamic
regions has not been identified. One possible source of innervation, however, is the vast continuum of cholinergic
neurons that populate the basal forebrain areas of the medial
septum, diagonal band nuclei, substantia innominata, and
ventral palladium. Although no distinct anatomical connection with preoptic and hypothalamic neurons has been discovered to date, cholinergic cells of the basal forebrain are
particularly intriguing since their neurochemical activity
can be influenced by gonadal steroids.

Choline acetyltransferase (CAT) is the major enzyme controlling the synthesis of acetylcholine. A variety of studies
have detailed alterations in CAT activity in the forebrain
region following treatment with steroid hormones. Work from
this laboratory (45) indicates that estradiol increases the
activity of CAT in the horizontal limb of the diagonal band
of Broca in female rats. In minimal treatment paradigms,
ovariectomized females are exposed to pure estradiol from
Silastic capsules (1 cm) for 6 to 24 hrs and sacrificed 24
hrs after capsule implantation. This elevation of CAT activity in the horizontal limb appears to reflect a protein
synthesis-dependent increase in the concentration of CAT (53).
Interestingly, a portion of the cholinergic neurons in this
region have been reported to concentrate estradiol (54).
Although male rats fail to show a similar increase in the
horizontal limb, estradiol was found to decrease the activity of CAT in the vertical limb of the diagonal band in males

(45). Several adjacent regions, including the bed nucleus, medial preoptic area, and anterior hypothalamus failed to exhibit any alteration in CAT activity following estrogen treatment of either sex (45). Estradiol treatment also did not affect CAT activity in the medial basal hypothalamus (55).

Similar elevations of CAT activity in the horizontal limb of female rats were not observed by Muth et al (56) following estrogen treatment; however, difference in tissue dissection and estrogen regimens may account for this discrepancy. These investigators did observe a significant reduction in CAT activity in the vertical limb of the diagonal band in castrate males following testosterone propionate treatment similar to that observed by this laboratory in the male vertical limb following estradiol administration (45).

In intact cycling female rats, the activity of CAT has been reported to be lower in the anterior portion of the hypothalamus during estrus compared to other stages of the cycle (57). A similar, though insignificant, reduction has been observed during estrus compared to diestrus in the preoptic suprachiasmatic area of intact female rats (58). At present, the relationship between these lower levels of hypothalamic CAT activity during estrus and increases in basal forebrain CAT activity following estradiol treatment of ovariectomized females is not understood.

Cholinergic neurons located in the horizontal limb are known to project to various telencephalic structures (59, 60) and two areas that receive such projections, the hippocampus and amygdala, also display small but significant increases in CAT activity after estrogen treatment of female rats (55). Since these areas probably do not contain cholinergic cell bodies, it is possible that the alterations in CAT activity arise from afferent projections from the cholinergic neurons

of the horizontal limb. Another area that receives projections from the horizontal limb, the cerebral cortex (59, 60),
does not appear to display changes in CAT activity over the
estrous cycle of female rats (58). However, James and Kanungo (61) have reported age-dependent increases in CAT activity in the cerebral cortex of male rats within four hours
after administration of testosterone or estradiol. Males
sacrificed more than 12 hours after hormone treatment failed
to exhibit increases in cortical CAT activity. This rapid
cortical effect appears to be quite different from the results obtained in the basal forebrain where alterations in
CAT activity are observed at least 24 hrs after the initiation of hormone treatment (45).

Acetylcholinesterase. Steroid hormones also have been found
to affect the activity of the major degradative enzyme of
acetylcholine, acetylcholinesterase (AChE), in several brain
regions. Work from this laboratory has demonstrated that
estradiol increases the activity of AChE in the horizontal
limb of the diagonal band in ovariectomized female rats,
an effect that parallels the actions of estrogen on CAT activity (45). Estrogen did not alter AChE activity in the
vertical limb of the diagonal band, the bed nucleus of the
stria terminalis, the medial preoptic areas, or the anterior
hypothalamus. Nor did estrogen affect AChE activity in any
brain area examined in castrated male rats.

In the cycling female rat, Libertun et al (58) reported significantly lower activity of AChE at estrus compared to diestrus in preoptic-suprachiasmatic area. No stage differences were detected in the cortex or arcuate-mammillary region.

Changes in AChE activity induced by gonadal steroids have
been observed in the cerebral cortex of male rats (61, 62),

a region that is devoid of cholinergic cell bodies but which receives cholinergic projections from basal forebrain neurons. Generally, gonadectomy was found to decrease the activity of AChE in male cortex while testosterone and estradiol increased enzyme activity 4 hrs after administration. Estradiol was also found to increase AChE activity in the cortex and cerebellum of ovariectomized females 4 hrs after treatment (62). These increases may have been mediated by induction of intracellular protein synthesis since actinomycin D, a protein synthesis inhibitor, prevented the elevations in AChE activity in both cortex and cerebellum when administered in conjunction with estradiol (62).

Using a similar hormone regimen, Iramain et al reported that estradiol increases AChE activity in the amygdala of castrated male rats and in the amygdala and adenohypophysis of ovariectomized females 4 hrs after injection (63, 64) while progesterone alone increased AChE activity in the amygdala, cerebral cortex, and mesencephalon of ovariectomized female rats 4 hrs after treatment (65).

Several investigators have noted various sex differences in baseline activity and distribution of AChE in certain brain regions. In this laboratory, the baseline activity of AChE was found to be significantly higher in the horizontal limb of long-term ovariectomized female rats when compared to long-term castrated males (45). AChE activity has also been reported to be significantly higher in the preoptic-suprachiasmatic area of intact female rats compared to intact males (58). In the gerbil, the distribution of cells that stain histochemically for AChE in the preoptic-anterior hypothalamic region is clearly different in males and females (66). Neurons in this preoptic-anterior hypothalamic region do not stain darkly enough to be classified as cholinergic cells, rather they may represent a population of cells that receive cholinergic innervation. Female gerbils display a rounder and more diffuse distribution and appear to possess a lower level of activity in this area compared to males as determined by densitometry. Gonadectomy reduced the activity of AChE in both sexes while treatment with testosterone stimulated the activity of the enzyme.

While gonadal hormones induce a variety of effects on CAT and AChE activities in a number of brain regions, the functional significance of these changes is unclear at present. Estrogen does not appear to alter the activities of these two enzymes in the preoptic area or medial basal hypothalamus (45,55), two regions where muscarinic receptor density changes following estradiol treatment. On the other hand, both enzymes display variations over the estrous cycle in the preoptic and anterior hypothalamic regions (57, 58). In addition, the existence of reliable sex differences in the activity, distribution, and hormone inducibility of these enzymes (45, 58, 66) may have important implications for the regulation of sexually-dimorphic functions, such as reproductive behavior.

Acetylcholine

The effect of gonadal steroids on the actual release of acetylcholine would be of particular value to the understanding of how hormones regulate cholinergic neural activity. However, the effects of steroids on the concentration of acetylcholine have not been well documented, partly due to the difficulties inherent in direct measurement of this transmitter. Furthermore, the turnover of acetylcholine which may represent a useful index of cholinergic activity, has proven to be even more difficult to measure. Using a radioenzymatic

technique, Muth, Crowley and Jacobowitz (56) found that cast-
ration of male rats elevated the level of acetylcholine in
three discrete brain areas; the rostral diagonal band, medial
preoptic nucleus, and ventral tegmental area. These increases were partially prevented by treatment of castrates with
testosterone propionate. In female rats, treatment with
estradiol benzoate in combination with progesterone reduced
the concentration of acetylcholine in periventricular nucleus
and ventral tegmental area compared to ovariectomized control
females. There were no changes observed in acetylcholine
level in either sex in a number of other brain areas that
concentrate testosterone and estrogen. The significance of
these results remains to be determined.

Functional implications

Although the precise nature of the changes in cholinergic
neurochemistry induced by hormones is controversial, the
major conclusion that emerges from these experiments is that
steroid hormones, acting as neuromodulators, are indeed capable of regulating cholinergic events within the central
nervous system. Perhaps, the variety of observations made by
investigators reflects the dynamic quality of this regulation,
which may be unusually sensitive to the subtle effects of
time and environment. In support of this suggestion, a wide
circadian variation in muscarinic binding in rat forebrain
has been observed (67). Additionally, significant strain and
species differences in cholinergic neurochemistry have been
demonstrated by a number of studies (68, 69). And, in a more
specific instance, the activity of the membrane-bound uptake
system for choline, a precursor for acetylcholine, has been
shown to be influenced by the simple act of handling the animals prior to sacrifice (70).

Evidence of a cholinergic component in hormone-dependent functions other than reproductive behavior, such as gonado-tropin release (71-74) and scent marking (75), indicates that this particular hormone-dependent interaction may have important implications for the regulation of certain complex systems of physiology and behavior. Clearly, the ability of hormones to alter the level of neurotransmission within the brain is a critical feature of central hormone action.

Modulation of steroid action by neurotransmitters

Overview

Behavioral, environmental and age related factors can influence steroid-dependent processes. Often, changes in steroid secretion mediate the effects of these factors. However, responses to steroid hormones are not "hard-wired"; and not all changes in steroid-dependent processes are accompanied by changes in circulating steroid levels. For example, time of day and season of year can have important effects on the sensitivity of reproductive processes to steroid hormones (76-85). Shifts in responsiveness to steroids also occur during early development, puberty and old age (86-91).

At present, only a few modulators of steroid action are known. One modulator of progestin action that has been extensively studied is estrogen. Exposure to estrogen increases the number of progestin receptors in some central and peripheral tissues (92, 93) and, thereby, plays a major role in regulating the sensitivity of those tissues to progestins. Some nucleotides can influence the binding of steroids to receptors and, therefore, might also modulate steroid action (94-98). In this section, we review recent evidence for another class of steroid modulator, neurotransmitters.

An obvious site for the modulation of steroid action by neurotransmitters is the brain, where steroid target cells receive many neural afferents of diverse origin. Surprisingly, however, much of the research in this area has been conducted with peripheral organs such as pineal, pituitary and uterus. This work has been discussed in detail elsewhere (99-102). Here, we focus on research concerning the regulation of steroid action by neurotransmitters in the brain. It should be kept in mind that the idea that neurotransmitters can affect steroid action in brain is relatively new and, therefore, there is not as yet incontrovertible evidence for any given neurotransmitter modulating the action of any particular steroid. However, taken together with findings with peripheral organs the existing evidence strongly supports the concept that neurotransmitters can modulate target cell sensitivity to steroid hormones.

Dopaminergic regulation of estrogen action

The hypothalamus is an important site of steroid action in brain. Interestingly, a number of cell bodies that concentrate radioactive steroid in hypothalamus appear to be surrounded by catecholamine terminals (103-104). One of the first indications that this catecholamine input might influence the sensitivity of the steroid concentrating cells to steroids was provided by experiments with the catecholamine neurotoxin 6-hydroxydopamine (6-OHDA). Marks et al (105) found that infusion of 6-OHDA into a lateral cerebral ventricle of rats caused a decrease in the concentration of a "soluble estrogen binding protein", presumably cytosol estrogen receptors. Later, Thompson et al (106) found a similar effect with the catecholamine synthesis inhibitor α-methyl-p-tyrosine.

Acute treatment of female rats with AMPT decreased receptor-mediated 3H estradiol uptake in anterior and basal hypothalamus (by 35-40%). Estradiol uptake in dorsal hypothalamus and in cerebral cortex and the level of radioactivity in plasma were not affected by AMPT.

Experiments with dopamine receptor agonists and antagonists indicate that the effects of 6-OHDA and of AMPT on hypothalamic estrogen receptors might be attributable to changes in dopamine function. Acute treatment with the dopamine agonist apomorphine or bromocriptine increased (by 60-90%) receptor-mediated 3H estradiol uptake in the nuclear fraction of anterior and basal hypothalamus of female rats. Estradiol uptake in cerebral cortex and plasma levels of radioactivity were not affected by the agonists (107, 108). Some caution should be exercised with regard to dopamine agonists. Some dopamine agonists bind to estrogen receptors (but not progestin or androgen receptors) with a relatively high affinity. For example, bromocriptine competitively inhibits 3H estradiol binding to hypothalamic estrogen receptors in vitro with a Ki of about 25 uM. Also, some agonists, including bromocriptine, might induce estrogen-inducible proteins such as progestin receptors through the estrogen receptor system although this has been tested only in gonadally intact immature rats thus far (109). Thus, it is conceivable that dopamine agonists might affect estradiol uptake in hypothalamus through an interaction with estrogen receptors rather than through dopamine receptors. However, pretreatment with the dopamine antagonist perphenazine blocked the agonist-induced increase in estradiol uptake in hypothalamus (107, 108). Phenothiazines such as perphenazine do not bind to estrogen receptors, at least up to a drug to 3H estradiol ratio of 1:100,000 (110, 111). Thus, it seems likely that the agonist-induced increase in estradiol uptake in hypothalamus and

gestin receptor dynamics in hypothalamic cells is sensitive to noradrenergic function.

Other neurotransmitters and steroids

Although most research on neurotransmitter modulation of steroid action in brain have been concerned with dopamine effects on estrogen action and noradrenergic effects on progestin action, there have been some experiments with other neurotransmitters and other steroids. For example, Clark et al (125) recently found that α_1-noradrenergic receptor blockade with prazosin decreases the concentration of nuclear estrogen receptors in hypothalamus and preoptic area of estradiol treated female guinea pigs suggesting that noradrenergic transmission might modulate estrogen action in those areas.

The sensitivity of brain regions to adrenal steroids might also be influenced by neural input. For example, Feldman and associates have postulated an important role for extrahypothalamic sites in modulating hypothalamic sensitivity to glucocorticoids in rat (126-130). Complete or posterior hypothalamic differentiation, dorsal hippocampectomy, or dorsal fornix section decreased the inhibitory effect of dexamethasone on the adrenal secretory response to ether stress. On the other hand, electrolytic lesions of the mammillary peduncle or the medial forebrain bundle or bilateral infusion of 6-OHDA into the medial forebrain bundle enhanced the inhibitory effect of dexamethasone (126-130). Various other CNS operations did not affect the feedback effect of dexathasone in rats (126-130). Experiments with species other than rats also indicate a possible role for extrahypothalamic sites in modulating hypothalamic sensitivity to glucocorticoids. Stith et al found that electrical stimulation

of the dorsal hippocampus, but not amygdala, increased the
uptake and nuclear binding of the glucocorticoid 3H hydrocortisone in hypothalamus of male and female cats (131). Also,
infusion of 6-OHDA into the 3rd ventricle of adrenalectomized
dogs has been shown to decrease the concentration of glucocorticoid receptors in hypothalamus with no effect in hippocampus (126).

There is much that is not yet known about the modulation of
steroid action by neurotransmitters. We know almost nothing
concerning the mechanism(s) of neurotransmitter effects on
steroid action although there has been speculation in this
area (100,106,133). We also know little about the functional
consequences of neurotransmitter-induced changes in sensitivity to steroids. There are, however, numerous known phenomena
that might be relatable to the operation of such a mechanism.
For example, neurotransmitter-induced changes in sensitivity
to steroids might underlie circadian and seasonal changes in
behavioral and endocrine responsiveness to steroids and, in
addition, shifts in sensitivity to steroids that occur during
early development, puberty and old age (76-91,134,135). From
the finding that neurotransmitters can influence the action
of steroids in postsynaptic cells, it also is not a large
conceptual jump to envisioning this as an important mechanism
by which environmental, behavioral and perhaps emotional
events can rapidly and selectively influence steroid-dependent processes.

Conclusions

In this chapter we have presented a view of steroid hormones
and brain function from the perspective of the interaction
of various "neuroactive" substances (sometimes called, collectively, "neuromodulators") on brain function, including

behavior and neuroendocrine responses. The picture which is beginning to emerge is of multiple interactions - of steroids upon neuromodulatory processes and neurotransmitters, and of neurotransmitters upon responsiveness to steroid hormones. These interactions are often highly specialized and localized within restricted regions of the brain. Their occurrence is also frequently dependent on the stage of development, with permanent effects occurring during early development and qualitatively different, reversible effects occurring in later life.

Many of the effects can be related to intracellular steroid receptors, which are produced by neurons in restricted brain regions. These receptors have characteristics which make them similar, if not identical, to receptors in other parts of the body. One of the challenges for future research is to understand the features of cellular differentiation which explain the diverse effects of steroids, acting via apparently identical receptors, on different tissues and different brain regions. Another important question for future research is to elucidate the mechanisms by which neurotransmitter activation can modify steroid receptor number or cellular uptake and cell nuclear binding of steroid hormones.

Acknowledgments

Research in the author's laboratory is supported by NIH grant NS 07080, by fellowships HD 06258 (Gary Dohanich) and NS 06966 (to Bruce Nock) and by an institutional grant RF 81062 from the Rockefeller Foundation for research in reproductive biology. We wish to thank Ms. Inna Perlin for editorial assistance.

References

1. Dismukes, R.K.: The Behavioral and Brain Sciences 2, 409-448 (1979).

2. Gudelsky, G.A., Simpkins, J., Mueller, G.P., Meites, J., Moore, K.E.: Neuroendo. 22, 206-215 (1976).

3. Fekete, M., DeWied, D.: Pharm. Biochem. Behav. 17, 177-182 (1982).

4. Markey, K.A., Sze, P.Y.: Neuroendo. 38, 269-275 (1984).

5. Delanoy, R.L., Kramarcy, N.R., Dunn, A.J.: Brain Res. 231, 117-129 (1982).

6. Wei, E., Sigel, S., Loh, H., Way, E.L.: Nature 253, 739-780 (1975).

7. Cott, J. M., Breese, G.R., Cooper, B.R., Barlow, T.S., Prange, A.J.: J. Pharm. Exp. Therap. 196, 594-604 (1975).

8. Kalivas, P.W., Horita, A.: Nature 278, 461-462 (1979).

9. Stumpf, W.E., Sar, M., Keefer, D.A.: In: Anat. Neuroendo. 104-119 (W.E. Stumpf and L.D. Grant, Eds.) S. Karger, Basel 1975.

10. Warembourg, M.: In: Biol. Cell. Proc. Neurosecret. Hypothal., 221-237 (J-D. Vincent, C. Kordon, Eds.) CNRS, Paris 1978.

11. Pfaff, D.W.: In: Estrogens and Brain Function, 281pp., Springer-Verlag, New York 1980.

12. McEwen, B.S., Biegon, A., Davis, P.G., Krey, L.C., Luine, V.N., McGinnis, M.Y., Paden, C.M., Parsons, B., Rainbow, T.C.: Rec. Prog. Horm. Res. 38, 41-92 (1982).

13. McEwen, B.S.: In: Current Topics in Neuroendocrinology, 1-22 (D. Ganten and D.W. Pfaff, Eds) Springer-Verlag, Berlin 1982.

14. McEwen, B.S., Parsons, B: Ann. Rev. Pharm. Toxicol. 22, 555-598 (1982).

15. McEwen, B.S., Davis, P.G., Parsons, B., Pfaff, D.W.: Ann. Rev. Neurosci. 2, 65-112 (1979).

16. Meyer, J.S., McEwen, B.S.: J. Neurochem. 39, 436-442 (1982).

17. Luine, V.N., McEwen, B.S., Black, I.B.: Brain Res. 120, 188-192 (1977).

18. Sar, M.: Science 223, 938-940 (1983).

19. Blum, M., McEwen, B.S., Roberts, J.L.: Abstr. Soc. Neurosci. 14th Annual Meeting, 308.3 (1984).

20. Biegon, A., Fischette, C., Rainbow, T.C., McEwen, B.S.: Neuroendo. 35, 287-291 (1982).

21. Fischette, C.T., Biegon, A., McEwen, B.S.: Science 222, 333-335 (1983).

22. Johnson, A.E., Nock, B., McEwen, B.S., Feder, H.H.: Brain Res., submitted (1984).

23. McEwen, B.S.: In: Biological Regulation and Development, 203-219 (R.F. Goldberger and K.R. Yamamoto, Eds.) Plenum Press, New York 1982.

24. Rainbow, T.C., Parsons, B., McEwen, B.S.: Nature 300, 648-649 (1982).

25. McEwen, B.S.: In: Fetal Neuroendocrinology (F. Ellendorff, N. Parvizi, P. Gluckman, Eds.) Perinatology Press, New York, in press 1985.

26. McEwen, B.S.: In: Reproductive Physiology IV, 99-145 (R.O. Greep, Ed.) University Press, Baltimore 1983.

27. Patterson, P.: Ann. Rev. Neurosci. 1, 1-17 (1978).

28. Sze, P.Y.: In: Serotonin: current aspects of neurochemistry and function, 507-523 (B. Haber, S. Gabay, M.R. Issidorides and S.G.A. Alivisatos, Eds.) Plenum Press, New York 1981.

29. Toran-Allerand, C.D.: In: Bioregulators of Reproduction, 43-57 (G. Jagiello, H.J. Vogel, Eds.) Academic Press, New York 1981.

30. MacLusky, N.J., McEwen, B.S.: Brain Res. 189, 262-268 (1980).

31. Azmitia, E.C.Jr., McEwen, B.S.: Brain Res. 78, 291-302 (1974).

32. Kelly, M.J., Moss, R.L., Dudley, C.A.: Exp. Brain Res. 30, 53-64 (1977).

33. McEwen, B.S., Biegon, A., Fischette, C.T., Luine, V.N., Parsons, B., Rainbow, T.C.: In: Frontiers in Neuroendocrinology, 8, 153-176 (L. Martini, W. Ganong, Eds.) Raven Press, New York 1984.

34. McEwen, B.S., Krey, L.C., Luine, V.N.: In: The Hypothalamus, 255-268 (S. Reichlin, R.J., Baldessarini, J.B. Martin, Eds.) Raven Press, New York 1978.

35. Luine, V.N., Rhodes, J.C.: Neuroendo. 36, 235-241 (1983).

36. O'Malley, B.W., Means, A.R.: Science 183, 610-620 (1974).

37. Boling, J.L., Blandau, R.J.: Endocrinology 25, 359-364 (1939).

38. Clemens, L.G., Humphrys, R.R., Dohanich, G.P.: Pharm. Biochem. Behav. 13, 81-88 (1980).

39. Clemens, L.G., Dohanich, G.P., Witcher, J.A.: J. Comp. Physiol. Psychol. 95, 763-770 (1981).

40. Dohanich, G.P., Clemens, L.G.: Horm. Behav. 15, 157-167 (1981).

41. Clemens, L., Dohanich, G., Barr, P.: Hormones and Behavior in Higher Vertebrates, Springer-Verlag, Berlin Heidelberg 1983.

42. Dohanich, G.P., Barr, P.J., Witcher, J.A., Clemens, L.G.: Physiol. Behav. 32, 1021-1026 (1984).

43. Clemens, L.G., Dohanich, G.P.: Pharm. Biochem. Behav. 13, 89-95 (1980).

44. Rainbow, T.C., Snyder, L., Berck, D.J., McEwen, B.S.: Neuroendo. 39, 476-480 (1984).

45. Luine, V.N., McEwen, B.S.: Neuroendo. 36, 475-482 (1983).

46. Rainbow, T.C., DeGroff, V., Luine, V.N., McEwen, B.S.: Brain Res. 198, 239-243 (1980).

47. Dohanich, G.P., Witcher, J.A., Weaver, D.R., Clemens, L.G.: Brain Res. 241, 347-350 (1980).

48. Olsen, K.L., Edwards, E., McNally, W., Schechter, N., Whalen, R.E.: Soc. Neurosci. Abstr. 8, 423 (1982).

49. Dohanich, G.P., Witcher, J.A., Clemens, L.G.: Pharm. Biochem. Behav., in press.

50. Egozi, Y., Avissar, S., Sokolovsky, M.: Neuroendo. 35, 93-97 (1982).

51. Avissar, S., Egozi, Y., Sokolovsky, M.: Neuroendo. 32, 295-302 (1981).

52. Egozi, Y., Kloog, Y.: 7th International Congress of Endocrinology 762 (1984).

53. Luine, V.N., Park, D., Tong, J., Reis, D., McEwen, B.S.: Brain Res. 191, 273-277 (1980).

54. Fallon, J.H., Loughlin, S.E., Ribak, C.E.: J. Comp. Neurol. 218, 91-120 (1983).

55. Luine, V.N., Khylchevskaya, R.I., McEwen, B.S.: Brain Res. 86, 293-306 (1975).

56. Muth, E.A., Crowley, W.R., Jacobowitz, D.M.: Neuroendo. 30, 329-336 (1980).

57. Kobayashi, T., Kobayashi, T., Kato, J., Minaguchi, H.: Endocrinol. Japon. 10, 175-182 (1963).

58. Libertun, C., Timiras, P.S., Kragt, C.L.: Neuroendo. 12, 73-85 (1973).

59. Saper, C.B.: J. Comp. Neurol. 222, 313-342 (1984).

60. Wenk, H., Meyer, U., Bigl, V.: Neurosci. 2, 797-800 (1977)

61. James, T.C., Kanungo, M.S.: Biochim. Biophys. Acta 538, 205-211 (1978).

62. Moudgil, V.K., Kanungo, M.S.: Biochim. Biophys. Acta 329, 211-220 (1973).

63. Iramain, C.A., Egbunike, G.N., Owasoyo, J.O.: Experientia 35, 1678-1679 (1979).

64. Iramain, C.A., Owasoyo, J.O., Egbunike, G.N.: Neurosci. Letts. 16, 81-84 (1980).

65. Iramain, C.A., Owasoyo, J.O.: Neuroendo. Letts. 2, 93-96 (1980).

66. Commins, D., Yahr, P.: J. Comp. Neurol. 224, 123-131 (1984).

67. Kafka, M.S., Wirz-Justice, A., Naber, D., Wehr, T.A.: Neuropharm. 20, 421-425 (1981).

68. Marks, M.J., Patinkin, D.M., Artman, L.D., Burch, J.B., Collins, A.C.: Pharm. Biochem. Behav. 15, 271-279 (1981).

69. Gilad, G.M., Rabey, J.M., Shenkman, L: Brain Res. 267, 171-174 (1983).

70. Burgel, P., Rommelspacher, H.: Life Sci. 23, 2423-2428 (1978).

71. Everett, J.W., Sawyer, C.H., Markee, J.E.: Endocrinology 44, 234-250 (1949).

72. Libertun, C., McCann, S.M.: Endocrinology 92, 1714-1724 (1973).

73. Libertun, C., McCann, S.M.: Proc. Soc. Exp. Biol. Med. 147, 498-504 (1974).

74. Bagga, N., Chhina, G.S., Mohan Kumar V., Singh, B.: Physiol. Behav. 32, 45-48 (1984).

75. Yahr, P.: Chemical Signals in Vertebrates, Vol. 2, Plenum Press, New York 1983.

76. Beach, F.A., Levinson, G. Proc. Soc. Exp. Med. 72, 78-80 (1949).

77. Goodman, R.L., Karsch, F.J.: In: Progress in Reproductive Biology (P.O. Hubinont, Ed.), Karger, Basel 1980.

78. Hansen, S., Soderten, P., Enroth, B., Serbro, B., Hole,K: J. Endocrinol. 83, 267-274 (1979).

79. Hansen, S., Sodersten, P. Serbro, B.: J. Endocrinol. 77, 381-388 (1978).

80. Harlan, R.E., Shivers, B.D., Moss, R.L., Shryne, J.E., Gorski, R.A.: Biol. Reproduction 23, 64-71 (1980).

81. Hinde, R.A., Steel, E.: In: Advances in the Study of Behavior, Vol. 8 (J.S. Rosenblatt, R.A. Hinde, C. Beer, M.-C. Busnel, Eds.) Academic Press, New York 1978.

82. Morin, L.P., Fitzgerald, K.M., Rusak, B., Zucker, I.: Psychoneuroendo. 1, 265-279 (1977).

83. Morin, L.P., Zucker, I.: J. Endocrinol. 77, 249-258 (1978).

84. Roberts, J.S.: Endocrinology 53, 1309-1314 (1973).

85. Ellis, G.B., Turek, F.W.: Neuroendo. 31, 205-209 (1980).

86. Davidson, J.M.: In: The Control of the Onset of Puberty (M.M. Grumbach, G.D. Grave, F.E. Mayer, Eds.) John Wiley, New York 1974.

87. Goldman, B.D.: In: Neuroendocrinology of Reproduction (N.T. Adler, Ed.) Plenum Press, New York 1981.

88. MacLusky, N.J., Lieberburg, I., McEwen, B.S.: In: Ontogeny of Receptors and Reproductive Hormone Action (J.H. Clark, T.H. Hamilton, W.A. Sadler, Eds.), Raven Press, New York 1979.

89. Roth, G.S.: Mech. Aging Develop. 9, 497-514 (1979a).

90. Roth, G.S.: Fed. Proc. 38, 1910-1914 (1979b).

91. Wise, P.M., Camp, P.: Endocrinology 114, 92-98 (1984).

92. MacLusky, N.J., Clark, C.R.: In: Proteins of the Nervous System (R.A. Bradshaw and D.M. Schneider, Eds.) Raven Press, New York 1980.

93. Muldoon, T.G.: Endocr. Rev. 1, 339-364 (1980).

94. Fleming, H., Blumenthal, R., Gurpide, E.: Endocrinology 111, 1671-1677 (1982).

95. Fleming, H., Blumenthal, R, Gurpide, E.: Proc. Natl. Acad. Sci. USA 80, 2486-2490 (1983).

96. Sando, J.J., Hammond, N.D., Stratford, C.A., Pratt, W.B.: J. Biol. Chem. 254, 4779-4789 (1979).

97. Toft, D., Moudgil, V., Lohmar , P. , Miller, J.: Ann. N.Y Acad. Sci. 281, 29-42 (1977).

98. Weigel, N.L., Tash, J.S., Means, A.R., Schrader, W.T., O'Malley, B.W.: Biochem. Biophys. Res. Commun. 102, 513-519 (1981).

99. Cardinali, D.P.: Trends Neurosci. 2, 250-253 (1979).

100. Nock, B., Feder, H.H.: Neurosci. Biobehav. Rev. 5, 437-447 (1981).

101. Carrillo, A.J., Steger, R.W., Chamness, G.C.: Endocrinology 112, 1839-1946 (1983).

102. Di Carlo, F., Rebani, Portaleone, P., Viano, J., Genazzani, E.: In: Pharmacological Modulation of Steroid Action (E. Genazzani, F. Di Carlo, W.I.P. Mainwaring, Eds.), Raven Press, New York 1980.

103. Grant, L.D., Stumpf, W.E.: In: Anatomical Neuroendocrinology (W.E. Stumpf, L.D. Grant, Eds.), S. Karger, Basel 1975.

104. Heritage, A.S., Stumpf, W.E., Sar, M., Grant, L.D.: Science 207, 1377-1379 (1980).

105. Marks, B.H., Wu, T-K., Goldman, H.: Res. Communs. Chem. Pathol. Pharmac. 3, 595-600 (1972).

106. Thompson, M.A., Woolley, D.E., Gietzen, D.W., Conway, S.: Endocrinology 113, 855-865 (1983).

107. Gietzen, D.W., Hope, W.G., Wooley, D.E.: Life Sci. 33, 2221-2228 (1983).

108. Woolley, D.E., Hope, W.G., Geitzen, D.W., Thompson, M.T., Conway, S.B.: Proc. West Pharm. Soc. 25, 437-441 (1982).

109. Liel, Y., Marbach, M., Aflalo, L., Glick, S.M., Levy, J.: Biochem. Pharm. 31, 707-710 (1982).

110. Shani, J., Givant, Y., Sulman, F.G., Eylath, U., Eckstein, B.: Neuroendocrinology 8, 307-316 (1971).

111. Shani, J., Roth, Z., Givant, Y., Goldhaber, G., Sulman, F.G.: Israel J. Med. Sci. 12, 1338-1339 (1976).

112. Feder, H.H.: In: Biological Determinants of Sexual Behavior (J.B. Hutchinson, Ed.), John Wiley, New York 1978.

113. Young, W.C.: In: Sex and Internal Secretions, Third Edition (W.C. Young, Ed.), Williams and Wilkins, Baltimore 1961.

114. Young, W.C.: In:Advances in the Study of Behavior, Vol. 2 (D.S. Lehrman, R.A. Hinde, Shaw, E., Eds.), Academic Press, New York 1969.

115. Crowley, W.R., Feder, H.H., Morin, L.P.: Pharm. Biochem. Behav. 4, 67-71 (1976).

116. Nock, B., Blaustein, J.D., Feder, H.H.: Brain Res. 207, 371-396 (1981).

117. Nock, B., Feder, H.H.: Brain Res. 166, 369-380 (1979).

118. Nock, B., Feder, H.H.: Brain Res., in press (1984).

119. Crowley, W.R., Nock, B., Feder, H.H: Pharm. Biochem. Behav. 8, 207-209 (1978).

120. Morin, L.P., Feder, H.H.: Brain Res. 70, 81-93 (1974).

121. Morin, L.P., Feder, H.H.: Brain Res. 70, 95-102 (1974).

122. Blaustein, J.D.: Brain Res., in press (1984).

123. King, W.J., Greene, G.L.: Nature 307, 745-747 (1984).

124. Welshons, W.V., Lieberman, M.E., Gorski, J.: Nature 307, 747-749 (1984).

125. Clark, A.S., Nock, B., Feder, H.H., Roy, E.J.: Brain Res., in press (1984).

126. Feldman, S., Siegel, R.A., Weidenfeld, J., Conforti, N., Melamed, E.: Brain Res. 260, 297-300 (1983).

127. Feldman, S., Conforti, N.: Horm. Res. 12, 289-295 (1980).

128. Feldman, S., Conforti, N.: Acta Endocrinol. 82, 785-791 (1976).

129. Feldman, S., Conforti, N.: Horm. Res. 7, 56-60 (1976).

130. Feldman, S., Conforti, N., Chowers, I.: Acta Endocrinol. (Kbh) 73, 660-664 (1973).

131. Stith, R.D., Person, R.J., Dana, R.C.: J. Neurosci. Res. 2, 317-322 (1976).

132. Stith, R.D., Person, R.J.: Neuroendocrinology 34, 410-414 (1982).

133. Nock, B.: In: Reproduction: A Behavioral and Neuroendocrine Perspective (B.R. Komisaruk, H.I. Siegel, H.H. Feder, M-F. Cheng, Eds.), New York Academy of Science, in press, 1984.

134. Roy, E.J., Wilson, M.A.: Science 213, 1525-1527 (1981).

135. Spelsberg, T.C., Boyd, P.A., Halberg, F.: In: Steroid Hormone Receptor Systems (W.W.Leavitt, J.H. Clark, Eds.) Plenum Press, New York 1978.

THE STEROID RECEPTOR OF ACHLYA AMBISEXUALIS

Robert M. Riehl, David O. Toft
Department of Cell Biology, Mayo Clinic,
Rochester, Minnesota, USA

Introduction

The mechanism of action of steroid hormones remains unclear despite the accumulation of studies on the individual steps involved in the molecular events associated with steroid-induced responses. Information relevant to the structure, stabilization and translocation of cytosolic receptors and some of the biochemical events associated with nuclear steroid-receptor complexes has been obtained from a number of model systems. These classical models are mainly composed of target tissues and/or cells from vertebrates which represent only a small fraction of the total population of known steroid responsive systems among the plant and animal kingdoms (1-3). Studies utilizing other nonclassical systems may provide new information or insight useful in defining the mechanism of action of steroid hormones in general and broaden our view of the biological role of steroidal compounds as intercellular communication molecules. In this regard, recent studies have shown that some eukaryotic microorganisms belonging to the kingdom Fungi possess steroid binding proteins (4-8). One of these, Achlya ambisexualis, is under study in our laboratory and is the subject of this chapter.

Background

A brief description of the relevant aspects of the biology of
Achlya will be presented here and the reader is urged to
consult the more extensive reviews to be found in the list of
references (3,9,10). Notably, Achlya is unique in its
ability to synthesize and respond to steroid hormones. It is
the only microbe known in which sexual reproduction is
controlled by steroid hormones.

Reproduction in Achlya is accomplished by either asexual or
sexual modes of sporulation. The asexual mode is thought to
be independent of the steroid hormones and occurs
predominantly in response to depletion of exogenous nutrient
supplies. Germination and culture of the asexual spores
(zoospores) is a common laboratory technique for obtaining
Achlya cultures in which the process of sexual reproduction
can be studied. Spore germination is evidenced by the
outgrowth of a small tube of protoplasm encased by the
plasmalemma and cell wall. The germ tube continues to
elongate and form apical branches that also grow and branch
to ultimately form a meshwork of interconnected tubes called
hyphae (somatic cell type) which are collectively known as a
mycelium. Sexual reproduction occurs when male and female
mycelia are in close physical proximity. Female hyphae
synthesize and release the steroid antheridiol (Figure 1)
into the environment from which it is detected by male hyphae
that respond by the growth and differentiation of the male
sex organs known as antheridial branches and by the
production and release of a second steroid, oogoniol.
Oogoniol acts upon the female hyphae inducing the formation
of the egg-bearing structures or oogonia. Chemotropic growth
of the male antheridial branches toward the oogonia along a
concentration gradient of antheridiol results in contact of
the two sex organs followed by syngamy and production of
oospores. The induction of antheridial branches can also be

observed by the addition of exogenous synthetic antheridiol
(and chemical analogs) to the culture medium. Within two
hours following exposure to antherdiol, male hyphae produce
thin, contorted subapical branches that are readily
observable with ordinary light microscopy (Figure 2).

The following characteristics confer exceptional advantages
to the Achlya steroid hormone system compared to the
classical vertebrate systems: 1) The somatic cells (hyphae)
of Achlya are a tubular coenocytium, consequently the entire
mycelium is composed of a single "cell" type and represents
the "target tissue". 2) One facet of the hormone response is
a rapid and readily observable morphological differentiation.
3) Male mycelia do not synthesize antheridiol; therefore,
when in axenic culture, there is absence of previous exposure
to the hormone. 4) Achlya possess a relatively simple
genetic endowment having three sets of chromosomes and a
genome size that is only a few times larger than that of
E. coli. 5) Cultivation of mycelia in the laboratory can be
accomplished with media of simple composition in ordinary
laboratory glassware and on the bench top.

The role of steroid hormones in the process of sexual
reproduction in Achlya has been well studied (3,9,10).
However, the mechanism of action of antheridiol in the male
strain has received the majority of experimental attention
because the chemical synthesis and availability of oogoniol
has only been of recent occurrence (11). Since chemically
pure antheridiol has been available (12), some of the
biochemical actions of this steroid have been studied (10).
The development of antheridial branches has been shown to be
dependent on continued RNA and protein synthesis (13,14).
The synthesis of RNA (14,15) and levels of specific
activities of RNA polymerase II (16) and cellulase (13,17)
are increased by antheridiol. From the results of indirect
studies, it was suggested that chemorecognition of

antheridiol could be mediated through a cytosolic receptor in a similar manner to the steroid hormone receptor systems of vertebrates (18).

In our studies, we have used a tritium-labeled analogue of antheridiol, 7-deoxy-7-dihydro-antheridiol (7dA), that is biologically active. Our objectives were to use the tritium-labeled ligand to detect the binding protein (7) and characterize the biological significance of binding by analysis of the saturability, specificity and affinity. Following identification of the receptor, the physicochemical properties of the macromolecule could be determined (8) and compared with those of steroid receptors in higher organisms.

Methods

Chemical

Nonradioactive antheridiol and its congeners were supplied by Trevor C. McMorris, Department of Chemistry, University of California-San Diego. The radioactive analog of antheridiol, $[1,2-^3H]$-7-deoxy-7-dihydro-antheridiol ($[^3H]$-7dA, specific activity = 40 Ci/mmol) was prepared as described elsewhere (Meyer et al., in preparation). The chemical structures of antheridiol and $[^3H]$-7dA are shown in Figure 1.

Cell culture

Achlya ambisexualis Raper strains E87 (male) and 734 (female) were cultured as previously described (7). Asexual spores (19) were germinated in PYG medium (20) for 18-24 hrs at 29°C and subsequently innoculated into 2 liters of M1 medium (14)

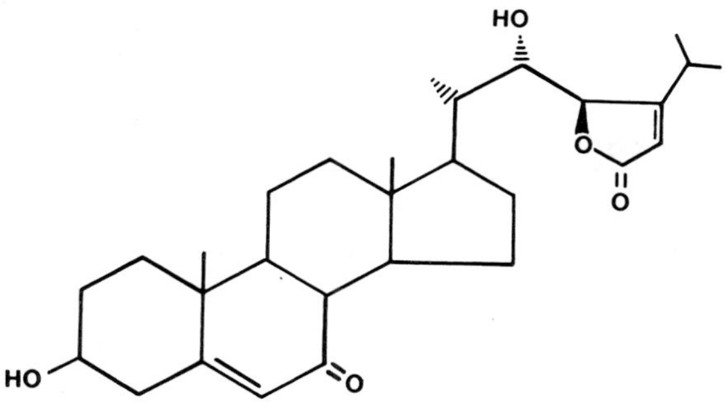

Antheridiol

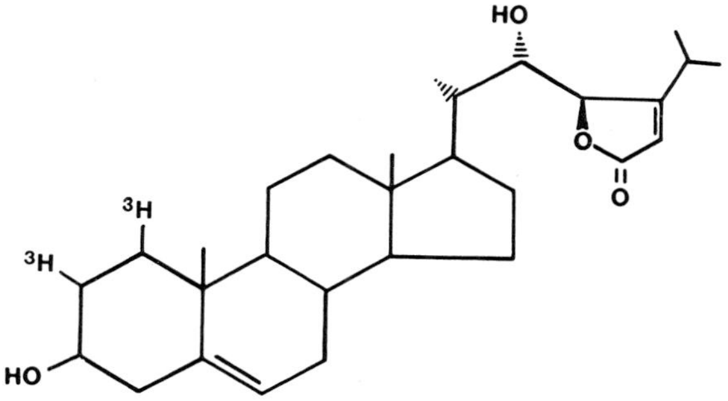

[1,2-³H]-7-deoxy-7-dihydro-Antheridiol

Figure 1. Chemical Structures of Antheridiol and the Tritium-labeled Analog Employed for Binding Studies.

for growth in aerated suspension culture at 24°C for various time periods. Mycelia were routinely harvested for study after 2-3 days of incubation except where described differently.

Preparation of fungal cytosol

The techniques for mycelial harvest and disruption are described in detail elsewhere (8). Because preliminary studies revealed that the antheridiol binding protein was unstable in vitro, considerable experimentation was performed to optimize the conditions and composition of buffers employed for homogenization and preparation of cytosol with optimum binding capacity. Preservation of cytosolic binding activity was highly dependent on the concentrations of sodium molybdate and mercaptoethanol in the homogenization buffer (8). Except where noted, most studies were performed using PM3 buffer consisting of 25 mM K_2HPO_4, 25 mM KH_2PO_4, 10 mM 4-morpholineethanesulfonic acid, 25 mM Na_2MoO_4 and 10 mM 2-mercaptoethanol, pH 7.5 at 0°C.

The mycelia were harvested by filtration, minced with scissors and added to PM3 buffer at a ratio of 1:4 wet weight to volume. Disruption of hyphae was accomplished by four ten second bursts of a polytron at the maximum setting while vessels were immersed in an ice/methanol slush. The homogenate was filtered through Miracloth (Calbiochem) and the filtrate centrifuged at 250,000xg for 1-2 hrs at 0°C. The supernatant was clarified by filtration (0.45 μ) and the resultant cytosol adjusted to pH 7.0 at 0°C. Alternatively, mycelia were frozen in liquid nitrogen, ground to a powder in a blender cup and thawed to 0°C in T buffer consisting of 100 mM KCl, 25 mM Na_2MoO_4, 10 mM 2-mercaptoethanol, 50 mM 4-morpholinepropanesulfonic acid, and 0.5 mM phenylmethyl-sulfonyl fluoride, pH 7.5 at 0°C. For some analytical procedures, the cytosolic binding activity was concentrated either by ultrafiltration using an immersible probe (Millipore Corp.) with a molecular weight limit of 10,000 or by precipitation with ammonium sulfate at 95% of saturation (8). The ammonium sulfate pellet was resuspended in a buffer consisting of 10 mM Na_2MoO_4 and 10 mM 4-morpholine-propanesulfonic acid, pH 7.0 at 0°C (MoM buffer) for further studies.

Analytical procedures

Radioligand binding assay. All steroid stock solutions were
stored at -20°C in redistilled ethanol and added to 12 x
75 mm disposable culture tubes immediately prior to addition
of sample. The final concentration of ethanol in the assay
volume was no greater than 1%. Incubation was routinely
performed at 0°C in an ice/water slush for the time periods
and at the steroid concentrations described in the legends to
the figures and tables. Unbound steroid was adsorbed to
dextran-coated charcoal over a 4-minute period after the
addition of a 200 μl aliquot of a dextran-coated charcoal
suspension (5% Norit-A, 0.5% Dextran T-70, 0.01% NaN_3) for
each ml of incubation volume and pelleted by centrifugation
at 2000xg for 4 min. The amount of bound tritium-labeled
steroid was measured in aliquots of the supernatant by liquid
scintillation spectrophotometry in Beckman Ready Solv-HP
cocktail at an efficiency of 33% determined by internal
standardization. Nonspecific binding was defined as the
amount of [^{3}H]-7dA bound in the presence of a fifty-fold
excess of unlabeled antheridiol. Specific binding was
calculated by subtracting the amount of nonspecific binding
from the total amount of [^{3}H]-7dA bound in the absence of
unlabeled antheridiol.

Determination of the steroid specificity of [^{3}H]-7dA
binding. The amount of [^{3}H]-7dA bound in the presence of
increasing concentrations of nonradioactive steroids was
determined to assess their relative binding affinities for
the receptor. Ammonium sulfate-precipitated receptor was
resuspended in MoM buffer pH 7.0 at 0°C and 1 ml aliquots
containing 280-320 μg protein were incubated in the presence
of [^{3}H]-7dA at a final concentration of 2.5 x 10^{-9} M.
Nonradioactive steroids were added at final concentrations
ranging from 1 x 10^{-11} to 1 x 10^{-5} M. The amount
of specifically bound [^{3}H]-7dA in the presence of each

Figure 2. Steroid-induced response of Achlya ambisexualis
male. Photographs (45x) were taken before (left) and 1.5 h
after (right) exposure to 1.2 nM [^{3}H]-7dA.

concentration of competitor was measured after 1.5 h of
incubation at 0°C. Relative binding affinities (RBA) were
calculated by determinations of the concentration of
competitor that reduced specific [^{3}H]-7dA binding to 50% of
the amount bound in the absence of competitor ($C_{0.5}$)
according to the equation

$$RBA = \frac{C_{0.5}\ 7dA}{C_{0.5}\ competitor}.$$

Sucrose density gradient sedimentation. Prior to layering on
gradients, the cytosol was concentrated approximately
six-fold by ultrafiltration using an immersible probe
(Millipore Corp.) with a molecular weight limit of 10,000.
[^{3}H]-7dA was then added to the cytosol at a final
concentration of 4 nM in the absence and presence of 200 nM

antheridiol. Sucrose was dissolved in PM3 buffer at pH 7.0
or in the same buffer without Na_2MoO_4 but containing 1 M
KCl and linear 5-20% w/w gradients formed. Aliquots of
concentrated cytosol (0.3 ml = 227 µg protein) and reference
proteins were layered on 4.5 ml gradients and centrifuged at
150,000xg for 16 hrs at 2°C. Fractions were collected from
the tube bottom with an ISCO fraction collector and the
radioactivity determined by liquid scintillation
spectrophotometry.

Results

The morphological response of an Achlya male mycelium to
exogenous [3H]-7dA is illustrated in Figure 2. The
photograph at the left was taken prior to exposure to
hormone. The photograph at the right was taken after 2 hours
of exposure to 1.2×10^{-9} M [3H]-7dA and shows the
extensive lateral branch formation induced by the steroid.
Additional studies have shown this radiolabeled analogue to
be biologically active at concentrations as low as 2 x
10^{-12} M. While it is not as potent as the natural
steroid (22), these results indicate that [3H]7dA should be
a very suitable ligand for receptor detection and analysis.

Our initial studies indicated that steroid binding activity
in Achlya cytosol was very low and variable. Therefore, we
tested a variety of conditions to optimize binding activity.
Sodium molybdate and a reducing agent such as mercaptoethanol
have been shown to be important stabilizing agents for
steroid receptors in general, and this was found to be true
for the Achlya system as well. Total exclusion of sodium
molybdate and mercaptoethanol from the method described for
preparation of the fungal cytosol resulted in an absence of
detectable binding sites. This requirement for Na_2MoO_4
in the buffer solutions is illustrated in Figure 3 which

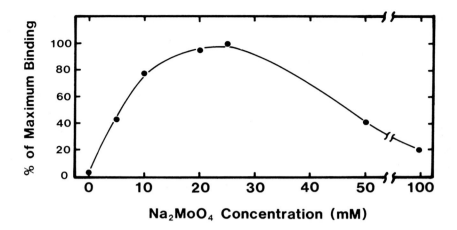

Figure 3. Effect of Sodium Molybdate on Specific Binding of
[³H]-7dA. The homogenate (●---●) was prepared as described
in Experimental Procedures and adjusted to the final
concentrations of sodium molybdate indicated on the abscissa.
Aliquots of each cytosol (1 ml = 595 g protein) were
incubated for 1.5 h at 0°C in the presence of 2 x 10⁻⁹ M
[³H]-7dA. Specific binding is shown as a percentage of the
maximum specific binding measured in the presence of the
optimum concentration of sodium molybdate. The mean values
(N = 2) for the maximum level of specific binding in the
cytosol was 15,303 dpm/ml.

depicts the results of adjusting the homogenate to contain a
range of Na_2MoO_4 concentrations prior to preparation of
the cytosol. Specific binding increased in direct relation
to an increase in Na_2MoO_4 concentration to an optimum of
25 mM Na_2MoO_4. Further increases in the Na_2MoO_4
concentration resulted in decreases in specific binding. In
contrast to the dramatic effect of Na_2MoO_4, the addition
of 5 mM, 10 mM and 20 mM mercaptoethanol resulted in
increased levels of cytosolic binding that were 93%, 100% and
98% of the maximum level, respectively (data not shown).

The total amount of [³H]-7dA bound at a constant protein
concentration was dependent on the pH of the buffer solution
but nonspecific binding was independent of the pH. Maximum
levels of specific binding were measured at pH 7.0.

Cytosolic specific binding expressed as a percentage of the maximum specific binding measured at pH 7.0, was 41%, 78%, 97% and 66%, at pH 6.0, 6.5, 7.5 and 8.0, respectively.

Figure 4A shows the results of incubating cytosol for 1 h at 0°C with a range of [³H]-7dA concentrations (0.1-4.5 nM). The level of nonspecific binding under these conditions was approximately 11% of the total [³H]-7dA concentration and ranged for 26-66% of the total amount bound. Saturation of the specific binding sites was achieved at approximately 3 nM with a plateau of specific binding at approximately 1200 fmoles/mg protein. Scatchard (23) analysis of the specific binding data in Figure 4A is shown in Figure 4B.

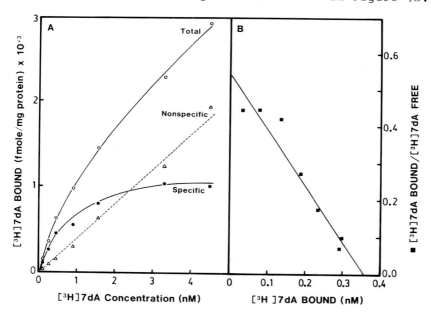

Figure 4. Amount of [³H]-7dA Bound as a Function of the [³H]-7dA Concentration in A. ambisexualis E87 Cytosol. Bound steroid was determined as described in Materials and Methods. (A) The amount of [³H]-7dA bound in the absence (o---o) and presence (△ --- △) of a 50-fold excess of unlabeled antheridiol and the amount specifically bound (●---●) calculated as the difference between the two. (B) Scatchard analysis of the specific binding data.

The mean equilibrium dissociation constant from 4 separate experiments was 0.73 nM $\pm$ .17 S.E. with a range of maximum binding capacities of 1100-2000 fmoles/mg protein.

Specific binding in the cytosol was destroyed by treatment with pronase or trypsin indicating that the binding site is proteinaceous. In addition, no specific binding of [^{3}H]-7dA was detected in cytosols prepared from cells of the female strain 734 of A. ambisexualis. Since females do not respond to antheridiol, these results indicate that the binding site has "target tissue" specificity. Thin layer chromatography of [^{3}H]-7dA extracted from male cytosol

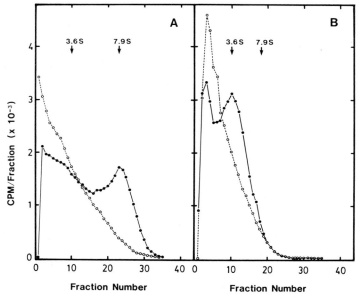

Figure 5. Sucrose gradient analysis of [^{3}H]-7dA Binding in Fungal Cytosol. Panel A: Sedimentation profile in low ionic strength gradients containing molybdate. Panel B: Sedimentation profile in high ionic strength gradients without molybdate. Symbols for both Panels A and B: (●---●) profile in the presence of [^{3}H]-7dA alone, (o---o) profile of [^{3}H]-7dA in the presence of a 50-fold excess of unlabeled antheridiol. Arrows denote fractions containing the peak level of radioactivity from [^{14}C]-ovalbumin (3.6S) and from [^{14}C]-aldolase (7.9S). Sedimentation was from left to right.

after 1 to 6 hours of incubation at 0-2°C or after 1 hour at
23°C revealed that no metabolism of [^{3}H]-7dA occurs
in vitro.

The sedimentation profile of [^{3}H]-7dA binding in sucrose
density gradients is shown in Figure 5. In low salt
gradients containing sodium molybdate, specific binding
appeared as a peak in the 8S region (Panel A). In the
absence of sodium molybdate and in the presence of 1 M KCl,
specific binding distributed as a peak in the 3.6S region
(Panel B). Additional experiments (data not shown) revealed
that an 8S form is observed when molybdate is in the sample,
but not in the low salt gradient. It was not possible to
test samples in the total absence of molybdate due to the
marked instability of the binding component. We have also
found that the bound steroid sediments at 3.6S in high salt
gradients (1 M KCl) in the presence of 10 mM sodium
molybdate.

The amount of [^{3}H]-7dA specifically bound in the presence
of various concentrations of nonradioactive steroids is shown
in Figure 6. Of the compounds tested, only antheridiol and
its analogs exhibited high affinity for the binding site.
The relative binding affinities, calculated as described in
Methods were as follows: 7dA = 1.0 (by definition);
22S,23R-antheridiol (natural pheromone) = 7.5;
22R,23S-antheridiol = 0.1 and 7dA-3-acetate = 0.03. A
significant inhibition of [^{3}H]-7dA binding by other
steroids and steroid hormones was detected only at
concentrations greater than 1×10^{-6} M. Some steroids
(e.g. cortisol and 7dA-3-acetate), at concentrations where no
competition occurred, were consistently found to enhance the
binding of [^{3}H]-7dA. The reason for this is unknown. One
possibility is that these steroids may increase the effective
concentration of [^{3}H]-7dA by reducing the association of

this hydrophobic compound with various components of the assay system.

When eluted from DEAE-Sephadex chromatography columns with a linear concentration gradient of KCl, bound [³H]-7dA elutes as a single peak at approximately 0.24 M KCl. The majority of cytosolic proteins (≅ 80%) do not bind tightly to DEAE and flow through the column or are removed by washing with

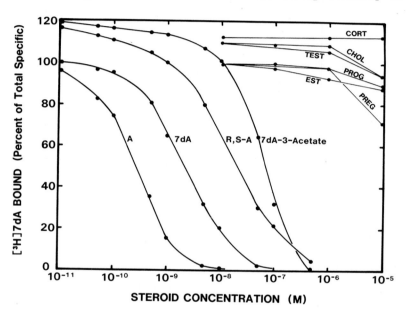

Figure 6. Specificity of [³H]-7dA Binding. Aliquots of the (NH₄)₂SO₄-precipitated receptor in MoM buffer were incubated in duplicate for 1.5 h at 0°C in the presence of [³H]-7dA at a final concentration of 2.5 × 10⁻⁹ M and increasing concentrations of the indicated steroids. The amount of [³H]-7dA specifically bound in the absence of any competitor (total specific = 15,500 dpm/ml) was defined as 100%. Nonspecific binding was determined as described in Experimental Procedures. Each point represents the mean value from two separate experiments. Symbols: A = (22S,23R)-antheridiol; R,S-A = (22R,23S)- antheridiol; 7dA = 7-deoxy-7-dihydro-antheridiol; 7dA-3-acetate = 7-deoxy-7-dihydro-3-β-aceto-antheridiol; Cort = cortisol; Chol = cholesterol; Test = testosterone; Prog = progesterone; Est = estradiol; and Preg = pregnenolone.

MoM buffer. The amount of $[^3H]$-7dA specifically bound per mg of protein is enriched approximately 7-fold after elution from DEAE columns with a dramatic decrease in the level of nonspecific binding (data not shown).

Gel filtration chromatography of the ammonium sulfate precipitated receptor on columns of Sephacryl S-300 was performed and each fraction of the eluate was assayed for $[^3H]$-7dA binding and protein content. The results of four separate analyses were similar. Specific binding of $[^3H]$-7dA was greatest at an elution volume corresponding to a K_{AV} value of 0.258. This K_{AV} value was fit to the linear regression line of the standard curve resulting in an estimation of a Stokes radius for the binding protein. The Stokes radius coupled with a sedimentation coefficient of 8.3S was used to calculate an apparent molecular weight of 192,000 by the method of Siegal and Monty (24). A summary of

Table 1. Physicochemical Properties of the Achlya Steroid Receptor

Sedimentation Coefficient	3.6S (High salt without Na_2MoO_4)
	8.3S (Low salt with $Na_2 MoO4$)
Stokes Radius	56.6 Å
Molecular Weight	192,000
Frictional Coefficient	1.5
Axial Ratio	8.9

Sedimentation coefficients were determined by centrifugation in sucrose gradients (5-20% w/w) prepared in PM3 buffer as described in Methods. The Stokes radius of the molybdate-stabilized (8.3S) form was determined by Sephacryl S-300 column chromatography in buffer composed of 100 mM KCl, 10 mM Na_2MoO_4, 20 mM 3-[N-morpholino] propanesulfonic acid, pH 7.0 at 4°C.

748

the molecular properties of the _Achlya_ steroid receptor is given in Table 1.

A very interesting aspect of the _Achlya_ steroid receptor system is the regulation of cytosolic receptor levels that can be achieved by alterations in the composition of the growth medium. A common method which we use for growing _Achlya_ in suspension culture involves the germination of asexual spores in PYG, a rich medium, for one day followed by dilution into a minimal medium (M1 medium) for a period of usually three days. This provides ample amounts of mycelia (about 18 g per 2-liter flask) with good binding activity and hormone responsiveness, as demonstrated above. Figure 7 illustrates the results of experiments in which the mycelial levels of cytosolic receptor were measured at 24-hour intervals during four days of growth in M1 medium (after one day of germination in PYG). Mycelia containing maximum levels of receptor after three days in M1 medium were transferred to an enriched medium (PYG) and the receptor levels were found to dramatically decrease. In contrast to this down-regulation of receptor, mycelia cultured in an enriched medium possess relatively low levels of receptor that can be increased by transfer and incubation in a nutrient-free salt solution (data not shown). Thus, the receptor levels in _Achlya_ show an inverse correlation with the supply of nutients. We have found that the visual response to hormone (Figure 2) is more obvious in cultures grown in a minimal medium than in an enriched medium. However, attempts to actually correlate binding and response have not been done and several factors in addition to receptor may be involved. The ability to manipulate receptor levels should prove valuable in future studies on receptor synthesis and regulation.

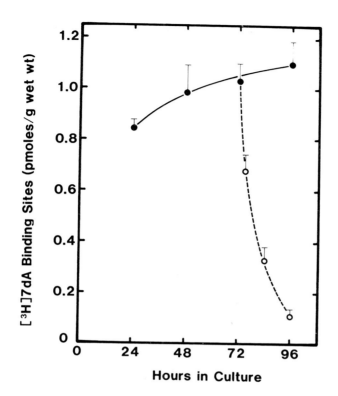

Figure 7. Mycelial content of [³H]-7dA Binding Sites.
Levels of binding sites (pmols/g wet weight) were measured at
24-hour intervals during 4 days of culture in Ml medium
(●---●). After 3 days in Ml medium, mycelia were transfered
to PYG medium and levels of binding sites measured at 3, 12,
and 24 h after transfer (o---o).

Discussion

The effects of Na_2MoO_4 in this fungal steroid binding
system deserve comment. Although the stabilizing effect of
Na_2MoO_4 on other steroid hormone receptor systems is well
documented (25-27), the presence of Na_2MoO_4 has not been
shown to be absolutely required to preserve binding activity
as observed in Achlya. In other systems, Na_2MoO_4 serves

to stabilize the steroid receptor in a nontransformed state
that does not bind to nuclei but retains the capacity to bind
hormone. This nontransformed state is commonly characterized
by a sedimentation coefficient that is larger (8 to 10S) than
that of the nuclear binding form of the receptor (3 to 5S).
A number of proposals regarding the mechanism of action of
Na_2MoO_4 on steroid hormone receptors have been made that
include either direct coupling to the receptor molecule,
inhibition of phosphatase activity or inhibition of protease
activity (26,27).

The mechanism of action of Na_2MoO_4 in Achlya is unknown
but may relate, in part, to inhibition of protease activity.
The Achlya binding protein is very sensitive to proteolytic
enzymes (7) and binding activity is destroyed by treatment
with pronase even at low temperatures. Since this organism
grows readily using complex protein as a main nutrient, it is
likely to contain an array of protease activities. Inclusion
of the protease inhibitors: phenylmethylsulfonylfluoride
(0.5 mM), leupeptin (10 µg/ml) or α_2-macroglobulin
(10 µg/ml) in homogenization buffers without molybdate did
not prevent the loss of cytosolic binding activity (data not
shown). Clearly, further research is required to define the
effect of molybdate in the Achlya steroid binding system as
well as in other systems.

It is also possible that molybdate interacts with the binding
protein directly and forms a stable or slowly dissociating
complex. With the avian progesterone receptor, the action of
molybdate is not diminished after extensive purification
indicating that it interacts directly with the receptor
protein (28).

In addition to the effects of sodium molybdate, the molecular
properties of the Achlya steroid binding protein are
remarkably similar to the molecular properties of the

well-characterized steroid hormone receptors of higher
organisms (25,27). It is an acidic protein with a molecular
weight of about 192,000 and it does not appear to be globular
since it has a frictional coefficient of 1.5 (Table 1). As
with other steroid receptors, the 8S form in cytosol can be
converted to a 4S form by high salt treatment.

Although the Achlya steroid binding protein and other steroid
receptor proteins are similar, the Achlya receptor is very
specific for fungal steroid ligands. The relative binding
affinities of antheridiol and its congeners are generally
consistent with their relative ability to induce sexual
morphogenesis in the Achlya male E87 (22). Also, the
affinity of [^{3}H]-7dA binding (Kd = 0.7 nM) measured
in vitro is consistent with our and other (22) observations
that the male E87 responds to a 7dA concentration of 0.24 nM
and the response increases within a 10- to 20-fold range
above this concentration.

As with other steroidal systems, the modulation of gene
expression is an early event in antheridiol action (10);
however, the existence of nuclear receptor forms has not yet
been tested in Achlya.

The present studies are of interest in light of recent
proposals regarding the evolution of cellular communication
molecules. Vertebrate hormones and their receptors have been
observed in microorganisms suggesting that these forms of
cellular communication might have arisen very early in the
evolution of eukaryotes and have been highly conserved (29).
To our knowledge, Achlya is the only fungal organism, and the
only primitive eukaryote below the insects, where a steroid
receptor has been described. However, recent investigations
by Feldman and coworkers have demonstrated the presence of
estrogen binding proteins in Saccharomyces cerevisiae (5),
and Paracoccidioides brasiliensis (6). They have also

752

identified a protein that binds glucocorticoids in <u>Candida albicans</u> (4). Unlike the antheridiol receptor, these binding proteins do not show a strong resemblance to steroid receptors in higher organisms. However, they are certainly of much interest in that they could be involved in the perception of environmental signals or they may represent evolutionary predecessors to steroidal control systems in higher organisms.

Because of its novelty, <u>Achlya</u> provides some unusual opportunities for investigation. The characterization of the antheridiol receptor is of clear significance to understanding the evolutionary aspects of steroidal control systems. Furthermore, the relative simplicity of this organism offers unique advantages for laboratory investigations on the mechanism of steroid hormone action.

References

1. Geuns, J.M.C.: Trends Biochem. Sci. 7, 7-9 (1982).
2. Callard, I.P., Klotz, K.L.: Gen. Comp. Endocrinol. 21, 314-321 (1973).
3. O'Day, D.H., Horgen, P.A.: Sexual Interactions in Eukaryotic Microbes, Academic Press, New York 1981.
4. Loose, D.S., Feldman, D.: J. Biol. Chem. 257, 4925-4930 (1982).
5. Feldman, D., Do, V., Burshell, A., Stathis, P., Loose, D.S.: Science 218, 297-298 (1982).
6. Loose, D.S., Stover, E.P., Restrepo, A, Stevens, D.A., Feldman, D.: Proc. Natl. Acad. Sci. U.S.A. 80, 7659-7663 (1983).
7. Riehl, R.M., Toft, D.O., Meyer, M.D., Carlson, G.L., McMorris, T.C.: Exp. Cell Res. 153, 544-549 (1984).
8. Riehl, R.M., Toft, D.O.: J. Biol. Chem. in the press.
9. Griffin, D.H.: in Fungal Physiology, pp. 286-291, Wiley and Sons, New York (1981).

753

10. Timberlake, W.E., Orr, W.C.: in Biological Regulation and Development, Vol. 3B, Hormone Action (Goldberger, R.F. and Yamamoto, K.R., eds.) pp. 255-283, Plenum Press, New York (1984).

11. McMorris, T.C., Le, P.H., Preus, M.W., Schow, S.R., Weihe, G.R.: J. Org. Chem. 48, 3370-3372 (1983).

12. McMorris, T.C., Sheshadri, R., Arunachalam, T.: J. Org. Chem. 39, 669-676 (1974).

13. Kane, B.E., Jr., Reiskind, J.B., Mullins, J.T.: Science 180, 1192-1193 (1973).

14. Timberlake, W.E.: Dev. Biol. 51, 202-214 (1976).

15. Silver, J.C., Horgen, P.A.: Nature (London) 249, 252-254 (1974).

16. Horgen, P.A., Iwanochko, M., Bettiol, M.F.: Arch. Microbiol. 134, 314-319 (1983).

17. Thomas, D. des S., Mullins, J.T.: Science 156, 84-85 (1967).

18. Horgen, P.A.: Biochem. Biophys. Res. Commun. 75, 1022-1028 (1977).

19. Griffin, D.H., Breuker, C.: J. Bacteriol. 98, 689-696 (1969).

20. Cantino, E.C., Lovett, J.S.: Physiol. Plant. 13, 450-458 (1960).

21. Barksdale, A.W.: Mycologia 62, 411-420 (1970).

22. Barksdale, A.W., McMorris, T.C., Seshadri, R., Arunachalam, T., Edwards, J.A., Sundeen, J., Green, D.M.: J. Gen. Microbiol. 82, 295-299 (1974).

23. Scatchard, G.: Ann. N. Y. Acad. Sci. 51, 660-672 (1949).

24. Siegel, M., Monty, K.J.: Biochim. Biophys. Acta 112, 346-362 (1966).

25. Niu, E.-M., Neal, R.M., Pierce, V.K., Sherman, M.R.: J. Steroid Biochem. 15, 1-10 (1981).

26. Housley, P.R., Grippo, J.F., Dahmer, M.K., Pratt, W.B.: in Biochemical Actions of Hormones, (Litwack, G., ed.) Vol. 11, pp. 347-376, Academic Press, Orlando (1984).

27. Sherman, M.R., Tuazon, F.B., Stevens, Y.-W., Niu, E.-M.: in Steroid Hormone Receptors: Structure and Function, (Eriksson, H., Gustafsson, J.-A., eds.) pp. 3-21, Elsevier, Amsterdam (1983).

28. Puri, R.K., Grandics, P., Dougherty, J.J., Toft, D.O.: J. Biol. Chem. 257, 10831-10837 (1982).

29. LeRoith, D., Shiloach, J., Berelowitz, M., Frohman, L.A., Liotta, A.S., Krieger, D.T., Roth, J.: Federation Proc. 42, 2602-2607 (1983).

THE RECEPTOR FOR 2,3,7,8-TETRACHLORODIBENZO-P-DIOXIN: SIMILARITIES AND
DISSIMILARITIES WITH STEROID HORMONE RECEPTORS

Lorenz Poellinger, Johan Lund, Mikael Gillner and Jan-Åke Gustafsson

Department of Medical Nutrition, Karolinska Institute, Huddinge University
Hospital F69, 141 86 Huddinge, Sweden.

Introduction

The receptor protein for 2,3,7,8-tetrachlorodibenzo-p-dioxin (TCDD), a
putative gene regulatory protein involved in the induction of specific
forms of cytochrome P-450, seems to share many characteristics with
steroid hormone receptors. The scope of the present review is to overview
and compare the present knowledge of the TCDD receptor to that of the
steroid hormone receptors. Topics for this comparison include current
models of gene regulation, physicochemical characteristics of the receptor
proteins, ligand binding specificities and receptor interaction with DNA.

Background

Steroid hormones seem to regulate the expression of specific genes by
their interaction via specific intracellular recognition sites, i. e.
soluble receptor proteins. In analogy to this endocrine model of gene
regulation, several lines of evidence indicate that intracellular, soluble
receptor proteins are essential mediators of the biological responses
produced by certain xenobiotics, i.e. halogenated or non-halogenated
polycyclic aromatic hydrocarbons (1, 2). TCDD is one of the most potent
agonists known today, both for these receptor-mediated biological responses and for receptor binding itself (2, 3). The chlorinated dibenzodioxins are formed as unwanted contaminants during the synthesis of
halogenated phenols. TCDD may accidentally be formed during the manufac-
ture of 2,4,5-trichlorophenol which is, in turn, used to synthesize the

herbicide 2,4,5-trichlorophenoxyacetic acid (2,4,5-T) and similar compounds (4). Furthermore, it appears that various polychlorinated dibenzodioxins, including TCDD, are formed as unwanted products during incomplete
combustion of organic chlorinated compounds (5). TCDD also seems to be a
remarkably persistent and metabolically inert compound (10) having a
half-life of more than 10 years in soil (11) and, furthermore, exhibiting
high biological availability after ingestion of TCDD-contaminated soil by
rats and guinea pigs (12). However, some metabolic alteration or biological degradation of TCDD has recently been reported to occur in vivo in
animals (10).

Investigations with laboratory animals have shown that TCDD and structurally related compounds, e.g. chlorinated or brominated dibenzo-p-di-
oxins, dibenzofurans or biphenyls, produce a similar characteristic
pattern of toxic responses (2, 6, 7). TCDD was shown to be the most toxic
compound of these congeners thus far examined and, furthermore, appears to
be one of the most potent toxic and teratogenic synthetic low-molecular
compounds known (2, 4, 8, 9). Thus TCDD serves as a prototype for these
toxic, structurally related halogenated aromatic hydrocarbons. Several
toxic lesions produced by halogenated aromatic hydrocarbons in the mouse,
such as thymic involution, cleft palate formation in fetuses, terato-
genesis, hepatic porphyria and epidermal hyperplasia and hyperkeratosis
appear to be mediated by the TCDD receptor (12, 14, 15). Furthermore, the
binding affinities of a large number of these compounds for the TCDD
receptor correspond well with the rank order of their toxic potencies (6).
Many of these quite characteristic lesions are reported to be relatively
species-specific and to occur in a limited number of species (4, 16). In
most species, however, administration of a single lethal dose of TCDD
leads to the same pattern of a prolonged "wasting" syndrome including loss
of adipose tissue and general debilitation of the animal leading to death
within a few weeks (2, 17). This extreme acute lethality of TCDD suggests
that TCDD is probably affecting some fundamental biological process within
mammalian cells. A very striking and consistent feature of TCDD-toxicity
is a depletion of lymphoid tissues in general and the thymus in particular
(18), an effect which closely resembles the effect of glucocorticoids on
the same tissues. It has also been reported that the induction of tyrosine

aminotransferase by dexamethasone can be inhibited by 3-methylcholanthrene and benzo(a)pyrene (19) - two well established ligands of the TCDD receptor (20-24). However, glucocorticoids do not compete with [3H]TCDD for TCDD receptor binding sites (20, 25-27), nor does TCDD compete for the glucocorticoid receptor binding sites (17, 23). Furthermore, adrenalectomized rats respond to TCDD with thymic involution (28) and no endocrine manipulation tested appears to have any effect on [3H]TCDD receptor binding in the rat liver (29).

Several endocrine effects have been described following exposure to halogenated aromatic hydrocarbons, e.g. lowered plasma concentrations of progesterone (30, 31), corticosteroids (32) and thyroxine (33), disturbances of the estrous cycle (30, 34) and impaired reproduction (30, 35).

One particularly striking and often studied biochemical effect produced by TCDD and related compounds is their potency to induce specific isozymes of cytochrome P-450 and the associated monooxygenase activity aryl hydrocarbon hydroxylase (AHH) (1, 36) together with several non-monooxygenase activities, e.g. UDP-glucuronosyltransferase, DT-diaphorase and ornithine decarboxylase (1). For chlorinated dibenzo-p-dioxin congeners, there exists a good correlation between their binding affinities for the TCDD receptor and their potencies to induce AHH activity in vivo (20). There also seems to exist a good correlation between the potency of these compounds to induce AHH activity and their toxic potency (2, 37). TCDD induced keratinization of a mouse teratoma cell line has been used as one in vitro model of toxicity (37). However, many TCDD receptor containing tissues in vivo and cells in vitro respond to TCDD with the induction of AHH activity but display no evidence of a toxic response (16, 38). A genetic model, where the TCDD receptor appears essential but not sufficient for the expression of toxicity has been proposed (15). In this model, two genetic loci are conceived: the Ah and hr loci, which determine the presence of the TCDD receptor and the expression of receptor mediated toxicity, respectively (15).

Gene Regulation by Steroid Hormones and TCDD - Level of Regulation

The synthesis of a wide variety of proteins has been demonstrated to be under hormonal control (39). For several of the genes encoding these proteins, the hormonal control of the observed alteration in gene expression has been attributed to the level of transcription, more specifically to an increased rate of transcription. This concept is, to a large extent, based on experiments where molecular cDNA probes were isolated from hormonally induced specific mRNAs and the radioactive cDNAs then used to quantitate specific mRNA levels, especially the kinetics of the induction process (40-42). The rapid hormonal induction of mRNA and the insensitivity of this response to inhibitors of protein synthesis have been taken as indications of a primary hormonal effect. A quantitative and temporal relationship between hormone-receptor complex formation, nuclear translocation and RNA induction have been taken as further support for this concept (40, 43). Also, sequences in the 5' flanking regions of hormonally regulated genes have been demonstrated to be required for the hormone responsiveness of these genes (44-55). As to the molecular mechanisms responsible for the hormone-receptor induced alteration in the transcription of certain genes, little is known. However, recent data from experiments where a glucocorticoid response element from murine mammary tumor virus (MMTV) has been inserted near originally hormone insensitive genes thereby rendering these genes hormonally controlled following transfection into glucocorticoid receptor containing cells (56, 57), may shed new light on this process and will be discussed in some detail later.

It should be pointed out that an increased rate of transcription after hormone administration is not the only mechanism proposed for the hormonal regulation of gene expression. Effects of steroids on the stability of mRNA molecules (40, 58, 59) as well as on protein-processing (60) have been proposed as additional mechanisms by which steroids may modulate gene expression.

Several studies have demonstrated that administration of TCDD or TCDD-like inducers leads to a large increase in translatable mRNA's encoding the TCDD induced cytochrome P-450 isozyme(s) (61-63). It has also been shown

by _in vitro_ nuclear transcription studies that this process reflects an
increased rate of transcription of the specific cytochrome P-450 gene(s)
(64-66) rather than an effect on mRNA stability - another plausible level
of regulation of gene expression (67; c.f. above). Nevertheless, the
latter mechanism cannot be completely ruled out in view of the limited
amount of data available. In cultured cells, it has been shown that
treatment with TCDD results in a large increase in the rate of transcription of specific cytochrome P-450 encoding RNA within 30 min (66). A
quantitative and temporal relationship between the nuclear accumulation of
the TCDD-receptor complex and the increase in synthesis of mRNA encoding a
specific form of cytochrome P-450 has also been demonstrated (68). Full
accumulation of mRNA also occured in the presence of cycloheximide (69).
Using variant hepatoma cells with specific cytochrome P-450 induction-re-
sponsive as well as induction-resistant phenotypes, it has also been shown
that the presence of a functional TCDD receptor constitutes an essential
component in mediating selective stimulation of the rate of cytochrome
P-450 transcription (66, 69). The rapidity of this induction is similar to
that observed with glucocorticoid activation of transcription of mammary
tumour virus (70). No specific data are available on the effect of TCDD on
cytochrome P-450 processing.

Current Models for the Mechanism of Action of Soluble Receptor Proteins

It is today widely accepted that specific intracellular recognition sites
are involved in gene regulation by steroid hormones and that all steroid
hormones act via a similar scheme (71, 72). This model was first proposed
by Gorski et al. (73) and Jensen et al. (74) and involves a) the uptake of
the hormone into the cell; b) the subsequent noncovalent binding of the
steroid hormone to specific, saturable and soluble receptor proteins; c)
an increased affinity of the hormone-receptor complex for the cell nucleus
induced by the receptor-ligand interaction itself. In this model, the
nucleus is believed to be the primary site of action and, furthermore,
cytoplasmic receptors are postulated to exist either occupied or non-occu-
pied by a steroid, whereas nuclear receptors are postulated to exist only
when occupied by a hormone. Recently, however, it has become clear that

several issues in this model, are somewhat controversial. Among such issues are e.g. a) the question concerning the intracellular distribution of steroid receptors in target tissues in the presence or absence of hormone (75-79); and b) the nature of the putative nuclear "acceptor" site of occupied steroid receptors (72, 79). Recent reports have indicated that, in fact, unoccupied steroid receptors may exist in a state of equilibrium between the cytoplasmic and nuclear compartment and that this equilibrium may be shifted in favor of the cytoplasm by manipulations such as tissue homogenization and subcellular fractionation (75, 76, 80, 81). Two independent studies using either immunohistochemical techniques (i.e. immunocytochemical staining using a monoclonal antibody against the estrogen receptor) (77) or cytochalasin B induced enucleation to obtain cytoplast and nucleoplast fractions from an estrogen responsive cell line (78) supported the notion that unoccupied steroid receptors predominantly reside within the cell nucleus. Based on these studies it was suggested that the classical "two-step" model for steroid hormone action requires some modification in so far as the steroid induced increased affinity of steroid receptor for DNA should be regarded as an intranuclear event, rather than as a step whereby cytoplasmic receptors are rendered capable of interacting with nuclear structures leading to a cytoplasmic - nuclear translocation.

It has been proposed by several authors that the unoccupied steroid receptor form with negligible affinity for nuclei, DNA or other poly-anionic resins may represent an oligomer of several steroid or nonsteroid binding entities. Not until after dissociation of this oligomer into a monomeric steroid binding form (for physico-chemical characteristics, cf. below), does the receptor exhibit a high affinity for nuclei or polyanions (82-84). This model, however, is based on observations in vitro and it remains to be proven whether it is valid for the situation in whole cells.

The nature of putative intranuclear "acceptor" sites for steroid hormone receptors has been the subject of intensive research efforts over the past decade (72, 85). Recently, however, reports that steroid receptors bind to specific DNA sequences and thereby enhance transcription of specific clusters of regulated genes (50, 52, 54, 86-98) have provided an attractive model to explain the extreme selectivity in protein induction by steroid hormones. This mechanistic model is particularly interesting in view of its analogy to the regulation of procaryotic genes by specific proteins, e.g. the lac repressor or the catabolite gene activator protein of Escherichia coli. Furthermore, certain features of procaryotic gene regulatory proteins - i.e. requirement of the ligand for DNA-binding and separateness of ligand- and DNA-binding sites - are shared by steroid hormone receptors (cf. below).

In analogy to the "two-step" model proposed for the mechanism of action of steroid hormones, an accumulation of TCDD-receptor complexes in the cell nucleus following occupation of cytosolic receptor sites has been reported by several authors (25-27, 99, 100). Furthermore, it has been suggested that transcription of TCDD-regulated genes requires nuclear localization of the TCDD-receptor complex (66, 68, 69). As is the case with the model for the mechanism of action of steroid hormones (cf. above), questions have been raised whether unoccupied TCDD receptors solely reside in the target cell cytoplasm as proposed in the "two-step" model of action (1, 2) or whether both unoccupied and occupied TCDD receptors reside within the nuclear compartment but in two affinity states for nuclear "acceptor" sites (101). In similarity to experiments carried out with genes regulated by steroid hormones, the identification of cis-acting regulatory elements within or near the specific cytochrome P-450 gene(s) should help to elucidate the nature of possible intranuclear target sites for occupied TCDD receptors.

Physicochemical Properties of Eucaryotic Soluble Receptor Proteins

Hydrodynamic Properties and Molecular Weights.
A comparison of available data on soluble receptors concerning even such basic characteristics as size and hydrodynamic properties is severely hampered by the great differences in experimental conditions used by different investigators. In addition, although a model for the struc-ture(s) of different soluble receptor forms extracted from mammalian tissues is beginning to evolve (102), virtually nothing is known about the

native form(s) of soluble receptors. Taking these limitations into consideration, it becomes necessary to define the basis for the selection of data for the comparison of receptors. In Table I we have selected data from the literature regarding the monomeric forms of soluble receptor proteins, preferentially from studies on purified preparations. Reports where inadequate precautions against proteolysis were taken, leading to registration of anomalously small receptor sizes, have been avoided.

As shown in Table I, the labeled glucocorticoid receptor, either in pure form or in crude cytosolic preparations, sediments as a 3.4 -3.7 S entity in hypertonic sucrose gradients (103, 104). During gel filtration, the glucocorticoid receptor displays a Stoke's radius of 5.6-6.0 nm (103, 104). This would imply an apparent molecular weight in the range of 85,000 to 96,000, a frictional ratio of 1.74-1.90 and an axial ratio of 15-20. These data appear to be confirmed by SDS-PAGE of either purified receptor preparations (103, 105, 106) or photoaffinity-labeled receptor in crude cytosol (107-109), where the molecular weights estimated range between 87,000 and 94,000.

In the case of the estrogen receptor, the monomeric form of the receptor sediments as a 4.2 S entity in hypertonic sucrose gradients (110, 111). If the incubation with ligand is performed at 20-37°C it appears that the ~4 S estrogen receptor forms a homodimer that sediments as a ~5 S entity (110). The Stoke's radius estimated for the monomeric form of the estrogen receptor ranges from 4.4 to 6.4 nm (110, 111) giving apparent molecular weights of 76,000 to 114,000. From these data it is possible to calculate frictional ratios of 1.45-1.84 and axial ratios of 8-20. By SDS-PAGE of the purified estrogen receptor its molecular weight was estimated to 70,000 (111).

Available evidence indicates that the progesterone receptor in chick oviduct (112-114) exists in the form of two subunits, A and B, whereas the progesterone receptor in rabbit uterus seems to exist as a hormone binding unit of one and the same size, not excluding, however, the possible existence of two subunits of equal size. The A subunit from chick oviduct sediments as a 3.6 S entity and has a Stoke's radius of 4.6 nm whereas the

B subunit sediments as a 4.2 S entity and has a Stoke's radius of 6.3 nm
(112). From these data, apparent molecular weights of 71,000 and 114,000
were calculated for the A and B subunits, respectively (112). It is also
possible to calculate frictional and axial ratios of 1.54 and 10 for the A
subunit and 1.81 and 15-20 for the B subunit. Due to the general availa-
bilty of a photoaffinity label for the progesterone receptor, R 5020,
extensive data is available on molecular weights as determined by SDS-PAGE
of the photoaffinity labelled receptor. These studies indicate that the A
subunit has a molecular weight of 79,000-80,000 and the B subunit a
molecular weight of 108,000-109,000 (113, 114). The rabbit progesterone
receptor seems to have a molecular weight of 70,000 as determined by
SDS-PAGE of a purified uterine receptor preparation (115).

The androgen receptor purified from rat ventral prostate sediments at 4.5
S in hypertonic sucrose gradients and displays a Stoke's radius of 4.8 nm
(116). These data suggest an apparent molecular weight of 83,000, a
frictional ratio of 1.41 and an axial ratio of 6-8. SDS-PAGE of the
purified androgen receptor indicated a molecular weight of 86,000 (116).
The same value was obtained when using a photoaffinity label for the
androgen receptor in the rat ventral prostate (117).

The vitamin D receptor, purified from chick intestine (118), has been
reported to sediment as a 3.3 S entity in hypertonic sucrose gradients and
a molecular weight of 68,000 was calculated from gel filtration experiments (118). From these data one may calculate a Stoke's radius of 4.9 nm,
a frictional ratio of 1.67 and an axial ratio of 12-15. SDS-PAGE of the
purified vitamin D receptor yielded a molecular weight of 55,000 (118).
Recently, higher molecular weights of 91,000 to 110,000 (119-121) have
been reported for the vitamin D receptor, a fact that the authors attribute to their precautions against proteolysis.

The data summarized above indicate that the monomeric forms of steroid
hormone receptors, during conditions minimizing proteolysis, exist as
components with sedimentation coefficients of 3.3 to 5.0 S, Stoke's radii
of 4.4 to 6.4, frictional ratios of 1.41 to 1.90, axial ratios of 6 to 20
and molecular weights in the range of 60,000 to 120,000. The frictional

Table 1. A comparison of hydrodynamic properties and molecular weights of soluble receptor proteins

Receptor*	Source	Purified	$S_{20,w}$	R_S	M_r,#	Frictional ratio¶	Axial ratio†	M_W††	Ref.
GR	Rat liver	Yes	3.4	60	85	1.90 §	15-20 §	89-94	103-105
	Human leukemia lymphocytes	No	3.7	56-60	90-96	1.74-1.83§	15§-20	–	106
	Rat hepatoma cells (HTC)	No	–	–	–	–	–	87-89	107-108
	Mouse lymphoma cells (S49)	No	–	–	–	–	–	94	109
ER	Rat uterus	No	4.2	44	77	1.45§	8-10§	–	110
			5.5	58	133	1.58§	10-12§	–	
	Calf uterus	Yes	4.2	64	114	1.84§	15-20§	70	111
PR	Chick oviduct A	Yes	3.6	46	71	1.54§	10§	79	112
	B	Yes	4.2	63	114	1.81§	15-20§	115	112

	Chick oviduct A	No	-	-	-	-	-	79-80	113
	B	No	-	-	-	-	-	108-109	114
	Rabbit uterus	Yes	-	-	-	-	-	70	115
AR	Rat ventral prostate	Yes	4.5	48	85	1.41	6-8§	86	116
	Rat ventral prostate	No	-	-	-	-	-	86	112
DR	Chick intestine	Yes	3.3	49§	68	1.67§	12-15§	55	118
	Chick intestine	No	-	-	99	-	-	-	119
TR	Mouse liver	No	5.7-7.5	60-75	196-245	1.40-1.67§	6-15§	-	21,25,68
	Rat liver	No	4.4-4.5	61-66	111-136	1.73-1.79	12-15§	-	23,123

* GR, glucocorticoid receptor; ER, estrogen receptor; PR, progesterone receptor; AT, androgen receptor; DR, vitamin D receptor; TR, TCDD receptor.

Calculated by using the equation $M_r = 424 \, S \, R_S$ (215), expressed in kilodaltons.

¶ Calculated by using the equation $f/f_o = 1.393 \, (R_S/M_r)$ (216).

† Determined from the frictional ratios, assuming the shape of a prolate ellipsoid (217).

†† Molecular weight as determined by SDS-PAGE expressed in kilodaltons.

§ These do not appear in the original work but have been calculated by using the equations above.

and axial ratios for these proteins imply a rather assymetric configuration and this is interesting in the light of reports suggesting that certain DNA binding proteins display similar assymetry (122). These authors speculate that this characteristic may explain the ability of these relatively low-molecular weight proteins to protect comparatively long DNA sequences in DNA foot-printing experiments.

Table I also presents comparative data on the physicochemical characteristics of the TCDD receptor. Data from our own laboratory indicate that the TCDD receptor in the rat sediments as a 4.4-4.5 S entity in hypertonic sucrose gradients, that it has a Stoke's radius of 6.1-6.6 nm, a frictional ratio of 1.73-1.79, an axial ratio of 12-15 and an apparent molecular weight of 111,000-136,000 (23, 123). The TCDD-receptor in the mouse has been estimated to sediment in the 5.7 to 7.5 S range in hypertonic sucrose gradients (21, 25, 68). Furthermore, Stoke's radii ranging from 6.0 to 7.5 nm have been described (ibid), and the apparent molecular weight has been estimated to be between 196,000 and 245,000 (21, 68). From these data a frictional ratio of 1.40-1.67 and an axial ratio of 6-15 may be calculated. However, in a recent study using identical experimental conditions for the rat and mouse TCDD receptor we were unable to detect any physico-chemical differences between the two receptors (23).

In summary, the hydrodynamic properties and molecular weights described for the different steroid hormone receptors show both similarities and dissimilarities; it is clear that the corresponding parameters estimated for the TCDD-receptor fall within this range of variation and that the TCDD receptor does not display any particular hydrodynamic property distinguishing it from the steroid hormone receptors.

Charge

DEAE-cellulose chromatography and isoelectric focusing are methods often utilized to assess differences in charge of proteins. Isoelectric focusing may be carried out in density gradients in columns, or more conveniently in flat-bed polyacrylamide gels (IFPAG). IFPAG-analysis requires considerably shorter separation times (2 h) than isoelectric focusing in

columns, thus receptor proteolysis and ligand dissociation may be minimized. In the following we have therefore, when possible, quoted data
obtained from IFPAG.

IFPAG-analyses have revealed apparent isolectric points(pI) for the
glucocorticoid receptor of 5 to 6 and 6.1-6.2 from human lymphocyte
cytosol (124) and rat liver cytosol (125), respectively. Similar pI-values
(5.9-6.4) have been reported for the estrogen receptor both in human
mammary tumor cytosol (126) and in rat liver cytosol (125). These data (pI
~6.4) were confirmed by isoelectric focusing in columns of a pure receptor
preparation from calf uterus (128). A pI of 6.2 has been reported for the
progestin receptor from rat uterus as well as human breast carcinoma
cytosol (129).

When the androgen receptor from rat prostatic cytosol was analyzed by
isoelectric focusing in sucrose density gradients the non-DNA-binding form
of the non-activated (c.f. below) receptor focused at a pH of 5.8, whereas
the DNA-binding form of the receptor focused at a pH of 6.5 (130). Chromatofocusing, a recently developed method for protein separation based on
differences in charge, has been used to estimate the pI of the vitamin D
receptor to 6.0-6.2 (131).

In the case of the TCDD receptor the apparent pI as determined by IFPAG is
6.0 in human lymphocyte cytosol (132) and 6.2 in rat liver cytosol (133).
At pH 7.2, the TCDD receptor from rat liver cytosol was reported to elute
from DEAE-cellulose at 0.2-0.3 M NaCl (23). DEAE- cellulose chromatography
at pH 7.4 has also been exploited to separate the DNA-binding form of the
rat liver glucocorticoid receptor, eluting at 0.06 M potassium phosphate,
from the non-DNA-binding form, eluting at 0.24 M at a pH of 7.4 (134).

In summary, steroid hormone receptor proteins seem to have isoelectric
points around 6. The same is the case with the native TCDD-receptor.
Limited proteolysis (135) is often used to improve the resolution of
soluble receptor preparations during IFPAG analysis. This treatment
affects the apparent pI of some receptor proteins (135). If subjected to
limited proteolysis, the apparent pI is increased for the estrogen

receptor of mammary tumours (126), is unaffected for the estrogen receptor from rat (127), and is decreased for the glucocorticoid (125) and TCDD receptor (133) from rat liver. It may be speculated that these differences are due to the loss of peptides with differing charges from different receptors. Both the TCDD and glucocorticoid receptors elute from DEAE-cellulose around a salt concentration of 0.2 M (23, 134).

Ligand Binding Specificity

Most of the information on the specificity of binding of steroid hormones to their receptor proteins has been derived from competitive binding experiments. In such experiments the affinity of an unlabeled competitor is estimated from its ability to displace a radiolabeled ligand for the receptor. The capacity of an agonist to elicit a biological response is not always directly correlated to its receptor affinity, since distribution factors, such as absorption, metabolism and plasma protein binding, determine the concentration of unmetabolized agonist available for receptor binding (136). It is thought that long-term retention of the agonist at the receptor sites, due to a low dissociation rate, is required for a sustained biological response (136)

From studies of substituent effects on the binding of adrenocortical hormones binding to the glucocorticoid receptor, it appears as the 3- and 20-oxo groups, and the 11- and 21-hydroxyl groups are essential for binding (137-139). Schmit and Rousseau (140) have studied fifteen glucocorticoid receptor ligands and concluded that the basic structure of ring A for high receptor affinity is 1α,2β-half-chair. Furthermore, it was concluded that the B and C rings are semirigid chairs, and that their conformation is not much affected by substituents. On the other hand, the receptor binding affinity may be affected by substituents in these two rings (142). The shape of the D-ring is critically dependent on the nature of the substituents. A 17-hydroxyl group reduces whereas a 17-methyl group increases the affinity for the receptor (141). Furthermore, these substituents influence the orientation of the pregnane side chain. However, the particular conformation of the side chain required for high affinity binding has not yet been established (142).

In a study of the thermodynamics of binding of 29 corticosteroids to the rat hepatoma cell glucocorticoid receptor, Wolff et al. (143) found that the changes in both enthalpy and entropy of binding decreased as the temperature was increased, which indicates that the steroid receptor binding mainly is of hydrophobic nature.

A phenolic ring seems to be a common feature of both estrogens and anti-estrogens, e. g. diethylstilbestrol and tamoxifen, respectively. Hähnel et al. (144) have suggested that the phenolic 3-hydroxyl group of estrogens is of greater importance for binding than the 17-hydroxyl group, although both are required for high-affinity binding of the estrogen receptor. Certain triphenylethylene derivatives hydroxylated in two of the rings have higher affinity for the estrogen receptor than estradiol, but it is not entirely clear how the hydroxyl groups of these ligands can be super-imposed on the hydroxyl groups of estradiol to depict common binding sites for these hydroxyl groups on the estrogen receptor (145).

Duax et al. (146) have found that the progestin receptor is able to bind a number of steroids with significant structural variations in the B-, C-and D-rings. The only structural feature that was common to all steroids with affinity for the progestin receptor was the 3-oxo-Δ^4 configuration al-though not all steroids with this structure bind to the receptor with a high affinity. Several of the 3-oxo-Δ^4-steroids with high affinity for the progestin receptor also had the 1β, 2α-inverted half chair conformation (146). These findings led Duax et. al. to propose that high binding affinity for the progestin receptor is due to a tight binding of the inverted A-ring to the binding site.

A relative flatness of the A-ring, as in 5α-reduced or Δ^4-structures, seems to be required for high binding affinity for the androgen receptor (147). A 17β-hydroxyl group also seems necessary for high affinity bin-ding, whereas structures with a 17α-hydroxy group are unable to bind to the receptor (147). A 3-oxo group increases binding affinity, but is not necessary (148, 149). 19-Nortestosterone binds with higher affinity than testosterone, a 17α-methyl group does not decrease binding affinity, and a 7α-methyl group further increases the binding affinity (147). Introduction of a 3,9,11-triene structure resulted in an increased binding affinity indicating that binding increases with increasing flatness of the steroid nucleus (150).

A problem in studies of the mineralocorticoid receptor has been the possible coexistence of mineralocorticoid and glucocorticoid receptors in mineralocorticoid target cells, since most ligands binding to one of these receptors also bind to the other receptor, albeit not with the same affinity (151). Because of this problem we have chosen not to discuss the properties of the mineralocorticoid receptor in this review. Fortunately, the problem of insufficient specificity of mineralocorticoid receptor ligands has recently been diminished by the synthesis of specific glucocorticoids, such as RU 26988, which do not interact with the mineralocorticoid receptor or corticosteroid-binding globulin and which may therefore be used to block the glucocorticoid receptor binding sites (152).

The B ring of the steroid nucleus is opened in the vitamin D secosteroids. In these, the 1α- and 25β-hydroxyl groups are reported to be the most important substituents for high affinity binding to the vitamin D receptor (153, 154). The binding is also reported to be sensitive to modifications in the A ring and the side chain (154).

The TCDD receptor binds TCDD with a high binding affinity ($K_d = 0.3 \times 10^{-9}$ M in mouse liver cytosol) (20). The TCDD receptor preferentially binds compounds known to induce microsomal AHH. These compounds are polycyclic aromatic hydrocarbons, e. g. β-naphthoflavone, 3-methylcholanthrene, benzo(a)pyrene, and chlorinated hydrocarbons, e.g. dioxins, dibenzofurans, and biphenyls (2). From studies of the binding of halogenated dibenzodioxins to the TCDD receptor it has become clear that at least 3 and preferentially 4 halogens in positions 2, 3, 7 and 8 are required for high binding affinity. The dioxin nucleus is not essential for binding since some other molecules, e. g. anthracene and biphenylene substituted with 4

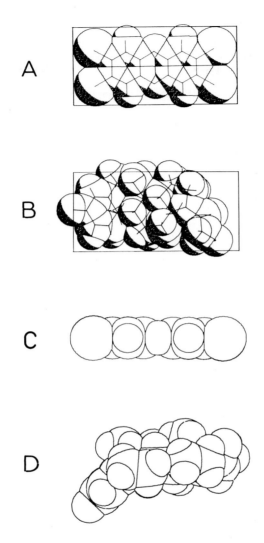

Figure 1. Plots of molecules with the van der Waals radii of the atoms
included. TCDD (2,3,7,8-tetrachloro-p-dibenzodioxin), top (A), and side
view (C), and budesonide (11β,21-dihydroxy-16α,17α[(22R)-propylmethyl-
enedioxy]-pregna-1,4-diene-3,20-dione) top (B) and side view (D).

chlorines at similar positions as in TCDD, also bind to the receptor with high affinity (6). Biphenyls chlorinated at similar positions as in TCDD binds to the TCDD receptor with a lower affinity than the corresponding dioxins (155). Planarity, or the ability to attain planarity, may therefore be a prerequisite for binding. It has been noted that these chlorinated ligands fit into a 3 x 10 Å rectangle where the centers of the chlorine atoms are situated in its corners. As pointed out (2), this concept does not account for the binding of unhalogenated ligands, like β-naphthoflavone, to the receptor. We have instead attempted to visualize the true three-dimensional space occupied by some receptor ligands. Therefore the molecular structures of these compounds were studied with a vector display driven by a VAX 11/750 computer running an interactive program using crystallographic data as inputs. All potent receptor ligands studied could be fitted into a rectangle of 6.8 x 13.7 Å, when the van der Waals radii of their atoms were included (156).

The affinity of TCDD for the TCDD receptor corresponds to that of steroid hormones for their receptors. To compare a high affinity ligand for the glucocorticoid receptor with TCDD, we have used the method described above to plot the (22R)-epimer of Budesonide (157), and TCDD (158) in two projections (Fig 1). Budesonide can be regarded as an analogue of triamcinolone acetonide, where the 9α-fluorine is replaced by a hydrogen, and the two methyl groups of the acetal are replaced by a hydrogen and a propyl group. It is evident that Budesonide fits quite well into the 6.8 x 13.7 Å rectangle. On the other hand, it can be seen that the overall thickness of the Budesonide molecule is considerably greater than that of TCDD (3.4 Å). The reason for this difference is that Budesonide is, due to its partially saturated structure, like other steroids, pleated, whereas TCDD due to its aromatic structure is planar. Since all known ligands of the TCDD-receptor are very lipophilic, it is probable that the main driving force for binding is of hydrophobic nature, as in the case of the glucocorticoid receptor (143).

It is interesting that the requirement for binding of chlorinated ligands to the TCDD-receptor is such that the chlorine atoms should be separated by certain distances, whereas the intervening structure is of less impor-

tance, as long as it is planar or may attain a planar conformation. This
structural requirement resembles that for ligand binding to the estrogen
receptor where hydroxyl groups separated by certain distances seem to be
required for binding, whereas the intervening structure appears less
critical. Furthermore it is interesting that planarity of ligands favors
TCDD receptor binding as is also the case with androgen receptor binding.
Steroid receptors exhibit some cross-specificity with regard to ligand
binding, especially in case of the glucocorticoid and mineralocorticoid
receptors. On the other hand, no steroid has yet been shown to bind to the
TCDD-receptor.

DNA-Binding Properties of Soluble Receptor Proteins

The interaction of steroid hormones and their receptor proteins with the
cell nucleus of target tissues is a presumed essential step in the mechanism by which these hormones modulate nuclear events such as gene expression (72). Nuclear steroid receptors may often be extracted from nuclei
with 0.3-0.6 M KCl or NaCl (73, 159, 160). The central issue about the
accumulation of soluble receptors in the nucleus is what defines a putative nuclear acceptor and/or biological effector site for these proteins.
Among the potential sites, DNA has been suggested to be of prime importance (72, 161).

The "nuclear transfer" phenomenon of steroid hormone receptors - in itself
a controversial issue, cf. above - is usually mimicked in vitro by the
addition of hormone to cytosol, followed by "receptor activation". This is
a poorly understood process in which the receptor is rendered competent to
bind to isolated nuclei or various nuclear target elements following
certain manipulations, such as prolonged storage, dilution, gel permeation
chromatography, warming, exposure to salts or precipitation by ammonium
sulfate (74, 160, 162-165). This process may involve a conformational
change of the steroid-receptor complex, resulting in the exposure of
positively charged regions on the surface of the molecule (166). After
"activation", the steroid-receptor complex displays an increased affinity
for both natural and synthetic polyanions including chromatin (128,

167-169), nucleosomes (170), purified DNA (166, 171-173), DNA-cellulose (174-177), RNA (178-180, phospho-cellulose (177, 181), heparin-agarose (111, 131), ATP-Sepharose (182, 183), carboxy-metyl(CM)-Sephadex (166, 184), sulfopropyl(SP)-Sephadex (166) and glass beads (166, 185). However, the overall K_d of the steroid receptor interaction with bulk DNA sequences has been estimated to only ~10^{-4} M (186).

Clearly, the DNA-binding property of steroid receptors seems to be physiologically significant. Yamamoto et al. (187) examined the differences in binding to DNA-cellulose of the glucocorticoid receptor from two mutant phenotypes of glucocorticoid-resistant S 49 mouse lymphoma cells in which the receptor appeared to be normal with respect to hormone-binding. One class of cells exhibited decreased nuclear binding (nt⁻) whereas the other showed increased nuclear binding (nt^i) of the mutant receptor complexes. The different nuclear binding properties of these receptors correlated well with their respective affinities for DNA-cellulose. A mutation affecting the polynucleotide binding domain of the receptor resulting in a glucocorticoid-resistant phenotype was suggested. The polynucleotide-binding domain was thus shown to be distinct and separated from the hormone-binding domain.

All studies on receptors associated with the nt^i-phenotype have revealed a molecular weight of the mutant glucocorticoid receptor of approximately 40,000 rather than 94,000 M_r characteristic of the wild-type receptor (109, 188, 189). Interestingly, α-chymotrypsin or trypsin cleavage of the 94,000 M_r rat liver glucocorticoid receptor leads to the formation of a 39,000 M_r fragment that retains both steroid- and DNA-binding activities (106, 190); like the nt^i receptor, this fragment binds with increased affinity to bulk DNA sequences (109, 187, 189). Accordingly, there seems to exist a third, non-steroid- and non-DNA-binding domain of the glucocorticoid receptor important for its biological activity (189, 191-193). Polyclonal antibodies raised against highly purified glucocorticoid receptor (194) have been used to detect and characterize this domain, which was shown to carry the main antigenic determinants (191). Furthermore, 40,000 M_r mutants of the glucocorticoid receptor as well as 40,000 M_r proteolytic fragments of wild-type glucocorticoid receptors lack this major immunoreactive region (194-196).

Limited proteolysis has also been used for the characterization of the progestin (198-203), estrogen (200, 204-208), androgen (209) and putative mineralocorticoid (200) receptors. Based on these findings and on studies performed on the glucocorticoid receptor, it has been proposed that all steroid hormone receptors may have the same basic structure (193): three protein domains separated by protease-sensitive regions.

It has been demonstrated that most classes of steroid hormone receptors (glucocorticoid, estrogen, progesterone and androgen receptors) have to undergo the losely defined process called "activation" (cf. above) in order to acquire affinity for polyanionic resins such as DNA-cellulose (160, 162, 165). Several molecular mechanisms leading to steroid receptor "activation" have been proposed: a) dimerization of receptor subunits (110, 176); b) limited proteolysis of "unactivated" receptor (204-206); c) conformational changes of the receptor molecule (138, 166, 210, 211); and d) the dissociation of receptor oligomers into constitutive subunits (82-84, 211). There has been some controversy regarding the existence of an "activation" process for vitamin D receptors, in part due to reports that both unoccupied (120, 212) as well as occupied (118, 212-214) vitamin D receptors readily interact with DNA-cellulose. Recently, however, it has been shown, by means of "mixing" experiments, that unoccupied vitamin D receptors exhibit a lower affinity for DNA than occupied receptors (120). The ionic strengths required to dissociate steroid hormone receptors from DNA-cellulose closely resemble those required to extract them from nuclear binding sites (i.e. ~0.1-0.5 M KCl or NaCl).

The concept that DNA may be an important component of genomic binding sites for steroid-receptor complexes is further strengthened by recent studies demonstrating selective binding of glucocorticoid and progesterone receptors to specific cloned portions of hormonally regulated genes (52, 54, 86-98). Several types of experiments have demonstrated that at least some of the cloned DNA-fragments that interact selectively with steroid receptors in vitro (89, 96) are capable of mediating hormonal responsiveness in vivo (46, 47, 50, 89, 97) leading to the formulation of the concept that these specific binding regions - subsequent to interaction with the receptor protein - might function as hormone- and receptor-dependent transcriptional enhancers (57).

It has been reported that less than 10% of protein-bound [3H]TCDD associates with DNA-cellulose without any preceding manipulations known to lead to "activation" of steroid receptors (123). However, upon incubation for 30 min at 25-37°C and/or gel permeation chromatography of TCDD-receptor complexes >50% of the specific [3H]TCDD binding in rat liver cytosol was retained on DNA-cellulose (R. Hannah, J. Lund, L. Poellinger, M. Gillner, J.-Å. Gustafsson, unpublished). DNA-binding of the TCDD-receptor required the presence of ligand, and limited proteolysis of the receptor by trypsin or α-chymotrypsin abolished the DNA-binding (123; Hannah et al., unpublished), in analogy to studies performed on the glucocorticoid receptor (190). The DNA-binding form of the TCDD receptor has, however, not yet been characterized. Furthermore, there is no consensus as to the nature of genomic target sites for the TCDD-receptor complexes (2, 68), and it remains to be established if the nuclear form of the TCDD receptor (cf. above) interacts with cloned portions of genes regulated by TCDD. There is also a paucity of data concerning the nature of the primary biochemical response to the "nuclear transfer" phenomenon of TCDD receptor-complexes. Clearly, further studies are needed in this field before any conclusions can be drawn about analogies between steroid receptors and the TCDD receptor as DNA-binding and gene-regulatory proteins.

Concluding Remarks

Apparently the steroid hormone receptors and the TCDD receptor share certain characteristics with regard to size, charge and DNA-binding. It is also thought that these soluble receptor proteins regulate the expression of certain genes in a similar fashion. However, to evaluate common features with regard to this receptor-mediated regulation of gene expression, further work is clearly needed on the interaction of both the TCDD receptor and steroid hormone receptors with regulatory elements of controlled genes. Such studies have been performed with the glucocorticoid and progesterone receptors (52, 54, 86-98).

In view of the many similarities between the the TCDD receptor and the steroid hormone receptors, it is tempting to speculate that the structural genes for all these receptor proteins have evolved from a common ancestral gene by gene duplication and subsequent divergent evolution. Based on DNA sequence homology such a concept has been proposed for certain subunits of an oligomeric steroid binding protein, the prostatic steroid binding protein (PSP) (218). Certain subunits of PSP have been shown to have amino acid homologies with another steroid binding protein, rabbit uteroglobin (219) and a common ancestor for these proteins has been suggested (219).

In order to test the validity of speculations regarding evolutionary relationships between soluble receptor proteins, the availability of a cDNA-probe corresponding to a portion of the rat glucocorticoid receptor coding sequence should prove extremely helpful (220). Using this cDNA probe it should be possibe to obtain the gene for the glucocorticoid receptor and perhaps also, by decreasing the hybridization stringency, to obtain the genes for other soluble receptor proteins.

Acknowledgements

This work was supported by grants from the Swedish Cancer Society and the Swedish Council for Planning and Coordination of Research. Dr. C. Cambillau (CRMC2-CNRS Campus Luminy - Case 913, 13288 Marseille, Cedex, France) is gratefully acknowledged for performing the computer supported plotting of the molecules in Fig. 1.

REFERENCES

1. Nebert, D.W., Eisen, H.J., Negishi, M., Lang, M.A., Hjelmeland, L.M., Okey, A.B.: Ann. Rev. Pharmacol. Toxicol. 21, 431-462 (1981).

2. Poland, A., Knutson, J.C.: Ann. Rev. Pharmacol. Toxicol. 22, 517- 554 (1982).

3. Kimbrough, R.D., ed.: Halogenated Biphenyls, Terphenyls, Naphthalenes, Dibenzodioxins and Related Products, 406 pp., Elsevier-North Holland, Amsterdam 1980.

4. Kimbrough, R.D.: CRC Crit. Rev. Toxicol. 2, 445-489 (1974).

5. Hay, A.: Nature 289, 351-352 (1981).

6. Poland, A., Greenlee, W.F., Kende, A.S.: Ann. N. Y. Acad. Sci. 320, 214-230 (1979).

7. Goldstein, J.A. In: Ref. 3, pp. 151-190.

8. Harris, M.W., Moore, J.A., Vos, J.G., Gupta, B.N.: Environ. Health Perspect. 5, 101-109 (1973).

9. McConnel, E.E., Moore, J.A., Haseman, J.K., Harris, M.W.: Toxicol. Appl. Pharmacol. 44, 335-356 (1978).

10. Neal, R.A., Olson, J.R., Gasiewicz, T.A., Geiger, L.E.: Drug. Metab. Rev. 13, 355-385 (1982).

11. DiDomenico, A., Silano, V., Viviano, G., Zapponi, G.: Ecotoxicol. Environ. Safety 4, 339-345 (1980).

12. McConnel, E.E., Lucier, G.W., Rumbaugh, R.C., Albro, P.W., Harvan, D.J., Hass, J.R., Harris, M.W.: Science 223, 1077-1079 (1984).

13. Jones, K.G., Sweeney, G.D.: Toxicol. Appl. Pharmacol 53, 42-49 (1980).

14. Poland, A., Glover, E.: Mol. Pharmacol. 17, 86-94 (1980).

15. Knutson, J.C., Poland, A.: Cell 30, 225-234 (1982).

16. Schwetz, B.A., Norris, J.M., Sparschu, G.L., Rowe, V.K., Gehring, P.J., Emerson, J.L., Gerbig, C.G.: Environ. Health Persp. 5, 87- 99 (1973).

17. Neal, R.A., Beatty, P.W., Gasiewicz, T.A.: Ann. N.Y. Acad. Sci. 320, 204-213 (1979).

18. Vos, J.G., Faith, R.E., Luster, M.I. In: Ref. 3, pp. 241-266.

19. Gayda, D.P., Pariza; M.W.: Carcinogenesis 4, 1131-1131 (1983).

20. Poland, A., Glover, E., Kende, A.S.: J. Biol. Chem. 251, 4936-4946 (1976).

21. Hannah, R.R., Nebert, D.W., Eisen, H.J.: J. Biol. Chem. 256, 4584-4590 (1981).

22. Okey, A.B., Vella, L.M.: Eur. J. Biochem. 127, 39-47 (1982).

23. Poellinger, L., Lund, J., Gillner, M., Hansson. L.-A., Gustafsson, J.-Å.: J. Biol. Chem. 258, 13535-13542 (1983).

24. Okey, A.B., Dubé, A.W., Vella, L.M.: Cancer Res. 44, 1426-1432 (1984).

25. Okey, A.B., Bondy, G.P., Mason. M.E., Kahl, G.F., Eisen, H.J., Nebert, D.W.: J. Biol. Chem. 254, 11636-11648 (1979).

26. Lund, J., Kurl, R.N., Poellinger, L., Gustafsson, J.-Å.: Biochim. Biophys. Acta 716, 16-23 (1982).

27. Poellinger, L., Kurl, R., Lund, J., Gillner, M. Carlstedt-Duke, J., Högberg, B., Gustafsson, J.-Å.: Biochim. Biophys. Acta 714, 516-523 (1982).

28. van Logten, M.J., Gupta, B.N., McConnel, E.E., Moore, J.A.: Toxicology 15, 135-144 (1980).

29. Carlstedt-Duke, J.: Cancer Res. 39, 4653-4656 (1979).

30. Jonsson, H.T., Keil, J.E., Gaddy, R.G., Loadholt, C.B., Hennigar, G.R., Walder, E.M.: Arch. Environ. Contam. Toxicol. 3, 479-490 (1976).

31. Barsotti, D.A., Abrahamson, L.J., Allen, J.R.: Bull. Environ. Contam. Toxicol. 21, 463-469 (1979).

32. Balk, J.L., Piper, W.N.: Biochem. Pharmacol. 33, 2531-2534 (1984).

33. Batomsky, C.H.: Endocrinology 101, 292-296 (1977).

34. Kociba, R.J., Keeler, P.A., Park, C.N., Gehring, P.J.: Toxicol. Appl. Pharmacol. 35, 553-574 (1976).

35. Murray, F.J., Smith, F.A., Nitschke, K.D., Humiston, C.G., Kociba, R.J., Schwetz, B.A.: Toxicol. Appl. Pharmacol. 50, 241-252 (1979).

36. Conney, A.H.: Cancer Res. 42, 4875-4917 (1982).

37. Knutson, J.C., Poland, A.: Cell 22, 27-36 (1980).

38. Knutson, J.C., Poland, A.: Toxicol. Appl. Pharmacol. 54, 377-383 (1980).

39. Dahlberg, E., Gustafsson, J.Å. In: Progress in Drug Research Vol. 29, in press.

40. McKnight, G.S., Palmiter, R.D.: J. Biol. Chem. 254, 9050-9058 (1979).

41. Palmiter, R.D., Moore, P.B., Mulvihill, E.R.: Cell 8, 557-572 (1976).

42. Hynes, N.E., Groner, B., Sippel, A., Jeep, S., Wurtz, T., Nguyen Huu, M.C., Giesecke, K., Schütz, G.: Biochemistry 18, 616-624 (1978).

43. Mulvihill, E.R., Palmiter, R.D.: J. Biol. Chem. 255, 2085-2091 (1980).

44. Ucker, D.S., Ross, S.R., Yamamoto, K.R.: Cell 27, 257-266 (1981).

45. Yamamoto, K.R., Chandler, V.L., Ross, S.R., Ucker, D.S., Ring, J.C., Feinstein, S.R.: Cold Spring Harbor Symp. Quant. Biol. 45, 687-697. (1981).

46. Lee, F., Mulligan, R., Berg, P., Ringold, G.: Nature 294, 228-232 (1981).

47. Huang, A.L., Ostrowski, M.C., Berard, D., Hager, G.L.: Cell 27, 245-255, (1981).

48. Renkawitz, R., Binetruy, B., Cuzin, F.: Nature 295, 257-259 (1982).

49. Fasel, N., Pearson, K., Buetti, E., Diggelman, H.: Embo J. 1, 3-7 (1982).

50. Chandler, V.L., Maler, B.A., Yamamoto, K.R.: Cell 33, 489-499 (1983).

51. Hynes, N., van Ooyen, J.J., Kennedy, N., Herrlich, P., Ponta, H., Groner, B.: Proc. Natl. Acad. Sci. USA 80, 3637-3641 (1983).

52. Renkawitz, R., Schuetz, G., von der Ahe, D., Beato, M.: Cell 37, 503-510 (1984).

53. Majors, J., Varmus, H.E.: Proc. Natl. Acad. Sci. USA 80, 5066-5870 (1983).

54. Karin, M., Haslinger, A., Holtgreve, H., Richards, R.I., Krauter, P., Westphal, H., Beato, M.: Nature 308, 513-519 (1984).

55. Dean, D.C., Knoll, B.J., Risen, M.E., O'Malley, B.W.: Nature 305, 551-554 (1983).

56. Ringold, G.M., Dobson, D.E., Grove, J.R., Hall, C.V., Lee, F., Vannice, J.L.: Rec. Prog. Horm. Res. 39, 387-424 (1983).

57. Yamamoto, K.R. In: Steroid Hormone Receptors: Structure and Function. Nobel Symposium 57 (H. Eriksson, J.-Å. Gustafsson, eds.), Elsevier, Amsterdam 1983.

58. Wiskocil, R., Bensky, P., Dower, W., Goldberger, R.F., Gordon, J.L., Deely, R.G.: Proc. Natl. Acad. Sci. USA 77, 4474-4478 (1980).

59. Brock, M.L., Shapiro, D.J.: Cell 34, 207-214 (1983).

60. Firestone, G.L., Payvar, F., Yamamoto, K.R.: Nature 300, 221-225 (1982).

61. Bresnick, E., Brosseau, M., Levin, W., Reik, L., Ryan, D.E., Thomas, P.: Proc. Natl. Acad. Sci. USA 78, 4083-4087 (1981).

62. Pickett, C.B., Telakowski-Hopkins, C.A., Donokue, A.M., Lu, A.Y.H.: Biochem. Biophys. Res. Commun. 104, 611-619 (1982).

63. Morville, A.L., Thomas, P., Levin, W., Reik, L., Ryan, D.E., Raphael, C., Adesnik, M.: J. Biol. Chem. 258, 3901-3906 (1983).

64. Tukey, R.H., Nebert, D.W., Negishi, M.: J. Biol. Chem. 256, 6969-6974 (1981).

65. Gonzales, F.J., Tukey, R.H., Nebert, D.W.: Mol. Pharmacol. 26, 117-121 (1984).

66. Israel, D.I., Whitlock, J.P., Jr.: J. Biol. Chem. 259, 5400-5402 (1984).

67. Darnell, J.E.: Nature 297, 365-371 (1982).

68. Tukey, R.H., Hannah, R.R., Negishi, M., Nebert, D.W., Eisen, H.J.: Cell 31, 275-284 (1982).

69. Israel, D.I., Whitlock, J.P., Jr.: J. Biol. Chem. 258, 10390-10394 (1983).

70. Ucker, D.S., Yamamoto, K.R.: J. Biol. Chem. 259, 7416-7420 (1984).

71. Gorski, J., Gannon, F.: Ann. Rev. Physiol. 38, 425-450 (1976).

72. Yamamoto, K.R., Alberts, B.M.: Ann. Rev. Biochem. 45, 722-746 (1976).

73. Gorski, J., Toft, D., Shyamala, G., Smith, D., Notides, A.: Rec. Prog. Horm. Res. 24, 45-80 (1968).

74. Jensen, E.V., Suzuki, T. Kawashima, T., Stumpf, W.E., Jungblut, P.W., DeSombre, E.R.: Proc. Natl. Acad. Sci. USA 59, 632-638 (1968).

75. Sheridan, P.J., Buchanan, J.M., Anselmo, V.C., Martin, P.M.: Nature 282, 579-582 (1979).

76. Martin, P.M., Sheridan, P.J.: J. Steroid. Biochem. $\underline{16}$, 215-229 (1982).

77. King, W.J., Greene, G.L.: Nature $\underline{307}$, 745-747 (1984).

78. Welshons, W.V., Lieberman, M.E., Gorski, J.: Nature $\underline{307}$, 747-749 (1984).

79. Gorski, J., Welshons, W., Sakai, D.: Mol. Cell. Endocrinol. $\underline{36}$, 11-15 (1984).

80. Walters, M.R., Hunziker, W., Norman, A.W.: J. Biol. Chem. $\underline{255}$, 6799-6805 (1980).

81. Walters, M.R., Hunziker, W., Norman, A.W.: Biochem. Biophys. Res. Commun. $\underline{98}$, 990-996 (1981).

82. Raaka, B.M., Samuels; H.H.: J. Biol. Chem. $\underline{258}$, 417-425 (1983).

83. Vedeckis, W.V.: Biochemistry $\underline{22}$, 1983-1989 (1983).

84. Sherman, M.R., Moran, M.C., Tuazon, F.B., Stevens, Y.-W.: J. Biol. Chem. $\underline{258}$, 10366-10377 (1983).

85. Thrall, C.L., Webster, R.A., Spelsberg, T.C. In: The Cell Nucleus, $\underline{6}$ (H. Busch ,ed.), 461-529, Academic, New York 1978.

86. Payvar, F., Wrange, Ö, Carlstedt-Duke, J., Okret, S., Gustafsson, J.-Å., Yamamoto, K.R.: Proc. Natl. Acad. Sci. USA $\underline{74}$, 6628-6632 (1981).

87. Mulvihill, E.R., LePennec, J.-P., Chambon, P.: Cell $\underline{28}$, 621-632 (1982).

88. Compton, J.G., Schrader, W.T., O'Malley, B.W.: Biochem. Biophys. Res. Commun. $\underline{105}$, 96-104 (1982).

89. Payvar, F., Firestone, G.L., Ross, S.R., Chandler, V.L., Wrange, Ö., Carlstedt-Duke, J., Gustafsson, J.-Å., Yamamoto, K.R.: J. Cell. Biochem. $\underline{19}$, 241-247 (1982).

90. Govindan, M.V., Spiess, E., Majors, J.: Proc. Natl. Acad. Sci. USA $\underline{79}$, 5157-5161 (1982).

91. Pfahl, M.: Cell $\underline{31}$, 475-482 (1982).

92. Geisse, S., Scheidereit, C., Westphal, H.M., Hynes, N.E., Groner, B., Beato, M.: EMBO J. $\underline{1}$, 1613-1619 (1982).

93. Compton, J.G., Schrader, W.T., O'Malley, B.W.: Proc. Natl. Acad. Sci. USA $\underline{80}$, 16-20 (1983).

94. Bailly, A., Atger, M., Atger, P., Cerbon, M.-A., Alizon M., Vu Hai, M.T., Logeat, F., Milgrom, E.: J. Biol. Chem. $\underline{258}$, 10384-10389 (1983).

95. Scheidereit, C., Geisse, S., Westphal, H.M., Beato, M.: Nature 304, 749-752 (1983).

96. Payvar, F., DeFranco, D., Firestone, G., Edgar, B., Wrange, Ö, Okret, S., Gustafsson, J.-Å., Yamamoto, K.R.: Cell 35, 381-392 (1983).

97. Pfahl, M., McGinnis, D., Hendricks, M., Groner, B., Hynes, N.E.: Science 222, 1341-1343 (1983).

98. Scheidereit, C., Beato, M.: Proc. Natl. Acad. Sci. USA 81, 3029-3033 (1984).

99. Greenlee, W.F., Poland, A.: J. Biol. Chem. 254, 9814-9821 (1979).

100. Okey, A.B., Bondy, G.P., Mason, M.E., Nebert, D.W., Foster-Gibson, C.J., Muncan, J., Dufresne, M.J.: J. Biol. Chem. 255, 11415-11422 (1980).

101. Whitlock, J.P., Jr., Galeazzi, D.R.: J. Biol. Chem. 259, 980-985 (1984).

102. Sherman, M.R., Stevens, J.: Ann. Rev. Physiol. 46, 83-105 (1984).

103. Wrange, Ö., Carlstedt-Duke, J., Gustafsson, J.-Å.: J. Biol. Chem. 254, 9284-9290 (1979).

104. Stevens, J., Stevens, Y.-W., Rosenthal, R.L.: Cancer Res. 39, 4939-4948 (1979).

105. Govindan, M.V., Sekeris, C.E.: Eur. J. Biochem. 89, 95-104 (1978).

106. Wrange, Ö., Okret, S. Radojcic, M., Carlstedt-Duke, J., Gustafsson, J.-Å.: J. Biol. Chem. 259, 4534-4541 (1984).

107. Nordeen, S.K., Lan, N.C., Showers, M.O., Baxter, J.D.: J. Biol. Chem. 256, 10503-10508 (1981).

108. Simons, S.S., Schleenbaker, R.E., Eisen, H.J.: J. Biol. Chem. 258, 2229-2238 (1983).

109. Gehring, U., Hotz, A.: Biochemistry 22, 4013-4018 (1983).

110. Notides, A.C., Nielsen, S.: J. Biol. Chem. 249, 1866-1873 (1974).

111. Sica, V., Bresciani, F.: Biochemistry 18, 2369-2378 (1979).

112. Schrader, W.T., O'Malley, B.W.: Cancer Res. 38, 4199-4203 (1978).

113. Dure, I.V., L.S., Schrader, W.T., O'Malley, B.W.: Nature 283, 784-786 (1980).

114. Gronemeyer, H., Harry, P., Chambon, P.: FEBS Lett. 156, 287-292 (1983).

115. Lamb, D.J., Holmes, S.D., Smith, R.G., Bullock, D.W.: Biochem. Biophys. Res. Commun. 108, 1131-1135 (1982).

116. Chang, C.H., Rowley, D.R., Tindall, D.J.: Biochemistry 22, 6170-6175 (1983).

117. Chang, C.H., Lobl, T.J., Rowley, D.R., Tindall, D.J.: Biochemistry 23, 2527-2533 (1984).

118. Pike, J.W., Haussler, M.R.: Proc. Natl. Acad. Sci. USA 76, 5485-5489 (1979).

119. Bishop, J.E., Hunziker, W., Norman, A.W.: Biochem. Biophys. Res. Commun. 108, 140-145 (1982).

120. Hunziker, W., Walters, M.R., Bishop, J.E., Norman, A.W.: J. Biol. Chem. 258, 8642-8648 (1983).

121. Kaetzel, D.M., Fu, I.Y., Christiansen, M.P., Kaetzel, C.S., Soares, J.H., Lambert, P.W.: Biochim. Biophys. Acta 797, 312- 319 (1984).

122. Biecker, J.J., Roeder, R.G.: J. Biol. Chem. 259, 6158-6164 (1984).

123. Carlstedt-Duke, J., Harnemo, U.-B., Högberg, B., Gustafsson, J.-Å.: Biochim. Biophys. Acta 672, 131-141 (1981).

124. Hansson, L.-A., Gustafsson, S.A., Carlstedt-Duke, J., Garton, G, Högberg, B., Gustafsson, J.-Å.: J. Steroid. Biochem. 14, 757-764 (1981).

125. Wrange, Ö.: Biochim. Biophys. Acta. 582, 346-357 (1982).

126. Wrange, Ö., Nordenskjöld, B., Gustafsson, J.-Å.: Anal. Biochem. 85, 461-475 (1978).

127. Wrange, Ö., Norstedt, G., Gustafsson, J.-Å.: Endocrinology 106, 1455-1462 (1980).

128. Molinari, A.M., Medici, N., Moncharmont, B., Puca, G.A.: Proc. Natl. Acad. Sci. USA 74, 4886-4890 (1977).

129. Wrange, Ö., Humla, S., Ramberg, I., Gustafsson, S.A., Skoog, L., Nordenskjöld, B., Gustafsson, J.-Å.: J. Steroid Biochem. 14, 141-148 (1981).

130. Mainwaring, W. P., Irving, R.: Biochem. J. 134, 113-127 (1973).

131. Simpson, R.U., DeLuca, H.F.: Proc. Natl. Acad. Sci. USA 79, 16-20 (1982).

132. Carlstedt-Duke, J., Kurl, R., Poellinger, L., Gillner, M., Hansson, L.-A, Toftgård, R., Högberg, B., Gustafsson, J.-Å. In: Chlorinated Dioxins and Related Compounds: Impact on the Environment., 355-365, (O. Hutzinger, ed.), Pergamon Press, Oxford 1982.

133. Carlstedt-Duke, J., Elfström, G., Snochowski, M., Högberg, G., Gustafsson, J.-Å.: Toxicol. Lett. 2, 365-373 (1978).

134. Sakaue, Y., Thompson, E.B.: Biochem. Biophys. Res. Commun. 77, 533-541 (1977).

135. Wrange, Ö.: Breast Cancer Res. Treatment 3, 97-102 (1983).

136. Raynaud, J.-P., Ojasoo, T., Bouton, M.M., Philibert, D. In: Drug design, Vol. 8 (E.J. Ariens, ed.), 169-214, Academic, New York 1978.

137. Baxter, J.D., Tomkins, G.M.: Proc. Natl. Acad. Sci. U.S.A. 68, 932-937 (1971).

138. Rousseau, G.G., Baxter, J.D., Tomkins, G.M.: J. Mol. Biol. 67, 99-115 (1972).

139. Ballard, P.l., Carter, J.P., Graham, B.S, Baxter, J.D.: J. Clin. Endocrinol. 41, 290 (1975).

140. Schmit, J.P., Rousseau, G.G. In: Glucocorticoid Hormone Action, (J.D. Baxter, G.G. Rousseau, eds.), 79-95, Springer, Berlin 1979.

141. Rousseau, G.G., Schmidt, J.-P.: J. Steroid Biochem. 8, 911-919 (1977).

142. Dahlberg, E., Thalén, A., Brattsand, R., Gustafsson, J.-Å., Johansson, U., Roempke, K., Saartok, T.: Mol. Pharmacol. 25, 70-78 (1984).

143. Wolff, M.E., Baxter, J.D., Kollman, P.A., Lee, D.L., Kuntz, I.D., Bloom, E., Matulich, D.T., Morris, J.: Biochemistry 17, 3201-3208 (1978).

144. Hähnel, R., Twaddle, E., Ratajczak, T.: J. Steroid Biochem. 4, 21-31 (1973).

145. Pons, M., Michel, F., Crastes de Paulet, A., Gilbert, J., Miquel, J.-F., Précigoux, G., Hospital, M., Ojasoo, T., Raynaud, J.-P.: J. Steroid Biochem. 20, 137-145 (1984).

146. Duax, W.L., Griffin, J.F., Rohrer, D.C., Swenson, D.C., Weeks, C.M.: J. Steroid Biochem. 15, 41-47 (1981).

147. Liao, S., Liang, T., Fang, S., Castaneda, E., Shao, T.-C.: J. Biol. Chem. 248, 6154-6162 (1973).

148. Dahlberg, E., Snochowski, M., Gustafsson J.-Å.: Endocrinology 108, 1431-1440 (1981).

149. Saartok, T., Dahlberg, E., Gustafsson J.-Å.: Endocrinology 114, 2100-2106 (1984).

150. Delettré, J., Mornon, J.P., Lepicard, G., Ojasoo, T., Rainaud, J.P.: J. Steroid Biochem, 13, 45-59 (1980).

151. Raynaud, J.-P., Ojasoo, T., Pottier, J., Salmon, J. In: Biochemical Actions of Hormones, Vol. 9 (G. Litwack, ed.), 305-341, Academic, New York 1982.

152. Moguilewski, M., Raynaud, J.P.: J. Steroid Biochem., 12, 309-314 (1980).

153. Wecksler, W. R., Okamura, W.H., Norman, A.W.: J. Steroid Biochem. 9, 929-937 (1978).

154. Procsal, D. A., Okamura, W.H., Norman, A. W.: J. Biol. Chem. 250: 8382-8388 (1975).

155. Poland, A., Glover, E.: Mol. Pharmacol. 13, 924-938 (1977).

156. Gustafsson, J.Å., Poellinger, L., Lund, J., Gillner, M., Hansson, L.-A. In: Banbury Report 18: Biological Mechanisms of Dioxin Action, (J. Blum, ed.), Cold Spring Harbor Laboratory 1984.

157. Albertsson, J., Oskarsson, Å., Svensson, C. Acta Crystallogr. B 34, 3027-3036 (1978).

158. Boer, F.P., Van Remoortere, F.P., North, P.P., Neuman, M. A.: Acta Crystallogr. B 28, 1023-1029 (1972).

159. Jensen, E.V., DeSombre, E.R.: Ann. Rev. Biochem. 41, 203-230 (1972).

160. Schmidt, T.J., Litwack, G.: Physiol. Rev. 62, 1131-1192 (1982).

161. Yamamoto, K.R., Alberts, B.M.: Cell 4, 301-310 (1975).

162. Grody, W.W., Schrader, W.T., O'Malley, B.W.: Endocrine Rev. 3, 141-163 (1982).

163. McBlain, W.A., Toft, D.O., Shyamala, G.: Biochemistry 20, 6790-6798 (1981).

164. Milgrom, E. In: Biochemical Action of Hormones (G. Litwack, ed.), Vol. 8, 465-492, Academic, New York 1981.

165. Schmidt, T.J., Barnett, C.A., Litwack, G.: J. Cell. Biochem. 20, 15-27 (1982).

166. Milgrom, E., Atger, M., Baulieu, E.E.: Biochemistry 12, 5198- 5205 (1973).

167. O'Malley, B.W., Spelsberg, T.C., Schrader, W.T., Chytil, F., Steggles, A.W.: Nature 235, 141-144 (1972).

168. Steggles, A.W., Spelsberg, T.C., Glasser, S.R., O,Malley, B.W.: Proc. Natl. Acad. Sci. USA 68, 1479-1482 (1971).

169. Simons, S.S., Martinez, H.M., Garcea, R.L., Baxter, J.D., Tomkins, G.M.: J. Biol. Chem. 251, 334-343 (1976).

170. Climent, F., Doenecke, D., Beato, M.: Biochemistry 16, 4694-4703 (1977).

171. Baxter, J.D., Rousseau, G.G., Benson, M.C., Garcea, R.C., Ito, J., Tomkins, G.M.: Proc. Natl. Acad. Sci. USA 69, 1892-1896 (1972).

172. Cake, M.H., DiSorbo, D.M., Litwack, G.: J. Biol. Chem. 253, 4886-4891 (1978).

173. Rousseau, G.G., Higgins, S.H., Baxter, J.D., Gelfand, D., Tomkins, G.M.: J. Biol. Chem. 250, 6015-6021 (1975).

174. King, R.J.B., Gordon, J.: Nature New Biol. 240, 185-187 (1972).

175. Yamamoto, K.R., Alberts, B.M.: Proc. Natl. Acad. Sci. USA 69, 2105-2109 (1972).

176. Yamamoto, K.R.: J. Biol. Chem. 249, 7060-7075 (1974).

177. Kalimi, M., Colman, P., Feigelson, P.: J. Biol. Chem. 250, 1080-1086 (1975).

178. Liao, S., Smythe, S., Tymoczko, J.L., Rossini, G.P., Chen, C., Hiipakka, R.A.: J. Biol. Chem. 255, 5545-5551 (1980).

179. Feldman, M., Kallos, J., Hollander, V.P.: J. Biol. Chem. 256, 1145-1148 (1981).

180. Chang, M.T., Lippman, M.E.: J. Biol. Chem. 257, 2996-3002 (1982).

181. Atger, M., Milgrom, E.: J. Biol. Chem. 251, 4758-4762 (1976).

182. Moudgil, V.K., Toft, D.O.: Proc. Natl. Acad. Sci. USA 72, 901-905 (1975).

183. Miller, J.B., Toft, D.O.: Biochemistry 17, 173-177 (1978).

184. Parchman, L.G., Litwack, G.: Arch. Biochem. Biophys. 183, 374-382 (1977).

185. Clark, J.H., Gorski, J.: Biochim. Biophys. Acta 192, 508-515 (1969).

186. Yamamoto, K.R., Alberts, B.M.: J. Biol. Chem. 249, 7076-7086 (1974).

187. Yamamoto, K.R., Stampfer, M.R., Tomkins, G.M.: Proc. Natl. Acad. Sci. USA 71, 3901-3905 (1974).

188. Yamamoto, K.R., Gehring, U., Stampfer, M.R., Sibley, C.: Rec. Prog. Horm. Res. 32, 3-32, (1976).

189. Dellweg, H.G., Hotz, A., Mugele, K., Gehring, U.: EMBO J. 1, 285-289 (1982).

190. Wrange, Ö., Gustafsson, J.-Å.: J. Biol. Chem. 253, 859-865 (1978).

191. Carlstedt-Duke, J., Okret, S., Wrange, Ö., Gustafsson, J.-Å.: Proc. Natl. Acad. Sci. USA 79, 4260-4264 (1982).

192. Stevens, J., Stevens, Y.-W. In: Biochemical Action of Hormones, Vol. 10 (G. Litwack, ed.), 383-446, Academic, New York 1983.

193. Vedeckis, W.V.: Biochemistry 22, 1975-1983 (1983).

194. Okret, S., Carlstedt-Duke, Wrange, Ö., Carlström, K., Gustafsson, J.-Å.: Biochim. Biophys. Acta 677, 205-219 (1981).

195. Okret, S., Stevens, Y.-W., Carlstedt-Duke, J., Wrange, Ö, Gustafsson, J.-Å., Stevens, J.: Cancer Res. 43, 3127-3131 (1983).

196. Westphal, H.M., Moldenhauer, G., Beato, M.: EMBO J. 1, 1467-1471 (1982).

197. Westphal, H.M., Mugele, K., Beato, M., Gehring, U.: EMBO J. 3, 1493-1498 (1984).

198. Sherman, M.R., Atienza, S.B.P., Shausky, J.R., Hoffman, L.M.: J. Biol. Chem. 249, 5351-5363 (1974).

199. Sherman, M.R., Tuazon, F.B., Diaz, S.C., Miller, L.K.: Biochemistry 15, 980-989 (1976).

200. Sherman, M.R., Pickering, L.A., Rollwagen, F.M., Miller, L.K.: Fed. Proc. (Fed. Am. Soc. Exp. Biol.) 37, 167-173 (1978).

201. Vedeckis, W.V., Freeman, M.R., Schrader, W.T., O'Malley, B.W.: Biochemistry 19, 335-343 (1980).

202. Vedeckis, W.V., Schrader, W.T., O'Malley, B.W.: Biochemistry 19, 343-349 (1980).

203. Hazato, T., Murayama, A.: Biochem. Biophys. Res. Commun. 98, 488-493 (1981).

204. Puca, G.A., Nola, E., Sica, V., Bresciani, F.: Biochemistry 11, 4157-4165 (1972).

205. Puca, G.A., Nola, E., Sica, V., Bresciani, F.: J. Biol. Chem. 252, 1358-1366 (1977).

206. Sica, V., Nola, E., Puca, G.A., Bresciani, F.: Biochemistry 15, 1915-1923 (1976).

207. Miller, L.K., Tuazon, F.B., Niu, E.-M., Sherman, M.R.: Endocrinology 108, 1369-1378 (1981).

208. Tilzer, L.L., McFarland, R.T., Plapp, F.V., Evan, J.P., Chiga, M.: Cancer Res. 41, 1058-1063 (1981).

209. Wilson, E.M., French, F.S.: J. Biol. Chem. 254, 6310-6319 (1979).

210. Samuels, H.H., Tomkins, G.M.: J. Mol. Biol. 52, 57-74 (1970).

211. Vedeckis, W.V.: Biochemistry 20, 7237-7245 (1981).

212. Pike, J.W.: J. Biol. Chem. 257, 6766-6775 (1982).

213. Franceschi, R.T., DeLuca, H.F., Mercado, D.L.: Arch. Biochem. Biophys. 222, 504-517 (1983).

214. Franceschi, R.T.: Proc. Natl. Acad. Sci. USA 81, 2337-2341 (1984).

215. Siegel, L.M., Monty, K.J.: Biochim. Biophys. Acta, 112, 346-362 (1966).

216. Sherman, M.R.: Methods Enzymol. 36, 211-234 (1975).

217. Schachman, M.K. In: Ultracentrifugation in Biochemistry p 239, Academic Press, New York (1959).

218. Parker, M., Needham, M., White, R.: Nature 298, 92-94 (1982).

219. Baker, M.E.: Biochem. Biophys. Res. Commun. 14, 325-330 (1983).

220. Miesfeld, R., Okret, S., Wikström, A.-C., Wrange, Ö., Gustafsson, J.-Å., Yamamoto, K.R.: Nature, in press.

SEPARATION AND CHARACTERIZATION OF ISOFORMS OF STEROID HORMONE RECEPTORS USING HIGH PERFORMANCE LIQUID CHROMATOGRAPHY

James L. Wittliff

Hormone Receptor Laboratory
Department of Biochemistry and
James Graham Brown Cancer Center
University of Louisville
Louisville, Kentucky 40292 USA

INTRODUCTION

Routinely, the analyses of estrogen receptors in biopsies of breast carcinoma are used as predictive indices of a patient's response to endocrine therapy. Reports from a multitude of investigators [cf 1-3] indicate that more than one-half of primary and metastatic lesions of the breast contain ten or more fmoles of estrogen receptors per mg of cytosol protein. Furthermore, 50-60 % of women with breast carcinomas containing estrogen receptors exhibit objective remissions to endocrine manipulation of either the administrative or ablative type [e.g., 1-3]. A summary of recent data is given in Table 1. Thus, more than one-third of patients presumably have breast tumors with only a portion of the cellular mechanism required to respond to hormonal stimulus. The association of estradiol-17ß with its receptor is merely the first step in the intracellular cascade of events necessary to exert the physiologic action of the hormone. The presence of the progestin receptor is now accepted as a marker that the estrogen response mechanism is intact (cf. 4).

As shown in Table 2, if the tumor biopsy contained both estrogen and progestin receptors, 78% of patients experienced objective remissions to endocrine manipulation (e.g. 2-4).

Molecular Mechanism of Steroid Hormone Action
© 1985 Walter de Gruyter & Co., Berlin · New York – Printed in Germany

Thus, both of these receptors may be considered predictive indices of breast cancer patients' response to hormone therapy.

Table 1. Relationship Between Estrogen-Receptor Status of Breast Tumor and Patient's Objective Response to Endocrine Therapy

Estrogen Receptor Status	
Responses/ER$^+$ Tumors	Responses/ER$^-$ Tumors
522/977 (53%)	36/567 (6%)

Adapted from the collective papers presented at the NIH Consensus Development Conference on Steroid Receptors in Breast Cancer. See reference (2).

Table 2. Relationship Between Steroid-Receptor Status of Breast Tumor and Patient's Objective Response to Endocrine Therapy

Steroid Receptor Status*			
ER$^+$/PR$^+$	ER$^+$/PR$^-$	ER$^-$/PR$^-$	ER$^-$/PR$^+$
135/174 (78%)	55/164 (34%)	17/165 (10%)	5/11 (45%)

Adapted from the collective papers presented at the NIH consensus Development Conference on Steroid Receptors in Breast Cancer. See reference (2).

*Number of patients responding to treatment/number of women with receptor status designated.

Recent studies with endometrial carcinoma suggest that the presence of the progesterone receptor in a tumor biopsy correlates with response to progesting therapy (e.g. 5-7). Our group (8) and the study of Mortel et al. (9) have demonstrated that the antiestrogen, tamoxifen, induces the formation of this receptor in uterine tumors. However some endometrial biopsies did not contain either the estrogen or progestin receptors suggesting a loss in the mechanism of endocrine responsiveness. Earlier our group (10) reported that normal endometrium was responsive to estrogen therapy in that both estrogen and progestin receptors were induced as an increase in the 8S specimen as determined by sucrose density gradient centrifugation. These data suggest a rational approach for developing therapeutic approaches in advanced endometrial carcinoma, which is consistent with present understanding of steroid hormone action in breast cancer (e.g. 3).

Current methods of assessing these hormone receptors in human tumor biopsies employ radioligand binding procedures usually with tritium labeled steroid hormones and analogs. The predominant assay used clinically is a multi-point titration analysis which provides a measure of the number of binding sites (specific binding capacity expressed as fmol/mg cytosol protein) and of the affinity constant of the steroid receptor complex often given as the Kd value. Procedures used in the clinical chemistry laboratory assess the presence of unoccupied estrogen-binding site in the cytosol (cell sap) of a tissue but provide no estimation of the biological integrity of the receptor.

For more than a decade, our laboratory has attempted to define each of the events initiated by interaction of estradiol-17ß with a target cell leading to the characteristic response of mammary gland differentiation and growth [e.g., 10-21]. It is our goal to discern defects in certain intracellular reactions of estrogen-receptor complexes that may explain the molecular basis of unresponsiveness in breast cancer patients with tumors containing estrogen receptors.

MULTIPLE FORMS OF STEROID HORMONE RECEPTORS

It is clear that steroid hormones are associated specifically
with a variety of components in extracts of endocrine target
organs. However, a central question relates to the origin of
these multiple forms of receptors and their physiologic
significance. We have been proponents of the view that there
are distinct physiologic species of estrogen receptors in
breast tissues [e.g., 16,17], in addition to steroid binding
componnents observed in cytosol preparations that may have
arisen due to proteolytic cleavage, as suggested by Sherman
and co-workers [22]. In contrast to our hypotheses, others
favor the idea that the 8S and 4S forms of estrogen receptors
identified on sucrose gradients may be artifacts from
degradation of the "native" species. Presumably this occurs
during homogenization, prolonged incubation, and
centrifugation. However to our knowledge, no one has provided
conclusive evidence of the "native" state of the estrogen
receptors in target cells.

Our laboratory has presented evidence that the larger
molecular weight species (8S) of the estrogen receptor as
defined by sucrose density centrifugation (Table 3), is a
predictive index of an endocrine responsive breast cancer
patient (e.g. 3, 16, 17). However, the appearance of the 4S
species alone was associated with a lower response rate to
hormone therapy (16,17) which was confirmed by McCarty et al.
(23). Recently, others (24) have suggested that the
concentration of the 8S form of the progestin receptor
measured by density gradient centrifugation using vertical
tube rotors (25) is a better indicator of disease-free
survival by breast cancer patients given adjuvant therapy.
These data and the earlier report Knight et al., (26) indicate
that steroid hormone receptors are prognostic indices as well.
Results from the NSABP adjuvant trials (27) also indicated a
relationship between an increase in both estrogen and

progestin levels and increased disease free survival in breast
cancer patients given tamoxifen and cytotoxic chemotherapy in
the adjuvant setting.

**Table 3. Relationship Between Patient Response to Endocrine
Therapy and Presence of Estrogen Receptor in Tumor Biopsy**

Therapy	Objective Remissions According to Estrogen-Receptor Species in Tumor		
	8S or 8S and 4S	4S	Undetectable
Hormone Adminstration	16/23	3/15	0/33
Endocrine organ ablation	17/21	1/8	0/11
Total	33/44	4/23	0/44

Adapted from Wittliff et al. (16).

*Nine additional patients exhibited remissions but had
   unclassified ER-positive tumors; five responded to
   estrogen, three to androgen therapy and one to
   oöphorectomy.

To circumvent the problem of prolonged manipulation of
receptor preparations, we developed the use of high
performance liquid chromatography in size exclusion (HPSEC),
ion-exchange (HPIEC) and chromatofocusing (HPCF) modes for the
rapid separation of isoforms of these receptors (e.g. 17-21).
Receptor isoforms are defined as protein components in a
target organ which exhibit a high ligand binding affinity and
specificity for a single class of steroid hormones (e.g.
estrogens) and may be identified based upon characteristics of
size, shape, and surface ionic properties.

With regard for other investigators who have either developed
or applied techniques and instruments for HPLC analyses of
steroid hormone receptor determinations, this paper will be
largely an account of the Hormone Receptor Laboratory at the
University of Louisville.

Preparation of Cytosols and Receptor Binding Reactions

All procedures were carried out at 0-4°. Tissues or frozen powders were homogenized using a Brinkman Polytron (two ten-sec bursts) in 2-4 volumes of Tris homogenization buffer (10 m$\underline{M}$ Tris-HCl, 1.5 mM EDTA, 10% glycerol, 10 mM monothioglycerol, pH 7.4 at 4°C) with or without 10 mM sodium molybdate (e.g. 18 more recent studies have employed phosphate buffers (e.g. 21). A thorough discussion of buffers and other conditions related to receptor characterization is given in a recent review of our investigations (28). Cytosols were prepared by centrifugation of the homogenates for 30-60 min at 40,000 rpm in a Beckman Ti 70.1 rotor. In certain cases, the supernatant lipid which appeared as a cap was separated from the cytosol layer.

Since the receptor is present in cytosol in very low amounts, its detection depends upon the formation of complex with its specific ligand, estradiol-17ß. To this end, the cytosols for HPLC studies of estrogen receptors were incubated at 4°C for 4-24 hr with 1-3 nM [16α-^{125}I]iodoestradiol-17ß in the presence (non-specific binding) or absence (total binding) of a 200-fold molar excess of an unlabeled competitor, such as diethylstilbestrol. For identification of progestin receptors using HPLC (29), the ligands, [^{3}H]R5020 and [^{3}H]ORG-2058 were employed. The incubations were terminated by removing unbound steroid with a pellet derived from an equal volume of a 1% dextran-coated charcoal suspension (1% charcoal, 0.5% dextran). The labeled cytosol was applied to the charcoal pellet, mixed briefly, allowed to stand for 5-10 min and then centrifuged at 600 xg for 5-10 min to sediment the dextran-coated charcoal. Cytosol protein concentrations were determined by the methods of Waddell or Bradford. Specific binding capacity was expressed as femtomoles of steroid bound per milligram of cytosol protein.

HIGH PERFORMANCE SIZE EXCLUSION CHROMATOGRAPHY (HPSEC)

All chromatography was performed in a cold room (0-5°)
utilizing the Spherogel TSK-3000SW size exclusion column (7.5
x 700 mm) with a Beckman Model 322 HPLC system equipped with
an in-line Hitachi Model 100-40 spectrophotometer (17,20).
The chromatographic column was comprised of two units, a short
(7.5 x 100 mm) TSK 3000SW guard column and, immediately
downstream, the longer (7.5 x 600 mm) TSK3000SW size exclusion
column. Reactions were applied in 20 to 250 µl volumes using
a Hamilton syringe and the Model 210 Sample Injection Valve.
Essentially no difference in resolution was noted when
injection volumes of 20 to 250µl and protein concentrations of
2 - 12 mg/ml were used. An additional aliquot was taken at
this time to estimate specific binding capacity and recovery.
The elution buffers were either TEGK$_{100}$ (10 mM Tris-HCl, pH
7.4 at 4°, 1.5 mM EDTA, 10% (v/v) glycerol, 100 mM KCl) or
PEGK$_{100}$ (25 mM sodium phosphate, pH 7.4 at 4° containing 1.5
mM EDTA, 10% (v/v) glycerol and 100 mM KCl). The PEGK$_{100}$ and
TEGK$_{100}$ buffers gave similar results on the HPSEC when used
for incubation and elution. All buffers were filtered
utilizing a 0.45 µm filter (Millipore Corp.). Elution was
carried out at a flow rate of 0.7 ml/min. Column effluent was
collected as either 0.5 or 1 min fractions. Following a day
of chromatography, the entire column was washed overnight with
filtered, distilled, deionized water. The entire column was
washed weekly with a filtered solution of 15% DMSO in methanol
whereas the TSK3000 SW guard column was washed periodically
with a solution of 6 M urea. The chromatography system was
stored in filtered, distilled, deionized water.

Most of our experiments have employed the TSK2000 SW, TSK3000
SW and TSK4000 SW columns manufactured by Toya Soda (supplied
by Altex/Beckman). The TSK3000 SW column quickly separates
estrogen receptor isoforms in cytosol from calf and human
uterus (Fig. 1). We have also separated receptor isoforms in

cytosols from human breast carcinomas as well as lactating mammary glands of rats and rabbit endometrial carcinoma (17,19,20). The size isoforms in the breast cancer exhibited stokes radii of 61A and 29-32A (20) identical to those of human uterus (Fig. 1). The principal estrogen receptor isoform in lactating mammary gland also gave a Stoke's radius of 61A although there was evidence of receptor heterogeneity by HPCF (18) to be discussed shortly. In contrast, the Stoke's radius of the estrogen receptor in rabbit endometrial carcinoma was 71A (19). To extend the versatility of the HPSEC columns, we recommend that they be used in series with various combinations (e.g. TSK4000 SW, then TSK3000 SW) to accommodate the receptor in question (28).

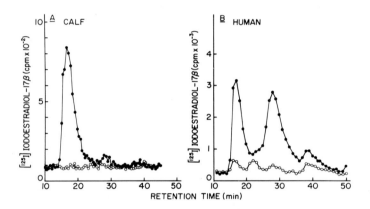

Fig. 1. Separation of estrogen receptor isoforms from uterine tissues by HPSEC. Cytosol was prepared from calf (A) or human (B) uterus and incubated with 5nM [^{125}I]iodoestradiol-17ß in the presence (O) or absence (●) of excess diethylstilbestrol. Aliquots of each reaction were cleared of unbound ligand with dextran-coated charcoal, applied to the TSK3000 SW column, and eluted using a Tris buffer fortified with 100 mM KCl. Reprinted from Wiehle et al., (20).

Preparations of monoclonal antibodies of the IgG class interact specifically with the estrogen receptor of various species (30). The receptor is not precipitated , but alters the sedimentation behavior of the receptor on sucrose density

gradient centrufugation. In particular, the D547 preparation
(provided courtesy of Drs. E.V. Jensen and G.L. Greene)
associated with **4S** isoforms of the estrogen receptor from
human breast cancer, which were extracted, then adjusted to
400 mM KCl. The resulting complex could be detected easily on
sucrose density gradients as a large molecular weight species
(Fig. 2). A similar shift in size was detected by HPSEC on
the TSK4000 SW column (Fig. 3). Interestingly, in addition to
the expected high molecular weight complex of antibody and
receptor, other complexes of greater size were detected. It
was also noted, a portion of the **4S** species did not react with
D547 monoclonal antibody. From studies in our laboratory (cf.
28) we suggest that caution must be observed in using
monoclonal antibodies in clinical assays, since certain
antigenic determinants may be either unrecognized or
inaccessible. The demonstration that receptors exhibit
polymorphism predicts a battery of monoclonal antibodies will
be necessary to measure estrogen receptors in a clinically
valid fashion.

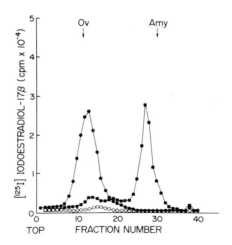

Fig. 2. **Influence of D547 monoclonal antibody on the**
sedimentation properties of the estrogen receptor on sucrose

density gradients. The estrogen receptor was extracted from human breast cancer and incubated with [^{125}I]iodoestradiol-17ß in the presence (O) or absence (●) of diethylstilbestrol. The incubate was adjusted to a final concentration of 400 mM KCl. Portions of the incubates were applied to 5-20% high salt (400 mM) sucrose density gradients. Ovalbumin (Ov) and Amulase (Amy) were applied as internal markers. The reactions incubated with nonimmune preparations (●,O) sedimented near ovalbumin while that reacted with D547 (■) sedimented in the region of amylase. Taken from (28).

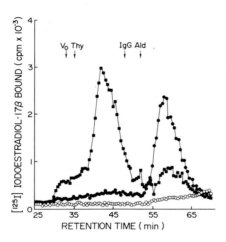

Fig. 3. Influence of D547 monoclonal antibody on the size of the estrogen receptor on HPSEC. The estrogen receptor was extracted from human breast cancer and incubated as described in Fig. 2. Portions of the incubate were separated on a TSK4000 SW column after treatment with non-receptor-reactive antibody (●,O) or with D547 monoclonal antibody (■) using Tris Buffer fortified with 400 mM KCl. Various marker proteins were separated as indicated: thyroglobulin (thy), human gammaglobulin (IgG) and aldolase (Ald). Blue Dextran was used to estimate the void volume (Vo). Taken from (28).

We have also utilized HPSEC to study the size isoforms o the progestin receptor (29) in human uterus and breast carcinoma. Both 30 cm TSK3000 SW as well as longer 60 cm columns have been employed. On the shorter column, receptor-bound ligand appeared as two peaks, using either [^{3}H]R5020 or [^{3}H]Org-2058 (Fig. 4). The primary peak associating specifically with R5020 appeared consistently between fractions 30 and 35 in many uterine cytosols (Fig. 4B). This receptor isoform represented the majority (>70%) of specific binding applied to the column. Recoveries on the 30 cm TSK3000 SW columns were consistently 87 to 93%. Column calibration with marker proteins suggested this component to be a very large species of >80°A.

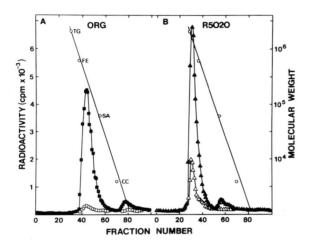

Fig. 4 Separation of progestin receptor isoforms from human uterus using HPSEC. Labeled cytosolic proteins were applied to and eluted from a 30 cm TSK3000 SW column as described (29). Progestin receptors labeled with [3H]ORG-2058 and incubated in the presence (□) and absence (■) of excess ORG-2058 are presented in A. The receptor isoform pattern eluting under identical conditions using [3H]R5020 as ligand in the presence (Δ) and absence (▲) of excess unlabeled steroid is presented in B. The HPSEC system was pre-calibrated with a series of pure proteins, thyroglobulin (TG), ferritin (FE), bovine serum albumin (SA) and cytochrome c (CC).

A small but distinct and reproducible secondary isoform (Fig. 4B) was demonstrable between fractions 50 and 60 with R5020, (ca. 50 A), but only represented 10 to 15% of the specifically bound radioactivity. No free steroid radioactivity appeared in these separations, indicating that dextran coated-charcoal clearance of the unbound ligand was complete and that no

discernible column-induced dissociation of steroid occurred.
[^{3}H]ORG-2058 also appeared bound specifically by two isoforms
with virtually identical ratios as observed for [^{3}H]R5020
(29). However, with ORG-2058 as ligand, the primary receptor
isoform was observed between fractions 40 and 47 (Fig. 4A)
representative of a protein of ca. 70 A. The smaller,
secondary receptor peak appeared between fractions 73 and 83
with ORG-2058. The nonspecific binding was minimal with ORG-
2058 when compared with that of R5020, similar to the density
gradient sedimentation data reported elsewhere (29).

Clinical application of the HPSEC mode for the analysis of
estrogen receptors in human tumor samples is rapidly evolving.
However, quantification is essential since the levels of
estrogen receptor have prognostic value in the determination
of hormonal response 2,3,24,27. At the same time, our
laboratory (e.g. 3,16) and others (24,25) have proposed that
the distribution of receptor isoforms has clinical
significance also. Clearly, if HPSEC analysis proves to
provide quantitative and qualitative information on hormone
receptors in human tumors, it will find wide application in
the clinical laboratory due to its speed. In this regard,
(21,28) suggested that an automated system employing high
performance ion-exchange chromatography (HPIEC) could be
highly useful in the determination of the profile of receptor
isoforms. The relationship of receptor isoform profiles
("fractionated receptors") to ultimate responsiveness has yet
to be established (3).

HIGH PERFORMANCE CHROMATOFOCUSING (HPCF)

As described earlier (18,29) all chromatography was performed
in cold-room at 0-4°C. Buffers were filtered under vacuum
through Millipore 0.45 μm HAWP filters before use. Free
steroid or the ligand-labeled cytosols were applied to
SynChropak AX-300 or AX-500 (250 x 4.1 mm I.D.) anion-exchange

columns (SynChrom) with an Altex Model 210 sample injection
valve (Beckman). Elution was carried out using Altex Model
112 pumps. The absorption profile of the eluate was monitored
at 280 nm with a Hitachi 100-40 spectrophotometer equipped
with an in-line flow cell (Beckman). pH was measured in-line
with a Pharmacia pH monitor.

Two different column equilibration and elution programs were
used depending upon the initial buffer conditions of the
receptor preparations. The columns were initially
equilibrated to the starting pH (slightly above the desired
upper limit) using a common cationic buffer. In the case of
high performance chromatofocusing on AX-300 and AX-500
columns, we have used 25 mM Tris-HCl containing 1 mM
dithiothreitol and 20% (v/v) glycerol adjusted to pH 8.1 - 8.3
at 0°C (18) or a similar phosphate buffer (29). For
chromatofocusing molybdate-stabilized receptor components, 10
mM sodium molybdate was included in the column equilibration
buffer. Cytosols prepared in homogenization buffer were
eluted with a 30:70 mixture of Polybuffers 96 and 74. This
polyampholyte solution was diluted 10- to 20-fold with 20%
glycerol, filtered with a 0.45 μm filter (Millipore) and
adjusted to between pH 4.0 and 5.0 at 0-4°C. For most
experiments, 1.0 ml fractions were collected at 1.0 ml/min.
Columns were regenerated to their starting pH (8.3) with
column equilibration buffer at 1-2 ml/min.

The [^{125}I]iodoestradiol-17ß-labeled receptor complexes, nonspecific binding components, and free steroid in each fraction
were detected radiometrically in a Micromedics 4/600 gamma
counter or with the new Beckman Model 170 flow-through
detector. [^{3}H]R5020 and [^{3}H]ORG-2058 were measured in Model
3801 liquid scintillation counter (Beckman). Sometimes the pH
of alternate fractions was determined at 0°C using a Beckman
Model 3500 pH meter with a combination glass electrode. The
counting efficiency of ^{125}Iodine averaged 65% in the

conventional counter, as judged by reference to independent determinations of disintegratins per minute using a Beckman 4000 two-channel gamma counter. Tritium counting efficiency was 35-42%.

Chromatofocusing is a technique which separates proteins on the basis of their surface charge properties and uses a column which is essentially a weak ion-exchanger. The enhanced ability to resolve ionic species which differ in charge by as little as 0.1 pH unit provide a unique method, especially in the HPLC mode to separate and charaterize proteins.

Our first experiments with estrogen receptor indicated that the AX-300 column formed a stable pH gradient with the polybuffers, and that a number of cytosolic proteins were well resolved within the gradient (18). We were concerned that the initial (i.e. "loading") peak may be composed of unresolved species, namely, that certain proteins would be excluded based upon size and charge properties. However, HPCF of labeled estrogen receptors from human uterus (Fig. 5) showed that isoforms were not eluted in the loading peak but were recovered in the gradient when the A-500 column was employed. Similar results were observed when estrogen receptors in lactating mammary gland of the rat were separated (Fig. 6).

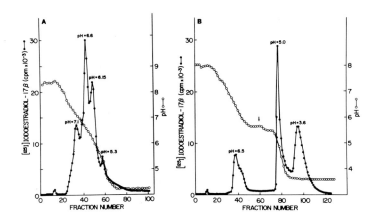

Fig. 5. Separation of estrogen receptor isoforms from human uterus in the presence or absence of molybdate by HPCF.
A. Cytosol was incubated with [125I]iodoestradiol-17ß in the presence   or absence (●) of excess diethylstilbestrol. Activity was eluted from the AX-500 column with a mixture of Polybuffers 96 and 74 adjusted to pH 4.5.
B. Cytosol was prepared in buffer containing 10 mM molybdate and incubated with [125I]iodoestradiol-17ß in the presence or absence (●) of excess diethylstilbestrol. The primary eluent was a mixture of Polybuffers 96 and 74 containing 10 mM sodium molybdate and adjusted to pH 5.0.   The secondary eluent (arrow) was Polybuffer 74 (no molybdate) adjusted to pH 3.5. Taken from (18).

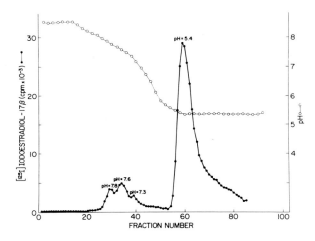

Fig. 6. Separation of receptor isoforms by HPLC chromatofocusing on AX-300. Cytosol was prepared from 14-day lactating mammary glands and incubated with [^{125}I]iodoestradiol-17ß as described earlier. For elution, a 30:70 mixture of Polybuffers 96 and 74, diluted 1:10 with 20% glycerol and adjusted to pH 5.0, was used. Taken from (18).

HPCF of progestin receptors was accomplished primarily on the AX-500 column as described previously (18). The AX-500 column in the HPCF mode exhibited problems found with the HPIEC system, namley that radioactivity appeared just after the void volume and prior to application of the pH gradient (Fig. 7). This peak was in the exact location in which free steroid eluted in the HPLC mode (29).

Even in the presence of 10 mM molybdate, the AX-500 column appeared to strip labeled-steroid from the receptor. However, a second peak appeared at a pH of 5.6 - 6.1 which contained specifically bound steroid (Fig. 7). The results presented with [^{3}H]R5020 in Figure 7 were virtually identical to those observed when [^{3}H]ORG-2058 was used as ligand (29). Thus, based on pH, the progestin receptor isoform focused at a pI value regardless of the ligand used in contrast to the HPSEC profiles (29).

The origin and significance of progestin receptor polymorphism remains obscure. Although certain components may represent distinct physiological species, proteolytic cleavage may occur with a labile receptor. Dougherty et al. (30) identified two 8S forms of the progesterone receptor from chick oviduct. Interestingly each form contained a 90,000 molecular weight component which did not associate with progestin and either a 75,000 or 110,000 molecular weight steroid binding species. Various combinations of these components could give rise to considerable size heterogeneity as we observed with receptors from human uterus (29).

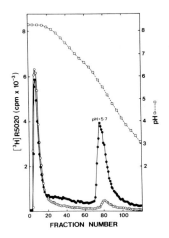

Fig. 7. HPCF of progestin receptor isoforms in human uterus.
Cytosol obtained from human uterus was incubated with
[^{3}H]R5020 in the presence (0) and absence (●) of excess
unlabeled R5020. Following removal of the free steroid, the
incubate was injected and eluted on an AX-500 column in a
chromatofocusing mode as described earlier (29).

One advantage of HPCF is that stabilizing agents such as
sodium molybdate may be included in the buffer systems.
Molybdate has several useful properties, including the
preservation (stabilization) of larger forms of the receptor
and the ability of block receptor activation (e.g. 31). Thus,
molybdate is a valuable tool in correlating the
interrelationships between receptor isoform structure and
biologic function.

HIGH PERFORMANCE ION EXCHANGE CHROMATOGRAPHY (HPIEC)

This is one of the most effective HPLC modes for the study of
receptor isoforms (21,29). The resolution of isoforms and
their high recovery provide an excellent means of
characterizing receptors for structure/function relationships.

Briefly, a portion (150-200 ul) of incubate cleared of unbound ligand is applied to an Altex 322 (Beckman, Berkeley, CA) chromatograph equipped with either AX-300, AX-500 or AX-1000 (SynChrom) anion exchange columns. All chromatography is performed in the cold room at 0-4°C. Each column was equilibrated previously with low ionic strength phosphate buffer. A wash (30 min) of the column with buffer was followed by elution with a linear gradient of potassium phosphate at pH 7.4 which approached 500 mM 90 min after gradient initiation (21,29). Subsequently the column was returned to starting conditions. All buffers were filtered prior to use with a 0.45um Millipore filter. The level of A_{280} nm absorbing species were detected as they emerged from the column by directing the eluate through a Hitachi 100-40 spectrophotometer equipped with a low volume flow cell. Approximately 1 ml fractions of the eluate were collected and counted for [16α - ^{125}I]iodoestradiol-17ß using a Micromedics gamma counter having a 62% counting efficiency or the Beckman Model 170 Flow-through Detector. [^{3}H]Ligands were measured by counting radioactivity in column fractions with a Model 3801 liquid scintillation counter (Beckman). The phosphate concentration was determined by measuring the conductivity of fractions with an in-line detector from Bio-Rad.

We have compared the use of the SynChropak AX-500 and AX-1000 columns in the HPIEC mode using human uterus and breast cancer (21), lactating mammary gland of the rat and endometrial carcinoma of the rabbit (19). A representative separation profile of estrogen receptor isoforms from human breast cancer is shown in Figure 8. The major isoform eluted at 190 mM phosphate while others were observed at 52 mM and 100 mM phosphate (21). The isoforms eluting at 100 and 200 mM phosphate have been observed in cytosols from mammary gland of the rat and human uterus (21) also. The isoforms in the cytosol of endometrial cancer fo the rabbit exhibit a 50 mM species and 175 mM component when separated on HPIEC (19).

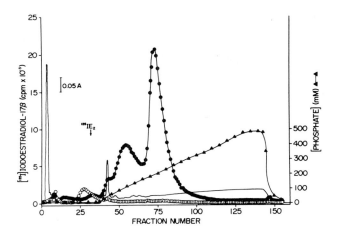

Fig. 8. HPIEC separation of ionic forms of the estrogen receptor from human breast cancer tissue on AX-1000. Cytosol was prepared and incubated in the presence (O) or absence (●) of 500-fold excess of inhibitor. Elution was performed at 1.0 ml/min using a gradient of potassium phosphate at pH 7.4. The elution of the labeled ligand alone was previously determined under identical conditions and is marked with an arrow. The recovery of radioactivity from the column was 91% for the aliquot of cytosol incubated in the absence of diethylstibestrol. A tracing of species absorbing at 280 nm is given by the continuous line. Taken from (21).

Additionally, the on-line method of analysis using the Model 170 Flow-Through Detector permitted the detection of very low levels of receptor isoforms in small quantities of cytosol (10-20 µl). Figure 9A and 9B compare the manual and on-line profiles of 6.9 fmol of total receptor-bound radioactivity from human uterine tissue separated by HPIEC. Measurements obtained manually are shown in panel A, with the continuous tracings presented in panel B. An elution pattern is similar to that for estrogen receptors in breast tissue emerged (32). Two non-specific binding components that did not intract with the column were also present in uterine cytosol. However, the two receptor isoforms were shown to have slightly different surface charge properties as characterized by an altered elution from the phosphate gradient. The first species of receptor eluted at a phosphate concentration of 150-180 mM and was equivalent to 1.4 fmol of bound steroid (22% of total). The second isoform eluted between 225-255 mM phosphate and was equal to 5.0 fmol of receptor (78% of total). A 93% recovery was observed in this representative experiment. The presence of different ionic isoforms of the receptor in breast and uterine tissues revealed by the rapid format with HPIEC allows the comparison required of clinical studies.

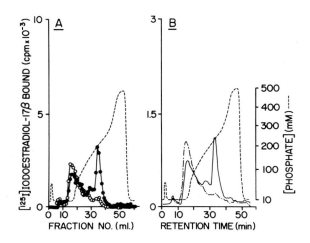

Fig. 9. HPIEC separation of micro quantities of ionic isoforms of the estrogen receptor from human uterus. The curves shown are the results of receptors separated in the presence (0) or absence (●) of 200-fold excess of diethylstibestrol. Elution was performed on 10 µl of cytosol (10 mg/ml) equivalent to 6.9 fmol receptor at 1.0 ml/min using a gradient of potassium phosphate (---). (A) 1 ml fractions were collected and radioactivity measured manually, or (B) radioactivity recorded continuously using in-line Model 170 Radioisotope Detector with conductivity flow cell. Total binding is indicated by (●) in A and by (—) in B, and nonspecific binding is indicated by (0) in A and by (–·—·) in B. Recovery of radioactivity from the column was 93% for the total bound curve determined by counting a 10 µl aliquot before sample injection. Specific binding was 30 fmol receptor/mg cytosol protein determined by multi-point titration analysis. Taken from (32).

SUMMARY

High performance liquid chromatography of steroid hormone receptors provides rapid analyses, sensitivity and high recoveries of these elusive, labile proteins. Based upon the demonstration that receptors exhibit polymorphism, we propose that their level of cellular organization and interrelationships are more complex than considered originally. Some of the cellular events which may give rise to receptor heterogeneity include proteolysis, phosphorylation and other post-translational modifications, protein-protein interactions as well as protein-nucleic acid interactions. Some isoforms may be generated due to handling artifacts while others may be the result of authentic physiologic processes. Regardless, HPLC in its various modes should be useful in future studies of receptor characterization. Although the biological significance of receptor polymorphism is not well understood currently, there are important biological implications which include the utility of receptor isoform profiles as new markers in the clinical setting.

ACKNOWLEDGMENTS

Studies from the author's laboratory have been supported in part by USPHS grants CA-19657, CA-34211, CA-32101, and CA-31946 from the National Cancer Institute and by grants from the American Cancer Society (PDT-210) and Phi Beta Psi Sorority. The important contributions of numerous research fellows are acknowledged, particularly those of Drs. R.D. Wiehle, G.E. Hoffmann, A. Fuchs, T.W. Hutchens, N.A. Shahabi and A. van der Walt. The author also expresses his deepest appreciation to Ms. Dana Gibson for her assistance in the preparation of this typescript.

1. McGuire, W.L., Carbone, P.P. and Vollmer, E.P., eds. Estrogen Receptors in Human Breast Cancer. Raven Press, New York (1975).

2. Anonymous Cancer 46, 2759-2963 (1980).

3. Wittliff, J.L., Cancer 53, 630-643 (1984).

4. McGuire, W.L., Raynaud, J.P. and Baulieu, E.E., eds. Progesteroine Receptors in Normal and Neoplastic Tissues. Raven Press, New York (1975).

5. Creasman, W.T., McCarty, K.S. Sr., Barton, T.K., and McCarty, K.S., Jr. Obstet. Gynecol. 55, 363 (1980).

6. Erlich, C.E., Young, P.C., Cleary, R.E. Am. J. Obstet. Gynecol. 141, 539-546 (1981).

7. Käuppila, A., Kujansuu, E., Vihko, R. Cancer 50, 2157-2166 (1974).

8. Carlson, J.A. Jr., Allegra, J.C., Day, T.G. and Wittliff, J.L. Am. J. Obstet. Gynecol. 149, 149-153 (1984).

9. Mortel, R., Levy, C., Wolf, J.P., Nicolas, J.C., Robel, P. and Baulieu, E.E. Cancer Res. 41, 1140-1145 (1981).

10. Daxenbichler, G., Grill, H.J., Geir, W., Wittliff, J.L. and Dapunt, O. In Steroid Receptors and Hormone Dependent Neoplasia (J.L. Wittliff and O. Dapunt, eds.) pp. 59-67, Masson Publishing USA, Inc., New York (1980).

11. Boylan, E.S. and Wittliff, J.L. Cancer Res. 33, 2903-2908 (1973).

12. Gardner, D.G. and Wittliff, J.L. Biochemistry 12, 3090-2096 (1973).

13. Goral, J.E. and Wittliff, J.L. Biochemistry 14, 2944-2952 (1975).

14. Wittliff, J.L. In Methods in Cancer Research (H. Busch, ed.), Vol. XI, pp. 293-354. Academic Press, New York (1975).

15. Wittliff, J.L., Mehta, R.G. and Kute, T.E. In Progesterone Receptors in Normal and Neoplastic Tissues (W.L. McGuire, E.E. Baulieu and J.P. Raynaud, eds.), pp. 39-57. Raven Press, New York (1977).

16. Wittliff, J.L., Lewko, W.M., Park, D.C., Kute, T.E., Baker, D.T. Jr. and Kane, L.N. In Hormones, Receptors and Breast Cancer (W.L. McGuire, ed.) pp. 325-359. Raven Press, New York (1978).

17. Wittliff, J.L., Feldhoff, P.W., Fuchs, A. and Wiehle, R.D. In Physiopathology of Endocrine Diseases and Mechanisms of Hormone Action (R. Soto, A.F. DeNicola and J.A. Blaquier, eds.), pp. 397-411. Alan R. Liss, Inc., New York (1981).

18. Hutchens, T.W., Wiehle, R.D., Shahabi, N.A. and Wittliff, J.L. _J. Chromatogr._ 266, 115-128 (1983).

19. Shahabi, N.A., Hutchens, T.W., Wittliff, J.L., Halmo, S.D., Kirk, M.E. and Nisker, J.A. _In_ Hormones and Cancer 2 (F. Bresciani, R.J.B. King, M.E. Lippman, M. Namer and J.P. Raynaud eds.), pp. 63-71. Raven Press, New York (1984).

20. Wiehle, R.D., Hofmann, G.E., Fuchs, A. and Wittliff, J.L. _J. Chromatogr._ 307, 39-51 (1984).

21. Wiehle, R.D. and Wittliff, J.L. _J. Chromatogr._ 297, 313-326 (1984).

22. Sherman, M.R., Pickering, L.A., Rollwagen, F.M., Miller, L.K. _Fed. Proc._ 37, 167-172 (1978).

23. McCarty, K.S. Jr., Cox, C., Silva, J.S., Woodard, B.H., Mossler, J.A., Haagensen, D.E., Barton, T.K., McCarty, K.S. Sr., and Wells, S.A. Jr. _Cancer_ 46, 2846-2850 (1980).

24. Clark, G.M., McGuire, W.L., Hubay, C.A., Pearson, O.H., Marshall, J.S. _N. Engl. J. Med._ 309, 1343-1347.

25. Powell, B., Garola, R.E., Chamness, G.C., McGuire, W.L. _Cancer Res._ 39, 1678-1682 (1977).

26. Knight, W.A., Livingston, R.B., Gregory, E.J. and McGuire, W.L. _Cancer Res._ 37, 4669-4671 (1977).

27. Fisher, B., Redmond, C., Brown, A., Wickerham, D.L., Wolmark, N., Allegra, J.C., Escher, G., Lippman, M., Savlov, E., Wittliff, J.L. and Fisher, E.R. et al. _J. Clin. Onc._ 1, 227-241 (1983).

28. Wittliff, J.L. and Wiehle, R.D. _In_: Hormonally Sensitive Tumors, (V.P. Hollander, ed.) Academic Press Inc. (1985) in press.

29. Van der Walt, A. and Wittliff, J.L. _J. Chromatogr._ (1984) in press.

30. Greene, G.L., Nolan, C.X., Engler, J.P. and Jensen, E.V. _Proc. Natl. Acad. Sci. U.S._ 77, 5115-5119.

31. Nishigori, H. and Toft, D.O. _Biochemistry_ 19, 77-83 (1980)

32. Boyle, D.M., Wiehle, R.D., Shahabi, N.A. and Wittliff, J.L. _J. Chromatogr._ (1985) in press.

SUBJECT INDEX

Walter de Gruyter
Berlin · New York

K. Fotherby
S. B. Pal
(Editors)

Hormones in Normal and Abnormal Human Tissues

Volume 1
1980. 17 cm x 24 cm. XIV, 658 pages with figures and
tables. Hardcover. DM 145,–; approx. US $48.40
ISBN 3 11 008031 1

Volume 2
1981. 17 cm x 24 cm. XII, 552 pages with figures and
tables. Hardcover. DM 135,–; approx. US $45.00
ISBN 3 11 008541 0

Volume 3
1982. 17 cm x 24 cm. X, 297 pages with figures and
tables. Hardcover. DM 150,–; approx. US $50.00
ISBN 3 11 008616 6

K. Fotherby
S. B. Pal
(Editors)

The Role of Drugs and Electrolytes in Hormonogenesis

1984. 17 cm x 24 cm. XII, 360 pages. Numerous
illustrations. Hardcover. DM 180,–; approx. US $60.00
ISBN 3 11 008463 5

K. Fotherby
S. B. Pal
(Editors)

Steroid Converting Enzymes and Diseases

1984. 17 cm x 24 cm. IX, 261 pages. Numerous
illustrations. Hardcover. DM 180,–; approx. US $60.00
ISBN 3 11 009556 4

Walter de Gruyter
Berlin · New York

K. Fotherby
S. B. Pal
(Editors)

Exercise Endocrinology

1985. 17 cm x 24 cm. XII, 300 pages. Numerous illustrations.
Hardcover. DM 230,–; approx. US $76.70   ISBN 3 11 009557 2

There has been a marked increase in the amount of interest
taken in exercise physiology during the past few years. This is
partly due to the higher standards demanded in most sports
and the most efficient use of strength, energy and stamina
required of the sports-person, which can have a significant
effect on the final result.
This book will be of importance to both "trained" and "untrain-
ed" subjects in helping them to understand the physiological
changes which take place during exercise.

M. K. Agarwal
(Editor)

Hormone Antagonists

1982. 17 cm x 24 cm. IX, 734 pages. Numerous illustrations.
Hardcover. DM 180,–; approx. US $60.00   ISBN 3 11 008613 1

M. K. Agarwal
(Editor)

Principles of Recepterology

1983. 17 cm x 24 cm. VII, 677 pages. Numerous illustrations.
Hardcover. DM 220,–; approx. US $73.30   ISBN 3 11 009558 0

M. K. Agarwal
M. Yoshida
(Editors)

Immunopharmacology of Endotoxicosis

Proceedings of the 5th International Conference of Immuno-
logy. Satellite Workshop. Kyoto, Japan, August 27, 1983

1984. 17 cm x 24 cm. XIV, 376 pages. Numerous illustrations.
Hardcover. DM 170,–; approx. US $56.70   ISBN 3 11 009887 3

M. K. Agarwal
(Editor)

Adrenal Steroid Antagonism

Proceedings · Satellite Workshop of the VII. International Congress of Endocrinology. Quebec, Canada, July 7, 1984

1984. 17 cm x 24 cm. VIII, 399 pages. With numerous
illustrations. Hardcover. DM 175,–; approx. US $58.30
ISBN 3 11 010090 8